SPECIAL EDITION USING MICROSOFT PROJECT 2000 KEYBOARD SHORTCUTS

While Project is menu-driven, there are a number of keyboard shortcuts you can also take advantage of.

EDITING SHORTCUTS

Activate entry bar to edit field	F2
Clear or reset contents of selection	Ctrl+Delete
Copy selection	Ctrl+C
Cut selection	Ctrl+X
Delete task, resource, or assignment	Del
Display Assign Resources dialog box	Alt+F10
Display Information dialog box	Shift+F2
Fill down	Ctrl+D
Insert hyperlink	Ctrl+K
Insert task or resource	Ins
Paste	Ctrl+V
Find	Ctrl+F
Find Again	Shift+F4
Replace	Ctrl+H
Spelling	F7
Undo editing	Ctrl+Z

LINKING SHORTCUTS

Link Tasks	Ctrl+F2
Unlink Tasks	Ctrl+Shift+F2

CALCULATING SHORTCUTS

Calculate active project	Shift+F9
Calculate all open projects	F9
Turn Auto Calculate on/off	Ctrl+F9

OUTLINING SHORTCUTS

Hide Subtasks	Alt+Shift+- (on number pad)
Indent task in outline	Alt+Shift+→
Outdent task in outline	Alt+Shift+←
Show all tasks	Alt+Shift+* (on number pad)
Show Subtasks	Alt+Shift++ (on number pad)

SCROLLING GANTT CHART SHORTCUTS

Timescale one minor time unit left	Alt+←
Timescale one minor time unit right	Alt+→
Timescale one screen left	Alt+Page Up
Timescale one screen right	Alt+Page Down
Timescale to beginning of the project	Alt+Home
Timescale to end of the project	Alt+End
Timescale to start of current task	Ctrl+Shift+F5
Zoom in	Ctrl+/ (on number pad)
Zoom out	Ctrl+* (on number pad)

CELL SELECTION SHORTCUTS

Extend selection to first field in a row	Shift+Home
Extend selection to last field in a row	Shift+End
Extend selection to entire column(s)	Ctrl+spacebar
Extend selection to entire row(s)	Shift+spacebar
Go to cell in first row	Ctrl+↑
Go to cell in first row, first column	Ctrl+Home
Go to cell in last row	Ctrl+↓
Go to cell in last row, last column	Ctrl+End
Move within a selection down one cell	Enter
Move within a selection up one cell	Shift+Enter
Move within a selection right one cell	Tab
Move within a selection left one cell	Shift+Tab

OTHER SHORTCUTS

Remove Filter	F3
Reset sort order to ID number	Shift+F3
Assign resources	Alt+F10
Display resource information	Shift+F2
Display Column Definition dialog box	Alt+F3
Display Visual Basic Editor	Alt+F11
Run macro	Alt+F8
Context-sensitive Help pointer	Shift+F1
Open Help topics	F1

Special Edition
Using
Microsoft®
Project
2000

Tim Pyron

A Division of Macmillan USA
201 W. 103rd Street
Indianapolis, Indiana 46290

CONTENTS AT A GLANCE

Special Edition Using Microsoft® Project 2000

TRADEMARKS

WARNING AND DISCLAIMER

Associate Publisher
Greg Wiegand

Acquisitions Editors
Laura Bulcher
Stephanie J. McComb
John Pierce

Development Editors
Laura Bulcher
Sean Dixon
Gregory Harris
Jill Hayden

Managing Editor
Thomas F. Hayes

Project Editor
Karen S. Shields

Copy Editors
Victoria Elzey
Kay Hoskin
Sossity Smith
Kelly Talbot
Megan Wade

Indexer
Sheila Schroeder

Proofreaders
Jeanne Clark
Harvey Stanbrough

Technical Editors
Brian Kennemer
Henry Staples

Team Coordinator
Sharry Lee Gregory

Media Developer
Jay Payne

Interior and Cover Designer
Anne Jones

Production
Darin Crone
Brad Lenser
Susan Geiselman

CONTENTS

ABOUT THE AUTHORS

Tim Pyron (tpyron@txdirect.net), besides writing for Macmillan, is an independent consultant and trainer for Microsoft Project. His previous Microsoft Project books include, among others, *Using Microsoft Project 4*, *Special Edition Using Microsoft Project 98*, *Sams Teach Yourself Microsoft Project 98 in 24 Hours*, and *Sams Teach Yourself Microsoft Project 2000 in 24 Hours*—all of which together have sold a quarter-million copies and have been translated into numerous languages. He is also editor of *Woody's Project Watch*, a free newsletter for Project users. To subscribe, go to http://www.woodyswatch.com/wpw/.

Ira Brown is the senior vice president of Project Assistants, Inc., a Microsoft Project Solution Provider specializing in training, consulting, and custom software development for Microsoft Project. He has extensive project management and application development experience, working in the healthcare information systems and financial services industries for over 15 years. Ira is recognized as a leading authority in integrating Microsoft Project with other products utilizing VBA, specializing in integration with the Microsoft Office suite of applications. He has many years of experience developing and implementing automated methodologies centered around Microsoft Project. He also has significant experience in helping organizations implement Microsoft Project across an enterprise, utilizing the workgroup features, Web publishing, and multiple project consolidation capabilities of the software. Ira, his wife, Diane, and their two children, Tara and Joey, reside in Philadelphia, Pennsylvania. Ira can be contacted by phone at (800) 642-9259, fax at (302) 477-9712, or email at ibrown@projectassistants.com. For more information about Project Assistants, visit its Web site at www.projectassistants.com.

Toby Brown, MCP PMP, is a full-time consultant and instructor specializing in project management, information systems, and curriculum development. He has more than 10 years' experience as a presenter, consultant, team builder, and project manager. Currently, he is employed with PMSI-Project Mentors (www.pmsi-pm.com), an Atlanta-based organization, part of Provant, Inc., dedicated to full-time project management services, training, and technology implementations. Toby is a member of the corporate training group responsible for conducting one-on-one and group classroom training sessions on project management processes, implementation, and systems design. When not teaching and consulting, Toby is an FAA commercial-certified hot air balloon pilot flying at select weekend events for Microsoft, The Weather Channel, and Home & Garden Television/Food Network.

Gus Cicala is the president and CEO of Project Assistants, Inc., in Wilmington, Delaware. Gus is an expert in project management and the use of Microsoft Project as a project management tool. He regularly delivers consulting and training on project management, Microsoft Project, contract administration, and custom methodologies for organizations across North America and Europe. He graduated Cum Laude from The Wharton School of the University of Pennsylvania, with dual majors in Operations Research and Management. Gus can be reached by phone at (302) 477-9711, by fax at (302) 477-9712, or by email at gcicala@projectassistants.com.

Rod Gill has been involved with project management for more than 20 years and has particular expertise in the creation and use of project management information systems. He is a Microsoft Most Valued Professional (MVP) for Project for Windows, an award and status given by Microsoft to those who have provided regular, accurate, and useful help on their Project Newsgroups. His company, Project Learning Ltd. (`www.projectlearning.com`), sells Microsoft Project Companion software and project management training videos.

Ron Hill is a graduate of West Point Military Academy and the U.S. Army Ranger and Airborne Schools. He has held various positions in Airborne and Mechanized Infantry units around the world. Ron is an expert in Internet and database application development, and specializes in creating VBA solutions and Web-based software for Microsoft Project. Ron is a senior technical analyst with Project Assistants, Inc., a Microsoft Project Solution Provider based in Wilmington, Delaware. He is the lead developer of several Microsoft Project add-on products from Project Assistants, including the ProjectCommander and TeamWork applications. You can reach Ron at `rhill@projectassistants.com`, call him at (800) 642-9259, fax him at (302) 477-9712, or reach him on the Web at `www.projectassistants.com`.

Thuy "Twee" Le is the president for Beyond Baseline in Austin, Texas. Beyond Baseline offers full-service training and consulting for Microsoft desktop applications, specializing in Project, Office, and FrontPage. Graduating with a BA in Psychology from the University of Texas at Austin, Thuy uses her people skills to develop and deliver customized training and consulting for various industries, including high-tech, education, medical, banking, construction, and government. If not working with computers, she is likely to be reading or dabbling with carpentry. Thuy can be reached at `thuyle@cheerful.com` or `thuyle@beyondbaseline.com`.

Winston Meeker is a training consultant and project manager for Productivity Point International. He enjoys translating complex and mysterious technological concepts into clear, practical terms that anyone can understand. Winston lives in San Antonio, Texas, with his wife, Tammy, and daughters, Charis and Montana. He holds a BA in English and Humanities from the University of Texas at San Antonio and is completing an MA in Biblical Studies at Reformed Theological Seminary in Oviedo, Florida. He strives to work and live *Soli Deo Gloria*.

Melette W. Pearce is an independent instructor and consultant in Dallas, Texas, where she teaches and crafts business solutions using tools ranging from simple spreadsheets and databases to Visual Basic applications. She has designed extensive supplemental courseware for numerous products, but specializes in MS Project and MS Access. Melette began as a presentation specialist in the MS-DOS environment; but, when she discovered her passion for teaching eight years ago, she has never looked back. A graduate of Eastfield College, she is also a Microsoft Certified Trainer. She can be contacted via the Internet at `gorgias@home.com`.

Patricia B. Seidl is an authority in project management with additional experience in application development and methodology development. She has seven years of project management experience and eighteen years of overall information technology experience. Patricia graduated Cum Laude from the College of St. Scholastica with a Bachelor of Arts degree with a major in Health Information Administration. She also holds an Associate of Applied Science degree in Computer Science Technology from the University of Southern Colorado, and she is a member of the American Health Information Management Association. Patricia is a project management consultant with Project Assistants, a leading Microsoft Solution provider specializing in Microsoft Project training, implementation services, and Web-based project management solutions. Patricia is a specialist on the use of Microsoft Project as a project management tool. She delivers training and consulting on project management, Microsoft Project, and custom methodologies for companies across the U.S. She can be contacted by phone at (800) 642-9259, by fax at (302) 477-9712, by email at pseidl@projectassistants.com, or on the Web at www.projectassistants.com.

Jo Ellen Shires is the owner of Common Sense Computing, a Portland, Oregon–based company that exclusively serves Microsoft Project users. She began her programming and training careers in 1974 and holds a B.S. in Economics and an M.S. in Biometry. A noted lecturer at regional and national gatherings, and founder of the Portland Project Users Group, Jo has contributed to *Special Edition Using Microsoft Project 98* and *Sams Teach Yourself Microsoft Project 2000 in 24 Hours*. She serves as an advisor to the Project development team at Microsoft and is participating in the launch of the Project certification testing program. Jo can be reached at jshires@cscservices.com.

Laurie Soslow is an expert at technical writing for computer-based tools and education. Laurie received her Bachelor of Arts degree in English and Political Science from the University of Vermont, and her Masters Degree in English and Creative Writing from Boston University. She develops software and training documentation for Project Assistants, a project management training, consulting, and Internet software development company based in Wilmington, Delaware. At Project Assistants, Laurie creates user documentation, online help systems, and custom training materials for Microsoft Project, as well as Project Commander and TeamWork, the popular add-on products for Microsoft Project. She can be contacted via email at lsoslow@projectassistants.com, by phone at (800) 642-9259, by fax at (302) 477-9712, or on the Web at www.projectassistants.com.

Laura Stewart is an experienced technical writer, software instructor, and award-winning Microsoft Office 2000 Beta tester. Laura has been a contributing author to *Special Edition Using Microsoft Project 2000*, *Special Edition Using Microsoft Project 98*, *Sams Teach Yourself Microsoft Project 98 in 24 Hours*, and *Special Edition Using Microsoft Project 95*. In addition to her contributions to these Microsoft Project books, Laura is the author of several computer reference books, including the *Platinum Edition Using Microsoft Office 2000* and *Migrating to Office 2000: A Corporate User's Desk Reference*. Laura is a certified Microsoft Office Expert Specialist in Excel and PowerPoint, and is a contributor to Woody's Project Watch (www.woodyswatch.com).

ABOUT THE TECH EDITORS

Brian Kennemer has worked in various project management roles for more than five years, including the development of a work management system at the Boeing Commercial Airplane Group. He has spoken around the United States for the Microsoft Project Users Group (www.mpug.org) on the uses of Project in the real world. Considered one of the leading experts on Microsoft Project, Brian is one of only seven Microsoft Most Valued Professionals for Project, volunteering his time in the Microsoft Support Newsgroups to help users with their everyday questions and issues with Project. He is also the Microsoft Project and Project Management writer for TechRepublic.com, an IT news and information portal. Brian is the Project Office program manager for Pacific Edge Software (www.pacificedge.com), a supplier of enterprise applications that automate and streamline project delivery within and between businesses. Brian lives near Seattle with his lovely wife, Alicia, and their three children, Riley, Jesse, and Alivia.

Henry Staples works at an Internet startup in the high-tech corridor outside Washington, DC. He has nearly 10 years of experience in the software development field and has several years of project management experience under his belt. Notable technical editing projects include books on the last three versions of Microsoft Project and several books on HTML and other Web-related technologies. In his spare time, he gallivants through museums with his girlfriend, plays volleyball, and trains for an annual 24-hour mountain biking race.

Dedication

As with all the previous editions, this book continues to be dedicated to Gerlinde K. Pyron—as do I. The dedication is only partly in appreciation for her support during the long process of bringing the book to completion. It's also in recognition of her contributions to the content, for she has taught me more valuable lessons about business, especially the importance of even-handed humanity in business, than I was ever taught in graduate management studies. Wise manager, cutting-edge e-commerce consultant, unstinting social volunteer, gifted artist, and adored grandmother—Gerlinde is a remarkable Renaissance woman for the new millennium.

—Tim Pyron

ACKNOWLEDGMENTS

When I wrote the first edition of this book nearly 10 years ago, I learned for the first time just how inadequate this Acknowledgements page of a book really is. Even though I was the sole author, the familiar phrases "couldn't have done it without…" and "…made it all possible" took on a deeply personal meaning. I must acknowledge that publishing a book is entirely a team project, and the author is just one of many links in the chain that stretches from supportive families through the publishing house to the bookstores and the readers who provide their valuable feedback.

Nowadays, it takes a team of writers to explore the depth and breadth of a new version of a complex software product like Microsoft Project and to capture that understanding in revised or new chapters, all in time to get to press as the software is released. There were a number of consultants and writers who contributed their expertise and insight to this revision. I encourage you to read about each of them in the section "About the Authors" in the preceding pages, as well as "About the Tech Editors." I'm sure you will be hearing more good things about these capable folks in the future. My thanks to each of them for their hard work.

I also want to thank **Laura Bulcher** at Macmillan who as development editor was responsible for seeing that the content met Macmillan's high standards. Laura also wound up playing the role of acquisitions editor, which means she had the added responsibility of helping find writers and give guidance and support to all of us. I would also like to thank **Victoria Elzey**, **Sossity Smith**, **Megan Wade**, **Kelly Talbot**, and **Kay Hoskin** for their diligent copy editing of this book; and to **Karen Shields**, **Jeanne Clark**, and all the other Macmillan folks who made this book actually happen. Thanks also to **Jay Payne** who developed the CD that accompanies the book.

Our technical editors for this book are **Henry Staples** and **Brian Kennemer**. They poured over and tested every list of instructional steps, every screen capture, and every other assertion to be sure that what is presented as fact is, in fact, fact. You owe them a debt of gratitude, for they rescued the truth more often than I, for one, would prefer to admit.

Finally, my special thanks go to **Adrian Jenkins** at Microsoft who served as the Microsoft Project Beta Coordinator. Adrian researched questions and provided answers to a wide range of questions about this new release for all of us. Congratulations to Adrian and the project team at Microsoft for a job very well done.

—*Tim Pyron*

TELL US WHAT YOU THINK!

As the reader of this book, *you* are our most important critic and commentator. We value your opinion and want to know what we're doing right, what we could do better, what areas you'd like to see us publish in, and any other words of wisdom you're willing to pass our way.

As an associate publisher for Que, I welcome your comments. You can fax, email, or write me directly to let me know what you did or didn't like about this book—as well as what we can do to make our books stronger.

Please note that I cannot help you with technical problems related to the topic of this book, and that due to the high volume of mail I receive, I might not be able to reply to every message.

When you write, please be sure to include this book's title and author as well as your name and phone or fax number. I will carefully review your comments and share them with the author and editors who worked on the book.

Fax: 317-581-4666

Email: desktop_pub@macmillanusa.com

Mail: Associate Publisher, Desktop Applications
          Que
          201 West 103rd Street
          Indianapolis, IN 46290 USA

INTRODUCTION

In this Introduction

Microsoft Project 2000 is an important new release of the best-selling and most widely used project management software product in the world. There are, of course, lots of exciting new tools in Project 2000 that will delight seasoned users. Moreover, Microsoft has made a number of fundamental technical changes that significantly extend the effectiveness and power of Microsoft Project.

WHY YOU SHOULD USE THIS BOOK

Almost anyone in the work place can make good use of Microsoft Project at one time or another, but for project managers it's a life-support system. Microsoft Project is adaptable to both large and small projects. Managers of large, decade-long projects rely heavily on project management software to keep track of all the interrelated tasks and phases of their projects. On a smaller scale, I have relied on Project to help me plan and coordinate software installations and upgrades over multiple corporate sites. And yes, I did rely on it to keep me on track while writing this book. Project was able to tell instantly that the publisher's deadlines were impossible. But by changing the scheduling calendar to include all evenings, weekends, and holidays, the goal became possible (if we assume family counseling can be delayed until after publication).

This book will give you direct answers about how to put a project schedule together with Microsoft Project 2000. It's organized to follow the project cycle of initializing and developing a plan, implementing the plan, tracking progress and adjusting to changes and unforeseen events, and preparing the final reports. You'll find step-by-step procedures for using Project's features, plus you'll get help with common problems (such as avoiding unintended constraints on tasks, adjusting task duration when resources are added, maintaining resource information among multiple projects, and many more). *Special Edition Using* books from Que offer comprehensive coverage of software. You can be sure you will find what you need in this book to make Project work for you.

WHY YOU SHOULD USE MICROSOFT PROJECT

Managing projects is a specialized field within management—and a rapidly growing field at that. There are professional associations, journals, professional certifications, and university courses and degrees for project managers. A project manager oversees all stages of a project, from concept and planning through the completion and drafting of final summary reports.

Note

One of the best Web sites for project management information is maintained by the Project Management Institute at http://www.pmi.org. Here you can find valuable references to publications, discussion forums on the Internet, other relevant Web sites, project management special interest groups (SIGs) in your area, educational opportunities, employment opportunities, Institute chapters in your area, and membership information. You can also download a free copy of the Institute's *Guide to the Project Management Body of Knowledge,* which documents the most up-to-date theory and best practices in project management.

Microsoft Project is, at its core, a scheduling and planning tool for project managers, providing easy-to-use tools for putting together a project schedule and assigning responsibilities; but, it also gives you powerful tools to carry you through to the end of the project.

After you have defined the scope and goals for your project, you can start putting Microsoft Project 2000 to use. Project is an invaluable planning tool for

- Organizing the project plan and thinking through the details of what must be done
- Scheduling deadlines that must be met
- Scheduling the tasks in the appropriate sequence
- Assigning resources and costs to tasks and scheduling tasks around resource availability
- Fine-tuning the plan to satisfy time and budget constraints or to accommodate changes
- Providing hyperlinks between the project schedule and related project management documents in other applications
- Preparing professional-looking reports to explain the project to stakeholders such as owners, top management, supervisors, workers, subcontractors, and the public
- Posting a copy of the project on the Internet or an intranet for review

When work begins on the project, you can use Microsoft Project to

- Track progress and analyze the evolving real schedule to see if it looks like you will finish on time and within budget
- Revise the schedule to accommodate changes and unforeseen circumstances
- Try out different what-if scenarios before making actual modifications to the plan
- Communicate with team members about changes in the schedule (even automatically notify those who are affected by changes) and solicit feedback about their progress
- Post automatically updated progress reports on an Internet Web site or a company intranet
- Produce final reports on the success of the project and evaluate problem areas for consideration in future projects

WHAT'S NEW IN MICROSOFT PROJECT 2000

Project 2000 extends the dramatic changes that were introduced in Project 98. If you are new to project management and its terminology, you might not be able to appreciate some of the items listed in this review of new features. On the other hand, if you are a seasoned user of Microsoft Project, you will be excited by these enhancements.

MANY OFFICE 2000 FEATURES ARE NOW IN PROJECT 2000

As in Office 2000, Help is now in HTML format, and Help also has much more project management content than before. Users can select the default directory for saved files and templates. The file Open and Save dialog boxes are designed like those in Office 2000: less cluttered and more functional. With Office Namespace Extensions, saving projects to a Web site is easy. There is also a new Auto Save option to save your active document at timed intervals. Project 2000 also supports Language Packs so that the same installed program can display menus and dialog boxes in different languages.

SCHEDULING CONTROLS ARE MORE COMPREHENSIVE

Upgrading the scheduling engine was the main thrust of the improvements in Project 98, and Project 2000 raises the bar even higher. The biggest improvement is the ability to contour resource availability over time, to forecast changes in the number of resources that will be available at future dates. If a task has special scheduling requirements, you can use a task calendar that affects only that task and overrides the assigned resource calendars. Project 2000 distinguishes between the traditional work resources and the new material resources, with the distinction being that with material resources you measure the units consumed and with other resources you measure the hours of work performed.

When entering durations you can now use the time unit month. You can also flag duration entries as estimates to be confirmed later. In addition to entering a traditional constraint date for a task, you can also enter a reference deadline date for a task. The deadline date doesn't affect the scheduling, but it does serve to notify you when a task misses a deadline.

The number of task priority levels you can use to control which tasks are leveled has increased from 10 to 1,000. Furthermore, you can assign project priorities to determine the order of task leveling when working with master projects or the order of leveling when multiple projects use the same resource pool. You also can control whether or not to clear existing leveling delays before calculating new leveling delays. Project 2000 also has a new command to clear the baseline or an interim plan.

Master projects now calculate their subprojects as though they were summary tasks; thus, you can now have a single critical path through the entire master project.

NEW CUSTOM FIELDS GIVE USERS MORE CONTROL

Perhaps the most popular new feature in Project 2000 will be the new custom fields, which the user can define to perform custom calculations based on data in other fields. You can also use the custom fields to provide pick-lists that help standardize data entry. Special indicators can be defined for the custom fields to flag values that fall within a specified range or above or below that range.

You can now define grouping criteria for displaying tasks or resources and choose summary statistics to be displayed for each group.

Project 2000 allows you to define the format for displaying WBS codes. A user-defined code mask guarantees that calculated or entered WBS codes conform to the defined standard. Project can also verify that entered WBS codes are unique.

New Outline Code fields enable you to define custom sorting orders and outline structures for your task list, independently of the real outline structure. As with the WBS codes, you can define a code mask that enforces the structure of the codes that are used.

THE PERT CHART HAS BEEN REPLACED BY THE NETWORK DIAGRAM

The network diagram is like the PERT Chart, but it has enhanced capabilities. You can now filter the diagram and hide or display subtasks. You also have extensive control over the format of the task nodes and the linking lines.

THE PROGRAMMING CONTROLS HAVE BEEN EXPANDED

To give programmers access to the new features in this release, there are new methods, properties, objects, collections, and events. The programmer now has control over the sub-projects in a master project as well as multiple projects that use the same resource pool. Project 2000 also allows COM add-ins to make custom applications more efficient.

PROJECT CENTRAL ENABLES WORKGROUP FUNCTIONALITY OVER THE WEB

You can easily save a project to a Web site using Project Central and members of your workgroup or other stakeholders can view the project using just a browser whether or not they have Microsoft Project installed on their machines. With the browser, users can take advantage of interactive features such as personal Gantt Charts, personal timesheets, and personal status reports. They can filter, sort, and group task or resource lists. They can also delegate tasks and run many reports.

THE INTERFACE IS MUCH MORE EFFECTIVE

Finally, there is a whole host of usage enhancements to make life easier for the user:

- More abundant ScreenTips explain data that is not self-evident on the screen.
- Like Microsoft Excel, in-cell editing and fill handles make data entry and editing easier.
- Clicking the taskbar in the Gantt Chart selects the task as it intuitively should.
- Hyperlinks can be assigned from a pick-list of recently visited sites, and you can control the ScreenTip accompanying the hyperlink.
- Project-level fields such as costs and earned-value fields can be displayed in headers, footers, or legends.
- In tables, you can set unique row heights for individual rows.
- You can select the outline level to display for the whole project from a pick-list.
- If you want taskbars to roll up to summary tasks, you can set that option for the whole project instead of having to set each task individually.
- You can display the fiscal year timescale alongside the calendar year timescale.
- The Copy Picture command produces a better picture that scales more effectively in other applications.
- You can convert a file into a template, choosing to include or exclude baseline values, actual values, resource rates, and fixed costs. Using the File New command displays a Templates tab with all your templates on it.
- Project 2000 uses the single document interface, which means that each open project appears on the Windows taskbar and can be switched using the Alt+Tab key combination.

How This Book Is Organized

This book is divided into nine parts, which take you from an overview of project management and Microsoft Project through programming and customizing Microsoft Project to suit your needs. Following is a brief review of these parts and the chapters you'll find in each part.

Part I: Getting Started with Microsoft Project 2000

Part I introduces you to Microsoft Project 2000 and shows you how to set up a new project document.

Chapter 1, "The Power of Microsoft Project 2000," introduces you to project management concepts and the major phases of managing a project with Microsoft Project.

Chapter 2, "Learning the Basics of Microsoft Project," introduces you to the Microsoft Project workspace. In this chapter, you learn to navigate the screen display, scroll and select data, and select different views of the project.

In Chapter 3, "Setting Up a New Project Document," you review the preliminary steps you take when creating a project. You learn how to specify the calendar of working days and hours, how to enter basic information about the project, and how to specify the planned date for starting or finishing the project. You also learn how to adjust the most critical of the default values that govern how Microsoft Project displays and calculates a project.

Chapter 4, "Working with Project Files," presents the information you need to work with project files. Included is a comprehensive discussion of the Global Project Template file and how you use it.

Part II: Scheduling Tasks

Part II shows you how to build the skeleton of the project plan.

Chapter 5, "Creating a Task List," explains how you define and enter the tasks, milestones, and recurring tasks that must be completed to successfully finish the project. You also learn how to enter the task list in outline form in accordance with top-down planning principles. You learn how to edit the data in a project and how to use different forms for editing the task data.

Chapter 6, "Entering Scheduling Requirements," shows you how to define the special conditions that govern the scheduling of tasks in your project: specific deadlines and sequencing requirements for the tasks.

Chapter 7, "Viewing Your Schedule," explains and compares the most popular views you can use in Microsoft Project to display the task list. The views covered are the Calendar view, the PERT Chart, and the special graphics capabilities of the Gantt Chart.

Part III: Assigning Resources and Costs

Part III shows you how to define and assign resources and costs to the tasks in your project.

Chapter 8, "Defining Resources and Costs," shows you how to define the resource pool that you plan to use in the project and how to define the working and nonworking times for those resources. You learn how to sort, filter, and print the resource list. You learn also how to save the resource pool as a template for use in other project documents.

Chapter 9, "Understanding Resource Scheduling," gives you an understanding of how Project calculates a schedule when resources are assigned to tasks—both when you first assign resources and when you change resource assignments. The detailed instructions for assigning resources are covered in the next chapter.

Chapter 10, "Assigning Resources and Costs to Tasks," shows you how to associate resources and costs with specific tasks. You also learn how to assign overtime for resources and how to assign fixed costs to parts of the project. Finally, you learn how to view the resources, costs, and task assignments in useful ways for auditing the project plan and how to print the standard views and reports.

Chapter 11, "Resolving Resource Assignment Problems," is a guide for troubleshooting problems in the schedule for assigned resources. Typically, some resources are scheduled for more work than they can possibly do in the time allowed; this is where you learn ways to resolve the conflicts.

PART IV: REVIEWING AND DISTRIBUTING THE PROJECT

Part IV covers that part of the project cycle where you have completed the initial planning and need to review the schedule and refine it to ensure that it meets the objectives of the project. Then you will want to publish the final plan in printed reports or on an intranet or the Internet.

Chapter 12, "Reviewing the Project Plan," introduces features that help you review your task schedule for completeness and accuracy. You learn how to get an overview of the project to see if you can complete the project plan in a timely fashion and at an acceptable cost. You also learn how to view the task list through filters that focus on important aspects of the project and to sort and print the task list. You learn how to spell check the schedule and how to view the summary statistics for the project.

In Chapter 13, "Printing Views and Reports," you learn how to use the standard views and reports to publish your plan for the project.

Chapter 14, "Publishing Projects on the Web," covers the new capability of Project to prepare its views for HTML display on Web sites and intranets.

Chapter 15, "Using Microsoft Project in Workgroups," will show you how to use Project's network workgroup features for communicating and coordinating the details of the project.

PART V: TRACKING AND ANALYZING PROGRESS

This part shows you how to keep track of actual work on the project and how to understand what is going on, with special emphasis on catching problems early so that corrective measures can be taken.

Chapter 16, "Tracking Work on the Project," deals with your role as project manager after work on the project begins. You learn how to save a copy of the finalized project plan to use as a baseline for comparisons. This chapter teaches you how to track the actual beginning and ending dates for tasks, the actual work amounts, and the actual costs.

Chapter 17, "Analyzing Progress and Revising the Schedule," is an important presentation of ways to look at the tracking information to see how well the project is meeting its objectives. Project offers many techniques and reports that you will learn to use in this chapter.

Part VI: Coordinating Projects and Sharing Data

The chapters in Part VI discuss more advanced topics that the beginning user will usually not encounter initially—therefore they are separated from the earlier Parts' flow covering the basic steps of developing and tracking a project schedule.

Chapter 18, "Working with Multiple Projects," explains how to link one or more subprojects to a master or summary project and how to link an individual task in one project to a task in another project. You also learn how to consolidate multiple projects and how to manage multiple projects that share a common resource pool.

Chapter 19, "Exporting and Importing Project Data with Other File Formats," shows you how to export and import task, resource, and cost data with other applications and file formats, including the database formats. You also learn how to save entire projects in database formats.

Chapter 20, "Copying, Pasting, and Inserting Data with Other Applications," shows you how to copy and paste selected data and objects between Project and other applications. You learn how to copy Project's timephased data into other applications and how to manage both embedded and linked objects in Project and in other applications.

Part VII: Working with Views and Reports

The chapters in Part VII teach you how to take advantage of the extensive options that Microsoft Project provides for displaying the data in your project. Some of the views and reports are mentioned in earlier chapters as the need arises. This section provides a comprehensive reference to all the major views and reports.

Chapter 21, "Using the Standard Views, Tables, and Filters," explains the many options for using tables, forms, graphic images, and filters to display your project in a view.

Chapter 22, "Formatting Views," provides all you need to know about the formatting options for all the major views. You'll also find procedures, including tips and techniques, for changing the appearance of graphic elements and text display for categories of items and individual items.

Chapter 23, "Customizing Views, Tables, Fields, and Filters," shows you how to create your own views, with custom tables and filters, to display just the detail that you want for your projects.

Chapter 24, "Using the Standard Reports," explains how to use the standard reports to supplement the printed views.

Chapter 25, "Customizing Reports," explains how you can change the display elements in reports.

Part VIII: Customizing and Programming Microsoft Project 2000

The chapters in Part VIII cover programming and customizing the Microsoft Project interface.

Chapter 26, "Customizing Toolbars, Menus, and Forms," is placed after the programming chapters only because you will typically customize a toolbar or menu to run your macros or Visual Basic procedures. This chapter explains the options for customizing the way Microsoft Project works. You learn how to change the standard toolbar buttons and how to attach commands and macros to a button. You learn also how to customize menus and how to create your own forms for data entry and review.

Chapter 27, "Introduction to Visual Basic Macros with Project 2000," is a basic guide for nonprogrammers who want to record and use simple macros.

Chapter 28, "Developing Visual Basic Macros," is for programmers or individuals who understand Visual Basic but want help in identifying the methods and properties available in Microsoft Project. This chapter walks you through situational macros that you can apply to your own day-to-day activities.

Part IX: Appendixes

The appendixes of Part IX provide reference material that applies to more than one chapter or section of the book.

Appendix A, "Reviewing the Basics of Project Management," is a brief introduction to project management for those who are new to the responsibility or profession.

Appendix B, "Microsoft Project 2000 Shortcut Keys," is a partial listing of the most commonly used special keys and key combinations in Microsoft Project.

Appendix C, "Companion Products for Microsoft Project 2000," describes some of the software products that you can buy to enhance Microsoft Project. The products are grouped by vendor and each is described briefly.

Last, there is a Glossary listing some of the most commonly used terms found in this book, and it is especially helpful to those who are new to project management. As an added bonus, you'll find a Field Reference document on the CD that accompanies this book. It's a comprehensive listing designed to help you understand how to use the Microsoft Project fields when using or customizing filters, tables, and forms; when using Import/Export maps; and when creating VBA macros.

There is also additional information, articles, sample Project files, and macros available to you at the Web site for this book. Please visit www.quepublishing.com and enter this book's ISBN number (0789722534) in the Search window.

SPECIAL FEATURES IN THIS BOOK

This book contains a variety of special features to help you find the information you need—fast. Formatting conventions are used to make important keywords or special text obvious. Specific language is used so as to make keyboard and mouse actions clear. And a variety of visual elements are used to make important and useful information stand out. The following sections describe the special features used in this book.

VISUAL AIDS

Notes, Tips, Cautions, and other visual aids give you useful information, and icons in the margin draw your attention to topics of special interest. The following are descriptions of each element.

 New features that are introduced in Microsoft Project 2000 are flagged with an icon in the margin.

Note

Notes provide useful information that isn't essential to the discussion. They usually contain more technical information, but can also contain interesting but less critical information.

Tip from Tim and the Project Team

Tips enhance your experience with Project 2000 by providing hints and tricks you won't find elsewhere.

Caution

Cautions warn you that a particular action can cause severe harm to your project schedule. Given the many not-so-obvious calculations that Project processes at every turn, you shouldn't skip the cautions in this book.

Cross-references point you to specific sections within other chapters so that you can get more information that's related to the topic you're reading about. Here is what a cross-reference looks like:

→ To learn more about working with your project plans, **see** "Starting and Exiting Microsoft Project," **p. 29**

Sidebars Are Interesting Nuggets of Information
Sidebars are detours from the main text. They usually provide background or interesting information that is relevant but not essential reading. You might find information that's a bit more technical than the surrounding text, or you might find a brief diversion into the historical aspects of the text.

SPECIAL FEATURES

You'll also find the following special features in this book:

Best Practice Tips from Toby Brown, PMP

Best Practice tips from Toby Brown, PMP, will help you learn the ins and outs of effective project management. These tips from Toby are related to the project management process recommended by the Project Management Institute. As a certified project manager and Project software user, Toby's tips will help you along with the responsibilities of managing projects both with and without software.

At the end of each chapter, there is a Troubleshooting section that highlights anticipated problems you might have and provides a solution. The problem is stated in bold type, and the answer or solution follows.

KEYBOARD CONVENTIONS

In addition to the special features that help you find what you need, this book uses some special conventions to make it easier to read:

Feature	Convention
Hotkeys	Hotkeys are underlined in this book, just as they appear in Windows 95 menus. To use a hotkey, press Alt and the underlined key. For example, the F in File is a hotkey that activates the File menu.
Key combinations	Key combinations are joined with the plus sign (+). Alt+F, for example, means hold down the Alt key, press the F key, and then release both keys.
Menu commands	A comma is used to separate the parts of a pull-down menu command. For example, choosing File, New means to open the File menu and select the New option.

In most cases, special-purpose keys are referred to by the text that actually appears on them on a standard 101-key keyboard. For example, press Esc, press F1, or press Enter. Some of the keys on your keyboard don't actually have words on them. So here are the conventions used in this book for those keys:

- The Backspace key, which is labeled with a left arrow, usually is located directly above the Enter key. The Tab key usually is labeled with two arrows pointing to lines, with one arrow pointing right and the other arrow pointing left.

- The cursor keys, labeled on most keyboards with arrows pointing up, down, right, and left, are called the up-arrow key, down-arrow key, right-arrow key, and left-arrow key.

- Case is not important unless explicitly stated. So "Press A" and "press a" mean the same thing.

FORMATTING CONVENTIONS

This book also uses some special typeface conventions to help you understand what you're reading:

Convention	Description
Italic	Italic indicates new terms. It also indicates place holders in commands and addresses.
Bold	Bold indicates text you type.
`Monospace`	This typeface is used for onscreen messages and commands that you type. It also indicates addresses on the Internet.
Myfile.doc	Windows filenames and folders are capitalized to help you distinguish them from regular text.

GETTING STARTED WITH MICROSOFT PROJECT 2000

THE POWER OF MICROSOFT PROJECT 2000

In this chapter

EXPLORING PROJECT MANAGEMENT

You were anxious to try out the new Microsoft Project software; to get your hands on keyboard and mouse and to see how it all works. So, you dove right in… and now you're looking for additional help. That's perfectly understandable, because becoming a confident user of Microsoft Project is not easy—especially if you don't have a project management background. There are many special terms to learn (such as *critical path*, *task dependencies*, and *leveling resources*), and most of the screens in Project are unlike any you've seen in Word or Excel. You will learn faster if you start with some understanding of the special requirements of project management. So, unless you're an old hand at project management, take the time to browse through this chapter.

Project management differs from conventional management in that managing a *project* is more limited and narrowly focused than managing an enterprise, or even managing a small department within an organization. Traditional management functions are concerned with managing the ongoing operations of an organization to assure its long-run success and survival. In contrast, project management is concerned with *temporary* goals of the organization.

PROJECTS ARE TEMPORARY

A project is a temporary assignment relative to the life of the organization, lasting only until the project's stated objectives are achieved. A project involves a one-time goal, produces a unique product or outcome, and has a defined start and finish date.

Managing a department or division is an ongoing assignment that extends into the future, perhaps for the life of the organization and the manager. Problems and challenges come and go; providing continuity is an inherent aspect of departmental management.

For example, selecting and installing a new word processor is a project; ongoing management of the word processing pool is not a project.

Defining projects and project management by the terms *temporary* and *short-term* is relative. A sales project might have a life of two weeks, and a project to build a nuclear power plant might have a life of twenty years. But both are shorter than the life span of the organization; both are temporary.

PROJECT OBJECTIVES ARE SPECIFIC AND MEASURABLE

Project goals are stated in terms of specific performance objectives. Vague generalities that call for unspecified improvements won't provide the focus needed for a project.

You can measure the success or failure of a project by the degree to which the measured performance satisfies the objectives set out in the goal.

Best Practice Tips from Toby Brown, PMP

It is often said that you can't manage what you can't measure. Project management offers the opportunity to improve on-going operations, fulfill the strategic vision of the organization, and rise above crisis management, a mode of "fire fighting" many of us constantly employ. It concentrates on organized task management by recognizing the details while still maintaining the big picture.

PROJECTS ARE CONSTRAINED BY TIME, COST, AND QUALITY

A project exists to deliver a specific performance objective, and the quality of the performance must be satisfactory while staying within the time allowed and without going over the budget.

Usually, either the project start or finish date (or both) must meet some time requirement. The overall time constraint needs to be explicitly incorporated into the project goal statement. Individual tasks of the project might also be subject to time constraints.

Projects are subject to resource or cost constraints because there is always a limit to how much money you can spend to achieve the project objectives.

Projects frequently require resources that are already in demand elsewhere in the organization. The project manager must compete for resources with other projects and with the ongoing operations of the organization. Resources are usually the main source of cost for a project.

Scholarly studies about project management usually define a *project* as a collection of activities or tasks designed to achieve a unique temporary goal of the organization, with specific performance requirements, and subject to time and cost constraints.

For an excellent paper on the full scope of project management, I recommend "A Guide to the Project Management Body of Knowledge," which you can download from the Web site of the Project Management Institute at `http://www.pmi.org`. PMI is the most important professional organization for project managers in general and the PMI Web site is the single most important site for project management information. PMI is also the organization responsible for administering the Project Management Professional or "PMP" certification exam.

A successful project must meet deadlines, stay within budget, and meet its performance objectives according to specifications.

The manager of a project is responsible for planning the actions or tasks that will achieve the project objectives and for organizing the resources of the organization to carry out the plan. He or she must apply management principles to plan, organize, staff, control, and direct resources of the organization to successfully complete the project. That includes, of course, keeping all participants in the project informed about the project plan.

The staffing function for project management is often a question of negotiating resource commitments with internal line managers instead of recruiting new employees. The personnel often come from the existing work force, and the facilities and equipment often must be shared with the regular operations of the organization. Moreover, the project manager is not necessarily the supervisor for the resources that are used in a project—this function is usually the job of a line manager.

Best Practice Tips from Toby Brown, PMP

The type of organization will greatly impact how resources are deployed. The organizational structure of the performing organization can run the spectrum from functional to projectized with various matrix structures in between. Details of key project-related characteristics of the major types of enterprise organizational structures are well-documented in PMI's Guide to the Project Management Book of Knowledge.

WHAT CAN MICROSOFT PROJECT 2000 DO FOR YOU?

Microsoft Project 2000 helps you achieve your project goal on time and on budget. Computer software can aid significantly in project management as a tool for recording, calculating, analyzing, and preparing presentations to help communicate the details of the project. However, Microsoft Project cannot produce or even guarantee a successful project plan any more than Microsoft Word can produce or guarantee a successful computer book. Still, Microsoft Project can be invaluable in planning and managing your projects:

- *Microsoft Project helps you develop a better plan.* Because the software requires you to specify precisely the tasks necessary for meeting the project goal, you must think carefully about the details of the project. The discipline imposed by entering these details helps you organize a better plan.

  The screen views provide an organized presentation of the details of your plan, which can improve your ability to visualize, organize, and refine the plan.

- *Microsoft Project makes calculated projections easier and more reliable.* Based on the data you enter, the computer calculates a schedule that shows when each task should begin and end and when specific resources are scheduled to perform specific tasks. If you have provided the necessary data, this schedule also shows the probable costs of the project.

- *Microsoft Project makes it easy to test various "what if" scenarios to search for the optimum project plan.* The computer lets you experiment with different elements of the plan to arrive at the best plan for your organization.

- *Microsoft Project helps you detect inconsistencies and problems in the plan.* The computer detects when resources are scheduled for more hours than they are available or when deadlines are impossible to meet given the constraints you've entered. The computer helps you find and resolve resource over-allocations and problems with deadlines.

- *Microsoft Project helps you communicate the plan to others.* The software provides printed reports and Internet HTML displays that make it easier to get the customer's or upper-level management's approval for the plan. Similarly, it makes it easier to communicate the plan to supervisors and workers, and that simplifies getting their approval and cooperation. The ease with which you can produce useful reports has been one of the main selling points for Microsoft Project over the years.

- *Microsoft Project helps you track progress and detect potential difficulties.* After the project is under way, you replace the projected dates for the tasks in the schedule with actual dates as work on the tasks is begun and completed. The software revises the schedule to incorporate these actual dates and it projects new completion dates and costs. This new projection provides you with valuable advance warning of potential delays or cost over-runs, so you can take corrective measures if necessary.

  If external circumstances change after the project is underway—for example, when new pay rates go into effect or your organization is subject to new regulations—the software makes it easier to adjust the plan and see the consequences.

It cannot be stressed too much, however, that project management software, like any soft-ware, is only as useful as the reliability and completeness of the data you supply. And that, my friends, takes lots and lots of time. So plan on it—or hire someone to take care of it for you.

Best Practice Tips from Toby Brown, PMP

"Buy-in" from the project stakeholders greatly insures the success or failure of a project. The stakeholders include not only the project manager and performing organization, but also the customer who ends up using the product of the project and the sponsor who is the individual or group within the performing organization who provides the financial resources for the project.

SOME GENERAL, COMMON-SENSE GUIDELINES FOR PROJECT MANAGERS

These guidelines are offered to help promote your success with your project. Most of them are common-sense management techniques, but reviewing them from time to time is always a useful exercise:

- Remember that your success as a project manager depends largely on your ability to motivate people to cooperate in the project. No software program or well-designed plan can compensate for ineffective people skills. Computers might respond to logic, but people respond to human emotions.

- Establish your authority as project manager and your role as coordinator of project planning at the outset. If you are appointed, ask the officer making the appointment to distribute a statement that validates your authority. Don't post it outside your door unless you provide cork backing as protection against sharp-pointed projectiles.

- Make the planning stage a group effort as much as possible. You're sure to find that you can't think of everything, and a wider base of experience and expertise is immensely helpful. And you will find it much easier to secure approval of the plan and to get peo-ple committed to the plan if they help in its formulation.

- Set a clear project goal:
    - State the goal of the project precisely and simply in a manner that everyone associated with the project can understand. This includes your supervisors who approve the project, managers who work with the project, and those who actually do the work. Prepare a concise summary statement of the project goal. State your goal in realistic and attainable terms that can be measured. It will then be possible to measure success.
    - Secure agreement on the goal by all who must approve the project or who must provide supervision during the execution of the project.
    - State a definite time frame in the goal—it should be part of the commitment to the project. The goal "Install a new word processor throughout the company," for example, is ill defined. "Select and install a new word processor throughout the company and train all personnel in its use by June 1" is measurable.
    - Define the performance requirements and specifications carefully.
    - Discover and record all fixed deadlines or time constraints.
    - Determine the budgetary limitations of the project.
    - State the performance or quality specifications of the project with great care. Write and then distribute these specifications, in a Statement of Work, to the creators of the specifications and to the supervisors and workers when they are assigned to tasks. Make sure no misunderstanding exists about what you expect. Misunderstood specifications can jeopardize the project's success.
- Organize the work of the project into major phases or components and establish *milestones*, or interim goals, to mark the completion of each of these phases. Milestones serve as checkpoints by which everyone can gauge how well the project is on target after the work begins. This is a *top-down* approach, and it provides organization for the project plan from the outset.

    For example, the conversion to a new word processing product might involve the following phases and milestones (the milestones are italicized):
    - Select the software

        Determine the features required

        Review available products

        Select the product

        Software selection complete
    - Acquire and install the software

        Buy the software

        Set up help desk

        Install software

        Software installed

- Convert to the new software

  Convert old documents

  Train users

  Conversion complete

- Define the work that must be completed to reach each milestone as distinct tasks and estimate how long each task will take. If a task takes too long (some say any more than 10 days!) you will probably be better off breaking it down into more components.

- Diagram the flow of activity to show the instances where tasks must be performed in a specific sequence.

- Distribute the project plan to all who are responsible for supervising or doing the work. Secure their agreement that the assumptions of the plan are sound and that all involved are willing to do their part. Revise the plan as needed to secure agreement.

- Distribute printed copies of the revised schedule with charts and tables to identify clearly the scope of the project and the responsibilities of all who must contribute to making the project a success.

- Secure from resources their firm commitment to do the work assignments outlined in the plan.

- After work on the project is under way, monitor progress by tracking actual performance and entering the results in the project plan. This is the best way to discover problems early so you can take corrective actions before disaster strikes.

  Tracking these performance details also helps document the history of the project so you can learn from the experience. It's especially helpful if you have problems meeting the goals, and will be valuable to you if you have to explain why the project goals are not met.

  If problems arise that jeopardize finishing the project on time or within budget, you can give superiors ample warning so they can adjust their expectations.

- After the project is completed, acknowledge all participants who made the project a success.

A CHECKLIST FOR USING MICROSOFT PROJECT

Microsoft Project is so rich with options you easily can lose sight of the forest as you explore all the interesting new trees. The following sections give you an overview of planning a project with Microsoft Project.

PRELIMINARIES

Before you start entering tasks in the computer, it's a good idea to define some basic parameters that govern how Microsoft Project treats your data. (These topics are covered in detail in Chapter 3, "Setting Up a New Project Document.")

1. Customize Microsoft Project's calendar of working time to define when the computer can schedule work on the project. This includes defining your organization's working days, non-working days, and regular working hours. And, while you're at it, be sure that you use the terms *day* and *week* to mean the same number of hours that Microsoft Project does.

Tip from Tim and the Project Team

> When you enter a task that you estimate will take a day or a week, Project translates those terms into hours (actually minutes, but hours will do for this explanation). If your "day" is not eight hours, or your "week" is not forty hours, you must define those terms for Project, or it will interpret your estimate incorrectly.

2. Enter some basic descriptions for the project: a project title, the name of the organization, the project manager, and the expected start or finish date. These descriptions will appear on reports.

3. Prepare a list of the resources you will use in the project. This includes defining resource costs and recognizing working days and hours when a resource is not available. You can add names to the list later, but most users like to have the list ready when they start entering the tasks in the planning phase.

PLANNING

Planning is the phase in which you outline the project plan, refine it, and distribute it to all who are involved in the project. These topics are explored in detail in Chapters 5 through 15.

1. List the major phases of the project in outline form and then fill in the detailed tasks and milestones in the project. Estimate how long each task will take or how much work is involved. This is the topic of Chapter 5, "Creating a Task List."

2. If the start or finish date of a task is constrained to a fixed date, enter the date at this point. Also define the required sequencing of tasks, that is to say where tasks must be scheduled in a certain order. These topics are covered in Chapter 6, "Entering Scheduling Requirements." You can view the schedule in several different ways. See Chapter 7, "Viewing Your Schedule," for a quick overview of the possibilities.

3. Define the resources and assign them to tasks. Defining and assigning resources is covered in Chapter 8, "Defining Resources and Costs," and Chapter 9, "Understanding Resource Scheduling."

4. Assign all fixed costs to the tasks. Fixed costs are covered in Chapter 10, "Assigning Resources and Costs to Tasks."

5. Review the schedule that Microsoft Project has calculated so far, and correct all problems by taking the actions discussed in the following list:

   - Identify and resolve scheduling problems where deadlines can't be met or where resources are assigned to do more work than they have the time to do. These problems are discussed in Chapter 6 and Chapter 11, "Resolving Resource Assignment Problems."

- Identify costs that are over budget and find ways to lower the costs as described in Chapter 12, "Reviewing the Project Plan."
- If the time constraint for the overall project is not met by the schedule, you must find ways to revise the schedule to meet the requirements of the project goal.

Auditing and refining the schedule are covered in Chapter 12.

6. Distribute the project schedule for review by the managers who must approve the plan and by project supervisors and workers who must agree to do the work. Publishing the project schedule and assignments is covered in Chapter 13, "Printing Views and Reports," Chapter 14, "Publishing Projects on the Web," and Chapter 15, "Using Microsoft Project in Workgroups."

7. Revise the plan, if necessary, to accommodate suggestions or changes submitted in the review (see Chapter 12).

8. Print and distribute the final schedule to all parties for final approval, and secure from each party a firm commitment to the plan.

MANAGING THE PROJECT

In this phase, you monitor progress on the project, recording actual experience and calculating a new schedule when actual dates fail to match the planned dates. These topics are covered in Chapter 16, "Tracking Work on the Project," and Chapter 17, "Analyzing Progress and Revising the Schedule."

1. Make a baseline (original) copy of the final schedule plan to use later for comparing actual start and finish dates with the planned dates.

2. Track actual start dates, finish dates, percentage of work completed, and costs incurred, and enter these details into the computer. Microsoft Project incorporates these changes in the schedule and calculates a revised schedule with revised cost figures.

3. Review the recalculated schedule for problems and, if possible, take corrective measures. Notify all participants about changes in the schedule that concern them.

4. After the project is completed, prepare final reports as documentation to show the actual work and costs and to compare those with the baseline copy of the plan you saved earlier.

Best Practice Tips from Toby Brown, PMP

Tracking progress moves the project manager into the Controlling process of the iterative process model of Project Management (Initiating, Planning, Executing, Controlling, and Closing). It ensures that the project objectives are being met by monitoring and measuring progress by comparing actual progress against the baseline and taking corrective action, if necessary.

PROJECT MANAGEMENT SCHEDULING TECHNIQUES

The methods used by project management software to schedule dates and times for tasks (and the resources assigned to them) is ingenious. You will need to understand the general concepts if you are to use Microsoft Project effectively. However, you don't need to master the details of how calculations are made. Although the applications of these methods are reviewed as needed in upcoming chapters, gaining an overview can be useful before you get into the details of planning and coordinating a project.

YOU MUST PROVIDE THE RAW DATA

You must provide accurate task information for Microsoft Project to calculate a schedule for your project. This usually requires a lot of guesswork; but without it, Project won't be as helpful to you. The less time you take in putting together reasonable task information, the less likely the computer projections will be reasonable.

- Enter a list of all the tasks that must be scheduled to complete the project. You must include the duration of each task (how long it should take to do the work). Include as milestones any major turning points in the project, such as the end of a major phase or a point where new decision making is called for.

Best Practice Tips from Toby Brown, PMP

> Estimating and entering how long it will take to complete a task can be represented several ways when assigning a duration to a task. The task duration may be thought of as the amount of expected effort a task may take to complete (regardless of how the duration is expressed—minutes, hours, days, or weeks) or it can be the allowable time for a task within the project. In other words, you might believe a task will take 40 hours of work to complete (one week) or you might not care how many hours of work is required, so long as it is completed within one week's time. Either way, the duration for the task would be expressed as one week.

- You also must include any sequencing requirements (dependencies) that will govern when the task can be scheduled. A *sequencing requirement* is a requirement that the scheduled date for a task has to be tied to the scheduled date for some other task. When you build a house, for example, you schedule the carpenters to start erecting the walls after the date the foundation has been finished. You link the date for starting the walls to the date when the foundation is scheduled to be finished.

- If a task must start or finish by a specific date, enter this requirement as a constraint on the scheduling of the task. For example, you might stipulate that a certain task can't start until the third fiscal quarter, due to cash flow problems. Or, you might have a contract that requires that a task be finished by a specific date. When calculating a schedule of dates for tasks, Microsoft Project normally schedules each task to begin as soon as possible, considering the task's position in the sequence of tasks. However, it will take note of your constraints and warn you if the schedule doesn't allow constraints to be met.

THE CALENDAR USED FOR SCHEDULING

Microsoft Project uses its internal standard calendar to calculate a schedule for the tasks. The default standard calendar has no holidays and assumes that work can be scheduled eight hours a day from 8:00 a.m. to 5:00 p.m., Monday through Friday, with one hour for lunch. You must customize the standard calendar to make it represent the workdays and shifts of your organization. This standard calendar will be used to schedule all tasks that do not have resources assigned to them.

HOW PROJECT CALCULATES THE SCHEDULE

Project starts calculating a schedule when you enter the first task. With each added detail, the schedule is updated. The primary method used in project management software for scheduling is called the Critical Path Method (CPM).

The CPM method calculates the overall duration of the project by chaining tasks together in their required sequences and then summing up the combined duration of all tasks in the chain.

Figure 1.1 illustrates a simple project that contains six tasks and a Project Finish milestone task. Tasks A, B, and C must be performed in sequence; tasks X, Y, and Z must also be performed in sequence. Both sequences can occur at the same time; however, both sequences must finish before the project is complete.

Figure 1.1
The longest sequence of tasks (the critical path) determines the finish date for the project.

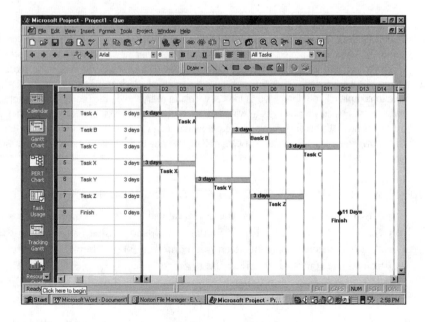

If parallel task sequences are in progress at the same time, the overall duration of the project is the duration of the longest of these task sequences. In Figure 1.1, the sequence A-B-C takes 11 days, and the sequence X-Y-Z takes nine days. It takes 11 days to complete the project—the duration of the longest sequence.

You cannot complete the project on schedule unless the tasks on the longest sequence are finished on schedule. These tasks, known as *critical tasks*, are vital to keeping the overall project on schedule. A sequence of critical tasks is called a *critical path*. All tasks on the critical path must be finished on time as scheduled or the finish date for the project will slip.

In Figure 1.1, tasks A, B, and C are critical tasks, and the sequence A-B-C is the critical path. The X, Y, and Z tasks are not critical to finishing the project on time. You could delay the completion of any one of these tasks for up to two days without causing a delay of the overall project. The X, Y, and Z non-critical tasks are said to have *slack*.

Critical tasks do not have slack. These tasks cannot be delayed if the project is to finish on schedule. So, having zero slack is one way to identify or define a critical task.

Best Practice Tips from Toby Brown, PMP

The term "critical" is often misused and misunderstood in traditional business practice. Many times when you hear someone refer to an important task as "critical," the perception is that the task has a higher priority within the project based on its content. However, "critical" does not necessarily mean "important" to a project manager. The term "critical" to a formally trained project manager means that it contributes to the longest path in the project, not only an important component or step. All tasks in a project are "important" or else they wouldn't be included and would, therefore, be outside of scope. However, not all tasks are "critical."

Why Should You Care About the Critical Path?

Identifying the critical tasks is an important time-saver in managing a project. Suppose you need to shorten the duration of the overall project (commonly known as *crashing* the schedule), and you're looking for tasks for which you can shorten the duration to accomplish that. (For example, you might add more resources to a task to finish its work sooner, or you might reduce the scope of a task or the quality of the work so that it takes less time to complete.) You don't have to look at each and every task in the project to find potential timesavings; you can safely limit your analysis to ways to shorten the critical tasks and not worry about shortening the non-critical tasks. That's because reducing the duration of non-critical tasks would have no effect on the finish date. This knowledge can save you a great deal of time in trying to find ways to shorten the project schedule.

HOW RESOURCE ASSIGNMENTS AFFECT THE SCHEDULE

If you assign resources to tasks, the calculated schedule can change dramatically. Every resource has its own scheduling calendar, which shows those times when the resource is not available (such as vacations or attending conferences) or when the resource is available in addition to the standard times for the organization. The project's base calendar is used to calculate schedules for tasks that have no resources assigned to them. When a resource is assigned, the task schedule will change to reflect the availability of the resource.

Changing the number of resources assigned to a task also affects its schedule. Some tasks have a *fixed duration*: no matter how many workers or resources you assign to the task, the duration remains unchanged. If you scheduled a task to deliver a small package to a customer in an outlying suburb, for example, you would assign a driver and a truck. You probably couldn't shorten the duration of the task by placing two drivers in the truck. In that case, the task would have a fixed duration. If, however, the task were to deliver a truckload of packages, a second driver could reduce the time it takes to load and unload the packages, and thus reduce the duration of the task. If changing the quantity of resources assigned to a task leads to a change in the duration of the task, the task's duration is said to be *resource driven* (also called *effort driven*). The schedule for the task is driven or determined by the quantity of resources assigned to the task.

Microsoft Project assumes that tasks are resource driven—that is, that they are *not* fixed-duration tasks. If a task has a fixed duration, you must define the task explicitly as fixed duration. The program assumes that you can shorten the duration of a task if you increase the resources assigned to do the work.

Note

> If you're experienced with Microsoft Project 98, scan Chapter 5 and Chapter 6 for some of the new features—especially task calendars. Spend some time in Chapter 9 and Chapter 11 to learn about the many changes in the way Project calculates schedules for resource assignments.
>
> If you're new to Project, go on to Chapter 2, "Learning the Basics of Microsoft Project," for a review of the Microsoft Project user interface and then continue with the chapter order that follows.

TROUBLESHOOTING

PROVIDING ACCESS TO RELATED DOCUMENTS

I already have a lot of documents about the project I am planning. Can I store those in Microsoft Project?

As you'll see in Chapter 3 and in Chapter 5 you can provide links to other documents in the notes you write about the project or about individual tasks.

DETERMINING THE LEVEL OF DETAIL TO INCLUDE IN THE TASK LIST

How do you decide how finely to subdivide the work into distinct tasks?

You will want individual tasks to be long enough to manage easily. A good general rule of thumb is to subdivide the work into tasks that are at least a day long and no more than two weeks long. If you have weekly status meetings for the project, you may want to create tasks that are no more than a week long. That makes it much easier to keep track of progress and to know very early when things are falling behind.

These are general guidelines. If a project is extremely time critical—for instance, a project like upgrading equipment which would necessarily disrupt other operations—you might want to subdivide the work into tasks that are as short as an hour.

CHAPTER

2

LEARNING THE BASICS OF MICROSOFT PROJECT

In this chapter

STARTING AND EXITING MICROSOFT PROJECT

You are undoubtedly anxious to build your first project (or work on one you have inherited). However, to get the most productivity out of Microsoft Project, you need to become familiar with initiating the program and all the screen elements you'll be working with.

When Microsoft Project is installed on a machine that uses Windows, the Setup program places Microsoft Project on the Start menu, under Programs. To start Microsoft Project, choose Start, Programs, Microsoft Project (see Figure 2.1).

Figure 2.1
You can add a short-cut on your Windows desktop to start Microsoft Project. Choose Start, Help and type **shortcuts** in the search keyword text box to learn how.

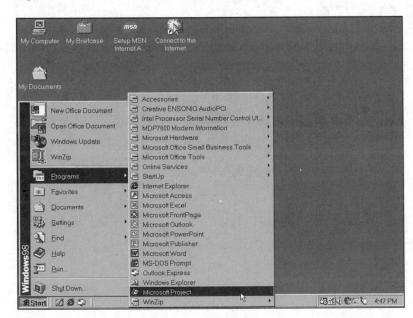

The program initially displays a new project window in the background and the new Microsoft Project Help window in the foreground (see Figure 2.2). The Help window is sometimes referred to as the *Help Home Page*, because it uses the same features found on a Web site home or default page. This window displays a number of built-in help features you can use to become more proficient with Microsoft Project. Even if you are an experienced Project user, the items in the Help window will be useful as you learn this version of Project.

Each of the items in the Help window is a link to a help feature in Microsoft Project. When you position the mouse pointer on a feature name, the pointer changes to a hand. Click the feature name to access the help information.

Note

Throughout this book you will see instructions to "click" or "right-click" with your mouse button. The instructions to "click" refer to using your primary mouse button. By default, this is the left mouse button. Instructions to "right-click" refer to using the other mouse button (sometimes called the *secondary* mouse button). If you have switched the mouse button settings (through the Control Panel), you will need to remember that instructions which will ask you to right-click are asking you to use the secondary mouse button.

Figure 2.2
The main Help window has been redesigned in Project 2000 to appear and function like an Internet Web page.

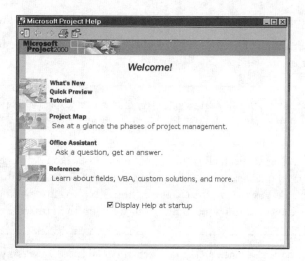

The following list briefly describes the choices in the Microsoft Project Help window:

- **What's New**—A list describing the most significant features that are new in Project 2000.

- **Quick Preview**—A short presentation (five screens) that provides a good introduction to Microsoft Project.

- **Tutorial**—A lesson-based approach to building and managing a project for people new to Microsoft Project.

- **Project Map**—More in-depth than the tutorial, this tool provides a road map of the steps you'll follow to create and manage a project. The Project Map outlines the three main phases of any project—Build a Plan, Track and Manage a Project, and Close a Project. Under each phase you'll find specific topics to help you progress through each of the phases.

- **Office Assistant**—When you have a specific question you need the answer to, use the Office Assistant. For example, when you type **create calendars** in the Office Assistant search box, a list of help topics relating to calendars appears.

- **Reference**—This feature contains a wealth of information about Microsoft Project, including descriptions of all the fields, troubleshooting tips, mouse and keyboard shortcuts, assistance with using Visual Basic for Applications (VBA) in Microsoft Project, a glossary of complex or confusing terms, and the Microsoft Project specifications and limits.

Each of these features is explained in more detail later in this chapter.

Note

If you don't want the Help window to display each time you open Microsoft Project, you can uncheck the Display Help at Startup box at the bottom of the window. You will still be able to display this window and access these features through the Help menu.

Use the Close button in the upper-right corner of the Help window to close the window.

To exit Microsoft Project, choose File, Exit or click the application Close button in the upper-right corner of the window.

Tip from Tim and the Project Team	You also can use the Alt+F4 shortcut key combination to quickly close an application. You will be prompted to save your latest changes before the application closes.

When you exit Microsoft Project, all open project files close. If any changes have been made in a project file since you last saved it, a dialog box prompts you to save the changes before closing the file. Choose Yes to save the changes; choose No to close without saving the changes; or choose Cancel if you want to return to work on the project.

Note	When you save a new project, the Planning Wizard appears and asks you about saving a baseline for the project. The *baseline* is a copy of the way the schedule looks at this moment, and is most useful for comparing later versions of the schedule with the original intentions.
	The Planning Wizard message that appears will vary, depending on whether or not the Office Assistant is active on the screen. See the section "Using the Office Assistant," later in this chapter, for an explanation and illustration of the message differences. For now, choose the option not to save a baseline.

Best Practice Tips from Toby Brown, PMP	A good practice of Project Management is to save a baseline when ready to commit to the schedule. Since baselining a project usually isn't done until the project is fully developed, it is suggested that you dismiss the Planning Wizard by checking the Don't Tell Me About This Again check box at the bottom of the Planning Wizard. Otherwise, you'll be prompted to save a baseline every time updates to the project are saved.
	You can always save the baseline when ready to do so as described later in this book. And turning the feature back on again is accomplished by placing a check mark under the options dialog box referring to advice about scheduling.

→ To learn how to effectively take advantage of the Office Assistant, **see** "Using the Office Assistant," **p. 41**

→ To understand what a baseline is, and why it is important to establish one for your project, **see** "Setting the Baseline or Plan," **p. 660**

EXPLORING THE MICROSOFT PROJECT WINDOW

After you've moved past the Help window, you see the Microsoft Project title bar at the top of the screen, along with the menu bar, two toolbars, and the Entry bar. In the center of the screen is an area used to display the data in your project, called the *view*. The term view refers to the way the project data appears. On the left side of the screen is the View bar (first introduced in Project 98). The View bar enables you to quickly switch between views and helps identify which view you currently have displayed. The status bar is visible at the bottom of the screen. Figure 2.3 shows a project displayed in the Gantt Chart view.

Figure 2.3
The Gantt Chart is the most commonly used view in Microsoft Project.

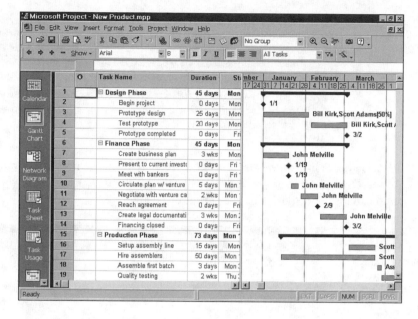

PART

I

CH

2

The default view is the Gantt Chart, which is divided into two parts: a table on the left showing a list of task names, and a timescale on the right where a bar chart will show the beginning and ending of each task.

Some views include graphic representations of your project data. For example, Figure 2.4 shows the new Network Diagram view. This is the same project data shown in Figure 2.3, but this view illustrates the sequencing of tasks in the project, similar to a flow chart.

Figure 2.4
The Network Diagram is a graphic view that shows the sequencing of tasks in the project.

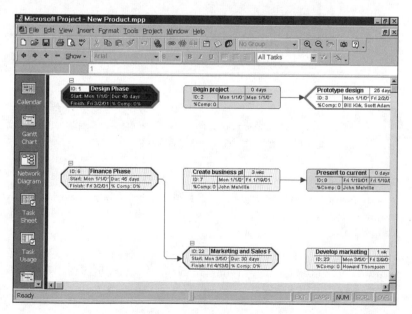

Best Practice Tips from Toby Brown, PMP

The Network Diagram replaces the PERT Chart view from previous versions of Project, which in fact was a misnomer. PERT, or Program Evaluation Review Technique, is a risk-analysis technique used to estimate project duration when there is a high degree of uncertainty with the individual activity durations.

Now correctly named, traditional project management refers to a network diagram as Precedence Diagramming Method, or PDM, notation. It is also known as an Activity-on-Node (AON) diagram.

Other views are like spreadsheets or database tables, where the data is arranged in columns and rows. An example of a spreadsheet-like view is the Resource Sheet, which displays information about the resources in your project (see Figure 2.5).

Figure 2.5
People, equipment, supplies, and facilities are considered resources in Microsoft Project.

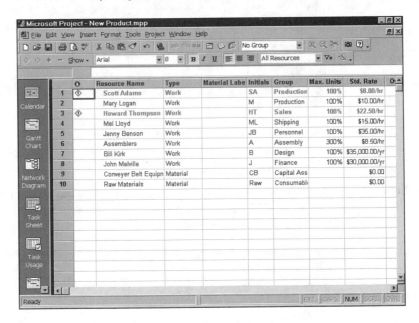

Best Practice Tips from Toby Brown, PMP

It's a good idea to consider materials along with supplies as resources, especially since units can be designated in the resource pool.

Some views are forms that show many details about one task or resource at a time. The Resource Form shows hourly rates and other details for Howard Thompson, one of the resources in this project, along with a list of all the tasks to which he is assigned (see Figure 2.6).

Still other views are combinations of these basic types. The Task Entry view shows the Gantt Chart in the top half of the screen and the Task Form in the bottom half (see Figure 2.7).

Figure 2.6
Among other things, the Resource Form view identifies how much of the resources' time will be devoted to this project (shown in the Max. Units field).

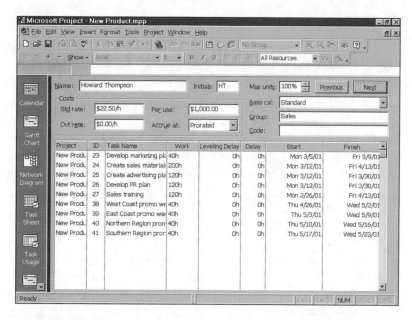

Figure 2.7
The Task Form view (in the bottom half) shows the details for the task selected in the Gantt Chart view.

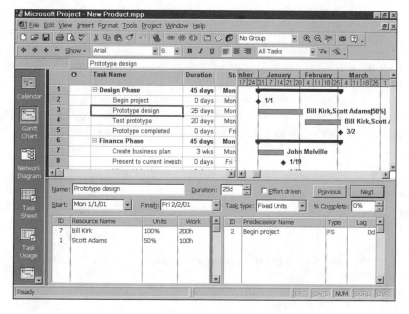

Each of these views draws on the same set of data, but presents it differently. Learning to make effective use of the different views is a key to successfully managing your projects in Microsoft Project. Later in this chapter, you learn how to display other views in Project.

THE MENU BAR

The menus in Microsoft Project are very similar to the menus in the other Microsoft Office products (Word, Excel, PowerPoint, and Access). The menu commands are defined and described in detail in later chapters, as the functions they perform are discussed.

In Project 2000 (as in Office 2000), the menus behave differently from previous versions of the software. When you first click a menu command, the menu initially displays a short subset of commands. As you use other commands, the menu automatically adjusts to show those commands you use frequently. This behavior is referred to as *personalized* menus. You can show the entire set of commands by double-clicking the menu instead of single-clicking.

➔ To turn off the personalized menu bar feature, **see** "Altering the Personalized Toolbar and Menu Behavior," **p. 1050**

THE TOOLBARS

Appearing below the menu bar are the Microsoft Project toolbars. These toolbars contain buttons (that you activate with the mouse) to use as shortcuts to menu commands or special functions. The buttons currently displayed are the most frequently used commands in Microsoft Project.

Like the menus, the toolbars behave differently than in previous versions of the software. By default, the Standard and Formatting toolbars share one row below the menu bar (see Figure 2.8), with the full Standard toolbar and a small portion of the Formatting toolbar displayed. You use the drop-down arrow at the end of a toolbar to see additional buttons. When you use one of the hidden buttons, the toolbar adjusts by hiding a button you haven't used. Thus the toolbars become "personalized" to fit your use. To see the entire group of buttons on each toolbar, they cannot share the same row. You can manually move a toolbar by dragging its move handle, or you can change the setting that controls this behavior in the Customize dialog box.

Note
If you are using Office 2000 and have turned off the personalized menu feature, it will be disabled in Microsoft Project as well. This setting can be changed on the Options tab of the Customize dialog box (Tools, Customize).

➔ To set the toolbars to appear on separate rows, **see** "Altering the Personalized Toolbar and Menu Behavior," **p. 1050**

Figure 2.8
The mouse pointer will change to a four-headed arrow when positioned on a move handle.

The individual buttons on the toolbar are described as you encounter them in the following chapters. When you rest the mouse pointer over the button for a second or two, a brief description (called a *ScreenTip*) appears beneath the toolbar button. For more complete descriptions of the toolbar buttons, use the Microsoft Project Help menu. Choose Help, What's This? and your mouse pointer will have a question mark attached to it. Simply click the toolbar button you are interested in learning more about and a mini help screen will provide you with additional information on that button.

There are nine toolbars provided with Microsoft Project 2000. The two displayed initially are the Standard toolbar and the Formatting toolbar. You can add and remove toolbars to the display, and create your own custom toolbars.

→ To alter the toolbar and menu settings, **see** "Customizing Toolbars and Menus," **p. 1053**

→ To create a custom toolbar that displays only the buttons you use regularly, **see** "Creating New Toolbars," **p. 1064**

The quickest way to show additional toolbars (or to hide ones that are currently displayed) is to use the shortcut menu. Position the mouse pointer over any visible toolbar and right-click to display the shortcut menu (see Figure 2.9). Toolbars that are checked are currently displayed. Choose a checked toolbar to hide it; choose an unchecked toolbar to display it.

Figure 2.9
You can use the short-cut menu to show or hide toolbars. Simply click the toolbar name to change its display status.

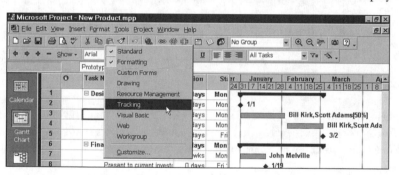

Note

You also can display and hide toolbars through several menu commands—View, Toolbars or Tools, Customize, Toolbars.

THE ENTRY BAR

The Entry bar is on the line below the toolbars (see Figure 2.10). The Entry bar performs several functions:

- The left end of the Entry bar displays progress messages that let you know when Microsoft Project is engaged in calculating, opening and saving files, leveling resources, and so on.

- The center and right portions of the Entry bar contain an entry area where data entry and editing takes place. When you are entering or editing data, Cancel and Enter buttons also appear.

Figure 2.10
The Entry bar is typically used to edit data in your project.

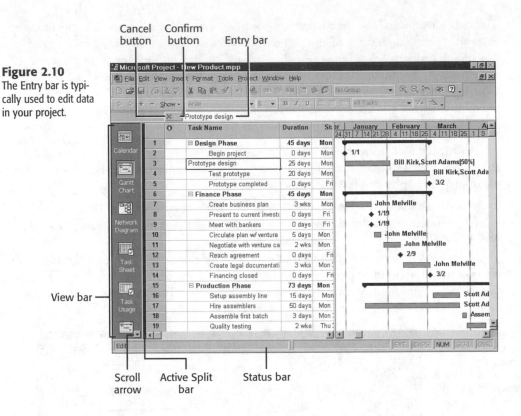

Use the entry area to insert data in a field or to edit data previously placed in a field. You use the entry area primarily when you change data in views that show a spreadsheet-like table, or when you enter task data in the Network Diagram view.

Note

When the Entry bar is active, many features of Microsoft Project are unavailable. Most menu commands, toolbar buttons, and shortcut keys also are unavailable. Make sure you close the Entry bar by pressing Enter or by selecting the Confirm button on the Entry bar (refer to Figure 2.10) after entering or editing data in a field.

THE VIEW BAR

The View bar (first introduced in Project 98) is a handy feature for quickly identifying which view you are looking at and provides you with easy access to switch to the most commonly used views in Project. There is a scroll arrow at the bottom of the View bar to see additional views (refer to Figure 2.10). When you scroll to the bottom of the View bar list there is a More Views option, which takes you to a dialog box listing of all the views available in Microsoft Project.

To show or hide the View bar, choose View, View Bar. Similar to the way views and toolbars are checked, choose the checked View bar to hide it; choose the unchecked View bar to display it.

PART

I

CH

2

Tip from Tim and the Project Team

You also can use the shortcut menu to show or hide the View bar. Right-click to display the shortcut menu and simply click in front of the name View Bar to change its display status.

Whenever the View bar is not being displayed, Project will still indicate which view you are in on the Active Split bar (the thick blue bar between the View bar and the active view). As there are more than 25 views you can work with in Project, the View bar and the Active Split bar will help you to quickly switch between the views and keep track of which view is being displayed. See the section "The Active Split Bar," later in this chapter, for more information.

For a view to appear on the View bar, the view has to be customized to display in the menu (which in turn displays it also in the View bar). Chapter 25, "Customizing Toolbars, Menus, and Forms," describes how to display views in the menu.

→ If you want to list a view you use regularly on the View menu, **see** "Adding Views to the View Menu," **p. 1074**

THE STATUS BAR

The status bar is located at the bottom of the window. It shows the status of special keys and displays advisory messages (refer to Figure 2.10). At the left end of the status bar is the *mode indicator*. This indicator says Ready when Microsoft Project is waiting for you to begin an operation. The mode indicator says Enter when you initially enter data, and it says Edit when you edit a field where you have already entered data. It also is used to provide information for whatever action is currently taking place, including messages when you have a dialog box displayed, when you are opening or saving a file, and when you are previewing the document before printing.

The middle of the status bar displays warning messages when you need to recalculate and when you've created circular relationships while linking tasks. The far right end of the status bar indicates the status of keys on the keyboard—the Extend (EXT), Add (ADD), Caps Lock (CAPS), Num Lock (NUM), Scroll Lock (SCRL), and Insert (OVR) keys. When you turn on one of these keys, the key name appears in the status bar. Use the Office Assistant to look up more information on these keys.

SCREENTIPS

When you rest the mouse pointer on certain items on the screen, a *ScreenTip* provides additional information about that item. In this version of Project you will encounter many more ScreenTips than ever before. These ScreenTips appear primarily in views that contain tables (such as the Gantt Chart and Resource Sheet views), or in graphic views like the timescale side of the Gantt Chart or the Network Diagram view. For example, when you position the mouse pointer in the upper-left corner of the Gantt Chart view (see Figure 2.11), a ScreenTip appears that provides information about the table and view displayed, and indicates you can right-click to select a different table.

Figure 2.11
Simply point to (do not click) an item on the screen to see the ScreenTip.

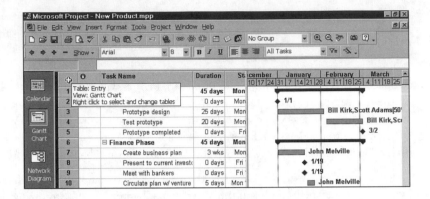

Although not an all-inclusive list, here are several other places you will notice these ScreenTips:

■ When a field in the table side of the Gantt Chart is not completely visible, you can point to the field to display the contents. This occurs when the column is not wide enough to display the data—such as when a task name is particularly lengthy, or when a date or cost figure displays a series of pound symbols (#) instead of the data.

■ When you point to a taskbar or milestone diamond in the timescale side of the Gantt Chart, a ScreenTip appears providing information such as Start Date, Finish Date, and Duration.

■ Pointing to the timescale heading in the Gantt Chart view displays the date range associated with the major or minor scale on which your mouse pointer is resting. So if the major scale is in Months and you point to the month of February, the ScreenTip will display the dates for that month (including February 29 if it is a leap year).

■ If you have zoomed out in the Network Diagram, when you point to a node, the node is magnified so that you can read its fields.

USING THE ONLINE LEARNING AIDS

Microsoft Project has an extensive online help facility, with many special new features to help you learn how to use Project. The learning aids range in complexity from the immediate and brief ScreenTips, to the analytical suggestions and warnings provided by the Planning Wizard, to the procedural steps contained in the Project Map, and a new sophisticated Tutorial to guide you through developing and managing your projects. Each of these online help features is described in the next few sections.

ACCESSING ONLINE HELP

Microsoft Project makes it very easy to get help online. When you start Project, the main Help window (discussed earlier in this chapter) automatically displays to provide assistance. If you have closed that window, there are many other ways to access help online:

■ **The Help Menu**—All your online help alternatives are listed under this menu. You can lookup information through the Contents and Index feature, ask questions of the Office Assistant, view a set of online tutorials, and browse the Microsoft Web site (if you are connected to the Internet) using the Office on the Web command.

- **The Office Assistant**—Instead of going through the Help menu, you can quickly activate the Office Assistant by clicking the Microsoft Project Help button on the Standard toolbar or pressing the F1 key.

- **Context-Sensitive Help**—To access context-sensitive help, choose <u>H</u>elp, What's <u>T</u>his or press Shift+F1. The mouse pointer changes into a question mark and an arrow. You can then choose a menu command or click an area of the screen (such as a toolbar button) about which you want help.

PART

I

CH

2

> **Note**
>
> Many dialog boxes provide context-sensitive help through a button (represented by a question mark) in the upper-right corner of the dialog box. When you click this Help button, the mouse pointer becomes a question mark with an arrow. Then click a feature of the dialog box to see an explanation of that feature.

USING THE OFFICE ASSISTANT

The Office Assistant is one of the quickest ways to get help in Microsoft Project. The Office Assistant will help find answers to your questions by interpreting the questions you ask it. It's based on Microsoft's IntelliSense technology, which means it can interpret questions you type in your own, non-technical words and provide a list of Help topics that might be relevant to your questions.

Additionally, the Assistant works closely with the Planning Wizard to help explain problems and offer shortcuts on working more effectively with Microsoft Project. If the Office Assistant is active, the suggestions and warnings offered by the Planning Wizard will be displayed through the Office Assistant. If you close the Office Assistant, then the Planning Wizard will use its own standard dialog boxes to display the messages.

For example, saving a new project file triggers the Planning Wizard to ask if you want to save a baseline with the project. If the Office Assistant is active, the Planning Wizard message appears in an Office Assistant pop-up, such as the one shown in Figure 2.12. If the Office Assistant is not active, a dialog box appears with the Planning Wizard message (as shown in Figure 2.13). Although different in appearance, the substance of the messages is the same.

Figure 2.12
When the Office Assistant is active, the Planning Wizard messages appear in the Office Assistant pop-up.

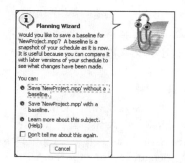

Figure 2.13
A similar (although not identical) message appears in a dialog box when the Office Assistant is not active.

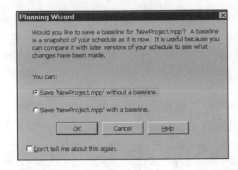

GETTING HELP WITH THE OFFICE ASSISTANT

 When you start Microsoft Project, the Office Assistant will be active. If you have hidden the Office Assistant, you can display it again by clicking the Microsoft Project Help button on the Standard toolbar, or by pressing F1.

To look up help information, type a question in the What Would You Like to Do? box, and press Enter or click Search. The Assistant will show several help topics that might answer your question (see Figure 2.14). You simply click the topic you want to display.

Figure 2.14
The Office Assistant looks up references from questions you pose in your own words.

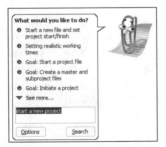

Sometimes there are so many Help topics that a See More option appears at the bottom of the list (as shown in Figure 2.14). Click this option to see the remainder of the list.

To close the Office Assistant's question box, press Esc or click away from the Assistant on a neutral part of the Project window (such as the empty area to the right of the toolbars).

The Office Assistant is designed to move when it's in the way. If you want to hide the Office Assistant, right-click the Assistant and choose Hide from the shortcut menu.

CHANGING THE OFFICE ASSISTANT OPTIONS

The Assistant is shared by all the Microsoft Office programs. Changes you make to the Assistant options while working in Project affect the Assistant in all the Microsoft Office programs, and vice versa. Click the Office Assistant and choose Options to display the Options dialog box. Figure 2.15 shows the default settings for the Assistant.

PART

I

CH

2

Tip from Tim and the Project Team

You can choose other symbols besides Clippit the paper clip to be your Office Assistant (such as Rocky the dog, Links the cat, or F1 the robot). To change the symbol, use the Gallery tab in the Office Assistant dialog box. Choose the Next button to see the other symbols. You might need the Microsoft Project CD or access to the installation files to make the change.

Figure 2.15
You can set the options for how the Office Assistant interacts with you.

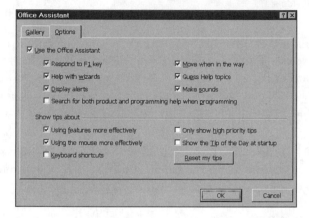

Tip from Tim and the Project Team

By default, the Assistant does not show tips about keyboard shortcuts. On the Options tab of the Office Assistant dialog box, you can activate this option.

CREATING CUSTOM HELP ARTICLES

Generally when users have a question in Project 2000, they can consult the Office Assistant. The Assistant provides responses, called *articles*, which match the question that was asked.

If you have Office 2000 and the Office 2000 Resource Kit, you can create custom help articles for Project 2000. You can either write easier-to-understand help articles for problems already covered in the help system, or create entirely new articles to answer questions about specific functions or custom applications that you use in your environment.

These custom help files are created using two basic tools: the Answer Wizard and an HTML editor. The Office help system is basically a database with an Answer Wizard file, which is an index of keywords and pointers to the related articles. These articles are located on the local hard drive, a network drive, the World Wide Web, or even some combination of locations.

The Microsoft Answer Wizard Builder depends on Hypertext Markup Language (HTML) answer files. These can be created in either HTML or Compressed HTML (CHM) format. What basically happens is that the Answer Wizard Builder creates an Answer Wizard project (AWB) file that contains your HTML or CHM help topics. The Answer Wizard Builder then uses the AWB file to create an Answer Wizard (AW) file that acts as an index to the help system. When a user types in a question, that index is searched and points to potential help topics.

An HTML editing tool is included for this purpose in the Office 2000 Resource Kit. It's called the HTML Help Workshop. This tool lets you edit existing help or create your own new help.

Note

To install the Answer Builder, go to the \ORK\PFILES\ORKTOOLS\TOOLBOX\ TOOLS\ANSWIZ directory of your Office Resource Kit CD and run the Setup.exe program.

If you have an intranet Web server set up for your company, you can use HTML and direct the user to your Web site for the help files. The good side of this is that you have only one location to maintain and it's not taking any disk space from the clients. The only drawback to this method is that the user must have connectivity to get there. The alternative is to create the CHM files and install them locally on the client machine or on a network share.

For more information on the exact mechanics of implementing this help enhancement, consult the Office 2000 Resource Kit. It contains the necessary tools, as well as extensive text on how to perform these enhancements and sample scenarios to assist in planning your Help rollout.

USING CONTENTS AND INDEX

Through the Contents and Index options on the Help menu, you can browse or search the entire contents of Microsoft Project Help. When you initially select Help, Contents and Index, the main Help window appears (see Figure 2.16).

Figure 2.16
Expand the Help window by selecting the Show button.

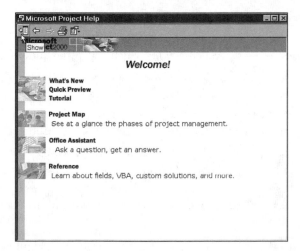

The first button on the toolbar toggles between two options—Show and Hide. You use this button to display or hide the Contents and Index help. After you've expanded the window (see Figure 2.17), there are three avenues for getting help: a table of contents, a text search capability, and an alphabetical index.

Figure 2.17
The expanded Help
window provides mul-
tiple ways to look for
help.

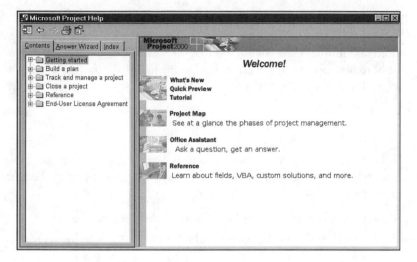

PART

I

CH

2

Using the Contents Tab

The Contents tab displays a list of topics organized into categories, which represent different project scheduling processes you might want help with. Each category is displayed with
a folder icon. To see a list of the items in a folder, double-click the folder or click the plus
sign next to the folder. Specific help topics have a document icon. You can drill down into
topics until you find a category that seems promising (see Figure 2.18).

Figure 2.18
Help topics are orga-
nized into procedural
categories on the
Contents tab.

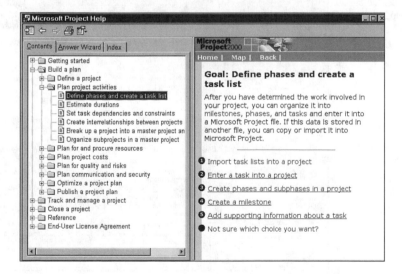

When you select a topic from the Contents tab, the text accompanying that topic appears
on the right side of the Help window.

USING THE ANSWER WIZARD TAB

You use the Answer Wizard tab in much the same way you use the Office Assistant. You type a question in the What Would You Like to Search box, and press Enter or click Search. A list of topics appears, which are related to the question you asked. Click the topic in the Select Topic to Display box and the text for that topic will appear on the right side of the Help window.

USING THE INDEX TAB

All Help topics have short index references. Use the Index tab to locate keywords in these index references. The easiest way to use this feature is to begin in the first text box (Type Keywords).

1. Type the first few letters of a keyword in the first text box.
2. As you type the letters, the second text box (Or Choose Keywords) lists the keywords that begin with those letters.
3. Double-click a keyword from the second text box and a list of Help topics that relate to that keyword appears in the third text box (Choose a Topic), along with a count of how many Help topics match the keyword (see Figure 2.19).
4. When you select a topic from the Choose a Topic text box, the text for that topic appears on the right side of the Help window.

Figure 2.19
Use the Index tab to search Help by keyword.

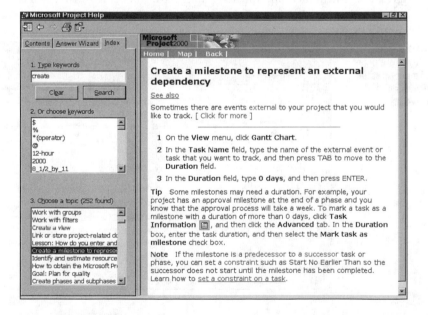

To start a new keyword search, click the Clear button just beneath the first text box and start again.

GETTING STARTED

 Microsoft has completely retooled the Getting Started help features in Project 2000 to provide more comprehensive information about using Microsoft Project, and more project management guidelines. To access these new help options, choose Help, Getting Started. A submenu listing the three menu choices appears. These choices are Quick Preview, Tutorial, and Project Map.

QUICK PREVIEW

The Quick Preview option on the Getting Started menu launches a brief five-step, Web-like introduction to the capabilities of Microsoft Project (see Figure 2.20). The Quick Preview is an excellent way to introduce new Project users to Microsoft Project.

Figure 2.20
The first screen of the Quick Preview begins your introduction to Project 2000.

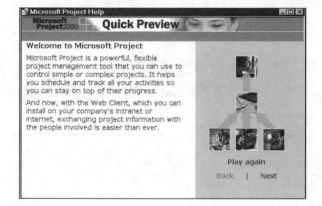

TUTORIAL

When you choose Tutorial from the Help, Getting Started menu, be prepared for a marvelous experience. Microsoft has designed a detailed tutorial to guide you through all the major tasks you are likely to want to use in Project. These tasks are divided into four groups: The Basics, Create Your Plan, Track and Manage, and Communicate. As you can see in Figure 2.21, when you click one of these groups, a list of tutorial lessons included in that group appears. You can follow the tutorial in sequence or skip to the topic you are most interested in learning.

When you select a lesson, the main Help window appears (as shown in Figure 2.22). Use the buttons at the top of the window to display the Home page of the main Help window, return to the list of lessons, go back one lesson, or advance to the next lesson.

The Tutorial is designed to provide users who are not familiar with Microsoft Project, or project management concepts, with sufficient information to initiate a project. The emphasis is on understanding the basic concepts necessary to accomplish the required tasks. The Project Map, described in the next section, provides more in-depth explanations and details for using the software.

Figure 2.21
Use the list of lessons from The Basics group of topics to help familiarize yourself with the major tasks you'll use in Project.

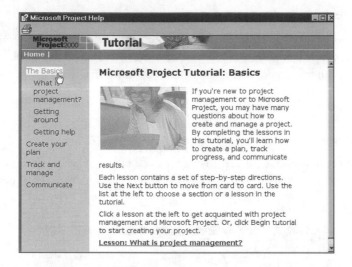

Figure 2.22
This is the first lesson in the Create Your Plan group of topics. The mouse pointer is on the Next button at the top of the Help window.

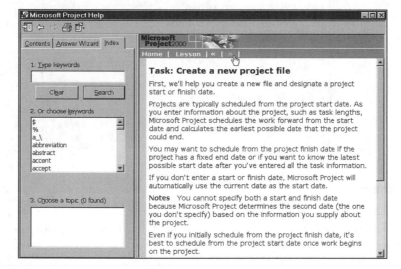

PROJECT MAP

Though it might appear similar to the Tutorial, the Project Map is in fact quite different. The Project Map is really designed for experienced project managers and people already familiar with the information presented in the Tutorial. The Project Map is a more detailed look at project management concepts and how to use Microsoft Project to accomplish your project management requirements.

The Project Map starts with a list of project management topics, as shown in Figure 2.23. When you select a topic, a detailed explanation appears, like the one in Figure 2.24.

Figure 2.23
The main topics included on the Project Map are listed.

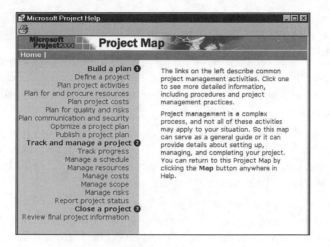

Defined term

Figure 2.24
The specific topics within the Project Map provide detailed information.

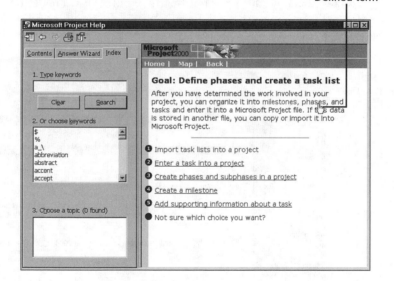

When you select a topic from the Project Map, the main Help window appears, as shown in Figure 2.24. Terms appearing in blue have hidden definitions that will display when you click the term. Additional help topics are underlined. Simply click a topic to view it. Use the buttons at the top of the window to display the Home page of the main Help window, return to the Project Map, or go back to the previous topic.

OFFICE ON THE WEB

If you have access to the Internet, use the Help, Office on the Web option to look up project information on the Microsoft Office Update Web site (see Figure 2.25). This site is designed to provide users with the latest information relating to all Microsoft Office products. Because you access the site through Microsoft Project, Project is selected from the software list on the left side of the window. There are four topics listed under Project:

- **Welcome**—As you can see from Figure 2.25, this topic contains a mixture of Project and general Office information. Check out the Important Updates area for the latest Project Service Releases (SRs), and make sure you scroll down for additional Project-related information.

- **Downloads**—As with the Welcome page, there is a mixture of Office and Project downloads available from this page. But it is worth taking the time to read through the list of downloads. Project-specific downloads include the Microsoft Project Guided Tour and the History of Project Management.

- **Assistance**—This page (shown in Figure 2.26) provides useful resources of information about Microsoft Project. You'll discover a series of How-To topics under the Articles for Microsoft Project, helpful Tips & Tricks, and information about the Microsoft Project Newsgroups.

- **Partners**—Check out the list of third-party resources listed under this page. Companies that develop tips, additional information, or downloads that work with Microsoft Project are listed here.

Figure 2.25
Office on the Web provides quick access to the Office Update Web site.

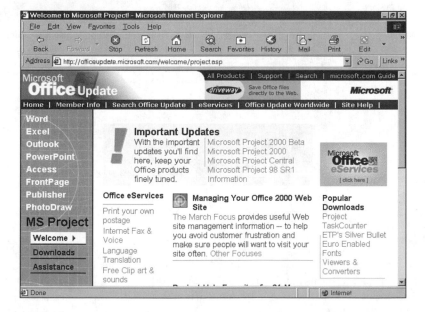

WORKING WITH THE PLANNING WIZARD

The Planning Wizard is a feature that continuously monitors your use of the program and suggests tips for easier ways to do things. It also warns you about potential problems you might create for yourself as a result of your current action and offers you solutions for avoiding the problems. For example, the message in Figure 2.27 appears when Planning Wizard detects that a task is being moved to a non-working day; it suggests appropriate ways to complete the procedure. The Planning Wizard is automatically turned on in Microsoft Project.

Figure 2.26
The Assistance page is the most useful, because it is devoted solely to Microsoft Project.

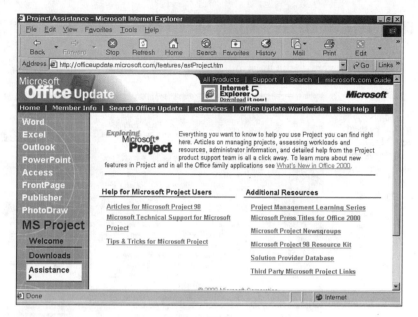

Figure 2.27
The Planning Wizard monitors your work and offers suggestions to improve your use of Microsoft Project.

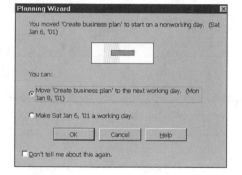

Note

If the Office Assistant is active, the suggestions and warnings offered by the Planning Wizard are displayed through the Office Assistant. Refer to Figure 2.12 for an example. If the Office Assistant is not active, the Planning Wizard will use its own standard dialog boxes, such as the one shown in Figure 2.27, to display the messages.

The Planning Wizard options are controlled on the General tab of the Options dialog box. To access the Options dialog box, choose Tools, Options.

There are other wizards active during specific activities to guide you through complex tasks. For example, the Gantt Chart Wizard helps you customize the graphics features of the Gantt Chart.

→ To change the appearance of the task bars, **see** "Using the Gantt Chart Wizard," **p. 912**

INTRODUCING THE GANTT CHART VIEW

The default view for a new project is the Gantt Chart view (shown in Figure 2.28). The Gantt Chart view is the most-often-used view for listing the project tasks.

Figure 2.28
The Gantt Chart is the view most often used in Microsoft Project because it shows both the outlined structure of the task list and the timescale for tasks.

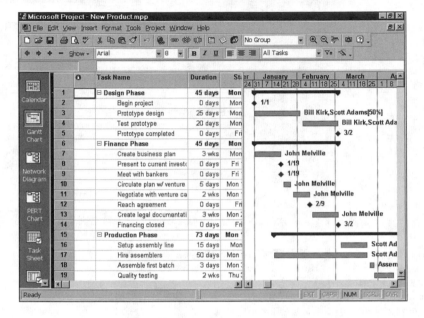

The Gantt Chart view is a graphical view that contains a spreadsheet-like *table* on the left side, and a bar chart (known as the *timescale*) on the right side. The table displays the task list, which includes by default the name and duration of each task. The table also contains additional columns hidden behind the bar chart. You can scroll the additional fields into view with the arrow keys or by using the horizontal scrollbar beneath the table. A task list can be created in an outline format to show the major phases of a project with subordinate details indented to the right.

The default Gantt Chart table (the Entry table) displays an interactive Indicators column. This column displays indictor symbols that provide you with additional information about each task. When you use your mouse to point to the indicator, a ScreenTip appears explaining the indicator. For example, if you have attached a note to a task, when you point to the symbol, the note appears (see Figure 2.29). There are symbols not only for notes, but symbols if the task has a constraint date, if the task is 100% complete, or when you insert one project into another.

*Best Practice
Tips from Toby
Brown, PMP*

Notes can be an effective way to communicate project rationale, including a scope statement, Statement of Work (SOW), constraints, limitations, and assumptions regarding the project or the scheduling of tasks within it. Many project managers include this information in the notes field of the start milestone, effectively communicating this information right from the start.

Figure 2.29
The ScreenTips associated with the indicators provide important task-related information.

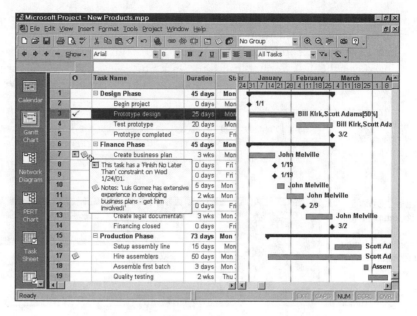

PART

I

CH

2

The bar chart on the right displays a timescale at the top and horizontal bars for each task in your project. Depending on the type of task you have created, the bars' shapes might vary. In Figure 2.29, the bars representing the phases (Design Phase, Finance Phase) are known as *summary taskbars*, and are typically displayed as thick black bars with triangular points on either end of each bar. The bars representing the detail tasks (Create Business Plan, Circulate Plan w/ Venture Capitalists) are known as *taskbars*, and are typically displayed as light blue, rectangular bars. The names of the resources assigned to the task are displayed at the ends of these bars. If a task has been started, it will have a *progress bar*, indicating how much of that task is complete. The Prototype Design task shows a progress bar across the entire taskbar and a check mark indicator, both of which indicate the task is 100% complete. Finally, you might have *milestones* in your project, which are commonly represented by black diamonds. Milestones also display the date of the milestone. In Figure 2.29, the Begin Project and Prototype Completed tasks are milestones.

The position of the bar indicates when the task starts and finishes. Use the horizontal scrollbar below the bar chart to scroll through the timescale. The vertical scrollbar to the right of the Gantt Chart enables you to scroll up and down the task list without affecting the selected task.

Tip from Tim and the Project Team

> If you drag the horizontal scroll button on the timescale, an information box identifies the date to which you are scrolling. If you drag the vertical scroll button, an information box tells you the task you will locate when you release the button.

Most views fill the entire window (as the Gantt Chart does in the initial display), or you can display a combination of views together—one in the top pane of the window and one in the bottom pane. Microsoft Project refers to these combination views as *dual-pane views*. You can split the Gantt Chart into a dual-pane view by choosing Window, Split. This places the Task Form in the bottom pane (see Figure 2.30). This particular combination, the Gantt Chart over the Task Form, is called the Task Entry view, and is useful for working with resource assignments or reviewing the linking relationships between tasks.

Tip from Tim and the Project Team

Many long-term users of Project do prefer to use the Task Entry view since it was the default view of the earliest versions of the tool. It can be set up as the default view under the View tab of the Options dialog box.

Figure 2.30
The bottom pane (the Task Form) shows additional detail about the task selected in the top pane.

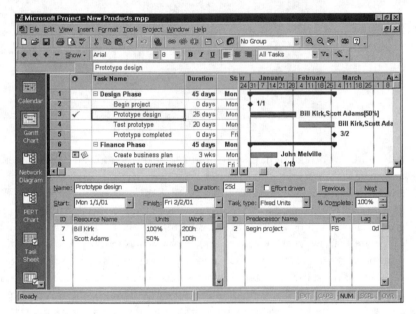

The bottom pane of combination views always displays details about the task you select in the view in the top pane. Therefore, the top view of a combination view is the main view, and the bottom view shows extra detail or a different perspective for the task selected in the top view. The same principle holds true when the top view displays resources rather than tasks; the bottom view shows details for the resource selected in the top view.

Tip from Tim and the Project Team

Use the F6 key to switch between panes in a combination view, or click the mouse pointer anywhere in the pane you want to activate.

THE ACTIVE SPLIT BAR

The active split indicator bar is a narrow vertical strip along the left edge of both top and bottom panes (see Figure 2.31). The active split indicator bar shows you which pane is active. When a pane is active, the corresponding active split indicator bar displays the same color as the window title bar. The color will be blue if you haven't changed the default Windows colors. When the pane is inactive, the bar displays the same color as an inactive window title bar. The color will be gray if you haven't changed the default Windows colors.

Tip from Tim and the Project Team

It's important to distinguish which pane is active in a split window. Many of the menu commands and tools on the toolbar are not active or available to be used if the bottom pane is active.

Figure 2.31
The pointer changes shape when the mouse locates the split bar.

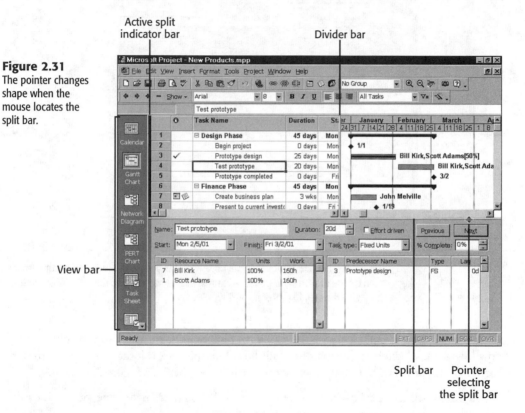

When the View bar is not displayed, Project will indicate the view you are in on the active split indicator bar by displaying the name of the view inside the active split indicator bar (see Figure 2.32).

THE SPLIT BAR AND THE SPLIT BOX

With combination views, a split bar separates the top and bottom panes. You can move the split bar up or down to change how much of each pane appears. To move the split bar, position the tip of the mouse pointer over the split bar until the pointer changes into the shape illustrated in Figure 2.31. Drag the split bar with the mouse to its new position.

Active split indicator
bar with view name

Figure 2.32
The active split indica-
tor bar displays the
name of the view you
are in when the View
bar is hidden.

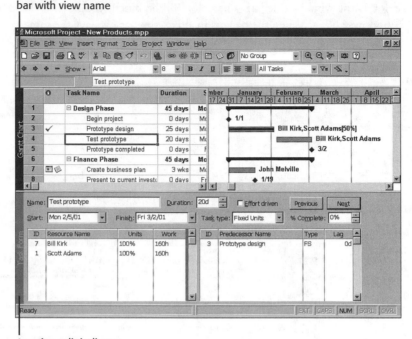

Inactive split indicator
bar with view name

Tip from Tim and the Project Team

You also can use Shift+F6 to move the split bar with the keyboard, and then use the arrow keys or the mouse to resize the panes. You must press Enter or click the left mouse button to finish moving the split bar after using Shift+F6.

One way to activate a split is to use the <u>W</u>indow, <u>S</u>plit command. You also can split a window by double-clicking or dragging the split box. The split box is located in the lower-right corner of the Project window, just below the vertical scrollbar (see Figure 2.33).

If you double-click the split bar, a combination view becomes a single-pane view (which displays only what was formerly in the top pane).

Tip from Tim and the Project Team

If there is a form in the bottom pane, you can use a shortcut menu to remove the bottom pane. Right-click in the bottom pane and choose Hide F<u>o</u>rm View.

Right-clicking the timescale (in a single pane or the upper pane of a split screen view) also will activate a shortcut menu. Choose <u>S</u>plit or Remove <u>S</u>plit as desired.

THE DIVIDER BAR

Some panes also have a vertical divider bar. The Gantt Chart, for example, has a vertical divider bar between the spreadsheet area and the timescale (refer to Figure 2.31). You can relocate the vertical divider bar just as you do the horizontal split bar by dragging with the mouse or by using Shift+F6 and the left and right arrow keys. This action enables you to display more of the table or the timescale area.

Figure 2.33
The split box is only available when there is only one view displayed.

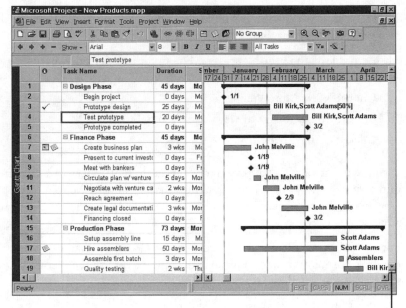

Split box

CHANGING VIEWS

There are many views you can use to display your project data. To display other views, you can use the View bar or the View menu. The View bar, described earlier in this chapter, is the quickest way to switch between the most commonly used views. The View bar lists the task views first, followed by resource views. If the view you are seeking is not on the View bar, you can scroll to the bottom of the list and choose More Views to display the More Views dialog box. You also can access the Project views through the View menu. The View menu lists the most frequently used views—an identical set of views displayed on the View bar. If you choose View, More Views, the More Views dialog box appears, showing the entire list of views available in Microsoft Project. Figure 2.34 shows the More Views dialog box.

Figure 2.34
Use the More Views dialog box to select from all the available views in Microsoft Project.

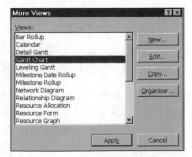

Most views listed in the menu display single-pane views that you can choose to place in the top pane or the bottom pane. When you choose a view from the menu, the view appears in the pane that was active when you accessed the menu. However, when you choose a combination view, such as the Task Entry view, the views in both panes will be replaced.

For example, if your screen is split in two panes and you want to display the Task Sheet view in the top pane, follow these steps:

1. Activate the top pane by pressing F6 until it is active or by clicking anywhere in the top pane.
2. Choose View, More Views.
3. Scroll through the list of views and choose Task Sheet.
4. Click the Apply button.

If your current view is dual pane and you want to replace it with a full-screen display of one of the views listed in the View menu, instead of removing the split, press the Shift key as you choose the View menu. Then choose a view from the menu. The view you select will be a full-screen view.

For example, if you're viewing Task Entry view (with the Gantt Chart in the top pane and the Task Form in the bottom pane) and you want to view the Network Diagram in a full-screen view, follow these steps:

1. Press Shift as you choose the View menu.
2. Choose Network Diagram from the menu. The Network Diagram appears in full-screen view.

Suppose your current view is a single-pane view and you want to split the screen and add a view from the menu in the bottom pane. Instead of adding the split, activating the bottom pane, and changing the view, you can employ the Shift key to accomplish this.

For example, if you're viewing the Resource Sheet as a full-screen view and you want to add the Gantt Chart to the bottom pane, follow these steps:

1. Press Shift as you choose the View menu.
2. Choose Gantt Chart. The screen splits into two panes, and the Gantt Chart displays in the bottom pane.

SCROLLING AND SELECTING DATA FIELDS

Unless a project is very small, you probably can't see more than a small portion of all the data onscreen at any one time. There are several ways to scroll through the data fields in a project.

Scrolling through the data fields differs from moving through the data fields. *Scrolling* changes the screen display to show new data fields without changing the field selected for data entry or editing. *Moving* changes the selected data field. Scrollbars are provided on all views except the forms. Forms typically fill the screen and there isn't a need to scroll. Forms use buttons to view the next screen worth of data.

The most widely used scrolling and moving methods are presented in this chapter. More specific methods are presented in the chapters that introduce the different views.

USING THE SCROLLBARS

You use the vertical scrollbar on the right side of a view to scroll through the rows of tasks or resources displayed in the view. If you drag the scroll box, you see a small box next to the top of the scrollbar that identifies the task or resource that will become active when you release the mouse button.

When a view displays data in a table (rows and columns), you can use a horizontal scrollbar along the bottom of the view to scroll through the columns of data. When a view displays data in a timescale, you can use the horizontal scrollbar beneath the timescale to scroll to different dates. If you drag the scroll box, you see a small box next to the scrollbar that shows the date that will appear when you release the mouse button. Drag the scroll box all the way to the left to go to the beginning date for the project, and drag it all the way to the right to go to the ending date for the project.

SCROLLING THE TIMESCALE WITH THE KEYBOARD

You can change the date displayed on the timescale by using the Alt key and the cursor movement keys on the keyboard. These key combinations and their functions are described in Table 2.1.

TABLE 2.1   KEYBOARD SHORTCUTS FOR NAVIGATING THE TIMESCALE

Key Combination	Result
Alt+Home	Beginning of project
Alt+End	End of project
Alt+left arrow	Left one unit of time on the minor scale
Alt+right arrow	Right one unit of time on the minor scale
Alt+Page Up	Left one screen
Alt+Page Down	Right one screen
Ctrl+Shift+F5	Beginning of selected taskbar

LOCATING A TASKBAR ON THE TIMESCALE

 In larger projects, it is often time consuming to scroll the timescale to display the taskbar that corresponds to a particular task. To quickly find the taskbar for a specific task name, select the task name in the table on the left of the Gantt Chart and choose the Go To Selected Task button on the Standard toolbar. The timescale scrolls to the beginning date for the selected task.

FINDING TASKS OR RESOURCES BY NAME

If you're looking for a task by name, choose Edit, Find (or choose Ctrl+F). In the Find dialog box, you can enter a keyword or string of characters that is part of the task name (see Figure 2.35). This search is not case sensitive; you don't need to be concerned with capital letters. Choose the Find Next button to initiate the search down the task list for the next task name that contains the values you entered. By default, the search always starts with the currently selected task (not with task number one) and searches down the list of tasks. You can change the Search option to Up to search up the task list.

Figure 2.35
Use the Find dialog box to search for text in any field for the character string you supply.

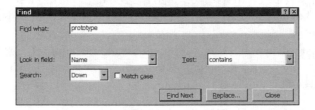

If a task is found that matches your search criteria but is not the task you were looking for, choose the Find Next button to locate the next task.

There are several other ways you can use the options in the Find dialog box to search for a task:

- **Match Case**—When you want the search to be case sensitive—to match the word or phrase exactly as you type it in the Find What text box—use the Match Case option in the Find dialog box.

- **Test**—The test setting tells Project the conditions under which it is to search for a word or phrase. Among the alternative conditions are *is greater than*, *is equal to*, and *is within*. For instance, you might search the Duration field for all tasks that have a duration that *is greater than* a week, or search the Start Date field for tasks whose start date *is within* a range from 1/1/01 to 2/15/01. To use the *is within* test, enter dates separated by a comma in the Find What text box.

SELECTING DATA FIELDS IN TABLES

You must select a data field if you want to enter data; edit the existing data in the field; or copy, move, or delete the data in the field. You can select data fields in any view or dialog box by clicking the mouse pointer on a field. In spreadsheet-like views, you also can use the arrow keys to select fields.

You can use the keyboard to move through the project data and select new data fields. The keys in Table 2.2 function in the same way in all views that contain spreadsheet-like tables.

TABLE 2.2   KEYBOARD METHODS FOR MOVING TO DIFFERENT FIELDS/ ROWS

Key Combination	Result
Up arrow	Up one row
Down arrow	Down one row
Left arrow	Left one field
Right arrow	Right one field
Home	Left end of a row
End	Right end of a row
Page Up	Up one screen
Page Down	Down one screen
Ctrl+Page Up	Left one screen
Ctrl+Page Down	Right one screen
Ctrl+Home	First field in first row
Ctrl+End	Last field in last row

When you're in a table view, you can extend the selection to include multiple data fields by dragging the mouse pointer through all fields you want to select. You also can hold down the Shift key as you use the arrow keys to extend the selection. Pressing the Extend key (F8) allows you to extend the selection without holding down the Shift key. When you press F8, EXT appears in the status bar. Use the arrow keys to extend the selected data fields. Then carry out the action you want to apply to all the selected data fields.

If you want to add fields that are not adjacent to the current selection, use the Ctrl key as you select the additional fields with the mouse. You also can use the Add key (Shift+F8) to extend the selection. Pressing the Add key keeps the current selection from going away while you move to the next fields. For example, after selecting the first group of fields, press the Add key. Then move to the next field you want to add. The status bar displays ADD in place of EXT. Then press the Extend key again and extend the selection, use the Shift key with arrow keys to extend the selection, or drag with the mouse to extend the selection.

SCROLLING AND SELECTING FIELDS IN FORMS

Form views display details about one task or resource at a time. You can move through the project's tasks or resources with the Previous and Next buttons that appear in most forms. Use the Tab and Shift+Tab keys in forms and dialog boxes to move to and select successive fields. The text next to each field in a form has an underlined character. Hold the Alt key and press the underlined letter to move the selection directly to that field. You cannot extend the selection in forms.

TROUBLESHOOTING

MISSING TOOLBARS

I seem to be missing a toolbar; only one is displayed on the screen. How can I see which one is displayed and add the one I'm missing?

The simplest way is to right-click on the toolbar or menu bar. A shortcut menu appears listing all the toolbars. The ones that are currently displayed will have a check mark beside them. The two toolbars that are displayed normally are the Standard and Formatting toolbars. If one of these does not have a check mark beside it, simply click on the toolbar name and the toolbar will appear. If both of these have check marks by their names, then they are sharing one row on the screen. To have them each appear on their own row, click Customize on the shortcut menu. Select the Options tab in the Customize dialog box and remove the check by the Standard and Formatting Toolbars Share One Row option.

NAVIGATION HOW-TO

What's the fastest way to get to the beginning of the timescale and the top of my task list?

Combine two keyboard shortcuts to accomplish this. Alt+Home will take you to the beginning of the timescale and Ctrl+Home will take you to the top of the task list.

CHAPTER 3

Setting Up a New Project Document

In this chapter

SUPPLYING INFORMATION FOR A NEW PROJECT

Creating a project with Microsoft Project involves more than just opening a blank document and typing a list of tasks. There are housekeeping chores to be done and choices to be made about how to calculate the project schedule. However, Project does not have rigid requirements about the order in which you deal with these preliminaries.

You can begin by jotting down some ideas about tasks you think might be required, and you can later adjust the scheduling calendar, enter the basic project information, revise the calculation and display options, and define the resources. In fact, you can execute all the previous steps in any order, and you can modify them as often as you like.

This chapter covers the preliminaries: You should consider these topics before you start entering tasks and resource assignments in a project file. By starting with the preliminary measures, it's more likely that Microsoft Project will process your data in a way that's consistent with your expectations. Remember though, you can still change these preliminary settings after you enter the project data without suffering loss or distortion of data.

Tip from Tim and the Project Team

Although you can address the preliminaries in any order, the order in which the topics are presented in this chapter is the order recommended when you begin developing your first project.

When you start a new project file, you need to indicate whether you plan to schedule your tasks based on a fixed start date or a fixed finish date; you cannot supply both dates. If you schedule from a start date, Project calculates the finish date. If you schedule from a finish date, Project calculates the start date. Project makes these calculations based on a number of factors, including the sequence you want the tasks performed and the availability of the resources assigned to the tasks. The project start or finish date is entered in the Project Information dialog box.

In addition, you should supply Project with some summary information regarding your project, such as the company name and project manager. The summary information can be used when printing reports and in searching for a project file among all the files on your computer, and is entered in the Properties dialog box. How to input data into the Project Information and Properties dialog boxes is described in the next few sections.

USING THE PROJECT INFORMATION DIALOG BOX

 To start a new file, choose File, New or click the New button on the Standard toolbar. Microsoft Project automatically displays the Project Information dialog box (see Figure 3.1).

Note

If this dialog box does not display, choose Tools, Options. On the General tab, mark the Prompt For Project Info for New Projects check box. Then start a new file; the Project Information dialog box should now appear.

Use the Project Information dialog box to record basic information about a project, such as the starting date and the base calendar to use for scheduling. To access the Project Information dialog box at any time, choose Project, Project Information.

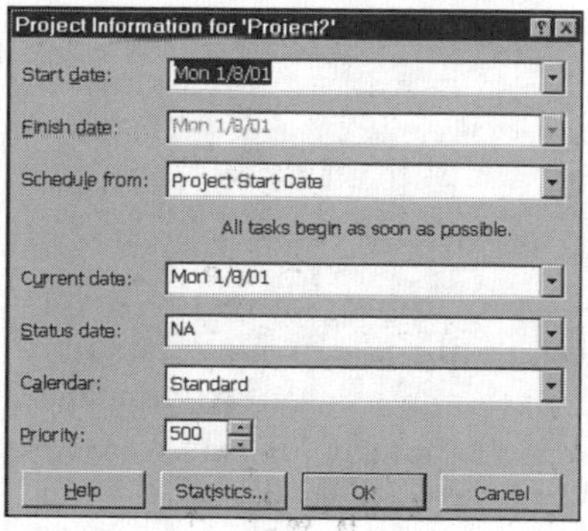

Figure 3.1
The Project Information dialog box defines the start date for the project.

Caution

Avoid the temptation to press Enter after you type a new entry; pressing Enter selects the OK button and closes the Project Information dialog box. To move to another field, use the Tab key or click with the mouse.

→ To learn more about moving around dialog boxes and forms, **see** "Scrolling and Selecting Fields in Forms," **p. 61**

The fields in the Project Information dialog box are described next. The following few sections explain in detail the implications of each field.

- **Start Date, Finish Date, and Schedule From fields**—To define a specific date when the project is scheduled to start, you can type the date in the Start Date text box, or click the Start Date drop-down button to choose a date on a calendar. If you must schedule the project to finish on a specific date, select the Schedule From list box and choose Project Finish Date. You can then type a specific date in the Finish Date text box.

- **Current Date and Status Date fields**—Microsoft Project looks to these fields to perform several date-related calculations. If you leave the Status Date set to NA, Project uses the Current Date as the Status Date—for example, if you want to see the values in the Earned Value fields calculated up through and including the current date or a date you specify. The date also is used as the date in the Complete Through field in the Update Project dialog box, and in the placement of progress lines in the Gantt Chart. See the section "Understanding the Current Date and Status Date Text Boxes," later in this chapter, for more information about under what circumstances you might want to use this text box.

→ To learn more about earned value calculations, **see** "Using the Earned Value Fields and Report," **p. 711**

→ To tell Microsoft Project that work on the current project is complete through a specific date, **see** "Updating the Schedule," **p. 725**

PART

I

CH

3

- **Calendar**—Select the Calendar list box if you want to choose a different base calendar to use for scheduling the project. The section "Scheduling with Calendars," later in this chapter, explains when you should use the default base calendar (Standard) and when you should consider using a different calendar.

Note

If the base calendar you want to use is defined in a different project file, you must use the Organizer to copy that calendar into the current project file before you can select it (see the section "Working with Calendars," later in this chapter).

- **Priority**—When you are sharing a pool of resources across multiple projects, you can identify which project has a higher priority by changing the Priority in the Project Information dialog box. You can set this project level priority between 0–1000.

→ When you have a resource spread too thin (overallocated), you can have Microsoft Project attempt to resolve the problem. **See** "Letting Project Level Overallocated Resources for You," **p. 490**

UNDERSTANDING THE START AND FINISH DATE TEXT BOXES

When starting a new project document, you enter either a start date or a finish date into the Project Information dialog box to function as an anchor point for scheduling the tasks in the project. Microsoft Project computes the other date. You cannot specify both a start date and a finish date.

If you enter the start date, Microsoft Project schedules the first task in the project to begin at that time and calculates the project's finish date based on that starting date and the sequence of tasks that come after the first task. New tasks added begin *As Soon As Possible* when you schedule from a start date.

If you enter the finish date, Microsoft Project schedules the tasks at the end of the project first and works backward. The final task is scheduled to end by the finish date; the task that precedes the final task is scheduled to end in time for the final task to begin, and so on. By the time Project schedules all tasks to end in time to meet the finish date requirement, the program has calculated a start date (the date by which the first task must begin for the project to be completed by the specified finish time). New tasks added begin *As Late As Possible* when you schedule from a finish date.

Prior to Microsoft Project 98, when a project was scheduled from a fixed finish date, new tasks, even when given an *As Soon As Possible* constraint, were still scheduled as if they were *As Late As Possible*. Now, on a project that is scheduled from a finish date, when a task constraint is changed to *As Soon As Possible*, Project schedules the task to begin as early as it can based on the projected start of the project. This is a significant enhancement to Microsoft Project.

You can change your choice in the Schedule From list box as often as you like. If you want to see when a project must start to finish by a deadline date, you can change the Schedule From option to Project Finish Date and enter the deadline date. When you choose OK, Project recalculates the schedule, calculating a new start date. View the Project Information dialog box again to see what the required start date is, given the new finish date deadline. While in the Project Information dialog box, you can then switch back to scheduling from a fixed start date.

To select a Start Date or Finish Date, you can either type the date or click the drop-down button to select a date from a calendar (see Figure 3.2).

To select a date in the current month, simply click that date. When you need to select a date in a different month, use the left and right arrows to select a different month and then click the date.

Best Practice Tips from Toby Brown, PMP

When managing a project, it's best to schedule forward based on a start date. If you schedule the project based on a fixed finish date, all activities must flow backwards based upon durations, linkages, and the calendars assigned–this is fine until you begin tracking the project. Once you schedule from a fixed finish date, the start date is set as a result of actual time needed to complete each phase. What's wrong with this picture? Since both the start and finish dates are fixed, the schedule cannot expand or contract.

Also, scheduling from the finish date assumes that there is no project buffer, or extra time added to the end of the project to allow for delays in completion of the project, unless you take that into consideration in selecting the finish date from which to schedule backwards.

Figure 3.2
Whenever you encounter a date field, you can use the built-in calendar to select a date.

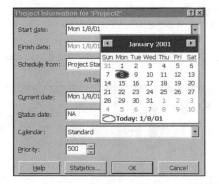

Note

If you change your mind about the date you selected, you can click the area designating Today at the bottom of the calendar to immediately return to today's date. This however closes the calendar pop-up.

UNDERSTANDING THE CURRENT DATE AND STATUS DATE TEXT BOXES

The computer's internal clock initially determines the date listed in the Current Date text box. Changing this text box has several implications:

- The date determines the location of the dashed (current) date line on the Gantt Chart timeline.
- The Current Date appears in the header of the Project Summary standard report as an As Of date. You also can display the Current Date text box in headers or footers on other reports by typing the appropriate code in the header or footer definition.

■ You can customize Project to start new tasks based on the Current Date instead of the project's Start Date. This is accomplished by changing a setting under Tools, Options, and selecting the Schedule tab.

While the Current Date also can be used for benchmarking the progress of tasks, you do have an alternative date you can use. If you specify a date in the Status Date field in the Project Information dialog box, it will be the date Project uses for placing the progress lines in the Gantt Chart. Additionally, if there is a Status Date, Project uses this date when calculating the Earned Value fields and for tracking purposes in the Update Project dialog box (used when you want to indicate tasks are complete through a given date).

To change the Current Date or enter a date in the Status Date field, select the field and type the date or click the drop-down arrow to pick a date from a calendar pop-up.

UNDERSTANDING THE PROJECT STATISTICS DIALOG BOX

 Use the Statistics button at the bottom of the Project Information dialog box to display the Project Statistics dialog box (see Figure 3.3). You also can display this dialog box with the Project Statistics button on the Tracking toolbar.

Figure 3.3 illustrates a project for which a baseline has been saved. Adjustments have been made to the schedule since the baseline was saved (which is why the Current and Baseline data do not match). The project has not yet started—the Actual fields display NA or zero.

Figure 3.3
Use the Project Statistics dialog box for a quick summary of the status of the project.

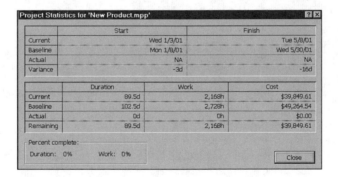

The Project Statistics dialog box displays summary information about the project. You cannot edit the data in this dialog box; you can only view it. See the tip at the end of this section for instructions on printing the information contained in the Project Statistics dialog box. The dialog box shows the current, or *currently scheduled*, values for five project parameters: the Start and Finish Dates and the total Duration, Work, and Cost. If you have saved the Baseline copy of the schedule then the Baseline (or original plan) values also are displayed for comparison.

In Figure 3.3, the baseline plan called for the project to begin on 1/8/01, but the schedule has subsequently been revised and the current schedule calls for the project to be started several days earlier, on 1/3/01. The current finish date is 5/8/01, 16 days before the planned finish. These differences are reflected in the Variance row, which measures the difference between the planned (baseline) values and the currently scheduled values. The Actual row of information is NA or 0, indicating the project has not started yet.

The first step in keeping track of what actually happens on the project is to update the Baseline. After you update the Baseline, the information in the Current fields and Baseline fields of the Project Statistics dialog box will match. After work begins on the project and you start tracking actual dates, duration, and work, the values in the Actual row will change from NA or zero to the actual recorded values.

In Figure 3.4, the project did not actually start until 1/5/01. There is no actual finish recorded yet. The actual duration, work, and cost also are displayed, along with the amount of duration, work, and cost that remain in the current schedule. The currently projected finish date is now 5/11/01, three days later than the baseline.

Figure 3.4
When the project begins, the Actual row of information is updated.

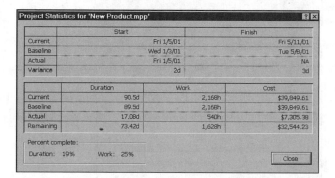

The Percent Complete of the project's duration and work is shown at the bottom of the dialog box. To close the Project Statistics dialog box, choose the Close button.

Tip from Tim and the Project Team

> Use the Project Summary report (in the Overview category) to print out the project statistics. Reports are accessed from the View menu.

USING THE PROPERTIES SHEET

Choose File, Properties to display the Properties sheet where you can view and edit a number of options that describe the project and the project document (see Figure 3.5). The Properties sheet is organized in five tabs. Click a tab to see its page. The Summary tab is the default tab.

Note

> You can display information from the fields in the Properties dialog box in the header or footer area of printed views or reports for the project, especially fields from the Summary tab. See Chapter 13, "Printing Views and Reports," for more information.

THE SUMMARY TAB

In the Summary page, you supply descriptive information about the project and the people associated with it (see Figure 3.5). You can include the options at the top of the tab (Title, Subject, Author, Manager, and Company) in reports as header or footer text. The remaining options (Category, Keywords, and Comments) are very useful when searching through the project files on your hard disk. Hyperlink Base can be used to indicate the main "address" or path of the hyperlinks you have in your project. This can be a link to another file on your computer or server, or a link to a location on the World Wide Web.

→ To learn more about linking files to a Web site, **see** "Publishing Projects on the Web," **p. 567**

Figure 3.5
The Summary page presents descriptive options that are useful in reports and when searching for files to open.

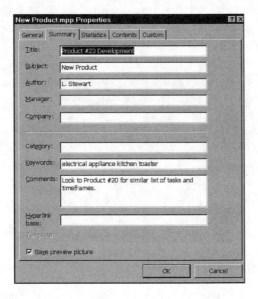

To change any of these options, select its text box and type your entry. Press the Tab key after you're finished typing your entry to move to the next option. Pressing the Enter key selects the OK button and closes the dialog box (except in the Comments list box).

If the file originated with a template, the template name appears at the bottom of the sheet.

Select the Save Preview Picture check box to have Project save a thumbnail sketch of the current view when you save the file. You can browse these preview pictures when searching for files with the File, Open command. The Save Preview Picture check box is not marked by default.

If you have trouble locating your files in the future, you can use the Open dialog box to search for words entered in these fields to find your files. Chapter 4, "Working with Project Files," provides more information on using the Find File capability in Microsoft Project.

→ To learn more about Project's Find File feature, **see** "Locating Files," **p. 109**

THE GENERAL TAB

The General page, illustrated in Figure 3.6, provides statistics about the project file: the file-name, type, location, and size as well as the dates when it was created, last modified, and last opened. This page is blank until the document is saved as a file.

Figure 3.6
The General page of the Properties sheet describes the file that stores the project document.

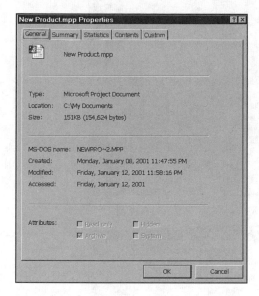

Part

I

Ch

3

THE STATISTICS TAB

The Statistics page provides useful statistics about your work with the project document: when it was created, last modified, last accessed, and last printed (see Figure 3.7). You also can see who last saved it, which is very useful with shared files in a workgroup. And, you can see how many times the document has been revised and the total amount of computer time spent editing the file.

THE CONTENTS TAB

The Contents page displays the most salient statistics about the current project schedule: the start and finish dates; the scheduled duration, work, and cost; and the percentage completed for both duration and work (see Figure 3.8).

Figure 3.7
The Statistics page summarizes your work on the project file.

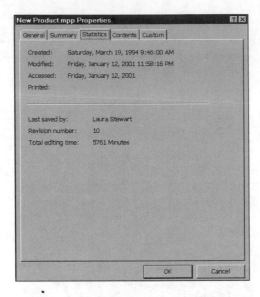

Figure 3.8
The Contents page displays summary statistics about the project schedule.

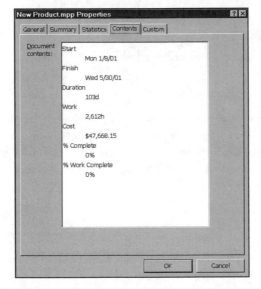

THE CUSTOM TAB

With the Custom page you can add additional properties to the file (see Figure 3.9). Then, you can search for files by the values of these properties. Based on the information in Figure 3.9, you could search for all projects having "Marketing" in the Department Value field.

Figure 3.9
The first row in the Properties list box shows that a property named "Department" has been created for this document with the text value "Marketing."

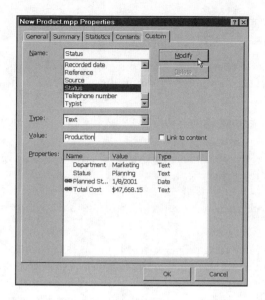

PART

I

CH

3

The Status property is being modified to show that the project has moved from the planning stage into the production stage. Thus, you could search for all projects that are in production if this property is defined for all your projects.

The Planned Start and Total Cost properties have been defined with links to actual values in the project. The Planned Start property is linked to the baseline start for the project, and the Total Cost property is linked to the currently scheduled cost of the project. Because these properties are defined as links, the property values change automatically as the schedule values change.

To create a Custom property for a project, follow these steps:

1. Choose File, Properties.

2. Choose the Custom tab.

3. Type a property name in the Name list box. In the drop-down list, there are commonly used properties. If you want to use one of these, select it and it appears in the Name list box.

4. If you don't link the value to a project field, use the Type drop-down list to define the type of data to place in the field. Use this option only when you will type the value of the property instead of linking it to a field in the project file. When you link the property value to a project field, the Type drop-down list is unavailable. The allowable data types are Text, Date, Number, and Yes or No (logical).

5. If you chose Text, Date, or Number previously, type a value in the Value text box. If you chose the Yes or No option in the Type list box, you see Yes and No buttons in the Value box. Select the one you want to use.

6. Choose the Add button (located where the Modify button is in Figure 3.9) to add the property to the list in the Properties list.

If you want to link the property value to a project field, follow these steps:

1. Follow steps 1–3 in the previous example.
2. Select the Link to Content check box (refer to Figure 3.9). The Type list box is dimmed and the Value text box becomes a drop-down list. The name of the text box changes to Source.
3. In the Source drop-down list, choose the field with the value you want the property to reflect.
4. Choose the Add button (located where the Modify button is in Figure 3.9) to add the property to the list in the Properties list.

If you want to delete one of the custom properties, select it in the Properties list and choose the Delete button.

If you want to modify the value for a property, select the property name in the Properties list. This places the current name and value in the text boxes at the top of the dialog box. Change the Type or Value as needed, and the Add button changes to Modify. If you change the Name, you have to use the Add button to include it as a new property. You could then use the Delete button to remove the original, leaving the newly named version. Then choose the Modify button to complete the change.

When you finish the custom properties list, choose the OK button unless you want to make additional changes on one of the other tabs.

SELECTING THE ENVIRONMENT OPTIONS

There are many assumptions Microsoft Project makes regarding projects. Most of these assumptions are found in the Options dialog box. The options are divided into two types: global and file specific. You can change these operating characteristics of Microsoft Project to suit your needs by choosing Tools, Options. Microsoft Project displays the Options dialog box (see Figure 3.10). The options are conveniently organized into categories on separate tabbed pages.

Most of the settings in the Options dialog box affect the way you view *all* projects, and are referred to as *global options*. Changes made to global options affect projects already created, the current project you are working on, and any future projects you create. For example, changing the setting for the way dates are displayed affects all projects, including those you originally created with a different date format. This format remains in effect for all projects until you change the setting again.

Some of the options are specific to the file you are currently working with. These options include the filename in the section title. For example, the dialog box in Figure 3.10 shows three sections that contain file specific options: *Cross Project Linking Options for 'New Product.mpp,' Currency Options for 'New Product.mpp,'* and *Outline Options for 'New Product.mpp.'* Changes made to these settings affect only the current project you are working on, in this case New Product.mpp. Any option that is not part of a section or for which the section title does not include the filename in the title (such as the Show section in Figure 3.10) are global options.

Figure 3.10
The View tab is the
default tab in the
Options dialog box.

PART

I

CH

3

The Cross Project Linking Options For section on the View tab controls links between projects. Figure 3.10 contains the Cross Project Linking Options for the *New Product.mpp* section. The settings in this section are set for the active file only—the default is to display all external links. Additionally, when you attempt to open a file that contains links to other projects, a dialog box will alert you that the file has external links (see Figure 3.11).

*Best Practice
Tips from Toby
Brown, PMP*

Selecting the Show Outline Number option will display the task list of the project in a traditional WBS (Work Breakdown Structure) format tying the schedule of the project to a previously defined scope of work. It is useful to ensure that all of the necessary work of the project has been captured.

Also, by selecting to display a project summary task, a roll-up summary will appear at the top of the project. Many times this is done manually by indenting, or demoting, all subsequent tasks to the first one, simply because the user is not aware of this feature.

Note

If the Office Assistant is active, the external link message will appear in an Office Assistant pop-up.

In some cases, file-specific options can be changed for the current file and new files if the section containing the file-specific settings has a Set as Default button (see Figure 3.12). If you choose the Set as Default button, Project updates a file called the Global template to reflect the option settings. The Global template controls the settings for all new project files. The current document, as well as all new project documents, will incorporate these options. However, previously created documents do not change.

→ For more information regarding template files and the Global template, **see** "Creating and Using Templates," **p. 124**

Figure 3.11
When you open a file that contains links to other projects, you are asked if you want to reestablish the links.

Figure 3.12
The Edit tab has two sections that include a Set as Default button.

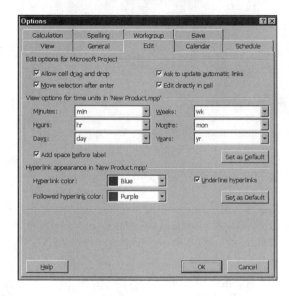

The following discussion focuses on a few choices in the Options dialog box that are critical in defining any new project and a few options of general interest.

Note
All changes you make in the Options dialog box are saved in the Windows Registry.

REVIEWING CRITICAL OPTIONS

There are several important settings on the Calendar tab that you should confirm are appropriate for your organization. These options determine how the calendar is used on printed reports, how your fiscal year is designated, and most importantly—how your use of the terms "day," "week," and "month" are interpreted by Microsoft Project. Figure 3.13 shows the settings on the Calendar tab.

DEFINING DAYS, WEEKS, AND MONTHS

The three most critical settings are those that define the meaning of the basic task duration units, *day*, *week*, and *month*. The fundamental unit of time in Microsoft Project is the *minute*.

When you enter any other unit for a task duration, these terms convert internally into minutes based on the definitions in the Options dialog box. All calculations dealing with the duration are carried out in minutes. When you ask Microsoft Project to display a task duration in days, weeks, or months, Project uses these settings for the conversion for the display. Therefore, the options Hours Per Day, Hours Per Week, and Days Per Month are crucial to the interpretation and display of your estimates of task duration (refer to Figure 3.12).

Figure 3.13
The Calendar tab enables you to customize the project plan settings to your organization's working hours.

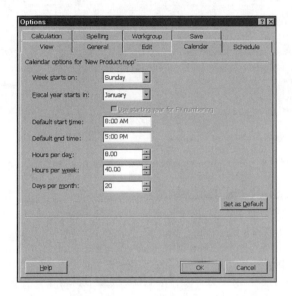

PART

I

CH

3

Thus, for example, if you estimate a task duration to be two days, Project uses the entry in the Hours Per Day text box to set the duration internally to minutes. If the Hours Per Day entry is "8.00," the duration is recorded as 960 minutes (2 days×8 hours/day×60 minutes/hour). If the Hours Per Day entry is "10.00" and you estimate the duration to be two days, then the task duration is recorded as 1,200 minutes, which is much more work.

Make sure these settings are appropriate for your organization. For example, if you work for an organization with a four-day work week (four, 10-hour days), change the Hours Per Day to "10" and leave the Hours Per Week at "40." If your organization is open eight hours a day, Monday through Friday, and half a day on Saturday, you might prefer to change the Hours Per Week to "44" so that when you estimate a task to take a week, the duration means the same thing to Microsoft Project as it does to you.

Note that the definition of the task duration is set at the time you estimate it, according to the definition of the terms you use (day, week, or month). If you later change the definition of a day, for example, to be 10 instead of 8 hours, Project does not change the minutes defined for each task duration. However, the display of those minutes in days or weeks is affected.

Best Practice Tips from Toby Brown, PMP

PMI suggests that no task be longer than 80 hours, or 2 weeks duration. In other words, the work should be broken down to increments no longer than this span of time.

Also, defining months can be difficult because it is typically an inconsistent measure of time, so it's best to use hour or week duration units.

Caution

If you change the definitions for a day, week, or month after entering the project data, Microsoft Project doesn't redefine the minute duration of tasks, but merely displays these minutes as a different number of days or weeks. For example, if you originally entered the duration of a task to be 1 week (40 hours per week) and later change the number of hours in a week on the Calendar tab from 40 to 44 hours per week, the duration for the task will read .91w. The task is still 40 hours, but 1 week is now equal to 44 hours, not 40. This is one reason for establishing your option settings *before* entering task and duration information.

→ To understand how Microsoft Project interprets duration, **see** "Entering Task Durations," **p. 161**

DEFINING THE DEFAULT START AND END TIME OF DAY

When you define the working days, hours, and months for your Standard calendar (see "Defining a Calendar of Working Time," later in this chapter), you define the hour when work normally begins and ends. It's important that you also record those standards in the Default Start <u>T</u>ime and Default <u>E</u>nd Time text boxes on the Calendar tab of the Options dialog box. Microsoft Project uses these settings in several places:

- When you specify the date but not the time for the start or finish date of the project in the Project Information dialog box.
- When you put a constraint on a task, such as Finish No Later Than.
- When you begin tracking the actual work on the project.

For example, say the normal work hours for an organization are 7:00 a.m. to 4:00 p.m. If you define these hours in your Standard calendar but leave the setting for Default Start <u>T</u>ime at 8:00 a.m., then Microsoft Project will schedule the first task in the project to start one hour later than the actual start of work.

Additionally, when you use the Tracking toolbar buttons to designate the percent completed for a task, the time a task started is assumed to be the Default Start Time from the Calendar tab in the Options dialog box. Even though time might not be displayed as part of the Start Date field format, it is stored with the date. So if the standard calendar hours are from 7:00 a.m. to 4:00 p.m., and you mark a task as 100% complete, the Actual Start date will record the task starting at 8:00 a.m. and the Actual Finish date will record the task ending the next day at 8:00 a.m. If only the dates and not the time are displayed in the Start and Finish Date field in the Gantt Chart table, it will appear there is an error—a task with a duration of 1 day (8 hours) starts on one day but ends on the next day. The culprit is typically an inconsistency between the time used on the standard calendar and the time designated on the Calendar tab of the Options dialog box.

| *Tip from Tim and the Project Team* | It is a good idea to display a date format that also displays time. The Date Format setting is on the View tab of the Options dialog box. |

If you change the default start and end times, be careful to coordinate these time settings with the Standard calendar you create for your organization.

DEFINING THE START OF THE FISCAL YEAR

The name of the month that begins the fiscal year is also a critical option. This choice affects displays and reports that show annual and quarterly amounts. If the fiscal year begins in October, for example, you might want all reports to include October through December figures in first quarter totals and the annual figures to be calculated by using the October through September figures. The Fiscal Year setting is on the Calendar tab of the Options dialog box.

By default, the fiscal year is assumed to be numbered by the year in which the fiscal year *ends*. Therefore, the year in which the fiscal year ends will be used with all months in that fiscal year. For instance, if the fiscal year begins October 2001 and ends September 2002, then the actual calendar month of November 2001 would belong in the fiscal year that ends in 2002.

On the Calendar tab, you have the option to have the fiscal year numbering use the starting year instead of the ending year (see Figure 3.14). If you select the Use Starting Year for FY Numbering check box, then a fiscal year running from October 2001 to September 2002 would have the calendar month of February 2002 belong in fiscal year 2001; the second quarter of fiscal year 2001 would be the calendar months of January, February, and March of 2002.

| *Tip from Tim and the Project Team* | The Fiscal Year Starts In and Use Starting Year for FY Numbering settings are file-specific settings. If you want to change these settings for the active file as well as all future project files, click the Set as Default button at the bottom of the dialog box. |

2000 Unlike previous versions of Microsoft Project, changing the Fiscal Year Starts In setting (refer to Figure 3.14) in the Options dialog box no longer changes the display of the calendar in the timescale of the Gantt Chart. A new feature enables you to retain the calendar year or show the fiscal year. To change this setting, you must access the Timescale dialog box. You can either choose Format, Timescale or right-click the timescale headings in the Gantt Chart and choose Timescale from the shortcut menu.

You can display the fiscal year on either the Major or Minor scale. A useful display would be to have the fiscal year on one scale and the calendar year on the other scale, using the same unit for both scales.

To display the fiscal year instead of the calendar year on the Major scale of the timescale, click the Use Fiscal Year check box (see Figure 3.15).

Figure 3.14
Change the Fiscal Year Starts In option if you want to set some month other than January as the beginning of the fiscal year.

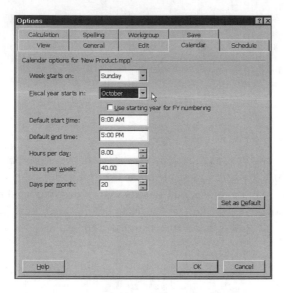

Note

Settings are only changed in the timescale of the current view. To update the timescale in another view, such as the Task Usage or Resource Usage view, you will have to display that view and change the Timescale settings.

Figure 3.15
The timescale headings display fiscal years instead of calendar years.

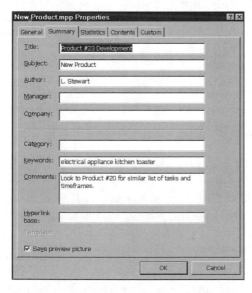

The timescale display in the Gantt Chart uses fiscal year numbers instead of calendar year numbers only when the timescale is formatted to display the year. In Figure 3.15, for example, the fiscal year begins in October and the time scale shows Sep '01 followed by Oct '02. This might be *very* confusing to people who receive your reports; you will want to remind them the printout represents fiscal, not calendar, year dates.

SETTING OPTIONS IN THE CALENDAR PAGE

To set critical calendar preferences, follow these steps:

1. Choose Tools, Options.

2. Click the Calendar tab.

3. If your fiscal year does not start in January, select the correct month from the Fiscal Year Starts In drop-down list. The default is for the next calendar year to be the fiscal year. Choose the check box to indicate the current year as the fiscal year.

4. If your work day doesn't start at 8:00 a.m., use the Tab key to advance to the Default Start Time text box and enter the appropriate time. You can enter time in the 12-hour or 24-hour format. If you use the 12-hour format, be sure to add p.m. to hours past noon (and noon itself is 12:00 p.m.).

5. Change the Hours Per Day, Hours Per Week, or Days Per Month, if necessary, to accurately represent your organization.

PART

I

CH

3

Tip from Tim and the Project Team

Some organizations change the hours to reflect the hours they expect to work on this project minus the hours needed for other activities—an example might be meetings that happen normally in the course of a 40-hour work week. You might change Hours Per Day to 6h, allowing 2 hours a day for other activities. This type of change is a judgment call on your part. If you do change the hours, make sure the Hours Per Week and Hours Per Month are changed as well.

Best Practice Tips from Toby Brown, PMP

Companies typically split the day as 75% (6 hours/day, 30 hours/wk) Productive time, or time worked on project-related tasks, and 25% (2 hours/day, 10 hours/wk) Administrative time, or time for office-related tasks. Some companies expect a 45-hour work-week where 8 hours per day are billable and one hour is set aside for administrative matters.

When planning your project, it's best to consider the specifics of how your organization operates—or how your particular project will operate.

6. Choose the Set as Default button to make the values you entered for Fiscal Year Starts In, Default Start Time, Default End Time, Hours Per Day, Hours Per Week, and Days Per Month the default values for all new project documents.

7. Choose the OK button (unless there are more settings you want to change).

SETTING OTHER USEFUL OPTIONS

There are other settings you can change to make your data entry easier. It is a good idea to review the current settings in the Options dialog box for each of the items in the following list:

- Click the General tab to confirm that your name is in the User Name text box. Project uses this name for the Author and Last Saved By properties of the document.

- Click the Schedule tab to select the time unit you plan to use most often when estimating task duration (see Figure 3.16). Choose the Duration Is Entered In drop-down list to select Minutes, Hours, Days, Weeks, or Months. The option to set Months as a duration unit is a new feature in Project 2000. The Duration setting provides Microsoft Project with instructions about the unit of time to use in case you enter a task duration without specifying the unit of time. For example, suppose most of your tasks will have the duration listed in days, and you have selected Days as the time unit in the Duration Is Entered In list box. On the Gantt chart, if you enter a **2** in the Duration column, Project records the task duration as 2d (two days). Any other duration type will have to be entered in. So a task with a duration of 3 weeks would be entered in as **3w**.

Figure 3.16
Set the default time unit you want used for displaying task duration.

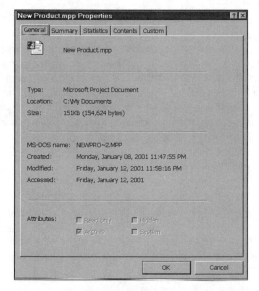

- Click the View tab to change the Default View for new projects. If you prefer to work in a view such as the Network Diagram or Task Sheet—rather than the Gantt Chart—when starting a new project, change the Default View setting (see Figure 3.17).

Figure 3.17
Set display options on
the View tab.

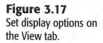

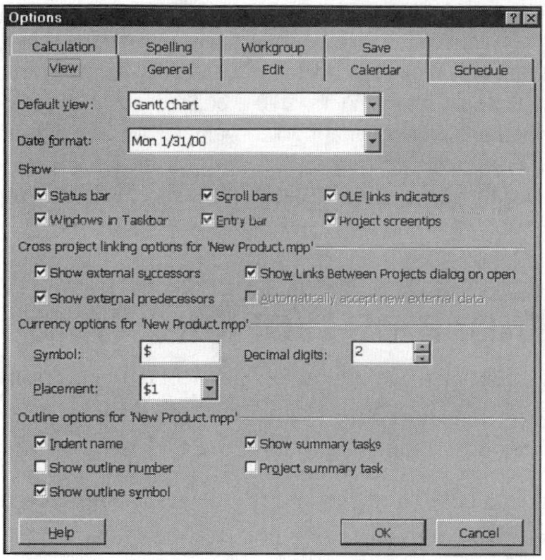

- On the View tab, choose Date Format to specify how to display dates. The default format displays the date, with the day of the week. The Date Format list box provides alternative format options (such as the date and time together or just the date).

Tip from Tim and the Project Team

> Use the Control Panel to set the international regional style for entering date and time. To change the regional date and time formats, open the Windows Start menu and choose Settings, Control Panel. In the Control Panel folder, choose Regional Settings to display the Regional Settings dialog box. Choose the Date and Time tabs to make your selections.

- Also on the View tab, choose the Currency Decimal Digits text box to specify the number of decimal points to use in displaying money amounts. The preset value is two decimal points, but you can change that to zero to suppress decimal-point display. As mentioned in the previous tip, use the Regional Settings dialog box in the Control Panel to select your currency unit and decimal display.

- In Microsoft Project views that contain tables (such as the Gantt Chart view), the Enter key causes the selection to advance automatically to the cell below—for example, when you type data in a sheet column, like the left side of the Gantt Chart or the Resource Sheet. You can turn off this feature by deselecting the Move Selection After Enter check box on the Edit tab.

- Click the Save tab to change the default save format and path. So if you want to save all your Project files as Microsoft Project templates or in the Microsoft Project 98 format, click the Save Microsoft Project Files As drop-down and choose one of the listed options. You also can designate the default path where your Project files should be stored. The current default is C:\My Documents. Select the file type you want to change from the File Locations list box, and click Modify to identify another path.

PART

I

CH

3

Tip from Tim and the Project Team

Many users enter their tasks by typing in the activity name, tabbing to the right to enter the duration, and then returning back to the left to enter the next task name. Since Project won't automatically return to the next line and requires the user to select the next task name field with the mouse or arrow keys, you might find it helpful to select the range of cells that you are entering tasks into. By doing so, the tab key will advance the selection to the right and then back to the left after the duration has been typed.

DEFINING A CALENDAR OF WORKING TIME

Microsoft Project use a calendar to define the default working and nonworking days used for scheduling tasks in your projects. This calendar is called the *base calendar*. Built into Microsoft Project are three base calendars: Standard, 24 Hour, and Night Shift.

All projects are assigned to a base calendar, and the default assignment is to the Standard base calendar. You can edit the Standard calendar, use one of the other built-in calendars, or create additional base calendars and assign the project to one of them if you want.

The Standard calendar assumes five working days per week, Monday through Friday, with eight hours of work per day (including an hour off for lunch). The default schedule is 8:00 a.m. to 12:00 p.m. and 1:00 p.m. to 5:00 p.m. No designated holidays are set in the original Standard calendar.

You can edit the Standard calendar to reflect your organization's regular working and nonworking days and hours. You also can designate the exceptions to the normal workdays, such as holidays, or time periods when the organization will be closed for remodeling, a company-wide meeting time when no work should be scheduled, and so on.

Base calendars also are used as the basis for resource calendars. Each resource has its own calendar, and the *resource calendar* is linked to a designated base calendar (by default the Standard calendar). The resource calendar inherits all the working days and hours of its base calendar, as well as all the holidays and other exceptions in its base calendar. The resource calendar can be edited to record the days and hours when the availability of the resource differs from the normal working times found in the base calendar. Examples of resource exceptions might be vacation days, sick leave, or unusual hours on particular days.

➔ To learn more about adjusting calendars to reflect your available resources, **see** "The Resource Availability Fields," **p. 331**

As an example, the base calendar for an organization in the United States might show that Thanksgiving Day, the last Thursday in November, is a company holiday. Suppose a security guard is scheduled to work on Thanksgiving Day and to have the following Friday off. The resource calendar for this worker will initially show the company holiday, Thanksgiving Day, as a nonworking day and the next Friday as a working day. For this security guard only, the resource calendar needs to be edited to reverse the status of both days.

If a resource has only a few exceptions to the Standard calendar, it's easy to edit the resource calendar. If the resource has working times that are radically different from the standard working times, the editing job can require a lot of work. If there are several resources with the same unique set of working times, it's easier to create an additional base calendar that has those unique working times and link each unique resource to that custom base calendar. For example, night and weekend security guards have unique days and hours. Instead of greatly altering a number of individual resource calendars, it's easier to create a Security Guard base calendar to reflect the special working times for security guards. Then, link each security guard to that base calendar.

Best Practice Tips from Toby Brown, PMP

With many organizations allowing people to have a flex-time schedule, you're likely to find an advantage to creating several variations of a base calendar. For example, you could configure base calendars for working hours of 6 a.m.–3 p.m., 7–4, 8–5, and so on. Once you've completed the calendars, you can assign them to the different resources that use those working hours. To keep this straight in your mind, think of the standard calendar as the hours of operation for the business, and think of the defined flex-time calendars as applying only to your resources.

Of course, many companies ignore the argument altogether by scheduling all tasks based on the standard calendar, suggesting that the task be scheduled to the day of the working calendar and not the hour of the working resource. In this case, the company is not interested in specifically which hour the task is worked, only that it is completed on the day that it is scheduled for completion.

Keep your organization's work environment in mind when you are configuring base calendars for your projects.

→ To adjust the resource calendars, **see** "The Resource Availability Fields," **p. 331**

SCHEDULING WITH CALENDARS

Project uses the base calendar for the project and the resource calendars to schedule the start dates for tasks. When Project schedules a task, it notes the earliest possible starting date, based on when the predecessors to the task will be completed. If no resources are assigned to work on the task, the project's base calendar is used to schedule the start and finish of the task. Otherwise, Microsoft Project checks to see what resources are assigned to work on the task and when the resource calendars for these resources show them available for work. The task is then scheduled to start on the next available working hour for the assigned resources.

Note

The resource calendars take precedence over the project's base calendar. In the absence of a resource calendar, the task is scheduled using the project base calendar.

To select a base calendar, choose Project, Project Information. Click the Calendar dropdown and choose one of the calendars—Standard, 24 Hour, and Night Shift—from the list:

- **Standard**—The five-day, 40-hour week with work from 8:00 a.m. to 5:00 p.m. that's standard in the United States.
- **24 Hour**—A round-the-clock operation from 12:00 a.m. to 12:00 a.m.

PART

I

CH

3

■ **Night Shift**—An example of a calendar for those whose work shift starts toward the end of one day and ends in the morning of the next day.

EDITING THE STANDARD CALENDAR

Changing the working days and hours on the Standard calendar affects the scheduled work time for all tasks that have no resources assigned to them and for all tasks whose resources are linked to the standard base calendar.

CHANGING WORKING AND NONWORKING DAYS

The original Standard calendar shows all weekdays, Monday through Friday, as working days and all Saturdays and Sundays as nonworking days. You can change the status of any day to make the day working or nonworking, and you can specify the number of hours available for work on any day by defining the starting and ending times for work shifts on that day.

To edit the Standard calendar, choose Tools, Change Working Time. The Change Working Time dialog box appears (see Figure 3.18). The Change Working Time dialog box can display a calendar of working and nonworking times for any of the base calendars and resource calendars defined for the project.

Figure 3.18
Use the Change Working Time dialog box to define the days and hours when work can be scheduled by Microsoft Project.

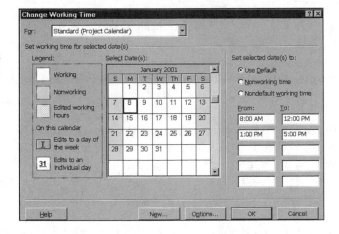

The dialog box contains a monthly calendar form, daily working times, buttons to change the calendar, and a legend. The legend (introduced in Project 98) indicates how working and nonworking days will be displayed, along with days that have different hours from the default hours. Each date that is modified from the default will have the date underlined. If you modify a day of the week for the entire project, such as making the working time on every Monday from 1 p.m. to 5 p.m., the letter **M** in the Working Time calendar is underlined. Use the calendar scrollbar to change months and years. The calendar spans the period from January, 1984, to December, 2049.

To change the status of a single day or a consecutive period of days from working to nonworking or vice versa, click the day with the mouse. You can select consecutive days by clicking and dragging. You can select multiple days that are not consecutive by pressing the Ctrl key as you click the extra dates. On the right side of the dialog box, there are several buttons in the Set Selected Date(s) To area to change the working or nonworking status of a day.

In the Set Selected Date(s) To area of the dialog box, select the Nonworking Time option button to make the selected day(s) nonworking. To make the selected day(s) working days, select the Nondefault Working Time option button.

Tip from Tim and the Project Team

To select days with the keyboard, use your arrow keys to move to the first day you want selected. Hold down the Shift key and use the arrow keys to select additional consecutive days.

You also can change the working status of any day of the week for all weeks throughout the year. If your organization works on Saturdays, for example, you will want to make all Saturdays working days.

To change the working status of a day for all weeks, select the day of the week by clicking the day letter at the top of the calendar (such as S for Saturday). Select the Nondefault Working Time or Nonworking Time option button in the Set Selected Date(s) To area of the dialog box.

After the working status of a day of the week is set, that becomes the *default* status for that day of the week. For example, suppose you have made every Friday a working day with the hours of 8:00 a.m. to 12:00 p.m. (noon). If you changed a particular Friday to either a full working day or a nonworking day and then want to change it back to the default hours for Fridays, select the Use Default option button to reset the hours from 8 a.m. to 12 p.m. Selecting any specific date and the Use Default option button sets that date's working hours to the default for its day of the week.

Figure 3.19 shows the month of December 2000. The company is having a Holiday party on Friday, December 15. They don't anticipate any work on this project will be accomplished in the afternoon, and this day has been marked as a partial working day. Because the company gives all its employees the afternoon of the 22nd and all of the 25th of December to celebrate Christmas, these days are marked accordingly. Partial working days are marked with slash marks; full nonworking days are marked in gray.

CHANGING THE STANDARD WORKING HOURS

You can define the work periods for each day by supplying up to five work periods in the From and To text boxes of the Change Working Time dialog box. The default eight-hour work time periods are 8:00 a.m. to 12:00 p.m. and 1:00 p.m. to 5:00 p.m., equaling 8 hours of work per day. Most of the time only the first four boxes are used. The remaining six boxes are typically filled in when the working times go across midnight, you want to account for several breaks or meal times, or for some other unusual work schedule. The section "Creating a New Calendar," later in this chapter, provides a good example of using six time boxes.

Figure 3.19
Use the Change
Working Time dialog
box to define the days
and hours when work
can be scheduled by
Microsoft Project.

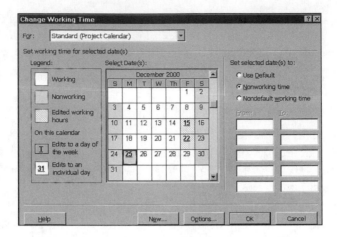

To change the working hours, follow these steps:

1. Select the From text box for the first time period you want to change.

Tip from Tim and the Project Team

You can use the Alt+F key to select the first From text box, and then use the Tab key to advance to the other time boxes. Use Shift+Tab to return to previous boxes.

---

2. Enter a time. For acceptable time formats, see the next section, "Entering Time Formats."

3. Select the To text box and enter a time.

4. Repeat this process, by clicking (or using the Tab key) on each subsequent From and To text box, to change the time in that box.

5. To stay in the Change Working Time dialog box, simply click any day in the calendar. Otherwise, click OK.

Note

Project checks all time entries for consistency. Each successive time must be later in the day than the preceding time text box.

You cannot leave a work period blank and put data in a work period beneath it. Therefore, you must use the top pair of From and To text boxes first; then you can fill in the next pair.

ENTERING TIME FORMATS

You can use several formats for entering times in these text boxes. You can use either the 12-hour clock or the 24-hour clock to enter times. If you enter times based on the 12-hour clock, make sure that you use the a.m. and p.m. suffixes to ensure that the program understands your intent. If you enter a time without using an a.m. or p.m. suffix, the computer uses the first instance of the time following 8:00 a.m. (or whatever time you designate as the Default Start Time on the Calendar tab of the Options dialog box).

If you enter 3:30 without a suffix, for example, the computer assumes that you want to use 3:30 in the afternoon and attaches the p.m. suffix. If you want to set a work shift to start at 5:00 in the morning, enter 5 a.m. instead of 5:00 because the program interprets 5:00 to mean 5:00 p.m. (If the time you want to enter is on the hour, simply enter the hour number. For example, you can simply enter **10** for 10:00 a.m., and **5 p.m.** for 5:00 p.m.)

Note

Noon is entered as 12:00 p.m., and midnight is entered as 12:00 a.m.

CLEARING THE WORKING HOURS TEXT BOXES

To remove a work period from the working hours text boxes, you need to delete both the From time and the To time for that period. Follow these steps:

1. Select the From text box for the work period you want to remove.
2. Press the Delete key to clear the text box.
3. Move to the To text box and select the time entry (the Tab key is useful to move and select the next entry). Press Delete to remove that time period.

RESETTING A CALENDAR

You can employ the Use Default option button in the Set Selected Date(s) To area of the dialog box to cancel changes you made for calendar days. Selecting individual days and choosing Use Default returns those days to the original working hours for those days of the week (as defined in the base calendar). Selecting the day of the week letters at the top of the calendar and choosing Use Default returns all days in the selected column to the standard eight-hour day, 8 a.m. to 5 p.m. (or whatever timeframes you designated for the calendar). Selecting all the weekday letters at the top of the calendar and choosing Use Default returns the working hours, and any other exceptions to the holidays and a 40-hour week, to the initial settings in the standard calendar. A warning message appears indicating that the calendar will be reset to the original settings.

CREATING A NEW CALENDAR

Suppose you have a processing crew that works from 5:00 p.m. to 2:00 a.m., Monday through Friday. You can create a Processing Crew calendar to use as a base calendar for the resources in that group. The regular shift begins at 5:00 p.m. and continues to 2:00 a.m. the following day. An hour break is scheduled from 9:00 p.m. to 10:00 p.m.

In this example, on Monday the crew starts at 5 p.m., breaks for dinner at 9 p.m., comes back to work at 10 p.m., and finishes that day at 12 a.m. (midnight). The work from midnight to 2 a.m. is entered on Tuesday. Tuesday through Friday the working times would show 12 a.m. to 2 a.m., then 5 p.m. to 9 p.m., and 10 p.m. to 12 a.m. Saturday would reflect the last hours (12 a.m. to 2 a.m.) of Friday night's shift. Figure 3.23 later in this section illustrates this example.

Create a new base calendar by following these steps:

1. Choose the New button at the bottom of the Change Working Time dialog box to create a new base calendar. The Create New Base Calendar dialog box appears (see Figure 3.20).

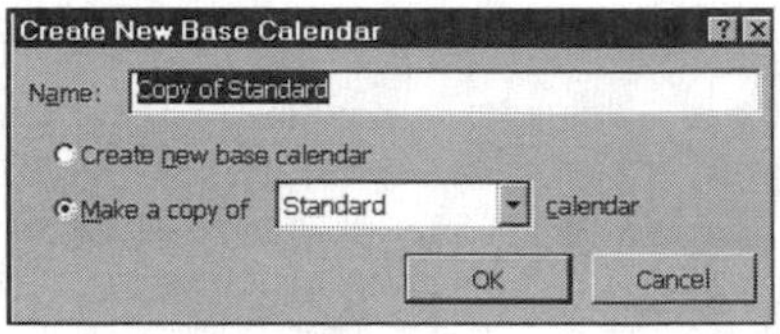

Figure 3.20
You can start a new calendar from scratch, or you can use a copy of any existing base calendar.

2. Choose the Name text box and type a distinctive name, such as **Processing Crew**, for the new calendar.

3. Click the Create New Base Calendar option button if you want to start with no holidays and the standard 40-hour week.

Or

Choose the Make a Copy of Calendar option button to start with a copy of an existing base calendar and all its holidays and exceptions. Select an existing base calendar from the drop-down list. If you have already defined all regular company holidays on the Standard calendar, start with a copy of it so you don't have to enter those holidays again.

4. Choose OK to start defining the new calendar. If you made changes in another calendar that you haven't saved, you see the warning shown in Figure 3.21 before you can proceed to make changes in the new calendar. Choose the Yes button to save the changes you made in the other calendar.

Figure 3.21
You must save or discard earlier, unsaved changes in another calendar before you can start working on a new calendar.

The new calendar name now appears in the For list box in the Change Working Time dialog box.

5. To change the hours for a weekday such as Monday, select the letter at the top of the day column and enter the shift hours for that day in the From and To text boxes (see Figure 3.22). The hours for Mondays are 5:00 p.m. to 9:00 p.m. and 10:00 p.m. to 12:00 a.m. The remainder of the shift will appear in the From and To boxes for Tuesdays.

Figure 3.22
Select the day letter at the top of a day column to change the hours for that day for every week.

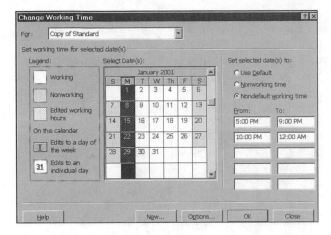

6. To change the hours for several days that have identical hours, drag from the letter for the first day to the last day in the group and enter the common hours in the Working Time group. The Tuesday through Friday schedules require three shifts, as shown in Figure 3.23. The first shift is the continuation of the previous evening's shift. The second and third shifts show the periods for the beginning of the next evening's shift.

Figure 3.23
You can select several days by highlighting the letters for the days at the top of calendar display. Here every Tuesday through Friday is selected so the working hours can be changed.

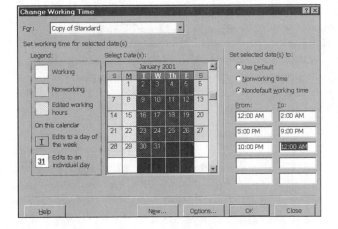

7. To set hours for a day that is currently a nonworking day, you first must make the day a working day. Then you can enter the hours in the From and To text boxes. The Saturday hours in the Processing Crew calendar are just from midnight to 2:00 a.m. (see Figure 3.24). First, select the S at the top of the Saturday column and choose the Nondefault Working Time button to make it a working day. Then you can enter the hours in the From and To text boxes.

Figure 3.24
You must first make a
day a working day
before you can define
working times for it.

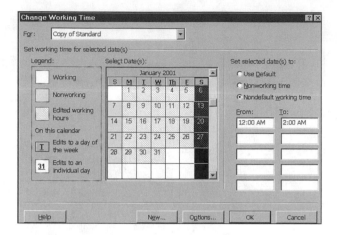

SAVING OR CANCELING YOUR CHANGES

To finish editing base calendars and save the changes you made, choose the OK button at the bottom of the Change Working Time dialog box. The Cancel button ignores all the changes you have made.

WORKING WITH CALENDARS

All the calendar information is saved along with the task and resource information in the project document. In earlier releases of Microsoft Project (Releases 1 and 3), the calendars were saved in a separate file named CALENDAR.MPC, and you had to copy the calendar file along with the project files to transfer a project document from one computer to another. Now you only have to copy the project file to transfer all information needed to process and display the project document.

If you create a base calendar in one project and want to use the same base calendar in future projects, you can use the Organizer to copy the calendar to the Global template (GLOBAL.MPT). The calendars in the GLOBAL.MPT file are automatically included in any new project file. You also can use the Organizer to copy a calendar to another existing project file, to delete a calendar from the active file, and to rename a calendar in the active file. The following section describes how to access the Organizer and how to use it.

Note

The GLOBAL.MPT template is stored in the directory with the Microsoft Project program files, usually in C:\Program Files\Microsoft Office\Office\1033.

WORKING WITH THE ORGANIZER

The Organizer is a feature that copies objects (such as calendars) from one project or template to another. You also use the Organizer to delete or rename a calendar. If you copy a calendar to the GLOBAL.MPT file (the template for all new projects), the calendar becomes part of all new project documents. For example, to customize the Standard calendar for all new projects, you must do the following:

1. Choose Tools, Change Working Times to edit the Standard calendar in an active project document to have the special working times, holidays, and hours that you want in the Standard calendar, as described in the previous section.

2. Use the Organizer to copy the customized Standard calendar to the GLOBAL.MPT file, replacing the existing Standard calendar in the GLOBAL.MPT file. The Standard calendar for all new projects will have your customized features. Specific steps to accomplish this are listed later.

You use the Organizer to manage not only calendars but also other customized elements (such as views, reports, macros, forms, tables, filters, toolbars, and menu bars). Therefore, you can activate the Organizer from several points in Microsoft Project—but not, unfortunately, from the Change Working Time dialog box where you define calendars.

Probably the most convenient way to access the Organizer is by choosing Tools, Organizer.

Note

The Organizer also can be accessed through several other dialog boxes:

- View, More Views, Organizer
- View, Table, More Tables, Organizer
- Project, Filter For, More Filters, Organizer

The Organizer can no longer be accessed by choosing View, Toolbars.

COPYING CALENDARS TO THE GLOBAL TEMPLATE

The following steps access the Organizer through the Tools menu. The active file, the file that contains the calendar, is referred to as the *source file*. The file in which you would like to place a copy of the calendar is referred to as the *target file*.

Follow these steps to copy a calendar to the GLOBAL.MPT template:

1. Choose Tools, Organizer to display the Organizer dialog box.

2. Choose the Calendars tab. Figure 3.25 shows the Calendars tab from the Organizer. The calendars in the active file are listed on the right. The calendars in the GLOBAL.MPT file are listed on the left.

3. Choose the calendar you want to copy from the list of calendars in your source file on the right side of the dialog box.

4. Choose the Copy button. If there is a calendar with the same name in the target file, such as the standard calendar, Project will ask you for confirmation to override the former calendar (see Figure 3.26).

Figure 3.25
The Organizer dialog box is used to make your customized calendars available to other projects you are working on.

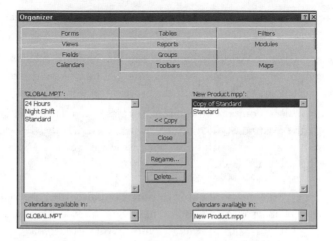

Figure 3.26
You must confirm that you want to replace the Standard calendar in the GLOBAL.MPT with the Standard calendar from the source file.

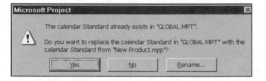

5. Choose the Yes button to replace the calendar in the target file with the new calendar from your active file.

   Or

   You can use the Rename button to copy the calendar to the target file by using a name that is not being used by another calendar.

6. Choose the Close button to exit the Organizer dialog box.

> **Note**
>
> You cannot edit the calendars in the GLOBAL.MPT template directly. To edit a calendar in the GLOBAL.MPT template, copy it to a project file with the Organizer. Edit the calendar in the project file, and then use the Organizer to copy it back to the GLOBAL.MPT template.

COPYING A CALENDAR FROM ONE PROJECT TO ANOTHER

You also can use the Organizer to copy a calendar from one project document to another. For example, if you want to place a copy of the Processing Crew calendar from the Building Construction file into the Business Park Construction file, follow these steps:

1. Open both the source and target files.

2. Choose Tools, Organizer to display the Organizer dialog box.

3. Choose the Calendars tab. The calendars in the active file, Building Construction in Figure 3.27, are listed on the right. The calendars in the GLOBAL.MPT file are listed on the left. However, the source file does not always have to appear on the right; you can copy from right to left or left to right.

4. Use the Calendars Available In drop-down list box on the bottom-left side to choose the target file, in this case the Business Park Construction project.

Figure 3.27
Display both the target and the source files in the Organizer dialog box.

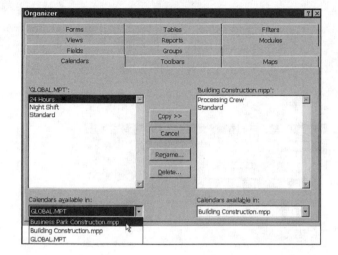

5. Choose the calendar you want to copy from the list of calendars in your source file.

6. Choose the Copy button. If there is a calendar with the same name in the target file, such as the standard calendar, Project will ask you for confirmation to override the former calendar.

7. Choose the Yes button to replace the calendar in the target file with the new calendar from your active file.

Or

You can use the Rename button to copy the calendar to the target file by using a name that is not already being used by a calendar in the target file.

8. Choose the Close button to exit the Organizer dialog box.

→ The Organizer is also used to share items you customize with other project files (such as views, reports, and tables). **See** "Using the Organizer," **p. 128**

USING CALENDARS FROM MICROSOFT PROJECT 3.0

Calendar files, and any other Project 3.0 files, cannot be brought directly into Project 2000. However, if your project files were saved in an .MPX format (either from Project 3.0, 4.0, or 4.1), you can open the project files in Project 2000, and the calendar information will be

PART

I

CH

3

included. The Organizer can then be used to copy the calendar(s) to the GLOBAL.MPT or to an .MPP file in Project 2000.

PRINTING THE BASE CALENDARS

You can print a report to show the details of each of the base calendars in the active project file. Printing reports is covered in detail in Chapter 13 and customizing the reports is covered in Chapter 25, "Customizing Reports." This section is a quick reference for printing the Working Days report, a report that provides information about the working and non-working days in all your base calendars.

To print the Working Days report, follow these steps:

1. Choose View, Reports. The Reports dialog box appears, shown in Figure 3.28.

Figure 3.28
The Reports dialog box organizes reports into five standard categories plus a Custom option for customizing reports.

2. Choose the Overview reports by double-clicking the Overview icon or by selecting the icon and choosing the Select button. The Overview Reports dialog box appears (see Figure 3.29).

Figure 3.29
The Working Days report prints all calendars for the active project.

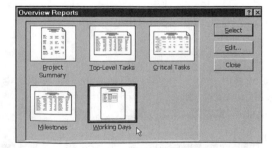

3. Click the Working Days report. Choose the Select button to preview the report (see Figure 3.30).

4. Choose the Print button to access the Print dialog box and send the report to your printer. Choose the Close button to return to the project workspace.

Figure 3.30
The print preview screen shows you the layout of the report.

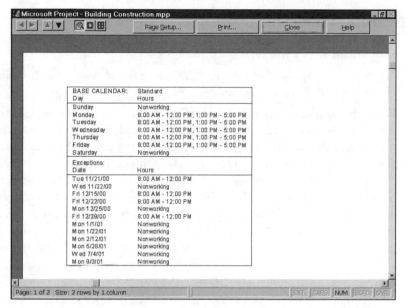

The report shows the standard working hours for each day of the week, followed by a list of the exceptions for individual days. Each base calendar prints on a separate page. Figure 3.31 is an illustration of the report for the Standard base calendar and the Processing Crew base calendar. Holidays are listed as exceptions below the standard days and hours.

Figure 3.31
The Working Days report shows the standard working times plus the exceptions (such as holidays).

BASE CALENDAR:	Standard
Day	Hours
Sunday	Nonworking
Monday	8:00 AM - 12:00 PM, 1:00 PM - 5:00 PM
Tuesday	8:00 AM - 12:00 PM, 1:00 PM - 5:00 PM
Wednesday	8:00 AM - 12:00 PM, 1:00 PM - 5:00 PM
Thursday	8:00 AM - 12:00 PM, 1:00 PM - 5:00 PM
Friday	8:00 AM - 12:00 PM, 1:00 PM - 5:00 PM
Saturday	Nonworking
Exceptions:	
Date	Hours
Tue 11/21/00	8:00 AM - 12:00 PM
Wed 11/22/00	Nonworking
Fri 12/15/00	8:00 AM - 12:00 PM
Fri 12/22/00	8:00 AM - 12:00 PM
Mon 12/25/00	Nonworking
Fri 12/29/00	8:00 AM - 12:00 PM
Mon 1/1/01	Nonworking
Mon 1/22/01	Nonworking
Mon 2/12/01	Nonworking
Mon 5/28/01	Nonworking
Wed 7/4/01	Nonworking
Mon 9/3/01	Nonworking

BASE CALENDAR:	Processing Crew
Day	Hours
Sunday	Nonworking
Monday	5:00 PM - 9:00 PM, 10:00 PM - 12:00 AM
Tuesday	12:00 AM - 2:00 AM, 5:00 PM - 9:00 PM, 10:00 PM - 12:00 AM
Wednesday	12:00 AM - 2:00 AM, 5:00 PM - 9:00 PM, 10:00 PM - 12:00 AM
Thursday	12:00 AM - 2:00 AM, 5:00 PM - 9:00 PM, 10:00 PM - 12:00 AM
Friday	12:00 AM - 2:00 AM, 5:00 PM - 9:00 PM, 10:00 PM - 12:00 AM
Saturday	12:00 AM - 2:00 AM
Exceptions:	
Date	Hours
Fri 12/15/00	8:00 AM - 12:00 PM
Fri 12/22/00	8:00 AM - 12:00 PM
Mon 12/25/00	Nonworking
Fri 12/29/00	8:00 AM - 12:00 PM

TROUBLESHOOTING

START TIMES DON'T MATCH

I've changed my default start time to be 7:00 a.m. and coordinated this change with my Standard calendar, but my first task is still starting at 8:00 a.m. What's wrong?

If you choose Project, Project Information, you'll notice the project starts at 8:00 a.m. This start time occurs because when you initially entered in the project start date (in the Project Information dialog box), Project also assumes a start time. The time was following the default hours of 8:00 a.m. to 5:00 p.m. The changes you make to the Calendar tab of the Options dialog box are not retroactive; you also have to change the start time for the project in the Project Information dialog box. This is one reason why I recommend formatting all dates to display time (through the Options dialog box). You can type a date and time in the Start Date field of the Project Information dialog box, even though time is not set to display in that field. Choose Project, Project Information to change the project start time.

MAKING START AND END TIME CHANGES PERMANENT

I've changed my default start and end times, but when I create a new project the times revert back to the default (8:00 a.m.–5:00 p.m.). How can I make this change permanent?

There are two types of environmental options in the Options dialog box: file-specific options and global options. The start and end times are file-specific options. However, if you click the Set as Default button on the Calendar tab of the Options dialog box (where you set the start and end times), your custom start and end times will be the default for any new files you create. The setting is changed for the current project file, as well as any new files you create. Any existing project files will not be changed.

CHAPTER 4

WORKING WITH PROJECT FILES

In this chapter

STARTING AND OPENING PROJECT FILES

Understanding how to effectively work with your project files is important for project managers. In this chapter we will discuss manipulating your project files, locating and opening files, saving your work, exploring the use of project templates, and using the Organizer.

When you need to create a new file or open up an existing one, use the File menu. Each open project file displays in its own document window, and you can easily switch between your open projects. There can be up to 50 project files open at the same time in Microsoft Project.

CREATING A NEW PROJECT DOCUMENT

 Chapter 3, "Setting Up a New Project Document," describes in detail how to set up a new project file. It involves more than choosing File, New, or using the New button on the Standard toolbar. When you create a blank project document, the new file inherits all the features of the Global project template (GLOBAL.MPT). All new documents, except those that are copies of templates, have generic document titles, such as Project1, Project2, and so on.

→ The most important decisions you need to make as you are starting a new project are discussed in the section "Supplying Information for a New Project," **p. 64**

→ To learn about the global and project specific options that effect your project files, **see** "Selecting the Environment Options," **p. 74**

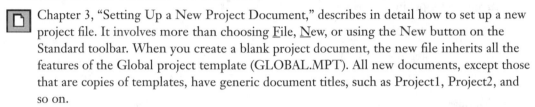

Note

The GLOBAL.MPT is the master project template. Changes made to the GLOBAL.MPT template affect all new project files. The Organizer is used to make changes in the Global template. For more information on working with the Global template and Organizer, see "Using the Organizer," later in this chapter.

For more information on the GLOBAL.MPT template, see the "Troubleshooting" section later in this chapter.

When you save a new document, Project opens the File Save dialog box, which enables you to assign a filename to the document. See the section "Saving a File" later in this chapter.

OPENING AN EXISTING FILE

Use the File menu to open an existing project file. Choose File, Open, or choose the Open button on the toolbar, to display the Open dialog box (see Figure 4.1). The Open dialog box is a powerful dialog box used by all Microsoft Office applications to locate and open files. It provides advanced search capabilities and is easy to use.

You can use the Places bar, the Look In drop-down, or the Up One Level button to navigate to the file you want to work with. Each of these options is described in the following sections.

When the name of the file you want appears in the Open dialog box list, double-click the name to open the file. Alternatively, you can select the name and choose the Open button.

Look In
drop-down

Up One
Level button

Figure 4.1
Use the Open dialog
box to locate a file
you want to open, or
to manipulate the
properties of an
existing file.

Places bar

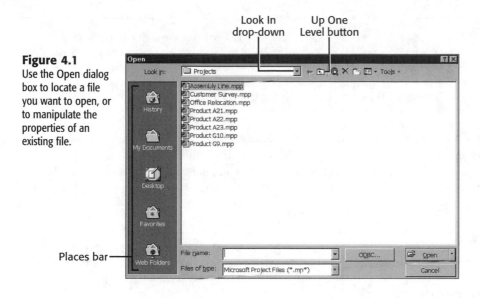

PART

I

CH

4

Note

You can customize the Places bar. The WOPR 2000 PlaceBar Customizer is a free COM add-in that allows you to customize the Office 2000 Places bar. The PlaceBar Customizer lets you specify new user-defined folder locations to replace the five standard locations listed by default on the Places bar. The PlaceBar Customizer also supports a Show Small Icons mode that adds five additional user-definable places to the Places bar.

Navigate to this site on the Web to download the free WOPR 2000 PlaceBar Customizer:

`http://www.wopr.com/officeupdate/`

Keep these things in mind when opening Project files:

- **Opening Multiple Files**—To open multiple files at the same time, those files must have been previously saved as a workspace. This feature is discussed later in this section.

- **Files with External Links**—If the file you want to open contains links to other documents, you will see a warning message appear before the file opens. This message alerts you that the file you are about to open has external links and asks you if you want to reestablish (update) the links.

Tip from Tim and the Project Team

When you activate the File menu, the pull-down menu displays a list of the four most recently saved project files below the list of commands. The most recently saved file is listed first. You can click one of these filenames to open a recently used file without having to use the Open dialog box.

The number of documents listed can be expanded up to nine. Choose Tools, Options, and on the General tab, change the number of entries in the Recently Used File List spinner box.

Note

If you open a project file created in a previous version of Microsoft Project, the PERT Chart view will be available in this file. The PERT Chart view has been replaced by the Network Diagram view in Project 2000. You can either leave the PERT Chart view in this file, or access the Organizer to remove the PERT Chart view. For more information, see the section "Using the Organizer," later in this chapter.

In addition to locating a file, many other file-related tasks can be accomplished from the Open dialog box. You can open files, print files, copy files, move files to another folder, delete files, rename files, send files to communication and network destinations, and edit the properties of Microsoft Office application files. You accomplish these tasks through the dialog box toolbar.

Note

If you've worked with previous versions of Project, you will notice the toolbar in this dialog box has been altered. Some of the features that were on the previous toolbar have been moved either to the Views drop-down menu or the Tools drop-down menu.

SELECTING A DIFFERENT FILE LOCATION TO BE SEARCHED

By default, when you access the Open dialog box, Windows looks in the My Documents folder. If the file you want to open is located in another folder or on another drive, there are several ways to change the folder you are viewing.

The left side of the Open dialog box displays a bar with a list of "places" from which you can locate files. The Places bar is a new feature in Project 2000 and has these five places:

- **History**—Displays the contents of the Recent folder, which lists shortcuts to the last 20 documents you accessed.

- **My Documents**—Lists the documents and subfolders in the My Documents folder, including the new My Pictures subfolder.

- **Desktop**—Displays the items on the desktop that are used to hold or to locate documents. These items include My Documents, My Computer, Network Neighborhood, My Briefcase, and files, folders, or shortcuts that are located on the desktop.

- **Favorites**—Lists the same folders and sites that appear in the Favorites list in your Web browser.

- **Web Folders**—Displays a list of the folders on Web servers that you have access to, making it easy to retrieve and store intranet and Internet files.

Simply click one of the locations on the Places bar to view the contents of that place.

Alternatively, the toolbar in the Open dialog box (see Figure 4.2) can assist you in changing the location of the files you are looking for.

Figure 4.2
The Open dialog box toolbar provides many alternatives for changing the file location.

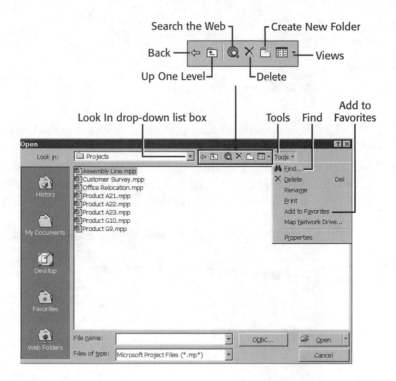

■ Use the Look In list box to select a different folder or disk drive to view. Choose the list box arrow to display a tree structure of your desktop, including all drives and CD-ROMs on your computer and all network or modem connections to your desktop. Select the location you want to view and all folders in that location display. All files in that location also appear as long as they match the criteria defined at the bottom of the dialog box (in the File Name and Files of Type drop-down boxes). Defining selection criteria is described in the section "Specifying Search Criteria for Finding Files," later in this chapter.

■ To return to the previous folder, use the left-pointing arrow or Back button.

■ Choose the Up One Level button to move up from the directory currently displayed in the Look In box.

■ Choose the Search the Web button to open the search page of your Internet browser.

■ Click the Tools drop-down and choose Find to search for the file. To learn more about using this feature, see the section "Locating Files," later in this chapter.

CHANGING THE FILENAMES DISPLAY

The filenames can be displayed in four different ways: List, Details, Properties, and Preview. The standard view, List, displays just the names of files or folders. You select the display by clicking the View drop-down button on the Open dialog box toolbar and choosing a display option from the list (see Figure 4.3).

Figure 4.3
The View drop-down button lists the alternatives for displaying folders and files.

- Choose <u>L</u>ist to view a simple listing of the files or folders in the Look In box. Figure 4.1 illustrates the List display.

- Choose <u>D</u>etails to display filenames in a table format with columns for the name, size, type (as defined by the filename extension), and date last modified (see Figure 4.4). You can adjust the width of the columns by dragging the divider lines in the column headings.

Figure 4.4
The Details view option displays more information about the folders and files.

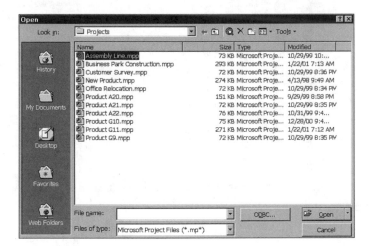

- Choose P<u>r</u>operties to display file details such as Title, Author, Date Created, Date Modified, and so forth (see Figure 4.5). These are properties from the Summary and Statistics tabs of the Properties dialog box. Additional properties—such as Percent Complete, Cost, and Duration—can be displayed if these items are added as custom properties. Chapter 3 discussed using the Property dialog box and adding custom properties in Project.

Tip from Tim and the Project Team

You can quickly access the Properties dialog box for a file by right-clicking the filename and choosing Properties from the shortcut menu. Other options on the shortcut menu are discussed in the next section.

→ To add author and company information to a file, **see** "Using the Properties Sheet," **p. 69**
→ Properties, including ones you create, can appear on printed project reports. **See** "The Custom Tab," **p. 72**, for more information on creating custom properties.

Figure 4.5
Use the Properties view option to display the Properties information for files.

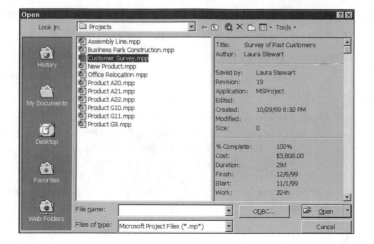

- Choose Preview to display a thumbnail sketch of Microsoft Project files (see Figure 4.6). The Microsoft Project preview shows the view that was active when the project was saved.

Note

To preview files, a properties setting must be established and saved with the file *prior* to using the Preview option. Choose File, Properties and on the Summary tab select Save Preview Picture. You must modify the properties for *each* file you want to be able to preview.

Figure 4.6
View the contents of the file with the Preview view option.

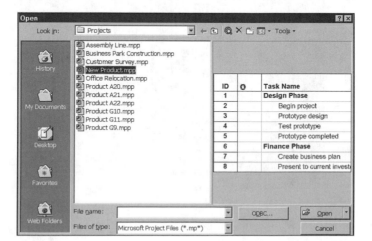

The list of filenames or folders can be sorted, regardless of which View option you have selected. Follow these steps to sort the files:

1. Click the View drop-down button on the toolbar.
2. Choose the Arrange Icons command to display the sorting options: By Name, By Type, By Size, and By Date. This sorts the project files in ascending order.

Tip from Tim and the Project Team

To quickly sort files in the Details view, click the column heading once for an ascending sort, and a second time for a descending sort. For the Size property, an ascending sort displays the smallest file size to the largest. A descending sort displays the largest file to the smallest. For the Data property, an ascending sort would display the most recently modified file first. A descending sort displays files that have not been modified recently at the top of the list.

ADDITIONAL OPTIONS FOR USING THE SELECTED FILE

Although the most common use of the Open dialog box is to retrieve a document for editing, you also can initiate a number of other file management actions after you select a file. Some file management actions, such as Create New Folder, are available directly from the dialog box toolbar or from the Tools drop-down menu (such as Rename and Print). Other actions are only available on the shortcut menu for the file. To access the shortcut menu, right-click the filename (see Figure 4.7).

Figure 4.7
A shortcut menu displays when you right-click the filename.

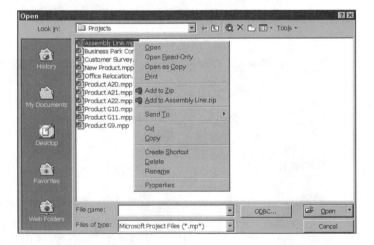

- You can open a file by choosing the Open button, the Open command on the shortcut menu, or by double-clicking the filename.
- You might want to allow others to modify a file while you are viewing it, to view a file without changing any of the values in the file, or to open a copy of the file. The Open Read Only and Open as Copy commands are available on the shortcut menu (see Figure 4.7).

Note

You also can use the Open Read Only or Open as Copy options from the drop-down on the right side of the Open button in the Open dialog box.

- You can send the file to the printer with the Print command on the shortcut menu. The view that was active when the file was saved will be the view that is printed.

- If you are using WinZip, you might have options on the shortcut menu (such as those displayed in Figure 4.7) to add a file to a list of documents to be zipped, or to create a separate .ZIP file for the selected project.

- The Send To option will copy (and in some cases move) a document to a different location, such as your floppy disk, My Documents, or My Briefcase. There also are options to route the project file to other users, create a shortcut to the file on the desktop, and publish the project file on the Web using the Web Publishing Wizard.

→ For more information on using the email and routing options, **see** "Using Microsoft Project in Workgroups," **p. 603**

- You can use the Cut and Copy commands to move or copy a project file to another folder location. Right-click the filename and choose Cut (to move the file) or Copy (to copy the file) from the shortcut menu. Choose another location in the Look In box and right-click the filename list area in that new location. Choose Paste from the shortcut menu that appears. The file is pasted in the new location.

- When you use the Create Shortcut option on the shortcut menu, a shortcut to the selected file is created in the same folder. You can then move the shortcut to another folder to allow access to the file from multiple locations.

- There are several ways to delete a file through the Open dialog box. You can delete a file by selecting it and clicking the Delete button on the toolbar, pressing the Delete key, or by choosing Delete from the shortcut menu for the file. Deleting a file moves it to the Recycle Bin. When you later empty the Recycle Bin, the Confirm File Delete dialog box appears; choose Yes to completely delete the file. Use Shift+Delete to immediately delete the file permanently, bypassing the Recycle Bin.

- You can change the name of a file by right-clicking the filename and selecting Rename from the shortcut menu, by choosing Tools, Rename from the toolbar, or by pressing F2. Edit the name and press Enter to complete the name change.

Tip from Tim and the Project Team

You can also rename a file by selecting the filename with two single clicks (clicking once, pausing, and then clicking again). Remember, a double-click opens the file!

Keep in mind that since the release of Windows 95, the number of characters to name files is 255, allowing the user to give a very descriptive project name to the file.

- You can edit the file properties of Microsoft Office application files without actually opening the files. Right-click the filename and choose Properties from the shortcut menu. The Properties sheet for the file appears. Edit the fields on the various tabs as desired and then choose the OK button.

PART

I

CH

4

→ Properties provide information about the project file, such as the number of times it has been revised. To learn more about file properties, **see** "Using the Properties Sheet," **p. 69**

Another action you can perform in the Open dialog box is to create shortcuts to files you use frequently and add the shortcuts to your Favorites list. Then when you want to access those files quickly, you click Favorites on the Places bar to see a list of your favorite files.

To add a file or folder to the Favorites list, follow these steps:

1. Find the location of the folder or file you want to add to the Favorites list and display the folder or filename in the file list box.

2. Select the file or folder.

3. Choose the Tools command on the Open dialog box toolbar and select Add to Favorites.

A shortcut to the item now appears when you choose the Favorites place on the Places bar.

To remove an item from the Favorites list, simply select the item and press the Delete key or click the Delete button on the toolbar. Choose Yes to confirm that you want to send the item to the Recycle Bin. Because the item is a Windows shortcut, deleting it does not delete the folder or file that it represents. You are only deleting the reference to the folder or file.

Caution

Check to be sure that "Favorites" is displayed in the Look In box before deleting an icon. The icons in the Favorites folder are shortcuts, but the file icons in other folders usually are for the files themselves. A shortcut icon can be distinguished from other icons by the small arrow in the lower-left corner of the shortcut image.

VIRUS PROTECTION

In this era of information exchange, files are frequently shared between people supporting a large project. When this happens, it is possible the file might pick up a computer virus. A *virus* is a computer program or macro that "infects" computer files by copying itself into your files and then, when you open the infected files, the virus executes. Part of a virus's execution might be to spread the infection to other files, or corrupting or deleting your files.

To safeguard against this, whenever you open something from someone else that contains macros in Microsoft Project, a warning is automatically displayed to alert you that the file contains one or more macros and reminds you that macros might contain viruses (see Figure 4.8).

You can choose to open the file with the macros enabled, open the file with macros disabled, or get more information from the Project help files. You also can close the dialog box thus canceling the action of opening the file.

You control the level of protection you want when you open files through the Tools, Macro, Security command.

Figure 4.8
Virus alert message
for files that contain
macros.

Locating Files

You can search for files by filename, by location, and by the date the files were created or last saved. Alternatively, files can be located by using the information you enter in the Properties dialog box for each file. You also can search for specific text that occurs in a project document. Specify search criteria as broadly or narrowly as you want. The more you narrow the search, the fewer number of files will be found.

The files found by using the search criteria are listed in the Open dialog box. As described earlier in this chapter, with this list, you can browse through the directories you included in the search, sort the files in the list, and preview any file without opening it in Microsoft Project. Furthermore, you can view summary information about a file—specifically the filename, title, size, author, and date last saved—or you can view the properties information entered for a file. See the section "Additional Options for Using the Selected File," earlier in this chapter.

If you know where the files you are looking for are located, you can indicate specific folders to search. This technique speeds up the process of finding the files because the program does not have to search the entire hard disk. For example, you might know that the files you want to find are in one of the subfolders of the My Documents directory. In this case, you can limit the search to this subfolder. You also can specify a different drive for a search, such as a floppy drive or a shared network folder.

Specifying Search Criteria for Finding Files

The methods for locating files in Microsoft Project have been refined in Project 2000. You can perform simple searches by filename (or partial name) and by file type using the two drop-down text boxes at the bottom of the Open dialog box (see Figure 4.9) or specify more complex criteria through the Find dialog box (see Figure 4.10). To access the Find dialog box, select the Tools drop-down menu on the Open dialog box toolbar, and choose Find.

Searching for Files of a Certain Type

By default, any file that has a Project extension (*.MP*) is displayed in the Open dialog box. The search pattern contains an initial asterisk to mean that the filename can be anything. The file extension must begin with the letters "MP" but the third character can be anything.

PART

I

CH

4

Figure 4.9
Use the text boxes in the Open dialog box to perform quick searches by filename and file type.

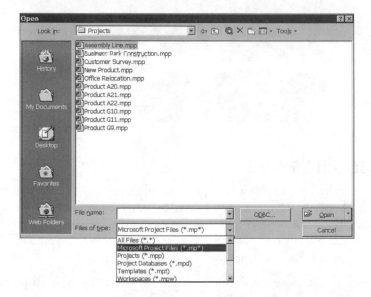

Figure 4.10
Use the Find dialog box to specify your search criteria.

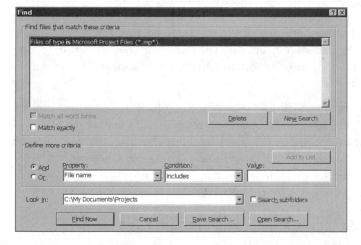

The file types that will be found by this pattern include all the extensions used by Project 2000, as well as those used in earlier releases, such as Project 98, 4.1, 4.0, and 3.0 (see Table 4.1).

TABLE 4.1 DIFFERENT TYPES OF FILES IN MICROSOFT PROJECT

Extension	Type of File
*.MPP	Microsoft Project project document
*.MPT	Microsoft Project template
*.MPW	Microsoft Project workspace
*.MPD	Microsoft Project database
*.MPX	Microsoft Project Exchange file for exchanging project data with older releases and with Microsoft Project on the Macintosh.

Note

> Microsoft Project 4.1 or earlier files (.MPP, .MPV, and .MPC) cannot be opened directly into Microsoft Project 2000. You can save these files as .MPX files in those versions of Project and then open them in Project 2000, or open and save these files in Project 98 and then bring them into release 2000 to convert them. Project 2000 does not directly support files from release 4.1 or earlier.

The .MPX file format continues to be available for working with previous versions of Project. This format does not incorporate any of the new features of Project 2000. A new file type, Microsoft Project Database (.MPD), was added in Project 98. The .MPD file format provides a more seamless transition between Microsoft Project and Microsoft Access and is a quicker way to export a project into Access.

→ To learn more about exporting data from Project to use with other programs, **see** "Exporting and Importing Project Data with Other File Formats," **p. 759**

To view a list of a particular file type, designate the file type by changing the entry in the Files of Type list box at the bottom of the Open dialog box (refer to Figure 4.9). Choose the drop-down arrow to show the file types that can be displayed in Project. Each file type mentioned in the list except the first (All Files *.*) can be imported into Microsoft Project to create new entries in a project document.

The other file types in the list include

- Text files (*.TXT)
- Comma Separated Value files (*.CSV)
- Excel worksheet files (*.XLS)—Excel 5.0 and later releases only
- Access database files (*.MDB)

PART

I

CH

4

SEARCHING FOR FILES BY THE CHARACTERS IN THEIR FILENAMES

You also can impose conditions on the filename itself by typing a criterion in the File Name text box. If you know the exact name, you can type it in. If you only know some of the characters in the name, you can use the traditional wildcards (* and ?) to specify a pattern search to find the filename. The asterisk (*) is used for finding multiple characters; the question mark (?) finds a single character. For example, to find all filenames containing the letters "plan" anywhere in the filename, type ***plan*** in the File Name text box. This would find files named Planning, Game Plan, and Construction Plan. To find all budget files for the nineties (named BUDGET90, BUDGET91, BUDGET92, and so on), type **budget9?**. All filenames matching the letters "budget9" exactly, plus one more unspecified character at the end of the name, will be listed.

Note

> You also can search for a project by filename in the Find dialog box by specifying the Property, Condition, and Value in the Define More Criteria section of the Find dialog box. See the next section, "Using the Find Dialog Box," for an explanation of how to locate files using this dialog box.

USING THE FIND DIALOG BOX

When you choose Tools, Find from the toolbar in the Open dialog box, the Find dialog box is displayed. Through this dialog box you can specify additional search criteria (see Figure 4.11). Each of the criteria fields used in the Open dialog box is represented as a criteria statement on a separate line in the list box at the top of this dialog box.

Figure 4.11
Use the Find dialog box to customize file search criteria.

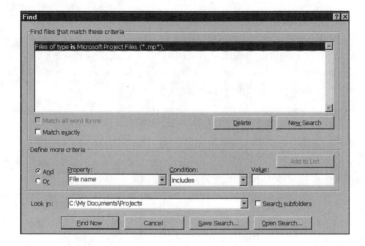

Use the Define More Criteria options to add more statements to the list of criteria:

1. First, indicate whether this new criteria is an And or Or condition. Choose the And option button if the new criteria must be satisfied in addition to the existing criteria. Choose the Or option button if the new criteria can be used to include a file even if the other criteria are not met.

2. Next click the Property drop-down arrow and select a property type from the list.

3. Then use the Condition drop-down list to specify how to use the entry in the Value text box. The options displayed in the Condition list box depend on what Property category you choose.

4. Enter a sample value in the Value text box.

As an example, Figure 4.12 shows a search for files that were last modified between 4/13/00 and 4/20/00. After you have your criteria selected, choose the Add to List button to add the criteria to the list.

You can edit criteria that has already been entered by double-clicking the criteria statement in the list. The criteria components are placed in the criteria boxes in the Define More Criteria group. Adjust the criteria definition and choose the Add to List button. Microsoft Project tells you if two conditions on the same property are not permitted, and lets you choose to replace the original criteria.

To remove a single criterion from the list, select it and choose the Delete button. To clear all criteria statements, choose the New Search button.

Figure 4.12
Compose criteria statements with the fields in the Define More Criteria group.

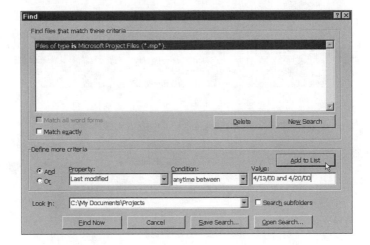

When your criteria involves searching for a specific word in the text of the file or its properties, select the Match All Word Forms check box to accept variations on the root word. For example, if you select this check box, a search for the word "write" would also accept "wrote" and "written."

If the upper- and lowercase spelling of a word must match exactly, select the Match Exactly check box.

You can use the Look In text box at the bottom of the dialog box to redefine the location for the search. Select the Search Subfolders check box to extend the search into subfolders that are found in the location you specify.

When you have set all the conditions, choose the Find Now button to initiate the search.

You can save the criteria set for future use by choosing; the Save Search button. The Save Search dialog box appears (see Figure 4.13). Supply a name for the set of criteria in the Name for This Search text box and choose OK.

You can reuse a previously saved search by choosing the Open Search button. The Open Search dialog box appears with the list of saved searches in a list box (see Figure 4.14). Select the search you want to use and choose the Open button to load the criteria in the Find dialog box.

If you want to rename a saved search, select the old name in the Open Search dialog box and choose the Rename button. Type the new name in the Rename Search dialog box and choose the OK button.

Use the Delete button to delete a saved search. Complete the deletion by choosing Yes in the confirmation dialog box.

SEARCHING FOR FILES THAT CONTAIN SPECIFIC TEXT

Choose Text or Property in the Property drop-down box to enter one or more words or character strings to be searched for in the body of the file or in its property fields.

PART

I

CH

4

Figure 4.13
Save customized searches for later use with the Save Search button.

Figure 4.14
Select the saved search whose criteria you want to use from the Open Search dialog box.

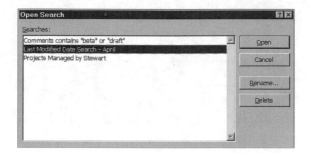

A few rules exist for entering the text string to be used in searching files. You can use partial words or any combination of upper- and lowercase letters. If you search for "an", for example, you get a list of files that contain the words *annual* or *bank*, as well as any other files that have the letters "an" in them. To search for a phrase, such as "subdivision finished", enclose it in double quotation marks. You can use wildcards in the search, and you can combine words, as the examples in Table 4.2 show.

TABLE 4.2   EXAMPLES OF SEARCHES LOOKING FOR WORDS OR PHRASES WHICH OCCUR IN THE PROJECT FILE

To Search For	Type
A phrase (such as "bank loan")	"" (quotation marks enclose the phrase) Example: type **"bank loan"**.
One word *or* another word	, (comma) Example: type **subdivision,county** to find files containing either "subdivision" or "county."
One word *and* another word	& (ampersand or space) Example: type **subdivision & county** or **subdivision county** to find files containing both "subdivision" and "county."
Files not containing	˜ (tilde) Example: type **subdivision˜county** to find files containing "subdivision" but not "county."

SEARCHING FOR FILES BY THE DATE SAVED

You can use the Last Modified property to search for files based on the date they were last saved. By default, there is no constraint; the default criteria is Anytime. When you choose Last Modified as the property in the Find dialog box, the choices on the Condition drop-down enable you to search for files that were last saved recently, such as yesterday, today, last week, this week, last month, and this month. There are also conditions that let you specify a date range: anytime between, on, on or before, on or after, and in the last.

To specify a date range, choose Anytime Between from the Condition drop-down and type the dates separated by commas in the Value text box. Refer to Figure 4.12 for an example of a date range search.

When you want to specify minutes, hours, days, or weeks, choose the In the Last condition. You simply type the time units followed by the first letter for the unit, much in the same way you enter units in the duration field in the Gantt Chart view. For example, if you want to search for files that were last modified in the past 2 weeks, type in **2w**, as shown in Figure 4.15.

Figure 4.15
If the Add to List button is grayed out, the unit you have entered is not valid.

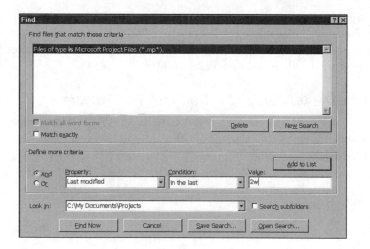

USING THE ODCB OPEN OPTION

ODBC, *Open Database Connectivity*, is an interface that allows developers to access data from both relational and non-relational databases. Through the Open and Save dialog boxes, Project 2000 can open and save entire projects in database formats. A database can be from any of three sources:

- **A Project 2000 or Project 98 database**—The file extension is *.MPD.
- **An Access 97 database**—The file extension is *.MDB.
- **An ODBC source**—An ODBC source looks like a long filename, but it is really an alias for a data collection managed by another computer with drivers that translate between the ODBC source and Project. The actual file format could be Access, SQL, Oracle's database, or a few others that have ODBC drivers already defined.

The ODBC buttons on the Open and Save dialog boxes just give you access to the sources that have been defined for your computer. The list of sources and drivers is managed by the ODBC applet in the Control Panel.

PART

I

CH

4

Note It is more reliable when you open a project from a database format that was saved by Project in the first place, such as a Project database or Access database format.

→ If the source of your data is not a Project or Access database, **see** "Exporting and Importing Project Data with Other File Formats," **p. 759**, and "Copying, Pasting, and Inserting Data with Other Applications," **p. 809**, to learn about other file formats Microsoft Project will accept.

SAVING AND PROTECTING FILES

When you create a new file or edit an existing one, you will want to save the project document. You can save files as project documents, HTML files, or workspace files. Additionally, if you are working with a group of people who need access to your project file, you might want to protect the file from accidental changes.

DESIGNATING A DEFAULT SAVE LOCATION AND FILE FORMAT

 When you save a project, the file is saved as a project (.MPP) file type in the My Documents folder. These are the default settings for file type and location. A new feature in Project 2000 allows you to designate a different default location and file type for your project files. Not only can you specify the default settings for your project files, but you also can designate default locations for your own templates (called User Templates) and templates you share with others.

To change these default settings, choose Tools, Options and click the Save tab (see Figure 4.16).

Figure 4.16
Workgroup templates are standardized project templates that you create for a team or organization to share.

To change the default file type, click the Save Microsoft Project Files As drop-down list and choose a type, as listed in Table 4.3.

TABLE 4.3   MICROSOFT PROJECT FILE TYPES

File Type	Description
Project (*.mpp)	Project is the standard file type used for individual project files.
Template (*.mpt)	Template is a special type of project file that contains either a standard set of tasks or group of resources used as a starting point for creating similar new project files.
Project Database (*.mpd)	Project Database is a file type used when you want to be able to export project data to other programs, including Microsoft Access. This format replaces the .MPX.
Project 98 (*.mpp)	Use the Project 98 format when you have Project 2000 but are sharing project files with others who have Project 98. Any features specific to Project 2000 will not be included in the file when you use this file format.
Microsoft Access Database (*.mdb)	Microsoft Access Database file format is convenient when you need to routinely use your project data in Microsoft Access.

→ If you need to share a Project 2000 file with people using older versions of Project, **see** "Exporting Project 2000 Data to Older Releases of Microsoft Project," **p. 763**

→ To learn about using Project with Microsoft Access, **see** "Using the Microsoft Access Format," **p. 769**

To change the location in which your project files are stored, select the file type from the File Locations box. For example, in Figure 4.16 the Projects file type is selected. Then click the Modify button. The Modify Location dialog box appears (similar to the Open and Save As dialog boxes) from which you can identify a different location. After you navigate to the folder you want to be the new default location, click OK. You will see the location change in the File Locations box.

ACTIVATING AUTO SAVE

A new feature in Project 2000 enables you to select a time interval during which Microsoft Project will automatically save your project files. You can choose to have the Auto Save feature save just your active project or all open project files.

To enable this feature, choose Tools, Options and click the Save tab in the Options dialog box (see Figure 4.17). Mark the Save Every check box and type the time interval or use the spinner arrows to select a unit of time. Then choose either Save Active Project Only or Save All Open Project Files as desired.

Best Practice Tips from Toby Brown, PMP

Project is not only a scheduling tool—it is an analysis tool for "what if" scenarios. This allows the user to make changes to task or resource information to see what the impact is to the project. Typically, you would not want to have these changes saved automatically. However, since you are prompted as to whether you wish to save or not, this shouldn't be a problem. Don't hesitate to use Project to help you play out various scenarios for your projects.

Figure 4.17
You must mark the Save Every check box to activate the Auto Save choices.

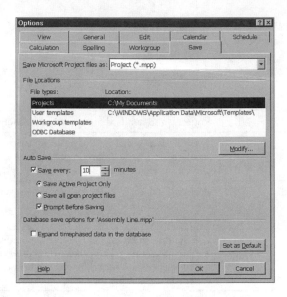

As a precaution, Project will prompt you each time it is preparing to Auto Save your files, as shown in Figure 4.18. However, Auto Save will only prompt you to save the file if you have made changes to it since the last time the file was saved. If no changes have been made, you will not receive this prompt.

You can deactivate this feature by removing the check from the Prompt Before Saving check box (refer to Figure 4.17).

Figure 4.18
The Auto Save prompt only appears if you have not saved your changes.

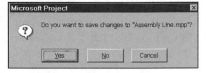

SAVING A FILE

The first time you save a file, the Save As dialog box appears, allowing you to specify the name and location you want to use to save the file (see Figure 4.19). Choose File, Save from the menu to save the file. The Save As dialog box is very similar to the Open dialog box.

Select the location in which you want to save the file using the Places bar, Save In drop-down, and Up One Level button. Then give the file a distinctive name (instead of Project1, Project2, and so on) that will help you distinguish this project from your other project files.

Note

Filenames can be up to 255 characters, including spaces. Certain characters are not permitted, including

/ ? \ : * , " < > |

Save In drop-
down list box   Back   Up One Level   Create New Folder

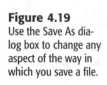

Figure 4.19
Use the Save As dia-
log box to change any
aspect of the way in
which you save a file.

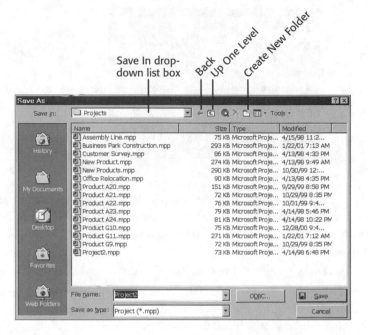

Sometimes you might want to create a new folder in which to store the project file.
Navigate to the location under which you want to create the new folder. Then click the
Create New Folder button on the Save As toolbar (refer to Figure 4.19). A pop-up box
appears in which you name the folder. The new folder becomes the active location. You can
then proceed to designate the name for the project file and save it in this new folder.

If you have entered tasks or resources into your file, you should see a dialog box from the
Planning Wizard that refers to saving a baseline when you save a document for the first time
(see Figure 4.20). If the Office Assistant is active, the message displays in a typical Office
Assistant pop-up.

Although it's very important that you save the baseline after you complete the project plan and
before actual work on the project begins, it isn't necessary to save the baseline in the early
stages of development. However, the Planning Wizard doesn't know when you add the final
touches to your project plan, so it displays the warning from the outset. The Planning Wizard
will continue to display this prompt as a reminder that you eventually need to save the project
with a baseline. This reminder is handy, especially if you are new to Microsoft Project. If you
don't want to be reminded about this each time you save the file, you have two choices:

■ You can check the option Don't Tell Me About This Again. Marking this option dis-
  ables this message. You can enable the warning again by going to the General tab in the
  Options dialog box (Tools, Options) and placing a check in the Advice About
  Scheduling option.

■ You can select the option to save the file with a baseline. There's no harm in choosing
  to save the project with a baseline at this point.

Figure 4.20
The Planning Wizard asks if you would like to save a baseline.

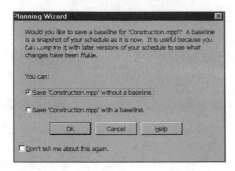

However, if you choose either of these options (disabling the message or saving a baseline), you must remember to save a baseline before actual work on the project begins. Also, there is a new feature in Project 2000 that lets you clear the existing baseline data in order to capture more accurate data.

→ To learn more about working with baselines, **see** "Setting the Baseline or Plan," **p. 660**

You must choose File, Save As if you later want to change any aspect of the way you saved a file. This includes changing the file's name, the location where it is saved, its password security, or the file format in which it is saved.

After you use the Save As dialog box once to establish the file name and location, you can choose File, Save or the Save button on the toolbar to save the file immediately—using its current save properties—without going through the Save As dialog box.

Caution

When working with programs (such as MS-DOS or Windows 3.1) which only support filenames of eight characters or less, a filename used in Windows 95, Windows 98, or Windows NT 4.0 will be truncated. The first six characters of the filename will be followed by a tilde (˜), and then by a number, usually a one (1). For example, the filename Office Move.MPP would be displayed as office˜1.mpp.

PROVIDING SECURITY FOR SAVED FILES

In the Save As dialog box, you can choose the Tools drop-down and select General Options to set the following security features for your file (see Figure 4.21):

- You can make a backup copy of the previous version of a file every time you save the file.
- You can password-protect the file. A user cannot access the file without knowing a password.
- You can write-protect the file so others can open and view the file under the original name—but cannot save any changes using the original filename. Changes can be saved under a different name. This feature protects the data you placed in the file, yet allows others to view the data.
- You can save the file with a warning message saying that you prefer users open the file as a read-only file.

Figure 4.21
You can protect your file from being changed by others or even from being read by others in the Save Options dialog box.

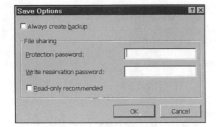

PASSWORD-PROTECTING A FILE

To protect a file, type up to 17 characters as a password in the Protection Password text box. You can enter any character, including spaces, numbers, and keyboard symbols. The password is case sensitive: If you enter capitals anywhere in the password, you must use capitals for those same characters when you supply the password to open the file. As you type the password, each character is represented onscreen by an asterisk. When you choose OK, you are prompted to confirm the password by typing it again (see Figure 4.22). You are notified if you fail to type it exactly the same and will have to reenter the password and confirmation. Choose OK to close the warning and try again.

Figure 4.22
You must type your password a second time to confirm it.

After you specify the security options, if any, choose OK to save the file. The password remains with the file each time you save the file.

When you attempt to open the file, you must enter the password exactly as typed when you saved the password (see Figure 4.23). If you do not enter the password correctly, including the upper- and lowercase of individual characters, you are warned and given another chance to type it correctly. There is no limit to the number of attempts you can make to type in the password.

Caution

It is important to use passwords you can easily remember. If you forget your password, there is absolutely no way to open the file. Not even the people at Microsoft can help you open the file with a lost password!

Figure 4.23
You must match the spelling of the pass word exactly to gain access to the file.

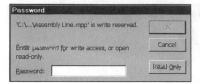

To remove a password, choose File, Save As. In the Save As dialog box, choose Tools, General Options. The Save Options dialog box appears. Delete all characters from the password field, and choose OK.

SAVING A READ-ONLY FILE

You also can save a file with a Write Reservation Password by selecting Tools, General Options in the Save As dialog box. The Write Reservation Password enables all users to open the file, but a warning appears stating that the file is write reserved (see Figure 4.24). If the user supplies the correct password in the Password text box, the file opens and the user has the right to make changes and save the file under the same name. If the user doesn't supply the correct password (or forgets the password), the user can only open the file as read only, and then save changes to the read-only file under a different name. Saving a file with a Write Reservation Password ensures that only users who have the password can replace the data in the file.

Figure 4.24
Unless you know the password, you cannot open a write-reserved file and save changes to it. You can only open it as read only.

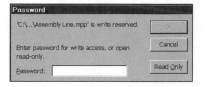

SAVING A FILE AS READ-ONLY RECOMMENDED

If you select the Read-Only Recommended check box in the Save Options dialog box (refer to Figure 4.21), users who try to open the file are warned that you want them to open the file as a read-only file (see Figure 4.25). Users can choose to accept the Read-Only default, or bypass the warning and open the file with read and write privileges. This option doesn't effectively prevent users from replacing the data in the file, but it does warn the users that the file is shared with others.

USING THE CREATE BACKUP FILE OPTION

If you select the Always Create Backup check box in the Save Options dialog box (refer to Figure 4.21), the original file is renamed by changing the extension from .MPP to .BAK each time you save the file. The revised version of the active file is then saved under the original name with the .MPP extension. This procedure retains a copy of the previous version of the file on disk. For example, suppose you created a project file named MOVE.MPP in April. It is now July, and you open the file to make several changes. If Always Create

Backup is active when the revised file is saved, the April version is saved as MOVE.BAK, and the revised file is saved as MOVE.MPP. If you make additional changes to the file in September, the July version *replaces* the April version and is saved with the .BAK extension; the September version will now have the .MPP extension. The April version is no longer available.

Figure 4.25
Choose Yes to open a file that was saved as Read-Only Recommended unless you must make changes and save them in the original filename.

SAVING FILES IN HTML FORMAT

Portions of your project files can be saved in the format (HTML) required by the World Wide Web. Your document can then be published on the Web. To save a file in HTML format, choose File, Save As Web Page. For information on Web capabilities, see Chapter 14, "Publishing Projects on the Web."

PART

I

CH

4

SAVING THE WORKSPACE

The File, Save Workspace command saves a small file that contains a list of the names of all the project files currently open in memory. When you open a workspace file, all the files contained in the list are opened. A workspace file acts as a *pointer* to the files; it does not contain a *copy* of the files.

Suppose you're working on three project files when you go to lunch. If you use the Save workspace command before you save and close the individual files, you can restore all the files to the screen just by opening the one workspace file. A workspace file also can be used to list files you work with routinely, so that each morning when you open the workspace all the files you need are opened.

The Open dialog box does not allow you to select multiple files to open; each file has to be opened separately. Creating a workspace file is the only way to open several project files at the same time and is a great feature for people who are managing multiple project files.

When you choose File, Save Workspace, the program displays the Save workspace As dialog box (see Figure 4.26). workspace filenames have the extension .MPW. Microsoft Project suggests a default workspace filename of RESUME.MPW, but you can change the name in the File Name text box. Unless you choose another drive or directory, the workspace file is saved in the current directory. Microsoft Project prompts you to save all open files that have changed since the last save. You also might see the Planning Wizard message about saving a baseline if tasks have been added that were not added to the baseline.

Note

If you have created a file but have not saved it, you will be prompted to make a decision about including that project file in the workspace file. New project files that are empty will not be added to the workspace file.

Figure 4.26
Create and save a workspace file when you want to be able to open all the Microsoft Project files that are currently open without having to open each individually.

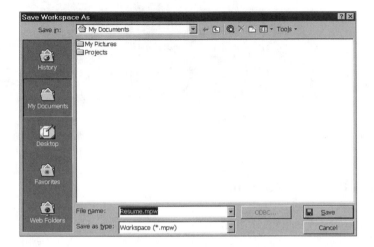

When you open a workspace file, all active files will be closed before the workspace file is opened. You will be prompted to save any active file in which changes have been made but not yet saved. Choose File, Open to open a workspace file and all the files contained in its list of filenames.

CREATING AND USING TEMPLATES

A *template* is a project file that contains a typical or standard set of tasks or resources that is used as a blueprint or starting point for creating similar new project files. Microsoft Project provides twelve sample templates, but you can create your own templates for repeating or similar projects. For example, you might create a template that lists a standard set of tasks common to a type of project you perform repeatedly. Likewise, if the same group of people are always involved in your projects, you can create a template containing the resource information so you won't have to enter it for each new project file. Template files have an .MPT extension.

OPENING TEMPLATE FILES

When you open a template, you are opening up a copy of the file, not the original template. You use this copy as a starting point for your new project.

 To open a template file, choose File, Open or click the Open button on the Standard tool-bar. Use the Places bar, Look In drop-down box, or the Up One Level button to navigate to the appropriate folder. You also can use the search criteria described in the "Locating Files" section earlier in this chapter to locate the template file you want to open. After you have selected the template you want to open, choose Open, or double-click the filename. The sample templates included with Microsoft Project are discussed later in this chapter.

With the exception of the GLOBAL.MPT, the copy of the template that appears will have the same name as the template. When you save the file, the Save As dialog box opens. The name of the template is the default project name, but the file type is changed to .MPP. You can use this name or supply a different name.

THE GLOBAL.MPT

When you create a new, blank project document, the new file is based on a default project template, the GLOBAL.MPT. The new file inherits all the features of the GLOBAL.MPT. All new projects have generic document titles: Project1, Project2, and so on. The GLOBAL.MPT is typically stored in the `\Program Files\Microsoft Office\Office\1033` or `Windows\Application Data\Microsoft\MS Project\1033` directory.

Note

To designate which language Windows and Office are installed in, Microsoft uses folders with numerical names. 1033 mentioned above designates English. If you have a different language version of Windows or Office installed, the folder name will be a different number.

PART

I

CH

4

Changes made to the GLOBAL.MPT affect all new project files. The Organizer is used to make changes in the Global template. See the "Using the Organizer" and "Trouble-shooting" sections later in this chapter for more information about modifying the GLOBAL.MPT.

USING THE MICROSOFT PROJECT SAMPLE TEMPLATES

Microsoft Project includes a wide range of sample files you can use as starting points for your own projects. The sample templates in Microsoft Project 2000 are unlike the templates provided with earlier versions of Project. Each template contains a detailed list of tasks, organized into phases appropriate for the type of project for which the template is designed. Each phase includes the typical activities with logical ties (links) to other activities in that phase or another phase.

For example, the Commercial Construction template specifies the common tasks required to construct a multiple-story commercial space and shows the relationships between those tasks. This template can be used as the foundation for a variety of commercial construction projects ranging from supermarkets and fast food restaurants to hotels and airports. The Commercial Construction Project template is organized into a number of phases: general conditions; long-lead procurement; site preparations; foundations; steel erection; floors; carpentry; masonry; roofing; windows and closures; elevators; plumbing; electrical; HVAC; and final cleanup and occupancy.

The list of sample project templates includes

- Commercial Construction
- Engineering

- Infrastructure Deployment
- MSF Application Development
- New Business
- New Product
- Project Office
- Residential Construction
- Software Development

Microsoft Project help contains detailed descriptions of each of these templates. Type **project templates** in the Office Assistant search box and choose the topic "Templates included with Microsoft Project" to learn more about these built-in templates.

There are three additional templates listed in the New dialog box for which there is no help. They are Microsoft Project 2000 Deployment, Office 2000 Deployment, and Windows 2000 Deployment. As the names imply, these templates are designed to help deploy Microsoft products within your organization.

The easiest way to access a sample template file is to choose File, New. Note—you *cannot* use the New button on the Standard toolbar to access the templates; you must use the New command on the File menu to display the New dialog box. In the New dialog box, click the Project Templates tab (see Figure 4.27). The sample templates are set up to install when you first attempt to use them. You will need to access the Project installation files to install these templates. These files are on the Project 2000 CD. Some organizations copy the installation files to a network server so users can access the installation files without the CD.

Note

If you have worked with previous versions of Microsoft Project, you will note that accessing templates in Project 2000 is more consistent with other Microsoft Office applications. In earlier versions of Project, you accessed the templates using the File, Open command. In Project 2000 you access templates through the File, New command.

Figure 4.27
You must use the File, New command to access the built-in Project template files.

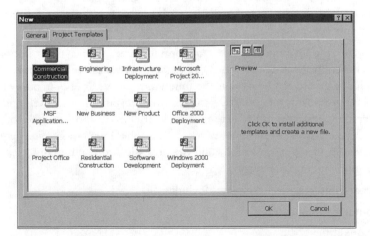

Select the template you want to use and click OK (or double-click the filename). When you create a new file based on one of Microsoft Project's templates, you are creating a copy of the file, not accessing the original template. Use this copy as a starting point for your own project.

> **Note**
>
> When you use a template to begin a file, the name of the template appears at the bottom of the Summary tab in the Properties dialog box (File, Properties).

CREATING A NEW TEMPLATE

Any of your existing project files can be saved as a template for similar or repeating projects.

Tip from Tim and the Project Team

> You can open the former project file, make your changes, and use the File, Save As command to save a copy of the new project with a different name. However, the advantage of creating a template is that when you save the file, because a template is a copy, you will automatically be prompted for the new filename. Thus you will avoid accidentally saving the new file over the former project file.

To save an active file as a template, choose File, Save As. Enter the filename you want to use, and choose Template from the Save as Type drop-down list at the bottom of the Save As dialog box. The filename extension changes to .MPT automatically. Microsoft Project stores templates in a default folder designated for User templates. The path to this folder is

`C:\Windows\Application Data\Microsoft\Templates\`

> **Note**
>
> You can designate a default location for your personal templates and for templates you share with other people. You can establish a default folder location for User templates and Workgroup templates through the Options dialog box. Refer to the section "Designating a Default Save Location and File Format" earlier in this chapter for the specific steps.

P 2000 When you save a project file as a template, a window appears (shown in Figure 4.28), which enables you to strip certain data from the template, such as baseline values, actual values, and so forth. This is a valuable new feature enabling you to use completed or active projects as the basis for new projects, removing data that is unique to each project.

→ Some data is not stripped out using this feature including task assignments, notes, and hyperlinks. **See** "Defining the Resource Pool," **p. 332**, and "Preparing a File for Use as a Resource Template," **p. 362**, for information on how to strip out this data before you save a file as a template.

When you use a template file as the basis for a new project, a copy of the file is displayed with the extension automatically changed to .MPP so you can save the working copy as a regular project file.

Figure 4.28
You can remove project-specific values from being saved with the template.

MODIFYING TEMPLATE FILES

If you would like the change a template file, there is no way to directly open the .MPT file. Instead, to make modifications to a template you must open a copy of the template, make the desired changes, and save the file under the default name, with the .MPT extension. You must make certain you choose Template from the Save as Type drop-down list to change the file type. The filename extension will change automatically.

USING THE ORGANIZER

When you modify an existing object—such as the Standard Base Calendar—or create a new customized view or report, the modified or custom object is only available to the project you are currently working with. The *Organizer* is a feature that lets you share objects in one project or template with another project or template. This is accomplished by copying the objects from one file to the other (see Figure 4.29).

The Organizer is most often used to copy modified or custom objects to other project files or to the GLOBAL template. You also use the Organizer to delete an object that is no longer needed or to rename an object. The Organizer is set up as a series of tabs, each tab focusing on a different type of object.

Figure 4.29
The Organizer dialog box provides access to all the items that can be customized and shared in Project.

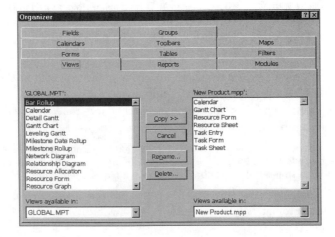

Table 4.4 lists the types of objects the Organizer keeps track of.

TABLE 4.4   OBJECTS IN THE ORGANIZER

Type	Description
Views	Views are screen displays used to enter, organize, and examine your project information. There are views designed to look at primarily task information and views for examining resource-oriented information. There are three types of views in Microsoft Project: charts or graphs; sheets; and forms. You can create custom views.
Reports	There are 29 predefined reports in Microsoft Project. You can create custom reports.
Modules	Modules are the location in which macros are stored. Microsoft Project uses Visual Basic to create macros. When you design your own macro, the macro is stored in a module.
Forms	A form is a specific type of view that provides detailed information about a task or resource. As with views, you can design your own custom forms.
Tables	Tables are used with views like Gantt Chart, Task Sheet, and Resource Sheet. Tables are similar to spreadsheets in that the data is organized in rows and columns. You can create custom tables.
Filters	A filter is a tool used to highlight specific information in a view. There are two types of filters—task filters and resource filters. You can create custom filters.
Calendars	A list of the base calendars for a project appears under this tab. You can create custom base calendars.
Toolbars	There are 11 toolbars in Project 98. These toolbars can be customized, or you can create your own custom toolbars.
Maps	The Maps tab is used track data exported to other programs. Export maps are sets of instructions that track exactly what types of data are to be exported, relating field to field or (when exporting to Excel) column to column.
Fields	The Fields tab lists any custom fields you have created in the project file. The GLOBAL.MPT file contains one custom field—WBS.
Groups	A group is a tool used to organize the display of your project information and see rolled-up totals for the grouped data. There are two types of filters—task groups and resource groups. You can create custom groups.

PART I

CH 4

The easiest way to access the Organizer is through the Tools menu—choose Tools, Organizer.

The Organizer also can be accessed through several other dialog boxes by choosing

- **More Views dialog box**—Choose View, More Views, Organizer.
- **More Tables dialog box**—Choose View, Table, More Tables, Organizer.
- **More Filters dialog box**—Choose Project, Filter For, More Filters, Organizer.
- **More Groups dialog box**—Choose Project, Group By, More Groups.

The Organizer can no longer be accessed by choosing View, Toolbars.

USING THE ORGANIZER TO MODIFY GLOBAL.MPT

New blank project documents are based on a Global template—the GLOBAL.MPT file. Changes you make to GLOBAL.MPT affect all new project files. If you want to customize GLOBAL.MPT, you can open the GLOBAL.MPT file directly, including earlier Global templates (from versions 98, 4.1, or 4.0), and transfer objects from your former Global templates into your Project 2000 Global template. When you open the file, it displays the Organizer. If you upgrade Microsoft Project 2000 over an older version of Microsoft Project (98, 4.1, or 4.0), customized items in the old Global template will automatically be included in the new GLOBAL.MPT file.

Best Practice Tips from Toby Brown, PMP

By customizing views and sharing these to a centralized global file, the organization goes a long way in presenting a concerted centralized Project Office effort. Customized views allow the organization to fully exploit the capabilities of the tool, not only in regards to formatting, but also the ability incorporate company logos, etc. This is a very effective way of standardizing the formatting of project plans for both internal and external communications.

Tip from Tim and the Project Team

If you make a copy of your former GLOBAL.MPT file (4.0, 4.1, 98)—naming it **GLOBAL98. MPT**, for example—and then open this file in Project 2000, you will be able to distinguish the two Global template files more easily in the Organizer. Otherwise, because the GLOBAL files in each version have the same name, it can be confusing as to which GLOBAL.MPT you are looking at.

COPYING OBJECTS WITH THE ORGANIZER

The steps that follow access the Organizer through the Tools menu. These steps are generic and can be used when copying any object managed by the Organizer. The active file, the file that contains the object, is referred to as the *source file*. The file in which you would like to place a copy is referred to as the *target file*.

Follow these steps to copy an object:

1. If you are copying an object to another file, rather than GLOBAL.MPT, make sure that both the source and target files are open.
2. Choose Tools, Organizer to display the Organizer dialog box.
3. Choose the tab that contains the object you want to copy. In Figure 4.30, the Tables tab is selected. The tables in the active file that have been used, altered, or newly created are listed on the right. The tables in the GLOBAL.MPT file are listed on the left.

   If you are copying an object to a file other than GLOBAL.MPT, use the Tables Available In drop-down list box on the bottom-left side to choose the target file. On the right side of the dialog box in Figure 4.31, the Entry Notes table is highlighted in the source file (New Product), and, on the left side of the dialog box, the target file (Product A24) is being selected.

Figure 4.30
The Tables tab in this figure shows the New Product file listed on the right.

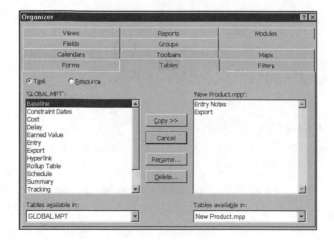

Source file   Object to be copied

Figure 4.31
To copy an object from one project document to another, display both the source and the target project files in the Organizer dialog box.

Target file

PART

I

CH

4

4. Choose the table you want to copy from the list of tables in your source file on the right side of the dialog box.

5. Choose the Copy button. If there is a table with the same name in the target file, Project will ask you for confirmation to override the former table (see Figure 4.32).

6. Choose the Yes button to replace the table in the target file with the new table from your active file.

    Or

    You can use the Rename button to copy the table to the target file by using a new name for the table, a name that is not already being used for another table.

7. Choose the Close button to close the Organizer dialog box.

Figure 4.32
You must confirm that you want to replace the table by the same name in the target file.

RENAMING AN OBJECT WITH THE ORGANIZER

You must use the Organizer if you want to rename an object you created in a project document. To rename an object, follow these steps:

1. Open the Organizer and choose the tab for the object you want to rename.

2. Select the object to be renamed.

3. Choose the Rename button. The Rename dialog box appears (see Figure 4.33).

Figure 4.33
Change the name of a project object in the Rename dialog box.

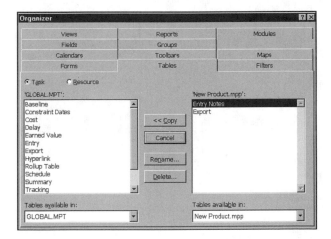

4. Type the new name for the object.

5. Choose the OK button to complete the name change.

6. Choose the Close button to close the Organizer.

DELETING AN OBJECT WITH THE ORGANIZER

Customized objects, such as tables, that you create in a project document cannot be deleted with the same menu or dialog box that you used to create them. You must delete them with the Organizer. To delete an object, follow these steps:

1. Activate the Organizer by choosing Tools, Organizer.

2. Choose the tab for the object you want to delete.

3. Select the object you want to delete.

4. Choose the Delete button. A confirmation dialog box appears (see Figure 4.34).

Figure 4.34
You must confirm the deletion of any object.

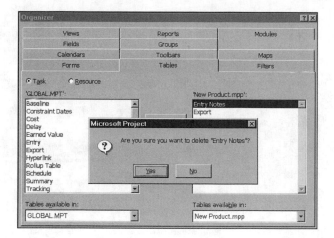

5. Choose the <u>Y</u>es button to confirm the deletion.
6. Choose the Close button to close the Organizer.

DISPLAYING AND CLOSING FILES

When you are working with more than one project file, you might want to alternate between your files, display them all at the same time, or close a file. Microsoft Project provides several alternatives for working with and closing your active files.

You can have up to 50 files open at the same time, each containing a separate project file. You can place one file at a time onscreen for viewing, or you can place all the files onscreen for simultaneous viewing by using the <u>W</u>indow, <u>A</u>rrange All command.

You can switch back and forth between your open project files several ways:

■ The Taskbar
■ The <u>W</u>indow menu
■ The Alt+Tab list
■ The Ctrl+F6 keyboard shortcut

USING THE TASKBAR AND ALT+TAB LIST

 If you have Internet Explorer (4.0 or higher) installed with Web Integration settings, you can use a new feature to easily switch back and forth between your open project files. This feature is called *Single Document Interface* (SDI). With SDI, each open project is displayed on the taskbar and in the Alt+Tab list.

To switch between any one of your open project files using the taskbar, simply click the project file you want to display. In Figure 4.35, the New Product file is displayed. There are two other project files open and listed on the taskbar. There is also an Excel file open. If there are so many files open that you cannot see the complete the name of the open files, you can position your mouse pointer on a file and a ScreenTip will display the entire name. In Figure 4.35 the mouse pointer is on the first file and the ScreenTip identifies this file as Assembly Line.mpp.

Figure 4.35
Each file you have open, regardless of the application, is listed on the taskbar.

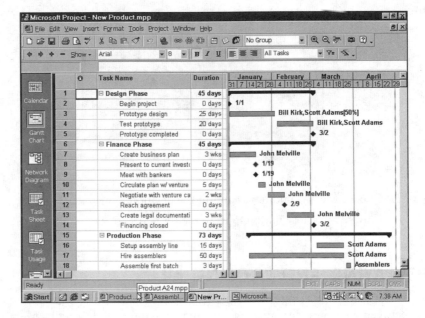

To use the Alt+Tab keyboard shortcut to switch between your open files, follow these steps:

1. Hold down the Alt key.

2. Press and release the Tab key once, keeping the Alt key held down. A pop-up appears, similar to the one shown in Figure 4.36. Each icon represents an open file. The name of the icon that is selected appears below the list. In Figure 4.36 the active icon is the Microsoft Project file New Product.

3. With the Alt key still held down, press Tab until the file you want to switch to is selected.

4. Then release the Alt key to display the file.

USING THE WINDOW COMMAND

The Microsoft Project Window menu lists up to nine open file windows at the bottom (see Figure 4.37). A check mark indicates the currently active file. You can choose the next file you want to activate by selecting a file from the list.

If more than nine file windows are open in memory, the More Windows command appears at the bottom of the Window menu, as shown in Figure 4.37. Choose the More Windows command to access the Activate dialog box (see Figure 4.38). The Activate dialog box enables you to choose the window you want from a list. Select the file you want to activate, and choose the OK button.

Figure 4.36
You must keep the Alt key held down until the file you want to view is selected from the list of icons.

Microsoft Project - New Product.mpp

Figure 4.37
Activate document windows by choosing from the list in the Window menu.

Figure 4.38
Use the Activate dialog box to scroll the entire list of open windows.

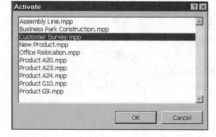

You also can use Ctrl+F6 to activate the next window. Pressing Ctrl+F6 again cycles through all the open windows until it returns you to the window you started with. Use Shift+Ctrl+F6 to cycle through the windows in the reverse direction. See Chapter 18, "Working with Multiple Projects," for more information on working with multiple files.

CLOSING FILES

Use the File, Close command to remove an active document from memory. If you have made changes to the document since you last saved it, you are prompted to save the contents before closing. Choose from one of the three choices: Yes, No, or Cancel. Choose Yes to save the file and close the file. Choose No to close the file without saving your changes. Choose Cancel to leave the document open on the workspace; the file is not saved or closed.

TROUBLESHOOTING

LOCATING THE GLOBAL.MPT

How do I copy my Global.MPT to a floppy disk so that I can share it with someone else?

Global.MPT may be installed in several locations on your hard drive, so it is important you check the date it was last modified to ensure you copy the correct one. Look in `C:\Windows\Application Data\Microsoft\MS Project\1033` or `C:\Windows\Profiles\`*Username*`\Application Data\Microsoft\MS Project\1033`, where *Username* is your name.

SPECIFYING WHERE PROJECT LOCATES GLOBAL.MPT

In Project 98, there were two places where Project looked for the Global.MPT file on startup: the current folder and the folder containing the winproj.exe file. So if I customized my Global.MPT and designated a specific folder to use on startup, I would be able to use my custom Global.MPT instead of the default Global.MPT. I understand this has changed in Project 2000. Can you explain how?

When Project starts, it first looks to see if there are any Registry policy keys. Organizations can add one or both of these keys to the Registry to control access to the Global.MPT file that is used by their users. This prevents users from making modifications to Global.MPT. The first key, RootKey, establishes the location where Microsoft Project will find Global.MPT (such as on a network drive). If this key exists, but the file or location named in the key doesn't exist, then Project displays an error message and will refuse to start. A second additional permissions key can be set to indicate whether Project users are restricted to using just the Global.MPT file in the RootKey location, or if they can use a Global.MPT file from another location—such as their own, customized Global.MPT located in the language folder (1033, for example).

```
HKEY_CURRENT_USER\Software\Policies\Microsoft\Office\9.0\MS Project\GlobalSearch

Data: RootKey

Value: <Full path to Global.MPT>

Type: REG SZ
```

```
HKEY_CURRENT_USER\Software\Policies\Microsoft\Office\9.0\MS Project\GlobalSearch

Data: Permission

Value: <0 or 1> // 0 = not restricted, 1 = restricted

Type: REG DWORD
```

If these registry keys don't exist, Project looks for the Global.MPT file in the following places in the order listed:

1. **In the current folder**—If you establish a shortcut to start Project, you can designate a default "Start In" folder. If there is a Global.MPT file in this folder, Project will use that Global.MPT file. Likewise, if you double-click on a project file in Windows Explorer, if a Global.MPT file resides in the same folder as the project file, then Microsoft Project will use that Global.MPT.

2. **In the user's profile folder**—For example, where *Username* is the user's name:

   `C:\Windows\Profiles\`*Username*`\Application Data\Microsoft\MS Project`

3. **In the user's profile language folder**—For example, where *Username* is the users name and *LanguageNumber* is the numerical folder name indicating the language of the version of the project installed (such as 1033 for English):

   `C:\Windows\Profiles\`*Username*`\Application Data\Microsoft\MS Project\`*LanguageNumber*

4. **In the same folder that contains the Winproj.EXE file**—By default this file (which is the main Project program file) is located in

   `C:\Program Files\Microsoft Office\Office`

5. **In the Winproj.EXE language folder**—Where *LanguageNumber* is the numerical folder name indicating the language of the version of project installed (such as 1033 for English). This is located in

   `C:\Program Files\Microsoft Office\Office\`*LanguageNumber*

6. If Global.MPT cannot be located, then the Windows Installer starts and attempts to restore a copy of the Global.MPT file to the Winproj.EXE language folder. If the Windows Installer is unable to restore a copy of Global.MPT (such as when the Project installation files are not available), a message appears indicating that a new Global.MPT file will be created, but that it may be missing some items.

SCHEDULING TASKS

CHAPTER 5

CREATING A TASK LIST

In this chapter

APPROACHING THE PLANNING PROCESS

After securing approval for a concise but comprehensive goal statement that defines the scope of the project, your next major planning function is to draw up a list of activities or *tasks* that must be completed to achieve the project goal. Using Microsoft Project to help create the task list can save a great deal of time and effort. At this stage of the process, the computer's major contribution is as a word processing tool to help you enter, annotate, revise, and rearrange your ideas. You take advantage of its impressive computational powers in later chapters when you tell it how to schedule the tasks and assign resources to them.

Best Practice Tips from Toby Brown, PMP

Starting the planning process typically follows completion of project initiation, the deliverables of which include the assignment of the project manager and the issuance of the project charter. Once created, the course of the project has been set and the product of the project has been defined.

There are two basic approaches to creating a task list: the top-down approach and the bottom-up approach. In the top-down approach, you start by listing the major phases of the project. Then you create an outline from the list of major phases by inserting and indenting under each major phase the detail tasks that make it possible to complete the phase. This method is probably the most common approach to project planning, and it provides an organizational structure from the outset that makes it easier to comprehend the scope of the project.

If you use the bottom-up approach, begin by listing all the task details. Although it is not required, many people prefer to have the list in a somewhat chronological order. If your project is not too complex, this list might be adequate for understanding the scope of the project. However, for more complex projects, finish by organizing the task list into an outline.

Outlining produces an organizational form that is functionally identical to the organization chart format traditionally used by project managers that is called the *Work Breakdown Structure* (see Figure 5.1). The Work Breakdown Structure identifies major components of a project and shows multiple levels of detail under each major component. Work Breakdown Structure codes (*WBS codes*) are traditionally used to number each task in such a way that the code identifies where the task fits into the hierarchical structure. These codes are by default identical to the outline numbers provided automatically by Microsoft Project and can be seen on the task list (see Figure 5.2).

Best Practice Tips from Toby Brown, PMP

Work Breakdown Structures (WBS) can appear in several formats, the most common of which include the chart format and the outline format. It doesn't matter which format is used, but rather the importance of capturing the entire scope of the project within the WBS. The chart format tends to be favored over the outline format simply because it is easier to add to the list under each element. However, Project doesn't support this type of charting function. Instead, you must do it manually or with some other software package. Using the more prevalent outline format requires pushing tasks down in order to insert additional tasks, regardless of whether the top-down or bottom-up approach is used.

Figure 5.1
Work Breakdown Structure diagrams organize the project tasks into phases or functional groups that help visualize the scope of the project.

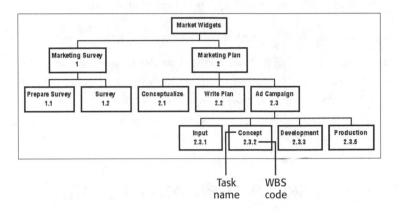

Figure 5.2
Project's outline numbers can be used as WBS codes.

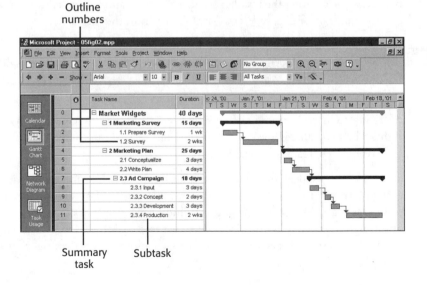

PART

II

CH

5

An outline is not necessary for a complete project plan. However, outlining has many advantages and can significantly enhance your plan's flexibility and usefulness as a planning and reporting tool:

■ Outlining encourages an orderly planning process, with less likelihood of leaving out crucial steps.

- You can display outlined projects with different levels of detail both on the screen and in printed reports. You can collapse the outline to major topics only, or to any level of detail, depending on the intended audience

- Summary tasks in outlined projects automatically provide summary calculations for the subtasks under them. The duration, cost, and work for all the tasks indented beneath them are summed ("rolled up") into the summary task.

Build your task list by creating three main types of tasks:

- *Normal tasks* are those that represent the actual work on the project.

- *Milestones* are tasks that represent a point in time in the project where a major goal is achieved or a significant decision point is reached.

- *Summary tasks* serve to group together and summarize other tasks that are related in some way. The tasks indented under a summary task are called *subtasks*.

ENTERING TASKS IN THE GANTT CHART

The initial view in Microsoft Project is the Gantt Chart view (see Figure 5.3), and it is the best view for creating the task list. To display the Gantt Chart, click the Gantt Chart icon on the View bar or choose View, Gantt Chart from the menu.

Note

You also can use other views for creating the task list, several of which are discussed later in this chapter in the section "Using Other Views to Enter Tasks."

The Gantt Chart displays a *task table* on the left side of the screen and a timescale on the right. The task table is a list of task names and related information about each task that is displayed in a spreadsheet-type format.

The task table is ideal for creating and editing the task list. You can edit the list of tasks and easily rearrange their order. You can enter a maximum of 1 million tasks in a single project, so the task table can be expanded to a million rows. You can include up to 65,000 levels of outlining indentation to organize the project into major phases or processes. Pop-up forms are easily accessible for any task to add or view more details than those provided in the table.

Tip from Tim and the Project Team

Microsoft Project also provides drag-and-drop features in the Gantt Chart view for moving, copying, outlining, linking, and assigning resources, all of which make editing the task list easier. (See "Working With the Gantt Chart View" in Chapter 7, "Viewing Your Schedule.")

Gantt
Chart
icon

Vertical
divider
bar

Figure 5.3
The Gantt Chart is
one of the most ver-
satile views in
Microsoft Project.

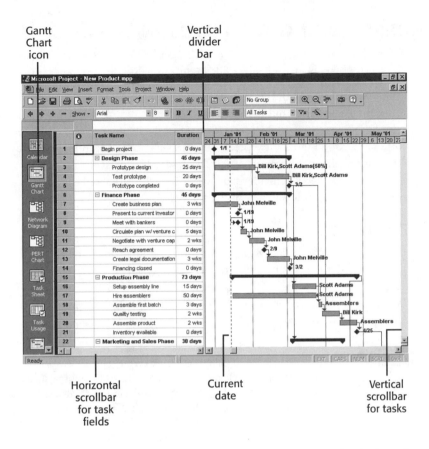

Horizontal
scrollbar
for task
fields

Current
date

Vertical
scrollbar
for tasks

PART
II
CH
5

The timescale on the right side of the Gantt Chart displays the start and finish dates for tasks as a bar chart. A horizontal bar begins at each task start date and ends at that task's finish date. The task bar is normally solid from the start to the end of the task, appearing in front of any shading on the Gantt Chart for nonworking time. The current date is displayed on the timescale as a vertical dashed line.

Tip from Tim and the Project Team

If you want task bars to only show working time, choose Format, Timescale from the menu and click the Nonworking Time tab. Change the Draw option from Behind Task Bars to In Front of Task Bars and click OK. This displays the nonworking-time shading in front of the task bar so that the solid parts of the bar reflect only actual working time.

The longer the task bar connecting the start and finish dates, the longer it takes to complete the task. By comparing the task bars for tasks, you can quickly see which tasks start or finish first and which take longer to complete. Text displayed next to each bar shows the resources assigned to the task. Lines with arrows connect tasks to show the sequence links between them.

→ There are many options for customizing the Gantt Chart display. If you want to learn more about using those options, **see** "Using the Common Format Options in the Standard Views," **p. 892**, and "Formatting the Gantt Chart," **p. 905**

UNDERSTANDING THE FIELDS IN THE TASK TABLE

Before you start creating your list of tasks, you should understand the columns you see in the Gantt Chart because Project fills in default values for them as you enter task names.

In the default version of the task table, you see four columns or *fields* (ID, Indicators, Task Name, and Duration) and these are the fields covered in this chapter. There are additional fields that you can scroll into view (Start, Finish, Predecessors, and Resource Names), but those are covered in later chapters. You can view these additional fields by using the horizontal scrollbar at the bottom of the task table. Alternatively, you can use the mouse to drag to the right the vertical divider bar that divides the table and the timescale. This displays more of the task table and less of the timescale.

THE ID FIELD

The column of row numbers at the left of the table is more formally known as the Task ID field. It shows the task's position in the task table and is also used to reference a task. References to a task use the ID number instead of the task name because duplicate task names are permitted. You can't edit the task's ID field directly, but it is automatically recalculated when a task moves to a different row.

> **Note**
>
> In addition to the ID number displayed on the screen, there is also a permanent ID number stored in the task field named *Unique ID*. Project assigns that number when the task is first created and that number never changes. If a task is deleted, its Unique ID is not reassigned. Internally, Project uses the Unique ID to identify and link tasks.

THE TASK NAME FIELD

The column headed Task Name contains the text you choose to describe the task. Task names can contain up to 255 characters and, as mentioned before, do not have to be unique. See "Displaying Long Task Names" later in this chapter for information about showing all of the text in long task names.

In creating your list of task names, you have to exercise judgement about how finely detailed you want your list to be. You should only list those tasks that you think it worthwhile monitoring to be sure that they are complete.

THE DURATION FIELD

The Duration field is one of the most important fields in calculating your schedule. In broad terms, this field is where you enter your estimate of how long it takes to complete a task. When you first enter a task name, Project supplies a default value of "1 day?" in the Duration field. The question mark is new in Microsoft Project 2000 and it flags this entry as a tentative estimate. Entering duration estimates is covered later in this chapter.

THE START AND FINISH FIELDS

These fields show the date and time when work on a task is scheduled to start or finish. The initial display format for the date fields shows only the date portion of the field. Instructions for displaying both date and time in date fields are given later in this section.

Generally, you want to let Project calculate the schedule of task dates for you—after all, that is one of the chief benefits of using project management software. However, you can also enter dates in these fields yourself, although doing so limits Project's ability to calculate a revised schedule if circumstances change. Generally, you should not enter dates in the Start or Finish fields but should instead provide Project with the information it needs to schedule the dates for you. Until you provide that information (which is the subject of the next chapter), Project arbitrarily sets the task at either the start or finish of the project.

Tip from Tim and the Project Team

By entering a date in the start or finish field, the task becomes constrained to the specified date. If you find yourself constantly entering a specific date for the tasks within the project, it becomes apparent that a scheduling tool, such as Microsoft's Outlook, may work better for you. In other words, you are not realizing the benefits of using a project management tool to build a schedule based on estimated durations, logical dependencies, resource assignments, and calendars. Specifying dates in the schedule defeats the purpose of doing the planning process.

THE DEFAULT START AND FINISH DATES

If you have chosen to schedule your project from a fixed start date, Project normally sets the start for new tasks to be the same as the date and time when the project starts. It then adds the task duration to derive the task finish date and time. If you have chosen to schedule the project from a fixed finish date, Project sets the finish for new tasks to be the date and time when the project finishes, and subtracts the task duration to derive the task start.

If the project start date is not the current date, the task bar might not be visible until you scroll to the date for the start of the project.

Tip from Tim and the Project Team

Move the button in the horizontal scrollbar beneath the timescale to the far left or right to go to the start or end of the project. Use the Go To Selected Task button on the Standard toolbar to go to the beginning date for the task that is currently selected.

Instead of scheduling new tasks at the project start or finish, you can optionally tell Project to start new tasks on the current date (the date when you are adding the new task to the project file). For instance, after a project is under way, you usually still have to add new tasks as circumstances change. In this case you probably want to have new tasks start on the current date, because the project start date is behind you at that point. But for creating a plan for a future project, you want to have new tasks initially set to the project start or finish date.

To set the default start date for new tasks, follow these steps:

1. Choose Tools, Options to display the Options dialog box and select the Schedule tab.

2. Using the drop-down list for New Tasks, choose the default schedule for new tasks:
   - For projects with fixed start dates, choose either Start on Project Start Date or Start on Current Date.
   - For projects with fixed finish dates, choose either Finish on Project Finish Date or Start on Current Date. (You wouldn't want Project to set the finish of the task on the current date because that would put the start in the past.)

3. Click OK to close the dialog box.

Note

Recall from Chapter 3, "Setting Up a New Project Document," that the project Current Date and either the Start Date or Finish Date are defined in the Project Information dialog box.

THE DEFAULT TIME OF DAY

All date fields in Project contain both date and time of day components, even when the display of the date is not formatted to show the time of day. The default start date for a task also includes the default start time of day for scheduling work on the project. The initial default time for starting work is 8:00 a.m., but you can change that in the Options dialog box (see Figure 5.4).

Tip from Tim and the Project Team

Even if date fields do not display the time of day, you can enter time along with the date in any date field. For example, to stipulate that a task should not start before 2:00 p.m. on January 1, 2001, you could enter **1/1/2001 2:00 PM**.

Figure 5.4
Set the default start and end of the working day to determine when Project starts and ends new tasks.

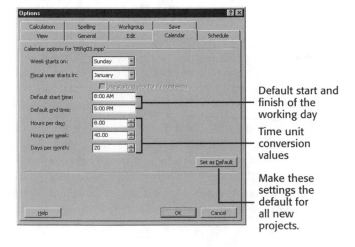

Default start and finish of the working day

Time unit conversion values

Make these settings the default for all new projects.

To set the default time of day for starting or finishing new tasks, you would follow these steps:

1. Choose Tools, Options to display the Options dialog box and select the Calendar tab.

2. In the Default Start Time field, enter the time of day to be used for starting tasks in projects with a fixed start date.

3. In the Default End Time field, enter the time of day to be used for finishing tasks in projects with a fixed finish date.

4. To make these the default values for all new project files that you create, click the Set as Default button. Note that this does not change any existing project files; it only ensures that new project files contain these values.

Note

The default start time for tasks must also be a working hour on the calendar or tasks can't actually be scheduled to start at that time. See "Defining a Calendar of Working Time" in Chapter 3 for help in defining the calendar.

Having set the task start date, Project calculates the task finish date by adding the duration (1 day) to the start date and enters that value in the Finish field. The finish date is usually the same date as the start date. However, the two dates contain different time elements: the start field refers to the start of the workday (for example, 1/1/2001 8:00 AM) and the finish field refers to the end of the work day (for example, 1/1/2001 5:00 PM).

DISPLAYING THE TIME OF DAY WITH DATES

If you want to display the time along with the date, use the Tools, Options command to display the Options dialog box. The Date Format list box on the View tab has a drop-down list of date formats, the first of which contains both date and time.

Tip from Tim and the Project Team

If you switch to a longer date format, the Start and Finish fields might display pound signs as an indication that they are not wide enough to display the longer format. You can widen the column by double-clicking the column heading for each field and choosing the Best Fit button.

You can enter time in the 24-hour format no matter which setting you have chosen in the Control Panel. For example, you can enter January 1, 2001, 3:30 p.m. by typing in either **1/1/2001 3:30 PM** or **1/1/2001 15:30**. If you want to display time in the 24-hour clock format, however, you must select that format in the Windows Control Panel for all applications to use. In the Regional Settings applet, select the Time tab and choose the HH:mm:ss style in the Time Style box.

THE PREDECESSORS FIELD

This field shows the ID numbers for any other tasks whose scheduled start or finish must be taken into account before calculating this task's start or finish. For example, if a task must be scheduled so as to start only after task number 5 is finished, the ID number 5 would appear in the Predecessor field. There is much more on coordinating task schedules in the next chapter.

THE RESOURCE NAMES FIELD

This field shows the names of the resources assigned to work on the task. Part III, "Assigning Resources and Costs," covers resource assignments in more detail.

ENTERING TASK NAMES

You create a task by typing a name in the Task Name field in one of the rows of the task sheet portion of the Gantt Chart. As soon as you press Enter or move to another cell, Project supplies a default duration of 1 day for the new task, and a default start and finish date for the task. It also displays a task bar starting at the project start date under the timescale in the Gantt Chart to the right.

Best Practice Tips from Toby Brown, PMP	A good practice in building projects is to name activities in a verb-noun format, such as Install Computers, Complete Design Specifications, or Move Warehouse. By using this concise call-to-action naming convention, it is easier to define the tasks and clearly communicate what work needs to be done in the project. It also makes it easier to estimate task durations by simply asking, "How long does it take to…".
Tip from Tim and the Project Team	Actually, if you make an entry in any field on a blank row of the task table, you have created a task, even if it has no task name yet. If you accidentally create a task this way, select any cell on that row and press the Delete key to remove the task.

To enter task names, you should

1. Select a cell in the Task Name column.
2. Type the task name, using any combination of keyboard characters and spaces and entering up to 255 characters.
3. Complete the cell entry by pressing Enter, by clicking the green check mark in the Entry bar, or by selecting another cell. You can cancel the cell entry before entering it by pressing the Esc key or by clicking the red "x" in the Entry bar. In that case, the field reverts to its former contents.

After completing the cell entry, Project fills in default values for the task duration and the start and finish dates for the task. Then it moves the selection to the next row for you to enter the next task.

Tip from Tim and the Project Team

If you don't want the selection to change when you press Enter, you can disable the feature in the Options dialog box. Choose Tools, Options and select the Edit tab. Deselect the Move Selection After Enter check box and click OK.

Note

See the section "Editing the Task List" later in this chapter for other tips for entering and editing the task list.

Caution

One more time: You should usually avoid entering start or finish dates in the date columns. They are intended to be calculated by Project based on the links between tasks that you create in the next chapter. If you enter dates here, a constraint is created that might limit Project's ability to reschedule the task as needed.

→ If you really do want to create a constraint for the task, **see** "Entering Task Constraints," **p. 239**

COPYING TASK NAMES FROM ANOTHER APPLICATION

If your task names have already been entered into another application such as a word processor, spreadsheet, or database, you can copy the list to the Windows Clipboard and paste it into Project. After the list of tasks arrives in Project, you want to organize the tasks into an outline.

To copy a list of task names from another application into Project, follow these steps:

1. Open both Project and the other application.

2. In the other application, select the list of names you want to copy. Note these requirements for the source list:

   • If the source is a word processing document or presentation document (such as Microsoft Word or Microsoft PowerPoint), each task name must be on a separate row of text.

   • If the source is a spreadsheet (such as Microsoft Excel), each task name must be in a separate cell in a column of entries, and all the names you want to copy must be adjacent to each other.

   • If the source is a database (such as Microsoft Access), the task names must be in a single field of the database. Select the cells in that field only—do not select the records because that would select other fields also and Project won't know what to do with the other fields.

3. Use the Copy command to copy the list to the Clipboard.

4. Select the cell in the Task Name field in Project where you want to place the first name in the list and use the Paste command.

PART
II

CH
5

DISPLAYING LONG TASK NAMES

If the task name is too long to see in the Task Name column, you can adjust the width of the column with the mouse. To change the width of a column, drag the right border of the cell that contains the column title to the right or left. You will see the pointer change into a double-headed right and left arrow when it's in position to change the column width. If you double-click instead of dragging, Project adjusts the column's width automatically to the longest entry it finds in the column.

Caution

If you don't place the mouse pointer directly on the title cell's border line, the pointer does not change into a double-headed arrow and double-clicking the mouse opens the Column Definition dialog box (shown in Figure 5.5). Select the Best Fit button to have Project adjust the column width to the widest entry.

Figure 5.5
Use the Column Definition dialog box for, among other things, adjusting the column width.

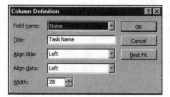

ADJUSTING THE HEIGHT OF TASK ROWS

Initially, all rows in a table display a single line of text. In that case the row height is said to be one (1). But you can adjust any or all rows to display variable numbers of text lines. The maximum row height is 20 (or 20 lines of text). Project automatically word-wraps text if extra lines are available and the text entry is longer than the column width can display. Figure 5.6 shows word-wrapped task names.

To adjust the height of a row, you drag the bottom (not the top) of the cell that contains the row number up or down: down to add lines and up to reduce lines. Note that row height is not infinitely variable; it can only be changed in increments of lines of text from 1 to 20.

To change the height of one row, follow these steps:

1. Position the mouse on the row divider line below the row number in the task ID column. The mouse pointer changes to up and down arrows.
2. Drag the divider line up or down until you reach the desired height for the row.

Note

Unlike adjusting column widths, you cannot double-click the line dividing row numbers to automatically set the best fit.

Select all
rows by
clicking
here.   Row height
of 1

Figure 5.6
You can use more
than one row to dis-
play each task in the
Gantt Chart. This
enables long task
names to word-wrap.

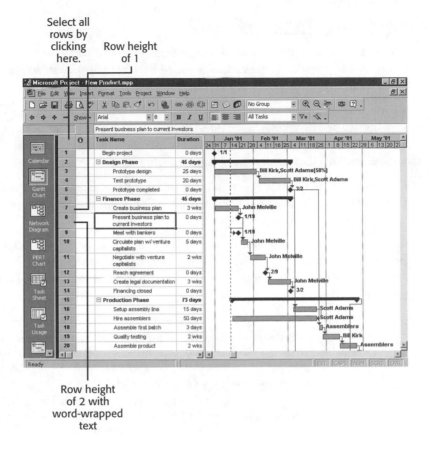

Row height
of 2 with
word-wrapped
text

To change the height of multiple rows at once, follow these steps:

1. Select the row numbers for the rows you want to change.

    • You can drag the mouse from the first row number to the last to select the rows if
      the rows are all together.

    • Use the Ctrl key to select row numbers that are not next to each other.

    • If you want to select all rows in the project, click the blank column header just
      above the column of row numbers.

2. Position the mouse on the row divider line beneath any one of the selected rows and
   drag to the desired the height. All the selected rows are adjusted to the same height.

→ For information about setting specific row heights for a table, **see** "Using and Creating Tables" **p. 949**

EDITING THE TASK LIST

After you start creating the task list, you inevitably need to edit your entries. This section is a collection of commands and techniques used for editing that apply to all views, not just the Gantt Chart.

 Microsoft Project 2000 has added *in-cell editing*, which means that you can choose to edit the contents of a cell by typing directly into the cell itself as an alternative to typing into the Entry bar. The difference is that the editing insertion appears within the cell text instead of in the Entry bar. Your typing is displayed in both places.

The simplest way to edit the entry directly in the cell is to select the cell and then press the F2 function key. The insertion point appears at the end of the text in the cell and you can reposition it by clicking elsewhere.

You can also initiate in-cell editing with the mouse. Select the cell by clicking it once. The mouse pointer should change into an I-beam when over the right side of the cell entry or when to the left of the beginning of the entry. When the pointer is an I-beam, click and the insertion point appears at the point in the entry where you clicked.

Tip from Tim and the Project Team

Activating in-cell editing with the mouse takes a little practice because the mouse pointer also displays a two-headed horizontal arrow (which is used to facilitate outlining) when over the first third of the cell entry. So, it shifts between being the I-beam and the outlining tool as you glide over the cell contents.

Also, if the pointer displays the white cross (the selection indicator), click the cell again and the I-beam should appear. Then click the I-beam where you want the insertion point to be.

UNDOING CHANGES IN THE TASK LIST

Although you are revising the task list, you can undo nearly any change made in the task list with the Edit, Undo command. However, you can only undo the most recent change. Also, you can usually reverse the last undo. When you use the Undo command a second time, Project calls the undo a "redo." When this is the case, the Undo command on the Edit menu is replaced by the Redo(u) command.

To undo or redo a change, follow these steps:

1. Choose Edit, Undo to reverse the most recent change in the project. You can also choose the Undo button on the Standard toolbar (or press Ctrl+Z).

2. Choose Edit, Redo (u) to reverse the undo you just executed, use the Undo button, or the shortcut key Ctrl+Z. These options all act as toggles.

INSERTING, CLEARING, AND DELETING TASKS

As you revise a project, you often need to insert new tasks or remove tasks from the task list.

To insert a task between other tasks

1. Select a cell in the row where you want the new task to appear. New rows are always inserted above the selected one. If you want to insert several tasks at the same location, extend the selection to include the number of rows that you want to add. All the details of the tasks included in the selection shift down to make room for new blank rows.

2. Choose Insert, New Task (or press the Insert key).

Deleting an entire task is different from clearing the data from one or more fields for the task.

Follow these steps to delete one or more entire tasks:

1. Select at least one cell in each of the tasks to be deleted.

2. Press the Delete key, or choose Edit, Delete Task. The rows for the selected tasks are removed from the task list, and the remaining tasks close the gaps.

You can undo the deletion if you choose Edit, Undo before making another change.

The Edit, Clear command leaves the task row in place but clears or removes selected characteristics of the task's fields. The Edit, Clear command displays a menu with the following choices:

- Choose Formats to clear only the formatting of the selected cells, leaving their content unchanged.

- Choose Contents to clear only the content of the selected field(s). If you have one or more individual cells selected, the command affects only the selected cells. If you have the task row selected (by clicking the task ID), the command is applied to all task fields, even those not displayed in the current view.

  The shortcut key for clearing contents only is Ctrl+Delete. The Clear Contents command also appears on the shortcut menu when you right-click a cell.

- Choose Notes to clear just the Notes field for the task, no matter which cell (field) you have selected. This is provided because the Notes field is not usually visible.

- Choose Hyperlinks to clear any hyperlinks that have been attached to the task. Again, the Hyperlinks fields are not readily available and this provides an easy way to clear an unwanted hyperlink.

- Choose the All command to execute all the above options at once, clearing the formatting, contents, notes, and hyperlinks. If you had the task row selected, this choice would cause Project to clear the contents of all fields but leave the row as a task. It would then immediately reapply the default duration and start and finish dates, even though the task now has no name.

- Choose Entire Task to clear all cells and fields for the task and leave a blank row that is no longer a task.

PART
II

CH
5

Note

> You can undo all the Clear commands except for Formats—you can't restore formats that have been cleared.

MOVING AND COPYING TASKS

You can copy or move cells or whole tasks to another location in the task list or to another project file. For both moving and copying, your selection must contain only adjacent cells or tasks. The Cut command removes the selected tasks or cells from their original location, whereas the Copy command just makes a copy of them. The Paste command is used with both Cut and Copy to insert the copy of the tasks or cells at the new location.

Caution

> If you want to cut or copy an entire task or group of tasks, you must select the task ID number (or press the Shift+spacebar shortcut key combination). Use the mouse to select the ID number, which selects all fields for the task (even those not displayed in the current view). If you select a limited number of cells in a task or group of tasks, only the data in these cells copies to the Clipboard.

To move a task or group of tasks, follow these steps:

1. Select the original task entries by clicking the ID number(s) for the tasks or by selecting all cells in a task row.

   Click the first task to be selected, press and hold the Shift key, and click the last task to be included. All tasks between those two points are included in the selection. You can also use the Shift key with the arrow keys to select adjacent task ID numbers.

2. Choose Edit, Cut Cell or Cut Task from the menu or use the Cut button on the Standard toolbar to cut the original data from the task list to the Clipboard.

3. Select the task row where you want to relocate the data. Even if you are moving more than one task, select only the first row of the new location.

   If a task already resides on the row you selected, this task and all tasks below it automatically shift down to make room for the task or tasks you're moving.

4. Choose Edit, Paste from the menu or use the Paste button on the Standard toolbar to paste the Clipboard contents into the task list at the selected row. The Paste command inserts a new row or rows at the target selection point and copies the tasks in the Clipboard to the inserted rows.

To copy a task or group of tasks, you should

1. Select the original task entries using the techniques previously described.

2. Choose Edit, Copy Cell or Copy Task from the menu or use the Copy button on the Standard toolbar to copy the selected data to the Clipboard.

3. Select the task row where you want the data duplicated. Even if you are copying more than one task, select only the first row at the new location.

   If a task already exists on the row you select, that task (and all tasks below it) shift down to make room for the new task or tasks you copy.

4. Choose Edit, Paste, or the Paste button on the Standard toolbar to copy the Clipboard contents into the task list at the selected row. The Paste command inserts a new row or rows at the target selection point and copies the tasks in the Clipboard to the inserted rows.

Note

Even if you don't like to try remembering shortcut keys, you should learn the three shortcut keys for Cut, Copy, and Paste because there are many situations where they can be used but there is no menu or toolbar active to use for those operations. For example if you want to move a paragraph in a task note, neither the menu nor toolbar is available.

The shortcut keys are: Cut (Ctrl+X), Copy (Ctrl+C), and Paste (Ctrl+V).

After you copy data to the Clipboard, you can paste the data multiple times. The task data remains in the Clipboard until another copy or cut operation replaces the current Clipboard contents with new data.

If you select just one or more fields for a task instead of selecting the entire task (for example, if you select just the Task Name field), the Paste command doesn't insert a new row to create a new task at the target location. Instead, Paste copies the text from the Task Name cell to the cell you have selected when you execute Paste. If no task exists on the target row, the new entry resulting from the Paste command creates a new task with a default duration.

Caution

Make sure you select the entire task or tasks—by selecting their ID numbers—before you begin a cut or copy operation if you intend to create new tasks at the paste site.

In addition to the cut-and-copy method for moving and copying tasks within the project, Project also includes a drag-and-drop feature to perform the same commands.

To *move* a task or group of tasks using the drag-and-drop feature, follow these steps:

1. Select the original task entries by clicking the ID number(s) for the tasks. Remember that they must be adjacent.

2. Position the mouse pointer over the ID number for any one of the tasks selected.

3. Hold down the mouse button and drag the pointer in the direction of the new location. A shadowed I-beam appears as you drag the pointer to its destination. Release the mouse when the I-beam is located where you want to insert the selected tasks. The selected tasks are inserted where the I-beam was located.

PART

II

CH

5

To *copy* a task or group of tasks using the drag-and-drop feature, follow these steps:

1. Select the ID numbers for the original tasks. You can click and drag to select multiple task ID numbers; or you can select the first ID number and use Shift as you select the last ID number in a group.

2. Move the mouse pointer over the ID number for any one of the tasks selected.

3. Press and hold the Ctrl key and then drag the mouse in the direction where you want to paste the copy. When you hold down the Ctrl key with the mouse button, a small plus symbol appears next to the mouse pointer. This symbolizes a copy command using the drag-and-drop feature, rather than a move. A shadowed I-beam follows as you drag the pointer to its destination.

4. When the I-beam is in the correct place, release the mouse to insert the copy at the I-beam.

USING THE FILL COMMAND

If you want several cells in a column to have the same entry (for example, many tasks with the same duration), you can place the entry in one cell and have Project fill the other cells with the same entry. To fill multiple cells with the same entry, follow these steps:

1. Type the entry in one cell.

2. Press and hold the Ctrl key as you click other cells below and in the same column. The cells do not have to be in adjacent rows.

3. Choose Edit, Fill and then the desired direction (Down, Right, Up, or Left) to fill the adjacent cells with the same entry that is in the selected cell. (For Fill Down copying you can also use the key combination Ctrl+D.)

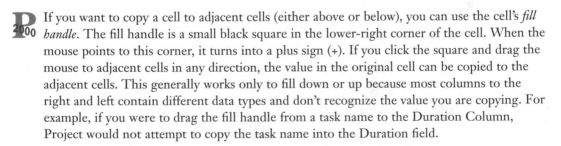

If you want to copy a cell to adjacent cells (either above or below), you can use the cell's *fill handle*. The fill handle is a small black square in the lower-right corner of the cell. When the mouse points to this corner, it turns into a plus sign (+). If you click the square and drag the mouse to adjacent cells in any direction, the value in the original cell can be copied to the adjacent cells. This generally works only to fill down or up because most columns to the right and left contain different data types and don't recognize the value you are copying. For example, if you were to drag the fill handle from a task name to the Duration Column, Project would not attempt to copy the task name into the Duration field.

USING THE AUTOCORRECT FEATURE WHILE TYPING

Microsoft Project 2000 includes an AutoCorrect feature that automatically corrects common typing errors as you type. These typing errors could be spelling, simple grammatical errors, or misplaced spaces. For example, if you type **comittee**, AutoCorrect replaces the word with the correctly spelled "committee" as soon as you press the spacebar or place a punctuation mark. In addition, if you type **might of been**, AutoCorrect replaces the phrase with "might have been."

AutoCorrect also automatically capitalizes the names of the days of the week. If you mistakenly hold the Shift key too long and capitalize two letters at the beginning of a word (such as PRoject), AutoCorrect changes the second letter to lowercase.

If AutoCorrect changes a word you want left unchanged, you can simply change it back and AutoCorrect leaves it alone. If you never want a particular change to be made, you can add the word to the exceptions list in AutoCorrect. Of course, you can still run the spell checker to locate spelling mistakes.

You can turn off all or part of the AutoCorrect features, and you can add your own frequent misspellings to the list of corrections to be made automatically. You also can use AutoCorrect to replace abbreviations to save time as you type. For example, you can set AutoCorrect to replace "abc" with "ABC Manufacturing Co." To make changes in AutoCorrect, follow these steps:

1. Choose Tools, AutoCorrect. The AutoCorrect dialog box appears (see Figure 5.7).

Figure 5.7
AutoCorrect can significantly speed up your typing because it corrects many of the most common typing mistakes.

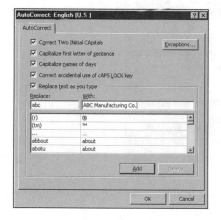

PART

II

CH

5

2. Deselect an option if you want to disable that AutoCorrect function.

   For example, deselect Replace Text as You Type if you don't want AutoCorrect to replace what you type with different spellings. (Select it again to turn it back on.)

3. In the Replace text box, type a word or character string you want to be replaced automatically each time you type it. For example, to replace "abc" with "ABC Manufacturing Co.", type **abc** in the Replace text box.

4. Press the tab key and type into the With text box the replacement word or phrase. For the "abc" example, type **ABC Manufacturing Co**.

5. Choose the Add button to add your replacement text to the list at the bottom of the dialog box. Add as many replacement text items as you want by repeating steps 3 through 5.

6. Delete an AutoCorrect entry by selecting the entry in the list at the bottom of the dialog box and then choosing the Delete button.

7. When all additions and deletions are completed, choose the OK button to close the AutoCorrect dialog box.

If you want to change the replacement text supplied by AutoCorrect, follow these steps:

1. Choose Tools, AutoCorrect to open the AutoCorrect dialog box.

2. From the list at the bottom of the dialog box, click the item you want to change. This places it in the Replace and With text boxes. Or, simply type the item in the Replace text box.

3. Enter or edit the text in the With box. The moment you add text to the With box, the Replace button becomes available (see Figure 5.8). In the figure, the abbreviation "Co." has been changed to "Company."

Figure 5.8
You can modify the replacement text supplied by AutoCorrect.

4. Choose the Replace button. A warning dialog box asks you to confirm the change (see Figure 5.9).

Figure 5.9
You must confirm any change to an AutoCorrect entry.

5. Choose Yes to confirm the change.

6. After you've entered all changes, choose OK to close the AutoCorrect dialog box.

If you want to change the way AutoCorrect makes changes to capitalization without turning the features off altogether, follow these steps:

1. Choose Tools, AutoCorrect to open the AutoCorrect dialog box.

2. Choose the Exceptions button.

3. Enter or edit the text in the D<u>o</u>n't Capitalize After box on the First Letter tab or in the D<u>o</u>n't Correct box on the INitial CAps tab.

4. Choose the OK button to close the AutoCorrect dialog box.

Note

The AutoCorrect list is shared among the various Microsoft products; therefore, any entries added or changed are also reflected in any other Microsoft products that you use. Likewise, any changes made in the AutoCorrect list of other products are also reflected in Project.

ENTERING TASK DURATION

The project calendar defines the hours and days when work can be scheduled on the project. The *duration* of a task refers to the amount of time that is scheduled on the project calendar for working on the task. A task with an estimated duration of 8 hours is scheduled for work during 8 hours of time on the project calendar. There might be one or many resources assigned during those 8 hours, but the duration is still 8 hours.

When you estimate the duration of a task to be, say, 8 hours, you should keep these points in mind:

- The duration hours do not have to be continuous, although Project initially assumes that they are the first available hours for work on the calendar after the start of the task. You can later modify the schedule so that the task could be worked on for 1 hour a day for 8 days. The duration (the amount of time spent working on the task) would still be the same.

- A task that is completed by one person working on it full-time for 8 hours has a duration of 8 hours. But so does a task that is completed by five people working on it full-time for 8 hours. Duration doesn't measure the total amount of work or effort needed to complete the task; it measures how many units of time on the calendar all that work takes.

- When estimating durations, you should consider past experience with similar tasks, the experience and skill level of the resources you plan to use, and the number of resources you plan to use. You need to remember these assumptions when you later assign the resources to the task, so you can assign the same number you counted on when estimating the duration. If you are not assigning resources as you estimate the task duration, you might want to use the Notes field to remind yourself of the resource configuration you assumed for the duration estimate. See the section "Entering Task Notes" later in this chapter.

PART
II

CH
5

Note

If you already have predetermined dates for starting and finishing all your tasks, you can enter those dates in the Task Form view and let Project calculate the duration implied by the dates (see "Project Extras. Letting Project Calculate Duration for You" at the end of this chapter). You can improve the reliability of your duration estimates by using Project's PERT Analysis toolbar. For additional information, see the "Using PERT Analysis" article available on the companion Web site for this book at www.quepublishing.com.

USING TENTATIVE DURATION ESTIMATES

When you create a task name, Project tentatively assigns the task a default duration of 1 day and displays the duration as "1 day?", with the question mark indicating that it is a tentative estimate. After you overwrite the default value with your own (hopefully) informed estimate of duration, the question mark goes away.

Tip from Tim and the Project Team

You can use the question mark with your own duration estimates. If you want to enter a tentative duration value (one that you want to consider further at a later time), you can add a question mark to your entry as a reminder. You can use the Tasks with Estimated Durations filter to display all those duration estimates that are tentative.

→ If you want to use the Tasks with Estimated Durations filter, or other filters for tasks, **see** "Working with the Gantt Chart View," **p. 260**

Note

If you have reliable duration estimates from past experience, you might want to use the more sophisticated statistical method of estimating duration with what is known as PERT Analysis. You can download the "Using PERT Analysis" article from the companion Web site for this book at www.quepublishing.com. Enter this book's ISBN number (0789722534) to access the supporting materials for the text.

UNDERSTANDING THE DURATION TIME UNITS

You have considerable flexibility in the unit of time with which you express duration. The default time unit is day, but you can also use minutes, hours, weeks, or (starting in Microsoft Project 2000) months. When you type in a duration value and attach one of these time units, Project displays the duration using the time unit you type in. However, if you enter a duration value without appending a time unit, Project appends the *default duration time unit* to your entry and displays the value with that time unit. The default time unit for duration is also used by Project when it creates the default duration value for a new task. Initially the default time unit is "day."

Caution

> Assume that you want to change the duration of a task from four weeks to five weeks and the default duration time unit is the day. If you type a "5" over the "4 weeks", Project changes the duration to "5 days" because it always appends the default duration unit when you fail to supply one. The result would be a gross understatement of the duration you wanted to enter. Always include the time unit unless you are positive that the default time unit is the one you want to use for that duration value.

If you want to change the default time unit for the Duration field, open the Options dialog box with the Tools, Options command and select the Schedule tab. The Duration Is Entered In field has a drop-down list of the possible time units that you can use (Minutes, Hours, Days, Weeks, or Months).

When you enter a duration estimate using day, week, or month units, Project internally converts these units to minutes because it does its calculations in minutes. Project bases its conversion to minutes on the assumption that an hour is always 60 minutes and on the definitions for the other time units found in the Tools, Options dialog box (refer to Figure 5.4). The default conversion rates are

- 1 day = 8 hours
- 1 week = 40 hours (or 5 8-hour days)
- 1 month = 20 days (or 160 hours)

If your organization works six 8-hour days a week, you would want to adjust the definition of a week to be 48 hours. Then, when you enter a duration of 1 week, Project knows what your frame of referenced is. Or, if your organization works four 10-hour days a week, you would want to change the definition of a day to 10 hours, but leave the definition of a week at 40 hours.

To redefine the conversion rates for duration time units, follow these steps:

1. Choose the Tools, Options command to display the Options dialog box.
2. Select the Calendar tab.
3. Enter the number of work hours in a day in the Hours Per Day field.
4. Calculate the number of work hours in a week and enter that number in the Hours Per Week field.
5. Decide on the number of days you want Project to use when you enter the month time unit and enter that number in the Days Per Month field.
6. Click OK to save your definitions.

USING TIME UNIT ABBREVIATIONS

When entering duration units, you can use the complete word or either one of two abbreviations. For example, to enter one day you can type 1 **d**, 1 **dy**, or 1 **day**. Project also supports plural versions of the time units. The full list of spellings Project supports for the time units is shown in the following list:

- m, min (or mins), minute (or minutes)
- h, hr (or hrs), hour (or hours)
- d, dy (or dys), day (or days)
- w, wk (or wks), week (or weeks)
- mo, mon (or mons), month (or months)

Although you can use any of the spellings when you enter duration values, Project uses a default spelling for displaying each of the time units. For example, if you set the default display for "weeks" to be "wk", no matter whether you enter "w", "wk", or "week", Project displays the result as "wk" or "wks".

You can select the default spelling for the time units by choosing Tools, Options to display the Options dialog box and selecting the Edit tab. Use the drop-down lists in the View Options for Time Units section to select the default spellings.

Note The Years field setting has nothing to do with duration time units. It is used exclusively to enter pay rates for resources who are paid on an annual basis.

DEFINING ELAPSED DURATION

The duration values discussed thus far referred to an amount of time to be scheduled on the project calendar. The project calendar has nonworking time (night, weekends, and holidays) that this regular duration must be scheduled around.

You can also schedule a task that has *continuous* or uninterrupted activity around the clock. For example, if a chemical process takes five hours, that usually means five continuous hours. If the process starts at 3:00 p.m., it needs to continue until 8:00 p.m. the same day. The Working Time calendar in Project might assume that work stops at 5:00 p.m. and Project would schedule the remaining work starting at 8:00 a.m. the following work day.

To schedule a task that should not be restricted by the working time calendar, enter the duration as *elapsed* time. To do this, insert the letter "e" before the time unit abbreviation. The duration estimate for the chemical process, for example, would be 5eh to represent five elapsed (continuous) hours.

Note The elapsed day is defined as 24 hours, and the elapsed week is 168 hours (seven 24-hour days).

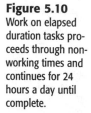

Best Practice Tips from Toby Brown, PMP

The use of an elapsed duration is typically confined to tasks that are not dependent upon resource scheduling, such as paint that is drying. These tasks are often necessary to realize a span of time that will usually not have a resource assigned to it and, therefore, are frequently excluded from the task list. Instead, lag is often used to impose a required time delay between activities.

From a project management standpoint, the rule of thumb is to ensure that every subtask has at least one resource assigned to it, which is why tasks might be intentionally omitted. However, from a communications perspective, there really is nothing wrong with including these types of tasks in the schedule. The point is to effectively communicate what is happening in the project, which is the whole reason for using the tool anyway.

Figure 5.10 illustrates the differences between normal and elapsed duration. Task ID number one is a task with a normal 5-day duration. Work begins on a Thursday but is interrupted by the weekend. Work is continued on the following Monday and continues through Wednesday for a total of 5 work days. The task bar looks longer (seven calendar days) than the actual working days because it spans the shaded nonworking days defined in the calendar. Total work during the period is 40 hours (five 8-hour work days).

Task ID number two is a task with an elapsed duration of 5 days. Project schedules work on the task around the clock for five 24-hour time periods. Work continues through the weekend days and the holiday. Total work during the period is 120 hours (five 24-hour work days).

Nonworking time
on the calendar
is shaded.

Figure 5.10
Work on elapsed duration tasks proceeds through nonworking times and continues for 24 hours a day until complete.

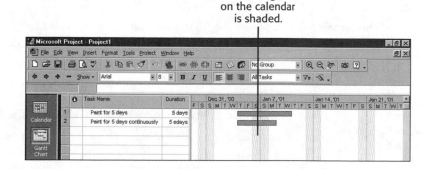

ENTERING MILESTONES

The *milestone* is a special type of task that represents a significant landmark, decision point, or turning point in the life of the project. You commonly use milestones to mark the completion of major phases or other major events in the project. A milestone is most easily defined by entering a task name and assigning it a duration of zero. Milestones typically do not represent *doing* work; they signal that some work has started or is completed. Milestones represent a point in time when something happens, whereas the ordinary tasks stretch out over time and represent continuing activity.

Best Practice Tips from Toby Brown, PMP

By definition, a milestone is a task that has a duration, cost, and resource assignment of zero, regardless of what the software allows you to do.

In the default Gantt Chart, milestones are formatted with the scheduled completion date displayed next to it. Also, milestones are often used to close the loop on a network schedule, providing both a starting point and ending point for the diagram.

At a minimum, it is good practice to ensure all of your projects have two milestones: project start and project complete.

You should create milestone tasks at points you want to monitor closely in the project. In a project to construct a building, for example, one milestone might be the completion of all the tasks involved in laying the foundation. The milestone could be named Foundation Complete and have a duration of zero. If you enter **0** in the duration field for a task, Project makes the task a milestone.

Note

You can mark any task as a milestone, even if it has a non-zero duration. To change a task to a milestone, or to remove its milestone designation, select the task and display the Task Information dialog box by clicking the Task Information button on the Standard toolbar, or by simply double-clicking the task name. Choose the Advanced tab and click the Mark Task as Milestone check box to change its milestone status. Choose OK to close the dialog box.

The Gantt Chart displays a milestone as a diamond shape, without a duration bar (see Figure 5.11). You can modify the symbol for a milestone and for all other task bars with the Format, Bar Styles command in the Gantt Chart view.

→ If you want to change the display for milestones, **see** "Formatting the Gantt Chart," **p. 905**

Figure 5.11 illustrates the power of using milestones. This view of the project displays the entire project on one screen and it shows only the milestones. In one glance you can see all the important dates for the project.

Figure 5.11
Milestones highlight major events in a project.

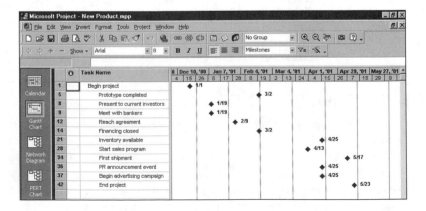

→ For instructions on creating a view like this, **see** "Working with the Gantt Chart View," **p. 260**

USING RECURRING TASKS

If you have one or more tasks that need to be repeated regularly during the life of the project, you can enter them as *recurring tasks*. For example, you might want to schedule weekly project status meetings every Monday from 2:00 p.m. to 5:00 p.m. Other examples could be monthly inspections or bi-weekly equipment maintenance.

Best Practice Tips from Toby Brown, PMP

Recurring tasks are a great way to capture time and effort on a project that is not specifically tied to work-related tasks. Since they occur at set intervals that you configure, they don't have to be linked to other tasks within the project. By definition, recurring tasks are constrained to the schedule and are not responsible to drive other task relationships. Status meetings are the most common use of this feature of the software, but other reasons include quality reviews, risk assessment, and scope change review meetings.

CREATING RECURRING TASKS

To insert a recurring task in your task list, follow these steps:

1. From any task view, select the Task Name field on the row where you want to insert the recurring task. You don't have to create a blank row for each recurring task, it is inserted automatically and the row you have selected is pushed down to make room for it.

2. Choose Insert, Recurring Task. The Recurring Task Information dialog box appears (see Figure 5.12).

3. Type the task name in the Task Name text box and the duration of each occurrence of the task in the Duration box.

4. From the Recurrence Pattern group of controls, choose a general frequency: Daily, Weekly, Monthly, or Yearly. In Figure 5.12, the Weekly option has been selected.

PART

II

CH

5

Duration of
each meeting

Figure 5.12
Use the Recurring
Task Information dialog box to add tasks
that repeat regularly.

General
frequency

Specific
frequency

Date and
time of 1st
meeting

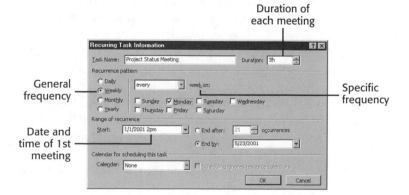

5. Define the specific frequency in the group of options to the right of the general frequency selection.

This group varies depending on the general frequency you choose. If you choose Weekly, you can use the *<every>* Week On drop-down list to specify a frequency ranging from every week to every 12th week. Then, select the day of the week on which you want to schedule the tasks. The specific frequency choices for Daily, Monthly, and Yearly are discussed later in this section.

6. Next, define how often the task is repeated by defining the date range within which the tasks should be scheduled, or by specifying the number of times you want the task scheduled.

> **Note**
>
> Initially, the Start and End By text boxes show the start and finish dates for the project, and the End After *<nn>* Occurrences box shows the calculated number of occurrences that can be scheduled in that date range.
>
> If you want the first occurrence of the recurring task to start sometime after the project starts, change the Start date. Specify a start date in the Start box. If you want the tasks to be scheduled at a specific time of day, enter the time as well as the date in the Start text box. To select a date from a calendar, click the drop-down arrow.
>
> Change the End By date if you want to specify when the last occurrence of the recurring task should be scheduled.
>
> Alternatively, select the End After *<nn>* Occurrences option and enter a number to specify how many occurrences are to be scheduled.

> **Caution**
>
> If you enter a number larger than the calculated default, Project schedules the number of occurrences you enter but the later occurrences are beyond the original finish date of the project and it extends the duration of your project.

7. If you have a special task calendar you have created for scheduling the recurring task, select its name in the Calendar box. Task calendars are covered in the next chapter.

→ If you want to create and assign a special calendar for a task, **see** "Creating and Using Task Calendars," **p. 252**

8. Each resource you assign to the task has its own calendar of available working times. If you assign a calendar to the task, you can select Scheduling Ignores Resource Calendars if you want Project to ignore the availability of assigned resources when scheduling the recurring task. This is useful when you expect resources to work on the task some but not all the time (for example, to attend some but not all the meetings).

→ To learn how to define resources and their working times, **see** Chapter 8, "Defining Resources and Costs," **p. 313**

9. Choose OK or press Enter to complete the recurring task definition.

Sometimes, your definition of a recurring task might lead Project to place a task on a nonworking day. If this occurs, Project warns you (see Figure 5.13) and asks you how to proceed.

- Choose the <u>Y</u>es button to let Project reschedule the affected tasks at the earliest available working time.

- Choose the <u>N</u>o button to skip those dates and leave those tasks out of the series of recurring tasks.

- Choose Cancel to stop the creation of the recurring tasks altogether.

Figure 5.13
Microsoft Project adjusts recurring tasks to the working calendar.

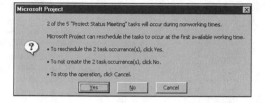

Note

Recurring tasks are automatically created as Fixed Duration tasks. This has implications for assigning resources to tasks. See the section "Choosing the Task Type" in Chapter 9, "Understanding Resource Scheduling," for details.

Once entered, the recurring task is placed in the task list as a specially formatted *summary task* (see Figure 5.14). Like all summary tasks, this one spans multiple subtasks; in this case, it extends from the beginning of the first meeting to the end of the last meeting. The formatting for this summary task is the special *rollup* formatting: Instead of being one solid bar, it shows short segments that represent the scheduled times for the subtasks.

Tip from Tim and the Project Team

An icon representing recurring tasks is displayed in the Indicators column to the left of the task name. If you point to the indicator with the mouse, Project displays a ScreenTip showing the number of occurrences and the overall date range for the group of tasks.

The duration of the summary task is the number of working calendar days that lapse between the start of the first occurrence and the end of the last occurrence of the recurring task. In Figure 5.14, the Duration column for the recurring task shows 100.38 days, but this doesn't mean that those who attend the meetings log a total of 100.38 days of meeting time. Rather, the last meeting ends 100.38 days after the first meeting begins.

In Figure 5.14, the task ID numbers 3 through 23 do not appear. That's because the summary task for the recurring task has hidden subtasks (the individual meetings that are currently hidden from view). Each of the subtasks is *rolled up* to the summary task bar.

Figure 5.15 shows the project with the subtasks displayed. To display the subtasks, select the summary task name and choose the Show Subtasks button on the Formatting toolbar. To hide the subtasks, choose the Hide Subtasks button. Complete instructions for working with outlines are covered later in this chapter.

Figure 5.14
The summary task for a recurring task displays the rolled-up schedule for all the subtasks on a single row of the Gantt Chart.

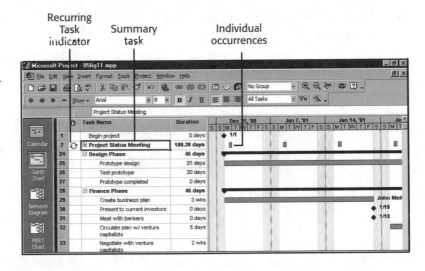

Figure 5.15
You can display and hide the subtasks (recurring tasks) by clicking the outline symbol to the left of the summary task or by double-clicking the task ID number.

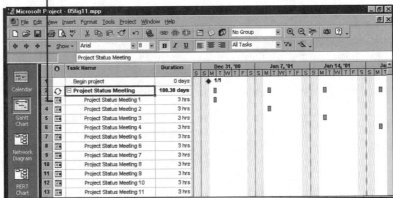

Caution

Each of the subtasks in a recurring task is constrained to start-no-earlier-than its scheduled date. Constraints can create problems in a schedule if you make major changes in the project schedule. To learn more about working with task constraints, see the "Entering Task Constraints" section in Chapter 6, "Entering Scheduling Requirements."

The previous steps describe how to create weekly recurring tasks. The process for creating daily, monthly, and yearly recurring tasks is very similar. The steps below describe the differences in defining the specific frequencies of these tasks.

To create a series of daily recurring tasks, follow these steps:

1. As with the steps for the weekly tasks, choose the task row where you want to insert the recurring tasks and choose Insert, Recurring Task.

2. Select the Daily option to display the Daily specific frequency group (see Figure 5.16).

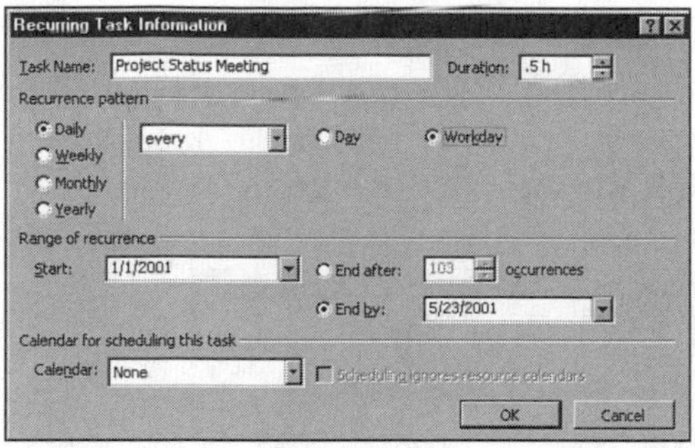

Figure 5.16
You can schedule daily recurring tasks at intervals on regular working days as well as on nonworking days.

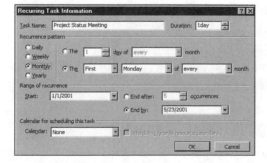

3. Choose a frequency interval ranging from every day to every 12th day from the *<every>* drop-down list box.

4. Select the Day option to schedule the tasks on working and nonworking days alike.

Or

Select the Workday option to schedule tasks only on days defined as working days on the calendar.

5. Choose OK to schedule the tasks.

You follow a similar procedure when you want to create a series of monthly recurring tasks. Simply select the task row where you want to insert the recurring tasks and choose Insert, Recurring Task. When you're given the option, select Monthly to display the Monthly specific frequency group (see Figure 5.17).

Figure 5.17
You can specify a specific month date or a recurring weekday for monthly tasks.

To pick a specific day of the month and specify which months to schedule the task in, select The *<nnth>* Day of *<every>* Month option. Fill in the *<nnth>* day of the month box and select an option from the *<every>* drop-down list to specify which months.

You can also choose to specify a particular weekday (such as the third Monday) of the month. Choose the option The *<nth>* *<weekday>* of *<every>* Month. Use the drop-down list boxes to specify the day and months that are scheduled. For example, Figure 5.17 shows the First Monday of every month displayed in the boxes. You can choose intervals from every month to every 12th month.

For creating a series of yearly recurring tasks, take a look at Figure 5.18. As with the previous examples, you choose the task row where you want to insert the recurring tasks and choose Insert, Recurring Task, and then select the Yearly option.

Figure 5.18
You can indicate a specific day of the year or a specific weekday in a specific month for yearly tasks.

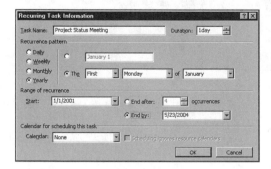

EDITING RECURRING TASKS

If you select the summary task for a recurring task and choose the Information button, the Recurring Task Information dialog box appears as though you were beginning to create the recurring task. After you make your changes, choose the OK button. A Microsoft Project warning message warns that Project changes the frequency of the recurring task (see Figure 5.19). Choose OK if you do not mind losing the existing subtasks that need to be deleted to change the frequency of the recurring task.

Figure 5.19
Project must delete the existing tasks if you change the frequency of a recurring task.

CREATING TASKS WITH THE MOUSE

You can use the mouse to create task bars on the Gantt Chart. You must then name the tasks, and you usually need to adjust the duration of tasks when they are created this way. Although this feature is easy to use, it has its hazards. When you drag the mouse to create a task bar, the task is automatically constrained to be scheduled no earlier than that date. If you drag from the start to the finish of the task, the task is constrained to start no earlier than the date you started the task bar on. If you drag from the finish to the start, the task is constrained to finish no earlier than the finish date you began with. These constraints can be very bothersome later as you edit the project, especially if you try to link subprojects to a master project. The best course is to rarely create tasks with the mouse.

→ If you have created a task constraint that you want to remove, **see** "Removing Task Constraints," **p. 247**

USING THE TASK INFORMATION DIALOG BOX

 You can quickly see more fields of information about a task in almost any view by selecting the task and then displaying the Task Information dialog box (see Figure 5.20). To display the Task Information dialog box, click the Task Information tool on the Standard toolbar, or choose Project, Task Information from the menu. You can also simply double-click the task name.

Five tabs organize the task fields in the Task Information dialog box: General, Predecessors, Resources, Advanced, and Notes. These tabs contain additional details about the task that is selected, and most of these fields are not immediately available on the Gantt Chart. In fact, no one view contains all the fields you find in the Task Information dialog box.

Figure 5.20
Use the Task Information dialog box for quick access to commonly used task fields that are not available in the view you are currently using.

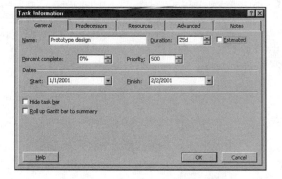

ENTERING DATA IN THE TASK INFORMATION DIALOG BOX

To review or change data in the Task Information dialog box, select the tab that contains the field you want. You can then move from field to field with the Tab and Shift+Tab keys or move directly to a field by clicking it. You can also move directly to a field by pressing the Alt key plus the underlined letter in the field label. Press Alt+D, for example, to move directly to the Duration text box.

Fill the Estimated check box on the General tab to add a question mark to the task duration to flag it as tentative. Clear the check box to remove the question mark.

Fill the Hide Task Bar check box to hide the task bar in the timeline display; clear the check box to let the task bar be displayed.

You can mark a task as a milestone by selecting the Mark Task as Milestone check box on the Advanced tab. When you enter a duration of zero, a task is automatically marked as a milestone. You can mark any task as a milestone by selecting this check box, even if the task's duration is not zero. You can also remove the milestone status by deselecting this check box.

When you are finished, click OK to accept the changes or click Cancel (or press Esc) to close the dialog box without changing anything.

ENTERING TASK NOTES

A hallmark of good project management is providing good documentation about the details of the project. Use the Notes tab of the Task Information dialog box to enter and display notes for each task (see Figure 5.21). These notes are invaluable to you in a complex project because you can easily forget why you made certain decisions earlier, especially if a superior wants an explanation. They also provide the essential information someone else would need if you must pass the project on to them to manage. Include in your notes any assumptions that you are making about this task and any reminders that you need to document. You can include the task notes in printed reports.

Best Practice Tips from Toby Brown, PMP

In addition to providing background information on a task, notes can be inserted regarding changes made to scope and the impact on the estimated durations. Scope creep is a significant cause of project overruns in both time and costs and should be well documented within the project, especially when examining variance (the difference between the current schedule and baseline). For this reason, notes can also be printed as an addendum page to the project plan.

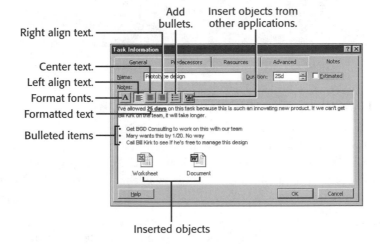

Figure 5.21
Use task notes to document details about the task that don't fit into one of the standard fields.

Right align text.
Add bullets.
Insert objects from other applications.
Center text.
Left align text.
Format fonts.
Formatted text
Bulleted items
Inserted objects

TYPING AND FORMATTING NOTES

To enter notes about a task, select the task and choose the Task Notes button on the Standard toolbar. This button takes you directly to the Notes tab of the Task Information dialog box. Type the note in the Notes text box. Notes can contain hundreds of thousands of characters.

A toolbar at the top of the Notes text box provides formatting options for the notes (refer to Figure 5.21). You can change the font and alignment for the notes, create a bulleted list, and even insert images or documents from other applications. You can also use the conventional Microsoft shortcut keys for bold (Ctrl+B), italics (Ctrl+I), and underline (Ctrl+U).

Project word-wraps in the Notes text box. If you want to force a new line or start a paragraph, press the Enter key. Use the following keys to move through the Notes text box:

Key	Effect
Home	Moves to the beginning of the current line
End	Moves to the end of the current line
Ctrl+Home	Moves to the beginning of the note
Ctrl+End	Moves to the end of the note
Ctrl+left arrow	Moves one word to the left
Ctrl+right arrow	Moves one word to the right

You can use drag-and-drop techniques to edit your notes. After selecting a word or group of words, you can click and drag the selection to a new location within the note. If you want to copy the selection, hold down the Ctrl key as you drag it to the new location.

Tip from Tim and the Project Team

The Tab key moves you out of the Notes text box. You can use Ctrl+Tab to insert a tab character in the note text—but you can't adjust the inherent tab stops which are set six spaces apart.

Tasks with notes attached display the Notes icon in the Indicators column to the right of the ID number in table views.

INSERTING OBJECTS IN NOTES

You can also insert data *objects* from other applications into a note. An object is a data file in the file format that another application maintains (pictures, spreadsheets, word processing documents, presentations, sound files, video clips, and so on). For instance, you could insert a blank Excel worksheet within a note and edit the worksheet to show calculations you need to keep handy. Or you can insert a copy of an existing worksheet. If you link the copy you have inserted to the original document, Project updates the copy in the note with the current contents of the original document.

The Task Information dialog box does not expand to provide an adequate display area for viewing large objects. Consequently, with large objects you probably only want to display an icon for the object in the note instead of the object itself. You can double-click the object or its icon and Project opens the application and lets you read or change the data as needed.

Best Practice Tips from Toby Brown, PMP

Other examples of objects that can be inserted include reference documents required at the start of a task and work products, which can be a deliverable of task completion. Including these items assists with the knowledge transfer processes often lacking within organizations. It also helps prevent re-inventing the wheel with each new project.

→ For more information on working with objects, **see** "Working with Objects," **p. 825**

To insert a data object in a note, you should

1. Select the location where you want to insert the object and click the Insert Object tool to display the Insert Object dialog box (see Figure 5.22).

2. Choose Create New to insert a blank object that you can design and edit from within Project (see Figure 5.22). Then use the Object Type list to select the application to create the object.

3. Choose Create from File to insert an object that is already saved as a file (see Figure 5.23). Type the path and filename for the object in the File box, or click the Browse button to select the file from your directory structure.

4. Fill the Link check box if you want to merely insert a link to the object. When you click the object or its icon, Project opens the current version of the file for you.

   Clear the Link check box if you want to store a permanent copy of the object as it now exists in the project file. This method not only takes up file space in the project file, but the version of the document you see later might not the most current version. You should usually just use a link to file objects.

5. Fill the Display As Icon check box to display an icon for the object in the Notes text box. Clear the check box if you want the contents of the object visible as you scroll the Notes text box. For most objects it is better to simply display the icon and double-click it when you want to see the contents of the object.

6. Click OK to store the object in the note.

Figure 5.22
You can create images or documents in a note and double-click the link to open the document.

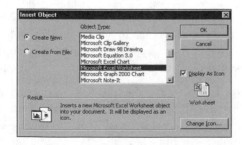

You can also store *hyperlinks* to Web sites in a note. However, Project does not help you create the hyperlink by displaying a browser history list or list of Favorites. You must type the text of the hyperlink into the note in the usual format (http://www.sitename). Project displays the hyperlink with the underline and color your machine uses for displaying hyperlinks, and when you click the hyperlink, your browser goes to that Web page.

Figure 5.23
You can also insert copies of files or links to the most current versions of files in a note.

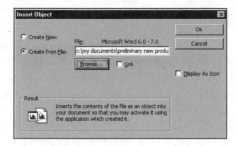

USING THE MULTIPLE TASK INFORMATION DIALOG BOX

An important feature of the Task Information dialog box is its ability to make an identical change in several tasks at once. If you select multiple tasks before activating the dialog box, the Multiple Task Information dialog box appears (see Figure 5.24). Any entry you make is copied to all the tasks you selected. For example, to assign a duration estimate of two weeks to several tasks at once, select the tasks and then choose the Task Information button on the Standard toolbar. (The double-click method does not work when multiple tasks are selected.) Enter the duration on the General tab and choose OK to close the dialog box. The duration for each of the selected tasks changes to 2 weeks.

Selected tasks   New duration entry

Figure 5.24
Enter or change several tasks at once with the Multiple Task Information dialog box.

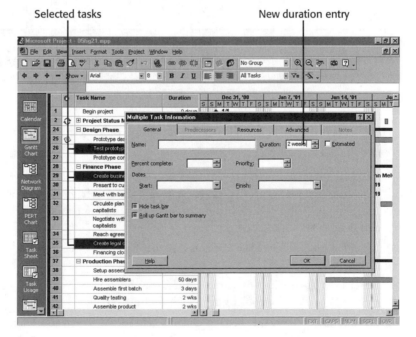

PART

II

CH

5

ATTACHING HYPERLINKS TO TASKS

In addition to storing hyperlinks to Web sites in the Notes field, there is also a Hyperlink field for storing a task's hyperlinks. These hyperlinks are more versatile than those you can store in Notes because they can jump not only to Internet or intranet sites but also to files on your computer or network and even to specific locations within those files.

When you insert a hyperlink in a task, a Hyperlink indicator appears next to the task. Simply click the indicator to jump to the target referenced in the link.

To store a hyperlink in a task, you can either use the Hyperlink command on the Insert menu or the Paste as Hyperlink command on the Edit menu.

- If you use the Insert, Hyperlink command, you can browse for the document or Web site that you want to link to, but you can't identify a specific location within the link.

- If you use the Paste as Hyperlink command, you must have already located the object and copied a part of the object to the Clipboard. However, with the Paste as Hyperlink command you get the added benefit of being able to link to the specific location within the object that you copied from. For instance, you could paste a link to a specific task in another project file, a specific cell in an Excel file, a word or section in a Word document, or a slide in a PowerPoint presentation.

Tip from Tim and the Project Team

Microsoft Project has 30 text fields that users can store miscellaneous information in. If you add one of these text fields to a view, you can store hyperlinks in any or all them. See "Using and Creating Tables" in Chapter 23, "Customizing Views, Tables, Fields, and Filters," for information about adding fields to a table.

To insert a task hyperlink to a file or Web site using the Insert, Hyperlink command, follow these steps:

1. Select the task you want to attach the link to.

2. Click the Insert Hyperlink tool to display the Insert Hyperlink dialog box (see Figure 5.25). You can also choose Insert, Hyperlink from the menu, or press Ctrl+K, to display this dialog box.

3. Click Existing File or Web Page to link to a file that's already stored on a Web site or disk drive.

4. Enter the full path and filename in the Type the File or Web Page Name box or use the File or Web Page buttons to browse to find the target.

5. Change the entry in the Text to Display field if you want a more familiar reference to appear for the link.

6. Click the ScreenTip button if you want to customize the ScreenTip that appears when the mouse points to the Hyperlink indicator.

7. Click OK to save the link.

→ For more features of the Insert Hyperlink dialog box, **see** "Adding, Modifying, and Deleting Hyperlinks in Your Project," **p. 594**

Figure 5.25
The Insert Hyperlink dialog box has been enhanced to help you locate browser sites or files you want to insert as hyperlinks.

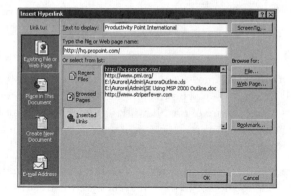

To create a hyperlink with the Paste as Hyperlink command, you should follow these steps:

1. Open the document and find the specific location you want to link to.
2. Select some part of the document at that location and choose the Copy command.

   In Excel, select a cell or group of cells.

   In Word, select a word or section title.

   In Project, select a cell in a task row.

   In PowerPoint, select a word or title in a slide or in the outline.

3. Return to Project, and select a cell in the row for the task you to contain the link.
4. Choose Edit, Paste as Hyperlink, and the link is established.

When you click the Hyperlink icon in the Indicators column, Project opens the necessary application, opens the target document, and then locates the exact word or cell you copied to paste the link.

USING OTHER VIEWS TO ENTER TASKS

Although the Gantt Chart is the most efficient view in Microsoft Project for creating a task list, some people prefer other views. Many people who were trained in engineering were taught to create the task list in the Network Diagram. Others like to split the screen and add the Task Form or Task Details Form to the Gantt Chart to facilitate adding resources and task linking as they enter the tasks. Instructions for using the other fields in these views are given in later chapters.

PART

II

CH

5

Note

If you enter or change a task name in any view, all other views that display the task name show the results of your entry. The views are just alternative ways of displaying the same information.

USING THE NETWORK DIAGRAM

P 2000 The Network Diagram (formerly known as the PERT Chart in Microsoft Project) is a time-honored way of displaying the tasks in a project and can also be used to create the task list (see Figure 5.26). The salient feature of the Network Diagram is that it provides a road map of the sequencing of tasks in the project. However, it does not address the time relationships of tasks like the Gantt Chart bar graph does.

Each task is represented on the Network Diagram by a box (called a *node*), and a line is drawn to *link* one task node to another to show that they are to be scheduled in sequence. If you print the Network Diagram, it generally takes many pages; but if you assemble the pages in order, you have a large diagram enabling you to see the progression of tasks from the start to the finish of the project. The Network Diagram is less useful onscreen because you can't see very much of the project at once. Most find it difficult to keep the overall structure in mind when using the screen version.

Figure 5.26
The Network Diagram shows clearly how one task follows another in sequence.

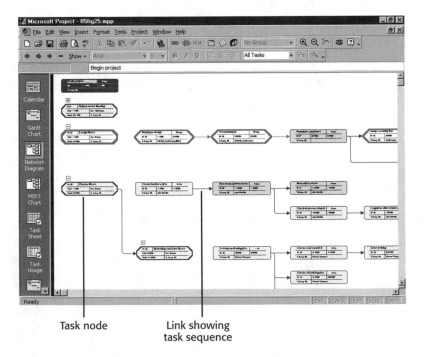

Task node   Link showing task sequence

→ If you want information about using the Network Diagram view, **see** "Working with the Network Diagram View," **p. 298**, and "Exploring the Standard Views," **p. 852**

Best Practice Tips from Toby Brown, PMP

> In project management terms, the Network Diagram is synonymous with the precedence diagramming method or PDM notation, which is any method using nodes to represent the activities and connect them with arrows. Finish-to-start is the most commonly used relationship employed by professional scheduling engineers. Start-to-start, finish-to-finish, or start-to finish relationships are not as common since they tend to produce unexpected results. Keep in mind that PDM notation does not allow for loops—non-sequential activities, such as a task(s) that must be repeated more than once, or conditional activities, such as a task(s) that might not be necessary.

USING THE TASK ENTRY VIEW

The Task Entry view is a combination view that displays the Gantt Chart in the top pane and the Task Form in the bottom pane. The Task Form in the bottom pane shows details for the task that is selected in the top pane (see Figure 5.27).

This view is not particularly useful if you are just typing task names and durations. But, it's very efficient if you want to assign resources and link tasks while you are creating the task list. Extensive use of the Task Entry view is covered in Chapter 10, "Assigning Resources and Costs to Tasks," in the sections covering assigning resources to tasks. Also, see "Project Extras: Letting Project Calculate Duration for You" at the end of this chapter for an example of using the Task Entry view.

Figure 5.27
The Task Entry view provides easy access to additional fields for defining a task.

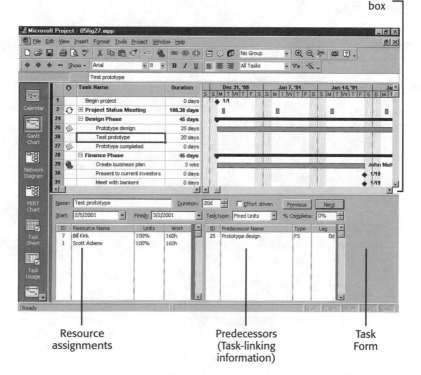

Resource assignments

Predecessors (Task-linking information)

Task Form

You can easily change the Gantt Chart view to the Task Entry view by merely splitting the screen. Project initially displays the Task Form in the bottom pane anytime you split the screen with a task view onscreen. To display the Task Entry view, follow these steps:

1. If the Gantt Chart is not currently displayed, choose <u>V</u>iew, <u>G</u>antt Chart.
2. Choose <u>W</u>indow, <u>S</u>plit.

Note

> You can also just double-click the split box located just below the vertical scroll bar to the right of the timeline. The <u>S</u>plit command also appears on the shortcut menu that is displayed if you right-click over the timeline area.

The Task Form view has fields for entering or editing the task name, duration, and task dates, plus other fields that don't appear on the standard Gantt Chart view. There are also fields to identify how the task should be treated when resources are assigned, and the percent complete field is useful when you begin tracking the actual work that has been done on the task.

Initially, the Task Form view displays tables for resource assignments and for predecessor relationships. The predecessor tasks are tasks whose scheduled dates must be considered before scheduling the current task. Use the Fo<u>r</u>mat, <u>D</u>etails command to display other information at the bottom of the Task Form. For example, you can display the notes text box, making it possible to add notes to tasks without using the Task Information dialog box (see Figure 5.28).

Figure 5.28
You can choose to display different details at the bottom of the Task Form. Here the Notes field is displayed instead of the Resources and Predecessors.

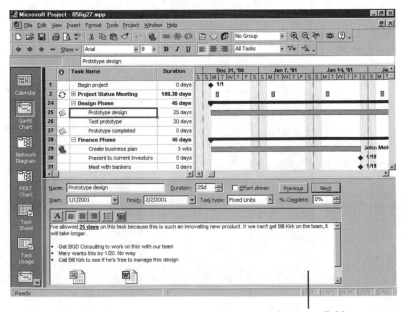

The Notes field

To display the Notes text box at the bottom of the Task Form, follow these steps:

1. If the Task Form is not already active, select it by clicking anywhere on the Task Form (or by pressing F6).

2. Choose Format, Details, Notes. (You can also right-click the form and choose Notes from the shortcut menu.)

USING THE TASK SHEET VIEW

The Task Sheet view displays the same task table that the Gantt Chart displays but without the Gantt Chart's timeline (see Figure 5.29). The Task Sheet view is a great tool for reviewing the major details of the task list, because you can see several columns for many tasks at the same time. It's also a good view to print if you just want to see the task outline without the timeline graphics.

At this point in the process, you won't have any entries in the Resource Names or Predecessors columns. You'll add that information in the ensuing chapters.

Figure 5.29
The Task Sheet view displays the essential task fields without the timeline graphics of the Gantt Chart.

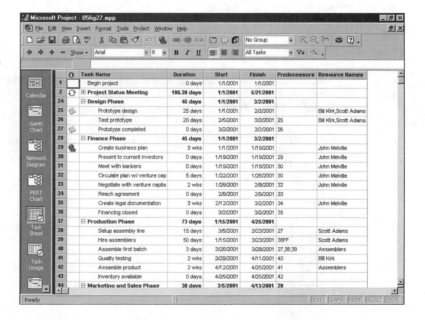

To display the Task Sheet view as a full screen view, follow these steps:

1. If the screen is split in a dual-pane view, remove the split by choosing Window, Remove Split; or just double-click the split box.

2. Choose View, More Views. The More Views dialog box appears.

3. Select Task Sheet from the Views list.

4. Choose Apply to display the view.

PART

II

CH

5

OUTLINING THE TASK LIST

Outlining is Microsoft Project's method of organizing the details of a project into groups of activities that correspond to the major phases of a project, and it is the equivalent of the traditional Work Breakdown Structure (refer to Figures 5.1 and 5.2). Each task has an outline number, which is calculated by Project using the so-called *legal numbering system*. For example, if a summary task has an outline number of 2, the subtasks directly under it would be 2.1, 2.2, and so on. The subtasks under the subtask 2.1 would be 2.1.1, 2.1.2, and so on. The outline number serves to identify the group containing the task in the overall structure of the project.

Like the Work Breakdown Structure, outlining organizes tasks into functional groups. Outlining usually is thought of in terms of its visual effect: You indent detail topics under major topics, creating *subtasks*. See the expanded task list in Figure 5.30. The major topics, called *summary tasks*, control and summarize the subordinate detail tasks. In project scheduling, indenting a task is called *demoting* the task, and the task you demote is a subtask. The task under which the task is indented automatically becomes a summary task that both controls and summarizes the subtasks.

Figure 5.30
Outlining helps you organize the details of the project.

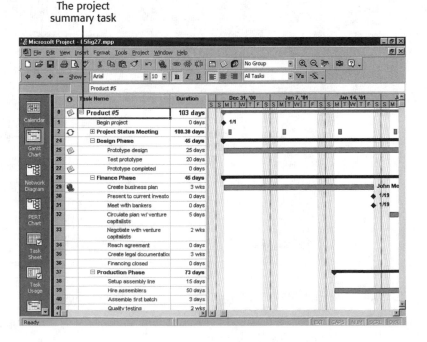

Note
What appears to be the first task in Figure 5.30 is actually a project summary task (notice that its ID number is 0). It is useful to summarize the entire project with one task. See the section "Selecting the Display Options for Outlining" later in this chapter for the instructions for displaying the project summary.

A summary task serves both to identify major groups of tasks and to summarize the duration, cost, and amount of work expended on its subtasks. When a task is transformed into a summary task, the task's start date is determined by the earliest start date of any of its subtasks, and the finish date is determined by the latest finish date of any of its subtasks. You cannot type a start date or finish date for a summary task. These dates can be calculated only from the related subtasks. The costs and amount of work associated with the subtasks are summarized in the cost and work fields of the summary task.

Caution
If you demote a summary task, its subtasks are demoted even further. In fact, all actions you apply to a summary task also apply to its subtasks. If you delete, copy, move, promote, or demote a summary task, all the subtasks—including subordinate summary tasks and their subtasks—are deleted, copied, moved, promoted, or demoted along with the summary task.

You can *promote* tasks already indented by *outdenting* them—shifting them to the left. When you promote an indented task, the tasks immediately beneath the promoted task are affected in one of the following ways:

- If the tasks below are at the same level of indentation as the new promoted task, the tasks become subordinate to the new summary task.
- If the tasks below are subordinates of the promoted task, these tasks remain subordinates but shift to the left to follow the summary task.
- If the tasks below are at a higher outline level (already further to the left than the promoted task), these tasks are unaffected by the promotion.

If you want to introduce a new task into the task list and make the new task a summary task, you must insert the task just above the task(s) you plan to make its subtasks. You can then indent the subtasks. Or, if the new summary task is not at the first outline level, you can outdent the summary task rather than indenting its subordinates.

Best Practice Tips from Toby Brown, PMP

Be careful when communicating task assignments based on task ID numbering. Any additions or deletions of tasks will renumber the entire project. In other words, if the project manager comments on task 9 and since that time another single task has been inserted before it, the ID changes to task 10. This problem is easily overcome with the new feature of custom WBS codes, described later in this chapter, along with the ability to renumber the project after making significant changes.

PART
II

CH
5

UNDERSTANDING DURATION FOR SUMMARY TASKS

Project calculates the duration for a summary task and does not let you modify it. The summary task start date is the earliest start date of any of its subtasks, and the summary task finish date is the latest finish date of any of its subtasks. The duration of the summary task is the amount of work time on the base calendar between that earliest start date and the latest finish date. A summary task whose first subtask starts at 8:00 a.m. one day and whose last subtask finishes at noon the next day would have a duration of 1.5 days (twelve working hours).

The duration for summary tasks is always displayed with the default setting for the Duration Is Entered In option on the Schedule tab of the Options dialog box. This is true even when the subtasks are expressed in other duration units. To change the duration units for summary tasks, you must change this setting.

INDENTING AND OUTDENTING TASKS

There are several methods that you can use to indent (demote) or outdent (promote) a task or group of selected tasks. First, you must select the task or tasks you want to indent or outdent. Then do one of the following:

- Choose Project, Outline, and then choose Indent or Outdent.

- Use the Indent or Outdent buttons on the Formatting toolbar to change the outline level of the selected tasks. The Indent button points to the right and the Outdent button points to the left.

- Use the drag-and-drop technique: Place the mouse pointer over the first letters of the Task Name field until it becomes a double arrow pointing left and right. Drag the pointer to the left or right to change the indent or outdent level of the task. If you select multiple tasks first, then all them are indented or outdented together.

- Use the task shortcut menu to indent and outdent. Select the ID number for a task or group of tasks. Right-click the ID numbers and choose Indent or Outdent from the shortcut menu.

- Use Alt+Shift+right arrow to indent a task or group of tasks. Use Alt+Shift+left arrow to outdent a task or group of tasks.

COLLAPSING AND EXPANDING THE OUTLINE

A major advantage of outlining is that you can collapse the outline by hiding subtasks to view only the major components of the project (see Figure 5.31). Collapsing an outline merely suppresses the display of the subtasks; it does not delete the subtasks.

You can also collapse all the outline and then expand just one part to focus on the details of that part and see how they fit into the overall picture (see Figure 5.32).

Figure 5.31
Look at the ID numbers to see which tasks are hidden (those are the missing row numbers).

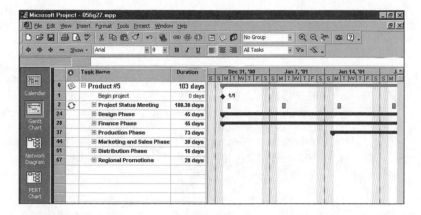

Figure 5.32
Show the subtasks in one section of the plan but hide all other subtasks to highlight how those tasks fit into the overall project.

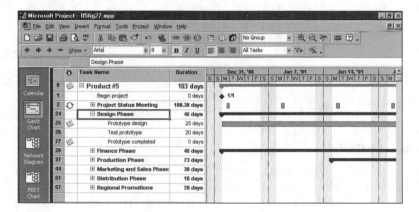

You can display all tasks or only selected levels of the outline with the Show command. Click the Show tool on the Formatting toolbar, or choose Project, Outline, Show to display the Show submenu. Select the outline level you want to be exposed. Select All Subtasks to display all levels; select Outline Level 1 to display only the top-level tasks (whether they have subtasks or not); select Outline Level 2 to display the top-level tasks plus the first level of subtasks; and so forth. The maximum number of levels you can control with this tool is nine.

You can hide or display subtasks for a selected summary task in a variety of ways. The simplest technique is to double-click the task ID to toggle between hidden and displayed subtasks.

If you select a summary task, you can hide its subtasks by clicking the Hide Subtasks tool, or (if they are already hidden) you can click the Show Subtasks tool to display them again. You can also use the menu to hide and show subtasks for individual tasks by following these steps:

1. Select the summary task or tasks whose subtasks you want to hide.

2. Choose Project, Outline to display the Outlining submenu.

3. Choose <u>H</u>ide Subtasks to collapse that part of the outline or choose <u>S</u>how Subtasks to expand that part of the outline.

Tip from Tim and the Project Team

If outline symbols are displayed (see "Selecting the Display Options for Outlining" later in this chapter) you see a small plus or minus to the left of each summary task. These outline symbols are miniature Hide Subtask and Show Subtask buttons that you can click to hide or display the subtasks. If the subtasks are currently displayed, a minus sign appears to the left of the summary task name and clicking it hides the subtasks. If the subtasks are currently hidden, a plus sign appears to the left of the summary task name and clicking it displays the subtasks.

Best Practice Tips from Toby Brown, PMP

In general, it is a good practice to have a minimum of three levels within your project: project level (a summary task over the entire project); phase level (summary tasks outlining the required project components); and work level (where the work package, or lowest level of the WBS, is located). Of course, it is possible to have more than three levels as a complex project is outlined. Regardless, the lowest indented level will always be where the work package is located. It is at this level that the tasks should be linked and the resources assigned to do the work.

EDITING OUTLINED PROJECTS

If you select a summary task and click the Task Information tool, Project displays the Summary Task Information dialog box (see Figure 5.33). Some fields are grayed-out (such as <u>D</u>uration) because they can't be edited for summary tasks, but you can edit all the other fields. Summary tasks have their own Notes field and you should make free use of notes to document important assumptions and background for summary tasks, just as you do for normal tasks.

Figure 5.33
Summary tasks have their own Task Information dialog box.

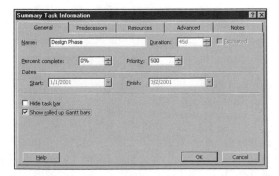

When you delete, copy, cut, paste, promote, or demote a summary task, all its subtasks are included in the same operation. For example, if you delete a summary task, you also delete all its subtasks. If you demote a summary task, you further demote its subtasks.

⚠ *If you want to delete, copy, cut, paste, promote, or demote a summary task without also affecting its subtasks, see "Moving Summary Tasks" in the "Troubleshooting" section near the end of this chapter.*

SELECTING THE DISPLAY OPTIONS FOR OUTLINING

There are several display options that Project provides for emphasizing the outline organization of your task list. Some of these are turned on by default. For example, by default Project displays summary tasks along with normal tasks and milestones, and it indents subtasks under their summary tasks.

The formatting options for displaying the outline structure of your project are

- Normally subtasks are indented to emphasize the organization of the outline. You can choose to display all tasks left justified, such as the top-level tasks. This might be useful to avoid taking up so much room on the screen or in a printed report.

- If you disable indenting, you probably want to display the task outline number next to the task name as a substitute for the visual reminder of the structure. Outline numbers are stored in the Outline Number field and cannot be edited. See "Using Custom Outline Numbers" later in this chapter for other outlining options.

- Normally Project displays outline symbols to the left of each summary task. These symbols are the minus sign (such as the Hide Subtask tool) and the plus sign (such as the Show Subtask tool). If the symbols are present, you can click them to hide and show subtasks for the summary task. They also serve as an indicator that a task is a summary task and, if a plus is showing, as a reminder that there are hidden subtasks. You can choose to hide these outline symbols.

- You can also hide the summary tasks themselves, leaving only the milestones and normal (working) tasks in the display. This option is especially useful when you want to sort normal tasks and milestones by start date, duration, or alphabetically by task name for a special report.

- Project can display an overall summary task for the entire project. Project displays it with the ID number "0" at the top of the task list. Note that all tasks are indented one level while the project summary task is displayed. The Task Name for the project summary task is taken from the project Title that is entered on the Summary page of the File Properties dialog box. Editing the project summary task name also changes the entry in the Properties dialog box. The Note field for the project summary task note is the Comments field in the Properties dialog box.

To change the outline formatting features, the active view must be a task view that must be the only pane or the top pane in the window. Follow these steps to select the outline options:

1. Choose Tools, Options to display the Options dialog box, and choose the View tab (see Figure 5.34).

2. Clear the Indent Name check box if you would prefer to left justify all task names.

3. Fill the Show Outline Number check box to display outline numbers to the left of task names.

4. Clear the Show Outline Symbol check box if you want to hide the plus- and minus-sign symbols next to summary task names.

5. Clear the Show Summary Tasks check box if you want to hide the display of summary tasks. Clearing this check box makes the following check box unavailable.

6. If the Show Summary Tasks check box is filled, you can fill the Project Summary Task check box to display a summary task for the overall project.

7. Click OK to display the new settings.

Figure 5.34
The Options dialog box regulates the display of outlined projects.

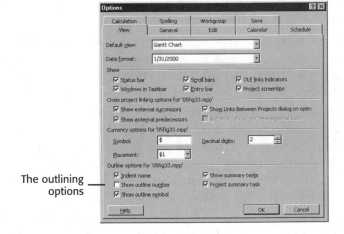

The outlining options

USING ROLLUP TASK BARS

The task bar for the summary task spans the bars for all its subtasks and is usually a solid bar. However, you can choose to "roll up" the subtask bars to the summary task bar. When you choose this option, each subtask's bar start and finish is marked on the summary task bar. Together, the rolled-up bars produce a segmented bar that shows how long each of the subtasks last.

To roll up all task bars to their summary task bars, choose Format, Layout to display the Layout dialog box, and fill the Always Roll Up Gantt Bars check box. The rollup bars appear in front of the standard summary task bar. If you want, you can choose to display the rollup bars only when their subtasks are hidden. Fill the Hide Rollup Bars When Summary Expanded check box to suppress their display when the outline is expanded.

Tip from Tim and the Project Team

You can also display the Layout dialog box by right-clicking in the bar chart area to display the short-cut menu and selecting Layout.

Figure 5.35
When you roll up task bars to the summary task, you see how the summary task is divided among the subtasks.

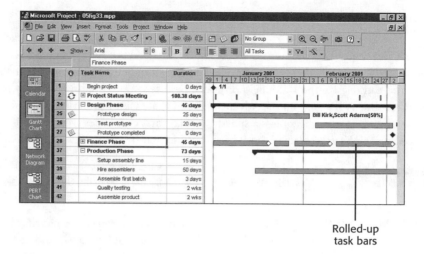

Rolled-up
task bars

Figure 5.36
The Layout command controls aspects of how the Gantt Chart is displayed.

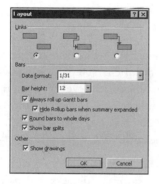

If you just want to roll up particular task bars, leaving others alone, you have to mark each subtask you want to be rolled up and you have to mark its summary task to display the rollup. Also, you must clear the Always Roll Up Gantt Bars check box described previously.

To mark a subtask for rollup, you should follow these steps:

1. Select the subtask you want to roll up and click the Task Information tool.

2. On the General tab, select Roll Up Gantt Bar to Summary and click OK.

3. Select the summary task you want to show the rollup. If the subtask's summary task is itself a subtask, the higher level summary task can display the rollup also (even if the lower-level summary task is not marked to display it). Each has to be selected separately to control the display of rollup bars.

4. Click the Task Information tool to display the Summary Task Information dialog box.

5. Fill the check box next to Show Rolled Up Gantt Bars if you want the summary task to display rolled-up task bars.

6. Click OK to save the setting.

7. Repeat this process for each summary task above the subtask that you want to display the rollup bar.

USING CUSTOM WBS CODES

Project automatically creates a default WBS code in the WBS field for each task. (See the beginning of this chapter for a description of the Work Breakdown Structure and the WBS codes.) The default WBS codes are identical to the outline numbers that Project generates. You can display the WBS field onscreen by inserting a column to display it. You can also view the WBS field on the Advanced tab of the Task Information dialog box. If your organization, or a client, requires a specific format for WBS codes, you can edit the codes in either of these places, replacing the Project outline number with your own WBS codes.

> **Note** Editing the WBS field does not change the entry in the Outline Number field.

 In Microsoft Project 2000, you can also define a customized format that Project uses to generate default codes for the WBS field. The custom format can include numbers, letters, and symbols (including ASCII characters).

CREATING CUSTOM WBS CODES

To customize the WBS code format, you create a *WBS code mask* that Project then uses to generate the codes. The mask contains numbers or characters for each outline level starting with level one, with separator characters in between each level. You can define code segments for as many levels as you want, except that the total length of the WBS code can't be greater than 255 characters. For example, if you created the code mask **"AAA-111.aa.***"** for the first four levels of the outline, it would mean the following:

- **"AAA-"**—Use three uppercase letters for top-level tasks (those with no summary task above them). Also use these codes as a prefix for all subtasks under the top-level task and follow them with a hyphen as a separator. You can edit and replace the letters Project initially supplies, but you must honor the mask and use three uppercase letters. If you edit these characters in the top-level task, the edited version will be used for all its subtasks.

- **"111."**—Use three numbers for second-level subtasks followed by a period separator for lower level tasks. Project numbers subtasks at this level "001", "002", and so forth, but you can edit those numbers.

- **"aa."**—Use two lowercase letters for third-level subtasks, followed by a period if needed as a separator.

- **"***"**—Use any mixture of characters on the keyboard for fourth-level subtasks. Project places the default characters "*1" in the code it generates, but you can change that to any characters you choose.

You can also include a project-level code to be used as a prefix for all tasks. This would be especially helpful to distinguish tasks from different subprojects in a consolidated (master) project.

I suggest that you display the WBS field as a column in the task table before creating the WBS mask. That way, you can see the effects of creating a WBS code mask immediately. To display the WBS code field, follow these steps:

1. Click the column heading where you want to display the new field. For instance, to display the new field where the Task Name field is now located, click Task Name.

2. Press the Insert key or choose Insert, Column from the menu to display the Column Definition dialog box (see Figure 5.37).

3. In the Field Name box, use the drop-down list to select WBS from the list of all fields.

4. For WBS codes, it's best to change the Align Data entry to Left.

5. Click Best Fit to create the new column and automatically adjust its width to accommodate the column title and any existing values in the column. The column whose heading you clicked to start with is pushed to the right to make room for the new column.

Figure 5.37
Use the Column Definition box to define the contents and display features of a column in the table.

Select field name here.

Change data alignment.

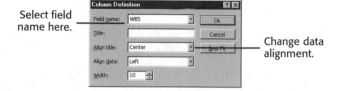

To create the WBS code mask, follow these steps:

1. Choose Project, WBS, Define Code to display the WBS Code Definition dialog box (see Figure 5.38).

2. Enter a code prefix for the project, if you would like, in the Project Code Prefix box. It's best to include a colon or other separator to show where the task code starts and the project prefix ends. The prefix appears in the sample display in the Code Preview box at the top of the dialog box.

3. In the Code Mask table, click the first blank row under the Sequence column to define the code format for top-level tasks. Use the pull-down arrow to display the options:

Choose Numbers (Ordered) to have Project insert sequential numbers in this part of the code. Remember you can edit the numbers at will.

Choose Uppercase Letters (Ordered) to use sequential uppercase letters.

Choose Lowercase Letters (Ordered) to use sequential lowercase letters.

Choose Characters (Unordered) to have Project insert the "*" character (which you can then change to any character on the keyboard).

4. In the Length column, use the pull-down arrow to display the options for how many characters are used for this part of the format:

Choose Any if you want to be able to edit this part of the code and use a varying number of characters.

Choose 1 through 10 to set a fixed number of characters for this section of the format.

5. In the Separator column, enter the symbol to use following the sequence code for sub-tasks You can use the pull-down arrow to display the most common separators (the period, hyphen, plus sign, or forward slash) or you can type from one to three symbols on the keyboard. If you don't want a separator, click the Edit bar just above the Sequence column and delete the default symbol. Note that you must have a separator if you have chosen Any as the code length.

6. Repeat steps 3, 4, and 5 for as many outline levels you want to specify in your mask.

7. Fill the check box Generate WBS Code for New Task if you want Project to calculate the WBS code for new tasks. If you leave it unfilled, you can type in WBS codes for new tasks, but you must honor the format of the mask.

8. Fill the check box Verify Uniqueness of New WBS Codes if you want Project to warn you if a new code is not unique. This only happens when you edit the codes, and you then need to modify the code to achieve uniqueness.

   If you leave this check box empty, Project does not detect duplication of codes. You should generally fill the check box.

9. Click OK to save the mask. Project automatically replaces the outline number codes that are displayed by default in the WBS field with codes that match the new mask.

10. You might need to widen the WBS column to see the new codes. To do so, just double-click the WBS column heading and choose Best Fit in the Column Definition dialog box.

Note   If your project has more outline levels than you have provided for in the mask, Project uses the conventional outline numbering system for the lower-level tasks that the mask doesn't cover.

Note   If you need to reduce the number of levels that are defined, click the bottom-most level you have defined and use the Delete key; then work your way up the list, deleting from the bottom. You can only delete the bottom-most level.

INSERTING, DELETING, AND MOVING TASKS WITH CUSTOM WBS CODES

When you insert a new task into a project, it is automatically given the next higher code for its level in the outline. If you delete a task, its WBS code is not reused unless you renumber the project.

Figure 5.38
Define a format mask for Project to create custom WBS codes for you.

Initial codes supplied by Project

WBS code mask

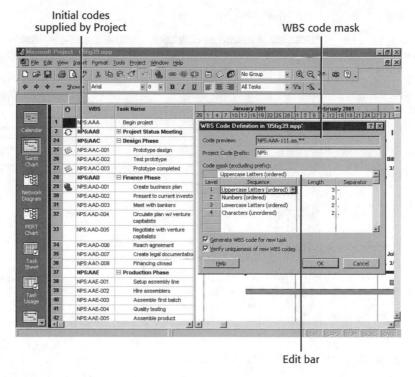

Edit bar

If you move a task to another row within its current summary task, it keeps its custom WBS code, even if it's now not in sequence. If you move a task from under one summary task to a different summary task, it automatically acquires the correct prefix codes for its new summary task. If the final part of its code would create a duplicate in its new subtask group, it will be changed to one number or letter higher than the highest existing number or letter in that subtask group. If no duplicate would be created, the final part of the code remains the same as it was before the move.

PART

II

CH

5

EDITING CUSTOM WBS CODES

After the mask is defined, you can edit the default codes for summary tasks. When you do that, the subtasks under those summary tasks automatically acquire the new letters as part of their code. For example, in Figure 5.39 the major phases have been edited to be abbreviations or acronyms for the name of the phase. The default WBS code for the Design Phase had been "AAA", but it has been changed to "DES" for easier identification. This makes recognizing a task's place in the WBS from its code much easier and is much closer to conventional practice. If you take the time to do this, however, pay attention to the troubleshooting section on preserving edited WBS codes when Project renumbers the tasks for you.

Figure 5.39
You can edit the default letters assigned by Project in the custom WBS codes to describe the task's place in the structure.

WBS codes have been edited.

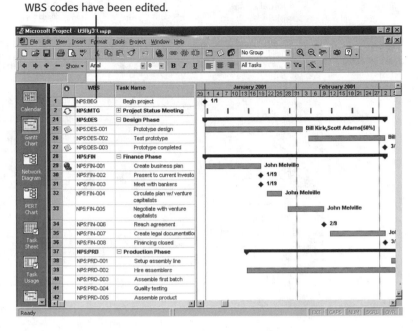

RENUMBERING THE CUSTOM WBS CODES

When you are designing your project, you might revise the task list quite a bit. If you have already defined custom WBS codes, they might not be in sequence after all the editing. You can have Project recalculate the WBS codes for the whole project to put them all in sequence. If you've only rearranged a small segment of the project, you can select those tasks and have Project recalculate the codes just for the selected tasks. To renumber the WBS codes, follow these steps:

1. If you want to renumber just a selected set of tasks, select those tasks first. The tasks must be adjacent to one another. The first of the selected tasks will not be renumbered but will serve as the starting point for renumbering the rest of the selection.

2. Choose Project, WBS, Renumber from the menu to display the WBS Renumber dialog box (see Figure 5.40).

3. Choose Selected Tasks or Entire Project according to your needs.

4. Click OK to start renumbering.

5. If you chose to renumber the entire project, Microsoft Project asks you to confirm your intent. Click Yes and the renumbering takes place.

Tip from Tim and the Project Team

Even though renumbering the entire project can change a lot of codes, you'll be relieved to know that you can use Undo to restore the original codes. As always, however, this must be done before any other changes are made.

Figure 5.40
You can have Project recalculate the WBS codes for the entire project or for just a set of selected tasks.

 If you edit customized WBS codes and then ask Project to renumber all tasks, Project overwrites your editing and reverts to sequential numbers and letters. See "Preserving Edited Custom WBS Codes" in the "Troubleshooting" section near the end of this chapter.

USING CUSTOM OUTLINE NUMBERS

Even when you customize the format of WBS codes, they are always tied to the outline structure. Each segment of the WBS code mask is linked to a specific outline level. If you want complete control over a coding system for tasks that is independent of the outline structure you have created, you can use any of 10 custom outline fields to create alternative labeling systems that you can use to sort and group tasks in different orders. For example, you could create a custom outline code field that is based on your organization's cost codes and sort the task list by that code when needed. You could also create another set of outline codes that is based on document numbers that provide specifications for the tasks and sometimes sort the task list by those codes. In Figure 5.41, the Accounts field is really one of the custom outline code fields with non-unique entries for accounting codes.

Tasks are sorted on this field.

Figure 5.41
The custom outline field can be used to sort the project in different ways independent of the outline.

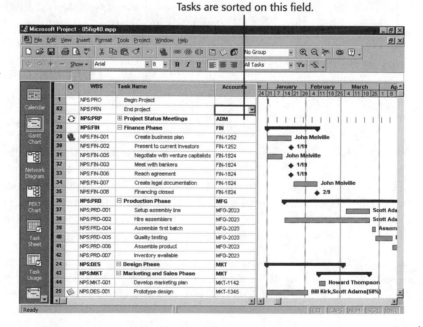

PART II
CH 5

CREATING CUSTOM OUTLINE CODES

As with the custom BS codes, you create a mask for the outline field you plan to use. However, Project doesn't populate the field with default codes—you must enter them manually. Therefore, you always need to add the field to the task view so it can be edited. Users can select the code for each task from a lookup table that you provide or they can type in outline codes, even creating their own codes (which you can optionally require to conform to the mask). The lookup table guarantees that the code conforms to the mask and it enables users to pick the correct codes by looking at descriptions for each code in the lookup table.

The instructions for creating an outline code mask are similar to the instructions for creating the WBS code mask. You can also create a custom lookup table that contains a description for each code as an aid to users in selecting the code for a task.

→ If you want to create a lookup table with descriptions of the choices for your custom outline code field, **see** "Creating and Using Custom Outline Fields," **p. 965**

WORKING WITH CUSTOM OUTLINE CODES

If you have defined one or more custom outline code fields, you can display the field in the task table for users to assign codes to the tasks. Project does not supply default values for you in the custom outline code fields as it does the custom WBS code field. You must manually enter the codes.

To display the custom outline code field, follow these steps:

1. Click the column heading where you want the field to be inserted and press the Insert key to display the Column Definition dialog box (refer to Figure 5.37).
2. In the Column Definition dialog box, use the drop-down list in the Field <u>N</u>ame box to select the outline code field you want to use. You can type the letter "o" to jump to the fields that begin with an "o" instead of having to scroll through all the fields. If you have assigned the field an alias (a name to call it by), that name also appears in the field list.
3. It is generally better to change the Align <u>D</u>ata selection to Left for outline codes.
4. Click <u>B</u>est Fit to display the field with a width sufficient to display the field name.

There are two options that can be selected when defining the custom field. One keeps users from using codes that are not provided in the lookup table. If that restriction is not in force, users can create new codes on the fly. The second option restricts any new codes by requiring that they match the include characters for all parts of the code mask.

Caution

If a user creates a new outline code on the fly, it is added to the lookup table for future use. However, the lookup table has to be edited to provide a description for the new code.

Both of these options are turned off by default, which means that users can create new codes on the fly, they do not have to include characters for all parts of the code mask, and the new code is added to the look-up table.

To enable or disable these options, follow these steps:

1. Choose Tools, Customize, Fields from the menu to display the Customize Fields dialog box (see Figure 5.42).

Figure 5.42
Use the Customize Fields dialog box to change the content and behavior of user-definable fields.

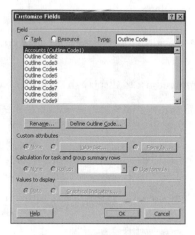

2. Choose Task and then select Outline Code in the Type pull-down list.

3. Select the outline code you want to work with in the Field list and click Define Outline Code to display the Outline Code Definition dialog box (see Figure 5.43). The two options are check boxes at the bottom of the dialog box.

Figure 5.43
The Outline Code Definition dialog box is a special form of the customize field definition.

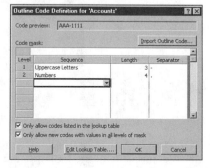

4. If you fill the check box Only Allow Codes Listed in the Lookup Table, users are not allowed to enter any codes but those defined in the lookup table. Users are unable to add new codes, intentionally or by mistake, when this option is selected.

If this first check box is clear, users can still view and use the lookup table, but they are not bound by its entries.

5. If the first check box is clear, users can enter new codes not included in the lookup table. By checking the second option, Only Allow New Codes with Values in All Levels of Mask, you can require that new entries must contain all parts of the code mask to be accepted.

6. Click OK twice to return to the task view.

If you need to edit the lookup table to provide a description for a new code, follow these steps:

1. Use steps 1–3 in the previous numbered list to display the Outline Code Definition dialog box.

2. Click the Edit Lookup Table button to display the Edit Lookup Table dialog box (see Figure 5.44).

3. Scroll down to find the code you need to document and enter the description in the column on the right.

4. Click the Close button when finished and click OK twice to return to the task view.

Figure 5.44
The lookup table for custom codes helps users select the correct code.

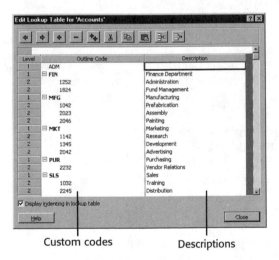

Custom codes   Descriptions

When a user needs to enter a custom code in this field, the lookup table provides the list of acceptable entries, and the description next to each entry helps the user pick the correct entry (see Figure 5.45).

Figure 5.45
The lookup table is available as a pull-down list when the user is entering a custom code.

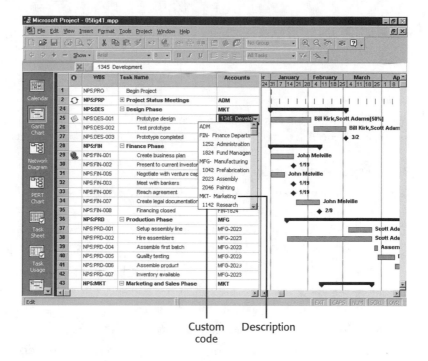

Custom   Description
code

PRINTING THE PROJECT TASK LIST

You can print the task list in a number of ways. You can print views like the Gantt Chart, the Network Diagram, or the Task Sheet view, all of which appear on paper much as they appear onscreen. You can also choose from among a number of standard reports. Note that you cannot print the task form views.

→ For full instructions on printing views of your task list, **see** Chapter 13, "Printing Views and Reports" **p. 537**

→ If you want to enhance the display before printing the view, **see** Chapter 22, "Formatting Views," **p. 891**, for ways to customize a view

There are six report categories available for printing standardized and custom reports in Microsoft Project. Chapters 24, "Using the Standard Reports," and 25, "Customizing Reports," explain how to use and customize these reports. These reports are mentioned here in case you want to experiment with standard reports. At this stage of developing your project, only the reports in the Overview category are useful. The reports in this category are as follows:

- The Top-Level Tasks report displays the task list but includes only those tasks in the first level of the outline.

- The Milestones report lists all milestone tasks.

- The Working Days report summarizes the calendar information, showing the normal working days and hours plus all exceptions to those normal working times.

TROUBLESHOOTING

MOVING SUMMARY TASKS

I don't understand how to move summary tasks without moving their subtasks…what do I need to do?

First, outdent the subtasks so that the summary task becomes a regular task. Then you can move, copy, cut, delete, promote, or demote the task without affecting its former subtasks.

PRESERVING EDITED CUSTOM WBS CODES

After I customize my summary task WBS codes, they seem to disappear when I have Project renumber tasks. What am I doing wrong?

If you have edited custom WBS codes for summary tasks and then want Project to renumber the tasks, your edited changes are lost unless you take the following special steps:

1. Choose Tools, Options to display the Options dialog box and select the View tab.
2. Clear the Show Summary Tasks check box and click OK to close the dialog box. Only normal and milestone tasks are then displayed.
3. Select one of the column headings to select all displayed tasks.
4. Select Project, WBS, Renumber to display the WBS Renumber dialog box.
5. Click the Selected Tasks button (instead of Entire Project).
6. Click OK to start the renumbering process.
7. Restore the display of summary tasks by choosing Tools, Options and filling the Show Summary Tasks check box on the View tab. Then click OK to close the dialog box. You can click any cell to deselect all tasks.

Your entire task list is displayed again and the summary tasks have not lost their edited codes, but all other tasks are renumbered based on their current order in the outline.

PROJECT EXTRAS: LETTING PROJECT CALCULATE DURATION FOR YOU

If you have start and finish dates already estimated for your tasks, and therefore implied durations, you can manually enter those dates and let Project calculate the Duration field for you. Even better, if the task names and dates are already in a file (like Excel or Word), you can paste the task values directly into Project to create the tasks and durations.

It's generally not a good idea to enter the dates for tasks; you should let Project schedule the task dates for you. However, in this case you can more quickly calculate and transfer duration estimates into Project by entering the dates. This produces constraints on the tasks, but you can remove the constraints after the duration estimates are in place and give Project the flexibility to create a new schedule of dates.

To manually enter predetermined task start and finish dates for tasks, follow these steps:

1. Display the Task Entry view by first displaying the Gantt Chart and then using the <u>W</u>indow, <u>S</u>plit command to display the Task Form in the bottom pane (see Figure 5.46).

Figure 5.46
The Task Entry view consists of the Gantt Chart in the top pane and the Task Form in the bottom pane. You can define tasks in the bottom pane as well as in the top pane.

Task name

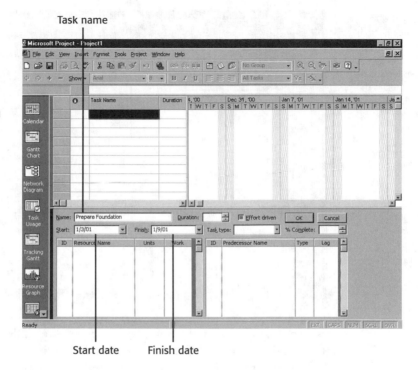

Start date   Finish date

2. Select the first row in the top pane, and then click in the bottom pane to activate its fields. From this point on, you can use the P<u>r</u>evious and Ne<u>x</u>t buttons in the Task Form to move up and down the rows of the top pane without having to switch panes.

3. Click in the <u>N</u>ame field (or use Alt+N to select it) and enter the first task name. Notice that the P<u>r</u>evious and Ne<u>x</u>t buttons have become OK and Cancel buttons. Don't click OK yet.

4. Click in the <u>S</u>tart field (or use Alt+S to select it) and enter the start date or date and time.

5. Click in the Finis<u>h</u> field (or use Alt+H to select it) and enter the finish date or date and time.

6. Now either press Enter or click OK to complete this task. Project posts your three entries in the Gantt Chart above and calculates the duration as the difference between the dates you entered (see Figure 5.47). The OK and Cancel buttons revert to P<u>r</u>evious and Ne<u>x</u>t.

7. Press Enter again, or click the Next button, to start the next task, and repeat steps 3 through 6 for all tasks.

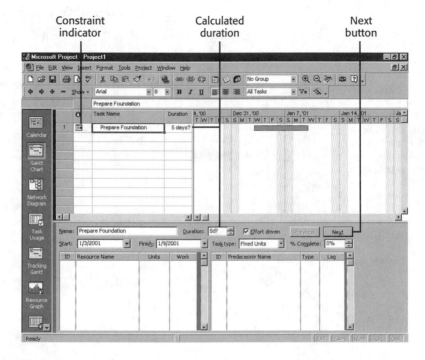

Figure 5.47
After entering both start and finish dates in the Task Form, the task has a calculated duration that is the difference between them.

Notice an indicator next to the task in the Gantt Chart view that reminds you that the task has a constraint. If you slide the mouse pointer over the indicator, it tells you that it is a Start No Earlier Than constraint: Project does not schedule the task any earlier than the start date.

After all the tasks are entered, the schedule should match the schedule you copied the tasks from. In the next chapter, you learn how to give Project the instructions it needs to schedule tasks for you. At that point, you might want to remove the constraints from the list and start the more elaborate scheduling process that Project makes possible.

You can remove all the constraints by clicking on one of the column headings (such as Task Name) to select all tasks. Then click on the Task Information tool to display the Multiple Task Information box and go to the Advanced tab. In the Constraint Task group of fields, select the constraint type As Soon As Possible (or, if the project is scheduled from a fixed finish date, select As Late As Possible). If the task names and dates are already stored in another document, you can copy the data into Project instead of manually typing all the data. The source task list can be in Excel, Word, Access, or PowerPoint, and your first step is to modify the source data (if necessary) to meet the following requirements:

■ Each task must be on a separate row.

- If the source is Excel or Access, the task names and dates must be in separate columns or fields. If the list is in Word or PowerPoint, tabs must separate the entries in each row.

  It's okay to use outlined text from Word or PowerPoint as the source, but the tasks will not be indented in Project and you will have to manually outline the task list after it's pasted.

- The dates must be in one of the formats that Project recognizes (for example, "1/20/2000" or "Thu 1/20/2000 4:00 PM").

- The task names and dates must be arranged in columns that are in the same order as the columns in the view you will be using when you paste them into Project. You can either adjust the source data or adjust the column order in Project. If you start with the standard Gantt Chart and hide the Duration column, the order for those columns in Project will be Task Name, Start, and Finish. So, the order of the columns in the source document should be the same: Task Name, Start, and Finish.

Next you must prepare the Project document to receive the list:

- Using the standard Gantt Chart as an example, hide the Duration column by right-clicking the Duration column heading and choosing Hide Column. The Task Name, Start, and Finish columns should now be next to each other and in just that order. After copying in the tasks, you can insert the Duration column again.

- If it's a new project document, you should establish the project start or finish date before you paste in the task list. This is especially important if the project will have a fixed finish date. Choose Project, Project Information and set the Start Date; or choose to Schedule from the Project Finish Date and set the Finish Date.

To copy the data, select the task rows and columns to be copied in the data source and use the Copy command to place the selection in the Clipboard. Then in Project select the single cell in the Task Name column on the row where you want the first imported task to appear and choose the Paste command. You may receive an error message to the effect that the date for the first task can't be pasted. You can usually just ignore this message and select the No option in the error dialog box to continue pasting without displaying the error messages for each task. As long as your dates were properly formatted in the source list, they should paste in correctly. If you did not include the time of day in the source dates, Project will apply its default Start Time for all the Start dates and the default End Time for all the Finish dates.

To display the Duration column again, you can right-click on the Start column heading and choose Insert Column. In the Field Name box, display the drop-down list and scroll to Duration. Click Best Fit to display the Duration column with a width sufficient to show the title and all values.

After linking the tasks, you can remove the constraints as described previously for the manually entered tasks with dates.

→ For more sophisticated importing of data from other applications, **see** Chapter 19, "Exporting and Importing Project Data with Other File Formats," **p. 759**

CHAPTER **6**

ENTERING SCHEDULING REQUIREMENTS

In this chapter

AN OVERVIEW OF SCHEDULING

After you enter project tasks and estimate durations, you must focus on developing the schedule of start and finish dates. Up to this point, you've used Microsoft Project as a basic word processor or spreadsheet program—entering tasks and durations in a task view. In this chapter, you take a look at how to link these tasks to define the logical sequence of activity, thus giving Project specific information for calculating the schedule. You also examine how you record constraints and deadlines, assign task calendars, and split tasks.

The *project schedule* depends on a number of factors:

■ *The project schedule either begins on a fixed start-date or is calculated to end on a fixed finish-date.* You determine which date by setting the start or finish date in the Project Information dialog box.

→ For more information on defining the start or finish of a project, **see** "Using the Project Information Dialog Box," **p. 64**

■ *Project schedules tasks only during the working times defined by the base calendar you select for scheduling the project, unless you assign a resource or a task calendar to a task.* If you assign resources to tasks, Project schedules work during the working times on the resource calendars. If you assign a task calendar to a task, Project schedules work during the working times on the task calendar. If there are both assigned resources and a task calendar, Project normally schedules work only during periods that are working times on both calendars, but you have the option to disregard the resource calendars and base the schedule only on the task calendar.

→ For guidelines on defining the project base calendar, **see** "Defining a Calendar of Working Time," **p. 84**

→ For information about task calendars, **see** "Creating and Using Task Calendars" **p. 252**

■ *The schedule depends heavily on the duration estimates for the individual tasks.* The duration of the tasks is one of the driving forces of the schedule. The longer the task duration for any given start date, the later the scheduled finish date for that task. Chapter 5, "Creating a Task List," covered estimating durations.

■ *The schedule also depends on the logical order or sequence in which tasks should be scheduled.* Typically, some tasks have start or finish dates that must be scheduled in relation to the start or finish date of another task. This chapter is largely devoted to topics about *sequencing*—the process of linking tasks in an appropriate order.

■ *The schedule can be affected by arbitrary limits or* constraints *you impose on the start or finish dates for individual tasks.* Imposing date constraints is covered later in this chapter.

■ *The task schedule can be governed by a task calendar.* Assigning calendars to tasks is covered in "Creating and Using Task Calendars" in this chapter.

■ *By default, tasks are scheduled without interruption for the duration of the task.* You can insert one or more interruptions in the work on a task by splitting the task schedule. See the section "Splitting Tasks" later in this chapter.

■ *The task schedule also depends on the availability of resources assigned to work on the tasks.* Chapter 9, "Understanding Resource Scheduling," explains the effects on the schedule of resource availability.

■ *The schedule will be affected if you delay a resource assignment to start after other resources have started, or if you "contour" the daily work assignment for a resource.* Chapter 9 discusses both contouring and delaying resource assignments and the effects they have on the task schedule.

In practice, after you learn to use Microsoft Project, you probably will outline, link, and impose constraints on the task list as you enter the tasks. The process is divided into separate chapters in this book to focus on all the options and techniques possible for each activity. Chapter 5 discussed entering and outlining your tasks. This chapter is devoted to linking tasks, adding constraints, and using other techniques for scheduling tasks such as using deadline dates, assigning task calendars, and splitting tasks.

By far, the most important topic in this chapter is linking tasks. The sequencing or linking of tasks makes it possible for Project to calculate your schedule. It is also what makes it possible for Project to identify for you the critical tasks—those that must finish on time if the project is to finish on time, and those it is worthwhile attempting to finish faster when you need to compress the overall duration of the project.

→ For a quick review of the terms *critical task* and *critical path*, **see** the overview topic "How Project Calculates the Schedule," **p. 25**

UNDERSTANDING DEPENDENCY LINKS

It's difficult to imagine a project in which no sequencing requirements exist for at least some of the tasks. Usually, one or more tasks cannot be scheduled to start until one or more other tasks have finished. One common reason for this requirement is a task using the output generated by another task. For example, in building a house, the task Frame the Walls requires the output of the task Lay the Foundation. This relationship between tasks is known as a *dependency relationship*—the scheduled start or finish of one task must be set to coincide with, or to be *linked* to, the scheduled start or finish of another task. One of the tasks is said to be dependent on the other.

DEFINING DEPENDENCY LINKS

When tasks are linked to show a dependency relationship, the dependent task is called the *successor* task and the task on which its schedule depends is called its *predecessor*. For example, in the most common type of dependency relationship, the successor is scheduled to start as soon as the predecessor finishes.

Suppose, for example, you need to schedule the application of two coats of paint, a first coat and a final coat, to the exterior walls of a small structure. There will be four tasks involved: Prepare Surfaces, Apply First Coat, Apply Final Coat, and Clean Up. You must prepare the surfaces before applying the first coat of paint; so Prepare Surfaces is the predecessor to Apply First Coat. Similarly, you must apply the first coat before you can apply the final coat; so, Apply First Coat is the predecessor to Apply Final Coat. The start date for the successor tasks should be linked to their predecessors, as illustrated in Figure 6.1. Project draws a small arrow from the finish of each predecessor task to the start of its successor task.

Figure 6.1
When you link a task, its schedule depends on the schedule of its predecessor.

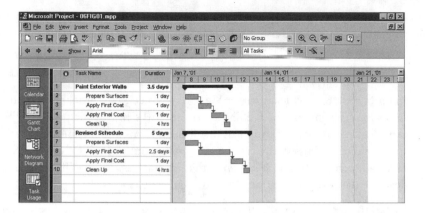

When you refer to a dependency relationship between tasks, the linked part of the predecessor task (either its start or its finish) is named first and then the linked part of the successor task is named. In the painting example in Figure 6.1, the dependency relationships are called *Finish-to-Start links* because the predecessor's finish determines the successor's start. Finish-to-Start is the most common type of link, but there are also three other types you can use: Finish-to-Finish, Start-to-Start, and Start-to-Finish. The section "Defining the Types of Dependency Link Relationships," later in this chapter, describes the use of each of these types of links. By establishing the link, you instruct Project to set the start date for Apply Final Coat based on the scheduled finish date for Apply First Coat. Any change that alters the calculated finish date for the predecessor causes Project to also reschedule the start date for the dependent or successor task. In Figure 6.1 the Apply First Coat task in the Revised Schedule on row 8 has been given a longer duration than the Apply First Coat task on row 3. Accordingly, the Apply Final Coat task on row 9 is scheduled to start and finish later than on row 4, reflecting the longer duration of its predecessor.

Note

Changes in the scheduling of a predecessor task result in changes to the scheduling of the successor (or dependent) task. The predecessor task is the catalyst for the scheduling of the successor task.

Tip from Tim and the Project Team

Do not link two unrelated tasks just to level out the work load for a resource (a worker or a piece of equipment) that is assigned to work on both tasks. True, the link forces Project to schedule the tasks one after the other, thus giving the resource enough time to complete all the work, and delaying tasks to level out the workload is standard practice. But, you should define the delay using Project's Leveling Delay field instead.

Delays created by an entry in the Leveling Delay field are easily identified as such and can be quickly removed if, for example, you later reassign one of the tasks to another worker and the delay is no longer necessary. Task links that are created to delay workloads, on the other hand, are not easily identified and tend to remain in place even though no longer needed, thus delaying the finish of the project for no good reason.

→ For the steps to follow in using leveling delays, **see** "Resolving Overallocations by Delaying Assignments," **p. 441**

USING THE TERM *Successor*

The terms *predecessor* and *successor* imply that the successor task takes place *after* the predecessor task. However, as used in project scheduling, the terms have a different meaning. When two tasks are linked in a dependency relationship, the dependent task is the one whose schedule can't be calculated until its predecessor's schedule is known. The predecessor task's schedule must be calculated before the successor task's schedule is calculated, but the predecessor doesn't necessarily have to take place before the successor.

Thus, the successor might be scheduled to take place at the same time or even *before* the predecessor task. It is easier to understand and use the types of dependency links if you think of the successor task as the *dependent* task in that its schedule is dependent on the schedule of its predecessor.

SELECTING THE DEPENDENT TASK

Deciding which of two tasks is the dependent task and which is the predecessor is often self evident. In many cases, the laws of physics decree the task sequence, and it is easy to decide which task is the predecessor and which the successor. Obviously, the final coat of paint always follows the first coat of paint, so Apply First Coat is the predecessor task and Apply Final Coat is the successor (dependent) task in Figure 6.1. Sometimes the situation is not so clear cut, however. Consider the following case where a person, not Microsoft Project, is doing the scheduling:

> Elaine is an on-the-job trainee for a residential construction project, and she is responsible for making sure that lumber and materials are on hand when the foundation is finished and it's time to frame the walls of the new house. Elaine is to watch the progress on finishing the foundation and call the lumber yard two days before the foundation is finished to schedule the delivery. Elaine's instructions are to avoid ordering the materials any earlier than necessary because that means paying interest on borrowed money for a longer period of time. Although the term "just-in-time scheduling" wasn't used in her instructions, this is, in fact, an example of that principle.
>
> As it happens, when it's just about time to call the lumber yard, Elaine learns that the carpenters are being diverted to another house that has a higher priority, and the framing phase of her project has been put on hold for a week. Elaine's common sense tells her that the materials order is really linked to the start of the framing, not to the finish of the foundation, and she delays placing the delivery order until two days before the new start date for framing.

If you were scheduling this example in Microsoft Project, you would want to give Project enough information to be able to do what Elaine did—to delay the start of the delivery task if the framing task is delayed. To do that you need to treat the delivery of materials as a task that is dependent on the start of the framing task. Therefore, the framing task is the predecessor for the delivery task (the successor), even though the successor in this case is to take place a day or so before its predecessor. Remember, the key to the predecessor and successor relationship is which task's schedule you want to be dependent on the other task's schedule—not which task comes first in time.

The decision as to which task should be the predecessor and which the dependent or successor task might hinge on which task you have more control over. If you have equal scheduling control over both tasks, make the task that must come first the predecessor and let the later task be the dependent successor. But, in cases where the schedule for one task is out of your control, you might want to arbitrarily make the more flexibly scheduled task the dependent task—regardless of which task actually must come first in time.

For example, suppose an office building project will have a world-famous artist paint a mural in the entrance to the building. The artist is only available at certain times, and a change in the artist's availability would mean a change in the schedule. The artist's task will likely be defined as the predecessor for other tasks that are more flexible—tasks such as having scaffolding erected for the artist to use.

When one of two linked tasks is a support function that merely facilitates the other task (such as ordering lumber and materials for framing, or erecting scaffolding for painting a mural), you will often make the main task the predecessor and the support function the dependent task.

ALLOWING FOR DELAYS AND OVERLAPS

Sometimes you might need to schedule a delay as part of the linkage between the predecessor and the successor task. For instance, in the painting example you need to allow time for the first coat of paint to dry before you apply the final coat. This kind of delay is known as a *lag* or as *lag time* in task scheduling, and you could add a one-day lag to the Finish-to-Start link between the Apply First Coat and Apply Final Coat tasks.

Other times you might want to allow the dependent task to overlap or start before the predecessor task is finished. You add *lead time* to a link when you want the successor task to anticipate its predecessor. For example, the cleanup crew can begin the Clean Up task when the painters are close to finishing the Apply Final Coat task.

Figure 6.2 shows the painting example again. The first set of tasks has no lead or lag defined; the Revised Schedule has lead and lag time added to the links. There is a lag added to the link between the first and final coats of paint, and there is lead time between the final coat and the clean up task. The lag adds to the overall duration of the painting project, but the lead allows the project to finish faster than it would otherwise.

Tip from Tim and the Project Team

Identifying task relationships where overlaps such as lead time are possible is one of the best ways to shorten the overall time it takes to finish a project.

→ For more information on compressing or crashing the schedule, **see** "Shortening the Critical Path," **p. 527**

Figure 6.2
You can use lag time to delay the successor task. Lead time, however, allows tasks to overlap, thereby finishing earlier than would be possible otherwise.

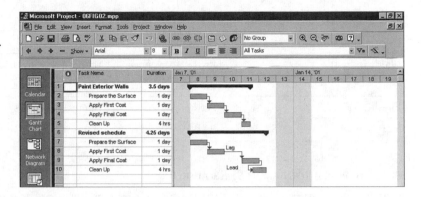

Lags and leads can be defined in ordinary duration units or in elapsed duration units. If you want Project to schedule the lag during working time on the calendar, use ordinary duration units. If Project can use nonworking time also for scheduling the lag, use elapsed duration units. For example, what if the Apply First Coat task were to finish on a Friday, the last working day of the week. If the one day lag for the Apply Final Coat task were defined as one ordinary day (typically 8 hours of working time on a standard calendar), Project would let one day of working time pass before scheduling the start of the Apply Final Coat task. The next working day after Friday is Monday; so the successor task would be scheduled for Tuesday. But if the lag were defined as one elapsed day (24 hours of continuous time), Project uses the weekend days for the lag and the final coat could begin on Monday.

→ For more information about using elapsed duration, **see** "Defining Elapsed Duration," **p. 164**

Although you will usually define lags and leads in fixed time units (such as 4 hours or 2 elapsed days), Project also allows you to define lags and leads as a percentage of the duration of the predecessor. With the percentage format, Project allows more or less time for the lag or lead as the duration of the predecessor increases or decreases. Using the different methods of entering leads and lags is discussed in the section "Entering Leads and Lags," later in this chapter.

DEFINING THE TYPES OF DEPENDENCY LINK RELATIONSHIPS

You can create four types of dependency relationships, depending on whether you use the start dates or finish dates when linking tasks. The name for each dependency type includes a reference to the linked date for the predecessor (either its start date or its finish date), followed by a reference to the linked date for the dependent task (either its start or finish date). Therefore, a *Finish-to-Start* relationship denotes the finish date of the predecessor task is used to schedule the start date of the dependent task. The predecessor is referenced first, and then the dependent or successor task.

Project uses two-letter code abbreviations for the four dependency types, as shown in the following table. The first letter in the code refers to the predecessor and the second refers to the dependent task. Thus, the code for Finish-to-Start is FS. Table 6.1 shows the different dependency types and their corresponding codes.

PART

II

CH

6

TABLE 6.1 LINKING RELATIONSHIPS AVAILABLE IN MICROSOFT PROJECT

Dependency Type	Code	Meaning
Finish-to-Start	FS	Predecessor's finish determines successor's start
Start-to-Start	SS	Predecessor's start determines successor's start
Finish-to-Finish	FF	Predecessor's finish determines successor's finish
Start-to-Finish	SF	Predecessor's start determines successor's finish

USING THE FINISH-TO-START (FS) RELATIONSHIP

In the Finish-to-Start relationship, the finish date of the predecessor determines the start date of the successor task. For example, framing the walls of a new house should be scheduled to start after the foundation is prepared. The links in the painting example in Figures 6.1 and 6.2 are all Finish-to-Start links. The linking arrow in the Gantt Chart is drawn from the finish of the predecessor task to the start of the dependent task. This is the most common dependency type and is the default relationship created by the Edit, Link Tasks command.

USING THE START-TO-START (SS) RELATIONSHIP

In the Start-to-Start relationship, the start date of the predecessor task determines the start date of the successor task. You are scheduling the two tasks to start at or near the same time with this link. Both the tasks are scheduled to run in parallel.

Note   A lag often is associated with Start-to-Start links. The start of the dependent task is delayed until sometime after the predecessor task is underway.

For example, suppose an organization leases new office space and moves to the new space when remodeling is completed. As part of the move from one office to another, several tasks need to be accomplished—packing boxes, disconnecting desktop computers, disassembling furniture, and loading the boxes and furniture into the moving van. You can approach this series of tasks in two ways. Because you can schedule the movers to start loading the vans almost immediately after the packing task starts, the start of the Load Vans task can be linked to the start of the Pack Boxes & Disassemble Furniture task, with a small amount of delay or lag time (see the tasks in Scenario A in Figure 6.3). Pack Boxes & Disassemble Furniture is the predecessor task; Load Vans is the successor task. The arrow is drawn from the start of the predecessor to the start of the dependent task.

In this example, you also could make Pack & Disassemble Furniture the dependent task, basing its start on the start of the Load Vans task, but with a small amount of lead time. The linking shown in the Scenario B task bars in Figure 6.3 illustrates this alternative. The start of the Pack & Disassemble Furniture task is linked to the start of the Load Vans task with a two-hour lead to ensure that packing starts shortly before the loaders are ready to start. The choice as to which task is the predecessor is often arbitrary.

Figure 6.3
You can link the start of the Load Vans task to the start of the Pack Boxes & Disassemble Furniture task, with a two-hour lag. Alternatively, you can link the Pack Boxes & Disassemble Furniture task to the Load Vans task with a two-hour lead.

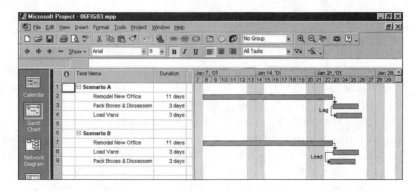

USING THE FINISH-TO-FINISH (FF) RELATIONSHIP

In the Finish-to-Finish relationship, the finish date of the predecessor determines the scheduled finish date of the successor task—you schedule two tasks to finish at or about the same time. For example, in remodeling a kitchen, the acquisition of the kitchen appliances should be completed by the time the cabinet makers finish installing the kitchen cabinets, so the cabinet makers can install the appliances in (and around) the new cabinets (see Figure 6.4).

Figure 6.4
The kitchen appliances should all be purchased by the time the kitchen cabinets are completed. This is a Finish-to-Finish relationship.

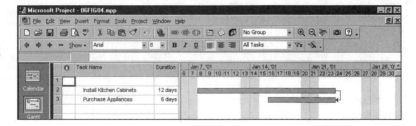

Note

The link types Start-to-Start or Finish-to-Finish with leads and lags can be used to schedule tasks to overlap and are standard techniques for *fast-tracking* a project—compressing the overall duration of the project by overlapping tasks.

PART

II

CH

6

USING THE START-TO-FINISH (SF) RELATIONSHIP

In the Start-to-Finish relationship, the start date of the predecessor task determines the scheduled finish date of the successor. You might be scheduling a task to finish just in time to start a more important task it supports. The following examples illustrate the Start-to-Finish relationship:

■ When preparing for an important exam, most students schedule their studying to finish approximately when testing begins!

■ When scheduling the delivery of merchandise to a new store, the Grand Opening date determines when the deliveries must be scheduled.

- "Just-in-time scheduling" in manufacturing is a policy that strives to stock raw materials just in time for the manufacturing process to begin. This policy saves money by not tying up cash in material inventories any longer than necessary.

- When throwing a party, the date of the celebration determines when the food and supplies are purchased.

Figure 6.5 illustrates a home building project that requires the framing materials to be purchased in time for framing the walls. In the first set of tasks (the original schedule), the Purchase Materials task is scheduled to finish just as the Frame Walls task begins. Purchase Materials is dependent on Frame Walls, making Frame Walls its predecessor. If the framing is delayed, the purchase of materials will be delayed, too. The link is a Start-to-Finish link, and the arrow is drawn from the start of the predecessor to the finish of the dependent task.

Figure 6.5
The Purchase Materials task must be completed in time for the Frame Walls task to begin, making its schedule dependent on the schedule for Frame Walls.

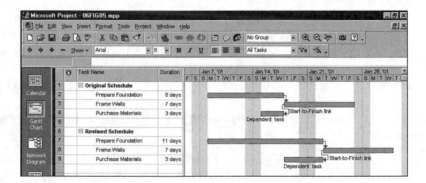

In the revised schedule in Figure 6.5, the Prepare Foundation task has a longer duration than in the original schedule, and that delays the scheduled start for Frame Walls. Automatically, Project delays the dependent task Purchase Materials just enough so it will still be finished just in time for the new start date of Frame Walls.

LINKING SUMMARY TASKS

Summary tasks can be linked to each other or to non-summary tasks. A summary task is already implicitly linked to its own subtasks, therefore Project won't let you establish an explicit link between a subtask and its summary task. If the summary task is linked to a predecessor, the predecessor relationship dictates when the summary task and its subtasks can begin. Likewise, as you will see later in this chapter, if the summary task has a date constraint, its subtasks are effectively constrained to that date also. If the summary task has no links or date constraints, its start date is derived from the earliest start of any of its subtasks, and its finish date is derived from the latest finish of any of its subtasks.

Linking in outlined task lists is more complicated than in non-outlined lists because more options are available. If the subtasks under one summary task are, as a group, the natural successors to the group of subtasks under another summary task, you could express that dependency in four different ways:

- You can link the first subtask in the successor group to the last subtask in the predecessor group. This method is illustrated by the first example in Figure 6.6 in the group of tasks labeled Linking Subtasks.

- You can link the successor summary task to the predecessor summary task and link the subtasks within each task group to each other. This method is illustrated by the second example in Figure 6.6 in the group of tasks labeled Linking Summary Tasks.

- You can link the first subtask in the successor group to the predecessor summary task.

- You can link the successor summary task to the last subtask in the predecessor group.

Figure 6.6
The two approaches to linking between phases—linking the summary tasks and linking the subtasks.

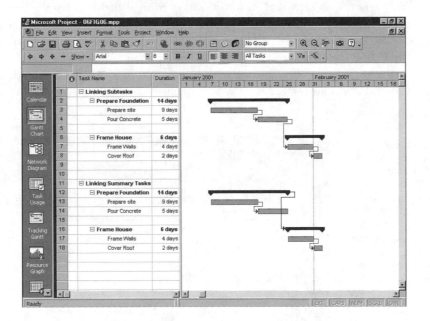

If, however, one or more subtasks in a summary group is uniquely dependent on tasks that lie outside the group, you might not be able to use links between the summary tasks.

If you select all tasks and let Microsoft Project link the tasks in an outlined project, it links all tasks at the first outline level to each other, whether they are summary tasks or not. It then links the next level of subtasks within any summary tasks to each other, until all outline levels in all summary tasks are linked at their own level. All links are the default Finish-to-Start link type.

The advantage of linking summary tasks is that you can change the subtasks in the summary groups without worrying about the link between the summary groups. The Linking Subtasks example in Figure 6.6 links the first task of the successor group (task 7, Frame Walls) to the last activity in the predecessor group (task 4, Pour Concrete). In the Linking

Summary Tasks example, the Frame House group is linked to the Prepare Foundation group, which means that no subtask in the Frame House group can begin until all tasks in the Prepare Foundation group are completed.

Note

If you create a task link that involves a summary task as the dependent or successor task, you can only use the link types Finish-to-Start and Start-to-Start. Project will not let you establish the other link types—where the summary task's finish date is linked. However if the link involves a summary task as the predecessor to a non-summary task, you can use any of the four possible link types. These rules apply the same in both fixed start-date and fixed finish-date projects.

In Figure 6.7, a new task (Get Inspection) is inserted at the end of the Prepare Foundation group in both examples. This task must follow Pour Concrete; therefore, it extends the duration of the first group of tasks. In the first example, where subtasks are linked directly, the Frame House task will remain linked to the Pour Concrete task unless you remember to link it to Get Inspection instead. In the second example, where the summary tasks are linked, Project automatically delays the Frame House task to allow for the Get Inspection task.

Figure 6.7
When new tasks are added to the end of the Prepare Foundation group, a different result will be produced, depending on the links you have originally created between the groups.

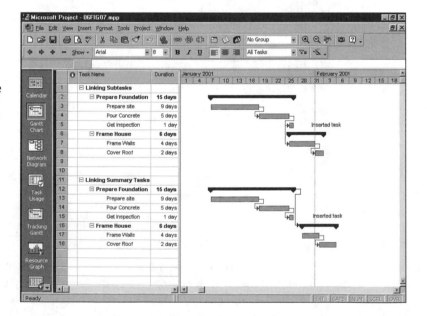

Another advantage to linking summary tasks is that, when you hide all the subtasks and display the summary task phases, they will have linking lines to show their logical order.

Caution

Be sure you establish no links between subtasks in the same group that try to schedule one of the subtasks to start before the first subtask in the summary group. For example, suppose subtask A starts when the summary task starts. If you link another subtask in the same group to subtask A with a Start-to-Start link and add lead time to the link, you would be telling Project to start the second subtask before the summary task begins. Project would ignore the lead time and schedule both tasks to start at the same time.

ENTERING DEPENDENCY LINKS

 You can create task links in Project in several ways. If the dependency is the default Finish-to-Start relationship without lag or lead, you can simply select the tasks you want to link and choose Edit, Link Tasks, or click the Link Tasks tool on the Standard toolbar. If the relationship is more complex, you must use another method, or you must edit the dependency link after it has been created.

Following is a brief listing of the different ways you can link tasks. Each of these methods is discussed in detail in the following sections. Some can be used only in very restrictive circumstances, so read about all the methods before you try just one.

- To create a link in a view with a task table, select the tasks to be linked and use one of these options:
  - The Menu command Edit, Link Tasks
  - The Link Tasks tool on the Standard toolbar
  - The Ctrl+F2 shortcut key
- To create a link in a view that represents tasks graphically, you can drag the four-arrow mouse pointer from the predecessor to the successor task to create a link. These views support linking tasks with the mouse:
  - Timescale side of the Gantt Chart view
  - Network Diagram view
  - Calendar view
- To edit a link—for example, to include lag time or lead time or to change the type of link—select the dependent (successor) task and use one of these locations:
  - The Predecessors tab in the Task Information dialog box
  - The Predecessors table in the Task Form in the bottom pane of a split screen
  - The Predecessors field in the Entry table of a task view like the Gantt Chart
  - The Task Dependency dialog box, which is activated by double-clicking the linking line in the Gantt Chart or Network Diagram

Each of these locations are described in the following sections.

PART

II

CH

6

CREATING LINKS USING THE MENU OR TOOLBAR

 The simplest and easiest way to link tasks is to select the tasks and then choose Edit, Link Tasks, or click the Link Tasks tool on the Standard toolbar. You also can press Ctrl+F2 to create a link. However, these links are always the default Finish-to-Start without lag or lead. You will have to edit the links if you want a different link type or to add lag or lead. In Figure 6.8, four tasks are selected and have been linked in series with the Link Tasks tool.

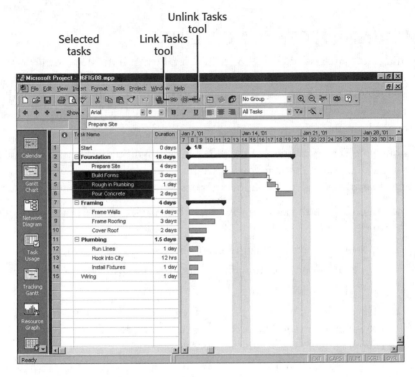

Figure 6.8
You can quickly link selected tasks with the Link Tasks button. This links the tasks in a Finish-to-Start relationship.

No limit exists to the number of tasks you can select for linking. You can link just one predecessor and one successor at a time, or you can link all the tasks in the project in the same operation.

To select multiple, adjacent tasks in the task list, drag the mouse pointer to extend the selection to as many tasks as you want to link or use the Shift+down arrow or Shift+up arrow key combinations. To select all tasks, click one of the column headings—for instance Task Name. When you link the tasks, those that are higher up on the task list (with lower ID numbers) are always predecessors to the selected task with the next higher ID number.

To select non-adjacent tasks for linking, select the first predecessor task and add tasks to the selection by holding down the Ctrl key while clicking additional tasks. With nonadjacent tasks, the first task selected will be the predecessor for the second task selected, and the second task selected will be the predecessor for the third. For example, if you select tasks 5, 2, and 12 in that order and then choose the Link Tasks tool, task 5 will become predecessor to task 2, and task 2 will become predecessor to task 12.

Tip from Tim and the Project Team	To select a task for linking, simply click any field in the task row or click the task bar. You do not need to select the entire task row.

 To remove a task link, select both tasks and either click the Unlink Tasks tool, use the Ctrl+Shift+F2 key combination, or use the Edit, Unlink Tasks command. To remove all links to a task and its predecessors and successors, select just the task alone and use the same options just mentioned.

CREATING LINKS USING THE TASK INFORMATION DIALOG BOX

You can also use the Predecessors tab of the Task Information dialog box to define and edit task links (see Figure 6.9). Unlike the Edit, Link Tasks command, the Task Information dialog box enables you to choose the type of link and to enter lag or lead time.

Dependent task selected   Type of link

Figure 6.9
Use the Task Information dialog box to define types of predecessor links and lag and lead times.

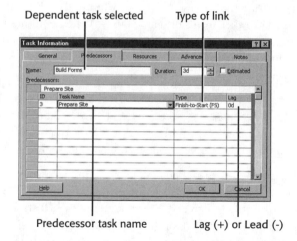

Predecessor task name   Lag (+) or Lead (-)

To create a dependency relationship using the Task Information dialog box, follow these steps:

1. Select the dependent (successor) task.

2. Click the Task Information tool on the Standard toolbar, or double-click the task to open the Task Information dialog box.

3. Click the Predecessors tab.

   The Predecessors tab features a table in which you can define predecessors, including the type of link and any lead or lag time (refer to Figure 6.9).

4. Activate the first blank cell under the Task Name field. Choose the name of the task to be the predecessor task from the drop-down list in the field. Project will automatically

supply the ID number and will supply the default Finish-to-Start link type with no lag, unless you choose otherwise.

Alternatively, if you remember the ID number for the predecessor task, you can enter it in the cell in the ID column. Press Enter to finish the cell entry or select the green check button on the Entry bar. Project automatically supplies the Task Name for that ID number and supplies the default Finish-to-Start link type with no lag.

5. Use the drop-down list in the Type column if you want to change the dependency type.

6. To create lag or lead time, click in the Lag field and type the amount of lag or lead time followed by a time unit (unless you want to use the default time unit). See the following section for more details about entering leads and lags.

7. If additional predecessors exist for this task, repeat steps 4–6 as needed for each predecessor.

8. Select OK or press Enter to accept the changes.

ENTERING LEADS AND LAGS

Entering leads and lags is done the same way whether you use the Task Information dialog box mentioned previously, or other forms or dialog boxes. When entering lags and leads, bear in mind that both are entered in the same Lag box on Microsoft Project forms. Positive numbers represent lag time and negative numbers represent lead time.

You can enter lag or lead as a number followed by one of the regular or elapsed time code letters you use for entering duration time (m or em, h or eh, d or ed, w or ew, or mo or emo). Lead time is entered as a negative lag. For example, enter **2d** to define a two-day lag and **–4h** to define a four-hour lead. Type **2ed** to schedule a lag of two elapsed days. If you type a number without a time unit, Project appends the default duration unit (initially days).

You can also express lag or lead time as a percentage of the predecessor's duration. Therefore, if you want a task to start when its predecessor is within 10% of being finished, you can enter a Finish-to-Start link with a 10% lead (entered as **–10%**). Project schedules the task to start so it overlaps the last 10% of the predecessor task duration. Using percentage lags and leads enables the amount of lag or lead to vary with changes in the duration of the predecessor. Thus, the longer the duration of the predecessor, the more time that a percentage lag or lead would entail.

When you use percentage lags and leads, Project uses the start or finish of the predecessor (as specified in the link type) for the starting point and offsets the start or finish of the successor from that point by the lag percentage times the duration of the predecessor.

For example, if the predecessor has a duration of 4 days, a Start-to-Start lag of 25% will cause the successor's start to be scheduled one day after the predecessor's start. A Finish-to-Start lead of 75% produces the same start date for the successor—as long as the duration of the predecessor remains unchanged. Subsequent changes in the duration of the predecessor, however, cause these two links to result in a different start date for the successor.

CREATING LINKS USING THE TASK FORM VIEW

With a task view such as the Gantt Chart in the top pane, you can split the window and use the Task Form in the bottom pane to define the predecessor and successor relationships. This is an easy way to define or edit complex dependency relationships. You select a task in the top pane and define its predecessor or successor link in the predecessor or successor details in the bottom pane.

To display the predecessor and successor details in the bottom pane of a task view such as the Gantt Chart, split the window, activate the bottom pane, choose Format, Details and select Predecessors and Successors.

Tip from Tim and the Project Team

You also can right-click the bottom pane and choose the details to display (see Figure 6.10).

Figure 6.10
The shortcut menu for the Task Form view offers several choices for displaying task link details in the bottom of the form.

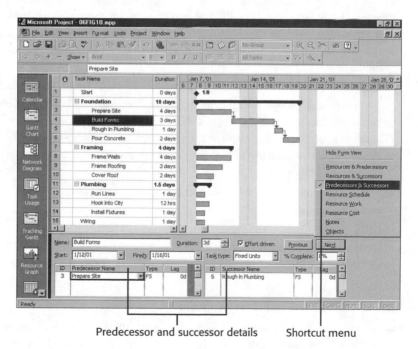

Predecessor and successor details   Shortcut menu

If you display the predecessor details, define a predecessor for the dependent task by following these steps:

1. Select the dependent task in the top pane or use the Previous and Next buttons in the lower pane to move to the desired task.

Note

If you want to enter the successor details in the Task Form, select the predecessor task in the top pane and use the successor detail fields in the steps that follow instead of the predecessor detail fields. The link is defined exactly the same in either details area.

2. In the bottom pane, activate the first cell in either the ID or Predecessor Name column.

3. If you selected the Predecessor Name field, use the drop-down list of task names to select the name of the task to be the predecessor. The Task Form view still shows the OK button because selecting the task name completes only the cell entry.

   If you selected the ID field, type the predecessor's ID number in the ID field and press Enter to complete the cell entry. Project automatically fills in the predecessor name when you click the OK button to complete the linking definition.

   If you do not know the ID number of the predecessor, you can use the vertical scrollbar in the top pane to view the predecessor task. The ID field remains selected while you scroll the task list. Do not select the predecessor, just view its ID number. Type this number into the ID field. You can then press Enter or click the green check button on the Entry bar to complete the cell entry for the ID number.

4. Select the predecessor Type field if you want to define a link type other than Finish-to-Start. If you leave the Type field blank, Project supplies the default Finish-to-Start type when you choose the OK button. Type in the two-letter code (FF, FS, SF, or SS) or use the drop-down list to select the code. Press Enter to complete the cell entry in the Type field.

5. Select the Lag field if you want to define a lag or lead time. The default of 0d (zero days, meaning no lag or lead time) is supplied automatically when you click the OK button if you leave this field blank. Use the spin control up to display lags (positive values) or down to display leads (negative values) in the default duration time unit. You can also type in a value using any of the duration or elapsed duration time units or using a percentage amount.

6. You can add more predecessors on the following rows in the Predecessors table by repeating steps 2–5.

7. Click the OK button to execute the changes you entered in the Task Form. Figure 6.11 shows the completed details for task 5's link with task 4 as a Start-to-Start predecessor with a 2-day lag.

CREATING LINKS USING THE ENTRY TABLE

You can also enter dependency relationships in the Predecessors field on the Entry table (see Figure 6.12). The Entry table is the default table displayed in the Gantt Chart. To see the Predecessors field on the table, either move the vertical split bar to the right or click the right arrow on the horizontal scrollbar at the bottom left side of the Gantt Chart.

You can enter the simplest relationship, the Finish-to-Start, by just entering the task ID number for the predecessor task in the Predecessors field. The other dependency relationships require a very specific pattern of coding that is explained below.

To enter one of the other relationships, you must enter the predecessor task ID number followed immediately by the abbreviation for the type of link followed immediately by the lag or lead if there is one. Begin a lag with a plus sign and a lead with a minus sign.

Selected task

Figure 6.11
You can use the predecessor fields on the Task Form to define a task's predecessor links.

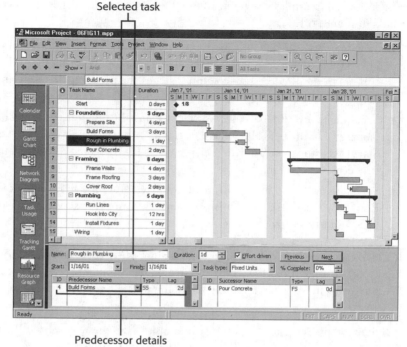

Predecessor details

Predecessors field

Figure 6.12
The codes entered in the Predecessors field define links just as do entries in the predecessor Details area of the Task Form.

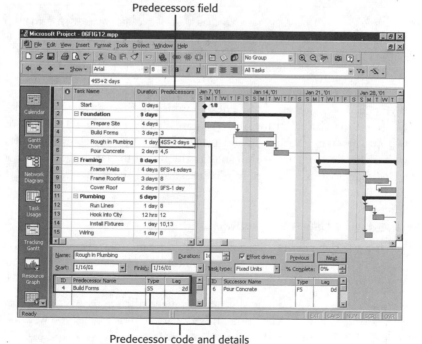

PART

II

CH

6

Predecessor code and details

The following examples show how to use these codes in the Predecessors column, as illustrated in Figure 6.12:

- Schedule task 5 (Rough in Plumbing) to start 2 days after the start of task 4 (Build Forms). In Figure 6.12, task 5 is selected in the top pane and the code 4SS+2d that appears in the Predecessors column matches the predecessor details in the Task Form below.

- Schedule task 8 (Frame Walls) to start 4 elapsed days after the finish of task 6 (Pour Concrete) in order to allow the concrete time to set properly. Make task 8 a Finish-to-Start successor to task 6 with 4 elapsed days lag by typing 6FS+4ed in task 8's Predecessors column.

- Schedule task 10 (Cover Roof) to start 1 day before the finish of task 9 (Frame Roofing). Make task 10 a Finish-to-Start successor to task 9 with a 1-day lead by typing 9FS–1d in task 10's Predecessors column.

If a task has more than one predecessor, separate the predecessor definitions by commas. In Figure 6.12, task 6, Pour Concrete, has two predecessors separated by a comma (tasks 4 and 5)—the forms must be built and the plumbing must be roughed in before you can pour the concrete.

To enter the predecessor relationship for a task in this view, select the Predecessors cell in the row for the successor task. Then type the codes for the relationship you want to create.

Tip from Tim and the Project Team

If you do not remember the ID number of the predecessor, leave the cell you are editing selected while you scroll the task list to find the predecessor task. Do not select the predecessor, just view its ID number. As you start typing, the ID number of the cell you are editing will return to the screen, and you can finish the link definition.

If you need a link other than the default Finish-to-Start, or want to add lag or lead time, type the abbreviation for the link type immediately after the ID number of the predecessor (with no separating space). To add a lag or lead, follow the abbreviation for the link type with a plus sign or a minus sign and the amount of the lag or lead, either in time units or as a percentage. To complete your link, press Enter or click the green check button on the Entry bar.

CREATING LINKS USING THE MOUSE

You can use the mouse to link task bars on the timescale side of the Gantt Chart or in the Network Diagram or Calendar view. You can also use the mouse to edit the linking relationship in the Gantt Chart or Network Diagram.

Using the mouse for linking is most convenient when you can see both tasks you are trying to link onscreen at the same time. If both bars are not visible, you will probably do better with one of the other methods of linking the tasks, such as using the Task Form View method described earlier in this chapter.

To link tasks with the mouse in the Gantt Chart, center the mouse over the predecessor task until the pointer changes into a four-arrows icon, and then click and drag the pointer (which should then turn into a linked-chain icon) over the center of the successor task. When Project interprets your action as creating a link, the mouse pointer will change into a linked-chain icon and Project will display the Finish-to-Start Link information box (see Figure 6.13).

Figure 6.13
Drag from the predecessor task bar to the dependent (successor) task bar to establish a Finish-to-Start link.

Successor task ID
Predecessor task ID

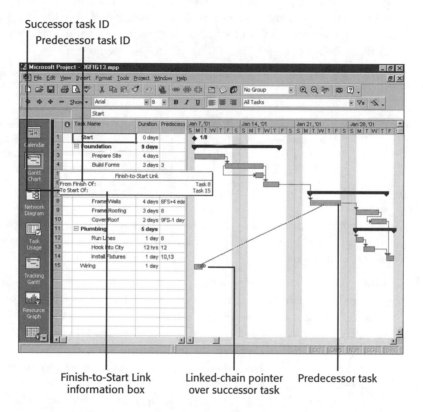

Finish-to-Start Link information box

Linked-chain pointer over successor task

Predecessor task

PART
II
CH
6

Caution

Be careful when creating links with the mouse! The mouse pointer is designed to perform a number of actions on tasks in these views. It is easy to accidentally move the task or mark the task as being partially complete. You must watch the shape of the mouse pointer carefully to ensure you're doing exactly what you intend to do.

In the Gantt Chart, the mouse must be the four-arrows shape when over the predecessor task, or it will not change into the linked-chain icon as you drag it to the successor, and you will not link the tasks. In both the Network Diagram and Calendar views, you must drag from the *center* of the predecessor task (where the pointer will be the normal white cross) to the *center* of the successor task, or the mouse will not change into the linked-chain shape, and you will not link the tasks. In all cases make sure that the mouse pointer is the linked-chain shape when you are over the successor task before releasing the mouse button (refer to Figure 6.13).

Tip from Tim and the Project Team

If you want to cancel the linking procedure, simply drag the mouse up to the menu or toolbar area of the Gantt Chart or the Calendar and release the button. In the Network Diagram, you must return the mouse to the task you started with before releasing the mouse button, or you will create a new task with a link.

Dragging the mouse pointer from one task bar to another task bar establishes a Finish-to-Start link between the tasks. The task you start on is the predecessor and the task you drag to is the dependent (successor) task. Make sure the mouse pointer has assumed the linked-chain shape shown in Figure 6.13 before you release the mouse.

 If Project scrolls too fast for you to see the task bar you are looking for, see "The Mouse and Task Links" in the "Troubleshooting" section near the end of this chapter.

Note

In the Network Diagram and Calendar views, you must drag from the *center* of the predecessor task's box or bar, and the pointer will be the plain white cross, not the four-arrow shape you look for in the Gantt Chart. In those views, the four-arrow shape appears when the pointer is over the border of the task box or bar and means that you will move the task if you drag the border.

The dependency type created with the mouse is always a Finish-to-Start relationship. You can change the link type, add a lag or lead, or even delete the link by displaying the Task Dependency dialog box with the mouse in the Gantt Chart or Network Diagram views.

To display the Task Dependency dialog box, scroll to display the linking line between the predecessor and dependent (successor) tasks. Position the tip of the mouse pointer on the line connecting the tasks whose links you want to edit. A ScreenTip should appear with the details of the link. Double-click the linking line. The Task Dependency dialog box appears, as shown in Figure 6.14. The From task in the dialog box is the predecessor, and the To task is the successor. You can change the dependency type with the drop-down list in the Type field. Choosing None removes the link, as does clicking the Delete button. You can redefine the lag or lead in the Lag field. Click the OK button to complete the change.

Note

You can't change the names of the linked tasks in the Task Dependency dialog box, nor which task is the predecessor and which is the successor.

 If you double-click a linking line but the wrong tasks are listed in the Task Dependency dialog box, see "The Mouse and Task Links" in the "Troubleshooting" section near the end of this chapter.

WORKING WITH THE AUTOMATIC LINKING OPTION

If you use only simple Finish-to-Start links in your project, Project's Autolink feature (which is enabled by default) can help you maintain the dependency link sequences when you move, delete, or insert tasks within a linked sequence of tasks. However, Autolink works only if the affected links are Finish-to-Start links.

Predecessor task

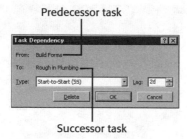

Figure 6.14
Double-click a task's linking line to display the Task Dependency dialog box for editing task links.

Successor task

When you change the order of tasks, and thus their ID numbers, in a task table (like the one in the Gantt Chart), Autolink acts as follows:

- If you cut or delete a task from within a chain of Finish-to-Start linked tasks, Autolink repairs the break in the chain by linking together the former predecessor and successor of the deleted task.

- If you insert a task in a chain of Finish-to-Start linked tasks, Autolink breaks the former link between the tasks. The new task is inserted between the existing tasks, and then the newly inserted task is linked to the task above and below it to keep the linked sequence intact.

- If you move a task from one Finish-to-Start sequence to another, Autolink repairs the chain at the task's old site and inserts the new task into the chain at the new site.

In the Network Diagram and Calendar views, Autolink behaves as above only when you delete a task or insert a new task (because you can't cut, copy, or move tasks to a different ID order in those views).

In Figure 6.15, the first group of tasks shows a series of tasks before a task is inserted. The second group of tasks illustrates what happens if you insert the Inspect Foundation task with Autolink enabled. Autolink inserts the Inspect Foundation task between Pour Foundation and Frame Walls, the new task automatically links to Pour Foundation as its predecessor and to Frame Walls as its successor, and the former link between those tasks is removed. The third set of tasks shows what happens if you insert the Inspect Foundation task with Autolink disabled. The new task is scheduled to start at the beginning of the project and is not included in the linked chain of tasks.

Note

If you add a task to or remove a task from the beginning or end of a linked chain, instead of in the middle of the chain, Autolink does not include the new task in the chain. Thus, inserting a task at the beginning of a series of linked tasks or after the last task in a linked sequence does not cause Autolink to extend the chain to include the new task.

To include a task in a sequence, when the task has been added either to the beginning or ending of the sequence, you must link the tasks yourself using one of the previously discussed methods.

PART

II

CH

6

Figure 6.15
Autolink retains the sequence of tasks when you insert or remove tasks from a linked chain of tasks.

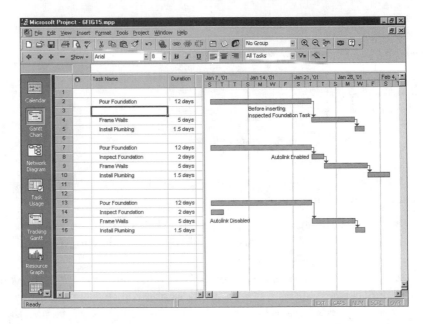

By default, Autolink is enabled, but you can disable it by changing the status of the Autolink option. Follow these steps:

1. Choose Tools, Options. The Options dialog box appears.

2. Choose the Schedule tab.

3. Deselect the Autolink Inserted or Moved Tasks check box. This disables Autolink. To turn it back on, select the check box again.

4. To set the option status as a global default for all new projects, choose the Set as Default button. Otherwise, the change you make will affect only the active project document.

5. Click the OK button to close the dialog box.

Tip from Tim and the Project Team

If you have disabled Autolink and need to insert or paste tasks into a Finish-to-Start sequence, you can quickly re-establish the sequence to include the new tasks. Select the tasks starting with the row above the insertion and including the row below the insertion and use the Unlink Tasks tool to break the original link. Then, with the tasks still selected, use the Link Tasks tool to include the new tasks in the sequence.

If you delete or cut tasks from a Finish-to-Start sequence, simply select the rows above and below the deleted rows and click the Link Tasks tool.

Caution

As convenient as Autolink can be when editing a simple task list, it can cause problems by creating unintended task links. Be extremely careful when this option is enabled, especially when inserting tasks. Double-check the links to ensure the links are as intended for the project. Unintended task links can become a vexing problem in a project schedule.

If automatic linking is enabled and you rearrange an outline, carefully review the links that result each time you move a task or group of tasks in the outline. You might have to edit the links to reflect exactly the relationship you want defined.

Tip from Tim and the Project Team

Personally, I leave Autolink disabled because it makes changes without asking for my approval, and I have found that I sometimes don't notice an unintended change in the linking for my task lists.

MODIFYING, REVIEWING, AND REMOVING DEPENDENCY LINKS

As you develop your project plan, you will inevitably make changes in the task list, and you will then have to adjust the sequence of links you have established. You might want to modify the type of link between tasks, insert lag or lead time, or remove the link entirely. You can modify existing links in the locations listed below, all of which were described in detail in previous sections of this chapter:

- Select the successor task and modify its predecessor links in the Predecessors tab of the Task Information dialog box.

- Split the window and display the Task Form in the bottom pane beneath a task view. With the predecessor and successor details displayed in the Task Form, select a linked task and modify its links in either the Predecessors or Successors table.

- Double-click a linking line in the Gantt Chart or Network Diagram to display the Task Dependency dialog box where you can modify the link.

 If two tasks are linked in the wrong direction—in other words the predecessor should be the successor— see "Reversing a Dependency Link" in the "Troubleshooting" section near the end of this chapter.

If you find that a link between tasks is no longer necessary, or you prefer to create a link to another task, you will want to remove the current link. Just as you can use several ways to create links, you can use many different methods to remove links. The following techniques will remove links:

- You can easily unlink tasks in any of the task views using the menu or toolbar. Select the tasks you want to unlink and choose Edit, Unlink Tasks or click the Unlink Tasks button on the Standard toolbar. You also can press Shift+Ctrl+F2.

  - If you select a single task and then choose Edit, Unlink Tasks or click the Unlink Tasks button, Project removes all predecessors for that task.

  - If you select multiple tasks, Project removes all links between any pair of the selected tasks.

- To remove all links from the project, display any view with a task table and select all tasks by clicking a field name, such as a Task Name.

■ Select a dependent (successor) task and remove its predecessor links with the Task Information dialog box. For each predecessor listed on the Predecessors tab that you want to remove, click the row for the predecessor and press the Delete key. Clicking OK closes the dialog box and removes those links.

■ With a task view in the top pane and the Task Form in the bottom pane, display the resource and predecessor—or predecessor and successor—details in the bottom pane. Select the dependent (successor) task in the top pane. For each predecessor link you want to remove, click its row in the details area and press the Delete key. Click OK to finish the deletion. If you display one of the details choices that includes successors, you can select the predecessor task in the top pane and delete the link in the Successors table in the bottom pane.

■ With a view that includes a task table, such as the Gantt Chart, click on the row for the dependent (successor) task and clear the entry in its Predecessors field by pressing Ctrl+Delete. Remember not to press the Delete key alone, for that deletes the entire task.

■ Double-click a linking line in the Gantt Chart or Network Diagram to display the Task Dependency dialog box and choose Delete to remove the link.

AUDITING THE TASK LINKS

The project schedule is heavily influenced by the linking relationships you establish among tasks. It is very easy to accidentally link tasks or break task links, and if you work with Autolink enabled there may have been changes you haven't noticed. Therefore, you should review the link relationships carefully before committing to the project schedule. Accidental links easily can skew the finish date of the project.

The Network Diagram and Descriptive Network Diagram views concentrate on the linking relationships by representing each task as a box or node with arrows from predecessor to successor tasks. (Chapter 7, "Viewing Your Schedule," is devoted to using and understanding the major task views, including the Network Diagram.) Because you see so few tasks on the screen in these views, it is best to print the views when using them to review all task links.

The Gantt Chart shows the task links as arrows connecting the task bars, with the arrow always pointing to the dependent (successor) task. The Gantt Chart view seen earlier in this chapter, with the predecessor and successor details in the Task Form in the bottom pane, provides a good review of the task links. For the task you have active, the predecessor and successor tasks are listed in the bottom pane, along with any lag or lead associated with the link. Use the Previous and Next buttons in the bottom pane to review the links.

Another useful view for auditing task links is the Relationship Diagram view. It shows the predecessors and successors for just the selected task as task nodes, like the Network Diagram view, and is useful for confirming that you defined the task relationships as intended (see Figure 6.16). You can display the Relationship Diagram view by itself, but it is most useful when displayed in the bottom pane beneath another task view in the top pane, such as the Gantt Chart or Network Diagram view.

The task you have selected in the top pane is represented by a box or node in the center of the Relationship Diagram in the bottom pane, with links to nodes for its predecessors and successors on the left and right. The type of relationship and any lag or lead is shown next to the linked task nodes. In Figure 6.16, the Relationship Diagram in the bottom pane makes it clear that there are three successors to the Frame Walls task, something that is not easy to see in the Gantt Chart in the top pane.

Figure 6.16
The Relationship Diagram view offers a good review of the predecessor and successor links for a task.

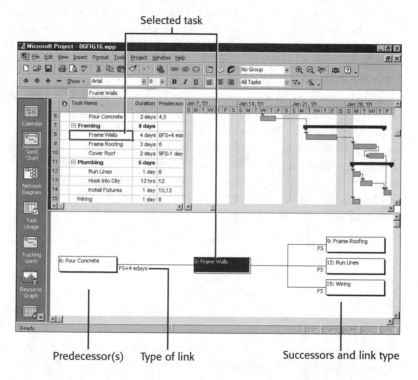

Selected task

Predecessor(s)   Type of link   Successors and link type

PART

II

CH

6

Note

The Relationship Diagram view is a display-only view. You can't make changes in this view, nor can you print it. You can, however, display the Task Information dialog box for the selected task and make changes there.

To display the Relationship Diagram below the Gantt Chart, split the window, and activate the bottom pane. Choose View, More Views, and select the Relationship Diagram in the More Views dialog box. Then click the Apply button to display the view.

Select tasks in the top pane to see their predecessors and successors displayed graphically in the bottom pane.

Tip from Tim and the Project Team

If you select multiple tasks in the top pane, you will see only one of the selected tasks in the center of the bottom pane at a time. You can use the horizontal scrollbar in the Relationship Diagram pane to scroll through all the selected tasks. Pressing the Home key displays the view for the first of the selected tasks, and pressing the End key displays the view for the last of the selected tasks. Use these same techniques to scroll through the tasks if you display the Relationship Diagram as a full-screen view.

WORKING WITH TASK CONSTRAINTS

Generally speaking you want Microsoft Project to schedule tasks as close as possible to the start of the project in order to minimize the overall duration of the project. For the same reason, if the project is scheduled from a fixed finish date, you want Project to schedule tasks as late as possible so they are close to the fixed finish date and keep the duration of the project as short as possible. However, there are many circumstances in which a task must be scheduled to start or finish by a specific date. These fixed-date requirements are called *task constraints* in Microsoft Project. They might be due to requirements from outside the project, or they might be the result of interim deadlines imposed by the project manager. External constraints might be deadlines imposed by customers, contractors, the government, or policies within the organization that are external to the project. Constraints that are internal to the project might be such things as progress reviews and reevaluations of the schedule as each major phase of the project nears completion. The following are some specific examples of task constraints:

- A manufacturing project contract might call for delivery of the product no later than a specific date; thus, the delivery task must finish on or before that date.

- A contract with a vendor might stipulate the earliest delivery date for some parts or finish date for a service; therefore, the finish of this task should be scheduled on or after that date.

- A government agency might require an environmental impact test at a specific point in time after the project starts, with the test results delivered by a specific date; therefore, the task to conduct the test must start on a specific date and the task to submit the results must be finished on or before another specific date.

- Senior management might require project progress reports to be delivered on specific dates.

- The project manager might want to create review or assessment deadlines at specific points once the work on the project is underway.

In all these cases, either the start or finish of a task is to be tied to a specific date in the schedule, and you will want Project to take this constraint into consideration when scheduling the task.

Constraints are defined by entries in the task Constraint Type and Constraint Date fields (see Figure 6.17). By default, new tasks you create have no constraint date. When you add a task to a project that is scheduled from a fixed start-date, Project supplies As Soon As Possible in the Constraint Type field as a default entry. This entry means that there is no fixed date requirement—in other words, no constraint—and the task will be scheduled as soon as possible after its predecessor requirements are met. The Constraint Date field for the task will have the default entry NA.

Figure 6.17
The default constraint type is As Soon As Possible and the default constraint date is NA, as seen on the Advanced tab of the Task Information dialog box.

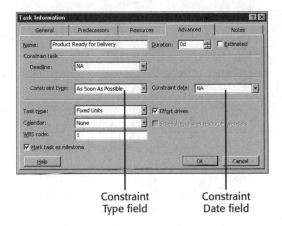

Constraint   Constraint
Type field   Date field

If the project is scheduled from a fixed finish date, Project supplies new tasks with the default entry As Late As Possible in the Constraint Type field. This entry also means that there is no constraint and the task will be scheduled as close to the finish date of the project as possible (considering the schedule for successor tasks, which must also finish before that date). Again, the Constraint Date field will have the default entry NA.

UNDERSTANDING THE TYPES OF CONSTRAINTS

The Constraint Type field is available on the Advanced tab of the Task Information dialog box. It provides a drop-down list of eight possible constraint types that you can use to define any possible date constraint. These types are described in Table 6.2. Constraint types are often referred to by the acronym shown in the second column of the table.

TABLE 6.2   THE CONSTRAINT TYPES AVAILABLE

Constraint Type	Acronym	Description
As Soon As Possible	ASAP	Marks a task as not constrained and does not require a constraint date. The task will be scheduled as soon as its predecessor requirements are met.
As Late As Possible	ALAP	Delays the task as long as possible, considering the scheduling requirements of its successor tasks, all of which must finish before the project finish date. This constraint type does not require a constraint date.

TABLE 6.2   CONTINUED

Constraint Type	Acronym	Description
Start No Earlier Than	SNET	This task must start on or after the defined constraint date.
Start No Later Than	SNLT	This task must start on or before the defined constraint date.
Finish No Earlier Than	FNET	This task must finish on or after the defined constraint date.
Finish No Later Than	FNLT	This task must finish on or before the defined constraint date.
Must Start On	MSO	This task must start exactly on the defined constraint date.
Must Finish On	MFO	This task must finish exactly on the defined constraint date.

The first two constraint types (ASAP and ALAP) in Table 6.2 are perfectly flexible because they have no constraint date associated with them—in fact, they are really nonconstraints. The duration of a sequence of tasks will expand when new tasks are inserted or when the existing tasks experience duration inflation. As a result, some tasks in the sequence will need to be rescheduled. If the tasks in the sequence have the constraint types As Soon As Possible or As Late As Possible, they can be rescheduled without limit as the sequence expands (or contracts).

The last two constraints in the table, Must Start On and Must Finish On (MSO and MFO), are considered to be inflexible—because they potentially can block the expansion of a task sequence in which they are defined for a task. If the linked sequence expands so much that it requires one of these tasks to move beyond its constraint date, Project must choose to honor the defined links or to honor the defined constraints, but it can't honor both. By default Project honors the defined constraint and ignores the defined sequence link, forcing the constrained task to overlap its linked task in a way that is contrary to the definition of the link. (See the section "Deciding to Honor Links or Constraints" later in this chapter for information about changing this default.)

Figure 6.18 illustrates the conflict between a task link and an inflexible constraint. The milestone Product Ready for Delivery must be completed by March 7, 2001. It has a Finish-to-Start link to its predecessor, Prepare for Shipping. The predecessor finishes in time for the milestone to meet its deadline in Scenario A. In Scenario B, however, the predecessor has been delayed because of duration inflation in an earlier task and now it is impossible to honor the link and to honor the constraint. Project schedules the milestone on its constraint date and ignores the link definition. The predecessor finishes after the milestone's date, causing the linking line to wrap back around as though the link were defined with lead time.

Figure 6.18
When a task's link definition and constraint definition are incompatible, Project normally honors the constraint.

Constraint Date

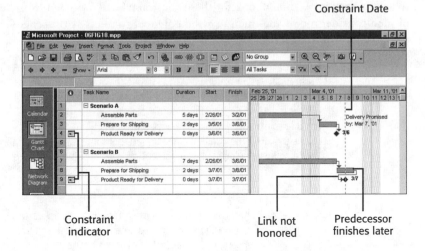

Constraint indicator

Link not honored

Predecessor finishes later

In a fixed start-date project, duration inflation in predecessor tasks tends to push successor tasks to later dates. Constraints that prohibit successor tasks from being rescheduled to later dates are therefore also also called inflexible constraints. Consequently, the Start No Later Than and Finish No Later Than constraint types are called inflexible in fixed start-date projects. But, the Start No Earlier Than and Finish No Earlier Than constraints are flexible in fixed start-date projects.

In a fixed finish-date project, duration inflation in successor tasks tends to push predecessor tasks to earlier dates. Constraints that prohibit predecessor tasks from being rescheduled to earlier dates are therefore also called inflexible constraints. Consequently, the Start No Earlier Than and Finish No Earlier Than constraint types are called inflexible in fixed finish-date projects. But the Start No Later Than and Finish No Later Than constraints are flexible in fixed finish-date projects.

Note

Though the Start No Earlier Than and Finish No Earlier Than constraints are flexible for the expansion of the fixed start-date schedule, they nevertheless do create a barrier if you are attempting to compress the project's duration. To shorten the overall project, you must shorten the critical path, and if a task with one of these constraints is on the critical path, it can block your efforts. Though you might shorten the duration of its predecessors, a Start No Earlier Than or Finish No Earlier Than task will not move to an earlier date and the critical path will not be shortened.

Similarly, in fixed finish-date projects, the Start No Later Than and Finish No Later Than constraints are called flexible because they don't inhibit the natural expansion of the project, but they can block compression of the project duration.

If you change a fixed start-date project to a fixed finish date, what were flexible Start No Earlier Than and Finish No Earlier Than constraints become inflexible. Similarly, the flexible Start No Later Than and Finish No Later Than constraints in a fixed finish-date project become inflexible if you switch to fixed start-date scheduling. If you do change the project

PART

II

CH

6

scheduling type you should look for those constraints that switched from flexible to inflexible and consider modifying them to avoid potential conflicts as the schedule changes.

Note

If you change a project from fixed start-date to fixed finish date, the As Soon As Possible constraint types for existing tasks will not be replaced with As Late As Possible constraints; however, all new tasks will be given the new default As Late As Possible constraint type. Likewise, changing a fixed finish-date project to fixed start date will leave the As Late As Possible constraints unchanged, but new tasks will be As Soon As Possible. Neither of these results will affect the duration of the project, but some tasks will be scheduled earlier or later than they could possibly be without affecting the start or finish of the project.

Tip from Tim and the Project Team

If you decide to permanently change a project from fixed start-date to fixed finish-date (or vice versa) and want to change all the old default constraints to the new default (for example, to replace As Soon As Possible with As Late As Possible), use Project's Replace command. For example, type **As Soon As Possible** in the Find What box, type **As Late As Possible** in the Replace With box, select the field Constraint Type in the Look In Field box, and select Equals in the Test box.

Creating constraints unwittingly is one of the most common mistakes made by novice users of Microsoft Project. Any time you type a date into the Start or Finish fields for a task, or drag the task bar to a new date in the Gantt Chart, Microsoft Project creates a constraint to honor that date. When you create a recurring task, Project also creates a constraint for each occurrence. Fortunately, Project always makes these flexible constraints. Thus, if you type in the start date for a task in a fixed start-date project, Project will change the Constraint Type to Start No Earlier Than and place the date in the Constraint Date field. The task will be scheduled to start on the date you typed (even if its predecessors would allow it to be scheduled earlier), but it can be freely moved to later dates if its predecessors experience duration inflation. Similarly, in a fixed finish-date project the flexible constraints Start No Later Than and Finish No Later Than will be supplied when you specify start or finish dates for tasks.

When a task has a constraint type other than As Soon As Possible or As Late As Possible, Project displays an icon in the Indicators field of the Gantt Chart view. The icon looks like a calendar with either a blue or a red "dot" in the calendar. The blue dot signifies a flexible constraint, and a red dot signifies an inflexible constraint. Table 6.3 summarizes the flexible/inflexible status for the eight constraint types in both fixed start-date and fixed finish-date projects and describes the indicators you will see for them.

TABLE 6.3   FLEXIBLE AND INFLEXIBLE CONSTRAINTS AND THEIR INDICATORS

	Projects Scheduled from a...	
Constraint Type	**Fixed Start Date**	**Fixed Finish Date**
As Soon As Possible	Flexible (no indicator)	Flexible (no indicator)
As Late As Possible	Flexible (no indicator)	Flexible (no indicator)

TABLE 6.3   CONTINUED

	Projects Scheduled from a...	
Constraint Type	**Fixed Start Date**	**Fixed Finish Date**
Start No Earlier Than	Flexible (Blue dot)	Inflexible (Red dot)
Finish No Earlier Than	Flexible (Blue dot)	Inflexible (Red dot)
Start No Later Than	Inflexible (Red dot)	Flexible (Blue dot)
Finish No Later Than	Inflexible (Red dot)	Flexible (Blue dot)
Must Finish On	Inflexible (Red dot)	Inflexible (Red dot)
Must Start On	Inflexible (Red dot)	Inflexible (Red dot)

ENTERING TASK CONSTRAINTS

Keep in mind that if you enter a date in a task's Start or Finish fields or drag the task bar in the Gantt Chart, you create a flexible constraint for the task. You can also create task constraints by filling in the Constraint Type and Constraint Date fields in the Task Information dialog box. If you want to create or modify many task constraints, you will want to add the constraint fields to the Entry table or to display the Task Details Form view, which makes the constraint fields available for editing.

Tip from Tim and the Project Team	When you type a constraint date, you can also include the time of day with the date. If you don't append the time of day, Project supplies one for you. Using the default values from the Calendar tab of the Options dialog box, it appends the Default Start Time for all constraint types that restrict the start of a task and the Default End Time for all constraints that restrict the finish of a task.

Note	No matter which method you use for creating constraints, if you create an inflexible constraint, the Planning Wizard will display a warning. Understanding how to deal with that warning is covered at the end of this section.

PART

II

CH

6

To enter task constraints in the Task Information dialog box, follow these steps:

1. Select the task you want to modify and display its Task Information dialog box.
2. Click the Advanced tab.
3. In the Constraint Type field, select the constraint type from the drop-down list.
4. For those constraints that require a date (which is all but As Soon As Possible and As Late As Possible), enter the constraint date in the Constraint Date box. Append the time of day if you want a time other than the Default Start Time or Default End Time.

   If you do not enter a date, Project will use the task's current start or finish date as the constraint date—the start date and time for start date constraints and the finish date and time for finish date constraints.

Tip from Tim and the Project Team

> It's a good idea to also click the Notes tab while in the Task Information dialog box and add a note explaining the reason for the constraint. This will be important information if you are sharing the project file with colleagues, and It's also a valuable reminder if there is a conflict later which you must resolve.

5. Click OK to complete the constraint definition.

If you need to create or edit a number of constraints, you can display the Constraint Dates table in the Gantt Chart (see Figure 6.19). This is also a good view to use when reviewing the constraints in your project.

Constraint Type field   Constraint Date field

Figure 6.19
Use the Constraint Dates table if you have many task constraints to create or to review.

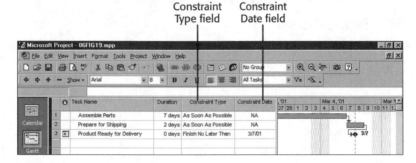

To create constraints in a task table, follow these steps:

1. Display a task view that includes a table, such as the Gantt Chart view with its Entry table.

2. Click the column title of the column where you want to insert the Constraint Type field and choose Insert, Column (or press the Insert key). Project will display the Column Definition dialog box.

3. In the Field Name box, choose Constraint Type from the drop-down list of field names and click Best Fit to display the column with the best width.

4. Insert the Constraint Date field using the same method shown in steps 2 and 3.

5. On the row for a task you want to constrain, use the drop-down list in the Constraint Type column to pick the type. Press Enter to assign the constraint. (As mentioned previously, if you have defined an inflexible constraint, the Planning Wizard will make you confirm that you want to keep the constraint.)

6. Unless the constraint type is As Soon As Possible or As Late As Possible, Project will supply a default date in the Constraint Date column—it will use the task's start date and time if the task's start is constrained and the finish date and time if its finish is constrained.

   If appropriate, type in a different date or use the drop-down calendar to pick one. Append the time of day if you don't want Project to supply the default time.

The Task Details Form also provides easy access to the constraint fields. It is best used in the bottom pane with the Gantt Chart or another task view in the top pane (see Figure 6.20). To enter task constraints in the Task Details Form, first display the Gantt Chart or other task view in the top pane and split the window. Once the window is split, you should activate the bottom pane and choose View, More Views to display the More Views dialog box. Next, select the Task Details Form view from the Views list and click Apply. Right-click over the Task Details Form and choose the Notes details for display. You should document the reason for adding a constraint along with its requirements in the Notes field.

After you have entered the information in the Notes field, click the task to be constrained in the top pane, or use the Previous and Next buttons in the bottom pane to scroll to the task. Then in the bottom pane, select the constraint type from the drop-down list in the Constraint box. You should enter the constraint date and time in the Date field, or you can let Project supply the default values as described previously.

Figure 6.20
Use the combination view of Gantt Chart and Task Detail Form to see the constraint fields along with other task details.

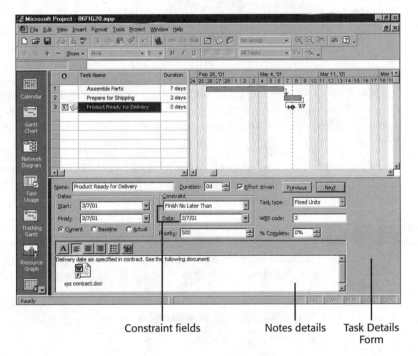

Constraint fields   Notes details   Task Details
                                            Form

As pointed out previously, if you define an inflexible constraint for a task that has dependency links, you create a potential conflict between the requirements of the constraint and the requirements of the links. When you create an inflexible constraint, the Planning Wizard warns you that your action could create a problem either now or in the future and makes you confirm the action. The Planning Wizard displays the dialog box in Figure 6.21 to warn you and give you three options:

- You can Cancel (which is the default). If you leave this option selected, you can click either the OK button or the Cancel button to cancel the action and no constraint will be set.

PART

II

CH

6

- You can Continue but avoid a conflict by changing the constraint to a flexible constraint. If you select this option and click OK, Project substitutes the flexible version of the same constraint. For example, if you define a Finish No Later Than constraint in a project that is scheduled from a fixed start-date, Project offers to change it to a Finish No Earlier Than constraint.

- You can Continue and create the inflexible constraint. You must both select this option and click the OK button to actually create the constraint.

Figure 6.21
The Planning Wizard alerts you when a constraint might cause a problem. This can save you from accidentally placing constraints you didn't intend.

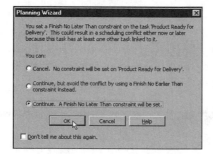

If you confirm the creation of the inflexible constraint and the constraint creates an immediate conflict with the task's dependency links, the Planning Wizard usually displays another warning that requests you to confirm that you want to go ahead and create the conflict (see Figure 6.22).

Your choices are to Cancel (the constraint will not be created) or to Continue (the constraint will be created and the scheduling conflict will exist). Again, you must both choose the Continue option and click OK to actually create the constraint.

Note

Project will not display this second warning if you have deselected the Tasks Will Always Honor Their Constraint Dates check box on the Schedule tab of the Options dialog box (which is explained in the next section, "Deciding to Honor Links or Constraints").

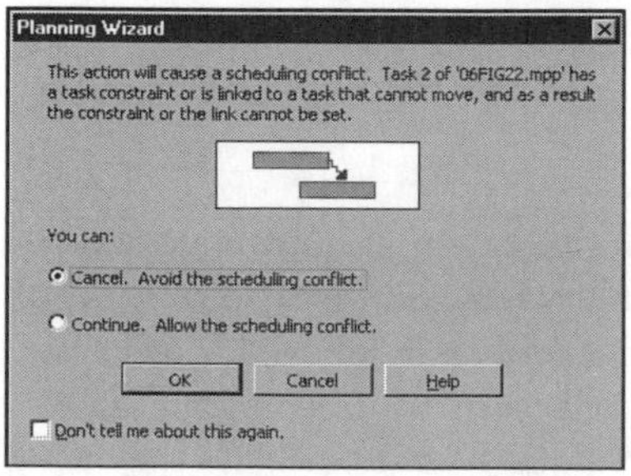

Figure 6.22
If a constraint creates an immediate conflict, you will usually be warned by this second Planning Wizard dialog box.

The Planning Wizard warning in Figure 6.22 will also be displayed by any other action that causes a constraint date to be in conflict with a dependency link. You will see it, for example, if you create new links or increase the duration of a predecessor task so much that the constraint date becomes a barrier.

The Planning Wizard warning that a constraint conflict has been identified will include a task ID number to help you troubleshoot the conflict (refer to Figure 6.22). The ID number is usually the ID for the predecessor to the task with an inflexible constraint. (In a fixed finish-date project, it would be the successor task.) However, in some instances the ID number is for the constrained task itself. Thus, in Figure 6.22 the message identifies Task 2, and that is the predecessor to the task that is being given an inflexible constraint.

If you see this warning from the Planning Wizard and choose to continue and allow the conflict to be created, you should make a note of the task ID number because you will not see this message again and you need to do something to resolve the conflict. (For ways to find and resolve constraint conflicts, see the sections "Finding and Reviewing Tasks with Constraints" and "Resolving Conflicts Caused by Constraints" later in this chapter.)

DECIDING TO HONOR LINKS OR CONSTRAINTS

As mentioned in the section "Understanding the Types of Constraints," when you define an inflexible constraint for a task, it might be impossible for Project to honor both the constraint and one or more links that you have defined for the task. When such a conflict presents itself, Project's default scheduling method is to honor the constraint definition and ignore the link definition, as you saw in Scenario B in Figure 6.18. When Project honors inflexible constraint dates, the constraints are sometimes called *hard constraints*. You can change Project's default behavior and force it to honor a task's links instead of its constraint by choosing Tools, Options, clicking the Schedule tab, and clearing the check box labeled Tasks Will Always Honor Their Constraint Dates. Then the constraints are *soft constraints* (see Figure 6.23).

Figure 6.23
Choose to make inflexible constraints soft constraints by clearing the Tasks Will Always Honor Their Constraint Dates check box.

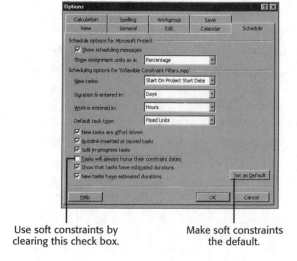

Use soft constraints by clearing this check box.

Make soft constraints the default.

In Figure 6.24 another set of tasks, Scenario C, is added to those from Figure 6.18 to show how Project schedules soft constraints to honor their links instead of their constraint date.

Inflexible Constraint indicator

Constraint date honored; task link ignored

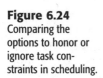

Figure 6.24
Comparing the options to honor or ignore task constraints in scheduling.

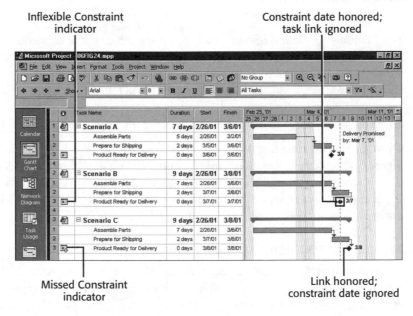

Missed Constraint indicator

Link honored; constraint date ignored

In Scenario B, the Product Ready for Delivery milestone is a hard constraint and is scheduled to honor its constraint date (as marked by the dashed line on March 7, 2001). In Scenario C, it is a soft constraint that is scheduled to honor its link; therefore, it falls on the day after the constraint date.

Notice the constraint icon in the Indicator column. This Missed Constraint indicator tells you that a task's schedule violates its constraint date. The constrained tasks in Scenarios A and B have the standard Inflexible Constraint indicator. There is nothing special to flag the conflict between the constraint and the link in Scenario B. The Missed Constraint indicator is the only flag that Project provides to identify constraint conflicts, and it will only appear if you have deselected Tasks Will Always Honor Their Constraint Dates.

If you go back into the Options dialog box and select the Tasks Will Always Honor Their Constraint Dates check box again (in other words, turn soft constraints into hard constraints again), the existence of any existing constraint conflicts in the project will cause Project to display the warning shown in Figure 6.25. You should make a note of the task identified at the start of this message so that you can find the tasks involved in the conflict and resolve the issue.

Assuming that all the links and constraint definitions are both appropriate and necessary to the project, it is best to use soft constraints (to have tasks honor their links) for the following reasons:

- *Honoring links is more realistic.* The project manager needs to revise the schedule so that the constraint can be met while honoring the links. This requires shortening the duration of the linked sequence of predecessors (or successors in a fixed finish-date project) that have caused the conflict.

- *Honoring links causes the Missed Constraint indicator to appear in the Indicators column.* This is the only reliable way to find constraint conflicts in your schedule. You can scan the Indicators column to see if you find tasks that have the indicator and then do something to the schedule to remove the indicator. Honoring constraints, on the other hand, merely causes the linking line to curve around the task that has a conflict, just as though the link involved lead time. These missed links are very difficult to find in the schedule—you have to manually scan over the entire timeline—and therefore the need for remedial action is often overlooked until too late.

Figure 6.25
Forcing Project to honor constraint dates when there are already constraint conflicts produces this warning.

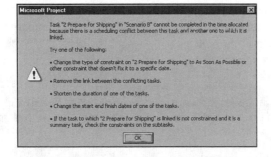

Tip from Tim and the Project Team

Based on these two points, I recommend that you clear the Tasks Will Always Honor Their Constraint Dates check box as described previously and make that the default for all your new projects by clicking the Set as Default button as shown in Figure 6.23. But be aware that doing this will mean that you no longer get the warning about incipient constraint conflicts. You will have to diligently search for them as described in the next section.

FINDING AND REVIEWING TASKS WITH CONSTRAINTS

Just as it is important to double-check the task sequencing links before committing to the project schedule, you should also review all the task constraints to ensure they are warranted and correctly defined. At the very least, you should attempt to identify any constraint conflicts and resolve them or your project schedule will be unrealistic.

To review the constraint conflicts, disable Tasks Will Always Honor Their Constraint Dates on the Schedule tab of the Options dialog box, as described in the previous section. Then scroll down the list of tasks in the Gantt Chart while you watch for the Missed Constraint indicator in the Indicators column. If your project is large, it will be easier if you also filter the task list for constrained tasks, as described next. When you find a task with the Missed Constraint indicator, follow the guidelines outlined in the section "Resolving Conflicts Caused by Constraints," later in this chapter.

If your project is scheduled from a fixed start date, you can use the Tasks with Fixed Dates filter to display the tasks with a constraint other than As Soon As Possible, for both flexible and inflexible constraints. This filter also selects tasks that have an Actual Start date entered; so, if you apply this filter after you start tracking work on the project, it will also select tasks that have started. However, if you use it during the planning stage of a fixed start-date project, it will select just the tasks with a nondefault constraint.

All Tasks	▾

To apply the Tasks with Fixed Dates filter, choose Project, Filtered For, More Filters, and select Tasks with Fixed Dates in the list of filters. Click Highlight to highlight the selected tasks, or click Apply to hide all but the selected tasks. You can also click the drop-down list arrow in the Filter tool on the Formatting toolbar and choose the Tasks with Fixed Dates filter, but you can't apply a highlight filter if you use that tool.

Project will select all tasks that do not have the constraint type As Soon As Possible (as well as those that have a start date entered). Project also displays the summary tasks for the selected tasks, which is helpful for remembering where the task falls in the outline in a large project. You can scroll through the filtered task list to easily review the constrained tasks.

Tip from Tim and the Project Team	A convenient view for reviewing constraints is the Gantt Chart with the Task Details Form and Notes field in the bottom pane, as described in the section "Entering Task Constraints."

When finished using the filter, press the function key F3 to clear the filter, or select All Tasks from the drop-down list on the Filter tool.

→ For help working with filters, **see** "Using Filters," **p. 512**

Tip from Tim and the Project Team	Another handy way to review tasks with constraints is to display the Constraint Dates table in the Gantt Chart, as described in the earlier section "Entering Task Constraints." Even better, you can create a customized version of this table that is more useful (see "Creating a Modified Constraint Dates Table" in the "Project Extras" section at the end of this chapter). Click the AutoFilter tool on the Formatting toolbar. In the title cell of the Constraint Type column, click the AutoFilter drop-down list arrow. The drop-down list will include the names of all constraint type names that appear at least once in that column. Click one of the constraint type names in the list and Project will display all tasks with that constraint type (along with their summary tasks).

You can create much more useful filters for finding inflexible constraints, for both fixed start-date and fixed finish-date projects. If you often work with fixed finish-date projects or want to be able to isolate constrained tasks after tracking has begun, or want to find scheduling conflicts, these filters are well worth adding to your Global Template. You will find files with these filters already defined on the companion Web site for this book at www.quepublishing.com. Use the Inflexible Constraint Filters.MPP file. Follow the instructions in the note attached to the project summary task to copy the filters to your GLOBAL.MPT.

REMOVING TASK CONSTRAINTS

To remove a task constraint, simply change the constraint type to As Soon As Possible or As Late As Possible, using one of the methods discussed earlier for creating constraints.

If you want to return several tasks to an unconstrained status, select all the tasks you want to change. Click the Task Information tool to display the Multiple Task Information dialog box. Choose the Advanced tab and select As Soon As Possible or As Late As Possible from the Constraint Type drop-down list. When you select OK, the changes are made in all the selected tasks. To remove all constraints in the project, select a column heading in the task list table and choose the As Soon As Possible or As Late As Possible constraint type in the Task Information dialog box.

RESOLVING CONFLICTS CAUSED BY CONSTRAINTS

When you add an inflexible constraint to a linked task, or link to a task with an inflexible constraint, the Planning Wizard displays the potential conflict warning that you saw in Figure 6.21. If Project is honoring task constraints (the default) and the potential conflict becomes a reality, the Planning Wizard gives you the warning that you saw in Figure 6.22. This can happen when you complete the constraint definition or the link definition, or it can happen later as a result of changes in the schedule that push the linked task past its constraint. If Project is not honoring task constraints, you will not receive the warning you saw in Figure 6.22, but you will see the Missed Constraint indicator that's displayed in Figure 6.24.

Caution

Notice that you can discontinue the display of Planning Wizard warnings by marking the Don't Tell Me About This Again check box. You should leave the Planning Wizard active to warn you about scheduling conflicts.

As mentioned previously, if you see the Planning Wizard warning and choose to create the constraint conflict, you should make a note of the task ID number mentioned in the message because you'll not see this warning again. You need to examine that task and the one to which it is linked to find a way to resolve the conflict.

Tip from Tim and the Project Team

When you first open a project document, you can press F9 (the Calculate key) to force Project to display its most recent scheduling error message. The message you see will be similar to the one displayed in Figure 6.25. However, you will only see one warning message like Figure 6.25, even if there are several constraint conflicts.

The three fundamental ways to resolve a constraint date scheduling conflict are as follows:

- Reassess the need for the constraint and the conditions that make the constraint necessary. Substitute a flexible constraint if possible.
- Reevaluate the dependency relationships in the sequence of tasks that are linked to the constrained task. Be certain that all links are necessary and defined so as to allow

maximum overlapping of tasks (using Start-to-Start, Finish-to-Finish, and lead time where reasonable).

■ Change the duration of individual tasks that are in the linked sequence using such techniques as those described in Chapter 12.

→ To learn how to change the duration of individual tasks, **see** "Reviewing the Project Plan," **p. 503**

You must choose the course of action that makes the most sense in your project. Frequently, a careful review of the tasks, constraints, and task relationships reveals that new definitions are called for—conditions might have changed since the original definitions were entered and the definitions are now more restrictive than they need be.

Tip from Tim and the Project Team
> Check to see whether a task note exists that might explain the need for the constraint. This might provide you with some guidance as to how you can resolve the conflict.

ENTERING DEADLINE DATES

2000 You saw in the previous section that you can define a constraint date for a task when it must be finished by a certain date. In Project 2000 you can also use the new Deadline Date field to record a task's finish deadline. The Gantt Chart shows a hollow arrow pointing down to the deadline date, and if the task finish is scheduled after the deadline date, a Missed Deadline icon (a red diamond containing an exclamation point) appears in the Indicators column to alert you that the task finish is scheduled after the deadline date.

2000 Unlike an inflexible constraint date, there are no conflict error messages or warnings when a deadline date is missed. However, you can apply the new Tasks with Deadlines filter to select all the tasks that have deadlines defined, and you can check the Indicators column for the Missed Deadline icon. To create a custom filter to select missed deadlines, see "Filtering for Missed Deadline Dates" in the "Project Extras" section at the end of this chapter.

An especially useful application of the Deadline Date field is for those tasks that have a constraint date defined for the task start and also a deadline for the task finish. Since you can only have one constraint date per task, the deadline date now allows you to define requirements for both the start and finish of a task.

Figure 6.26 shows the same sets of tasks you saw in Figure 6.18, except that the milestone in both scenarios has a deadline date instead of a constraint date on 3/7/01. In Scenario A, the milestone is scheduled for 3/6, which falls to the left of the deadline as represented by the downward pointing arrow. In Scenario B, the milestone is scheduled after the deadline and the Missed Deadline indicator appears in the Indicators column. If you pause the mouse over the Missed Deadline indicator, the ScreenTip message will be "This task finishes on 3/8/01 which is later than its Deadline on 3/7/01."

Figure 6.26
Notice the Missed Deadline icon in the Indicators column and the task bar.

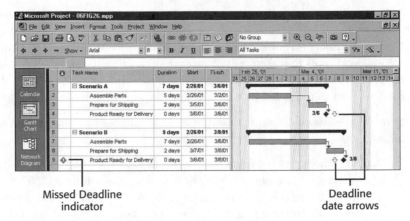

Missed Deadline indicator

Deadline date arrows

To define a deadline date for a task, follow these steps:

1. Select the task and activate the Task Information dialog box by either double-clicking the task or using the Task Information tool.

2. Click the Advanced Tab (see Figure 6.27).

3. Type a date, including the time of day if appropriate, in the Deadline field, or activate the drop-down box and choose the date in the calendar control. If you don't specify a time of day, Project will add the default end time of day (as defined on the Calendar tab of the Options dialog box) to the date you enter.

4. Click OK to complete the definition.

Deadline field

Figure 6.27
Enter the Deadline date on the Advanced tab of the Task Information dialog box.

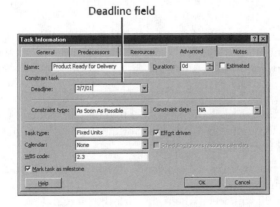

PART

II

CH

6

Tip from Tim and the Project Team

If you need to remove a deadline date, type **NA** in the Deadline field.

SPLITTING TASKS

Normally Project schedules work on a task to continue uninterrupted until the task is complete. If you know that there will be interruptions or periods of inactivity on a task or, having started work on the task you find that you must interrupt the work and resume at a later date, you can split the task into two or more scheduled segments.

Several examples of tasks that would be good candidates for task splitting include the following:

- *Suppose someone is scheduled to work on a task, but a week-long business trip is planned during the time she is scheduled to work on this task.* The work on the task is going to stop during the week she is gone and will resume when she returns. You can incorporate the interruption in the planning stage of your project by splitting the task around the business trip.

- *Suppose that a specialized employee is working on a low-priority task when a task with a higher priority requires his or her attention.* You can split the low-priority task and reschedule the remainder of its work after the higher-priority task is completed.

- *Suppose the project has already begun.* In a status meeting, it is decided to redefine all the project's remaining tasks. It might be necessary to interrupt any in-progress tasks to incorporate the revisions to the project. You can interrupt these ongoing tasks and then reschedule the remaining work.

Note

A task can have an unlimited number of splits. When you link to a task that is split, the link is to the task; you cannot create a link to a split segment of a task.

The easiest way to split a task is in the Gantt Chart, where you use the mouse to split a task bar and drag the segment on the right further to the right to resume at a later date. To split a task in the Gantt Chart, follow these steps:

1. Activate the Gantt Chart view.

2. Choose Edit, Split Task; or click the Split Task tool on the Standard toolbar; or right-click the task and select Split Task from the shortcut menu. The Split Task information box will appear (see Figure 6.28).

3. Position the mouse pointer over the task bar you want to split. As you slide the pointer right and left over the task bar, the Start date in the Split Task information box tells you the date where the split will occur when you click the mouse.

4. When you locate the correct Start date, you can either click the task bar or click and drag. The different results will be as follows:

    - If you just click the task bar, Project will insert a split in the schedule starting on the date in the Split Task information box, at the default start time of day (normally 8:00 a.m.). The length of the split or interruption will be one unit of the time unit used in the minor scale of the timescale. If the minor scale is days, even if it displays every third day, the split will be one day.

- If you click and drag, you insert the split as above, but you also drag the remainder of the task on the right to begin on another date (thus modifying the length of the split). As soon as you start dragging, the Split Task information box is replaced by the Task information box (see Figure 6.29), which tells you the start date for the new segment (the date where the task will resume) and the finish date for the task. Release the mouse when you reach the date where you want the new segment to start.

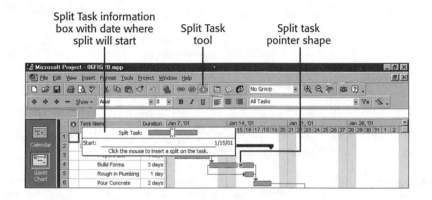

Figure 6.28
The Split Task information box guides you in selecting the date where you will split a task.

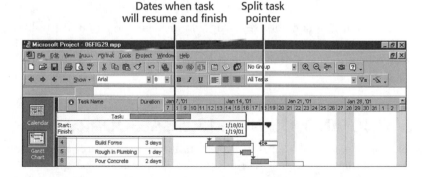

Figure 6.29
When splitting a task, the Task information box tells you when the task will resume and finish.

Caution

If Calculation is set on Manual, a task split will not appear graphically on the Gantt Chart until you press F9 to recalculate and refresh the screen. To check the calculation settings, go to Tools, Options, Calculation, Calculation Options for Microsoft Project. The default setting is Automatic.

Tip from Tim and the Project Team

Watch the start and finish dates in the Split Task information box carefully to determine when this segment of the split task resumes.

If your timescale units are minutes or hours, or if you want to control the exact time of day when a split begins, see "Splitting Tasks with Precision" in the "Troubleshooting" section near the end of this chapter.

Note

You can also split tasks in the Task Usage view, and if resources are assigned to a task, you can split the resource assignments to the task in the Resource Usage view. If all assignments are split at the same point, it effectively splits the task itself.

→ For instructions on creating splits in tasks and assignments with the Task and Resource Usage views, **see** "Resolving Overallocations by Delaying Assignments," **p. 441**

After you have split a task, resting the pointer over a split segment will display the Task information box for just that segment, telling you the start date, finish date, and duration for that segment.

Dragging the first segment of a split task moves all segments of the task together. Holding down the Shift key as you drag a later segment also moves all segments together.

You can drag any but the first segment to the right or left to change the start and finish of that segment of the task (as long as you don't touch another segment of the task).

To remove a split (to rejoin segments of a split task), drag the segment on the right left until it touches the next segment on the left.

Caution

Do not drag a middle segment to the right to touch a later segment. Project often loses track of part of the task duration.

To change the duration of a segment (and thus the duration of the task), drag the right end of the segment right or left. The pointer changes into the same shape you saw in Figure 6.28—a vertical bar followed by a right arrow—to indicate that you are changing the duration.

CREATING AND USING TASK CALENDARS

 In earlier versions of Microsoft Project, tasks without resource assignments were scheduled according to the working time on the project calendar (as specified in the Project Information dialog box). Tasks with resource assignments were scheduled according to the working time on the resource calendars. In Project 2000, you can also assign base calendars to individual tasks to replace the project calendar for scheduling those tasks. Typically you create a special base calendar that reflects the schedule you want to use for the task and assign that calendar to the task.

A task calendar provides specific control over the dates and hours when a task can be scheduled, and it affects only the task or tasks to which it is assigned. Task calendars are ideally suited to tasks that involve equipment resources that must be scheduled outside the normal working hours of the project calendar.

Tip from Tim and the Project Team

A task calendar might be a viable alternative to task splits when there are many interruptions in the planned schedule for a task.

If a resource is assigned to a task that also has a task calendar, Project normally takes the task calendar and the resource calendar into account and schedules the assignment only during periods that are working times on both the task calendar and the resource calendar—during the intersecting working times on both calendars. Project gives you the option, however, of ignoring the resource calendar and using only the task calendar for scheduling the assignment.

In additional to normal tasks, you can also assign task calendars to recurring tasks and to summary tasks. Assigning a task calendar to a recurring task affects the scheduling of the individual instances of the recurring task. Thus, you could use a task calendar to schedule regular maintenance on equipment during the off hours of a project. Assigning a calendar to a summary task, however, does not affect the schedule for any subtasks—it would only affect the schedule for any resources that you might assign to the summary task.

→ For more information about resources and task calendars, **see** "Scheduling with Task Calendars," **p. 397**

To assign a calendar to a normal, summary, or recurring task, follow these steps:

1. Create a base calendar containing the working days and hours when you want the task to be scheduled. Refer to the section "Defining a Calendar of Working Time" in Chapter 3, "Setting Up a New Project Document," for details on creating new base calendars.

Tip from Tim and the Project Team

If you are using many task calendars, you might distinguish them from other base calendars by starting the calendar name with an identifier like "TC:" and including some wording to identify the task or set of tasks for which it is designed. This will make it easier to find the calendar you want when assigning calendars.

2. Select the task and display its Task Information dialog box by double-clicking the task or by clicking the Task Information tool. Figure 6.30 shows the Task Information dialog box for a normal task.

3. For normal tasks and summary tasks, activate the Advanced Tab. For recurring tasks, all fields are on the same tab.

4. Change the selection in the drop-down list in the Calendar field from None (the default) to the base calendar you created for the task. In Figure 6.30, the selected calendar is TC: Upgrade Servers.

5. Fill the check box labeled Scheduling Ignores Resource Calendars if you want Project to ignore the working and nonworking time on the resource calendars and schedule the task by the task calendar alone.

6. Click OK to finish assigning the calendar.

PART

II

CH

6

Figure 6.30
Assign task calendars in the Task Information dialog box.

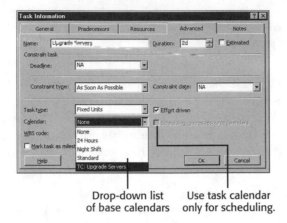

Drop-down list of base calendars

Use task calendar only for scheduling.

As an example, suppose that as part of deploying Microsoft Project 2000 an organization plans to upgrade its servers. The Upgrade Servers task is to be scheduled over a weekend while most users are normally offline. You could create a task calendar named Upgrade Servers that defines Saturdays and Sundays as working days and Mondays through Fridays as nonworking days. Figure 6.31 shows the Upgrade Servers task scheduled for Saturday and Sunday (even though its predecessor finished two days earlier) because the TC: Upgrade Servers calendar has been assigned to the task.

Tip from Tim and the Project Team

Notice the Task Calendar indicator in Figure 6.31. If you pause the mouse over the indicator, the ScreenTip will tell you the name of the calendar that is assigned to the task.

Task Calendar indicator

Predecessor finishes earlier.

Figure 6.31
The Upgrade Servers task is scheduled on the weekend because its task calendar only has weekend working days.

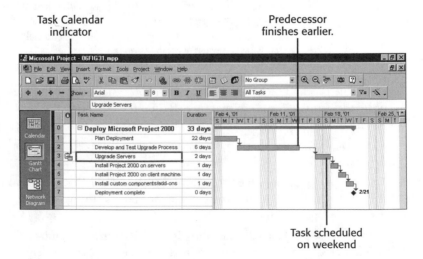

Task scheduled on weekend

If you assign a calendar to a task that has resources assigned, or assign a resource when there is already a task calendar assigned, and Project discovers that there are no intersecting working time periods for the task calendar and the resource calendar, then an error message will display (see Figure 6.32). The message tells you that the resource calendars will be ignored and the task will be scheduled during the working times on the task calendar and an indicator (see Figure 6.33) will flag the task as having inconsistent calendars assigned to it.

Figure 6.32
If a task calendar and the calendars for assigned resources have no intersecting working times, Project will use the task calendar and ignore the resource calendars.

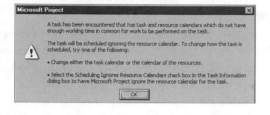

Insufficiently Intersecting Task and Resource Calendars indicator

Figure 6.33
A special indicator flags those tasks that have inconsistent task calendars and resource calendars.

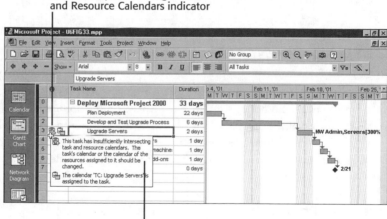

ScreenTip identifies the indicators.

TROUBLESHOOTING

THE MOUSE AND TASK LINKS

When I try to link tasks with the mouse, the screen scrolls too fast for me to find the successor task. What can I do?

When tasks you want to link aren't close enough for both to be visible, you can try to make them both visible at the same time by using the Zoom Out tool to compress the timescale, or by hiding subtasks under summary tasks that lie between the two tasks in the task list to place both task bars onscreen.

If that doesn't work, or is too much trouble, it's usually simpler to just select the tasks and use the Link Tasks tool. You can select both tasks by clicking the predecessor task (or its task bar) first to select that task, using the scrollbars to bring the dependent task into view, and then holding down the Ctrl key as you click the dependent task or task bar. Then click the Link Tasks tool.

TASK LINKING MISTAKES

What can I do if I make a mistake linking tasks using drag-and-drop?

The answer is almost always Undo the action immediately. Because Project supports only one level of Undo, you should verify the results of a drag-and-drop operation immediately while you can still take advantage of Undo. The shape of the pointer always advertises the type of action you will perform when you release the mouse button. Learn the various shapes to help avoid making mistakes. Returning the pointer to the point of origin will usually void the action. In the Gantt Chart and Calendar views, you can drag the pointer to the menu or toolbar area and the action will be voided when you release the mouse button. In the Network Diagram, however, you must return to the point of origin before releasing the button if you want to void the action.

TASK DEPENDENCY TROUBLES

No matter where I double-click on the dependency link line, the Task Dependency box doesn't display the task names of the two tasks whose link I want to modify. What am I doing wrong?

There must be more than one linking line where you are clicking. Project frequently draws them on top of each other to simplify the display. Find a point where the two lines separate, usually near one of the linked tasks. Otherwise, use another method to change the link. For example, click on the dependent task's bar (or node in the Network Diagram view) and click the Task Information tool to display the Task Information dialog box and change the link on the Predecessors tab.

REVERSING A DEPENDENCY LINK

I linked two tasks and accidentally got the wrong task as the predecessor. How do I reassign the predecessor to be the successor and vice versa?

You can't reverse the direction of the dependency relationship once it's created. You must delete the link and create it again.

LINKING TASKS FROM DIFFERENT PROJECTS

I want to link a task in one project to a task that is in another project. How do I do that?

To link tasks that are in different projects, you need to put both projects in a consolidated file. Open a blank project document and use Insert, Project for each of the projects that contain tasks you want to link. Expand the outlines for each project so that you can select the individual tasks to be linked. Click on a predecessor task and use the Ctrl key as you click on its successor. Then click the Link Tasks tool. Alternatively, you can drag from the predecessor task bar to the successor task bar to create the link. These are the only simply methods for creating external links—all the other methods involve special codes that are easily typed incorrectly.

→ For more information about linking tasks between projects, **see** Chapter 18, "Working with Multiple Projects," **p. 735**

USING THE ADJUST DATES MACRO

I have a project with constraints, and now I need to change the start date for the project. I want all the constraints to change by the same number of days as the change in the project's start date. How do I do that?

Use the Adjust Dates tool to reschedule the start or finish of the project. It also changes all constraint dates by the same number of days.

To use the Adjust Dates tool, follow these steps:

1. Open the project document whose dates you want to adjust. Don't adjust the project start or finish date yet; let the tool do that for you.
2. Display the Analysis toolbar by right-clicking over the toolbars and choosing Analysis from the shortcut menu.
3. Select the Adjust Dates tool to display the Adjust Dates dialog box.
4. Enter the new start date or finish date in the input box.
5. Click the OK button. Project will enter the new date in the Start Date (or Finish Date) field of the Project Information dialog box and adjust all task constraint dates by the same number of days.

SPLITTING TASKS WITH PRECISION

I want to specify the exact time of day when a split begins. How do I do that?

Normally, Project lets you pick the date when a split begins. If you want to control the hour when the split starts, you must adjust the timescale to show individual hours on the minor scale (the second row of the timescale). Choose Format, Timescale (or double-click the timescale itself) and change the Minor Scale Units to Hours with a Count of 1. If you have displayed hours in the timescale minor units, start the split under the hour you want the split to begin. If the minor scale is less than a day, the split will start at the start of the minor unit over the point where you clicked.

PROJECT EXTRAS

Creating a Modified Constraint Dates Table

It is easier to analyze constraint conflicts if you modify the standard Constraint Dates table to include the Indicators, Predecessors, and Successors fields. The Indicators field allows you to see the Constraint conflict indicators (if Project is honoring task links instead of constraint dates). The Predecessors field allows you to identify the link(s) that conflict with the constraints in a fixed start-date project and the Successors field serves the same function in a fixed finish-date project.

To customize the table, follow these steps:

1. In a task view like the Gantt Chart, right-click over the Select All cell (the table's upper-left cell over the ID number column) and choose More Tables from the shortcut menu.

2. In the Tables list in the More Tables dialog box, select Constraint Dates and click the Copy button.

3. In the Name box, change the name for the new table if desired.

4. To insert the Indicators field, click on the row below ID in the Field Name column and click the Insert Row tool to insert a blank row.

5. Type in into the blank cell in the Name column and Project will supply indicators. Press Enter to add the field.

6. Repeat step 5 in the blank rows at the bottom of the list of field names to add the fields Predecessors and Successors. You may want to change the Align Data entry to Left for both these fields.

7. Fill the Show in Menu check box if you want this table to appear on the menu of table names.

8. Click OK to create the table, and click Apply to display it.

Filtering for Missed Deadline Dates

The standard Tasks with Deadlines filter selects all tasks with deadline dates, whether the deadlines are missed or not. The deadline is missed when the task's Finish date is later than the date in the task's Deadline field.

To create a filter that only selects missed deadline dates, follow these steps:

1. Choose Project, Filtered For and select More Filters.

2. Select the Tasks with Deadlines filter name and choose the Copy button.

3. Type **Missed Deadline Dates** or another suitable name in the Name text box.

4. In the table of criteria, select the first blank cell on the second row (under the column named And/Or) and type **and**.

5. In the Field Name column, type **Finish**.

6. In the Test column, type **is greater than**.

7. In the Value(s) column, type **[Deadline]**.

8. Fill the Show in Menu check box if you want this filter on the Filtered For menu.

9. Click OK to complete the filter and click Apply if you want to apply it immediately.

CHAPTER 7

VIEWING YOUR SCHEDULE

In this chapter

WORKING WITH THE GANTT CHART VIEW

The previous chapters in this book discuss creating projects and establishing a task list. Most of these discussions are centered around the Gantt Chart view—probably the most widely used view in Microsoft Project. This chapter is devoted to expanding your knowledge of the Gantt Chart view (and several other views) to effectively work with your project schedule. You'll find a number of cross-references in this chapter pointing you to other sections of the book, which provide more detailed information on scheduling and customizing the views.

One of the reasons the Gantt Chart view is so widely used is the array of information readily available in this view. The Gantt Chart is divided into two components: the task table and the timescale. The task table is similar to a spreadsheet. It displays your task data in columns and rows. The default table is the Entry table, although other tables are available for you to view.

➜ For a complete discussion of the task tables, **see** "The Task Tables," **p. 875**

COMPONENTS OF THE TASK TABLE

As you can see from Figure 7.1, each row in the task table represents a separate task. Each column in the table displays some information about that task. The columns are *fields* in the project database. Typically you enter new tasks and their durations. Then, based on the project start date and the links between the various tasks, Project calculates the start and finish dates for that task.

OUTLINED TASK LISTS

As you build a project schedule, you typically have phases and specific tasks underneath each phase. These phases, or main tasks, are called *summary tasks* and are displayed in bold in the task table. Project indents the specific tasks, called *subtasks*, under the summary tasks. Any task that has subtasks displays an outline symbol in front of the task name. Collapsed summary tasks display a plus (+) sign; expanded summary tasks display a minus (–) sign (refer to Figure 7.1).

➜ To learn more about working with your task list, **see** "Outlining the Task List," **p. 184**, and "Collapsing the Task List Outline," **p. 507**

TASK INDICATORS

Other features you might see in the Gantt Chart are task note and constraint indicators (refer to Figure 7.1). The note indicators appear similar to yellow sticky notes in the Indicators column. These notes are task-specific notes. You enter notes through the Task Information dialog box, which can be accessed via the Task Notes button on the Standard toolbar.

Constraint indicators are symbols that alert you a task has a date constraint associated with it. Constraints are either something you intentionally add for a particular purpose (such as a Finish No Later Than constraint to indicate a deadline) or appear as a result of some action you have taken (such as entering the start and/or finish date for a task). You set and modify task constraints through the Task Information dialog box. Chapter 5, "Creating a Task List," discusses how to use the Task Information dialog box and enter task notes. Chapter 6, "Entering Scheduling Requirements," describes and explains task constraints.

→ For more information on using the Task Information dialog box, **see** "Using the Task Information Dialog Box," **p. 173**

→ To learn more about task constraints and how to work with them, **see** "Working with Task Constraints," **p. 234**

Additionally, there are other types of indicators that you might encounter. For instance, some indicators alert you when a task is complete, when the task has a hyperlink attached to it, or when the task has been assigned to a resource but the resource has not yet confirmed the assignment.

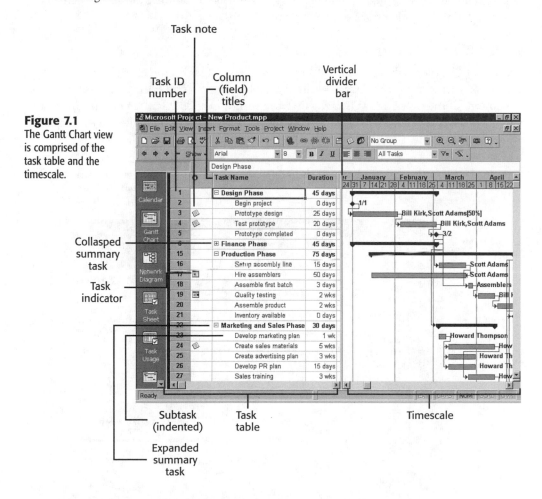

Figure 7.1
The Gantt Chart view is comprised of the task table and the timescale.

MOVING AROUND IN THE TASK TABLE

As you enter tasks and work with your task list, it is useful to understand how to move from row to row and column to column. Likewise, in a large project, it is helpful to be able to locate tasks quickly. You can move around the task table using some of your keyboard movement keys:

- **Arrow Keys**—Pressing the arrow keys moves the active cell (indicated by the heavy, dark border) in the direction of the arrow you press: up, down, left, or right.

- **Page Up and Page Down**—These keys move you up or down one screen's worth of tasks. If you are viewing tasks 1–18, for example, Page Down will display tasks 18–35. The last visible task (18 in this example) is displayed as the first task when you Page Down.

- **Home and End**—Home moves the active cell to the first column in the current row and End moves the active cell to the last column in the active row.

Other techniques for moving around include scrolling and using the Edit, Find command. These techniques are described in the next two sections.

SCROLLING IN THE TASK TABLE

The Gantt Chart view has three scrollbars: a vertical scrollbar on the far right of the view, a horizontal scrollbar at the bottom of the task table, and a second horizontal scrollbar at the bottom of the timescale. When you drag the vertical scrollbar box, a pop-up appears to indicate what task will be listed at the top of the view when you release the mouse (see Figure 7.2).

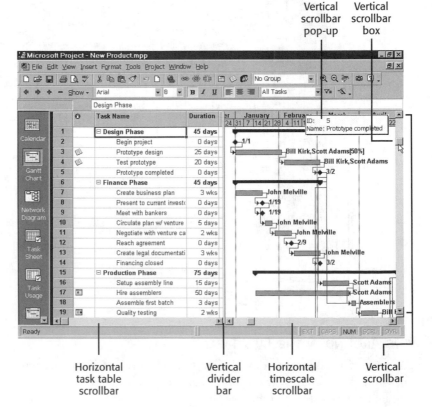

Figure 7.2
Drag the scrollbar box to quickly move down or up the task list.

Vertical scrollbar pop-up

Vertical scrollbar box

Horizontal task table scrollbar

Vertical divider bar

Horizontal timescale scrollbar

Vertical scrollbar

The task table comprises a series of columns, or *fields*. Initially, just a few columns are visible when you display the Gantt Chart view: ID, Indicators, Task Name, and Duration. However, several other columns are hidden underneath the timescale. There are two ways to see the data in these columns—you can use the horizontal task table scrollbar or move the vertical divider bar.

When you drag the horizontal scrollbar in the task table, it does not display a pop-up or even move the display. You have to guess when to release the mouse. As a result, it becomes a little tricky to figure out just how far to scroll to see additional columns.

Using the scrollbar is described here; the section "Viewing More Columns in the Table" later in this chapter will show you how to use the vertical divider bar.

USING FIND TO LOCATE TASKS

When you have a long list of tasks, and you want to find all the tasks that contain a specific word in the task name, you can use the Find command. To find a task by searching for one or more words in the task name, follow these steps:

1. Select any task. If you want to search from the beginning of the task list, press Alt+Home to scroll to the beginning of the project and then select the first task bar displayed.

2. Choose Edit, Find (or press Ctrl+F). The Find dialog box appears, as shown in Figure 7.3.

Figure 7.3
Search for a task by name or any other field value with the Find command.

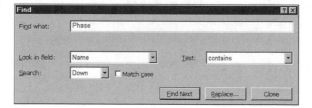

3. In the Find What text box, type the characters you want to search for. You can enter whole words or phrases, or just parts of words. In Figure 7.3, the word **Phase** is being located.

4. By default, the Name field is searched. However, you can select any task field to search. Select the Look In Field box and use the drop-down list box to choose the task field you want to search. Figure 7.3 has the Name field selected.

5. The Test box provides the criteria for the search. The default is Contains. Other options include Equals, Is Greater Than, Is Greater Than or Equal to, and so forth.

6. Choose the direction to be searched from the Search drop-down list box. The choices are Down or Up from the selected task.

7. You can further tailor the search by making it case sensitive. Marking the Match Case option requires the results to match the text typed in the Find What text box.

PART

II

CH

7

8. Click Find Next to locate the first task the matches your criteria. Each time you click Find Next, it will advance to the next task that matches your criteria.

You might have to move the dialog box to see the selected task. Position the mouse pointer on the dialog box title bar and drag to move the dialog box. After you have located the task(s) you are looking for, click the Close button to close the Find dialog box.

Tip from Tim and the Project Team	If you've closed the dialog box, you can use your last Find criteria again by pressing Shift+F4 to search farther down the task list, or press Ctrl+Shift+F4 to search back up the task list.

The Find command locates tasks, one at a time, that match your criteria. You can also use the Filter command. The main difference between the Find and Filter commands is that the Find command is primarily designed to perform text searches and the Filter command searches for tasks with a particular status: tasks that are summary tasks, tasks that fall within a specified date range, or tasks that have been completed.

ALTERING THE TASK TABLE DISPLAY

As you work with your project in the Gantt Chart view, there will be times when you want to change the display of the task table to show more data or change the appearance of the data. One of the changes you might want to make is to the font and font attributes of the tasks. For example, while the default settings have summary tasks in bold, you can customize the appearance to display in other colors, in italic, or in a different font.

If you want to apply a different table all together, you can choose a table using the View, Table command.

→ For additional information about the tables in the Gantt Chart view, **see** "The Task Tables," **p. 875**

Other display changes you might want to make include showing more of the built-in columns in the task table, adjusting the height of individual rows, using the new rollup task feature, altering the date format, and inserting new columns in the task table. These display options are illustrated in the next few sections.

VIEWING MORE COLUMNS IN THE TABLE

When you want to see the task table columns hidden beneath the timescale, you have to move the vertical divider bar. To move the vertical divider bar, position the mouse pointer on the bar; the mouse pointer changes to the shape of two vertical parallel lines with arrows pointing left and right. Hold the mouse button down and drag right to the desired position. A thick gray line appears, indicating the bar's position (as shown in Figure 7.4).

Figure 7.4
Drag the vertical divider bar to adjust the view of the task table columns.

Mouse shape to move divider bar

Widened row heights (two places)

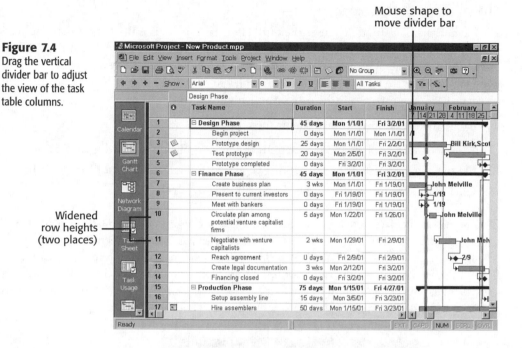

Tip from Tim and the Project Team

If you get the vertical divider bar in the middle of a column, double-click to move the bar to the border of the column to the closest border.

Note

You can also adjust the widths of columns displayed in the task table. Position the mouse pointer on the right-column border, up next to the column name. The mouse pointer changes to double vertical lines with arrows pointing left and right. Hold and drag to widen or narrow the column width, or double-click and the column will adjust to the longest entry.

ADJUSTING ROW HEIGHT

In previous versions of Project, adjusting the height of the rows in the task table was limited to setting one height for all the rows. A new feature in Project 2000 lets you adjust the height of each row independently, identical to the way you adjust row heights in an Excel worksheet. Position the mouse pointer on the bottom row border, beneath the row number. The mouse pointer changes to a plus sign with arrows pointing up and down. Hold and drag to widen or narrow the row height. Figure 7.4 shows a few rows that have been adjusted; the text will automatically word-wrap in the cell to fit the new height.

→ To learn how to work with row size, **see** "Adjusting the Height of Task Rows," **p. 152**

PART
II

CH
7

CHANGING THE DATE FORMAT

The default date display format uses the mm/dd/yy pattern. This is the format that you see in the Start and Finish columns of the task table. You can add the time of day to the display, or switch to any one of a number of data format options. Be aware, however, that changes you make to the date format affect the date display in all your project files—not just the active project. You can change the date display at any time.

To change the date display format, follow these steps:

1. Choose Tools, Options and the Options dialog box will appear (see Figure 7.5).
2. On the View tab, select the format that you want in the Date Format drop-down box.
3. Click the OK button to make the change effective.

Depending on the date format you select, you might see a series of # symbols displayed in the cells in the Start and Finish columns. This indicates you need to widen the column to display the date in the new format. To quickly widen a column, position the mouse pointer in the column title area on the right border of the column you want to widen. Then double-click to adjust the column width to the longest entry. For example, if the Start column needs to be adjusted, double-click the line separating the Start and Finish titles.

Figure 7.5
You can change the date format in this dialog box.

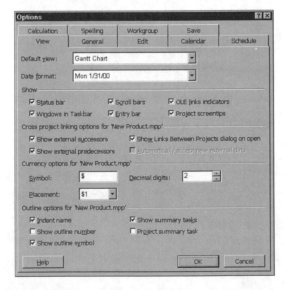

Note

If you want to use an international date or time format, you must set this through the Regional Settings applet in the Microsoft Windows Control Panel.

INSERTING AND CHANGING COLUMNS IN THE TASK TABLE

Sometimes, you might want to change the column titles to match some more common names used within your organization, or you might even want to change the contents of a column. For example, you could change the title of the Task Name column to "What has to be done," or you could display the Notes field instead of the Resource Names field in the last column of the table. To modify the column, simply double-click the column title and Project displays the Column Definition dialog box (see Figure 7.6). The following list describes the options in the Column Definition dialog box:

- If you want to change the data displayed in a column, select a different field from the Field Name drop-down box.

- Change the entry in the Title box to modify the column title. If you don't supply an entry in the Title box, Project displays the field name as the column name. Note in Figure 7.6 that the field name is Name and the title is Task Name.

- You can select the alignment (left, center, right) for the title with the Align Title drop-down box and for the data with the Align Data drop-down box.

- When you widen or narrow a column in the task table, the Width box reflects the current width. You can also adjust the width from here by clicking the spinner buttons.

- Clicking the OK button implements the changes you have selected.

- Clicking the Best Fit button applies the changes like the OK button does, but it also adjusts the column width to the longest cell entry.

Figure 7.6
You access this dialog box by double-clicking the column title in the task table.

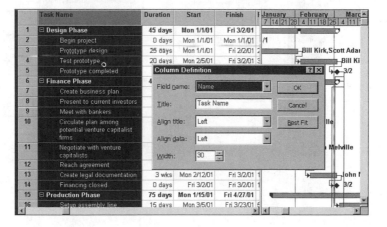

If you don't want to see a column in the task table, you can delete it from the table without losing the data that it displays. Simply click the column title to select the entire column and then press the Delete key.

To insert a new column in the table, select the title of the column that is the position where you want the new column to be, and press the Insert key. The Column Definition dialog box appears, and you can select the column options as described previously.

PART

II

CH

7

> **Caution**
>
> If you use the methods described earlier to delete and insert columns in the task table, you are in fact *customizing* the table for the active Project.

→ For specific information about customizing tables and sharing those custom settings with other project files, **see** "Using and Creating Tables," **p. 949**

COMPONENTS OF THE TIMESCALE

The timescale is the graphic portion on the right side of the Gantt Chart view. The timescale displays several items: a timeline, task bars, bar text, and linking lines. These items are identified in Figure 7.7.

Figure 7.7
The timescale is the right portion of the Gantt Chart view.

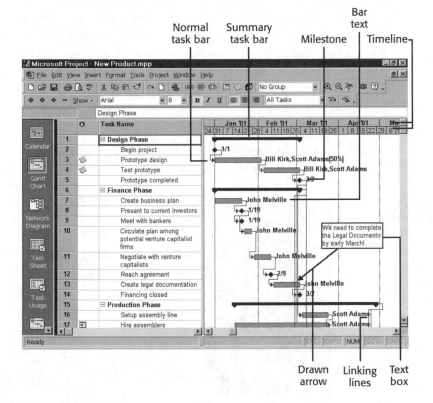

Additionally, you can also add graphic drawing objects to the timescale, such as text boxes, arrows, and the like. Placing graphic objects on the timescale is discussed later in this chapter.

→ To learn more about objects and Gantt Charts, **see** "Working with Drawing Objects in the Gantt Chart View," **p. 278**

TASK BARS

There are three types of task bars in Project: Summary, Normal, and Milestone. The default display of these bars was shown in Figure 7.7. However, using the Gantt Chart Wizard, you can significantly alter the display of the task bars, as shown in Figure 7.8.

Figure 7.8
You can significantly alter the display of the timescale using a number of tools; the easiest one is the Gantt Chart Wizard.

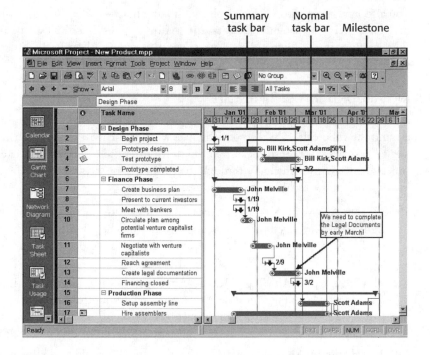

You access the Gantt Chart Wizard through the button on the Formatting toolbar, or by choosing Format, Gantt Chart Wizard.

→ To learn more about using the Gantt Chart Wizard and other options for formatting the timescale, **see** "Using the Gantt Chart Wizard," **p. 912**

BAR TEXT

The default settings for the timescale task bars display the name of the resource at the end of Normal tasks and the start date next to Milestones. You can designate the data and placement that appear with a task bar in the Bar Styles dialog box. Choose Format, Bar Styles, and select the bar type at the top of the dialog box. The bottom of the dialog box displays the Text and Bars settings for the selected bar type. The bar text and placement options are on the Text tab.

LINKING LINES

The lines that connect the task bars represent links between tasks, defining the order in which the tasks must be done. The position of the line indicates the type of link. If the linking line extends from the end of one task to the beginning of another, there is a Finish-to-Start link between the tasks. There are four different link types. Additionally, you can build in lead time and lag time between linked tasks.

→ If you would like more information about the link types, as well as lead and lag time, **see** "Understanding Dependency Links," **p. 209**

→ For more on working with your task layout, **see** "Selecting Layout Options," **p. 922**

PART

II

CH

7

You also have three options for displaying linking lines—to display no linking lines, to display lines that wrap around task bars, and to display lines that don't wrap. You establish these settings in the Layout dialog box (Format, Layout). Altering the timescale display is discussed later in this chapter.

MOVING AROUND IN THE TIMESCALE

After you have created your project schedule, it is useful to understand how to quickly move around the timescale. This is especially true when you have a large, extensive project. With a few keystrokes or mouse clicks, you can move from the beginning to the end of the timescale, move incrementally through the timescale, or scroll to a specific task. Below is a list of some of the techniques you can use:

■ **Alt+Up Arrow or Alt+Down Arrow**—Holding down the Alt key and pressing the right arrow key scrolls the timescale one unit (on the minor scale) to the right. Using the left arrow key with the Alt key scrolls the timescale one unit (on the minor scale) to the left.

■ **Alt+Page Up or Alt+Page Down**—Alt+Page Down scrolls you to the right one screen's worth on the timescale. So, if you are viewing the weeks of January 7 through January 21, Alt+Page Down will display the weeks of January 28 through February 10. Alt+Page Up scrolls you to the left one screen's worth on the timescale.

■ **Alt+Home or Alt+End**—Alt+Home scrolls the timescale to the beginning of the project, the time frame that shows the first project tasks. Alt+End scrolls the timescale to the end of the project, the time frame that shows the last project tasks.

Other techniques for moving around include using the scrollbars and the Go To Selected Task button. These techniques are described in the next few sections.

SCROLLING IN THE TIMESCALE

The timescale uses two scrollbars: the vertical scrollbar on the far right of the view and a horizontal scrollbar at the bottom of the timescale portion of the Gantt Chart view. The vertical scrollbar is used primarily to scroll to a specific task and see its corresponding task bars, links, and so on.

When you drag the horizontal scrollbar in the timescale, it displays a pop-up to indicate the date you will be scrolling to when you release the mouse button (see Figure 7.9).

LOCATING A TASK BAR OR SPECIFIC DATE IN THE GANTT CHART

Often when you are working in the Gantt Chart view, you have a task selected but the corresponding task bar is not visible on the screen. This is especially true when you zoom in to see minutes, hours, or days in the timescale.

 To have the timescale scroll to show the task bar associated with a specific task, select the task in the table and click the Go To Selected Task button on the Standard toolbar. Project scrolls to show the beginning of the task bar.

Figure 7.9
Drag the horizontal scrollbar box to move quickly to a specific date.

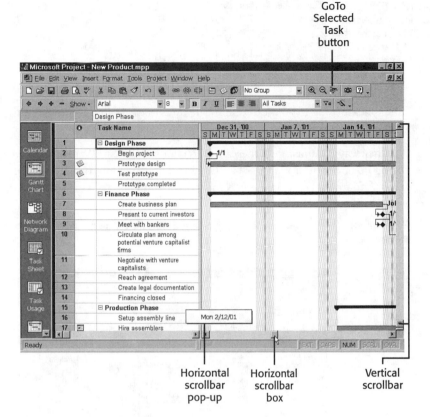

Use the Edit, Go To command (or Ctrl+G) to display the Go To dialog box (see Figure 7.10) if you want to jump to a specific date in the timescale. Enter a date in the Date box or click the drop-down to select a date from a calendar that appears. You can click the arrows next to the month in the calendar to scroll to see other months. Click the date you want to view, and then click OK. You can also just type in a number to go to that date in the current month.

> **Note**
>
> The Date box also accepts words like **today**, **yesterday**, or **tomorrow** and jumps to the corresponding dates.

ALTERING THE TIMESCALE DISPLAY

The actual timescale in the left side of the Gantt Chart view is the two rows at the top of the view. The top row is the *major scale*, and the bottom row is the *minor scale*. The units on the major scale run down the screen. You can customize the amount of time encompassed by the units on each of the scales and you can change the labels that appear in the units.

Figure 7.10
You can also type in a task ID to go to the task with that particular ID number.

The quickest way to adjust the timescale units is to zoom in or zoom out using the buttons on the Standard toolbar.

Another way to adjust the timescale is to choose Format, Timescale to access the Timescale dialog box (shown in Figure 7.11). Use the Timescale tab to establish the settings for the major and minor scale. Use the Nonworking Time tab to set the display options for nonworking days, such as weekends.

→ To learn how to effectively use the settings in the Timescale dialog box, **see** "Formatting Timescales," **p. 900**

Figure 7.11
Individual adjustments to the timescale can be set using this dialog box.

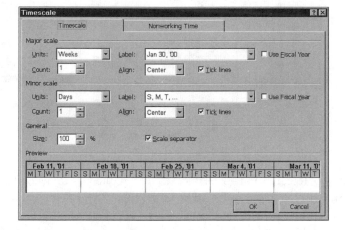

ROLLING UP THE TASK BARS

A new feature in Project 2000 lets you roll up subtasks to appear on the summary task bars. The advantage of this feature is the capability to hide the subtasks, but still see some information about those tasks displayed on the summary task bars. The rollup bar feature must be turned on in the Layout dialog box (see Figure 7.12). Choose Format, Layout and select Always Roll Up Gantt Bars.

→ To learn more about the rollup bar feature, **see** "Using Rollup Task Bars," **p. 190**

This feature rolls up all tasks in the project. Use the option Hide Rollup Bars When Summary Expanded to only show the rollup bars when summary tasks are collapsed (indicated by a plus sign in front of the summary task name). To roll up individual tasks to their summary tasks, use the Task Information dialog box (see Figure 7.13).

Figure 7.12
The Layout dialog box is also used to establish the display for the linking lines.

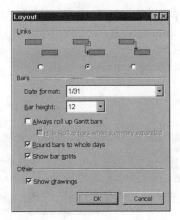

VIEWING MORE TASK DETAILS

While the Gantt Chart contains a lot of information, you can see even more details about individual tasks either with the Task Information dialog box or by splitting the screen and viewing the Task Form.

USING THE TASK INFORMATION DIALOG BOX

 Click the Task Information button on the Standard toolbar to display a pop-up dialog box that displays many details about the selected task (see Figure 7.13). The five tabs in the dialog box provide access to many additional fields. If you have a summary task selected, the Summary Task dialog box appears. Some fields are unavailable on the Summary Task dialog box because those fields are calculated by Project from the subtasks for the summary task.

Figure 7.13
The Task Information dialog box shows quite a lot of task information that isn't visible in the Gantt Chart view.

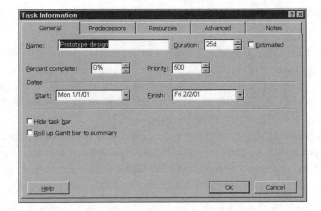

USING COMBINATION VIEWS

One of the most useful and powerful display techniques that Microsoft Project provides is the capability to split the screen in half (top and bottom) to see two different views of the project simultaneously. Choose <u>W</u>indow, <u>S</u>plit to split the screen (see Figure 7.14).

PART
II

CH
7

The window splits into two panes: the top pane shows the view you were working in before splitting the screen and the bottom pane shows either the Task Form (if you started with a task view) or the Resource Form (if you started with a resource view). Figure 7.14 shows the Gantt Chart in the top pane and the Task Form in the bottom pane.

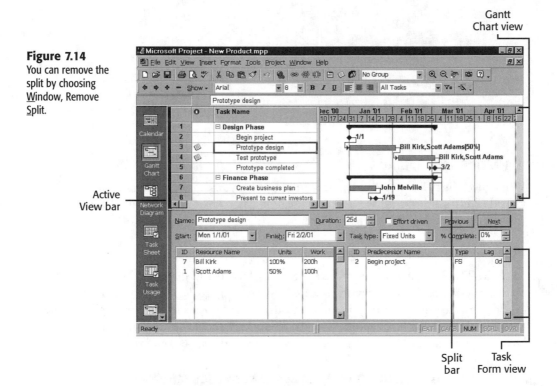

Figure 7.14
You can remove the split by choosing Window, Remove Split.

Task 3, "Prototype Design," is selected in the top pane in Figure 7.14. The bottom pane shows detailed information about task 3. The bottom pane displays all the fields that are in the columns in the Gantt Chart view, including the ones hidden beneath the timescale (unless you have customized the view). This screen arrangement enables you to see the values in those fields, eliminating the need to display a large number of columns in the task table. More of the timescale can be viewed. You are also able to see additional fields—Effort Driven, Task Type, and % Complete—as well as much more detail about resources and predecessors. This screen arrangement lets you see how the task fits into the overall scheme of things in the top pane, and you can see many significant details in the bottom pane.

You can enter task information in either pane, but you must activate the pane before you can use it. To activate the bottom pane, simply click anywhere in the bottom pane. You can also use the F6 function key to toggle back and forth between panes. The pane that is active displays a dark blue color on its half of the Active View bar (see Figure 7.14).

The two mini-tables at the bottom of the Task Form initially display resource and predecessor details. You can select different details to display in these areas. First, activate the bottom pane. Then choose Format, Details. A submenu appears with alternative data you can display.

> **Note**
> You can display other views in the top and bottom panes. Throughout this book you will encounter examples of useful combination views.

Adding Graphics and Text to Gantt Charts

The Gantt Chart view can be significantly enhanced through graphic and text objects, which are used to draw attention to or explain particular events within the project. Microsoft Project provides a set of drawing tools to help you enhance the appearance of your Gantt Charts. The drawing tools produce graphic objects that can be moved, resized, placed in front of, along side of, or behind the task bars.

 Included among the drawing tools is a Text Box tool that lets you place free text anywhere in the Gantt Chart display. This section shows you how to create and modify graphics and text on the Gantt Chart.

> **Note**
> Graphic objects can only be placed in the timescale side of the Gantt Chart view. Graphic objects you place on the Gantt Chart are not displayed when the Gantt Chart is in the bottom pane of a combination view.

Introducing the Drawing Toolbar

Text and graphic objects are created on the Gantt Chart with the Drawing toolbar. When the toolbar is displayed, you can create objects by selecting an object button and creating an example of the object on the Gantt Chart area. After they are created, you can modify the objects to create the effect you desire. Figure 7.15 shows an example of a text message overlaid on the Gantt Chart. An arrow directs your attention to the circled tasks that the message describes.

To display the Drawing toolbar, choose Insert, Drawing. Initially the Drawing toolbar is displayed floating on the screen. When a drawn object is selected, the Drawing toolbar automatically appears.

Tip from Tim and the Project Team

> You can also display the Drawing toolbar by right-clicking on any toolbar and choosing Drawing from the shortcut menu.

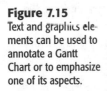

Figure 7.15
Text and graphics elements can be used to annotate a Gantt Chart or to emphasize one of its aspects.

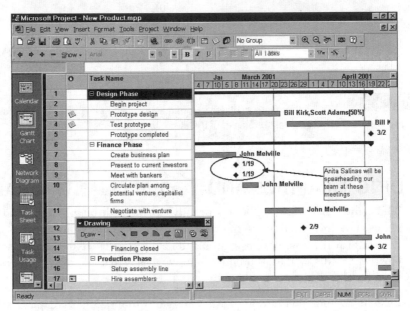

DESCRIPTIONS OF THE DRAWING BUTTONS

The first button on this toolbar is a drop-down menu providing options for arranging and editing the objects you draw. The next seven buttons on the toolbar are used to create objects on the Gantt Chart. These buttons create lines, arrows, rectangles, ovals, arcs, polygons, and text boxes. The remaining two buttons provide access to various editing possibilities.

THE DRAW DROP-DOWN MENU

Use the Draw button when you want to arrange and edit the objects you draw. From its drop-down menu, it includes options to

- **Bring to Front**—Bring a selected object to the forefront, placing it before all other objects that originally overlaid it.

- **Send to Back**—Send an object to the back, placing it behind all other objects in the same area.

- **Bring Forward**—Move an object in front of other objects, one at a time, toward the viewer. Objects in front hide objects that are behind them.

- **Send Backward**—Move an object behind other objects, one at a time, away from the viewer.

- **Edit Points**—Change the shape of a polygon.

THE DRAWING OBJECTS BUTTONS

When you choose one of the seven drawing buttons, the mouse pointer becomes a set of crosshairs. Position the pointer where you want to begin drawing an object and drag it to create the object. After it has been created, the object has small black resizing handles at each corner and along each side. The handles are used to change the dimensions of the object. Remember, as stated earlier, graphic objects can only be added to the timescale portion of the Gantt Chart view.

Figure 7.16 shows samples of the figures that you can draw. The buttons that draw the objects are described in the following sections. Table 7.1 shows each of the seven drawing buttons and describes its use.

Figure 7.16
You can draw a variety of geometric figures, lines, and arrows, in addition to placing text among the other figures.

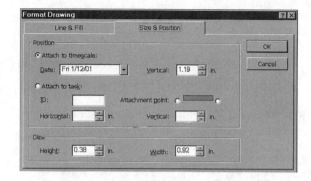

Tip from Tim and the Project Team

With some objects, the Shift key can be used to create a perfectly symmetrical object—for example, a perfect square, a perfect circle, or a perfect arc. To draw a square or circle, select the appropriate drawing button, and then hold down the Shift key as you begin to drag the mouse to create the object.

TABLE 7.1   DRAWING BUTTONS ON THE DRAWING TOOLBAR

Button	Name	Click and drag to draw...	Shift+Click and drag to draw...
	Line	A line without arrowheads	(n/a)
	Arrow	A line with arrowheads	(n/a)
	Rectangle	A rectangle	A perfect square
	Oval	An elliptical figure	A perfect circle
	Arc	An elliptical arc	A symmetrical arc from circles
	Polygon	A many-sided figure of any configuration	(n/a)
	Text Box	A rectangle box for typing text	A perfect square for typing text

To add a drawing object to the Gantt Chart timescale, follow these steps:

1. Display the Gantt Chart view, if it is not already displayed.
2. Choose Insert, Drawing to display the Drawing toolbar
3. Click the button for the object you want to draw.
4. Move the mouse to the place you want to draw the object; the mouse pointer should be the shape of a crosshair.
5. Hold the mouse button down and drag to create the object. Remember, you can press Shift as you drag to create a symmetrical object.
6. When you release the mouse button, the object is drawn.

 The last two buttons on the toolbar are the Cycle Fill Color button and the Attach to Task button. The Cycle Fill Color button allows you to change the fill color of the selected object, cycling through the palette of color choices each time you click the button. With the Attach to Task button, you open the Format Drawing dialog box to change how an object is anchored to the Gantt Chart or to modify the attributes of the object.

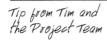 **Double-click the Polygon button to have the computer draw the final line that connects the last point to the starting point, producing a closed figure.**

WORKING WITH DRAWING OBJECTS IN THE GANTT CHART VIEW

When you have drawn an object in the Gantt Chart view, you might want to modify the object. You can attach an object to a specific task or date so that when you zoom out, the object stays with the task or date it is attached to. You can hide, move, resize, copy, or delete objects you have drawn. The color of the border surrounding the object and the inside of the object can be changed to enhance its visual appearance.

However, before you can make any of these changes, you must first select the object you want to modify.

SELECTING OBJECTS

In the Gantt Chart view, you can select task fields in the table area; you can select a task bar (when you use the mouse to modify the task); or you can select objects that you have drawn in the timescale.

You can use the mouse to select objects in the timescale if you watch the mouse pointer carefully. Move the tip of the mouse pointer to an object's line or border. When a small cross appears below and to the right of the pointer arrow, click to select the object. When the object is selected, small black resizing handles appear around it. Only one object can be selected at a time.

Tip from Tim and the Project Team	For solid figures (rectangles, ellipses, arcs, or polygons with a fill pattern), you can point to the interior of an object to select it. This is easier than pointing to the border.

You also can use the keyboard to select objects. The F6 function key toggles back and forth between selecting the task table and a graphic object in the timescale. (If a combination view is displayed, the bottom view is also selected in turn by the F6 key.)

Tip from Tim and the Project Team	If you have created multiple drawing objects, when one of them is selected, you can use the Tab key to cycle the selection to the other drawing objects one at a time. Shift+Tab can be used to cycle backwards through the drawn objects.

ATTACHING OBJECTS TO A TASK BAR OR A DATE

When you create an object, it is automatically attached to a date on the timescale where you created it on the Gantt Chart. Along with the date, there is a vertical offset that dictates how far down from the date it should be displayed. The vertical offset is more visible when you zoom in the timescale. Drawn objects stay with the date they are associated with as you scroll or zoom the timescale.

Caution	Be aware that if you zoom out in the Gantt Chart, your objects might be placed on top of each other due to the compressed timescale.

 If an object is attached to a date in the timescale, when you move the object, it remains attached to the timescale but at the new date and vertical position where you move it. You can see the attachment by examining the Size & Position tab of the Format Drawing dialog box for the object (see Figure 7.17).

Figure 7.17
Use the Format Drawing dialog box to attach an object to a task or to the timescale.

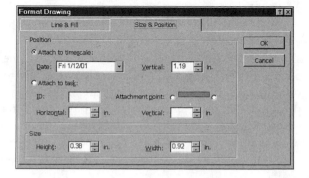

To view the Format Drawing dialog box, you can simply double-click the object. Be sure to double-click the border of text boxes, because double-clicking the center of the box opens the text area for editing.

There are several other ways to display the Format Drawing dialog box. You can select the object and use the Attach to Task button on the Drawing toolbar. If you prefer to use the menu bar, choose Format, Drawing and choose Properties from the submenu. Or, to use the shortcut menu (see Figure 7.18), position the mouse pointer over the object so that the pointer displays the small cross to its right. Right-click to see the shortcut menu; select Properties. Selecting Properties will open the Format Drawing dialog box shown previously in Figure 7.17.

Figure 7.18
The drawing objects shortcut menu is a quick way to work with drawn objects.

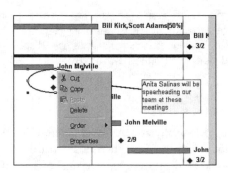

Rather than have a drawn object attached to a date, you can attach it to a task in the table portion of the Gantt Chart view. To attach an object to a task, follow these steps:

1. Make a note of the ID number of the task to which you want to attach the object. You will need to enter the ID number on the dialog box, and there is no way to browse or search for the ID number after the dialog box is active.

2. Activate the Format Drawing dialog box and choose the Size & Position tab.

3. Choose the Attach to Task option button.

4. Enter the task number in the ID text box. If you do not remember the ID number, you will have to close the dialog box, find the number, and then come back to the dialog box.

5. Attach the object to the beginning or the end of the task bar by choosing the Attachment Point at the beginning or the end of the sample task bar.

6. The Horizontal and Vertical fields show the offset from the attachment point where the object's top-left corner will be placed. Positive offset values are to the right horizontally and down vertically. Negative offset values are to the left horizontally and up vertically. Enter zero in both these text boxes unless you are absolutely certain that you know the values that will look best. The zero values ensure that the drawing object is displayed next to the task bar when you finish this procedure, and you do not have to search the Gantt Chart to find it. You then can use the mouse to reposition the drawing as desired.

After the object is attached to the task, you can move it with the mouse, and the horizontal and vertical offset values are recorded automatically. The object remains attached to the task as you move the task (unless you come back to the Size & Position tab and attach it to the timescale).

7. Choose OK to return to the workspace.

If you later decide to unlink the object from the task to fix it at a particular date, return to the Size & Position tab and choose the Attach to Timescale button. Then move the task with the mouse to the preferred position.

HIDING OBJECTS ON THE GANTT CHART

The drawn objects you place on the Gantt Chart remain visible and print with the Gantt Chart unless you elect to hide them. You can hide them for a printing, for example, and then display them again later.

To hide the drawing objects, use these steps:

1. Choose Format, Layout. The Layout dialog box is displayed (see Figure 7.19).

2. Clear the Show Drawings check box at the bottom.

3. Choose OK to implement the change.

Figure 7.19
Graphic objects are hidden from view if you clear the Show Drawings check box on the Layout dialog box.

MOVING OBJECTS

You can move an object by moving the mouse pointer over the object, away from the selection handles. Watch for the small cross to appear to the right of the pointer arrow. Then drag the object to a new position.

Caution

It is very easy to accidentally move a task bar or create a new task bar when your intention is to move or resize a graphic object. If the mouse pointer does not have the cross beside it, you are not moving the object. Do not click the mouse until the cross appears.

RESIZING OBJECTS

Although you can size an object with the Height and Width fields at the bottom of the Size & Position tab in the Format Drawing dialog box (refer to Figure 7.17), it is much easier to use the mouse to achieve the same end.

When a two-dimensional object is selected, its selection handles are evident in a rectangular array around the object. Line and arrow objects display selection handles at each end of the object. You can change the size of the object by moving the mouse pointer over one of the selection handles until the pointer changes into a pair of opposing arrows. Drag the handle to the position you desire (see Figure 7.20).

Figure 7.20
Use the selection handles to resize an object.

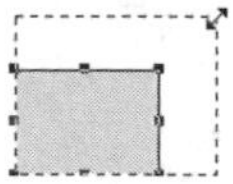

The corner handles resize both sides that meet at the corner. For instance, if you use the selection handle in the lower-right corner, you will be resizing the right and bottom sides of the object. The handles along the top and bottom midpoints resize vertically, and the handles along the sides resize horizontally.

Tip from Tim and the Project Team

Use the Shift key with one of the corner handles to resize the object proportionally along both horizontal and vertical dimensions.

Polygons are a special case. Because they have multiple sides, you can reshape the polygon by adjusting its points. The *points* on a polygon are the locations where the shape changes direction. Sometimes points are called *nodes*.

To reshape a polygon, you must first select it. Then click the Draw button on the Drawing toolbar and choose Edit Points. The selection handles of a polygon disappear when you click the Edit Points option on the Draw drop-down list on the Drawing toolbar (see Figure 7.21). Instead, you see reshaping handles at the connecting nodes of its line segments. Use these handles to reposition the connecting nodes and thus change the shape of the drawing. To move a connecting node, position the mouse pointer directly over the handle (it turns into a large plus sign). When you are finished reshaping the figure, click the Edit Points tool again to display the selection handles again.

Caution

It is just as easy to accidentally move a task bar or create a new task bar when you are trying to resize an object, as it is when moving an object. If the mouse pointer has not become opposing arrows, you will not be resizing the object, and you should refrain from clicking the mouse.

Figure 7.21
The Edit Points option on the Drawing toolbar allows you to edit the points on a polygon.

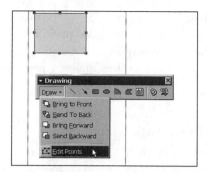

If you want to increase or decrease the size of a polygon without changing its shape, you can make proportional changes to its Size fields on the Format Drawing dialog box. For example, to double the size of a polygon, follow these steps:

1. Select the polygon.
2. Activate the Format Drawing dialog box by double-clicking the polygon, or by right-clicking the polygon to activate the shortcut menu and selecting Properties.
3. Choose the Size & Position tab.
4. Double the values entered in the Height and Width fields.
5. Choose OK to close the dialog box.

COPYING OBJECTS

There might be times when you draw an object in the Gantt Chart that you want to copy to another area of the Gantt Chart or to another Project document. If the place you want to copy the object is visible on the screen, it is quite easy to use the mouse to drag a copy to the new location. However, if the place you want to copy the object is not visible, or you want to copy the object to another file, you're better off using the traditional methods for copying and pasting.

Follow these steps to copy an object with the mouse:

1. Select the original object.
2. Use the Ctrl key as you drag away from the original object. You will be dragging a copy of the original.
3. Continue dragging the copy until it is in its new position. The copy appears as an outline until you release the mouse button.
4. Release the mouse button when the copy is in position.

The traditional copy and paste techniques use the Clipboard to copy an object; this method must be used if you are copying the object to another file:

1. Select the original object.
2. Choose Edit, Copy.

PART
II

CH
7

3. If you want to place the copy in the same project document, choose Edit, Paste. A copy of the object appears at the top-left corner of the visible part of the Gantt Chart timescale area. If you want to place the copy in another document, you must activate that document and then choose Edit, Paste to place the copy in the new document.

4. Drag the copy of the object into its desired position.

CHANGING THE LINE AND FILL STYLE OF AN OBJECT

To enhance the appearance of a drawn object, you can change the thickness and color of the object's lines and borders. You can also apply a background pattern or color that fills the interior of the drawn object. Both the line and fill options are selected on the Line & Fill tab of the Format Drawing dialog box (see Figure 7.22).

Figure 7.22
You can customize the attributes of lines and the interior fill of objects.

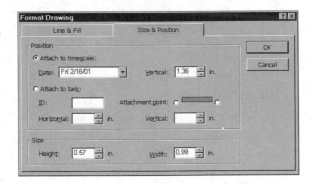

To change an object's line and fill attributes, use these steps:

1. Select the object and display the Format Drawing dialog box by double-clicking the object or by choosing Format, Drawing, and selecting Properties to display the dialog box.

2. Click the Line & Fill tab.

3. If you want the line or border to be invisible, choose the None button in the Line section. If you select a line color or line style, the Custom button is activated automatically.

4. To select the color for a line, choose a sample color band from the drop-down list below the Color label.

5. To select the thickness of a line, choose a sample line from the drop-down list below the Line label.

6. If you want the background of the object to be transparent so that you can see task bars or other objects behind this object, choose the None button in the Fill section of this tab. If you choose a Color or a Pattern, the Custom button is activated automatically.

7. The default fill pattern is solid; the default color is white. If you want to display a different color in the interior of the object, simply select a different color from the

drop-down list below the Color label. Selecting the object and using the Cycle Fill Color button on the Drawing toolbar can also change the color of an object.

8. Whatever is black in the pattern is displayed in the color you select. Whatever is white in the pattern remains white. If you leave the default white color selected and select a pattern, you will have a white pattern color on a white background. Select a color for the pattern to see the pattern on the object.

9. Choose a pattern by selecting a sample from the drop-down list below the Pattern label. The first pattern in the entry list appears white. It is a clear pattern, equivalent to choosing the None button in the Fill section. The second pattern in the entry list is solid black. Choose the solid band to display a solid background using the color you selected from the Color field. The remaining patterns are displayed against a white background, with the pattern appearing in the foreground in the color you selected from the Color field.

10. Use the Preview box at the lower-right corner of the tab to assess the choices you have made. Change the choices until the Preview box looks the way you want the object to look.

11. Choose OK to implement the changes. Choose Cancel to leave the object unchanged.

DELETING OBJECTS

You can delete objects by simply selecting them and then pressing the Delete key on your keyboard.

PLACING INDEPENDENT TEXT ON THE GANTT CHART

Use the Text Box drawing button to place independent text in the Gantt Chart timeline. After you draw the text box on the screen, enter the text into the box. You can change the line and fill attributes, as well as the position of the text box, as described in the preceding sections. You can also edit the text and select the fonts for the text display.

CREATING A TEXT BOX

To display a text message in the Gantt Chart, you need to bring into view the area of the timeline where the message is to appear and then follow these steps:

1. Click the Text Box button on the Drawing toolbar.
2. Drag the mouse in the Gantt Chart to create a box at the approximate location and of the approximate dimension you need. You can adjust the box to fit the text later. An insertion point cursor will blink in the text box.
3. Type the text you want to appear in the box. The text automatically word-wraps within the current size of the text box. It also word-wraps automatically when you resize the text box later. Press Enter when you want to start a paragraph on a new line in the text box.
4. When you finish entering text, click outside the text box.

EDITING THE TEXT IN A TEXT BOX

Periodically, it might become necessary to modify the text in a text box. Click to select the text box, and then click again to activate the edit mode. Make sure you don't double-click the text box, as this displays the Format Drawing dialog box. When the edit mode is active, the mouse pointer appears as a capital I (sometimes referred to as the I-beam) within the text box. The flashing cursor indicates the keyboard position within the text—if you begin typing, the text will be entered at the point of the flashing cursor (see Figure 7.23).

You can use many of the text-editing techniques with which you are already familiar: Double-click a word to select it; press the delete key to remove characters to the right of the flashing cursor; and press the Backspace key to remove characters to the left of the flashing cursor.

After you edit the text, click outside the text box.

Figure 7.23
You can use normal editing techniques in a text box.

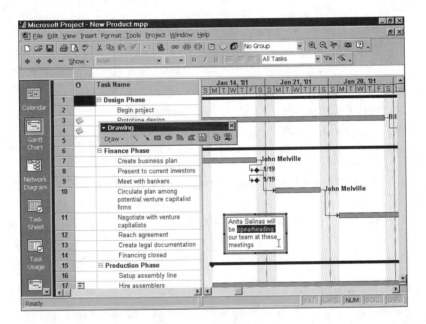

Tip from Tim and the Project Team

If you want to move a text box, position the mouse pointer over the text box and the mouse pointer will display as an arrow with an X at the stem (bottom) of the arrow. Hold the mouse button and drag to move the text box. Unlike the other drawn objects, selecting the interior of the text box does not allow you to move it. Instead, you are allowed to select formatting options for the entire text box or edit the text.

CHANGING THE TEXT FONT

The only method for changing the font or font attributes of text in a text box is through the menu; the formatting options on the Formatting toolbar are deactivated when the text box is selected. You choose the font or font attributes for the text by selecting the text box and choosing Format, Font. Choose the font type, color, style, or size desired.

Your selections are applied to all text within the text box. You cannot apply different fonts or font attributes to individual words or phrases within the text box. Text within a text box is left aligned. It cannot be centered or right aligned.

CHANGING THE PROPERTIES OF THE TEXT BOX

When you create a text box, it is automatically given a lined border and a white background fill. If you want the text to float freely without lines and so the Gantt Chart shows through the text box, you must choose the None button in both sections of the Line & Fill tab on the Format Drawing dialog box.

First double-click the text box to display the Format Drawing dialog box. Then choose the None button in the Line section and the None button in the Fill section. Click OK to effect the change.

WORKING WITH THE CALENDAR VIEW

You will often find it useful to display your project on the familiar monthly calendar background. After creating a project file using the other views provided by Microsoft Project, it can be very helpful to distribute reports showing all tasks or selected tasks in the calendar format. Although it isn't the best view for designing and creating lengthy or complex projects, you can use the Calendar view to create simple, short-duration projects.

UNDERSTANDING THE CALENDAR VIEW

Display the Calendar view by clicking the Calendar button on the View bar or by choosing View, Calendar. The standard Calendar view appears (see Figure 7.24). You should note that the Calendar view cannot be displayed in the bottom pane of a split screen view.

The Calendar view features a month and year title, and shows one or more weeks of dates with task bars stretching from their start dates to their finish dates. The default display shows four weeks at a time and includes bars or lines for all tasks except summary tasks. You can include summary tasks and you can change many other features of the display by customizing the Calendar view. Milestone tasks are represented by black task bars with white text. As you can see in Figure 7.24, the Begin Project milestone task is displayed.

In some cases, there isn't enough room in the calendar to display all the tasks whose schedules fall on a particular date. When this happens, you see an overflow indicator in the left corner of the date box (refer to Figure 7.24). The overflow indicator is a black arrow with an ellipsis that indicates there is more data to see.

PART

II

CH

7

Figure 7.24
Present your project in Calendar view; most people are familiar with this format and can easily decipher your data.

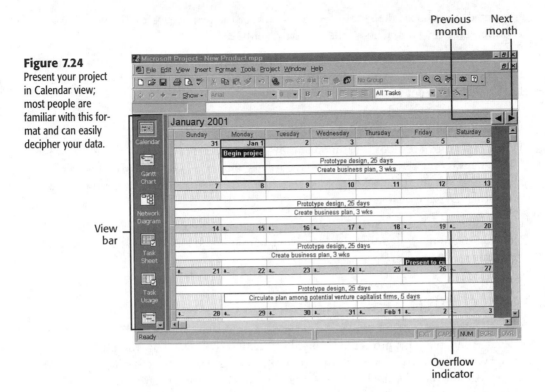

You can see all the tasks scheduled for a given date by displaying the Tasks Occurring On dialog box for that date (see Figure 7.25). To display the Tasks Occurring On dialog box, double-click the gray band at the top of the date box, or follow these steps:

1. Position the mouse pointer over any portion of the gray band at the top of the date box. (The day number appears at the right of this gray band in the default calendar layout.)

2. Right-click to display the shortcut menu for dates.

3. Choose Task List from the shortcut menu. The Tasks Occurring On dialog box appears for the specific date you pointed to.

After you have the Tasks Occurring On dialog box displayed, you can double-click a task to see the Task Information dialog box for that task. The Task Information dialog box shows specific information about a particular task, including start and finish dates, duration, assigned resources, task constraints, and notes.

→ To learn more about the Task Information dialog box, **see** "Using the Task Information Dialog Box," **p. 173**

Click the OK button to close the Task Information dialog box and return to the Task Occurring On dialog box. After reviewing the list of tasks, click Close to close the dialog box.

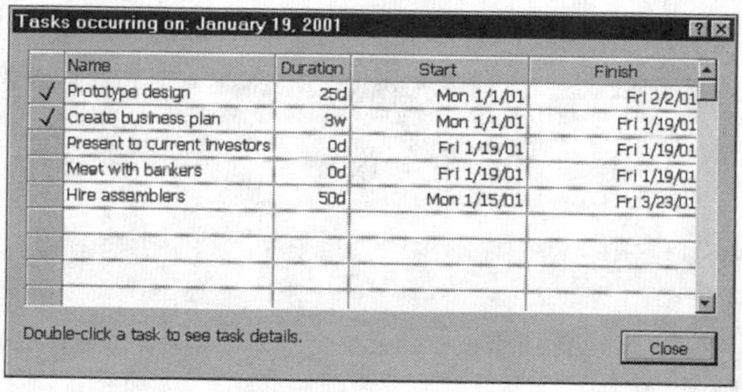

Figure 7.25
All tasks that occur on a specific date are shown in a list. Double-click any of the tasks to see details for that task.

The Tasks Occurring On dialog box lists all tasks whose schedule dates encompass the date you selected. Those tasks whose bars appear in the calendar have a check mark to the left of the listing. To increase the number of tasks that appear on the calendar, you can use the Zoom command (see "Using Zoom" later in this chapter) or you can make changes in the calendar format.

The Calendar view, like other views, has a number of shortcut menus available. One approach to learning about this view is to just start right-clicking different spots on the view. There are navigation options such as Go To and Zoom on shortcut menus. Additional shortcut menus offer access to the Task Information dialog box, a list of tasks occurring on specific dates, and formatting options for virtually every element of the calendar.

MOVING AROUND IN CALENDAR VIEW

As with other views, your effective use of the Calendar view depends on your ability to move around and find the information you want to focus on. It's helpful to know how to change the display of the calendar to show only selected information.

SCROLLING THE CALENDAR

Use the scrollbars to move forward and backward in time on the calendar. When you drag the scroll box on the vertical scrollbar, a date indicator pop-up box helps you locate a specific date (see Figure 7.26). The beginning and end points on the scrollbar are approximately the start and end dates of the project.

Press Alt+Home and Alt+End to jump to the beginning and ending dates of the project, respectively. You also can use the Page Up and Page Down keys to scroll through the display showing successive weeks in the life of the project.

Scroll through the months of the year with the left and right arrow buttons to the right of the month and year title. As you scroll through the months, the beginning of each successive month appears in the first row of the calendar, no matter how many weeks you displayed in the view. The Alt+up arrow and Alt+down arrow keys also scroll by months through the project calendar.

Scroll box

Figure 7.26
Drag the scroll box to move quickly to a specific date.

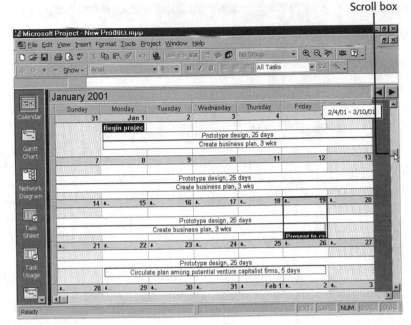

LOCATING A SPECIFIC TASK OR DATE

You can quickly move to a specific date anywhere in the calendar, including dates outside the date range of the project. You can also locate a specific task by specifying its task ID or by searching for tasks by name.

Use the Go To command to move directly to a specific task ID or date. You access the Go To command by right-clicking the month and year title or a date in the calendar. Then choose Go To from the shortcut menu that appears. The Go To dialog box appears, as shown in Figure 7.27.

Figure 7.27
You can also use Edit, Go To to access this dialog box.

Caution

By default, the summary task bars do not display in the Calendar view. The Go To command (and the Find command described later in this section) cannot select tasks that don't display task bars in the Calendar view. Therefore, you can't go to a summary task. You can change the Calendar view to display summary task bars through the Format, Bar Styles command.

→ To learn more about working with your project calendars, **see** "Formatting the Calendar," **p. 914**

With the Go To dialog box displayed, you enter a date or task ID and click OK.

When a given date has more tasks than can be shown in the Calendar view display, it shows the first few tasks and indicates there are more by an arrow next to the date. If you enter an ID for a task whose task bar is not visible on that date, Project selects the task, and its beginning date scrolls into view—but you can't see the task or a selection marker to indicate which date is the beginning date.

 However, because the task is selected, you can choose the Information button on the toolbar to view its Task Information dialog box. The task start date is on the General tab. Close the Task Information dialog box by choosing the Cancel button. Double-click the start date for the task to see the other tasks scheduled on that date.

Another way to locate tasks is with the Find command. Use Find to locate tasks by their field values, usually by the value in the Name field. As with the Go To command, if the task you find is not currently displayed in the calendar, you cannot see it.

Tip from Tim and the Project Team

You must select a task bar in the Calendar view before you can use the Find command.

To find a task by searching for one or more characters in its name, follow these steps:

1. Select any task. If you want to search from the beginning of the task list, press Alt+Home to scroll to the beginning of the project and then select the first task bar displayed.

2. Choose Edit, Find (or press Ctrl+F). The Find dialog box appears, as shown in Figure 7.28.

3. In the Find What text box, type the characters you want to search for. You can enter whole words or phrases, or just parts of words. In Figure 7.28 the word **Inspection** is being located.

4. By default, the Name field is searched. However, you can select any task field to search. Select the Look in Field box and use the drop-down list box to choose the task field you want to search. Figure 7.28 has the Name field selected.

5. The Test box provides the criteria for the search. The default is Contains. Other options include: Equals, Is Greater Than, Is Greater Than or Equal to, and so forth.

6. Choose the direction to be searched from the Search drop-down list box. The choices are Down or Up from the selected task.

PART

II

CH

7

Figure 7.28
Search for a task by name or any other field value with the Find command.

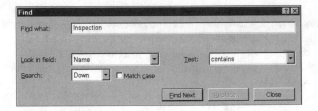

7. You can further tailor the search by making it case sensitive. Marking the Match Case option requires the results to match the text typed in the Find What text box.

Tip from Tim and the Project Team

If you've closed the dialog box, you can still use your last Find criteria. Press Shift+F4 to search farther toward the end of the task list, or press Ctrl+Shift+F4 to search farther toward the beginning of the task list.

Note

If the bar for the task is not visible, try using the Zoom In button to see more task bars for each day or use the Task Information button to see details for the task. Both of these features are described in the following section.

USING ZOOM

You might want to look at your calendar from different perspectives, backing away at times to see the big picture (although this has practical size limitations) or zooming in on the details for a specific week. To change the perspective, use the Zoom In and Zoom Out buttons on the Standard toolbar, or choose View, Zoom. Each click on one of these buttons displays one, two, four, or six weeks in ascending or descending order, depending on the button you use.

The calendar in Figure 7.29, for example, is zoomed in to a two-week view to get a good understanding of the tasks going on during that time.

Tip from Tim and the Project Team

You often have more options when accessing the dialog box for a feature than you do when using the toolbar button.

Choose View, Zoom to display the Zoom dialog box (see Figure 7.30). You can also right-click an empty spot on the calendar, and choose Zoom from the shortcut menu that appears. You have many options in the Zoom dialog box. You can zoom to a Custom level specified in weeks, or you can designate a From date and a To date.

Figure 7.29
Click the Zoom In button to display fewer weeks and more tasks per day.

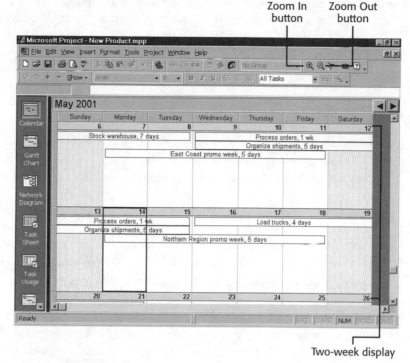

Zoom In button   Zoom Out button

Two-week display

Figure 7.30
Use the Zoom dialog box to customize the number of weeks to display in the Calendar.

Using the Zoom command on the Calendar view has no effect on the printed Calendar view; it only affects the screen display.

→ For more information about using the Page Setup dialog box to control the printing of calendars, **see** Chapter 13, "Printing Views and Report," **p. 537**

USING FILTERS TO CLARIFY THE CALENDAR VIEW

When a project has many overlapping tasks, the Calendar view can quickly become very cluttered and difficult to read. As previously discussed, you can zoom in to see more detail, but you can also use *filters* to narrow the list of tasks that display at one time. A filter limits the display of tasks to just those that match the criteria defined in the filter. For example, you can have Project display only the critical tasks in the project by applying the Critical filter. You might also choose to display tasks that a specific resource is working on by applying the Using Resource filter.

To apply a filter to a Calendar view, do one of the following:

- Choose the Filter button on the Formatting toolbar. Select from the available filters on the drop-down list.

- Choose Project, Filtered For and choose from the predefined filters.

- If you want to highlight a particular category of tasks, choose Project, Filtered For, More Filters. Select the filter you want to apply and then choose the Highlight button.

When you need to focus on the project deadline and, therefore, the critical path, use the Critical filter. When you want to give each resource a list of their assigned tasks, choose the Using Resource filter. When the project is underway and you want a record of what has been accomplished so far, use the Completed Tasks filter.

→ To learn more detailed information about filters, **see** "Using Filters," **p. 512**

EDITING A PROJECT IN THE CALENDAR VIEW

As mentioned in the section "Working with the Calendar View" earlier in this chapter, it isn't recommended to use the Calendar view to create a complex project. After the project is created, this view really is more useful to review and print tasks and the time frames in which they occur. However, you can use this view to edit task data. This section includes techniques for looking up and modifying task information. For example, this section will show you how you can add and modify task notes when reviewing the calendar.

VIEWING TASK DETAILS IN THE CALENDAR VIEW

The display of individual task information is minimized in the Calendar view; it is not displayed by default onscreen. You can view and edit details about a task by selecting the task and opening the Task Information dialog box. Alternatively, you can use the Calendar view as the top part of a dual-pane view, and then select a task in the calendar and view its task details in the lower pane.

You can open the Task Information dialog box, shown in Figure 7.31, for a task in the Calendar view in several ways. You can use any of the methods listed here for tasks that display task bars. If the task bar is not displayed, you must use one of the last two methods described in the following bulleted lists.

To display the Task Information dialog box for tasks that display task bars, use one of these methods:

- Double-click the task bar to both select the task and display the Task Information dialog box.

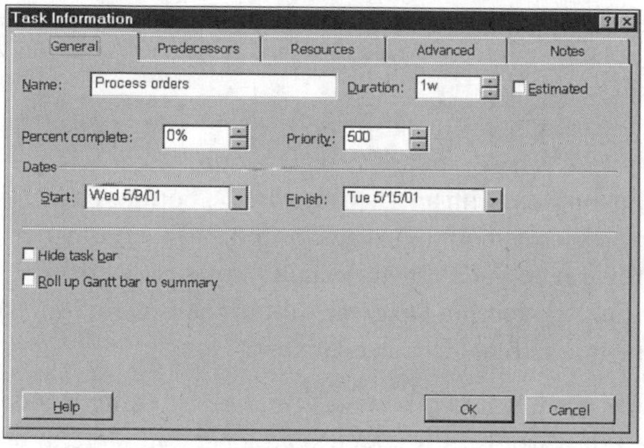

Figure 7.31
The Task Information dialog box offers easy access to most of the data fields for a task.

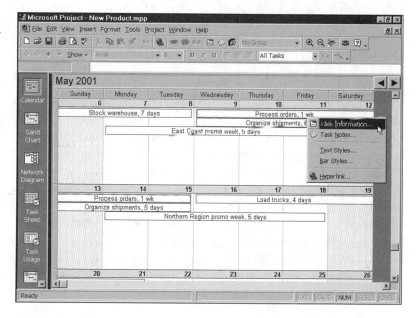

- Right-click the task bar. This selects the task and displays the shortcut menu (see Figure 7.32). Choose Task Information to see the General tab of the Task Information dialog box, or choose Task Notes to go directly to the Notes tab of the Task Information dialog box.

Figure 7.32
The shortcut menu for a task is helpful for displaying task information.

If the task bar is not displayed, you must first select the task using the Go To command or the Find command as described in the earlier section "Locating a Specific Task or Date." After you select the task, you can use one of the following methods to display the Task Information dialog box:

- Choose Project, Task Information. (Choose Project, Task Notes if you want to go directly to the Notes tab of the Task Information dialog box.)

■ Choose the Information button on the Standard toolbar to view the General tab of the Task Information dialog box. (Choose the Task Note button if you want to go directly to the Notes tab.)

Another way to view task details is to use a combination view where you display the Calendar view in the top pane with another view in the bottom pane. For example, if you put the Task Form view in the bottom pane, it displays task information for a task selected in Calendar view. You can choose Format, Details, Notes to see the notes for the selected task. If you display the Relationship Diagram view in the bottom pane, it illustrates task dependencies for the task selected in Calendar view.

You can split the view window into two panes either by choosing Window, Split or by right-clicking anywhere in the calendar (except a task) to open the shortcut menu and choose Split.

When you choose the Split command, Project puts the Task Form view in the bottom pane by default. You can replace the Task Form view with any view you want. Note: Displaying the Network Diagram in the bottom pane is not particularly useful. When a specific task is selected in the Calendar, only the node for the selected task appears in the bottom pane. Selecting a date in the Calendar will result in no tasks displayed in the bottom pane. Your best view choices here are Task Form, Task Details Form, and Task Usage.

INSERTING TASKS IN CALENDAR VIEW

Although it's easy to create tasks in the Calendar view, you might not want to use the Calendar view in this manner for two reasons:

■ With the Gantt Chart view, as well as other views, you can insert a new task in the middle of the project and near other tasks to which the new task is related. The task is given an ID number where it was inserted. When creating a task in Calendar view, however, it is always given the next highest ID number in the project, regardless of where the task was inserted. If you view the new task in Gantt Chart view (or any view with a table), the task is at the bottom of the list—even if its dates fall in the middle of the project or you link it to tasks in the middle of the task list.

■ The task you create in Calendar view is often automatically given a date constraint. You would want to remove the constraint as soon as you create a task in the Calendar view. To remove the constraint, set the constraint type to As Soon as Possible in the Advanced Tab of the Task Information dialog box.

Caution

Adding tasks to a project in Calendar view can result in task constraints that, unless removed, needlessly produce scheduling conflicts.

Whether tasks created in the Calendar view are constrained depends on what you have selected when you create the new task: a task or a date.

- If you select a task and you insert the new task using the Insert menu or the Insert key, the new task will not be constrained (its constraint type will be As Soon As Possible).

- If you select a date when you create the new task, or if you create the task by dragging with the mouse (which automatically selects the date where you start dragging), the new task will be constrained.

If the task is constrained when you create it, the constraint type depends on whether you schedule your project from a fixed start date or a fixed finish date. If you create the task by dragging with the mouse, the constraint type also depends on the direction you drag the mouse: from start to finish or from finish to start. Remember to check the constraint type of any task you create in the Calendar view (following the steps that are outlined below) and change it appropriately.

To insert a task in the Calendar view, follow these steps:

1. Select the date for the start of the task if you want the start date constrained, or select any task if you do not want the new task to be constrained (and the task will be added to the end of the project).

2. Choose Insert, New Task. You can also simply press the Insert key that is the shortcut key for the Insert Task command. Project inserts a new, untitled task in the project with a default duration of one day. Because the task has no name yet, its task bar only displays its duration. If there is no room to display the bar for the new task, it seems to disappear. Regardless, the new task is selected.

 3. Choose Project, Task Information (or choose the Information button on the Standard toolbar) to open the Task Information dialog box.

4. Provide a name and any other information for the task. For example, you probably need to enter the Duration. You might also want to choose the Notes tab and type comments about the task.

5. Because most tasks created in Calendar view are automatically given a date constraint, choose the Advanced tab and change the entry in the Constrain Task Type field as appropriate. For example, to remove the date constraint, change the constraint to As Soon As Possible.

6. Choose OK to close the dialog box.

As an alternative, you can insert a task with the mouse. First scroll the Calendar until you see the start date (or finish date) for the task. Drag the mouse from the start date to the finish date for the task (or from the finish date to the start date). Click the Information button on the Standard toolbar to display the Task Information dialog box and supply the task name (and any other information you want to specify). Then choose the Advanced tab and correct the Constrain Task Type as appropriate. Click OK to close the dialog box.

DELETING TASKS IN CALENDAR VIEW

To delete a task, simply select it and choose Edit, Delete Task or press the Delete key. If the task bar is not displayed, you must use the Go To command or the Find command to select it. (See the section "Locating a Specific Task or Date" earlier in this chapter.) If you accidentally delete a task, use the Undo feature to get it back. Just click the Undo button; choose Edit, Undo; or press Ctrl+Z.

Tip from Tim and the Project Team

You must do this right away though, because Undo can only undo your last action.

CREATING LINKS BETWEEN TASKS IN CALENDAR VIEW

There are several ways to create task dependency links in Calendar view. One method is to select the tasks you want to link (use the Ctrl key to add tasks to the selection). Then choose the Link button on the Standard toolbar.

You can also use the mouse. Simply click the *center* of the task bar for the task that will be the predecessor task and hold down the mouse button until the mouse pointer turns. Drag down to the intended successor task. The mouse pointer changes into a chain links symbol and a pop-up box indicates the creation of a Finish-to-Start relationship between the two tasks.

To change to a different kind of relationship or to add lag or lead time, you must display the Task Information dialog box for the dependent (successor) task and choose the Predecessors tab.

→ To learn more about linking tasks, **see** "Understanding Dependency Links," **p. 209**

WORKING WITH THE NETWORK DIAGRAM VIEW

A new view called the Network Diagram has been added to Microsoft Project. As you can see from Figure 7.33, the Network Diagram is a graphic display of tasks in a project, in which each task is represented by a small box or *node*. Lines connect the nodes to show task dependencies. The Network Diagram is most useful for an overall view of how the process or flow of task details fit together. You can also use the Network Diagram to enter your task list and create your project schedule.

The task nodes in the Network Diagram differ considerably both in their look and in the data they present from the former PERT Chart nodes. In this view you now have extensive formatting options (including the ability to format by task category or by individual boxes), and more fields are displayed in each task box. Additionally you now have a number of alternatives for displaying the layout of the task boxes and selectively displaying task boxes via filtering—a feature never available in the PERT Chart view.

Note

While in the Network Diagram view, you cannot use the Clipboard to copy or move entire tasks. You can, however, use the Clipboard to cut, copy, and paste individual field entries.

Figure 7.33
The Network Diagram view focuses on the links between tasks; use it as a road map for the flow of work in the project.

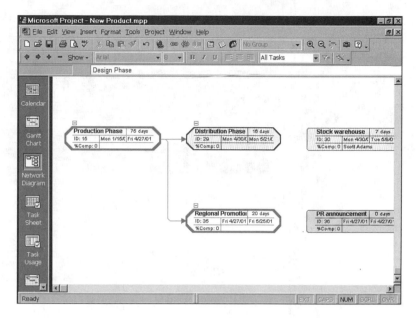

UNDERSTANDING THE NETWORK DIAGRAM VIEW

The Network Diagram is a flow chart view of your project. The Network Diagram reveals information about the individual task, as well as information about the task's place in the flow of activity. Figure 7.34 shows the default Network Diagram view of the New Product project. In this figure, Design Phase is the currently selected task. The default format for nodes displays six fields: the task name, task ID, duration, start, finish, and resources assigned to the task.

Note

You can select other fields to display in the node; in fact, there is a great deal of flexibility in the customization you can perform on these nodes. You can use one of the default fields to add fields or substitute a field that is more useful to you. For example, you might add the Cost field to the node, or substitute the resource name field with the resource group field. You can even design your own node templates that display primarily cost or work information in the nodes, thus designing your own custom Network Diagrams, which display the information in which you are most interested.

→ To learn more about customizing the Network Diagram nodes, **see** "Formatting the Network Diagram View," **p. 917**

Each node represents a task, which is connected to predecessors and successors by lines. In the default layout of the diagram, dependent (successor) tasks are always placed to the right of or beneath predecessors. Different border styles or colors distinguish summary tasks, critical tasks, and milestones. Summary tasks are above and to the left of subordinate tasks.

Table 7.2 describes a few of the most common task types and the node borders displayed earlier in Figure 7.34.

PART

II

CH

7

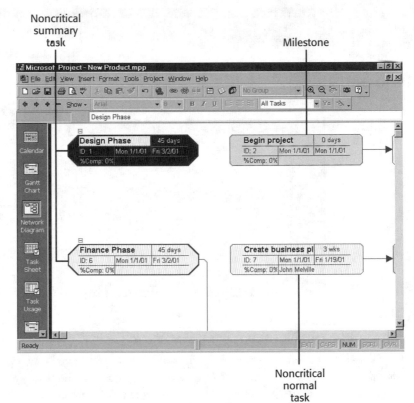

Noncritical
summary
task

Milestone

Noncritical
normal
task

Figure 7.34
You can create a project in the Network Diagram view just as you can in the Gantt Chart view.

TABLE 7.2   EACH TYPE OF TASK HAS A UNIQUE NODE BORDER

Type of Tasks	Node Shape and Color
Noncritical Summary Tasks	Elongated Stop-sign shape, with a thin blue border and aqua background.
Critical Summary Tasks	Elongated Stop-sign shape, with a thick red border and white background.
Milestones	Rectangle with rounded corners, with a thin blue border and silver (gray-blue) background. This shape and color are used for both critical and noncritical milestones.
Critical Normal Tasks	Elongated diamond shape, with thick red border and white background.
Noncritical tasks	Rectangle with rounded corners, with a thin blue border.

To view the Network Diagram, click the Network Diagram button in the View bar or choose View, Network Diagram.

Note

If you have a split screen and want the Network Diagram to be in the top half of the screen, you must make that the active pane before you change to the Network Diagram view. You cannot display the Network Diagram in the bottom pane in a split screen.

ZOOMING THE NETWORK DIAGRAM VIEW

In the Network Diagram in Figure 7.34, shown previously, each node is large enough to read the field data easily. If you want to get an overview of the links among more tasks, you can zoom the view to show more tasks. Figure 7.35 shows the same task selected, Design Phase, as in Figure 7.34. When the view is zoomed out, you get a better feel for how that task fits into the overall project.

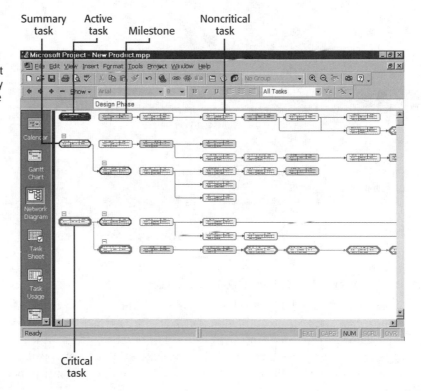

Figure 7.35
The default box layout has the main summary tasks appearing in the far left side of the Network Diagram, with the sequence of tasks associated with each summary flowing out to the right.

 You can zoom out to view more tasks using the Zoom Out button on the Standard toolbar. Zoom in to see the task details using the Zoom In button. The Zoom In and Zoom Out buttons increment and decrement the zoom percentage using preset percentages of 25%, 50%, 75%, 100%, and 200%. Each time you click one of the Zoom buttons, the percentage increases or decreases using the preset percentages. The normal magnification is set to 100%.

PART

II

Cн

7

However, the supported zoom range is from 25% to a maximum of 400%. You have more options for zooming when you choose View, Zoom. The Zoom dialog box appears (see Figure 7.36). To change the zoom percentage, select one of the percentage buttons or fill in the Custom text box with a value between 25 and 400%. Select the Entire Project button to select the percentage (between 25% and 400%) that just fits the entire project in the window. If the entire project cannot be displayed in one screen at 25%, the Zoom command displays a warning (see Figure 7.37). Choose OK to close the alert.

Figure 7.36
The Zoom dialog box gives you precise control over the scope of the view.

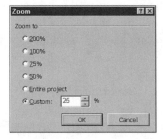

Note

Using the Zoom command affects only the screen view in the Network Diagram. It does not affect how much of the chart is printed.

Figure 7.37
This warning appears if the entire project cannot be displayed on one screen.

OUTLINING IN THE NETWORK DIAGRAM VIEW

One new feature in the Network Diagram view is the capability to collapse and expand the summary task nodes as you would in the Gantt Chart view. The summary task boxes are represented by elongated Stop-sign shapes. The outline buttons, which are initially minus signs, appear just above these boxes (refer to Figure 7.35). Click to an outline button to collapse or hide the tasks under a summary task. The outline button then becomes a plus sign.

SCROLLING AND SELECTING IN THE NETWORK DIAGRAM

You can use the horizontal and vertical scrollbars or the movement keys (the arrow keys, Page Up, Page Down, Home, and End) to scan through the Network Diagram view. However, the rules for each method are quite different.

Scrolling does not change the currently selected node. After you scroll, you probably cannot see the selected node, although the selected field in that node still displays in the Entry bar.

To put the selected node back in the screen where you can see it, press the Edit key (F2) as though you plan to change the selected node. To cancel the editing, press the Esc key. To select one of the visible nodes after scrolling, just click the node.

You can also use the selection keys to move around the Network Diagram, selecting different nodes as you go. The rules that the selection keys follow in selecting the next node are not apparent. The following list defines the rules of the selection keys:

- **Right arrow key**—Selects nodes to the right until there are no more nodes directly to the right. It then selects the next node down and to the right and continues to the right.
- **Down arrow key**—Selects nodes directly below until there are no more nodes. Then selects the next node that is down and to the right and continues down.
- **Left arrow key**—Selects nodes to the left until no more nodes lie directly to the left. It then selects the next node up and to the left and continues to the left.
- **Up arrow key**—Selects nodes directly above until there are no more nodes. Then selects the next node above and to the left, and continues up.

The rest of the selection keys behave as they do in other applications, such as Excel; here's what the other selection keys do:

- **Page Down**—Displays a screen's worth of data down from the group of tasks you are viewing.
- **End**—Selects and displays the last task in the project.
- **Page Up**—Displays a screen's worth of data up from the group of tasks you are viewing.
- **Home**—Selects and displays the first task in the project.
- **Ctrl+Page Down**—Scrolls a screen's worth of data to the right.
- **Ctrl+Page Up**—Scrolls a screen's worth of data to the left.
- **Ctrl+End**—Makes the first box in the last horizontal row of boxes the active task.
- **Ctrl+Home**—Makes the first task in the Network Diagram the active task—the first box in the first horizontal row of boxes.

EDITING A PROJECT IN THE NETWORK DIAGRAM

Some people prefer to use the Network Diagram to create and edit their project tasks. You can use the Network Diagram view to change task data, add and delete tasks, and create and modify task links.

CHANGING TASK DATA IN THE NETWORK DIAGRAM VIEW

To change the field data displayed in a node, you must first select the task to edit by clicking the mouse pointer on the node or by using the selection keys. When you click to select a task, it also selects the field at which your mouse was pointing.

If necessary, you can select another field using the Tab and Shift+Tab keys or by clicking the field.

- If you're replacing the entire entry, type the new data directly in the selected cell.
- If you simply need to edit part if the existing data, or add to the existing date, use the Entry bar.

Complete the change by pressing Enter, by selecting the Enter box in the Entry bar, or by selecting a different field or node.

 If you want to change data in fields that don't appear in the node (such as constraints, fixed duration, and so on), you must use the Task Information dialog box. Select the node you want to edit and click the Task Information button on the Standard toolbar, or choose Project, Task Information to display the Task Information dialog box.

 *Tip from Tim and the Project Team*	You can also double-click the center of the node to display the Task Information dialog box. Double-clicking the border of a node takes you to a formatting dialog box.

Then select the tab in the Task Information dialog box where you want to make your changes. Choose the OK button to apply the changes.

ADDING TASKS IN THE NETWORK DIAGRAM VIEW

You can add tasks directly to the project in the Network Diagram view. Project inserts a task you add in the Network Diagram view just after the currently selected task. So, to insert a task just after a specific task, first select the task you want the new task to follow.

Note

If you are upgrading to Project 2000 from a previous version, you will undoubtedly be glad to learn that when you insert a task in the Network Diagram view, the ID number assigned to that task is the number that immediately follows the task that was selected when you inserted the new task. In other words, if there are 20 tasks in the project and task 4 was selected, the newly inserted task would be 5 and the subsequent tasks would automatically be renumbered. In the PERT Chart view in previous versions of Project, the new task would be inserted at the position following the selected task, but would be numbered 21. And when the task list was viewed in the Gantt Chart view, the task would be at the bottom of the list.

To add a new task, simply select the task you want the new task to follow. Then choose Insert, New Task (or press the Insert key) to insert a blank node to the right of the selected task.

This behavior is different from the Gantt Chart view, which inserts the task at the position of the active task and renumbers the active task (and subsequent tasks) by one number. In Figure 7.38, task 7 (Create Business Plan) was selected before the new task was inserted. The new task is numbered 8 (notice it does not have a task name) and the task that was formerly 8 is now 9 (Present to Current Investors).

Figure 7.38
Insert a new task by selecting the task that is to precede it and pressing the Insert key.

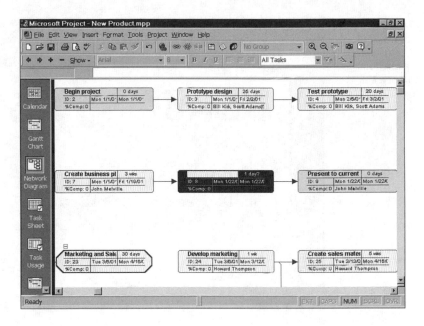

After you have inserted the new task, enter a new name for the new task. Tab to the Duration field and estimate the duration. Do not enter the start or finish date unless you want the task constrained to one of those dates.

You can also create a new task node by dragging the mouse pointer to form a rectangle in an empty area of the Network Diagram (see Figure 7.39). The ID number of the new task is still one greater than the currently selected task. In Figure 7.39, task 3 (Prototype Design) is selected; so, the new task will be 4. It's important for you to note that the default layout settings for the Network Diagram view are set to automatically position boxes when they are added to the view. In other words, where you draw the node might not be exactly were it will end up. If you want Microsoft Project to position the boxes in the exact position you draw them, you will need to change this setting in the Layout dialog box (Format, Layout).

Note

Automatic linking of tasks is not enabled while you add, delete, or move tasks in the Network Diagram view.

DELETING TASKS IN THE NETWORK DIAGRAM VIEW

You can delete tasks while in the Network Diagram view, just as you would in the Gantt Chart view. If you delete a task in the middle of a linked chain of tasks, it will automatically extend the link to maintain an unbroken sequence of tasks. When you attempt to delete a summary task in the Network Diagram, you will see a warning message confirming the deletion—because deleting a summary task also deletes the subtasks underneath it.

To delete a task, select the task and choose Edit, Delete Task (or press Delete).

PART

II

CH

7

Figure 7.39
Drag the mouse to create a rectangle in the position you want the new task to occupy.

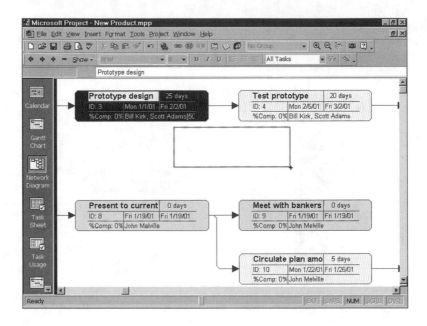

In previous versions of Project, you could not undo a deleted task in the Network Diagram view. Starting with Project 98, you can undo your deletions, but only your last action.

LINKING TASKS IN THE NETWORK DIAGRAM VIEW

You can create task links in the Network Diagram view by dragging the mouse from the predecessor task to the successor task. Make sure you start in the middle of the predecessor task node. Dragging the border of a task node merely repositions the node. The task relationship is Finish-to-Start with no lead or lag. If you want to change the relationship, enter lead or lag time. If you want to delete the task link, you must activate the Task Dependency dialog box, and then double-click the line that links the two tasks. The Task Dependency dialog box appears, allowing you to redefine the task relationship.

To redefine a task relationship in the Network Diagram view, follow these steps:

1. Double-click the line between the tasks to display the Task Dependency dialog box. Make sure the very tip of the mouse pointer is on the line that links the tasks when you double-click. In Figure 7.40, the link between Test Prototype and Prototype Completed is being edited. The Task Dependency dialog box shows the predecessor and successor task names in the From and To fields.

2. Change the relationship in the <u>T</u>ype list box.

3. Enter a lead or lag in the <u>L</u>ag text box, if needed.

4. Choose the <u>D</u>elete button if you want to remove the link altogether.

5. Choose OK to complete the change.

Figure 7.40
The Task Dependency dialog box can be used to edit or remove task links.

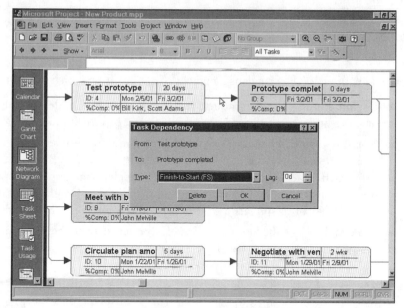

REARRANGING TASK NODES IN THE NETWORK DIAGRAM VIEW

You can change the layout of the Network Diagram nodes by accessing a special dialog box from which you can customize the layout of the task nodes. To display the Layout dialog box, choose Format, Layout (see Figure 7.41).

Figure 7.41
The Layout dialog box contains all the formatting options for the task boxes in the Network Diagram view.

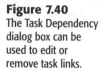

PART

II

CH

7

Tip from Tim and the Project Team

> You might find it useful to zoom out so you can see an overview as you redesign the layout of the Network Diagram.

The Layout dialog box contains a number of options from which you can choose:

- **Layout Mode**—Project automatically arranges the task nodes. If you want to move one or more nodes manually, choose Allow Manual Box Positioning.

- **Box Layout**—Click the Arrangement drop-down box to select from one of seven arrangements, including Top Down From Left, Top Down By Week, and Centered From Left. The Top Down By Week, for example, arranges the task starting the first week of the project in the first column in the Network Diagram. Tasks that start the second week of the project are in the second column in the Network Diagram.

- **Link Style**—Use the Show Link Labels to insert dependency, lead, and lag indicators on the task linking lines (see Figure 7.42).

Figure 7.42
For the link labels to be readable onscreen, you need to zoom in to 100%.

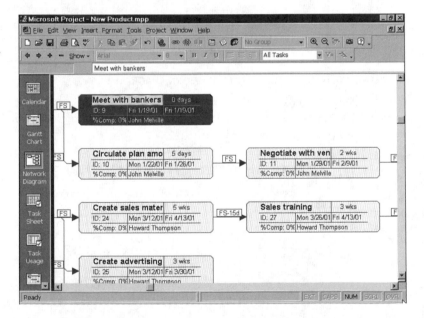

- **Link Color**—These settings allow you to customize the linking line color for critical and noncritical tasks. The default setting is for the lines to display the same color as the border of the predecessor tasks.

- n Diagram Options—Mark the Show Page Breaks check box when you want to see the delineations for standard 8.5×11-inch printed pages in the Network Diagram view.

You can select multiple task nodes by drawing a selection box around them. This is sometimes called *lassoing* the items to be selected. Imagine a rectangle that encloses only the nodes you want to select. Move the mouse pointer to one of the corners of this imaginary rectangle. Hold down the mouse button and drag the mouse pointer diagonally to the opposite corner of the imaginary rectangle, creating the rectangle. All task nodes that fall even partly in the area of the rectangle are selected.

Note
Press the Shift key as you select a task, and Project selects that task plus all its dependent (successor) tasks. This is a quick way to select all the subtasks under a summary task.

TROUBLESHOOTING

ATTACHING TO A TASK BAR

My drawing won't stay with the task bar I want it associated with. What should I do?

Just choose Format, Drawing, Properties to attach the drawing to the task.

MISSING TASK BAR

The task bars are hidden by the drawing and I can't see them.

You need to select the drawing and use the shortcut menu to move the drawing back.

If an object seems to disappear after you attach it to a task bar, open the Format Drawing dialog box again and change the Horizontal and Vertical offset values to zero. Then the object appears right next to the task bar, and you can reposition it with the mouse.

PART III

ASSIGNING RESOURCES AND COSTS

CHAPTER 8

DEFINING RESOURCES AND COSTS

In this chapter

UNDERSTANDING HOW PROJECT USES RESOURCES AND COSTS

This chapter focuses on resources and costs—understanding what resources are, how to create a resource pool, and how resource costs are calculated in Microsoft Project. You will learn how to define resources and their costs and how to define costs that are not associated with a particular resource. With this foundation you will then be ready in ensuing chapters to assign resources and costs to tasks, modify those assignments, and resolve conflicts that arise with overallocated resources.

List of resource names

Figure 8.1
The list of resources includes information about the availability and cost of using the resources.

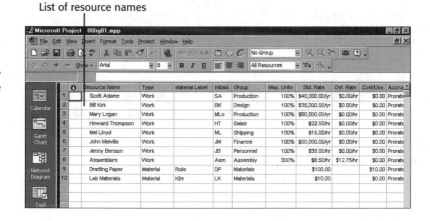

You can create a project schedule in Microsoft Project without assigning resources or costs to the tasks. You can enter all the task information and let Project schedule the tasks based on the factors discussed in Chapter 6, "Entering Scheduling Requirements."

That schedule, however, will be based on the assumption that you will have all the necessary resources on hand whenever you need them, an assumption which is rarely realistic. People take vacations, have sick leave, or have unique work schedules. Machinery and equipment need downtime for maintenance. Employees leave the organization and new ones arrive. New facilities are not ready for occupancy until midway through a project. All these are examples where the resource that is necessary to complete a task might not be available when Project schedules the task.

There are several major benefits of including your resources in the project file:

■ At the very least, you can attach the name of the person or persons responsible for the completion of each task.

■ If you provide the availability information for each resource, Project automatically schedules tasks only during the dates and times when the assigned resources are available.

■ Every project manager needs to know how much the project will cost. If you include the cost information for each resource, Project can automatically calculate the cost of each resource assignment to an individual task and sum those costs to show you the total cost of each task and the overall cost of the project. You can use these cost calculations in creating the budget for the project.

You can define a comprehensive list of resources at the outset, including resource cost rates and availability information, and then later assign these resources to the respective tasks; or you can define the resources as you create the tasks (while you are thinking about how the work will be done). When you assign new resource names to a task, Project adds these names to the roster of resources. If you create resources on the fly, you must remember to go back later and enter the resource cost rates and availability information.

Note

The Automatically Add New Resources and Tasks option (available on the General tab of the Options dialog box) determines how Project treats undefined resources that you assign to tasks. See the section "Setting the Automatically Add New Resources Option" later in this chapter to learn about the hazards of using this option.

UNDERSTANDING RESOURCES AND COSTS

Although the most important resources for your project are the people who do the work, you have to provide those people with the facilities in which to do the work and the equipment and materials they need to do their jobs. The cost of your project will usually be based on the sum cost of all the resources needed to complete each task.

DEFINING RESOURCES

The term *resource* refers to the people and assets that must be assigned to work on a task until it is completed. Resources will include workers, supervisors, managers, plant and equipment, facilities, supplies, and materials. You also might choose to assign as resources people who don't actually work on the task or whose work you do not need to measure (such as outside contractors or vendors), but whose name you want associated with the task. The list of resources available for work on a project is known as the *resource pool*.

Best Practice Tips from Toby Brown, PMP

Resources are typically defined as one of three types necessary to complete activities within a project.

People are the most common resource tracked and are usually listed one of three ways. First is by name (with the last name used since there is no defined first name field); second by type, which can be listed in the pool as a skill-set of multiple units; or, third, by outsourced vendor, providing an indication of accountability or responsibility for the task.

The next most common resource tracked is equipment. Sometimes use of a truck, crane, or computer might be necessary to complete work within a project.

Last, the tracking of materials or supplies can be closely monitored.

SINGLE RESOURCES AND RESOURCE SETS

Some resource names you add to the resource pool represent a single individual or asset. You can use a person's name, for example, as a resource name, or you can name a single piece of equipment as a resource. You can also define a *group resource* that represents multiple people who are similarly skilled, or multiple pieces of similar equipment. For example, you might define a group of five electricians as the Electricians resource and the set of four forklifts in the warehouse as the Forklift resource. Group resources are also called *resource sets* in Microsoft Project.

Caution

All the individuals in a group resource must share a common cost rate and will be scheduled by a single resource calendar that is defined for the group. You cannot assign unique cost rates to individual members of a resource group, and you cannot recognize individual vacation days or other nonworking times for members of the group.

WORK RESOURCES AND MATERIAL RESOURCES

Microsoft Project 2000 enables you to distinguish between what it defines as work resources and material resources. *Work resources* contribute part of their total time and effort (meaning, their work) to a task; but when the task is completed they have not been consumed by the task and they have future time that they can devote to other tasks. People, facilities, and equipment are examples of work resources. *Material resources*, however, are consumed or used up when they are assigned to a task and are no longer available to be assigned to other tasks. Concrete, lumber, and camera film are examples of material resources. Chapter 9, "Understanding Resource Scheduling," covers the way Project handles resource availability and costs for both resource types.

DEFINING COSTS

Project stores and calculates a number of different measures of cost. It is important that you understand what the different terms mean.

RESOURCE COSTS, FIXED COSTS, AND TOTAL COSTS

Most of the costs of a project are due to the cost of using resources to complete the project, and these costs are called *resource costs*. The cost of each work resource assigned to a task is generally based on the hours of work or effort associated with the assignment and the hourly cost of using the resource. If the duration of the task changes, the hours of assigned work changes and the cost of the resource assignment changes. Thus, Project adjusts costs as you revise the project schedule. For material resources, the cost is based on the cost of a unit of the material and the number of units assigned to the task.

If there are costs which are not specifically related to any one named resource, you can attach that amount of cost directly to the task. These costs are called *fixed costs*.

The sum of the resource costs and fixed costs is called *total cost*.

*Best Practice
Tips from Toby
Brown, PMP*

Sometimes a resource is procured at a fixed cost to the contract, like a consultant, for example. Many types of contracts have work performed according to a fixed-price or lump-sum agreement and, therefore, the project manager is usually not interested in tracking the hours worked or resource's hourly rate. In cases such as these, the contract-consultant can be listed in the resource pool and assigned to tasks for which he is responsible, but no costing is defined in the resource pool for these types of resources. Instead, a fixed cost is assigned directly to the task. Various accrual methods might also be defined which control when the cost is incurred against the project (at the start, prorated over the duration, or upon completion of the task).

RESOURCE COST CALCULATIONS   When you assign a work resource to a task, Project calculates the cost of the task by multiplying the cost rate per unit time for the resource by the amount of time the resource spends on the task. Thus, if a work resource costs $10 per hour and it spends 2 hours on a task assignment, Project calculates $20 as the cost of that assignment. If you assign multiple resource names to a task, the sum of all the individual resource assignment costs is totaled as the resource cost of the task.

Note

Resource rates can be defined as an amount per minute, hour, day, week, month, or year. The month time unit is new to Project 2000.

Material resource costs, on the other hand, are based solely on the number of units consumed or used up by the task and only indirectly, if at all, on the duration of the task. If the material resource goes directly into the output of the task, like lumber goes into framing a house, then the duration of the task has no effect on the number of units of material required for the task. If it takes carpenters longer to frame a house than anticipated, that would not change the amount of lumber that is needed. The material cost is simply the number of units of the resource (the board feet of lumber) multiplied by the per unit cost of the resource (the cost per board foot of lumber).

If the material resource is consumed by a work resource, like diesel fuel is consumed by a bulldozer, then the number of units consumed can be affected by the duration of the task. The longer the task, the more hours of work required from the work resource (the bulldozers) and therefore the more of the material resource (the fuel) that is needed. In this example the material cost is calculated by multiplying an estimate of the number of units consumed per unit of time (gallons of fuel per hour) by the cost per unit (cost per gallon).

FIXED COSTS   Fixed costs are costs incurred in completing a task but that are not attributable to any of the named resources assigned to the task. The legal fees associated with a contract or construction permit fees could be treated as fixed costs. Fixed costs are entered in the task table as a lump-sum amount.

*Tip from Tim and
the Project Team*

You should always document the reasons for the fixed-cost amount in the task note.

→ The steps you take to actually assign fixed costs to tasks is covered in Chapter 10. **See** "Assigning Fixed Costs and Fixed Contract Fees," **p. 435**

TOTAL COST   Together, the resource costs and the fixed costs add up to what Project displays as Total Cost. The actual field name is just Cost, but it is titled Total Cost in many views. Figure 8.2 shows the Gantt Chart with the Cost table displayed in the top pane and the Task Form in the bottom pane. The details of the resource costs are shown in the bottom pane. Note that the column titled Total Cost in the top pane is the total cost for the task, whereas the column titled Cost in the bottom pane is the cost of the individual resources assigned to the task.

To display the Cost table, right-click the blank space at the left end of the column header row (the space above the ID column). The shortcut menu that appears lists tables that can be displayed in the current view. Click Cost.

Figure 8.2
The Cost table displays Fixed Cost and Total Cost, with the difference between them being Resource Cost.

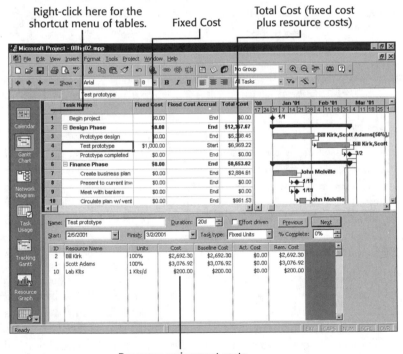

In Figure 8.2 the Test Prototype task is selected in the top pane. Its Fixed Cost and Total Cost appear in the top pane and the details for the assigned resources are shown in the bottom pane. Table 8.1 shows the way the costs in the view are connected.

TABLE 8.1 COST OF THE TEST PROTOTYPE TASK

	Amount
Top Pane	
Task Total Cost	$6,969.22
Fixed Cost	1,000.00
(Sum of Bottom Pane)	($5,969.22)
Bottom Pane	
Bill Kirk	$2,692.30
Scott Adams	3,076.92
Lab Kits	200.00

The cost of the work by Bill Kirk and Scott Adams plus the cost of the Lab Kits brings the resource cost to $5,969.22 for the task. There is also a $1,000.00 fixed cost for the task that brings the task's total cost to $6,969.22.

SCHEDULED COSTS, BASELINE COSTS, ACTUAL COSTS, AND COST VARIANCES

The Total Cost described in the last section (the sum of resource and fixed costs) is calculated as part of the current schedule and is sometimes also called the *scheduled cost*. At the end of the planning stage, just before starting the actual work on the project, the Project schedule will contain your final projections or estimates of what the project should cost. You will use the Save Baseline command to make a copy of these final cost estimates, called the *baseline costs* (also called the *budgeted costs*). You will use the baseline costs later for benchmark comparisons with the scheduled costs.

The reason you need to set aside the baseline copy of the scheduled costs is that the scheduled costs will probably change because of revisions in the schedule after work gets under way. For example, if you find that a task is going to take longer to finish than originally estimated and you change the duration of the task in the schedule, Project calculates new scheduled costs because of the additional work resources must now complete. But the baseline costs you set aside will remain unchanged as a record of the planned cost.

As work is completed on the project, you will track that information on a regular basis, marking some tasks as completed and others as partially complete. The cost of work that is completed on a task is accumulated as the task's *actual costs*. (See the next section, "Accrued Costs," for more information about calculating actual costs.) If unforeseen costs arise during the work on a task, you can add those to actual costs when the task is completed. Updates to actual costs are automatically copied to the scheduled costs to keep the schedule as accurate as possible. The baseline costs retain the original planned costs throughout this process.

The difference between the scheduled cost and the budgeted cost is called the *cost variance*. The actual calculation is Total Cost (scheduled cost) minus Baseline Cost (budgeted cost).

Thus, if the currently scheduled Total Cost is greater than the budgeted cost, the variance is a positive number. A positive cost variance means costs are over budget.

These additional cost fields are displayed in Figure 8.3 where the vertical divider bar has been moved to the right to display more of the Cost table. In the lower pane the scheduled cost is the column titled Cost and the actual cost is the column titled Act. Cost.

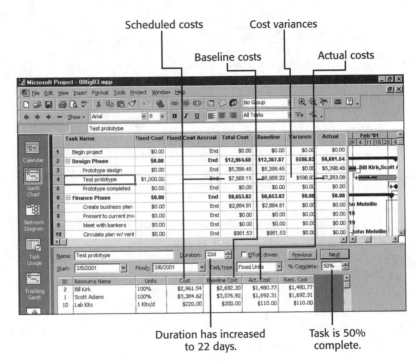

Figure 8.3
The Cost table also displays the Baseline Cost, Actual Cost, and Cost Variance (the difference between scheduled and baseline costs).

In order to illustrate the baseline and actual costs, some actual work has been marked as completed in Figure 8.3. Although you don't see the Percentage Complete field in this figure, the Prototype Design task has been marked as 100% complete and its actual cost is now the same as the scheduled and baseline costs with zero variance. After working on the Test Prototype task a bit, its estimated duration was increased from 20 days to 22 days—a change that has increased the scheduled cost of the resources that are assigned to the task. Also, the work on the Test Prototype task has now been marked as 50% complete.

The increase in the duration of the Test Prototype task in Figure 8.3 has increased the Cost entries for the assigned resources in the bottom pane. You can tell this because their scheduled costs (Costs) are greater than their baseline costs (which remain the same as they were in Figure 8.2).

Table 8.2 reproduces the cost details from Figure 8.3 to show you how the amounts are related. The task level totals and the Fixed Cost component from the top pane of the figure are in the first two rows. Then the resource cost subtotals are given followed by the individual resource details from the bottom pane of the figure. The Resources subtotals plus the Fixed Cost amounts add up to the Task Totals.

TABLE 8.2 RESOURCE COSTS WITH INCREASED DURATION AND 50% OF WORK COMPLETE

	Total Cost	Baseline	Variance	Actual Cost
Task Totals	$7,566.15	$6,969.22	$596.93	$3,283.08
Fixed Cost	1,000.00	1,000.00	+ .00	.00
Resources	6,566.15	5,969.22	+ 596.93	3,283.08
Bill Kirk	2,961.54	2,692.30	+ 269.24	1,480.77
Scott Adams	3,384.62	3,076.92	+ 307.69	1,692.31
Lab Kits	220.00	200.00	+ 20.00	110.00

Note that the actual costs for the resources are 50% of their scheduled costs (Total Cost), but the actual cost for the fixed cost is zero. The way Project calculates the actual costs when a task is started but not complete is discussed in the next section.

ACCRUED COSTS

When you mark a task as partially complete, Project must calculate the amount to be added to Actual Cost. These costs are called *accrued costs* and the way Project calculates them is governed by the *accrual method* selected for the resources or for the fixed cost. By default, if you mark a task partially complete, Project prorates the scheduled resource costs. In Figure 8.3, for example, the task is marked 50% complete and Project has applied 50% of the scheduled resource costs to actual cost. In Figure 8.3 the Fixed Cost Accrual setting for this task is End; so, Project applies all $1,000 of the fixed cost to actual cost only when the task is marked 100% complete.

When you define a resource or enter a fixed cost, you also specify the accrual method for determining when the cost will be recognized as actual cost. You can choose one of the following three methods for accruing costs as work on a task progresses:

- **Prorated**—The default accrual method for both material and work resources is *Prorated*. Project recognizes a prorated portion of the cost of the scheduled work as actual cost based on the percent complete entered for the task.

- **Start**—You can treat the resource cost as being fully expended the moment work on the task starts—the *Start* accrual method. For example, if the resource must be paid in full up front before it starts an assignment, you could recognize the full cost as expended as soon as work on a task starts.

- **End**—You can withhold recognition of the cost until the task is completed—the *End* accrual method. For example, if the resource will only be paid if the finished work on tasks is satisfactory, you might withhold recognition of the cost until the task is finished.

Note that the choice of the accrual method is only significant when tasks have started but are not complete. All three accrual methods yield the same result after tasks are completed.

DEFINING THE RESOURCE POOL

At first, you will probably define a separate resource pool in each project file. If you have multiple projects that use the same resources, however, you can design project files that use a resource pool—already defined in another project—that can be shared by all your projects. Using a shared resource pool has the advantage that Project can then show you the total demands being made on the shared resources from all projects sharing that pool.

→ To learn more about working with resources across multiple overlapping projects, **see** "Sharing Resources Among Projects," **p. 751**

Note

Many users create a project template containing no tasks but that defines a standard set of resources. When a new project file is started, it is created from a copy of this template, which then provides a ready-made resource pool. See "Preparing a File to Use as a Resource Template" in the Design Corner at the end of this chapter for the steps on creating a resource template file.

You can create the resource pool at any time, before or after you define the tasks. You can also add resources to the pool on-the-fly, so to speak, by assigning new (not previously defined) resources to tasks. By default, Project automatically adds new names to the resource pool.

Tip from Tim and the Project Team

You can elect not to automatically create new resources when you assign a new resource name. See the section "Setting the Automatically Add New Resources Option" later in this chapter. It is important to understand how this option works before you assign previously unnamed resources to tasks.

You can type the resource pool information into Project, or you can import resource names from another application. If you plan to use email to communicate with your resources, you can import their names and email addresses directly from the email Address Book.

 If you try to copy a list of resources from another application and paste it into Project, you might encounter some unexpected results. See "Pasting a Resource List from Another Application" in the "Troubleshooting" section near the end of this chapter for instructions on doing it successfully.

There are several views and view combinations you can use to create the resource list. This section briefly reviews those views and tools you are most likely to use without pausing to provide a full explanation for the many fields you can use. Then it uses those views to show you how to better use the individual fields.

USING THE RESOURCE SHEET

The Resource Sheet is perhaps the most effective view you can use for manually entering the names in the resource pool. The Resource Sheet enables you to see many resources in the pool at once, and you can see a number of important fields for each resource (see Figure 8.4). Indicators serve to notify that there is critical information in other fields. To display the Resource Sheet, choose View, Resource Sheet.

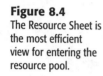

Best Practice
Tips from Toby
Brown, PMP

Although not obvious, the resources defined within the Resource Sheet create what is referred to as the resource pool. This pool details what resources are available within the specific project you are working on, or within the projects that are connected in the case of a shared resource pool solution. This pool does not specifically define which resources are assigned to tasks, but rather which ones are available to be assigned.

Overallocation   Notes
indicator   indicator

Figure 8.4
The Resource Sheet is the most efficient view for entering the resource pool.

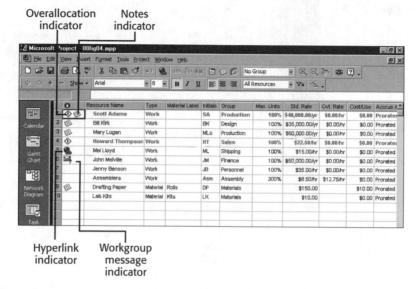

Hyperlink   Workgroup
indicator   message
                 indicator

If your video resolution is 800-by-600 pixels or less, you will not be able to see all the columns of the Resource Sheet without scrolling to the right. You might find it convenient to use the Window, Split command to have Project display the Resource Form in the lower pane (see Figure 8.5). The Resource Form shows details for the resource that is selected in the top pane. In the form you can see the additional fields that are not visible in the sheet above unless you were to scroll to the right.

You can also use the Resource Form to display and edit the Notes field. To display the Notes in the form, activate the Resource Form, choose Format, Details and select Notes. Figure 8.5 shows the Notes field in the details section of the Resource Form.

To add a resource in the Resource Sheet, follow the steps below. Remember that the full meaning and use of the fields is explained later in this chapter.

1. Select an empty cell in the Resource Name column and type in a descriptive name for the resource. Project will automatically supply default values for a number of fields to the right.

2. Replace the default values or fill in the blanks for the rest of the fields using the definitions and instructions in the "Using the Resource Fields" section that follows.

Figure 8.5
With the Resource Form in the lower pane, you can see the Notes field and other fields that are off the screen in the top pane.

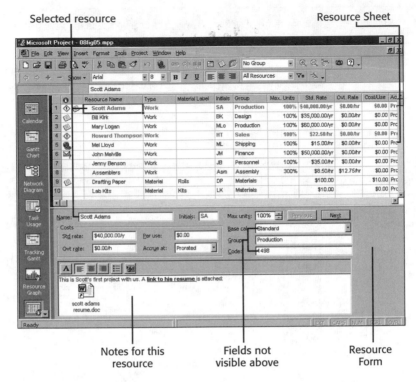

Selected resource — Resource Sheet

Notes for this resource — Fields not visible above — Resource Form

USING THE RESOURCE INFORMATION DIALOG BOX

There are several important resource fields that are not available on the Resource Sheet or the Resource Form. The Resource Information dialog box, on the other hand, contains almost all of the important resource definition fields (see Figure 8.6). The additional fields on the Resource Information dialog box supply information such as:

- When the resource is normally available for work
- When the normal working times are changed for vacations or other exceptions
- Alternative cost rates to use for different types of work
- When different cost rates for the resource will become effective
- How to provide electronic communication with the resource
- Notes about the resource

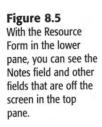 You can use the Resource Information dialog box with the Resource Sheet to complete the definition of the resource. Enter at least the resource name on the Resource Sheet. Then use the Resource Information tool on the Standard toolbar to display the Resource Information dialog box for that resource and fill in the rest of the fields. When finished with the dialog box, click OK to return to the Resource Sheet.

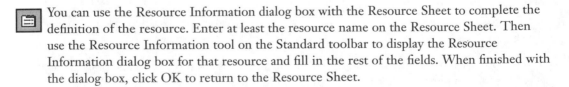

Figure 8.6
The Resource
Information dialog
box contains all the
important resource
definition fields on
four tabs.

Availability
table

Resource
calendar

Alternative cost rate
tables and cost
increases

Notes

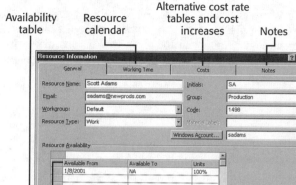

USING THE ASSIGN RESOURCES DIALOG BOX

 If you are using a task view such as the Gantt Chart, you can add names to the resource pool
with the Assign Resources dialog box (see Figure 8.7), and from there you can open the
Resource Information dialog box to add the rest of the resource fields.

Assign Resources tool

Assign Resources
dialog box

Figure 8.7
The Assign Resources
dialog box lets you
view the list of
resources and can be
used to view the
Resource Information
dialog box.

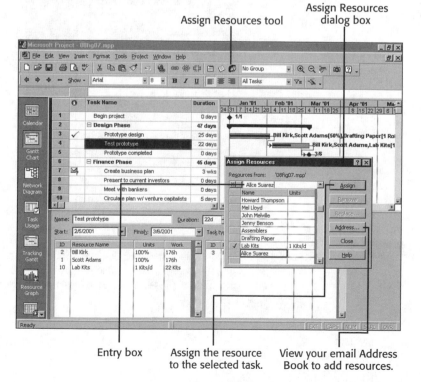

Entry box

Assign the resource
to the selected task.

View your email Address
Book to add resources.

Tip from Tim and the Project Team

The Assign Resources dialog box is one of the few dialog boxes in Microsoft Project that can be left open on the workspace as you switch between it and an underlying view. You can only display the Assign Resources dialog box when the active underlying view is a task view. After it is displayed, however, you can use it to create resource names no matter what the underlying view.

To add resource names with the Assign Resources dialog box, follow these steps:

1. With a task view active, choose the Assign Resources tool on the Standard toolbar to display the Assign Resources dialog box.

2. Select a blank cell in the Name column and type the name. The name will appear in the cell and also in the Entry box at the top of the dialog box as you type. Press Enter once, or click the green check mark next to the Entry box to add that name to the resource pool.

3. Alternatively, if the resource name is in your email Address Book, click the Address button to display the Address Book (see Figure 8.8) and select the name from the list in the Address Book. Click the Add button and then OK to add the name to your resource pool.

Figure 8.8
Use your email Address Book to import names and email addresses into Project as resources.

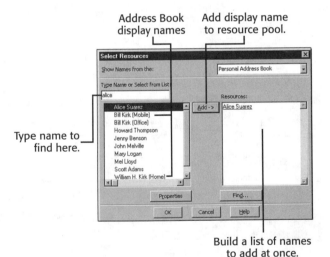

Address Book display names

Add display name to resource pool.

Type name to find here.

Build a list of names to add at once.

Caution

Be careful if you are just creating the resource name and don't intend to assign it to the task that is selected in the underlying view. When you press Enter after typing the name, the Assign button becomes activated—pressing Enter again would assign the resource to the currently selected task.

After you add a name in the Assign Resources dialog box, you can double-click the name to view the Resource Information dialog box for that resource and fill in the additional resource definition fields.

USING THE TASK FORM

The Gantt Chart with the Task Form in the lower pane is one of the popular views for assigning resources. You can also add resources to the resource pool in that view, using the Resource details in the lower pane. To add resources in the Task Form, follow these steps:

1. Display the Gantt Chart and then choose Window, Split to display the Task Form in the lower pane.

2. If the resource details are not displayed in the Task Form, click anywhere in the lower pane to activate it and then choose Format, Details from the menu and select one of the resource listings—for example, Resources and Predecessors (see Figure 8.9).

3. Select a task in the top pane.

4. Click in the Resource Name column in the Task Form where you can select an existing resource to assign to the task, or you can type in the name of a new resource to assign. In Figure 8.9, "John Melville" is being typed in to add to the resource pool. If you type in a new name and click the OK button, Project adds the resource to the resource pool and supplies default values for the assignment Units and Work if you didn't. Chapter 10, "Assigning Resources and Costs to Tasks," discusses how to use the Units and Work fields.

5. Double-click the resource name to display the Resource Information dialog box where you can fill in the rest of the fields that define the resource.

→ For a full discussion of the assignment fields, **see** "Understanding the Resource Assignment Fields," **p. 369**

Figure 8.9
Use the Resource Name column to both enter a new resource name and assign it to a task at the same time.

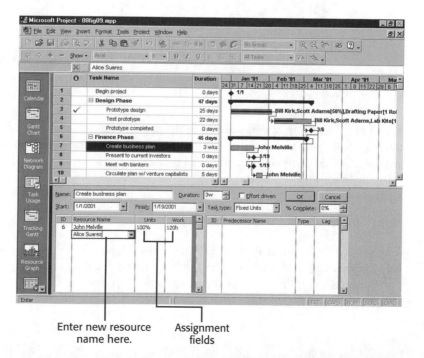

Enter new resource name here.

Assignment fields

Now that you have seen the views that are most useful for defining the resource pool, the next sections explore the various resource fields in detail to show you how to use them to define your resources to get the most out of Microsoft Project.

USING THE RESOURCE FIELDS

As stated before, the best view for typing and reviewing the list of resources is the Resource Sheet. It can be used in combination with the Resource Information dialog box to enter all the important fields of information that define a resource. The Resource Sheet and Resource Information dialog box are shown in Figure 8.10.

Selected resource   Resource Information dialog box

Figure 8.10
The Resource Sheet is the primary data-entry view for defining resources.

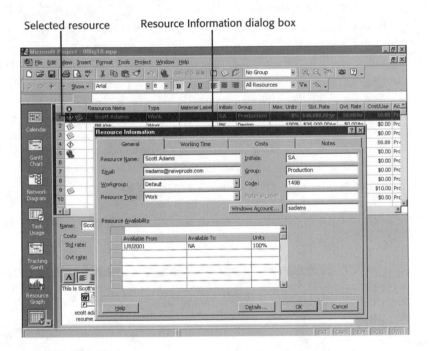

When you define a resource, you should provide a resource name and information about the availability and cost of the resource. The fields commonly used in defining resources are listed in the following sections. The order of the listing is based mainly on the order of the columns in the Resource Sheet and on the related fields in the Resource Information dialog box.

ID

The row numbers on the Resource Sheet are the *ID numbers* for the resources. As with task ID numbers, you cannot edit this field, but if you move a resource on the list it automatically acquires the ID number for the row number you move it to. The ID number does not appear in the Resource Information dialog box.

INDICATORS

The *Indicator* field displays icons representing the status of critical fields that might not normally be displayed. For example, the overallocated indicator for Scott Adams in Figure 8.10 means that Scott's time has been overallocated at some point in the project (he has been booked in two places at the same time). The note indicator for Mary Logan indicates that there is text in her Notes field. The hyperlink indicator for Mel Lloyd indicates a hyperlink associating Mel with a Web site or a document file. The TeamAssign workgroup indicator next to John Melville indicates that he has not responded to one or more messages notifying him of task assignments. Indicators only appear on resource table views such as the Resource Sheet.

NAME

Use the *Resource Name* field to provide a descriptive name for the resource. The name can contain any characters except the Windows separator character (by default the comma) and the square brackets ([]). Resource names can be up to 255 characters long and they don't have to be unique (because resources are identified by their ID numbers). However, if you assign a non-unique resource name to a task, Project uses the first resource it finds with that name in the resource list. The resource name can be a specific name, such as Anita Salinas, or it can describe a group of resources, such as Electricians.

Best Practice Tips from Toby Brown, PMP

> For a larger pool of resources, it might be preferable to list them by last name instead of by first name. Many times, the first name might be "Bill" but listed as "William" in the pool. Without obvious naming conventions, scrolling through a list of hundreds of names can be tedious, at best.

TYPE

 As stated previously, Project 2000 distinguishes between *work resources*—those that contribute their work to tasks but are not thereby consumed in the process—and *material resources*, those resources that are consumed in the process. The cost of the work resources is based on the number of hours they work on a task and the hourly cost for the resource. The cost of the material resources is based on the cost of a unit of the resource and how many units are consumed. The default resource type is Work, but you can use the drop-down arrow to select either Work or Material.

Caution

> When you assign a resource to a task, its type determines how the assignment affects the schedule for the task. If it is a work resource, the resource calendar determines when work can take place; if it is a material resource, there is no resource calendar to consider. Thus, if you try to change the type of a resource after it has been assigned, Project warns you that the schedule will be affected and that the changes cannot be undone (see Figure 8.11). Be cautious about changing resource types after they are assigned to tasks.

Figure 8.11
Changing the type of a resource that is already assigned to tasks can affect the task schedule with changes that can't be reversed with the Undo command.

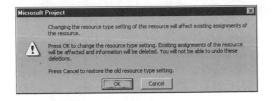

MATERIAL LABEL

 Use the *Material Label* field to define the unit of measure used for material resources (for example, gallons, bushels, tons, liters, and so on). You use that unit when you assign the resource to tasks and when you define the unit cost of the resource. This field is unavailable for work resources.

If the amount of the material resource that is consumed doesn't depend on the duration of the task, it is said to have a *fixed consumption rate*. For example, the amount of concrete used in pouring a foundation does not depend on the duration of the task and its material label could be Cubic Yards.

If the amount of the material resource consumed varies with the duration of the task, it is said to have a *variable consumption rate*. In calculating the cost of using a variable consumption rate material resource, Project factors the duration of the task into the calculation.

In order to tell Project that it should factor duration into the calculated cost for a material resource, you have to append a time unit abbreviation when you enter the assignment units. For example, to assign 5 gallons of diesel fuel per hour to a task, you would enter the units as 5/h.

→ For details on assigning material resources to tasks, **see** "Assigning Material Resource Units," **p. 370**

INITIALS

The *Initials* field provides a place for a shortened form of the resource name that can be used in views such as the Gantt Chart or Network Diagram to save space and reduce the clutter that using the full names sometimes creates. When you first enter the resource name in a new row, Project supplies the first character of the name as the default initial and makes no attempt to keep it unique. You should edit the initial to make it uniquely identify the resource.

GROUP

The *Group* field provides a place to enter an identifying label or number that you can use for sorting, grouping, or filtering resources. For example, you could identify all management personnel by entering Management; all equipment resources by entering Equipment; and all vendors and contractors by entering Vendors. Some users put the name of the department that manages a resource in the Group field. With these labels entered, you can then use the Resource Group filter to view only the resources that have one of those values in this field.

If a resource belongs to multiple groups, or if you want to be able to group the resources in several different ways, you can enter multiple labels in the Group field as long as they are separated by a comma or space. You can enter any combination of letters, numbers, spaces, or other characters, up to a total of 255 characters.

For example, suppose you want to identify resources by the department managing them (Production, Marketing, Finance, and so on), their job title (Manager, Foreman, Carpenter, Driver, and so forth), and the skill level they bring to their task assignments (Trainee, Semi-Skilled, Skilled, Expert). For a trainee electrician in the production department you could enter this text string in the Group field: Production, Electrician, Trainee.

→ You could also use separate custom text fields for each of the categories described in the example. For information on creating and using custom fields, **see** "Customizing Fields," **p. 956**

Tip from Tim and the Project Team	When applying a filter to locate one label in a list in the Group field, use the logical test "contains" rather than "equals." See the "Filtering Resources" section toward the end of this chapter for an example of using filters.

 If you have put multiple group labels in the Group field and want to filter the resource pool for one of the labels, see "Filtering for Labels Contained in the Group Field" in the "Troubleshooting" section at the end of this chapter.

Tip from Tim and the Project Team	Don't confuse the Group field with the concept of a *group resource*. A group resource is a resource representing a set of multiple resource units that all serve the same function and are identified with one ID and name.
	Also, don't confuse the Group field with the Group By command on the Project menu. That command can sort and group records based on the entries in any field (including the Group field). See "Grouping Resources" later in this chapter.

THE RESOURCE AVAILABILITY FIELDS

There are several fields that together define the *availability* of the resource—exactly how many units of the resource are available for work and how many hours of work can be assigned to the resource on any given date:

- The Max Units field specifies the number of units of the resource that are normally available on any given date.

- If that number will be changing over time during the project, the changes will be listed in the Resource Availability table in the Resource Information dialog box.

- One of the project's base calendars is designated as the source of the normal working days and hours for the resource calendar.

- The Working Times in the resource calendar define for individual days any exceptions to the base calendar's normal schedule.

You can enter the Max Units and the Base Calendar to which the resource is linked on the Resource Sheet, but you must use the Resource Information dialog box to enter the rest of the availability information.

MAX UNITS

Use the *Max Units* field to enter the maximum number of units that can be assigned to tasks at any one time. Project uses the Max Units field to determine when more units of the resource have been assigned than are available—in other words, when the resource is overallocated. Because you can assign resources to multiple tasks (in multiple projects), it's possible to assign a given resource to tasks that are scheduled at the same or overlapping times. If the sum of the resource units assigned to all tasks at a given moment exceeds the entry in the Max Units field, Project calculates that the resource is overallocated, and displays a symbol in the Indicator field to flag the overallocated resource for you.

The Max Units field can be formatted as a percentage or as a decimal, with the default being the percentage format. The next chapter—when discussing assigning resources to tasks—explains why the percentage format is used as the default.

Note You can change the format for the Max Units field in the Options dialog box. Choose Tools, Options, and select the Schedule tab. Use the drop-down list in the Show Assignment Units As A box, and select either Percentage or Decimal.

By default the resource is assumed to be available 100% of the available time on its calendar for the duration of the project. Resources that work half-time would only be available for 50% of the hours on the calendar. Group resources could work a multiple of the hours on the calendar in any one day. For example, five electricians could work 500% of the hours on the calendar in one day.

Project supplies a default Max Units value of 100% (or 1 in decimal format) when you create a resource. However, you can enter any value between 0% and 6,000,000,000% (between 0 and 60,000,000 in decimal format). For a single unit resource, the default value of 100% means that this resource is available to work 100% of the hours on its calendar on this project. If you are grouping resources into a set, you would enter a value greater than 100%. Thus, if you have five electricians in an Electricians resource, you would enter 500% (or 5 in decimal format).

Tip from Tim and the Project Team There is no Max Units value for material resources. Project assumes that you will acquire as many units as you have assigned.

RESOURCE AVAILABILITY

New to Microsoft Project 2000 is the capability of defining different Max Units values for different time periods. For example, sometimes a resource won't be available until after the project starts and up until that date its Max Units is 0%. Or a resource might leave the organization before the project is completed and after its final date the Max Units is 0%.

You also might intend to add more units of the resource over the duration of the project and would need to record the dates when the additional units would come on board. Use the *Resource Availability* table on the General tab of the Resource Information dialog box to define the time periods and the Units (Max Units) for each time period (see Figure 8.12).

The Max Units field on the Resource Sheet and on the Resource Form displays the Max Units value for the *current date* on the Resource Availability table. The current date is normally the computer's current date, but it can be any date you choose to enter into the Current Date field in the Project Information dialog box.

In Figure 8.12, for example, Scott Adams's Resource Availability table shows that he will not start work until 1/8/2001, even though the project starts on 1/1/2001. The "NA" in the Available To column indicates that a date is not applicable because there is no ending date foreseen. If you look at his Max Units field on the Resource Sheet on any date prior to 1/8/2001, the value will be 0%; after that date, it will be 100%.

Figure 8.12
The Resource Availability table shows dated changes in the availability of a resource.

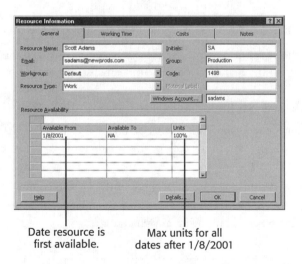

Date resource is first available.

Max units for all dates after 1/8/2001

The default values in the Resource Availability table are "NA" for both the Available From and Available To columns and the Units (Max Units) is 100%. This means that there are no applicable starting or ending dates for the Units value.

Figure 8.13 shows the Resource Availability table for the Assemblers resource. The "NA" in the Available From field means that there is no beginning date for the 300% units. But, starting on 4/1/2001 an additional assembler will be hired, bringing the Max Units to 400%; and a new hire is scheduled for 7/1/2001, bringing the total to 500%.

Figure 8.13
Use multiple Resource Availability rows to show how the Max Units of a resource will be "ramped up" over time.

Starting at these dates the units change.

NA means no set date.

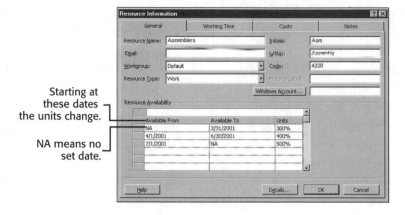

When Project examines this project schedule to see if the Assembler resource is overallocated, it shows the overallocated indicator if the total assignments for the Assembler resource exceeds 300% on any date to 3/31/2001, or exceeds 400% on any date thereafter until 6/30/2001, or is more than 500% on 7/1/2001 and later dates.

To change the Resource Availability table for a resource, follow these steps:

1. In a view that shows resource names, select the resource and click the Resource Information tool on the Standard toolbar. You can also just double-click the resource name.

2. Click the General tab if it is not displayed.

3. Click the cell for the date you want to change under the Available From or Available To column. You can either type in the date or use the drop-down arrow to display the date-picker and select the date.

4. Enter the Max Units for that row's date range in the Units column.

5. After all entries are completed, click OK to save the changes. You can also click Cancel to close the dialog box without saving any changes.

Tip from Tim and the Project Team

Be sure that the dates in the Resource Availability table are in sequential order and that you leave no gaps in the dates from one row to the next. If you have an Available From date that is more than one day later than the Available To date on the previous row, Project will use 0% as the Max Units for the dates in the gap.

If you have more than one row in the Resource Availability table, you shouldn't have an "NA" entry in the Available From column except on the first row, and you shouldn't have an "NA" entry in the Available To column except in the last row.

BASE CALENDAR

Use the *Base Calendar* field to name the project calendar on which the working time in the resource's calendar is based. The Base Calendar field is available on both the Resource Sheet and on the Working Time tab of the Resource Information dialog box.

Note

Material resources do not have a calendar because they are assumed to be always available. The Working Time tab in the Resource Information dialog box is unavailable for a material resource.

Use the drop-down arrows to show a list of all the base calendars that have been defined, and select the one that most closely fits this resource. The resource calendar inherits all the working days and hours as well as the individually marked nonworking days and hours that are defined in its base calendar. The default base calendar is Standard.

Tip from Tim and the Project Team

If you have more than one named resource with the same set of exceptions to one of the standard base calendars, you might want to create a special base calendar for those resources. Otherwise, you will have to mark the same exceptions in each of the resource calendars. For example, if a number of resources will be assigned to work on a project on a night shift, and they all have the same basic schedule of night work hours, creating a base calendar for night shift work and then using that base calendar for all workers with those hours saves you time. With this method, you only define the hours once, instead of customizing each night-shift worker's resource calendar.

Tip from Tim and the Project Team

If you create additional base calendars in your project that resources or tasks are linked to, remember to make organizationwide changes in working days and hours to all base calendars. If your company decides to make December 24 a holiday, for example, you need to edit each base calendar used by resources or tasks in order to apply the holiday to all schedules.

→ For instructions on creating base calendars, **see** Chapter 3, "Setting up a New Project Document," **p. 63**

WORKING TIME

As mentioned above, the resource calendar is based on one of the base calendars and it inherits all the normal working times per week as well as all the holidays or other exceptions to the normal working times. You use the resource calendar to enter exceptions for the resource to the working time on the base calendar. Use the date and time fields on the Working Time tab of the Resource Information dialog box to enter the resource's exceptions. For instance, in Figure 8.14 the resource calendar for Bill Kirk shows that he will not be working March 26–30. This is a week of vacation he has scheduled.

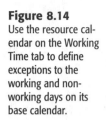

Figure 8.14
Use the resource calendar on the Working Time tab to define exceptions to the working and nonworking days on its base calendar.

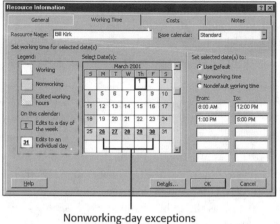

Nonworking-day exceptions
(vacation days)

Note You can also edit a resource calendar from the Change Working Time dialog box, although you can't change the base calendar it's linked to there. Choose Tools, Change Working Time to display the Change Working Time dialog box and use the drop-down list in the For box to select the resource name.

To edit the calendar days and hours, use the techniques described in Chapter 3, "Setting Up a New Project Document," in the section "Defining a Calendar of Working Time." Follow these additional steps to edit a resource calendar:

1. Select the resource in a resource view or on the Assign Resources dialog box and double-click the resource name to display the Resource Information dialog box. Select the Working Time tab to display the resource calendar and time fields.

2. You can use the Base Calendar drop-down list to select the base calendar for the resource.

3. To give the resource time-off on dates that are normal working dates on the base calendar, select the dates and click the Nonworking Time button. For example, in Figure 8.15 the date November 9 is a standard working day but Mary Logan has chosen to take the day off. On her calendar the date is shaded to show it is nonworking and the date is underlined to show that it is an exception to the base calendar. You would click on November 9 and then click the Nonworking Time button to turn it into a nonworking date. Note that you would have to select a different date to change the selection highlight before you can see the shading on November 9.

4. To schedule a resource for work on dates that are normally nonworking dates, select the dates (they are shaded before you select them) and click the Nondefault Working Time button. The dates are no longer shaded but the underlined date numerals indicate that they are an exception.

For example, Mary Logan has agreed to work on a date that is normally a holiday (November 30) to make up for the nonworking day on November 9. To show this on her calendar, you would select November 30 and click the Nondefault Working Time button.

5. Modify the hours of work on any date as needed. The date appears with a diagonal shading pattern to indicate that the hours are non-standard for that day of the week, and the date will be underlined to show that it is an exception to the base calendar.

6. If a date is marked as an exception on the resource calendar, but you want to remove the exception and return it to the default for the base calendar, select the date and click the Use Default option button.

7. Choose the OK button to save your changes in the resource calendar, or choose the Cancel button to abandon the changes without saving them.

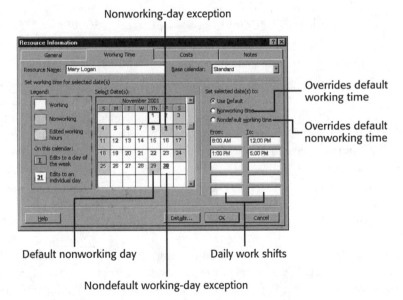

Figure 8.15
Use the Working Time tab to record exceptions to the base calendar on which the resource calendar is based.

Nonworking-day exception

Overrides default working time

Overrides default nonworking time

Default nonworking day

Daily work shifts

Nondefault working-day exception

THE RESOURCE COST FIELDS

You can associate three cost measures with a resource: its Standard Rate (for work during normal working hours), its Overtime Rate (for work during overtime hours), and its Cost Per Use (a special one-time cost per assigned unit without regard to the number of hours worked). Each of these cost measures has a default rate which you can define in the Resource Sheet.

If you want to charge different rates for different kinds of work, you can create four additional sets of the three rates in the Resource Information dialog box. For example, you might want to charge different standard rates and overtime rates for an electrician depending on whether the task involves new residential wiring, new commercial wiring, modifying existing residential wiring, or modifying existing commercial wiring.

Finally, Project recognizes that you might have planned changes in these rates that will take place over the duration of the project. For example, you might plan to increase each cost by 5% a year. Consequently, you can define rate changes and the dates when those changes become effective for all of the rates described above. If the task schedule causes an assignment to extend into one of the higher-cost periods, Project uses the higher cost for that portion of the assignment that falls in that period.

STANDARD RATE

Use the *Standard Rate* field to show the current default cost of each unit (each 100% of a unit) of the resource assigned to a task:

- For work resources the standard rate is the amount to charge per unit of normal working time. Enter the rate as a number, followed by a forward slash, and one of the following time units or its abbreviation: minute(m), hour(h), day(d), week(w), month(mo) or year(y). If you type just a number (without a time unit), Project assumes it's an hourly rate. For example, type **600/w** for $600 per week, **35000/y** for $35,000 per year, or just **15.5** for $15.50 per hour.

  For example, suppose that you were to rent a bulldozer for $1,200 per week. You could create a resource named Bulldozer with a standard rate of 1200/week.

- For material resources, the standard rate is the amount to charge tasks per unit of the resource consumed. There is no time unit appended to the dollar amount. The Standard Rate is entered just as an amount, with no time unit, and is understood to be the amount per unit of the resource, where the unit to use is defined in the Material Label field.

  For example, if you include Diesel Fuel as a material resource for the bulldozer, its Material Label might be Gallons and the Standard Rate might be 1 (which means $1 per gallon).

If the standard rate is entered with a time unit, the rate is converted to an hourly rate and is applied to the number of hours of work it takes to complete the task. For annual rates, the hourly rate is calculated by assuming 52 weeks in a year, and the number of hours per week is that which is defined on the Calendar tab of the Options dialog box. For the standard workweek of 40 hours, for example, the annual rate is divided by 2,080 (52 times 40) to get an hourly rate. For monthly rates the hourly rate is calculated using the Calendar tab's definitions for days in a month and hours in a day.

In addition to the default standard rate, you can define four additional rates that can be used for assignments when you want to charge more or less than the default rate. See the "The Cost Rate Tables" section later in this chapter for details.

Best Practice Tips from Toby Brown, PMP

Although the standard rate is frequently the salaried rate for an associate, organizations often define the standard rate as the billed-at rate. Defined in this manner, a project plan serves as an estimate for the work to be performed under contract.

Many times, a defined project plan demonstrates to a client early in the proposal stage that their needs are recognized and acknowledged. Expectations are then set for the project in the early stages of planning, right from the beginning. And estimates of costs and work are based on defined work rather than ball-park estimates, mitigating some of the risks in contracting for work.

OVERTIME RATE

Project uses the entry in the *Overtime Rate* field when calculating the cost of overtime hours that you schedule for a work resource. There is no overtime rate for material resources. The default overtime rate is zero (0.00), so for salaried employees you can leave the zero value if they are not paid for their overtime hours. If the rate for overtime work is the same as the regular rate, you must enter that amount again in the Overtime Rate field or overtime hours will be charged at the zero default rate.

Tip from Tim and the Project Team

You can also use the overtime rate to reflect the opportunity cost of using a resource in overtime. For example, if a salaried employee with an overtime rate of zero were to be assigned to do all the work on a task in overtime, the cost of the task would be zero and the task will add nothing to the cost of the project! This seems like a great way to lower costs.

Though the time spent working overtime on a task might not add to payroll costs, that time could have been used on completing other tasks or other projects, and the failure to complete those other tasks is an opportunity cost to the organization.

By this logic, the overtime rate should never be zero but at least as much as the standard rate to reflect the opportunity cost to the organization of using the resource to complete the task.

As with the standard rate, you can define four additional overtime rates for each resource and use them for special tasks. See the "The Cost Rate Tables" section later in this chapter.

Note

You can set default values for the Standard and Overtime Rates for all new resources in the Options dialog box. Choose Tools, Options and click the General tab. Enter an amount per time unit in both the Default Standard Rate and the Default Overtime Rate fields. All resources added from that point on initially show these default rates.

COST PER USE

The *Cost Per Use* field (which is titled Cost/Use on the Resource Sheet and Per Use Cost on the Resource Information dialog box) contains any cost that is to be charged once for each unit (each 100% of a unit) of the resource assigned to a task, regardless of the duration of the assignment. It was designed to be used for material resources before there was a Type field to distinguish material and work resources. With the new resource type designation for material resources, you can use the Standard Rate field to show the cost of each unit of a material resource.

You should always be careful with the Cost Per Use field with work resources. The amount entered in that field will be charged once for each 100% of the resource that is assigned to any task. For example, if you rent a piece of equipment by the hour but also have to pay a flat charge of $200 for having it delivered to your work site, you could treat the delivery charge as a Cost Per Use. If you assign the equipment to more than one task, however, the delivery charge would be charged multiple times (once for each assignment), which would overstate the true costs. It would be better in this example to record the delivery charge as a Fixed Cost attached to one of the tasks that use the resource or to a summary task that includes all the tasks that are affected.

Best Practice Tips from Toby Brown, PMP

Be sure to take advantage of Cost Per Use when you're laying out your project plans. One example of this would be a required trip charge for deploying that resource. Perhaps a refrigerator repair man charges $50 to examine a problem with your ice-box regardless of the number of hours spent and the materials necessary to fix the problem. Cost Per Use allows you to assign flat-rate costs to various tasks.

THE COST RATE TABLES

The Costs tab of the Resource Information dialog box contains five Cost Rate Tables (A through E) which show the default cost rates (Table A) plus four other levels of cost that you can define for different types of assignments. For example, an Electrician resource's Table A would contain its default rates, which might be for new commercial wiring assignments. Table B might contain the rates for new residential wiring assignments, Table C might show rates for modifying commercial wiring, and Table D might contain the rates for modifying residential wiring. You can select the rate to apply to an assignment in the Assignment Information dialog box.

→ For use of the cost rate tables in assignments, **see** "Assigning Resources and Costs to Tasks," **p. 401**

Tip from Tim and the Project Team

Because you can't change the labels on the five cost tabs to something more descriptive than A–E, you should document what each rate is to be used for in the resource Notes field.

Figure 8.16 shows cost rate table A for Scott Adams. This table defines the default cost rates to use for his assignments.

Figure 8.16
Use the cost rate tables to show different cost rates for different types of work and to show planned changes in the rates.

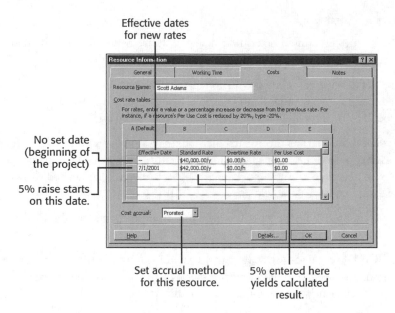

Effective dates
for new rates

No set date
(beginning of
the project)

5% raise starts
on this date.

Set accrual method
for this resource.

5% entered here
yields calculated
result.

You can also allow for changes over time in these rates. For example, if you assume that inflation will cause your costs to rise by 5% per year, you could show different rates for each of the years during which the project lasts. In Figure 8.16, Scott Adams will get a raise on 7/1/2001, which is the end of his probationary period.

The entry in the first cell of the Effective Date column is always two dashes, signifying that there is no set start date for that level of rates. To enter additional levels for subsequent dates, enter the change date in the Effective Date column and then enter the values for the Standard Rate, Overtime Rate, and Per Use Cost. You can enter up to 25 dated rate changes in each tab.

If you want Project to calculate a percentage increase or decrease in one of the rates, just enter the plus or minus percentage (with a percent sign) and when you leave the cell Project applies that increase to the value in the cell just above, displaying the result instead of the percentage you had entered. For example, the entry for Scott Adams in Figure 8.16 for 7/1/2001 was created by typing "+5%" into the second row cell under Standard Rate. As soon as the next cell was selected, Project calculated a 5% increase over the $40,000 amount in the first row (which is an increase of $2,000 to $42,000) and replaced the 5% entry with $42,000.

Best Practice Tips from Toby Brown, PMP

Often times, the various cost tables allow for the use of a resource that might serve various functions within the project and be billed at different rates for various services. Say, for example, that your resource pool has a programmer who is billed at one rate for programming in Visual Basic, but charges a different rate for programming in Java. By factoring in the resource's competency in using each programming language, a different rate can be charged for utilizing the same resource with various skill-sets within the same project.

COST ACCRUAL

The Cost Accrual field determines when costs are recognized for Standard and Overtime costs. Choose one of the three options: Start, End, and Prorated.

The default accrual method is Prorated, which means that if you mark a task as 25% completed, the actual standard and overtime costs for all assigned resources would be estimated to be 25% of the scheduled or estimated cost of those assignments.

If you choose Start as the accrual method, then as soon as you indicate that any of the task work has been done, Project considers the entire standard and overtime costs of the assignment as actual cost. Any report generated after the task has started shows the entire cost of the assignment as already incurred.

If you choose End, Project defers recognition of the actual cost until you enter a finish date and the assignment is 100% complete.

The Cost Accrual setting only matters when printing interim reports and work on a task assignment has started but is not finished. The Cost Per Use is always added to actual cost the moment work starts on a task, no matter what the Cost Accrual setting happens to be.

Note

The Cost Per Use is always accrued at the Start of an assignment, no matter which accrual method you choose for the resource. Only the standard and overtime rates are affected by the accrual method you choose.

CODE

The Code field can be used to enter any arbitrary code that you want to associate with a resource. It was used in earlier versions of Project to show cost accounting codes so that you could relate assignment costs to the organization's accounting system. The new Outline Codes discussed in Chapter 5, "Creating a Task List," now provide better functionality for that purpose because they allow you to create lookup lists to use when filling in the codes. You can enter any kind of information and can use any combination of up to 255 symbols and characters in this field.

Tip from Tim and the Project Team

You can use the code field to help you keep track of miscellaneous information about specific resources. For example, you can use this field to include Employee ID number, Social Security number, or phone number for the resource.

WORKGROUP FIELDS

Project can help you communicate with your human resources either through email messages or by posting information to a Web site that the resource can access with a browser. You will need to define for each resource the type of workgroup communication to use. If it's to be email, you will also need to let Project know the email address. If you will be using Project's new Project Central workgroup feature, you will also need to let Project know the resource's account name on the server.

The workgroup fields are on the General tab of the Resource Information dialog box (see Figure 8.17).

Figure 8.17
Use the Email and Workgroup fields on the Resource Information dialog box to define workgroup messaging for the resource.

Workgroup communication method

Email address field

Windows account

Details button

WORKGROUP

Use the Workgroup field to define the type of communication you will use for this resource: Default, Email, Web, or None.

The project has a default messaging method which is set in the Options dialog box. To set the default messaging method for the project, choose Tools, Options and click the Workgroup tab. In the Default Workgroup Messages field, choose None, Email, or Web. For the individual resource, as in Figure 8.17, the default value for the Workgroup field is in fact "Default"—which means use the project's default messaging method.

If a particular resource does not have access to the project's default communication method but can take advantage of a different method, indicate that choice in the resource Workgroup field. For example, if the default method for the project will be a Web site on the organization's intranet, most of the resources who are employees have access to the intranet site and you can leave the Workgroup field set at Default for those resources. However, an outside resource or one who travels might have to use email, and for that resource you would set the Workgroup field to Email.

→ For more information on setting up and using workgroup communications, **see** Chapter 15, "Using Microsoft Project in Workgroups," **p. 603**

EMAIL

If the workgroup communication method for the resource will be email, Project needs to know the email address for the resource. If you enter an email address in the Email field, Project uses that address when it sends a message to the resource. For example, if Bill Kirk's email address is "bkirk@newprods.com", you can enter that in the E<u>m</u>ail field and Project always addresses his messages to that address.

You can also enable Project to look up the address in an email address book. Your email software has an organizational or personal Address Book that contains *display names* and *email addresses* for email recipients (see Figure 8.18). For example, the resource shown in Figure 8.17, Bill Kirk, might be listed in the Address Book with the display name "Bill Kirk (Office)". You can enter into the E<u>m</u>ail field for Bill Kirk the display name "Bill Kirk (Office)" and Project looks up the address for that display name each time it sends an email message to the resource.

Type name to find here.

Figure 8.18
Project can look for a resource's name among the display names in your email software's Address Book.

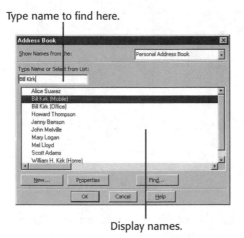

Display names.

Tip from Tim and the Project Team

If the email address for a resource were to change and you rely on Project to look up the address in the Address Book, you only have to enter the change in the address in one place, the Address Book. If you have placed the email address in the E<u>m</u>ail field, you must remember to change it in both the Address Book and in the E<u>m</u>ail field on the Resource Information dialog box.

Note

If you have created the resource by using the A<u>d</u>dress button on the Assign Resources dialog box to choose a name from the email Address Book (see "Using the Assign Resources Dialog Box" previously in this chapter), then Project automatically puts the display name you chose from the Address Book into the E<u>m</u>ail field.

When you instruct Project to send an email message to a resource, it searches for an email address for the resource using the following rules:

- First, Project checks the E<u>m</u>ail field to see if it contains what looks like a valid email address format. Valid addresses contain a user name, the "@" symbol and a mailbox name; for example, "bkirk@newprods.com" is a valid email address format. If the entry looks like a valid email address, Project will send the message to that address.

- If there is an entry in the E<u>m</u>ail field but it doesn't look like an email address, Project assumes that the entry is a display name and attempts to find it among the display names in the email Address Book. In searching for a match, Project looks for display names that contain the text string it found in the E<u>m</u>ail field. For example, if you put just "Kirk" in the E<u>m</u>ail field, Project would consider display names such as "Bill Kirk", "Kirk, Bill", and "William B. Kirk" as legitimate possibilities.

- If there is no entry in the E<u>m</u>ail field, then Project attempts to find the resource name itself within one of the display names in the Address Book.

Tip from Tim and the Project Team

> If you think you might ever use the project file to send messages when the Address Book is not available, then you should put the actual email address in each resource's E<u>m</u>ail field. This would be necessary, for example, if you use a mobile computer and do not always have access to the organizational Address Book. It would also be necessary if you are using the personal Address Book on your computer and the project file is copied to a different computer where the display names are different or non-existent.

Thus, if Project doesn't find a valid email address in the E<u>m</u>ail field, it searches for a matching display name in the Address Book using the entry in the E<u>m</u>ail field or, if that's blank, using the resource name. What happens next depends on what Project finds in the Address Book—whether it finds just one match, no match, or multiple matches. Project takes the following actions:

- If Project finds a single match among the display names, it uses that display name's email address without prompting you for assistance. For example, if it found "Bill Kirk (Office)" in the address list and no other display name containing "Bill Kirk", it uses the address for that listing.

- If Project finds no matching display names, it prompts you to intervene. You need to either create a new listing in the Address Book or manually browse through the display names and pick the one that you want to use.

  You do not want this to happen each time you send email to the resource; so, you want to provide an entry in the E<u>m</u>ail field that tells Project the email address to use or create a listing in the Address Book that Project can find.

  In the previous example where Bill Kirk's display name in the address book is "Kirk, Bill", you could put either "Kirk, Bill" or his address "bkirk@newprods.com" in the E<u>m</u>ail field.

- If Project finds more than one matching display name, it prompts you to choose the one you want to use. For example, if it finds "Bill Kirk (Office)" and "Bill Kirk (Mobile)" in the address list, it prompts you to select the one to use for the message.

  If you always want to use just one of the display names, you should copy that address or its display name to the E<u>m</u>ail field. On the other hand, if you want to select the address each time you send a message, leave the E<u>m</u>ail field blank so that you are prompted for the choice each time you send a message to this resource.

In summary, then, you only need to place an entry in the Email field under the following circumstances:

- If the resource is not in the Address Book (a contract consultant, for example) and you don't want to add a record to the Address Book for the resource, then you should put an email address directly in the Email field for Project to use.

- If you want to use a different address than the one in the Address Book, enter it directly into the Email field.

- If Project can't find the display name in the Address Book because it's spelled differently than the resource name, then enter the display name or the email address itself in the Email field.

- When there are multiple listings for the resource in the Address Book, you can put the display name for the listing that you want to use in the Email field. You could also just put the email address itself in the Email field.

- If you anticipate that the project file might be used to send messages when the Address Book is not available, place the actual email address in the Email field.

Using the Details Button

The Details button on the Resource Information dialog box helps you verify that Project can find an email address or helps you determine the display name or address to place in the Email field. When you click the Details button, Project attempts to find a matching display name for the Email field entry or, if that's blank, for the resource name.

If Project finds a single match, it shows the display name and email address for that entry in the address book. For example, in Figure 8.19 Project found a single listing for Mary Logan and displays the properties dialog box for that listing.

Figure 8.19
The SMTP–Internet tab on the Email Properties dialog box shows the Display Name and Email Address for entries in the Address Book.

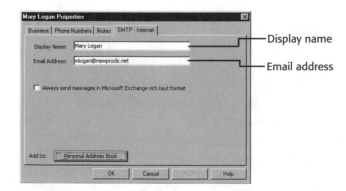

If you want to use a different email address for this resource than the one in the Address Book, you have to add a new entry for the resource using your email software product. If the address book is your personal address book, you could also just edit the display name or email address in this dialog box, but be aware that you are really editing the Address Book itself.

If after clicking the D̲etails button on the Resource Information dialog box Project has not found any matches, it will display the Check Names dialog box with the message that it doesn't recognize the resource name. In Figure 8.20 the selected resource is Mel Lloyd and Project says it doesn't recognize "Mel Lloyd" and has placed the text "[No Suggestions]" in the C̲hange To list box. You will need to create a new address or look at the list of names in the Address Book to see if you can find a match.

Figure 8.20
The Check Names dialog box prompts you to resolve the search for a display name in the Address Book.

Create a new email address listing.

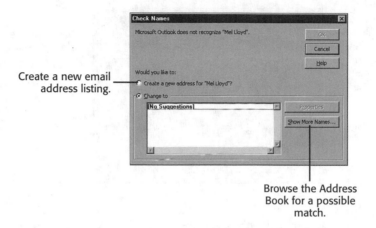

Browse the Address Book for a possible match.

Use the S̲how More Names button to display the Address Book (see Figure 8.21) when you have to locate the spelling of the resource name yourself.

Search text.

Figure 8.21
The S̲how More Names button opens the email Address Book for you to man-ually locate resource email names.

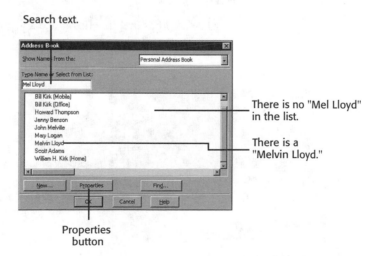

There is no "Mel Lloyd" in the list.

There is a "Melvin Lloyd."

Properties button

In Figure 8.21 there is no "Mel Lloyd" in the Address Book because his name is spelled "Melvin Lloyd." If you are able to locate a display name for the resource in the address list, you should click the name and then click the P̲roperties button to display the full information for that name. Project displays the SMTP—Internet tab (see Figure 8.22), which shows the properties for the address. You need to copy either the display name or the email address to the resource's Email field. Select the full text in either the Display Name or Email Address box and press the Ctrl+C shortcut key combination to copy the text to the Clipboard. Then Cancel three times to return to the Resource Information dialog box and paste the text into the Email field using the Ctrl+V shortcut key combination.

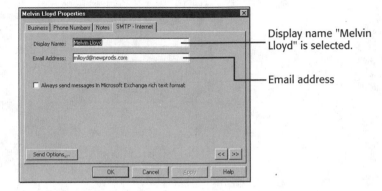

Figure 8.22
The Properties display for the email address shows both the display name and the email address. Copy one of them to the Email field on the Resource Information dialog box.

Display name "Melvin Lloyd" is selected.

Email address

If you were unable to find a display name for the resource in the Address Book, then you need to create a new one in your personal Address Book or have the email administrator create one in the organizational Address Book. In the Check Names dialog box (refer to Figure 8.20), you would select the Create a New Address For button and follow the instructions of your email software for creating a new listing.

If, after pressing the Details button, Project finds multiple possible display name matches, it displays the Check Names dialog box with the matches it has found listed in the Change To list box (see Figure 8.23).

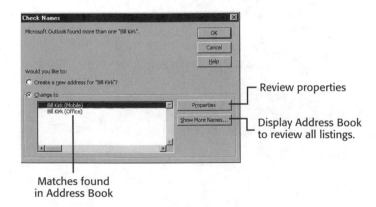

Figure 8.23
The Check Names dialog box prompts you to select a name when Project finds multiple matches in the email Address Book.

Review properties

Display Address Book to review all listings.

Matches found in Address Book

The Check Names dialog box message says that it has found more than one "Bill Kirk" and shows the display names it found in the change To list box. Use the Properties button to review the email address for each listing (as in Figure 8.22). If you want to make one of these display names the permanent address for messages to the resource, select all the text in its Display Name or Email Address box and copy it to the Clipboard with the Ctrl+C short-cut key combination. Then click the Cancel buttons until you return to the Resource Information dialog box where you can paste the text into the Email field with the Ctrl+V shortcut key combination.

WINDOWS ACCOUNT

If your communication method is via a Web page on an intranet, use the Windows Account button to find the resource's account name in the NT directory of users and place it in the box (refer to Figure 8.13).

SETTING THE AUTOMATICALLY ADD NEW RESOURCES AND TASKS OPTION

The setting of the Automatically Add New Resources and Tasks option determines how Project reacts when you assign a resource to a task and the resource is not currently in your pool of resources.

When you assign a resource name to a task, Project checks the resource pool for the name you have entered. By default, if it doesn't find it in the resource pool, it adds it to the pool. The default is also that Project does not ask you to confirm the addition. All resource fields for the new name have the default values and you must remember to update those fields later. This can be the cause of miscalculations in your costs if you neglect to go back and fill in the data for the new resource because the default cost rates are usually zero.

This feature can also be the cause of multiple resource names for the same resource. For example, suppose you have created a pool of resources which includes: Peter, Maria, and Ivan. As you are assigning resources to tasks, you type in **Pete** instead of Peter. A new resource (Pete) has been added to your list of resources; you now have Peter, Maria, Ivan, and Pete. You now have no comprehensive list of the assignments for this resource, because they are split between Peter and Pete.

If the Automatically Add New Resources and Tasks option is disabled, Project prompts you to decide if you want the resource added to the resource pool. In Figure 8.24 the resource name "Bill Kirkk" was accidentally typed in an assignment and Project is prompting you to decide whether or not this is a new resource you want added to the pool or not. If you con-firm that you want to add the resource, the resource is added and you must remember to define the rest of the resource fields. In this example, you would choose the No button to avoid adding a misspelled version of Bill Kirk's name to the pool.

Figure 8.24
Disable the Automatically Add New Resources and Tasks options so that you will be prompted if you attempt to assign a non-existent resource.

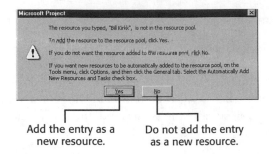

Add the entry as a new resource.

Do not add the entry as a new resource.

→ To see how resource assignments work, **see** "Assigning Resources and Costs to Tasks," **p. 401**

Tip from Tim and the Project Team

I always disable the Automatically Add New Resources and Tasks option to avoid the possibility of creating new resources if I enter a typing error. If you are going to leave the option enabled, I suggest that you always use the pick list of resource names that is available when you assign a resource to a task to avoid typographical errors instead of typing in the name.

To set the Automatically Add New Resources and Tasks option for automatic addition of resources, follow these steps:

1. Choose Tools, Options to display the Options dialog box.

2. Choose the General tab (see Figure 8.25).

3. Clear the Automatically Add New Resources and Tasks check box (near the bottom section of the dialog box) if you do not want Project to add resource names to the resource pool unless you have confirmed that you want that to happen.

   Or

   Fill the check box if you want Project to add resources without asking for confirmation.

4. Click OK to close the dialog box.

Figure 8.25
Turn off automatic adding of new resources in the Options dialog box.

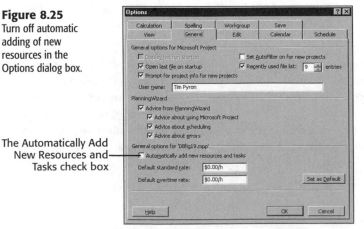

The Automatically Add New Resources and Tasks check box

SORTING RESOURCES

The normal order of the resource names in the Resource Sheet is by ID number, which initially reflects the order in which you enter the resources. You can temporarily sort the resource list for a special report or for purposes of analysis. You can also sort the list and have Project permanently change the row ID numbers to match the new order.

For example, after entering all the resources, you could sort the list so that all the work resources are listed first—in alphabetical order by name—and then the material resources are listed in order by name (see Figure 8.26). As another example, you might want to see which resources add the most cost to the project; so, you could apply the Cost table to the Resource Sheet, showing the cost of all their task assignments for each resource, and then sort the resource list by the Total Cost field in descending order (see Figure 8.27).

You can sort a table on up to three fields at a time, and each of those fields can be sorted in ascending or descending order. For example, to produce the sort order in Figure 8.26 you would sort first on the resource Type field, in descending order (to put Work resources before Material resources). Then you sort on the Resource Name field in ascending order (to list the names in normal alphabetical order).

Note

If you sort the resource table on the Standard Rate field, Project sorts the work resources on the hourly equivalent of the entry in the Standard Rate field.

Sorted first
by Type in
descending order

Then sorted by
Name within
each type

Figure 8.26
You can sort the resource pool by type and by name for special reports or as a permanent order with new ID numbers.

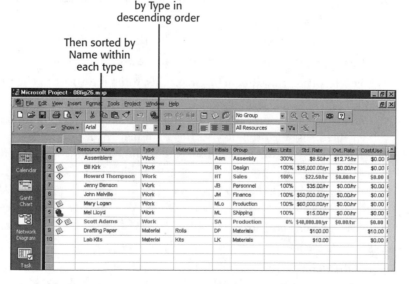

Cost table fields

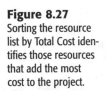

Figure 8.27
Sorting the resource list by Total Cost identifies those resources that add the most cost to the project.

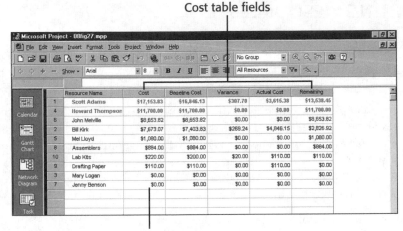

Sorted by Cost in descending order

Sort resources by choosing Project, Sort to display the Sort submenu. Sorting by Cost, Name, or ID is used so often that these options appear on the submenu. If you choose Cost, the sort order is in descending order, but both Name and ID sort in ascending order. These three choices use the current settings at the bottom of the Sort dialog box.

If you choose Sort By, you can define up to three fields to use for sorting, and each can be sorted in either ascending or descending order (see Figure 8.28).

To produce the sort order by Type and then by Name as illustrated in Figure 8.26, follow these steps:

1. Display the Resource Sheet (you can choose View, Resource Sheet).

2. Choose Project, Sort, Sort By to display the Sort dialog box.

   You can sort on a maximum of three fields, using the Sort By, Then By, and Then By fields.

3. Enter the first sort field in the Sort By box. In this example the field is the resource Type field. Use the drop-down arrow to display the list of fields. Type the first letter of the field name (in this case "t") and Project highlights the first field that begins with that letter. Scroll down to select the Type field.

4. Click the Ascending button if you want the field sorted in normal order. In this example, you click the Descending button to list Work before Material resources.

5. In the Then By box, select the "Name" field.

6. Select Ascending to sort the names in normal order.

7. Fill the Permanently Renumber Resources check box if you want Project to change all ID numbers to match the new sort order. See the following Caution if you elect to fill this check box.

8. If you have combined several project files into a consolidated display, the Sort Resources By Project check box keeps the resources for each project together and sorts them within that grouping.

9. When all settings are ready, click the Sort button to close the dialog box and execute the sort, or click the Cancel button to close the dialog box without sorting the resources.

Caution

If you fill the Permanently Renumber Resources check box in a sort operation, then as soon as the sort is completed you should immediately open the Sort dialog box again and clear the check box or click the Reset button. You can then click Cancel because you don't need to sort at this time—you just needed to clear the check box. If you don't take this extra step, the check box remains filled and any future sorting with the Sort submenu also permanently renumbers your resources.

If you decide to cancel a sort operation and you have already filled the Permanently Renumber Resources check box, be sure to clear the check box (or click the Reset button, which also clears it) before clicking the Cancel button.

Note

You can undo the sort operation, even after permanently renumbering the resources. Of course, you have to do it before making any other changes. Just as a precaution, you might be wise to save a copy of the file before permanently renumbering the resources just in case you want to undo it later.

Figure 8.28
The Sort dialog box lets you customize the sort order for the resources.

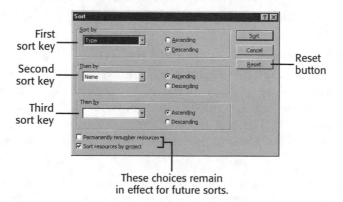

To produce the sort order by descending total costs for assignments, as illustrated in Figure 8.27, follow these steps:

1. Display the Resource Sheet by choosing View, Resource Sheet.

2. Display the Cost table by choosing View, Table, Cost.

3. Choose Project, Sort, Cost to sort the list by Cost in descending order.

Note, if the Sort dialog box has the Permanently Renumber Resources box filled, the row ID numbers are permanently renumbered to match the new sort order.

When you are ready to return the list to the ID order, you can either press Shift+F3 or choose Project, Sort, ID from the menu.

Tip from Tim and the Project Team

If you have sorted the resource list in a special order and have made changes that might make the sort order no longer valid, you can press Ctrl+Shift+F3 to reapply the last sort instructions. For example, if you had sorted by resource Type and Cost and then make task assignments or change some resource cost rates, the list might no longer be in descending cost order within each Type. Press Ctrl+Shift+F3 to sort by Type and Cost again.

→ If you frequently use a custom sort order and would like to place it on the Sort submenu, you have to create a macro and customize the menu. **See** "Recording and Saving a Macro," **p. 1098**, for the steps to create the macro. **See** "Customizing the Menu Bar," **p. 1072**, for information about customizing the menu.

GROUPING RESOURCES

In Project 2000, you can use the Group By command to sort tasks or resources into groups based on the entries in one or more of the fields. For example, you could group resources by resource types (see Figure 8.29) or by the entries in the Group field, among others. At this stage in the development of your project, without resource assignments to tasks, there are not many uses of the Group By command that yield interesting displays. You can find the full treatment of the Group By command in Chapter 23, "Customizing Views, Tables, Fields, and Filters."

→ For a full discussion of using the Group By command, **see** "Creating Custom Groups," **p. 979**

The difference between sorting and grouping is that a Group By record is inserted at the start of each group as a pseudo summary task. Project calculates totals for any numeric fields in this record for the records grouped beneath it. In Figure 8.29, the cost table has been applied and the numeric fields various measurements of the cost of assignments for the resources. You can see that the total cost of assignments for work resources is $47,144.71, whereas that for material resources is only $330.

The inserted record has no resource ID or row number and is a temporary row that disappears when you remove the grouping. Until you assign resources to tasks, the Group By command offers little added information to the Resource Sheet.

Summary rows
for groups

Total scheduled
cost for all work
resource assignments

Figure 8.29
Use the Group By
command to sort
resources and show
summary totals for all
resources in each
group.

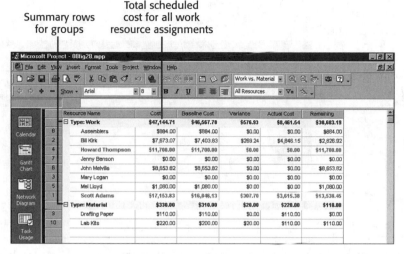

To group resource records on the resource type as in Figure 8.29, choose Project, Group By, Work vs. Material Resources. To remove the grouping, choose Project, Group By, No Group (or press Shift+F3).

You can change the sort order while the resources are grouped. The sort settings are applied within each group—in other words, resources do not move to a different group as a result of the new sort order. You can also apply filters while the resources are grouped. See the next section for a discussion of filters.

FILTERING RESOURCES

You can use filters to select all of those resources that meet some condition which you specify. For example, you might want to select all of your material resources. The condition in this instance—that the resource Type must be "Material"—is called the filter *criteria*. Project has a built-in filter named the Resource—Material filter that imposes this criterion for you (see Figure 8.30).

Tip from Tim and the Project Team

Filtering for specific resources is a great way to isolate only those resources that meet specific criteria that you've defined and to temporarily omit the other ones. By doing so, you can apply a change that impacts an entire group of resources instead of having to find each one independently in order to make the change.

All work resources are hidden.

Figure 8.30
The resource pool is filtered to show only the material resources.

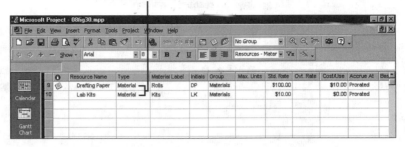

After Project has selected the resources that meet the criteria, it normally changes the display to show only the selected resources, temporarily hiding all those that don't meet the criteria. However, you can also choose to use the filter as a *highlight filter*, and Project merely highlights the selected resources without hiding all the others. In Figure 8.31 the Resource—Material filter has been applied as a highlight filter. The highlight includes underlining in this example to make it stand out more in the illustration.

Material resources are highlighted.

Figure 8.31
The filter has highlighted all the material resources without hiding the resources that don't match the filter criterion.

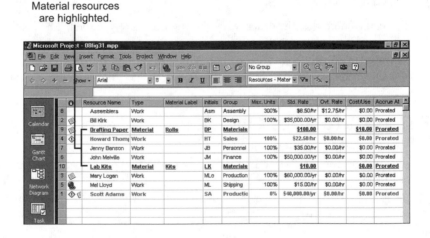

→ If you want to customize the highlight that is used for filters, **see** "Formatting Text Displays for Categories of Tasks and Resources," **p. 894**

When you have finished using the filtered display, you must apply the All Resources filter to return to the normal display, or simply press the F3 function key.

Another useful filter for reviewing how you categorized your resources is the Group filter. If you have entered category labels in the Group field, you can quickly filter the list to show all the resources that have a certain label in the Group field. For example, if you entered department names in the Group field, you could filter the list for "Production" to identify all the resources managed by the Production department.

If you have multiple group labels in the Group field and want to filter resources for one of the group labels, see the instructions in "Filtering for Labels Contained in the Group Field" in the "Troubleshooting" section near the end of this chapter.

After work on the project has begun, you can use filters to quickly check on the status of resources, to see at a glance where problems might lie. The following partial listing illustrates how useful filters can be in managing your project. There are built-in filters that allow you to identify those resources

- That are overallocated—that are assigned to more work than they can possibly finish in some specific time period.

- Whose scheduled costs are more than you had budgeted.

- Who have finished all their work.

- Who have not started work that should have started by now.

- Who are taking longer than planned to finish their assignment.

- Who have been assigned overtime work.

- Who have not responded to workgroup messages about their assignments.

→ For a complete listing of the built-in filters and how to use them, **see** "Exploring the Standard Filters," **p. 881**

→ For instructions on creating your own filters, **see** "Creating Custom Filters," **p. 968**

Note

You can only apply filters to full screen views or views that are in the top pane of a combination view. They can't be applied to views in the bottom pane because those views are already filtered for the task or resource that is selected in the top pane.

You can apply a filter with the menu or by using the Filter tool on the Formatting toolbar. If you want to apply the filter as a highlight filter, you must use the menu.

For example, if you want to display only your material resources in a resource view, you would follow these steps:

1. Display one of the resource views that has a table of resources in the top pane.

    All Tasks ▾

2. Click the Filter tool to display the drop-down list of resource filters and click on Resources—Material.

    Or, choose Project, Filtered For: to display the Filter menu and click on Resources-Material.

    Whichever method you use, Project hides all but those resources that have Material in the resource Type field.

Tip from Tim and the Project Team	To use a filter that is on the menu as a highlight filter, simply hold down the Shift key as you select the menu choices and Project highlights the filtered (selected) records without hiding the other records.

Tip from Tim and the Project Team	If you have applied a filter and then have made changes that might alter which resources are selected by the filter, use Ctrl+F3 to reapply the filter.

PRINTING THE RESOURCE LIST

You can get a printed copy of your resource pool either by printing the Resource Sheet view or by printing one of the resource reports. The resource reports offer more detail than you can see in the Resource Sheet.

→ For complete instructions on printing views and reports, **see** Chapter 13, "Printing Views and Reports," **p. 537**

If you want to print the Resource Sheet with special formatting, sorting, grouping, or filtering, you must apply those to the Resource Sheet view before you start printing. You can also apply a different table to the Resource Sheet view, but the other tables are not very interesting until you have assigned resources to tasks and Project has calculated the cost and work fields. If you just want to print out the list of resources that you have added, the default Entry table is the best to use because it shows the most common resource fields.

To print the Resource Sheet view, follow these steps:

1. Display the Resource Sheet either in the top pane or as fullscreen. You cannot print a view displayed in the bottom pane.
2. Select a filter, grouping, or sort order before starting the Print command.

3. Preview how the report is going to look by choosing File, Print Preview (or by clicking the Print Preview button).
4. Choose the Print button to open the Print dialog box.
5. Click OK to start printing.

There are three resource reports. All three of them print the rows of the Entry table in the Resource Sheet. But below each resource row you can also include additional details from the Resource Information dialog box. For example, you can include the cost tables, calendar details, and the resource notes. The following list describes the three resource reports:

■ The Resource (Material) report is filtered to show only material resources and omits columns that are not used for material resources (such as the overtime rate and base calendar).

■ The Resource (Work) report is filtered to show only work resources and omits the Material Label column.

- The Resource report displays all resources and all the columns contained on the other reports.

The additional details you can include in these reports are the

- Resource calendar and its exceptions
- Cost rate tables with dated rate changes
- Resource notes
- Objects attached to the resource

→ For an understanding of objects, **see** "Working with Objects," **p. 825**

→ For an understanding of objects, **see** "Working with Objects," **p. 825**

Note   Unfortunately, the new Resource Availability table is not available on the resource reports.

After you've made task assignments, you can also include the list of tasks assigned to each resource along with details about each assignment, such as

- The cost of each assignment
- The amount of work in each assignment
- Schedule details for each assignment
- Notes attached to any assignments

To print one of the resource reports, follow these steps:

1. Choose View, Reports to display the Reports dialog box.
2. Select Custom to display the Custom Reports dialog box.
3. Scroll the Reports list and select either Resource, Resource (Material), or Resource (Work).
4. Choose the Edit button to display the Resource Report dialog box where you can click the Details tab to specify the details you want to include in the report.
5. Fill the check boxes in the Resource group for those resource definition details that you want to include (Notes, Objects, Calendar, and Cost Rates).
6. If you have assigned resources to tasks, you can fill the check boxes in the Assignment group for the assignment details you want to include (Notes, Schedule, Cost, and Work).
7. Use the Sort tab to sort the resource list in the printed report.
8. Click OK to save the report definition.
9. Click Preview to get an idea of what the report will look like. From the preview screen you can click the Page Setup button to modify the page setup if needed, and you can click the Print button to open the Print dialog box.

TROUBLESHOOTING

PASTING A RESOURCE LIST FROM ANOTHER APPLICATION

You can easily copy and paste a list of resources into Project from another application, but you might have to prepare the list correctly and prepare Project to receive the data or you will not get the results you intended.

→ For a much more comprehensive discussion of importing data into Project, **see** Chapter 19, "Exporting and Importing Project Data with Other File Formats," **p. 759**

If you have a list of resource names in another application that you would like to copy into Project, and the list contains nothing but a column of resource names, then the process is very simple if you follow these steps:

1. Select the list in the other application and use the Edit, Copy command (or press Ctrl+C) to copy the list to the Clipboard.

   It's important to note that the source list must be in separate rows in the other application—separate cells in the same column of a spreadsheet, or separate lines in a text document.

2. Select a cell in the Resource Name column of the Resource Sheet in Project 2000. The pasted list begins in this cell.

3. Choose Edit, Paste and Project copies the list into the Project document. All the new resources are given default values for the other resource fields.

However, if your list contains more columns than just the names, copying the list into Project is a little more complicated. For example, if the source list also contains a column with a money amount that you want to use as the standard rate for the resources, you must prepare the source list and also prepare the Resource Sheet to accept the list when it is copied.

To prepare the source list, you must do these things:

- In a spreadsheet, you must arrange the data so that each resource is in a separate row and the data you want to copy are in adjacent columns. For example, the money amount column should be just to the right of the resource names column.

- In a text document, the resource name and the money amount must be on the same line, separated by a tab character or in adjacent cells of a table.

- If the money amounts are all hourly rates they do not have to have a time period appended to them. But if they are rates for any other time period you must append a slash and the word or abbreviation for the time period. For instance, if they are annual salaries, you must append "/y" or "/year" to each of them. Without the appended time period, Project treats them as hourly rates.

To prepare the Project file to receive the resources, you must set up a table that has columns in the same order as the data you are pasting. To prepare the resource table, follow these steps:

1. Display the Resource Sheet. Add temporary columns to receive the pasted data.
2. Click the column title for the column immediately to the right of the Resource Name column (by default it is the Type column).
3. Select Insert, Column to display the Column Definition dialog box.
4. Select the Standard Rate field in the Field Name box.
5. Click OK to insert the column.
6. Repeat steps 2 through 5 for each column of data you are pasting in, being careful that the order of the columns matches the order of the data you are pasting.

After the source and the target location are prepared, select the source data and copy it to the Clipboard. Then select the blank Resource Name cell below any existing resource names and choose Edit, Paste.

After you have copied the data in, you should remove the columns you added to the display by selecting the column titles and choosing Edit, Hide Column.

FILTERING FOR LABELS CONTAINED IN THE GROUP FIELD

If you put multiple group labels in the Group field and wish to filter the resource pool for one of those labels, you need to modify the standard Group filter to use the "contains" test.

The standard Group filter uses the "equals" test when it searches for the label you ask it to filter for. The "equals" test requires that the entire entry in the Group field contains exactly the label you tell it to search for—no more and no less. If you create a copy of the Group filter that uses the "contains" test, it selects all resources whose Group field *contains* the label you are searching for.

If you choose Project, Filter For, you will display the Filters menu. Notice that the Group... filter is on the menu and that its first letter is underlined. The underlining signals that the user can simply type the underlined letter (the "hot" key) to select the item. The three periods at the end of the filter name are a convention that signals the user that the filter asks for input before executing; in this case, the filter asks the user to type in the group label that the user wants the filter to find.

The steps that follow will add the Group Contains... filter to this menu and underline the first "n" as the hot key. They start with a copy of the Group filter and merely change the name and the logical test from "equals" to "contains".

To create a copy of the Group filter named the Group Contains filter, follow these steps:

1. Choose Project, Filter For, More Filters to display the More Filters dialog box.
2. Select the Resource button to display the list of defined resource filters.
3. Select the Group... filter in the Filters list.

4. Click the <u>C</u>opy button to display the Filter Definition dialog box for a new filter. The default name for the new filter will be "Copy of &Group" and you will change that.

5. Change the entry in the <u>N</u>ame field to "Group Co&ntains..." with the ampersand before the first "n" and three periods at the end. The ampersand causes the following character to be the hot key.

6. Leave the Show in <u>M</u>enu check box filled so that this filter appears on the Filter menu.

7. Click the "equals" entry in the Test column and either type in **contains** or use the drop-down list to select it.

PROJECT EXTRAS: PREPARING A FILE TO USE AS A RESOURCE TEMPLATE

If you plan to use the same set of resources in multiple project files, you'll save time by defining these resources and their associated costs in a template document. When you want to start a new project file, just open the template file and Project creates a new project document containing all the data in the template so you don't have to key it in again. You can then add your tasks for the new project, without having to define the project resources and costs.

→ For a complete discussion of working with project templates, including options not covered here, **see** "Creating and Using Templates," **p. 124**

If you use an existing project file as the basis for a template, there might be data in the file that you don't want in the template. For example, if you include tasks in the project as standard tasks in the template and have already captured baseline data or actual costs and start and finish dates, you would want to remove that information before starting a new project with the template. You might also want to remove fixed costs that you have associated with tasks. Project 2000 offers to strip out this data for you when you save the file as a template. It also offers to strip out the cost rates for resources; but if you're creating the template because it contains the resource pool, you probably will not choose to delete the resource cost rates.

There are other fields that Project 2000 doesn't offer to clear for you, and if you want those fields cleared, you have to do that manually. For example:

- Project doesn't remove notes or hyperlinks that are attached to tasks or resources.

- If you leave both the tasks and resources in the file when you create the template, Project doesn't remove the assignments of resources to tasks nor, if you have used workgroup messaging, does it remove the messaging flags that show up as indicators for tasks and resources.

→ For an understanding of the workgroup messaging fields, **see** Chapter 15, "Using Microsoft Project in Workgroups," **p. 603**

If these values remain in the template, a new project that is based on the template opens with task assignments in place—possibly with resources already overallocated—and indicators appear for all the notes, hyperlinks, and workgroup messaging flags that were attached to the resources.

Although you can remove this information by editing each resource individually, that would take a very long time in a large project. The instructions below show you how to quickly remove all notes, hyperlinks, assignments, and message tracking from a project.

To save a file as a template and remove unwanted field values from the template, start by saving the template:

1. Open the project file that contains the resources you want to store in the template.
2. Choose File, Save As.
3. Type the template name in the File Name box.
4. In the Save as Type list box, choose Template. When you choose template as the file type, Project appends the .MPT file extension to the filename and changes the file location to the directory where user templates are stored.
5. Click the Save button. Project displays the Save As Template dialog box, where you can instruct Project to scrub some of the unwanted data from the template.
6. Select the data you want to Project to remove from the template and click the Save button.

Project saves the file as a template and leaves it open on your screen. You can now remove the unwanted field values manually and then save the template again.

To remove all task assignments and all workgroup message flags pertaining to those assignments, follow these simple steps:

1. View the Gantt Chart in the top pane and click on the Task Name column title to select all tasks.
2. Click the Assign Resources tool to display the Assign Resources form and click on the Name column title to select all resource names in the form.
3. Click the Remove button to remove all resource assignments.

To remove all notes and hyperlinks for tasks and resources, follow these steps:

1. For resource notes and hyperlinks, display the Resource Sheet.
2. Click on any column title to select all rows.
3. Choose Edit, Clear, Hyperlinks to clear the hyperlinks and choose Edit, Clear, Notes to remove all notes.
4. If you need to remove all task notes or hyperlinks, display the Gantt Chart view and repeat steps 2 and 3 above.

After you have removed the unwanted data, save the template file one more time to overwrite the initial version.

UNDERSTANDING RESOURCE SCHEDULING

In this chapter

LEARNING ABOUT RESOURCE SCHEDULING

This chapter prepares you for the next several chapters, in which you will be assigning resources to tasks and dealing with the changes in the schedule and the scheduling problems that normally arise from including resource assignments in your project. This chapter gives you the background and understanding you need to use resource scheduling successfully. The details of using different views both to enter assignment information and to deal with changes and problems in the schedule are covered in the next two chapters.

This chapter explains how Microsoft Project calculates resource assignments and schedules and reviews the controls you can exercise over those calculations. There are numerous calculations that Project performs in the background as you edit the data for resource assignments, and many of them are not obvious—especially if you're not trained in project management software. It can be very frustrating to make a change that you assume will have only a small effect on one resource's schedule and then to find that Project has amplified that small change into a chain reaction that affects many other resources and costs. This chapter helps you understand how Project proceeds with its calculations, helps you understand and predict the consequences of your data entries, and therefore helps you achieve the scheduling results you're looking for.

You have already seen, in Chapter 8, "Defining Resources and Costs," the data fields that you use in Microsoft Project to define resources and costs. This chapter shows you how those fields influence the way Project schedules work when you assign a resource to a task. The resource fields that are used in this chapter include the following:

- The resource name
- The working hours on the resource calendar
- The maximum number of units of a resource that can be assigned to tasks

Note

Technically speaking, you will not use the Max Units field itself in assigning resources to tasks; it's listed here because you will use the same "units" measure that the Max Units field uses when you define how many resource units are actually assigned to a task.

Project does not enforce the maximum number of available units when you make resource assignments. Project enables you to assign more units than the Max Units when you are planning your project, but if you do exceed the maximum, Project warns you so that you can revise the assignments or the schedule. For example, you might then consider increasing the maximum units (by acquiring more resource units) or reducing the number of units assigned to various tasks.

With the topics in this chapter under your belt, you will be better able to focus on the many views, tools, and features of Project that you will see in the next two chapters as you go through step-by-step instructions for actually entering the details of resource assignments and correcting problems in the schedule.

REVIEWING THE ESSENTIAL COMPONENTS OF RESOURCE ASSIGNMENTS

When a work resource is assigned to work on a task (in other words, to spend time or effort on the task), Microsoft Project initially schedules work for the resource in specific time periods based on several controlling factors that are outlined in the discussion that follows. Note that material resources do not "work," and therefore this discussion is about scheduling work resources. I will deal with material resources in the section "Assigning Material Resource Units." Before you assign resources to it, a task already has scheduled dates that are derived from its duration, its links to other tasks, and any date constraint that might be imposed on it. There can also be task splits that interrupt the task schedule, providing periods of inactivity between the start and finish dates for the task.

P **2000** Starting with Project 2000, the task can also have a special calendar attached to it that regulates the specific days and working times when the task will be scheduled. In Figure 9.1 the calendar icon in the indicator column signifies that the Test Prototype task has a special calendar attached to it.

PART

III

CH

9

Task calendar icon   Task split

Task constraint icon   Task links

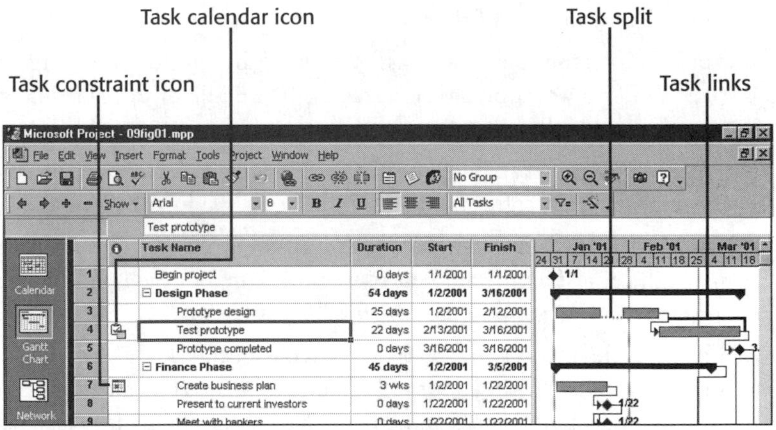

Figure 9.1
The start and finish dates in the task schedule are the basis for scheduling a resource when it is assigned to a task.

The schedule of work for an assigned resource is initially built around the task schedule based on the following factors:

- When you assign a resource to a task, Project schedules the resource's work to start at the time that the task is scheduled to start and schedules the work to continue uninterrupted and at a constant rate during the times the task is scheduled until all the work assigned to the resource is completed.

- Normally, Project only schedules work during the dates and times that are defined as working time on the resource's calendar. Therefore, Project does not schedule work for a resource during weekends, vacations, or other times that have been marked as nonworking on the resource calendar. Therefore, the task schedule changes to reflect the available working times on the resource calendar.

If there is also a task calendar attached to the task, Project only schedules work during those times that are working times on both the task calendar and the resource calendar.

Project also enables you to disregard the resource calendar and schedule work for the resource whenever the task is scheduled.

■ The amount of work scheduled on any given day is the number of working-time hours defined for that day in the relevant calendar multiplied by the number of resource units that are assigned to the task.

Project runs through all the calculations mentioned previously when you assign a resource to a task, and it calculates the dates and hours of work that constitute the initial assignment schedule. You can then modify the initial schedule to suit specific requirements or the needs of your resources. The following list describes the types of adjustments you can make to the assignment schedule:

■ You can introduce a scheduled delay in the start of the work for one resource, leaving other resources to start the task as originally scheduled.

For example, if a resource performs a specialized function on the task that is not needed until the task is almost finished, the work schedule for that resource can be delayed until toward the end of the task.

■ You can interrupt the flow of assigned work by splitting the assignment, setting periods of no work for this resource in the middle of the schedule while other resources continue to work.

For example, you can pull a resource off a long task temporarily to work on something more pressing by splitting the assignment on the long task to allow for the interruption.

■ You can override the even distribution of the work that Project normally schedules by manually adjusting the amount of work assigned in each period, thus creating periods of high and low activity on the task for the resource.

For example, if you know that a resource is needed only part-time on a task during the second week on the task, but full-time otherwise, you can edit the assignment for the resource during that week to be fewer hours per day than Project assigned.

■ You can instruct Project to apply one of its predefined work contours that vary the amount of effort scheduled during the assignment.

For example, the *front-loaded* contour schedules the resource to put its full effort into the early periods of the assignment but to taper off to part-time involvement as the task nears completion.

■ If the schedule has *overallocated* a resource (assigned units of the resource to various tasks at a moment in time that exceeds the maximum units for the resource), you can add a *leveling delay* to one of the assignments. This delay is similar to the scheduled delay mentioned previously, except that it serves a different purpose. The scheduled delay likely remains in place permanently because that's the way the task should be completed. The leveling delay might become unnecessary if other ways are found to eliminate the resource's overallocation. For instance, you could substitute a different resource for the one that is overallocated to reduce its workload during the time of the overallocation.

Before tackling these more advanced topics of customizing a resource assignment, you must first understand the basic assignment fields and how the initial schedule is calculated.

UNDERSTANDING THE RESOURCE ASSIGNMENT FIELDS

When you assign a resource to a task, you must at least identify the resource that is being assigned. You can optionally also specify the number of resource units to dedicate to the task and the amount of work that the assignment entails. The fields in which you enter this information are described in the following list and can be seen in the Task Form illustrated in Figure 9.2.

PART

III

CH

9

Figure 9.2
The Task Form displays all three key assignment fields in the Resource details area.

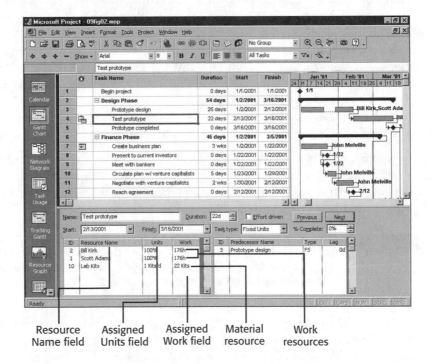

ASSIGNING A RESOURCE NAME

You must identify the resource by its resource ID number or by its name. In most instances the Resource Name field offers a drop-down list of the names that are already defined in the resource pool. You can select one of those names, or you can type a new resource name, and Project adds that name to the pool as it assigns the name to the task.

As you saw in Chapter 8, you should require that Project alert you before a new name is added to the resource pool because it is possible that you accidentally mistyped an existing resource name. If you don't have the chance to intervene, Project creates a new variation of the same resource in the pool with a slightly different spelling. Furthermore, the workload of the correctly spelled resource is misrepresented because it does not include the assignments that were given to its typographically challenged alter-egos.

→ To learn more about why and how Project adds to your resource pool, **see** "Defining Resources and Costs," **p. 313**

ASSIGNING THE UNITS

 Both the Units and Work fields have been updated to provide for the new material resource type. For both resource types, the Units field defines the number of resource units to be assigned to the task. If you don't enter a value for Units, Project supplies a default value.

ASSIGNING WORK RESOURCE UNITS

The term *units* is actually something of a misnomer in Project. The word itself tends to make you think it means "physical units" of a resource. Indeed, it does mean that for material resources, and this book sometimes uses that meaning for work resources as well. What Project does with this value is to use it as a multiplier to calculate the number of hours of work that can be scheduled for a resource on a given day. Project looks up the number of hours that are available on that day in the resource calendar and multiplies that number of hours by the units value to get the work scheduled for that task on that day. Thus, if a physical resource unit is assigned 100% to a task, Project schedules 100% of the hours in the calendar for that resource. However, if that physical resource unit is assigned to a task at 25%, Project only schedules 25% of the available hours on any given day.

As an example, if two electricians are scheduled to work on a task on a given day, the units assigned are 200% in percentage format or 2 in decimal format. If the electricians calendar has only 4 hours of working time on that particular day, the resource's scheduled hours for the day are 8 hours (200% of the 4 hours of available time).

> **Note**
>
> If the task is being scheduled exclusively by a task calendar that allows 8 hours to be scheduled on that date and if the option to disregard resource calendars has been selected, Project schedules 200% × 8, or 16 hours, for the day.

Therefore, when you enter the units for an assignment, you need to think not "How many physical resource units do I have to work with?" but "What multiple of the available working time on the calendar should be scheduled as work for the resource?" If 1 physical unit is working half-time, enter 50%. If 2 physical units are working full-time, enter 200%.

For work resources, the default Units value for an assignment is 100% (or 1 in decimal format), or the maximum units available if that is less than 100%. The value 100% or 1 means you are assigning the equivalent of the full-time effort of one physical unit of the resource. You can enter any value between 0% and 6,000,000,000% (between 0 and 60,000,000 units in decimal format). (See Figure 9.3 in the next section.)

Tip from Tim and the Project Team

> To view Units in decimals instead of percents, choose Tools, Options, select the Schedule tab, and in the Show Assignment Units as A field, select the Decimal setting.

Project now uses the percentage format by default because formerly (when it used the decimal format) users tended to mistakenly accept the default units value of 1 when assigning human resources to tasks. The internal dialogue must have gone something like this: "I'm assigning Mary to this task. How many Marys will I assign? Well, there's only one Mary, so I'll leave the default 1 in the Units field." However, in actuality, you often expect human resources to multitask—to work on a number of tasks simultaneously and therefore to spend only part of each day on any one task. If you're using the percentage format and assign Mary to a task that you expect her to spend only 10% of her time on each day, the default 100% units should remind you that Project assumes that Mary devotes all of her time to that task until it's finished. Hopefully, you are more likely to remember that this field is the multiplier for calculating work and to recognize that you need to reduce the units to 10% if you expect Mary to spend only 10% of her daily time on this task.

If you use group resources, you have multiple physical resource units grouped together under one resource name. You can then have multiple physical units assigned to work on a task. In that case, enter the units as a multiple of 100%. For example, if you want to assign the full-time services of three forklifts to move inventory in a warehouse, enter 300% in the Units field. If you want to assign the three forklifts half-time to the task (that is, to spend only 50% of each day on this task), enter 150% (3 × 50%) in the Units field.

Obviously, the percentage format is cumbersome when you have to assign 50,000 units of a resource as 5,000,000%. If very few of your resources are individuals who work on many tasks at the same time, you will probably want to revert to the decimal format.

You can also assign a resource to a task with 0% units. In that case, Project calculates the work as zero and consequently calculates the cost of the work as zero also. For instance, you could assign zero units when you assign a contractor to a task and the contractor agrees to complete the task for a fixed fee. The amount of work is the responsibility of the contractor. All you need to record is the fee, which you would enter in a cost field.

→ For more information about assigning resources to tasks and entering costs, **see** "Assigning Fixed Costs and Fixed Contract Fees," **p. 435**

Note

> You can enter fractions of a percent in the Units assignment, but they display as rounded whole percent numbers. If you want to specify that a worker spends 1 hour per 8-hour day on a task (one eighth, or 12.5%, of a day), you see 13% displayed after you enter 12.5%. Project actually uses fractional percents in its calculations (down to tenths of a percent); it just doesn't display them.

ASSIGNING MATERIAL RESOURCE UNITS

For material resources, the Units value is always formatted as a decimal. If you fail to enter the assigned units, Project supplies the default value of "1" followed by the material label you defined for the resource. For example, if you defined the material resource Concrete with the label "Yd" (for cubic yard), the default units supplied by Project would be "1 Yd". This means that the task consumes exactly 1 yard of concrete.

ASSIGNING FIXED CONSUMPTION RATES   If you enter just a numeral in the Units column for a material resource assignment (or a numeral with the material label), it is called a *fixed consumption rate* for the resource. The amount consumed is fixed and independent of the task duration. For example, to assign 4 yards of concrete to a task, you could type "4" or "4 yd"; either way, Project responds with the value "4 Yd". If the task duration changes, this consumption rate does not change.

Note that if you type something Project doesn't understand, such as "4 yards" when the material label is "Yd", Project displays a warning that it is not a valid units value (see Figure 9.3).

Figure 9.3
Entering an unrecognized units value causes Project to display this warning.

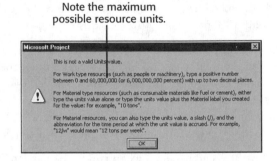

Note the maximum possible resource units.

The simplest remedy is to enter just the numeral and let Project provide the label.

ASSIGNING VARIABLE CONSUMPTION RATES   You can also assign material resource units with a variable consumption rate, where the total amount consumed is a function of the task duration. To create a variable consumption rate, simply enter the units with a slash and the abbreviation for the time period (for example "4/d" or "4 Yd/d" for 4 yards per day).

For example, suppose that you are using a bulldozer on a task that consumes about 6 gallons of fuel an hour. You can define a material resource "Diesel Fuel" with the label "Gal" (for gallons). Then, you can assign the fuel to the task by entering "6/h" or "6 gal/h" in the Units field. For either entry, Project displays either "6 Gal/h" or "6 Gal/hour" in the Units field (depending on the view you are using). Project then calculates the total number of units consumed by multiplying this rate times the task duration.

ASSIGNING THE WORK

As with the Units field, the addition of the new material resource type has required some alteration in the way the Work field is used.

A work resource spends hours of time or effort attending to the task, and you measure its contribution in *hours*. It is this effort of the work resources that causes a task to have duration in the first place: It takes time to complete the necessary work on a task. In fact, when you estimate the duration for a task, you are really thinking about how long it will take the work resources to complete the task. A material resource, on the other hand, doesn't expend effort: It's rather passively consumed by the task. You measure its contribution in physical units consumed. Both the hours for the work resource and the units of the material resource are calculated in the Work field. The total work for the task, however, is the sum of the hours of work for the work resources.

ASSIGNING WORK WITH WORK-TYPE RESOURCES

For work-type resources, the term *work*, which is also called *effort*, measures the time actually expended by a resource on the task during the assignment. Work is always measured in hours in Microsoft Project, and it can be entered by the user or, if not, is automatically calculated by Project. The hours of work assigned to the work resources is summed to provide the total work for the task.

If a work resource is scheduled full-time (100%) on a task that has a duration of 1 week (40 hours), the resource is assigned to 40 hours of work (100% of 40 hours). However, if the resource is only assigned half-time to the task (Units is 50%), it is only assigned 20 hours of work. If 2 resource units work full-time (200%) all week, there are 80 hours of work. Other things being equal, the following holds true:

> The longer the duration of the task, the more work is scheduled.

> The larger the resource units assigned, the more work is scheduled.

The amount of work that Project schedules for the resource is tied to the duration of the task and the number of units assigned to the task. This relationship is defined more precisely in the section "Understanding the Work Formula" later in this chapter.

ASSIGNING WORK WITH MATERIAL RESOURCES

For the new material-type resource, the Work field shows the total number of physical units of the resource that are consumed in completing the task. If you enter the units, Project calculates the work units for you.

For fixed-rate consumption assignments, the Work field is the same as the Units field. If you assign "4 Yd" of concrete, the Work field shows "4 Yd". If, however, you assign "48 Gal/d" to a 10-day task, Project places the value "480 Gal" in the Work field. The work units for material resources are not included in the total work for the task.

The next section describes how Project calculates Work and how the interdependence of task Duration, assigned Units, and assigned Work operates to determine resource and task schedules.

UNDERSTANDING THE WORK FORMULA

The formula for calculating work is the following:

> Duration × Units = Work

In symbols, it is represented as this:

$$D \times U = W$$

In words, multiply the task duration by the assigned units to calculate work.

Note

These formulas do not apply to material resources with a fixed consumption rate. For those resources, the value in the Work field is identical to the value in the Units field. The formulas are applicable to material resources with variable consumption rates. However, these formulas were developed and implemented before the material resource type was introduced, and the following discussion makes more sense if you think in terms of work resources.

Simple algebra can be used to reformulate this equation to calculate values for Duration when Work and Units are given:

Duration = Work / Units

In symbols, it is represented as this:

$$D = W / U$$

Also, when Duration and Work are given, Project can calculate Units with this variation of the formula:

Units = Work / Duration

In symbols, it is represented as this:

$$U = W / D$$

Although Duration can be displayed in minutes, hours, days, weeks, or months, Project converts Duration to minutes when calculating work and then displays it in the default unit for work which is normally the hour. Thus, if a 1-day task has 100% units assigned to it (1 full-time unit of the resource), the work is calculated as follows:

$$D \times U = W$$
$$8 \text{ hrs} \times 100\% = 8 \text{ hrs}$$

APPLYING THE WORK FORMULA IN NEW ASSIGNMENTS

The duration for a task is already defined before you assign the first resource to the task. Therefore, one of the values in the work formula (task duration) is already established. Your entries in assigning a new resource are handled slightly differently by Project for work and material resources, so I will discuss them separately.

ENTERING NEW ASSIGNMENTS FOR WORK RESOURCES

The following cases show what happens for new assignments to work resources. The distinctions are based on which fields you fill in: Units, Work, or both Units and Work. The task in these examples has a Duration of 1 day (8 hours).

- If you just enter the resource name but don't provide either the Units value or the Work value of the assignment, Project defaults the Units value to 100% and calculates the Work from the Duration and Units. For example, if you assign a work resource to a 1-day task without specifying the Units, Project supplies 100% to the Units field and calculates 8 hours for the Work field as follows:

  $D \times U = W$

  $8 \text{ hrs} \times 100\% = 8 \text{ hrs}$

- If you enter the Units value, Project uses that value with Duration to calculate Work. For example, if you assign a resource to the 1-day task and enter 50% in the Units field, Project calculates Work as follows:

  $D \times U = W$

  $8 \text{ hrs} \times 50\% = 4 \text{ hrs}$

  The task Duration is still 1 day.

- If you enter the Work value but do not supply the Units, *Project assumes that you want the default Units (100%)* and calculates a new value for Duration based on the specified Work value and the assumed value of 100% for Units. For example, if you assign a resource to the 1-day task and enter 16 hours in the Work field but nothing for the Units, Project calculates a new Duration value using this variation of the Work formula:

  $D \times U = W$

  $D \times 100\% = 16h$

  $D = W / U$

  $D = 16h / 100\% = 16 \text{ hours (or 2 days)}$

Now, you might wonder why Project chose to recalculate the Duration value instead of calculating a value for Units. The reason is that Project does not calculate new values for Units except in rare circumstances (where you leave it no alternative). It will help you predict what Project will recalculate when you make changes by remembering this set of "biases" that are inherent in Microsoft Project.

Note

When it has the choice, Project is programmed with a bias to calculate changes in Duration before changing Work, and to calculate changes in Work before changing Units.

- If you enter both the Units and Work values, Project recalculates the previously entered task Duration using the new entries. (There is one exception to this rule, which is explained in the section "Choosing the Task Type.") For example, if you assign Units the value 200% and Work the value 32 hours, Project calculates a new task Duration using this variation of the Work formula:

  $D \times U = W$

  $D \times 200\% = 32h$

  $D = W / U$

  $D = 32h / 200\% = 16 \text{ hours (or 2 days)}$

If you use the Task Form to assign resources, you can prepare a list of resources to assign to the task and then execute all assignments at once. In this event, Project calculates each of the assignments independently as outlined previously and then calculates the task duration to be equal to the longest duration needed by any one of the resources to complete its work. (See the section "Understanding the Driver Resource Concept" later in this chapter.)

Entering New Assignments for Material Resources

When the resource is a material resource, there are fewer alternatives to consider. Again, assume that the task is a 1-day task. This time, the resource is the material resource Concrete and its label is "Yd".

- If you just enter the material resource name but don't provide either the Units value or the Work value of the assignment, Project assumes the Units value is 1 and calculates the Work to be 1 Yd. For example, if you assign the Concrete resource to a 1-day task without specifying the Units, Project supplies 1 Yd to both the Units field and the Work field.

- If you enter the Units value as a numeral (in other words, as a fixed consumption rate), Project enters that value into both the Units and the Work field. For example, if you assign the Concrete resource to the 1-day task and enter 2 in the Units field, Project supplies 2 Yd to both the Units and the Work fields.

- If you enter the Units value as a variable consumption rate, Project uses that rate with the task duration to calculate the Work field. For example, if you enter 2/d in the Units field, Project converts that to 2 Yd/day and multiplies that by the duration (1 day) to calculate the Work field entry of 2 Yd.

- If you enter the Work value but do not supply the Units, Project assumes it is a fixed consumption rate assignment for the amount you entered and puts that amount in both the Units and Work fields.

- If you enter both the Units and the Work, Project ignores the entry in the Units field and places the Work field entry in both the Units and Work fields.

Applying the Work Formula to Changes in Existing Assignments

These arithmetic examples have assumed that Project is free to recalculate any of the three variables in the work formula. However, if you modify an existing assignment by changing one of the three values, Project accepts the new value you enter and has to calculate a change in one of the other values to maintain the equation.

You will see in the next section, however, that one of the three work equation variables (Duration, Units, or Work) is always "fixed" for the task's assignments, and Project avoids changing that value when it has to recalculate the work equation. For example, by default, tasks are created as fixed Units tasks, so if you change the Duration, Project leaves the Units unchanged and recalculates the Work. If you designate a task as having a fixed Duration and change the Work for an assignment, Project has to adjust the Units to keep the equation in balance; it can't change the work because it's fixed.

However, if the task has a fixed duration and you change the Duration itself, Project has to decide whether to adjust Units or Work because neither is fixed. Recalling the inherent bias described in the previous note, you can predict that Project adjusts Work and leaves Units unchanged.

CHOOSING THE TASK TYPE

Suppose that you add a task to the project whose duration must remain fixed, such as a conference or a meeting. You wouldn't want Project to change the duration as you change resource assignments for that task. Alternatively, you might want to edit an assignment to a task, and just for this particular change, you don't want Project to change the duration as it normally would. As you will see in this section, you can select the appropriate task type to keep Project from recalculating either Duration, Work, or Units as you change resource assignments.

By selecting a task type, you choose how you want Project to calculate changes in the task assignment schedule as it keeps the resource work formula in balance. You can leave the task type as a permanent attribute of the task, but you can also change the task type temporarily at any time to control how Project treats a particular change in one of the work equation variables.

As an example of how you can use this powerful tool, suppose that you want to force Project to calculate how many resource units you need to assign when you know the duration of the task and the amount of work you want done. You can tell Project that the task has a fixed duration, and when you enter the work required, Project has to calculate the necessary units to keep the work formula in balance.

Each of the task types listed defines one of the three variables, Duration, Work, or Units, as fixed in assignment calculations:

- **Fixed Duration**—Some tasks have a defined duration that should not be changed. Perhaps the duration is set by a client, by the government, or by another organization, and you must work within that time frame. If a task's duration must not be changed, select the task type Fixed Duration. Of course, *you* can change the Duration value, but Project avoids recalculating it if you define the task as the Fixed Duration type. Then, if you change the Work value in the equation, Project adjusts the Units; or if you change the Units, Project adjusts the Work value. If you change Duration itself for a Fixed Duration task, Project recalculates Work (because of its bias against recalculating Units).

- **Fixed Units**—The default task type is Fixed Units because Project assumes that you generally want to be the sole decision maker about how many units of each resource are assigned to the task. For those tasks, if the Work value is changed, Project recalculates Duration, and if Duration is changed, it adjusts Work. Of course, *you* can change the Units value, and if you do, Project recalculates Duration (because of its bias for recalculating Duration before Work).

- **Fixed Work**—For some tasks, you might want to stipulate that the total Work is fixed. As an example, you might contract to provide a fixed amount of work for a client. If the amount of Work is not to change even though Duration or Units change, define the task as a Fixed Work task, and Project does not adjust Work to keep the equation in balance. If you change the Duration of an assignment to a Fixed Work task, Project recalculates the Units. If you change the Units, Project recalculates the Duration. If you change the assigned Work itself, Project recalculates Duration (because of its bias against recalculating Units).

You can define a task's type in the Task Information dialog box, in the Task Entry or Task Details views, or by adding a column for the field Type to any task table. Figure 9.4 shows the Task Type field on the Task Information dialog box. Figure 9.5 shows the field on the Task Entry view.

Figure 9.4
The Task Type can be set in the Advanced folder tab in the Task Information dialog box.

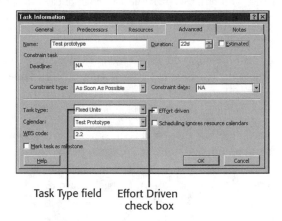

Task Type field   Effort Driven check box

Figure 9.5
Task Type can also be defined in the Task Entry view.

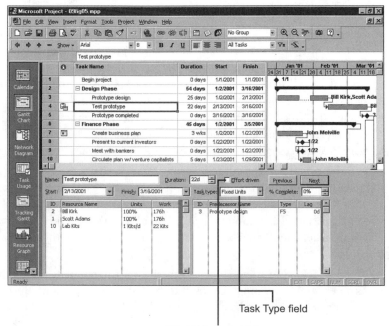

Task Type field

Effort Driven check box

As mentioned previously, the default task type for Project is Fixed Units, which means that new tasks are automatically assigned the Fixed Units task type. Thus, Project normally leaves it up to you to change the units assigned and recalculates Duration if you change Work or recalculates Work if you change Duration. You can change the default type for new tasks in a project with the Tools, Options menu. In the Options dialog box, select the Schedule tab and the type you want as the default in the Default Task Type field (see Figure 9.6).

Figure 9.6
You can change the default task type in the Options dialog box.

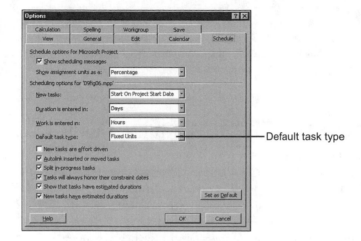

Default task type

When Project processes your work resource assignments, it must maintain the Work equation (Work = Duration × Units), but the task type governs how Project chooses to keep the equation in balance. Project responds in the following ways when you create a new assignment for a task:

- If you enter a value in Units and leave the Work field blank, Project calculates the unknown Work (because both Units and Duration have been given values). This is true no matter what the task type is.

- If you enter a value in Work and leave the Units blank, Project's calculation depends on the task type because Project is programmed to leave changes in Units up to the user if at all possible.

  - If the task is not a Fixed Duration task (if it's Fixed Units or Fixed Work), Project adjusts the Duration value. It assumes that the Units are the default (100% or less if the Max Units is less) and calculates the Duration that is necessary for the resource to complete the amount of work you assigned.

  - However, if the task is a Fixed Duration task, Project cannot change the Duration entry and calculates the Units needed to complete the Work you entered and places that value in the Units field.

- If you entered values in both Units and Work, Project again bases its calculations on the task type.
  - If the task is not a Fixed Duration task, Project adjusts the Duration to accommodate the Work and Units you entered.
  - If the task is a Fixed Duration task, Project keeps the Work amount you entered and calculates a new Units value that can do the specified work in the given (fixed) Duration.

Note

The previous example is an exception to the rule that Project avoids calculating Units if it can choose to recalculate Work. When the task type is Fixed Duration and you change both the Work and Units for an assignment, Project keeps your Work entry and recalculates the Units within the fixed duration.

UNDERSTANDING EFFORT-DRIVEN TASKS

You saw in the previous sections that if a task is marked as Fixed Work and you change the number of units in a resource assignment, Project leaves the work amount unchanged and adjusts the duration of the task. If you increase the units, Project decreases the duration. What do you want Project to do if you increase the number of resources assigned to a task by listing more resource names to work on the task? That constitutes more units also. The answer depends on the nature of the work for the new resources.

As an example, suppose that Sam and Bob are individually named resources (not members of a group resource) and that it's reasonable to expect them to be able to load 100 boxes into a delivery van in 1 hour. Each man has to move 50 boxes to finish the task. If you were to give them some help by assigning Juan and Bill to help with the task and you add their names to the list of assigned resources, each of the four men would have only 25 boxes to move, and the task could be finished in half the time. The amount of work or effort involved in completing this task is fixed, and increasing the number of resources who are named to work on the task should reduce the time it takes to complete the task. In this case, you would want Project to manage the calculations just like it did for increasing the units of a single resource.

This is an example of an *effort-driven* task calculation. You want the total amount of work for the task to be fixed so that when you add resource names to the assignment list, Project reduces the workload for those already assigned to the task. By the same token, if you have to remove a resource from the assignment, it means more work for those resources that remain assigned to the task, and Project calculates increased amounts of work for them.

On the other hand, suppose that you decide to add Andy to the box-loading task to monitor the work and make sure inventory records are accurate. This is not the same work; it is an additional aspect of the task, and you want Project to add Andy's work to the total of the work done by the two men who are moving the boxes. This is an example of a calculation that is not effort-driven: You do not want the work to remain the same after adding the new resource name to the task.

By default, Project makes all new tasks effort-driven, but you can change the effort-driven status of a task when you change the list of resources assigned to the task to govern how Project calculates the change. The Effort Driven field is a check box on the Task Information dialog box and on the Task Form (see Figure 9.7).

Effort Driven check box

Figure 9.7
The Effort Driven check box is available on the Advanced tab of the Task Information dialog box as well as on the Task Form.

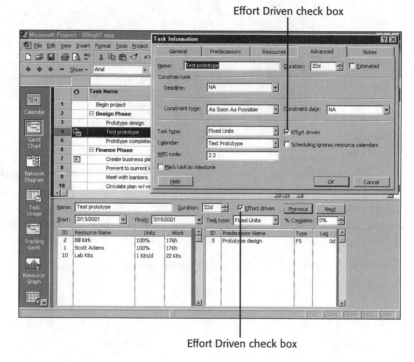

Effort Driven check box

Tip from Tim and the Project Team

Adding or removing material resource names to the list does not affect Effort Driven calculations because the work for material resources is not hours of effort but units consumed.

Note

When you make a task a Fixed Work task, it automatically becomes an Effort Driven task. Project automatically fills the Effort Driven check box and dims it so that you can't clear it.

The Effort Driven status is not a factor in the calculations when you first assign resources to a task because there is no work defined for the task until after the first work assignment. Thus, if you are using the Task Form and you create a list of resource names with assignments before clicking the OK button, Project calculates the hours of work for each of the work resources and sets the sum as the total work amount for the task.

The default status for new tasks in Project is Effort Driven, but you can change the default in the Options dialog box, right next to where you change the default Task Type (see Figure 9.8). Choose Tools, Options from the menu and select the Schedule tab on the Options dialog box. Deselect the New Tasks Are Effort Driven check box to change the default setting.

Figure 9.8
Set the default Effort Driven status for new tasks on the Options dialog box.

Default Effort Driven status

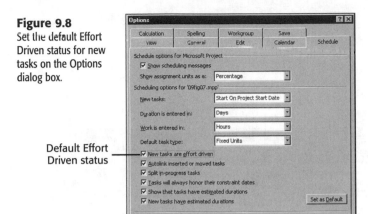

If, after the initial assignment of resources to a task, you add more work resources or remove some of the work resources, Project must consider the Effort Driven status of the task in its calculations. If Effort Driven is on, as it is by default, Project redistributes the total work for the task across the revised work resource list, prorating the work for each resource according to its share of the total number of work resource units assigned to the task.

For example, suppose that Mary and Scott are assigned to a 5-day (40 hour) Effort Driven task, as shown in Table 9.1.

TABLE 9.1 EFFORT DRIVEN TASK—THE INITIAL ASSIGNMENT

Resource	Units	Work	Duration
Mary	50%	20 hours	5 days
Scott	100%	40 hours	5 days
Task Total	150%	60 hours	5 days

Then, Pat is assigned to the task at 100% units. The total work is assumed by Project to remain unchanged at 60 hours (because this is an Effort Driven task). Project shifts some of the 60 hours of work to Pat and reduces the amounts assigned to Mary and Scott. The total units assigned has increased from 150% to 250%, as you can see in Table 9.2.

TABLE 9.2 EFFORT DRIVEN TASK—AFTER ADDING A NEW RESOURCE

Resource	Units	New Share of Task	Total Work	Duration
Mary	50%	50%/250% (1/5 of 60) =	12 hours	3 days
Scott	100%	100%/250% (2/5 of 60) =	24 hours	3 days
Pat	100%	100%/250% (2/5 of 60) =	24 hours	3 days
Task Total	250%		60 hours	3 days

Mary's 50% is 1/5 of the total units assigned, and her assigned work now is 1/5 of the 60 hours total or 12 hours. Similarly, Scott and Pat's units are both now 2/5 of the total units, and their work assignment is now 2/5 of 60 or 24 hours.

Each of the resources can now finish their work in 3 days, so the duration of the task is changed from 5 days to 3 days.

If Effort Driven is off, Project assumes that the work of a newly assigned resource is to be added to the existing work of all other named resources. The assignments of the existing resources are not changed. Table 9.3 shows how Project calculates work if Pat is added to a task that is not Effort Driven. The total work on the task rises from 60 to 100 hours, all due to adding Pat's 40 hours of work to the total. The task duration does not change.

TABLE 9.3   NON-EFFORT DRIVEN TASK—AFTER ADDING A NEW RESOURCE

Resource	Units	Work	Duration
Mary	50%	20 hours	5 days
Scott	100%	40 hours	5 days
Pat	100%	40 hours	5 days
Task Total	250%	100 hours	5 days

Similarly, if you remove a named resource from a task, Project reduces the total work for the task by that resource's work assignment and does not recalculate other resource assignments.

Note

The Effort Driven setting only regulates calculations when you add to or subtract from the list of assigned resources. For example, if you change the *duration* of an Effort Driven task, Project does not keep the work of the assigned resources the same but does change their work to fit the new duration.

You should feel free to temporarily change the Effort Driven field for a task if you need to. For example, suppose that you created a task for 20 hours of work moving stock in a warehouse and assigned warehouse workers to the task but forgot to assign the forklifts they would be using. If the task is Effort Driven and you add forklifts to the list of resources, Project reduces the current duration of the task and reassigns work from the warehouse workers to the forklifts. However, you simply want to add the forklifts without changing the duration because your original estimate of 20 hours of work was made assuming that the workers would have the forklifts to use. Before adding the forklifts, turn off the Effort Driven field. Then add the forklifts with Effort Driven off. Then you can turn Effort Driven back on for future calculations.

UNDERSTANDING THE DRIVER RESOURCE CONCEPT

The *driver resource* refers to the fact that, in some cases, one or more resources are fully occupied with work throughout a task's duration (the driver resources), and other resources have less work to do during the same period (the nondriver resources).

For example, if you create a task with the default duration of 1 day and then assign Mary, Scott, and Pat to the task with the work amounts given in Table 9.4, Project calculates the task duration to accommodate the longest time needed by any one of the resources. In this case, both Mary and Pat need 5 days to complete their assignments, so the task duration is changed by Project to 5 days. Scott only works the first 2 days on the task.

TABLE 9.4   DRIVER RESOURCES

Resource	Work	Units	Duration	Driver Resource
Mary	40 hours	100%	5 days	Yes
Scott	16 hours	100%	2 days	No
Pat	20 hours	50%	5 days	Yes
Task Duration			5 days	

Note

Note that Scott is assigned full-time, 100%, but because he only has 16 hours of work assigned, he will be finished in 2 days. Had he been assigned 16 hours at 40% units, it would take him all 5 days to complete his work, putting in a little over 3 hours each day.

In a case like this example, Mary and Pat are said to be *driver resources* because their assignments drive or determine the task duration. If you change the assigned work or units for Mary and Pat, it will likely have an effect on the duration of the task. For example, if you increase Mary's workload to 50 hours, she needs a longer time to complete it, and the task duration has to increase. However, you can make changes in Scott's assignment, within limits, without affecting the duration of the task:

- You can increase the work assigned to Scott from 16 hours to 40 hours without needing to increase the task's duration.

- You can also change Scott's Units from 100% down to as low as 40% before it impacts his ability to complete his assignment in the current duration.

- Similarly, you can reduce the task duration from 5 days down to 2 days without affecting Scott's ability to do the work currently assigned to him (16 hours at 100% effort).

If you change either the assigned units or the assigned work for a resource that is not a driver resource (a resource such as Scott that doesn't need the entire task duration to complete its assigned work) and the duration required by that resource after the change is still less than the task duration, Project does not need to change the task duration.

If there are multiple resources assigned to a task when you change the task Duration field entry, only the *driver resources* (those that must work for the full task duration to complete their work) are affected. However, if you shorten the task duration so much that nondriver resources cannot complete their work, they are affected also.

To summarize these points, consider the following:

- When you change the duration for a task, only the assignments for driver resources (those who need the full duration to complete their assignments) are affected. Project applies the work formula to calculate changes in the assignments. Nondriver resources are not affected as long as the change in duration still leaves them enough time to complete their assignments.

- When you change the assigned units or work for driver resources, task duration is affected, and Project recalculates the assignment values for all driver resources but not those for nondriver resources.

- When you change the assigned units or work for a nondriver resource without making it a driver resource, Project does not recalculate the assignment for that resource or for any other resources assigned to that task.

CALCULATING TASK DURATION WITH MULTIPLE RESOURCES ASSIGNED

When there are multiple resources assigned to a task, they might not all have the same work schedule. Some resources might not be available during the entire task duration. Individual schedules for some resources can be modified to delay an assignment or to split the assignment with a period of inactivity.

Duration in the simplest cases is just the number of work days between the start and finish of a task. This definition assumes that work goes on continuously during that time. Duration is now defined by Microsoft Project as the number of time periods during which any work resource is working on a task.

Note

The consumption of material resources is not considered in calculating duration.

As an example, suppose Bill Kirk and Mary Logan are both assigned 5 days of work preparing for a conference. The task duration is 5 days if they do their work during the same time periods. Suppose that Bill is taking 2 vacation days when the task starts, so Mary starts working on the task alone. He also has scheduled 2 more vacation days at the beginning of the following week. Bill starts working on the task 2 days later than Mary does. Then, they work together for 3 days, at which time Mary has completed her part of the task. Bill still has 2 days of work to do, but he doesn't do those days until after his second set of vacation days.

Bill's work schedule does not match Mary's. Mary's earlier start date and Bill's later finish date define the task's start and finish dates. The task duration is the number of time periods during which anyone is working on the task. In this case, the task duration is 7 days—2 days when Mary worked alone, 3 days when they were both working on the task, and 2 days when Bill worked alone after Mary finished her part.

Figure 9.9 illustrates this example and introduces you to the Task Usage view. I will use this view extensively later in this and the next several chapters. The top pane in Figure 9.9 displays the familiar Gantt Chart, but the bottom pane displays the Task Usage view. The Task Usage view shows tasks with their resource assignments indented beneath them. Because the Prepare for Conference task is selected in the top pane, you only see that task and its assignments in the Task Usage view in the bottom pane. If I had displayed the Task Usage view in the top pane, you would see all tasks and all assignments in that view.

Figure 9.9
The Task Usage view can show assigned work on a day-by-day basis.

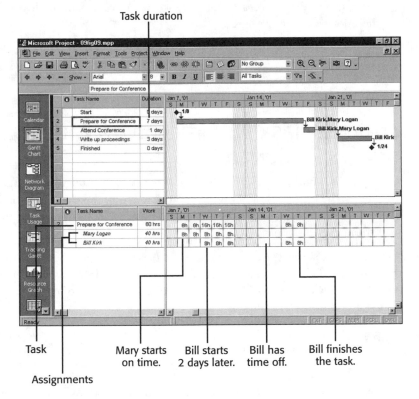

The Task Usage view replaces the Gantt Chart task bars in the timescale with a grid of cells that show work and other details during each period in the timescale. Figure 9.9 shows the hours of work that are scheduled for each date. You can edit the cells to change work assignments for individual time periods. Each task row is a kind of summary row for all the resource assignments that are indented beneath it. The task row provides totals in its grid cells for the assignment cells below it.

Figure 9.9 illustrates the duration example above very well. You can see that Bill and Mary work independently some days and together some days. If you count the number of days in the task row where total work is a full day or more (8 hours or more), you see that there are 7 such days and that is what determines the task duration of 7.

MODIFYING RESOURCE ASSIGNMENTS

You have seen that you can define a resource assignment by specifying the task duration, the assignment units, and the work for the assignment. You have seen that your choice of the task type and its Effort Driven status also impact resource assignments. In this section, you will examine other options you have for fine-tuning resource assignments. Your choices include the following:

- Assigning overtime work on a task.
- Applying one of the predefined work contours to an assignment.
- Manually adjusting a resource contour on a task.
- Splitting a resource's schedule on a task to accommodate time when she is needed elsewhere.
- Splitting an entire task and rescheduling the remaining work.
- Adding a delay to a resource's start date for working on a task.
- Scheduling the resource based on a task calendar instead of the resource calendar.

USING OVERTIME TO SHORTEN DURATION

You can reduce the duration for a task by allowing some of a resource's work to be scheduled as overtime work. To Microsoft Project, *overtime* work means work that is scheduled sometime other than during the working times defined on the resource calendar. If you assign overtime work, the total work to be done on the assignment remains the same, but the amount of work that is scheduled during regular working-time hours is reduced by the amount of the overtime. Also, the overtime rate for the resource is charged for the overtime work.

For example, suppose that Bill Kirk has been assigned full-time (100% units) to write a report that is scheduled to take 60 hours of work and requires a duration of 7.5 days to complete. Bill is scheduled to start on a Monday and finish at mid-day on Wednesday, 1 week later. The Cost of the task is $1,200 (based on Bill's standard rate of $20/hour). However, Bill's manager decides she must have the report in no more than 5 days, so she authorizes 20 hours of overtime work for Bill on this task. Bill still spends 60 hours on the report, but 20 hours are overtime hours and only 40 hours are scheduled in the regular working time made available by his resource calendar.

This example is illustrated with the "before and after" tasks Write Report (No Overtime) and Write Report (with Overtime) in the Task Usage view at the top of Figure 9.10. The assignment details on the right have been increased to show not only Work (which is total work per period), but to break that down into Regular Work and Overtime Work. In the figure, the work amounts are in bold. The Cost of the work in each time period is also included. The value in the Cost column on the left is the sum of the italicized daily costs in the grid.

Note

Bill's assignment rows are hidden in Figure 9.10 because he is the only resource assigned to each of these tasks and therefore the task totals for work and cost that you see are the same as Bill's values. This makes the figure easier to read.

Work details
by category

Figure 9.10
Scheduling overtime
work shortens task
duration but can lead
to increased cost.

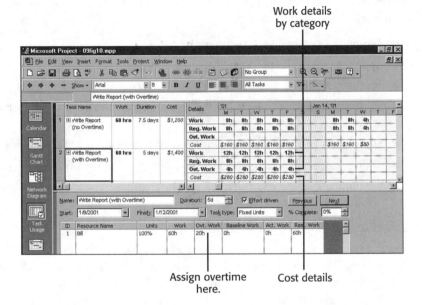

Assign overtime
here.

Cost details

For Task 1 (no overtime), the total work is 60 hours, which is the sum of the Work hours in the grid. You can see that the total Work for each day is made up of Regular Work only. The duration of Task 1 is 7.5 days, and that is due to the fact that there are 7 full days of work and 1 half day of only 4 hours. The total cost of the task is $1,200, which is the sum of the daily Cost values in the grid.

For Task 2 (with overtime), the total in the Work column on the left is the same as for Task 1, but the grid shows that Bill now does 12 hours of work a day—8 hours of regular work plus 4 hours of overtime. All 60 hours of work are completed in just 5 days; thus, the task duration is 5 days. The cost in each day is $280. This is made up of $160 of standard rate hours (8 hours at $20/hour) plus $120 of overtime rate hours (4 hours at $30/hour).

The bottom pane shows the Task Form with the Resource Work (or assignment) details displayed at the bottom. Because Task 2 is selected in the top pane, the details show the values with overtime assigned. Note that the Ovt. Work field displays 20 hours. The Work field shows the total work, 60 hours, which includes overtime.

Tip from Tim and the Project Team

The cost figures in Figure 9.10 do not display decimal digits, and this helps make columns narrower to display more days in the grid. To hide the display of decimal digits, choose Tools, Options to display the Options dialog box, and select the View tab. Use the spin control in the Decimal Digits box to select 0.

The easiest way to assign overtime hours for a resource is to display the Task Form or the Resource Form in the bottom pane and to display the Resource Work details (or Work details in the Resource Form) at the bottom of the form. Figure 9.10 shows the Task Form in the lower pane with Resource Work details displayed.

Note

Overtime work that is scheduled by Project cannot be adjusted manually. That is, you can't edit the cells in the grid to change the number of overtime hours scheduled on a particular day. However, when you are tracking progress on the task, you can enter the amount of actual overtime work in each time period to show exactly when the overtime work was performed.

CONTOURING RESOURCE USAGE

The traditional resource work pattern is the so-called *flat pattern*. The flat pattern schedules a resource's work to begin when the task begins, using the same units assignment every day until the assigned work is completed. Sometimes, you might want a resource to put greater effort into a task at the outset and then to taper off the daily effort until the task is finished. In that case, you want to assign more units and hours at the beginning of the task and then use a reduced number of units and hours each day to complete the task. This is called *front loading* the work on the task. Other times, you might want to *back load* the work by starting with a small number of hours and assignment units up front and then increasing the work as the task nears completion. Varied scheduling patterns like these are available in Project as *work contours*. The default resource schedule is the flat contour pattern, but you can have Project modify an assignment schedule by applying one of seven predefined work contours.

To change the scheduling pattern, you display either the Task Usage view (see Figure 9.11) or the Resource Usage view (see Figure 9.12). The Resource Usage view is similar to the Task Usage view in that it displays all the resources with their assignments indented beneath them and provides assignment details for each period in the timescale in a grid of cells. Both these views enable you to apply contoured assignments, either by applying one of the built-in contours or by editing the work assigned in any given time period in the grid.

Suppose that Bill is assigned another report to write that's estimated to take 40 hours to complete. He needs to concentrate completely on the report to start with, but he can start spending more time on other tasks once it's underway. You could schedule his assignment like the example in the Task Usage view in Figure 9.11 (which is again a "before and after" example). Task 1 is named Write Report (Flat Contour), and it shows the standard assignment schedule.

Note that the grid in Figure 9.11 shows a new detail field, Peak Units. The Peak Units field shows the maximum units that are assigned to the task at any moment in time during the time period covered by the cell. You can see from the Units field in the bottom pane that Bill's initial assignment to the task was at 100%. In the standard schedule, that means his Peak Units is 100% in all 5 days and he is assigned 8 hours of work each day.

Task 2 shows Bill's assignment schedule after applying the front-loaded contour. Note the icon in the indicator column that flags this assignment as having a front-loaded contour. His assignment units start at 100% but soon drop to lower and lower levels until all the work is completed, and consequently the value for the hours of work scheduled for each day becomes less and less. Bill still does 40 hours of work, but it takes longer now. Note that the duration for Task 2 is 8.33 days instead of 5 days.

Figure 9.11
The Task Usage view displays all the resource assignments indented under each task.

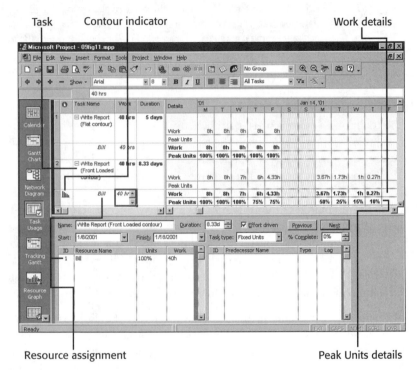

Figure 9.12 shows the Resource Usage view of Bill's front-loaded task. The main record is now the resource, Bill, instead of the task, but indented under it is the same assignment record, now labeled with the associated task name, Write Report (Front Loaded contour). The details in the grid are the same as those for Task 2 in Figure 9.11. However, the detail labels are missing because the bottom pane shows another view with a timescale. Project leaves off the detail labels so that the two timescales are aligned.

The view in the bottom pane of Figure 9.12 is the Resource Graph. This view displays a histogram (a vertical bar chart) to give a graphical image of the resource assignment detail that you select. In this case, the Peak Units detail is graphed and illustrates very nicely the declining nature of the front-loaded work contour. In fact, this graph is the source of the image that is used in the indicator for front-loaded contours.

→ For more information about the Resource Graph, **see** "The Resource Graph," **p. 867**

Figure 9.12
The Resource Usage view displays all task assignments under each resource name.

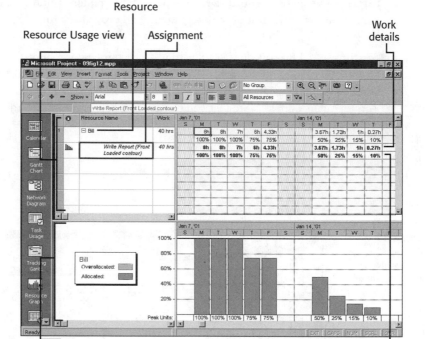

Resource Usage view · Resource · Assignment · Work details

Resource Graph · Peak Units details

Project 2000 provides seven predefined work contour patterns that you can apply to a resource assignment. These are in addition to the default assignment pattern, called *flat*, which is used when Project initially calculates an assignment. The contour patterns are illustrated in Figure 9.13 and are listed as follows:

- **Flat**—This is the pattern used in the initial assignment calculation by Project. All work is assigned as soon as the task starts and continues until the assignment is completed. There is no icon for this pattern.

- **Back Loaded**—The daily workload starts light and builds to the end of the task.

- **Front Loaded**—Heaviest daily load is at the beginning of the task and tapers off continuously to the end of the task.

- **Double Peak**—The daily workload starts low, builds to an early peak, drops off, builds to another peak, and then tapers off to the end of the task.

- **Early Peak**—The daily workload starts light, builds rapidly to a peak, and then tapers off to the end of the task.

- **Late Peak**—The daily workload starts light, builds slowly to a peak near the end of the task, and then drops off somewhat at the end.

- **Bell**—The daily workload starts light, builds to a peak in the middle of the assignment, and then tapers off to the end of the assignment.

- **Turtle**—The daily workload starts somewhat light, builds rapidly to a plateau, remains there for most of the rest of the assignment, and drops back to a somewhat light level at the end.

- **Contoured**—This row does not illustrate a predefined contour; rather, it illustrates the fact that you can edit the work assignments to produce your own work pattern. The indicator, with a pencil on the bar chart, serves notice that the work assignment has been manually edited. Note that you can only edit the Work cells. You cannot edit the Peak Units values directly.

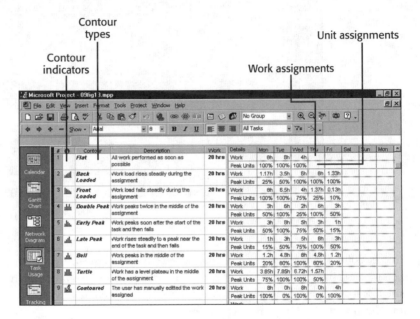

Figure 9.13
Work contours redistribute assigned work over a longer duration.

Figure 9.13 illustrates the contour types in an actual calculation by Microsoft Project. The first row, labeled Flat, shows how an initial assignment of 20 hours of work to a 5-day task was scheduled for a resource with a unit assignment of 100%.

In the timescale on the right, you can see the Work and Peak Units for each day. The resource is assigned 100% to the task, and for the all 3 days, 100% of its time is allocated to the task. There are 8 hours of work for the first 2 days but only 4 hours on Wednesday because the assignment is completed after 4 hours of work.

Each of the other rows shows how Project would schedule the work if one of the other contours is applied. The Total Work remains 20 hours in all cases, as seen in the Total Work column. The Work assignment for each day varies depending on the contour pattern, as does the Peak Units.

Each of the contours reduces the unit assignment during selected days in the assignment; the choice of which days determines the pattern that is the source of the different contour names. Because less work is scheduled in some days, the total assignment necessarily takes longer to complete. Note that the duration of the task is extended when the contours are applied. Instead of completing the task on Wednesday, work must continue until Friday.

The last row in Figure 9.13 is labeled Contoured and represents a case where the user has manually created a unique contour, in this case by scheduling the work for Monday, Wednesday, and Friday only (scheduling no work on Tuesday and Thursday). In either the Task Usage or Resource Usage view, you can edit the assigned hours in the Work details cells.

 To apply a contour to an assignment, you should display either the Task Usage or Resource Usage view and then select the indented assignment that you want to change. Double-click the assignment row or use the Assignment Information tool on the standard toolbar to display the Assignment Information dialog box (see Figure 9.14). Display the pull-down list of contours in the Work Contour field and select the one you want to apply. Note that the first contour is the flat contour. Select Flat to reset an assignment back to a standard schedule with no contour.

Figure 9.14
The Assignment Information dialog box displays settings that affect the scheduling of the assignment.

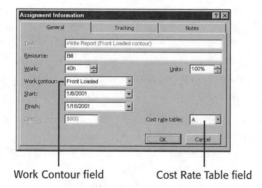

Work Contour field   Cost Rate Table field

Tip from Tim and the Project Team

Note that the Assignment Information dialog box is where you assign a different cost rate table for an assignment. Use the pull-down list in the Cost Rate Table to select tables A through F.

Tip from Tim and the Project Team

If you change the work contour or the cost rate table for an assignment, it's a good idea to document why you made the choices you made in the assignment Notes field. Click the Notes tab in the Assignment Information dialog box (refer to Figure 9.14) and enter supporting documentation about an assignment, including links to external documents such as job specifications or standards.

Note

If overtime hours are assigned to the task when you apply a contour, Project spreads the overtime out evenly over the duration of the assignment, no matter which contour is applied.

Tip from Tim and the Project Team

If you want to add a resource with a contoured assignment to an existing task that has other resources already assigned and if you don't want the task duration or the other resource schedules to change when you apply the contour to the new resource's assign ment, make the task a Fixed Duration task before assigning the contour. You can later return the task to its previous task type. Project applies the contour but has to stop scheduling hours when it reaches the end of the task duration. As a result, the new resource has a lower total amount of work than it initially did.

SPLITTING A TASK ASSIGNMENT

 Splitting an assignment means that you schedule an interruption in the work, usually extending the duration of the assignment to make up for the time lost to the interruption. There are two basic methods for splitting a work assignment:

■ You can split the task, and Project automatically splits each resource assignment for the task, with zero work scheduled during the period of the split.

■ You can split an individual resource assignment by inserting one or more periods of zero work in the middle of the assignment.

If you introduce a split in an individual resource assignment, Project does not show a split in the task unless it is the only resource assignment for the task or unless you introduce the same split in all assigned resources.

Figure 9.15 shows three tasks to which both Mary Logan and Bill Kirk are assigned. The view has a Gantt Chart in the top pane and the Task Usage view in the bottom pane. The work detail in the bottom pane for their assignments to the Prepare for Conference task shows a split in the assignment on Wednesday. This split was the result of splitting the task; thus, all assigned resources receive a split in their schedules.

Figure 9.15
Introduce a split in a task assignment when the resource needs to work on another task temporarily.

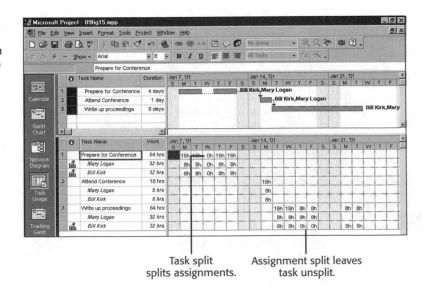

Task split
splits assignments.

Assignment split leaves
task unsplit.

Bill Kirk also has a 2-day split in his assignment to the Write Up Proceedings task. However, the task bar in the top pane of Figure 9.15 is not split because Mary Logan, who is also assigned to the task, continues to work on those days, while Bill is diverted to another task.

SCHEDULING A LATE START FOR AN ASSIGNMENT

Sometimes, one of the resources assigned to a task is expected to perform a function that is needed not at the beginning of the task, but only after some work on the task has been completed. For example, a group charged with proposing a new product might need to run its preliminary ideas for a proposal by technical experts for feedback on the feasibility of the ideas. If an expert is too expensive to engage in the preliminary debates, the expert's assignment to the task can be delayed to start only after the task has been underway for an appropriate amount of time.

You also need to delay an assignment if one of the resources assigned to a task is needed more urgently elsewhere in the project at the time that the task is scheduled to start.

You can delay the start of an assignment by entering a value in any one of several places in Microsoft Project:

- The assignment Delay field is displayed in the Resource Schedule details of both the Task Form and the Resource Form. In Figure 9.16, the Task Form is displayed in the bottom pane. Mary Logan's assignment has 1d entered in the Delay field. As a consequence, although the Start date for the task is January 16, 2001, the Start date for her assignment is January 17, 2001.

  If you enter a value in the Delay field, Project automatically calculates the delayed dates for the Start and Finish date fields.

Note
> The default entry in the Delay field is 0d, which means no delay. The Delay field is never blank. You can remove a delay by entering zero in the Delay field; you cannot erase an entry and try to leave the field blank.

- You can also enter a delayed start date in the Start field to the right of the Delay field. Project automatically calculates the value for the Delay field.

Note
> If you enter a date in the Finish field to the right of the Delay field in the Task Form or in the Finish field in the Assignment Information dialog box, Project does not calculate a delay for the Start date. Instead, it recalculates the amount of work that is completed between the (unchanged) start of the assignment and the new finish you just entered.

- You can enter a delayed start date in the Assignment Information dialog box. The Assignment Information dialog box in Figure 9.16 was displayed by double-clicking the assignment row for Mary Logan in the Task Usage view in the top pane. The Start field is on the General tab. Click the calendar control to the right of the field to select a start date.

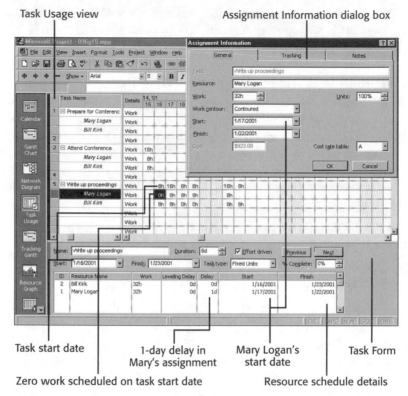

Figure 9.16
Create a delay in an assignment to recognize the fact that the resource is not necessary at the start of the task.

Task Usage view

Assignment Information dialog box

Task start date

1-day delay in Mary's assignment

Mary Logan's start date

Task Form

Zero work scheduled on task start date

Resource schedule details

The Delay field does not appear on the Assignment Information dialog box, but its value is recalculated if you enter a new date in the Start field.

- You can also create a delay for an assignment by editing the work details in the timescale of the Task Usage view or the Resource Usage view. Figure 9.16 shows the Task Usage view in the top pane with Mary Logan's assignment selected. The timescale shows 0h highlighted on the Monday for her assignment. The delay could have been created by inserting this day of zero work in the timescale. Project would then have automatically calculated the value displayed in the Delay, Start, and Finish fields in the Task Form in the bottom pane and in the Assignment Information dialog box.

This discussion about delaying assignments has been presented in terms of projects that are scheduled from a fixed start date. In those projects, Microsoft Project schedules tasks and assignments as soon as possible, calculates the start date for both tasks and assignments first, and then calculates their finish dates. A delay in an assignment is tantamount to a late start, and it offsets that assignment schedule from other resource assignment schedules on the same task.

If your project is scheduled from a fixed finish date, Microsoft Project first schedules the last tasks in each chain of linked tasks to end on the fixed finish date. Task and assignment finish dates are calculated first and then their start dates are calculated. Project then works backward along the chain of linked tasks, scheduling later tasks before earlier tasks until the start of the project is reached and a project start date is calculated.

You cannot introduce delays (late starts) for assignments in fixed finish date projects because that would delay the project finish date, which is fixed by definition. You can, however, modify assignments to show that some resource assignments are offset from others by introducing an early finish for an assignment.

An early finish for an assignment in a fixed finish date project is entered in the same Delay field I used previously, but it is entered as a negative number. Alternatively, you can enter an early finish date in the assignment's Finish field, and Project calculates the (negative) Delay value for you and a new date for the Start field.

As a corollary to the note, if you enter a different date in the assignment Start field, Project does not adjust the Delay value but calculates a new amount of work for the assignment based on the (unchanged) finish date and the start date you enter.

> **Note**
>
> You can enter negative amounts in the assignment Delay field only if the project is scheduled from a fixed finish date. You can enter positive amounts only if the project is scheduled from a fixed start date.

SCHEDULING WITH TASK CALENDARS

 If a task has its own special calendar assigned to it, Project schedules work for the resources only in those times where the working times for both the task calendar and the resource calendar intersect. Project displays the Assigned Calendar indicator (see Figure 9.17) for the task.

> *Tip from Tim and the Project Team*
>
> If the task and resource calendars do not intersect for enough hours to complete the task, Project displays an indicator to alert you that there are insufficient intersecting working times. You need to modify one of the calendars or tell Project to ignore the resource calendar (see the following text).

This facility is useful when there are special nonworking times associated with the task but you don't want to enter those nonworking times on the resource calendars because they would interfere with scheduling other task assignments for the resources.

For instance, a key resource for the task might have unique nonworking times, and no other resources can work when that key resource is unavailable. The equipment on an assembly line, for example, might need to be offline for four hours every week for maintenance. You could create an Assembly Line Maintenance base calendar to define these nonworking hours and assign it to the task. The alternative would be to add the nonworking times for this key resource to the calendars for all the other resources assigned to the task. Again, that could interfere with scheduling the other resources for other tasks.

Figure 9.17
Attach a base calendar to a task to limit the working time for scheduled work on the task.

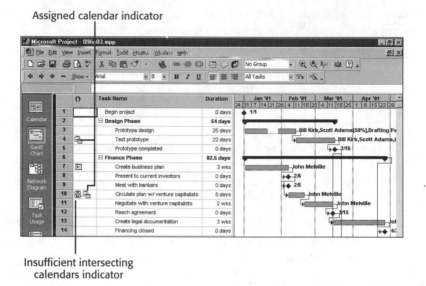

Assigned calendar indicator

Insufficient intersecting calendars indicator

To assign a calendar to the task, you have to create the special base calendar first, using the Tools, Change Working Time command. Then select the task and display the Task Information dialog box. On the Advanced tab, display the drop-down list of base calendars in the Calendar box and select the appropriate calendar (see Figure 9.18).

→ For instructions on creating base calendars, **see** "Defining a Calendar of Working Time," **p. 84**

Figure 9.18
Assign task calendars in the Task Information dialog box.

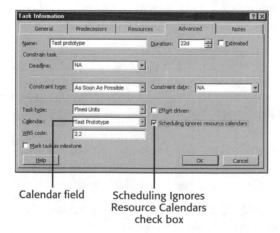

Calendar field

Scheduling Ignores Resource Calendars check box

If you want Project to ignore the resource calendar working times, fill the Scheduling Ignores Resource Calendars check box. In that case, the number of hours of work scheduled for a resource on any given day depends on the units assigned and the work hours defined on the task calendar, not the resource calendar. It is up to you to verify that the resources can, in fact, meet this schedule.

TROUBLESHOOTING

RESOURCE POOL LISTS

My resource pool list keeps growing, but I don't remember adding to it myself. What's happening?

It's possible that you have accidentally mistyped existing resource names. If you don't have the chance to intervene, Project creates a new variation of the same resource in the pool with a slightly different spelling. You should require that Project alert you before a new name is added to the resource pool to cut down on misspellings being entered into your resource pool.

CONTROLLING TASK TYPES

I added to my project plan a 2-hour weekly meeting that is attended each week by different people depending on the project stage. Each time I assign new resources to the meeting task, Project tries to change the duration. Am I doing something wrong?

You should select the appropriate task type—either Fixed Duration, Fixed Units, or Fixed Work. By selecting a task type, you choose how you want Project to calculate changes in the task assignment schedule as it keeps the resource work formula in balance. You can leave the task type as a permanent attribute of the task, but you can also change the task type temporarily at any time to control how Project treats a particular change in one of the work equation variables.

CHAPTER 10

ASSIGNING RESOURCES AND COSTS TO TASKS

AN OVERVIEW OF ASSIGNING RESOURCES

You usually assign resources to tasks because you want Microsoft Project to help you schedule and monitor the work the resource does on the task. You can also use resource assignments to associate a cost with the task, such as the contract fee of a vendor who will deliver the completed task without requiring you to schedule and monitor the work. Finally, you can use a resource assignment to associate a name with the task just for reporting purposes. This chapter shows you how to use Microsoft Project's views and tools to assign resources and to modify resource assignments. To benefit the most from this chapter, you should understand the contents of Chapter 8, "Defining Resources and Costs," and Chapter 9, "Understanding Resource Scheduling." There are intricate relationships among task and resource fields that are covered in those chapters.

When assigning resources to tasks, there are a number of data fields you can use to give Microsoft Project the information it needs to calculate schedules and costs as you intend:

- You can choose the task type and effort-driven settings at the task level to control how Project calculates changes in the schedule due to resource assignments.

- You *must* identify the name when you assign it to a task.

- You can define the units assigned or let Project assign the default number of units.

- You can define the amount of work the resource performs or let Project calculate that from the task duration and number of units.

- You can let Project use the default cost rates for the resource or select a special Cost Rate table you have defined if the task is to be charged different rates from those normally used for this resource.

- To speed up progress on the task, you can assign the resource overtime work or modify the resource calendar to provide additional available hours on specific days.

- You can accept the default work pattern for the assignment, which is an even amount of work each day until the task is complete, or you can modify the work contour to schedule more work at different times in the assignment. You can also delay the start of the assignment beyond the start of the task and split the assignment to work around interruptions in the availability of the resource.

As you can see, Project provides you the opportunity to fine-tune resource assignments so that schedule and cost calculations can be very precise. On the other hand, you can also get by with just the minimum amount of definition if you don't need all that sophistication.

This chapter shows you how to enter all the information listed above. You will also see how to use quick tools that record the minimum amount of information needed to get the job done. There are a number of different views and tools you can use to assign resources, and you will see how to use all of them. Each has its advantages.

SELECTING THE APPROPRIATE TASK SETTINGS

If you don't assign resources to tasks or if you only assign material resources, you do not have to be concerned with selecting the task type or whether the task is effort-driven. Most resource assignments are for work resources, and for those you need to consider the task type and the effort-driven setting for a task each time you make or change resource assignments for the task.

The effort-driven setting and the task types were defined and explained in detail in Chapter 9. Only a summary of the distinctions among the task types is given here. Similarly, the data fields that define a resource were covered in detail in Chapter 8 and are not explained again in detail here.

→ For more information about task types, **see** "Choosing the Task Type," **p. 377**
→ For more information about effort-driven tasks, **see** "Understanding Effort-Driven Tasks," **p. 380**
→ For detailed explanations of the use of the resource fields, **see** "Using the Resource Fields," **p. 328**

By selecting a task type, you choose how you want Project to calculate changes in the task schedule when any one of the three variables in the resource Work formula is changed. The Work formula, you will recall, is as follows:

$$\text{Duration} \times \text{Units} = \text{Work}$$
$$D \times U = W$$

The elements of the equation are as follows:

- Duration is the task duration.
- Units is the number of units of the assigned resource.
- Work is the number of hours the resource is scheduled to devote to the task.

When one of these values is changed, either one or both of the other values *must* change to keep the equation valid. Project automatically recalculates the values in the equation any time one of the values changes.

By choosing a task type, you let Project know which value you want it to leave undisturbed—which value it should leave *fixed*. You must choose one of the three task types:

- Choose *Fixed Units*, which is the default for Project, if you want Project to leave the assigned Units unchanged when you change either Work or Duration. Duration and Work then respond to changes in each other. If you change the fixed Units yourself, Project recalculates Duration, not Work, to keep the equation in balance. Project's response to your changes in a Fixed Units task will be as follows:

    Changing Duration causes Project to change Work in the same direction (both increasing or decreasing together).

    Changing Work causes Project to change Duration in the same direction (both increasing or decreasing together).

PART III · CH 10

Changing Units causes Project to change Duration in the opposite direction (increasing when Units decreases and vice versa).

■ Choose *Fixed Duration* if you want Project to leave the task's Duration unchanged when either Work or assigned Units is changed. Work and Units are then linked so that changing one changes the other for this task. If you change the fixed Duration yourself, Project recalculates Work. Project's response to your changes in a Fixed Duration task will be as follows:

Changing Units causes Project to change Work in the same direction (both increasing or decreasing together).

Changing Work causes Project to change Units in the same direction (both increasing or decreasing together).

Changing Duration itself causes Project to change Work in the same direction.

■ Choose *Fixed Work* if you want Project to leave assigned Work unchanged when you change either Duration or Units. Changing Duration leads to a change in Units and vice versa. If you change assigned Work for a Fixed Work task, Project recalculates Duration. Project's response to your changes in a Fixed Work task will be as follows:

Changing Duration causes Project to change Units in the opposite direction (decreasing when Duration increases and vice versa).

Changing Units causes Project to change Duration in the opposite direction (decreasing when Units increases and vice versa).

Changing Work causes Project to change Duration in the same direction.

The default type for new tasks in Microsoft Project is *Fixed Units*, which means that Project normally enables you to change the units assigned and recalculates Duration if you change Work or recalculates Work if you change Duration.

You can make any one of the three task types the default for new tasks by following these steps:

1. Choose Tools, Options to display the Options dialog box.
2. Select the Schedule tab.
3. In the Default Task Type field, use the drop-down list to select the type you want to be the default.

To verify or change the Task Type setting, follow these steps:

1. Select the task.
2. Click the Task Information tool to display the Task Information dialog box.
3. Select the Advanced tab.
4. Set the Task Type by choosing the list arrow and selecting Fixed Duration, Fixed Units, or Fixed Work (see Figure 10.1).

Task duration

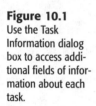

Figure 10.1
Use the Task
Information dialog
box to access addi-
tional fields of infor-
mation about each
task.

Task constraint

Task type

Task calendar

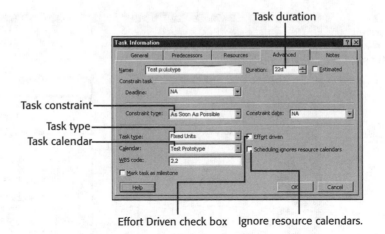

Effort Driven check box   Ignore resource calendars.

PART
III
CH
10

5. Choose OK.

You can also select the task type on the Task Form (see Figure 10.2), which is the view displayed in the bottom pane when you split a full-screen task view. To change the task type
settings using the Task Form, follow these steps:

1. If not already displayed, choose a task view such as the Gantt Chart, the Task Sheet, or
   the Task Usage view.

2. Split the view by choosing Window, Split. The bottom pane displays the Task Form
   view.

3. Activate the bottom pane. If resource details are not visible, choose Format, Details,
   and select one of the options that includes resources, such as Resources & Predecessors.

4. Use the Task Type list box to choose a new task type.

Closely allied to the choice of a task type is the choice of whether a task is *effort-driven*. The
default for new tasks in Microsoft Project is Effort Driven, but you can change that to
non–Effort Driven. This choice only has importance when you change the number of work
resource names assigned to a task. It does not have any effect if you merely change the number of assigned units for an already assigned resource or if you change the material resources
assigned to the task.

If the task is effort-driven, when you add new work resource names to the assignment list,
Project divides the preexisting work among all the resources, which results in less work for
the preexisting resources and a shorter duration for the task. Conversely, if you remove a
named work resource from a task, Project assigns its work to the remaining resources, and
the task duration increases.

If a task is not effort-driven, Project does not change the workloads of existing resources
when you add a new work resource, and task duration does not change. Total work for the
task increases due to the addition of a new work resource.

Figure 10.2
The Task Type field can also be accessed on the Task Form.

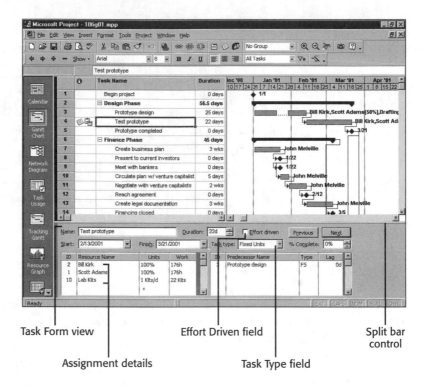

Task Form view   Effort Driven field   Split bar
                                                      control

Assignment details   Task Type field

To verify or change the Effort Driven setting for a task, follow these steps:

1. Select the task.

2. Click the Task Information tool to display the Task Information dialog box. The Effort Driven field also appears on the Task Form (refer to Figure 10.2).

3. Select the Advanced tab.

4. Look at the Effort Driven check box to change its status (refer to Figure 10.1). If the check box is filled, the task is Effort Driven; if empty, the task is not Effort Driven. Click the check box if you want to change its status.

5. Choose OK.

The default status for new tasks in Project is Effort Driven, but you can change that default on the Options dialog box. Choose Tools, Options and select the Schedule tab on the Options dialog box. Deselect the New Tasks Are Effort Driven check box to change the default setting.

Remember, before making any change in resource assignments, ask yourself these two questions:

■ What do I want Project to leave unchanged when I enter this new information: Duration, Units, or Work?

■ Am I changing the number of named work resources that are already assigned to this task, and if so, do I want the total work for the task to remain the same or to be changed? If you want the total work to change, be sure you uncheck the Effort Driven field for the task.

Then make sure that the task type and the effort-driven status is appropriate for the result you want to see.

ASSIGNING RESOURCES TO TASKS

There are a variety of views and dialog boxes you can use to assign resources to existing tasks. These include the following (in increasing order of usefulness):

- You can use the task sheet to enter assignments in the Resource Names column, but the syntax is strict, and you can't control the calculations very well.

- The Assign Resources dialog box, where drag-and-drop is available, is the quickest way to assign resources, but it provides you only limited control over how Project calculates the assignment.

- Similarly, the Task Information dialog box enables you to assign resources but only offers limited control over the calculation.

- Using the Task Form view, especially in the bottom pane of a task view such as the Gantt Chart or the Network Diagram, gives you almost total control over the resource assignment calculations. The Task Form enables you to change the Task Type and Effort Driven status of the task, and you can specify the Duration, Units, and/or Work for the assignment.

- You get the most control over the assignment process when you use the Task Usage view in the top pane with the Task Form in the bottom pane. The Task Usage view replaces the Gantt Chart task bars in the timescale with a grid of cells that show details about the assignment during each period in the timescale. You can edit the cells to change work assignments in individual time periods. Plus, you can access the Assignment Information dialog box from this view to specify work contours, to assign different standard costs, and to document the assignment with notes.

The Assign Resources dialog box and the Task Information dialog box offer pop-up accessibility from any task view, but they accept and display a limited amount of data. They enable you to change the Work or the Units for an assignment, but not both.

The Task Form gives you access to most of the important task, resource, and assignment fields that govern resource assignments. It is especially useful in the bottom pane under a task view such as the Gantt Chart, the Network Diagram, or the Task Usage view. The latter view, Task Usage, adds accessibility to the Assignment Information dialog box and to the timephased details of the work schedule for the ultimate control over resource assignments.

You will use the Gantt Chart over the Task Form first to see how to assign resources because the timephased data in the Task Usage view can be distracting at first. Then, you will put the Task Usage view in the top pane and look at fine-tuning assignments. Later, you will also see how to use the other views and dialog boxes mentioned previously in case you want to use them also.

ASSIGNING RESOURCES WITH THE TASK ENTRY VIEW

The Task Entry view, with the Gantt Chart in the top pane and the Task Form in the bottom pane, is one of the best combinations for assigning resources. You have access to the important fields that govern the task, and the form can display resource assignment details in a table at the bottom of the form. The most commonly displayed details are ID Resource, Name, Units, and Work for each assigned resource, but you can also display the overtime work fields and the scheduled delay fields for fine-tuning individual assignments. This is a convenient place for assigning resources because it enables you to enter resource Units, Work, or both for each resource assignment.

The Task Entry view is the view you get when you display the Gantt Chart and use the Window, Split command. The Task Form is displayed in the bottom pane with one of eight possible sets of details. For assigning resources you will want to use either the default details, Resources and Predecessors, or Resource Work. To set up this view, follow these steps:

1. Choose View, Gantt Chart, or click the Gantt Chart icon on the View bar.

2. Split the view by choosing Window, Split. You can also double-click the split bar control below the vertical scrollbar.

3. Right-click anywhere in the bottom pane to display the details shortcut menu and choose Resources & Predecessors, Resources & Successors, or Resource Work (see Figure 10.3).

    The assignment details in these three choices include the Units field, along with Name and Work. The Resource Schedule details do not include Units, so you can't manage assignment units in that display.

Figure 10.3
The Details menu for the Task Form shows the current display with a check mark and enables you to select a new display.

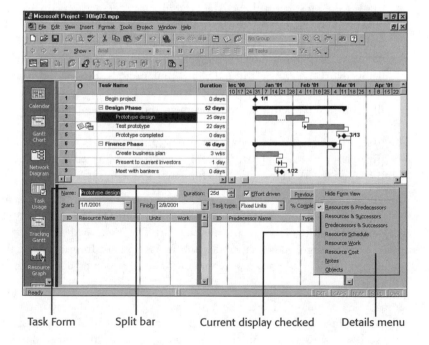

Task Form   Split bar   Current display checked   Details menu

ENTERING THE ASSIGNMENT VALUES

To assign resources using the Task Form, follow these steps:

1. Select the task in the top pane.

Tip from Tim and the Project Team

If the bottom pane is active, you can change the task selection in the top pane with the Previous and Next buttons in the lower pane. If the task you want to select is near to the currently selected task, this is faster than activating the top pane, selecting the task, and then activating the bottom pane again.

2. Check the Task Type field to be sure that it is set appropriately to manage the calculations for the assignments you are about to enter. If you are adding work resources and you want to be sure duration doesn't change, make the task a Fixed Duration task for this assignment and then return it to its prior setting after completing the assignment. For example, if you plan to enter Work amounts and want Project to calculate the Units needed to complete that work within the duration time period, make the task Fixed Duration.

3. If you are adding new work resource names to (or deleting existing resource names from) an existing list of resource name assignments, check the Effort Driven field for its appropriateness. If the changes you are about to enter change the total work associated with the task, clear the Effort Driven check box. However, if the changes simply redistribute the existing total work among the resources assigned to the task, leave the field checked.

4. Select the Resource Name field and identify the resource by selecting the resource name from the drop-down list. You can also type the name, but if you misspell it, Project might create a new resource for the misspelled name.

5. If you leave the Units field blank, Project assigns the default (the lesser of 100% or the Max Units for the resource). If you want to specify the units for the assignment, select the Units field and enter the units you want to assign as follows:

    - For work resources, type a units value as a percentage (for example, **200%**) unless you have chosen to use decimal format for units (for example, **2**).
    - For material resources with a fixed consumption rate, type a decimal number that represents the total units to be consumed by the task. For example, if 20 gallons of fuel (where "gal" is the material label for the resource) are to be assigned, enter **20**. Project replaces your entry with 20 gal.
    - For material resources with a variable consumption rate, type the number of units as a decimal followed by a slash and a time unit to indicate a rate of consumption. For example, to assign 20 gallons of fuel a week enter **20/wk**. Project replaces your entry with 20 gal/wk.

6. If you leave the Work field blank, Project calculates the work based on the task duration and the assigned (or default) units. If you want to specify the amount of work for the assignment, select the Work field and type the work amount. For work resources, work

must be entered with a number plus the unit of measure—minute(m), hour(h), day(d), week(w), or month (mo). For material resources, simply enter a decimal value, and Project uses this value as the fixed consumption rate for the task.

Note

Recall that if you enter both Units and Work, Project will recalculate the Duration (except for Fixed Duration tasks, in which case it keeps the Duration and Work values and recalculates Units).

7. If you are assigning multiple resources, you can enter additional resources in the next rows of the Resource Name column before you click the OK button. For instance, Figure 10.4 shows the resources to be assigned to the Prototype Design task.

8. After all resource assignments are made for the task, choose the OK button. Figure 10.5 shows the result when the OK button is clicked and Project has calculated the fields that were left blank.

Figure 10.4
If you initially enter all the resources that are to be assigned to a task at once, it makes the calculations easier to manage.

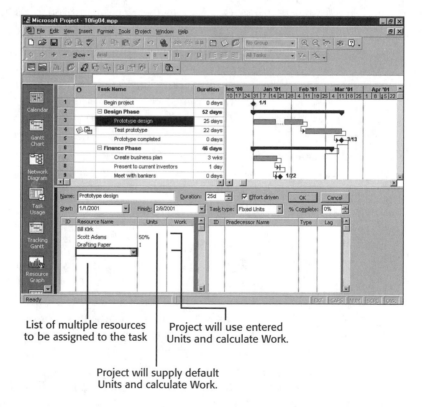

List of multiple resources to be assigned to the task

Project will use entered Units and calculate Work.

Project will supply default Units and calculate Work.

When you click OK, Project calculates the values for those fields you did not fill in, in accordance with the principles discussed in Chapter 9 (see Figure 10.5).

Figure 10.5
Project calculates all
the initial assignments
at once.

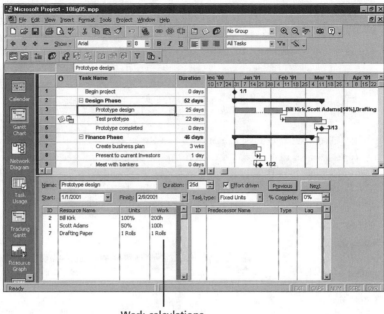

Work calculations

ADDING DELAY TO AN ASSIGNMENT

When you assign a resource to a task in a project that has a fixed start date, Project schedules the work to start when the task starts. Sometimes, however, one or more of the resources assigned to a task might be allowed to delay starting until after the task is partly completed by other resources.

> **Note**
> This discussion is presented in terms of *forward scheduled* projects—projects with fixed start dates. The case of the project with a fixed finish date is explained later in this section of the chapter.

For example, if you assign a marketing manager, an engineer, and a draftsman to draw up a preliminary design for a product, the draftsman's work on the task doesn't really start until some design details have already been proposed. To accurately schedule the draftsman's work, Project needs to delay the start of the draftsman's scheduled work to some time after the task starts.

Microsoft Project provides an Assignment Delay field, which you can use to force a delay in the scheduled work for a resource beyond the start of the task. If you want to enter a value in the Delay field on the Task Form, you need to display the Resource Schedule details where the Delay field is available for editing.

PART
III

CH
10

Note

You can also get to the Delay field by replacing the Task Form with the Resource Form and displaying the Schedule details (which is just like the Resource Schedule details on the Task Form).

You can also enter delays on the Task Usage and Resource Usage views. The Task Usage view is discussed in a later section of this chapter. The Resource Usage view is explored in greater detail in Chapter 11, "Resolving Resource Assignment Problems."

Figure 10.6 shows the Task Form with the Resource Schedule details displayed. The Prototype Design task is selected, and the three existing assigned resources are listed in the assignment details with the draftsman added at the bottom of the list. The draftsman is only scheduled to work 16 hours, much less than the hours for the other work resources. Note that there is already a split in this task, and that explains the later-than-expected finish date of the assignments.

Figure 10.6
The Resource Schedule details enable you to control when assigned work begins.

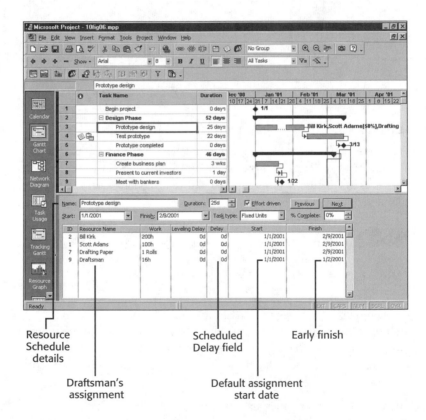

Resource Schedule details

Draftsman's assignment

Scheduled Delay field

Default assignment start date

Early finish

You can also see in Figure 10.6 that Project has scheduled all resources to start at the start of the task, which is 1/1/2001. In reality, the draftsman is expected to execute his assignment in the last 16 hours of the task, after the other resources have completed most of their work.

Figure 10.7 shows a delay of 28 days entered for the draftsman's assignment. Note that the Start and Finish dates for the assignment have been changed and that all three resources finish their assignments on the same date (which is also the finish of the task). Of course, if the delay causes the draftsman's assignment to finish after all the other assignments are finished, it also delays the finish of the task and increases the task's duration.

Figure 10.7
Delaying the start of the draftsman's assignment by 28 days places his work at the end of the task.

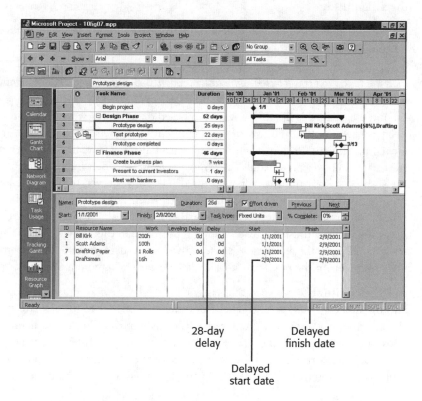

28-day delay

Delayed start date

Delayed finish date

To enter a delay in an assignment, you can follow these steps:

1. Display the Task Form or Task Details Form in the bottom pane of a task view, as described in the numbered steps at the beginning of this section.

2. Activate the form in the bottom pane and display the Schedule details by choosing Format, Details, Resource Schedule.

3. Select the task for the assignment in the top pane.

4. Select the cell in the Delay field for the resource name you want to delay.

5. Enter a Delay value, using a number followed by the measurement units for the delay (minutes, hours, days, weeks, or months). Alternatively, you can enter a delayed start date for the assignment in the Start field and Project calculates the Delay.

6. Click the OK button to complete the entry.

As pointed out in step 5, instead of entering the Delay value and having Project calculate a new assignment start date, you can also enter a new start date in the Start field and Project calculates the Delay value and the new Finish date. Don't attempt, however, to enter a delayed date in the Finish date column because Project doesn't treat that as a "delaying tactic." Instead, it treats it as an extension of the assignment and recalculates the Work value of the assignment.

To remove a delay for an assignment, enter a zero value in the Delay field and click the OK button. Project reschedules the assignment at the start of the task.

 If you have delayed an assignment in a Fixed Duration task, even though the assignment is shorter than the task, Project will increase the task duration! See "Scheduling Short Assignments in Fixed Duration Tasks" in the "Troubleshooting" section at the end of this chapter.

As noted earlier, this discussion has been based on a project with a fixed start date, and the delay is used to offset the *start* of an assignment from the start of the task. If your project has a fixed finish date, Project schedules the finish dates for tasks first and then calculates the start date. Likewise, it schedules assignments to finish when the task finishes and calculates the start of the assignment. Whereas the delays above served to offset the assignment start until after the task start, in a fixed finish date project the assignment finish is offset from the task finish so that the assignment finishes before the task finishes. Thus the concept of a delay becomes an early finish. Instead of adding the value in the Assignment Delay field to the task start to calculate the assignment start, in fixed finish date projects the Assignment Delay value is *subtracted* from the task finish to calculate an early assignment finish.

For fixed finish date projects, the Assignment Delay field accepts only negative numbers, and the delay amount is subtracted from the task finish date to calculate an early finish for the assignment. You can also enter an earlier date in the Finish date field, and Project calculates the negative delay and new start date for you. If you enter a new date in the Start date column, Project recalculates the Work value of the assignment instead of calculating a delay. As before, to remove a delay set the entry in the Assignment Delay field to zero.

ASSIGNING OVERTIME WORK

Recall that Project schedules work during the working times that are defined in the resource calendar (or in the task calendar if one is assigned and you have elected to ignore the resource calendars). Work that is scheduled during calendar working times is called *regular* work in Microsoft Project. If you want a resource to complete more work than can be done in regular time for a given period, you can assign part of the work as *overtime*. Project reduces the amount of the assignment's work that is scheduled during the regular hours, but the total work, regular plus overtime, remains the same.

Note that when you enter overtime work hours, you do not designate the exact days and hours when the overtime work takes place; you just tell Project that a certain number of hours on the task are overtime hours. Project schedules the overtime work by spreading it out evenly over the duration of the assignment. Later, when you enter actual work completed, you can specify exactly how many hours of overtime were completed in any given time period.

The cost of the overtime hours is calculated by using the overtime rate that you defined on the Resource Information dialog box for the period in which the work took place.

Another way to schedule more work during a specific time period is to change the resource calendar and increase the working time hours for that time period. You can edit the resource calendar and change nonworking days or hours into working times. Be aware, however, that Microsoft Project charges the Standard Rate for work scheduled during the regular working time hours. If the overtime rate for the resource is not zero, this is not a good solution because the cost is misrepresented. However, if you don't pay for overtime, editing the calendar is satisfactory. Indeed, editing the calendar gives you the ability of stating explicitly when the extra work time takes place. The drawback in this situation is that if you were to reassign the resource to different tasks, or if the task gets rescheduled to a different date range, you no longer need the extra working time. Project will use the time for other assignments unless you remember to remove the extra working time.

PART

III

CH

10

Scheduled overtime can be viewed in the Task and Resource Usage views, but you cannot enter overtime in those views unless you add a column for the Overtime Work field. The Overtime Work field appears on three forms for you to view and edit, and in each case, you must use the Format, Details command to apply the Work table at the bottom of the form. You can enter overtime in these standard views:

- The Task Form, with the Resource Work details table displayed at the bottom of the form

- The Task Details Form, with the Resource Work details table displayed at the bottom of the form

- The Resource Form, with the Work details table displayed at the bottom of the form

Note

If you assign all the work to be done in overtime, Project reduces the duration of the task to zero and automatically flags the task as a milestone. You can remove the milestone flag by opening the Task Information dialog box and clearing the Mark Task as Milestone check box on the Advanced tab. The milestone symbol no longer appears in the Gantt Chart for the task, although its duration still is zero.

To enter overtime in the Task Form, follow these steps:

1. Choose a task view such as the Gantt Chart from the View menu for the top pane.

2. Select the task for which you want to schedule overtime.

3. Display the Task Form in the bottom pane by choosing Window, Split.

4. Press F6 to activate the Task Form in the bottom pane.

5. In the bottom pane, choose Format, Details and select Resource Work, or right-click the Form and select Resource Work from the shortcut menu, to display the Resource Work fields in the entry table (see Figure 10.8).

Figure 10.8
You can enter over-time hours and reduce task duration with the Task Form.

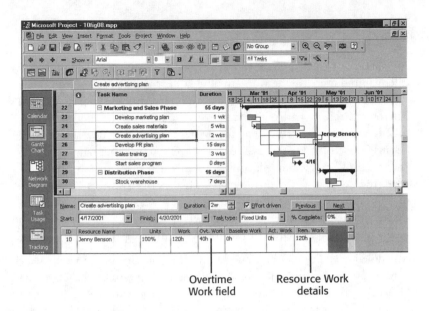

Overtime Work field

Resource Work details

6. Select the Ovt. Work field and enter the amount of work that you are scheduling in overtime. Enter a number followed by a time unit abbreviation (m, h, d, w, or mo), and then press Enter.

Do not reduce the entry in the Work field. That field's entry must show the *total* amount of work to be done, including both the regular work and the overtime work.

7. Choose OK to complete the overtime assignment.

Tip from Tim and the Project Team

If you want to eliminate overtime, you must enter a zero in the Overtime field. You cannot leave the field empty because this field must contain a value.

In Figure 10.8, overtime has been entered for Jenny Benson's assignment to the Create Advertising Plan. The total workload for this assignment is 120 hours, which was scheduled to take 3 weeks, but after recording 40 hours of overtime, the regular hours are only 80 and the task duration is reduced to 2 weeks. Usually, overtime is scheduled for just this reason—to reduce the calendar time required to complete a task.

ASSIGNING RESOURCES WITH THE TASK USAGE VIEW

Everything you accomplished in the previous section with the Gantt Chart in the top pane can be done with the Task Usage view in the top pane. In fact, you can do much more:

- You can display the Assignment Information dialog box where you can apply work contours and different Cost Rate tables to an assignment and where you can write documentary notes about the assignment.

- You can view the *timephased* work schedule. The timephased view shows work broken down into specific time periods.

- You can display a number of timephased work and cost measures.

- You can edit many of the timephased values directly in the grid cells. For example, you can reapportion work among the time periods or create and fine-tune splits or delays in an individual assignment.

Figure 10.9 shows the Task Usage view in the top pane and the Task Form in the bottom pane.

Figure 10.9
The Task Usage view offers timephased detail about individual task assignments for viewing and editing.

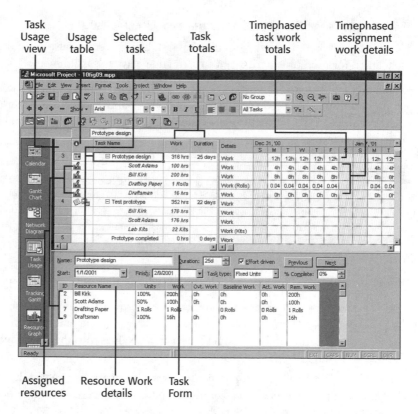

To display the Task Usage view, click the icon for the view on the View bar or choose View, Task Usage from the menu.

The table area of the Task Usage view displays all the tasks in the project using, by default, the Usage table. Indented under each task are rows for each resource that is assigned to that task. You can hide or show the assignments using the outline icons to the left of each task name. The Work field for the task is the sum of the Work field values for the assigned resources.

The right side of the view is a timescale grid of cells that show timephased assignment details. In Figure 10.9, the Work details are displayed in the grid. This is the default assignment detail, but you can display other details if desired. However, for creating and editing assignments, the Work detail is the most important.

The value in the Work field for each resource in the table on the left is the sum of the timephased values displayed in the cells on that row in the timescale.

You can edit the entries in the cells to change the work assigned for specific time periods. In Figure 10.9, the contoured indicators show that all the resource assignments have been adjusted. This task has a split in it, and that triggers the contour indicator. The draftsman also has a delay, which would trigger the contour indicator as well.

→ To learn more about displaying tasks, **see** "Using the Task Usage View," **p. 864**

MODIFYING WORK SCHEDULES WITH THE TASK USAGE VIEW

As mentioned previously, you can use the Task Usage view to customize the amount of work scheduled for each time period and to split and delay task assignments.

To change the amount of work scheduled for any given time period in the Task Usage view, simply select the timephased cell, type a new value, and either press Enter or select another cell. When you type a value, Project assumes the unit is hours unless you provide a different measurement unit.

Note

If you type a value with a time unit that is not hours, Project converts the value to hours in the display. For example, if the timescale unit is days (each cell is one day) and you type **1 week**, Project displays 40h (40 hours) in that cell. If the assignment units is 100%, this is too many hours for that one day. This example also serves to warn you that you should not enter a work value in a cell that represents more hours than is available for that time period.

There are several techniques you can use for editing the cells in the timephased grid:

- If you select a cell or group of consecutive cells in a row, you can use Ctrl+C to copy those values or Ctrl+X to cut those values from the grid, and you can then select a cell at a new location and use Ctrl+V to paste the values into the cell at that location. If you chose to cut cells, they display 0h.

- If you select a cell or group of consecutive cells in a row, you can drag the border around the selection to a new location and drop the cells into that new location. The original location cells display 0h.

Caution

If you drop a cell with a work value in it onto a nonworking time period (such as a weekend), the work in the cell you were dragging is lost. Project does not find the next working period for you. Therefore, if you are dragging a group of cells, be sure that there are enough working periods following the target cell you drop the group onto.

- If you select a cell or group of consecutive cells in a row, you can drag a copy to a new location by holding down the Ctrl key as you drag the selection border to the new location. The caution about dropping cells on nonworking days applies here also.

- The bottom-right corner of the cell selection border displays a small black square, which is called the *fill handle*. You can drag this handle to bordering cells in the same row to copy the value in the selection into those cells.

- If you select a cell or group of consecutive cells in a row, you can press the Insert key to insert nonworking time (**0h**) in place of the selection, pushing the selected values to the right. Thus, you effectively introduce a split.

- If you select a cell or group of consecutive cells in a row, you can press the Delete key to remove that work from the assignment. Project shifts any cells to the right that contain work leftward to fill in the space you deleted.

For example, if you want to increase the work and duration of an assignment, you can select the last cell in the assignment and drag its fill handle to the right to fill as many additional work periods as you choose. Also, if you want to introduce a split in an assignment, you select the cells where the split is to occur and press the Insert key. To remove the split, you can select the cells that display 0h and press the Delete key.

If you modify a timephased cell on the task Work row, the new value is apportioned among all the work resource assignments that had work scheduled for that time period. The relative proportions of the total work for each resource are kept the same. If you modified a timephased cell on an assignment row, the new values change the sum in the row for the previously mentioned task.

As soon as you complete a cell modification, Project immediately recalculates the task and assignments as follows:

- If you modified a cell on the task row, the changes are applied to all assignments that were scheduled during that time period.

- If you modified a cell on a row for a work resource, the summary value for that time period on the task row above the assignment is updated.

- The Work column entries for assignments in the table on the left are updated. These are the totals for all time periods for each assignment.

- The Work column entry for the task in the table on the left is updated. This is the total for all assignments for all time periods.

- The Duration for the task is updated. If you have not changed the number of time periods in which work is scheduled, there is no change in the Duration.

> **Note**
>
> Be very careful when using the above editing techniques when you have a project with a fixed finish date. The results are not the same as for the fixed start date project and therefore will likely cause you to lose a lot of time trying to correct the changes.

Figure 10.10 illustrates an earlier example in which you had a split in the Prototype Design task. You can create that split by inserting **0h** value cells in the timephased data for the task in the Task Usage view. All assignments are automatically split also.

PART
III

CH
10

Figure 10.10 shows before-and-after versions of the same task, with Task 2 showing the results of inserting the split. Because both tasks are selected in the top pane, you can see both task bars in the Gantt Chart in the bottom pane. Task 2 shows the 1-day split that has been created in the top pane by inserting a nonworking day into the row for Task 2.

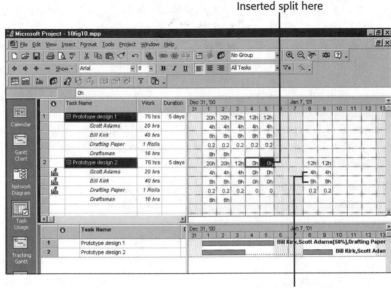

Figure 10.10
The timephased distribution of work can be edited directly in the Task Usage view.

Notice that the draftsman is not affected because there was no scheduled work for the period covered by the split.

To introduce a split in a task or in an individual assignment using the Task Usage view, follow these steps:

1. Display the Task Usage view in the top pane. You can type changes into timephased cells in the bottom pane, but you can't use drag-and-drop techniques in that pane.

2. Select the cell or cells that currently have work in them where you want to insert the split. If you select cells on the task row, the split is applied to all the resource assignments indented under that row. If you select cells on an assignment row, only that assignment is affected.

3. Press the Insert key. Project shifts the work values to the right, leaving the selected cells with no scheduled work during that period.

Figure 10.11 shows how drag-and-drop can be used to create a delay. Again, Task 2 shows Task 1 after adding the delay. The draftsman's assignment needs to be delayed until the end of the task duration. You can select all the cells from the start of the task up to the point where the assignment should start and then press the Insert key.

To use drag-and-drop, select the cells you want to drag to a new location and drag the selection border to the new location.

Figure 10.11
You can create a delayed assignment by dragging the work to a later date.

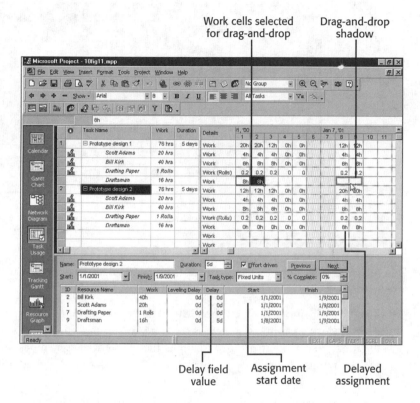

The bottom pane in Figure 10.11 shows the Resource Schedule details with the assignment delay and delayed start date calculated for Task 2. You can create a delay either in the Task Usage timephased grid or in the Resource Schedule details of the Task Form.

USING THE ASSIGNMENT INFORMATION DIALOG BOX

The Assignment Information dialog box can be displayed by selecting an assignment row in either the Task Usage or the Resource Usage view and then choosing Project, Assignment Information. You can also display the dialog box by clicking the Assignment Information tool on the Standard toolbar or by simply double-clicking the assignment row.

Figure 10.12 shows the Assignment Information dialog box for the draftsman's assignment from the previous example. As you can see, the dialog box provides several fields that you have already worked with on forms and tables, including the assigned Work, the assigned Units, and the Start and Finish dates for the assignment. The Cost field is a read-only total cost for the assignment. You can also change the name of the assigned Resource here, but there is no drop-down list to pick the correct spelling, so you must know how to spell the name, or you might wind up creating a new resource out of a typographical error.

Work contour
selection

Notes tab

Figure 10.12
Use the Assignment Information dialog box to enter assignment notes, to choose the Cost Rate table for the assignment, or to apply predefined work contours.

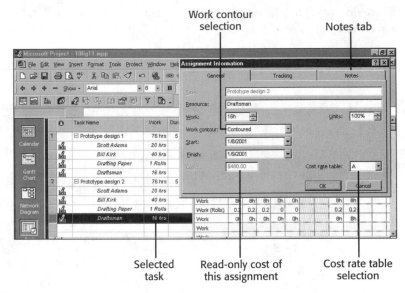

Selected task

Read-only cost of this assignment

Cost rate table selection

There are three fields in the Assignment Information dialog box that you won't find on any other standard view or dialog box:

- The Work Contour field, on the General tab, enables you to choose from a set of predefined work contours. A *contour* is a planned pattern of scheduled work spread over the duration of an assignment. For example, the bell contour schedules few hours per day at the beginning and end of an assignment, but increases the assigned hours toward the middle of the assignment.

  The default contour is *flat*, which means that the resource is scheduled to work the number of hours each day called for by the assigned units and the hours available on the resource calendar. Thus, the workload tends to be the same every day until the assignment is finished. If you have edited the assignment or applied one of the other contours, you can return the assignment to the standard schedule by applying the flat contour.

  The only other way to access and select the predefined contours is to display the Work Contour field as a column in the Usage table.

- The Cost Rate Table field, on the General tab, enables you to select one of the five different Cost Rate tables that you can define for a resource as the standard and overtime rates for this assignment. The default assignment is Table A. The Cost Rate Table field can also be displayed as a column in the Usage table. (The Usage table is the table displayed on the Task Usage and Resource Usage views.)

- On the Notes tab, the Notes field enables you to record notes about an assignment. For instance, you might record a note about why you delayed an assignment or chose a different Cost Rate table. You could also embed links to other documents such as specification texts, cost worksheets, or Web sites.

The Tracking tab has fields you will use if you monitor work progress and record when work starts, how much work has been done so far, and when work is completed. See Chapter 16, "Tracking Work on the Project," for an explanation of using those fields.

SELECTING A PREDEFINED CONTOUR   By default, the work that Project schedules for an assignment is evenly distributed across the available time periods of the assignment. As you've already seen, you can edit the assignments in individual time periods to customize the schedule. You can also choose one of eight predefined contour patterns for Project to apply to an individual assignment. Figure 10.13 shows the eight predefined contours, the indicators that identify them, and a sample work distribution over a ten-period assignment. The last row, labeled Contoured, is included to show the indicator for manually edited assignments.

→ For more information about predefined contours, **see** "Contouring Resource Usage," **p. 389**

Thus, if a resource schedule needs to show lots of hours up front with a tapering off toward the end, you can assign the front loaded contour to the assignment, and Project changes the work in the individual periods to reflect that pattern.

Figure 10.13
The predefined assignment contours feature work patterns that rise, peak, and taper at different stages in the assignment.

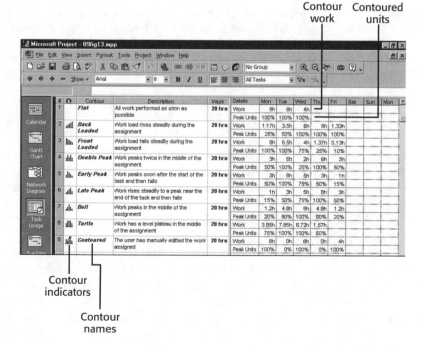

To select a contour for an assignment, follow these steps:

1. Select the assignment in the Task Usage view or the Resource Usage view.

2. Display the Assignment Information dialog box by choosing Project, Assignment Information, by clicking the Assignment Information tool, or by double-clicking the assignment row.

3. On the General tab, use the drop-down list in the Work Contour field to select one of the predefined contours.

4. Click OK to have Project calculate the new assignment pattern.

When you apply a contour to an assignment, Project keeps the total work of the assignment constant (see the following Caution for an exception). The units assigned in some time periods are reduced below the original assigned units to produce a varying amount of work in different time periods. Thus, it normally takes more time periods to complete the assignment than before the contour was applied, and the duration of the task has to be extended to allow the resource enough time to complete its assigned work.

Caution

If you assign a contour to an assignment for a Fixed Duration task, the task duration cannot change. Because the predefined contours reduce the work in some periods, you will usually find that not all the work will have been assigned by the end of the task. The total work for the assignment will normally be less after applying a contour with a Fixed Duration task.

Tip from Tim and the Project Team

Suppose that you have assigned a resource to work only half-time on a task, with Units of 50%, and now want to contour the assignment so that the assigned units will *average* 50%. The assigned Units value (in this case, 50%) is the maximum units assigned by the contour calculations for any time period. Thus, to average 50% units, you have to increase the Units assigned before applying the contour.

If you want to restore the assignment to the default schedule, whether changed by an assignment contour or edited by you, apply the Flat predefined contour.

Selecting a Cost Rate Table for an Assignment One of the important features in Project is the ability to define a graduated scale of standard and overtime cost rates for a resource so that work on assignments can be charged at different rates for different types of work. For example, a law firm might assign a seasoned lawyer to some highly technical cases at exorbitant rates, but to other more mundane tasks at lower, merely outrageous rates.

The only convenient way to select the Cost Rate table for an assignment is through the Assignment Information dialog box, and the only way to display the Assignment Information dialog box is with either the Task Usage or Resource Usage views. Choose one of the lettered tables in the drop-down list in the Cost Rate Table field to assign the standard rate and overtime rate on that table to the assignment. If there are dated changes in the rates, Project applies the rates that are defined in the table for the dates in which the task is scheduled.

Note

The Cost Rate tables can be edited only in the Resource Information dialog box. Display a view with fields for resources and either double-click a resource name or click the Information tool on the standard toolbar to display the Resource Information dialog box. Click the Costs tab to display the five Cost Rate tables, A through E.

CREATING ASSIGNMENT NOTES   Use the Notes tab of the Resource Information dialog box to document the assignment. You can type and format the note text just as you do task notes and resource notes. You can insert documents into the note or insert links to documents that are stored outside the Project file. You can also insert hyperlinks to Web sites.

→ To learn more about using the Notes field, **see** "Entering Task Notes," **p. 174**

USING THE ASSIGN RESOURCES DIALOG BOX

 The Assign Resources dialog box is a versatile tool for creating resource assignments, but you have much less control over the scheduling calculations than with the Task Form or the Task Usage view. You must have a task view (other than one of the forms) active to display the Resource Assignment dialog box, and, generally speaking, it should be in the top pane. To display the dialog box, click the Assign Resources tool or choose Tools, Resources, Assign Resources.

Tip from Tim and the Project Team

Because you might need to change the task type or effort-driven status of the task before making or changing a resource assignment, you will usually want the Task Form in the bottom pane of the underlying view. Remember to consider the settings for those parameters before making any changes in assignments.

Caution

The Undo command is not available for resource assignment actions you take with the Assign Resources dialog box.

The Assign Resources dialog box is the only pop-up dialog box that you can leave on the workspace, switching back and forth between the dialog box and the underlying views. When displayed, the dialog box remains accessible even if the underlying active view is not a task view. Other features include the following:

- You can use the dialog box to add resource names to the resource pool, regardless of whether the active underlying view is a task view.

- You can use the Address button to look up names in the address book for your email service.

- You can double-click a resource name in the dialog box to view and edit the Resource Information dialog box for that resource, no matter what underlying view is active.

- If the underlying active view is a task view (other than one of the forms), you can use the dialog box to assign resources to one task at a time or to multiple selected tasks at the same time.

- If the underlying active view is a task view, you can use the dialog box to remove resources from selected tasks.

- If the underlying active view is a task view, you can use it to replace one resource with another resource for selected tasks.

If you would like to control the order of the resource names in the Assign Resources dialog box, see "Sorting the Resource List" in the "Troubleshooting" section at the end of this chapter.

Figure 10.14 shows the Assign Resources dialog box over the Task Entry view in the background. The selected task is Test Prototype. You can see in the Assign Resources dialog box which resources are assigned to the task because they have check marks next to their names when that task is selected. The underlying view shows more detail about the assignments in the Resources area of the Task Details Form in the bottom pane.

Figure 10.14
Use the Assign Resources dialog box to assign resources to selected tasks.

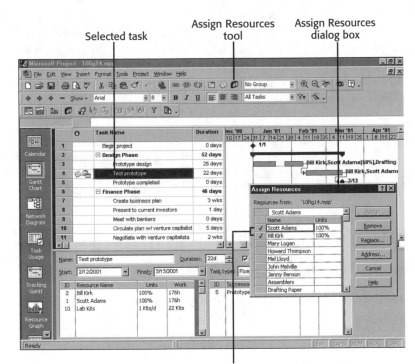

Selected task   Assign Resources tool   Assign Resources dialog box

Check mark signifies assigned resources for selected task.

ASSIGNING RESOURCES

To add a resource assignment to a selected task or group of tasks, follow these steps:

1. Select the task or tasks to which you want the resource assigned.

 2. Display the Assign Resource dialog box by choosing Tools, Resources, Assign Resources or by clicking the Assign Resources tool on the Standard toolbar.

3. Select the resource name from the Name list or type the name for a new resource.

4. If the resource is a work resource, the default for the Units field is 100%. If you want to assign a different number of units, select the Units cell to the right of the resource name and enter the new value. Remember that a smaller percentage means that a resource devotes only the designated fractional part of each day to the task. If you enter **0** as the units value, neither work nor resource cost is calculated for the resource for

this task. The cost fields described later in this chapter are used to record costs for the tasks that do not depend on the amount of work a resource performs.

If the resource is a material resource, enter the number of units to be consumed by the task in the Units cell. If you enter just a numeral, Project schedules that total number of units to be consumed by the task no matter what the length of the task duration. If you enter a number with a time period appended (for example, **2/d**), Project schedules that number to be consumed per time period as long as the duration of the task lasts.

Tip from Tim and the Project Team

For work resources, the units should be no greater than the maximum units available for this resource at the time the task is scheduled. If you do not know the maximum units available, double-click the resource name to see the Resource Information dialog box (see Figure 10.15). The Resource Availability table shows the maximum units for different time periods.

Figure 10.15
The Resource Information dialog box shows additional information about resources.

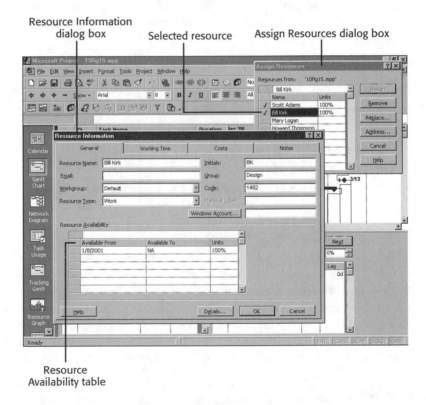

Resource Information dialog box

Selected resource

Assign Resources dialog box

Resource Availability table

5. Click the Assign button or press Enter to assign the resource and unit information to the selected tasks.

Note

When you click the Assign button, a check mark appears to the left of the resource assigned, as shown in Figure 10.14. This check mark appears any time the task is selected in the underlying view.

6. If you are adding more resources to the same tasks, select the next resource name to be assigned, type the number of units in the Units field, and select Assign to assign this resource to the selected tasks.

7. After the resource assignments are completed, you can hide the Assign Resources dialog box by selecting the Close button.

SCHEDULING RESOURCES FOR A SPECIFIC AMOUNT OF WORK

For work resources, the Assign Resources dialog box can also be used to calculate the number of units needed to complete a specified amount of work within the task's current duration. Normally, you enter a simple percentage in the Units column of the Assign Resources dialog box. If you enter a work amount in the Units column (a number followed by a time unit, such as **40h** for 40 hours), Project calculates the number of units of that resource needed to do that much work within the current duration for the task. This procedure does not work if the task is effort-driven and this is the initial assignment of the resource to the task. You can use the technique to recalculate an existing working resource assignment, however, even if the task is effort-driven.

To assign resources using a work amount, follow these steps:

1. Select the task or tasks to which you want the resource assigned.

2. Display the Assign Resources dialog box.

3. Select the resource name from the Name list.

4. Select the Units field and type the work amount followed by the unit it's measured in: m (min), h (hour), d (day), w (week), or mo (month).

5. Click the Assign button or press Enter to assign the resource and unit information to the selected tasks. Project automatically replaces the work value with the units value.

ADDING RESOURCES USING DRAG-AND-DROP

With the Assign Resources dialog box, you can assign resources to a task by using the drag-and-drop method as well. An advantage to using the drag-and-drop assignment feature is that you do not have to preselect the task for which a resource should be assigned. This provides a quick and efficient way of assigning different resources to one task at a time. However, Project gives you no choice but to use a unit value of 100% for the resource assignment you create with this technique. Of course, you can change the units assignment later, but that can lead to other automatic calculations that might not be intended.

> **Caution**
>
> Do not use drag-and-drop assignments unless you want the unit assignment to be the default (the lesser of 100% or the Max Units for the resource).

To assign resources to a task by using the drag-and-drop feature, perform the following steps:

1. Display the Assign Resources dialog box by clicking the Assign Resources tool.

2. Select the resource by clicking the Name field.

3. Position the mouse pointer in the gray rectangle just to the left of the resource name. The Assign Resources graphic appears below the mouse pointer. You can see the pointer and graphic in Figure 10.16, where Jenny Benson is being assigned to a task.

Figure 10.16
When you point to the gray button beside a selected resource, the mouse pointer appears as a selection arrow carrying a resource.

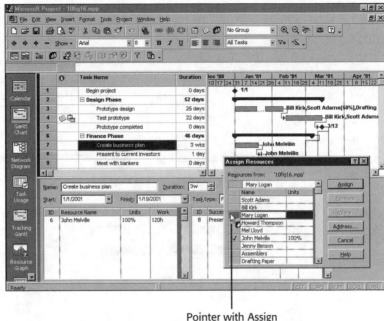

Pointer with Assign
Resources graphic

PART

III

CH

10

4. Hold down the mouse button (a plus sign appears next to the pointer graphic) and drag the mouse pointer to the task for which the resource should be assigned.

5. When the task is highlighted, release the mouse button to assign the resource.

Tip from Tim and the Project Team

To assign multiple resources to a task using the drag-and-drop feature, hold down the Ctrl key while selecting the resource names in the Assign Resources dialog box. When you drag the mouse pointer to the task, all selected resources are assigned at once.

REMOVING RESOURCE ASSIGNMENTS FROM ONE OR MORE TASKS

To remove a resource assignment from one or more selected tasks, perform the following steps:

1. Select the task (or tasks) in the view that has resource assignments you want to remove. In Figure 10.17, the task is West Coast Promo Week.

2. Display the Assign Resources dialog box by clicking the Assign Resources tool.

3. Select the resources you want to remove from assignments by clicking the check mark or the resource name. The draftsman, who is mistakenly assigned, is selected in Figure 10.17.

Note

Resources assigned to the selected task are identified by check marks to the left of the resource name. If a check mark is gray instead of black, your task selection in the view includes some tasks that have that resource assigned and some that do not.

4. Choose the <u>R</u>emove button. The resources that are selected in the Assign Resources dialog box are removed from any assignments they might have with the tasks that are selected in the view.

Figure 10.17
Delete unwanted assignments with the Remove button on the Assign Resources dialog box.

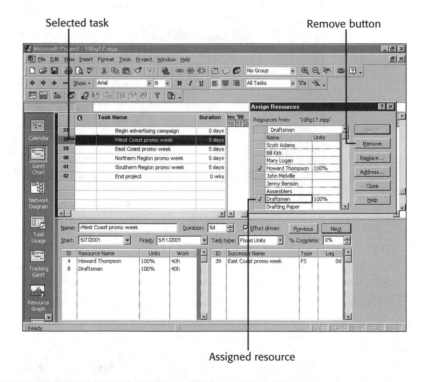

Tip from Tim and the Project Team

To remove a group of resources from the selected tasks, hold down the Ctrl key while you select the resources.

MODIFYING AN ASSIGNMENT

Use the Assign Resources dialog box to replace one resource with another, to change the assigned units for a resource, or to change the amount of work assigned to a resource. Each assignment should be modified individually, and different techniques are used depending on what you want to modify.

To replace an assigned resource with another resource name, follow these steps:

1. Select the task. You can select multiple tasks by using the Ctrl key if you want to make an identical assignment change in all of them. In Figure 10.18, the Prototype Design task is selected, and Mary Logan will replace Bill Kirk in the resource assignments.

2. Display the Assign Resources dialog box by clicking the Assign Resources tool.

3. Select the Resource Name to be replaced.

4. Click the Replace button. Project displays the Replace Resource dialog box over the Assign Resources dialog box. In Figure 10.18, the Replace Resource dialog box has been moved to show both dialog boxes.

5. Select the new resource name.

6. Select the Units field for the selected resource and enter the value if you want it to be something other than 100%. Note that Project does not preserve the units from the first resource. If the first resource units was not 100%, you need to enter that value again for the new resource.

7. Choose OK or press Enter.

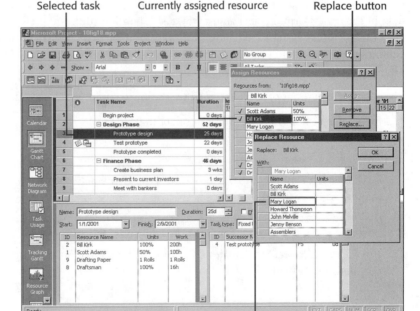

Figure 10.18
A second dialog box, Replace Resource, provides a list of replacement resources to choose from.

Note

The Replace Resource dialog box lists all resources on the project. Microsoft Project does not filter the list for availability during the dates for the task or suitability to the task. Therefore, many of the names in the list might not be available or appropriate to the task assignment.

To replace the number of units in a resource assignment, follow these steps:

1. Select the task in the view. You can select multiple tasks if you plan to make an identical assignment change in all of them.

2. Display the Assign Resources dialog box by clicking the Assign Resources tool.

3. Select the Units field for the resource whose assignment is to be changed.

4. Type the new unit assignment for the resource.

5. Choose Close or press Enter.

Note

Changing the number of resource units assigned to a task causes Microsoft Project to recalculate the task duration (unless the task is a Fixed Duration task).

When you change the assigned work for a resource using the Assign Resources dialog box, Project uses a unique set of rules for calculating the work formula. If you change the Work field in the Task Form, Project adjusts the task Duration (unless the task is a Fixed Duration task, in which case it must change the Units). If you enter a new work amount in the Units column in the Assign Resources dialog box, Project adjusts the Units and not the Duration, no matter what the task type setting is.

To replace the amount of work assigned to a resource, follow these steps:

1. Select the task in the view. You can select multiple tasks if you plan to make an identical assignment change in all of them.

2. Display the Assign Resources dialog box by clicking the Assign Resources tool.

3. In the Assign Resources dialog box, select the Units field for the resource whose assignment is to be changed.

4. Type the new amount of work for the assignment as a numeral with a time unit (minute, hour, day, week, or month). For example, to enter 16 hours, type **16h**.

5. Press Enter. Project recalculates the number of resource units needed to complete the new amount of work.

Note

Although you cannot enter work amounts in the Assign Resources dialog box for effort-driven tasks when assigning the first resource, you can do so for subsequent assignments or for changes in the original assignment.

ASSIGNING RESOURCES WITH THE TASK INFORMATION DIALOG BOX

You can use the Resources tab on the Task Information dialog box to add, change, or delete the resource assignment information for the selected task. Like the Assign Resources dialog box, you can use the Units field to enter either Units or Work. If you enter Work (using a numeral followed by a time unit), Project treats the task as a Fixed Duration task and adjusts the Units to accommodate the Work.

To change assignments using the Task Information dialog box, follow these steps:

1. Select the task for which you want to add or change a resource assignment.

 2. Display the Task Information dialog box by choosing Project, Task Information. You can also click the Task Information tool on the toolbar. The fields in the dialog box show the current data for the task (see Figure 10.19).

Tip from Tim and the Project Team
> You can also access the Task Information dialog box by selecting the task, clicking the secondary mouse button, and choosing Task Information from the pop-up shortcut menu. Still another method is to use the shortcut key Shift+F2.

3. Select the Resources tab to assign or view the resource information for the selected task.

Selected task   Task Information dialog box

Figure 10.19
The Task Information dialog box contains a Resources tab that can be used to assign or edit resource assignments.

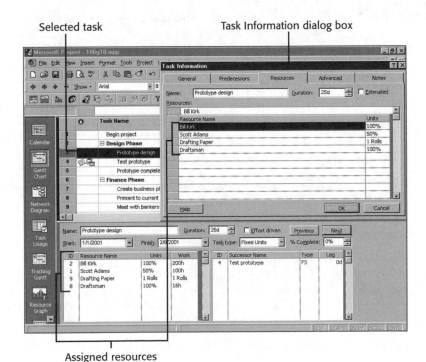

Assigned resources

4. In the Resource Name box, edit an existing entry or choose a blank row to add a new resource. To add or change the resource, select a resource from the drop-down list in the field.

5. Type the unit assignment for the resource in the Units field. If you leave the Units field blank, Project supplies the default value (the lesser of 100% or the Max Units for the resource).

   You can also modify an existing assignment by entering a work amount followed by a time unit in the Units field. If you enter a work amount, Project adjusts the assigned units, not the duration of the task.

6. To add additional resources to the selected task, click the next Resource Name field and repeat the preceding steps.

7. After you complete all resource assignments for the task, choose OK.

If you use the Ctrl key to select more than one task before opening the Task Information dialog box, Project displays the Multiple Task Information dialog box so that any resource you select automatically is assigned to all selected tasks.

The resource assignment entries you make in the Multiple Task Information dialog box are added to existing resource assignments for the selected tasks.

Note You cannot change existing resource assignments for multiple tasks by using the Multiple Task Information dialog box.

ASSIGNING RESOURCES WITH THE TASK TABLE

You can also use the Resource Name field on the task table to assign resources to a task. However, entering the resource assignment data in the Resource Name field requires a text entry with a different and very specific syntax. The entry must follow this notation pattern:

```
ResourceName1[Units],ResourceName2[Units], ResourceName3[Units] ...
```

When entering data using this format, note that the Units value follows immediately after the resource name, without an intervening space, and is placed in square brackets. Units values of 100% do not need to be included. Notice, too, that multiple resource assignments are separated by commas.

Tip from Tim and the Project Team

If you want to import a list of tasks with resource assignments, you must have used this format in the source data to identify the resource assignments. For information about importing data, see Chapter 19, "Exporting and Importing Project Data with Other File Formats."

To assign resources to tasks in the Task Sheet view, perform the following steps:

1. View the Gantt Chart.

2. Choose View, Table and apply any table that includes a Resource Name column, such as the Entry table.

3. Select the Resource Names column of the task table for the task to which you want to assign resources.

4. Enter the resource name. You can select the name from the drop-down resource list, which appears in the cell when the Resource Names column is active.

5. If the number of units is other than 100%, type the units, enclosed in square brackets, immediately after the name in the Edit bar.

6. If you want to assign more resources to the same task, use the list separator (a comma in North America) to separate each resource and repeat steps 4 and 5 until all resources are complete.

Tip from Tim and the Project Team

To change the list separator, open the Control Panel, use Regional Settings (in Windows 95) or International (in Windows NT 3.51), and select the Number tab.

7. Press Enter or select any other cell to complete the resource assignment.

Selected task

Figure 10.20
Use the Resource Names field to review or enter resource assignments.

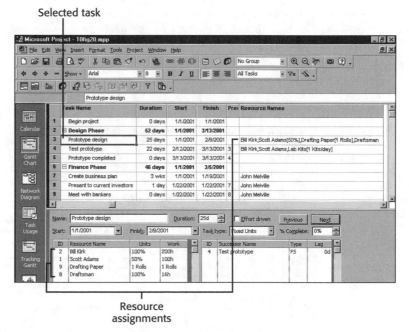

Resource assignments

ASSIGNING FIXED COSTS AND FIXED CONTRACT FEES

For some tasks, you might have costs that aren't linked to a particular resource you have named. This type of cost is called a *fixed cost* and is entered in the Fixed Cost column of the Cost table on a task view such as the Gantt Chart. You can also have a cost that is associated with a resource but that is not affected by the task duration or any variations in work for the resource. For instance, the resource might be a contractor or vendor who is to deliver the completed task at a fixed cost. In these cases, the cost is entered as part of the assignment information on the Task Form.

If there is a cost associated with the task that is not affected by the task duration and you have not named a resource that is associated with this cost, you can enter the amount in the Fixed Cost field for the task. Project adds the fixed cost amount to the total of the resource costs and displays the sum in the Cost (Total Cost) column of various views.

To display the Fixed Cost field, display a task view such as the Gantt Chart in the top pane. To display the Cost table, right-click over the blank area just above the row numbers and choose Cost (see Figure 10.21).

Tip from Tim and the Project Team

If you enter an amount in the Total Cost (Cost) field to overwrite the calculated value displayed there, Project treats this as the sum of the calculated resource costs and a new fixed cost amount. It then changes the entry in the Fixed Cost column to support this interpretation.

Tip from Tim and the Project Team

You should document any fixed cost amounts in the task Notes field so that you and others will always know what the cost represents.

Figure 10.21
Enter costs that are not associated with a particular resource and that do not change with the task duration in the Fixed Cost column of the task Cost table.

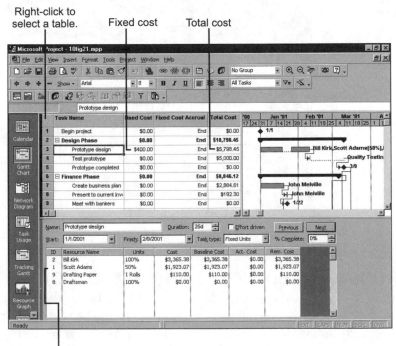

Right-click to select a table.   Fixed cost   Total cost

Resource Cost details

If a resource that is assigned to a task is working for a fixed fee (such as a contractor or vendor), you will want that cost to remain fixed no matter what happens to the task duration. In this case, you do not need Project to track the hours of work for the resource because those hours are important to the contractor or vendor but not to you. Your cost isn't affected if the job takes more work or money than estimated. For these tasks, make the task a Fixed Duration task and assign the contractor or vendor as a resource to the task, but enter a 0 in the Units field for the assignment. The work amount is calculated as 0; therefore, the hourly resource cost values for this resource are also 0. After you click OK to complete the assignment, Microsoft Project enables you to enter the contract amount in the resource Cost field, and that will not be overwritten by Project's calculations.

Suppose that the Test Prototype task is to be contracted out to Quality Testing Labs for a fixed cost of $5,000, and it promises to complete the tests in 20 days (see Figure 10.22). To record this in Project, you follow these steps:

1. Display the Gantt Chart and split the window to display the Task Form.

2. Make the task a Fixed Duration task of 20 days.

3. If there are other resources assigned to the task, you also need to clear the Effort Driven check box so that the resources are independent of each other.

4. In the Task Form, assign the resource to the task, but enter 0 in the Units column and then click OK. With 0 units, Project does not calculate work for the task and does not calculate resource costs.

   Note that you must click OK before you can enter values in the Cost field.

5. Display the cost details in the Task Form by right-clicking over the form and choosing Resource Cost.

6. Enter the fixed cost of the task in the assignment Cost field and click OK again.

Note

If you have cleared the check box in the Options dialog box, Calculation tab, that is labeled Actual Costs Are Always Calculated By Microsoft Project, you have to enter the fixed resource cost in the Actual Cost field instead of the Cost field. See Chapter 16 for more information about entering and calculating actual costs.

Figure 10.22
Enter fixed fees or contract amounts in the Cost field for the resource.

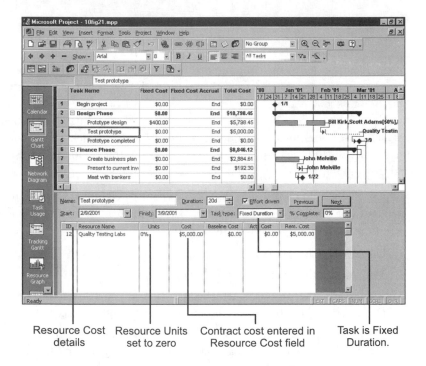

Resource Cost details

Resource Units set to zero

Contract cost entered in Resource Cost field

Task is Fixed Duration.

PRINTING RESOURCE WORK AND COST REPORTS

Several report formats are available to help you monitor and evaluate the scheduled tasks for the resources and resource costs for the project (see Figure 10.23). Reports are covered in more detail in Chapter 24, "Using the Standard Reports."

Figure 10.23
The Reports dialog box groups reports into categories.

Reports that reflect resource information are included in the following report categories:

- The *Costs* reports provide budget information for the resources as well as for tasks. Special reports are designed to display specific information. One reports only those resources currently over budget, whereas another displays tasks over budget, and a third monitors the weekly cash flow of the project.

- The *Assignments* reports are designed to identify each resource and the tasks to which the resource is assigned. One report design lists only the resources, a second report design adds a timescale for each task, whereas a third identifies only overallocated resources. The fourth report format creates a weekly To-Do list for each resource.

- The *Workload* reports include a Resource Usage report, which resembles the Resource Usage view. It lists the resources and tasks assigned to each resource along with their work assignment over a time period.

To choose one of these report formats, follow these steps:

1. Choose View, Reports.
2. Choose the report category containing the desired report format.
3. Select the report design.

When you select a report, the report automatically is displayed in the Print Preview window. From this screen, you can zoom the report to see the data close up, choose Page Setup to format the report layout, or choose Print to send the report to the printer.

 If you find that Project says it can't display the print preview of a report, see "Using Filters in Reports" in the "Troubleshooting" section at the end of this chapter.

TROUBLESHOOTING

SORTING THE RESOURCE LIST

How can I change the order of the list of names in the Assign Resources dialog box?

The Assign Resources dialog box displays resource names in ID order. If you want a different order you have to sort the list of resource names in a resource table such as the Resource Sheet with the Permanently Renumber Resources option turned on. Display the Resource Sheet by choosing the view in the View menu. Choose Project, Sort, Sort By to display the Sort dialog box. Choose the fields and sort order you want to use and fill the Permanently Renumber Resources check box. Click Sort to change the order of the records. Remember to open the Sort dialog box again and click Reset or clear the Permanently Renumber Resources check box manually so that your next sort operation won't inadvertently change the number order again.

SCHEDULING SHORT ASSIGNMENTS IN FIXED DURATION TASKS

How can I schedule a short assignment in a Fixed Duration task without extending the duration of the task?

When you add a short assignment (one that could be finished before the other assignments to the task finish) to a Fixed Units or Fixed Work task, Project schedules all the work at the beginning of the task and the assignment finishes before the task finishes. But when you add a short assignment to a Fixed Duration task, Project spreads the work out evenly over the duration of the assignment and reduces the units to reflect the reduced workload during each period.

If you want to concentrate the short assignment's work to the start, finish, or other point in the task duration, you will have to edit the assigned work in the Task Usage or Resource Usage view. With one of the usage views displayed, select the short assignment and note the total work for the assignment in the Work column of the table on the left. Click the Go To Selected Task tool to scroll the timephased data for the assignment into view. You need to replace the distributed work in the grid with work concentrated in the periods you choose. The fastest method is to clear all the current work entries by typing a zero into the Work column for the assignment in the table. Then, type the work amounts you want to schedule into the time periods of your choice until the total in the Work column is back to the original amount.

USING FILTERS IN REPORTS

When I use a filter in a report, an error message tells me there is no data to report; but I know there are tasks or resources that match the filter. What's wrong?

A filter in a report will only select records that are visible in the current view. If you have collapsed the outline in the active view, or applied a filter to that view, then the report filter can only select records from those that are visible. If no visible records match the report filter, you will get the error message. You must either remove the filter from the report or change the current view to display all records.

CHAPTER 11

RESOLVING RESOURCE ASSIGNMENT PROBLEMS

In this chapter

UNDERSTANDING HOW RESOURCE OVERALLOCATIONS OCCUR

A resource is overallocated when assigned to work more hours during a given time period than the resource has available for work on the project. The number of hours that the resource has available for the project during any given time period is determined by two values that you define:

- The *units* of the resource that are available during the time period. You define time periods and units in the Resource Availability table on the General tab of the Resource Information dialog box.

- The number of *working time hours* the resource has for the time period in the resource calendar. You define working time on the Working Time tab of the Resource Information dialog box.

Multiplying the units available for the resource by the calendar working hours in a given time period determines the hours of work the resource has available for that time period. Table 11.1 shows several examples of the work availability calculation. A single employee resource typically has 8 hours available per day and has maximum units available of 100% (one full-time unit). Case A shows that this employee can be assigned to up to 8 hours of work a day. But, if the employee has only 4 hours of working time in a day on the calendar, Case B shows that you are limited to assigning no more than 4 hours a day to that resource. Case C shows a group resource with 300% units available and 8 hours of working time on the calendar. This resource can deliver up to 24 hours of work in the time period.

TABLE 11.1 DETERMINING THE WORK HOURS AVAILABLE FOR A RESOURCE

Case	A	B	C
Maximum Resource Units Available	100%	100%	300%
Calendar Working Hours for the Period	8 hrs	4 hrs	8 hrs
Maximum Work Hours Available for the Period	8 hrs	4 hrs	24 hrs

Overallocations generally occur for only two reasons:

- A resource will be overallocated if you assign more units of the resource to a single task than the maximum units available for that resource. For example, if you assign a group or team resource that has five units available (500%) to a task by entering six units (600%), you would automatically overallocate that resource.

- A resource will also be overallocated if you assign the resource to multiple tasks that happen to be scheduled at the same time period and that in combination have more units assigned than the maximum units available. This second case is the most common cause of overallocated resources.

When Microsoft Project calculates the task schedule for you, it can easily create an overallocated resource by scheduling multiple-task assignments for a resource during the same time period. Before resource assignments are made, Project schedules tasks in forward-scheduled projects to start as soon as possible based on three factors: the first possible date (as determined by the start of the project and any predecessors for the task), the earliest date that leaves constraints satisfied, and the next available working time on the project base calendar (or task calendar if one is assigned).

Note

Forward-scheduled projects are those that are scheduled from a *fixed start date*, leaving Project to calculate the finish date of the project. This explanation and most others in this chapter are worded in terms of forward-scheduled projects. Microsoft Project automatically schedules tasks in such projects *As Soon As Possible* to minimize the project duration and achieve the earliest finish date for the project.

If a project is scheduled from a *fixed finish date*, tasks are automatically scheduled *As Late As Possible* in order to minimize the overall duration for the project and achieve the latest project start date.

When you assign a resource to work on the task, Project substitutes the resource calendar for the project base calendar, and schedules the task assignment on the first available date on the resource calendar that meets the conditions described above. However, Project does not normally look to see whether the resource is already assigned to other tasks during the times it schedules for the new assignment. Because Project ignores existing assignments when scheduling new assignments, it is easily possible for a resource to be overallocated.

Note

If there is an assigned task calendar, the dates that are scheduled must be working dates on both the task calendar and the resource calendar. If the task field labeled Scheduling Ignores Resource Calendars has been checked, the resource calendar will be ignored and the task calendar will be the only calendar considered. If this results in work scheduled during periods that are nonworking times on the resource calendar, Project will not consider it to be an overallocation of the resource.

Tip from Tim and the Project Team

The *default* behavior for Project is to ignore other assignments. However, you can change the default behavior and have Project check for other assignments each time it schedules a resource and, if necessary, delay the new assignment until the resource is free to work on it. Before you decide to change this default, however, you should read the rest of this chapter, especially the section "Understanding the Pitfalls of Automatic Leveling."

If there is more than one assignment for a resource during a given time period, the combined work and units for that period might exceed the resource availability, as illustrated in Table

11.2 for Scott Adams. The first two rows in the table spell out the resource availability: Scott has 100% units available for assignments and 8 hours of working time on each day; thus, his available work is 8 hours each day.

Scott has three assignments during this week and on Thursday two of them overlap. Task C starts before Task B is completed. The total assigned units on Thursday is 150% (which exceeds his Max Units) and the total assigned work on that day is 12 hours (which exceeds the 8 available hours on the calendar). Therefore, Scott is overallocated on Thursday.

Note that this example involves only 36 hours of work for the week and that's less than the 40 hours of work available for the week; so, on a weekly basis you could say he is not overallocated. In fact, if we could just reschedule 4 hours of work that is assigned for Thursday to take place on Friday, there would be no overallocation. More about these ideas later.

TABLE 11.2   SCOTT ADAMS'S ASSIGNMENTS FOR ONE WEEK

		Mon	Tue	Wed	Thu	Fri	Weekly Total
Max Units		100%	100%	100%	100%	100%	
Working Time		8h	8h	8h	8h	8h	40h
Task A	Units	100%	100%				
	Work	8h	8h				
Task B	Units			100%	100%		
	Work			8h	8h		
Task C	Units				50%		
	Work				4h		
Combined	Units	100%	100%	100%	150%	0%	
	Work	8h	8h	8h	12h	0h	36h
Overallocated		No	No	No	Yes	No	(No)

IDENTIFYING RESOURCE OVERALLOCATIONS

Project alerts you to overallocated resources by highlighting them in any view that displays a resource table. For example, the Resource Sheet, Resource Usage, and Resource Allocation views all highlight overallocated resource names in a red font. In the Resource Sheet in Figure 11.1, three resource rows are highlighted: Scott Adams, Mel Lloyd, and Howard Thompson.

Note

By default Project uses a red font to highlight overallocated resources. Since that color doesn't show up well in this book's figures, I've used a bold black font as the highlight in the figures. Where I mention highlighted overallocations, look for red text on your screen and for bold text in these figures.

PART

III

CH

11

Tip from Tim and the Project Team

You can modify the format for overallocated resources in any resource table by choosing Format, Text Styles to display the Text Styles dialog box. In the Item to Change box, select Overallocated Resources from the drop-down list. Use the other controls in the dialog box to create the style you want. When finished, click OK to implement the change.

Figure 11.1
Resource views that display a table highlight the names of overallocated resources in red (here in bold).

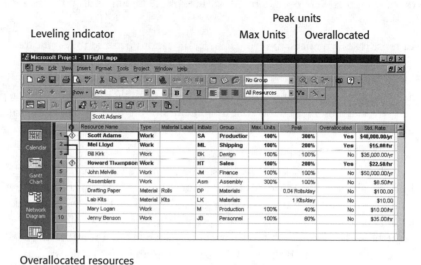

Peak units

Leveling indicator   Max Units   Overallocated

Overallocated resources

Recall from Table 11.2 that an overallocation is due to more work being scheduled in a given time period than the resource can deliver, and the cause of that is the fact that the sum of the assigned units exceeds the Max Units for the period. Project maintains a calculated field named *Peak* which shows for any designated time period the largest number of simultaneously assigned units during that time period. The Max Units field on the Resource Sheet in Figure 11.1 displays the maximum units for the *current date* from the Units column of the Resource Availability table in the Resource Information dialog box. Project also maintains a calculated resource field named Overallocated that contains Yes if Peak is greater than Max Units at any moment in time and No if otherwise. If the Overallocated field contains Yes, the resource is highlighted in red on your screen.

Tip from Tim and the Project Team

The current date is normally determined by the computer's internal clock, but you can set the Current Date to any date in the Project Information dialog box (choose Project, Project Information), using the Current Date field.

Figure 11.1 shows the Resource Sheet with both the Peak and Overallocated fields displayed to the right of the Max Units field. The column for Peak in this figure shows the peak units for the life of the project; so the value displayed is the largest simultaneous amount of assigned units at any time in the project. Thus, the peak of 300% for Scott Adams means that at some point during the project his simultaneous assignments total 300% units. Mary Logan, on the other hand, is never at any moment during this project required to provide more than 40% units.

Three of the first four resources are flagged as overallocated because the Peak value exceeds the Max Units value. If the Overallocated field were not displayed, you would still know these resources were overallocated because of the highlight used for the overallocated resources.

In most cases, you need to reconcile overallocations because they indicate that the schedule is a fiction—the resource can't possibly do what is scheduled. The way you reconcile overallocations is to level the workload for the resource by reassigning tasks to other resources, delaying tasks until the resource is available, or by other adjustments to the schedule that we will cover in a moment. However, intelligent leveling takes a lot of the project manager's time and you may decide to let the workers make minor adjustments in their schedules themselves.

Sometimes you can view the overallocation as a mere technicality that's a product of the way Project calculates the schedule. For example, suppose a regular full-time employee is scheduled to work 100% on two tasks on a given day, and each task will only take an hour to complete. That's only two hours of work for the day and is hardly an overallocation for an eight-hour day. But if both tasks have been scheduled by Project to begin first thing in the morning at 8:00 a.m., Project would flag the resource as overallocated, because the schedule calls for Peak Units of 200% at that time. In reality, the resource could easily finish both tasks in the day by delaying one task until the other is finished. The project manager may prefer not to be bothered by dealing with overallocations like this when the conflict is small enough that the resource can adjust the schedule and finish its assigned work for the day.

To help you focus only on those overallocation cases that you think really warrant your rescheduling efforts, Project lets you choose a leveling *sensitivity* that it uses to flag those overallocations that are considered too severe to ignore. In the example just given, the project manager would need to do something about the schedule if it is important that the project be on schedule on an hour-by-hour basis. But the manager might be content to let resources manage the conflicts as long as they can be on schedule on a day-by-day basis. If the manager chose the Hour By Hour sensitivity setting (meaning assigned work must be completed within the assigned hour), Project would display the Leveling indicator that you see in Figure 11.1. But if the manager chose the Day By Day setting, then there would be no indicator because the work will be completed within the assigned day.

In Table 11.2 we saw an example where Scott Adams was overallocated for the day on a Thursday, but his workload for the week was OK. If the manager is content to let Scott manage the conflict by pushing back his Task C work until Friday when he has finished Task B, the sensitivity setting can be defined as Week By Week and there would be no Leveling indicator.

You can choose the sensitivity setting for Project to use when evaluating overallocations on the Resource Leveling dialog box. Your choices are Minute by Minute, Hour by Hour, Day by Day, Week by Week, and Month by Month.

Project displays a Leveling indicator in the Indicators field for any resource that has an overallocation judged excessive according to the leveling sensitivity setting. All resources with any overallocation still appear highlighted in resource tables, but if you don't see the Leveling indicator, the overallocation is acceptable within the boundaries of the leveling sensitivity setting.

Tip from Tim and the Project Team

Rest the mouse pointer over the Leveling indicator to see the time period covered by the current sensitivity setting. This is quicker than opening the Resource Leveling dialog box where the leveling sensitivity is defined.

Note

If the task that is rescheduled by the worker is a critical task (a task whose delay will delay the completion of the project), there are consequences to the finish date of the project. For this reason you do not want to select an overly long sensitivity setting.

In Figure 11.1 the resource names Scott Adams, Mel Lloyd, and Howard Thompson are highlighted to indicate that there is at least one time period in which their workloads exceed their availability. Both Scott and Howard have the Leveling indicator, and the project manager needs to look at the overallocations for those resources.

Figure 11.2 shows the same resources in the Resource Usage view. If you rest the mouse pointer over an indicator, Project displays the meaning of the indicator. In Figure 11.2 you can see the ScreenTip where the mouse is resting over the indicator next to Howard Thompson. The ScreenTip explains that "This resource should be leveled based on a Week by Week setting."

Instead of emphasizing the resource definition fields, the Resource Usage view emphasizes a timescale with the scheduled activity for each resource broken down into discrete time periods—what Project calls "timephased" assignment data. In this example, the Work and Peak Units fields are displayed for each day in the timescale.

Mel Lloyd is overallocated because his Max Units for the period shown is 100% and he is assigned for 200% units on Tuesday. He does not have a Leveling indicator because the leveling sensitivity setting is Week by Week (see the ScreenTip in Figure 11.2), and Mel has less than 40 hours of assigned work for the week. Although Mel is overallocated on Tuesday, his assignment does not need leveling because he can do the weekly work he has been assigned. Howard Thompson on the other hand has far more than 40 hours of work assigned during the week; therefore, on a Week by Week basis, his assignments need leveling.

VIEWING RESOURCE OVERALLOCATIONS

To identify all the overallocated resources by name, you need to use one of the three resource views that display a table: the Resource Sheet, the Resource Usage view, or the Resource Allocation view. Figure 11.1 shows the Resource Sheet, and Figure 11.2 shows the Resource Usage view. The Resource Allocation view includes the Resource Usage view and will be discussed more in later sections of this chapter. If a resource is overallocated during any period in the life of the project, the resource name will be highlighted in any of these views.

Leveling indicator

Not highlighted timephased data

Figure 11.2
The Leveling indicator appears in the Indicators column in resource views with a table, such as the Resource Usage view shown here.

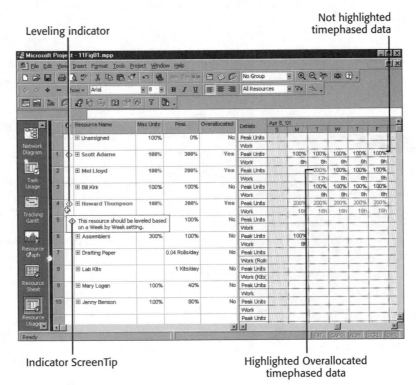

Indicator ScreenTip

Highlighted Overallocated timephased data

FILTERING OVERALLOCATED RESOURCES

If your resource list is extensive, you can filter the resource list to display only those resources with an overallocation. This will display all overallocated resources, not just those with the Leveling indicator. In Figure 11.3, the Resource Sheet is filtered for overallocated resources; in this case, only three resource names appear.

Note

There is no way to filter for just those resources that have the Leveling indicator displayed. That indicator is calculated by Project "on-the-fly" and there is no field that shows the result of the calculation other than the Indicators field; and you can't apply a filter to the Indicators field.

To apply the Overallocated filter, select the top pane view if you are in a combination view, and choose Overallocated Resources in the Filter tool drop-down list. Or, you can use the menu to choose Project, Filtered For, Overallocated Resources. Filters affect only the top pane, because the bottom pane is already filtered to show details for the selection in the top pane.

Filter tool

Figure 11.3
Applying the Overallocated Resources filter reduces the display to just those resources that are overallocated.

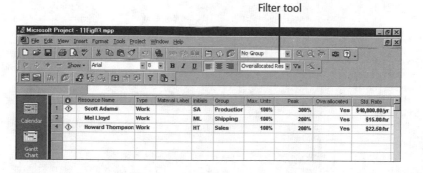

Tip from Tim and the Project Team

> If you correct the overallocation problem for one of the resources displayed by the filter, the resource remains in the display until the filter is applied again. This is because the display of Project filters is not automatically refreshed. You can press Ctrl+F3 to refresh the filtered list.

To remove the filter, choose <u>P</u>roject, <u>F</u>iltered For, <u>A</u>ll Resources, or press the F3 function key.

WORKING WITH THE RESOURCE USAGE VIEW

You must use a resource view with a timescale if you want to see assignment data for each time period or to see exactly when a resource overallocation occurs. The Resource Usage view is a standard view that can display a wealth of assignment information, including timephased details for each time period displayed in the timescale. In addition to listing all the resources, and highlighting those that are overallocated, you can display rows indented under each resource for all the resource's assignments (see Figure 11.4). Furthermore, you can display multiple timephased assignment field values for each of the assignments, and some of the fields can be edited right in the cells of the timescale grid. In Figure 11.4, both the Peak units and the Work values are displayed for each assignment and summarized for each resource. The cells in the timescale grid break down the assignment values into discrete time periods. Since you can choose the time unit displayed in the timescale, you can zoom in to view the assignment details minute by minute or zoom out to see summaries for months, quarters, or years.

The Resource Usage view in Figure 11.4 shows the individual assignments for Mel Lloyd and Scott Adams. The individual assignments for Howard Thompson are hidden from view, but they are summarized on the rows for Howard Thompson. You can click the outline symbol that appears to the left of a resource name to hide or display the assignments for that resource. If there are undisplayed assignments, the outline symbol will be a plus sign (see Howard Thompson and Bill Kirk in Figure 11.4). If the assignments are displayed, the outline symbol will be a minus sign (see both Mel Lloyd and Scott Adams in Figure 11.4). If a resource has no assignments, there will not be an outline symbol next to the name.

PART

III

CH

11

Figure 11.4
The Resource Usage view allows you to view all assignments under each resource.

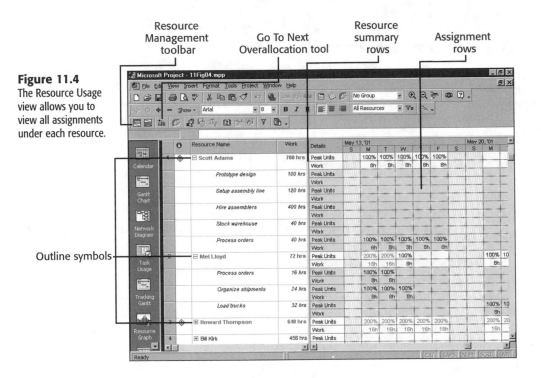

You can also use the Hide Assignments tool on the Formatting toolbar to hide or display the assignments for one or more resources that you have selected. To hide or display all assignments, select one of the column headings, like Resource Name, to select all resources and then click the Hide Assignments tool.

For each assignment row in the Resource Usage view, the default display in the cells in the timescale is the timephased Work for the time period spanned by that cell. You can also add additional rows to display other timephased values such as Overtime Work, Cost, Available Units, Peak Units, Baseline Work, Actual Work, and so on. In Figure 11.4, for example, there are five assignments listed under Scott Adams in the table on the left. Each assignment has two timephased rows in the timeline, one for Peak Units and one for Work. There are also timephased Peak Units and Work rows for Scott Adams that serve to display the totals of the Peak Units and Work cells for his assignments.

Note
The timephased rows for the assignments have a different background color in the figures in this book to help you distinguish them from the summary timephased rows for the resources. The default background color is the same for resources and assignments.

If any assignment value in a cell in the grid is itself greater than the resource availability for the time period, the assignment value will be highlighted. For example, if you assigned 200% units of a resource with only 100% Max Units for that time period, the values in the assignment timephased cells for that assignment would all appear highlighted.

Note

Unfortunately the figures do not adequately show the highlighted text in the grid for over-allocations because you can't apply a bold font to overallocations in timephased data. On your screen the highlight will be red, but not bold red as is the default for text in the table.

The cells in the rows for the resource name contain the sums of the values in the assignment rows beneath them. If a resource is overallocated during any time period, the resource name will be highlighted and the summary values in the timephased cells for those periods in which the overallocations occur will be highlighted also. This allows you to locate the exact time periods when overallocations occur.

Tip from Tim and the Project Team

If you see a highlighted value in a cell and want to know exactly when during the period spanned by the cell the overallocation occurred, you can drill down by using the Zoom In tool to view shorter and shorter time periods until you find the exact time when the overallocation occurs. If there is an overallocation at any time during the period spanned by a cell, Project will highlight text in that time period's cells in red no matter how far you may zoom out to compress the timescale.

USING THE GO TO NEXT OVERALLOCATION TOOL

If you are in a the Resource Usage view and have displayed the Resource Management toolbar, you can use the Go To Next Overallocation tool to find the next time period in which a resource has an overallocation (refer to Figure 11.4). The timescale automatically scrolls to the beginning of the next overallocation and selects the resource that is associated with that overallocation. Click the Go To Next Overallocation tool again to find the next overallocation. It will select the next resource that is involved in the current overallocation or move on to the next date where an overallocation occurs.

If you use the Go To Next Overallocation tool in a view with a task list, such as the Gantt Chart or the Task Sheet, the task list will scroll to the first task associated with an overallocation and select that task. Successive use of the Go To Next Overallocation tool selects other tasks assigned to overallocated resources during the same time period. When all tasks associated with overallocations for that time period have been identified, the Go To Next Overallocation tool will identify the next time period with an overallocated resource and select the first associated task for that time period.

CHANGING THE TIMEPHASED DETAILS

The Resource Usage view displays rows for all resources with their assignments indented beneath them. You can choose different timephased field values to display in the timescale grid. Each timephased field you choose to display will have its own rows in the display, once for each resource and once for each resource assignment. For example, if you choose to display four timephased field values, there will be four summary rows for each resource and four detail rows for each assignment. The default timephased value displayed is the Work field, which shows the total hours of assigned work per unit of time.

The display of the timephased details is governed by the Detail Styles and the Details commands on the Format menu. The Details command is a short selection menu of timephased fields to display or remove from the display. All fields that are currently displayed will be listed on the Details menu with a check mark next to their name. You can click the field to remove it from the display. The Details menu also contains a standard list of fields that can be added to the display by clicking. The list of fields to be included in this standard list is governed by the Detail Styles dialog box.

To remove a timephased field from the display, or to display one of the fields on the standard selection menu, choose Format, Details from the menu and click the field you want to add or remove from the display. You can also just right-click over the timescale grid to display the Details short-cut menu which includes the selection list as well as the command to open the Detail Styles dialog box (see Figure 11.5).

Figure 11.5
The Details shortcut menu displays check marks for the fields that are currently displayed and lets you change the display by clicking a field name.

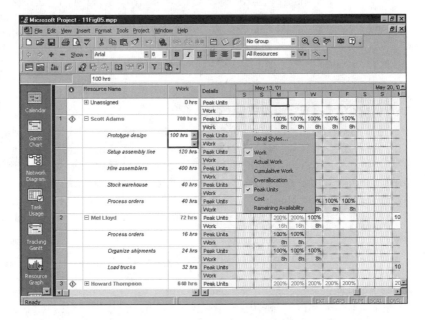

→ If you need to manage the timescale units, **see** "Formatting Timescales," **p. 900**

To display the Detail Styles dialog box, choose Format, Detail Styles (see Figure 11.6). You can also right-click over the timephased grid and choose Detail Styles from the shortcut menu.

The Usage Details tab contains a full list of all the timephased assignment fields that can be displayed in the view. If they are already displayed, they will be listed in the Show These Fields list on the right; otherwise, they will appear in the Available Fields list on the left. You can select a field from either list to define its formatting or to assign it a place on the standard Details selection menu.

Figure 11.6
The Usage Details tab of the Detail Styles dialog box governs which timephased details are displayed in the Resource Usage view, how they are formatted, and which appear on the Details standard shortcut menu.

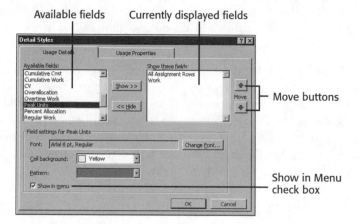

The list of timephased fields includes a wide range of actual, baseline, and scheduled values for work and cost, as well as availability and assigned values for units and work:

- The cost fields include Actual Cost, Baseline Cost, (scheduled) Cost, Cumulative (scheduled) Cost, and the earned value fields (ACWP, BCWP, BCWS, CV, and SV).

- Work fields include Actual Work, Actual Overtime Work, Baseline Work, (scheduled) Work, (scheduled) Regular Work, (scheduled) Overtime Work, Cumulative (scheduled) Work, Work Availability, Remaining Availability, Overallocation, and Percent Allocation (percent of available work that is assigned already).

- Units fields include Peak Units and Unit Availability.

Note

For detailed descriptions of these fields, take a look at the Microsoft Project 2000 Fields reference that is available on the CD accompanying this book, as well as the companion Web site for the book at www.quepublishing.com.

The list of fields also includes the entries All Resource Rows and All Assignment Rows. These are not fields but are included so that you can define separate formatting for the resource rows and assignment rows in the grid.

To add a timephased field to the standard selection list displayed by the Details command, select the field (whether it's in the Available Fields list or in the Show These Fields list) and fill the Show in Menu check box. Note that this does not display the field; it just adds it to the standard list in the Details menu.

To display a field that is not currently in the Show These Fields list, select the field in the Available Fields and click the Show button. The field will be added to the Details selection menu until you remove it from the display (unless its Show in Menu check box has been filled, in which case it will remain on the Details menu).

To move a field that is currently in the Show These Fields list, back to the Available Fields list select the field and click the Hide button.

PART
III
CH
11

The order of the fields listed in the Show These Fields list is the order in which their rows will appear in the grid. You can change the order with the Move arrows. Select a field name and move it up or down in the list with the arrows.

You can define distinguishing formats for individual timephased fields in the resource summary rows, but the format you choose will not be applied to a field's rows for assignments. To change the display characteristics of a resource field row, click the field (in whichever list it appears) and click the Change Font button to select a different font format. Select the Cell Background drop-down list to change the color of the row of cells or the Pattern drop-down box to change the fill pattern for the cells in that row. The selected format remains defined for the field no matter which list it appears in.

Tip from Tim and the Project Team

If you design special formats for the Resource Usage view and want to use those format settings for all projects, use the Organizer to copy the view into other projects and into the Global template for all new projects.

However, you can assign distinct formats to all resource rows or to all assignment rows. For example, in Figure 11.6 the assignment rows have a different background to distinguish them from the resource rows in the grid. To define a general font or background for the assignment rows or for the resource rows, select the All Assignment Rows entry or the All Resource Rows entry (in whichever list it appears) and use the Change Font button, the Cell Background drop-down list, or the Pattern drop-down list to define the format. To apply the format, you must move the All Assignment Rows or the All Resource Rows entry to the Show These Fields list. If you apply a special format to All Resource Rows, it will override any special formats you may have defined for individual timephased fields.

The Usage Properties tab controls the display of row titles in the grid and the alignment of data within the cells (see Figure 11.7). The controls are as follows:

- Use the Align Details Data drop-down list to select Right, Left, or Center alignment of timephased data within the grid cells.

- Select Yes or No in the Display Details Header Column list box to display row headers for each assignment field row. Without these headers, you cannot tell what the value display represents.

If the headers don't appear on your screen for the details rows in the timephased data, see "Displaying Detail Headers" in the "Troubleshooting" section at the end of this chapter.

- Select the Repeat Details Header on All Assignment Rows check box to display the headers on every row in the display, for resource and assignment rows alike. Leave the check box empty if you want the row headers to appear next to the resource rows but not for each assignment row.

- Select the Display Short Detail Header Names check box to use shorter names for the detail headers. Leave the check box empty to use the long names.

Figure 11.7
The Usage Properties page of the Detail Styles dialog box governs how the details are displayed.

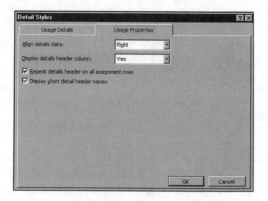

STRATEGIES FOR ELIMINATING RESOURCE OVERALLOCATIONS

The existence of overallocated resources in your project plan means that the resources will not be able to complete all their assignments in the scheduled time period. Some of the assigned work will not be completed within that time period—either the work will not be done, it will not be done thoroughly, or it will have to be done at a later time. If the work is never done or is not done well, the full scope of the project delivery will not be realized. If the work is done later, the project finish date may well be delayed, and you won't meet your final deadline.

You can resolve the overallocation by looking for ways to do either or both of the following: You can increase the availability of the resource during the time period in question, or you can reduce the total work assigned to the resource in that time period.

INCREASING AVAILABILITY OF OVERALLOCATED RESOURCES

If you want to try to increase the availability of an overallocated resource, remember that the availability during any time period depends on the settings in both the Resource Availability table in the Resource Information dialog box and the Resource Calendar (the Working Time tab).

- The Resource Availability table in the Resource Information dialog box lets you define when the resource is available and how many units are available during each time period. The resource will be overallocated if the assigned units exceed the available units for any time period. You might be able to change the available units for the period to encompass the overallocated assignment. The units available is typically 100% (or one) for individual resources and a larger number than that for group or team resources. If an individual resource has less than 100%, you can see if the resource can work full-time. If a group resource is overallocated, you can increase the number of units available by adding more units to the group.

Tip from Tim and the Project Team

Although part-time workers can be given a Max Units Available setting of less than 100% to show that they are part-time, it is generally best to enter the units as 100% and modify their available working hours on the calendar to reflect exactly *when* they are available each day. In that way, they are available 100% during those hours when they are scheduled to work. If the part-time resource uses flexible working hours, however, and works at different times as needed, you could give that resource a regular 8-hour calendar setting and enter 50% in the Max Units field.

If additional workers have to be hired to increase the number of units, you must consider the substantial added costs of searching, hiring, increased payroll, fringe benefits, and all the other factors associated with permanent employment. This solution is generally not feasible unless there is a demonstrated need for a permanent increase in the employment roster. If additional workers can be added as temporary employees, the added cost is probably less than a permanent hire, but still must be figured into the decision. If the group resource already is made up of nonemployees—for example, contract workers or workers supplied by a vendor for an out-sourced task—then requesting additional units to work during the peak demand time is not necessarily an added cost to the project. If those workers were going to be paid for completing this task anyway, although over a longer duration, you can just as easily pay them for a shorter duration to meet the demand.

- If the overallocation is not substantial, you can see if the resource is willing to work more hours during the period of overallocation. One way to show this in Project is to schedule overtime hours for the overallocated resource. Overtime hours are charged to the task at the overtime rate defined for the resource and, therefore, potentially increase the cost of the task since Project substitutes these hours for hours during the regular calendar hours.

- Alternatively, you can increase the working time temporarily by changing the working hours on the resource calendar during the overallocation time period. Use this alternative instead of assigning overtime when the resource is not paid a premium wage rate for working overtime. You can control exactly when the additional hours are available with this solution, but you cannot specify when overtime hours will be worked in the schedule.

Tip from Tim and the Project Team

As in earlier releases of Project, you cannot schedule overtime hours for specific dates or time periods. You assign the resource to work overtime on a specific task, and Project schedules the overtime work. Project spreads the overtime evenly over the duration of the task. When tracking actual work in you can, however, record the actual overtime work in the time period when the work was done.

REDUCING THE WORKLOAD FOR THE OVERALLOCATED RESOURCE

If a resource has peaks of activity which result in overallocations during those peaks, you can remove the overallocations by leveling—the process of reducing the workload during the peaks to level out the amount of work expected from the resource. To reduce the workload for a resource in an overallocated period, you can

- Reduce the total work defined for one or more task assignments during the period.
- Reduce the number of tasks assigned to the resource during the period.
- Shift the workload for one or more assignments to other periods by delaying assignments or by changing the contour of assignments to shift work to later time periods.

If you reduce the total work defined for a task, that can help ease the overallocation for the resources assigned to the task. This reduction might result from lowering the performance requirements for completing the task, removing unnecessary work or frills from the task definition, or reassessing the work estimate for completing the task. But you must consider the effect of this downscaling of the project on the scope and goal expectations of the project.

You can reduce the number of tasks assigned to the resource during the overallocated period in several ways:

- You can cancel one or more tasks. This option may reduce the scope of the project's delivered outcome. But, to the extent that the task list included unnecessary elements or frills, you will have some latitude in removing tasks without seriously affecting the project scope.
- You can substitute other resources for the overallocated resource in the assignments for the task. This is frequently the most satisfactory solution for resolving resource overallocations. However, this solution requires more investigative work for the project manager.
- You can keep the resource assigned to all the tasks if you can postpone or delay the assigned work for some of the tasks to a later period when the resource has more availability for the work. Delaying any of the assigned work in the project schedule naturally extends the duration for the task and may compromise finishing the overall project on time.

To delay some or all work on an assignment, you can try one of the following solutions:

- You can delay one or more tasks to start at a later date in order to free the overallocated resource to work on higher-priority tasks. This may not be a viable option when deadlines are important because delaying tasks may extend the project finish date. If critical tasks are delayed, the project finish date will by definition be delayed.
- Instead of delaying the entire task, and therefore delaying the assignments for all resources assigned to that task, you can delay just the overallocated resource's assignment to a task. Other resources may continue to work as scheduled, but the overallocated resource will do her part later in the project.
- If work on the task has already begun, you can split the task to stop work temporarily, thus freeing the resource for other tasks during the overallocation period. Splitting the

task will stop work for all resources assigned to the split task. This will not change the task duration or the total work for the task.

- Instead of splitting the task, and therefore interrupting all resource assignments for the task, you can split just the assignment for the overallocated resource, thus leaving other resources to continue their work as originally planned. This will increase the duration of the task, but not the total work for the task.

- You can change the contour of the overallocated assignment to shift more of the work to later time periods. The default assignment contour is *flat*, which means that work is evenly distributed throughout the duration of the task. You can choose one of several other predefined contours that set higher workloads at later points in a task's schedule. You can also edit the resource's work assignment on each task yourself to reduce the workload during the overallocated time period.

ELIMINATING RESOURCE OVERALLOCATIONS YOURSELF

The previous section provided an overview of the possible ways to resolve resource overallocations. This section shows you how to use Microsoft Project's views to analyze the facts and use your own judgment to implement the strategy you think best fits the situation. The last section shows how Microsoft Project's Leveling command can eliminate overallocations using the sole strategy of delaying assignments.

INCREASING THE AVAILABILITY OF THE OVERALLOCATED RESOURCE

The first set of strategies revolves around increasing the availability of the resource that is overallocated. After negotiating with the resource, you can use the tools in this section to implement the changes.

 The best place to change the availability of a resource is in the Resource Information dialog box because more of the fields that govern availability are accessible there. To display the dialog box, you must be in a view that contains resource data fields or you must have the Assign Resources dialog box open on the workspace. The best overall view for dealing with overallocations is the Resource Allocation view, which places the Resource Usage view in the top pane and the Leveling Gantt in the bottom pane. After selecting a resource name, click the Resource Information tool to display the Resource Information dialog box.

Tip from Tim and the Project Team

You can access the Resource Information dialog box by double-clicking the resource name in most views where the resource name is displayed and in the Assign Resources dialog box. The views where this doesn't work are the Resource Form and Resource Name Form.

INCREASING THE RESOURCE AVAILABILITY SETTINGS

To change the dates when a resource is available (assuming that it is not available for the entire project), you will need to modify the Resource Availability table on the Resource Information dialog box for the resource.

→ For a thorough explanation of working with the Resource Availability table, **see** "The Resource Availability Fields," **p. 331**

To change the units available for a resource, follow these steps:

1. Select the resource name in a view onscreen, as discussed in the introduction to this section.

2. Click the Resource Information tool (or double-click the resource name) to display the Resource Information dialog box. Choose the General tab (see Figure 11.8).

Figure 11.8
Use the Resource Information dialog box if you want to increase either the time periods when the resource is available or the units available during those time periods.

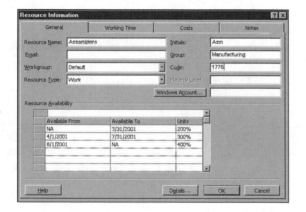

3. Select the row for the appropriate time period in the Resource Availability table and enter a new value in the Units column.
4. Choose OK to accept the changes.

SCHEDULING OVERTIME FOR THE RESOURCE

You also can schedule overtime hours for the resource to supplement the regular calendar working hours. If you enter overtime hours, Microsoft Project subtracts this number of hours from the total amount of work that was to have been scheduled during the regular working hours. The regular working hours are those that are defined as working time on the resource calendar. The total work will still be the same; so, don't change the total amount of work for the task when adding overtime hours—simply enter the quantity of hours that will be assigned as overtime. Of course, overtime hours are frequently paid for at premium hourly rates. Using overtime to solve overallocation problems may be a costly method of solving the problem, but not usually as costly as hiring new resources.

Before you enter overtime hours for an assignment, all the work will be scheduled as Regular Work. When you enter overtime hours for an assignment, Project performs these calculations:

- It first calculates a new value for regular work hours by subtracting the overtime hours from the total hours for the assignment.
- It schedules the new regular work hours in the available working time on the calendar, reducing the duration of the assignment.
- It then spreads the overtime hours equally over the new time period for the assignment.

If the work assignment is contoured, the overtime hours will still be evenly distributed over the duration of the regular hours, no matter which contour is applied.

Note that you cannot directly enter the number of overtime hours to be scheduled during specific time periods in the timephased grid. You can, however, manually contour the regular work hours in individual cells. In fact, as you will see, Project's calculations almost always leave the resource overallocated even after you apply overtime because of the way it distributes the work. You will need to manually contour the assignment to show Project how to remove the overallocation indicator when you apply overtime.

You can enter overtime on the Task Form or on the Resource Form. In either case, you need to display the Work details to see overtime. If you use the Task Form, you see only one task listed at a time. If you use the Resource Form, all tasks to which the resource is assigned are displayed in the Work fields listing, and you can assign overtime to multiple tasks from the same screen. You can also enter overtime in the Resource Usage view if you add a column to display the Overtime Work field.

Look at these two examples of using overtime to solve a scheduling problem: 1) you need to shorten the duration of a task without reducing the work, and 2) you use overtime to deal with overlapping assignments.

Figure 11.9 shows a before-and-after version of an assignment for Mel Lloyd to load trucks. The original task is represented by the first resource "Mel Lloyd (no overtime)" and is scheduled to take four days. If the task needs to be finished in two days instead of four, and if other resources are not available to help, the scheduler could ask Mel to work a lot of extra hours to complete the task earlier. The second resource shows how overtime can shorten the duration of the task without overallocating the resource.

The figure displays the Resource Usage view in the top pane and the Resource Form in the bottom pane. In the Resource Form, the Work details table is displayed at the bottom to make the Ovt. Work field available for entering overtime.

The timephased data in the top pane displays details for Work (which is total work for the task), Regular Work (which is work during working times on the calendar), and Overtime Work. The Overtime Work field has also been added to the table on the left as an alternative way to schedule overtime for assignments.

The second resource, "Mel Lloyd (with overtime)," has 16 hours of overtime scheduled and Project has shortened the duration of the task to two days. The overtime could have been entered either in the Overtime Work column in the top pane, or in the Ovt. Work column in the Resource Form at the bottom of the screen.

Overtime Work column   Ovt. Work colum

Figure 11.9
Use the Resource Usage view to apply and fine-tune scheduled overtime.

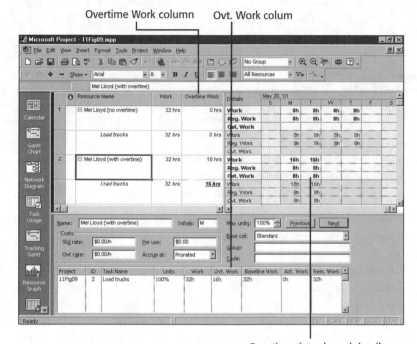

Overtime timephased details

To enter overtime hours for a task using the Resource Form, follow these steps:

1. Select the pane in which to place the Resource Form. In this example, the bottom pane is used. With the Resource Usage view in the top pane, you can just double-click the split box to display the Resource Form (this always works when a resource view is in the top pane).

2. Make the Resource Form the active pane.

3. Choose Format, Details, Work. Or right-click in the Resource Form and choose Work from the shortcut menu.

    The Resource Work fields are displayed at the bottom of the form (refer to Figure 11.9).

4. If the Resource Form was placed in the bottom pane, as it is in this example, you can select the resource in the top pane or use the Next and Previous buttons on the Resource Form until you find the resource. If the Resource Form is in the top pane, use the Next and Previous buttons to select the resource name.

5. Select the task for which you want overtime hours scheduled.

6. In the Ovt. Work column, type the amount of overtime work. You must use a number, followed by a time unit. If you don't specify a time unit, Microsoft Project assumes that the time unit is hours.

   If you want to remove the overtime, you must type a zero into the overtime field. Don't press the Delete key, because that will delete the assignment.

7. Choose OK to complete the entry.

Note
If the resource is paid for overtime work, be sure that the resource doesn't have a zero overtime rate in the cost fields of the Resource Form. Some Project users mistakenly leave the overtime rate zero if overtime is paid at the same rate as regular hours.

If you have displayed the Overtime Work column in the Resource Usage view, you can enter overtime on the rows for assignments (the rows for resources will not allow data entry) just as you do in the Ovt. Work column of the Resource Form.

In those cases where an overallocation has resulted from overlapping assignments, you can assign overtime work to one or more of the tasks to remove the overallocation. If you have two or more tasks that are assigned to one resource and that are scheduled at the same time, the simplest method is to assign all the work of one or more of the assignments (usually the shorter assignments) to overtime. This will leave the assignments that have overtime work with zero hours of regular work, and it will eliminate the overallocation. However, if the resource is the only resource assigned any of those tasks, the zero hours of regular work cause Project to treat the task as having no duration and to display it as a milestone. Although you can use the Format, Bar command to give the milestone a distinctive appearance, it is nevertheless confusing to see a milestone graphic on the Gantt Chart when the task will really be ongoing until the overtime work is completed.

A better solution is to assign some overtime to both (or all) the tasks that are competing for the resource's work. As an example, suppose that Mel Lloyd has two task assignments, Process Orders and Organize Shipments, which are competing for his time and which create an overallocation. Figure 11.10 shows two versions of the assignments, without and with overtime. The top resource (simply named Mel Lloyd) shows the original situation. Process Orders will take one week or 40 hours and Organize Shipments will take 3 days or 24 hours. The total work for the week is 64 hours, which is 24 hours more than he has available per week. During the time that Organize Shipments is scheduled, Mel is overallocated by 8 hours per day for 3 days, or, as just pointed out, a total of 24 hours of overallocation.

The second resource listing in Figure 11.10, "Mel Lloyd (with overtime)," shows how Project calculates the assignments if you assign 12 hours of overtime to both tasks. With 24 hours of overtime assigned, the regular work for the week is now just 40 hours for the week, but the regular work for Monday and Tuesday is still excessive at 16 and 12 hours, respectively, because Project still schedules 8 hours of regular work for both tasks until the task is completed. The Leveling indicator is still displayed because the sensitivity setting is Day by

Day. In fact, even if you changed the sensitivity setting to Week by Week, Project would still (mistakenly) display the Leveling indicator.

Figure 11.10
Split the overtime assignment between the competing tasks.

Before assigning overtime

After assigning overtime

Leveling indicator still shows.

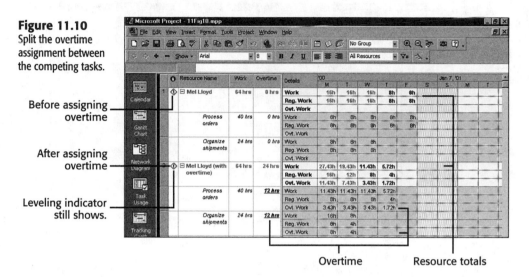

Overtime   Resource totals

To get Project to remove the Leveling indicator, we must reduce the units assigned to each task to 50% so that the total units is 100% (the units available) and no more than 4 hours of regular work is scheduled per day for each task. Figure 11.11 shows this change. The top resource repeats the bottom resource in the previous figure. The bottom resource shows what happens when the units assigned are reduced to 50% for each task. The Leveling indicator is gone, but the duration of the longer task, Process Orders, has been increased and work is scheduled for Monday and Tuesday of the following week. The reason is that, with the 50% units assignment, the scheduling calculations keep the regular hours down to 4 hours per day, even on Thursday and Friday when the Organize Shipments task is completed and Mel could work 8 hours a day instead of just 4. That lost time is scheduled the following week.

The final adjustment that is needed is to compact the regular work for the Process Orders task at the end of the task where the reduced units has resulted in unused available hours. On both Thursday and Friday the 50% units assignment causes only 4 hours to be scheduled, but 8 hours is available now that the Organize Shipments task is finished. The reduced hours has made it necessary to schedule work on Monday and Tuesday of the following week. Figure 11.12 shows the effect of manually adjusting the regular work schedule for those days. The top resource is a copy of the bottom resource in Figure 11.11, and the bottom resource shows the edited schedule. The regular work cells for Thursday and Friday for the Process Orders assignment were selected and 8h was typed in to replace the 4h that Project scheduled. Then the regular work cells for the following Monday and Tuesday were selected and the Delete key pressed to remove work for those days. Because of the editing, the Contour indicator is displayed for the Process Orders task. The final result shows the two tasks with the same duration and total work we started with, but the Leveling indicator is gone.

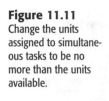

Figure 11.11
Change the units assigned to simultaneous tasks to be no more than the units available.

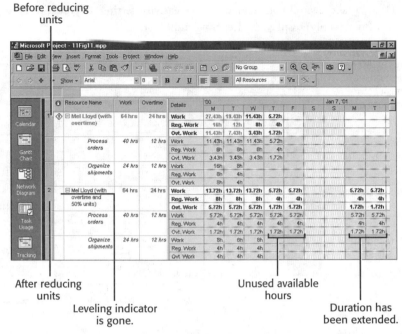

Before reducing units

After reducing units

Leveling indicator is gone.

Unused available hours

Duration has been extended.

Figure 11.12
Manually contour the schedule to keep the task durations at the same length.

Before contouring

After contouring the remaining work

Contour indicator

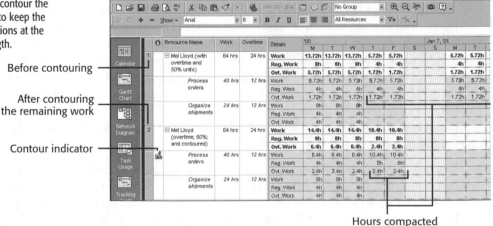

Hours compacted

EXTENDING THE AVAILABLE HOURS ON THE RESOURCE CALENDAR

If you want resources to work extra hours, you can adjust the calendar for the resource to add extra hours on specific days instead of assigning overtime. Unlike assigning overtime, you can specify precisely when the extra work will take place. However, you cannot specify which task assignments will be scheduled during the extra time unless you manually contour the assignments. Project will use the extra hours for any assignment that has started at that point in time, and you may have to edit the assigned work for tasks it has scheduled but which you don't want scheduled during those extra hours.

> **Note**
>
> Remember that all working hours on the calendar are charged at the standard rate for the resource; so, if these hours are really overtime hours and there is a premium rate for overtime, you should assign overtime instead of adding hours to the calendar.

If only certain resources work the added hours, make the change on the individual resource calendars. If the added hours are to be worked by all resources, you can make the change on the base calendar (or calendars) for resources in the project.

To extend the normal working hours for one or all resources, follow these steps:

1. Choose Tools, Change Working Time to display the Change Working Time dialog box (see Figure 11.13).
2. Select the resource calendar or the base calendar whose hours you want to extend in the For drop-down list.
3. Select the date or dates on which you want the extra hours worked. Use click-and-drag to select adjacent dates. Use the Ctrl key to add non-adjacent dates to the selection.
4. Enter the extra time in the From and To text boxes.
5. Click OK to close the dialog box and execute the changed hours.

> **Tip from Tim and the Project Team**
>
> If the Change Working Time command is grayed out (unavailable), you probably have the lower pane of a combination active. Activate the top pane and it will be available. As an alternative, you can click in any Resource field that is visible, in either the top or bottom pane, and click the Resource Information tool on the Standard toolbar to view the Resource Information dialog box for that resource. Click the Working Time tab to modify that resource's calendar.

In Figure 11.13, Mel Lloyd's resource calendar is being modified to extend his hours during the week of January 1, 2001, by adding five hours of work for each of those days, from 6:00 PM to 11:00 PM. Figure 11.14 shows the before-and-after effects of extending Mel's regular hours in the same situation we used to illustrate overtime in Figure 11.10. Resource 1, labeled "Mel Lloyd", has 8 available hours per day (or 40 hours per week) as shown in the Work Availability detail row. The total work required for the two tasks is 64 hours, which is 24 hours more than the hours available. Mel is overallocated, even on a Week by Week basis (which is the setting in the illustration), and the Leveling indicator is displayed next to his name.

Figure 11.13
You can increase the working hours on the calendar to extend a resource's availability.

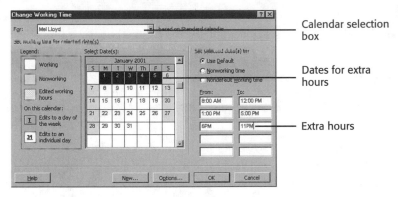

Calendar selection box

Dates for extra hours

Extra hours

Figure 11.14
Increasing the working hours enables the resource to do more work, but it won't remove the overallocation.

Total work to be scheduled

Available work hours

Before adding extra working time

After adding extra working time

No Leveling indicator

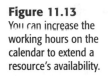

Resource 2, labeled "Mel Lloyd (more working time hours)," shows that Mel's availability after adding the extra hours has risen to 13 hours per day (or 65 hours for the week). With the extended hours, Project is able to schedule all 64 hours of the work during regular hours. And, since the Leveling indicator sensitivity setting is Week by Week, the Leveling indicator is not displayed. However, the schedule is totally unrealistic, for Mel is assigned to both tasks at 100% and is scheduled for 26 hours of work on Monday and 24 hours on Tuesday. To make the schedule realistic, and to remove the overallocation highlight, the units must be reduced so that they total no more than 100%.

Figure 11.15 shows the before-and-after effect of reducing the units assigned to 50% for each task. Resource 2, labeled "Mel Lloyd (more working time hours)," is the same resource schedule you saw in the last figure. Resource 3, labeled "Mel Lloyd (adjusted units)," shows the schedule that Project calculates when the unit assignments are changed to 50%. The resource name is no longer highlighted as an overallocated resource because the daily work is no greater than the work availability.

Figure 11.15
Reducing the units to match the resource availability resolves the overallocation.

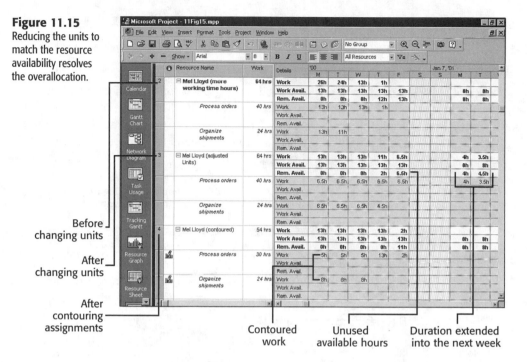

Before changing units

After changing units

After contouring assignments

Contoured work

Unused available hours

Duration extended into the next week

However, due to the reduced units Project's new schedule has increased the duration of the Organize Shipments task (assigning only 6.5 hours per day instead of 13 hours as before), and Project doesn't use all the available hours for the Process Orders task when it is the only task needing work. The Remaining Availability detail row shows that 2 hours is not used on Thursday and 6.5 hours goes unused on Friday. Since the Process Orders task is not finished, the remaining work has been pushed back to the following week. As with scheduling overtime, the final step to make the schedule reflect your real intentions is to manually edit the assignment contour to take advantage of all the available hours at the end of the longer task.

Resource 3 in Figure 11.15, labeled "Mel Lloyd (contoured)," shows the results of editing the timephased work assignments to take advantage of all available hours. The Work cells for the Organize Shipments task have been restored to 8 hours per day and that task still finishes in 3 days as it did in the original schedule. During those three days, the remaining 5 available hours are assigned to the Process Orders task. The Remaining Availability details calculate how many hours can be assigned to the Process Orders task on Thursday and Friday and those cells were edited to finish the task by Friday.

REDUCING THE WORKLOAD OF THE OVERALLOCATED RESOURCE

Instead of increasing the availability of the resource that is overallocated, we can look for ways to reduce the demands on the resource during the overallocated period. We can cancel nonessential tasks, reassign tasks to other resources, or delay one or more assignments until the resource has time to work on them. We will first look at the Resource Allocation view, which is an efficient view to use for all these strategies.

USING THE RESOURCE ALLOCATION VIEW

The Resource Allocation view provides a good starting point for tackling the problem of reducing the demand for an overallocated resource. The view has its own tool on the Resource Management toolbar, offering easy access, or you can access it by choosing View, More Views and choosing Resource Allocation from the Views list. Once it is selected, click the Apply button to display the view (see Figure 11.16).

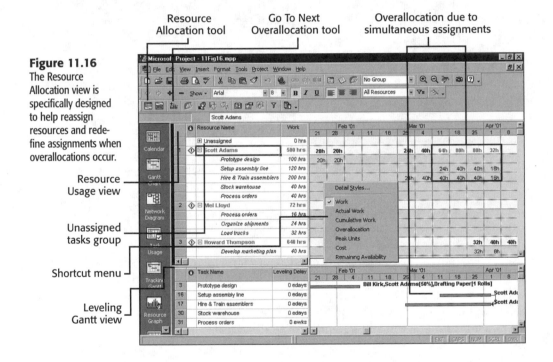

Figure 11.16
The Resource Allocation view is specifically designed to help reassign resources and redefine assignments when overallocations occur.

This composite view shows the names and task assignments of all resources in the Resource Usage view in the top pane, it highlights overallocated resources, and it displays the Leveling indicator for those resources that need your attention. Timephased assignment details in the timeline grid on the right let you edit assignment schedules down to the hour or the minute. The bottom pane displays the Leveling Gantt that shows, for the resource name you have selected in the top pane, all the tasks to which the resource is assigned. The Leveling Gantt has special formatting that will be especially helpful when we discuss leveling resource assignments.

You can use the Go To Next Overallocation tool in either pane to pinpoint overallocated resource assignments. In the top pane, which is a resource view, the Go To Next Overallocation tool scrolls the timeline to the next date when an overallocation begins and selects the resource that is associated with the overallocation. Clicking the tool again finds the next overallocation in the timeline and selects its associated resource.

The bottom pane is a task view that only shows the set of tasks that are assigned to the resource that is selected in the top pane. When the bottom pane is active, the Go To Next Overallocation tool finds the next overallocation associated with one of the tasks in the restricted set. Clicking the tool again causes Project to select the next task associated with that same overallocation or to find the next overallocation in the timeline associated with one of the tasks in the restricted set.

If you are trying to locate the overallocations for a particular resource, you will find that using the Go To Next Overallocation tool in the top pane can be pretty tedious because it finds overallocations for all resources. Selecting the resource in the top pane, activating the bottom pane, and using the tool there will narrow the search considerably. However, the overallocation that Project finds may be for a different resource that is also assigned to one of the tasks in the restricted set. To confirm that the overallocation is for the selected resource, check the grid in the top pane to see if there is highlighting in the timephased data for that resource.

You can use the top pane to remove a task assignment from an overallocated resource, either by reassigning the task to another resource or by leaving the task unassigned for the time being. If you want to remove an assignment from a resource without designating another resource to take its place, you can simply select the assignment and choose Edit, Delete Assignment (or press the Delete key). The assignment will disappear from under the resource and will reappear in the Unassigned category at the top of the Resource Usage view. You can move the assignment to another resource later. You can also select the row for the assignment and drag the assignment to the Unassigned group.

 If you want to redefine a task—for example, by reducing its duration to help deal with an overallocation—you can select the overallocated resource in the top pane and then select the task in the bottom pane. Either double-click the task or use the Task Information tool to display the Task Information dialog box, where you can modify the task definition.

SUBSTITUTING UNDERUSED RESOURCES FOR OVERALLOCATED RESOURCES

Probably the most conventional method of dealing with the problem of overallocated resources is to find substitute resources to take some of the load off the overallocated resources. To use this approach in a cost-effective manner, you need to consider a number of things, including the following:

- **The list of overallocated resources and their current work loads per time period**—This tells you when the overallocations occur. These resources are identified in the Resource Usage view, the top pane of the Resource Allocation view. Use the Go To Next Overallocation tool to identify overallocations.

- **The tasks that each overallocated resource is currently assigned to work on during the periods of overallocation**—This identifies the tasks for which you may seek substitutes. These tasks are identified in the top pane by the timephased data in the grid and in the bottom pane by the taskbars.

PART

III

CH

11

- **The total work commitment for each of the tasks for which resources may be substituted**—This helps you decide which of two tasks to give to a substitute and which to keep for the overallocated resource. You can give the task that involves the most total work to the cheaper resource to keep costs low. The total work for each assignment is displayed by default in the Usage table's Work column that displays on the left of the top pane.

- **The availability of other resources during the overallocated time periods**—This helps you find resources that may be used as substitutes. Although not displayed by default in the Resource Usage view, the Remaining Availability detail is one of the details you can choose to display in the timescale grid. Because the bottom pane of the Resource Allocation view has a timescale, the detail labels will not be displayed. But you can assign a distinctive format to any of the details to help identify those values easily. For example, in Figure 11.18 later in this section the Remaining Availability has been formatted in **bold underlining** to distinguish it from the Work field.

- **The standard rate cost for using each of the resources**—This tells you the cost of substituting other resources for those currently assigned to the tasks. Although not in the default display of the table in the Resource Usage view, the Standard Rate field can be added as a column in the table. In Figure 11.17, it is being added to the right of the Work field.

- **The skill level of other resources available to do the work and the time it may take them to learn the tasks that need to be done**—The comparative skill levels of resource substitutes can be used to estimate how many units of the substitute resource should be assigned and to reassess how long the assignment will take. This is not a standard field in Microsoft Project, but you can use one of the custom resource text or number fields to hold this data and then display it in the table on the Resource Usage view for reference when reassigning tasks.

It is certainly not required that you add the information suggested in the previous list (standard rate, remaining availability, and skill rating), but the additional information promotes more cost-effective assignments.

Since the default table for the Resource Usage view is the Usage table, you can add the Standard Rate field to that table. The following steps show the quickest method of adding this column:

→ For more options about customizing tables, **see** "Using and Creating Tables," **p. 949**

1. Click the column heading for the Work column. In this example, we will insert a column to the left for the Standard Rate field.

2. Choose <u>I</u>nsert, <u>C</u>olumn to display the Column Definition dialog box (see Figure 11.17).

3. Type an **s** in the Field <u>N</u>ame field to jump to the field names in the list that start with an S, and Standard Rate will appear since it is the first S field in the list. Click Standard Rate or press Enter.

4. Select the <u>T</u>itle text box and type a shorter name. Std. Rate is used in this example.

5. Click the Best Fit button to insert the column with the width adjusted to the widest entry.

6. If necessary, adjust column widths and the vertical divider bar so you can see both the Std.Rate and Work columns.

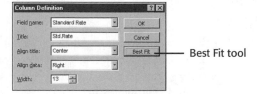

Figure 11.17
Insert columns in your tables to show field values that aid your decisions.

Best Fit tool

Displaying details in the Resource Usage timescale is described earlier in this chapter in the section "Working with the Resource Usage View." See that section for instructions on displaying and formatting the Remaining Availability field in the timescale. The resulting view will be similar to the one in Figure 11.18.

Standard Rate field   Work detail   Zoom Out tool   Remaining Availability detail

Figure 11.18
This modified Resource Allocation view displays the cost and availability of potential substitute resources.

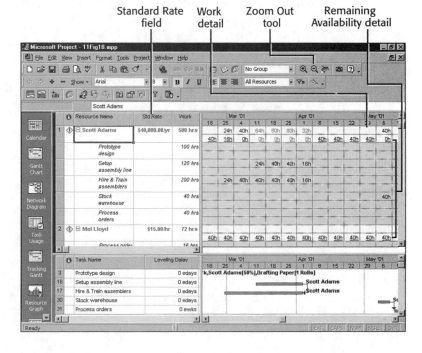

 To substitute another resource for one of the assignments of an overallocated resource, first select the overallocated resource in the top pane and scroll the timescale to the start of the project. (In Figure 11.18 Scott Adams is selected in the top pane.) Then activate the bottom pane and use the Go To Next Overallocation tool to find the next time period when the selected resource is overallocated. In the figure, the first overallocation for Scott is in the week of March 11, 2001, where he is scheduled to work on the Setup Assembly Line task and the Hire & Train Assemblers task at the same time. The Zoom Out tool was used to compress the minor timescale in Figure 11.18 to weeks in order to get a better perspective on the length of the tasks. Decide which task will be reassigned to another resource. The shorter and least work of the two tasks in this example is Setup Assembly Line; so, let's look for a suitable substitute resource for that task.

By double-clicking the Setup Assembly Line task in the bottom pane to display the Task Information Form, we can tell that the task is scheduled from 3/14/2001 to 4/3/2001. To see what other resources might have available hours during that period, you can scroll down the list of resources and look at the Remaining Availability values for other resources. We need to find a resource with at least as many hours available during each week as the work for the task requires: 24 hours the first week, 40 hours the next two weeks, and 16 hours the final week.

| *Tip from Tim and the Project Team* | If the list of resources in the top pane is long, you will find it helpful to highlight the time periods when the substitute must have available hours. Click and drag across the time units in the minor scale of the timeline to highlight those weeks for all resources (see Figure 11.19). Then scroll down the list looking for available hours in the highlighted range. |

| *Tip from Tim and the Project Team* | You may also find it helpful to hide the assignments in the top pane so that you only see the rows for resources (see Figure 11.19). To hide all assignments, click one of the column headings to select all rows and then click the Hide Subtasks button. If you want to continue to view the work hours for the assignment, you're looking for a substitute for, click the plus-sign outline symbol next to the resource currently assigned to the task. |

| *Tip from Tim and the Project Team* | If you have placed labels in the Group field (or in any text field) that identify resources that are qualified substitutes for Scott, you can filter the resource list in the top pane to focus on those resources. For example, the Setup Assembly Line might be a task requiring a manager resource. If managers are identified in the Group field, you could filter the list for managers to shorten the list of potential substitutes. |

Both Mel Lloyd and Mary Logan have enough available time during the period shown, and Mary's standard rate is greater than Mel's. However, we will assume that the task is better suited to Mary's abilities and assign her to the task. Mary's standard rate is also higher than Scott's; so, the substitution is going to increase the cost of the task.

After a task and resource combination is selected, you can use the Resource Assignment dialog box to replace one resource with another:

1. Select the task for the substitution in the lower pane. In this example the task will be Setup Assembly Line (see Figure 11.20.)

Hide Subtasks tool Work hours to be reassigned Drag here to highlight the target time period. Possible substitutes

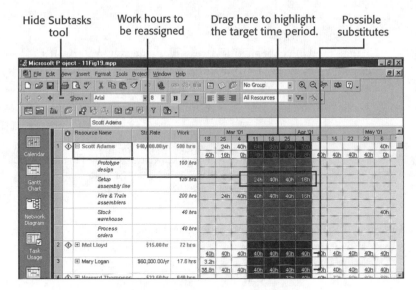

Figure 11.19
Highlighting the time periods in question and hiding the assignments makes it easier to find available substitutes.

Work for task Assign Resource tool Replace button

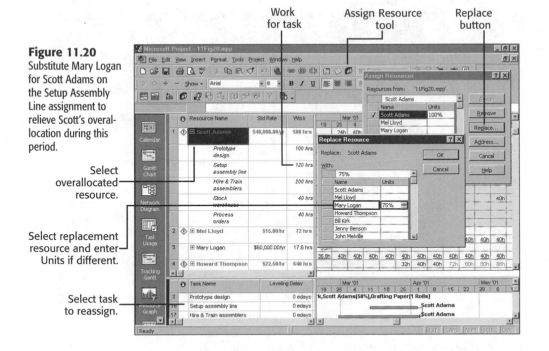

Figure 11.20
Substitute Mary Logan for Scott Adams on the Setup Assembly Line assignment to relieve Scott's overallocation during this period.

Select overallocated resource.

Select replacement resource and enter Units if different.

Select task to reassign.

2. Click the Assign Resource tool to display the Assign Resources dialog box. (You can also use Alt+F8 to open this same dialog box.)

3. First, select the resource you want to replace (Scott Adams) and click the Replace button to display the Replace Resource dialog box.

4. Select the name of the resource that you want to assign as a substitute in the With list box.

5. Change the Units assigned if necessary. By default, Microsoft Project 2000 will assign the same number of units for the new resource as were assigned for the original resource.

6. Choose OK to complete the substitution.

Tip from Tim and the Project Team

If the new resource is more or less efficient or skilled in the task than the original resource, you should manually adjust the assignment after the replacement to show how many hours it will take the new resource to complete the task.

Figure 11.21 shows the schedule after substituting Mary Logan for Scott Adams. Scott's workload is reduced, and he is no longer overallocated in this period.

New assignment for Mary   Mary's workload increased   Scott's workload reduced

Figure 11.21
The schedule after substituting Mary Logan for Scott Adams.

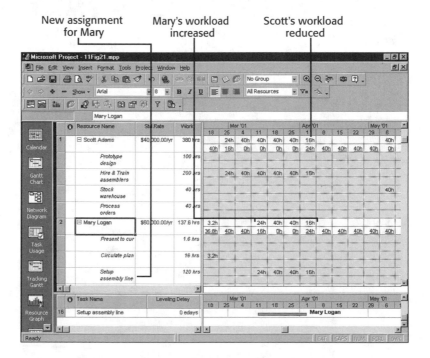

Once the new assignment has been added to the replacement resource, you can modify the assignment with the Assignment Information dialog box. You would select the assignment row in the top pane and click the Assignment Information tool, or simply double-click the assignment.

RESOLVING OVERALLOCATIONS BY DELAYING ASSIGNMENTS

If resource overallocation is the result of scheduling multiple tasks at the same time, you can delay one or more task assignments to a later date to spread out the demands on the resource over a longer period of time, and thereby reduce the demand in the overallocated period. You can delay assignments yourself by examining the schedule and selecting the assignments to delay, or you can have Microsoft Project choose the assignments to delay—either on your command or automatically as task assignments are added to the schedule. This section shows you how to level assignments yourself, on a case-by-case basis. Using Project's Leveling command is reserved for a later section.

> **Note**
>
> This discussion is built around the case of forward-scheduled projects—projects that are scheduled from a fixed start date. Delaying to resolve overallocations means to offset one or more tasks that would otherwise be scheduled at the same time. In forward scheduled projects, you add a delay to a task's start date to push it back to a later date. In projects that are scheduled from a fixed finish date, however, you insert an offset at the finish of the task to cause it to be scheduled for earlier dates. Delay values are entered as positive numbers in forward-scheduled projects and as negative numbers in projects that are scheduled from a fixed finish date.

PART

III

CH

11

If you choose to delay assignments yourself, there are several ways you can go about it:

- You can use the Delay field of the task database to enter a delay in the start date for a task, thus delaying all assignments to that task.

- You can use the Assignment Delay field to delay the start of the assignment for just the resource that is overallocated, leaving other resources' assignments for the task unchanged.

- If work on a task is scheduled to have started already when the overallocation begins, you can split the task at that point and resume the task when the overallocated resource is available again. Of course, other resources assigned to the task will have their assignments split also.

- Instead of splitting the task, and all assignments, you can split just the assignment for the overallocated resource, leaving other resource assignments unchanged.

- Instead of delaying all the work on the overallocated resource's assignment, you can merely reduce the hours assigned during the period of overallocation and increase the hours at a later period. This is called *contouring* the assignment and can be done by manually editing the assigned work in each period or by choosing one of the predefined contour patterns to apply to the assignment.

 DELAYING A TASK   Use the Resource Allocation view when leveling resource work loads manually. With the Resource Usage view in the top pane to help you select the overallocated resources, the bottom pane displays the Leveling Gantt with the Leveling Delay field in the table next to the task name (see Figure 11.22). The Leveling Delay field is zero by default, but if you enter an amount of time in the field, Project delays the start of the task—and therefore all assignments to the task—by the amount of that delay value.

For forward scheduled projects (those with fixed start dates), the delay value is a positive number which, when added to the task's original start date, makes it a later start date. For projects with fixed finish dates, the delay value is a negative number which makes Project push the task finish date back to an earlier date.

Delay amounts are shown in elapsed time. Elapsed time ignores the distinction between working time and nonworking time on calendars. Using elapsed time makes it easier for you to estimate the amount of time you should enter in this field. You can count the time units in the timescale of the Gantt Chart and enter that number without having to check to see if any of those units fall on nonworking days.

→ For more information about using elapsed duration, **see** "Entering Task Duration," **p. 161**

The Delay table also includes the Successors field to give you information about what tasks are directly affected if you delay the selected task. You must scroll the columns in the table to see the Successors field. The taskbars display the names of assigned resources to the right of the bar.

The Leveling Gantt shows the amount of any *free slack* (the amount of time between the end of a task and the start of a successor task) as a thin teal-colored Slack bar extending to the right beyond the bottom edge of the taskbar. You can delay a task by as much as the free slack, without affecting the scheduling of other tasks. Of course, if you delay tasks beyond the free slack, the start and finish of successor tasks will also be delayed; if you delay a task beyond the total slack (not shown in this view), the finish of the whole project would be delayed.

Tip from Tim and the Project Team

ScreenTips will identify any taskbars that appear in the view. In Figure 11.22, the pointer rests over the Slack bar and the ScreenTip names the bar along with information about the task.

Note

Free slack is the amount of time that a task can be delayed without delaying successor tasks. *Total slack* is the amount of time that a task can be delayed without delaying the project.

As shown in Figure 11.22, Mel Lloyd is an overallocated resource in the week of May 13, 2001. Selecting his name in the top pane causes the tasks to which he is assigned to appear in the bottom pane. After using the horizontal scrollbar in the timeline to move to the beginning of the project, click the Go To Next Overallocation tool to locate the first time period during which Mel is overallocated. The overallocation is due to the overlapping assignments for Process Orders and Organize Shipments. We could delay either of these tasks to remove the overallocation for Mel.

Figure 11.22
The Leveling Gantt is especially helpful when delaying tasks to level resource assignments.

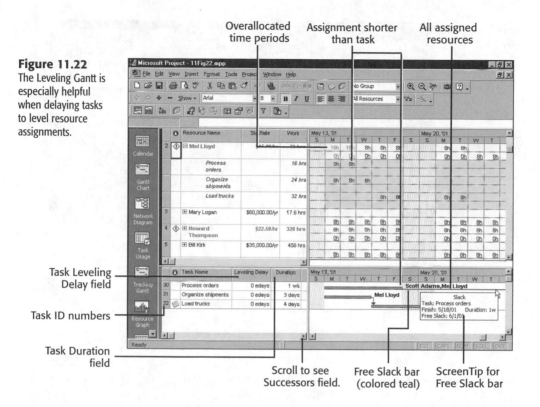

Overallocated time periods

Assignment shorter than task

All assigned resources

Task Leveling Delay field

Task ID numbers

Task Duration field

Scroll to see Successors field.

Free Slack bar (colored teal)

ScreenTip for Free Slack bar

Scott Adams is also assigned to the Process Orders task, and if we delayed the task, both Mel's and Scott's assignments would be delayed. However, the existence of the Slack bar to the right of the Process Orders task shows that delaying the task will not delay any other tasks or the project. If we were to delay the Organize Shipments task to resolve Mel's overallocation, the absence of a Slack bar for the task tells us that other tasks and the overall project would be delayed as a result. We will delay the Process Orders task.

To delay the task, select the Leveling Delay field for the task and estimate the amount of delay. It appears from the Duration field in the lower pane that Organize Shipments is a 3-day task, so entering "3 days" for the Process Orders task should remove the overallocation.

In Figure 11.23, you see the results of entering the delay. The Leveling Gantt displays the amount of the delay in the Leveling Delay field on the left, and it displays the Delay bar to the left of the taskbar to show the amount of the delay graphically. The tasks no longer overlap, and Mel's initial overallocation period is now free of overallocation. However, he now has a 3-day conflict with his Load Trucks assignment. If that conflict is resolved by delaying the Load Trucks assignment, it will mean a 3-day delay in the completion of the project. Also, since the entire task was delayed, the assignment for Scott Adams was delayed also and that could possibly create an overallocation for Scott.

Figure 11.23
The Leveling Gantt shows the amount of the delay as a thin bar to the left of the main taskbar.

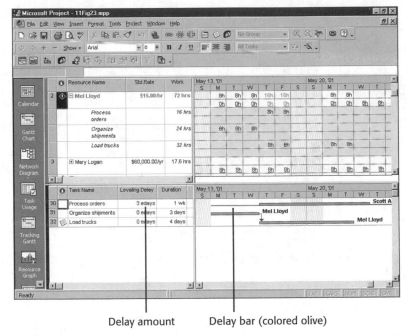

Delay amount   Delay bar (colored olive)

You can use Undo (Ctrl+Z) immediately after entering a delay amount to restore the previous values to the delay field entries. You also can remove a delay by entering a zero in the delay field. Note that you can't leave the Leveling Delay field blank. If there are many delay values to be cleared, you may want to use the Clear Leveling command. To use the menu to return the delay values to zero for a single task or group of tasks, follow these steps:

1. Select the tasks for which you want to reset the delay to zero. Click and drag to select adjacent tasks. Press Ctrl while clicking to select nonadjacent tasks.

2. Choose Tools, Resource Leveling.

3. At the bottom of the Resource Leveling dialog box, click the Clear Leveling tool to display the Clear Leveling dialog box.

4. Choose the Selected Tasks option to change the values for only the tasks that you selected. If you want to remove all delay values for all tasks, use the Entire Project option.

5. Choose OK. All tasks with nonzero delay values will be reset to zero delay.

DELAYING INDIVIDUAL ASSIGNMENTS   When tasks have multiple resources assigned to them, it may be better to resolve an overallocation for just one of the resources by delaying the assignment for just that resource, leaving the other resources unaffected. Of course, if the delayed assignment now has a finish date that is later than the task finish date before the delay, the task duration will be increased. This section will show you how to delay individual assignments for tasks.

Returning to the previous example, we can delay Mel Lloyd's assignment to that task instead of delaying the task and Scott's assignment also. In the Resource Allocation view, you can delay an assignment in one of four ways:

- You can add the Leveling Delay field to the Usage table in the top pane and enter the amount of the delay in that column.

- You can manually edit the timephased work data in the top pane to shift work hours to the right to later dates and times.

- You can change the assignment's start date in the Assignment Information dialog box.

- You can add the Assignment Delay field to the Usage table in the top pane and enter the amount of the delay in that column.

If the purpose for delaying an assignment is to avoid an overallocation, you should use the Leveling Delay field. This field is specifically designed to show delays due to overallocations. Furthermore, if you later want to remove all the leveling delays that you or Project have inserted, the Clear Leveling command (which is discussed later in this chapter) will remove the delay if it's in this field.

The Leveling Delay field is not included in the standard Usage table, but you can easily add it to the table by clicking the column heading where you want the field to go and choosing Insert, Column. In the Column Definition dialog box, choose Leveling Delay in the Field Name box and click the Best Fit button to adjust the column width to the widest entry. You may need to adjust the vertical divider bar so that you can see the new column.

Note

Unlike task delay values, which are *elapsed* time periods, leveling delay values are regular, nonelapsed, time periods.

Figure 11.24 shows the Leveling Delay field added to the table in the top pane. Note the delay in Mel's Process Orders assignment.

To remove the delay, type a zero or use the spin control to select zero. Do not press the Delete key, for that will delete the assignment.

Caution

Do *not* press the Delete key to clear a field in an assignment row. Like task tables and resource tables, the Delete key removes the row that contains the selection.

Note

The Leveling Delay field only accepts zero or positive numbers for projects that are scheduled from a fixed start date. It only accepts zero or negative numbers for projects that are scheduled from a fixed finish date.

Leveling Delay field   Work details   Remaining Availability details

Figure 11.24
You can use the Leveling Delay field in a Usage table to enter and remove assignment-leveling delays.

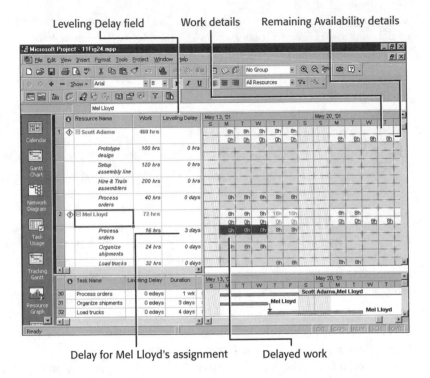

Delay for Mel Lloyd's assignment   Delayed work

To edit the timephased data, select the cells that contain work that is to be delayed and press the Insert key. The cells you selected will shift to the right, also pushing rightward all later work cells for the assignment. The Contour indicator will appear in the Indicators column for the assignment.

Tip from Tim and the Project Team

You may need to Zoom In to see smaller time units to detect exactly how many days and hours the assignment needs to be delayed. Zoom In until you can see clearly exactly when the task that is not being delayed finishes. Then shift the work for the delayed task one cell further to the right.

To remove the delay, select the assignment cells that have 0h in them and press the Delete key. All work cells to the right of the selection will be shifted leftward.

If you want to delay the assignment by modifying the start date and time for the assignment until just after a conflicting assignment is completed, you will need to be able to determine exactly when the conflicting assignment finishes. To determine the finish time, you will need to first instruct Project to display time along with dates. To display dates with the time of day appended, choose Tools, Options and display the View tab. In the Date Format box, select one of the formats from the drop-down list that includes the date and time of day.

In this example, we will delay Mel's Process Orders assignment to start immediately after the conflicting assignment Organize Shipments finishes. You can find out when the

Organize Shipments assignment finishes by double-clicking that assignment to display its Assignment Information dialog box. In Figure 11.25, the Assignment Information dialog box for Organize Shipments shows that the task finishes on 5/16/01 at 5:00 PM. The Process Orders task would be delayed to start on 5/17/01 at 8:00 AM to resolve the conflict.

Figure 11.25
Use the Assignment Information dialog box to find out when an assignment finishes.

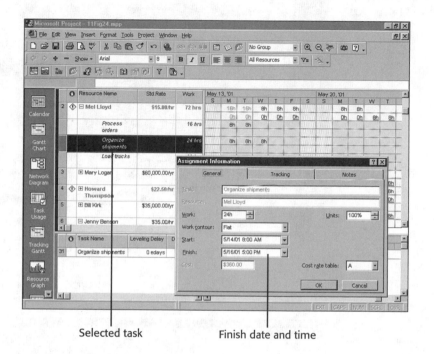

Selected task   Finish date and time

To delay the start of an assignment, follow these steps:

1. Double-click the assignment you want to delay to display its Assignment Information dialog box (see Figure 11.26).

2. Enter the delayed start date and time in the Start field or click the date control and select the date from the calendar and then append the time.

3. Click OK to complete the entry.

Figure 11.27 shows the effect of delaying Mel's assignment on the Process Orders task from Monday to Thursday. The original cells for his assignment now have 0h in them, and Mel is no longer overallocated during that period. You can also see that Scott Adams's assignment on that same task continues to start on Monday.

Figure 11.26
Use the Assignment Information dialog box to delay the start date and time for an individual assignment.

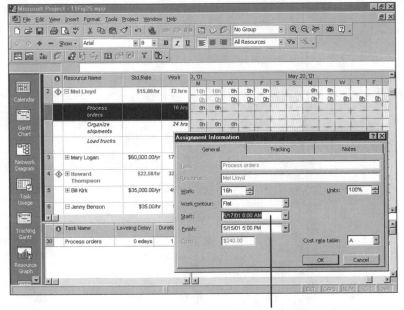

Delayed start date and time

Scott Adams's start unchanged | Work details | Remaining Availability details

Figure 11.27
The timephased data in the Resource Usage view shows the delayed start of the assignment with 0h entries in the delay periods.

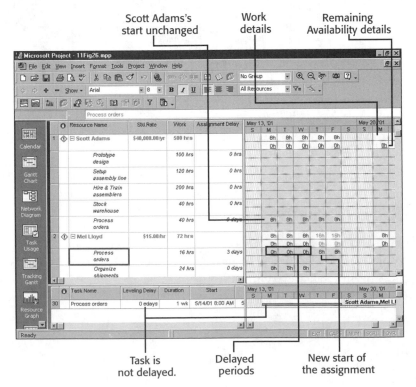

Task is not delayed. Delayed periods New start of the assignment

When you delay an assignment by editing the Start field of the Assignment Information dialog box, or by editing the timephased data in the grid, Project translates the difference in the previous start date and the new one as an *assignment delay* and stores that value in the Assignment Delay field. You can also delay an assignment by entering the amount of the delay directly into the Assignment Delay field. However, as pointed out above, if the purpose of the delay is to level resource usage, the assignment Leveling Delay field is a better field to use.

Note

The Assignment Delay and Leveling Delay fields both produce the same result—the start of the assignment is delayed. The difference is that the Leveling Delay field is used by Project to enter a delay when you use the Level Now command to resolve resource overallocations. There is also a Clear Leveling command that will reset all Leveling Delay values to zero.

Project does not make entries in the Assignment Delay field, nor is there a command to clear those entries. The Assignment Delay field is intended to be used to delay one resource's assignment when there is a valid operational reason for the delay. For example, if one resource contributes finishing touches on a task and should be scheduled at the end of the task.

The Assignment Delay field is not included in the standard Usage table, but you can easily add it to the table by clicking the column heading where you want the field to go and choosing Insert, Column. In the Column Definition dialog box, choose Assignment Delay in the Field Name box and click the Best Fit button to adjust the column width to the widest entry.

The Clear Leveling command does not reset assignment delays to zero. Perhaps the easiest method to use if you want to remove an assignment delay is to display the Assignment Delay field in the Resource Usage view, or in the Task Usage view, and change delay values to zero. You can also find inserted nonworking time periods in the grid and delete them, but it's easier to identify nonzero values in the Assignment Delay field.

Tip from Tim and the Project Team

If you want to review all your assignment delays or leveling delays, you can design a filter to display only those tasks where the Assignment Delay field is not equal to zero or the Leveling Delay field is not zero. Using the criterion Not Equal to Zero instead of Greater Than Zero will allow the filter to serve both projects with positive delay values (scheduled from a fixed start date) and projects with negative delay values (those scheduled from a fixed finish date).

→ For detailed help in creating a filter, **see** "Creating Custom Filters," **p. 968**

SPLITTING A TASK   Suppose that an overallocation occurs because an assignment starts while another assignment that has already started is not yet finished. We could, as in the preceding examples, delay all work on the new assignment until the already started assignment is finished. But you can also interrupt the work on the already started assignment (*split* the assignment) until the new assignment is completed. If you introduce the split at the task level, all assignments to the task will be split at the same point. If you just split the assignment itself, other resource assignments to the task will not be split.

In Figure 11.28, the Create Advertising Plan task is assigned to both Howard Thompson and Mary Logan. It is scheduled to be already started when the Sales Training task starts. Howard Thompson is assigned to both tasks, and he is overallocated during the period when the tasks overlap.

Figure 11.28
When two tasks contend for the same resource, you can split one task to work around the other.

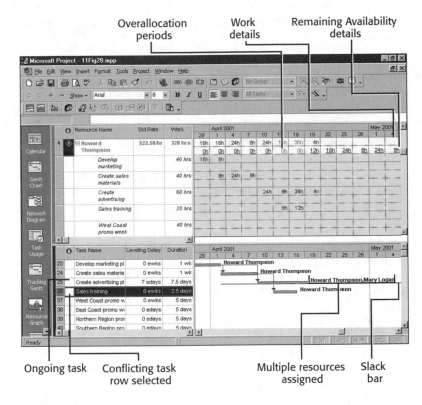

The ongoing task, Create Advertising Plan, has slack (as evidenced by the Slack bar in the lower pane) and its finish can be delayed without affecting the project finish date. However the new task, Sales Training, does not have a Slack bar and should not be delayed if you want to avoid delaying the finish of the project. We could split Howard's assignment to the Create Advertising Plan task and avoid delaying the project. If we split the task, it will split both Howard's and Mary's assignments. If we just split Howard's assignment, Mary will continue her work as scheduled and Howard will complete his after the Sales Training is finished. The duration for the Create Advertising Plan task will be increased to incorporate Howard's delayed work.

 If you are using the Resource Allocation view, you must split tasks in the Leveling Gantt in the bottom pane because only resources and assignments (not tasks) are displayed in the top pane. You will use the Split Task tool to split a taskbar in the Leveling Gantt, thus splitting the task and all its assignments.

PART

III

CH

11

Tip from Tim and the Project Team	If you were to display the Task Usage view in the top pane, you could split a task by inserting nonworking cells in the timephased data for the task. Select the cell or cells for the time period when the split should occur and press the Insert key.

We first need to determine exactly when the split should start and when it should end. We want the split to start when the new task starts and to end when the new task finishes. You can determine the start and finish of the new task by double-clicking it in the lower pane to view its Task Information Form. The Start and Finish dates are on the General tab. You could also scroll the table in the lower pane to the right to see the Start and Finish fields for the task. In Figure 11.29 you can see the Start and Finish dates for the Sales Training task in the table. The task starts 4/13/01 at 8:00 AM and finishes at noon on 4/17/01.

Tip from Tim and the Project Team	When scrolling tables horizontally where the Name field will scroll out of view, select the row ID to highlight the entire row (as was done previously in Figure 11.28). Then you can identify the row easily when you get to the column you want to examine (as in Figure 11.29).

Tip from Tim and the Project Team	It's worth your while to have the time of day included in the date format so you can coordinate the timing of the tasks.

 If you want to split a task down to the hour, you must format the timeline to show hours. In Figure 11.29, the Zoom In tool has been used to display quarter-days, which is a format that includes hours on the minor scale.

To split a task in the Leveling Gantt chart, follow these steps:

1. Activate the pane with a task view—in this case, the Leveling Gantt in the lower pane.

2. Determine the exact date and time when the split should start and end. In Figure 11.29, the dates are seen on the highlighted row in the bottom pane.

 3. Click the Split Task tool to activate the Split Task ScreenTip. As you move the pointer over the taskbars, the ScreenTip shows the date and time for the pointer's position on the screen. When you click over a taskbar, this will be the date and time when the split will start. Do not click anywhere until you are in position over the taskbar you want to split and the ScreenTip shows the date and time you want the split to start.

Tip from Tim and the Project Team	If at this point you decide to abandon the split operation, simply press the Esc key to cancel the split command. If you decide to cancel the command after you have started dragging the split in the following steps, drag the pointer to an area where it is not over the taskbar and release the mouse button.

Figure 11.29
Use the Split Task tool to split taskbars in the lower pane of the Resource Allocation view.

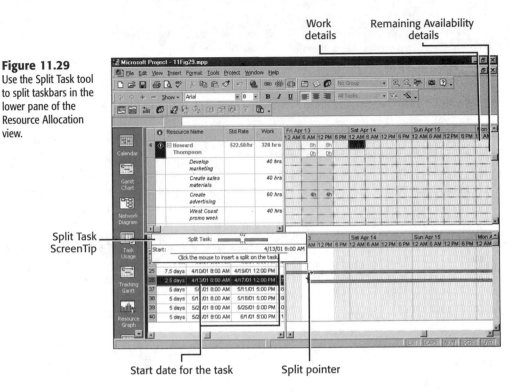

Work details

Remaining Availability details

Split Task ScreenTip

Start date for the task

Split pointer

4. When you are over the correct taskbar and the ScreenTip shows the date and hour you want the split to start, click and hold down the mouse button to start dragging the remainder of the task to the right to locate the date and time when work should resume.

The Split Task ScreenTip will disappear and a Task ScreenTip will appear. The Start field in this ScreenTip shows the date and time where the pointer is currently located. This will be the date and time when work on the task will be scheduled to resume.

5. Drag the remainder of the task to the correct date and time (as shown in the Task ScreenTip) to resume work on the task. Figure 11.30 shows the pointer in position to resume after noon on 4/17/01.

Tip from Tim and the Project Team

When dragging part of the task to a new date, if the destination date is off the screen, drag the pointer just beyond the edge of the screen slowly and the timescale will scroll until you reach the destination.

Figure 11.31 shows the task after the split has been created, with the timescale formatted the same as in Figure 11.28. In Figure 11.31, you can see both assignments to the task that was split. Mary Logan and Howard Thompson both have a "0h" cell in the middle of their assignments during the period where the taskbar shows the split.

Work details

Remaining
Availability details

Figure 11.30
Drag the remaining
portion of a split task
to the date and time
when you want work
to resume.

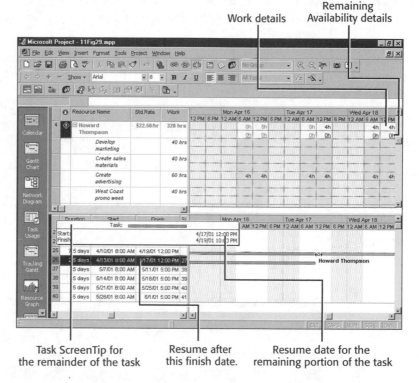

Task ScreenTip for
the remainder of the task

Resume after
this finish date.

Resume date for the
remaining portion of the task

Interrupted assignments

Work details

Figure 11.31
Splitting the task also
splits all assignments
to the task.

Contour
indicators

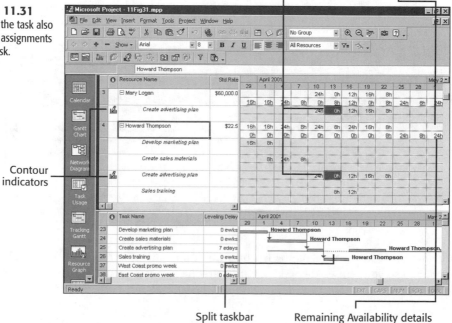

Split taskbar

Remaining Availability details

To remove a split in a task, simply use the mouse to drag part of the task on the right toward the part on the left. When they touch, Project will remove the split and rejoin the taskbar.

SPLITTING INDIVIDUAL ASSIGNMENTS   In Figure 11.31, we split the task to resolve an over-allocation problem and that split all resource assignments for the task, whether they were overallocated or not. Now we will split just the assignment for the resource that is overallo-cated (Howard Thompson), thus leaving other assigned resources (Mary Logan in this case) on their existing schedule. To split an assignment, you must view either the Resource Usage view or the Task Usage view and edit the timephased work cells for the assignment. Select the cells where the interruption will take place and press the Insert key to shift those work amounts to later dates.

In Figure 11.32, the Zoom In tool has been used to view quarter-days since we need to reschedule the assignment to stop at 8:00 AM and resume at 12:00 PM (noon). If those par-ticular hours were not shown on the timeline, we would need to zoom in further until the time periods we need to schedule appear in the timeline.

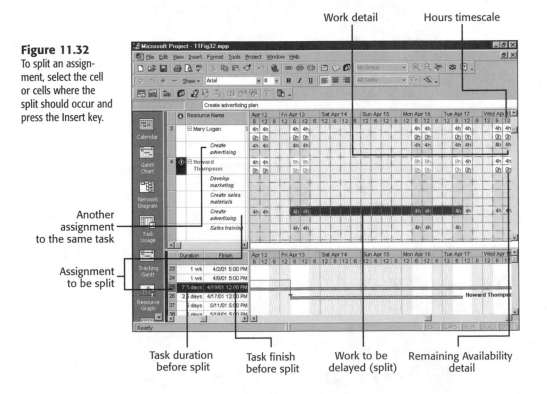

Figure 11.32
To split an assign-ment, select the cell or cells where the split should occur and press the Insert key.

In Figure 11.32 in the table on the left of the bottom pane, the columns have been rearranged so you can see the task's duration and finish date. Before the assignment is split, the task duration is 7.5 days and the finish date is 4/19/01 at noon.

The timephased work cells where the split will occur are selected in the figure. With the cells selected, you can create the split by pressing the Insert key or by choosing Insert, Cell from the menu. The contents of the selected cells will be shifted to the right, and all cells to the right of the insertion cells will be shifted also.

Caution

If you type a zero into an assignment work cell, instead of pressing the Insert key, you will likewise create a split in the assignment, but the work scheduled for that day will be lost.

Figure 11.33 shows the assignment schedule after the split has been inserted. The cells that were selected now have zero hours of work for Howard Thompson, but Mary Logan still has work scheduled in those same time periods. The taskbar in the Gantt Chart does not show a split because Mary Logan is continuing to work during the period of the split. The total work for the assignment has not changed, but the duration of the task has increased from 7.5 days to 9.5 days and the finish date is pushed back from 4/21/01 to 4/23/01. Notice the Contour indicator on the assignment row, indicating that the timephased values for the assignment have been edited.

Figure 11.33
The split appears as cells with zero work in the assignment row.

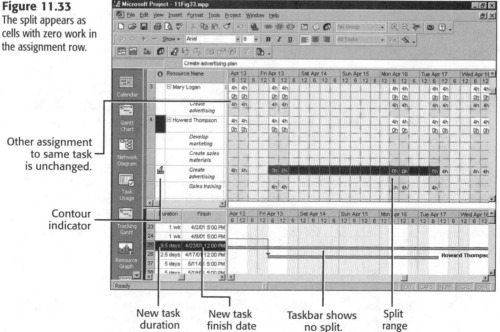

Other assignment to same task is unchanged.

Contour indicator

New task duration

New task finish date

Taskbar shows no split.

Split range

Tip from Tim and the Project Team

To select a series of assignment cells, drag the mouse across them or, after selecting the first cell, hold down the Shift key as you click the last cell to select. You can then press the Insert key to shift work assignments past the last selected cell.

To remove the splits in an assignment, select the cell or cells that have 0h in them and press the Delete key. Unfortunately there is no easy way to identify those assignments that have been edited, other than the existence of the Contour indicator on those assignment rows. You have to scroll the timeline for the contoured assignment to find cells that contain 0h to find the edited cells.

Tip from Tim and the Project Team	If you select and remove 0h cells by pressing Delete, the Contour indicator will still be displayed. If you have deleted a delay or split and you're sure there are no other edited changes you want to preserve, you can remove the Contour indicator by double-clicking the assignment to display the Assignment Information dialog box and selecting Flat on the drop-down list in the Work Contour box.

LETTING PROJECT LEVEL OVERALLOCATED RESOURCES FOR YOU

Instead of delaying, or *leveling*, individual tasks and assignments on your own, you can instead have Project calculate task or assignment delays to remove resource overallocations. Project will search through the project looking for those resources that display the Leveling indicator. Using the settings in the Resource Leveling dialog box, which is described shortly, Project will select tasks to be delayed in order to resolve overallocation for those resources that display the Leveling indicator.

Note	Project doesn't delay material resource assignments. However, if the leveling operation changes the duration of the task, the material assignments may be contoured also.

If the project is scheduled from a fixed start date, Project adds *positive* delays to tasks to remove overallocations. If a critical task is delayed, the leveling procedure causes the project to finish later. If the project is scheduled from a fixed finish date, Project adds *negative* delays to tasks to remove overallocations. A negative delay causes a task to finish *earlier*, and therefore to be scheduled to start earlier. If the task is a critical task, the effect of leveling on a fixed finish date project is to schedule an earlier start date for the project.

Tip from Tim and the Project Team	Do not attempt to use the Leveling command until after you enter all the tasks and all the information about each task and resource. If you do use leveling prior to entering all information, you will need to repeat the leveling operation after adding more tasks or redefining resources and resource assignments to accurately reflect the changes.

CONFIGURING SETTINGS IN THE RESOURCE LEVELING DIALOG BOX

There are a number of settings you should confirm or change before using Project's Leveling command. The Resource Leveling dialog box contains the controls for the leveling operation (see Figure 11.34). You should generally open this dialog box when a task view is active because then you will have access to all the buttons and fields.

The Leveling indicator that displays on resource tables depends on your selection in the Look for Overallocations on a list box. As you change this selection, the highlight for over-allocated resources will not be affected, but the Leveling indicator appears less often if you select larger time units. Thus, if you increase the time basis from Day by Day to Week by Week, some Leveling indicators may disappear.

Figure 11.34
The Resource Leveling dialog box has many settings that determine how Project calculates the schedule when it does leveling calculations for you.

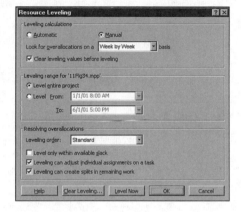

Table 11.3 outlines the choices and tools in the Resource Leveling dialog box and provides a brief description of each choice.

TABLE 11.3   THE LEVELING OPTIONS

Option	Description
Automatic	Instructs Project to level tasks the moment one or more overallocated resources is detected. Automatic leveling takes place as you enter the tasks into the project or change the schedule in other ways.
Manual	Leveling is executed only when you choose Tools, Resource Leveling, Level Now. Manual is the default status for leveling.
Look for Overallocations an a *x* Basis	This setting determines the timescale sensitivity of leveling calculations. The choices in this drop-down list box are Minute by Minute, Hour by Hour, Day by Day, Week by Week, and Month by Month.
Clear Leveling Values Before Leveling	If this check box is filled, Project will remove all leveling delays from tasks before calculating new ones. Otherwise, Project leaves all leveling delays in place and adds to them.

TABLE 11.3   CONTINUED

Option	Description
Level Entire Project	With this option, Project searches for overallocations that need leveling from the beginning to the end of the project. This choice does not keep you from choosing to level just selected resources or all resources.
Level From, To	You can limit the date range that Project scans for overallocations to be corrected. Overallocations outside this date range are allowed to remain.
Leveling Order	This option provides three choices for establishing how Project decides which of several tasks to delay when the tasks cause a resource overallocation conflict. The choices are ID Only, Standard, and Priority, Standard. A description of these choices follows this table.
Level Only Within Available Slack	If this box is selected, tasks are delayed only within the amount of total slack, and the finish date of the project is not delayed. With this setting constraining the amount of leveling delay that Project can add, the leveling operation may not resolve the overallocation problem. If you clear this box, and no task constraints exist to serve as impediments, Project can resolve the resource overallocation through leveling, although often with a delay in the finish date of the project.
Leveling Can Adjust Individual Assignments on a Task	With this feature checked, Project can delay just the assignments for resources that are overallocated on a task instead of delaying the task and consequently all assignments. The task duration will be increased because the total work effort is more spread out. This setting affects all tasks unless the task's Level Assignments field is set to No. This field is discussed later in this chapter.
Leveling Can Create Splits in Remaining Work	If a resource assignment is delayed, Project can split the remaining work into pieces that can fit into available time slots for the resource, thus working around later task assignments that have constraints. This choice affects all tasks unless a task's Leveling Can Split field is set to No. This field is discussed later in this chapter.

The Leveling Order drop-down list box has three possible values, as described in the following list:

■ **ID Only**—If the ID number is the only basis for selecting which of several tasks will be delayed, tasks with higher ID numbers (those that are further down on the task list) are always delayed before tasks with lower ID numbers (those higher up on the task list). If the task list is created in chronological order—with earlier tasks listed at the top of the list and with one sequence of tasks leading to the finish date—the ID Only scheme essentially delays tasks with the later start dates. Delaying the tasks with later start dates minimizes the number of successor tasks affected by imposing leveling delays.

- **Standard**—The Standard order, which is the default leveling order for Microsoft Project, uses seven factors to determine which of several conflicting tasks is to be leveled first. One of those factors is the Priority rating which you can assign to tasks. In the Standard order, your Priority rating has relatively less weight than most of the other factors.

- **Priority, Standard**—The same factors considered in the Standard order are used for the Priority, Standard order. Primary weight is given to the Priority assignment of each task (a factor which you can control).

In deciding which of two tasks is delayed and which is left unchanged, both the Standard and Priority, Standard orders use the same set of seven factors, the difference being only in the greater weight assigned to the tasks' Priority value in the Priority, Standard order. The factors, listed in descending order of importance, are

- **Predecessor**—Tasks that do not have successor dependencies are picked before those that have successor dependencies.

- **Amount of total slack**—Tasks with more total slack are chosen before those with less slack.

- **Start date**—Tasks that start later are delayed before those that start earlier.

- **Priority value**—You can raise or lower each task's priority value to affect the selection of those to delay. Lower-priority tasks are chosen for delay before the higher-priority tasks. In the Leveling Order choice named Priority, Standard, this factor is moved to the top of the list. Entering priority values for tasks is discussed later in this chapter.

- **Constraints**—Tasks with constraints are less likely to be delayed than those without constraints.

- **Weighted slack**

- **Potential Delay**

There are other fields that influence how Project treats tasks and resources when the Level Now command is applied. These fields determine how likely it is that a task or an assignment will be delayed or split. With these fields, you can instruct Project to exempt a specific resource or task from being delayed or split by the Level Now command:

- **Can Level**—This resource field contains a Yes or No value. If the value is the default Yes, Project can delay assignments for that resource if it needs to in its leveling calculation. If the value is No, Project will not delay the resource's assignments. The field does not appear on any prepared views or information forms. You can add the field to any resource table and enter No for those resources whose assignments you want to keep from being delayed.

- **Level Assignments**—This task field contains a Yes or No value. If the value is the default Yes, Project can delay assignments to the task if it needs to in its leveling calculation. If the value is No, Project will not delay the task's assignments. This field overrides the check box in the Resource Leveling dialog box labeled Leveling Can Adjust Individual Assignments on a Task. You must add this field to a task view since it doesn't appear in any standard tables.

- **Leveling Can Split**—This task field also contains a Yes or No value. If it's the default Yes, Project can split tasks in its leveling calculations. This field overrides the check box in the Resource Leveling dialog box labeled Leveling Can Create Splits in Remaining Work. You can add this field to a task view that contains a table.

- **Priority**—This task field lets you assign priority values to tasks ranging from a high of 1,000 to a low of zero. In the leveling operation, Project uses the priority value to choose between two tasks to delay, delaying the task with the lower priority value. In general, those tasks with lower priority values (closer to zero) are given leveling delays before those with high priority values when Project selects tasks to be delayed.

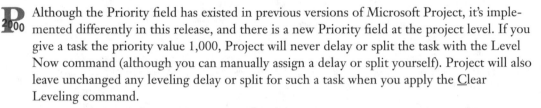 Although the Priority field has existed in previous versions of Microsoft Project, it's implemented differently in this release, and there is a new Priority field at the project level. If you give a task the priority value 1,000, Project will never delay or split the task with the Level Now command (although you can manually assign a delay or split yourself). Project will also leave unchanged any leveling delay or split for such a task when you apply the Clear Leveling command.

You can assign priority values to projects as well as to tasks. When leveling resources that are assigned to multiple projects, tasks in those projects with lower priority values are chosen for delay before tasks in projects with higher priority values. The priority value 1,000 assures that no task in that project will be given a leveling delay by the Level Now command.

The priority value for the project overrides the relative priority values for tasks. For example, if one project has a higher-priority value than the other, all tasks in the higher priority project (even those with priority values close to zero) will have higher priority than any task in the lower-priority project (except for those that have a priority value of 1,000, which are never delayed).

To assign a priority value to a task, follow these steps:

1. Select the task in a view that displays one or more task fields. You can select multiple tasks if you want to set them all to the same priority value with one step.

 2. Click the Task Information tool on the Standard toolbar to display the Task Information dialog box (see Figure 11.35) or the Multiple Task Form if more than one task has been selected.

3. Select the General tab and type the priority value into the Priority box using values between 1,000 (highest priority—least likely to be delayed) and zero (most likely to be delayed). Or use the spin control to raise or lower the default priority value of 500. Remember: the higher the number, the less likely the task will be delayed in leveling operations; and tasks with the priority value of 1,000 are never delayed.

4. Click OK.

Task Priority field

Figure 11.35
Setting priorities for a task controls how likely it is to be delayed in leveling.

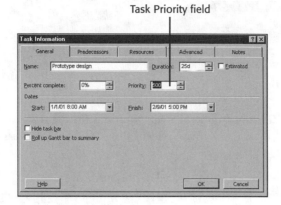

To change the priority level for a project, follow these steps:

1. Open the project.

2. Choose Project, Project Information to display the Project Information dialog box.

3. In the Priority box, enter the priority level using values between 1,000 (highest priority—least likely to be delayed) and zero (most likely to be delayed). Or use the spin control to raise or lower the default value of 500.

4. Click OK to close the dialog box.

Figure 11.36
Setting a different priority value for one of multiple projects determines which project's tasks are leveled first.

Project Priority field

USING THE LEVEL NOW COMMAND

After establishing your choices in the Resource Leveling dialog box, you can instruct Project to level the project with the Level Now command. If you select this command from a task view, the leveling occurs immediately, without prompts. If you select the command from a resource view, you see the Level Now dialog box (see Figure 11.37), which prompts you to choose between leveling all resources or only those that you have selected.

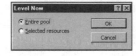

Figure 11.37
You can level assignments for all overallocated resources or for just those you have selected.

If you choose Selected Resources, only the overallocations for the resources in the selection are reviewed for leveling operations. If you select Entire Pool, all resources and all tasks are reviewed.

When you choose OK, Project tries to resolve the resource overallocations by adding leveling delays to tasks—within the bounds you specify in the Resource Leveling dialog box. For the first overallocation problem it encounters, Project identifies the tasks causing the overallocation and notes tasks that *cannot* be delayed. These include tasks that have hard constraints, tasks that have higher priority assignments, and tasks that are already started. Note that task deadline dates do not keep Project from delaying a task. If more than one task exists that can be delayed, Project uses the set of seven factors previously discussed to select one or more of the tasks to delay.

Tip from Tim and the Project Team

You can undo the changes made by the Level Now command if you choose Edit, Undo Level before changing anything else in your project.

In Figure 11.38, you see the result of the leveling operation for the resource Howard Thompson. A deadline date has been added to the Create Advertising Plan task to illustrate how Project respects deadlines when leveling (it doesn't).

Only one delayed task is seen in this figure—Sales Training is delayed by 6 days. However, Howard's assignment to the Create Advertising Plan task was also delayed (see the highlighted timephased work data in Figure 11.38), while Mary Logan's assignment was not delayed. This combination of assignments extended the task's duration past the deadline date for the task (note the deadline date marker in the figure) and the Missed Deadline indicator appears in the Indicators column to alert you that the task deadline will be missed in the current schedule.

Note the new taskbars in the Gantt Chart. When the Level Now command is executed, Project saves the current (before leveling) start and finish dates of all tasks into fields called Preleveled Start and Preleveled Finish. The Leveling Gantt displays these dates as *preleveled* taskbars above the *scheduled* bars for tasks so that you can easily see the scheduled dates before and after the leveling operation. Notice in Figure 11.38 that the lower bar for Sales Training is shifted to the right of the preleveled bar just above it (thus reflecting the leveling delay).

Figure 11.38
After the Level Now command has changed the schedule, the Leveling Gantt displays preleveled taskbars for comparing the original schedule with the delayed schedule.

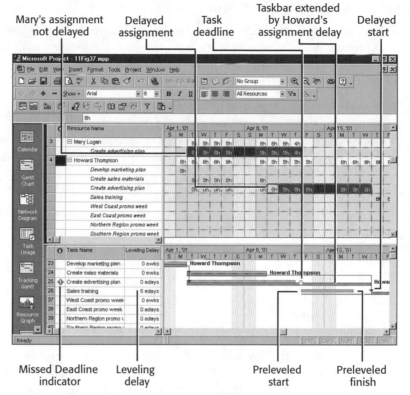

Mary's assignment not delayed · Delayed assignment · Task deadline · Taskbar extended by Howard's assignment delay · Delayed start

Missed Deadline indicator · Leveling delay · Preleveled start · Preleveled finish

If one or more assignments are found where overallocations can't be resolved, you will see a message similar to the message in Figure 11.39.

Figure 11.39
Sometimes the Level Now command can't resolve all the overallocation problems and it prompts you for directions.

To respond to the Unresolved Overallocations message, do one of the following:

- Choose Skip to have Microsoft Project skip this resource and continue looking for other overallocations.

- Choose Skip All to have Project skip this resource and all others that cannot be resolved without pausing to alert you to those that cannot be resolved.

- Choose Stop to stop the leveling process and erase all the delays that have been entered so far.

PART

III

CH

11

CLEARING THE EFFECTS OF LEVELING

You can use the Clear Leveling tool in the Resource Leveling dialog box to have Project reset leveling delays to zero for all tasks or just those for the selected tasks. As mentioned previously, Project will not clear the leveling delay for tasks that have a priority setting of 1,000.

To use this command, you must be in a task view. Choose Tools, Resource Leveling, Clear Leveling. The Clear Leveling dialog box will display (see Figure 11.40). Select Entire Project or Selected Tasks and click OK. All Leveling Delay fields will be reset to zero for the entire project or for the selected tasks.

Figure 11.40
You can quickly remove all leveling delays from the entire project or from selected tasks with the Clear Leveling command.

UNDERSTANDING THE PITFALLS OF AUTOMATIC LEVELING

The first option on the Resource Leveling dialog box is Automatic leveling. If you select this option, Microsoft Project will watch for resource overallocations as you assign resources and as the project schedule changes. The moment Project detects an overallocation, it will quietly attempt to resolve it by delaying tasks in the background as you go on building the schedule. This seems like a powerful and useful option, but it has very clear drawbacks.

Most importantly, you are a far better judge of the best choices for your schedule. You can't provide Microsoft Project with all the information you bring to the decision-making process as you make scheduling choices. If you use Automatic leveling, you will not be aware of the leveling decisions going on in the background. Had you seen a Leveling indicator, you might well have had an alternative that doesn't require delaying tasks and, most often, the project finish. It's not uncommon to wind up with a bloated schedule that has lots of unproductive time because of all the leveling delays.

You also should note that Project doesn't optimize the leveling strategy. The program doesn't examine all possible combinations of task delays in order to choose the best solution in terms of lowest cost, earliest project finish date, or any other consideration.

TROUBLESHOOTING

DISPLAYING DETAIL HEADERS

I can't tell what data field is displayed in the timephased data of the Resource Usage view because there are no headers for the rows. How can I tell which rows contain which fields?

There are two reasons why you might not see the detail headers:

- The detail headers will not be displayed in a split window that has a timescale in both panes. Display the Resource Usage view as a full screen view and you will see the headers.

- You might have suppressed the display of the headers in the Detail Styles dialog box. With the Resource Usage view active, choose Format, Detail Styles and click the Usage Properties tab. The Display Details Header Column box must contain Yes to display the headers.

You can figure out which rows are which even without displaying the headers, however, by following these steps:

1. Right-click over the timephased data and note the fields that are checked in the shortcut menu. This tells you which fields are included, but they will not necessarily be in the same order as they are in the shortcut menu.

2. Choose Detail Styles from the shortcut menu and note the order of the fields in the Show These Fields list. This is the order of the rows on your screen.

SORTING ASSIGNMENTS IN THE RESOURCE ALLOCATION VIEW

In the Resource Allocation view, the list of assignments in the top pane under a resource name is not in the same order as the list in the bottom pane, and it makes it hard to find the task in the bottom pane. How can I get them in the same order?

Activate the top pane and choose Project, Sort, By ID to have Project sort the top pane by ID number. The lists should then be in sync. If not, activate the bottom pane and sort it by ID also.

LEVEL NOW SEEMS NOT TO BE WORKING

I used the Level Now command, but there are still overallocated resources, even though Project didn't give me any alerts saying it was unable to resolve an overallocation. What did I do wrong?

The Level Now command tackles only overallocations that trigger the Leveling indicator. So if your project has the leveling sensitivity setting Week by Week, for example, there might still be resources that are overallocated on an Hour by Hour or Day by Day basis.

Managing Preleveled Taskbars

I entered a leveling delay for a task in the Leveling Gantt view, but Project doesn't show the preleveled taskbar for the task.

The preleveled taskbar is based on the dates in the Preleveled Start and Preleveled Finish fields. These fields contain NA until you use the Level Now command for the first time; therefore, you won't see these bars until you use the Level Now command. You can't edit the dates in these fields because they can only be calculated by Project. You can hide the Preleveled bar if you use the Format, Bar Styles command and delete the bar from the display or choose a clear bar style that will not show onscreen.

REVIEWING AND DISTRIBUTING THE PROJECT

CHAPTER 12

REVIEWING THE PROJECT PLAN

In this chapter

LOOKING AT THE BIG PICTURE

Once you have defined the tasks, assigned the resources involved in the project to their respective tasks, and Project has calculated costs, it is a good time to step back from all the details and look at the overall project. You need to evaluate how successfully the project plan meets the objectives of the project, as stated in the project goal. Microsoft Project offers many tools to make this evaluation easy.

Often, the first draft of a project plan includes costs that exceed budget limits, or the scheduled finish date of the project is later than acceptable. There also might be inconsistencies in the plan. For example, deadlines for individual tasks might not be met. This chapter shows you how to get an overview of your project, identify and shorten the critical path, and identify and reduce costs for the project.

Some of the things you can do to review your project plan are

- View your project to get the overall picture. You need to have a good working knowledge of the various views in Microsoft Project and when they are most appropriate. There are also many display options that allow you focus on a careful review of the project plan.

- Use filters to focus on the tasks and resources that need special attention before the project plan can be finalized.

- Control the sort order of task and resource lists to provide a better order when reviewing tasks and resources.

- Before circulating project printouts, ensure accuracy by spell-checking the project plan.

- In between planning and starting work on a project, print reports that are useful to the people who are involved in or will be monitoring the project plan.

- Identify the critical path and reduce its duration. Part of the review process often includes attempts to reduce the duration of the project to meet deadlines. First you must identify the critical path, then you can test out different strategies for reducing its duration.

- Identify associated project costs and review strategies for reducing costs. If the calculated project budget exceeds expectations, Project offers ways to test strategies for reducing costs. It is better to test out these strategies with a computer model than in the real world while the project is underway.

You probably feel overwhelmed by the multitude of details in a large project. From time to time, you might need to step back and look at the overall project to keep a global perspective. There are several ways to gain a global perspective. You can review the Project Statistics sheet to note specifics about the scheduled start and finish dates and the planned costs. You can collapse the timescale when viewing the Gantt Chart to get a macro time perspective. You can filter the summary tasks and milestones, or collapse the outline to view and compare the schedules and costs of the major phases of the project.

After you define the tasks, durations and constraints, dependency relationships, and resource assignments, Microsoft Project calculates the scheduled start and finish date for each task and also the scheduled finish date for the project. You can use the Project Statistics dialog box shown in Figure 12.1 to view the scheduled start and finish dates for the project. To display the Project Statistics dialog box, choose the Project Statistics button on the Tracking toolbar (if you have that toolbar displayed), or choose Project, Project Information to display the Project Information dialog box; then choose the Statistics button. All the data in the Project Statistics dialog box is calculated—you cannot edit any of the fields on the form.

Figure 12.1
Examine the Project Statistics dialog box for a quick summary of the project's start and finish dates.

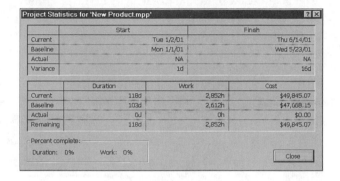

At a glance, you see the Current Start and Finish dates, the Duration for the project, and the planned amount of Work and Cost. If you have saved a baseline copy of the schedule, you see the Baseline Start and Finish dates. After you start work on the project and enter tracking information, you also see the Actual Start of the project, the Variance for the Start and Finish dates, and the Actual and Remaining Duration, Work, and Cost.

Note

Notice at this point the baseline information in Figure 12.1 does not match the current information. In Chapter 16, "Tracking Work on the Project," you will learn how to update the baseline. If baseline data does not appear in the Statistics dialog box, Chapter 16 will show you how to capture a baseline.

→ To establish a baseline for your project, **see** "Setting the Baseline or Plan," **p. 660**

If the project is scheduled from the Start date, use the Project Statistics dialog box to identify the currently calculated Finish date; if the project is scheduled from the Finish date, use the Project Statistics dialog box to view the currently calculated Start date. If the calculated date is inconsistent with the project goal statement, you need to find ways to shorten the life of the project.

The scheduled cost figure in the Project Statistics dialog box tells you at a glance the sum of all resource costs and fixed costs that you previously defined for the project. If this figure is too high to be consistent with the goals of the project, you need to search for ways to reduce costs without sacrificing the time objectives of the project goal.

PART
IV
CH
12

Best Practice Tips from Toby Brown, PMP

To reduce costs, remember where costs are derived from: resource assignments and fixed costs assigned to the tasks. To reduce costs associated with the project, the user is going to have to remove a fixed cost assigned to a task, remove a resource assignment altogether, reduce the number of hours a resource is working on a task, or reduce the cost of the resource within Resource Information.

COMPRESSING THE TIMESCALE

You usually can gain an overview of the flow of activity in the project by viewing the Gantt Chart with the timescale compressed. In Figure 12.2, for example, the project is displayed with the timescale compressed to show months in the major scale and weeks (every 7 days) in the minor scale. (For clarity, resource names have been removed from the taskbars using the Format, Bar Styles command).

Figure 12.2
Compress the timescale to get an overall view of the time dimension of the project.

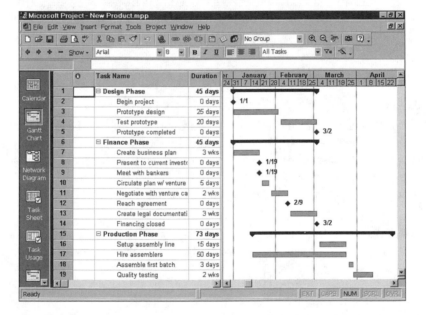

 To compress the timescale with the toolbar, click the Zoom Out button on the Standard toolbar to automatically select larger time units represented in each unit of the timescale. Use the Zoom In button on the Standard toolbar to subdivide time into smaller units of time.

→ To learn more about ways you can alter the appearance of view, **see** "Formatting Views," **p. 891**

To make more explicit changes than these toolbar buttons provide, choose Format, Timescale. To make references easier to follow in the discussion, for example, the illustrations in this chapter label the days on the timescale with the day number rather than with the weekday letter. To learn more about these types of customizations, see the instructions in Chapter 23, "Customizing Views, Tables, Fields, and Filters."

It is also useful to Zoom the screen to view the whole project at once. You can do this by choosing View, Zoom, Entire Project. To return the screen to the default timescale of months and weeks, choose View, Zoom and select the Reset button.

Tip from Tim and the Project Team | You can double-click any part of the timescale headings in the Gantt Chart to access the Timescale dialog box.

COLLAPSING THE TASK LIST OUTLINE

The compressed time display might be more meaningful if you also collapse the outline or filter the task list to view only the summary tasks or the milestones. In Figure 12.3, the task list is collapsed to show only the first-level summary tasks (all subtasks are hidden). This view provides an overview of the start and finish dates of the major phases of the project. You can collapse the outline to any level of detail clicking the Show button on the Formatting toolbar and choosing the outline level you want to view. This is a new feature in Project 2000.

Figure 12.3
Hide the subtasks in an outlined project to focus on the major phases of the project.

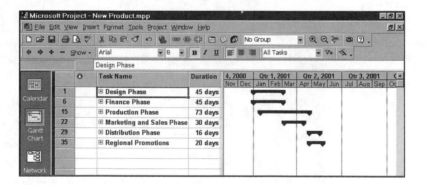

To collapse the outline to the first level, follow these steps:

1. Activate a pane that displays a task list table (the Gantt Chart, for example).

`Show ▾`

2. Click the Show button on the Formatting toolbar and choose Outline Level 1 from the list that appears.

You also can collapse and expand the outline by using the Hide Subtasks button (minus sign) and Show Subtasks (plus sign) button on the Formatting toolbar. These buttons hide or show the subtasks for the selected task.

Similarly, you might find it constructive to view just the summary tasks or milestones to focus on the completion dates of the important sections of the project. The next few sections show you how to display rollup taskbars and filter the display to show just certain tasks or resources.

PART
IV

CH
12

Best Practice
Tips from Toby
Brown, PMP

Realize that summary tasks within the Gantt chart view should correspond to the WBS (Work Breakdown Structure) previously created. Remember that the WBS is not a time-drive schedule, like the Gantt Chart, but rather a method to ensure that all the necessary work to complete the project is included. PMI defines the WBS as "a deliverable-oriented grouping of project elements which organizes and defines the total scope of the project with each descending level representing an increasingly detailed definition of a project component."

USING ROLLUP TASKBARS

P A particularly useful new feature in Project 2000 is the ability to display the individual bars **2000** associated with a summary task when the summary task is collapsed. Typically when you collapse a summary task, only the summary taskbar displays. For example, Figure 12.4 shows the Design Phase expanded and the Finance Phase collapsed. When the subtasks indented under a task are hidden, only the summary taskbar displays.

Figure 12.4
Use the minus and plus signs next to summary tasks to quickly hide or show the subtasks.

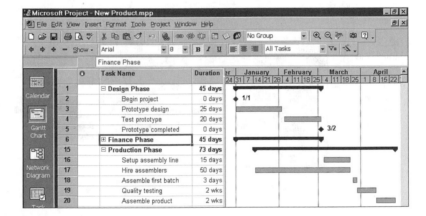

You can, however, tell Project to display the rolled up taskbars instead of the summary taskbar. Figure 12.5 shows the rolled up taskbars for the Finance Phase. You implement this display through the Format, Layout command.

Figure 12.5
The rolled up taskbars provide an alternative display for the summary taskbars.

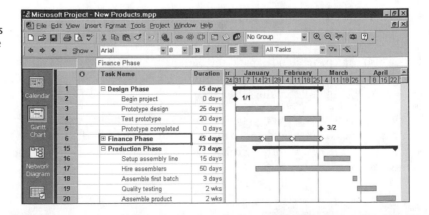

In previous versions of Project, you could display multiple Gantt bars on a single task line, but had to apply this feature to each individual task. In Project 2000 the Rollup Task Bars feature affects your entire task list, not just the active task.

USING THE CUSTOM WBS CODE FORMATS

WBS stands for *Work Breakdown Structure*. In previous versions of Microsoft Project, there wasn't a convenient way to set your own numbering for the WBS codes. The WBS numbering was based on the task list outline. For example if Planning was the first task in the list, it would have WBS number 1. If Review Impact Study was the second task in the list, indented under Planning, it would have WBS number 1.1.

A new feature in Project 2000 allows you to specify the format for the WBS codes. The WBS format now allows both numbers and letters. So if you want the code to combine a number and letter format (such as 1, 1.A, 1.A.1, 1.A.2, 1.B, 1.C, 1.C.1, 1.C.1.a) you can designate that format.

To see the WBS codes currently being used in your project task list, you will need to display the WBS field in a view that displays task information. There are several views that are ideal for this—the Gantt Chart view and the Task Sheet view. After you have added the WBS field to a view, you can use the <u>P</u>roject, <u>W</u>BS, <u>D</u>efine Code command to designate the WBS format. Chapter 23 provides the specific steps for customizing views and formatting the WBS field.

→ To learn how to create and use custom WBS code formats, **see** "Customizing Fields," **p. 956**

Unfortunately, the WBS codes remain tied to the task list sequence. The good news is that Microsoft Project includes a fully customizable Outline Codes feature where you can specify your own codes. This feature is described in the next section.

USING THE CUSTOM OUTLINE CODES

When you need to apply a code to a task or resource, such as an internal accounting code or a pre-designated organizational code, use the Outline Code fields instead of Project's WBS field. There are ten Outline Code fields (named Outline Code 1, Outline Code 2, and so on) available in Project 2000. These new fields enable you to apply your own codes to tasks or resources. The advantage is you can then sort the task or resource list by this code and print the results. For instance, you can create a code that designates the department responsible for the task and the type of work that the task entails (say for billing purposes). After you've applied a code to each task, you can sort the list by department and type of work, thus providing each department head with a clear picture of the tasks assigned to the department and the type of work involved.

The Outline Code fields provide a drop-down list from which users can look up authorized codes. By limiting users to the codes on the list, you prevent inadvertent errors that arise when codes are manually typed in.

And although the default field name is Outline Code, you can change the displayed field name to reflect the actual name you want to use for the code. Turn to Chapter 23 for detailed steps on working with the Outline Code fields.

→ To learn how to alter the properties of Outline Code fields, **see** "Creating and Using Custom Outline Fields," **p. 965**

FILTERING THE TASK OR RESOURCE LIST

When you filter the task list, you impose conditions that must be met to display a task. All the tasks that meet the conditions are allowed to filter through and are displayed. These are known as *filtered tasks*. All those tasks that fail to meet the conditions are not displayed. You can apply a filter, for example, to display only the milestones (as shown in Figure 12.6), only the critical tasks, or only the summary tasks. You also can use the filters to just highlight the tasks selected by the filter, leaving the rest of the tasks displayed but not highlighted (see Figure 12.7). When this type of filter is used, the tasks that meet your filter conditions are displayed in blue. You can use the Text Styles dialog box (Format, Text Styles) to alter the highlighted tasks color. Filters also can be used in resource views to display specific resources.

Figure 12.6
A filtered task list that shows only milestones lets you focus solely on important completion dates.

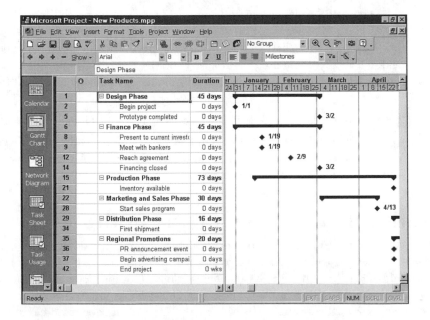

> **Note**
>
> The summary tasks for filtered tasks will display based on a setting in the Filter Definition dialog box. If you don't want to display summary tasks when filtering, edit the filter by choosing Project, Filtered For, More Filters. Select the filter and then click the Edit button. Clear the Show Related Summary Row check box.

Figure 12.7
Having filtered tasks appear highlighted makes them stand out in the display.

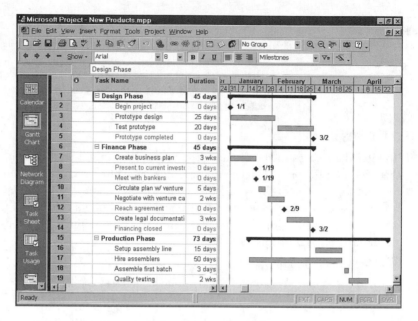

Microsoft Project has many predefined task filters, and you can add custom filters to the list. Some are interactive filters: When you select the filter, a dialog box with the name of the filter in the title bar appears from which you specify values to use in selecting the filtered tasks. The Date Range filter, for example, prompts you for two dates, the beginning and ending dates for the range. It then displays all tasks whose schedules include dates that fall within those two filter dates. The Using Resource filter prompts for a resource name and then only displays the tasks assigned to that resource.

You might find the following list of task filters useful for reviewing the project after the tasks are all entered:

Filter	Description
Critical	Displays only critical tasks
Date Range	Displays only those tasks scheduled for work between the two dates that you enter when prompted
Milestones	Displays only milestone tasks
Summary Tasks	Displays only summary tasks
Tasks with Deadlines	Displays tasks for which you have set a deadline date. This is a new feature in Project 2000
Tasks With Fixed Dates	Displays all tasks that have any date constraint other than As Soon As Possible

PART

IV

CH

12

Note

The Summary Tasks filter is not usually a good substitute for collapsing the outline, as described earlier in this chapter. The Summary Tasks filter shows only summary tasks, but all levels in the outline are displayed. Furthermore, if any first-level task in the outline is not a summary task, the task is not included in the list of tasks filtered by the Summary Tasks filter. If you want to focus only on the tasks up to a certain level in the outline, collapsing the entire outline to that level of tasks is the preferred method.

USING FILTERS

To filter the task list or the resource list, choose Project, Filtered For and choose the filter that you want to apply. If you choose an interactive filter, such as the Date Range filter, respond to the prompts by typing the requested information and choose OK. The list of filters on this menu represents the most frequently used filters. Additional filters are available when you select the More Filters option. You also can use the Filter drop-down box on the Formatting toolbar to apply a filter.

Note that the currently applied filter appears in the Filter drop-down box on the Formatting toolbar. When no filter is applied, All Tasks (or All Resources) appears in the Filter box.

You can use filters to merely highlight the tasks that meet the filter criteria without hiding the other tasks. If you want to apply one of the filters as a highlight filter, hold down the Shift key as you select the Filtered For menu option. You can then select the filter that you want to apply, and it will be implemented as a highlight filter. This technique works whether you are opening the menu from the keyboard or using the mouse. You must hold down the Shift key until you have selected the Filtered For menu option. After that, you can release the Shift key.

You also can apply a highlight filter by following these steps:

1. Choose Project, Filtered For and choose More Filters.
2. Select the filter you want to use in the More Filters dialog box.
3. Click the Highlight button.

When you finish using the filter, you can remove it by pressing F3, or by choosing Project, Filtered For, and selecting the All Tasks filter.

Caution

If you edit the tasks or resources while a filter is applied, you might change an element of a task or resource that impacts whether the task meets the filter conditions. For example, suppose you apply the Date Range filter to display only those tasks in the month of April. If you then make a change to the project that alters the start and finish dates of several tasks (causing the dates to no longer fall in the month of April) the filter does not automatically refresh. You must then reapply the filter to make the filtered display accurate. Use Ctrl+F3 to reapply the current filter.

One of the most useful filters is Tasks With Fixed Dates. This filter is used to identify all the tasks that have constrained dates. Users new to Microsoft Project often inadvertently place constraints on tasks, and then don't understand why Project doesn't recalculate start and finish dates as expected. Use the Tasks With Fixed Dates filter to display tasks that have constraints. You can then review the tasks and be certain that the constraints are in fact necessary.

→ To make sure you understand what Project defines as "constraints," **see** "Working with Task Constraints," **p. 234**

To apply the filter for constrained tasks, follow these steps:

1. Choose <u>P</u>roject, <u>F</u>iltered For, and choose <u>M</u>ore Filters from the menu. The More Filters dialog box is displayed (see Figure 12.8).

Figure 12.8
The More Filters dialog box displays the entire list of filters available in Project.

2. Scroll down the list and select the Tasks With Fixed Dates filter.

3. Choose the Apply button to activate the filter.

Note

If a task has a fixed date constraint, a constraint symbol appears in the Indicators column of the Gantt Chart view.

To clear a filter, you have several options. You can use the Filter drop-down button on the Formatting toolbar. When you open the drop-down list, choose All Tasks at the top of the list. A quick alternative is to press the F3 key.

→ Learn more about the built-in filters; **see** "Exploring the Standard Filters," **p. 881**

VIEWING THE COSTS

The Gantt Chart focuses on the time relationships among the tasks. If you want to focus on the costs of the major phases of the project or on the amount of work scheduled for each major phase, switch to the Task Sheet view and apply the Summary table. To display the Task Sheet with the Summary table, follow these steps:

1. Display the Task Sheet by choosing <u>V</u>iew, <u>M</u>ore Views, and select the Task Sheet from the resulting More Views dialog box. Then click the Apply button.

2. Choose <u>V</u>iew, Ta<u>b</u>le, and choose S<u>u</u>mmary from the drop-down list of tables.

The Summary table (see Figure 12.9) shows the duration, cost, and work of all the tasks in the project. With a very large project, you might find it easier to see the duration, cost, and work associated with just the summary tasks in your project. You can accomplish this by applying the Summary Tasks filter to the project, as shown in Figure 12.10.

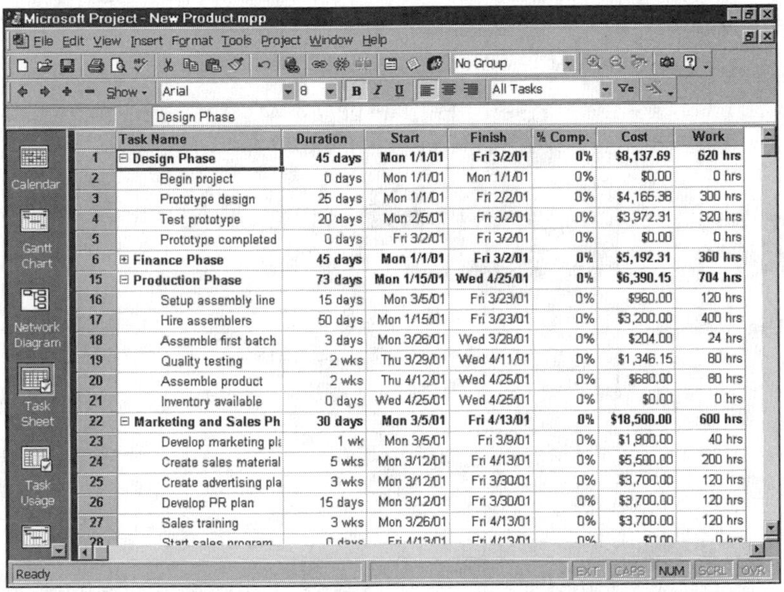

Figure 12.9
The Summary table includes the Duration, Cost, and Work fields, providing a good overview for the entire project.

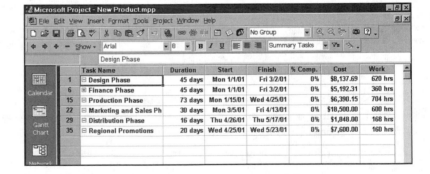

Figure 12.10
With the Summary Tasks filter applied, the same data from Figure 12.9 is collapsed to focus on work and cost amounts for the major phases of the project.

The Summary Table view of the project affords an opportunity to see the project from a larger perspective and to see which tasks or phases entail the most work, cost, and duration.

The Cost field displays the total of both the resource costs and any fixed costs associated with each task. The section "Reducing Costs," later in this chapter, will outline strategies you can use to reduce your project costs.

Best Practice Tips from Toby Brown, PMP

There are filters to view the broad scope of the project (Summary) and the specific deliverables of the project (Milestone), but there is no filter to display just the detail or subtasks, also known as the "work packages" of the project. However, it is easy enough to create one. You simply create a filter that excludes both summary and milestone tasks (Summary = no and Milestone = no) within the same filter definition. What remains in this filtered view are only the tasks at the lowest level of the WBS outline which allows the user to view only the specific detailed work of the project.

SORTING AND GROUPING YOUR PROJECT DATA

You can reorganize the list of tasks or resources in your project by sorting or grouping the data. *Sorting* involves rearranging the rows of information. You can design a sort that uses up to three fields to sort by. For example, using a single field sort you might order the resource list by Resource Name to have an alphabetical list of your resources. Alternatively, you can use a multi-field sort to order the resource list first by Resource Group to display everyone from a particular department together, and then by Resource Name.

Grouping, on the other hand, can both sort and summarize a list of task or resource information. With this powerful new feature in Project 2000, you can designate the groups you want to create. For instance, you can group a task list by Critical and Non-critical tasks and then group the list by Resource Group. An example of how a task list will appear when grouped this way is shown in Figure 12.11. The Critical tasks are listed first, grouped by Resource Group. You would scroll to see the Non-critical tasks and the Resource Groups associated with those tasks.

Figure 12.11
The grouping feature also lets you select from several formatting options to alter the appearance of the grouped data.

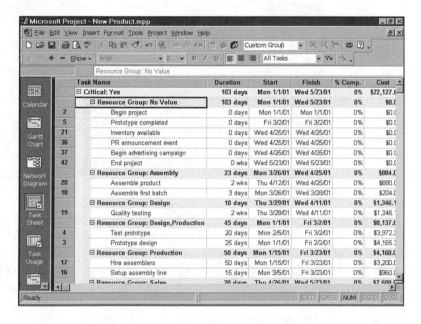

PART

IV

CH

12

The next few sections explain how to use the sort and group features in Microsoft Project.

SORTING THE TASK AND RESOURCE LISTS

You can sort the task list or the resource pool to view the rows of data in a different order. There are two choices for the order in which data will be sorted, ascending and descending. *Ascending* will sort text alphabetically (A–Z); numbers are sorted from lowest to highest (0–9) and dates from oldest to most recent date. *Descending* is not particularly useful for most text (such as Task Names), as it sorts Z to A. Most often descending is used to sort numbers (such as Cost, Work, and Duration information) from highest to lowest (9–0) or dates (such as Start and Finish) from most recent to oldest date.

Although the tasks or resources are displayed in a different order after sorting, by default the ID numbers do not change and the schedule is unaffected. For example, in Figure 12.12 the task list is sorted by the Start field, but the tasks retain their original ID numbers. When you finish using the sorted order, you can return the task list to the original order (by ID number). However, you also have the option of instructing Microsoft Project to permanently renumber the task IDs according to the current sort order. Before you permanently renumber a task list, make sure you read the caution later in this section.

Figure 12.12
Summary tasks have been omitted from the list to see a chronological list of actual tasks, sorted by Start Date.

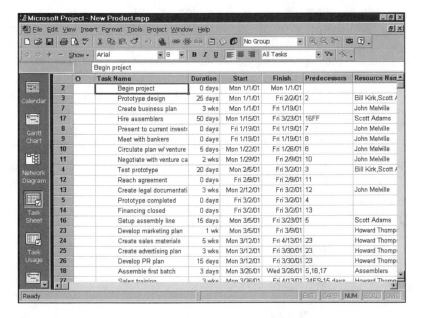

When you sort an outlined project, you can retain or ignore the outline structure. If you retain the outline structure, all tasks at the first outline level are sorted (carrying their subtasks with them); then within each summary task all subtasks at the next outline level are sorted (carrying their subtasks with them), and so forth. If you choose not to keep the outline structure, subtask groups are broken up and dispersed throughout the task list independent of their summary task. If you do not keep the outline structure, you will probably want to suppress the display of summary tasks and the indentation of subtasks, as shown in Figure 12.12. The steps for suppressing summary tasks and indentation are listed later in this section.

Note

If you choose to ignore the outline structure during sorting, you cannot permanently renumber the tasks to match the new sort order—that would restructure the outline. See the Caution later in this section.

Normally, the task and resource lists are sorted according to the numbers in the ID field, and the default sort order is ascending order. When you choose Project, Sort, Sort By, you are asked to identify the field to use for sorting and the direction of the sort—whether to sort in ascending (normal) order or in descending (reverse) order. For example, you could sort the resource list by the Resource Group field, and for duplicates within a group, sort by the Standard Rate paid to the resources, with the highest pay rates listed first. The sort fields in this instance are Group (Ascending) and Standard Rate (Descending), as shown in Figure 12.13.

Figure 12.13
The resource sheet will first be sorted in ascending order by the resource group and then in descending order by the standard pay rate.

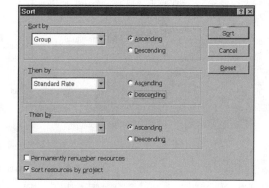

You can use up to three sort fields, which enables you to apply a second and third sort order for groups of tasks or resources that have the same entry in the first sort field. If, for example, you sort tasks by Start Date and many tasks have the same start date, you might use the second sort field to sort all the tasks with the same start date by their estimated duration. If several tasks have the same start date and duration, you can use a third sort field to arrange the tasks within this similar group according to the percent completed on each task. The process is the same as when you sort a mailing list by state, and within states by city, and within cities by name.

Note

If the tasks are filtered when you sort or if some tasks are hidden because the outline is collapsed, the suppressed tasks remain suppressed and are not displayed after sorting.

To sort tasks or resources, follow these steps:

1. Choose File, Save to retain any changes you have made to your file up to this point.
2. Choose Project, Sort, Sort By. The Sort dialog box appears (see Figure 12.14).

PART

IV

CH

12

Caution

Some of the most commonly used fields for sorting appear in a short list when you choose Project, Sort. Although you can select a field from this list when you only want to sort on that one field (the list will be sorted in ascending order), it is always best to use the Sort By command.

The reason has to do with the setting for the Permanently Renumber Tasks (or Resources) option at the bottom of the Sort dialog box. If this option was selected the last time the Sort command was used, it will be used when you sort by selecting from the short list of fields and the original ID numbers for each task or resource will be lost. Unless you immediately undo the renumbering, you will not be able to return the list to its original order.

Figure 12.14
This figure displays the default settings in the Sort dialog box.

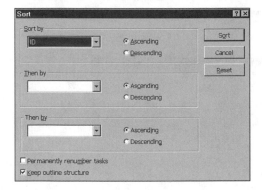

3. Choose the Sort By drop-down to identify the name of the field that you want to serve as the primary sort key. You can scroll in the list view the field names or type the first letter of the field name to quickly move to the section of this field list that contains the field you are looking for.

Note

Don't be confused! Some of the names that appear above the columns of information in a view are slightly different from the actual field names Project uses. For example, the Task Name field displayed in the Gantt Chart or Task Sheet view (refer to Figure 12.14) will actually be the Name field in the Sort drop-down list. Another example can be found in the Resource Sheet view. The Resource Group field is actually the Group field. The rationale for using slightly different names is to provide you the user with more descriptive names when viewing the data.

4. Choose Ascending or Descending order for the first key.

5. To sort by a second field, choose the Then By drop-down and select another field from the field list. This field will be used for sorting if duplicates are found after the list is sorted on the first field you designate.

6. Choose Ascending or Descending order for the second field.

7. To sort by a third field, choose the second Then By drop-down and select another field from the list. Then choose Ascending or Descending as necessary.

8. Clear the Keep Outline Structure check box to sort tasks independently of their summary task groups if desired. (This also makes it impossible to permanently renumber the tasks.)

   If you leave this check box marked, first-level tasks in the outline are sorted, then second-level tasks in the outline are sorted within their summary tasks, and so on.

9. After you have made your selections in the Sort dialog box, click the Sort button to initiate the sort.

If you are sorting a list of tasks, you might want to hide the display of summary tasks and remove the indentation from the display of subtasks.

1. Choose Tools, Options.
2. Click the View tab on the Options dialog box.
3. Clear the check boxes for Show Summary Tasks and Indent Name.
4. Choose OK to close the Options dialog box.

If you edit a list that has been sorted, the list doesn't automatically re-sort based on your changes. You might want to sort the modified list again to take into account the values that have changed, as the changes might affect the sort order. To sort the list again using the current sort keys, press Ctrl+Shift+F3, or you can activate the Sort dialog box again. The sort keys are still defined as you last set them, and you can simply select the Sort button again.

To reset the list to normal order (by ID number), press Shift+F3, or access the Sort dialog box and choose the Reset button and then the Sort button.

There might be times when you want to permanently renumber a list after it has been sorted. This option is used almost exclusively with the resource list, and almost never with the task list. To permanently renumber a list, follow these steps:

1. Choose the sort keys as in the preceding steps. If you are renumbering a task list, double-check that the Keep Outline Structure check box is active. You cannot renumber tasks unless Keep Outline Structure is turned on.
2. Choose the Permanently Renumber Tasks check box for tasks or the Permanently Renumber Resources check box for resources.
3. Click the Sort button to apply the sort.

PART

IV

CH

12

Caution

You can undo the renumbering, provided you act immediately. Choose Edit, Undo Sort. If you don't undo the sort immediately, you can always close the file without saving and then open it again. However, any changes you made to the file that have not been saved will be lost. This is why it is suggested that you always save your project file before performing any kind of sort.

GROUPING THE TASK AND RESOURCE LISTS

 Grouping, a new feature in Project 2000, lets you reorder the task or resource list to better assess how your project is proceeding When you organize the list into groups, the individual data for each item in that group is rolled up into totals for the entire group. Grouping project data is an excellent way to generate summary information that would otherwise be difficult to ascertain.

PREDEFINED GROUPS IN PROJECT

Microsoft Project contains several predefined groups, or you can create your own. The predefined groups you can apply to task and resource information are listed in Tables 12.1 and 12.2.

TABLE 12.1   PREDEFINED TASK GROUPS

Group Name	Description
Complete and Incomplete Tasks	Organizes tasks into three groups: 0% complete, 1%–99% complete, and 100% complete.
Constraint Type	Groups tasks by type of constraint, such as Start No Earlier Than, As Soon As Possible, Finish No Later Than, and so on.
Critical	Separates critical and non-critical tasks. Remember, the status of a task is not fixed. Therefore, tasks that were not critical previously might become critical as you update the project data.
Duration	Groups tasks having the same duration together, regardless of the duration timeframe used. For example, tasks that have durations of 8 hours or 1 day are in one group, and those that have durations of 5 days or 1 week are in another group. This is assuming that you have left the default durations—that 1 day equals 8 hours and 1 week equals 5 days.
Duration then Priority	Groups tasks first by Duration and then, using a subgroup, organizes the tasks by Priority.
Milestones	Separates tasks that are milestones from tasks that are not milestones.
Priority	Organizes tasks by Priority, from lowest to highest priority (0–1,000). The default priority is 500.
Priority Keeping Outline Structure	Organizes subtasks by Priority, within each Summary task; the outline structure remains intact.
TeamStatus Pending	Separates tasks that have a status request pending, from those that do not. See Chapter 15, "Using Microsoft Project in Workgroups," for more information on using the TeamStatus features.

TABLE 12.2 PREDEFINED RESOURCE GROUPS

Group Name	Description
Complete and Incomplete Resources	Organizes resources into three groups: 0% work complete, 1%–99% work complete, and 100% work complete.
Resource Group	Lists resources by the departments, types, or categories you designate in the Group field.
Response Pending	Separates resources that have a response pending from those that do not. The Response Pending field shows you the resources from whom you still need responses to complete the task assignments.
Standard Rate	Groups together resources that receive the same standard pay rate. You can use this information to substitute resources without changing the overall cost of your project.
Work versus Material Resources	Separates the Work and Material Resource Types. Work is the type used with individuals or groups of people working on the project. Material is the type used with raw materials and supplies.

To apply one of these predefined groups, display the view you want to group; the most effective views are the Task Sheet and Resource Sheet. Then click the Group By drop-down on the Standard toolbar and choose a group.

For example, suppose a project is underway and you want to know which of your resources might be available to take on additional work. By applying the Complete and Incomplete Resources group to the Resource Sheet (see Figure 12.15), you will immediately know the percent of work each resource has completed on the project. Those in the 100% group are good candidates to which you might assign additional tasks.

Figure 12.15
By default the percents are listed in ascending order, lowest percent complete to highest percent complete.

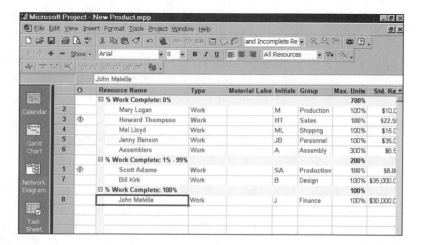

CUSTOMIZING PREDEFINED GROUPS

In addition to using the predefined groups, you can customize these existing groups. There are two ways to customize groups:

- **Customize Group By**—If you have applied a group to your data and now want to customize the active group, use the Project, Group By, Customize Group By option. This displays the Customize Group By dialog box showing the specific settings for the active group (see Figure 12.16). In this dialog box you can specify the Field Name; Sort Order; Text Font and Color; Background Color and Pattern; and (where applicable) Group Intervals.

Figure 12.16
The Customize Group By dialog box appears when you have already applied a group and want to modify the group settings.

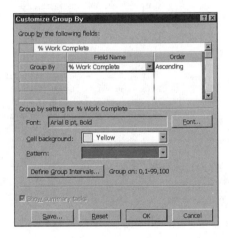

- **Edit**—If you have not applied a group to your data (or you want to alter a group other than the one that is active), use the Project, Group By, More Groups option. This displays the More Groups dialog box from which you can choose a group and click Edit. A dialog box virtually identical to the one shown in Figure 12.16 appears, where you can edit the settings for an existing predefined group.

If you alter a predefined group, the changes you make are temporary. To retain the changes, you must save the revised group under a different name. Click the Save button in the Customize Group By dialog box (refer to Figure 12.16) to save the group.

Caution The Reset button in the Customize Group By dialog box removes all the settings in the dialog box—it does not restore the original settings to the group.

Some fields that you can group on allow you to designate *intervals*, or ranges for the group. For example, the Complete and Incomplete Resources group (which uses the % Work Complete field) has only three intervals: 0, 1–99, and 100. If you want to expand the number of intervals, click the Define Group Intervals button (refer to Figure 12.16) to display the Intervals dialog box shown in Figure 12.17.

Figure 12.17
Use commas to separate the intervals.

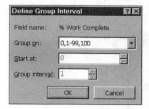

Other fields that allow you to designate intervals are Cost fields, Integer fields, Duration fields, Work fields, Date fields, and Text fields.

CREATING NEW GROUPS

Alternatively, you can create your own custom groups, by following these steps:

1. Choose Project, Group By, More Groups.

2. In the More Groups dialog box (shown in Figure 12.18), select either Task or Resource to designate which type of group you are creating. Then click the New button to define a new group.

Figure 12.18
Designate the type of group (task or resource) you want to create in the More Groups dialog box.

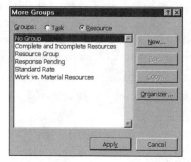

3. Replace the default name, Group 1, with the name you want to give the group.

4. If you want the new group to appear on the Project, Group By list, mark the Show in Menu check box.

5. Click in the Field Name area of the dialog box and choose a field from the drop-down list.

6. Select either ascending or descending from the Order section of the dialog box.

7. Choose the font, cell background, and pattern you want displayed with the group.

8. If applicable, click the Define Group Intervals button to designate a range of intervals for the group.

9. If you are creating a task group, the Show Summary Tasks option will be active, but not marked. If you want the summary tasks to be included with the group, click this option.

10. After you have completed the Group Definition dialog box click OK to create the new group.

Figure 12.19 shows a new group created that groups the resource list first by the Resource Group field, then by the % Work Completed field.

Figure 12.19
The new group will appear in the Project, Group By list because the Show in Menu option is checked.

Like many other custom project items, new groups you create are only attached to the active project. If you want to use a custom group in another project file, copy the group to the other project through the Organizer. If you want to make it available to all project files use the Organizer to copy the group to the GLOBAL template file. Refer to Chapter 4, "Working with Project Files," for more information on using the Organizer and the GLOBAL template.

→ To copy your custom groups to other project files, **see** "Using the Organizer," **p. 128**

→ To make sure any custom items you create in a project will be available in all your other projects, **see** "The GLOBAL.MPT," **p. 125**

Note To delete a custom group, you must use the Organizer.

 You can print a view to which a group has been applied just as you would print any view. Start by selecting File, Print Preview (or clicking the Preview button on the Standard toolbar). Depending on the amount of data to be printed you might want to change the Page Setup options to change the page layout to Landscape instead of Portrait.

→ To discover the printing options you have access to, **see** "Printing the Project Task List," **p. 201**, and "Printing the Resource List," **p. 358**

CHECKING FOR SPELLING ERRORS

Before you show any project information to colleagues or clients, it's a good idea to run a spell check on the file. Microsoft Project has a spelling checker that you can use to verify spelling in all names, notes, and special text fields for both tasks and resources.

USING THE SPELLING COMMAND

 To activate the spelling checker, click the Spelling button on the Standard toolbar or choose Tools, Spelling. When Project cannot find a word in the dictionary, the Spelling dialog box appears (see Figure 12.20).

Figure 12.20
Use the Spelling dialog box to decide how to treat words that are not in the dictionary.

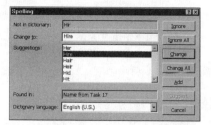

The text boxes in the Spelling dialog box identify the problem word and where the word is found and offer options for responding to the problem. These text boxes are defined in the following list:

Field	Definition
Not in Dictionary	Display-only field that shows the problem word.
Change To	Text entry field in which you type a replacement for the word. If Always Suggest is enabled on the Spelling tab of the Options dialog box, a suggested replacement from the Suggestions list is placed in the field automatically.
Suggestions	Optional list of possible replacements culled from the master Office dictionary (and from your Custom dictionary).
Found In	Display-only field that shows the field and task or resource where the problem word is found.

The following list defines the action buttons found on the right side of the Spelling dialog box:

Button	Use
Ignore	Select Ignore to ignore the problem word in this instance.
Ignore All	Select Ignore All to ignore the word here and anywhere else it appears.
Change	Select Change to have the entry in the Change To field replace this instance of the problem word.
Change All	Select Change All to have the entry in the Change To field replace this and all other occurrences of the problem word.
Add	Select Add to add the problem word to your custom dictionary. The spelling checker ignores this occurrence and all future occurrences with the same exact spelling.
Cancel (Close)	Select Cancel to quit the spelling checker before any words are changed. If any words have changed, the Cancel button changes to a Close button. Select Close to quit the spelling checker immediately. Words that you changed remain changed.
Suggest	Select the Suggest button to display a list of suggested alternatives for the problem word when the Suggestions list is not already displayed. This button is only available when the Always Suggest option is not selected in the Spelling tab of the Options dialog box (see the following section) or when you type into the Change To field.

SETTING THE SPELLING OPTIONS

The Spelling tab of the Options dialog box (shown in Figure 12.21) provides you with an opportunity to determine some characteristics of the spell check operation. To display this tab choose Tools, Options and click the Spelling tab.

Figure 12.21
Use the Spelling tab in the Options dialog box to regulate how spell-checking works.

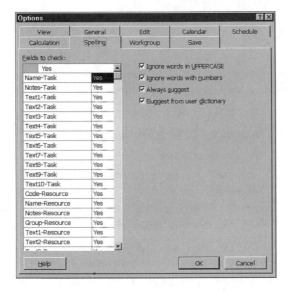

The Spelling tab provides the following options:

Option	Description
Fields to Check	Contains a selection list of text fields in the task and resource databases. All fields are initially marked Yes to be included in the spell-checking operation. Change any field settings to No if you don't want the field checked.
Ignore Words in Uppercase	Causes uppercase words to be ignored.
Ignore Words with Numbers	Causes words that contain numbers to be ignored.
Always Suggest	Activates the Suggestions list each time the spell-checker is used.
Suggest from User Dictionary	Along with the standard dictionary, this checks problem words against the user Custom dictionary.

Tip from Tim and the Project Team

The Ignore Words in Uppercase option is handy if you use a lot of acronyms or abbreviations. However, if you always enter text in uppercase, this would be a good option to turn off.

There will be times when a word you intend to use regularly is not in the master dictionary and appears as a possible misspelled word when you run the spell-checker. When you click

Add to include the word in the dictionary, it does not add it to the master dictionary (that is shared by all Microsoft Office applications including Microsoft Project). Instead, the word is added to a separate user dictionary called CUSTOM.DIC. The Custom dictionary is associated with the computer you are using, not with you as a specific user. So for instance, suppose your project file contains the Resource Group Pub. Rel., your abbreviation for Public Relations. You spell-check the project file and add the abbreviation to the Custom user dictionary on that machine. When you copy the file to another machine and spell-check it, the Pub. Rel. phrase will appear again as a misspelled word. The Pub. Rel. phrase is in the Custom dictionary on your machine, not on this other machine.

Note

On Office 2000, the Custom dictionary is stored in the folder `Windows\Application Data\Microsoft\Proof`. In Office 97 the Custom dictionary is stored in the folder `Program Files\Microsoft Office\Office`. You can edit the Custom dictionary with a text editor. Make sure, however, that the entries are in alphabetical order before you save the edited file.

SHORTENING THE CRITICAL PATH

The preceding sections looked at the project plan from a variety of perspectives: changing the timescale, zooming in or out for more or less detail, filtering the list to only see certain tasks, and rearranging the task list in a different order. This section turns its attention to making some changes that might have been identified as a result of the earlier work and reducing the overall duration of the project to schedule the finish date sooner (or the start date later for a project that is scheduled from the finish date). The popular phrase for this process is *crashing the schedule*.

PART

IV

CH

12

To reduce the duration of the project, you must reduce the duration of the tasks or overlap the tasks so that the combined duration of all the tasks is not as great. Reducing the duration of individual tasks might be no more complicated than reassessing the estimated duration and entering a more optimistic figure. Often, however, to reduce the overall duration of the project requires much more effort:

- You might need to increase the quantity or quality of the resources assigned to the task.

- You might be able to schedule overtime to shorten the duration of a task.

- By changing the relationships among tasks, you might be able to realign the task dates to allow for more overlapping of tasks. You might define lead-time for some Finish-to-Start relationships, or you might be able to redefine a Finish-to-Start relationship to be a Start-to-Start or Finish-to-Finish. If tasks that were originally scheduled end-to-end are allowed to overlap in time, you probably can shorten the project schedule by redefining the task relationships.

Of course, working on shortening noncritical tasks, or scheduling these tasks to overlap, would be a waste of your time. Instead, you should focus your attention only on critical tasks—tasks in the schedule that directly impact the finish date of the project. Only critical tasks count when trying to crash the schedule. By definition, delays to critical tasks impact the end date of the project; delays to noncritical tasks do not.

Keep in mind that changes you make in the schedule might change the status of a task from noncritical to critical. So it is important that you can clearly identify the critical tasks at all times.

Best Practice Tips from Toby Brown, PMP	Within the discipline of Project Management, there are three ways considered to "crash the schedule," and one way to "fast-track." Crashing can be accomplished one of three ways, with each having a downside in doing so. The three techniques of crashing are as follows: 1. Changing Scope—Changing or re-estimating the duration of critical tasks, which means that you are changing the scope of the project. Essentially you are saying that you will be doing the same amount of work in less time. Assuming that your duration estimates are not padded, changing scope in a well-defined, closely assessed project typically means compromising content or quality. Basically, you will be removing tasks from the project or cutting corners to get the work done. 2. Assigning Resources—Assigning additional resources allows you to do the same amount of work in less time. This suggests that if one resource can do a task in one week, two resources can do it in half a week, three in a third, etc. However, the "law of diminishing returns" (or "too many cooks spoil the soup") actually prevents this from happening, giving an unrealistic schedule. 3. Work More Hours—Working overtime makes more working time available over the period of time that the project occurs, but affects worker morale and quality.

Best Practice Tips from Toby Brown, PMP	Overlapping tasks, in Project Management terms, means "fast tracking." This multitasking approach which PMI considers different from "crashing" means not waiting for one task to finish before starting a subsequent task. However, keep in mind that when you fast track a project, risk goes up. There are more opportunities for things to go wrong requiring task durations to slip, as well as the possibility of rework. It's crucial that you use caution when overlapping tasks.

IDENTIFYING THE CRITICAL PATH

 You can use any task view to identify the critical tasks. The basic Task Entry view on the More Views menu is popular because this view displays many fields relevant to crashing the schedule, and can be displayed in the top or bottom pane. (This view also is accessible using the Task Entry View button on the Resource Management toolbar. Turn on the Resource Management toolbar by right-clicking any portion of a displayed toolbar.) You also can use the Network Diagram to identify the critical tasks. However, it's not as easy to get to all the fields you might want to change as you revise the project.

Probably the most dramatic way to identify the critical tasks is to use the Gantt Chart Wizard (Format, GanttChartWizard). When you elect to view the Critical Path on the second step of the wizard, the taskbars in the timescale side of the view change color. Figure 12.22 shows a project in the Gantt Chart view that is formatted to show the critical path.

Best Practice Tips from Toby Brown, PMP

Although the Project software does calculates the critical path automatically, it is important to understand how it is calculated. The calculation involves a forward and backward pass. The forward pass calculates an activity's early dates which are the earliest times an activity can start and finish once its predecessors have been completed (Early Start + Duration – 1 = Early Finish). The backward pass then happens which calculates an activity's late dates which are the latest times an activity can start and finish without delaying the end date of the project (Late Finish – Duration + 1 = Late Start). Float, or slack as it is called in Project, is the amount of time an activity can slip from its early start without delaying the project. It is the difference between the late finish and early finish dates of an activity. Activities with zero total float are defined as critical.

It is also important to distinguish between "critical" activities and "important" ones. Many times the terms are used interchangeably but mean different things to a formally trained project manager. Critical tasks are important to a project because they contribute to the longest path through the project and, thereby, dictate the earliest possible finish date. Important tasks, however, might or might not be "critical."

Figure 12.22
Critical tasks are displayed in red when the Gantt Chart is formatted to display the Critical Path.

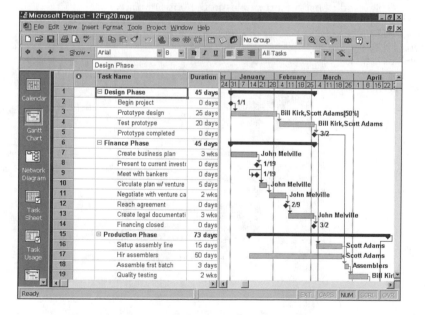

→ Formatting the Gantt Chart to display the Critical Path is easy with the Gantt Chart Wizard; **see** "Using the Gantt Chart Wizard," **p. 912**

Another alternative is to filter the task list in the Gantt Chart view or the Task Sheet view to show only the critical tasks. However, as you redefine the project, some tasks might change from noncritical to critical (and vice versa). The filter does not automatically recalculate, although you can use Ctrl+F3 to quickly reapply the current filter.

PART

IV

CH

12

To filter the critical tasks, follow these steps:

1. Select the top pane if a combination view is in place.

2. Display a task list view by choosing Gantt Chart from the View menu or Task Sheet from the View, More Views menu.

3. Choose Project, Filtered For, and then Critical from the drop-down menu.

Another popular combination view for crashing the schedule places the Task Details Form in the top pane and the Task Name Form in the bottom pane (see Figure 12.23). To create this combination view, follow these steps:

1. Choose View, More Views and select Task Details Form. Then click Apply.

2. Choose Window, Split to split the screen into two panes.

3. Click in the bottom pane and choose View, More Views, and select Task Name Form. Then click Apply.

4. Click in the top pane and choose Format, Details, Predecessors & Successors to display the tasks that are linked to the active task.

5. Click in the bottom pane and choose Format, Details, and select Resource Work to display additional resource fields in the bottom pane.

Figure 12.23
Use two task forms to display task and resource information.

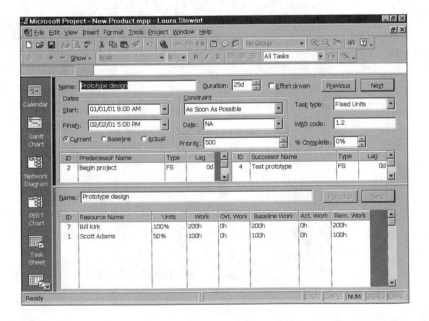

You can filter the top pane to display only Critical tasks (but note that you need to recalculate the filter fairly often). Use the P̲revious and Ne̲xt buttons in the top pane to change the tasks as you review the task definitions. You can change task definitions, relationship definitions, and resource assignments (including overtime) all on the same screen. You will not have the benefit, however, of the graphical displays (such as the Gantt Chart taskbars and Network Diagram nodes) that can help you keep the project organized in your head.

STRATEGIES FOR CRASHING THE SCHEDULE

No matter which view you use, move through the project from one critical task to the next, looking for the opportunities from the following list:

- Review with intent to reduce task durations that are unnecessarily long. Assigning more resources or more skilled resources might be one way to do this.
- Examine the predecessor and successor relationships and try to identify the relationships that you can change from Finish-to-Start to one of the overlapping relationships (Start-to-Start, Finish-to-Finish, or Finish-to-Start with lead-time). This strategy usually is one of the most fruitful because many users hastily define all relationships as Finish-to-Start when more lenient definitions can be applied. Ask the question: Does the predecessor to this task really have to be 100 percent complete before this task can start, or would almost finished or partially finished be good enough?
- Schedule overtime to reduce the number of regular work hours that a task might take. This is discussed in the section "Assigning Overtime Work" in Chapter 10, "Assigning Resources and Costs to Tasks."

You might find it easier to concentrate on each of these strategies if you go through the project task list once for each of the areas identified in the preceding list. Remembering what you are looking for is sometimes easier if you look for the same thing as you examine task after task. Make one complete pass through the project, looking for duration estimates that you can trim. Then make another pass through the complete list of critical tasks, looking for changes in task relationships. Finally, do the same for changing resource assignments and scheduling overtime.

After you make changes, remember that some formerly noncritical tasks now might be critical and that these tasks should be reviewed along the same lines for possible duration reductions.

A useful combination view at this point is the Gantt Chart or Task Sheet in the top pane and the Relationship Diagram view (formerly the Task PERT Chart view) in the bottom pane. You can move from one task to another easily in the top pane and view the task relationships for the selected task in the bottom pane.

→ To learn how to more about the Relationships Diagram, **see** "The Relationship Diagram," **p. 862**

→ To create custom views that consist of one view in the top pane and another view in the bottom pane, **see** "Creating a Combination View," **p. 948**

PART **IV**

CH **12**

Figure 12.24
The Relationship Diagram view in the bottom pane provides a visual verification of task predecessors and successors.

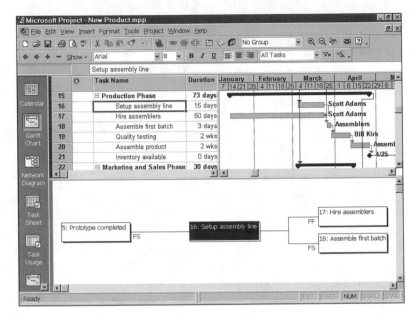

REDUCING COSTS

If the project costs are above expectations, you can examine the project schedule for possible cost savings. There are two types of costs associated with each task: variable costs and fixed costs. Because variable costs all derive from resource assignments, you might want to focus on ways to reduce the cost of the resources assigned to individual tasks.

→ To learn more about how Microsoft Project determines cost, **see** "Understanding Resources and Costs," **p. 315**, and "Fixed Costs," **p. 316**

REVIEWING THE COST SCHEDULE

You can see the cost and total amount of work for each task if you display the Task Sheet and apply the Summary table. If you display the Task Form in the bottom pane and choose the Resource Work fields from the Format menu to appear at the bottom of the form, you can see the resource assignments, including overtime work, in detail.

You also might use the Resource Substitution view, discussed in the section titled "Reducing the Workload of the Overallocated Resource" in Chapter 11, "Resolving Resource Assignment Problems," to identify less expensive resource substitutes to assign to tasks.

To display the Summary table in the top pane and the Resource Work table in the bottom pane, follow these steps:

1. Select the top pane if currently displaying a combination view.

2. Choose View, More Views.

3. From the More Views dialog box, choose Task Sheet.

4. Click the Apply button.

5. Choose <u>V</u>iew, Ta<u>b</u>le, <u>S</u>ummary.

6. If you are not currently displaying a combination view, choose <u>W</u>indow, <u>S</u>plit.

7. Select the bottom pane. The Task Form appears in the bottom pane because it is the default view when you split a window underneath the Task Sheet or Gantt Chart.

8. Choose F<u>o</u>rmat, <u>D</u>etails, Resource <u>W</u>ork to display the work fields.

If you only want to focus on tasks with costs in excess of some determined amount, you can create a filter to display only these tasks.

➔ To build your own filters, **see** "Creating Custom Filters," **p. 968**

STRATEGIES FOR REDUCING COSTS

Less expensive resources that perform the same quality of work in the same amount of time obviously will lower your costs if you substitute the currently assigned resources with these less expensive resources.

You also can reduce costs if you can substitute more expensive but more efficient resources. You can justify the extra cost if the number of hours of work that complete the task is more than reduced proportionally. For example, if the standard rate of the new resource is 20% higher than the old resource, but you can reduce the work hours by 25%, this substitution would result in a cost savings. Let's suppose you have an eight-hour task with a $10/hr resource assigned to it. This task would cost $80. What if a $12/hr resource could accomplish the same task in six hours? The task would only cost $72, a savings of $8.

You also might be able to assign tools or equipment to the task and thereby increase the efficiency of the labor so that reduced hours of work result in reduced total labor costs. If the reduction in labor time and costs is enough to match the cost of the tools or equipment, the added capital expense results in a cost savings overall.

DISTRIBUTING COPIES OF PROJECT WITH EMAIL

As part of the review process, you might want to let others look at the project schedule. One way to accomplish this is to electronically distribute a copy of the project file. You can send it directly to each person who needs to review it, or by routing a single copy of the file sequentially from one person to another.

To send a copy of the file to one or a group of people, choose <u>F</u>ile, Send To, M<u>a</u>il Recipient (As Attachment). You then complete the addressing information just as you would any other email. To route a copy of the file through a series of people, choose <u>F</u>ile, Send To, <u>R</u>outing Recipient. A routing slip appears from which you identify the order in which the recipients review the file. Chapter 15 contains detailed steps on sending and routing project files via email.

➔ One way to sharing project files is to route them via email. **See** "Communicating by Email," **p. 604**

PRINTING SUMMARY REPORTS

Several overview reports are available for printing at this point in your project review process. You can run these reports by choosing View, Reports. A dialog box appears that displays an icon for each category of reports (see Figure 12.25).

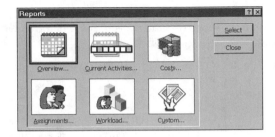

Figure 12.25
The Reports dialog box offers a variety of report categories.

Double-click the icon for the category desired and another dialog box appears with the reports included in that category. Figure 12.26 displays the reports in the Overview category. Click a report, and it is displayed in print preview format.

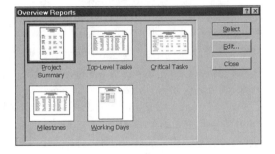

Figure 12.26
The reports provided in the Overview category are useful when auditing the task schedule.

Each report in Microsoft Project is described in detail in Chapter 24, "Using the Standard Reports." Customizing reports is covered in Chapter 25, "Customizing Reports." A brief discussion is included here of the reports that are most useful at this stage of project development.

The Overview Report category offers several reports that are helpful in documenting this stage in project design:

- The Project Summary offers a one-page snapshot view of the project, including start and finish dates, total duration of the project, total hours of work, and dollar costs. It shows the same information that is displayed in the Project Statistics dialog box. It also includes the Comments you enter on the Summary tab of the File Properties dialog box.

- The Top-Level Tasks report displays the summary duration, cost, and work information for the top-level summary tasks.

- The Critical Tasks report identifies all critical tasks of the project, noting their dependencies and any lag or lead times. It is here that you can start to pinpoint inconsistencies behind the logic of the project plan.

- The Milestones report highlights the major landmarks of the project. This report is useful in communications with members of the project team and other interested parties.

- The Working Days report documents the calendars defined in your project. It lists the normal working days and hours and any exceptions for all defined base calendars and resource calendars.

The Cost Reports category of reports also includes two reports that are helpful when completing the design phase of the project.

- The Cash Flow report is instrumental in providing information needed in funding the project—planning to have the correct amount of money at the correct time.

- The Budget report also might be helpful at this point, listing each task and its fixed and variable costs. If the project is over budget, it is easy to pinpoint the most expensive tasks with this report.

When you finish the initial design of the project, use these tools to step back from the details and look at the big picture. Does it make sense? Is the project going to finish on time? Are costs within budget? If not, then you have the tools to decide where changes are necessary.

Before you can call the project plan complete, a careful review is in order. This chapter introduces a variety of ways to modify the display of the project plan to explain it to others, to identify potential problems, and to improve its efficiency. The following chapters provide more information depending on the direction you seek:

- Chapter 13, "Printing Views and Reports," shows you how to transfer your project plan onto paper.

- Chapter 14, "Publishing Projects on the Web," shows you how to transfer your project plan to others via the Internet.

- Chapter 16, "Tracking Work on the Project," provides the steps necessary to keep track of activities on the project as they occur as well as the reasons for doing so.

TROUBLESHOOTING

USING A ROLLED UP TASKBAR

I told Project to collapse my summary tasks, but I don't want to see the summary taskbar. How can I make Project show me a rolled up taskbar instead?

A feature new in Project 2000 is the ability to display the individual bars associated with a summary task when the summary task is collapsed. When the subtasks indented under a task are hidden, only the summary taskbar displays. If you'd rather see a rolled up taskbar instead, you can tell Project to do so through the Format, Layout command.

GENERATING REPORTS

I need to generate a report but I don't seem to be able to print out the information in Project Statistics box. Am I doing something wrong?

In the Overview Report category, choose the Project Summary report. It's a one-page snapshot view of your project, and it shows the same information that is displayed in the Project Statistics dialog box.

PRINTING VIEWS AND REPORTS

In this chapter

USING THE PRINT COMMANDS

One of the main functions of project management software is to print reports that will communicate your project plan to others in a clear and informative format.

There are two ways to print your project data:

- Many times you just want to print the view of the data that appears onscreen. The printed version is nearly identical to the display format onscreen. A few views cannot be printed, however, including combination views (a split screen with one view in the upper pane and another in the lower pane), the Relationship Diagram, and the forms (such as the Task Form, the Resource Form, and the Tracking Form).

- Microsoft Project also provides 25 predesigned reports for printing. The report formats include a monthly calendar with tasks shown on the scheduled dates, comprehensive lists of tasks and resources, and a summary page that resembles the Project Statistics dialog box.

 Selecting the Print button sends a copy of the current view to the printer immediately; you do not have a chance to exercise control over the way the report looks. Through the commands introduced in this chapter, you will learn how to make changes to the page setup before using the Print button.

 Choosing the Print Preview button allows you to see what the printed copy will look like and also gives you access to the Page Setup and Print commands. You should almost always start a print job with the Print Preview button instead of the Print button.

As in all Windows applications, the printer commands are located on the File menu (see Figure 13.1). The Page Setup command defines headers, footers, page orientation, and so on, for printed views. You also can use Page Setup to select the printer and to change any printer-specific options available for your printer. The Print Preview and Print commands are used to print views. Additionally, there are 25 predesigned reports in Microsoft Project that are accessed by choosing View, Reports. The Page Setup and Print buttons displayed when viewing a report work the same way the commands on the File menu do.

Figure 13.1
You can establish the print settings, using the Print Setup command, before or after you enter the project data.

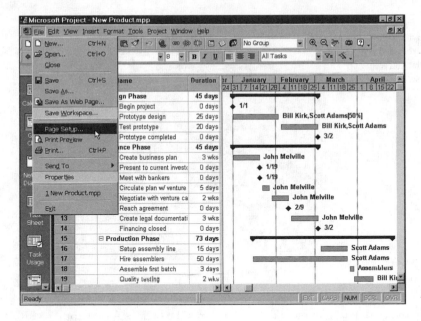

CHANGING THE PRINTER SETUP

Make sure that you select the correct printer before you start a print job. You can select the default printer for any Windows application by selecting the Start button on the taskbar and choosing Settings, Printers.

The default printer is selected when you start to print in Microsoft Project. If you want to use a printer other than the default printer, you can select the printer by choosing File, Print. The Print dialog box appears (see Figure 13.2). From this dialog box, choose the Printer Name drop-down button to select the printer.

The list of installed printers appears in the Printer Name drop-down list. If you only want to change the printer you are printing to, simply click the printer you want to use. If you want to change the way the printer is set up, choose the printer you want, and then click the Properties button. The Properties dialog box for the selected printer appears.

PART

IV

CH

13

Figure 13.2
From the Print dialog box, choose the printer you want to use.

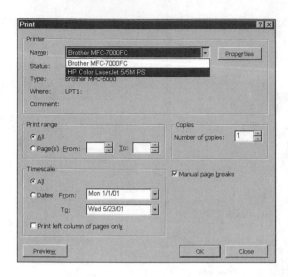

The options listed in the Properties dialog box differ depending on which printer you selected. For example, Figure 13.3 shows the options for a Brother MFC 7000 printer and Figure 13.4 shows the options for a Hewlett-Packard Color LaserJet 5/5M PS printer.

Some of the settings include selecting the paper size, selecting a paper feeder source, and changing the resolution of graphics objects. You also can change the orientation of the report on the paper from portrait (upright) to landscape (sideways).

Your printer might have different options. Select the options you want and choose OK when finished. Until you change the printer or the options, Microsoft Project will use this printer and its settings as the default.

Figure 13.3
The Brother MFC 7000 Properties dialog box contains some basic printer options.

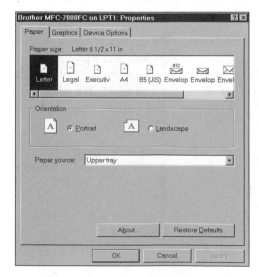

Figure 13.4
The HP LaserJet 5/5M PS Properties dialog box lists other, more extensive printer options.

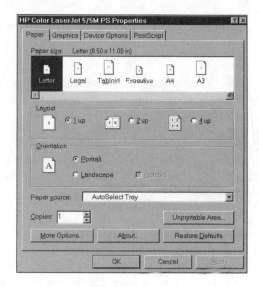

PRINTING VIEWS

Most of the time you will be printing views, such as the Gantt Chart view or the Resource Sheet view. This section provides a few pointers about preparing the screen view for printing. Chapter 7, "Viewing Your Schedule," Chapter 22, "Formatting Views," and Chapter 23, "Customizing Views, Tables, Fields, and Filters," contain detailed instructions for refining the display with special formatting and graphics features. This chapter focuses on the use of the print commands after the screen presentation is established.

→ To add text boxes and arrows to the Gantt Chart, **see** "Introducing the Drawing Toolbar," **p. 275**

→ Format your views before you print. **See** "Using the Common Format Options in Standard Views," **p. 892**

→ You can print the Gantt Chart view using any of the built-in tables. **See** "Using and Creating Tables," **p. 949**

PREPARING THE VIEW FOR PRINTING

The first step is to set up the screen to display the project data just as you want the information to appear on the printed report. You use the View menu, the Tools menu, and the Format menu to get the combination of data and display features that presents your data in the best way.

CHOOSING THE VIEW FUNDAMENTALS

You first must choose the appropriate view to print. You can view tasks or resources in either a worksheet table layout or a graphic layout. In views that contain timescales, the timescale displayed is printed. For instance, in the Gantt Chart view, the timescale can be displayed using the following:

Minutes	Weeks	Quarters
Hours	Thirds of Months	Half Years
Days	Months	Years

 Using the Zoom In or Zoom Out buttons on the Standard toolbar adjusts the timescale to show most of these time measurement units. To select a specific time unit, choose Format, Timescale. The Thirds of Months and Half Years (new units in Project 2000) are only available through the Timescale dialog box.

Best Practice Tips from Toby Brown, PMP

A common way to view project-related information on a quarterly basis is to customize the timescale to quarters over weeks.

If you filter the tasks or resources, only the data displayed is printed. Moreover, if you have split the screen into panes, you must choose the pane from which the view is printed. If the top pane is active, all tasks or all resources are printed unless you filter the data. If the bottom pane is active, only the tasks or resources associated with the selection in the top pane are printed. You might decide to print from the bottom pane, for example, if you want to isolate all the resources assigned to a selected task, or you might want to print a list of all the tasks to which a selected resource is assigned.

To display a view, select the View menu and choose the desired view from the list (or click More Views if the view you want is not on the menu). If the screen is split into panes, the active pane will have a colored bar on the far left side of the screen next to the pane. So if you are using the standard Windows color scheme, the default color for the active pane is dark blue; light gray is used to designate the inactive pane. To select a different pane, click (with the mouse) on the desired pane or use the F6 key to toggle between the upper and lower panes.

If the view contains spreadsheet-like columns of data, you might need to choose View, Table to select the most appropriate set of data columns. The various tables were introduced in previous chapters as tools to use in the process of building and managing a project. To simply change the table currently displayed, choose View, Table, and choose the table you want to use.

→ To learn about which tables are useful for viewing baseline data and tracking work on your project, **see** "Tracking Work on the Project," **p. 659**

→ If you want to learn more about Project's built-in tables, **see** "Using the Standard Views, Tables, and Filters," **p. 851**

→ To create your own custom tables, **see** "Using and Creating Tables," **p. 949**

Finally, if you want the printed view to focus on just part of the project, you might want to use a filter to display only a subset of the tasks or resources. Most of the filters are useful tools in building and managing a project. To apply a predefined filter, choose Tools, Filtered For, and choose the appropriate filter.

Note

In views that show a table to the left of a timescale, check the columns of the table that are visible onscreen. By default, the rightmost column that is *completely* visible is the last column of the table that appears on the printed report. For example, in the initial Gantt Chart view (where ID, Task Name, and Duration are the only columns visible), the printed report doesn't show the other columns in the table. You must move the dividing line between the table and the timescale to display more columns, or choose the Print All Sheet Columns option on the View tab of the Page Setup dialog box to print all the table columns.

→ The general use of filters, including how to use the AutoFilter capability, is discussed in Chapter 12. **See** "Filtering the Task or Resource List," **p. 510**

→ To learn about Project's built-in filters and their uses, **see** "Exploring the Standard Filters," **p. 881**

→ To create your own custom filters, **see** "Creating Custom Filters," **p. 968**, and "Creating Custom Filters with AutoFilter," **p. 978**

Tip from Tim and the Project Team

A quick way to apply a filter is to use the Filter drop-down list box or AutoFilter button on the Formatting toolbar.

SORTING AND GROUPING THE DISPLAY

2000 After displaying the data you want to print, you might want to rearrange the order of the tasks or resources. You can sort or group the data. Grouping, a new feature in Project 2000, sorts and summarizes a list of task or resource information. If you have not used the Sort or Group By commands before, see Chapter 12, "Reviewing the Project Plan," for a comprehensive discussion of sorting and grouping in detail.

→ To reorganize and summarize your project data, **see** "Sorting and Grouping Your Project Data," **p. 515**

The basic steps for sorting table lists are

1. Choose Project, Sort. From the drop-down list, choose the Sort By option. The Sort dialog box appears.

Caution

Most of the time you will sort tasks or resources temporarily to display or print project information differently from how it appears in the view. Make sure the Permanently Renumber Tasks check box is deselected if you are only temporarily sorting the data.

2. Choose the Sort By list box, and select the column on which to sort the records.

3. Choose Ascending or Descending for the order of the sort. If you anticipate duplicates to occur in the first column you are sorting on, use the two Then By list boxes to create second- and third-level sorts, if necessary.

4. Choose the Sort button to execute the sort.

PART

IV

CH

13

Note

Ascending will sort text alphabetically (A-Z). Numbers are sorted from lowest to highest (0–9) and dates from oldest to most recent date. Descending is not particularly useful for sorting text (such as Task Names), as it arranges text from Z to A. Most often descending is used to sort numbers (such as Cost, Work, and Duration information) from highest to lowest (9–0) or dates (such as Start and Finish) from most recent to oldest date.

Figure 13.5 shows the Sort dialog box where all the tasks will be sorted by Cost in descending order, from highest to lowest cost. One of the choices at the bottom of the dialog box is Keep Outline Structure. This would result in a sort where the detail tasks remain with their summary tasks and are only sorted within the "phase" they are in.

Figure 13.5
The Sort dialog box provides three levels of sorting.

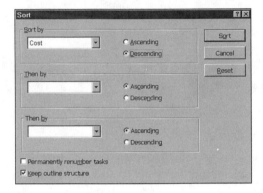

If you print the report, it shows the data in the order displayed onscreen. If at some point you want to return to the default sort order, choose the Reset button in the Sort dialog box.

You also can use the new grouping feature in Project to alter the display of the project information. There are several predefined groups or you create your own custom group. To apply one of the predefined groups, display the view you want to group. The most effective views for seeing the grouped information are the Task Sheet and Resource Sheet. Then click the Group By drop-down on the Standard toolbar and choose a group. Figure 13.6 shows an example of how the Resource Sheet will appear when arranged by Resource Group.

ENHANCING THE DISPLAY OF THE TEXT DATA

You can format text data to emphasize or highlight selected categories of tasks or resources. For example, you might want to display summary tasks in bold, milestones in italic, or overallocated resources (in a resource view) as underlined. The display of the gridlines and the column and row separator lines can be customized as well. In views with a timescale, you can customize the time units and labels used to represent the time units. In graphic views, special graphical features from a palette might be selected. All these customizing features are covered in detail in Chapter 23. Use these display enhancements selectively to improve the presentation quality of your printed reports.

Figure 13.6
The grouping feature also enables you to select from several formatting options to alter the appearance of the grouped data.

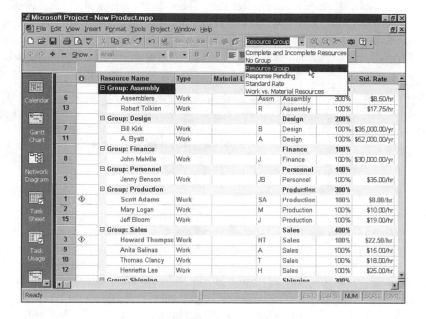

SETTING AND CLEARING PAGE BREAKS

You can force a page break when printing task and resource lists so that a new page starts at a specific task or resource—even if the automatic page break doesn't occur until further down the list. Page breaks are tied to the task or resource you select when you set the page break. Even if you sort the list or hide a task by collapsing the outline, a new page starts at the task or resource where the page break was set.

Page breaks also affect the printing of the built-in reports. The final dialog box you see just before printing offers an option to use or ignore the page breaks you set manually. This feature prevents you from having to remove all page breaks for one special printout and later having to replace the breaks. You can remove one page break or all page breaks with relative ease.

Note

The Manual Page Breaks setting in the Print dialog box is retained when you save your project file. This is a new feature in Project 2000.

To set a page break, select the row just below the intended page break. This row becomes the first row on a new page. Choose Insert, Page Break. A dashed line appears above the selected row to indicate the presence of a manually inserted page break.

To remove a page break, reselect the row just below the page break. Choose Insert, Remove Page Break. (Notice that when a page break row is selected, the menu choice changes from Page Break to Remove Page Break.) The selected page break is removed.

To remove all page breaks, select all the rows in the active view by clicking the first column heading on the far left of the view. Typically, this is an empty gray rectangle above the task or resource ID number. Choose Insert, Remove All Page Breaks. (The wording of the Page Break command changes to Remove All Page Breaks when all rows are selected.)

Best Practice Tips from Toby Brown, PMP

Page breaks are a great way to create several "separate" projects within one master one. By properly placing page breaks, project managers can effectively print different parts of a project, perhaps assigned to different resources on a team responsible for different phases of the project, and still maintain managing the project within a single file. This makes it much easier to distribute hard copies of the project without having to cut and paste into different files.

 In the Network Diagram view, page breaks are automatically displayed, but you might have to zoom out to see them. Choose View, Zoom or choose the Zoom Out button to see the page breaks in the Network Diagram view. You cannot set the page breaks in the Network Diagram view. However, you can move the task boxes to either side of the automatic page breaks. To do this, select Format, Layout. Then choose Allow Manual Box Positioning and click OK. When you choose this setting, Project will allow task boxes to be placed on a page break. The option Adjust for Page Breaks in the Layout dialog box will correct this, but only after you redraw the Network Diagram view by choosing the Format, Layout Now command.

Best Practice Tips from Toby Brown, PMP

If the project manager has access to a plotter, printing the Network Diagram will be much easier then having to tape numerous 8.5" × 11" sheets of paper together. Plus, you will be able to take advantage of the colored pens typically available with a plotter, allowing you to highlight important elements of the project, including the critical path.

Note

Page breaks are automatically displayed in the Network Diagram. If they have been turned off, you can display page breaks by selecting Format, Layout and marking the Show Page Breaks check box.

→ To learn more about the moving boxes and formatting the Network Diagram, **see** "Working with the Network Diagram View," **p. 298**

CHANGING THE PAGE SETUP

You can change the appearance of the printed pages for any view with the Page Setup command. For example, the margins, orientation, headers and footers, and legend for graphic views can be modified. A separate page setup configuration is available for each of the views and reports. This means that changing the header and footer you design for Gantt Charts does not change the header and footer you design for Task Sheets.

To change the page settings for the active view, choose File, Page Setup or choose the Page Setup button in Print Preview. (If the active view cannot be printed, the File, Page Setup command is not available.) The Page Setup dialog box is displayed for the active view.

Figure 13.7 shows the Page tab of the Page Setup dialog box for Gantt Charts. Use the Page tab in the Page Setup dialog box to set the page orientation for printing and to designate the starting page number.

Figure 13.7
The name of the active view appears in the title bar.

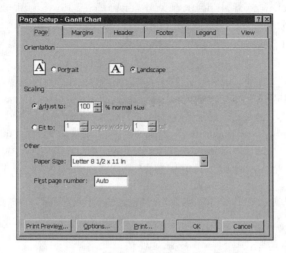

Note

In this version of Project, a number of the print settings you select in the Page Setup and Print dialog boxes are saved with the project, including the setting for manual page breaks, the range for views containing a timescale, and the Print Left Column of Pages Only setting.

The following sections describe the print settings in the Page Setup dialog box.

USING THE PAGE SETUP DIALOG BOX

The current settings on the Page Setup dialog box for any view are saved with the project file; they are available when you print the same view using another project file. To use those custom settings in another project file, the custom item (in this case the view) has to be copied to the other file. This is accomplished though the Organizer.

→ To copy custom views from one project file to another, **see** "Using the Organizer," **p. 128**

As with other dialog boxes, the Page Setup dialog box has multiple tabs (refer to Figure 13.7). Each tab at the top accesses a different collection of settings. To see the settings for a particular topic, choose the appropriate tab.

SELECTING THE ORIENTATION

The Page tab shown in Figure 13.7 contains options used to set the page orientation to Portrait (upright) or Landscape (sideways). This setting overrides the default orientation set in the Print Setup dialog box. If you intend to add the printout to another document or if you have a number of tasks and a short timescale, the Portrait orientation would be best. If on the other hand you have a longer timescale, the Landscape orientation would display more of the timescale per printed page.

SCALING THE PRINTOUT

Scaling options are available for all printers; you don't need a PostScript printer to take advantage of scaling. *Scaling* can be used to reduce or enlarge your printout. These options allow you to scale the printouts either by a specified percentage or by a given number of pages.

In Figure 13.8, a project is being previewed, showing multiple pages, to see how the project will appear when printed. Four pages will be printed, two pages wide by two pages tall. The final task is being printed on the bottom two pages. Instead of printing the bottom pages for just one task, you can adjust the printout to compress the pages so the last task is included in the top two pages. Select the Fit To option in the scaling area of the Page tab (refer to Figure 13.7). In this case, you would set the printout to fit to two pages wide by one page tall.

Figure 13.8
Four pages will be printed unless you use the Fit To option on the Page tab to compress the printout.

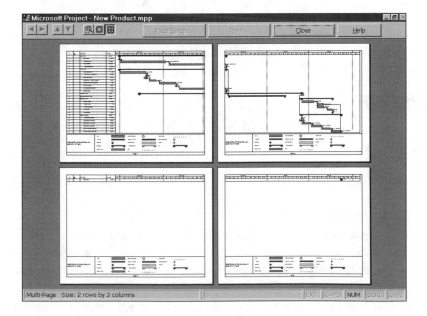

DESIGNATING THE PAPER SIZE

You can now set the paper size in the Page Setup dialog box instead of having to go into the printer Properties dialog box. The Paper Size option is located at the bottom of the Page tab in the Page Setup dialog box (refer to Figure 13.7).

Note

You also can choose the paper size in the printer Properties dialog box, which is accessed several ways: through the Options button in the Page Setup dialog box (refer to Figure 13.7) and through the Properties button in the Print dialog box (refer to Figure 13.2).

SETTING THE PAGE NUMBERING

Another new feature in Project 2000 is the ability to designate the first page number for the printed pages. For example, suppose two pages you print from your project will be the fifth and sixth pages in a document. You can set First Page Number to start at 5 for the printed pages.

SPECIFYING THE MARGINS

Choose the Margins tab in the Page Setup dialog box to set the margins as appropriate (see Figure 13.9). The default margin is half an inch (.5) for the top, bottom, left, and right margins. Microsoft Project prints with a quarter-inch (.25) margin, even if you reduce the margin to zero (0). If a header or footer is added or if borders are displayed on every page, the margin automatically expands to fit the text, though no change is displayed in the Page Setup dialog box.

Figure 13.9
The Margins page is used to change the width of the margins of your printout.

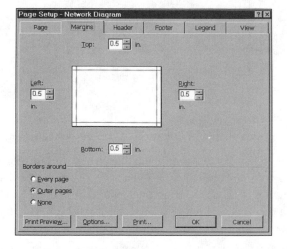

PART
IV
CH
13

PLACING BORDERS

Also on the Margins tab of the Page Setup dialog box are options for placing borders on the printed view. You can use borders to surround the page and separate the body of the report from the header, footer, and legend. By default, borders are printed with every page. For multiple-page Network Diagrams that you want to tape together, this capability makes cutting and pasting easier if you place borders around the outer pages only.

To enclose each page in a lined border, choose Every Page in the Borders Around section on the Margins tab of the dialog box. To place borders on the outside pages only, choose Outer Pages (for Network Diagrams only). To suppress all borders, choose None.

DESCRIPTIONS OF THE HEADER AND FOOTER BUTTONS

On the Header and Footer tabs of the Page Setup dialog box are seven buttons that can be used to format, insert system codes, or insert pictures into the header or footer (see Figure 13.10).

Figure 13.10
Most views do not have a default header; however, most views have the printed page number as the default footer.

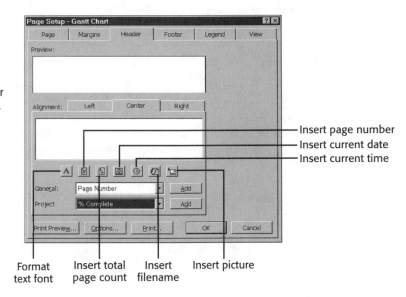

From left to right, the buttons shown in Figure 13.10 are described in the following list:

- **Format Text Font**—Displays the Font dialog box, where options for formatting font, font style, size, and color are available. Text you type, system codes inserted, or any of the project information items added from the General or Project Fields list boxes might be formatted using the Text Styles button. You must first highlight the text or code to be formatted before choosing the Font button.

- **Insert Page Number**—Inserts the code &[Page] for the current page number. Only the page number is printed. If you want the header or footer to display Page 2 where 2 represents the number of the page, you must type the word **Page** followed by the code. The header or footer would show Page &[Page].

- **Insert Total Page Count**—Inserts a code &[Pages] for the total number of pages. Only the number representing the total number of pages is printed. If you want the header or footer to display Page 2 of 10, where 2 represents the current page and 10 the total number of pages, you must type the word **Page** followed by the Page Number code; then type the word **of** followed by the Total Page Count code. The header or footer would show Page &[Page] of &[Pages].

- **Insert Current Date**—Inserts a code &[Date] in the header or footer that is based on the date in your computer system. This is used when you want to indicate the date your view or report was printed.

- **Insert Current Time**—Inserts a code &[Time] in the header or footer that is based on the time in your computer system. This is used when you want to indicate the time your view or report was printed.

Note

> It is very useful to print the date and time on your view and reports, especially if you are producing several revisions in a single day or over several days.

- **Insert File Name**—Inserts a code &[File] in the header or footer that reflects the name of the project file. The file extension (.MPP) is not displayed with the filename, unless you have Windows set to display file extensions.

- **Insert Picture**—Inserts any type of picture file including wmf, pcs, cgm, tif, bmp, and gif. This is particularly useful for inserting your company logo.

Best Practice Tips from Toby Brown, PMP

> Many times, a project plan is used during the initial proposal stage of a project as part of the Scope Statement, outlining the work that is going to be performed on behalf of a client. Including the client's company logo, downloaded from a Web site or scanned in to create a file, can easily customize and spruce up a proposal.

ENTERING HEADERS AND FOOTERS USING THE DROP-DOWN LIST BOXES

In addition to the header and footer buttons, you also can use the General or Project Fields drop-down list boxes to enter project data in the printed header and footer. These drop-down boxes are located toward the bottom of the Page Setup dialog box (refer to Figure 13.10).

The General drop-down list box contains the same data as provided by the Header and Footer insert buttons (such as Page Number), as well as data that comes from the Project Properties dialog box (such as Company Name).

Tip from Tim and the Project Team

P 2000

> If you want to insert the name of the project file, as well as the path to its location, use the new Filename and Path option in the General drop-down list. This option inserts the &[Filename and Path] code in your header or footer.

To access and fill in the Properties dialog box, choose File, Properties. The Properties dialog box was discussed in detail in Chapter 3, "Setting Up a New Project Document."

→ To learn how to effectively use properties, **see** "Using the Properties Sheet," **p. 69**

Using the Project Fields drop-down list box enables you to insert information specific to the project. It lists fields from your project that contain information about cost, duration, work, dates, and custom text and number fields.

The next section describes how to insert data from these lists into the header and footer.

ENTERING HEADERS AND FOOTERS

You can enter up to five lines of header text and three lines of footer text to repeat on each page of the printed document. You can type in the text you want to appear in the header and footer, or you can place codes that are replaced with system variables, such as the &[File] code that is replaced by the actual filename when the pages are printed.

Headers and footers can be aligned to the left, center, or right, by adding the text or code to the desired alignment tab (refer to Figure 13.10). In either the Header or Footer tab of the Page Setup dialog box, the Sample text box at the top of the tab shows what your header or footer will look like.

To enter a header or footer, follow these steps:

1. Select either the Header or Footer tab of the Page Setup dialog box.
2. Choose the desired Alignment tab (Left, Center, or Right).
3. Use the box below the Alignment tabs to type the appropriate text you want to appear on the header or footer.

   Or, choose one of the buttons to insert a system code—for example, page number, total page count, date, time, or filename.

   Or, select either the General or Project Fields drop-down box below the buttons to insert information from the project—for example, project name, project manager, project start date, or the name of a filter applied to the view. Scroll through the list, as there are many options to choose from. If you use one of the items in a drop-down box, click the Add button associated with that list box to insert the information into the header or footer.

4. If you want to format any of the text or codes in the header or footer, highlight the text or code and use the Font button. See Figure 13.11 for a sample header.

Best Practice Tips from Toby Brown, PMP

There are also keyboard shortcuts for applying formats. Select the text or code and use Ctrl+B to apply bold formatting. Ctrl+I italicizes, and Ctrl+U underlines the selection.

→ Appendix B contains a list of keyboard shortcuts you can use in Microsoft Project. **See** "Microsoft Project 2000 Shortcut Keys," **p. 1175**

The header in Figure 13.11 contains the Project Title, from the General drop-down list box, in the first line. In the second line, the word **Company:** was typed, followed by the Company Name code inserted from the General drop-down list box. The third line is blank to create some space in the header text area. In the forth line, **Project Length:** was typed followed by the Duration field code from the Project Fields drop-down list. After all the text was entered into the header, each line was selected and formatted using the Format Text Font button. Note: you are not restricted to applying the same format for the entire line. Line two in the header has the label Company: formatted with bold italic and the actual company name just bold.

Figure 13.11
Format the text using the Format Text Font button.

Using Legends

If the view you are printing has graphic elements (as do the Network Diagram, the Gantt Chart, and the Resource Graph), you can place a legend in the printout to explain the graphic elements used. Choose the Legend tab to display choices for configuring the display of the legend (see Figure 13.12).

Figure 13.12
The Legend tab of the Page Setup dialog box provides you with options for customizing the legend in your printout.

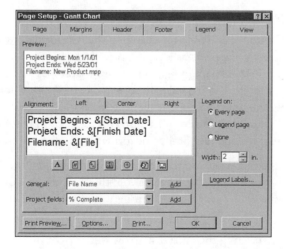

PART
IV

CH
13

You can enter up to three lines of legend text in each of the three alignment areas to repeat on each page of the printed document. Just as with the Header and Footer tabs, seven buttons on the Legend tab of the Page Setup dialog box can be used to format, insert system codes, or insert pictures into the legend. Additionally, the two drop-down list boxes enable you to insert information specific to the project.

The default legend displays the project title and the date the view or report was printed in the Left alignment tab.

The text area can occupy up to half the legend area. You regulate the width of the legend text area by typing a number from 0 to 5 in the Width box; the number represents how many inches of the legend area are devoted to the text. Typing a **0** means all the legend area is devoted to the graphical legends. Typing a **5** means five inches of the area is reserved for text. The default is two inches.

The formatting of the legend text is controlled through the Format Text Font button on the Legend tab, in the same manner as header and footer text.

The Legend On option enables you to select where to display the legend. Choose from the following:

- **Every Page**—Prints the legend at the bottom of each page.
- **Legend Page**—Prints the legend once on an extra page at the end of the report.
- **None**—Suppresses the display of a legend entirely.

Figure 13.12 shows a sample legend. The legend will be placed at the bottom of all pages. The start and finish dates for the project, as well as the project filename, will be printed in the legend text area. The text area occupies two inches of the legend area width. (Skip to Figure 13.20 for a sample legend that has a picture and the start date in the legend text area.)

FORMATTING HEADER, FOOTER, AND LEGEND TEXT

The Format Text Font button is available for changing the text formatting of header, footer, and/or legend text. This button appears as a capital A (refer to Figure 13.12) and is just to the left of the code buttons for inserting file and system variables, as discussed in the previous sections on headers, footers, and legends. To format any of the text or codes in the header, footer, or legend, you must first select the Alignment tab that has the text you want to format. Project gives you the options of formatting all the text on that tab the same, applying a different format to each line of text, or formatting individual words or codes.

It is necessary to select the text you want to format before you choose the Format Text Font button. When you click the Format Text Font button, the Font dialog box appears (see Figure 13.13).Use this dialog box to apply formatting to the text in the header, footer, or legend.

You can choose a font by selecting the entry list arrow to the right of the Font box. Choose the print attributes you want (bold, italic, or a combination) by selecting from the Font Style list box. Turn on underline by checking the Underline check box. After you choose the font and the font styles, choose the font point size (if multiple sizes are available) by selecting from the Size list box. If you are using a color printer or plotter, you also can choose the Color of the text. After all items are formatted, choose OK to return to the Page Setup dialog box.

Figure 13.13
The Font dialog box enables you to format all the text or apply a different format to each select line or words.

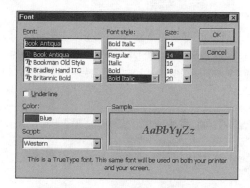

Tip from Tim and the Project Team

If the point size you want doesn't appear to be available, highlight the current font size and type the size in the box directly below the <u>S</u>ize heading for a custom font size.

Figure 13.13 shows the font as Book Antigua, with a font style of Bold Italic. The size is 14-point font with a blue color. Figure 13.14 shows these settings in Print Preview applied to the top line of a header.

Figure 13.14
A preview of the header, zoomed in. Each line or part of a line can be formatted differently.

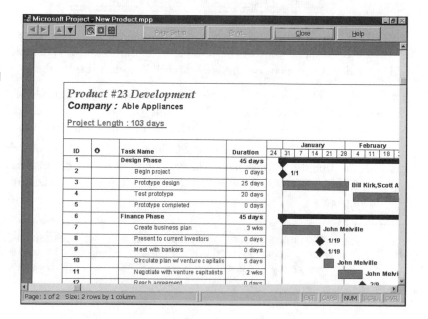

PART

IV

CH

13

After you configure all page setup options, choose OK to close the Page Setup dialog box. Alternatively, you might choose to preview your changes (as shown in Figure 13.14) or print directly from the Page Setup dialog box by using the Print Previe<u>w</u> or <u>P</u>rint buttons.

SELECTING SPECIAL OPTIONS FOR VIEWS

Choose the View tab in the Page Setup dialog box, shown in Figure 13.15, to see options specific to the view being printed. These settings are for all views except the Calendar view. Some options on the View tab do not apply to all views and are dimmed to indicate they are inactive for these views.

Figure 13.15
The View tab of the Page Setup dialog box, for all views except the Calendar view.

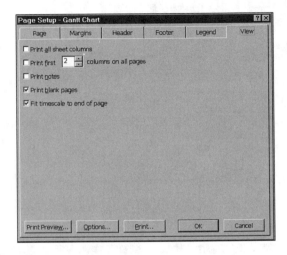

The View tab displays some of the most valuable print settings. When printing the Calendar view, the options on the View tab will be different from those listed here:

- For views with sheets—such as the Gantt Chart, Delay Gantt, Detail Gantt, Task Sheet, and Resource Sheet—click the Print All Sheet Columns check box to print all columns of the sheet, regardless of whether they are completely visible on the screen.

- Select the check box for Print First *x* Columns on All Pages to override the default of only printing the ID numbers, indicators, and task names on the first column of pages (refer to Figure 13.15). This option allows you to print a specified number of columns on all pages.

Best Practice Tips from Toby Brown, PMP

> This feature allowing you to print a specified number of columns on all pages is especially useful if you don't have access to a plotter, or if you don't intend to tape a multiple-page project together to make one large sheet. Also, printing blank pages as outlined below might also be unchecked for the same reason.

- Select the Print Notes check box to print notes that have been entered for tasks or resources.

Best Practice Tips from Toby Brown, PMP

Printing out the notes for your project plan creates a separate addendum page along with the chart that is being printed. This is particularly important to communicate the scope, constraints, assumptions, and limitations of the project if they have been included in the Notes field of the start milestone. (Thus, a good rule of thumb is to include these important pieces of information along with your start milestone.)

- Uncheck the Print Blank Pages option to suppress the printing of blank pages. The default is for all pages to print.

- Leave the check box for Fit Timescale to End of Page checked to ensure that a timescale unit (a week, for example) does not break across pages.

The following options are available for the Calendar view on the View tab of the Page Setup dialog box (see Figure 13.16):

- Select Months Per Page and choose either 1 or 2 months on a page.

- Marking the Only Show Days in Month check box will display a blank box indicating a day from another month, like a placeholder. However, the calendar will not display the dates or tasks in boxes for days in other months. For example, if September is the current month and the 1st of September begins on a Tuesday, then the dates and tasks for Sunday and Monday of that week (August 30th and 31st respectively) do not display on the printout.

- If you mark the Only Show Weeks in Month check box, only those weeks from the month are displayed. Weeks from other months are not printed. If the Calendar view is displaying six weeks—all five weeks in September and a week in October—only those weeks in September will print. The printout will not reflect the sixth week (in October).

- Select Weeks Per Page and type the number of weeks in the entry box. This is very useful if you have many tasks and want to print one or two weeks on a page. If you have more than eight weeks per page, the information becomes unreadable.

Figure 13.16
The View tab of the Page Setup dialog box, for the Calendar view.

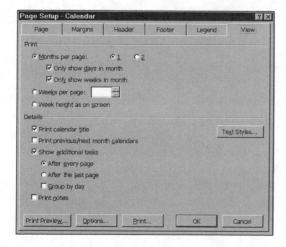

- Use the Week Height as on Screen option if you want the printed calendar to match the week height on the screen display of Calendar view.

- The calendar title is printed at the top of each page when the Print Calendar Title check box is marked. You can change the format of the title by choosing Format, Timescale.

- Select the Print Previous/Next Month Calendars option to have miniature calendars of the previous and next months appear in the upper-left and upper-right corners of the printed calendar. Only the dates are printed for the miniatures; no project information is displayed.

- The Show Additional Tasks option is used when more tasks exist than can be displayed on the calendar. You have the choice of printing these overflow tasks After Every Page or After the Last Page. The default for displaying additional tasks is After Every Page.

  The Group by Day check box displays the overflow page with each day listed. If a task occurs across several days, it will be listed beneath every date the task is being worked on. By default this check box is not selected, and the additional tasks are listed once, based on the day the task starts.

- Check the Print Notes option to print the notes for the tasks. The notes are printed on a separate page after the calendar or overflow page. The task ID and name appear with the note.

- The Text Styles button allows you to format the font type; font style, size, and color for all printed text; monthly titles; previous/next month miniature calendars; or overflow tasks (see Figure 13.17).

Figure 13.17
For Calendar view, you have the option to format the way certain text appears when printed.

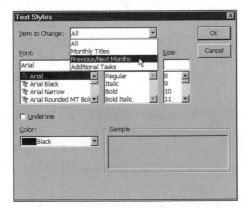

USING PRINT PREVIEW

 You can choose File, Print Preview (or the Print Preview button from the toolbar) to preview onscreen the look of the printed document. You also can choose the Print Preview button in the Page Setup dialog box. Figure 13.18 shows the Print Preview screen for the settings illustrated to this point in this chapter.

Figure 13.18
Always preview before you print.

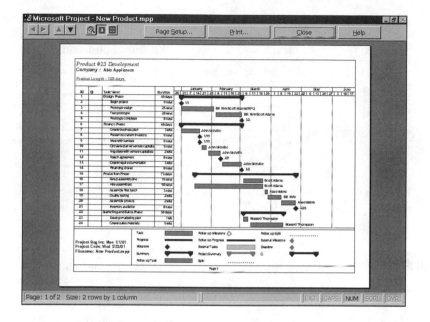

The initial preview screen shows the entire first page of the view being printed. If multiple pages exist, you can use the buttons at the top left of the preview screen to scroll left, right, up, and down one page at a time (see Table 13.1). You can zoom in on the details of a page by choosing the Zoom button or by using the mouse pointer, which changes to a magnifying glass when positioned over a page. Simply click the part of the page you want to see in greater detail. The magnifying glass only appears while the pointer is over the page (otherwise, the pointer is an arrow).

Best Practice Tips from Toby Brown, PMP

This is particularly important on larger projects that have been created. Within the status bar in the lower-left corner of the screen, the total number of pages to be printed will be displayed. It is important to ensure that what is being printed is precisely what is required by the project manager in order to avoid wasting paper and tying up a network printer.

PART

IV

CH

13

TABLE 13.1   THE PRINT PREVIEW BUTTONS

Button	Effect	Keyboard Shortcut
◀	Move left one page	Alt+left arrow
▶	Move right one page	Alt+right arrow
▲	Move up one page	Alt+up arrow
▼	Move down one page	Alt+down arrow

TABLE 13.1 CONTINUED

Button	Effect	Keyboard Shortcut
	Zoom in on one page	Alt+1 (one) (Click area of page to zoom in to.)
	View one full page	Alt+2 (Click specific page to view.)
	View multiple pages	Alt+3 (Click area outside of page.)

Use Alt+Z to switch between the Zoom, One Page, and Multiple Page views. The Alt+1, 2, and 3 shortcuts only work with the numbers above the alphanumeric keys, not those on the number pad.

Note

If the Print Blank Pages option on the View tab of the Page Setup dialog box is not checked, blank pages are displayed with a gray shaded background and are not printed.

Figure 13.19 shows the zoomed-in view of the title area of the first page 1 of a Gantt Chart view, and Figure 13.20 shows the zoomed-in legend text area in the bottom-left corner of the same page, which includes a picture in the legend text area. Figure 13.21 illustrates the multiple-page preview of the same report. Note that Figure 13.21 shows eight pages and the status line indicates that the size of the printout will be two rows by four columns. Pages are numbered down the columns, starting from the left. Therefore, page two of the report is the bottom page in the left column onscreen.

Figure 13.19
A preview of a Gantt Chart, zoomed in to show the title area.

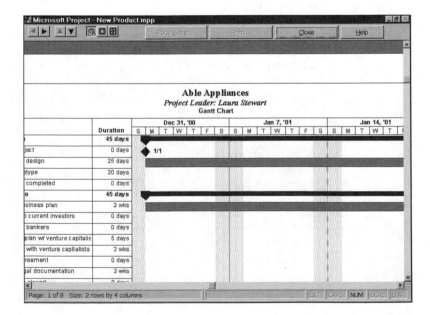

Figure 13.20
A preview of a Gantt Chart, zoomed in to see the legend area.

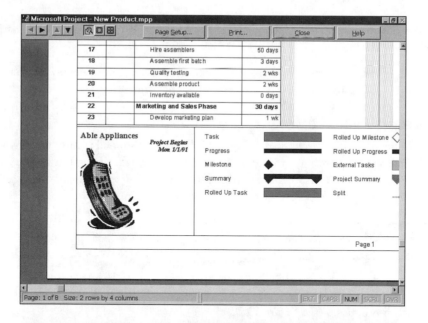

Figure 13.21
The multi-page view of a Gantt Chart, in the preview screen.

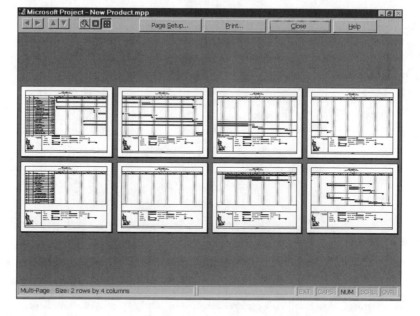

You can open the Page Setup dialog box from the Print Preview screen by choosing the Page Setup button at the top of the preview screen. If you have a question about one of the available options, choose the Help button for context-sensitive online help. When you are ready to print, choose the Print button (see the following section). To make modifications, or if you decide against printing at this time, choose the Close button to return to the project view.

Tip from Tim and the Project Team

Ctrl+P is a shortcut key combination that you can use instead of choosing File, Print.

After you have established the print options, these settings become a permanent part of the project file. You can change the settings at any time.

USING THE PRINT COMMAND

When the view is refined onscreen and the page setup and printer options are selected, the final step in printing is to choose File, Print. The Print dialog box appears and presents you with choices for printing the current screen view. You also can choose the Print button from the Print Preview screen or the Print button from the toolbar.

Caution

The Print button on the toolbar sends the view to the printer directly, without first presenting the dialog box where you choose your print options.

When you choose File, Print or select the Print button in the preview screen, the Print dialog box appears (see Figure 13.22).

Figure 13.22
Choose what to print, the quality of the printout, and the number of copies from the Print dialog box.

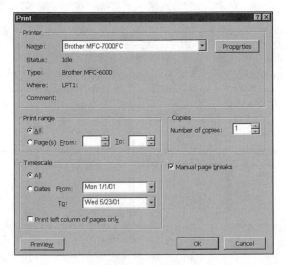

Some options on the Print dialog box do not apply to all views and might be dimmed to indicate they are inactive for the view you are printing.

SELECTING THE PAGES TO PRINT

In the Preview screen, you can see the number of pages that will print. When you display the Print dialog box, the default is to print all pages, as indicated in the All option of the Print Range area. If you only want to print some of the pages, enter the starting page number in the Page(s) From box and the ending page number in the To box. To reprint just page five of a view, for example, type **5** in both the Page(s) From and To fields. On views that include a timescale, the default is to print from the start date of the project through the finish date. You can limit the printed output to a specific time span. See the upcoming section, "Printing Views with a Timescale," for details.

If you embedded manual page breaks in a task list or a resource list, these page breaks are not used in printing unless the Manual Page Breaks check box is marked. Unmark the check box if you want to ignore the manual page breaks.

Note

Printing with manual page breaks is inappropriate if you previously sorted the list for a particular report, because the manual page breaks make no sense in the sorted order. See earlier sections in this chapter—"Sorting and Grouping the Display" and "Setting and Clearing Page Breaks"—for more information.

SELECTING THE NUMBER OF COPIES

For multiple copies of a view, enter a number in the Number of Copies box. You must collate the multiple copies by hand because Microsoft Project instructs the printer to print all copies of the first page, and then all copies of the second page, and so on.

PRINTING VIEWS WITH A TIMESCALE

For views that contain timescales, you can print the full date range of the project, from the start date to the finish date of the project, which is the default setting. Alternatively, you can print the timescale data for a limited range of dates. Choose the All option button to print the entire project, or choose the Dates From option button to specify a limited range of dates. Enter the starting date in the Dates From box and the ending date in the To box.

 Reminder—the screen display dictates whether the information is printed showing weeks, months, quarters, or years. Choose View, Zoom or choose the Zoom In/Zoom Out buttons on the Standard toolbar to change the timescale on the screen.

Choose the Print Left Column of Pages Only check box to print only the pages on the far left in Print Preview, Multi-Page Layout. If you refer to Figure 13.22, for example, the two pages that contain the task names are the left column of pages.

SENDING THE VIEW TO THE PRINTER

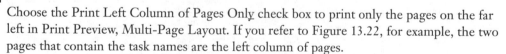 Before you print the document, you should preview it, especially if you have made changes in the Print dialog box. You can choose the Preview button in the Print dialog box or the Print Preview button in the Page Setup dialog box to review the effects of the choices you made. If you are not currently viewing the Print or Page Setup dialog boxes, you also might access Print Preview by using the Print Preview button on the Standard toolbar. If you selected a limited number of pages to print, the Print Preview screen still shows the entire report. Nevertheless, when you are actually printing, only the selected pages are printed.

To start the print job, choose OK in the Print dialog box . Or you can use the Print button on the Standard toolbar.

Note

The Print button causes data to be sent to the printer immediately; you do not get a chance to make selections in the Print dialog box.

PRINTING STANDARD REPORTS

Project has designed reports for you to use; you can customize these reports, or create your own reports. The 25 predesigned reports have been divided into five standard categories of reports and are available by choosing View, Reports. Choose this command to display the Reports dialog box shown in Figure 13.23.

Figure 13.23
Select one of the categories on the Reports dialog box to choose from several impressive built-in reports.

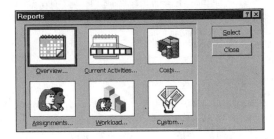

Double-click the category of reports that you want to view, or click a category and choose Select. A subsequent dialog box lists the individual reports available for each category. Table 13.2 lists those individual reports.

TABLE 13.2 THE STANDARD, PREDEFINED REPORTS

Category	Report Name
Overview	Project Summary
	Top-Level Tasks
	Critical Tasks
	Milestones
	Working Days
Current Activities	Unstarted Tasks
	Tasks Starting Soon
	Tasks In Progress
	Completed Tasks
	Should Have Started Tasks
	Slipping Tasks
Costs	Cash Flow
	Budget
	Overbudget Tasks
	Overbudget Resources
	Earned Value
Assignments	Who Does What
	Who Does What When
	To-do List
	Overallocated Resources
Workload	Task Usage
	Resource Usage

The Custom category accesses a dialog box with numerous preformatted reports, many of which were in the categories previously discussed.

After a report has been selected, you are taken into the Print Preview screen. From there, you can access the Page Setup and Print dialog boxes. To print a report, simply choose the Print button in the preview screen.

The Page Setup dialog box, the Print Preview screen, and the Print dialog box options are used the same way for reports as for the views, as discussed in earlier sections of this chapter. Due to the nature of the reports, some of the Page Setup and Print options might not be available. See the earlier sections "Changing the Page Setup" and "Using the Print Command" for more information on these options.

→ To learn more about the built-in reports in Microsoft Project, **see** "Using the Standard Reports," **p. 987**

→ To alter the existing reports or create your own reports, **see** "Customizing Reports," **p. 1013**

TROUBLESHOOTING

VIEW APPEARANCE AND PRINTOUT DON'T MATCH

I've changed the display in the Gantt Chart view to view only the task ID by moving the partition to the far left. Yet both the ID and the Indicator columns continue to be printed.

By default, the ID and Indicator columns are both printed on the Gantt Chart even if you change the screen display to show only the ID column. First make sure that only the ID column is being displayed on the screen. Then edit the table that is currently being used in the view by choosing View, Table, More Tables. Choose the Edit button to display the Table Definition dialog box. You need to uncheck the Lock First Column check box. When this box is not checked, only the first column, ID, will print.

USING MANUAL PAGE BREAKS

Project is ignoring the manual page breaks I have set.

Check the Print dialog box and make sure that there is an X in the Manual Page Breaks check box.

AVOID GANTT CHART TIMESCALE TRUNCATION

When I print my Gantt Chart view, the timescale begins flush to the task names columns. It also chops off my resource names on the last few tasks of the printout because they extend beyond the finish date. How do I avoid this?

By default, the start and end dates of the project are displayed in the Timescale section of the Print dialog box. This causes the printout to display the beginning of the Gantt Chart bars flush against the task names on the left side of the printed view. It also has the printout stop when the last task is completed, regardless of whether or not the resource names printed to the right of the last few taskbars can be seen.

You will want to display a gap between the table-side of the Gantt Chart and the beginning of the taskbars and leave a few extra days at the end of the printed project view. You can accomplish this by changing the Dates From entry to a date slightly earlier (two or three days) than the beginning of the project. This starts the Gantt Chart timescale at that date, which pushes all taskbars slightly to the right for better display on paper. If you can't see the resource names on the last few tasks, extend the Dates To entry slightly (two or three days). Use the Preview button to see how this will look before you begin printing your pages.

CHAPTER 14

PUBLISHING PROJECTS ON THE WEB

In this chapter

OVERVIEW OF PROJECT 2000'S INTERNET FEATURES

Project 2000 has many powerful features that integrate it with the Internet. Consistent with Word, PowerPoint, Excel, and Access, Microsoft Project includes a Save As Web Page feature that lets you save your project as an HTML document that can be published to your Internet Web site or corporate intranet (see Figure 14.1).

Figure 14.1
Select Microsoft Project 2000's Save As Web Page menu item to save your project as a Web document.

In addition, Project 2000's other Web features include

- The ability to create an Import/Export map, which allows you to select the specific task, resource, and resource assignment fields to be included in your HTML document.

- The ability to set up templates for your Microsoft Project Web pages to include graphics for your company logo, custom backgrounds and colors, and fonts that you specify.

- Several Web-related task and resource fields that store information as hyperlinks, which can be used to navigate to Web sites on the Internet or to documents stored on your Web server.

- The ability to communicate project information via the Internet or your corporate Intranet using Project 2000's new Web client (for more information on this topic, see Chapter 15, "Using Microsoft Project in Workgroups").

- The ability to save your project as a Microsoft Project Database (MPD) file, which can be used to generate Web pages that contain dynamic content from your project plan.

- A Microsoft Project template which includes all the tasks for designing, rolling out, and supporting a corporate intranet.

The remainder of this chapter describes in detail each of these topics, including many real-world examples of how you can integrate Microsoft Project 2000 with the Internet.

NAVIGATING WITH HYPERLINKS

The purpose of this section is to introduce you to some basic Internet concepts and terminology, which provide the foundation for moving forward with how Microsoft Project 2000 integrates with the Web.

Applications that are used to view documents on the Internet are called *Web browsers*. The two most popular Web browsers that dominate the industry are Netscape Navigator and Microsoft Internet Explorer. The latest version of the Microsoft Web browser, Internet Explorer, is included free on the Project 2000 CD. A browser lets you navigate to a specific Internet site by referencing its Web address, also known as its *URL (Uniform Resource Locator)*. For example, the URL for Microsoft's home page is `http://www.microsoft.com/`. By typing this URL in the address field of Internet Explorer (see Figure 14.2), the browser will navigate you directly to this site.

Figure 14.2
Microsoft's home page as viewed through Internet Explorer 5.0.

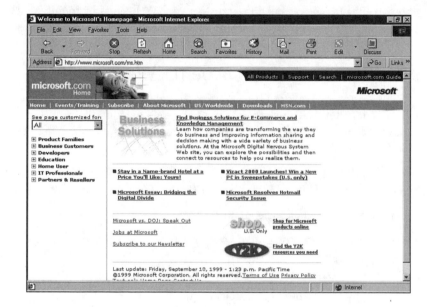

Hyperlinks provide the capability to quickly and easily jump from one document to a related document by simply clicking a graphic or underlined text. For example, Windows Online Help frequently uses hyperlinks to jump from one topic to another within the help file.

The Internet has expanded the concept of hyperlinking in that a Web page on the Internet can navigate someone to another Web page stored on a server anywhere in the world.

A Web page (or Web document) is formatted using *Hypertext Markup Language*, or *HTML*. The HTML code contains all the text, formatting, font and color information, and references to graphics that determine how a document will display in a Web browser. In addition, the HTML code might include hyperlinks that can navigate someone to another location on the Web.

PART

IV

CH

14

Note

Just a few years ago, the only way to create documents for a Web site was to become an expert in writing HTML code (or hiring someone to do it for you). Fortunately, Microsoft Project (as well as the other Office 2000 applications) will automatically generate the HTML code for you when you select the Save As Web Page option. After the HTML document is created, it can be opened directly into Internet Explorer (or any other Web browser) so you can immediately see how your documents will look when they are published on the Web.

Later in this chapter, in the section "Modifying Project's HTML Templates," you will learn how to enhance the overall appearance of your Web pages by modifying the HTML code created from Project 2000 to include specific font references and background graphics.

EXPORTING PROJECT DATA TO WEB PAGES

In this section, we will step through several examples of saving your project as an HTML document. After we complete each example, we'll open up the resulting HTML file in Internet Explorer so we can immediately see what it would look like if it were published on the Web.

For each of the following examples, we will be using the `New Product.mpp` file that is included on the *Special Edition Using Microsoft Project 2000* CD in the following location:

    \source\chap01\New Product.mpp

If you prefer, you can use one of your Project files for these examples.

SAVING YOUR PROJECT AS AN HTML DOCUMENT

To save a project as an HTML document, follow these steps:

1. Open your Project file, and select File, Save As Web Page. This will open the Save As dialog box (see Figure 14.3).

Figure 14.3
The Microsoft Project Save As dialog box allows you to save your project as an HTML document.

2. Navigate to the directory where you want to save the document, and type the name of the HTML document in the File Name field. The document will automatically be assigned the .HTML extension.

3. Click the Save button, and the Export Mapping dialog box will open (see Figure 14.4).

Figure 14.4
Microsoft Project 2000's Export Mapping dialog box allows you to select an Import/Export map on which to base your HTML document.

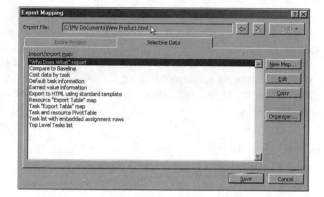

4. Click the New Map button, and the Define Import/Export Map dialog box opens (see Figure 14.5).

Figure 14.5
The Define Import/Export Map dialog box allows you to define the type of project data (tasks, resources, and assignments) you want to export to your HTML document.

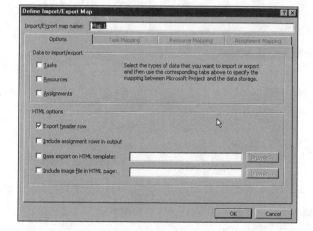

Note

An Import/Export map allows you to define the type of information to be included in your HTML document. You can create an Import/Export map that exports task data, resource data, resource assignment data, or any combination of the three. After you select which type of data to export, you will then select the specific fields you want to export to your HTML document.

5. In the Import/Export Map Name text box at the top of the dialog box, type a descriptive name for the Import/Export map. For example, if this map will contain task schedule information, type **Task Schedule Map** in this field.

6. In the Data to Import/Export section, select one or more check boxes for the type of data you want to export (refer to Figure 14.5).

Note

For each type of project data you select in the Define Import/Export Map dialog box (Tasks, Resources, or Assignments), the corresponding tab on the dialog box will be enabled (Task Mapping, Resource Mapping, or Assignment Mapping). When you select the Task Mapping, Resource Mapping, or Assignment Mapping tab of the dialog box, you will be presented with a screen that gives you the ability to select the specific fields to be exported for that type of project data.

7. Select the tab corresponding to the type of data you are exporting (for example, Task Mapping), and the Define Import/Export Map dialog box will display the mapping options for that type of data (see Figure 14.6).

Figure 14.6
This figure shows Microsoft Project 2000's Define Import/Export Map dialog box displaying Task Mapping options. This dialog box is used to select the specific task, resource, or resource assignment fields to be exported to your HTML document.

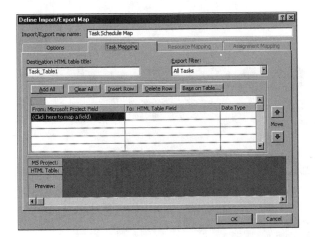

Note

Each type of data you export (tasks, resources, and assignments) will be displayed in a separate table in the HTML document.

8. In the Destination HTML Table Title field, type a descriptive name for the table, which will be generated in the HTML file for this data type. For example, if you are defining task fields to be exported for a new widget development project, you could type the name **New Widget Project Tasks**. This descriptive name will be displayed above the corresponding table in the HTML file (see Figure 14.7).

Figure 14.7
The Destination HTML Table Title text box shows the title "New Widget Project Tasks." This title will display above the task table in your HTML document.

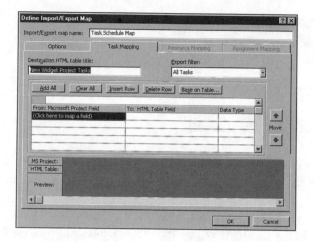

9. From the Export Filter drop-down list, select the filter to be used for the tasks or resources you are exporting to an HTML file. If you want to export all the tasks or resources from your project, select the corresponding filter (All Tasks or All Resources).

Note

The Export filter only applies to Task Mapping and Resource Mapping, because filters do not exist for assignments in Microsoft Project.

Tip from Tim and the Project Team

If you have not yet created the task or resource filter to be used with this Import/Export map, you can click the OK button to close the dialog box, create the filter, and select Save As Web Page once again to continue where you left off.

10. The next step in setting up your Import/Export map is to define which fields you want to export to your HTML document. For example, to create a task schedule table, you would most likely select the ID, Name, Start, Finish, and Duration fields to be exported to the HTML document.

Tip from Tim and the Project Team

If you have an existing Microsoft Project table that contains the same fields you want to export to your HTML document, click the Base on Table button and select the existing table on which you want to base your HTML table (see Figure 14.8).

PART

IV

CH

14

Figure 14.8
The Select Base Table for Field Mapping dialog box allows you to select an existing Microsoft Project table on which to base your HTML table.

11. In the From: Microsoft Project Field column, click the (Click here to map a field) cell. From the drop-down list, select the first field you want to include in your table.

Tip from Tim and the Project Team

A quick way to select the field you want from the drop-down list is to type the first letter of the field name after you have clicked the list. This will navigate you directly to the fields that start with that letter, rather than having to scroll down the entire list. This technique will work on any drop-down list in a Windows application.

12. If you would like to display a header for this field other than the Microsoft Project field name in your HTML document, click the To: HTML File Field column, and type the new name you would like to use. For example, you might want to display Task ID as the column header instead of ID in your HTML document.

13. Repeat steps 11 and 12 for each field you want to export to your HTML document (see Figure 14.9).

    Also, you can change the order of the fields in your table by clicking the Move Up and Move Down arrows on the right of the dialog box.

Figure 14.9
This figure shows the Define Import/Export Map dialog box with several task-related fields selected.

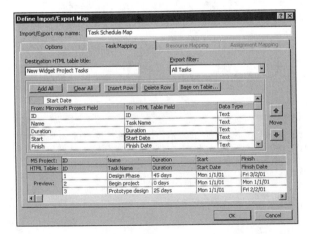

Note

As you build your table, you can use the Insert Row and Delete Row buttons to add or delete fields to your table. Or, you can use the Add All button to add every field for the corresponding data type to the table. Although this sounds intriguing, it is unlikely you will want to create a huge table in your HTML document containing every field available in Microsoft Project for that data type!

14. After you have selected the fields you want to export for this data type, repeat steps 7 through 13 for each of the other data types you are exporting.

15. Click the OK button to close the Define Import/Export Map dialog box, and click the Save button to save your project as an HTML document.

Note

The Import/Export map is automatically saved in your GLOBAL.MPT file, and will be available for all your other future projects.

VIEWING YOUR PROJECT AS AN HTML DOCUMENT

Now, you get to view the HTML file that was created in your Web browser. Start up your Web browser. For this example, we will be using Internet Explorer, but Netscape has a similar option.

To view your project, follow these steps:

1. Select File, Open, and the Open dialog box will open. Click the Browse button to navigate to your HTML file and click Open.

2. From the Open dialog box, click the OK button (see Figure 14.10), and your Web browser will display the HTML document you created in Microsoft Project (see Figure 14.11).

Figure 14.10
The Microsoft Internet Explorer Open dialog box allows you to open a Web document by referring to its Internet address or filename.

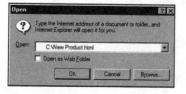

Figure 14.11
This figure shows Microsoft Internet Explorer displaying the HTML document created from your project.

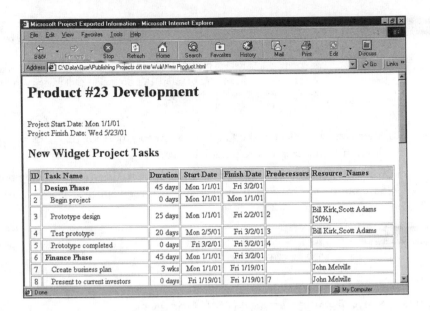

DEFINING IMPORT/EXPORT MAP HTML OPTIONS

Now that you have created your first HTML document from Microsoft Project, let's examine some of the other available options you can choose when exporting your Project:

1. Open a plan in Microsoft Project, and select File, Save As Web Page.

2. From the Save As dialog box, navigate to the directory in which you want to save the document.

3. Type the name of the HTML document in the File Name field.

4. Click the Save button, and the Export Format dialog box will open (see Figure 14.12).

Figure 14.12
The Export Format dialog box allows you to select the Import/Export map on which you want to base your HTML document.

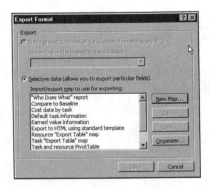

5. From the Import/Export Map to Use for Exporting list box, select the Task Schedule Map used in the previous example and click the Edit button. The Define Import/ Export Map dialog box will display.

Note

If you prefer to keep your original map intact, you can click the Copy button to make an exact copy of your first map.

6. The Export Header Row option on the Define Import/Export Map dialog box will export the HTML file field names to the first row of the table in your HTML document (see Figure 14.13). If you do not check this option, the first row of the table will contain the actual data (see Figure 14.14).

Figure 14.13
This figure shows the HTML document displayed with the task field names in the first row of the table (for example, Task ID, Task Name, and so on) because the Export Header Row option was checked in the Define Import/Export Map dialog box.

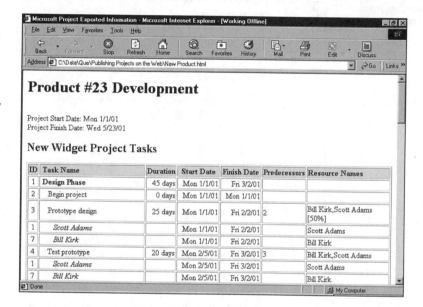

Figure 14.14
This figure shows the HTML document displayed without the task field names in the first row of the table because the Export Header Row option was not checked in the Define Import/Export Map dialog box.

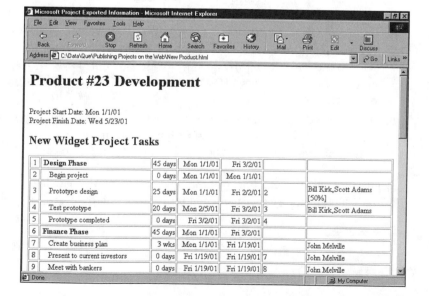

7. If you want to include the resources assigned to each task directly below the task row in your HTML document, check the Include Assignment Rows in Output option in the Define Import/Export Map dialog box. Figure 14.15 shows the results of selecting this option as displayed in Internet Explorer 5.0.

Figure 14.15
The task table in your HTML document displayed with resource assignments below each task.

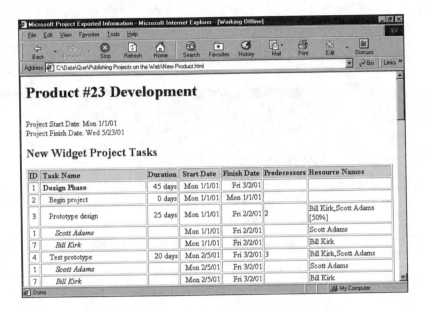

8. Microsoft Project includes several HTML templates on which you can base your HTML document. These templates contain formatting and other information that determine how your document will display in your Web browser.

The Base Export on HTML Template option in the Define Import/Export Map dialog box allows you to select the HTML template on which you want to base your HTML document. To select a template for your HTML document, check the Base Export on HTML Template option. Then, click the Browse button to select the template you want to use for your HTML document. These templates are typically stored in the `Program Files\Microsoft Office\Templates\1033\Microsoft Project` Web directory on your computer.

9. After you have selected the appropriate options in the Define Import/Export Map dialog box, click OK, and the Export Format dialog box will display. Click the Save button, and your project will be saved as an HTML document.

The next section discusses how you can modify the HTML templates that come with Project 2000 to improve the layout and format of a Microsoft Project Web page.

MODIFYING PROJECT'S HTML TEMPLATES

In this section, you will explore some of the ways you can change the HTML templates that come with Microsoft Project 2000. You can actually modify the HTML code that is contained within a template to change several characteristics of the template's appearance, including

- The background color of the HTML document
- Defining a background graphic for the template
- Adding graphic images, such as a company logo, to your Web page
- Changing the text that appears in the title bar of your browser when displaying your Web page
- Defining the font type, color, size, and justification of the HTML header
- Adding hyperlinks to other Web pages on the Internet or your corporate intranet
- Adding the capability to send an email directly from your Web page

In each of the following examples, you will walk through the process of modifying the `Centered Mist Dark.html` template that comes with Project 2000. The `Centered Mist Dark.html` template is a text document that can be edited in any text editor such as Notepad, or if you prefer, a Web design program such as Microsoft FrontPage or a word processor such as Microsoft Word.

As you proceed through each of the following examples, you will continue to add modifications to the `Centered Mist Dark.html` template to create a highly customized, professional-looking Web page.

CHANGING THE BACKGROUND COLOR OF YOUR WEB PAGE

In the first example, you will change the background color of the template to a light blue. Use the following steps to edit the `Centered Mist Dark.html` template:

1. From your text editor, open the `Centered Mist Dark.html` file, typically located in the `Program Files\Microsoft Office\Templates\1033\Microsoft Project` Web directory (see Listing 14.1).

LISTING 14.1 HTML CODE FROM THE `Standard Export.html` FILE

```
<!--      MICROSOFT PROJECT HTML EXPORT TEMPLATE

     TEMPLATE NAME     : Centered Mist Dark.html
     TEMPLATE STYLE    : Centered
     COLOR SCHEME      : Mist Dark
     IMAGE PLACEHOLDER : Yes
     TABLE PLACEHOLDERS : Task/Resource/Assignment
-->
```

LISTING 14.1 CONTINUED

```html
<HTML>
<HEAD>
<META HTTP-EQUIV="Content-Type" CONTENT="text/html; charset=windows-1252">
<TITLE>Microsoft Project Exported Information</TITLE>
</HEAD>

<!-- ******* BACKGROUND, LINK, AND FONT COLORS ******* -->

<BODY BGCOLOR="#336666" TEXT="#336666" LINK="#ADA990" VLINK="#D6E0E0" ALINK=
"#ADA990" TOPMARGIN="30" LEFTMARGIN="5">
<DIV ALIGN="CENTER">

<!-- ******* PROJECT TITLE ******* -->

<FONT COLOR="#ADA990" SIZE="7" FACE="Arial Narrow">
<B>
<!--MSProjectTemplate_ProjectTitle-->
</B>
</FONT>
<BR><BR>
<HR NOSHADE WIDTH="75%" COLOR="#ADA990">

<!-- ******* PROJECT IMAGE ******* -->

<BR>
<!--MSProjectTemplate_Image-->
<BR>

<!-- ******* START AND FINISH DATE ******* -->

<BR>
<TABLE>
<TR>
    <TD ALIGN="RIGHT">
    <FONT COLOR="#ADA990" SIZE="2" FACE="Arial">
    <B>
    Project Start:
    <BR>
    Project Finish:
    </B>
    </FONT>
    </TD>
    <TD ALIGN="LEFT">
    <FONT COLOR="#D6E0E0" SIZE="2" FACE="Arial">
    <B>
    <!--MSProjectTemplate_StartDate-->
    <BR>
    <!--MSProjectTemplate_FinishDate-->
    </B>
    </FONT>
    </TD>
</TR>
</TABLE>
```

LISTING 14.1   CONTINUED

```
<BR><BR>

<!-- ******* TASK TABLE TITLE ******* -->

<P ALIGN="CENTER">
<FONT SIZE="5" COLOR="#D6E0E0" FACE="Arial Narrow">
<B>
<!--MSProjectTemplate_TaskTableTitle-->
</B>
</FONT>
</P>
<HR NOSHADE WIDTH="50%" COLOR="#D6E0E0">

<!-- ******* TASK TABLE ******* -->

<DIV ALIGN="CENTER">
<TABLE BORDER="2" CELLPADDING="2" BGCOLOR="#ADA990" BORDERCOLOR="#ADA990"
BORDERCOLORDARK="#ADA990" BORDERCOLORLIGHT="#ADA990">
<TR>
    <TD>
    <!--MSProjectTemplate_TaskTable-->
    </TD>
</TR>
</TABLE>
</DIV>
<BR>

<!-- ******* RESOURCE TABLE TITLE ******* -->

<P ALIGN="CENTER">
<FONT SIZE="5" COLOR="#D6E0E0" FACE="Arial Narrow">
<B>
<!--MSProjectTemplate_ResourceTableTitle-->
</B>
</FONT>
</P>
<HR NOSHADE WIDTH="50%" COLOR="#D6E0E0">

<!-- ******* RESOURCE TABLE ******* -->

<DIV ALIGN="CENTER">
<TABLE BORDER="2" CELLPADDING="2" BGCOLOR="#ADA990" BORDERCOLOR="#ADA990"
BORDERCOLORDARK="#ADA990" BORDERCOLORLIGHT="#ADA990">
<TR>
    <TD>
    <!--MSProjectTemplate_ResourceTable-->
    </TD>
</TR>
</TABLE>
</DIV>
<BR>

<!-- ******* ASSIGNMENT TABLE TITLE ******* -->

<P ALIGN="CENTER">
```

Listing 14.1   Continued

```
<FONT SIZE=5 COLOR="#D6E0E0" FACE="Arial Narrow">
<B>
<!--MSProjectTemplate_AssignmentTableTitle-->
</B>
</FONT>
</P>
<HR NOSHADE WIDTH="50%" COLOR="#D6E0E0">

<!-- ******* ASSIGNMENT TABLE ******* -->

<DIV ALIGN="CENTER">
<TABLE BORDER="2" CELLPADDING="2" BGCOLOR="#ADA990" BORDERCOLOR="#ADA990"
BORDERCOLORDARK="#ADA990" BORDERCOLORLIGHT="#ADA990">
<TR>
    <TD>
    <!--MSProjectTemplate_AssignmentTable-->
    </TD>
</TR>
</TABLE>
</DIV>
<BR>

<!-- ******* MICROSOFT LINKS ******* -->

<P ALIGN="CENTER">
<BR>
<FONT FACE="Arial" SIZE="1">
<A HREF="http://www.microsoft.com/isapi/redir.dll?prd=msft&plcid=0x0409&ar=
home">
Microsoft Home Page
</A>
<BR>
<A HREF="http://www.microsoft.com/isapi/redir.dll?prd=msproject&sbp=&plcid=
0x0409&pver=8.0&ar=home">
Microsoft Project Home Page
</A>
</FONT>
</P>

</DIV>

</BODY>
</HTML>
```

2. From your text editor, save this file with the name Export Project with Custom Options.Html, or you can save the file using any name you want.

3. In the HTML template, look for the section that begins with the heading <!-- ******* BACKGROUND, LINK, AND FONT COLORS ******* -->. Immediately following this heading, you will see a line that begins with the text <BODY BGCOLOR="#336666". Change the BGCOLOR setting from "#336666" to "#CCFFFF".

Note

The BGCOLOR= parameter tells your Web browser the background color to use when displaying your HTML document. If you leave out the BGCOLOR= parameter, your browser will typically display the Web document with a gray background. The #CCFFFF used in the previous example is the hexadecimal representation of the light blue color for the background of the Web page.

Tip from Tim and the Project Team

A great way to figure out the hexadecimal value for your desired background color is to create a new document using Microsoft Word (version 97 or later), and save it as an HTML file. Then, select Format, Background, and Word will display a dialog box, which will allow you to graphically select a background color for your document (see Figure 14.16). After you have selected the background color, select View, HTML Source. Microsoft Word will display the source for the HTML document (see Listing 14.2).

From the line <body bgcolor="#99ccff" lang=EN-US style= 'tab-interval:.5in'>, copy the hexadecimal value or name of the BGCOLOR setting and set the BGCOLOR in your Microsoft Project template equal to the same value.

Figure 14.16
You can select a background color in Microsoft Word to help figure out the hexadecimal value of the background color for your HTML document.

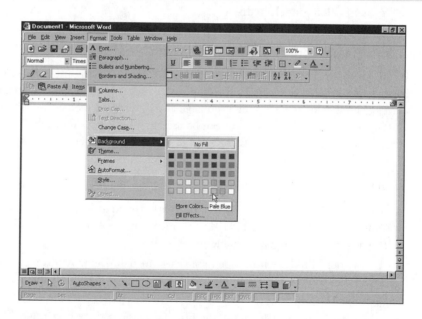

LISTING 14.2   PARTIAL HTML SOURCE FROM A MICROSOFT WORD 2000 HTML DOCUMENT

```
<body bgcolor=lime lang=EN-US style='tab-interval:.5in'>
```

4. After you have selected a background color for your HTML document, save and close the file in your text editor.

5. Open the project you want to save as an HTML file in Microsoft Project, and select File, Save As Web Page.

6. From the Save As dialog box, navigate to the directory where you want to save the document.

7. Type the name of the HTML document in the File Name field.

8. Click the Save button, and the Export Format dialog box will open.

9. From the Import/Export Map to Use for Exporting list box, select the Task Schedule Map used in the previous example and click the Edit button.

10. Select the Base Export on HTML Template check box, and click the Browse button to select the template you created in step 2.

11. Click the OK button to close the Define Import/Export Map dialog box, and from the Export Format dialog box, click Save.

12. Now, open the HTML document in your Web browser to see the result of changing the background color. Start up your Web browser, and open the HTML document you created in this example. Notice how the Web page now displays with the custom background color you selected.

DEFINING A BACKGROUND GRAPHIC FOR THE TEMPLATE

In this example, we will modify the template we created in the previous example to add a background graphic to the HTML template. A background graphic is often used instead of a background color to give your Web page a rich, textured look. The Microsoft Office 2000 CD includes several GIF files that can be used as a background graphic for your Web page. These graphic files are typically installed in the `Program Files\Microsoft Office\Office\Bitmaps\Styles` directory.

To add a background graphic to your Project template, follow these steps:

1. Copy the file you want to use for your background graphic into the same directory where you will save your HTML document. In this example, we will use the file `Acsndstn.gif` as the background graphic.

2. From your HTML editor, open your customized Microsoft Project HTML template created in the previous example (or any other Project HTML template you want to modify).

3. About six lines down from the top of the code, locate the text `<BODY...` (the exact text after the word `BODY` will vary depending on any other changes you might have already made to the template).

4. Change the text inside the brackets (<>) to `<BODY BACKGROUND="xxxxxx.gif">`, where `xxxxxx.gif` represents the name of the background graphic file you want to display on your Web page. In this example, set the text inside the brackets to `<BODY BACKGROUND=" Acsndstn.gif">`.

5. Save the template, and close the file in your text editor.

6. Open the project you want to save as an HTML file in Microsoft Project, and select File, Save As Web Page.

7. From the Save As dialog box, navigate to the directory where you want to save the document.

8. Type the name of the HTML document in the File Name field.

9. Click the Save button, and the Export Format dialog box will open.

10. From the Import/Export Map to Use for Exporting list box, select the Task Schedule Map used in the previous example and click the Edit button.

11. Select the Base Export on HTML Template check box, and click the Browse button to select your customized Project HTML template.

12. Click the OK button to close the Define Import/Export Map dialog box, and from the Export Format dialog box, click Save.

13. Now, open the HTML document in your Web browser to see the result of changing the background graphic. Start up your Web browser, and open the HTML document you created in this example (see Figure 14.17). Notice how the Web page now displays with the custom background graphic you selected.

Figure 14.17
This HTML document displays a custom background graphic.

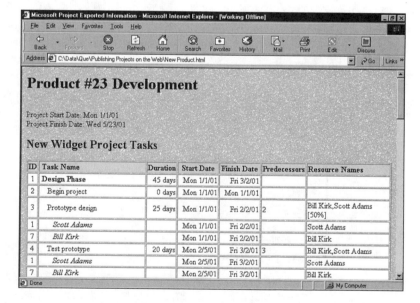

DISPLAYING A GRAPHIC IMAGE IN YOUR PROJECT TEMPLATE

Microsoft Project allows you to easily include a graphic image in your template without having to make any modifications to the HTML source code. You might want to include your company logo or other graphic to enhance the appearance of your Web page.

To add a graphic to your Project HTML template, do the following:

1. Open the project you want to save as an HTML file in Microsoft Project, and select File, Save As Web Page.

2. From the Save As dialog box, navigate to the directory where you want to save the document.

3. Type the name of the HTML document in the File Name field.

4. Click the Save button, and the Export Format dialog box will open.

5. From the Import/Export Map to Use for Exporting list box, select the map you want to use for this export, and click the Edit button (or you can create a new map, if you prefer).

6. Select the Base Export on HTML Template check box, and click the Browse button to select the Project HTML template you want to use for this export.

7. Select the Include Image File in HTML Page check box, and click the Browse button to select the graphic you want to use in your template.

8. Click the OK button to close the Define Import/Export Map dialog box, and from the Export Format dialog box, click Save.

9. Now, open the HTML document in your Web browser to see the result of adding the new graphic. Start up your Web browser, and open the HTML document you created in this example (see Figure 14.18). Notice how the Web page now displays with the graphic you selected.

Figure 14.18
This figure shows the HTML document displayed with a graphic image.

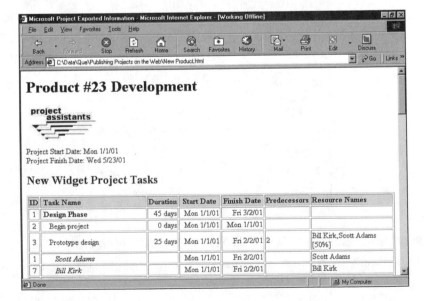

CHANGING THE TITLE BAR TEXT

Another way you can customize your Microsoft Project Web page is to change the text that will display in the title bar of the Web browser when your page is opened. By default, Microsoft Project displays the text `Microsoft Project Exported Information` in the title bar of the browser.

To change your HTML template to display your company name or the name of your project in the title bar text of your Web browser, do the following:

1. From your HTML editor, open your customized Microsoft Project HTML template created in the previous example (or any other Project HTML template you want to modify).

2. About three lines down from the top of the code, locate the text `<TITLE>Microsoft Project Exported Information</TITLE>`.

3. Replace the text `Microsoft Project Exported Information` with the text you want to display in the title bar of the Web browser. For example, you could change the title bar text to display `ABC Corporation New Widget Project`. Be careful not to change the `<TITLE>` and `</TITLE>` tags that surround the title bar text.

4. Save the template, and close the file in your text editor.

5. Open the project you want to save as an HTML file in Microsoft Project, and select File, Save As Web Page.

6. From the Save As dialog box, navigate to the directory where you want to save the document.

7. Type the name of the HTML document in the File Name field.

8. Click the Save button, and the Export Format dialog box will open.

9. From the Import/Export Map to Use for Exporting list box, select the map you want to use for this export, and click the Edit button (or you can create a new map, if you prefer).

10. Select the Base Export on HTML Template check box, and click the Browse button to select the Project HTML template you want to use for this export.

11. Click the OK button to close the Define Import/Export Map dialog box, and from the Export Format dialog box, click Save.

12. Now, open the HTML document in your Web browser to see the result of changing the title bar text. Start up your Web browser, and open the HTML document you created in this example (see Figure 14.19). Notice how the Web page now displays the text `ABC Corporation New Widget Project` in the title bar of the window.

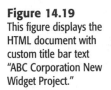

Figure 14.19
This figure displays the HTML document with custom title bar text "ABC Corporation New Widget Project."

Custom title bar text

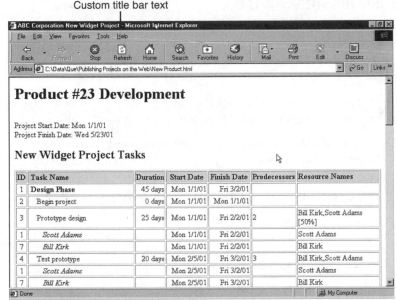

FORMATTING TEXT IN YOUR PROJECT HTML TEMPLATE

In this next example, you will modify the formatting of the header text that displays at the top of the Standard Export.html template. Specifically, we will define the font, size, color, and justification of the header text. These same techniques can be used in other places in your template as well.

The Standard Export.html template will automatically include the project title at the top of the HTML document.

> **Note**
>
> You can easily change the project title in Microsoft Project by selecting File, Properties, and typing the new project title in the Title field on the Summary tab. If you do not select the project title yourself, Microsoft Project will automatically use the name of the file as the project title.

To format the header text in your HTML template, do the following:

1. From your HTML editor, open your customized Microsoft Project HTML template created in the previous example (or any other Project HTML template you want to modify).

2. About 23 lines down from the top of the code, locate the text <!-- ******* PROJECT TITLE ******* -->.

3. Directly below this line, modify the line with the following HTML code in Listing 14.3.

LISTING 14.3   HTML CODE FROM CUSTOMIZED PROJECT HTML TEMPLATE

```
<FONT COLOR="#ADA990" SIZE="7" FACE="Arial Narrow">
```

Note

You can choose any Windows font next to the FACE= parameter, but you should try to avoid nonstandard fonts that a user might not have installed on her computer. Also, you can select any color for the text that you want (the one in the previous example is blue) by specifying the hexadecimal code for the color. To determine the hexadecimal code for the color, follow the tip given in step 3 in the section "Changing the Background Color of Your Web Page," earlier in this chapter. The <CENTER> tag that appears in the previous code will center all text and graphics that follow it, up until the </CENTER> tag.

4. Save the template, and close the file in your editor.

5. Open the project you want to save as an HTML file in Microsoft Project, and select File, Save As Web Page.

6. From the Save As dialog box, navigate to the directory where you want to save the document.

7. Type the name of the HTML document in the File Name field.

8. Click the Save button, and the Export Format dialog box will open.

9. From the Import/Export Map to Use for Exporting list box, select the map you want to use for this export, and click the Edit button (or you can create a new map, if you prefer).

10. Select the Base Export on HTML Template check box, and click the Browse button to select the Project HTML template you want to use for this export.

11. Click the OK button to close the Define Import/Export Map dialog box, and from the Export Format dialog box, click Save.

12. Now, open the HTML document in your Web browser to see the result of formatting the header text. Start up your Web browser, and open the HTML document you created in this example (see Figure 14.20). Notice how the header text displays the title of your project with center justification and a blue Arial font!

ADDING HYPERLINKS TO YOUR PROJECT HTML TEMPLATE

Another useful customization you can make to a Project HTML template is to include hyperlinks to other Web pages. For example, you can include a link that will navigate visitors to your company's home page on the Internet or Microsoft's Internet Explorer home page, or even allow a visitor to download a demo file that describes your company's products or services.

PART
IV

CH
14

Figure 14.20
This figure shows the HTML document with the customized header text "Product 23 Development."

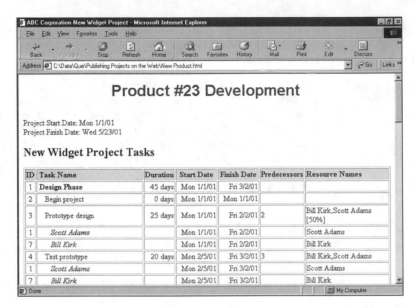

Another type of hyperlink you can add provides visitors to your site the ability to send an email to the Webmaster of your Web site or president of the company. This type of hyperlink is referred to as a *mail link*.

To add hyperlinks to your Microsoft Project HTML template, do the following:

1. From your HTML editor, open your customized Microsoft Project HTML template (or any other Project HTML template you want to modify).

2. Toward the bottom of the HTML code in Listing 14.1, locate the section that begins with the comment `<!-- ******* MICROSOFT LINKS ******* -->`, shown in Listing 14.4.

LISTING 14.4 HTML CODE INCLUDING A HYPERLINK FROM CUSTOMIZED PROJECT HTML TEMPLATE

```
<!-- ******* MICROSOFT LINKS ******* -->

<P ALIGN="CENTER">
<BR>
<FONT FACE="Arial" SIZE="1">
<A HREF="http://www.microsoft.com/isapi/redir.dll?prd=msft&plcid=
0x0409&ar=home">
Microsoft Home Page
</A>
<BR>
<A HREF="http://www.microsoft.com/isapi/redir.dll?
prd=msproject&sbp=&plcid=0x0409&pver=8.0&ar=home">
Microsoft Project Home Page
</A>
</FONT>
</P>
```

Note

The templates that come with Microsoft Project 2000 include hyperlinks to the Microsoft Project home page, as well as the Microsoft Corporation home page. Let's examine the syntax of a hyperlink so we can add two additional links to your template:

<A HREF="*xxxxxxxx*">*yyyyyyyy*</A>

The *xxxxxxxx* represents the address of the site you want to navigate to, and *yyyyyyyy* represents the displayed text that the visitor will click to navigate to the site.

3. Add an additional hyperlink to the Project HTML template that will navigate to ABC Corporation's home page on the Internet. Directly below the link to the Microsoft Project home page and above the </FONT> tag toward the bottom of the Project HTML template, add the following:

```
<A HREF="http://www.abc-corporation.com"><B>ABC Corporation
Home Page</B></A>
```

The HTML code should now appear as shown in the following example (see Listing 14.5).

LISTING 14.5   HTML CODE WITH A HYPERLINK TO ABC CORPORATION'S HOME PAGE

```
<A HREF="http://www.microsoft.com/isapi/redir.dll?
prd=msproject&sbp=&plcid=0x0409&pver=8.0&ar=home">
Microsoft Project Home Page
</A>
<BR>
<A HREF="http://www.Projectassistants.com/isapi/redir.dll?
prd=msproject&sbp=&plcid=0x0409&pver=8.0&ar=home">
Project Assistants Home Page
</A>
```

Let's add one more hyperlink to the template. It is very common to provide visitors to your home page with the ability to send an email to someone in your organization, such as the Webmaster of your Web site or a technical support engineer. When a visitor to your home page clicks this hyperlink, it will automatically start up his or her email application and create a new email message addressed to this individual.

An email hyperlink (also referred to as a *mail link*) uses the structure <A HREF="mailto: *xxxxxxxx*">*yyyyyyyy*</A>, where *xxxxxxxx* represents the email address you want to send mail to, and *yyyyyyyy* represents the displayed text that the visitor will click to start his or her email application with the new email message.

To create a mail link that will send an email to the Webmaster of ABC Corporation when the visitor clicks it, follow these steps:

1. Directly below the link to the ABC Corporation Home Page and above the </TABLE> tag toward the bottom of the Project HTML template, add the following:

```
<TD ALIGN=CENTER>
<A HREF="mailto:webmaster@abc-corporation.com"><B>Click
here to send email to the ABC Corporation
Webmaster</B></A></TD>
```

The HTML code should now appear as shown in Listing 14.6.

LISTING 14.6   HTML CODE WITH AN EMAIL HYPERLINK

```
<BR>
<A HREF="http://www.ProjectAssistants.com/isapi/redir.dll?
prd=msproject&sbp=&plcid=0x0409&pver=8.0&ar=home">
Project Assistants Home Page
</A>
<BR>
<A HREF="mailto:webmaster@abc-corporation.com"><B>Click
here to send email to the ABC Corporation
Webmaster</B></A>
```

---

2. Save the template, and close the file in your text editor.

3. Open the project you want to save as an HTML file in Microsoft Project, and select File, Save As Web Page.

4. From the Save As dialog box, navigate to the directory in which you want to save the document.

5. Type the name of the HTML document in the File Name field.

6. Click the Save button, and the Export Format dialog box will open.

7. From the Import/Export Map to Use for Exporting list box, select the map you want to use for this export, and click the Edit button (or you can create a new map, if you prefer).

8. Select the Base Export on HTML Template check box, and click the Browse button to select the Project HTML template you want to use for this export.

9. Click the OK button to close the Define Import/Export Map dialog box, and from the Export Format dialog box, click Save.

10. Now, open the HTML document in your Web browser to see the result of adding the new hyperlinks. Start up your Web browser, and open the HTML document you created in this example (see Figure 14.21). Scroll down to the bottom of the Web page, and you will see the two new hyperlinks you added to your Project HTML template.

DISPLAYING A GANTT CHART IMAGE IN YOUR PROJECT WEB PAGE

In addition to publishing your project data to an HTML file, you might also want to include a picture of your project's Gantt Chart with your Web page. In this section, we will walk through all the steps that allow you to accomplish this.

To add a picture of your project's Gantt Chart to your HTML file, do the following:

1. Open the project you want to save as an HTML file in Microsoft Project.

2. Click the Select All button to highlight every task in your project, and click the Copy Picture button in the Standard toolbar. The Copy Picture dialog box will be displayed (see Figure 14.22).

Figure 14.21
This HTML document has hyperlinks to ABC Corporation's home page and a mail link to the Webmaster of ABC Corporation.

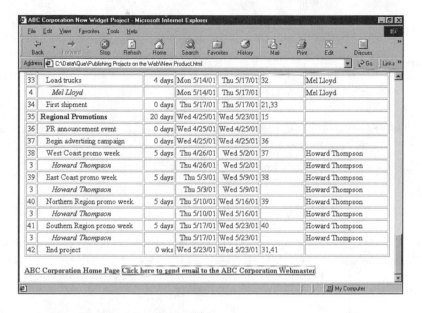

Figure 14.22
The Copy Picture dialog box allows you to create a graphic of your project's Gantt Chart to display on your Web page.

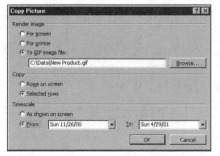

3. On the Copy Picture dialog box, set the Render Image option to To GIF Image File. By default, Microsoft Project will set the path for the image to be the same location as where you saved your project file. The filename for the image will be set to the name of your project with the extension GIF. If you wish, you can change the name and location for the file, but the default path and filename should be fine as is.

4. Since you selected all rows in step 2, if you want to create a picture of your Gantt Chart that displays every task in your project, select the Copy Selected Rows option. If you only want to display the tasks that are visible on the screen, select the Rows on Screen option.

5. To include the timescale that is currently displayed on your screen, from the Timescale option, select As Shown on Screen. If you want to display the timescale for a particular date range, set the From and the To dates to the desired dates.

6. Click OK, and Microsoft Project will create a GIF image file of your Gantt Chart.

PART
IV

CH
14

7. From the Save As dialog box, navigate to the directory in which you want to save the HTML document. Type the name of the HTML document in the File Name field, click the Save button, and the Export Format dialog box will open.

8. From the Import/Export Map to Use for Exporting list box, select the map you want to use for this export, and click the Edit button (or you can create a new map, if you prefer).

9. Select the Base Export on HTML Template check box, and click the Browse button to select the Project HTML template you want to use for this export.

10. Select the Include Image File in HTML Page check box, and click the Browse button to select the graphic of your Gantt Chart.

11. Click the OK button to close the Define Import/Export Map dialog box, and from the Export Format dialog box, click Save.

12. Now, you should open the HTML document in your Web browser to see the result of adding the Gantt Chart graphic. Start up your Web browser, and open the HTML document you created in this example (see Figure 14.23). Notice how the Web page now displays with the graphic you selected.

Figure 14.23
This figure shows the HTML document displayed with a graphic image of your Gantt Chart.

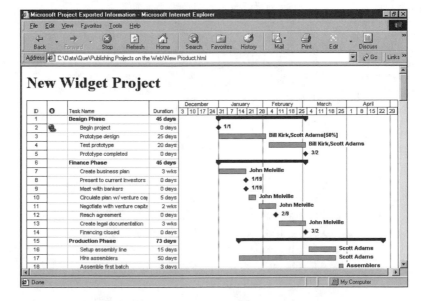

ADDING, MODIFYING, AND DELETING HYPERLINKS IN YOUR PROJECT

Microsoft Project 2000's Insert Hyperlink feature has been enhanced significantly from Project 98 in several ways. In addition to being able to navigate to a Web page or document, you now have the ability to navigate to a different view in your project, or even to a task or resource within that view. You can also create a new document that can be accessed via a hyperlink, as well as insert a hyperlink that will create a new email message to the designated recipient.

In this section, you will take a look at the many hyperlink features available in Microsoft Project 2000. In addition, you will see some practical examples of how hyperlinks can help you work more effectively when managing a project.

MANAGING A PROJECT WITH HYPERLINKS

Hyperlinks can be very useful in helping you manage a project by allowing you to associate specific references to information stored on the Internet or your corporate intranet to a task or resource in your plan. For example, you might have developed a PowerPoint presentation that is always delivered when you kick off a new project in your organization. By creating a hyperlink from this task in your plan, you can easily navigate a user directly to this presentation (or even a specific slide within the presentation) at the click of a mouse.

Another example of how a hyperlink can be effective is the capability to associate detailed reference information for a task to help a person successfully perform the task in your project. A hyperlink could navigate a person to a Word document that details the step-by-step instructions on how to complete a task in your plan, or even to a Web site that is always being updated with the latest information on a particular topic.

ADDING A HYPERLINK TO A TASK OR RESOURCE

To create a hyperlink to open a Microsoft Office file from a task or resource in your project plan (in the following example, we will open a Word document), do the following:

1. Select the task or resource to which you want to add a hyperlink, and click the Insert Hyperlink button on the Standard toolbar (or if you prefer, select Insert, Hyperlink from the menu). The Edit Hyperlink dialog box opens (see Figure 14.24).

Figure 14.24
Microsoft Project's Edit Hyperlink dialog box gives you the ability to add a hyperlink to a task or resource in your project.

2. Click the Existing File or Web Page button, and in the Type the File or Web Page Name field, type the file path of the Microsoft Word file you want to navigate to from this task or resource. You can also click the Browse button to select a file from your hard drive or network.

PART

IV

CH

14

Note

The Edit Hyperlink dialog box includes three new buttons that make it easier to insert a hyperlink in your project:

Recent Files—Click the Recent Files button to display a list of Microsoft Office files you have worked with recently.

Browsed Pages—Click the Browsed Pages button to display a list of Web sites you have visited recently.

Inserted Links—Click the Inserted Links button to display a list of links you have added to Project files recently.

3. In the Text to Display field, type the text that you want to use to describe the hyperlink. For example, if we were creating a hyperlink to a business plan document, we would type Business Plan in this field.

4. To add a more detailed description of your document, which will display when you hold your mouse over the hyperlink indicator in Project, click the ScreenTip button, and enter your description in the ScreenTip Text field (see Figure 14.25).

Figure 14.25
Microsoft Project 2000's Edit Hyperlink feature gives you the ability to add a ScreenTip to a hyperlink that you will see when you hold your mouse over a task's or resource's hyperlink graphical indicator.

5. Click OK, and the hyperlink definition will be complete.

6. To test the hyperlink, click the hyperlink icon in the Indicator column. Project will launch Microsoft Word and open your document (see Figure 14.26).

NAVIGATING TO A HYPERLINK

Project 2000 provides you with the ability to reference a bookmark within your Word document when you set up your hyperlink. A *bookmark* is a placeholder that provides an easy way to navigate to a particular section of a document. For example, you might want to create a Word document that provides detailed, step-by-step task procedures for every task in your project. Within this Word document, you could create a separate bookmark for each section that documents an individual task in your project. Then, in Project, insert a hyperlink for each task that references the appropriate bookmarked section in the Word document.

Figure 14.26
Click the hyperlink graphical indicator to open your Word document.

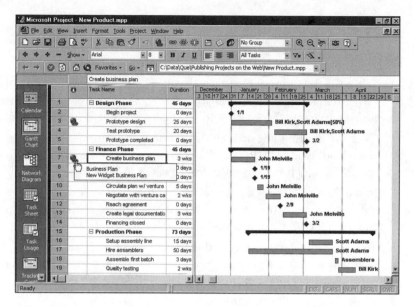

To reference a bookmark in your hyperlink, follow these steps:

1. Select the task or resource to which you want to add a hyperlink, and click the Insert Hyperlink button on the Standard toolbar (or if you prefer, select Insert, Hyperlink from the menu). The Edit Hyperlink dialog box opens.

2. Click the Existing File or Web Page button, and in the Type the File or Web Page Name field, type the file path of the Microsoft Word file you want to navigate to from this task or resource. You can also click the Browse button to select a file from your hard drive or network.

3. Directly after the filename entered in the previous step, type the pound sign (#) followed by the name of the bookmark that you want to navigate to, and click OK.

4. From the Insert Hyperlink dialog box, click OK. The hyperlink definition will be complete.

5. To test the hyperlink, click the hyperlink icon in the Indicator column. Project will open your document in Microsoft Word and navigate you to the bookmarked section of your document.

Note

In addition to being able to navigate to a bookmarked section of a Word document, the Bookmark feature allows you to quickly navigate to specific locations—such as to a cell or named range in an Excel file, a specific slide number in a PowerPoint presentation, a table in an Access database, or a particular section of a Web page (known as an *anchor*).

ADDING A HYPERLINK TO A WEB PAGE

To create a hyperlink to access a Web page from a task or resource in your project plan, do the following:

1. Select the task or resource to which you want to add a hyperlink, and click the Insert Hyperlink button on the Standard toolbar (or if you prefer, select Insert, Hyperlink from the menu). The Edit Hyperlink dialog box opens (refer to Figure 14.24).
2. Click the Existing File or Web Page button, and in the Type the File or Web Page name field, type the URL for the Web page you want to navigate. You can also click the Browsed Pages button to select from a list of Web pages you have visited recently.
3. In the Text to Display field, type the text that you want to use to describe the hyperlink. For example, if we were creating a hyperlink to our company's home page, we could type **ABC Corporation Home Page** in this field.
4. To add a more detailed description of your document that will display when you hold your mouse over the hyperlink indicator in Project, click the ScreenTip button, and enter your description in the ScreenTip Text field.
5. Click OK, and the hyperlink definition will be complete.
6. To test the hyperlink, click the hyperlink icon in the Indicator column. Microsoft Project will launch your browser, and navigate you to your Web page.

EDITING A HYPERLINK FOR A TASK OR RESOURCE

To edit a hyperlink to a task or resource in your project plan, do the following:

1. Select the task or resource for which you want to edit a hyperlink, and click the Insert Hyperlink button on the Standard toolbar (or if you prefer, select Insert, Hyperlink from the menu). The Edit Hyperlink dialog box opens.
2. Enter the hyperlink information as described in the previous sections.
3. Click the OK button, and the hyperlink will be modified with your new information.

DELETING A HYPERLINK FOR A TASK OR RESOURCE

To delete a hyperlink from a task or resource in your project plan, do the following:

1. Select the task or resource for which you want to delete a hyperlink, and click the Insert Hyperlink button on the Standard toolbar (or if you prefer, select Insert, Hyperlink from the menu). The Edit Hyperlink dialog box opens.
2. Click the Remove Link button, and the hyperlink will be deleted from your task or resource.

NAVIGATING TO A HYPERLINK USING PROJECT'S HYPERLINK FIELDS

After you have set up a hyperlink in your project, you can very easily navigate to the associated document or Web site by simply clicking the Hyperlink field from the task or resource in your project.

An easy way to display the hyperlink fields in your project is to display the Hyperlink table (available from both a task view and a resource view).

To navigate to a hyperlink from a task or resource, follow this step:

1. From either a task view or a resource view in Project, select View, Table, Hyperlink. The Hyperlink table will open (see Figure 14.27).

Figure 14.27
This figure shows a hyperlink from a task to the Microsoft Project home page on the Web.

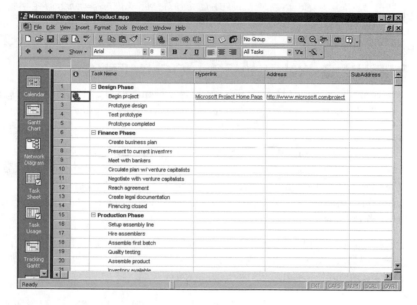

CREATING WEB PAGES FROM MPD FILES

One of the most exciting aspects of being able to save your project data to a MPD file is that you can utilize the Internet features of Microsoft Access to create static or dynamic Web content from your Microsoft Project data.

Microsoft Access includes a very robust wizard that lets you create HTML pages from any Access object. For example, you can create an Access report to generate HTML pages of your Project data, you can publish data from any Access table of query, and you can even generate a Web page from an Access form to collect Project data from project team members on a Web server.

UPDATING YOUR PROJECT WEB PAGES

With Microsoft Access 2000, it is possible to create a dynamic Web page in which the content is generated by connecting to an Access database and executing a query on the database. The advantage of a dynamic Web page is that that it is not necessary to re-create HTML pages with fresh content, because the page is automatically generated with the latest information whenever someone accesses it.

PART

IV

CH

14

Because a Microsoft Project MPD file is actually an Access database, you can create dynamic Web pages that query the MPD file to refresh the content of the Web page. Furthermore, you can create a dynamic Web page to update the Project MPD file with the latest information from Project team members.

Note

For more information on how to set up a dynamic Web page from an Access database, refer to Que's *Special Edition Using Microsoft Access 2000* (0-7897-1606-2).

PUBLISHING YOUR WEB DOCUMENTS

After you have created your Web assets (for example, HTML documents, graphic files, and so on), the next step is to publish those assets on the Internet or corporate intranet.

If your Web documents will be viewed from a corporate intranet, all you need to do is copy the files to the required location on a server (as specified by your intranet administrator). If your files will be viewed from an Internet Web site, you will need to upload the files to the Web server of your Internet service provider. As your Project HTML documents change over the course of a project, it will be necessary to copy the latest files to the server to refresh the content.

An easy way to publish your Web assets is to use the Web Publishing Wizard, which ships as part of Windows 98. The Web Publishing Wizard will literally walk you through the entire process of publishing your files to your server.

To publish your Project Web pages using the Web Publishing Wizard, do the following:

1. Start up the Web Publishing Wizard by selecting Start, Programs, Accessories, Internet Tools, Web Publishing Wizard. The Web Publishing Wizard dialog box opens (see Figure 14.28). Click the Next button to start this wizard.

Figure 14.28
The Microsoft Web Publishing Wizard will lead you through the process of publishing your HTML documents on the Internet or corporate intranet.

2. From the next screen of the wizard, select the Web document you want to publish (see Figure 14.29). Or, if you will be publishing several files, select the directory where the files are stored and click Next.

Note

If you will be including any graphics files on your Web page, such as a picture of your Gantt Chart, make sure you publish these files along with your HTML file.

Figure 14.29
This screen from the Web Publishing Wizard allows you to select the files or folders you want to publish.

3. Enter a descriptive name for the Web server, such as New Product, and click Next.

4. Enter the name of the URL or Internet address to be used to access your Web page at the URL or Internet Address prompt. Then, type the path for the local directory on your PC where these files are stored (see Figure 14.30).

Figure 14.30
This screen from the Web Publishing Wizard allows you to specify the URL or Internet address where your files should be published, as well as the local directory where they are stored on your PC.

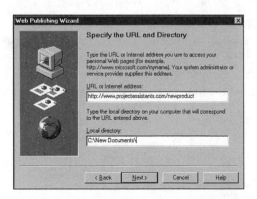

5. Click Next, and the Web Publishing Wizard will lead you through the specific steps required to transfer files to that Web server.

6. After your files have been transferred, use your Web browser to make sure you are able to access and view your files from the server.

PART

IV

CH

14

TROUBLESHOOTING

USING THE BOOKMARK FEATURE WHEN CREATING A HYPERLINK

I am trying to reference a bookmark within a Word document when creating a hyperlink to a task. When I click the Bookmark button and enter the name of the bookmark, I receive the message "Microsoft Project could not open this file or could not parse a file of this type." What am I doing wrong?

In Project 2000, you can only use the Bookmark button to create a bookmark reference to a Microsoft Project file. For example, you can create a hyperlink that references a particular task or resource within another project file. If you want to reference a bookmark within a Word document or a named range within an Excel spreadsheet, you need to append the name of the file with a pound sign (#) followed by the name of the bookmark or named range. For example, if you were referencing a Word document in your documents folder named Status Report.doc with a bookmark named CurrentAccomplishments, you would enter the following text in the Type the File or Web Page Name field:

```
C:\My Documents\Status Report.doc#CurrentAccomplishments
```

PROBLEMS WITH THE COPY PICTURE FEATURE

When trying to use the Copy Picture feature of Microsoft Project to capture an image of my Gantt Chart, I am not seeing all of my tasks in the image. What am I doing wrong?

In order to include all of your tasks in the image of your Gantt Chart, first you must select all of your project's tasks by clicking on the Select All button on the upper-left corner of the Gantt Chart. After you have selected all of the tasks, click the Copy Picture button on the Standard toolbar. Then, on the Copy Picture dialog box, select the Selected Rows option. Because you have selected all of the rows in your project, the entire task list will be included in the Gantt Chart.

CHAPTER 15

USING MICROSOFT PROJECT IN WORKGROUPS

In this chapter

EXPLORING PROJECT'S WORKGROUP FEATURES

Since projects are group endeavors, they require extensive communication between project team members. Microsoft Project 2000 supports this communication with workgroups. There are two workgroup methods in Microsoft Project 2000—email messaging and Project Central. The email messaging method requires a 32-bit MAPI-compliant mail application.

P The second method takes advantage of the new Project Central companion product. Project **2000** Central greatly enhances the Project 98 Web-based functionality with expanded messaging, new project views, and new status reporting capabilities.

This chapter describes the features of both workgroup methods from the standpoint of the project management process. You have the option of using one method exclusively or you can set up workgroups to use email messaging for some resources and Project Central for others.

COMMUNICATING BY EMAIL

All members using email messaging need to have access to a MAPI-compliant, 32-bit email system, such as Lotus Notes, Groupwise, Microsoft Exchange, or Microsoft Outlook. Additionally, each member of the project team must have a unique email address. While the project manager needs to have Microsoft Project 2000 installed, this is not a requirement for the team members. If the team members do not have Project, they will need to install the Workgroup Message Handler from the Microsoft Project CD to enable workgroup messaging.

CONFIGURING THE PROJECT CENTRAL SERVER

Project Central messaging consists of two parts—a server and a client. The server uses Internet Information Server (IIS) and a database (Oracle, SQL Server, and Microsoft Database Engine are supported). The setup program makes the necessary connection between IIS and the database and also installs any needed server-side files.

On the client side, each project team member will need a browser such as Microsoft Internet Explorer. As an alternative to Explorer, a browser module is shipped with Project Central.

The details for setting up the Project Central server are contained in a document available on the Project Central CD. You can find the document in PJCNTRL\HELP\1033\SVRSetup.htm. You can also use the new HTML-based Help engine to find extensive information on setting up and using Project Central.

SETTING UP WORKGROUP OPTIONS IN THE PROJECT PLAN

To enable the workgroup features, the project manager sets the appropriate Workgroup options and values in the project plan. The next few sections will take a look at what features must be configured.

VALUING THE OPTIONS

For both email and Project Central Workgroup methods, you need to value the options. To do so, follow these steps:

1. On the Tools menu, click Options, and then click the Workgroup tab (see Figure 15.1).

Figure 15.1
Tools (Options/
Workgroup) enables
you to set up your
workgroup properties.

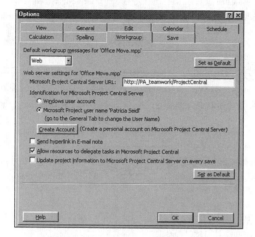

2. In the Default Workgroup Messages list, select Web or Email.

*Tip from Tim and
the Project Team*

If you will be using both the Web and Email methods, select the one that will be most common for the team members. Then you simply need to modify the value for any resource using the alternative method in the Resource Sheet view.

Complete the following additional steps if you are using Project Central. These options are noneditable if you selected email as the default workgroup message option.

1. In the Microsoft Project Central Server URL box, type the URL for the Microsoft Project Central server. (It'll probably be something similar to
   `http://machinename/WebClient.`)

Note

Get the URL for the Microsoft Project Central server from your system administrator. If you happen to be the first one in the office to adopt the Web interface, your system administrator will have to do some installing and configuring to get things off the ground.

2. Under Identification for Microsoft Project Central Server, choose an identification method. This option determines how your name will display for the messages you generate. You can choose your Windows user account name or the Project username specified on the General tab.

3. To perform work on the Microsoft Project Central server (such as customizing Microsoft Project Central or creating reports for your team) without first having to send a workgroup message, click Create Account.

> **Note**
> This step is optional. An account does need to be created for you before you can work with Microsoft Project Central, but that happens automatically when you send a workgroup message. Follow this step only if you want to work with Microsoft Project Central without sending a workgroup message.

4. If you select the Send Hyperlink in E-mail Note check box, an email notification will be sent to the team member whenever a message is posted on Project Central. The email message will contain the Project Central URL to accommodate easy navigation to Project Central.

> **Note**
> If you use this feature, be sure the email address field has been defined for each resource. The email address is accessible through Resource Information.

5. To allow a resource to delegate tasks to another resource, select Allow Resources to Delegate Tasks in Microsoft Project Central.

6. To automatically send updated project summary information, such as the project start and finish dates, from the project plan to Microsoft Project Central, select Update Project Information to Microsoft Project Central Server on Every Save. If you do not select this option, you must periodically perform the function Update Project to Web Server located under the Workgroup menu.

DEFINE RESOURCE WORKGROUP VALUES

By default, all of the resources in the project plan will use the workgroup messaging option as defined on the Workgroup tab under the Options dialog box. If some resources will use a different method, you need to value that method for each resource in its Workgroup field. Keep in mind that if you are using the email messaging option, you should be sure all resources have an email address defined in their email Address fields. There is not a standard Resource table that contains these fields. You can access the fields under Resource Information or by adding the fields to a table.

Tip from Tim and the Project Team

> If there are some resources who won't be using the workgroup features (for example, resources who are external to your organization), value their Workgroup fields to None.

Introduction to Microsoft Project Central

P Microsoft Project 2000 builds on the exciting Web-based workgroup features from
2000 Microsoft Project 98 with the Project Central companion product. With the expanded features in Project Central, the project manager can communicate task assignments and task updates with the project team quickly and easily. The project team, in turn, can send timesheets containing actual work values and project status reports back to the project manager. Plus, the project team members can access their task information in a variety of ways, including a Gantt Chart view.

Updating the Project Plan to Project Central

This function will either send a new project file to the Project Central server or will refresh a project file that already exists on the server. To perform the function, choose Tools, Workgroup, Update Project to Web Server. You'll receive two messages—one indicating the update is occurring and one when the update is complete.

If you did not select the option on the Workgroup tab (under Tools, Options) to automatically send an update whenever the project file is saved, you must remember to routinely perform this function.

Accessing Project Central

After you have set up your project plan, you are prepared to start using Project Central. To access Project Central, follow these steps:

1. Start your browser and enter the Project Central URL in the address field. You will be presented with the Microsoft Project Central Log On Web page (see Figure 15.2).

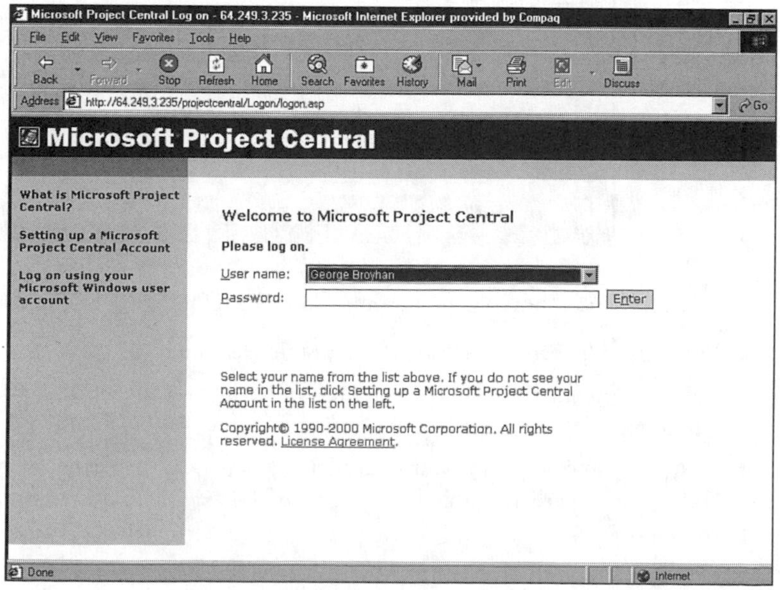

Figure 15.2
The Microsoft Project Central Log On enables you to log on to your personal Project Central home page.

Note

You can also access Project Central directly from the project plan. From the Tools menu, click Workgroup and then click TeamInbox.

2. Select your name from the User Name drop-down list.

3. Enter your password and click Enter.

THE PROJECT CENTRAL HOME PAGE

After you log on to Project Central, you will be presented with your personal home page (see Figure 15.3).

Note

The first time Project Central is presented, a security warning dialog box will appear for the ActiveX Control being installed into the browser.

Figure 15.3
The Project Central home page provides an overview of messages, tasks, and status reports.

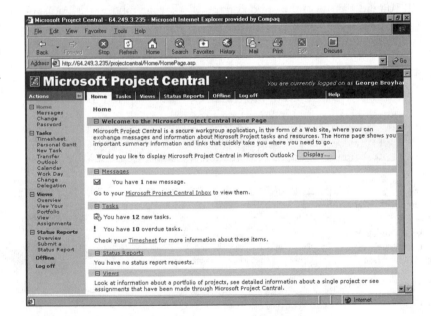

The Project Central home page is comprised of the following elements:

- **Banner**—The banner section displays the username.

- **Menu**—The menu provides a method of navigating the various Project Central functions.

- **Help**—Online help can be displayed as a sidebar on the Project Central screen. The Help contents are available by topic. The Help sidebar will continue to display until you close it.

- **Actions**—The Actions bar is an alternative to the menu for navigating through the Project Central functions. By selecting the left-pointing arrow button that resides next to the Actions header, you can hide the bar. When the bar is hidden, a right-pointing arrow appears. This arrow button can be used to toggle the Actions bar on and off.

- **Welcome**—The Welcome section provides an overview of Project Central and the home page.

- **Messages**—This section shows you how many new messages you have received. You can see a listing of all your messages by selecting the Messages hyperlink, by selecting Home, Messages from the menu, or by selecting Messages from the Actions bar.

- **Tasks**—This section gives you an overview of the number of new tasks you have been assigned and a notice of the number of tasks that are overdue. You can see your task detail by selecting the Tasks hyperlink, by selecting the Timesheet hyperlink, by selecting Tasks, Timesheet from the menu or by selecting Timesheet from the Actions bar. After you have looked at the task detail on the timesheet, the Number of New Tasks indicator on the home page will be reset to zero.

- **Status Reports**—This section provides a listing of the status reports that have been requested by the project manager and status reports that have been submitted. To see the status report detail or to work with any of the status reports, select the Status Reports hyperlink, select Status Reports from the menu, or select the appropriate function from the Actions bar.

- **Views**—Views allow team members to see more than just the tasks they are working on and allow managers to communicate critical information about projects throughout the organization.

MESSAGES

After selecting to view your messages from your Project Central home page, you will see the Message Inbox (see Figure 15.4). Messages are generated as a result of performing the various Project Central functions. For example, when the project manager sends a TeamUpdate, a message will appear in each team member's Inbox.

You have two options for displaying the message detail. As you place your mouse over the message line, you will see that each piece of information for the message becomes a hyperlink. By double-clicking on any of the pieces of information, the message detail will be displayed. Another option for viewing the detail is to select the message (a dark-shaded double arrow will appear next to that message) and select the Open Message icon. The detailed message will be displayed (see Figure 15.5).

Figure 15.4
The Message Inbox is a one-line display of your messages.

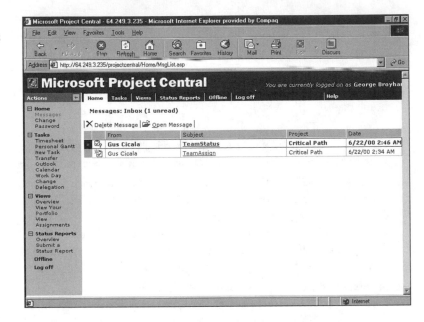

Look here to see if you
must reply to the message.

Figure 15.5
From the detailed message screen, you can reply to the message.

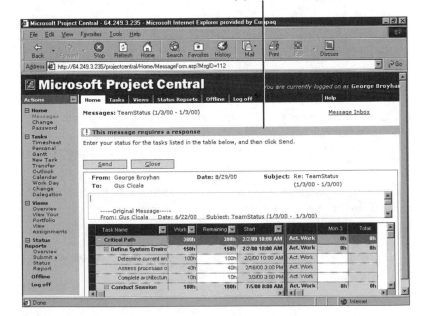

USING WORKGROUPS IN THE PLANNING PROCESS

During the planning process, the project manager creates a project plan that outlines the tasks to be completed along with the estimated work effort and resource assignments. The project manager can then use the Project workgroup functionality to notify the team members of their task assignments. Each team member has the option of accepting or declining the assignment.

COMMUNICATING RESOURCE ASSIGNMENTS WITH TEAMASSIGN

The project manager will use the TeamAssign function to communicate the task assignments to the team members.

Tip from Tim and the Project Team

If you want to communicate assignments for a subset of tasks, select these tasks prior to accessing the TeamAssign function.

Create and send a TeamAssign message by following these steps:

1. Choose the TeamAssign button, or choose <u>T</u>ools, <u>W</u>orkgroup, <u>T</u>eamAssign. You will be prompted to send team assignments for all tasks or just the tasks you selected.

2. Next, the TeamAssign Form appears (see Figure 15.6).

Team members with
unconfirmed task
assignments

Figure 15.6
The TeamAssign Form
enables you to assign
tasks to resources.

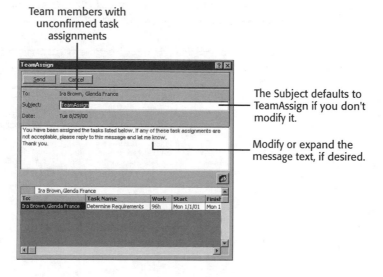

The Subject defaults to
TeamAssign if you don't
modify it.

Modify or expand the
message text, if desired.

3. Complete the TeamAssign Form as shown in Figure 15.6.

4. You also can add to the task assignments with the Assign Resources button above and to the right of the task list.

Caution

> If you add a resource to a task under TeamAssign, Project will assign the work based upon the task type. This might result in changes to the task duration.

5. When the TeamAssign Form is complete, choose the Send button to transmit the message to the resources.

6. You will briefly see a series of Send Message dialog boxes that indicate the assignments are being transmitted.

After the TeamAssign function is completed, some of the project plan task fields are updated. The values of the fields varies depending on whether workgroup messages are sent via email or the Web. The fields and their values are summarized in Table 15.1.

TABLE 15.1   THE TEAMASSIGN TASK FIELD VALUES

	Before TeamAssign Confirmed	Pending Response	After TeamAssign Confirmed	Pending Response
Email	No	No	No	Yes
Web	No	No	Yes	No

If you are using email-based messaging, a TeamAssign icon appears in the Indicators column of the project plan. This icon tells you that the resources assigned to a task have not all responded to the task assignment (see Figure 15.7).

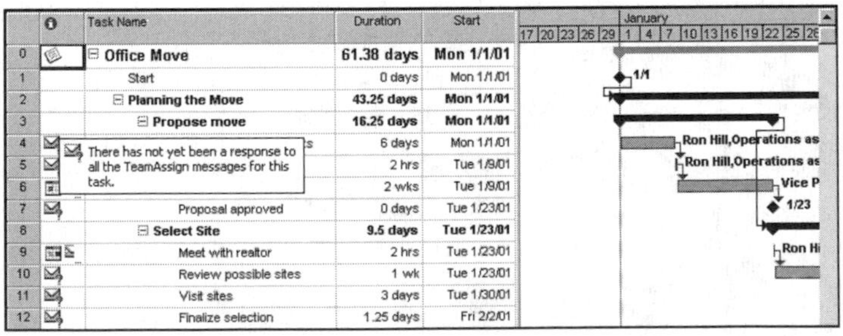

Figure 15.7
Unconfirmed team assignments will be flagged in the Indicators column.

Note

If you are using Project Central messaging, Project assumes the task assignments are accepted. If you are using email-based messaging, Project requires an acceptance of the team assignment.

Replying to Resource Assignments

After the project manager has sent the resource notification information via TeamAssign, each team member will receive a message in either his Project Central Inbox or his email inbox. The subject of the message reflects what was entered by the project manager. (For the purposes of illustration, the rest of this section assumes the subject of the message remained TeamAssign.)

Using Project Central to Reply to Resource Assignments

Figure 15.8 shows the Project Central Inbox with the TeamAssign message.

Figure 15.8
The TeamAssign message displays in the team member's Project Central Inbox.

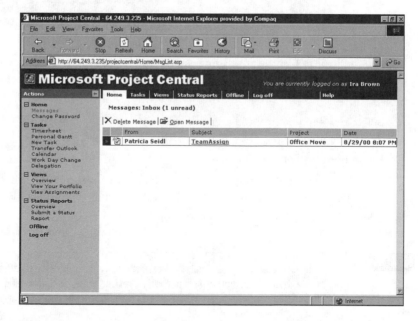

The team member can see a list of the task assignments by viewing the message detail (see Figure 15.9). (For a description of the features of Project Central Messages, refer to the "Messages" section earlier in this chapter.)

Figure 15.9
The detailed message displays the task assignments for the resource.

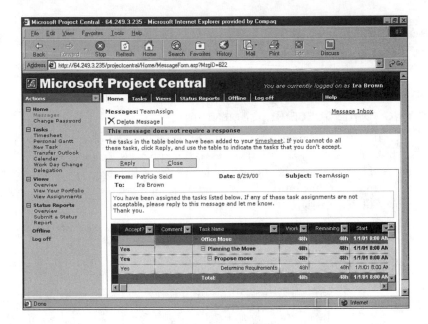

Because the Project Central messaging assumes that task assignments are accepted by the team member, it is only necessary to respond to the message if you must decline a task assignment. Follow these steps to respond to a task assignment message:

1. Select the Reply button to enter your response. A message with the subject Re: TeamAssign will appear (see Figure 15.10).

2. If you must decline a task request, change the Yes in the Accept? column to No.

3. Enter an explanation in the Comments column. The information you enter in the Comments field will be appended to the Notes field in the project plan.

4. Choose the Send button to send your reply.

Note

The estimated work, start dates, and finish dates cannot be revised through the TeamAssign reply. If you think these values need to be revised, enter the information in the Comments field. The project manager will be able to view these comments in the TeamAssign reply and the Notes field for the task.

USING EMAIL TO REPLY TO RESOURCE ASSIGNMENTS

Team members who are using email for workgroup messaging will receive the detailed message as shown in Figure 15.11.

Figure 15.10
The Reply message, in this case, is used to decline task assignments.

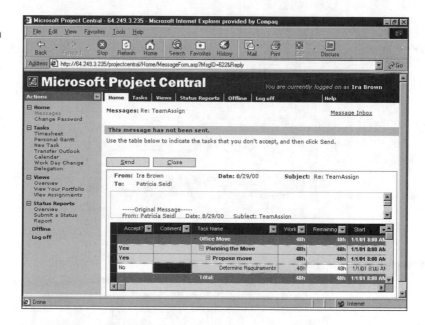

Figure 15.11
The detailed message displays the task assignments for the resource.

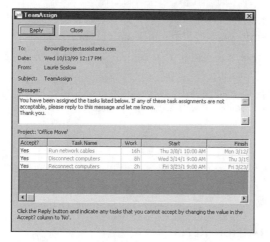

A response will be returned to the project manager by performing the following steps:

1. Choose the Reply button. A Reply Form will be displayed (see Figure 15.12).

2. Enter No in the Accept? column for any tasks you feel you cannot perform.

3. Enter an explanation in the Comments column. The information you enter will be appended to the Notes field in the project plan.

Figure 15.12
Task assignments are accepted or declined on the TeamAssign reply.

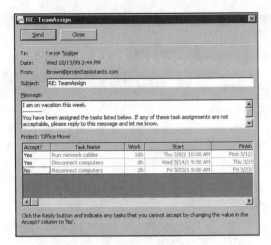

> **Note**
>
> To access the Comments column, you might need to scroll to the right of the task list. You can also resize the column widths by placing the mouse pointer over the column dividers. The pointer will turn into a double-headed arrow. Drag the column divider to the desired width.

4. Enter any additional information in the message text section.

5. Choose the <u>S</u>end button to transmit your reply.

In email-based messaging, Project automatically generates Outlook tasks from the team assignments. The tasks are located under a category (also created by Project) with the same name as the project.

> **Note**
>
> The ability to see task assignments in a personal management system is a feature only available if you are using Outlook.

RESPONDING TO THE TEAMASSIGN REPLY

After the project manager receives the reply to the TeamAssign message, she can incorporate the updates into the project workplan, or she can continue the dialogue by sending a Reply to the team member. Figure 15.13 shows the detailed message that is received by the project manager for Project Central messaging and Figure 15.14 shows the message that is received from email messaging.

> **Note**
>
> Keep in mind that the email message is actually an email message with an attachment, which appears as a dialog box. The dialog box has the message about the project inside it, and that dialog box requires an installation at the client desktop to handle it. It would be a good idea to check with your system administrator with any questions.

Figure 15.13
The project manager receives this message when a task assignment is declined via Project Central messaging.

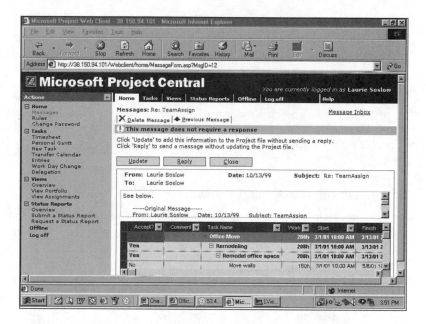

Figure 15.14
The project manager receives the TeamAssign reply as an attachment with email-based messaging.

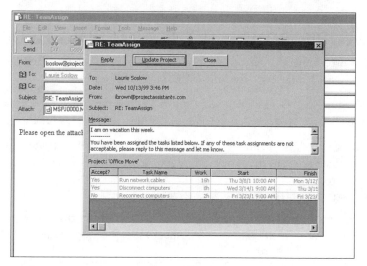

UPDATING THE PROJECT PLAN WITH TEAMASSIGN REPLIES

The project manager can have the project plan automatically updated by selecting Update Project. If the project plan isn't active, Project will be started and the workplan will be opened. For Project Central messaging, a dialog box will confirm the update and give the project manager the option of deleting the Reply message from his Project Central message box.

When the project plan is updated, the TeamAssign icon on the Indicators field is removed and the Confirmed and Response Pending fields are updated as appropriate (refer to Table 15.1). Any comments submitted by the team member will be appended to the Notes field for the task.

Tip from Tim and the Project Team	As a project manager, you'll want to keep abreast of declined task assignments. You can add the Confirmed field to a task sheet and you can use the Unconfirmed filter to help you manage these tasks.

CONTINUING THE TEAMASSIGN DIALOGUE

In some cases, the project manager might not want to automatically update the project with the declined team assignment. In those cases, he or she will want to continue to correspond with the team member to determine what alternatives are available. The project manager would select the Reply button (refer to Figures 15.13 and 15.14) to continue this dialogue. Pressing the Reply button will initiate a message to the team member. This messaging can continue until there is agreement on the resolution of task assignment and the project plan is updated as needed.

USING WORKGROUPS IN THE TRACKING PROCESS

After the project gets underway, the project manager will be tracking the actual progress of the tasks (see Chapter 16, "Tracking Work on the Project").

For both email-based messaging and Project Central messaging, the project manager can solicit a project progress update by completing the TeamStatus function.

In Project Central, the team members can track their actual and remaining work in a timesheet that is sent to the project manager for an automatic update to the project plan.

REQUESTING ACTUALS THROUGH TEAMSTATUS

When the project manager requests a TeamStatus from her team members, each team member receives a message containing a timesheet for capturing actuals.

Tip from Tim and the Project Team	If you want to request a status for a subset of tasks, select these tasks prior to accessing the TeamStatus function.

You create and send a TeamStatus message by following these steps:

1. Choose the TeamStatus button, or choose Tools, Workgroup, TeamStatus. You will be prompted to request a status for all tasks or just the tasks you selected.
2. Next, the TeamStatus Form appears (see Figure 15.15).

Team members receiving
the TeamStatus message

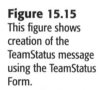

Figure 15.15
This figure shows
creation of the
TeamStatus message
using the TeamStatus
Form.

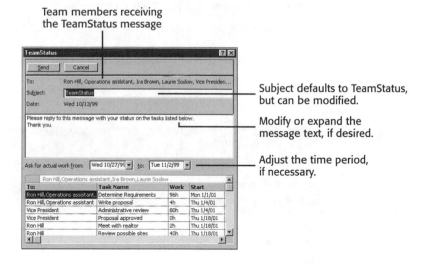

Subject defaults to TeamStatus,
but can be modified.

Modify or expand the
message text, if desired.

Adjust the time period,
if necessary.

3. Choose the Send button to complete the process.

4. You will briefly see a series of dialog boxes that indicate the messages are being sent to the team members.

When the project manager completes the TeamStatus function, the Indicators column in the project plan contains an icon that indicates the TeamStatus has been requested (see Figure 15.16).

Figure 15.16
The project manager
can easily see which
tasks have a pending
TeamStatus.

	🛈	Task Name	Duration	Start	17 20 23 26 29
12	✉	Finalize selection	1.25 days	Fri 2/2/01	
13		Site selected	0 days	Mon 2/5/01	
14		⊟ Design space	6.5 days	Mon 2/5/01	
15	✉	Meet with architect	4 hrs	Mon 2/5/01	
16	✉	Review architect's propose	1 day	Fri 2/8/01	
17	✉	There has not yet been a response to all the TeamStatus messages for this task.	1 day	Tue 2/13/01	
18			0 days	Wed 2/14/01	
19	✉	Notes: 'Expect about 3 days wait for Architect to return with the drawings.'	2 wks	Wed 2/14/01	
20			0 days	Wed 2/28/01	
21		⊟ Select furnishings	1 day	Wed 2/28/01	
22	✉	Inventory old furnishing	4 hrs	Wed 2/28/01	
23	✉	Identify new needs	2 hrs	Wed 2/28/01	
24	✉	Order new furnishings	2 hrs	Thu 3/1/01	

REPLYING TO THE TEAMSTATUS REQUEST

Each team member will receive a TeamStatus message either in their Project Central Inbox or email inbox. The subject of the message reflects what was entered by the project manager. (For the purposes of illustration, the rest of this section assumes the Subject of the message remained TeamStatus.) The detail of the message contains a timesheet. The team members will enter their actual work, update the remaining work, and add any pertinent comments regarding the task. Team members then must send the timesheet update back to the project manager.

USING PROJECT CENTRAL TO RESPOND TO THE TEAMSTATUS REQUEST

For team members who are using Project Central, their detailed TeamStatus message will appear as shown in Figure 15.17.

Figure 15.17
The TeamStatus function creates a timesheet message for the team members.

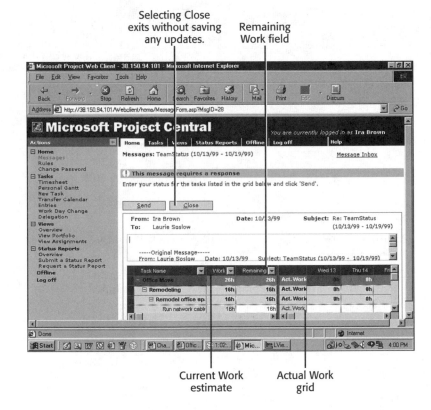

Complete the TeamStatus timesheet. As you see in Figure 15.17, you have the following items to update:

- Actual Work needs to be entered in the appropriate time phase on the grid.
- Update the Remaining Work field if the current Work field should be recalculated.
- Enter comments about the task. You might need to scroll to the right of the table side of the timesheet to see the Comments field.

You can update the Actual Work, Remaining Work, and Comments fields. The Remaining Work will be automatically calculated based on the current Work field. Revise the Remaining Work field if necessary to indicate a modification to the estimated Work.

> **Caution**
>
> If the remaining work is calculated or entered as zero, Project will assume your work for the task is complete. If all other resources have completed their work or if you were the only resource on the task, Project will set the task as completed (if the Updating Task Status Updates Resource Status option is turned on). When updating your TeamStatus timesheet, be sure to accurately estimate the remaining work.

> **Note**
>
> The task table portion of the TeamStatus timesheet can be modified. You can move columns, resize the column width, sort the tasks, apply an AutoFilter, and resize the row height. See the "Modifying the Timesheet Table" and "Grouping and Sorting Tasks" topics in the section "Modifying the Timesheet" in this chapter for details on performing these specific view changes.

USING EMAIL TO RESPOND TO THE TEAMSTATUS REQUEST

Team members who are using email for workgroup messaging will receive the detailed TeamStatus timesheet shown in Figure 15.18.

Figure 15.18
The TeamStatus function creates a timesheet message for the team members.

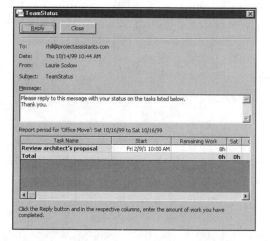

A response will be returned to the project manager by performing the following steps:

1. Enter your Actual Work in the appropriate timephase grid cell.

2. Update the Remaining Work. In the email timesheet, this field will not be automatically calculated based on the estimated and actual work. Enter a value of zero if the task is complete.

3. Enter any pertinent information in the Comments field. The information you enter will be appended to the Notes field in the project plan.

Note

To access the Comments, you may need to scroll to the right of the task list. You can also resize the column widths by placing the mouse pointer over the column dividers. The pointer will turn into a double-headed arrow. Drag the column divider to the desired width.

4. Enter any additional information in the Message text section.

5. Choose the Reply button to transmit your update to the project manager. You can also elect to delay the response by choosing the Save and Send Later button. If you choose the Close button, you will exit the message and will be prompted to save any updates.

Note

Although it appears you can modify the Start date in the TeamStatus timesheet, this will not update the Start date field in the project plan. The Start date for the task will be updated based on the date associated with the actual work entered.

COMPLETING THE PROJECT CENTRAL TIMESHEET

The Project Central timesheet provides an alternative to the TeamStatus timesheet for collecting actual work. The project manager can procedurally determine how often the timesheets will be completed. The team members will then have the responsibility to submit the timesheets in a timely fashion. The team member can use the timesheet to update the Actual Work, Remaining Work, Actual Overtime Work, and Comments. Any comments will be appended to the Notes field in the project plan.

To update the timesheet, perform the following steps:

1. Select Timesheet from the Tasks menu or Actions bar.

2. You will be presented with the timesheet (see Figure 15.19). The timescale will default to Days and the timescale period will default to five working days starting with the current day's date. See the "Modifying the Timesheet" section later in this chapter for details on the options for changing the display of the timesheet.

Note

Actual progress on the task is either entered via the Actual Work field or the % Work Complete field. When you enter one of those values, the alternate fields become non-editable.

3. Enter your Actual Work in the timescaled grid or enter the % Work Complete.

4. The Remaining Work will be automatically calculated based on the current Work field. Revise the Remaining Work field if necessary to indicate a modification to the estimated work.

Figure 15.19
The timesheet is used by the team member to supply actual and remaining work for each task.

Noneditable fields (gray)   Editable fields (white)

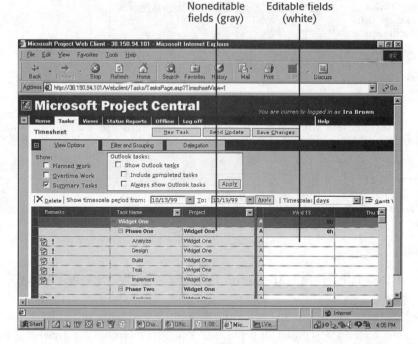

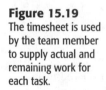

Caution

If the remaining work is calculated or entered as zero, Project will assume your work for the task is complete. If all other resources have completed their work or if you were the only resource on the task, Project will set the task as completed (if the Updating Task Status Updates Resource Status option is turned on). When updating your timesheet, be sure to accurately estimate the remaining work.

5. Enter Overtime Work if appropriate.

6. Enter any pertinent comments for the task. For example, note if the task will not be completed by the estimated Finish date.

Tip from Tim and the Project Team

To view the entire comment, point to the Comments cell.

7. When you have completed entering the actual and remaining hours, choose the Send Update button. You'll receive the message shown in Figure 15.20. If you would like to make additional updates to the timesheet before submitting it to the project manager, select the Save Changes button instead.

Figure 15.20
This message alerts you that the update has been successfully sent to the project manager.

The Timesheet display now shows an icon in the Remarks column for the updated tasks. The icon tells you that the information has been sent to the project manager but has not yet been updated in the actual project plan (see Figure 15.21).

Figure 15.21
This icon displays the tracking status of the task.

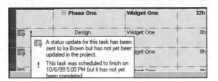

UPDATING THE TEAMSTATUS AND TIMESHEET DATA IN THE PROJECT PLAN

After the team member completes and sends his timesheet information, the project manager will receive a message in either the Project Central Inbox or email inbox. If TeamStatus is the method being used for project tracking, the subject of the message is Re:TeamStatus. For Project Central timesheet tracking, the subject of the message is Task Update.

The project manager will display the detailed message and either select Update to post the actuals information in the project plan or Reply to continue a dialogue with the team member regarding his timesheet. The detailed message from the TeamStatus timesheet is shown in Figure 15.22. The detailed message from the Project Central timesheet is displayed in Figure 15.23.

Figure 15.22
The project manager can choose to have the timesheet information automatically update the workplan.

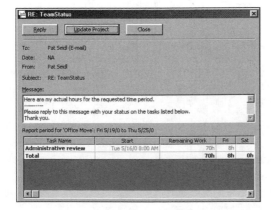

Figure 15.23
The Task Update message requires a response by the project manager.

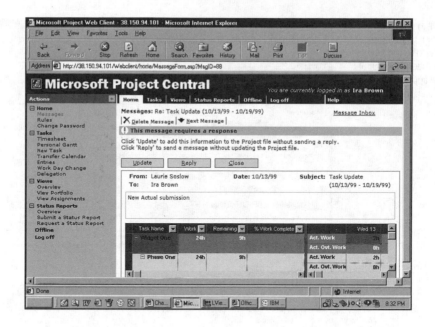

If the project manager selects the Update button, the actuals information is automatically updated in the project plan. For Project Central messaging, the project manager will be prompted to delete the Task Update message. The icon that appeared in the team member's Project Central timesheet (refer to Figure 15.21) will no longer appear because the project plan has been updated to reflect the posted actuals.

USING PROJECT CENTRAL TO REQUEST A NEW TASK

As work progresses on the project, a project team member might find himself in a situation where he is working on a task that is not in the workplan. You can communicate this information to the project manager via Project Central. To create the new task, select the New Task function from the menu, the Actions bar, the Timesheet view, or the Personal Gantt view. You will be presented with the screen displayed in Figure 15.24.

For the task to be added to the project plan, several pieces of information are required. You will supply this information by completing the New Task screen as follows:

1. Determine whether the task should be created at the highest outline level or as a subtask to an already existing summary task. The drop-down box next to the summary selection will display the summary tasks across all the project plans you are assigned to.

2. You must identify the project plan that the task is associated with. The Project drop-down box will display all the projects available in Project Central.

3. Enter a free-form task description in the Name field.

4. Enter the Start date and estimated Work. You can optionally enter Comments. Anything you document in the Comments field will be appended to the Notes field for the task.

Figure 15.24
When requesting a new task, the team member must supply the appropriate information for the task.

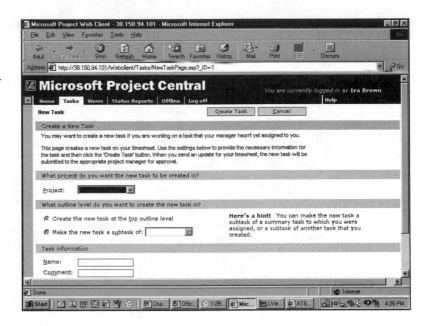

Note

If you enter a Work value without specifying a measurement (for example, hours, days, weeks), the value will be assumed to be hours. You can override this default by keying in the measurement. For example, if you enter a value of 2d, the work will be assigned as 16 hours.

5. When you have entered all the information, choose the Create Task button. The task will be added to your timesheet with two icons added to the Remarks column (see Figure 15.25).

6. To finalize the process, choose the Send Update button. This will send the new task request to the project manager.

The request for a new task will be submitted to the project manager. When the project manager opens the New Task message, a detailed message will appear, as shown in Figure 15.26.

You have the option of updating the project plan with the new task or updating the plan and sending a reply to the team member. The Comments field can be modified on this screen but the Task Name, Work, and Start fields cannot be changed.

Caution

The new task will be added to the project plan with a constraint type of Start No Earlier Than. Keep in mind that the task is added at the bottom of the section of the project plan where the resource requested it to be added, such as a subsection or at the top level.

Figure 15.25
A new task request from a resource must be approved by the project manager.

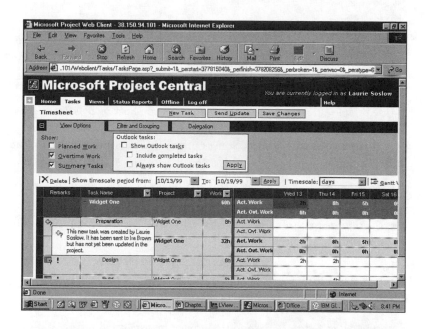

Figure 15.26
The project manager can add the task to the project plan by choosing the Update button.

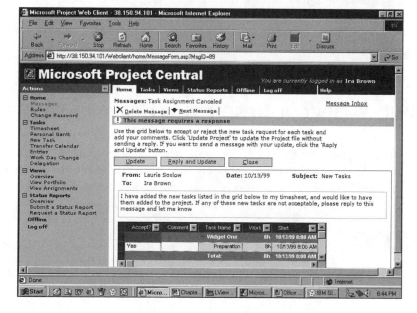

DELEGATING TASKS IN PROJECT CENTRAL

On large projects, there often is a need to have team leaders in addition to the project manager. Project Central supports this need by providing the ability to delegate tasks and designate a lead person for those delegated tasks.

Tip from Tim and the Project Team

> There is an option that controls this functionality. To use it, go to Tools, Options, select the Workgroup tab, and check the Allow Resources to Delegate Tasks in Microsoft Project Central option.

Tasks are delegated from the team member's timesheet or by selecting Delegation from the Tasks menu. You'll be prompted through the steps to complete the delegation. At the time you delegate the task, you have some options that determine your continued responsibility for the task:

- *Transfer the task.* The task will be displayed in your timesheet with a different background color but you won't be able to edit it.

- *Continue to track the task.* With this option, you can't edit the task but you will see the most recent updates to it.

- *Designate yourself as the lead resource.* As lead resource, you have the ability to request a task status from the delegated resource and have responsibility for approving the resource's actuals prior to submitting them to the project manager.

Both the delegated resource and the project manager will receive a Task Delegation Request message in their Message Inbox. When the project manager retrieves the delegation message, a function can be invoked to update the project plan. This replaces the resource assignment on the delegated task with the delegated resource. In addition, the task appears on the delegated resource's Project Central timesheet.

USING WORKGROUPS IN THE UPDATE PROCESS

As the project progresses, changes will be occurring in the project plan. Project workgroups support these changes through several functions. The project manager will use the TeamUpdate function to communicate changes to task start or finish dates. The team members will be sending status reports to the project manager. A resource can also notify the project manager of changes to her availability.

> **Note**
>
> As you update the project plan, you might also be adding tasks or adding resources to existing tasks. Both of these situations will require you to perform the TeamAssign function. In these cases, even if you select to send the assignments for all tasks (refer to Figure 15.5), Project knows to only send the information for these new task assignments.

COMMUNICATING TASK UPDATES USING TEAMUPDATE

Certain changes, such as a task's start or finish date, will flag the task as one that needs to be communicated to the team using TeamUpdate (see Figure 15.27).

Figure 15.27
The icon in the Indicators column informs the project manager that the TeamUpdate function should be performed.

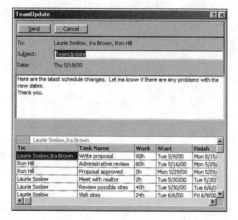

The project manager completes the TeamUpdate process by performing the following:

1. Choose the TeamUpdate button, or choose <u>T</u>ools, <u>W</u>orkgroup, <u>T</u>eamUpdate. The TeamUpdate Form appears (see Figure 15.28).

Figure 15.28
The project manager creates the TeamUpdate message utilizing the TeamUpdate Form.

2. When the dialog box is complete, choose the <u>S</u>end button to transmit the message to the resources.

3. You will briefly see a series of dialog boxes that indicate the messages are being sent to the team members.

After sending the message, the TeamUpdate icon that appeared in the Indicators column of the project plan will be removed.

Note

Project only allows you to use the TeamUpdate function if there are tasks flagged for communication to the team. If there haven't been any of these types of task changes and you try to execute the TeamUpdate function, you'll receive a message from Project informing you that there are no tasks to update.

RECEIVING TEAMUPDATES

After the project manager sends the TeamUpdate, each team member will receive a message in either his Project Central Inbox or email inbox. The subject of the message reflects what was entered by the project manager. (For the purposes of illustration, the rest of this section assumes the subject of the message remained TeamUpdate.)

The team member can see a list of the task changes by viewing the message detail. The team member's task list consists of only the changed tasks he is assigned to.

RECEIVING TEAMUPDATES IN PROJECT CENTRAL

For team members who are using Project Central, their detailed TeamUpdate message will appear as shown in Figure 15.29.

Figure 15.29
The detailed message displays the resource's tasks that had changes.

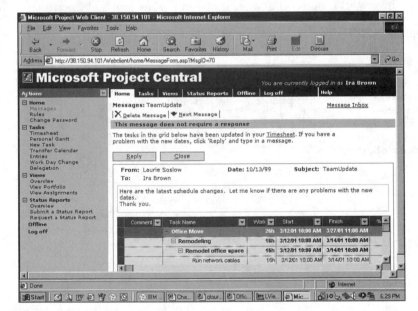

It is not necessary to respond to the message. However, if you need to communicate any information to the project manager about the changed dates, you may do so by selecting the Reply button. This will send a message back to the project manager.

Note

In the response to the TeamUpdate message, you cannot key any information into the task listing box. All comments need to be entered into the message text.

The project manager and team members can continue to carry on a dialogue regarding these task changes via the Reply functionality until all issues are resolved.

RECEIVING TEAMUPDATES VIA EMAIL

Team members who are using email for workgroup messaging will receive their TeamUpdate messages through their email inbox. The detailed message received is shown in Figure 15.30.

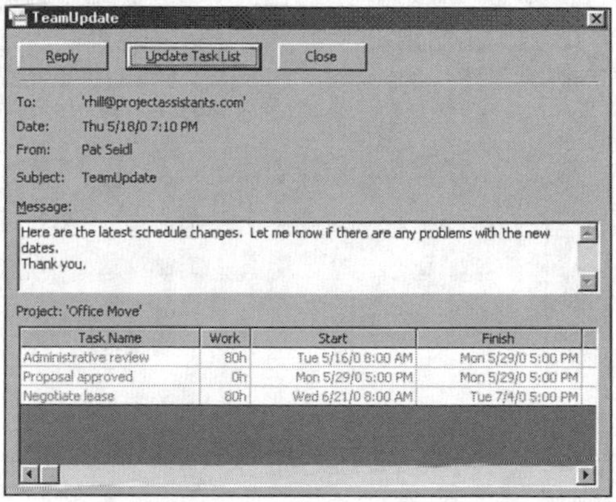

Figure 15.30
You can reflect the revised information in your Outlook task or reply to the project manager.

If you need to continue to communicate with the project manager about the changed dates, you may do so by selecting the Reply button. If there are no questions or issues surrounding the task revision, you can incorporate the change in your Outlook tasks by choosing the Update Task List button.

CREATING STATUS REPORTS IN PROJECT CENTRAL

Project Central can be used to formally report the status of the project. The project manager can initiate this process by requesting that a status report be submitted on a recurring basis by a particular date. Another option is for the project team member to submit a status report on an ad-hoc basis. This would be useful in a situation where critical events have occurred outside of the preset status reporting period.

REQUESTING A STATUS REPORT

When a project manager requests a status report from the project team members, he or she can specify a time cycle, a due date, and the format of the report. After the project manager submits the request, it will appear on the team member's Project Central home page. The responses from the team members can be consolidated into a group report.

To initiate this process, the project manager selects the Request a Status Report function from the Status Reports menu or from the Actions bar. The process is shown in Figures 15.31–35.

Selecting these screens takes you to a specific step.

Figure 15.31
You can request a new status report, edit a current request, or delete a request on this screen.

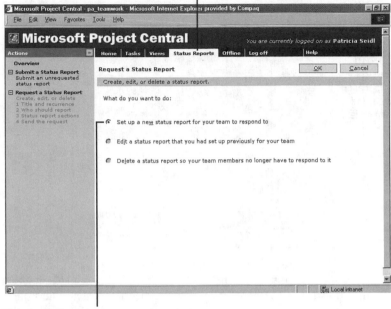

Click the option to set up a new request.

Type a name for the status report.

Use these button to navigate the four steps.

Figure 15.32
The status reporting cycle is defined in this step.

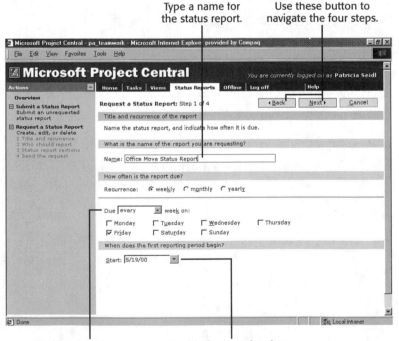

Set the report frequency.   Modify the start date here.

Figure 15.33
The resources who should submit status reports are designated in this step.

All resources defined in Project Central are displayed here.

Resources who must submit the status report

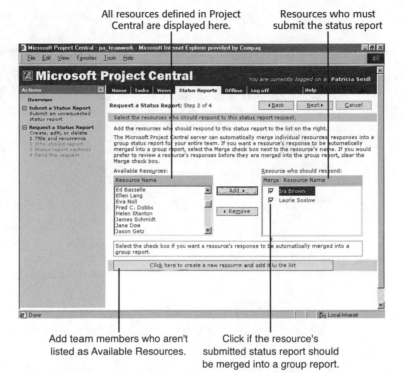

Add team members who aren't listed as Available Resources.

Click if the resource's submitted status report should be merged into a group report.

Three topics are predefined in Project Central.

Click here to add a topic in a specific order.

Figure 15.34
In this step the topics for the status report are defined.

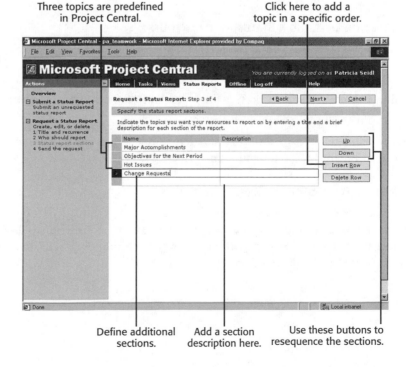

Define additional sections.

Add a section description here.

Use these buttons to resequence the sections.

Either send or save the
status report request.

Figure 15.35
The status report request can be sent to the team members or can be saved for future modifications.

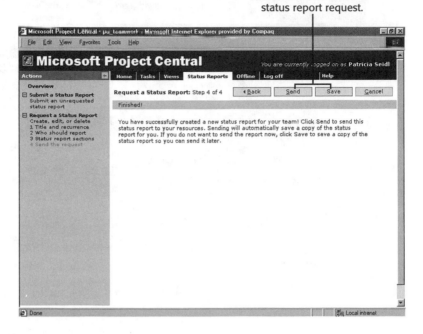

After the project manager submits the status report request, each team member will see a line item under the Status Report section of the home page (refer to Figure 15.3).

EDITING OR DELETING A STATUS REPORT REQUEST

A saved status report request can be edited prior to being sent to the project team members. The project manager will choose the Request a Status Report function from the Status Reports menu or from the Actions bar. From this point they can maneuver through the editing process by either selecting the Next and Back buttons or by selecting the appropriate screens from the Actions bar.

If the status report is no longer required, the project manager will use the delete option (refer to Figure 15.31) to remove this request.

RESPONDING TO A STATUS REPORT REQUEST

The project team member can respond to the requested status report by selecting it from his home page, from the Actions bar, or from the Status Report menu. It will be listed under the Submit a Status Report section. After selecting the report, the team member will be presented with the screen shown in Figure 15.36.

Figure 15.36
The status report detail is documented in the appropriate topic section.

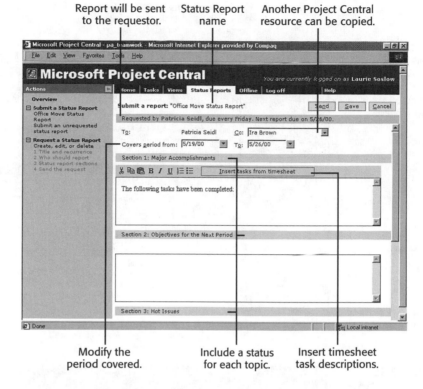

Report will be sent to the requestor.

Status Report name

Another Project Central resource can be copied.

Modify the period covered.

Include a status for each topic.

Insert timesheet task descriptions.

When submitting the status report, you can only select one resource to be copied. However, after submitting the report, you will be able to forward it to additional team members.

You have the option of including specific task names in the section by choosing the Insert Tasks from Timesheet button. Figure 15.37 shows the screen that is used to select the tasks.

After selecting the Insert Tasks button, the task descriptions will be pasted into the status report, as shown in Figure 15.38.

Figure 15.37
Scroll down in the bottom pane to select the different status report sections.

Choose which tasks to select.

This button incorporates task names into the status report.

Click here to return to the status report.

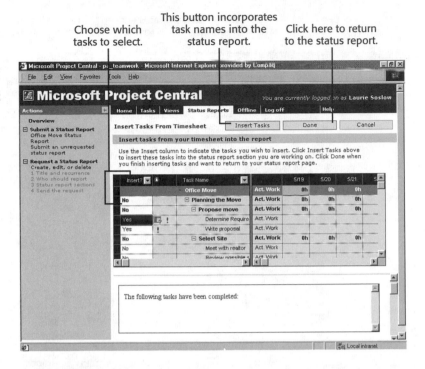

Figure 15.38
The task description for the selected tasks will be included in the status report.

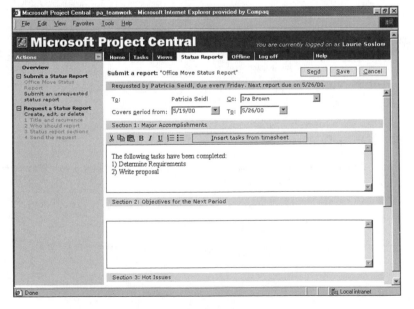

After documenting the status for each section topic, you have the option of including a new topic by choosing to add a section (see Figure 15.39).

Figure 15.39
Add a new section if you have additional information for the report.

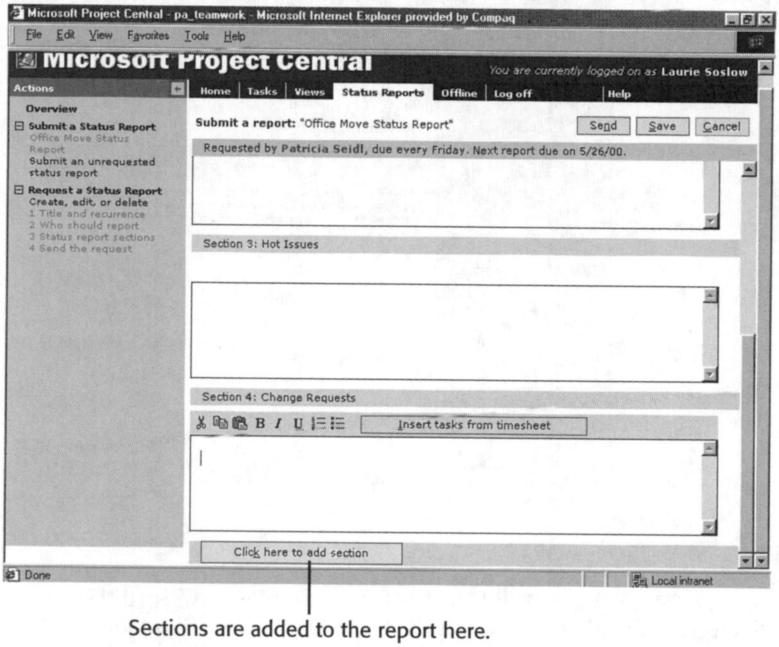

Sections are added to the report here.

Type in a description for the new section and select OK to complete the information for the added topic.

Note

You can choose to delete any sections that you added; however, you cannot delete a section that was requested by the project manager.

When you have completed the status report and are ready to submit it to the project manager, choose the Send button. If you haven't finished the report choose the Save button.

SUBMITTING AN UNREQUESTED STATUS REPORT

There could be situations where a team member would like to communicate with the project manager outside of the regular status report schedule. This can be accomplished by using the Create/Submit an Unrequested Status Report function. The steps for completing the report are very similar to those for a requested report. For an unrequested report, the team member also determines the name of the report, who receives the report, and all the section topics (see Figure 15.40).

Figure 15.40
There are no prede-
fined section topics in
an unrequested
report.

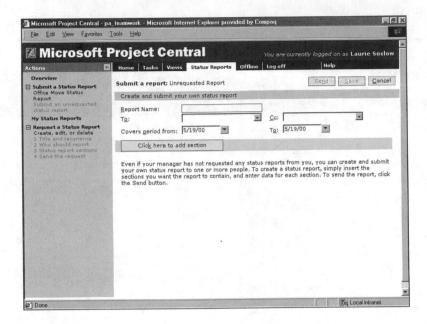

VIEWING STATUS REPORTS

The project manager will view the status reports under the Group Status Report display.
Each team member can view his submitted or saved reports under My Status Reports.

THE PROJECT MANAGER VIEW OF STATUS REPORTS

After submitting the request for a status report, the report will be listed on your home page
or under the Status Reports menu. You can track the responses to the report and select a
report to view on the screen shown in Figure 15.41.

The icon next to the team member's name indicates whether or not the requested report
has been received. It will also indicate if the team member submitted an update to a previously submitted report. Any updates to a status report are automatically merged into the
original status report.

You can select a single status report to view or can select the compiled group report. You
can also choose to merge status reports that were not originally designated to be included
in the group report.

*Tip from Tim and
the Project Team*

If you need to send the status report to someone who doesn't have access to your Project
Central site, you can email it by selecting the Mail icon on your Internet browser.

Figure 15.41
This screen provides a
way to access and
monitor status
reports.

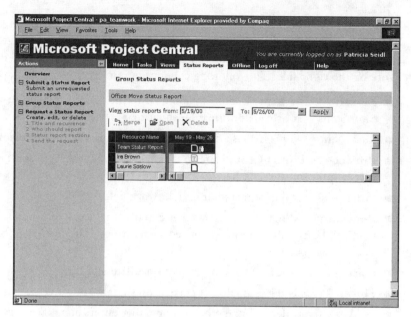

THE TEAM MEMBER VIEW OF STATUS REPORTS

Each team member can access his status reports (submitted and unsubmitted) through the
My Status Reports function.

You can use the Filter and Group By drop-down boxes to limit and rearrange the listing of
the reports. If you need to modify a status report that has already been submitted to the
project manager, you can select the report and select the Update function. This will append
the new information to the status report that has already been sent. You can also forward
your status report to additional individuals.

The Miscellaneous Report view shows you status reports that you have been copied on.

OTHER FUNCTIONS IN PROJECT CENTRAL

There are several other Project Central features and functions that may be used throughout
the duration of the project. The team members have the ability to modify the Project
Central views to better accommodate their working styles. They also have access to project
information across the organization—not just projects they are assigned to. There are also
other communication features for the project team members.

MODIFYING VIEWS

In Project Central, each team member has access to his task list in Timesheet and Personal
Gantt views. There are various display customizations you can use to make the views more
applicable to the way you work.

MODIFYING THE TIMESHEET

The Timesheet view is laid out in a similar fashion to the Resource Usage view in Project. On the left side is task information in a table format. The timescale grid displays the Actual Work on the right side. The following columns of information are displayed for each task:

- **Remarks**—The Remarks column is similar to the Indicators field. It will contain indicator icons that provide information about that task.

- **Task Name**—This is a task description as defined in the project plan.

- **Project**—In Project Central a team member sees the tasks across all his projects, so it is very helpful for the timesheet to include this field.

- **Work**—This is the estimated or current work field.

- **Remaining**—When the team member enters actual work in the timescale grid, this field will be calculated based on the estimated work. The team member should update the field as needed.

- **Start**—This is the estimated or current start date and time.

- **Finish**—This is the estimated or current finish date and time.

- **% Work Complete**—When the team member enters actual work in the timescale grid, this field will be calculated based on the estimated work.

- **Comments**—Anything entered here will be appended to the Notes field for the task in the project plan.

- **Assigned to**—Name of the resource assigned to the task. If the task assignment has been delegated, this column will reflect the name of the delegated resource.

- **Lead Name**—Resource name who is designated as the lead when the task has been delegated to another resource.

Tip from Tim and the Project Team

You might need to move the vertical bar that separates the table and the timescale grid to see all the columns.

There are several ways you can modify your timesheet. You can

- Modify the timescale grid by selecting the fields that appear and by designating a particular timeframe.

- Rearrange the columns of data that display in the table and apply groupings and sorts to the tasks.

- Include and exclude tasks from displaying, with the option of showing Outlook tasks.

MODIFYING THE TIMESCALE GRID   Figure 15.42 shows the options that control the display of the timescale grid.

Add currently scheduled work to the timescale grid.

Configure the timescale format.

Figure 15.42
There are several options for displaying the data in the timescale grid.

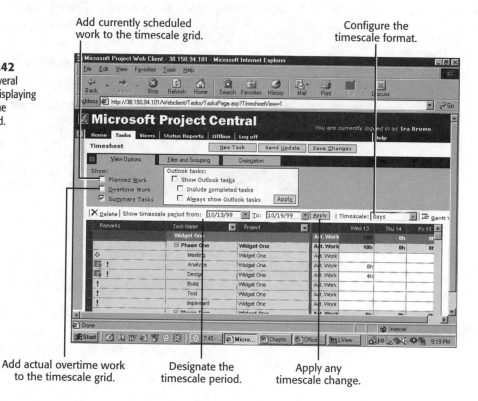

Add actual overtime work to the timescale grid.

Designate the timescale period.

Apply any timescale change.

Note

The Entire Period timescale option will display one time period that spans the earliest start date through the latest finish date for the particular team member's tasks.

Note

When you select the options on the timesheet, these options will remain in effect until you turn them off. For example, the default for the Timescale is days. If you change it to be weeks, every time you access the timesheet it will be displayed in weeks.

MODIFYING THE TIMESHEET TABLE   Figure 15.43 shows the options that control the display of the Timesheet tasks.

Include Outlook tasks and configure which tasks appear.

Click here to process your selections.

Figure 15.43
There are several options for displaying the task information.

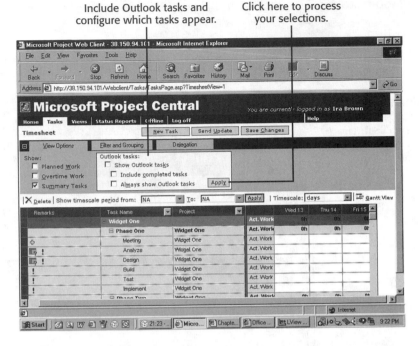

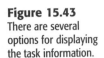

There is a difference between the two selections for displaying Outlook tasks. The Show Outlook Tasks option only applies to your current session. Select the Always Show Outlook Tasks to have this option remain in effect every time you log in.

The width of the columns can be resized by placing the mouse on the vertical bar that separates the column headings. When the mouse pointer is a double-headed arrow, drag and drop the vertical line to the desired column width.

You can move the entire column to another location in the table by selecting the column heading and then holding down the left mouse button until it is a double-headed arrow. Drag and drop the column to the new location.

The row height is also modifiable in the same manner as the column width. The row height must accommodate the fields in the timescale grid.

GROUPING AND SORTING TASKS When the timesheet is first displayed, it is grouped by the Project field. Figure 15.44 shows the options that are available to you for grouping and sorting the tasks, as well as for filtering the tasks that are displayed.

Figure 15.44
The Filter and Grouping tab provides options for the task display.

Filter drop-down box

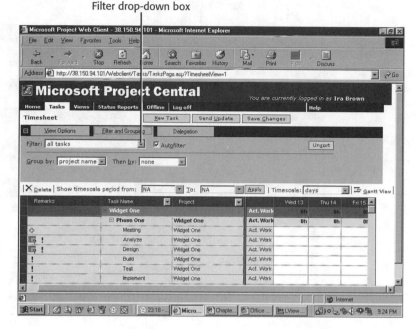

At least one level of grouping must be selected. The second level is optional. A group row is displayed prior to the detailed tasks for that grouping.

You might also want to apply a sort within the group. You can apply one sort to the timesheet. Click in the column heading for the field that will be used as the sort value. An ascending arrow will appear in the column heading and the tasks will be sorted in the appropriate order. If you click the column heading, the sort will be switched to a descending sort.

To remove the sort, select the Unsort button.

MODIFYING THE PERSONAL GANTT

The Personal Gantt view is like the Gantt Chart view in Project. The task table resides on the left side of the screen while the right side displays the timescaled bar chart.

The options available for displaying the Personal Gantt are comparable to the Timesheet view options. There are some differences on the View Options tab, as shown in Figure 15.45.

Each time you click the Zoom In or Zoom Out options, the Gantt timescale is incrementally changed. Table 15.2 summarizes the timescale levels.

Figure 15.45
The Personal Gantt has different options that control the bar chart section of the display.

Filter drop-down box

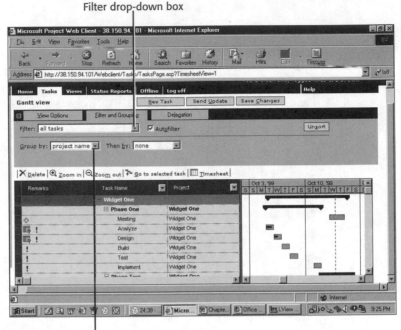

Choose task grouping levels.

TABLE 15.2   THE PERSONAL GANTT TIMESCALE LEVELS

Major Scale	Minor Scale
Year	Half Year
Year	Quarter
Year	Month
Quarter	Month
Month	Week
Month	Three-day increments
Week	Day
Day	Six-hour increments
Day	Two-hour increments
Hour	Fifteen-minute increments

VIEWING OTHER PROJECT PLANS

One of the collaborative features of Project Central is the ability to see project and resource information for projects you might not be assigned to. The Project Central Administrator is responsible for setting the security to determine the projects and resource assignments you are authorized to see. There are two functions available to you. The first is View Your

Portfolio, which displays a list of projects. You can select a project to see more detail, such as the tasks and resources.

The second function is View Assignments. This view shows the timephased breakdown of work and actuals for the resource assignments.

USING PROJECT CENTRAL TO SUBMIT CHANGES IN AVAILABILITY

Project Central provides two methods for a team member to communicate changes in their availability. The first method is to submit a work day change. This method can be used by team members who are not using Outlook as their personal management system. The second method is to transfer calendar entries directly from Outlook. Both methods create a message in the project manager's Inbox and provide an automated way to post the availability change in the resource's calendar.

NOTIFYING THE PROJECT MANAGER OF WORK DAY CHANGES

In Project Central a project team member can alert the project manager to changes in his availability and those changes can automatically update the selected project plans. The project team member selects the Notify Manager of a Work Day Change function from the Tasks menu or Actions bar. There are three steps in this process. Step 1 is shown in Figure 15.46, step 2 in Figure 15.47, and step 3 in Figure 15.48.

Figure 15.46
The team member designates the type of change and dates affected in the first step of the process.

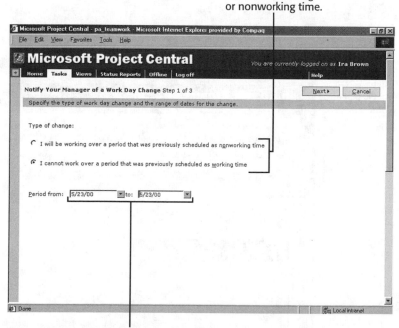

Indicate working
or nonworking time.

Enter dates affected by this change.

Note

You do not have the ability to select time blocks. Project Central assumes the documented change is for the entire calendar day.

Project managers as
defined in Project Central

Figure 15.47
Select the project managers who will receive the notification.

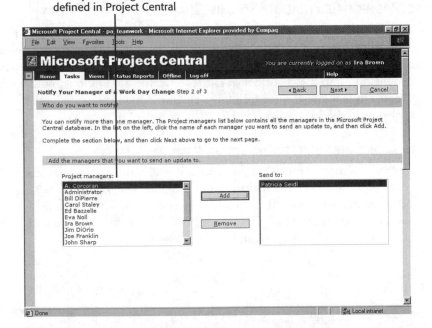

Figure 15.48
This screen provides a review of the notification information.

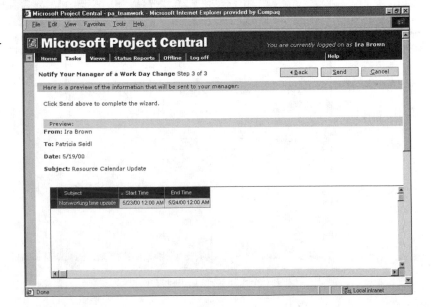

After the team members complete this function, the project manager(s) will receive a message in their Project Central Inbox (see Figure 15.49). You can have the notification automatically update the resource's calendar for the selected project plan (see Figure 15.50). Figure 15.51 displays the resource's revised calendar.

Note

If Project is not active, it will be opened when you perform the function.

Figure 15.49
The working day change notice is communicated to the project manager via his Project Central Inbox.

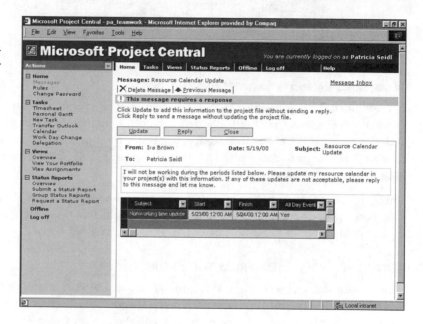

Active project files displayed here

Figure 15.50
The project manager selects a project plan to be updated with the revised resource calendar information.

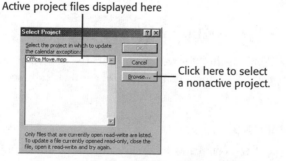

Click here to select a nonactive project.

Tip from Tim and the Project Team

You can only select one project file to be updated. If this resource is on more than one of your projects, do not delete the message when Project prompts you that the update has been completed. You can then repeat this process until all project files have been updated.

Figure 15.51
The resource calendar reflects the working time change.

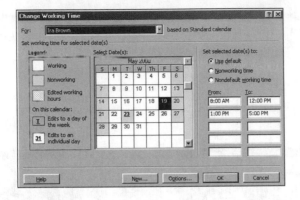

TRANSFERING CALENDAR ENTRIES FROM OUTLOOK

If a team member is using the Outlook Calendar to enter events, the dates and times of these events can be automatically updated in nonworking time in either the resource's calendar or his Project Central timesheet. A five-step wizard will guide you through the process of transferring these calendar entries. The wizard selects calendar entries that are assigned a status of Busy or Out of Office.

After you submit the transfer to the project manager, she will have the ability to automatically post the nonworking time in the project plan in the same manner as described in the topic "Notifying the Project Manager of Work Day Changes."

ACCESSING THE TEAMINBOX FROM THE PROJECT PLAN

The TeamInBox selection on the Workgroup menu and toolbar allows you to access Project Central directly from the project plan. When you choose this function, your browser will automatically start and you will be presented with the Project Central sign onscreen.

OTHER FUNCTIONS IN WORKGROUPS

If you are using the Email method for workgroups, there are several functions that give you the ability to share project information. You can also automatically set task reminders in Outlook.

USING THE SEND COMMAND

The Microsoft Project Send command is similar to the Send command in the other applications in the Microsoft Office group. The Send command opens a new mail message form where you can compose and address a message, and the currently active project is automatically attached to the message. Each addressee will get a copy of the project file in Microsoft Project. You can, if you want, remove the attached project file and send the message without it.

The steps that follow assume that you have not previously attached a routing slip to this project and that you must address the message before you can send it. See the next section ("Using a Routing Slip") for information about creating and using routing slips.

To address and send a copy of a project file through electronic mail, follow these steps:

1. Choose File, Send To, Mail Recipient, or choose the Send To Mail Recipient button on the Workgroup toolbar.

2. The Outlook mail message form will appear (see Figure 15.52). There will be an icon in the message area representing the attached project file. You will need to address the message and add appropriate text (if desired) in the message area.

Figure 15.52
Here is the Outlook mail message form with the project file-name in its title bar and a Project icon representing the attached Project file.

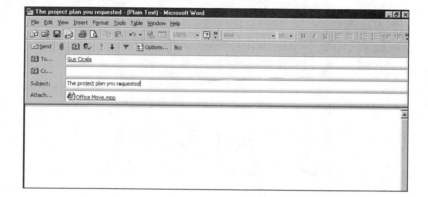

3. When the addresses and message are complete, choose the Send button to transmit the message with the accompanying copy of the project file.

When the addressees receive the message, they can double-click the file icon in the message area to open Microsoft Project with the project file displayed.

Note

For more information on using Outlook, you should take a look at Que's *Special Edition Using Microsoft Outlook 2000* by Gordon Padwick.

USING A ROUTING SLIP

If you will be corresponding regularly with the same group about the project, you will want to prepare a routing slip to attach to the project file. The routing slip can be used repeatedly to circulate the same file from one recipient to another, accumulating suggested changes in the project file. You also will be notified automatically as each recipient forwards the message and file on to the next person on the routing slip list. These status notes will keep you informed of the progress of the message.

You can reuse the routing slip to send later messages and new versions of the project. You also can change the names on the list and change the message text. You can choose to have the project and message sent to all names on the address list simultaneously, or one after another in the order they are listed. If you route the message to one recipient after another, you can choose to have tracking notices sent to you each time the message is forwarded to the next name on the list.

To attach a routing slip to a project file, follow these steps:

1. Choose File, Send To, Routing Recipient, or choose the Send to Routing Recipient button on the Workgroup toolbar. The Routing Slip dialog box appears (see Figure 15.53). You can use the Cancel button to close the dialog box without changing anything.

Figure 15.53
Create a permanent address list and an accompanying message with the Add Slip command.

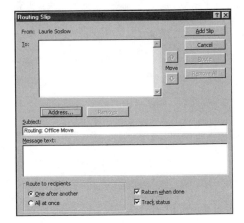

2. Add to the address list and remove names from the list with the Address and Remove buttons. You can remove all names from the list (and clear the message area) by choosing the Remove All button).

   If you are routing the message to recipients one after another, you can move names up or down in the list to alter the routing order. Move a name by selecting the name and then clicking one of the arrows above or below the Move label. Sally Campetti is currently first on the list to receive the message. Sally Campetti is selected and the down arrow can be used to move her down the list. In Figure 15.54, Sally Campetti has been moved to the bottom of the list and will be the last to receive the message, enabling her to review all comments and changes.

3. The Subject text box will contain a default that can be modified if you desire.

4. Type the message you want delivered with the file in the Message Text box.

Figure 15.54
This figure shows the routing slip with Sally Campetti moved to the last position using the Move button.

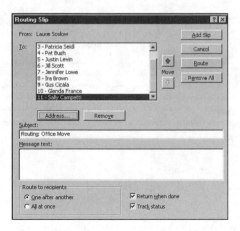

5. In the Route to Recipients area, choose how you want the message routed. Choose <u>O</u>ne After Another to let one copy of the message make the circuit of all recipients, accumulating responses and changes in the project file as it moves down the list in the order you have entered the names. Choose A<u>l</u>l at Once to send a separate copy of the message and file to each recipient.

6. If you route the message one after another, you can choose to receive tracking notices as each recipient passes the message on to the next name on the list. Fill the Trac<u>k</u> Status check box to receive progress messages.

7. Fill the check box for Return <u>W</u>hen Done if you want the project file, including modifications by the people on the routing list, to be returned to you after all others on the routing slip have seen it.

8. If you are ready to send the message immediately, choose the <u>R</u>oute button. If you want to attach the routing slip to the project but are not ready to send the message just yet, choose the <u>A</u>dd Slip button.

After a routing slip has been attached to a Project file, the labels of two buttons on the Workgroup toolbar change: The Send to Mail Recipient button label changes to Next Routing Recipient, and the Send to Routing Recipient button's label changes to Other Routing Recipient. After the file has been sent to all recipients, the labels of these buttons change back to Send to Mail Recipient and Sent to Routing Recipient.

Note
If you selected <u>A</u>dd Slip instead of <u>R</u>oute when you created the routing slip, choose Other Routing Recipient to either modify or send the message.

When you send the message with the routing slip, each recipient will be able to double-click the Project file icon to open Microsoft Project and the attached Project file. Recipients can make changes in the project if they choose. Figure 15.55 shows the message that Patricia receives. The message about the routing slip and how to continue the routing is supplied automatically by Microsoft Project and the mail application.

Figure 15.55
The mail message contains the routed project file, with instructions to use the Send To, Next Routing Recipient command to continue the routing.

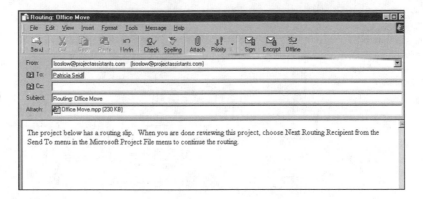

To forward the message and file on to the next name on the routing slip (or back to the originator when the route is complete), the recipient must open the project and use the Send To, Next Routing Recipient command. The Routing Slip dialog box will appear (see Figure 15.56). You can choose to continue the routing (Andrea Hamilton is the next name on the list), or you can choose to send the project to an address you supply.

Figure 15.56
The Routing Slip dialog box has the next recipient's name automatically filled in.

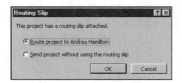

To review and forward a project you have received as a recipient on a routing slip, follow these steps:

1. Open the mail message that contains the routed project file.

2. Double-click the icon for the Microsoft Project file.

3. Review the project, making changes and adding notes to tasks or resources as you think appropriate.

4. Choose File, Send To, Next Routing Recipient (or click the Next Routing Recipient button on the toolbar) to forward the message and the edited file to the next name on the routing slip. The Routing Slip dialog box appears (refer to Figure 15.56).

5. Choose the option button next to Route Project to *nextname*, and choose the OK button to send the message.

6. Close the project file and save the changes.

When routing slip recipients forward the message to the next name on the list, a status message is automatically sent to the originator of the routing slip if the Track Status check box is filled on the routing slip.

When the last recipient of the routed message sends the file on, the file is returned to the author of the routing slip. Figure 15.57 shows the message that indicates the routing is completed.

Figure 15.57
Here is the message sent to the originator of the routing after all messages have been routed.

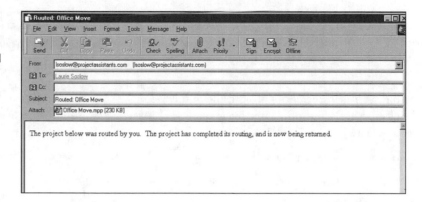

Send Schedule Note

The Send command described in the section "Using the Send Command" earlier in this chapter sends the entire project file to the recipients of the message. If you would like to send a message about a limited selection of tasks, or if you want to send a special copy of the project file without losing your routing slip, you can use the Send Schedule Note command by choosing Tools, Workgroup, Send Schedule Note.

The Send Schedule Note dialog box appears (see Figure 15.58) to offer you choices about creating the message. Fill the check boxes at the top to have the message addressed automatically to the Project Manager, the assigned Resources for the tasks that are included, or the Contacts that have been named for the tasks. Choose the Entire Project button to select those recipients for all tasks in the project, not just those currently selected. Choose the Selected Tasks option button to choose the resources and contacts for only the selected tasks.

Figure 15.58
Use the Send Schedule Note dialog box to select the attributes of the message.

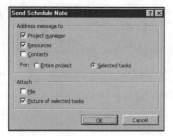

Note

In order for the Send Schedule Note function to work properly, an email address has to be defined for each resource and contact name. For resources, you can either value the email field on the Resource Information dialog box or you can add them to your email address file.

Because the Contact field does not appear on standard forms or views, you will have to add the field to a table to assign Contact names to tasks. Any name you type in the Contact field must be in your email address book.

You can attach the entire project File to the message. You also can choose the Picture of Selected Tasks button to attach a graphic of the way the active view displays the tasks that are selected.

To send a schedule note, follow these steps:

1. If you plan to attach a picture of selected tasks, apply the appropriate view and select the tasks.

2. Choose Tools, Workgroup, Send Schedule Note. The Send Schedule Note dialog box is displayed (refer to Figure 15.58).

3. If you want names of people who are defined in the project file to receive copies of the message, fill the check boxes for the appropriate categories to be selected: Project Manager, Resources, or Contacts.

4. If you fill one or more of the category check boxes, choose whether names are to be selected for those categories from the Entire Project or only from the Selected Tasks.

5. If you want to attach the project file, fill the File check box.

6. If you want to attach a picture of the selected tasks as displayed in the active view, fill the Picture of Selected Tasks check box.

7. Choose OK to continue assembling the message. An Outlook Mail Message dialog box will appear (see Figure 15.59). The dialog box is initially titled to match the project file, but the title will change to match the subject of the message.

Figure 15.59
Finalize the message from the Send button in the mail message dialog box.

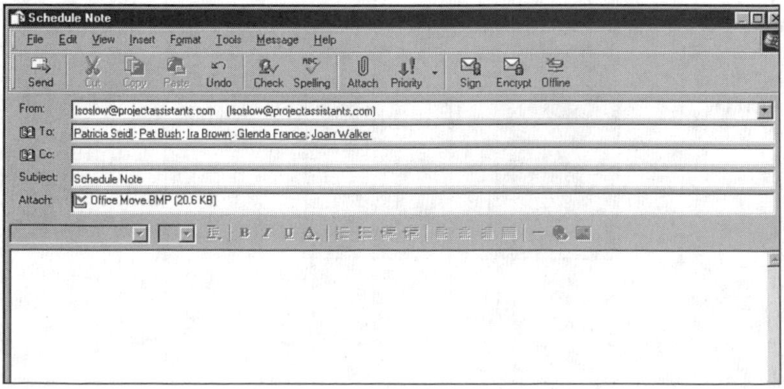

8. You are free to add or remove names from the To list of direct recipients and the Cc list of copied recipients. Use the Address Book button to help select mail addresses.

9. Type the message Subject. The Subject will replace the dialog box title as soon as you leave the field.

10. Type the message text before or after the attachment icons (if there are any).

11. Choose the Send button to send the message.

RESEND ALL MESSAGES

The Resend All Messages function is similar to the TeamUpdate function. However, instead of just sending task information for changed tasks, information for all tasks will be forwarded to the team members.

SET REMINDER

Use the Set Reminder command to place alarms on tasks in Outlook. You can choose to have the reminder alarm set to the start or finish dates for the selected tasks, and you can choose how long in advance of the event the alarm will sound.

Caution

If the tasks are subsequently rescheduled, the alarm is not adjusted in Outlook. Although you can use the Set Reminder command again to capture the new scheduled date, you must manually remove the old alarms in Outlook.

To set alarms in Outlook to give a warning before a task's start or finish date, follow these steps:

1. Select the tasks you want to set alarms for.

2. Choose the Set Reminder button on the Workgroup toolbar, or choose Tools, Workgroup, Set Reminder. The Set Reminder dialog box appears, as shown in Figure 15.60.

Figure 15.60
You can set reminders for the start or finish of tasks.

3. In the Set Reminders For field, type a number of units and select the unit to be used from the entry list to the right.

4. In the Before The field, select Start or Finish to indicate where the reminders should be placed.

5. Choose the OK button to set the reminders.

SEND TO EXCHANGE FOLDER

The Send to Exchange Folder function allows you to copy the project file into Exchange or Outlook. After the project file has been copied, it can be viewed, grouped, categorized, or sorted by its properties. Choose File, Send To, Exchange Folder (or select Sent to Exchange Folder from the Workgroup toolbar). You will be presented with the dialog box shown in Figure 15.61.

Figure 15.61
Select the personal folder that will contain the project file.

TROUBLESHOOTING

WORKGROUP MESSAGES DON'T APPEAR IN PROJECT CENTRAL

I just sent a TeamAssign from my project plan but the message doesn't appear in the team member's Project Central Inbox. What happened?

Most likely an error occurred in the transfer of the message from Project to Project Central.

Messages are conveyed by the Project Central spooler. As soon as you submit a workgroup message, the spooler begins running and its icon appears in the Windows status bar. If it encounters an error, a red exclamation mark appears next to the icon. Double-click the icon to open the Project Central spooler.

The error will be displayed. After the error is resolved (it could be something as simple as the URL being spelled incorrectly on the Workgroup tab), you can resubmit the message from the Action menu. If you select Rollback Project, the project plan is reset as if no messages were sent.

TRACKING AND ANALYZING PROGRESS

CHAPTER 16

TRACKING WORK ON THE PROJECT

In this chapter

SETTING THE BASELINE OR PLAN

After you finalize the planning of the project, set aside a copy of the finalized project schedule for future reference. Actually, the *final plan* is considered final only because it represents the final product of the initial planning effort. The copy you make of the finalized plan is the baseline you use to compare actual performance with planned performance. As work progresses on the project, you might have to modify the plan to respond to changing circumstances or as a result of new information. Resource availability can change, duration estimates can change, and so on. You also begin to record the actual start and finish dates for tasks. If actual dates match the planned dates exactly, you have performed a miracle. In all probability, some tasks will finish late, and other tasks will finish early. As you enter these actual dates, Microsoft Project reschedules successor tasks to reflect the changed circumstances.

The *planning stage* culminates in a finalized plan, the copy of which is known as the *baseline*. As the *execution stage* gets underway, changes and revisions in the plan often are necessary. These changes are added to the computer version of the plan, and Microsoft Project recalculates the schedule to incorporate the revisions. As work on the project progresses, the actual dates and durations of tasks are entered into the computer version of the plan, and Microsoft Project replaces the calculated start and finish dates with the actual dates and recalculates the remaining schedule. Therefore, with the progression of the project, the current schedule is revised by the addition of changes and actual data. You can print reports that show the variances or differences between the planned dates and the actual dates, the planned amount of work and the actual amount of work, and the planned cost and the actual cost.

The baseline is similar to an architect's final drawings for a building project. After construction gets underway, plan changes are penciled in, and some features are whited out. If changes are significant, new plans are drawn. By setting aside a clean copy of the original plans at the start of construction, you can compare the original intentions with the final result.

In managing your project, you can set aside copies of the printouts from the original plan for comparison purposes. You might find, however, that having an electronic set of the plan dates, planned work, and planned cost is more useful. This enables the computer to print comparisons or variances to show how work is progressing, how well the plans are being realized, and how likely you are to meet the project goals.

Best Practice Tips from Toby Brown, PMP

There is a Zen Buddhist philosophy that says, "no matter where you go, there you are." This saying reminds me of an ever-changing schedule. If you never set a baseline, changes to a project allow for nothing to measure performance against, and you never have a sense of how well you are progressing.

The PMBOK Guide defines the baseline as the original plan plus or minus approved changes, and it usually has a modifier along with it (for example, cost baseline, schedule baseline, performance measurement baseline, and so on). When setting the baseline, all schedule elements (start date, finish date, duration, cost, and work) are captured for variance analysis to determine how well the work is being performed and if the project is proceeding according to plan.

After the project baseline has been captured, the stage is set for you to take advantage of the forecasting powers of Microsoft Project by implementing the following procedures:

- *Track actual events on your project.* Recording facts about what actually happened on a task-by-task level is a worthwhile endeavor, especially if your projects are similar.

- *Examine the revised schedule to identify potential problems.* If you have a baseline and you've entered information about what is actually happening on your project tasks, Microsoft Project provides a variety of views to compare the two. If you can identify problems early enough in the process, you can make adjustments in the plan to keep the problems from getting bigger.

- *Modify the plan to adjust for events that are throwing your project off track.* If everything happens exactly as you planned, you have no need to reschedule subsequent tasks. If the actual finish dates for tasks differ from the planned dates, however, Microsoft Project can use the real dates to reschedule the remaining tasks in the project.

If you fail to use the forecasting powers, you miss some of the greatest benefits Project can provide.

CAPTURING THE BASELINE

Microsoft Project provides two ways to capture the baseline. The first is with a Planning Wizard. The first time you save a file, the Planning Wizard asks whether you want to save the file with a baseline (see Figure 16.1). If you select the option to save the baseline and click OK, Project will save a second set of start and finish dates for each task, duplicating the currently calculated start and finish dates. This second copy of dates is called the *baseline*. As you enter actual information about each task—such as when it started and finished, how long it actually took to complete, or how much work has been completed on the task— Project will recalculate the start and finish dates of all successor tasks. Because of this continual recalculation, you need those baseline dates to compare reality with what you had planned.

Figure 16.1
The Planning Wizard stands ready to save baseline information when you first save a project file.

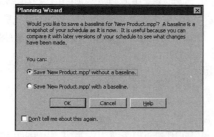

→ For more information on saving project files, **see** "Saving and Protecting Files," **p. 116**

As with other Planning Wizards, you can elect not to be reminded of this in the future. If you mark the Don't Tell Me About This Again check box and later want to turn the feature back on, use the General tab in the Options dialog box. The Advice About Scheduling option is unchecked or might be gray. Re-check the box to again have the Planning Wizard prompt you for updating the baseline.

Best Practice Tips from Toby Brown, PMP	Rarely do you completely define a project in the first sitting, so "dismissing" the Planning Wizard for this feature is probably appropriate. Otherwise, it will constantly remind you to set a baseline every time you save work on the project. Remember that a baseline is considered a final commitment of the project and is often referred to as the plan. It is not very often that the first pass at creating a schedule is the one which you wish to commit to.

Caution	The Planning Wizard updates the project baseline for all tasks, not just new or modified tasks. Any existing baseline values for every task in the project are overwritten and lost.

The second method of saving the baseline enables more flexibility. It is performed by choosing Tools, Tracking, Save Baseline. This command, just like using the wizard, copies the currently calculated start and finish dates, duration, work, and cost data into a set of fields, respectively known as Baseline Start, Baseline Finish, Baseline Duration, Baseline Work, and Baseline Cost. You can execute the Save Baseline command from any task view, but not from the resource views.

The Save Baseline command offers an option of copying data for the entire project or for selected tasks. Use the Selected Tasks option when you want to correct mistakes for selected tasks or add data for tasks that you added to the plan after the baseline was captured. Use the Entire Project option when you create the baseline for the first time or when you want to update the baseline for all tasks. Typically, using either method, the baseline is set only once for each task, unless there is a major rescheduling of the entire project.

To save a baseline plan, you should follow these steps:

1. Activate any task view, such as the Gantt Chart or the Task Sheet.
2. Choose Tools, Tracking, and then Save Baseline. The default settings for the Save Baseline dialog box appear in Figure 16.2.
3. Choose OK to save the baseline. You will see no evidence that the field data was copied until you look at views that display baseline data fields. The following section explains how to view and verify the baseline data.

CLEARING THE BASELINE

 A new feature in Project 2000 is a command used to easily clear the baseline fields of all values. If, for example, you inadvertently agreed to let the wizard save the baseline for you, you can reopen the file and clear the baseline fields in all or selected tasks. Select Tools, Tracking, and then Clear Baseline to display the dialog box in Figure 16.3. This capability also enables Project to clear out any baseline data when saving a file to be used as a template. See the "Creating and Using Templates" section of Chapter 4, "Working with Project Files," for information about creating templates.

Figure 16.2
The Save Baseline dialog box enables you to specifically save the baseline information.

Figure 16.3
Remove all baseline data for some or all tasks with the new Clear Baseline feature.

VIEWING THE BASELINE

The fields that are changed with the Save Baseline command are the Baseline Duration, Baseline Start, Baseline Finish, Baseline Work, and Baseline Cost. These fields are displayed in the Baseline table (see Figure 16.4).

Figure 16.4
The Baseline table applied to the Task Sheet view displays baseline information.

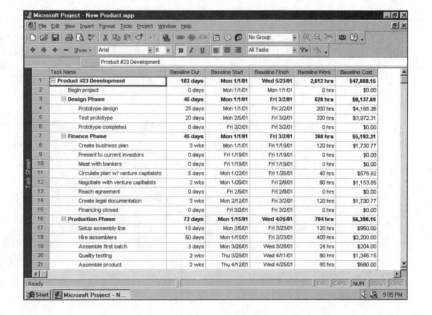

To view the baseline fields in a task view, follow these steps:

1. Be sure that you are in either the Task Sheet view or the Gantt Chart view. If you are in a combination view and you want to see all tasks, you must be in the top pane.

2. Choose View, Table, and then More Tables to see the full list of standard tables.

3. From the More Tables list, select the Baseline table.

4. Click the Apply button to display the table.

CORRECTING THE BASELINE

If you want to correct the entries for any task, or if you need to add tasks to the baseline because they were not in the plan as originally conceived, select the tasks to be added or corrected to the baseline plan and choose Tools, Tracking, Save Baseline. This time, however, choose the Selected Tasks option button in the Save Baseline dialog box rather than the Entire Project option button.

You also can make changes directly to the Baseline table. Be careful when you use this option, though, because Microsoft Project doesn't check entries for consistency. Typographical and calculation errors are not corrected by Project. If you change the baseline duration, for example, Project doesn't change the baseline finish date. For most changes, the best option is to use the Save Baseline command for Selected Tasks to ensure that all the data entries are consistent.

You also can view the baseline dates in the Task Details Form as shown in Figure 16.5. To display this form, choose View, More Views, and then Task Details form and Apply.

Best Practice Tips from Toby Brown, PMP

Remember that a good practice of project management is to save and establish the baseline only once for the project. In fact, changing a baseline that the stakeholders agreed to is considered inappropriate. The purpose of the baseline is to evaluate variance, which is an inevitable part of an ever-changing schedule.

Figure 16.5
Verifying baseline dates on the Task Details Form.

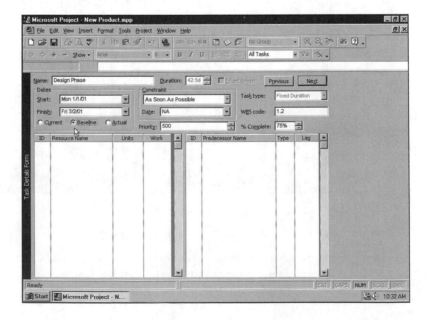

Baseline information is also captured on a per resource basis. Again, use the Task Details form to verify the baseline work or cost for resource assignments. With the Task Details Form displayed and active, choose Format, Details to view the Resource Work or Resource Cost fields. To see the Baseline Work or Cost fields from the perspective of a resource rather than a task, display the Resource Form instead (as shown in Figure 16.6) with Format, Details, set to Work or Cost. Again, Microsoft Project does not automatically recalculate related fields when you make a manual entry in a baseline field such as Baseline Work. Add the resource to the task as you normally would, make sure the task remains selected, and then update the baseline by choosing Tools, Tracking, Save Baseline for modified task. All related fields will be automatically recalculated.

PART

V

CH

16

Figure 16.6
The Resource Form with details set to Work or Cost shows baseline information from the resource's perspective.

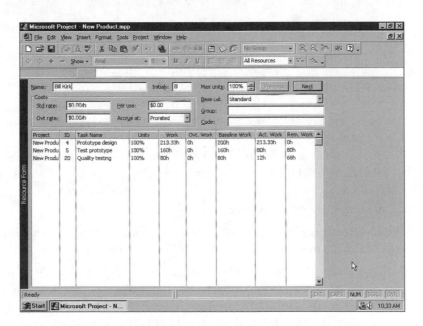

The Task Usage and Resource Usage views also have the capability of showing baseline work and cost information.

→ For more information on using the supplied Project views, **see** "Exploring the Standard Views," p. 852

SAVING INTERIM SCHEDULES

At key points during the project, either during the planning stages before the baseline plan is saved or, more typically, after work is underway on the project, you might want to make a record of the current (calculated) dates for tasks at this point in the evolution of the project plan. A common use for interim plans is enabling the comparison of how the project has progressed from one month to the next or one quarter to the next.

Tip from Tim and the Project Team

Capture interim dates at regular intervals to create custom Gantt Charts commonly known as *slip diagrams*. A series of bars is drawn for each task, visually tracing the evolution of the task's schedule.

Ten sets of baseline date fields are available for each task, which represent 10 sets of Start and Finish dates, aside from the date fields saved in the baseline. Because each date set is numbered, you will see fields named Start1 through Start10 and Finish1 through Finish10 for each task. By using the Save Baseline command, you can capture interim date schedules by copying the Current Start and Finish dates into one or more of these sets of date fields. Note that only the date fields are copied for each task—the work and cost values are not copied.

To save interim project dates, follow these steps:

1. Choose a task view.
2. Choose Tools, Tracking, Save Baseline.
3. Choose the Save Interim Plan option button. The Copy and Into date fields are then available.
4. Select the Entire Project option button (although you also can choose to copy only selected tasks).
5. Both sets of date fields have a list of 10 sets of Start/Finish date fields. Do not use the Baseline Start/Finish fields because performing this process wipes out the original baseline dates. Choose an appropriate set of dates from each entry list.
6. Choose OK to copy the date values.

You can use the copies of the dates in reports or display them in customized views. You also can control the titles that are visible in the selected task view.

In long projects, the project plan can change so dramatically over time that a new baseline is considered worthwhile. Although you can keep as many as 10 sets of date values for comparison purposes, you can maintain only one set of baseline duration, work, and cost figures. If a new baseline is needed, and you want to preserve the work and cost estimates of the old baseline, you must find a creative solution to the problem of saving data for which no automatic-saving provision exists. Several options are available to achieve this task. One option is to save a copy of the project file under a different name, and then open the originally named file again and continue setting a new baseline.

Best Practice Tips from Toby Brown, PMP

In the case of significant scope creep of a project (or feature creep in the case of a product development), it is sometimes necessary to create another baseline but still retain the ability to review previous baseline commitments.

Preserving the original baseline cost, duration, and work estimates has always been a challenge in all versions of Project, including Project 2000. Although the scheduled baseline dates are important, these other elements might be even more so, particularly when changes to the scheduled dates do not impact the critical path. This is why I encourage a user to simply save the project as a first revision using Save As and then resave the baseline for the entire project. This way, it is possible to review previous versions of the project plan saved as separate files that include cost, duration, and work values in addition to baseline dates.

Another option for preserving baseline information is to copy the baseline field data to unused custom fields in Project. Copy Baseline Duration and Baseline Work into separate custom Duration fields (Duration1–Duration10 are available) and Baseline Cost into a custom Cost field (Cost1–Cost10). This can be particularly useful with the new custom field calculations in Project 2000.

If you want to preserve only the dates of the original baseline and are not concerned about the work and cost estimates, you can copy the dates to one of the 10 sets of interim dates.

To copy the baseline dates to an interim set of dates, follow the preceding steps for saving interim dates, except you should choose Copy, Baseline Start/Finish when you reach step 4.

No standard views or reports are available that display the interim date fields. However, you can create views and reports or modify any view or report that displays the baseline dates and substitute the interim dates for the Baseline date fields.

→ For detailed information on replacing fields in a table, **see** "Using and Creating Tables," **p. 949**
→ For more information on creating custom reports, **see** "Customizing Specific Report Types," **p. 1022**

COMPARING THE BASELINE WITH THE CURRENT SCHEDULE

Because comparing what you planned to what is actually happening is such a useful project management task, several views and reports are available that enable you to see baseline data next to the currently calculated plan. You can use the Task Usage view, which enables you to turn on the display of Baseline Work. You can use the Task Sheet view with three different sets of predefined tables. You also can use the Tracking Gantt for a more graphical view. The Gantt Chart Wizard has five different predefined options for formatting the baseline information. Many of the reports in the Current Activities and Costs categories compare actual progress to baseline information.

USING THE TASK USAGE VIEW TO SEE BASELINE INFORMATION

The Task Usage view enables you to turn on the display of some baseline data. By default, the timescale portion of the view displays planned hours of work for each task, spread across the days when the work is planned to occur. If you right-click the timescale portion of the view, you can also turn on the display of Baseline Work and Actual Work. Figure 16.7 shows the Task Usage view with the baseline work values displayed, as well as the current scheduled and actual work values.

→ For more information on the elements of Project views, **see** "Exploring the Standard Views," **p. 852**

USING TABLES TO VIEW BASELINE DATA

The baseline data is displayed beside the currently calculated data in three separate task tables—the Variance table, the Cost table, and the Work table. You can display each table in the Task Sheet or in one of the Gantt Chart views. In addition, you can use all three tables to print progress reports.

Figure 16.7
The Task Usage view with baseline work displayed enables you to compare when work was supposed to occur with when it actually occurred.

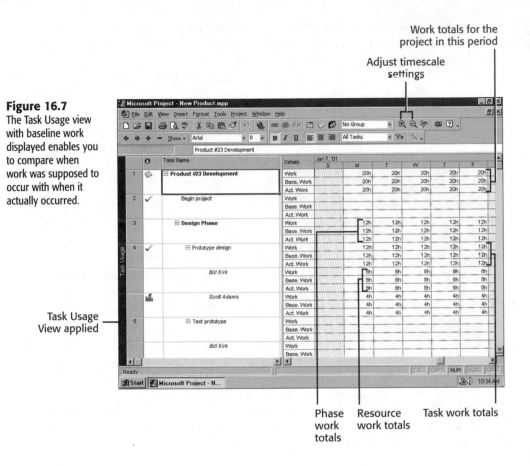

In each table, the currently calculated field values are displayed along with the baseline field values. Variances are calculated to show the difference between the current and the baseline data.

The current values represent predicted or anticipated values until actual tracking data is entered. Actual data always replaces the currently calculated data, so the schedule always contains the most accurate information available. Therefore, after tracking begins, the current fields show anticipated values for tasks that have not yet begun and actual values for tasks that already have actual data recorded.

Tip from Tim and the Project Team

To quickly choose different tables, right-click the button at the top of the task IDs, just to the left of the Task Name column.

Best Practice Tips from Toby Brown, PMP

Variance analysis in Microsoft Project is the opposite of traditional project management practices. In variance analysis in Project 2000, a scheduled date that is beyond its baseline is displayed as a positive value. Project works like accounting: If it is over (credit), it is a positive value; if it is under (debit or shortfall), it is a negative value.

In traditional project management, however, the values would be opposite of this. I remember it this way: If it is over or finishes late, it is negative, or bad; if it is under or finishes early, it is positive, or good.

The point is that there is variance, not necessarily how the variance is reported. Unless, of course, you are preparing for the PMP examination, in which case you had better keep it straight!

VIEWING THE TASK VARIANCE TABLE

The Baseline Start and Baseline Finish date fields are displayed in the task Variance table (see Figure 16.8). The Variance table focuses on dates only. The start and finish dates are calculated dates until actual dates are entered. Therefore, the Start Variance and Finish Variance columns show anticipated variances based on the actual information entered for predecessor tasks. After actual information has been entered for tasks, these variances are real. Incidentally, it is impossible to tell from the Variance table alone whether the current start and finish dates are actual dates or just the currently planned dates.

Figure 16.8
The Variance table applied to the Task Sheet concentrates on date differences in the schedule.

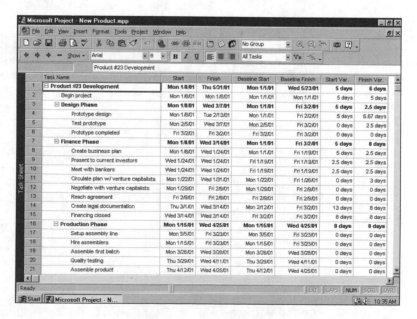

To display the task Variance table, choose <u>V</u>iew, <u>M</u>ore Views, <u>T</u>ask Sheet, and then <u>A</u>pply to display the Task Sheet in the active pane. Then choose <u>V</u>iew, Ta<u>b</u>le, <u>V</u>ariance to display the Variance table. For a detailed discussion of variances, see Chapter 17, "Analyzing Progress and Revising the Schedule."

VIEWING THE TASK COST TABLE

The Baseline Cost field appears in the task Cost table (see Figure 16.9). The Total Cost values in the Cost table equal the actual values if tracking data was already entered for the tasks. In addition, variances are either anticipated or actual, depending on whether actual data was entered.

Project calculates Actual Cost by the following rules:

- For tasks that have not yet begun, the values in the Actual column are zero, and the values in the Total column are the currently calculated data. The Remaining cost equals the Total Cost.

- For completed tasks, the Total and Actual data is the same, and the Remaining cost is zero.

- For tasks still in progress, the Actual cost plus the Remaining cost equals the Total Cost.

An unexpected Fixed Cost of $1,000 was entered for task 4, as shown in Figure 16.9. As a result, the Total Cost field becomes $1,000 greater than the Baseline Cost, and the Variance field shows the $1,000 disparity.

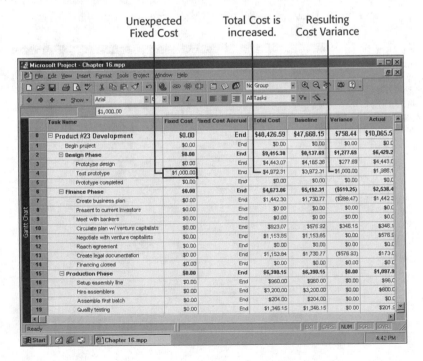

Figure 16.9
The Cost table applied to the Task Sheet focuses on differences in costs than what was planned.

To display the task Cost table, display the Task Sheet. Then, display the Cost table by choosing View, Table, Cost.

VIEWING THE TASK WORK TABLE

The Baseline Work field is displayed in the task Work table (see Figure 16.10). The values in the Work column equal the actual work amounts if tracking data was already entered for the tasks, and variances are either anticipated or actual, depending on whether actual data was entered.

Figure 16.10
The Work table applied to the Task Sheet displays differences between the actual number of hours worked and what was planned.

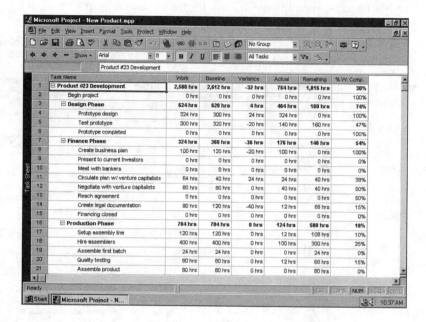

PART
V
CH
16

Project calculates Actual Work by the following rules:

- For tasks that have not yet begun, the Actual work amount is zero, and the Work amount is the current Baseline amount. The Remaining work equals the value in the Work column because all the work remains to be done.

- For completed tasks, the Work and Actual work amounts are the same, and the Remaining work is zero. The %W.Comp. (percent of work completed) field is 100%.

- For tasks still in progress, the Actual work plus the Remaining work equals the Work. The percent of work completed (%W.Comp.) reflects the completed portion.

The Work field was increased for task 4 from 320 hours to 400 hours in Figure 16.10, and because Work is now greater than Baseline work, the Variance field shows the 80-hour difference. The Actual field is updated during tracking of the project.

To display the task Work table, display the Task Sheet. Then, display the Work table by choosing View, Table, Work.

VIEWING THE TRACKING GANTT CHART

An extremely informative graphic view of baseline values compared to the current schedule is called a *Tracking Gantt* (see Figure 16.11). It is accessible from the <u>V</u>iew menu or from the View Bar. The Tracking Gantt view shows two task bars for each task. The upper bar represents the baseline start and finish dates for a task, whereas the lower bar represents the currently calculated start and finish dates for the same task.

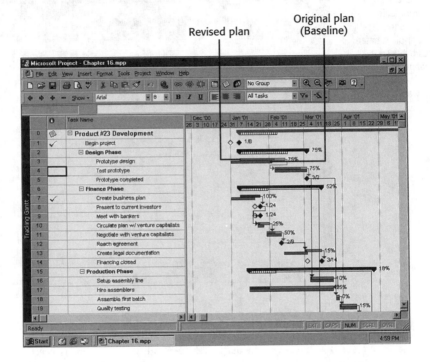

Figure 16.11
The Tracking Gantt displays two sets of bars for each task, one for the original plan and one for the current schedule.

You also can use the Gantt Chart Wizard to display baseline information. In step 2 of the Gantt Chart Wizard, select the Baseline option to have Project draw two bars for each task, one with baseline information and one with calculated dates. Instead of the Baseline option, you can also choose from one of four baseline formats under the Other option (see Figure 16.12). The preset colors and positions of each bar are the only differences.

→ For more information on using the Gantt Chart Wizard, **see** "Formatting the Gantt Chart," **p. 905**

As long as the project proceeds according to the plan, the dates on the two bars will match. When the dates of any task deviate from the baseline, however, you can see the discrepancy immediately. In Figure 16.11, for example, the added work that was imposed on task 4 is reflected in the even further shift to the right of the scheduled finish date.

Figure 16.12
The Gantt Chart Wizard will display baseline information for you.

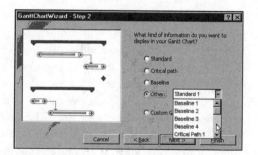

PRINTING THE VIEWS THAT SHOW BASELINE COMPARISONS

Each of the views that displays comparisons between baseline values and values in the current schedule can be printed without extensive adjustments. The default print settings are adequate for simple reports.

To print any of these views, display them onscreen and choose File, Print. Some predefined reports print current activities compared to baseline values. Choose View, Reports to display the Reports dialog box. For example, the Slipping Tasks report in the Current Activities category prints baseline and planned start and finish information.

TRACKING ACTUAL PERFORMANCE AND COSTS

After the project gets underway, you might find that some tasks start or finish early or late, or that completing a task takes longer or costs more than expected. As you respond to these unexpected changes in the project, you might need to adjust estimated durations for later tasks—based on the experience of the earlier tasks—and you might want to change task relationships. If the cumulative effects of the changes threaten the cost and finish date as set forth in the project goal, you might need to crash the schedule again and find ways to reduce costs.

If you record the actual dates, durations, and work for tasks as events unfold, Microsoft Project uses this data to reschedule tasks affected by the changes. You can see right away the implications for the rest of the project when the actual work doesn't go according to plan. With this knowledge beforehand, you can take corrective measures to minimize unwanted consequences. By entering actual performance data in the computer on a timely basis, you can predict problems and do something about them early in the project. You also can use the project schedule to try *what-if* tests to measure the effects of alternative compensating actions.

The frequency with which you update the project is determined by the criticality of the project. A project plan is similar to a financial plan or budget in that the plan is a blueprint for reaching a goal. If accounting data is not recorded in a timely fashion, management does not have the accounting reports that can warn of possible problems in meeting budgeted profits. Similarly, if the project data is not recorded regularly, the project manager doesn't have reports that can warn of problems with the project. Therefore, the project can't be completed on time and within budget.

Updating the project schedule can be a time-consuming task and, probably for this reason, it is often neglected by project managers. A lot depends on how much detail you intend to track. The level of detail you intend to track is determined by how much information you need back and how much time you can spend on tracking. You can choose to track dates and durations carefully but not spend the time needed to track individual resource work and cost. You must base this decision on the usefulness of the data, as opposed to the cost of gathering and entering the information. If you use this approach, Microsoft Project still can help warn you about tasks that slip (are not on schedule) and can help you keep the project on course. The work and cost data, however, will be less accurate at any point in time because actual work will be an estimate based on time lapsed in the task duration and cost will be primarily calculated from the work.

A wide variety of views, tables, and forms can be used to enter actual data. The ones you choose depend to a large degree on what kind of information you are entering and how much information you need to see as a result of the actual information. It also depends on whether you prefer working with sheet views, forms, or graphic views. As with the entering of the original project data, information you enter in one view is automatically reflected in all other relevant views.

In addition to the views that display baseline information, several views exist that display progress on a task—for example, work that has occurred during the completion of the task. The Gantt Chart displays a progress bar in the middle of the task bar for tasks that have already begun. The progress bar appears differently depending on whether you are showing baseline bars. If you are displaying baseline bars (as discussed in the previous section), the progress bar is overlaid on the scheduled task bar and is a solid dark bar of the same color (see task 3 in Figure 16.11). If you are not displaying baseline bars (as in a standard Gantt Chart), the progress bar is a narrower black bar inside the task bar that represents the percent complete. Figure 16.13 shows the progress in tasks 10 and 11 and 100% completion for task 7.

The Network Diagram (formerly referred to in Project as the PERT Chart) also can display a record of progress, but only in a general way (see Figure 16.14). If a task is completed, the task node (the box representing the task) shows crossing diagonal lines (as though the node was crossed out). If the task is in progress but not complete, you see a single diagonal line drawn through the node. No diagonal lines appear in tasks that are not yet started.

The sections that follow describe views you can use to enter and review actual progress data.

Completed task

Figure 16.13
The progress bars indicate tasks that have already started.

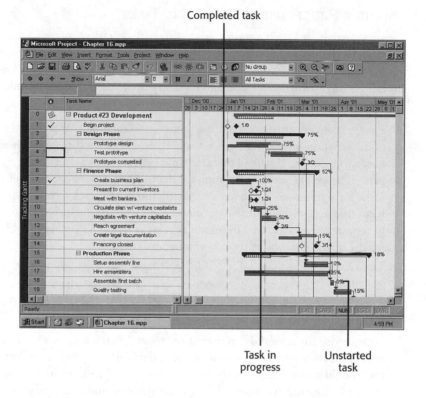

Task in progress

Unstarted task

Completed task   Task in progress

Figure 16.14
Progress marks on the Network Diagram nodes indicate tasks that have started or are complete.

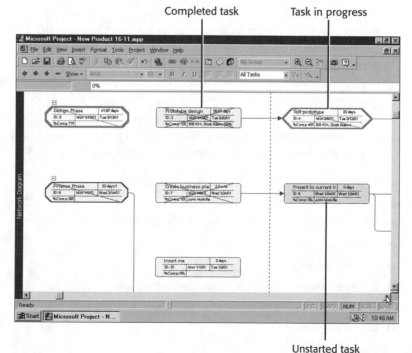

Unstarted task

ESTABLISHING A PROCEDURE FOR UPDATING TASKS

The updating procedure is a simple process if work on tasks proceeds according to the schedule. Updating becomes progressively more time-consuming when dates, work amounts, durations, and costs differ from the schedule. A well-established procedure for gathering actual performance data and regularly updating the computer files is necessary to keep the project file current, as shown in the following steps:

1. First, gather information about the progress on each task. You should gather two pieces of information—both what was actually done and new estimations about what still needs to be done. You need to know what progress was made during the reporting period, as well as whether duration estimates were revised or the estimated amount of work for a resource on a task was revised. You might want to print a progress report form that you distribute to all personnel who work on the project. You also might want to require these personnel to submit regular updates. This data should provide the basis for the actual data you enter as you track progress.

Tip from Tim and the Project Team

The Tracking table applied to the Task Sheet, filtered by the Using Resource filter, is a useful tool here. Give each resource a printed copy to keep track of their work on the project.

2. Next, revise the *scheduled* description of tasks to match the revised estimates before you record that *actual* work was begun or completed. If the progress reports suggest that you should make changes in the planned schedule for unfinished or unstarted tasks, enter adjustments to the scheduled duration, work, and costs before you enter actual dates and percents completed.

3. If work on tasks in progress was as scheduled, you can enter changes to Percent Complete and other tracking tool shortcuts to force Microsoft Project to compute and enter values in Actual fields. For more control over individual fields, enter actual start, finish, and duration values manually using one or more of the views, forms, and tools described in the following section.

4. When you enter the dates and Percent Complete for tasks, Microsoft Project can calculate the interim and completed work and cost figures. If necessary, you can enter your own figures for work and cost after tasks are completed.

UNDERSTANDING THE FIELDS USED IN UPDATING

You can enter one or more of the following tracking fields for tasks. Many of these fields are calculated by Microsoft Project when an entry is made in one of the others in the list:

- Actual Start date
- Actual Finish date
- Percent Complete (percent of the task's duration)
- Actual Duration (to date)
- Remaining Duration

- Scheduled Duration, revised
- Actual Work
- Percent of Work Completed
- Remaining Work
- Actual Fixed Cost
- Actual Cost
- Remaining Cost

No one view displays all these fields—with the possible exception of the Export table. Some of these fields lead to automatic recalculation of other fields. Some fields are calculations only, and your entries are ignored. The Work and Cost fields are special cases; if you are tracking work and cost carefully, you do not enter actual in-progress work or costs for the task, but rather you enter the in-progress work for the resources assigned to the task. The work you enter for the resources is the source of the cost calculations.

You can save time if you understand how these fields are interrelated. You then can select the fields to update and select the view or form that provides the fields you want to use. The tracking fields are described in the following sections, with emphasis on the impact made by entering a change in one of the fields. You will become more successful in tracking projects if you understand these relationships.

ACTUAL START DATE

Prior to having an actual date entered, the Actual Start field value is NA. When you record actual dates, Microsoft Project replaces the current calculated Start and Finish dates with the actual dates. Therefore, as the project progresses, your entries of actual dates replace the calculated (predicted) entries for task dates, and the schedule contains more and more reality, as compared to prediction.

You can enter the Actual Start date on all the tracking views and forms directly or you can enter them indirectly by setting some other field value. For example, if you set a Percent Complete other than zero, Microsoft Project assumes the task actually started when it was scheduled to start, and the calculated Start date is automatically recorded as the Actual Start date. Similarly, if you set the Percent Complete to 100, the Actual Start and Actual Finish are set to the current scheduled dates.

ACTUAL FINISH DATE

This field displays NA until the task finish date is entered or calculated. You can enter the Actual Finish date on all the tracking views and forms, either directly or indirectly, by having the finish date calculated. If you enter a date in the Actual Finish date field, Microsoft Project performs the following procedures:

- Moves the Actual Finish date to the current Finish date.
- Sets the Percent Complete (of the Duration) to 100%.

- Sets the Actual Start date to equal the current Start date, if no Actual Start date is entered.
- Calculates the Actual Duration field and changes the Duration, if necessary, to match the Actual Duration.
- Sets the Remaining Duration field to zero.
- Calculates the Actual Work and Actual Cost fields, based on the Actual Duration. If the Actual Duration differs from the original Duration, Work and Cost are adjusted proportionally.
- Changes the task status to non-critical if it was critical (its completion can no longer endanger the finish date of the project).

PERCENT COMPLETE

After a task has started, you can track the progress of the task by entering the percent completed on a regular basis. You also can track progress by entering either the actual duration to date for the task or the remaining duration. See the "Actual Duration" and "Remaining Duration" sections later in this chapter. The relationships among these three variables (Percent Complete, Actual Duration, and Remaining Duration) are defined by these equations:

Percent Complete = Actual Duration/Duration

Remaining Duration = Duration–Actual Duration

When you record an actual finish date for a task, Microsoft Project displays 100% in the Percent Complete field for the task. If you want to track interim progress on a task, you can enter partially completed percent numbers. The Percent Complete field is available on the General tab of the Task Information dialog box (double-click on a task or choose Project, Task Information).

It is important to understand that the Percent Complete field applies to task duration, which is calendar time. The Percent Work Complete field is a separate and distinct field related to resources. By default, changes to Percent Complete also change Percent Work Complete values. But that might not reflect reality. For example, one full-time resource on a 1-week task is scheduled by Project to work 40 hours on that task. A value of 50% Complete really says that we have consumed 2.5 days of calendar time allotted for the task. But has the resource completed the scheduled 20 hours of work? You can break that link and track actual values for duration and work separately, but it does require entering more detailed progress reports data.

The link between duration and work is controlled by the setting of an option called Updating Task Status Updates Resource Status. The Updating Task Status Updates Resource Status option on the Calculation tab of the Options dialog box instructs Microsoft Project as to whether it should translate actual duration into actual work and actual work into actual costs. If the option is set to Yes, Microsoft Project applies the task percent complete to scheduled work and scheduled cost for each resource on the task and calculates the

Actual Work and Actual Cost per resource for each task. The total Actual Work for the task is the sum of the resource actual work; the total Actual cost for the task is the sum of the resource costs plus a percent of any fixed costs on the task. Therefore, you will see prorated cost figures appear as you indicate progress on the task (if the Accrue At field for the resources has been set to Prorated). See the section "Recording Actual Work and Costs" later in this chapter.

Best Practice Tips from Toby Brown, PMP

In a poorly scoped project, it is sometimes necessary to break the linkage between actual work performed and the percent complete. In fact, in many organizations, progress is reported strictly in terms of percent complete, and time is captured elsewhere, often outside of the program. As the company matures and becomes a more projectized organization, the project teams will become better at estimating task durations based on realized work performance and not on arbitrary values.

PART

V

CH

16

When the Percent Complete field is changed, Microsoft Project performs the following procedures:

- **Sets the Actual Start date to equal the current start date, unless an actual start date was already entered**—If the task did not start on schedule, first update the start date with the actual start date, and then enter the Percent Complete.

- **Sets the Actual Finish date to match the current Finish date if 100% is the percent value entered**—If the Actual Finish date is not the same as the calculated date, type the Actual Finish date instead of entering 100%.

- **Sets the Actual Duration field to equal the Percent Complete figure times the scheduled duration**—Therefore, if a task is marked 60% complete when the scheduled Duration was 10 hours, the Actual Duration field is calculated and set to 6 hours.

- **Sets the Remaining Duration field to equal the scheduled Duration minus the Actual Duration**—Using the preceding example, the Remaining Duration field is calculated as 10 hours minus 6 hours and set to 4 hours.

- **Sets the Actual Work and Actual Cost fields to match the Percent Complete times the scheduled Work and Cost amounts, but only if the check box for Updating Task Status Updates Resource Status is marked**—You can find this check box on the Calculation tab of the Options dialog box.

- **For summary tasks, sets each of the subtasks with the same value entered for the summary task**

ACTUAL DURATION

This field is available on the Tracking table and in the Update Tasks dialog box, which you can access by choosing Tools, Tracking, Update Tasks. When you enter a value in this field that is less than or equal to the scheduled Duration, Microsoft Project assumes work on the task is progressing according to plan. Accordingly, the program automatically sets the Actual Start date as scheduled (unless it has been set previously) and calculates the Percent Complete and the Remaining Duration fields by comparing the Actual Duration with the originally entered or calculated Duration.

If you enter an Actual Duration that is greater than the original Duration, Microsoft Project assumes that the task is finished and took longer than scheduled. The current Duration is changed to match the new, longer duration, and then the Percent Complete and Remaining Duration fields are set to 100% and 0, respectively, to indicate that the task is complete.

If the Updating Task Status Updates Resource Status option is on, the work and cost figures for resources also are updated based on the task information entered.

Remaining Duration

If you enter a value in the Remaining Duration field, Microsoft Project assumes that work has begun as scheduled, and that all but this amount of the scheduled Duration has been completed. The program calculates and sets the Actual Duration and the Percent Complete based on the new value and the original Duration. If not already set, Microsoft Project sets the Actual Start date as whatever was scheduled. If the option Updating Task Status Updates Resource Status is on, and resources were assigned to the tasks, work and costs are updated for the resources and summed for the task.

If you enter **0** in the Remaining Duration field, it is the same as entering **100%** in the Percent Complete field. The Actual Finish date will be updated as originally scheduled.

If you enter a figure in the Remaining Duration field that is larger than the existing figure, Microsoft Project assumes that you are simply entering a new estimation of the total duration and not tracking actual progress. If no entry has been made to show that the task has started, this new Remaining Duration value is used to increase the scheduled duration of the task. If the task has already been marked as started, the new Remaining Duration entry is used to extend the scheduled Duration. The new scheduled Duration will be equal to the Actual Duration already shown, plus this new estimate of the amount of time left to complete the task. Percent Complete is recalculated to show the Actual Duration figure as a percent of the new, longer total Duration, and the work and cost figures are recalculated proportionally.

For example, suppose that a task with an estimated Duration of 10 days has already had 3 days of Actual Duration recorded. The Remaining Duration field shows 7 days, and 30% displays in the Percent Complete field. If the entry in the Remaining Duration field is changed to 9 days, Microsoft Project takes that to mean 9 more days (after the 3 days already recorded) are necessary to complete the task instead of just 7. The total Duration is changed automatically to 12 days, and the Percent Complete is reduced to 25% (3 days of 12 total days).

The Scheduled Duration

Revised estimates of the scheduled (originally planned) Duration can be entered in any of the locations discussed in previous chapters for defining a task.

If you change the scheduled Duration after a task has already started and the Actual Duration is greater than zero, the already recorded Actual Duration is left unchanged and the Percent Complete and Remaining Duration fields are adjusted to reflect the new estimate of total Duration.

RECORDING ACTUAL WORK AND COSTS

Work and cost values are calculated by Microsoft Project for individual resources and summed for the tasks to which the resources are assigned. If a task has no resources assigned, you must manually enter the work and cost values when the task is completed. However, you can enter the work and cost values for individual resources while work is in progress. You are allowed to edit the Actual Work field on a summary task. In previous versions it was only a calculated field. As you enter work for the summary task, the subtasks are allocated their portion of the work, depending on how the tasks are linked. If the subtasks are not linked, as you enter work hours for the summary task, the hours are split equally between the subtasks until any of the subtasks reach their total originally calculated hours of work. Thereafter, the work hours are split between the remaining subtasks that are not yet complete. If the tasks are linked, the hours of work entered for the summary task are allocated to the first task in the link. If that task has two successors, after the first task is complete, additional hours are split between the two successors. For example, you can see in Figure 16.15 that 60 hours of actual work have been entered for the summary task, Regional Promotions. The first 40 were allocated to task 37 because it was the first to be performed. Both tasks 38 and 39 are Finish to Start successors to task 37, so the remaining 20 actual work hours were split between them.

Best Practice Tips from Toby Brown, PMP

It is good practice to record actual work performed at the activity level, not at the summary level. By definition, the summary will display the overall work progress for that component of the project, but only by managing at the activity level where the work package is located can a project manager truly monitor what is happening within the project. As the saying goes: The devil is in the details.

Figure 16.15
Actual Work data entered on summary tasks is distributed to its subtasks.

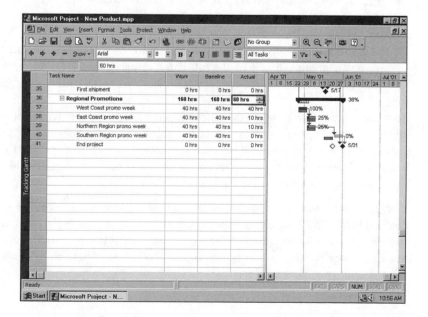

PART

V

CH

16

You cannot increase the work on a summary task beyond the total calculated work for the subtasks. Figure 16.16 displays the error message that appears if you try to increase the work beyond the calculated work for the subtasks. If the actual work for the summary task was greater than that originally calculated, you would have to enter the actual work for each of the subtasks and have the summary task's work calculated.

Figure 16.16
You can't enter total work for a summary task that exceeds what was originally calculated.

To successfully update work and cost amounts, you must understand the following points:

- If no resources are assigned to a task or if resources are assigned and the Updating Task Status Updates Resource Status check box on the Calculation tab of the Options dialog box is *not* marked, you can enter actual work and cost amounts directly into the Actual Work and Actual Cost fields for the task (or for each resource), just as you can enter actual dates and duration.

- If resources are assigned and the Updating Task Status Updates Resource Status check box *is* marked, Microsoft Project translates each resource assignment's Actual Duration into Actual Work and Actual Work into Actual Cost. If you enter Actual Work for a resource while this setting is marked, Microsoft Project translates this into Percent Complete for the task.

- If resources are assigned and the check box for Actual Costs Are Always Calculated by Microsoft Project is turned on, you cannot enter Actual Cost values into the task tracking fields while the task is in progress (before it is marked completed). The values are being calculated from the Actual Work data for each resource, and all entries you make are replaced immediately by the calculated value. After the task is marked as completed, however, you can override the calculated work and cost figures with your own entries.

To track work and costs while the task is in progress, you can enter the actual work and cost amounts for the resources or for the task itself. If you enter work for the task, Project assumes that the work was split between resources assigned to the task. If the resources worked a different number of hours on the task, it is better to enter the hours worked for the resources. Project will sum the hours for the task total.

The Task and Resource Usage views are good choices for entering this information at a detailed level. The Task Usage view is best when you are looking at work from the perspective of the task. The Resource Usage view is best when you are working from the perspective of the work performed on many tasks by a resource. These views enable you to enter work details on a timescale basis.

If you are not interested in that level of detail and want to enter the total hours worked on a task, without regard to when they were performed, use the Task Form, or Resource Form, to enter actual work and cost values for each resource. The work and cost fields are available at the bottom of these forms by selecting the appropriate format choice from the menu when the form is displayed. If the check box for Updating Task Status Updates Resource Status is checked, the Percent Complete field is calculated accordingly.

USING THE FACILITIES PROVIDED FOR UPDATING TASKS

Several views, menu commands, tools, and custom forms are available for updating tasks. This section starts with the facilities that provide the greatest detail and greatest range of options. The shortcut tools and commands are covered at the end of this section. Before using shortcuts, you should understand the details of the operation and the results of using the shortcut tools.

Facilities that can be used for tracking actual performance are described in the following list:

- *The Task and Resource Usage views both enable the entering of actual data at either the task level or resource level.* You can either enter the hours worked into the timescaled grid or double-click a resource assigned to the task and use the Tracking tab in the Assignment Information dialog box.

- *The Task Sheet, with the Tracking, Variance, Work, or Cost tables applied, provides access to all the fields described in the preceding section "Understanding the Fields Used in Updating."* The Tracking table focuses on only the tracking or actual fields. The other tables show scheduled, baseline, actual, remaining, and variance values.

- *The Task Form provides the Duration and Percent Complete tracking fields.* The Task Details Form provides the actual date fields. Both forms provide entry fields for resource work and resource costs, which you can access by choosing the appropriate option from the Format, Details menu command.

- *The Resource Form with the details set to Work provides a column for Actual Work and, with details set to Cost, provides a column for Actual Cost.*

- *The Tools, Tracking menu command has two commands relevant to tracking tasks: Update Tasks and Update Project.* Update Tasks enables you to enter very specific actual information when the task is not proceeding according to plan. Update Project provides a date-sensitive facility for updating the actual dates, duration, and percent complete for tasks with scheduled dates that fall before a designated *as of* date.

- *The Tracking toolbar has a series of buttons that can make tracking progress easier, including a button to access the Update Tasks dialog box.*

USING THE USAGE VIEWS

The usage views provide the greatest level of detail on a per-resource, per-task, day-by-day basis. When resources use timesheets to keep track of their work, these are the best views to capture that information. If you are tracking exact hours of work and subsequent costs, these are probably the best views to use.

By default the Task Usage view displays a timescaled work value for each task with a break-down by resource assigned to the task. You can add a row for each assignment on each task that displays an editable region for actual work (see Figure 16.17). Right-click anywhere in the timescale portion and choose Actual Work from the shortcut menu. You also can choose Format, Details from the menu and choose Actual Work from the cascading menu. As you enter actual hours for resources, the task work hours are totaled from the assigned resources. If you enter actual hours for the task, they are distributed to the resources assigned in a smart way. If all resources are working on the task for the whole duration of the task, the hours are split between the resources according to each resource's percent con-tribution to the work total for the task in the timeframe of the actual hours entered. If a delay has been placed on when a resource begins work on the task, that resource is not given any actual hours until the delay has been covered.

Figure 16.17
The Task Usage view with an Actual Work row displayed enables detailed tracking of work.

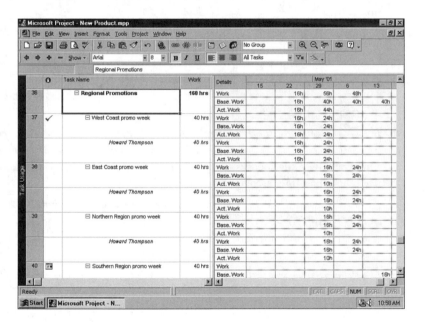

The Resource Usage view (as shown in Figure 16.18) works much the same way but from the perspective of the resource. The Actual Work rows allow entry of work performed per person per task. This is a better view to use when a resource hands in a timesheet with hours performed for various tasks.

USING THE TRACKING TABLE

The Task Sheet view can display a Tracking table that provides columns for tracking the percent complete, actual dates, and so on. To view the Tracking table, choose View, Task Sheet. Again open the View menu, but this time choose Table and then choose Tracking (see Figure 16.19).

Figure 16.18
The Resource Usage view enables you to enter detailed work hours from a resource's timesheet.

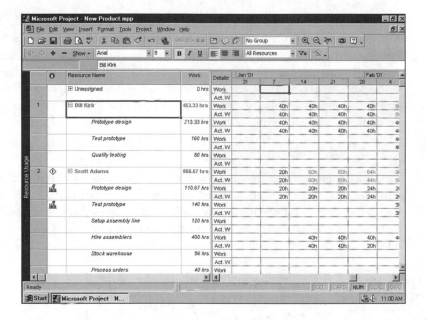

The Tracking table has fields for entering progress on tasks. Note that the Actual date fields in the Tracking table display NA when no actual date is yet recorded. This table also displays the Percent Complete, Actual Duration, Remaining Duration, Actual Cost, and Actual Work fields. You see the values in these fields calculated immediately after you enter any of the fields that signal work has been done on the task. The calculated entries are the same proportion of their scheduled values as the value displayed in the Percent Complete field. For example, if you enter a Percent Complete of 60% on a 10-day task, it will calculate an Actual Duration of 6 days and a Remaining Duration of 4 days.

Figure 16.19
The Tracking table provides a spreadsheet format for collecting data on tasks that are in progress.

	Task Name	Act. Start	Act. Finish	% Comp.	Act. Dur.	Rem. Dur.	Act. Cost	Act. Work
1	⊟ Product #23 Development	Mon 1/8/01	NA	28%	28.92 days	75.08 days	$0.00	824 hrs
2	Begin project	Mon 1/8/01	Mon 1/8/01	100%	0 days	0 days	$0.00	0 hrs
3	⊟ Design Phase	Mon 1/8/01	NA	75%	31.69 days	10.81 days	$0.00	464 hrs
4	Prototype design	Mon 1/8/01	Tue 2/13/01	100%	26.67 days	0 days	$0.00	324 hrs
5	Test prototype	Mon 2/5/01	NA	44%	10 days	12.5 days	$0.00	140 hrs
6	Prototype completed	Fri 3/2/01	Fri 3/2/01	100%	0 days	0 days	$0.00	0 hrs
7	⊟ Finance Phase	Mon 1/8/01	NA	54%	26.07 days	21.93 days	$0.00	176 hrs
8	Create business plan	Mon 1/8/01	Wed 1/24/01	100%	2.5 wks	0 wks	$0.00	100 hrs
9	Present to current investors	NA	NA	0%	0 days	0 days	$0.00	0 hrs
10	Meet with bankers	NA	NA	0%	0 days	0 days	$0.00	0 hrs
11	Circulate plan w/ venture capitalists	Mon 1/22/01	NA	36%	3 days	5 days	$0.00	24 hrs
12	Negotiate with venture capitalists	Mon 1/29/01	NA	50%	1 wk	1 wk	$0.00	40 hrs
13	Reach agreement	Fri 2/9/01	NA	50%	0 days	0 days	$0.00	0 hrs
14	Create legal documentation	Thu 3/1/01	NA	15%	0.3 wks	1.7 wks	$0.00	12 hrs
15	Financing closed	NA	NA	0%	0 days	0 days	$0.00	0 hrs
16	⊟ Production Phase	Mon 1/15/01	NA	18%	12.86 days	60.14 days	$0.00	124 hrs
17	Setup assembly line	Mon 3/5/01	NA	10%	1.5 days	13.5 days	$0.00	12 hrs
18	Hire assemblers	Mon 1/15/01	NA	25%	12.5 days	37.5 days	$0.00	100 hrs
19	Assemble first batch	NA	NA	0%	0 days	3 days	$0.00	0 hrs
20	Quality testing	Thu 3/29/01	NA	15%	0.3 wks	1.7 wks	$0.00	12 hrs
21	Assemble product	NA	NA	0%	0 wks	2 wks	$0.00	0 hrs

PART

V

CH

16

You have some control over whether actual costs can be entered manually. You can use an option on the Calculation tab of the Options dialog box: Actual Costs Are Always Calculated by Microsoft Project. If resources are assigned to tasks and this check box is marked, you cannot change the entries in Actual Cost. If you clear the check mark, you will be able to enter your own cost figures but Project will not calculate any. Be careful about turning the option back on again after manually entering any cost figures. They will be overwritten, as shown in the warning box displayed in Figure 16.20.

USING THE TASK FORM FOR TRACKING

The Task Sheet and Task Details Form both provide fields for entering tracking information. However, the Task Details Form offers much more flexibility, partly because you can enter actual dates. You first must activate the actual fields by choosing the Actual option button. Figure 16.21 shows the Tracking table applied to the Task Sheet in the top pane and the Task Details Form in the bottom pane.

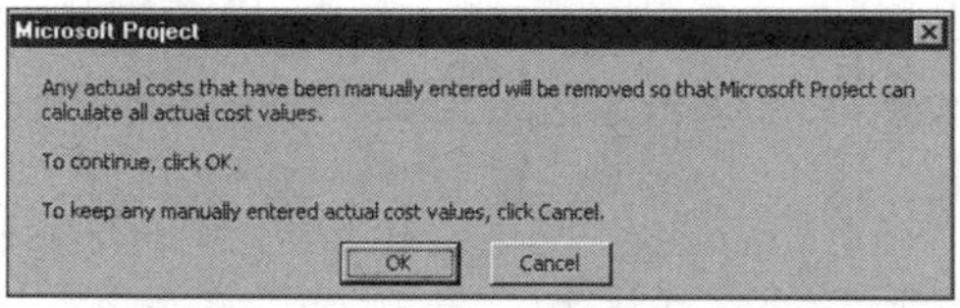

Figure 16.20
Project advises that manually entered cost figures will be over-written if you turn on the Actual Costs Are Always Calculated by Microsoft Project option.

Figure 16.21
Combining the Task Sheet with the Tracking table applied and the Task Details Form provides many fields necessary for tracking.

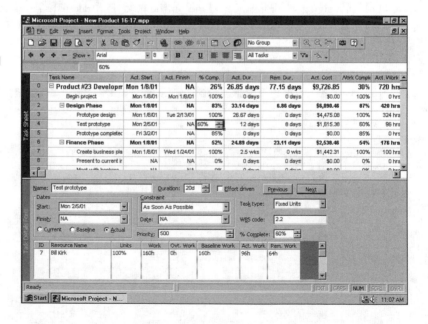

In Figure 16.21, task 4 was updated to show that the task is 60% complete, which means that the duration is 60% complete. As a result, in the Tracking table, you can see that Microsoft Project calculated that the actual duration is 12 days (60% of 20 days); the remaining duration is 8 days; and the Start date have been placed in the Actual Start column. Notice that the Actual Work field shows that 96 hours of work have been performed (60% of the 160 hours assigned to Bill Kirk), and the Actual Cost is set to $1,615.38, which is based on the standard rate for Bill Kirk and the actual work value. With the Task Details Form set to display work, you can enter total hours of work performed by each resource, but not on a timescaled basis as in the usage views. With the usage views (either Task Usage or Resource Usage), you can track actual hours of work on a day-by-day or other timeframe basis.

→ For additional information on the Task and Task Details Forms, **see** "Formatting the Task and Resource Forms," **p. 927**

Project uses the work data to calculate the resource costs for each task. If actual costs differ from the scheduled cost for the values entered in the Actual Work fields, you need to have a way to enter actual costs. To do this, display the Resource Cost fields at the bottom of the Task Details Form and record actual costs by resource for each task (see Figure 16.22). This method will work only if the option Actual Costs Are Always Calculated by Microsoft Project is not on in the Options dialog box (Calculation tab).

Figure 16.22
Fields for Resource Cost also can be displayed on the Task Details Form.

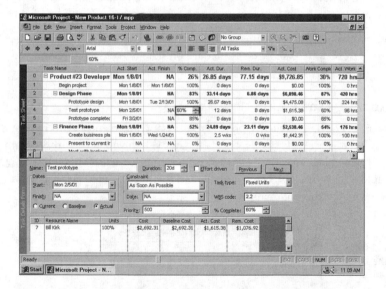

USING THE UPDATE TASKS DIALOG BOX

 Access the Update Tasks dialog box by using either the Tools, Tracking, Update Tasks menu command or the Update Tasks button on the Tracking toolbar. Use this dialog box to enter all the tracking fields discussed in this section except the actual work and cost (see Figure 16.23). The logic and order of calculations for affected fields are exactly the same whether the information is entered in a dialog box or on a table or form. For example, as would happen on a Tracking table, if you use the Update Tasks dialog box to enter 100% complete, Project sets the Actual Start and Actual Finish to what they were scheduled to be. If you set an Actual Duration of 6 days on a 10-day task, Project calculates Percent Complete to be 60%, with a Remaining Duration of 4. On the other hand, if you enter a Percent Complete of 60%, Project calculates the Actual Duration to be 6, with a Remaining Duration of 4.

Figure 16.23
Use the Update Tasks dialog box to enter actual dates and duration information for selected tasks.

If you select several tasks before accessing the Update Tasks dialog box, the dialog box appears blank. Any change you enter here is added to all the selected tasks. You could record, for example, all tasks completed yesterday by selecting the tasks and typing yesterday's date in the Actual Finish date field.

USING THE PERCENT COMPLETE BUTTONS

If one or more tasks have started and are *on schedule*, you can select the tasks and use the various percent complete buttons to copy the scheduled start and finished dates to the actual dates and to enter the appropriate percent in the Percent Complete field.

You also can use the following methods to mark a task as completed; these buttons, however, are the fastest way to show tasks that are on schedule either as completed or in varying stages of completion.

USING THE UPDATE PROJECT COMMAND

Choosing Tools, Tracking, Update Project is a convenient way to update a group of tasks scheduled to start or finish by a certain date. When you choose this command, the dialog box displayed in Figure 16.24 opens. Either enter or select a date in the Update Work as Complete Through text box. Only the tasks with scheduled activity before the update date are affected by this command.

Figure 16.24
A group of tasks progressing in the same timeframe can be updated together in the Update Project dialog box.

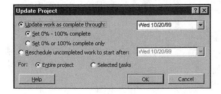

The Update Project dialog box offers choices for updating tasks that are on schedule and tasks that are slipping. The updating options you can choose in this dialog box are as follows:

■ **Set 0%–100% Complete**—Sets the actual dates as originally scheduled and also calculates the Percent Complete. The Percent Complete is calculated as the percent of the duration that was scheduled for completion by the update date.

■ **Set 0% or 100% Complete Only**—Leaves the Percent Complete field at zero until the Actual Finish date is updated, at which time the percent is set to 100%. This option is useful for cases where the Percent Complete is to be either 0% or 100%.

Best Practice Tips from Toby Brown, PMP

Reporting of percent complete is often preferred at an executive level where there's little room for analysis and interpretation into the why's and how's of performance. In the strictest sense, this information is for the benefit of the project manager to take corrective action, when necessary. At a higher level, it becomes more of a bottom-line interpretation of project performance. In other words, it's either done or not done, and no in-between.

PART

V

CH

16

- **Reschedule Uncompleted Work to Start After**—Reschedules slipping tasks to start on the update date as entered in the top-right corner of the dialog box. If the task already has some amount of actual duration recorded for it, the remaining duration is split off from the part already completed and rescheduled to begin on the update date. If a task has not yet started but should have, Project moves the start of the task to start on the update date.

Best Practice Tips from Toby Brown, PMP

I often refer to this feature as "the bulldozer of time." In other words, whatever work is not completed is automatically moved (or rescheduled) to the current date entered. This procedure ensures that the work is constantly moved forward and accounted for within the project.

Note

The Split In-Progress Tasks check box must be marked (the default) on the Schedule tab of the Options dialog box before you can use the Reschedule Uncompleted Work to Start After option in the Update Tasks dialog box.

To use the Update Project command, follow these steps:

1. Select the task or tasks you want to update, if only selected tasks are to be updated. If you want to include all tasks that start before the update date, it doesn't matter whether you have multiple tasks selected or not.

2. Choose Tools, Tracking, Update Project. The Update Project dialog box opens (refer to Figure 16.23).

3. Choose the Entire Project or Selected Tasks option button, depending on whether you want all tasks considered for updating or only tasks that you selected.

4. Choose the operation you want performed. Select one of the options as described in the previous list.

5. Change the date field to the date you want to use as a cut-off date—all uncompleted tasks *before* the update date are processed by the command. By default, the update date is the status date, as set in the Project Information dialog box. Access this dialog box by choosing Project, Project Information.

6. Choose OK to execute the update.

The Update as Scheduled toolbar button behaves much the same way as making updates through the Update Project dialog box. But as with most toolbar shortcuts, you lose flexibility by bypassing the dialog box options. Figure 16.25 shows the results of applying this button command to tasks 19–28. Note that all those tasks' bars that cross or lie to the left of the status date (April 1, 2001, in this example) now show progress bars right up to the update line.

Caution

The Update as Scheduled button uses the status date for updating, as specified in the Project Information dialog box (choose Project, Project Information). Be sure to enter a status date before using this button.

Figure 16.25
All selected tasks have been automatically updated as of an update date.

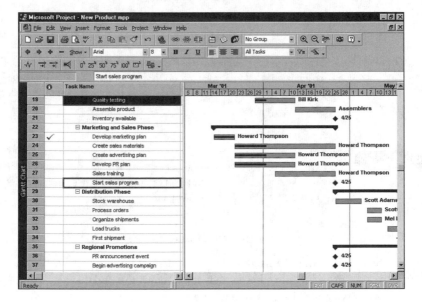

USING THE RESCHEDULE WORK BUTTON ON THE TRACKING TOOLBAR

 The Reschedule Uncompleted Work to Start After option in the Update Project dialog box is useful when the scheduled start date falls before the status date and the task has not yet started; the task is then rescheduled to start on the status date. If the task has started but the actual duration is less than expected by the current date, the remaining duration of the task is split off and scheduled to start on the current date. The two fields controlled by this button are Stop and Resume. In earlier versions, these fields were calculated fields but can now be edited.

USING THE MOUSE IN THE GANTT CHART

You can use the mouse in the Gantt Chart to drag the progress bar from the start date of a task to the percent-completed point on the task bar. To enter Percent Complete with the mouse, follow these steps:

1. View the Gantt Chart by choosing View, Gantt Chart.

2. Move the mouse pointer to the beginning of the task bar for a task you want to update. The pointer changes to a percent sign (%).

3. Click and drag the mouse to the right to increase the Percent Complete. As you move the mouse, an information box appears to the left of the task bar to indicate the date the task is complete through a certain date, which is specified as you drag the mouse. When the correct date is reached, release the mouse button. Drag the mouse all the way to the finish date to indicate 100% complete.

The actual start date is set to the date on which the task was scheduled to start. The Percent Complete changes to a value determined by the date chosen with the mouse; these computed percents can't be a "whole" number such as 50% or 75%. Manually changing the Percent Complete later, by any method, will redraw the progress line on the Gantt Chart.

PART

V

CH

16

Tip from Tim and the Project Team

Increase your accuracy in dragging the mouse to a Percent Complete date by zooming in the timescale setting for finer granularity.

You can extend the duration of a task by dragging the scheduled end date to the right. Move the mouse pointer to the right end of the task bar until the pointer changes to a right-pointing arrow. As you drag the pointer to the right, an information box appears to let you know the duration that will be set when you release the mouse button.

After you record an actual start date for a task, you can use the mouse to change the date. Move the mouse pointer to the left end of the task bar until it turns into a left-pointing arrow. Then, click and drag to the right as the information box indicates an actual start date. Release the mouse button when the start date indicated is what you want.

Be careful when using the mouse to update tasks on the Gantt Chart. If the mouse is in the middle of the task bar, the pointer turns into a double-arrow symbol, and if you drag the mouse, you move the task and set a task constraint of Start No Earlier Than. These constraints are insidious because you probably will not be aware that you have set a constraint.

→ For more information on the effects of setting task constraints, **see** "Working with Task Constraints," **p. 234**

If you accidentally start any of these mouse actions in the Gantt Chart and want to escape, you can drag the mouse down from the task bar before releasing the button to prevent any changes. Depending on where you pointed when any of these actions were initiated, the mouse pointer can change to a chain link. If this happens, make sure that you drag to an open space sufficiently away from other task bars so as not to inadvertently create a task link.

Tip from Tim and the Project Team

Don't forget about Undo if you inadvertently make a change to a task with the mouse.

The tracking facilities presented so far are used for the more difficult cases, which actually might be the more common cases. When tasks start on time and finish within the scheduled duration, quicker ways exist to record the actual data. You also can update many tasks at the same time (refer to the section "Using the Update Tasks Dialog Box" earlier in this chapter).

USING TIMESHEETS

One common method for collecting hours worked on project tasks is requiring team members to complete and submit timesheets at regular intervals. However, several obstacles are involved:

- Workers not used to completing timesheets might exhibit strong resistance to this requirement on their time.

- Workers might resist the increased visibility of time reporting.

- Any new system might be an overlap with an existing system.

- Time reporting might have been tried in the past, which increases objections to "new and improved" efforts.

- Compliance is frequently an issue unless mandated by management.

- Incomplete records from previous reporting periods might communicate false information about the present work status.

- Any system might require high maintenance time or costs to keep all work assignment lists current, given the fluid nature of most projects.

Microsoft Project as a tool can do very little to overcome human resource issues involved with time reporting. It can, however, help provide an environment in which the reporting is more complete, more accurate, and less time consuming. Via email or Web technology, project managers can take advantage of electronic submissions of work data and maintain Project as a central data repository for their projects. Even without electronic communication, tables from Project can be customized and then standardized for distribution to team members as data collection vehicles.

Electronic time reporting in Project involves the use of TeamAssign, TeamStatus, and TeamReport messages. The default TeamAssign message appears in Figure 16.26. The resources assigned to the selected task will be notified via Web or email that these assignments have been made. As work progresses on the task, the resources will send Status messages to the project manager. After the status information has been reviewed, the project manager can accept the reported work values as valid and they are immediately recorded in the project plan. Microsoft Project also automatically recalculates all related fields, such as remaining work values and cost data.

Figure 16.26
Electronic time reporting begins with notifying resources of their assignments.

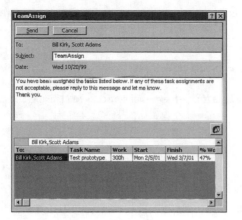

The electronic timesheet reporting capabilities are greatly enhanced in Project 2000. New intranet features in Project Central can form the basis of a highly personalized and customized timesheet reporting system. These features are covered in detail in Chapter 15, "Using Microsoft Project in Workgroups."

The more manual approach to capturing actual work data is creating a customized table to be printed and distributed to team members. Figure 16.27 shows one example of using a table as a data collection tool. In this format, resources would be asked to supply the amount of work completed this period on each task as well as to note any changes that need to be made in the total work estimate or finish date for the task. They also can review and update their work progress, expressed as % Work Complete.

Baseline Work values   Actual Work values   Inserted Custom fields

Figure 16.27
Predefined and custom fields can be displayed and printed together on a custom table to aid time reporting.

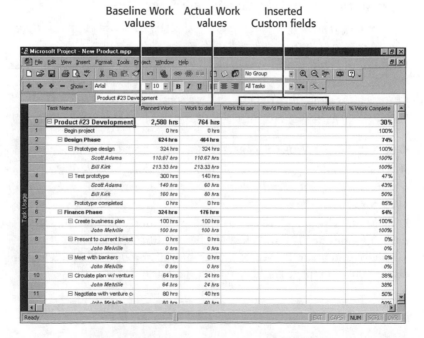

With the new custom field calculation capabilities in Project, importing periodic information from another application, such as Excel, and performing the necessary update calculations in Project are also possible.

→ For more information on creating and using custom fields in Project, **see** "Customizing Fields," **p. 956**

→ For more information on updating data from an external source, **see** "Linking Selected Data Between Applications," **p. 819**

TROUBLESHOOTING

ADDING TASKS TO A BASELINED PLAN

I've already saved the baseline and begun work on the project; then I get a new set of tasks assigned. What do I do?

Add the new tasks and make sure to link them to the rest of the project as necessary. Then, select the tasks and choose Tools, Tracking, Save Baseline. Be sure you mark the option button for selected tasks.

CAPTURING MULTIPLE BASELINE PLANS

The project's baseline has already been saved and initial phases of the project have begun. Now the project has been delayed. How can I reset the baseline without losing the one I have already?

Choose Tools, Tracking, Save Baseline as before, but be sure to mark the Save Interim Plan option button, and then choose one of the alternative sets of dates—for example, Start1, Start2, Start3, and so on.

CREATING HARD COPY DATA COLLECTION FORMS

I get tracking information from people out in the field. How can I provide them with a tool that enables them to capture the information I need?

Print out the project using the Task Sheet with the Tracking table applied. The Task Sheet has several blank columns into which information can be entered as soon as it is available. If the project is long, filter the project for a specific date range. The Using Resource filter also is helpful for printing only the tasks for which a particular resource is responsible.

TRACKING ACTUAL WORK SEPARATELY FROM PERCENT COMPLETE

As I track my project, I want to manually track the actual time worked on a project rather than have the software do it, but when I indicate that a task has started, the work and cost fields are filled in and I can't change them.

Unmark the Updating Task Status Updates Resource Status option on the Calculation tab of the Options dialog box. When you deselect this option, the work and cost fields are not calculated automatically; you can enter information of your own. Or simply wait until the task is 100% complete and then enter your data.

CHAPTER 17

ANALYZING PROGRESS AND REVISING THE SCHEDULE

In this chapter

ANALYZING VARIANCES AND REVISING THE SCHEDULE

As you might recall, the initial project definition stage culminates in the development of what is commonly referred to as the project business plan, proposal, or statement of work. In this all-important first developmental milestone, you'll typically determine the project budget, schedule, and scope, in addition to goals, objectives, approach, and project completion criteria. In order to ensure successful completion, it is important to maintain project control through sound project management practices. Project control is typically attained through tracking, analysis, revision, scope management, and communication.

Best Practice Tips from Toby Brown, PMP

> The iterative process model of project management supported by PMI is Initiating, Planning, Executing, Controlling, and Closing. The Controlling aspect of the model requires the project manager to step back from the project and ask, "How are we doing?" After evaluation, it is often necessary to implement a change control which requires a return to planning before re-executing work. This then completes the feedback loop of the process model.

As we execute our project plans, we find it necessary to track and analyze actual progress to ensure that our goal of on-time, on-budget completion remains achievable. If tasks are being completed late or in excess of their original work estimates, we have to spot these trouble signs sooner rather than later to be sure that we proactively revise our project plan to adjust to the day-to-day realities of the project. If progress is not as expected, we have to start to think about revising our plans to extend the scheduled finish date, adjust resource assignments, modify the budget, or reduce scope.

Best Practice Tips from Toby Brown, PMP

> The process of adjusting the project schedule to align it again with the baseline, which is evaluated through variance analysis, is called *corrective action*.
>
> As a project manager, you should expect to make changes to control the schedule, as changes are an inevitable part of managing a project. In other words, you will always have variance because projects rarely proceed exactly as planned. In the project manager role, you are most interested in what the tolerance is for making changes to the schedule to ensure conformity to the baseline, and what the impact is to the project in terms of dates, durations, costs, and work estimates.

We can begin the process of analysis by regularly looking for tasks that are not progressing as originally planned. You'll typically start to analyze progress after you have captured tracking information by entering Percent Complete or keying the Actual Work, Remaining Work, Actual Start, and Actual Finish. After you have captured this information, you're ready to analyze plan *variances*, that is, tasks where progress is out of sync with the baseline (original estimates).

ANALYZING PROGRESS

The easiest way to hone in on unfavorable variances is to apply a set of tables, filters, views, or reports to quickly locate these variances. Let's take a look at the different techniques we can use to catch trouble early.

Predicting the future is risky, even for a skilled project manager. The foundation of project control is to know which of your predications are proving to be inaccurate. Analyzing progress, part of the Controlling process of project management, and revising the schedule are important pieces of your project management process. If you spot trouble in your project (unfavorable variances), the next step is to figure out how you will revise your work plan to complete the schedule within the available time and budget.

There are two primary ways to make sure your plan remains dynamic and up-to-date: rescheduling unstarted or slipping tasks and rescheduling remaining work on in-progress tasks. These rescheduling steps help you avoid stagnant work plans, a common problem for late, overbudget projects. In the last sections of this chapter (see "Revising the Schedule to Complete on Time and on Budget"), we'll review how to use Project to achieve a realistic, revised schedule.

PART V CH 17

DEFINITIONS

Before we perform our first work plan analyses, let's take a look at how Project calculates and stores information that will help to analyze the plan.

Project automatically calculates the difference between current progress and original estimates. The calculated values are the schedule variances and Project places the results into fields labeled as *variance* fields.

You might find it easier to remember these fields as follows: Think of work as Current Estimated work and baseline work as Original Estimated work. The work variance then is the difference between your Current Estimated work and your Original Estimated work. The same holds true for the other four variance fields listed later.

Anytime the Current Estimated values are higher than the Original Estimated (baseline) values, the resulting variance will be a positive number. This means that any variance that is greater than zero is exceeding your original estimates and is considered unfavorable. A list of how Project calculates variances follows:

Work Variance = (Work–Baseline Work)

Cost Variance = (Cost–Baseline Cost)

Finish Variance = (Finish–Baseline Finish)

Start Variance = (Start–Baseline Start)

Duration Variance = (Duration–Baseline Duration)

In addition, Project automatically calculates two types of percent complete: Percent Complete and Percent Work Complete. It is important to understand the differences between these two fields because they give you two different flavors of project progress:

- Percent Complete is the percentage of calendar time expired, based upon the tasks' actual duration divided by estimated duration times 100. If you key directly into the Percent Complete field, Project calculates the Actual and Remaining Duration for the task.

- Percent Work Complete is the percentage of completion based upon the task's actual work divided by total estimated work times 100. If you key directly into the Percent Work Complete field, and the option for Updating Task Status Updates Resource Status is turned on, Project calculates the Actual and Remaining Duration for the task, and sets the Percent Complete to be equal to the Percent Work Complete.

Note

One important setting in Project controls the relationship between task completion and actual work. To change this setting, choose Options from the Tools menu, click the Calculation tab, and locate the option box for Updating Task Status Updates Resource Status. With this option turned on, as it is by default, Project automatically updates Percent Work Complete, Actual and Remaining Work, and Actual and Remaining Duration when Percent Complete changes. Conversely, with this option turned off, Project will not change your Actual Work and Remaining Work with changes to %Complete.

Caution

If you set this option, any changes to Percent Complete or Actual or Remaining Duration will cause Project to overwrite your Actual Work and Remaining Work, even if you have keyed values in these fields.

REVIEWING SUMMARY PROGRESS INFORMATION

There are two easy ways to analyze how your entire project is performing against your original plan. The first method is to display the Project Summary Task, combined with the Work, Variance, or Tracking table. To display the Project Summary task, choose Tools, Options. Move to the View tab and note the Project Summary task option in the bottom of the screen under Outline Options. Check this option and Project automatically displays a summary task for the entire plan.

Best Practice Tips from Toby Brown, PMP

As a rule, it is a good practice to have a Project Summary task on all of your projects. You can create it by "turning on" the option outlined in the previous paragraph. Or you can create a project summary task by defining the first task as a Project Summary and then indenting, or "demoting," all subsequent tasks underneath.

There is no real difference in the approaches other than the numbering of the tasks. By using the software feature, the numbering of the tasks is maintained with the first task being "0." Otherwise, it will be numbered task one. Regardless of how you wish to add it, the important thing is to create a Project Summary task within all of your projects, as it provides a quick summary view of the entire project.

ANALYZING THE WORK VARIANCES FOR THE ENTIRE PROJECT

After you've displayed the Project Summary task, try applying the Work table. Choose View, Table, Work.

Figure 17.1 shows that for the New Product project, the total Work Variance is –16 hours (favorable).

Figure 17.1
Work table values roll up to the Project Summary task.

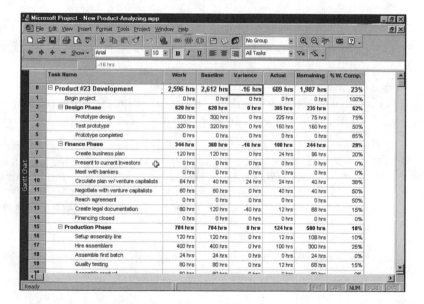

	Task Name	Work	Baseline	Variance	Actual	Remaining	% W. Comp.
0	⊟ Product #23 Development	2,596 hrs	2,612 hrs	-16 hrs	609 hrs	1,987 hrs	23%
1	Begin project	0 hrs	0 hrs	0 hrs	0 hrs	0 hrs	100%
2	⊟ Design Phase	620 hrs	620 hrs	0 hrs	385 hrs	235 hrs	62%
3	Prototype design	300 hrs	300 hrs	0 hrs	225 hrs	75 hrs	75%
4	Test prototype	320 hrs	320 hrs	0 hrs	160 hrs	160 hrs	50%
5	Prototype completed	0 hrs	0 hrs	0 hrs	0 hrs	0 hrs	85%
6	⊟ Finance Phase	344 hrs	360 hrs	-16 hrs	100 hrs	244 hrs	29%
7	Create business plan	120 hrs	120 hrs	0 hrs	24 hrs	96 hrs	20%
8	Present to current investors	0 hrs	0 hrs	0 hrs	0 hrs	0 hrs	0%
9	Meet with bankers	0 hrs	0 hrs	0 hrs	0 hrs	0 hrs	0%
10	Circulate plan w/ venture capitalists	64 hrs	40 hrs	24 hrs	24 hrs	40 hrs	38%
11	Negotiate with venture capitalists	80 hrs	80 hrs	0 hrs	40 hrs	40 hrs	50%
12	Reach agreement	0 hrs	0 hrs	0 hrs	0 hrs	0 hrs	50%
13	Create legal documentation	80 hrs	120 hrs	-40 hrs	12 hrs	68 hrs	15%
14	Financing closed	0 hrs	0 hrs	0 hrs	0 hrs	0 hrs	0%
15	⊟ Production Phase	704 hrs	704 hrs	0 hrs	124 hrs	580 hrs	18%
16	Setup assembly line	120 hrs	120 hrs	0 hrs	12 hrs	108 hrs	10%
17	Hire assemblers	400 hrs	400 hrs	0 hrs	100 hrs	300 hrs	25%
18	Assemble first batch	24 hrs	24 hrs	0 hrs	0 hrs	24 hrs	0%
19	Quality testing	80 hrs	80 hrs	0 hrs	12 hrs	68 hrs	15%

ANALYZING THE DATE VARIANCES FOR THE ENTIRE PROJECT

Now try applying the Variance table instead of Work. Choose View, Table, Variance.

Figure 17.2 shows the date variance fields for the project. You can see that even though the project is tracking ahead of plan on work estimates, the project has a Start Variance of positive 4 days (unfavorable). This means the project started later than expected.

It can be tempting to focus too heavily on analyzing work variances. If you analyze your work variances and your work estimates are accurate, you might assume that you would meet your objective of on-time delivery. It's possible to be completing tasks according to the original (baseline) work estimates, but miss your objective of on-time delivery due to these tasks starting or finishing late.

Figure 17.2
Project variances are shown on the Project Summary task with the Variance table applied.

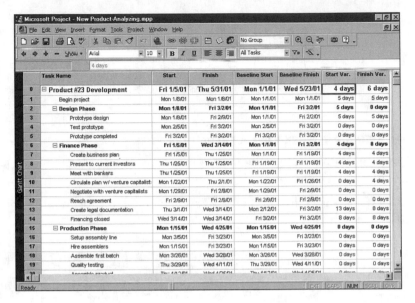

As we can see in the current example, the Work Variance is favorable (refer to Figure 17.1), but if we look at the Finish Variance, the entire project is forecasted to complete 6 days later than originally estimated (refer to Figure 17.2).

Tip from Tim and the Project Team

During the tracking process, you should consistently update Actual Start and Actual Finish dates for each task. When you key an Actual Finish date that is later than originally estimated, your project's overall Finish Date can be pushed to a later date. When this happens, it means that slipping tasks have extended the critical path for the project.

ANALYZING COST VARIANCES FOR THE ENTIRE PROJECT

To analyze your overall project costs, try applying the Cost table. Choose <u>V</u>iew, Ta<u>b</u>le, <u>C</u>ost.

Figure 17.3 shows the Cost Variance field for the New Product project. The project summary task shows a total Cost Variance of –$230.77 (favorable). The original estimated Cost (baseline) was $47,668.15 but based on current progress, the project is expected to be completed under budget at a Total Cost of $47,437.38.

Figure 17.3
The Summary Project task shows the Cost table applied.

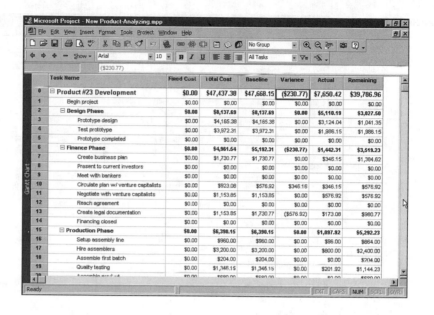

Task Name	Fixed Cost	Total Cost	Baseline	Variance	Actual	Remaining
0 ⊟ Product #23 Development	$0.00	$47,437.38	$47,668.15	($230.77)	$7,650.42	$39,786.96
1 Begin project	$0.00	$0.00	$0.00	$0.00	$0.00	$0.00
2 ⊟ Design Phase	$0.00	$8,137.69	$8,137.69	$0.00	$5,110.19	$3,027.50
3 Prototype design	$0.00	$4,165.38	$4,165.38	$0.00	$3,124.04	$1,041.35
4 Test prototype	$0.00	$3,972.31	$3,972.31	$0.00	$1,986.15	$1,986.15
5 Prototype completed	$0.00	$0.00	$0.00	$0.00	$0.00	$0.00
6 ⊟ Finance Phase	$0.00	$4,961.54	$5,192.31	($230.77)	$1,442.31	$3,519.23
7 Create business plan	$0.00	$1,730.77	$1,730.77	$0.00	$346.15	$1,384.62
8 Present to current investors	$0.00	$0.00	$0.00	$0.00	$0.00	$0.00
9 Meet with bankers	$0.00	$0.00	$0.00	$0.00	$0.00	$0.00
10 Circulate plan w/ venture capitalists	$0.00	$923.08	$576.92	$346.16	$346.15	$576.92
11 Negotiate with venture capitalists	$0.00	$1,153.85	$1,153.85	$0.00	$576.92	$576.92
12 Reach agreement	$0.00	$0.00	$0.00	$0.00	$0.00	$0.00
13 Create legal documentation	$0.00	$1,153.85	$1,730.77	($576.92)	$173.08	$980.77
14 Financing closed	$0.00	$0.00	$0.00	$0.00	$0.00	$0.00
15 ⊟ Production Phase	$0.00	$6,390.15	$6,390.15	$0.00	$1,097.92	$5,292.23
16 Setup assembly line	$0.00	$960.00	$960.00	$0.00	$96.00	$864.00
17 Hire assemblers	$0.00	$3,200.00	$3,200.00	$0.00	$800.00	$2,400.00
18 Assemble first batch	$0.00	$204.00	$204.00	$0.00	$0.00	$204.00
19 Quality testing	$0.00	$1,346.15	$1,346.15	$0.00	$201.92	$1,144.23

DISPLAYING PROJECT STATISTICS

 Another quick way to see your project's progress in a single view is to display the Project Statistics dialog box. You can show this view from the Tracking toolbar by clicking the Project Statistics tool button. When you click this tool button, you'll see the entire project summarized as shown in Figure 17.4. This dialog box summarizes project start and finish dates, duration, work, and cost for the project. You also can display this summary box by choosing Project, Project Information. In the Project Information dialog box, click the Statistics button.

Figure 17.4
The Project Statistics dialog box shows a snapshot of progress.

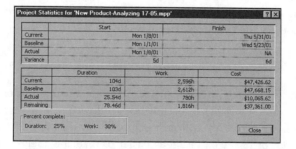

THE PROJECT SUMMARY REPORT

Project also provides a convenient report, called Project Summary, that shows a summary analysis of the entire project. Choose View, Reports. On the Reports dialog box, click Overview, and then Select. Choose the report called Project Summary, and then click Select. You'll be presented with the report, as shown in Figure 17.5. This report provides a summary of your overall project dates, duration, work, costs, and summary task status.

PART
V
CH
17

Figure 17.5
Print out a snapshot of progress with the Project Summary report.

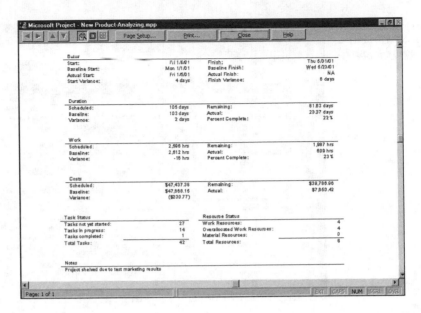

Now that you've seen how to analyze the overall project, go to the next level of detailed analysis: analyzing the highest-level summary tasks in your project. These high-level summary tasks are often called *phases*. Instead of focusing only on the Project Summary task, we can apply the Cost, Work, or Variance tables combined with the filter called Top Level Tasks. The Top Level Tasks filter chooses all tasks with an outline level of 1, that is, the next highest outline level after the Project Summary task. These tasks will usually be summary tasks but there also might be individual tasks at a high outline level.

To apply the Top Level Tasks filter, open the filter drop-down list on the Formatting toolbar and select Top Level Tasks. Figure 17.6 shows the results of applying the Top Level Tasks filter. Try applying the Cost, Work, or Variance tables combined with this filter to analyze how the phases in your project are progressing.

Show ▾

A new button on the Formatting toolbar provides another way to focus on tasks at a certain outline level. The maximum number of outline levels allowed in a project is the unfathomable number of 65,535. Typically a Project plan will include less than 10 levels; keeping the outline to five levels or less makes it much easier to read and analyze. The Show button opens a drop-down list, letting you choose an outline level number. All tasks at the chosen outline number or less will be displayed; tasks with higher outline numbers (and more indentation) will be hidden. Be sure no filter has been applied before selecting the Show button; All Tasks should be visible on the Formatting toolbar filter drop-down list.

Filter results
displayed

Filters
drop-down list

Apply Top-Level
Tasks filter

Figure 17.6
Apply the Top Level
Tasks filter to analyze
values at the first out-
line level.

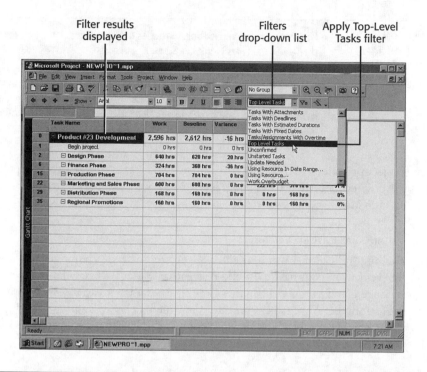

PART
V
CH
17

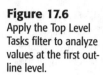
*Best Practice
Tips from Toby
Brown, PMP*

It is good practice to have a minimum of three levels within your project. They are typically identified as project level, phase level, and work (or activity) level.

The project level summary task would be at level one, as outlined earlier in this chapter.

Level two defines the phases of work to be completed and typically corresponds to a WBS, or Work Breakdown Structure, which is the skeletal structure of the project, each defining a unique deliverable for that component of the project. Examples would include Design Phase, Production Phase, Financing Phase, and so on.

Finally, the work level is the lowest level, where the activity is identified, the resource is assigned, and dependencies are established.

REVIEWING PROGRESS INFORMATION AT THE TASK LEVEL

It's a good idea to prepare to analyze variances in your work plan at least as often as you track progress. If you apply actual and remaining work on a weekly basis, plan to analyze variances on a weekly basis. It doesn't do much good to key in actuals every week, and then not see what these numbers are telling you. Subtle increases of work and costs over your original baseline can add up quickly. The sooner you spot trouble and revise your plan, the more likely you are to achieve your project's objectives of on-time, on-budget completion.

Best Practice Tips from Toby Brown, PMP

Remember that a "revised" plan includes not only scheduled dates, but also includes changes in estimates of durations, work, and costs.

Costs can be adjusted one of two ways: changes made to resource assignments and/or the additions or deletions of fixed costs. Also, changes to calendars can modify the schedule as to when work is performed on the project. These changes can be made to the overall project calendar or to specific resource calendars. Either one can impact the scheduling of the remaining tasks within the project.

Project provides a number of views, filters, and reports to assist you in spotting trouble at the task level of detail. Let's take a look at how we can analyze variances that are occurring on individual tasks in your plan.

FINDING TASK WORK VARIANCES

You might recall that work variances are created whenever your current work estimates are different from your baseline work. A negative work variance is favorable and a positive work variance is unfavorable. The fastest way to see the work variances for each task in your plan is to apply the Work table. From the View menu, choose Table, Work. Figure 17.7 again shows the Work table. The Variance column displays the work variances for each task in your plan.

Work table applied

Project overall has favorable work variance.

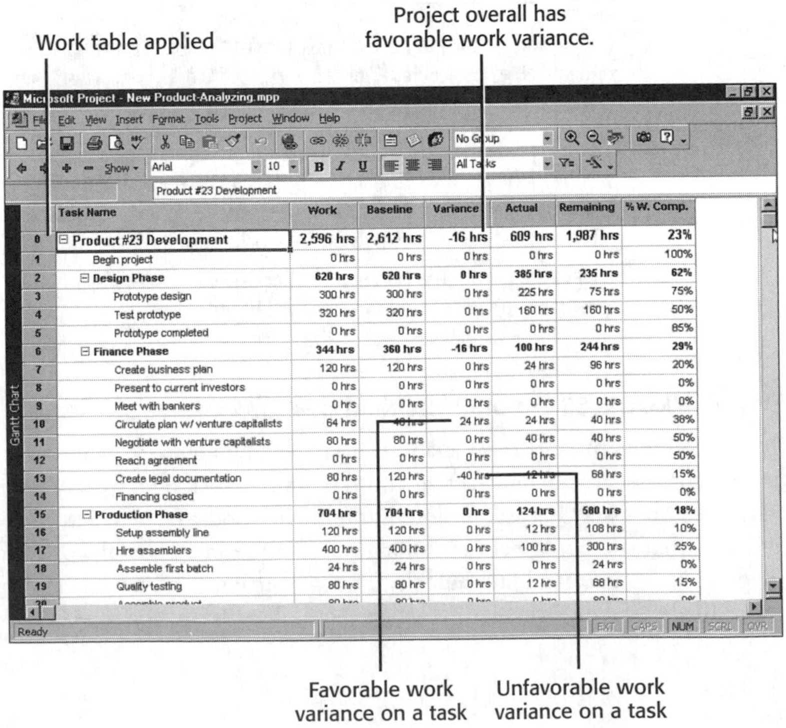

Figure 17.7
Gantt Chart with Work table applied and all tasks displayed.

Favorable work variance on a task

Unfavorable work variance on a task

To focus on trouble spots, you'll want to look at tasks with unfavorable work variances. Project provides a filter, called Work Overbudget, for this purpose. Figure 17.8 shows the contents of this filter. The tasks will be selected if *Actual* Work is in excess of Baseline Work and the task was baselined with some amount of work (Baseline Work not equal to zero).

Figure 17.8
The contents of the Work Overbudget filter show the logic used to select tasks that have actually exceeded their baseline estimates.

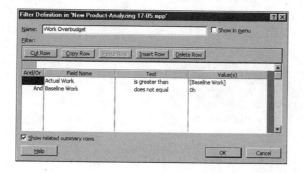

PART
V
CH
17

Tip from Tim and the Project Team

You might be more interested in seeing tasks that are currently scheduled to exceed their original work estimates but have not yet done so. Modify the Work Overbudget filter to compare Work to Baseline Work instead of the supplied setting of comparing Actual Work to Baseline Work.

→ For more information on customizing filters, **see** "Creating Custom Filters," **p. 968**

Applying the Work Overbudget filter to a Gantt Chart results in the display seen in Figure 17.9.

Figure 17.9
The results of applying the Work Overbudget filter, showing those tasks that have exceeded their original (baseline) estimate.

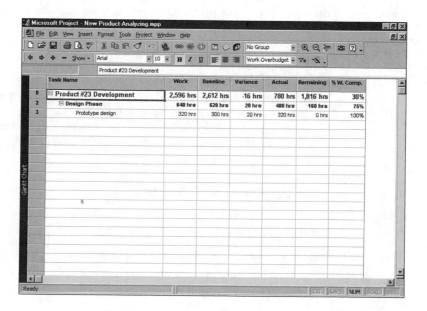

You can combine the Work table and Work Overbudget filter into a new single view. Begin the process of creating a customized view by choosing View, More Views and clicking New to display the Define New View dialog box. This new view can be applied anytime you want to quickly spot tasks that are forecasted to exceed their original work estimate. Figure 17.10 shows the new Work Variance view definition. This same configuration can be used to build an Underestimated Tasks report. To build this view or report, see Chapter 23, "Customizing Views, Tables, Fields, and Filters," and Chapter 25,""Customizing Reports."

Figure 17.10
The newly created Work Variance view, which combines the Work table with the Work Overbudget filter.

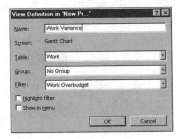

Variances are meaningless unless your work plan has been baselined. If you haven't baselined your plan, all of your work variances will be equal to your work. If you see this happening, you need to baseline your plan. If you've already keyed in actuals, re-baselining your plan may cause your baseline to be different from what you originally intended, especially if some of your work or date estimates are proving to be inaccurate.

A second option for recovering from a problem like this requires a backup of your plan that reflects the condition of your plan before you keyed in your first actuals. Open your backup copy of the plan, baseline the plan, then re-key the actuals. One last option is to continue working with the current plan, but manually enter estimates into the Baseline fields.

Best Practice Tips from Toby Brown, PMP

Typically, you should avoid making changes to the baseline once it is set. The baseline usually has "buy-in" from stakeholders on the project. Efforts to change the baseline after it is set are usually attempts to "make it look good" by "tweaking" the numbers (changing the plan to match the schedule instead of the other way around). As in financial accounting, such practices are frowned upon. A better practice is that corrections should be made to the schedule to bring it back in line with the baseline. These types of actions demonstrate a reactive response and attentive maintenance of the schedule by the project manager.

FINDING TASK START AND FINISH DATE VARIANCES

Date variances are created whenever your current start and finish estimates are different from the baseline dates. This can happen in a variety of ways:

- A predecessor task is delayed or completed early, forcing a successor task to be rescheduled.

- You set a new start or finish date for a task because it could not be completed as originally scheduled.

- You set an actual start or finish date that's different from the baseline date.

- Actual work is higher or lower than originally planned, causing the task's duration and dates to change.

To see all date variances for your project, display the Variance table. Choose View, Table, Variance. Figure 17.11 shows the work plan with the Variance table displayed. You can see the start and finish date, baseline start and finish dates, and date variances.

Figure 17.11
The Variance table shows the current estimated start and finish dates, the original (baseline) start and finish dates, and any variances from the baseline start and finish dates.

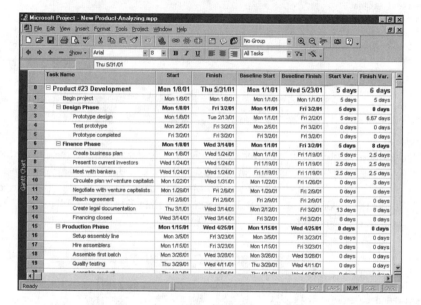

PART

V

CH

17

Next, you might want to focus on tasks that are forecasted to finish later than originally estimated. To do this, you'll look for tasks with finish variances greater than zero that have not yet finished. Project provides the Slipping Tasks filter for this purpose. Figure 17.12 shows the contents of the Slipping Tasks filter. To view the contents of this filter, choose Project, Filtered For, More Filters and select the Slipping Tasks filter from the list. Edit the filter or make a copy to view.

This filter shows you tasks that are not yet finished, that have a baseline finish date, and have a current estimated finish date later than the baseline finish date. This filter can be used to find tasks that you can still do something about. They're forecasted to finish late, but they're not finished yet.

Best Practice Tips from Toby Brown, PMP

When analyzing slipping tasks, special attention should be given to tasks that are critical. Critical tasks contribute to the longest path in the project and will pushout the expected finish date. Identifying these will allow the project manager to concentrate on shortening those tasks (crashing) in order to ensure the project finishes on time. Of course, the critical path may change to another "longer" path following crashing, so attention should be given to how it can be redefined.

Figure 17.12
The Slipping Tasks filter shows tasks that are currently scheduled to complete later than originally planned.

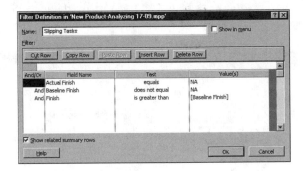

Project supplies another filter that looks for similar problems with tasks forecasted to start by a certain date, called the Should Start By filter. Figure 17.13 shows the contents of the Should Start By filter. The filter prompts the user to supply the start date of interest, then looks for tasks that are scheduled to start by that date and that have no actual start date (the task has not started)

Figure 17.13
The Should Start By Filter shows tasks that are scheduled to start by a user-supplied date but have not started yet.

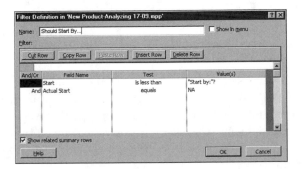

You might want to view all tasks that have either a late start or a late finish date. Project 2000 supplies a filter named Should Start/Finish By for this purpose. Figure 17.14 shows the definition of the filter. Display this filter with the Variance table and you'll quickly isolate all the tasks in your plan that have unfavorable date variances. The filter prompts the user to supply both the start and finish dates of interest.

Figure 17.14
Apply the Should Start/Finish By filter to find tasks with a late start or late finish.

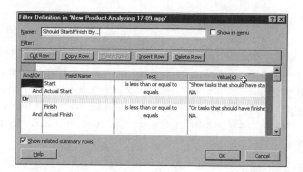

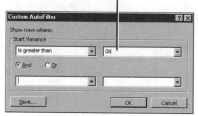

To isolate unfavorable values for a variance field, you can quickly apply an AutoFilter. First apply the Variance table. Then run an AutoFilter by clicking the AutoFilter button on the Formatting toolbar or by choosing Project, Filtered For, AutoFilter.

Select any cell in a variance column, such as Start Variance. Click the AutoFilter drop-down list on the Start Variance column heading and choose a variance value from the list. You also can create a custom filter to display only positive variances. Select Custom from the AutoFilter drop-down list. Set the test to Is Greater Than and set the value to 0 (zero). The resulting Custom AutoFilter will appear, as shown in Figure 17.15.

Testing for a positive start variance

Figure 17.15
The Custom AutoFilter is showing unfavorable start variances.

The same concept can be applied to the Finish Variance field for your project, or for Work Variances if you first apply the Work table.

You might not see date variances for a large number of the tasks in your project. Whenever a task Percent Complete is greater than zero, Project automatically copies the estimated task Start date to the Actual Start date. If you don't explicitly key an Actual Start date, Project will assume it started on the estimated Start date. Project will also insert an Actual Start date if any Actual Work is entered for the task or for a resource assigned to the task.

Applying similar logic to Actual Finish dates, Project automatically copies the estimated task Finish date to the Actual Finish date when either the task Percent Complete or the Percent Work Complete is set to 100%. Project will also insert an Actual Finish date when Remaining Work or Remaining Duration is set to zero. If you don't explicitly tell Project when the task actually finished, Project will assume it finished on the estimated Finish date. You can, however, find the Actual Finish or Actual Start fields and change them if needed. An easy way to view and edit these date fields is by applying the Tracking table.

FINDING TASK COST VARIANCES

Cost variances are created whenever your current cost estimates are higher than your baseline cost estimates. Tasks can start and finish on time and complete within their original estimates, but still have cost variances. For example, if you estimated that the programming would be completed with a VBA programmer at $50 per hour but you're forced to re-assign the task to a programmer whose rate is $60 per hour, your costs will be over budget even if the hours remain constant. Hopefully, the programmer with the higher rate can complete the task in fewer hours, but this will not always be the case.

Tip from Tim and the Project Team

> Project does not take into account the competencies of resources available to the project, so assigning a different resource will not automatically shorten the duration of the task. Factoring this element into re-estimating the duration for the task will sometimes be necessary on many skill-based assignments.

To spot problems with unfavorable costs, you can apply the Cost Overbudget filter. Figure 17.16 shows the contents of the Cost Overbudget filter. This filter looks for tasks that were baselined and that have a current estimated cost greater than the baseline cost (or original estimate).

Figure 17.16
The Cost Overbudget filter is useful for quickly finding tasks where the current estimated cost is greater than the originally estimated cost.

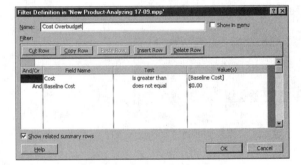

You can combine the Cost table and Cost Overbudget filter into a new view. This new view can be applied anytime you want to quickly spot tasks that are currently predicted to exceed their original cost estimate. Figure 17.17 shows the new Cost Overbudget view definition. To build this view, see Chapter 23.

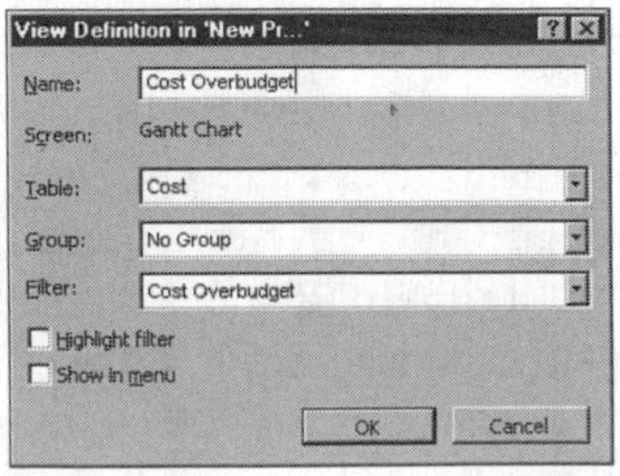

Figure 17.17
Custom Cost Overbudget view combines the Cost table and Cost Overbudget filter for quickly spotting tasks that are exceeding their original budgets.

REVIEWING PROGRESS INFORMATION AT THE RESOURCE LEVEL

You also can analyze progress and variances for resources. The concept is very similar to many of the analyses that you performed on tasks in the previous section. By analyzing resources, you might determine that the reasons for task variances are related to human, or work-type, resources:

- Resources arrived late onto the project.
- Tasks were assigned to resources with the wrong skills to perform the task.
- Work on tasks for one resource was consistently underestimated.
- Resources have not been able to apply the percentage of time to the project that was originally anticipated.
- Tasks that are slipping seem to be assigned to the same resource or combination of resources.
- The original cost of a resource was under- or overestimated.
- Customer or user resources are not applying the appropriate effort to the project.

To find these kinds of patterns, you can view variances for resources. Rather than repeat the previous steps that we performed on tasks for work, date, and cost variances, Table 17.1 shows the variances you can select.

TABLE 17.1   SUGGESTED VARIANCE ANALYSES FROM TABLES APPLIED TO RESOURCE SHEET

Table	Filter	Shows You
Cost	Cost Overbudget	Resources whose current estimated cost is higher than the originally estimated baseline cost
Entry	Slipping Assignments	Resource assignments that are forecasted to finish later than originally estimated
Entry	Should Start/Finish By	Resource assignments that should have started or finished by dates that you specify (an interactive filter)
Entry	Should Start By	Resource assignments that should have started by a date that you specify (an interactive filter)
Work	Work Overbudget	Resources whose current estimated work is higher than originally estimated baseline work

ANALYZING VARIANCES AT THE RESOURCE ASSIGNMENT LEVEL

You might be interested in viewing specific tasks with resource assignments that are currently calculated to finish late or overbudget for a specific resource. To view late or overbudget assignments, you apply the Late/Overbudget Tasks Assigned To filter. From the Project menu, select Filtered For, More Filters. From the More Filters dialog box, choose Late/Overbudget Tasks Assigned To. Because this filter is interactive, you will be prompted to enter the name of the resource you want to analyze. Figure 17.18 shows the contents of the Late/Overbudget Tasks Assigned To filter.

Figure 17.18
The Late/Overbudget Tasks Assigned To filter provides detailed variance information about specific resources assigned to specific tasks.

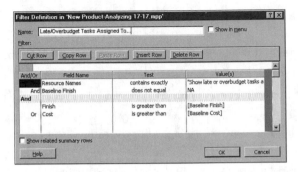

You also can compare baseline work to currently scheduled work at the detailed resource assignment level in your plan. Use the following steps:

1. Display the Task Usage View by clicking the Task Usage icon on the View bar or by choosing View, Task Usage.

2. On the Task Usage timescale grid, click your right mouse button. Choose Baseline Work.

3. You are now able to review the current work estimate against the baseline work estimate at the detailed resource assignment level of detail.

Figure 17.19 shows the Task Usage view with Work and Baseline Work displayed.

You can perform this same analysis from the Resource Usage view. The information presented is basically the same, except that the information is presented by task within resource, instead of resource within task.

THE EARNED VALUE FIELDS AND REPORT

One of the best ways to analyze variances in your plan is to compare how much of your budget you should have spent compared to how much you've actually spent. This concept is sometimes referred to as Estimated Burn Rate versus Actual Burn Rate. Project supplies a number of fields that are automatically calculated and collectively called Earned Value fields. In its simplest form, Earned Value Analysis answers the question "Are we getting what we paid for?"

The main goal behind Earned Value is to analyze differences between planned and actual work progress, and how those differences are affecting the costs (and therefore *value*) of the work product. All three key types of Project fields are used in various calculations: baseline (also called planned), actual, and current estimates.

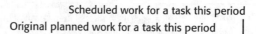

Scheduled work for a task this period
Original planned work for a task this period

Figure 17.19
Task Usage comparing scheduled work to baseline work at the resource assignment level.

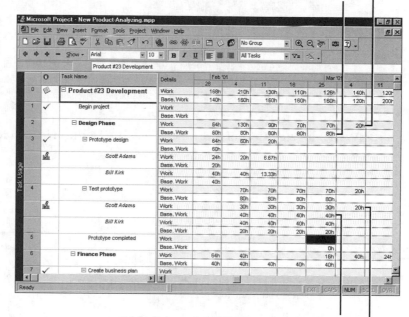

Original planned work for an assigned resource
Scheduled work for an assigned resource

The following is a list of definition fields used on the Earned Value table and report:

- **BCWS (Budgeted Cost of Work Scheduled)**—The planned (or scheduled) earned value of the task. Project first determines the planned completion percentage based on today's date and the task's baseline start and finish dates.

  BCWS = Planned Completion Percentage×Planned Cost

  The BCWS field shows how much of the budget should have been spent on a task or resource by now.

> **Note**
>
> The planned completion percentage is an internally calculated field that cannot be displayed. Project calculates this field by figuring out what the percent complete should be for a task by taking the difference between the planned start date for the task and the project status date.

Tip from Tim and the Project Team

You can calculate the planned completion percentage for a task by using some algebra on the BCWS calculation:

Planned Completion Percentage = BCWS/Planned Cost

Sample calculation of planned completion percentage: The baseline cost for an assignment is $100, and is evenly distributed over its scheduled time on the task. The baseline start for the assignment is September 1 and the baseline finish is September 30. If today's date is September 15, then the BCWS for the assignment is $50. By dividing the planned cost of $100 into the BCWS of $50, you can calculate a planned completion percentage of 50%.

■ **BCWP (Budgeted Cost of Work Performed)**—This field is often referred to as the earned value of the work that has been performed on the task.

BCWP = Percent Complete×Baseline Cost

Example, if the baseline cost for a task is $100 and the task is now 75% complete, the BCWP is $75.

Tip from Tim and the Project Team

Because you can calculate planned completion percentage and Project stores the task's actual percent complete, try comparing these two numbers. If a task's planned completion percentage is 75% and the percent complete is 50, you are running 25% behind the planned burn rate for that task.

■ **ACWP (Actual Cost of Work Performed)**—This field represents the cost of actual work plus any fixed costs for the task, up to the project status date. The calculation of the ACWP depends on each resource's Accrue At settings in the Resource Information dialog box (or Resource Sheet). The resource's cost accrual method is used in conjunction with the actual work recorded for each resource, any fixed costs for the task, and the status date or today's date.

Actual Cost = (Actual Work×Standard Rate) + (Actual Overtime Work×Overtime Rate) + Resource Per Use Costs + Fixed Cost

■ **SV (Schedule Variance**—The difference between the current schedule and the baseline schedule. If the schedule variance is negative, the project is ahead of schedule; if the schedule variance is positive, the project is behind schedule.

Current Schedule–Baseline Schedule

■ **CV (Earned Value Cost Variance)**—The difference between the baseline costs and the scheduled costs (current estimate). If the cost variance is negative, the cost is currently under the budgeted (or baseline) amount; if the cost variance is positive, the task is over budget.

Earned Value Cost Variance = Cost–Baseline Cost

■ **EAC (Estimate at Completion**—This field is simply an alternate column heading for the Cost field.

- **BAC (Budgeted at Completion**—This field is simply an alternative column heading for the Baseline Cost field.

- **VAC (Variance at Completion)**—This field is simply an alternative column heading for the Cost Variance field.

Time-phased Earned Value fields provide enhanced information about data that is spread over some period of time. For example, the BCWS (budgeted Cost of Work Scheduled) field contains the cumulative time-phased baseline costs up to the status date or today's date. This time-phased field shows cumulative BCWS as distributed over time, up to the status date or today's date.

Because Earned Value Analysis draws from so many fields, it is imperative that detailed and accurate work and cost records be kept and entered into the plan. The calculations required to populate the Earned Value fields are automatically handled by Project; no additional steps are required on the part of the project manager. However, some independent research into the use, value, and application of Earned Value Analysis is highly recommended.

See "The Cost Reports Category" section of Chapter 24, "Using the Standard Reports," for a description of the included Earned Value report. Also, see "Exploring the Standard Tables" section of Chapter 21, "Using the Standard Views, Tables, and Filters," for a discussion of the Earned Value task and resource tables.

Sometimes you will find variances in your favor. Managing a project that is ahead of schedule is an enjoyable, though sometimes rare, position to be in. It's very tempting to tell everyone when you find yourself in this enviable position. Before you do, consider what sometimes happens if you report that you're ahead of schedule:

- **Scope**—Because you have extra time on your hands, your project scope might be increased.

- **Budget**—Because you don't need all the money you originally asked for, your budget might be cut to be in line with current projections.

- **Schedule**—Because you're ahead of schedule, your project finish date can be adjusted to complete earlier than originally planned.

- **Resources**—Because you're completing tasks early, in fewer hours than originally predicted, some of your resources can be diverted to other efforts.

Carefully consider the right time and method to report favorable variances. Full and accurate disclosure of project progress is essential for managing the plan as well as keeping the team on track. In practice, it may be necessary to report favorable status in the context of "wait and see" to be certain that a trend is developing instead of revising the plan based on a single positive result.

*Best Practice
Tips from Toby
Brown, PMP*

Many organizations consider favorable variances to be poor project management. Increased scope encourages *gold-plating*, a practice of delivering more than expected with little added value to the customer. Under-budget expenses and finishing early implies excessive padding to both time and costs and will be scrutinized by a project's sponsor in future projects. Additionally, the early release of resources means under-utilization since people can rarely start right away on their next assignment. It's like a plane arriving early at an airport: It typically means waiting on the tarmac for the assigned gate to become available or an extended wait for passengers making connections. Experience shows that customers are most appreciative for delivery of what is expected—no more, no less.

Be aware that anytime you set the baseline for a task, or the entire project, you will reset the variance fields to zero (or NA for dates). If your project is already underway, you might not want to lose your variances when you reset the baseline. Before resetting the baseline, use the custom Duration fields to store intermediate variances.

*Tip from Tim and
the Project Team*

You might want to take an extra step and capture current information before resetting the baseline. Use Tools, Tracking, Save Baseline, Save Interim Plan to copy and save start and finish dates into custom date pairs. Also, manually copy work and duration values into custom duration fields (Duration1–Duration10) and cost values into custom Cost fields (Cost1–Cost10). Using the new calculated values feature for custom fields, you can then compute a variety of variance values for later comparisons.

→ For more information on creating calculated custom fields, **see** "Customizing Fields," **p. 956**

On the other hand, you might find that resetting variances to zero is just what you want. Maybe your original estimates were incorrect, but you were just given permission to re-estimate the unfinished tasks in your plan. You can apply a filter for Uncompleted Tasks, select those uncompleted tasks, and set the baseline For Selected Tasks.

GRAPHICALLY ANALYZING TASKS IN YOUR PLAN

The analysis methods described so far present the project manager with raw numbers to review. In some cases it might not require any more than a glance at a Gantt Chart to spot developing problems. Different team members and managers might actually spot trends in visual displays that are not apparent to them by looking at the numbers. This section discusses formatting options to help highlight potential problem areas.

ADDING PROGRESS LINES

The progress line is a line drawn vertically down the Gantt Chart. You specify a progress date (an *as of* date) and Project draws a line connecting the actual duration of each task to the date you have specified. There are two ways to display a progress line:

- Using the Add Progress Line button on the Tracking toolbar.
- Choosing Tools, Tracking. Select Progress Lines.

USING THE ADD PROGRESS LINE TOOL BUTTON

When you click the Add Progress Line tool button, the mouse pointer changes shape to look like a progress line and the Progress Line ToolTip box pops up as you move your cursor over the Gantt Chart area. The ToolTip displays the date it will use to display the progress line. Figure 17.20 shows the ToolTip box that will pop up.

Figure 17.20
The Progress Line ToolTip box will display the date on which the progress line will be placed.

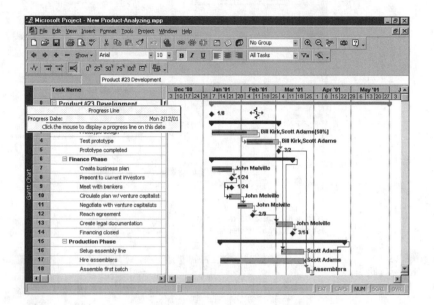

PART
V
CH
17

When you have moved your mouse pointer to the desired date, click the mouse button and the progress line will display. The line connects each task's Percent Complete at the progress date you specify. If a task has not started, it will have a 0% Complete and the progress line connects to the task's start date. The progress line passes straight through tasks progressing ahead of schedule and does not draw through tasks whose schedule does not include the progress line date. Figure 17.21 shows a resulting progress line. The progress line is drawn using 2/12/01, because this is the date that was displayed in the ToolTip pop-up box when the Gantt Chart was clicked.

DISPLAYING PROGRESS LINES FROM THE TOOLS MENU

Project provides many additional options for displaying progress lines from the Tools menu. From the Tools menu, choose Tracking, Progress Lines. You are then presented with the Progress Lines dialog box (see Figure 17.22).

Figure 17.21
The progress line will display, connecting the current progress within each Gantt Bar in the date range.

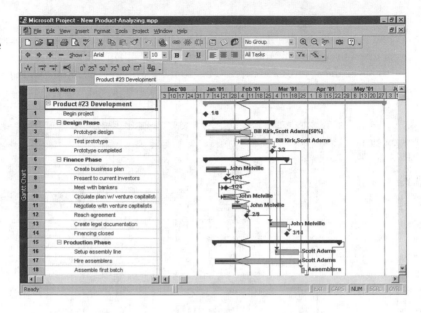

Show progress as of last project status date.

Insert lines from specific dates.

Figure 17.22
The Progress Lines dialog box provides numerous options for controlling formatting and placement of one or more progress lines.

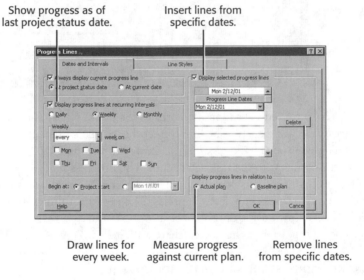

Draw lines for every week.

Measure progress against current plan.

Remove lines from specific dates.

The most common way to show a progress line is at the current status date. As discussed in Chapter 16, "Tracking Work on the Project," the status date is a date you select that signifies the date you consider to be current for your project. The status date will not change unless you change it. (Select Project Information on the Project menu to view or modify your project's current status date.)

To display a progress line at the status date, check the option in the Progress Lines dialog box titled Always Display Current Progress Line, and then check the option At Project Status Date. The progress line displays in red on the Gantt Chart by default. You can choose instead to display the current progress line At Current Date. This option will use the Current Date setting to display the progress line. The Current Date can be changed, but by default is set to the date on your system clock.

Note the option boxes at the bottom right of Figure 17.22. You can Display Progress Lines in Relation To one of two options: Actual Plan or Baseline plan. The default setting, Actual Plan, shows the progress line based on the actual progress of the tasks. If you choose the Baseline Plan option, the progress line connects the baseline Start date for any task with 0% Complete instead of the current scheduled start; some connection points on this progress line might actually be before the Gantt bar.

Note

The progress line does not stretch and connect Gantt lines with future dates. It always shows progress up to, but not past, the project status date.

DISPLAYING PROGRESS LINES AT REGULAR INTERVALS

Figure 17.22 also shows an option called Display Progress Lines at Recurring Intervals. This option enables you to display multiple recurring progress lines on the Gantt Chart. This option can be used for what–if scenarios. For example, if you choose the Monthly option, you'll see what the progress lines will look like with each passing month on your project. You might recognize these recurring option settings if you've ever used a recurring task.

Choosing Daily enables you to select either every day of the week or only the working days. The drop-down list provides many more options than every day (every other, every 3rd, and so on). If you choose Weekly, the options automatically change to specific days of the week to use and again offers a drop-down list with options for every other, every 3rd, and so on. If you choose the Monthly display, the options now change to options for the day of the month on which you want to show the progress line. Table 17.2 shows these intervals and their options.

Note

You can use both the Always Display Current Progress Line and Display Progress Lines at Recurring Intervals options. If you choose both options, the current progress line will display in red, by default.

TABLE 17.2   OPTIONS FOR PROGRESS LINES AT RECURRING INTERVALS

Interval	Options
Daily	Every Day Every Work Day Drop-down allows every day through every 12th day.
Weekly	You can choose any day of the week (Mon through Sun). You are not limited to only one day of the week. You can choose one day, through all seven days of the week. Drop-down list allows every week through every 12th week.
Monthly	You can choose day 1 through 31 of every month. Drop-down list allows every month through every 12th month. or You can choose the first or last day (or workday or nonworking day or any day of the week). Drop-down allows every month through every 12th month.

You might prefer to see progress lines at irregular intervals over the time span of the project. If you select the Display Selected Progress Lines in the Progress Lines dialog box, Dates and Intervals tab, you can type the dates directly into the list of progress line dates. You also can use Date Picker control to graphically select dates from the drop-down list on each line of the selected progress lines grid. Delete progress lines from these custom dates by clicking the date of the line you want to remove and then clicking the Delete button.

Tip from Tim and the Project Team

After you show a progress line, you might want to change the options you originally selected. One easy way to do this is to double-click anywhere on the progress line. Project then automatically displays the Progress Lines dialog box.

CHANGING THE LOOK OF PROGRESS LINES

The Line Styles tab on the Progress Lines dialog box provides numerous options for displaying progress lines. These display options give you a high degree of control over the types, colors, shapes, and date interval of the progress line. Figure 17.23 shows the Progress Lines dialog box with the Line Styles tab selected.

REMOVING PROGRESS LINES

There is no method for deleting progress lines directly on the screen; you must remove them through the Progress Lines dialog box (select Tools, Tracking, Progress Lines). To remove the current progress line and lines being displayed at recurring intervals, simply deselect those options. If the Tracking toolbar button was used to graphically create progress lines, the display dates for those lines will be listed in the Progress Line Dates area. Select a date and choose Delete to remove a single line; remove all lines drawn at a fixed date by deselecting the Display Selected Progress lines option.

Figure 17.23
The Line Styles tab in the Progress Lines dialog box allows you to format the look of progress lines.

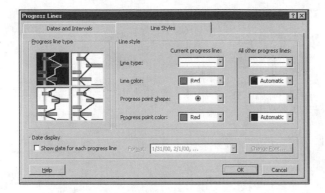

USING GANTT CHART BARS TO ANALYZE PROGRESS

You can analyze your project progress by simply looking at the standard Gantt Chart. View the standard Gantt Chart and look for tasks with a progress bar that is to the left of the current date line. Figure 17.24 shows a project plan with the current date set to 2/10/01. The progress lines for tasks 3 and 11 are left of the current date, indicating that they're behind schedule. Task 4 is ahead of schedule.

Figure 17.24
Horizontal progress lines in Gantt bars show tasks ahead and behind schedule.

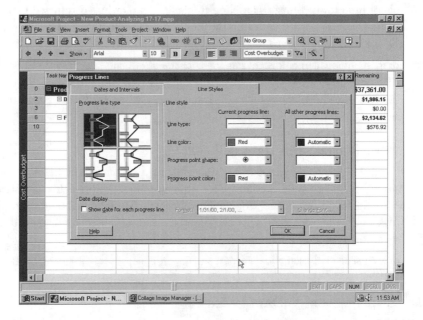

Besides the standard Gantt Chart view, Project also supplies a different view called the Detail Gantt, which can be used to see slack and slippage. Access the Detail Gantt through View, More Views and choose Detail Gantt. Figure 17.25 shows the Detail Gantt chart. Tasks that are slipping have a line to the left of the progress bar and the number of days of slippage is also displayed. For example, task 3 has slipped five days.

Figure 17.25
The Detail Gantt shows the amount of slippage for each task by displaying a thin line to the left of the Gantt bar.

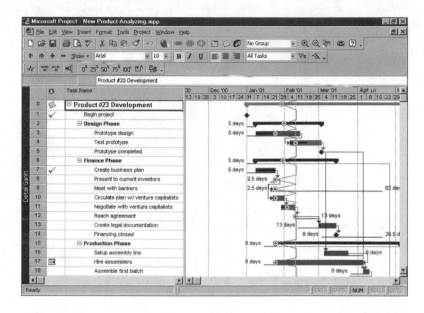

You also can use the Gantt Chart Wizard to build customized Gantt Chart views. One useful configuration compares baseline to plan. To build this customized Gantt Chart, click the Gantt Chart Wizard tool button on the Standard toolbar. When you run the wizard, choose Baseline for step 2.

→ For more information on customizing the appearance of Gantt Charts, **see** "Formatting the Gantt Chart," **p. 905**

Figure 17.26 shows the resulting Gantt Chart. Task 4 has started and is proceeding as planned; task 7 started and finished late.

ANALYZING TIME-SCALED DATA IN EXCEL

For more extensive analysis of raw Project data, you can export fields of interest into Microsoft Excel. Good candidates for exporting include cost fields, variances, and Earned Value fields. Once in Excel, the data can be analyzed, modified, and plotted. If needed, worksheet and graphing results can then be imported, inserted, or pasted back into Microsoft Project.

→ For a detailed discussion of data export and import options, **see** "Saving Project Data as an Excel Worksheet," **p. 791**

ANALYZING TIMESCALED DATA IN EXCEL

Project has a macro that allows you to export the timescaled data from Project for analysis in Microsoft Excel. To initiate this function, display the Analysis toolbar and click the Analyze Timescaled Data in Excel tool button.

Figure 17.26
A Gantt Chart with Baseline task bar makes it easy to graphically analyze your plan.

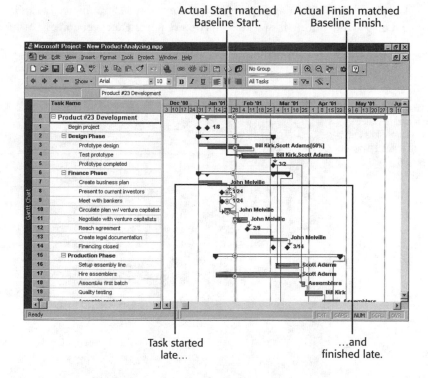

After you click this tool button, Project starts a macro that presents the options to you in a wizard format with steps 1 through 5 as follows:

1. In the first wizard step, pick whether you want to export all tasks in the project or only the currently selected tasks. If no tasks are currently selected, the second choice is deactivated.

2. Next, select the fields to be exported. On the left side of the screen (available fields), all of the fields stored at the resource assignment level are offered for export to Excel. Click the field you want to add and click the Add button. The field selected is then displayed on the right side of the screen (fields to export). If you decide you don't want a field you've already selected, select it on the right side of the screen and click Remove.

3. Set the date range and units you would like to use for the export. The default date range is the project start and finish dates. The default unit is Days.

4. You can choose to automatically graph the timescaled data in Excel. Choose Yes or No.

5. For the final wizard step, click the Export Data button to begin the export process.

Note

You can select Finish at any one of the previous steps and accept the defaults without going through all five steps.

After you select Finish or Export Data, the macro will automatically export the data to Excel and display the information. This function requires Excel version 5.0 or higher.

Figure 17.27 shows the sample graph that is drawn in Excel. In step 2 of the export wizard, Total Work was chosen as the export field, and in step 3 a graph was requested.

Figure 17.27
Graph of timescaled data in Excel plots the amount of total work for each day of the project.

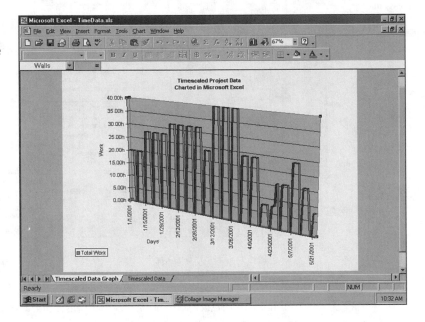

Two Excel sheets are created by the macro: Timescaled Data Graph and Timescaled Data. Click the Timescaled Data worksheet tab to see the data sheet with the numbers that were used to draw the data graph.

Figure 17.28 shows a sample data sheet. If you scroll to the bottom of the data sheet, you'll see totals for each time-period column in the sheet, based on the units you selected in step 3 of the wizard.

Note

For information on manipulating information in Excel, refer to Que's *Special Edition Using Microsoft Excel 2000* or your Microsoft Excel User's Guide.

CAPTURING AND REVIEWING WEEK-TO-WEEK TRENDS

The information that has been covered so far in this chapter deals with analyzing variances as a snapshot in time. These snapshots only tell part of the story. The full story involves watching what your project variances are doing over time. A project that has a total work variance of 100 hours this week might appear to be in trouble, but what if the total work variance was 500 hours last week? Despite the current 100-hour work variance, it looks like the situation has improved significantly over last week.

Figure 17.28
Sample data sheet created by the Analyze Timescaled Data in Excel Wizard.

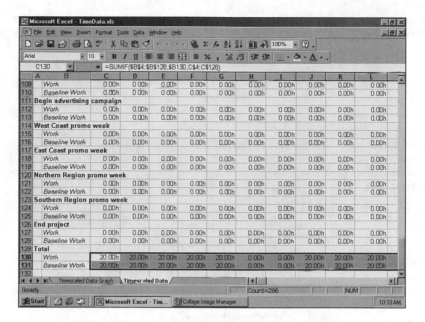

If you want to watch variance trends over time, you can keep track of these changes in Excel. By filling in a simple spreadsheet in Excel with the week-ending dates of your analyses (Finish), the total baseline work (Baseline Work), total work (Work), and work variances (Work Variance), you can calculate the percent variances and graph them using the Chart Wizard in Excel. For more information on using graphs to plot Project data in Excel, refer to Que's *Special Edition Using Microsoft Excel 2000* or your Microsoft Excel User's Guide.

UPDATING THE SCHEDULE

As your project progresses, you'll find that it becomes necessary to update your project's schedule. These next two sections review the different techniques you'll employ to keep your schedule in sync with what's really happening on your project. This part of the chapter covers techniques for updating your schedule, whereas the final section covers techniques for modifying the results of your updated schedule to ensure that you deliver within your original project objectives, schedule, and budget.

RESCHEDULING REMAINING WORK

Whenever you key in actual and remaining work, Project assumes that the remaining work will continue as originally scheduled. Unfortunately, tasks get interrupted and it is sometimes necessary to reschedule the remaining work for a task to a date that is later than originally planned. Project provides an easy way to reschedule remaining work.

Note

Before you try to reschedule remaining work for a task, be sure your project options are set to allow this activity.

Choose Tools, Options. The Schedule tab in the Options dialog box has an option called Split In-Progress Tasks. This option must be checked to be able to use the reschedule remaining work functions. Figure 17.29 shows the Split In-Progress Tasks option.

Figure 17.29
Use the Options dialog box for splitting in-progress tasks.

You can reschedule remaining work in one of two ways: from the Tracking toolbar or from the Tools menu.

- **Rescheduling remaining work from the Tracking toolbar**—The Reschedule Work button on the Tracking toolbar automatically reschedules all remaining work for the selected tasks to start on the status date as set in Project, Project Information.

- **Rescheduling remaining work from the Update Project dialog box**—If you don't want remaining work to be rescheduled to the status date, you can use the Update Project command on the Tools, Tracking menu. Figure 17.30 shows the Update Project dialog box. You can set the date when you want the remaining, rescheduled work to start.

Figure 17.30
The Update Project dialog box offers more options for rescheduling uncompleted work on one or more tasks.

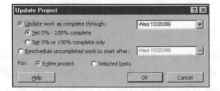

For tasks that are partially complete, Project automatically splits the task between the completed work and the remaining work. Figure 17.31 shows that task 4, Test Prototype, was split to show interruption of work.

Split task

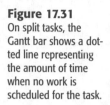

Figure 17.31
On split tasks, the Gantt bar shows a dotted line representing the amount of time when no work is scheduled for the task.

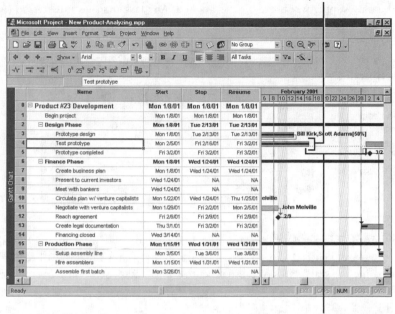

No work scheduled or performed in this period

Caution

Rescheduling the remaining work might change task constraints. For example, on a task with a Must Finish On constraint, rescheduling the remaining work task causes the task finish date to go beyond the constraint date. Project displays a Planning Wizard warning message describing the conflict created by rescheduling work.

When you reschedule remaining work for a task, Project sets the Stop date to the date when the last actual work was applied and the Resume date is set to the date you specified in the Update Project dialog box. Figure 17.31 shows the Stop and Resume fields for task 4 from the previous example. The last actual work concluded on 2/16/01 and the task's remaining work is scheduled to resume on 3/2/01.

Rescheduling remaining work is conceptually the same as setting a second Start date for a task. The Resume date is the date when the remaining work will start. A task with rescheduled remaining work looks the same as a split task on the Gantt Chart.

RESCHEDULING TASKS THAT HAVEN'T STARTED

Besides rescheduling the remaining work for a task, you might sometimes be forced to reschedule an entire task. Any task that was scheduled to start before a specified date that has not yet started should be rescheduled. To identify these tasks, try applying the Should Start By filter. Figure 17.32 shows the selection criteria for this filter. This filter allows you to specify a date by which tasks should have started. The tasks in your plan are compared to the date supply when the filter is applied. Any task that has not started (Actual Start = NA) by the date you supply is displayed by this filter.

Figure 17.32
The Should Start By filter helps to quickly find tasks that need to be rescheduled because they did not start as originally planned.

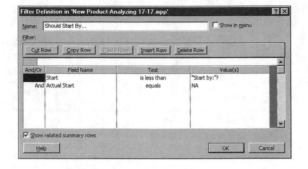

This filter basically shows you unstarted tasks that were scheduled to start on a date that has already passed. This is a sign of a plan that is not reflective of reality. You should change the start dates of these tasks to a new date when you think they can be performed.

REVISING THE SCHEDULE TO COMPLETE ON TIME AND ON BUDGET

After you have determined that your plan is encountering unfavorable variances, you have to do something about it. If the project is in trouble, it's important to remember one thing: Use the plan to manage the project. Don't deviate from the plan; change it! Depending on the type of problem you are having, there are different strategies you'll need to employ to get your plan back on track. The bottom line is that something needs to change if you still plan to deliver on time and on budget with high quality and all expectations met.

Project provides many tools to help you revise your schedule, but first you have to know what will work for you, on this project, in your particular situation. Remember that, when it comes to revising a project plan, there are limited options: scope, schedule, and resources (people, machines, and money). Some project managers fail to recognize the need to adjust one of these factors and end up cutting something that should not be touched—quality.

Best Practice Tips from Toby Brown, PMP

Making trade-offs to maintain a schedule is known as the "good, fast, or cheap" argument. "Balancing competing demands" requires careful assessment of which element the customer is willing to compromise on. In other words, pick two of three.

Good encompasses both scope and quality, which means that what is good to one in terms of features and benefits might not be good to someone else. *Fast* means time in regards to schedule. Perhaps more work can be done in less time. Usually, it requires an increase in the third consideration, which is cost (*cheap*). Money might not be a first factor, but it always remains in the formula.

The answer is often a compromise on all three to arrive at an acceptable project plan.

Before you even begin to modify the plan in Project, chances are that there are users, customers, sponsors, and management that you'll need to talk to before you can reflect your strategy in Project. Whatever you decide, you are likely to be forced to make trade-offs. If you use a cheaper resource to stay within budget, the work estimates might increase due to lack of experience of the less expensive resource. If you reduce scope, you are probably sacrificing some of your objectives to stay within schedule and budget. If you overlap tasks to meet deadlines, you increase the risk of failing to meet other objectives. The harsh reality is that, if there were serious oversights when the plan was developed, the chances of completing your plan according to all of its original expectations will take quite a bit of creativity on your part.

The following sections describe what these options mean in Project.

REDUCING SCOPE

When you cut scope, you're reducing function, taking something out of your project objectives, or delivering less than originally committed. You might also be compromising on the quality of the project goal. Reducing function in Project can be deployed in limited ways:

- Deleting tasks
- Reducing work

Negotiating a reduction in scope or a redefinition of project quality can be among the more difficult tasks you'll face as a project manager. After you define your initial project objectives, removing functions from your deliverables is often technically complicated, requiring advice from many different members of the team. It's hard to decide what you can take out and still have everything function smoothly. Add to this dilemma a group of sponsors who have had high expectations, and you'll find yourself in a pretty tough situation. Assuming you're able to overcome these hurdles, here are some ways to reduce the scope of your project.

Project provides an easy way to delete tasks: Highlight the tasks you want to delete and press the Delete key or choose Edit, Delete Task.

Caution

Recall that pressing the Delete key on the keyboard completely and permanently removes the selected task (or tasks) from the project.

Here are two suggestions for displaying views to modify work by task. Display the Task Entry view (View, More Views, Task Entry), and apply the Work table to the top Gantt Chart (View, Table, Work) and the Resource Work format to the bottom Task Form (Format, Details, Resource Work). Another good approach is to display the Task Usage view (View, Task Usage). Read more about setting up specialized views in Chapter 22, "Formatting Views."

Reducing Cost

Your project might be on target for the completion date, and meeting scope and quality requirements, but running over budget to achieve those goals. Typically, if you "throw money" at a project, anything is possible. But if staying within the project budget is the most important consideration, you will need to find ways to conserve expenditures. Possible options include the following:

- Substitute less expensive workers for more expensive ones. The less expensive resource also might be less experienced, however, causing a reworking of hours required on the tasks. A bonus here is that the more expensive resource might now be available to work on another task and actually reduce its duration.

- Reduce allowable overtime for resources billed against the project at an increased overtime rate.

- Schedule resources with a per-use fee to work on their assigned tasks simultaneously. For example, if a delivery fee is associated with a resource, schedule all deliveries together to avoid being charged multiple delivery fees.

- Negotiate with suppliers, if possible, to reduce fixed costs and materials costs.

- Reducing project scope might be the only option for reducing overall cost of the project.

Reducing Scheduled Duration

If your targeted project finish date is in jeopardy, reducing the project scheduled duration means you first have to find out which tasks are extending the schedule, and then figure out some way to make those tasks finish sooner. In Project, you can reduce the schedule by

- Adding more resources to your project, so that some tasks can be completed sooner.

- Breaking links between tasks and allowing them to occur simultaneously, usually a risky proposition.

- Overlapping dependent tasks by introducing lead (the opposite of lag).

- Reducing duration by increasing a resource's percent commitment to tasks or allowing overtime.

- Replacing inexperienced resources with more experienced resources. You might be able to reduce work estimates, thereby completing tasks in less time.

- Using resources more efficiently; underallocated resources are a problem, too.

Schedule reductions can be accomplished in a variety of ways, but the decision to do so needs to be made with great caution. Many elements of risk are introduced to your project plan when you agree to reduce work, overlap tasks, add resources, and maintain scope. Reducing the schedule might lower your confidence in completing on time while increasing your risk of delivering quality. Despite these concerns, we are sometimes forced to revise the plan and bring it in early. Here are some ways to reduce the schedule:

- Overlap dependent tasks. If two tasks are linked, Project sets the default relationship to Finish-to-Start and the Lag to 0d. You can overlap tasks by setting the lag to a negative number. A negative lag is usually referred to as *lead*. If you introduce lead for tasks on the critical path, the project finish date will be recalculated to an earlier date.

- Increase a resource's percent commitment to a task. For tasks with fixed work, increasing the resource units on a task will reduce the task's duration. To display a unit as a percent, refer to the Schedule tab on the Options dialog box. Project shows resource units as a percentage, by default.

- If a resource is already 100% committed to a task, consider using the Overtime Work field to reduce duration. The overtime field can be viewed for each resource assigned to a task on the Task Form with details Resource Work displayed.

- Look for underallocated resources. The Resource Usage view is often used to look for resource overallocations. This view also can be used to look for underallocated resources by setting the display to Remaining Availability (View, Resource Usage; Format, Details, Remaining Availability). Keep your resources assigned up to their maximum availability to ensure that your schedule is as efficient as possible.

PART
V
CH
17

Tip from Tim and the Project Team

> When you reduce schedule, Project will not automatically remove unneeded occurrences of a recurring task. Don't forget to get rid of unneeded tasks, such as weekly status meetings, by modifying the number of occurrences on your recurring tasks (on the Task Information dialog box) or by deleting individual occurrences.

- Add more experienced resources to your tasks. If you decide to replace a resource with a different, more experienced resource, you can use the Resource Assignment dialog box. In this case, the trade-off is usually higher cost versus lower work estimates. For a detailed discussion of changing resource assignments, see Chapter 10, "Assigning Resources and Costs to Tasks."

Tip from Tim and the Project Team

> After you have revised your plan, it might be appropriate to re-baseline, if setting your variances back to zero is what you want.

Adding resources is sometimes an effective way to recover a schedule that is falling behind, but usually comes at a price—the budget. Adding resources is easy in Project (View Resource Sheet, Insert Resource). Finding the right resource at the right time for the right price can be pretty challenging.

If you do add resources, there are some things you might need to do:

- Reassign work to the new resource.
- Modify task duration to reflect redistribution of work on the task (effort-driven scheduling).

- Split complex tasks into smaller, more manageable tasks with less work and less complex resource assignments on each.

- Modify work estimates so that they are realistic for the new resource.

- Re-baseline, if setting your variances back to zero is what you desire.

When you're done revising your schedule, chances are that your resources might have become overloaded. Load leveling is the final step to ensuring that a revised schedule remains realistic.

Many of these strategies are easy to implement in Project. The hard part is likely to be convincing your project team and sponsors that your strategies for adjusting the plan are viable and acceptable to all involved.

Tip from Tim and the Project Team

> Before you adjust your project plan, it's a good idea to take frequent backups of your Project's .MPP file. You might decide that the changes you are making to your schedule are not working out. Rebuilding the plan without a good backup can be pretty painful if you're not careful.

TROUBLESHOOTING

OVERWRITTEN DATA

Every time I make changes to Percent Complete or Actual or Remaining Duration, Project overwrites the data I already had in Actual Work and Remaining Work. Am I doing something wrong?

Project has an important setting that controls the relationship between task completion and actual work. To change this setting, choose Options from the Tools menu, click the Calculation tab, and locate the option box for Updating Task Status Updates Resource Status.

With this option turned on, as it is by default, Project automatically updates Percent Work Complete, Actual and Remaining Work, and Actual and Remaining Duration when Percent Complete changes. If this option is turned off, Project will not change your Actual Work and Remaining Work with changes to %Complete.

THE SLIPPING TASKS FILTER

I'd like to be able to have Project show me what tasks are sliding away from their schedules. Is there a way to do this?

Project has a filter known as the Slipping Tasks filter. This filter shows you tasks that are not yet finished, that have a baseline finish date, and have a current estimated finish date later than the baseline finish date. To view the contents of the Slipping Tasks filter, choose Project, Filtered For, More Filters and select the Slipping Tasks filter from the list. Edit the filter or make a copy to view.

COORDINATING PROJECTS AND SHARING DATA

CHAPTER **18**

WORKING WITH MULTIPLE PROJECTS

In this chapter

USING THE WINDOW COMMANDS

There are several instances where working with one project file does not allow you to accomplish your objectives. Working in a Windows environment typically offers the capability to work with more than one file at a time, and this is certainly true with Microsoft Project.

With this in mind, consider the following situations where it would be beneficial to work with more than one file at a time:

- A task in one project might depend on a task in another project. For example, the start date for one task might need to be linked to the start or finish date for a task in another project.

- Several projects, managed by different people, might be placed under the supervision of a manager who provides coordination of dates and resources between the various projects.

- A project might be so large that it is easier to organize and manage by breaking it into several smaller, more manageable units. These separate files can then be linked back together to be able to see the whole project. This benefit is similar to that gained by outlining a project, but on a larger scale.

- Several projects might use the same group of resources and need to be coordinated so that the right resources are available to each project at the right time.

- A project might be too large to fit into the computer's memory at one time. Breaking it into smaller projects can overcome the memory limitations.

In this version of Microsoft Project, you can have 50 files in separate windows open at the same time. If you are using inserted projects, you can have up to 1,000 in any one file. When there are multiple files open at the same time, the Window menu is used to control and move between the various open windows. You can also use the Ctrl+F6 shortcut key combination to move between active project windows. As shown in Figure 18.1, a list of open project files appears at the bottom of the Window menu. A check mark appears in front of the name of the active window. When more than nine files are open at the same time, there will be an additional More Windows option at the bottom of the Window menu. When chosen, More Windows displays all project files that are open. Choose the project file that you want to make active. Other files are not closed; they are simply moved to the background.

Note	This list of files is different from the one displayed at the bottom of the File menu, which is simply a list of the last four files that were opened, but which are not necessarily open now.

Figure 18.1
The Window menu includes a list at the bottom that you can use to locate other open project files.

The Window, Split command, discussed previously, is used when dividing the screen for a combination view. Combination views can be very helpful during many different stages of a project's life.

→ For more information on the views supplied with Project, **see** "Using the Standard Views, Tables, and Filters," **p. 851**

→ To learn about creating custom views, **see** "Customizing Views, Tables, Fields, and Filters," **p. 943**

VIEWING ALL THE FILE WINDOWS AT THE SAME TIME

The Window, Arrange All command is useful when you want to view more than one project file in its own distinct window at the same time. Open the projects that you want to see onscreen at the same time and then choose this command. Depending on how many project files are open, each window will be sized and moved (tiled) so that each file can be seen onscreen simultaneously. As you can see in Figure 18.2, the name of each file will be displayed in its title bar, with the active window having the brighter color title bar as well as the active pane indicator (the colored narrow bar at the left side of the active pane). The title bar of the inactive files will be gray (assuming the default Windows colors). This is obviously only practical when a small number of project files are open at one time or when some of the project files are hidden (see the next section).

PART

VI

CH

18

Figure 18.2
Several windows displayed at the same time can be very convenient when coordinating several project files.

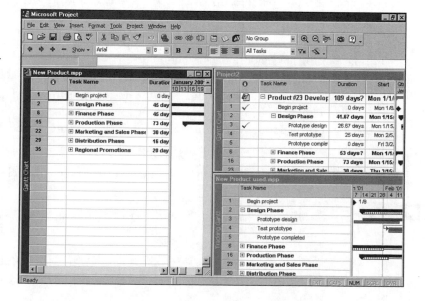

Tip from Tim and the Project Team	Whichever window is active when you choose the Window, Arrange All command will appear at the top left-corner of the screen and will remain active.

Tip from Tim and the Project Team	When a project file is not maximized, there is a handy shortcut menu that appears when you right-click the title bar of the file. Useful commands on this shortcut menu include Save, Print, Spelling, Project Information, and most of the Window commands.

When you maximize any one window, all other windows will become maximized as well. You won't be able to see them because the active file is covering the full screen, but when you move to any other file, it will already be maximized.

HIDING AND UNHIDING OPEN WINDOWS

If there are any project files that are open that you don't want included in the Arrange All display, instead of closing them, you need only temporarily hide them using the Hide command. To redisplay the hidden window, choose the Window menu again. If any files have been hidden, an Unhide command is now on the menu. If you choose the Unhide command, the Unhide dialog box opens and displays a list of files that have been hidden. Choose the file you want to unhide and choose OK. If you exit Project with windows hidden, you will be prompted to save them if necessary.

USING THE SAVE WORKSPACE COMMAND

If you have been working on a several files at the same time, and you want to be able to resume your work by opening the same files together, you can save the workspace in addition to saving the individual files. To save the workspace, follow these steps:

1. Choose File, Save Workspace.
2. If any files have unsaved changes, you are prompted to save the individual files. In the File Save dialog box, choose the Yes button.
3. The Save Workspace As dialog box displays. Select the directory for the workspace if you want to store it somewhere other than the default directory. The name of the workspace file will initially be resume.mpw (so that you can resume later with the same files), but you can change it by typing a new name in the File Name text box.
4. Click the Save button to complete the operation.

To open all the files, choose File, Open. Select the workspace file and click OK.

Note	Workspace files are automatically saved with the extension .MPW.

DISPLAYING TASKS FROM DIFFERENT FILES IN THE SAME WINDOW

The Window, New Window command deserves special attention. Combined with the Insert, Project command, you can merge multiple project files into one window to edit, view, print, or even link their tasks in one view. Each task retains its native ID number, so you will see more than one task with ID number 1. You can modify the display to add a column that identifies the file that each task came from. You can sort the task list as if it were one file; you can filter the merged list in the same way you use filters in one file. You can apply any table or view to see the merged view, including the Network Diagram. You can print views or reports from the merged window as though it were a single project file. You can even insert and delete tasks.

There are two basic approaches to combining projects together into one window. One is with the Window, New Window command. This approach assumes that all the files to be combined are already open. The second is with the Insert, Project command and allows access to files that are not currently open.

USING THE NEW WINDOW COMMAND

To combine the tasks from multiple projects that are currently open into the same view, follow these steps:

1. Choose Window, New Window to display the New Window dialog box (see Figure 18.3).

Figure 18.3
In the New Window dialog box, choose the projects that you want to combine into one window.

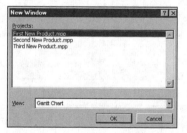

2. From the Projects list, select all the filenames you want to include in the new window. Use the Ctrl key to add non-adjacent filenames to the selection.

3. Choose the View list box located at the bottom of the dialog box and change the view if you want. You can change the view later, after the new window is displayed.

4. Click OK to display the new window.

The merged window has the title Project#, where # is a consecutively assigned number for each time that you create a new project file. When you open the Window menu, you see that the Project# choice is now a separate entry on the open projects list, whereas the individual project files have been left open. You can save the merged window for further use with the regular File, Save command.

As you can see in Figure 18.4, when any of the task sheet views are active (including any of the Gantt Charts), the Indicators column will display an icon for an inserted project. Point at the icon to display a message with the name of the source file. An inserted project is simply a copy of all the tasks from another file inserted into this new window.

At the beginning of each file's tasks there will be a Project Summary task added. The task ID for this Project Summary task indicates the order in which the selected files were merged. You can use the Outline symbol in front of the Project Summary task name to hide the details of the task, just like working with the tasks in an outline. On the timescale side of the Gantt Chart, there will be a gray bar that appears much like a summary task bar.

Figure 18.4
There are several ways to get information about an inserted project.

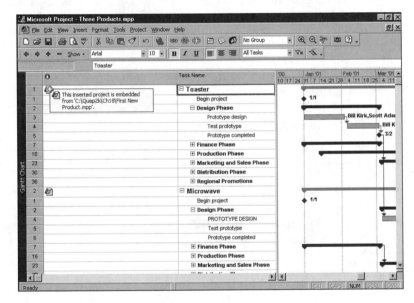

Tip from Tim and the Project Team

The new <u>S</u>how drop-down list on the Formatting toolbar lets you easily choose the level of outline detail to be displayed.

Tip from Tim and the Project Team

You also might use the <u>W</u>indow, <u>N</u>ew Window command when you want to see two window views of the same project. This, in essence, allows you to see more than the standard combination view. Using this method, you could see two separate combination views, two full-screen views at the same time, or one combination view and one full screen, all of the same project. To do this, choose <u>W</u>indow, <u>N</u>ew Window, but select only one project file. The title bar of the new window has the project name followed by a colon and a number, indicating the second instance of this project file. You can use either the <u>W</u>indow menu or Ctrl+F6 to move between them. Any changes that you make and save to one instance of the project file will be saved in the other window as well. There is only one file open here: It's simply displayed in two separate windows, much like the combination views you have already seen.

FILTERING AND SORTING THE COMBINED TASKS

Initially, all the tasks are grouped by the file from which they came. For the most part, you can sort or filter the list in the normal way. When sorting, you must choose Project, Sort, Sort By to gain access to the check box that keeps the outline structure. You will most likely want to be able to sort by start date, for example, and allow the tasks to move out of their original project order. The predefined sort options on the Sort menu are set to retain the outline structure. When you allow the sort not to retain the outline structure, the outlining tools in the Formatting toolbar are not available.

The task list in Figure 18.5 includes two inserted projects whose tasks have been sorted in start date order. A column for the Project field has been added to the table to display the name of the source project for each task. The summary tasks and the Project Summary tasks have been temporarily hidden, and the outline indenting option has been turned off. These outline display options are available on the View tab of the Options dialog box.

Figure 18.5
Sorting a file with inserted projects can make it easier to see when tasks from several projects are scheduled.

Combined projects sorted by start date...

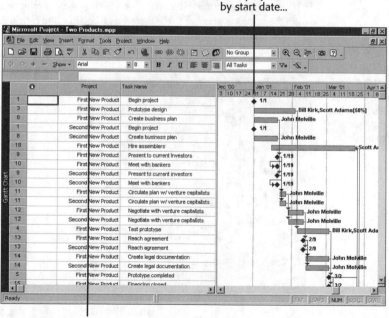

...then by project name

Note the duplication of task names in Figure 18.5. Most managers find that some common tasks occur in almost all projects of a similar type. If you are following good project management practices and creating project files from existing files or templates, there will undoubtedly be some repetition of task names in a combined master file. The inclusion of the Project column is one way to identify the source of each task.

Tip from Tim and the Project Team

If you have created and entered a task identification scheme of your own—for example, a work breakdown structure—display that information in the combined file instead of or in addition to the Project file source name.

→ For more information on creating and using custom fields, **see** "Customizing Fields," **p. 956**

→ To learn about working with customized tables, **see** "Using and Creating Tables," **p. 949**

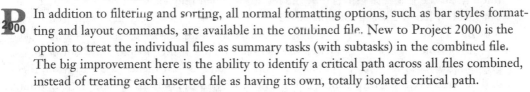 In addition to filtering and sorting, all normal formatting options, such as bar styles formatting and layout commands, are available in the combined file. New to Project 2000 is the option to treat the individual files as summary tasks (with subtasks) in the combined file. The big improvement here is the ability to identify a critical path across all files combined, instead of treating each inserted file as having its own, totally isolated critical path.

To see a critical path across all projects and tasks in a combined file, you turn on an option under <u>T</u>ools, <u>O</u>ptions. On the Calculation tab of the Options dialog box, turn on the <u>I</u>nserted Projects Are Calculated Like Summary Tasks feature (shown in Figure 18.6). The files do not have to be linked in any way to use this feature.

Tip from Tim and the Project Team

Cross-project task dependencies are important if the project manager is truly interested in managing to the critical path. Otherwise, the critical path simply will be displayed at the point where two projects just happen to converge. For a project manager to truly appreciate the impact of changes to the project and, possibly, the critical path, task dependencies must be established.

Figure 18.6
Display a critical path across combined files by treating inserted files as summary tasks.

CREATING SUBPROJECTS AND MASTER PROJECTS

Certainly there are advantages to managing a large or complex project in smaller, separate files. Computing speed, file sharing among co-workers, and faster printing and transmitting of smaller files are a few of the advantages. When the time comes to review, analyze, and report on the plan across all individual files, you create a master project/subproject structure to combine the files of interest in one window. This combined file can be saved and used again later; it does not have to be recreated for each use.

The first method for combining files into a master/subproject structure—using the <u>N</u>ew Window command—was discussed previously. The following sections describe a second method for combining files—inserting files stored on disk into a new master project plan. Key master file issues, such as maintaining the combined file, removing a subproject, and linking between combined files, also are discussed in the following sections.

COMBINING PROJECTS INTO ONE FILE

If a project that you want to combine with another is not already open, you will need to use the <u>I</u>nsert, <u>P</u>roject command. To insert an entire project into another, follow these steps:

1. Select the task below where you want the new inserted project to be placed.

2. Choose <u>I</u>nsert, <u>P</u>roject to access the Insert Project dialog box (see Figure 18.7).

Figure 18.7
Use the Insert Project dialog box to identify the file to be inserted into another.

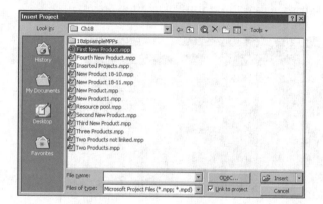

PART

VI

CH

18

3. Locate and select the file to be inserted.

Tip from Tim and the Project Team

If inserting multiple files, click to select them in the order you want them displayed in the master file.

4. Use the Insert drop-down list to select the <u>R</u>ead Only check box to open this copy as one that is read-only. You will not be able to make changes to the source copy—more specifically, you won't be able to save changes back to the source copy.

5. Create a link to the inserted project by choosing the <u>L</u>ink to Project option. Changes to inserted and master files also are made to the other file. (You still have the option of not saving changes and closing the files.)

6. Select OK when you are finished. The tasks of the inserted project will now be available in the original file as if they had been entered there.

Note

The ODBC button in the Insert Project dialog box allows you to insert a file that is stored in a database. This topic is covered in detail in Chapter 19, "Exporting and Importing Project Data with Other File Formats."

WORKING WITH INSERTED PROJECTS

You can see information about the inserted project by choosing the Advanced tab in the Task Information dialog box. Access the dialog box using the Task Information button in the Standard toolbar, double-click the task, or right-click any portion of the inserted project task and choose Task Information from the shortcut menu. Then choose the Advanced tab. When you access the Task Information dialog box for a task that represents an inserted project, the title of the dialog box changes to Inserted Project Information. Notice in Figure 18.8 that the title bar indicates that this is an inserted project.

Figure 18.8
The Task Information dialog box for an inserted project displays information about the link back to the source file and offers access to project information for that file.

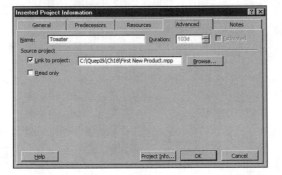

You can choose whether to maintain a link with the individual source files. The Link to Project check box determines whether or not changes made in this file should be linked back to the original file. If checked, any content-related changes that you make to the new file also will be made in the original source file. By default, there is a link between the inserted project and the original file that it came from. Regardless of your choice, any changes made to the formatting in the new window will not be reflected in the source files. The obvious advantage here is that you can make formatting changes in the new window for the purpose of printing reports for different audiences without having those changes reflected in the original working file.

By default, files are opened as read-write, but you can change that to read-only. Select the Read Only check box if there is a link maintained and you prefer to protect the original source files. If the inserted file is set to read-only, the icon in the Indicators column of the Gantt Chart will show an exclamation mark, and the message will indicate that it is read-only.

Use the Browse button to change the link to another file or to restore the link when the file has been moved or renamed. See upcoming sections on moving, deleting, and renaming inserted projects for detailed information.

You can access the Project Information dialog box for the source file by using the Project Info button in the Inserted Project Information dialog box.

Note

> The reference to the location of the original source file is stored in the Subproject field for the inserted project task. If the Read Only check box is active, a Yes is stored in the Subproject Read Only field. You will only see these fields if you add them on your own to a table.

Project 2000 now stores the relative path to linked or inserted projects. In previous versions, the absolute path to these files was stored, causing users to save files to inconvenient locations simply to maintain links.

Note

> It's important to note that, when you combine project files by choosing Window, New Window or Insert, Project, these project files are only displayed together in one window, but so far are not linked to each other.

You can create inserted projects at any level of an outline, as well as inserting a project into a project that is itself inserted into another. Microsoft Project checks to be sure that no circular references exist within the levels.

BREAKING A LARGE PROJECT APART USING INSERTED PROJECTS

You can create inserted projects by moving tasks from a large project into new project files, and then defining the new files as inserted projects. Some preparation is involved in making the move as easy and successful as possible.

If you move one or more tasks that are linked to tasks that will remain behind, you will lose the links and have to redefine them later. It is easier to copy the tasks that are going to become a new project file rather than cut them, save the copied tasks as a new file, insert the new project file, change the links, and then delete the original copied tasks.

To move tasks to a new project file, follow these steps:

1. Select the task IDs of the tasks that you plan to move. This ensures that all fields will be selected and that all relevant data will be copied. If the tasks to be moved include a Summary and all the subtasks indented underneath it, you need only select the summary task.

2. Choose Edit, Copy Task (or press Ctrl+C) to copy the task data to the Clipboard.

3. Choose File, New to create a new project file. If the Prompt for Project Info for New Projects check box is checked on the General tab of the Options dialog box, the Project Information dialog box will open.

→ For more information on creating a new project file, **see** "Supplying Information for a New Project," **p. 64**

PART

VI

CH

18

4. With the Name field of the first task selected in the new file, choose <u>E</u>dit, <u>P</u>aste (or press Ctrl+V). The task data is copied.

5. Choose <u>F</u>ile, <u>S</u>ave to save the new file. Fill in the dialog box to save the file and click OK.

6. Return to the original file by choosing the filename from the list at the bottom of the <u>W</u>indow menu. Alternatively, press Ctrl+F6 until the project document reappears.

7. Select the task in the row below where the inserted task will be placed and create the inserted project as described in the section "Working with Inserted Projects," earlier in this chapter.

Best Practice Tips from Toby Brown, PMP

Maintaining a library of subprojects allows the project manager to incorporate the best practices of an organization and incorporate standard methodologies into all of their projects. These linked methodologies can be previously completed projects and can also include the best lessons learned of how it was done before.

MAINTAINING INSERTED PROJECTS

You can replace the inserted project by changing the name in the Source Project area on the Advanced tab of the Task Information dialog box. You can use the <u>B</u>rowse button to locate the file instead of typing it in. If the filename is simply deleted, the link between the two projects is severed, and the inserted project task becomes a single task with the default 1-day duration. If the new filename exists, it will be used as the source project file instead of the one just replaced. If you type the name of the file to be inserted and Microsoft Project can't find the file, a warning message appears, as shown in the title bar of Figure 18.9.

Figure 18.9
You need to re-identify an inserted project when the original is moved, deleted, renamed, or simply can't be found.

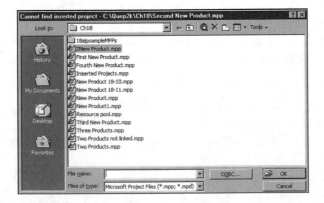

Be careful about moving or renaming projects that are used as inserted projects. When you open a project that contains an inserted project, if Microsoft Project can't find the file, it again displays the message shown in the title bar in Figure 18.9. To maintain the link, you would need to locate the file before proceeding.

Caution

You will not be made aware of problems with linking to lost inserted project files until the outline for the file is expanded in the combined file. The combined file always opens collapsed down to a single summary line for each inserted project, even if the outline was expanded when the combined file was last saved and closed.

Tip from Tim and the Project Team

If the project manager will be maintaining multiple subprojects rolled up into a master project, time should be invested on how best to organize and catalog the repository of files. Not unlike your desk filing cabinet or computer hard drive, creating the appropriate filing system will save a lot of time in not only organizing your files, but maintaining the linkages built into a master project.

IDENTIFYING TASKS THAT ARE INSERTED PROJECTS

In addition to the indicator for inserted projects in the Indicators column, you can use the Subproject File field, where the name of the inserted project is stored. You can design a table to display that field and thereby identify the tasks.

Tip from Tim and the Project Team

All Subproject File field entries must contain a filename and extension that are separated by a period. Figure 18.10 shows a filter definition for displaying inserted projects by filtering the Subproject File field for entries that contain a period. Use the "contains" test and enter a period as the Value to look for.

PART

VI

CH

18

Figure 18.10
Filter for inserted projects by searching the Subproject field for a "." (period).

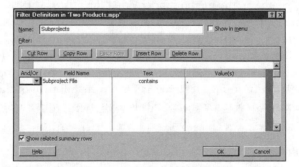

→ For more information on filter definitions, **see** "Creating Custom Filters," **p. 968**

DELETING INSERTED PROJECTS

You delete an inserted project in much the same way as you delete a summary task. Simply select it and then press the Delete key on the keyboard, or right-click the task ID and choose <u>D</u>elete Task from the shortcut menu. You will be warned about deleting more than one task with the warning message shown in Figure 18.11. When the Office Assistant is being used, the warnings will appear in the Office Assistant's question box rather than the standard Windows dialog box.

Figure 18.11
Deleting an inserted project deletes all the tasks that were part of that project.

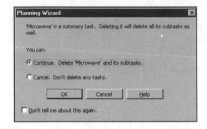

CREATING LINKS BETWEEN TASKS IN SEPARATE PROJECTS

There are two basic types of links that you can create between projects. One is when all the tasks of one project taken together are the predecessor or successor to a group of tasks in another project. For example, in the New Product project file, the design phase is probably handled by a completely separate department also using Microsoft Project. Many other tasks in the New Product project can't proceed until the design phase is complete. You could insert the entire project for the design phase and link it as you would link any other task.

A second kind of link occurs when a specific task in another project, not the project start or finish, needs to be linked to a specific task in the current project file. For example, in the design phase, there is a task called *Prototype Complete*. Although the design phase as a whole might not be complete, some sales and marketing tasks could begin after the prototype is complete.

 Whichever situation you have, the method for creating the links is the same: Simply select both tasks and use the <u>E</u>dit, <u>L</u>ink Tasks command or the Link Tasks tool on the Standard toolbar. If you have inserted a whole project into another project, you can easily expand the inserted project task list and select the tasks to be linked. You should use the <u>W</u>indow, <u>N</u>ew Window command described earlier to display tasks from both projects together and then select the tasks to be linked. Alternatively, you can enter the full path of the project file and task ID in the Predecesors or Successors task fields using this format:

```
drive:\directory\sudirectory\filename.ext\taskIDnumber
```

For example, if the predecessor is task 6 in the project file `ProductX.MPP`, which is stored in the directory `C:\Manufacturing\Development`, you would enter the following into the Predecessors field:

`C:\Manufacturing\Development\ProductX.MPP\6`

Note

On networked computers, in Windows 95, 98, NT, or 2000, it's not necessary to use a drive name; a network share can be used instead. The format would be

```
\\sharename\directory\subdirectory\filename.ext\taskIDnumber
```

Files can even be stored on FTP sites and then inserted through the Insert Project dialog box by pulling up the predefined FTP site under the drop-down list box for the Look <u>I</u>n field.

These cross links between files can use any of the standard task relationships (FS, SS, FF, and SF), as well as support lag and lead time.

→ To learn more about creating links between tasks, **see** "Entering Scheduling Requirements," **p. 207**

When the link is established, the name of the task being linked to appears in the task list in gray text. The duration, start, and finish also display in gray. No other information will be immediately available. If the task that is linked to has a duration, the task bar appears in gray as well. If the task being linked to is a milestone, the milestone marker will be gray. If you double-click the linked task, it opens the project plan that contains the linked task. In the source project for the linked task, the task that was linked to from the destination project plan also appears in gray, and you can double-click it to return to the original project plan. If you access the Task Information dialog box for either of the two grayed tasks, you will be able to view information about the task but you will only be able to change Note entries.

Caution	Project will allow you to enter a note about a grayed task but it will not be linked back to the original task.

Tip from Tim and the Project Team	When you create a link to a task in another Project file, the External Task field is set to Yes. This means that you can create a filter for all tasks that have an external link. This filter, combined with a table including the predecessors and successors columns, would provide a view of all external links and their source.

PART
VI
CH
18

For example, using separate files for two new products in development, suppose that design work for the second product prototype can begin when the prototype for the first product is finished. When the two tasks from separate files have been linked together, Project will include placeholder tasks in both files. The external successor task in the First New Product file would appear as illustrated in Figure 18.12.

Notice the gray text of the task Prototype Design (in all capitals). This task is only part of the First New Product plan to the extent that it is a successor to Prototype Completed. If you double-click the gray Prototype Design task, the Second New Product project file is opened, as shown in Figure 18.13. Notice the gray text of the first Prototype Completed task. This task is only part of the Second New Product plan to the extent that it is predecessor to beginning the Prototype Design. If you double-click the gray Prototype Design task, you will be returned to the First New Product file.

From here on out, any changes in the First New Product project plan that cause the Prototype Completed task to change will have an impact on the Second New Product project plan. Otherwise, the two project plans function independently of each other.

When you open a file that has cross-linked predecessors, a Links Between Projects dialog box will automatically appear if any changes have taken place to the external tasks. You can access this dialog box at any time by choosing Tools, Links Between Projects. Use this dialog box not only to refresh any changes made to the external files, but also to reestablish file locations or delete links. The Differences column shows what kind of changes have taken place. Notice in Figure 18.14 the full path is shown for the selected task in the title bar of the dialog box.

External task name is gray.   **External task bar is gray.**

Figure 18.12
A predecessor or successor that refers to a task in another project creates a cross-linked task.

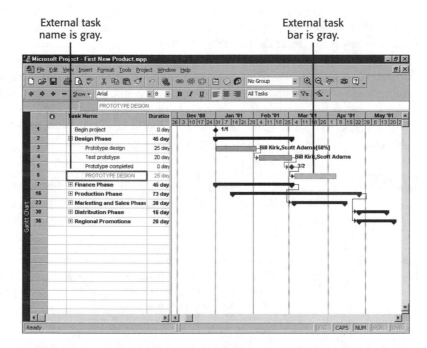

Figure 18.13
Grayed task names indicate cross-linked tasks and allow easy movement back and forth between files.

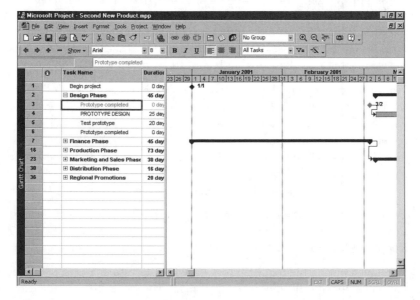

Task in
current file

Linked filename

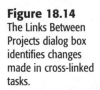

Figure 18.14
The Links Between
Projects dialog box
identifies changes
made in cross-linked
tasks.

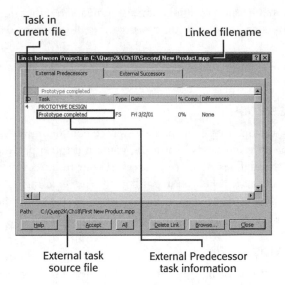

External task
source file

External Predecessor
task information

If you create links that would cause a circular relationship between tasks, one task acting as a predecessor and a successor of another, the dialog box in Figure 18.15 will open. You will need to explore the relationships between the linked tasks, locate the erroneous link, and remove it.

Figure 18.15
Project displays an
error message if any
cross-linked tasks cre-
ate a circular relation-
ship.

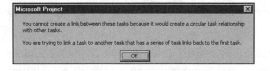

SHARING RESOURCES AMONG PROJECTS

It is not unusual to have several projects that use the same set of resources. When this is the case, it's cumbersome to manage the same resources in several different project files. You can't easily see what each resource is doing for all projects. You might want to have Microsoft Project store the resource information in one file and only the assignment information in the project files. You do this by entering all resources in one project file (which might not even have any tasks) and by instructing the other project files to use the resources defined in the file with the resources.

If projects share the same list of resources, you can open all the projects at the same time and view the allocation of resources across the projects. Microsoft Project warns you when a resource is overallocated because of conflicting assignments in different projects, and you can use the leveling command to resolve the resource overallocation by delaying tasks in different projects.

→ For more information on managing resource allocations, **see** "Strategies for Eliminating Resource Overallocations," **p. 455**

CREATING THE RESOURCE POOL

Any project file can be the one that contains the resource pool definitions. If your resources typically work on many different kinds of projects, you can create a project file that has no tasks defined in it but that defines all your resources. If your resources typically work on many projects of the same basic type, you might benefit from creating a template that contains the basic tasks as well as the setting to use the resources in another file.

→ For more information on Project templates, **see** "Creating and Using Templates," **p. 124**

USING THE RESOURCE POOL

By choosing Tools, Resources, Share Resources, you can define any project file to use the resources of another project file. If both files have resources defined in them at the time the link is established, the resource pool will be enlarged to include all resources defined in both files. If the same resource is defined in both files and there is a difference in the definition between the two files, you must tell Microsoft Project which file takes precedence in settling definition conflicts. The Share Resources dialog box provides a check box for this purpose.

Tip from Tim and the Project Team	Maintaining a clean pool should be a significant concern to the project manager or resource manager. The default option is for the pool to take precedence and should probably be the button of choice for every project link that is established. This way, each new sharer can be assured of having the most current resource data available. It will help prevent inconsistencies between projects that utilize the same set of resources.

After the sharing link is established, you can look at the Resource Sheet in either file to see the complete list of resources, and you can change the resource definitions in either file. When you close the files, each includes a copy of the entire resource pool. In this way, you can open the project file that uses the resource pool independently of the file that actually contains the resources, if needed, to modify and manage that project file.

To enable a project file to use the resources of another file, follow these steps:

1. Open both project files: the one containing the resource pool and the one that is to share that pool. Make sure that the active project is the one that is to use the other project's resources.

2. Choose Tools, Resources, Share Resources to display the Share Resources dialog box (see Figure 18.16). Choose the Use Resources option button and use the From drop-down box for a list of currently open files from which you can choose.

Figure 18.16
Use the Share Resources dialog box to link to a resource pool in another project file.

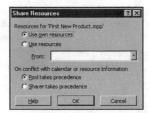

3. Select the Pool Takes Precedence option button if you want conflicting definitions to be settled by the entry in the file that contains the resource pool. Select the Sharer Takes Precedence option button if you want resource definition conflicts to be settled by the entry in the file that uses the resource pool.

4. Click OK to complete the link.

If the file containing the resources is not open when you open a connected file that shares its resources, an Open Resource Pool Information dialog box opens (see Figure 18.17). You can choose to have Project open the resource pool as well as all other project files that use the resources. However, you can work on the file even if you do not have the resource pool project open, because a copy of the pool is saved with each file that uses the common resource pool.

Figure 18.17
Microsoft Project offers to open the file containing the resources.

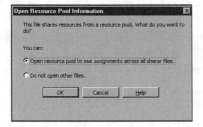

P2000 The options in the Open Resource Pool Information dialog box have changed in Project 2000. If you choose the first option, to open the resource pool and see assignments across all sharer files, both files will be opened and any changes made to the sharer file is reflected immediately in the pool. The pool file is opened read-only, but this is misleading. The pool can accept changes to resource assignment information, so it isn't read-only; but it is locked to prevent other sharer files from making immediate changes to the pool.

The other option in the Open Resource Pool Information dialog box allows you to open and work on a project file without also opening the resource pool. This lowers the computing overhead and increases work speed.

Caution

If you open a shared file without also opening the pool and make changes to the file, the changes are saved with the file but the pool is not immediately updated. Your changes will not be incorporated into the pool until the pool itself and all sharer files have been opened at one time. Options for opening the resource pool file are shown in Figure 18.18.

Figure 18.18
Access and behavior of the resource pool file are affected by how the pool was opened.

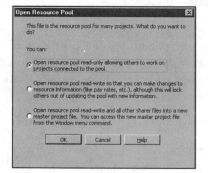

When opening the resource pool file directly, the option you choose on the Open Resource Pool dialog box determines the accessibility and updating behavior of the pool. The read-only option allows you to make changes and see the results immediately in a copy of the last-saved version of the pool file but changes made in real time by any other user are not reflected until the pool is closed and reopened. However, there are commands that will refresh the pool with current information while multiple users are working in it. Under Tools, Resources, choose the Update Resource Pool option to save your changes out to the stored resource pool, and then use the Refresh Resource Pool option to load a fresh copy of the pool into the open pool window. If these two options are not available (they will be gray), then the file-sharing environment is such that updating and refreshing the pool are not necessary.

The second option for opening a resource pool file is to open the file read-write. The descriptive text in the Open Resource Pool dialog box informs you that this option will give you complete editing control over the pool file but other users are completely locked out while you have the file open. Use the third option—open the resource pool and all sharer files—to force the pool file to retrieve the latest saved versions of all attached files and essentially rebuild the pool.

Tip from Tim and the Project Team

It is good computing practice to periodically open the resource pool file and all sharer files, forcing the most up-to-date information into all files. This procedure also will alert you to files with lost or corrupted links.

After a project is defined to use another project's resource pool, changes you make to the resource pool while both files are open are recorded directly into the shared pool and are shared by both files immediately. If you work with the dependent file alone, however, and you make changes in the copy of the resource pool, the changes might not be saved back to the resource pool. If you merely add new resources with different names, the resources are added to the resource pool when both files are open together the next time.

If you change the definition of the resource (for example, the pay rate, maximum units, or working days on the resource calendar), the changes might be lost when both files are loaded in memory together the next time. If you marked the Pool Takes Precedence option button in the Share Resources dialog box, the changes are lost; if you left the check box unmarked, the changes are recorded in the resource pool.

Tip from Tim and the Project Team

For consistency, the resource pool should be the only file where underlying resource details are changed. Typically, one or two people in a company are made custodians of the resource pool, entering all changes to pay rates and other resource details. The sharer files should be connected to the pool with the Pool Takes Precedence option turned on.

SAVING MULTIPLE FILES IN A WORKSPACE

The pool and resource sharing files can be saved simultaneously into a workspace file. This workspace file is assigned the default filename of Resume.MPW. Choose the File, Save Workspace command to save all open pool and sharer files together.

An easy way to open files attached to a resource pool is by opening the pool file first, and then opening the Share Resources dialog box (choose Tools, Resources, Share Resources). The Share Resources dialog box presents a list of all sharing files. Open all sharing files by clicking the Open All button (see Figure 18.19). You can also open each individual sharing file by selecting the filename in the Sharing links area and clicking Open.

PART

VI

CH

18

Figure 18.19
Open all sharing files from within the Share Resources dialog box in the pool file.

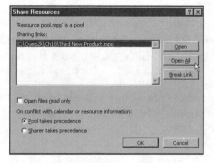

DISCONTINUING RESOURCE SHARING

You can discontinue the sharing of resources at any time. Simply open the file that uses another file's resources, open the Share Resources dialog box (choose Tools, Resources, Share Resources), and choose the Use Own Resources option button. The resources in the resource pool are no longer available to the file. However, any resources that were assigned to tasks in the file are copied into the file's resource list and are saved with the file. Likewise, any resource in the file that was sharing the resource pool of another project is copied into the pool and remains there, even after sharing is discontinued.

To discontinue a project file's dependence on another file's resource pool, perform the following steps:

1. Open the file that is to become independent (and use its own resources).
2. Make the file that is to use its own resources the active file window.
3. Choose Tools, Resources, Share Resources.
4. Choose the Use Own Resources option button in the Share Resources dialog box.
5. Click OK to execute the new definition.

The message in Figure 18.20 confirms the removal of the connection between the two files.

Figure 18.20
Microsoft Project confirms that you want to remove the connection between a project file and a resource pool.

> **Note**
>
> You also can break the sharing link from the other direction. Open the pool file, and display the Share Resources dialog box. As seen in Figure 18.19, a Break Link option is available.

IDENTIFYING RESOURCE POOL LINKS

The resource-sharing connection is recorded in the file that contains the resource pool and in the file that uses the resource pool. The Share Resources dialog box displays linking information is both file types, and the layout of the dialog box tells you which of the two file types is active.

Figure 18.16 displays the Share Resources dialog box in a file that uses the resource list from another file. Contrast that illustration with Figure 18.19. Project "knows" which file is acting as the pool file and changes the Share Resources dialog box to offer file link management options.

Tip from Tim and the Project Team

> When you first begin to experiment with inserted projects, cross project links, and sharing resource pools, it would be worth your while to create a table that includes the following columns: External, Linked Fields, Predecessors, Successors, Sub Project File, Sub Project File Read Only, and Notes. As you begin working with the files, you can see exactly what is happening and where Project is storing the information. Change the column titles to an abbreviation so that you can make the columns narrow to see more onscreen without scrolling.

→ For more information on customizing tables, **see** "Using and Creating Tables," **p. 949**

VIEWING RESOURCE LOADS WITHOUT SHARING A POOL

In a larger organization, it might not be desirable to have multiple project managers attaching their files to a single resource pool. Performance can be affected and other managers might be prohibited from making and saving changes to their files if someone has inadvertently opened all of the sharer files. If your main reason for pooling is to summarize and report on resource assignments across multiple files, it is not necessary to maintain file links to a resource pool.

When two or more Project files have been consolidated, as discussed earlier in this chapter, Project can create a combined list of resources assigned to those files. Breaking the link to all underlying files causes Project to recreate a list of resources from all consolidated files. Resource names from each file are matched and the assignments totaled. Then the Resource Usage view, among others, will show the distribution of work by resource across all projects consolidated in this particular file.

To create this combined resource list, open the Task Information dialog box for the project summary line of each inserted project. Move to the Advanced tab, and, in the Source Project area, turn off the Link to Project option, as shown in Figure 18.21. Now the Gantt Chart will display tasks renumbered consecutively; duplicate task IDs no longer exist. The individual files cannot be edited within this revised consolidation because the links no longer exist. Create a separate consolidated file, including file links, to edit projects from this level.

PART VI
CH 18

Figure 18.21
Unlink consolidated files to create a combined resource list across projects.

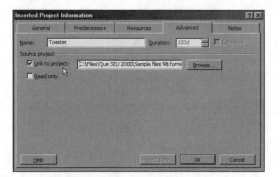

Tip from Tim and the Project Team

When using this method to create a consolidated resource list, a separate file acting as a resource information repository should still be maintained. Designate someone to keep the resource detail information—pay rate, nonworking time, and so on—up to date in a single file. When updates are made, notify all project managers to open their Project files, link them to this resource file to bring down the most recent resource information, and then simply break the resource sharing link and save their files.

TROUBLESHOOTING

VIEWING TASK INFORMATION FROM MULTIPLE PROJECTS

When I use the Window, New Window command, I can't tell which task is from which file, especially if I have sorted the tasks by their start date. Can I change that?

Modify the table that you are using to also display the project filename, which is most likely just before or just after the ID number for the task. This way you can see the filename and the task ID together to distinguish between files. Right-click a column heading and choose Insert Column. Then choose Project for the Field Name.

TURNING OFF RESOURCE SHARING

My project plan is sharing resources with several other plans—how do I make it stop sharing?

Open the file that uses another file's resources, open the Share Resources dialog box (choose Tools, Resources, Share Resources), and choose the Use Own Resources option button. The resources in the resource pool are no longer available to the file. Remember that any resources assigned to tasks in the file are copied into the file's resource list and get saved with the file. Likewise, any resource in the file that was sharing the resource pool of another project is copied into the pool and remains there, even after sharing is discontinued.

CHAPTER 191

EXPORTING AND IMPORTING PROJECT DATA WITH OTHER FILE FORMATS

In this chapter

EXCHANGING PROJECT DATA WITH OTHER APPLICATIONS

There are many reasons why you might find it useful to be able to share all or part of a Microsoft Project 2000 document with another software application. One common reason is the desire to prepare reports in other applications. Other purposes include using another application for additional analysis or processing of Project data and archiving an organization's history of projects. Similarly, it is often useful to copy data from other applications into Microsoft Project, especially to avoid retyping large amounts of data. The following scenarios illustrate some of the uses for a data-exchange capability:

- You might want to copy some of your Project information to a PowerPoint presentation or to a report that you want to put together in Word or Excel (or other similar office software applications).

- You might have a list of tasks or resource names in Word or Excel that you want to use in a Project document. It is faster and more accurate to import the data than to key it in again in Project.

- You might want to process some of your Project data using the special facilities or calculating power of Microsoft Excel.

- There might be others in your organization who want to query aspects of the project but who don't know how to use Project. If the project is saved in a database, you can work on it in Project and they can use Access-aware applications to view the Project data details.

- You might want other applications to be able to query the data in a Project file directly using the data-sharing capabilities of Microsoft's OLE DB.

- You might want to keep an archive of all projects for a department or organization, which can be used to review the history for a resource or to calculate performance statistics over a longer time period.

- You might need to make the project available to someone who has an older version of Microsoft Project, or to someone who uses another project management application.

- You might prefer to distribute new schedule notices or other reports on a corporate intranet or on the Internet, via Web pages.

This chapter will help you choose the best method for exchanging data between a Microsoft Project 2000 data file and other software applications. As illustrated by the previous examples, you can transfer all the Project data or only a part of it. For small amounts of data, you may well just use the copy-and-paste facilities of the Windows Clipboard. Chapter 20, "Copying, Pasting, and Inserting Data with Other Applications," will show you how to copy-and-paste data between Project files and other file formats. For larger transfers, it will be easier to export and import data files as described in this chapter.

FILE FORMATS SUPPORTED BY MICROSOFT PROJECT 2000

You can import and export entire projects or selected sets of project data using the File, Open and File, Save As menu commands. These commands allow you to read and write the project data in formats other than Project's native MPP format. After an overview of the file formats supported by Microsoft Project 2000, we will examine in detail exporting and importing with each of the formats.

→ For information about using the File commands, **see** Chapter 4, "Working with Project Files," **p. 99**

Microsoft Project supports three native formats that store all Project data, including views, filters, and field data. Additional formats are supported for exchanging selected data with other applications that don't read the Project native formats. Table 19.1 summarizes the list of file formats that you can use with Microsoft Project 2000. In general, if the format can handle the entire set of Project data, Microsoft Project will create copies of all its tables and fields in the new format. If only part of the Project data is to be exchanged, you will need to use an Import/Export map to match Project fields with the fields in the other format.

Note

The file extensions referred to in Table 19.1 and the text will only be visible in Project's Open and Save As dialog boxes if Windows is displaying file extensions.

TABLE 19.1   FILE FORMATS SUPPORTED BY MICROSOFT PROJECT 2000

File Format	Extension	Description
Native Formats		
Project	MPP	This is the standard format for Project document files. It saves the complete set of project data. However, previous versions can't open these files because those versions don't support the new fields and processes in Project 2000.
Template	MPT	Templates save standard or *boilerplate* information that you use frequently for your Projects. When opened, the template produces a new Project document.
Project Database	MPD	This format is based on the Microsoft Access 2000 (version 9.0) file format. The entire project data set is saved in this format, including field data, views, calendars, and formatting. The files can be queried, opened, modified, and saved either in Microsoft Project or Microsoft Access.

Table 19.1 Continued

File Format	Extension	Description
Other Formats		
MPX 4.0	MPX	The MPX format was used in past versions of Microsoft Project to exchange data between versions of Project or with other project management software. The MPX 4.0 format does not include the fields and features introduced in either Project 98 or in Project 2000. You can open an MPX file in Project 2000 but you can't save your Project 2000 documents in the MPX format.
Microsoft Access Database	MDB	This is the Microsoft Access 2000 database format. You can save all or part of the project data in this format, and any application that recognizes this format can open the file or query it for reports. An Import/Export map can be used with this format if you want to save only portions of the project.
ODBC		ODBC databases are data storage sources that can be accessed by a wide variety of applications, both commercial software products and custom applications developed within the organization. You can store entire projects or selected project data in ODBC data stores. The use of an Import/Export map is optional.
Microsoft Excel Workbook	XLS	Project can export to the Microsoft Excel 5.0/95 format. You can export field data in this format but not project elements such as calendars and views. The resulting file can be opened directly in Microsoft Excel 2000 as a workbook or in any application that supports the Excel 5.0/95 format. Although you can read Excel 2000 data into Microsoft Project 2000, you cannot save data in the Excel 2000 format from Project 2000. An Import/Export map is required for exchanging data in this format.
Microsoft Excel PivotTable	XLS	This is the format used in Excel for its PivotTable. You only export field data to a PivotTable, not all the Project data. You cannot import from an Excel PivotTable into Microsoft Project. An Import/Export map is required for exporting data in this format.
HTML	HTM	This is the HTML Markup format used by browser programs on the World Wide Web and intranets. You can export field data, but not an entire project, to the HTML format; and you cannot import from HTML files into Microsoft Project. An Import/Export map is required for exchanging data in this format.

TABLE 19.1   CONTINUED

File Format	Extension	Description
Other Formats		
ASCII Text	TXT	This is a generic text format that is widely used for data transfers between applications and platforms. Field data is tab-delimited. You can only transfer field data for a single Microsoft Project table in this format. An Import/Export map is required for exchanging data in this format.
Comma Separated Value	CSV	This is another generic text format widely used for transferring data between applications and platforms. Originally, field values were separated by commas, but now the format uses the default system list separator. You can only transfer field data for a single Microsoft Project table in this format. An Import/Export map is required for exchanging data in this format.

Note

The Project Workspace format, with the extension MPW, also appears in the list of file types in both the Open and Save As dialog boxes. However, this is not really a data file format. It merely saves the *workspace settings* (the names of the files that are open, not any field data) so that you can open all those same files in the same window arrangement by simply opening the Workspace file.

The sections that follow will examine all these file formats except the standard Project document (MPP), Project template (MPT), and Project Workspace types. These were covered earlier in Chapter 4, "Working with Project Files."

Most of the non-native formats require that you use an Import/Export map to define which field values in Project are to be associated with data locations in the other format. The creation and use of a map will be presented in detail with the first file format that requires it (see the section "Creating Import/Export Maps for Access and ODBC Sources" later in this chapter).

EXPORTING PROJECT 2000 DATA TO OLDER RELEASES OF MICROSOFT PROJECT

In the past, the most comprehensive exchange of data between Microsoft Project and other products was through the MPX (Microsoft Project Exchange) format. However, MPX has been replaced by the Microsoft Project Database format as the preferred vehicle for exchanging all project data. Project 2000 will open MPX files, but it cannot create them.

To open a file in Microsoft Project 2000 that was saved in the MPX format, choose File, Open. After selecting the search directory in the Look In text box, the list of files you can

PART
VI

CH
19

open will include any MPX files in that directory along with the rest of the Project files. To see just the MPX files, select MPX in the Files of Type list box. Select the MPX filename that you want to open and choose the Open button.

SAVING THE ENTIRE PROJECT IN A DATABASE

Examine the options you have for saving the entire Project data set in other formats, namely the Microsoft Project Database format, the Microsoft Access Database format, and other ODBC database sources. All aspects of the Project document can be saved, including all the field data, calendars, views, filters, and format settings.

> **Note**
>
> When you create a file in one of these foreign formats, Microsoft Project creates many new tables and fields in the external database to hold copies of the data from its internal tables and fields. However, the table and field names are very different from the names you see in Project when you place fields in views or reports. To work with the data in these foreign formats, you need to read the document titled "Microsoft Project 2000 Database Format," which is saved in a file named ProjDB.HTM. This file is copied during installation into the 1033 folder under the folder where Project is installed. For example, in the standard installation, this document would be found in
>
> `C:\Program Files\Microsoft Office\Office\1033\ProjDB.HTM`
>
> You can open the file in a browser or any word processor (such as Microsoft Word) that can work with HTML files.

USING THE MICROSOFT PROJECT DATABASE FORMAT

The Microsoft Project Database format saves the entire project to a Microsoft Access 2000 database format with the extension MPD. This format has replaced the MPX format as the standard interchange format for project data. You can store multiple projects in the same MPD file, which facilitates analysis of resources, tasks, or assignments spanning many different projects. You can open individual projects from the MPD file in Microsoft Project, or in Microsoft Access, or any application that supports the Microsoft Access format. You can query the MPD file with any application that can query an Access database directly or with an ODBC data source.

> *Tip from Tim and the Project Team*
>
> To see a list of Project database files in Access, you must type ***.mpd** into the File Name box in the Open dialog box. The file extension MPD is not on the list of default data source extensions displayed by Access—nor is it on the list of options in the Files of Type pull-down list.

SAVING A PROJECT IN A MICROSOFT PROJECT DATABASE

When you save a project in the Microsoft Project Database format, you have the choice of creating a new MPD file that initially contains just that one project or of adding the project to an existing MPD file that may contain related projects you want to keep together. When you open an MPD file that contains multiple projects, you are asked to select the project that you want to retrieve.

You cannot save just selected parts of a project in a Microsoft Project database—the entire project is saved, including all field data for tasks, resources, and assignments, plus all other information such as views, formats, calendars, and so forth.

Tip from Tim and the Project Team

P2000

Project's timephased assignment data is normally saved in a binary file instead of in a table in the database to improve performance. If you want the timephased assignment data to be available in a table in the database, you must choose Tools, Options and select the Save tab. Fill the check box labeled Expand Timephased Data in the Database. Note that this is a project-level setting—it only affects the current project.

Tip from Tim and the Project Team

It's a good idea to supply the project with a title in the Properties dialog box before starting to save it to a database, especially when saving it to a database that already contains other projects. Project will suggest the properties title as the name for the project you are saving during this process, and having that identifying name in place will help you avoid confusion when saving to a database.

To save a Project file as a new Microsoft Project database, follow these steps:

1. Choose File, Save As to display the Save As dialog box.
2. Select the location for the new database file in the Save In box.
3. Pull down the list of file types in the Save as Type list box and select Project Database (*.MPD).

    If there are any MPD files in the location you have selected, they will appear in the file list at this point. The extension on the project filename will also change to MPD.

    In Figure 19.1, the project document was originally named NewProduct.MPP, but the extension is changed to NewProduct.MPD when the MPD file type is selected. Since this is to be the name of the database, not just one project in the database, the filename has been changed to New Products.MPD. An existing Project database named Software Conversions appears in the file list.

Tip from Tim and the Project Team

When choosing the name for a new Project database, bear in mind that you might decide to store many project documents in the database. Unless you know that you will only store one project in the database, choose a generic name that will help you identify the current project you are saving and all others that you will likely store in the same database file.

An existing database name

Figure 19.1
Selecting Project Database as the file type changes both the list of files in the location and the extension on the default filename.

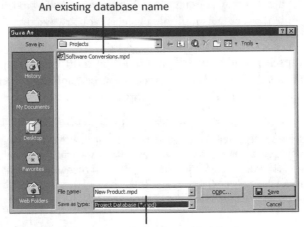

Replace the current project name with a database name.

4. Supply the name for the database in the File Name text box. Note that this does not necessarily have to match the name of the project; the database can potentially contain many projects. The default database name is the same name that was attached to the project file. To give the database a more general name, you must type in the new filename.

5. Choose the Save button to start saving the data. The Save To Database dialog box will appear (see Figure 19.2). The Entire Project tab is the only available option when saving a Microsoft Project Database.

Database filename

Figure 19.2
Provide the name to identify this project within the database in the Project Name box of the Save To Database dialog box.

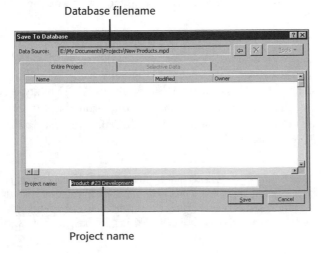

Project name

6. Select the text box labeled Project Name if you want to change the name of the project and type in a new name.

The project title will appear as a default name for the project. The project title is maintained in the File Properties dialog box, on the Summary tab. (See Chapter 3, "Setting Up a New Project Document," for information about the file properties.)

7. Choose <u>S</u>ave to begin creating the database. A Saving progress bar will appear on the left of the status bar to let you know the file is being saved.

To save your project in an already existing database requires a few additional steps:

1. Choose <u>F</u>ile, Save <u>A</u>s to display the Save As dialog box.

2. Use the Save <u>I</u>n box to select the location where the database file is stored.

3. Pull down the list of file types in the Save as <u>T</u>ype list box and select Project Database (*.MPD). This will display the Microsoft Project Database files already stored in that location.

4. Choose the database name in the list. Note that the original project name in the File <u>N</u>ame text box disappears and the database name replaces it. You will restore the project's unique name in a moment.

5. Choose the <u>S</u>ave button to start saving the project. Because you are adding a project to an existing database, Microsoft Project needs to know if you are replacing that database or just appending another project to those already stored there. A dialog box appears to let you choose the next step (see Figure 19.3).

Figure 19.3
When adding a project to a Project database, you can append the project to those already in the database, or you can replace the existing projects in the database with the new project you are saving.

6. Choose the <u>A</u>ppend button if you want to add this project to those already in the database. Also choose the <u>A</u>ppend button if you want the project you are saving to replace another project already saved in the database. You will have to give the new project the same name in the database as the project that it replaces and choose to overwrite the existing project in the database.

or

Choose the <u>O</u>verwrite button only if you want to remove all existing projects from the database and save only the new project in that file.

or

Choose the Cancel button if you want to back out of the process and leave the database file unchanged. If you choose Append or Overwrite, the Save to Database dialog box will appear as in the previous example.

7. Review the names of other projects stored in the database file (see Figure 19.4). If you are replacing a project, select that project's name in the list. Otherwise, you can keep the default name of the new project or change its name by typing a new name in the Project Name list box.

Note that other buttons let you return to the previous dialog box and delete the selected project from the database. You can also use the Tools button to delete or rename a selected project.

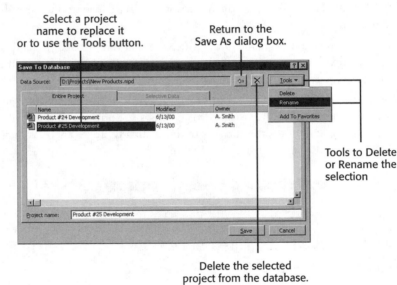

Figure 19.4
Review the list of projects stored in the database in the Name list box.

Select a project name to replace it or to use the Tools button.

Return to the Save As dialog box.

Tools to Delete or Rename the selection

Delete the selected project from the database.

8. Choose Save to begin saving the project in the database.

OPENING PROJECTS FROM A MICROSOFT PROJECT DATABASE

Use the File, Open command to open a project that was saved in a Microsoft Project Database:

1. Choose File, Open.

2. Select the location of the database file you want to open in the Look In box. The Microsoft Project Database files in that location will be displayed along with other project files stored there. If you want to see only project database files listed, choose Project Databases in the Files of Type box.

3. Choose the database name from the list and choose the Open button. The Open From Database dialog box will appear (see Figure 19.5).

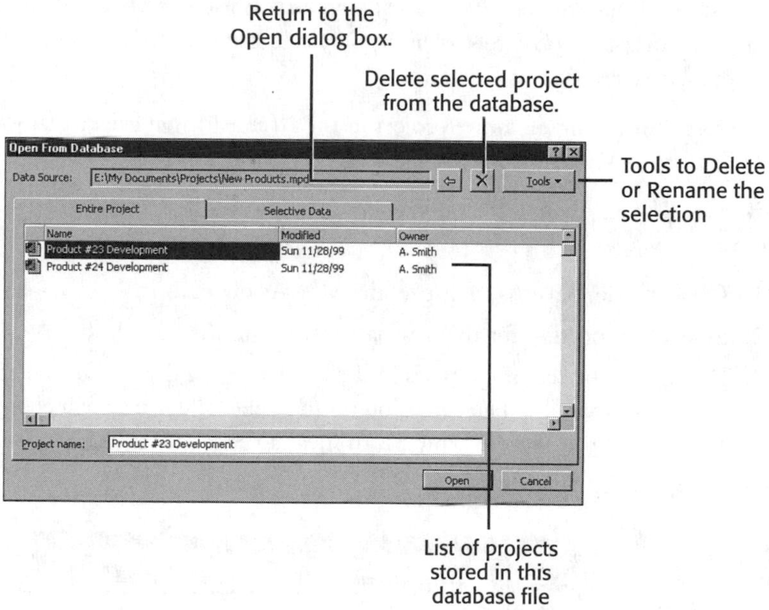

Return to the
Open dialog box.

Delete selected project
from the database.

Figure 19.5
Select the project
name to be opened
from a Microsoft
Project database file.

Tools to Delete
or Rename the
selection

List of projects
stored in this
database file

4. Use the list arrow to display the names of the projects stored in the database and choose the project you want to open from the list.

5. Choose the Open button to begin loading the project from the database. Note that other buttons let you return to the previous dialog box and delete the selected project from the database. You can also use the Tools button to delete or rename the selected project.

If project data has been changed by another application in the MPD file, then when it is imported into Project 2000 the program will attempt to determine which field was changed and will make appropriate adjustments to other data that may rely on the changed field.

After opening and working with a project stored in an MPD file, you can save your work as you would with any other file: Simply choose File, Save from the menu or choose the Save button on the Standard toolbar. The project will be saved in the database it came from, replacing the older version of the project.

Tip from Tim and the Project Team

If you choose the File, Save As command instead of the Save command, Project will change the extension of the project file to MPP and, unless you correct it, the project would be saved in a new standard project document instead of back in the database it came from.

USING THE MICROSOFT ACCESS FORMAT

You can also save the entire project in a standard Microsoft Access 2000 database. The Microsoft Project database is also stored in the native Microsoft Access 2000 format. You

PART

VI

CH

19

must save all the project data when you choose to use the Microsoft Project Database format, but you can choose to save all or only selected parts of the project when you choose to use the Microsoft Access format.

The steps for saving an entire project in the Access format are virtually the same as those used to save a Microsoft Project database.

To save all of an open project document in a Microsoft Access 2000 database, follow these steps:

1. Choose File, Save As to display the Save As dialog box.
2. Select the location for the new database file in the Save In box.
3. Pull down the list of file types in the Save as Type list box and select Microsoft Access Databases (*.mdb). The extension on the default filename will change to .MDB also (see Figure 19.6). If there are any MDB files in the location you have selected, they will appear in the file list at this point.

Figure 19.6
Save a project in an Access 2000 database the same way you save one in a Project 2000 database.

Existing Access database

Name for new Access database

4. To create a new database, supply the name for the database in the File Name text box. The default database name is the same name that was attached to the project file. To give the database a distinct name, you must type in the new name. Remember that if other projects are to be stored in this database, an inclusive name might be better than the current project's name. Previously in Figure 19.6 the project name was New Product but the database file has been renamed New Products. To add the project to an existing database, select the database name from the file list.
5. Choose the Save button to start saving the data.
6. If you are adding to an existing database file, the dialog box you saw previously in Figure 19.3 will prompt you to choose what will happen to the existing database. You have three choices:

Choose Append to add this project to the others contained in the database, or to replace one of the existing projects in the database with the data in this project.

or

Choose Overwrite to replace the database file, and all the projects contained in it, with a new database that contains only the project you are saving.

or

Choose Cancel to stop saving the project.

7. When the Save To Database dialog box appears, be sure that the default tab Entire Project is selected. When saving to an Access database you also have the option to save just selected data; so, the Selective Data tab is also available.

8. Supply the name given to this project by typing it into the Project Name text box. You can accept the default name, type in a new name, or use the name of one of the existing projects in the database (if you want to replace that project's data with the data in the project you are saving). Click one of those names in the project list if you want to replace that project.

9. Choose Save to begin saving the project in the database.

You open a project that was saved in a Microsoft Access database with the File, Open command:

1. Choose the File, Open command from the menu to display the Open dialog box.

2. Select the location of the database file you want to open in the Look In box.

3. Pull down the list of file types in the Files of Type list box and select Microsoft Access Databases (*.mdb).

4. Choose the database name from the file list and click the Open button. The Open From Database dialog box will appear (see Figure 19.7).

Entire Project tab   Database filename

Figure 19.7
Choose one of the complete projects stored in an Access database to open it as a project document.

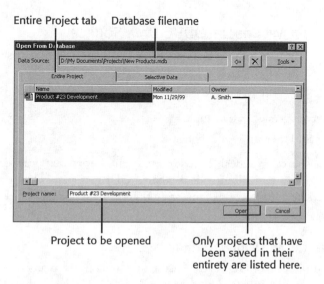

Project to be opened   Only projects that have been saved in their entirety are listed here.

Caution

If the database does not contain any complete project files (in other words, it only contains parts of one or more projects), the Entire Project tab will be dimmed and Project will display the Selective Data tab. You can import selected data from the tables in the database, but you must create a map to access it (see the section "Creating and Using an Import Map," later in this chapter).

5. Select the project you want to open from the list.

6. Choose the Open button to begin loading the project from the database.

After opening and working with a project stored in an Access database, you can save your work as you would with any other file by choosing File, Save or selecting the Save button on the Standard toolbar. The project will be saved in the database it came from, replacing the older version of the project.

Note

After saving or opening a project in a Project database or an Access database, you will find the project name in the list of files at the bottom of the File menu. The listing will include the database name in angle brackets followed by a backslash followed by the project name. For example, if you save a project in the NewProducts.MPD database in the Projects directory of your D: drive, giving the project the name Product#24, you would see the following in the file list on the File menu:

`<D:\Projects\NewProducts.MPD>\Product#24`

Clicking this file listing will create a new project document named Product#24.MPP that contains all the information for that project in the database.

SAVING PROJECTS IN A MICROSOFT ODBC DATA SOURCE

You can store and retrieve project data with these ODBC (Open Database Connectivity) data sources:

Microsoft Access 2000

Oracle Server, version 8.0 or higher

Microsoft SQL Server 7.0 or higher

ODBC database sources are ideal for customized applications that draw data and reports from many different organization-wide databases. ODBC is not a file format; it is a set of protocols, drivers, and instructions for storing the way to access and work with different data sources.

SAVING A PROJECT IN AN ODBC DATABASE

You can save a project in an ODBC database almost as easily as in any other format. There are a few additional steps involved in identifying the ODBC data source. The data source definition is not a database itself, but a reference to a database. You can create some databases on-the-fly in which to store your project. Others must be created by server administrators. See your database administrator if you need help with the data sources available to you.

To save an entire project in an ODBC database, follow these steps:

1. Choose File, Save As.

2. Choose the ODBC button on the right side of the Save As dialog box. This will display the Select Data Source dialog box (see Figure 19.8).

Selected data source

Figure 19.8
The Select Data Source dialog box lets you create a new data source definition or use an existing one.

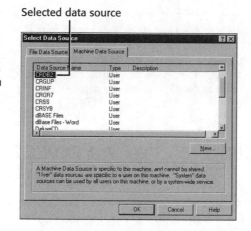

3. Choose either the File Data Source tab or the Machine Data Source tab to show the list of data sources (databases) already defined on your system. If you want to create a new data source, choose the New button and follow the instructions for defining a new data source.

4. If required by the data source you selected, enter your logon ID and password and then click OK. The Save To Database dialog box will be displayed.

5. Be sure the Entire Project tab is selected.

6. Provide the name you want to use for this project in the database.

7. Choose the Save button.

IMPORTING A COMPLETE PROJECT FROM AN ODBC SOURCE

You must be careful when importing a project from an ODBC source that was not originally created in Microsoft Project. The source database must have been carefully structured to parallel the database structure used by Microsoft Project. See the Project database document ProjDB.HTM referenced previously for the required structure.

To open a project from an ODBC database:

1. Choose File, Open.

2. In the Open dialog box, choose the ODBC button.

3. Select the tab (File Data Source or Machine Data Source) that lists the data source you want to open.

PART

VI

CH

19

4. Choose the data source and then click OK.

5. In the Open From Database dialog box, select the Entire Project tab if necessary.

6. Choose the project you want to open.

7. Click the Open button to open the project data.

Note

After saving or opening a project in an ODBC data source, you will find the project name in the list of files at the bottom of the File menu. Like projects saved in Project or Access databases, the listing will include the ODBC data source name in angle brackets followed by a backslash followed by the project name, and clicking the listing will create a new project document that contains all the information in the database for that project.

EXCHANGING SELECTED PARTS OF A PROJECT WITH OTHER FORMATS

For some file formats, you are only allowed to store selected field values from a Project file. This is true for the Microsoft Excel format, the HTML format for Web browsers, and the text formats. In other instances, you simply may not want to store all the Project information. For example, a colleague might ask you to supply an Access database that records just the task names, scheduled work, and actual work for your project as a source to help that person estimate task work in a similar project.

When you save an entire project in a database, Microsoft Project automatically creates a standard set of tables in the database with standard Microsoft Project database field names. If you save only part of a project's data to a database, you will need to provide the name of the new or existing table(s) that will receive the data.

If you choose to save only parts of the project in one of the export formats, you must use an export format map to define which fields you want to export from Project and what you want to call the table or tables in which they will be stored. If you plan to change the values in the other format and then import the data back into Project, you must use that same map or a similar map to tell Project where the imported data is to be inserted in the Project data structure.

WORKING WITH IMPORT/EXPORT MAPS

All Import/Export maps are similar in design: They specify tables and fields in a foreign data format that will be matched with tables and fields in Microsoft Project's native format. A map allows you to define tables in the foreign format to match the data in Project's native tables. The tables you can define in an Import/Export map are

- A task table for values that match Project's task fields
- A resource table for values that match Project's resource fields
- An assignment table for values that match Project's assignment fields

You cannot import or export Project's timephased data with Import/Export maps.

For each table in the map, you specify the field name in Project and the corresponding data location in the foreign format. Option buttons make it very easy to add all Project fields to the table, or to add the same set of fields that appear in one of the already defined tables in Microsoft Project.

For export maps, you can choose to export a subset of the tasks or resources in the project by applying one of the already defined Project filters.

For import maps, you can choose how the imported data will fit into the open Project file. Your options are as follows:

- You can place the imported records into a new Project document. Project will create a new MPP document file with the field values you have selected. This file is a standard Project MPP file that has no links to the source of the imported data—saving it does not update the source data.

- You can have the imported records appended to the tasks, resources, or assignments already in the open project. Project will add new tasks, resources, or assignments below the existing tasks, resources, or assignments.

- You can have the values in the imported records merged into the existing project to update the existing tasks, resources, or assignments. This means that Project will attempt to match the records coming in with those already in the open document. Where there is a match, the field values coming in will replace the existing field values. For Project to match the records coming in with those in the current file, you will have to define one field as a key field to be used for matching records. For example, you could import resource names and standard rates to update the pay rates in the resource table. In this case, you would probably use the resource names as the key field to match records.

The maps are not file format specific; that is, if you design a map to export data to Access, you can also use the same map to export data to an ODBC data source, to a text file, or to an Excel worksheet. However, the different file formats often convert nontext fields into different field types and different values. For example, the same export map will save 8 hours of work to an Excel worksheet as text (as "8 hrs") and to an Access database as the number 480,000 (1,000 times the number of minutes in 8 hours). Furthermore, some maps export more data to one format than to another. For example, the Who Does What Report map exports more data to an HTML document than it does to an Access database (see the section "Using the Who Does What Report Map," later in this chapter).

When you choose to save Project data in a non-Project format, Project will modify the options that are shown on the Import/Export map to match the format you chose. For example, if you choose Save <u>A</u>s for an HTML format, and then choose an Import/Export map that was originally designed for exporting to an Excel worksheet, the worksheet options will be replaced by HTML options.

PART

VI

Cн

19

You must be very careful when using a map to import data into Project. A map designed for one database or worksheet may specify tables or fields that are not used in another data source. Always check the structure of the map before applying it to import.

Import/Export maps are saved in the GLOBAL.MPT file, not in the Project file that is open when you create them. You can rename a map without having to go to the Organizer; however, when you edit a map, you have the option to change its name. You must, however, use the Organizer to delete a map.

→ For information on using the Organizer to delete objects such as Import/Export maps, **see** "Deleting an Object with the Organizer," **p. 132**

Tip from Tim and the Project Team

To share a map with another user, you can use the Organizer to copy the map into an open project file and then save the project. The other user can then open the saved project file and use the Organizer to copy the map into his or her GLOBAL.MPT.

REVIEWING THE PREDEFINED IMPORT/EXPORT MAPS

Microsoft Project 2000 includes 11 predefined Import/Export maps for general-purpose use. Some are like predefined Project reports, views, or tables. The predefined maps are listed in Table 19.2. Some are intended for a specific file format and references are given to the intended file format.

TABLE 19.2 THE PREDEFINED IMPORT/EXPORT MAPS

Map	Description
"Who Does What" Report	Use to save an HTML table that lists resources and their task assignments.
Compare to Baseline	Use to export a table that lists all tasks with scheduled and baseline values.
Cost Data by Task	Use to export a table that lists task costs.
Default Task Information	Use to export or import the basic task fields that are included in the task Entry table.
Earned Value Information	Use to export the task earned value fields.
Export to HTML Using Standard Template	Use to export basic task, resource, and assignment values to an HTML document.
Resource "Export Table" Map	Use to export all the fields in the predefined resource Export table.
Task "Export Table" Map	Use to export all the fields in the predefined task Export table.
Task and Resource PivotTable	Use to create Excel PivotTables for tasks and resources.
Task List with Embedded Assignment Rows	Use to export an HTML table of tasks and their assigned resources.
Top Level Tasks List	Use to export a table with data for outline level 1 tasks.

The sections that follow explain how these maps are put together and how they are to be used. All the predefined maps were designed for exporting selected data from Project to another file format. Some were designed with specific file formats in mind—for example, HTML or Excel PivotTables—but any map can be used to export to any of the formats. They generally work best, however, if used with the format for which they were designed.

Note that in all cases the exported values for the duration and work fields are exported as text (not as numeric data) with the time unit attached as part of the text value.

Although some maps are designed for exporting and some for importing, any map can be used for either export or import operations. Suppose that a map is designed to export Project data to another format for building a report. If that map is used to import data into a Project document, the result might not make sense. Be very careful about using a map to import data into Project.

When you use an Import/Export map to exchange data with an another file format, the external file that supplies or receives the data will be added to the list of recently saved or opened files that appears at the bottom of Project's File menu. For example, if you export (save) data to an Excel worksheet named "TaskCosts.xls" using the map named "Cost Data by Task," you will see the entry "TaskCosts.xls(Cost Data by Task)" on Project's File menu. Because clicking a file listing causes Project to open the file, clicking the listing would cause Project to import (open) the Excel file TaskCosts.xls and copy data into a Project document using the "Cost Data by Task" map to determine which Project fields receive the imported data.

By default, Project's predefined maps all place imported data into a new Project document that is created on the fly. Therefore, clicking the file listing will cause Project to create a new document that has the Excel data in it. You will want to close this new project file without saving it because the map was designed for exporting, not for importing, and the new project file will not be a complete project file.

When imported data is placed in a new Project document, there is no harm done because you can simply close the new document. But import maps can also be defined so that they append the imported data to the active file or merge the imported data into existing task or resource records, updating existing field values with the values stored in the external document. If the map named in the file listing is set to append or merge, clicking the file listing will alter the data in the document that is active when you click the listing. If the active document has unsaved data in it, you could lose some or all of that data as a result of clicking the listing on the File menu.

PART

VI

CH

19

Caution

You should never open a foreign format map file from the File menu's file list unless you're absolutely sure that you want that data imported. Even then, be sure that you save the active document beforehand, just in case.

USING THE "WHO DOES WHAT" REPORT MAP

This map is best used to save an HTML table of resource assignments. The resulting table is named Who Does What and is similar to the Who Does What report you can print in Project by choosing View, Reports, Assignments, Who Does What. Like the Resource Usage view in Project, the HTML table lists resource names and task assignment names in the same column with the assignment names indented under their resource names. There are columns for the Start, Finish, and Work field values for each assignment. The data for Work is text data (not numeric) with the unit "hours" appended as part of the text value.

Although the map works best when saving to HTML format, you can also use it to save to an Excel workbook or to one of the text file formats. When saving to Excel or one of the text formats, the resource rows will be indistinguishable from the assignment rows because the assignments will not be indented as they are in the HTML format. If you open the HTML document in Excel, however, the resources and assignments will be formatted distinctively.

Tip from Tim and the Project Team

> When saving the data to Excel or a text format, you should modify the map and add the field named Assignment to the table to distinguish resource names from task assignment names. Those rows in the list that are resources will have "No" in the Assignment field, whereas rows for assignments will have "Yes." You could apply Excel's conditional formatting to bold the resource rows based on the value "No" being found in the Assignment column. See the section "Saving Project Data as an Excel Worksheet," later in this chapter, for more information.

If you attempt to use the map to create a database table, you will find that Project doesn't include the associated assignment rows for each resource. To create database tables, you would have to add to the map an additional table for the assignments and then link the tables on the resource names within the database application.

See "Exporting Project Data to the Internet or an Intranet," later in this chapter, for more details about the HTML format.

USING THE COMPARE TO BASELINE MAP

Use this map to export a table named Baseline Comparison that lists all tasks with their Start and Finish dates along with their scheduled, baseline, and variance values for Duration, Work, and Cost. This map works the same for database, worksheet, or text formats.

USING THE COST DATA BY TASK MAP

Use this map to export a table named Task Costs that lists all the tasks with their cost values (Fixed Cost, Total Cost, Baseline Cost, Cost Variance, Actual Cost, and Remaining Cost).

USING THE DEFAULT TASK INFORMATION MAP

This map can be used to export or import the basic task fields that are included in the task Entry table: ID, Name, Duration, Start and Finish Dates, Predecessors, and Resource Names. It works the same with all file formats.

USING THE EARNED VALUE INFORMATION MAP

Use this map to export the earned value fields for tasks to any of the file formats. It includes these fields: task ID, task Name, BCWS, BCWP, ACWP, SV, CV, EAC, BAC, and VAC.

For more information about these fields, see "The Earned Value Fields and Report" in Chapter 17, "Analyzing Progress and Revising the Schedule."

USING THE EXPORT TO HTML USING STANDARD TEMPLATE MAP

Use this map to export basic task, resource, and assignment values to an HTML document. The task table includes the ID, Name, Duration, Start, Finish, Resource Names, and % Complete fields. The resource table includes the ID, Name, Group, Max Units, and Peak fields. The assignment table includes the Task ID, Task and Resource Names, Work, Start, Finish, and % Work Complete fields.

See "Exporting Project Data to the Internet or an Intranet," later in this chapter, for more details about the HTML format.

USING THE RESOURCE "EXPORT TABLE" MAP

Use this map to export the fields that are included in the predefined resource Export table. The resource Export table is a fairly comprehensive set of 24 resource fields that covers the definition of the resource as well as scheduled, baseline, and tracking sums for work and cost for each resource.

USING THE TASK "EXPORT TABLE" MAP

Use this map to export nearly all the fields that are included in the predefined task Export table. The 74 fields that are exported include task definition fields; values for scheduled, baseline, and actual work, cost, duration, start, and finish; and a large number of the user-definable text, cost, duration, number, and flag fields.

USING THE TASK AND RESOURCE PIVOTTABLE MAP

Use this map to create an Excel document with two PivotTables that summarize the total cost of resource assignments. Both PivotTables are organized by resource groups and within each group by resource names. The resulting Excel file will contain four sheets in all:

- The Tasks sheet provides the data for the Task PivotTable and includes these columns: Resource Group, Resource Name, Task Name(s), Duration, Start, Finish, and Cost. If your project is outlined, there is a Task Name column for each outline level and all summary task names for a subtask will appear on the row for the subtask. Its outline level 1 summary task will be in the column named Task Name 1, its outline level 2 summary task will be in the column named Task Name 2, and so forth.

- The Task PivotTable sheet shows for each resource the tasks to which it is assigned along with the task duration, start, and finish. The Cost for each assignment is the data field in the PivotTable and there are summary costs for each task and summary task, for each resource, and for each resource group.

- The Resources sheet provides the data for the Resource PivotTable and includes the Resource Group, Resource Name, Work, and Cost.

- The Resource PivotTable shows the cost totals for each resource without the breakdown by task, with subtotals for each resource group.

Note

If your project has more than two outline levels, Project will create the data sheets and the PivotTables but it will not be able to perform the layout of fields for the Task PivotTable, and that sheet will appear to be empty. You will have to manually do the layout within Excel.

See the section "Exporting to an Excel PivotTable," later in this chapter, for more information about working with PivotTables.

USING THE TASK LIST WITH EMBEDDED ASSIGNMENT ROWS MAP

Use this map to export an HTML table of tasks and their assigned resources. This map is best used to export a table that, along with all the resource assignments to each task, also includes the Work, Duration, Start, Finish, and % Work Complete fields for each assignment. All the caveats about exporting to Excel or Access that were mentioned earlier for the "Who Does What" Report map apply to this map as well.

USING THE TOP LEVEL TASKS LIST MAP

Use this map to export a table that shows only the outline level 1 tasks. The fields include the task ID, Name, Duration, Start and Finish dates, % Complete, Cost, and Work. This map works for all file formats.

CREATING IMPORT/EXPORT MAPS FOR ACCESS AND ODBC SOURCES

Creating an Import/Export map is fairly straightforward, once you understand the mechanism. Project does most of the work, at least if you stick to general cases. To illustrate, we will first create an export map to send selected cost data for tasks, resources, and assignments to an Access database. Then we will modify the same map to import a more limited set of data from the Access database. The same map could be used for an ODBC database as well.

CREATING AND USING AN EXPORT MAP

Export maps are easier to create than import maps for the simple reason that the Project field names are the source of the data, and you can create field names in the target format that are similar to the Project field names. With import maps, the field names in the source may not be as easy to relate to the field names in Project.

To create a map for exporting some of Project's cost data to an Access 2000 database, follow these steps:

1. Open the Project file whose data you want to export.

2. Choose File, Save As.

3. Select the directory location in the Save In list box.

4. In the Save as Type list box, select the Microsoft Access Databases (*.mdb) file type.

5. If you are creating a new database, type its name in the File Name text box.

Tip from Tim and the Project Team

If you are going to append data to an existing database, I recommend that you create a copy of the database for testing while creating the new map. Then, when the map behaves as you want, you can use it to append to the intended database and you can delete the test database.

Tip from Tim and the Project Team

In general, I suggest that you do not add partial project data sets to an Access database that already contains complete projects. Project will not let you add selective data to the tables it has already created in the database; so, you would have to create your own named tables to hold the data, which you might as well do in a special database that is dedicated to partial data sets.

6. Click the Save button to display the Save To Database dialog box.

7. Click the Selective Data tab to display the list of maps and the tools for managing them (see Figure 19.9).

You can select an existing map to use, create a New Map, Edit an existing map, Copy a map as a starting point for a map to edit, or open the Organizer to copy maps from other Project files and other templates to this list.

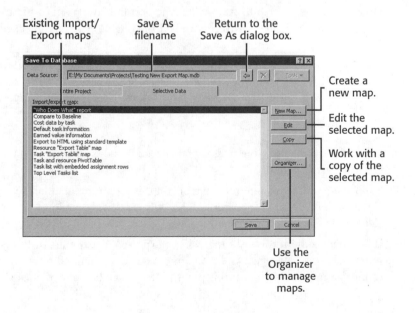

Existing Import/
Export maps

Save As
filename

Return to the
Save As dialog box.

Figure 19.9
Use the Save To
Database dialog box
to manage the maps
that determine how
data is exchanged
with other formats.

Create a
new map.

Edit the
selected map.

Work with a
copy of the
selected map.

Use the
Organizer
to manage
maps.

8. Choose the New Map button to advance to the Define Import/Export Map dialog box (see Figure 19.10).

Assign a name to the new map

Figure 19.10
Use the Options tab of the Define Import/Export Map dialog box to assign a name to the map and to choose what type of data tables will be created.

Select data table types.

9. On the Options tab, type a name for the map that will help you remember the map's focus in the Import/Export Map Name text box. Also, select one or more of the check boxes for the types of data you want to store in the new format. When you check a table check box, the tab for that table type becomes available. In Figure 19.11 the map name will be Cost Data for Access and all three table types are checked.

Tip from Tim and the Project Team

If you design a map for use with one file format—for instance, with HTML—and then use the map to exchange data with another application, such as Access, the results might be very different. For specialized maps it's a good idea to include the application name in the map name.

10. Select the tab for the table type(s) you checked on the Options tab. We will start with the Task Mapping tab.

11. Supply a descriptive name for the table on this tab in the field labeled Destination Database Table Name. In Figure 19.12, you see that the table to be created will be called Cost Summary by Task.

12. If you want to limit the tasks that will be exported, use the list of filters in the Export Filter field to select a task filter. Any of the currently defined filters can be chosen. You cannot design a new filter at this point. Filters must be defined ahead of time.

Figure 19.11
This map will be called Cost Data for Access and will include fields from the task, resource, and assignment tables in Microsoft Project.

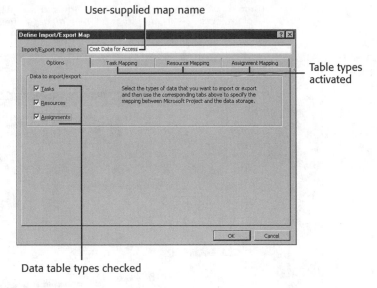

User-supplied map name

Table types activated

Data table types checked

Supply this table's name.

Select a predefined filter here.

Figure 19.12
Use a Project filter to control which tasks will be exported; but you must already have defined the filter before starting the export.

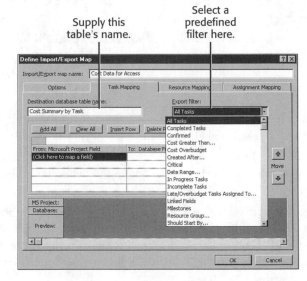

PART

VI

CH

19

13. Now you must define the task fields that will be exported in the mapping table. You must list each of the Project fields that are to be exported in the column labeled From: Microsoft Project Field. You must create a name for the database field that will hold that data in the column labeled To: Database Field. The data type will be filled in automatically from the Project field types.

Click the list arrow in the first cell in the left column—the cell that displays the prompt Click Here to Map a Field. The complete list of Microsoft Project task fields will be displayed (see Figure 19.13).

Drop-down list
of Project's
field names

Names for
exported fields

Tools to
help manage
the field list

Move selected
field up or down
in the list.

Figure 19.13
Select a Project field
name to be exported
from the list.

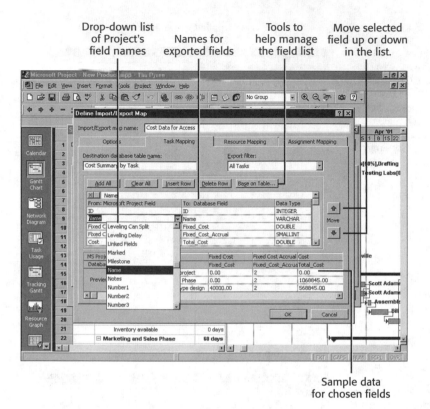

Sample data
for chosen fields

14. Select the field to be exported from the list of Project fields and press Enter to complete the selection. A default field name is inserted in the second column (for the exported database) and the field data type will be inserted in the third column.

Below the mapping table, you will see a sample of the fields you have added and the data they contain.

You can change the export field name to suit your tastes. Be sure, however, that you don't violate any field-naming rules of the format you are creating. For example, for an Access database field names can't have leading spaces or include periods, exclamation marks, or square brackets. You can, however, replace the underscore word separator in the field names suggested by Project.

Note

When exporting to Access you should leave the underscore word separators that Project supplies in place. Although Access will accept (nonleading) spaces in field names, the Microsoft Project procedure that creates the table for Access thinks that spaces are not allowed and will display the error message seen in Figure 19.14.

Figure 19.14
Improper field names for the fields to be created in Access tables will keep Project from completing the creation of an Access database.

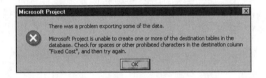

15. Continue this process for each field you want to export.

    There are several buttons that can speed the process of managing the field mapping table (refer to Figure 19.13):

    - To move a field row in the list, select the row to be moved and use the Move arrows on the right side of the mapping table to move the row up or down in the list.

    - To insert all the task fields in Microsoft Project, select the Add All button.

    - To clear the mapping table, select the Clear All button.

    - To insert a blank row for a new field in the middle of the list, select the place where the row should be inserted and click the Insert Row button.

    - To remove a field row, select the row to be removed and click the Delete Row button.

    - To populate the mapping table with the same fields that are contained in one of the task tables in Microsoft Project, select the Base on Table button. The Select Base Table for Field Mapping dialog box will appear (see Figure 19.15) with a list of all the currently defined task tables. Select the table you want to use and click OK. The field list will be cleared from the mapping table, and the fields that are defined in the table you selected will be inserted in the mapping table.

Predefined list
of task tables

Figure 19.15
You can fill the mapping table with the fields defined in a Project table by using the Base on Table button.

16. When the task mapping table is completed, move on to the next table you have elected to include in the database export. In the example, the Resource Mapping tab is selected (see Figure 19.16). The table name will be Summary by Resource and the fields were filled in by selecting the Cost table from the list displayed by the Base on Table button.

Note that you can also apply a resource filter to select a subset of the resource records to be included in the Export table.

Resource table name

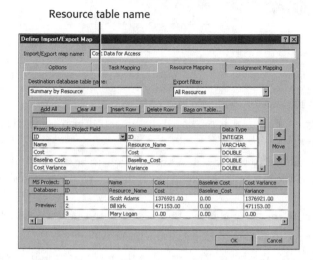

Figure 19.16
The resource mapping table is defined in the same way as the task mapping table is defined.

17. Finally, if you are including assignment fields, choose the Assignment Mapping tab and repeat the process (see Figure 19.17).

The assignment records are the details that are combined for the task and resource cost summaries. Because there is no table in Microsoft Project for assignments (they only appear in the Task Usage and Resource Usage views and on certain forms), you cannot choose a table as a template for the fields to be included. Also, there are no filters for assignments. Both these options are dimmed on the Assignment Mapping tab.

Assignment table name

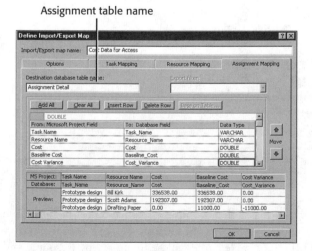

Figure 19.17
The assignment mapping table has fewer options than the task and resource mapping tables.

18. When all the tabs are filled in, click OK to save the export map. You will be returned to the Save To Database dialog box, and your new map will be selected in the list of maps.

19. Choose the Save button to export the selected data to the database name you entered in the Save As dialog box at the beginning of these steps.

CREATING AND USING AN IMPORT MAP

When you want to import data into Microsoft Project from another source, you must find a workable import map or create one of your own. If the data was originally exported from Microsoft Project, use the same map for the import that you used for the export. Or, if you want to make slight changes, it is easy to copy the export map and edit the copy to produce the new import map.

The options for an import map are slightly different from those found on the export map:

- The source tables are already defined (whereas you defined the target tables in the export map). For example, there may be many tables in the source database that have task information in them. You must choose the table containing the task data you need. Similarly, you must identify the source tables that are appropriate for supplying resource or assignment fields.

    If you created the source by exporting fields from Project, it will be much easier because the field names will be recognizable. But, if the source table was created from a source other than Project, the field names will have to be matched with Project's internal fields.

- You cannot import only a portion of the records using any of the Project filters. If you want only part of the records from the source, you will have to filter the source first to produce a new database and then import the resulting tables into Project. Alternatively, you could import all the data into Project and then delete the unwanted records.

- When importing, you can choose whether the imported data will be stored in a new project file or merged into an existing Project document. You can append the imported records to the records already existing in a Project document. You can also choose to merge the imported data by using it to update selected fields for already existing tasks or resources.

To illustrate importing from another file format, we will import from the cost database that was created earlier in explaining the export map process.

1. If you intend to add the imported data to an existing Project document, then you must open that project before starting the import process. Otherwise, it doesn't matter which project documents are open when you import, because Project will create a new document.

2. Choose File, Open or click the Open tool.

3. Select the location of the data source in the Look In list box.

    If you are importing from an ODBC data source, choose the ODBC button instead and select the data source in that dialog box.

4. In the Files of Type list box, select the format of the data source.

5. Choose the data source file from the file list and click the Open button.

6. In the Open From Database dialog box, choose the Selective Data tab (in many cases it will be your only choice).

7. Select the map that you plan to use for importing. Or, start a New Map (following the same techniques outlined for creating an export map). If there is an existing map that is similar to the map you need, then Copy it and Edit the copy.

8. You should always Edit the map you plan to use to be sure that it defines the desired import process. Figure 19.18 illustrates the errors you will see in the mapping tables if you choose the wrong map. If the map names source fields that don't exist in the file you have started to open, the field name entries will be in red and will have an OUT OF CONTEXT: prefix in the From: Database Field column.

Wrong map selected

Figure 19.18
If you have chosen the wrong predefined map for an import file, it will be apparent if you examine its tabs.

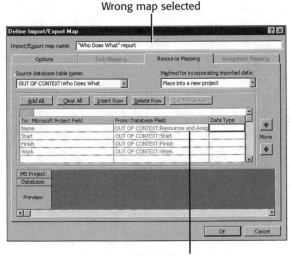

Field names in map are
not found in the source data.

9. Look at each tab to verify the settings. You should pull down the list of names in the Source Database Table Name field to verify that the appropriate table has been chosen for each tab. If you don't want the data from one of the tables, clear the check box for that table on the Options tab.

Figure 19.19 shows the import map that is derived from the export map we created earlier, with the Task Mapping tab selected. The Source Database Table Name list is pulled down to show the tables that are found in the source database.

Source database table names

Figure 19.19
The map that you defined as an export map will have a few different options compared to the original export map.

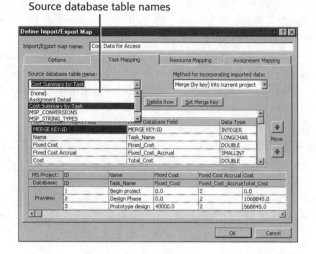

Note

The list of source database table names will contain more tables than those you explicitly defined in your export map. These extra table names have an MSP_ prefix and they are there to help the user decipher the data values that were exported.

10. Examine the option labeled Method for Incorporating Imported Data (see Figure 19.20).

- Choose Place Into a New Project to start a new Project document with the imported data.

- Choose Append to End of Current Project to add these records (task records in this case) beneath the task records already in the project.

- Choose Merge (By Key) Into Current Project to have Microsoft Project match incoming records with existing records and update the fields with the imported values.

Drop-down list for methods of incorporating imported data

Figure 19.20
You can start a new project file with the imported data, or you can incorporate the imported data into an existing project file.

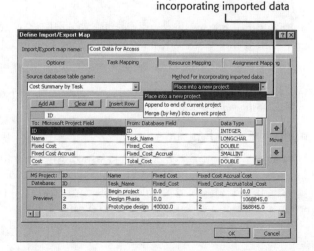

11. If you choose to merge the imported data, the Set Merge Key button becomes active. Select a field that will have the same values in both the existing Project file and the imported table.

For example, the task ID field would match tasks as long as the task list has not been edited since the exported data was created. It would have been better to include the Unique ID field in the export because that ID number doesn't change after a task is created and is a more reliable key field.

After you have selected the key field, click the Set Merge Key button. The field name will change to MERGE KEY: field name (for example, MERGE KEY: ID in Figure 19.21). If you need to change the MERGE KEY field, simply select the new key field and click the Set Merge Key button again.

Note

If you want to merge assignment data, you must use the Unique ID field for assignments.

Selected key field   Set Merge Key tool

Figure 19.21
One field must be selected as the Merge Key field to identify matching records when imported data is to be merged with existing data.

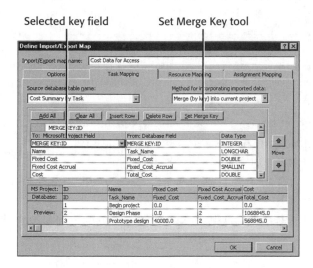

12. Repeat the process outlined previously for all the tabs to verify that they have been set correctly. When finished, choose the OK button to save the import map.

13. Choose the Open button on the Open From Database dialog box to begin the import.

If you don't see the imported data in Project after the import operation is finished, see "Missing Imported Data" in the "Troubleshooting" section at the end of this chapter.

WORKING WITH MICROSOFT EXCEL FORMATS

You can export field data to Microsoft Excel workbooks as worksheet data or as PivotTable data, and you can import table data, but not PivotTables. When you export to Excel, Microsoft Project creates an Excel file in the Excel 5.0/95 format which makes the data available to that version and all later versions of Excel. You can import from Excel documents that were saved in Excel 4.0 format or any later format, including Excel 2000.

There are a few options that are different on the Import/Export map for working with the Excel format:

- You can choose whether or not to export field names as the first row of the worksheet. If you choose not to export field names, the field data will go in row 1 of the worksheet and there will be no column titles unless you add them later.

- You can instruct Project to include assignment rows such as those displayed in the tables of the Task Usage and Resource Usage views. The worksheet rows will not be automatically outlined and indented in the Excel workbook as they are in Project.

  Of course, you can use Excel's Outlining command to group assignments under the task or resource, and this will make it possible to hide and display the assignment rows at will (as in Project). But, you will have to do this by hand, and when the assignment rows are displayed, they still will not be indented.

Tip from Tim and the Project Team

> Remember to change Excel's default grouping direction. Choose Data, Group and Outline, Settings and clear the Summary Rows Below Detail check box.

SAVING PROJECT DATA AS AN EXCEL WORKSHEET

You can use an Import/Export map you created for other formats to export Project data to Excel. You might want to create a copy and save it with a name that indicates it's for Excel. In the following example, the map for exporting to Excel is based on the Cost Data map developed previously for exporting to Access.

To export Project data to an Excel workbook, use these steps:

1. Open the Project document that you want to export.
2. Choose File, Save As to display the Save As dialog box.
3. Select the location for the new file in the Save In list box.
4. Change the Save as Type selection to Microsoft Excel Workbook (*.XLS).
5. Supply the name for the file in the File Name text box.
6. Choose the Save button. Project will display the Export Mapping dialog box.
7. Select or create a map to use for exporting the data. Be sure you open the map for editing if it was created earlier. There are options for Excel that don't appear on maps when used for Access, for example. Figure 19.22 shows a copy of the Cost Data for Access map open for editing. The name is changed to reflect its use with Excel.
8. On the Options tab, in the Microsoft Excel Options group, fill the check box labeled Export Header Row/Import Includes Headers. If filled, the first row on each sheet in the workbook will display field names as column headers. If this check box is empty, there will be no labels at the top of the columns in the workbook.
9. If you want tasks and resources to show details by assignment (as in the Task Usage and Resource Usage views), fill the check box labeled Include Assignment Rows in Output, and remember to include the field named Assignment so you can distinguish assignments from tasks or resources.

Figure 19.22
You can include assignment rows with task and resource data to identify which records are tasks or resources and which are assignments.

Default name for copied map

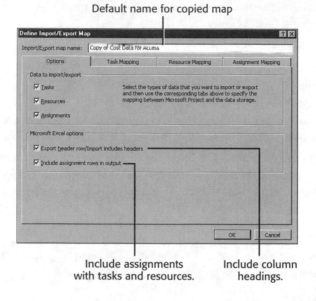

Include assignments with tasks and resources.

Include column headings.

> **Caution**
>
> If you export the rows for the assignment details in a task mapping, the assignment rows will appear to be just additional tasks in the workbook that is created. If you imported that workbook back into Project, the resource assignments would indeed be listed as tasks, even if you included the task Assignment field in the exported data. Similarly, exported assignment details in a resource mapping result in the assignments being treated as additional resources, and they cannot be imported back into Project satisfactorily.

10. Click OK to save the revised map.

11. Choose the Save button on the Export Mapping dialog box to initiate the export.

When the exported data is opened in Excel, there is a worksheet for each of the tables that were defined in the export map in Project (see Figure 19.23). As specified in the export map, the field names appear in the first row of the worksheet and the assignments for each resource are listed under the row for the resource.

> **Caution**
>
> If you sort the rows in the worksheet, you will not be able to tell which assignments go with which tasks or resources. Be very careful about sorting.

EXPORTING TO AN EXCEL PIVOTTABLE

Excel PivotTables summarize data in crosstab calculations, and they offer truly impressive flexibility for easily changing which calculations will be presented and in what level of detail. When you export to the Excel PivotTable format, the export map will let you choose the fields to be included for one or more of the three categories—tasks, resources, and assignments. A separate PivotTable will be created for each category and all will be stored in the same Excel workbook. The save operation will not only copy the selected data into Excel data sheets but will also create separate sheets for the PivotTables that are based on the data sheets.

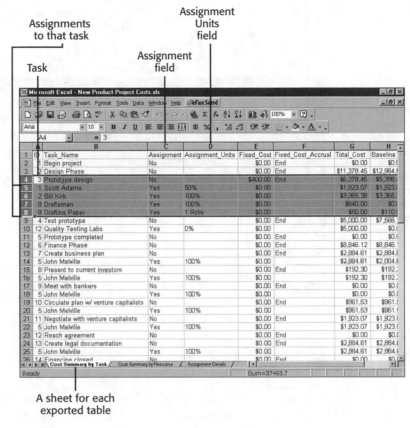

Figure 19.23
The Excel file shows the Project data that was exported. The Prototype Design task and its assignments are selected on the Cost Summary by Task worksheet.

For example, we will export task and resource assignment costs to an Excel PivotTable. Each record will contain the name of a top-level task (a phase of the project), the name of a resource assigned to a task in that phase, and the scheduled cost of the assignment. The resulting PivotTable usually needs editing to produce the results you want, but with a little effort in Excel you can produce a useful report. In Figure 19.24, the edited PivotTable for our example displays the data in a compact table that neatly summarizes the following items:

- The total cost for any phase of the project along with the distribution of that cost among contributing resources in dollar amounts and in percentage terms

- The distribution for each resource of cost in the different phases of the project

The row headings shown in Figure 19.24 are the top-level tasks—in this case, the phases of the project. The column headings are the resource names. The summary data (the numbers in the body of the table) are calculated by Excel by

- Summing the cost amount from all assignment records that have the same combination of phase task name and resource name

- Expressing the sum as a percentage of the total for its row

Figure 19.24
Reading across the PivotTable, you see which resources worked on each phase and the percentage distribution of costs among resources for that phase. Reading down, you see the phases on which a given resource worked.

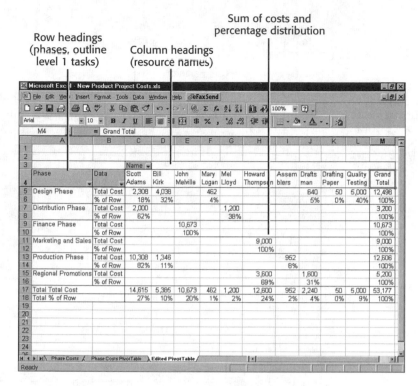

Creating a PivotTable such as this involves exporting the data and then fine-tuning the PivotTable in Excel to produce the results you want. The export operation creates only the simplest of PivotTables. For example, there will be no column headings like those in Figure 19.24, and there will be only one data item in the body of the table. You can edit the PivotTable yourself to add these and other enhancements.

To export Project data to an Excel PivotTable, follow these steps:

1. Open the Project file from which you want to export data.

2. Choose File, Save As.

3. Select the location for the new Excel file in the Save In list box, and provide a name for the file in the File Name text box.

4. Choose the file type Microsoft Excel Pivot Table (.XLS) in the Save as Type list box.

5. Choose the Save button.

6. In the Export Mapping dialog box, choose New Map to display the Define Import/Export Map dialog box.

7. On the Options tab, provide a name for the map in the Import/Export Map Name text box. Because PivotTable maps are so distinctive, I suggest including the word PivotTable in the map name, as in Figure 19.25.

8. Select one or more of the data category check boxes in the Data to Import/Export group: Tasks, Resources, and Assignments.

   You can only use one category for each PivotTable. If you export fields from all three categories, you will produce three separate, unrelated PivotTables in the same Excel workbook. The Task table data will be exported to create a Cost PivotTable similar to the one illustrated previously in Figure 19.24.

9. Click the tab for the data category you have selected.

10. Provide a name for the worksheet in the Destination Worksheet Name text box (see Figure 19.26).

Only task
category selected   New map's name

Figure 19.25
You can include tasks, resources, and assignments when exporting to a PivotTable, but each category will be a separate PivotTable in the resulting Excel workbook.

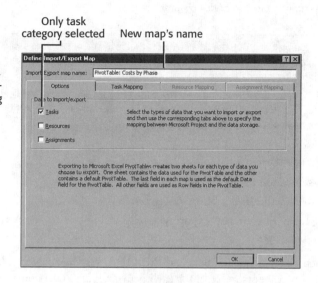

Sheet name   Last field is the field
for Excel   for the data area in
                    the PivotTable.

Figure 19.26
The last field in the mapping table will appear in red with the prefix Pivot Data Field: to remind you that this field will be the calculated body of the PivotTable.

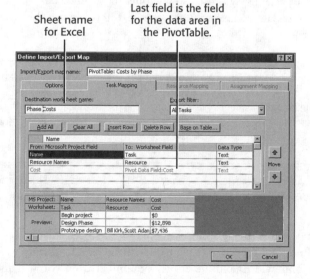

11. Enter the names of the Project fields you want to export in the From: Microsoft Project Field column. When you enter a Project field name, Project will supply the field name for the worksheet in the To: Worksheet Field column. Feel free to modify the worksheet field names.

The last field entered in the mapping table will be the field that Excel uses for the table data (the calculated summary numbers in the body of the PivotTable). To remind you of this, Project displays the last field row in red, and adds the prefix Pivot Data Field: before the export field name. If you edit the export field name, Project will replace the prefix as long as it is the last field name row.

⚠ *If the last field row is not red in your PivotTable map, see "Malfunctioning PivotTable Map" in the "Troubleshooting" section at the end of this chapter.*

Tip from Tim and the Project Team	If you plan to group the data in the PivotTable by major categories with minor category details listed under them, put the major category fields above the minor category fields in the field mapping.
	Always make the field you want to be used for calculations the last field in the field mapping list. In this example, Cost is the last field listed because you want calculations based on its values to appear in the body of the PivotTable.

12. When the field map is completed, repeat the process for any other data category tab you have chosen to use in the export.

13. Choose OK to save the Import/Export map.

14. Choose the Save button on the Export Mapping dialog box to begin saving the exported data into Excel.

Now, you can open Excel to see the data and PivotTable you have created (see Figure 19.27). You will see two sheets in Excel for each data category (tab) you exported. In this example, only the Task category is used so you only see a single pair of sheets. The first sheet contains the raw data you exported in a table. You could use this data to create a PivotTable on your own.

Tip from Tim and the Project Team	If you include the task Name field in the Task Mapping list of fields, Project will create multiple Task Name columns in the worksheet—one for each outline level. For any subtask, its outline level 1 summary task will appear in the Task Name 1 column, its outline level 2 summary task will appear in the Task Name 2 column, and so forth (refer to Figure 19.27).

Tip from Tim and the Project Team	If you include the Resource Names field in the Task Mapping list of fields, Project will create a separate record for each resource name assigned to the task (refer to Figure 19.27).

The second sheet contains the default PivotTable that Project created (see Figure 19.28). You will need to fine-tune the PivotTable in almost all cases. Not only will you need to format things like column widths and the display of numbers, but you will also need to adjust the layout of the PivotTable. Specifically, there are no column categories in the default PivotTable, and we want the resource names to appear as column headings. Also, there is only one calculation in the data area and we want to show the percentage distribution in addition to the sum of the costs.

Figure 19.27
Project places all the data you export into a plain worksheet that is the source for the PivotTable.

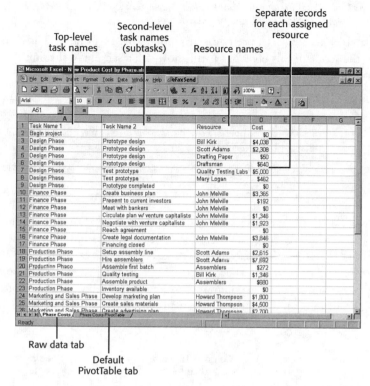

Top-level task names — Second-level task names (subtasks) — Resource names — Separate records for each assigned resource

Raw data tab
Default PivotTable tab

Figure 19.28
The default PivotTable that Project creates is rarely satisfactory as is—you will need to use Excel to create the finished product.

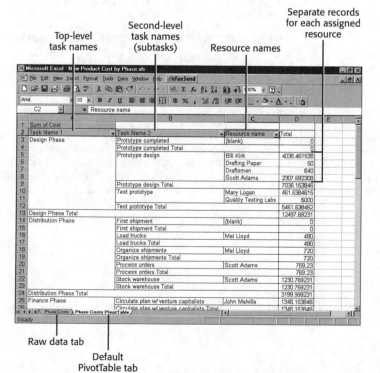

Top-level task names — Second-level task names (subtasks) — Resource names — Separate records for each assigned resource

Raw data tab
Default PivotTable tab

If the PivotTable sheet in your workbook is blank, see "Empty Exported PivotTable" in the "Troubleshooting" section at the end of this chapter.

Fortunately, Excel makes it pretty easy to modify the PivotTable. Those techniques are beyond the scope of this book but I will show you a sample of the finished result after I edit the PivotTable in Figure 19.28.

Note

For information about using PivotTables, see Chapter 20, "Using PivotTables and PivotCharts," in *Special Edition Using Microsoft Excel 2000* (0-7897-1929-8) by Patrick Blattner (also published by Que).

Also, there is an entire section of help articles within Excel 2000. See "Analyzing Data with PivotTable Reports" in the Excel Help contents.

The PivotTable in Figure 19.29 shows only the top-level tasks that are summary tasks (in other words, top-level tasks that do not summarize phases have been hidden). The resource names appear across column headings with data for each resource in the column below its name. A second calculation has been added to show the percentage of the phase costs attributable to the resource in that column. This figure also shows a few minor formatting changes (zero values are suppressed, decimals are removed, and so forth) just to improve the readability.

Figure 19.29
With task details suppressed, and a few other formatting changes, the PivotTable is presentable. With a relatively small effort, you can export Project data to Excel PivotTables for a powerful reporting tool.

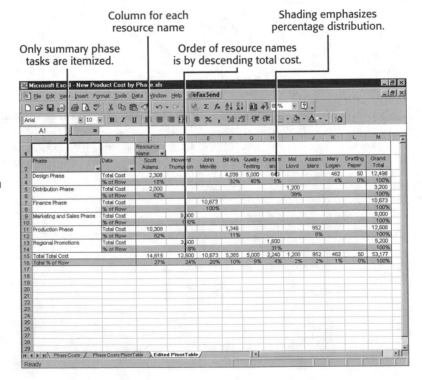

IMPORTING PROJECT DATA FROM THE EXCEL FORMAT

Importing data from original sources outside Microsoft Project into a Project document has to be done with extreme care. You will have to be sure that the data is mapped to the correct Project fields and that the data type is appropriate for those fields.

Caution

As explained earlier, if the Excel workbook was created by exporting tasks or resources from Microsoft Project, and if the option to include rows for resource assignments was selected, then some of the rows in the workbook will be tasks (or resources) and others will be assignment details. Do not attempt to import data from a workbook like this. Identify and remove the assignment details before attempting to import the data back into Project.

The simple example that follows shows how to add a list of new employees to the resource roster in a Project file. The list is stored in Sheet 1 of an Excel worksheet. The names are to be added to the Resource data in the New Product project file where a new product development is being planned. The column headings are not exact matches for Project field names, and there are text entries in the overtime rate field where Project expects to find only numbers. Figure 19.30 shows the data from the worksheet.

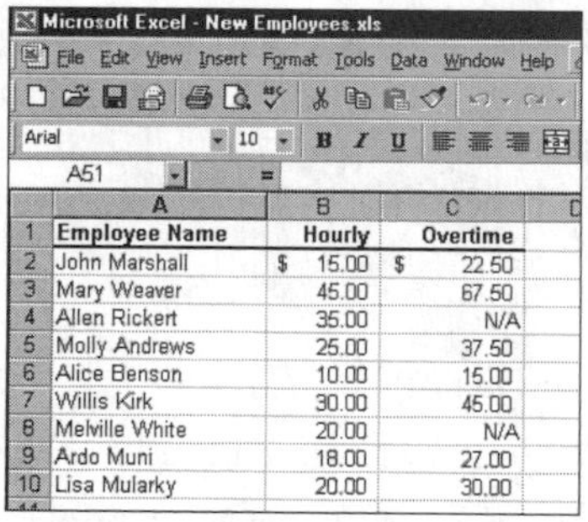

	A	B	C
1	Employee Name	Hourly	Overtime
2	John Marshall	$ 15.00	$ 22.50
3	Mary Weaver	45.00	67.50
4	Allen Rickert	35.00	N/A
5	Molly Andrews	25.00	37.50
6	Alice Benson	10.00	15.00
7	Willis Kirk	30.00	45.00
8	Melville White	20.00	N/A
9	Ardo Muni	18.00	27.00
10	Lisa Mularky	20.00	30.00

Figure 19.30 The New Employee worksheet contains new resources and their pay rates, which we can import into Project.

To import the data from Excel into the Project file, follow these steps:

1. Open the Project file into which you want to import the data, unless you plan to have Project create a new document file for the imported data. Figure 19.31 shows the Project Resource sheet before the import.
2. Although not necessary, choose a view in Project that will show the data when it is imported. This is especially helpful if you're not sure what Project field names to use for some of the imported data. For example, in the Resource sheet the employee's name should go in the column labeled Resource Name, but the actual name of that field is just Name. Similarly, the real field name for the Std. Rate and Ovt. Rate columns are Standard Rate and Overtime Rate. You must know these field names when you map the imported data.

Figure 19.31
The current resource roster in the New Product Project file contains 12 names.

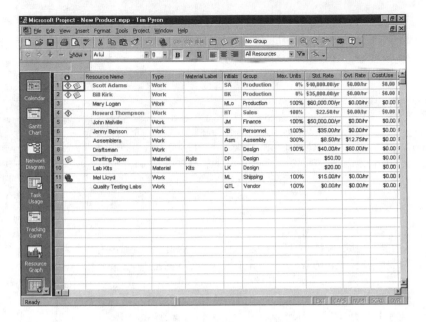

Tip from Tim and the Project Team

To see the real field name for a column, double-click the column heading for the field to display the Column Definition dialog box. Figure 19.32 shows the column definition for the column labeled Resource Name. Resource Name is the Title for the column, but the Field Name is Name. Choose Cancel to close the dialog box without changing the column definition.

3. Choose File, Open to display the Open dialog box.

4. Use the Look In list box to select the location in which the Excel workbook is saved.

5. Change the Files of Type selection to Microsoft Excel Workbooks.

6. Select the Excel file from the file list and choose the Open button.

7. Choose the New Map button in the Import Mapping dialog box to display the Define Import/Export Map dialog box.

8. On the Options tab, provide a name for the map and select the check boxes for the type of data you are importing. In this example, we are importing only resource data (see Figure 19.33) and the map name will be New Employees.

   Also, be sure there is a check mark in the box labeled Export Header Row/Import Includes Headers. If you don't check the Headers box, the map's field list will not display the Excel column headers (it will just number the columns) and that will make it difficult for you to know which Excel column maps to which Project field.

   Note that the option to import assignment detail rows is not available. Project has no way of knowing which rows are tasks (or resources) and which are assignment details.

Title displayed
in this table

Official name
of the field

Figure 19.32
The column definition
for the Resource
Name column shows
that the name of the
field is Name. Be sure
to click Cancel to
avoid changing the
column definition.

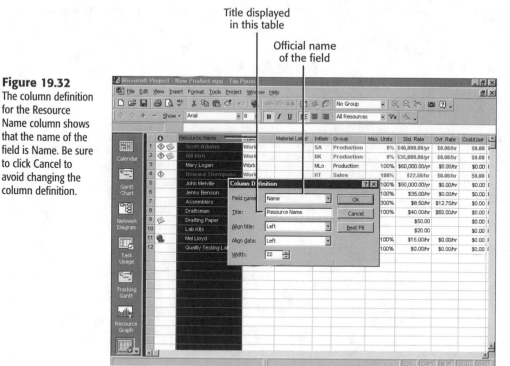

Project table to
receive the data

Map name

Figure 19.33
You will need
the headers to be
imported to help you
match the imported
data with Project
fields.

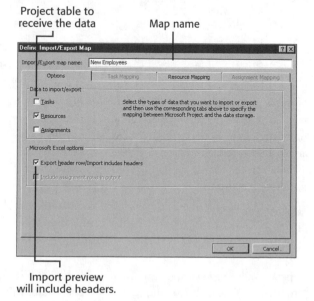

Import preview
will include headers.

9. Choose the tab for the data types you are importing. In this example, the Resource Mapping tab is selected (see Figure 19.34).

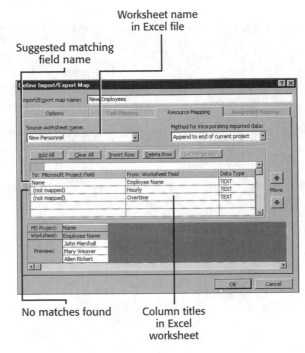

Figure 19.34
You must select which sheet in the workbook contains the data you want to import.

10. Use the list arrow in the Source Worksheet Name list box and select the worksheet you want to use. In this case, we will use a sheet that is named New Personnel.

    When the source worksheet is selected, Project fills the From: Worksheet Field column in the center of the mapping table with the column headings from the worksheet (but only if you checked the Export Header Row/Import Includes Headers box on the Options tab) and attempts to find a matching field name from Project in the left column. As you saw in Figure 19.34, Project suggests a close match for the first field (it offers Name as the Project field for Excel's Employee Name column), but it found no match for the other two columns.

11. Supply the correct field names in the first column of the mapping table (see Figure 19.35). You can type the field name into the Edit bar just above the table, or you can use the in-place arrow control to display the list of all Project field names and select the correct one from the list.

12. Select the appropriate method for importing the data in the list box labeled Method for Incorporating Imported Data. In this example, the imported data will be appended to the bottom of the existing resource sheet.

13. Choose OK to save the import map.

Figure 19.35
Use the drop-down list of field names to select the correct field to receive the imported data.

14. Choose the <u>O</u>pen button in the Import Mapping dialog box to begin the import.

15. If there is a problem with the data types being imported into any field, you will see a warning message like that displayed in Figure 19.36.

    - Choose <u>Y</u>es to continue importing and to continue seeing error messages. You should generally choose this option unless you know what the problems are and what corrective action you will need to take in the Project document as a result.

    - Choose <u>N</u>o to continue importing without seeing further error messages.

    - Choose Cancel to stop importing.

Caution

The mismatched data will not be imported into Project, and the affected field in Project will display a default value. You will need to find these holes in the data and manually supply the correct information.

It's a good idea to jot down the source references in the warning message (refer to Figure 19.36). If you are importing a lot of data at once, the references will help you locate the problem in the source file so you can determine where you need to look in the Project file to fill in the missing information.

16. Review any data type mismatches and correct the entries in the Project file.

    The imported resource names will be added below the existing names in the resource pool (see Figure 19.37) and Project has changed the Overtime Rate values for the "N/A" values to zero.

PART
VI

CH
19

Location of error
in source file

Figure 19.36
If there is a data mis-
match during import-
ing, Project will warn
you and let you
choose how to pro-
ceed.

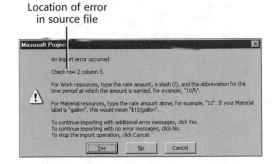

Caution

When importing task start or finish dates, Project treats the imported dates as though you
had typed them instead of letting Project calculate them. In other words, the tasks are
assigned the soft constraint Start No Earlier Than (for fixed start date projects) or Finish No
Later Than (for fixed finish date projects). You can reset these task constraints to As Soon
As Possible or As Late As Possible after the tasks are imported into Project.

*Tip from Tim and
the Project Team*

If you are importing dates and there is no time of day attached to the source date, Project
will assign the time of midnight to the date, for both start and finish date fields. If there is a
time of day attached to the date, Project will keep the time unless it falls before the default
start time or after the default end time (as defined on the Options dialog box, Calendar
tab); in which case, Project will substitute the default time of day.

"N/A" values set
to default (zero)

New imported records

Figure 19.37
The imported names
are appended to the
bottom of the
resource roster.

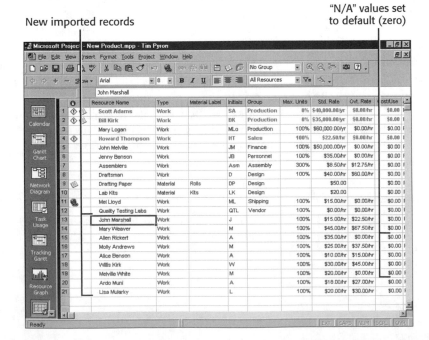

EXPORTING PROJECT DATA TO THE INTERNET OR AN INTRANET

You can create pages for your intranet or the Internet by exporting Project data to the HTM format. HTML (Hypertext Markup Language) is currently the standard format for Internet browsers. You can save Project data to the HTML format, but you cannot import Project data from the HTML format.

Exporting to the HTML format was covered in detail in Chapter 14, "Publishing Projects on the Web."

WORKING WITH TEXT FILE FORMATS

Project supports two ASCII text formats: tab-delimited and CSV (comma-separated value). The Import/Export maps for both these formats are almost the same as the Import/Export maps for Excel. However, you can import or export with all three of Project's data field tables at once in Excel (Tasks, Resources, and Assignments), but you can only import or export one Project table at a time with the text formats.

EXPORTING PROJECT DATA IN THE TEXT FORMATS

Suppose you want to export a list of project milestones to a text file. Follow these steps:

1. Open the project file you want to export from.
2. Choose File, Save As.
3. Select the directory for the new text file in the Save In list box.
4. Select the file format in the Save as Type list box. For a tab-delimited file, select Text (Tab delimited) (*.TXT). This format places tab characters between each field of data in a record (with quote marks surrounding field values that contain commas) and separates the records with a paragraph mark (carriage return and line feed).

   For a comma-delimited file, select CSV (Comma delimited, *.CSV). This format places commas between each field of data in a record (with quote marks surrounding field values that themselves contain commas) and separates the records with a paragraph mark (carriage return and line feed).
5. In the Export Mapping dialog box, choose New Map if you do not have a map for this purpose.
6. The Define Import/Export Map dialog box has option buttons instead of check boxes for selecting the data type (Tasks, Resources, or Assignments) to export or import. The Milestones map in Figure 19.38 shows the Tasks data selected.
7. Leave Export Header Row/Import Includes Headers checked so that the exported data will be labeled.
8. Check Include Assignment Rows in Output if you want assignments to be included. Remember that assignments will be indistinguishable from tasks or resources unless you include the Assignment field to identify them.
9. Use the Text Delimiter drop-down list if you want to use either the Space or Comma as a delimiter instead of the Tab character.

Export field labels.

Select only one data type.

Text Delimiter

Figure 19.38
The Define Import/Export Map dialog box allows you to work with only one table at a time.

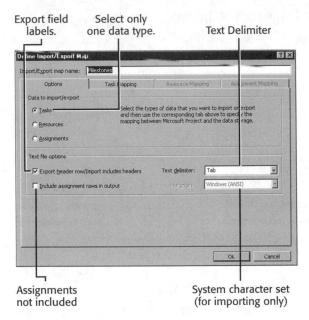

Assignments not included

System character set (for importing only)

10. Select the tab for the data type you have chosen to export and define the fields you want to export just as described for an Excel map.

In Figure 19.39 only two fields are to be exported, the task name and the finish date, and the Milestones filter has been selected. Notice that the Destination Table Name text box is not available for exporting or importing text formatted data.

Exported field labels

Project field names

Milestones filter

Figure 19.39
The Milestones filter will limit the tasks that are exported to just those that are mile-stones.

11. When the map is complete, choose OK to save the map.

12. Choose the <u>S</u>ave button on the Export Mapping dialog box to create the file.

IMPORTING PROJECT DATA FROM THE TEXT FORMATS

Importing from a text file is similar to importing from an Excel workbook, except that you can only import one type of data at a time—you must import tasks, resources, and assignments separately. (See the previous section "Importing Project Data from the Excel Format.") The same problems in matching field names are likely to occur with text files that are found with Excel formats when the import source file was not originally exported from Project.

When importing from a text format you have an additional option, which was grayed-out for exporting in Figure 19.38. You can use the File <u>O</u>rigin text box to specify a different system character set for the source data. The default is Windows (ANSI), but you can also select DOS or OS/2 (PC-8), or you can select Unicode.

TROUBLESHOOTING

MISSING IMPORTED DATA

I imported data into Microsoft Project but I can't see the data in Project. What have I done wrong?

Make sure you have used an appropriate import map. If the field names in the map don't exist or are mismatched with Project fields, you might not have imported any data. Also, make sure you are using the appropriate view or table. If you imported resource data and are using a task view, you would not see the data. Likewise, if the Project table in the current view does not include the fields you imported, you will not see the imported data.

MALFUNCTIONING PIVOTTABLE MAP

The last field row is not red in my PivotTable map and it doesn't display the Pivot Data Field prefix. Can I fix it?

Even though a map might be designed for exporting to a PivotTable, if you start the Save <u>A</u>s command by choosing any format other than Microsoft Excel Pivot Table, the map will not display the last field in red and will generate a regular worksheet instead of a PivotTable. Of course, you can manually create a PivotTable based on the worksheet in Excel.

EMPTY EXPORTED PIVOTTABLE

I think I'm doing something incorrectly. After exporting project data to an Excel PivotTable, I find that the PivotTable sheet has no data in it.

Project cannot format an Excel PivotTable if there are more than eight fields in the data set. If your export map includes more than eight fields, Project will export the field data but will be unable to create the initial PivotTable. However, you can use Excel's PivotTable Wizard Layout dialog box to place the fields in a PivotTable.

Remember that, if you include task names, Project will add a field for each outline level that is used in your project; so, it's easy to exceed the maximum fields that Project can handle if your project has multiple outline levels.

CHAPTER **20**

COPYING, PASTING, AND INSERTING DATA WITH OTHER APPLICATIONS

In this chapter

Copying Selected Data Between Applications

In the preceding chapter you learned to export and import Project data in other file formats using Project's File Open and Save commands. You learned to exchange whole projects and to use Import/Export maps to work with selected blocks of data. In this chapter you will learn how to exchange individual field values as well as objects between files using the Copy and Paste commands and the Insert Object command. Both data that you paste into Project and objects that you insert into Project can often be linked to the original source to enable you to update the Project document to show the most current values in the source file.

> **Note**
>
> Using Copy and Paste is the only easily accessible way to copy Project's timephased data into other applications. Import/Export maps don't handle timephased data and Project's timephased reports can only be sent to the printer or viewed onscreen in Project. See the section "Placing Project Objects into Other Applications" for the steps to accomplish this.

If you do not need to transfer all the information in a file (for example, you need just one or a few values from the source document), you can use the Windows Clipboard to copy and paste the data from one application's document (the source) to another application's document (the destination). Project can be the source or destination for exchanging data this way. You can choose to simply paste a copy of the values, or you can paste a permanent link that displays the current value from the source document but also can be updated on demand to display revised values if the source document is changed.

The term *link* is also used for dependency (predecessor) relationships. When the linked tasks are in separate project documents, the concept is similar to the external links discussed in this section.

→ For information about using external dependency links, **see** "Creating Links Between Tasks in Separate Projects," **p. 748**

When pasting Clipboard data into a Project document, it is very important that you select the correct field(s) to receive the data. With importing files, the Import/Export map defines where the field data will be pasted. But with the copy/paste procedure, it all depends on where you click the mouse to make a selection just before you use the Paste command.

If you are pasting a single value, it's easy to select a recipient field that is appropriate for the value you are copying. If you are copying a block of two or more columns of values, however, you will need to have a table view in Project that has the appropriate columns next to each other to receive the block of copied values.

Frequently, this means that you must define a special table in Project to display the data field columns in the same order as the data that you are copying. When you paste the data into Project, the special table must be displayed in the current view.

 If you change the columns in the standard table for the current view and then find that you don't want the changes in all views that use that table, see "Restoring Standard Tables That Have Been Customized" in the "Troubleshooting" section at the end of this chapter. Also see "The Efficient Way to Customize a Table" in the "Troubleshooting" section for steps for creating customized tables.

The Excel worksheet in Figure 20.1 is laid out with resource names next to the cost rates for the resources. The standard Resource Sheet Entry table seen in the top window of Figure 20.2 has five other columns between the Resource Name and the Std. Rate. You should create a copy of the Entry table and hide those five columns to allow the data to be pasted; that is what you see displayed in the bottom window of Figure 20.2. The data was pasted into the bottom window and it was received successfully by Project, as you can see in both windows.

Figure 20.1
If you paste the resource names and cost rates in this table to the Project Resource Sheet in the top pane in Figure 20.2, the rate values will fall into the wrong columns.

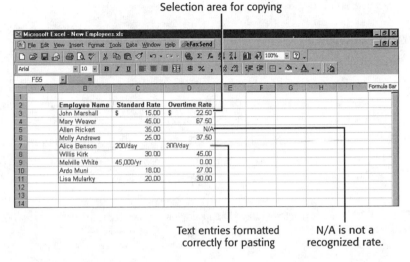

Selection area for copying

Text entries formatted correctly for pasting

N/A is not a recognized rate.

Figure 20.2
The order of the columns in the bottom pane is designed to accept pasting the block of data shown in Figure 20.1.

Normal Resource Entry table

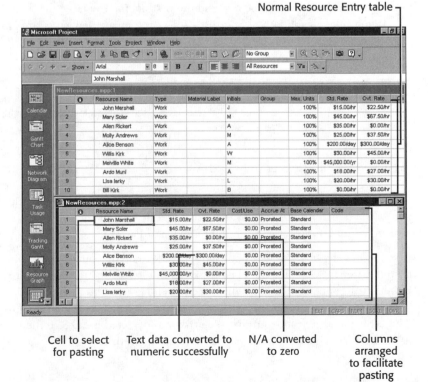

Cell to select for pasting

Text data converted to numeric successfully

N/A converted to zero

Columns arranged to facilitate pasting

Note

To create Figure 20.2, I used the Window, New Window command to display a second window for the same project and chose a different table for the display in the window at the bottom. The Window, Arrange All command displayed the two windows simultaneously.

You must also be sure that the cell you select before executing the Paste command is the cell that should receive the upper-left cell of the pasted block. The cell containing John Marshall was selected before pasting.

COPYING DATA FROM OTHER APPLICATIONS INTO PROJECT

To copy data from another application into Microsoft Project, follow these steps:

1. Select the source data. You can select a single value or several values, as in Figure 20.1. If you select several values, be sure that the layout of the values matches the order of the values in the Microsoft Project table that will serve as the destination.

2. Place the data in the Clipboard by choosing Edit, Copy or by pressing Ctrl+C.

3. Move to Microsoft Project and select a view with a table containing columns in the same order as the data you are copying, as in Figure 20.2.

Tip from Tim and the Project Team

Do not close the other application if more data is to be moved. Use Alt+Tab to switch between Project and the other open application.

4. Select the task or resource row and the first field in the table that is to receive the data. If you select blank rows, Microsoft Project will create new tasks or resources with the data you copy. If you select rows that already contain data, Project will replace the existing data with the newly copied data.

Note

If you overwrite an existing resource, you are simply changing field values for that resource. Any tasks assigned to that resource are still assigned to it—even though the resource name may have been changed.

5. Choose Edit, Paste (or press Ctrl+V).

Paste places a static copy of the current value from the source document in the field that you selected. Microsoft Project cannot update this value if the value in the source document is changed (unless you execute another Copy and Paste).

If you selected a field that does not support the data type you are importing, you will see a pasting error message like the one illustrated in Figure 20.3. In this case the data from Figure 20.1 contained the text value N/A in cell D5 (the third row of the selection) and Project let us know that it was unclear what to do with that value in the Overtime Rate field. The error message points out that the error was detected in ID 3 in the Overtime Rate column. The error dialog box offers you these option buttons:

- If you want to continue pasting and continue receiving error messages, choose <u>Y</u>es. The mismatched value will be pasted into the cell and Project will attempt to make sense of it.

- If you want to continue pasting but without having to deal with any more error messages, choose <u>N</u>o.

- If you want to stop the pasting operation, choose Cancel. Note that you were pasting a block of values and several have already been pasted. They will remain in the Project document but no more will be added.

Location where data error was detected

Figure 20.3
The pasting error message tells you where the error occurred and gives you clues about the type of data that is expected.

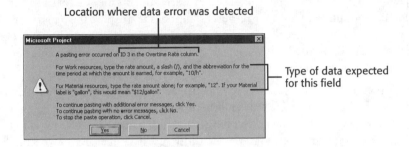

Type of data expected for this field

> **Caution**
>
> Note that pasting dates into the Start or Finish fields for tasks creates soft constraints for those tasks (Start No Earlier Than constraints in fixed start-date projects and Finish No Later Than constraints in fixed finish-date projects). You can correct the constraint on the Advanced tab of the Task Information dialog box.

→ For more information about removing constraints and the types of constraints, **see** "Working with Task Constraints," **p. 234**

COPYING MICROSOFT PROJECT DATA INTO OTHER APPLICATIONS

To copy data from Microsoft Project to another application, follow these steps:

1. Place a view onscreen with a table that displays the data you want to copy to the other application.

2. Select the source data. You can select a single value, several adjacent values, whole rows or columns, or all cells in the table.

   - To select entire rows, click the ID number for the row or rows.
   - To select entire columns, click the column headers.
   - To select all cells in the table, click the blank space above the ID numbers (to the left of the other column headers).

3. Place the data in the Clipboard by choosing <u>E</u>dit, <u>C</u>opy or by pressing Ctrl+C.

4. Move to the other application and select where you want to place the data.

5. Choose <u>E</u>dit, <u>P</u>aste.

The <u>P</u>aste command places a static copy of the current value from the project file. This value is not updated if the value in the project is changed.

EXPORTING TIMEPHASED DATA TO OTHER APPLICATIONS

As mentioned earlier, there is no standard report or Import/Export map for exporting the timephased resource assignment work and cost data you see in the Resource Usage or Task Usage views. Import/Export maps can include assignment data but not the timephased details. The Analyze Timescaled Data in Excel tool on the Analysis toolbar exports timephased summary data for resources but does not export the details for each assignment. Yet the timephased cost data can be very useful for further analysis and processing in Excel or other applications. Many users like to pair this data with other values not captured in Project for management reports.

This section will show you how to copy timephased assignment data to Excel. You will have to copy and paste the table data and the timephased data separately and align the two blocks of data when you paste them into Excel, but with a little care you can duplicate the Resource Usage or Task Usage view with Project data in an Excel workbook.

Figure 20.4 shows the Resource Usage view with timephased resource costs in the grid on the right. The table on the left is the Cost table for resources; there are more columns hidden behind the grid than those seen in the figure—columns for baseline and actual costs plus the cost variance.

You can use simple <u>C</u>opy and <u>P</u>aste to copy the data in the Resource Usage view to a worksheet. You have to copy the table data on the left separately from the timephased data in the grid. However, the timescale won't be included in the copy so you will have to manually add dates above the grid once the data is in Excel.

Tip from Tim and the Project Team

When you copy all the timephased data in the grid using the steps outlined next, Project will actually copy a block of grid cells starting with the time period for the earliest start date for any task in the project. To be certain that the time period Project starts the block with is also the time period for the beginning of the project, be sure that there is at least one task that has the project start date as its start date: for example, a milestone at the start of the project that has no predecessors, constraints, resources, or task calendar to keep it from starting when the project starts.

First, you must prepare the view in Project to show the table columns, the time periods, and the data details that you want to export. Follow these steps to prepare the Resource Usage view for copying:

1. Click the outline icon to the left of Unassigned in the first row of the table to hide the unassigned tasks. There will not be any resource costs associated with these tasks.
2. Display the columns in the table on the left that you want to export. You will want to copy at least the column titled Resource Name (the Name field) to identify the resources and task assignments; and you will probably want a column for the field whose timephased details you will copy.

Also, unless you include the Assignment field in the copied data, you will not be able to distinguish resources from assignments once the data is pasted. In Figure 20.4 the Assignment field is also included. Rows for assignments display Yes in this field and rows for resource names display No.

Figure 20.4
The Resource Usage view contains timephased work and cost data by resource assignment, which you can copy and paste in another application like Excel.

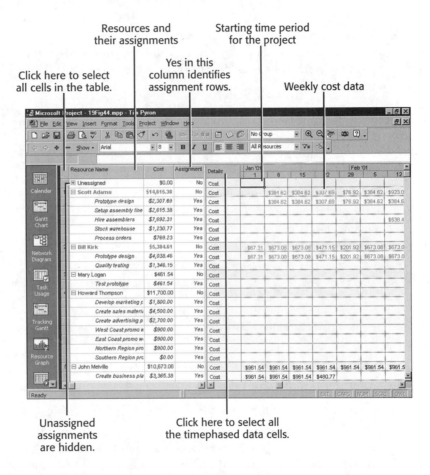

Resources and their assignments

Starting time period for the project

Yes in this column identifies assignment rows.

Click here to select all cells in the table.

Weekly cost data

Unassigned assignments are hidden.

Click here to select all the timephased data cells.

→ For help with modifying the Resource Usage view, **see** "Formatting the Resource Usage View," p. 938

In Figure 20.4, the Resource Name, Cost, and Assignment columns are displayed. We will copy the data in these three columns in this example.

3. Display the timephased details in the grid that you want to copy. In Figure 20.4, the grid shows the Cost details.

Tip from Tim and the Project Team

To avoid confusion, you should only display and copy one timephased detail field at a time. If you display multiple timephased details in a Usage view, there will be multiple rows of data in the grid for each row in the table on the left. Therefore, the rows you copy from the table and the rows you copy from the grid will not line up when you paste them into Excel.

Tip from Tim and the Project Team

> Work values can also be copied to Excel instead of costs, but work values by default have the time unit label "h" appended to the work value and will not support arithmetic operations in Excel without further processing. You can use Excel's Replace command to replace all instances of "h" with nothing (leave the Replace With box blank).

4. Choose the timescale settings to match the time periods that you want in the worksheet you are creating. If you want to export daily data, display days in the timescale; if you want to export weekly data, display weeks in the timescale as shown previously in Figure 20.4.

Tip from Tim and the Project Team

> Notice that Monday is the beginning of the week in Figure 20.4. That isn't necessary, but it makes the timescale label for the major units coincide with the first minor unit's label and therefore promotes clarity.

5. Make a note of the starting time period for the timephased data—-the first time period in the grid that contains a cell with data in it. Normally, this will be the time period that contains the start of the project.

Tip from Tim and the Project Team

> The quickest way to identify the timescale column for the beginning of the project is to click on a cell in the grid and then press the Home key. Project will jump the selection to the column that contains the start date of the project as shown in the Project Information dialog box. You can slide the mouse pointer over the date label in the timescale for the period and the ScreenTip will show you the date range covered by that time period.

Once the view is prepared for copying, and you know the date for the first time period that contains timephased data, copy the view's data to Excel with these steps:

1. Select the table data that you want to copy.

   If you want to copy all columns, click on the blank button that is above the row numbers and to the left of the column headings (refer to Figure 20.4). If you want to copy only selected columns, you can click on the column title for the first column and then use the Ctrl key as you click on other column titles to add them to the selection. In this example, I have selected the three columns Resource Name, Cost, and Assignment.

Note

> The selection does not really include the column titles, just all the data cells below the titles. You will have to manually type the column headings into the Excel worksheet.

2. Use the Copy command (Ctrl+C) to copy all the selected data to the Clipboard.

3. Select cell A2 in the worksheet (leave the first row blank for adding column titles) and use the Paste command (Ctrl+V) to paste the data into the worksheet starting in cell A2. The column titles will not be pasted and will have to be typed above the pasted data manually. They have already been typed into Figure 20.5.

Manually entered titles

Figure 20.5
Paste the table data
into the worksheet
first and fill in the
column headings
for the data.

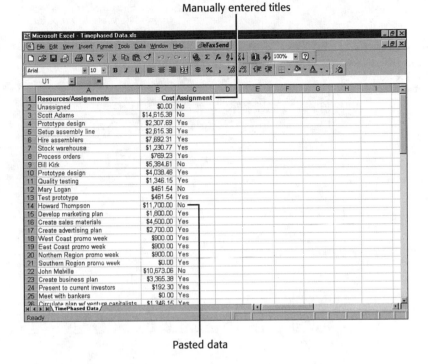

Pasted data

4. Fill in the column titles on row 1 by referring to the selected columns in the table in the Resource Usage view.

5. Switch back to Project and select all of the timephased data cells by clicking the Details column heading to the left of the timescale (refer to Figure 20.4).

 If you don't see the Details column headers, see "Restoring the Details Column Header" in the "Troubleshooting" section at the end of this chapter.

 6. Choose the Copy command.

7. Switch to the Excel worksheet and select the cell in row 2 in the first column to the right of the table data you have already pasted. The timescale dates will start in row 1 above this cell.

8. Use the Edit, Paste Special command and choose the Text format option to copy all the timephased data (see Figure 20.6).

Tip from Tim and the Project Team

You must use the Paste Special, Text option if you want to be able to sum the numbers once they're pasted into Excel.

9. Select the cell in row 1 above the cell you just selected to paste the timephased data and enter the starting date (the date you identified in the steps listed above for preparing the view for copying). In this example, the starting date is 1/1/2001 (refer to Figure 20.6).

PART

VI

CH

20

Figure 20.6
Paste the timephased data to the right of the table data.

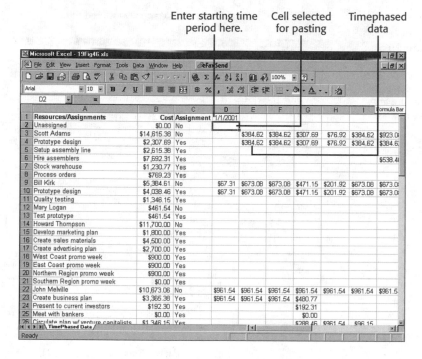

Enter starting time period here.

Cell selected for pasting

Timephased data

10. Starting with the cell you entered the starting date into, select the rest of the cells in row 1 above the timephased data.

11. Use Excel's Edit, Fill, Series command to fill in the dates for each period, using the date unit and step value that match your choices in setting up the timescale in the Resource Usage view.

In this example, the time period for incrementing the dates is the day (there is no week choice), and the step value is 7 (see Figure 20.7).

The data type is Date.   The Date Unit is Day.

Figure 20.7
Excel's Fill Series command will populate the column headings for the timephased data's dates.

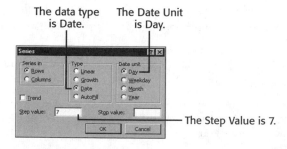

The Step Value is 7.

After filling in the dates and adding formatting to emphasize the data, the final worksheet looks similar to the Resource Usage view in Project.

Figure 20.8
The final copy in Excel has the timephased data of Project and can be used for further analysis.

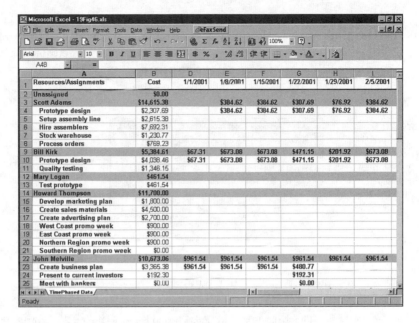

LINKING SELECTED DATA BETWEEN APPLICATIONS

LINKING SELECTED DATA BETWEEN APPLICATIONS

The copy operations described in the preceding section produce static copies in the destination document; the pasted copy of the data will not change if the source data changes. However, you can also paste a value from another application that is a *linked reference* to the data location in the source document. The linked reference can be updated to reflect changes in the value stored in the source document.

Use Edit, Copy in the source document and use the Edit, Paste Special command in the target document to create the dynamic link.

LINKING MICROSOFT PROJECT DATA FIELDS TO EXTERNAL SOURCES

You can paste a link to an external data source into a Microsoft Project table. The external source can be another application (such as Excel or Word) or another Project document. For example, we will use an Excel worksheet as the source for resource names and cost rates in a Project document. You could also link the constraint date for a task to a date in another file if you want the task to start or finish on that date.

To link Microsoft Project field values to values stored in other sources:

1. Select the source data—for example, a cell or range of cells in an Excel worksheet. You can select a single value or several values. If you select several values, be sure that the order of the values matches the order of the values in the table that you view when you paste the values into Microsoft Project.

2. Copy the data to the Clipboard by choosing Edit, Copy or by pressing Ctrl+C.

3. Move to Microsoft Project and select a view that has a table with the columns arranged to match the order of the data that you are copying.

4. Select the row in the table that is to receive the data. If you select a blank row, Microsoft Project creates new tasks or resources with the data that you are copying into the file. If you select rows in which data already exists, Microsoft Project replaces the existing field data with the data being pasted.

5. Choose <u>E</u>dit, Paste <u>S</u>pecial. The Paste Special dialog box appears (see Figure 20.9).

Figure 20.9
The Paste Special dialog box lets you specify the format for the data that will be pasted into the receiving file.

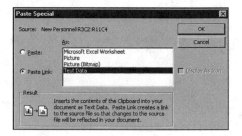

6. Choose the Paste <u>L</u>ink option button.

7. In the <u>A</u>s box, choose Text Data as the type of link if you want the data to become text in a table. Project attempts to convert text data into number data in a number field or a date in a date field.

If you are in a Gantt Chart, there are more options for the format in which the data is pasted (as shown earlier by the graphics options in Figure 20.9). Choose the Worksheet or Picture option if you want the data to be a picture object in a graphic area. (See the section "Placing Objects into Microsoft Project" later in this chapter.) In the Gantt Chart view, for example, both those options would create a graphic object in the bar chart area of the view.

8. Click OK to establish the link. By default Project will display a small triangle in the lower-right corner of each cell that is linked to a source for its data. You can see the link indicators in the Standard Rate and Overtime Rate values in Figure 20.10. The cost rate table is linked to an Excel worksheet in which the cost rates are maintained.

Figure 20.10
Linked cells in a table view display a link indicator, a small triangle in the lower-right corner of the cell.

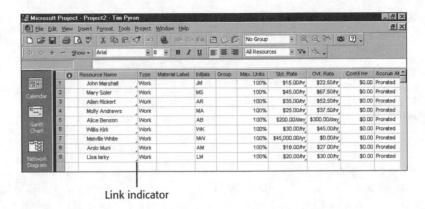

Link indicator

If you don't see the link indicator where it should be displayed, choose Tools, Options, and select the View tab in the Options dialog box. Fill the OLE Links Indicators check box.

If you attempt to paste a link with mismatched data, you will receive an OLE error message that the operation cannot be completed (see Figure 20.11). Unlike the regular Paste command, if there is a data mismatch while pasting a block of values, Project halts the operation and removes all values pasted in during that operation. These values are removed because a block of cells is considered one link. If one cell contains a mismatch, the entire paste link will be ignored.

Figure 20.11
Unlike pasting static values, if you paste a linked value that is a data mismatch, Project will reject the paste operation and will not attempt to interpret the mismatched data.

PART
VI

CH
20

REFRESHING LINKED DATA IN MICROSOFT PROJECT

If you save a project file that contains linked values, Project saves the current values of the linked fields along with the reference to the source for the value. That way, when you open a file with linked values, Project can display the most recent values.

When you open a Project document that contains links to other files, Project asks you if you want to reestablish the links, which means to refresh the values in the linked cells in Project with the current values in the source files (see Figure 20.12). If you select Yes, Project will quickly look into the source files and retrieve the current or saved values of each link's source. If you select No, Project will open the Project document and display the last saved values for the linked cells. You can update the links yourself later.

Figure 20.12
When opening a Project file with links to other files, you can have Project refresh the links or use the values that were saved in the Project file.

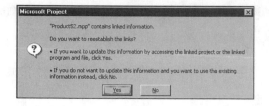

You can update the linked values in a Project document at any time with the Edit, Links... command. The source application does not need to be open for the linked values to be refreshed. The Links dialog box lists all the external links in the current document (see Figure 20.13).

Selected link

Figure 20.13
All external sources of linked data are identified in the Links dialog box.

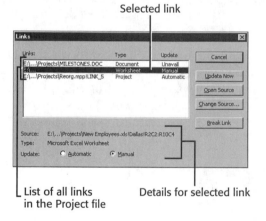

List of all links in the Project file   Details for selected link

The Links list (usually) displays the path to the source, the document type of the source file, and the update status of each link. These three items are displayed in greater detail at the bottom of the dialog box for the selected link. If the filename and link reference are too long, the path to the source will be truncated.

In Figure 20.13, the selected item in the Links list shows the path to the file truncated (because it's too long for the display), but the details below show the filename (New Employees.xls) and the location of the linked data within the file to be in the sheet named Dallas, the cell range R2C3:R10C4 (or C2:D10 in standard A1 notation). The Type is identified as a Microsoft Excel Worksheet. The Update status is Manual, which means that you must choose the Update Now tool to the right to refresh the values in Microsoft Project.

If the Update status is Automatic, and if the file is open in memory and supports automatic updating, changes in the source will appear immediately in the Project document while it's also open in memory. Even if you select the Automatic update choice, some source applications don't support automatic updates and the Update column at the top of the dialog box will display Unavail, like the Milestones.doc source did earlier in Figure 20.13. The Update status will also be Unavail when the Project document has not been updated during the current editing session.

Caution

If an object's Update field at the bottom of the dialog box has the Automatic button selected and you want to select the Manual button, do not make the change if the Update status for the link in the list of Links above is Unavail. You need to update the link with the Update Now button before you change the update method or Project will usually hang and you will have to shut it down, losing any unsaved data.

Note

Notice in this example that there is just one link reference in the Links dialog box for the whole range of Excel cells that was pasted in the link operation. If you need to maintain each of the cells as separate links, you should copy and paste each of the cells individually.

To work with the links to external sources, follow these steps:

1. Choose Edit, Links... from the menu to display the Links dialog box (refer to Figure 20.13).

Tip from Tim and the Project Team

If the Links command is dimmed, then the document has no linked values.

2. Select all links that you want to refresh. To select all links, click the first link and hold down the Shift key as you click the last link. To add nonadjacent links to the selection, hold down the Ctrl key while making the additional selections.

3. Choose the Update Now button to refresh all the data links you have selected. The source for each link that you select will be searched for the current values.

4. If you want to open the application document named in the selected link reference, choose the Open Source button. You can open only one link source at a time.

5. If you want to remove the selected link, choose the Break Link button. The current value will remain in the link location, but the reference to an external source will be gone.

6. If you want to change the source of the linked data, you can do so in the Change Source dialog box. Choose one of the links in the Links box and choose the Change Source button. The Change Source dialog box appears (see Figure 20.14), in which you can choose another file to link to.

Tip from Tim and the Project Team

Although you can browse through the directory of files to find the filename of a new source to link to, you must know the location within the new source file to complete the change. For that reason, it is usually better to paste new links over the old instead of using this dialog box.

Figure 20.14
The Change Source dialog box can be used to redefine the link source—but only if you know the address of the specific location within the file.

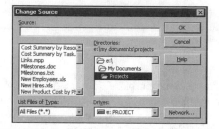

DELETING LINKS TO EXTERNAL SOURCES

As pointed out in step 5 above, if you break the link to an external source, Project retains the current value that was linked but disassociates the value with the external source. If you attempt to type over a field value that is linked to an external source, you will be warned that the link will be lost (see Figure 20.15) and you will be offered the opportunity to proceed or to cancel the data entry. Choose No to abandon the editing change and preserve the link. If you choose Yes (to proceed with the change), the DDE link reference will be lost. Fortunately, you can undo the change with the Edit, Undo command.

Figure 20.15
If you edit or clear a cell that contains a linked value, you will lose the link.

To delete the data and its link to an external source, you can select the field whose link you want to remove and choose Edit, Clear (or press Ctrl+Delete). Then select the Contents option. You are then asked to confirm the deletion. Choose Yes to complete the deletion.

Caution

If you delete the link in a cell that is part of a block of linked values, the link for all cells in the block will be removed, not just the link for the one cell. The Edit, Undo command will restore the links.

IDENTIFYING TASKS OR RESOURCES WITH LINKS ATTACHED

You can filter task or resource tables to determine which tasks or resources use linked data from other sources. For either a task view or a resource view, choose Project, Filtered For, More Filters to display the More Filters dialog box, and choose the Linked Fields filter. Choose the Apply button to display only the tasks or resources that have one or more linked fields. Choose the Highlight button to highlight those tasks or resources that have linked values in one or more fields. To find the linked values, search for the links indicator in the lower-right corner of the cells.

PASTING LINKS TO MICROSOFT PROJECT DATA IN OTHER APPLICATIONS

Both Microsoft Excel and Microsoft Word will accept pasted links to individual data cells in Microsoft Project tables. If you want to copy a single linked value to one of these applications, you only have to display a table that has a cell for the value you want to use, select the cell, and use the Copy command. Then, in Word or Excel use the Edit, Paste Special command and use the Paste Link option to paste the data as text. If you want to copy a block of values, you ought to modify a table in Project, if necessary to put the values you want to copy adjacent to each other. Select the block and, as with a single value, use the Edit, Paste Special, Paste Link commands to paste the block of values in Word or Excel. The pasted block of data is a single entity in both applications and, when you update the links in the other application, all the values in the block will be updated. That is why you should arrange the data in Project before copying so that it only includes the values you want to see in the other application.

USING MICROSOFT PROJECT 2000 AS AN OLE DB PROVIDER

 Project 2000 is now an OLE DB provider, albeit a read-only provider. That means you can read the current project data with another application, thus making it possible to integrate project data across the organization. However, you can't modify the Project data with the OLE DB client. For example, you can use Microsoft Access Data Access Pages to build dynamic reports that allow the viewer to drill down into the current project data. Creating this link occurs entirely within the client application (for example, within Microsoft Access). Your Project 2000 CD has the documentation you will need for accessing the Project data in the following HTML document:

```
<CD>\PFILES\MSOFFICE\OFFICE\1033\OLE_DB.htm
```

> **Note**
>
> For information about creating Data Access Pages, see Que's *Special Edition Using Microsoft Access 2000* (0-7897-1606-2) by Roger Jennings.

> **Note**
>
> There are significant formatting issues in displaying the Project data in other applications. For example, duration fields will display the duration in minutes multiplied by 10 (an hour will appear as 600) and work fields will display the work as minutes multiplied by 1,000 (an hour will appear as 60,000). The data will have to be processed to provide a meaningful display for users.

WORKING WITH OBJECTS

The preceding sections focused on sharing data values as text between applications. As we saw, a group of cell entries in an Excel workbook can provide the task names and durations in a Microsoft Project document. Or, if you paste Excel data as text into Project's Resource Sheet view, each cell will be placed in a separate field in the table, as you saw in Figure 20.10.

An *object*, on the other hand, is a representation of data (usually a group of data or a special format for data) that is formatted by another application. The most frequent use of objects is to show graphic data (for example, Excel charts, artwork, PowerPoint slides, or special displays such as the Network Diagram or the Gantt Chart from Microsoft Project) in an application that doesn't normally generate similar formats. You can also paste media formats such as sound files or video clips.

It is common to refer to the application that generates an object as the *server* application and the application that has the object pasted in it as the *client* application. The client document is also sometimes called the *container* document. These terms will be used in the following discussion where they help clarify.

PASTING OBJECTS

As with text data, you can copy data from an external application and paste it as an object in Project using the Edit, Paste or Paste Special commands. For example, an Excel chart can be pasted into the Gantt Chart. If you use the Paste Special command, the chart can be linked to the Excel document in which it was created. Like linked text data, a linked object can be updated automatically or manually, depending on the settings in the Links dialog box.

Tip from Tim and the Project Team

If a pasted object is not linked, it cannot be automatically updated to show changes in the original source document. To update the image in that case, you would have to copy and paste the image again.

If the object is not linked, it is said to be *embedded* in the client document. An embedded object is stored entirely in the client document. Since the format is foreign to the client application, editing the object will necessitate activating the application that created the object (the server application). Once editing is finished and the server application is closed, the revised object will still reside in the client application.

For example, if you paste an Excel chart into the Gantt Chart view as an object, either linked or embedded, it will appear in the timeline area of the Gantt Chart along with the task bars (see Figure 20.16). The Excel document in this instance would be the server and the Project document would be the client or container.

You can usually position and resize the object within Project after it is pasted. Many object formats, including those from Excel, can also be edited directly from within Project. If the Excel chart or worksheet were pasted as a linked object, then double-clicking the object would open Excel with the source document open for editing. On closing Excel and saving any changes, the revised object would be visible in Project. If the chart or worksheet were embedded, then double-clicking would open the object for editing and you would see

Excel's menu and toolbars instead of Project's menu and toolbars. However, you would still be working within Project. After making your changes, you could click outside the object on the Project workspace and the Project menu and toolbars would return. The revised embedded object would only exist in Project.

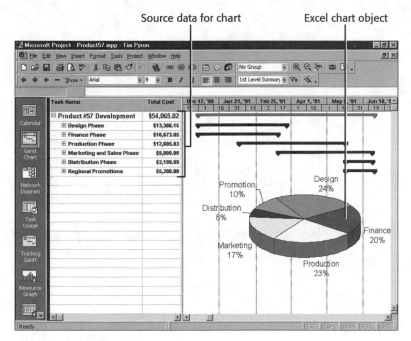

Figure 20.16
For this illustration the Project data was first paste-linked into an Excel worksheet, then the worksheet data was used to generate an Excel chart, and finally the chart was paste-linked back to Project as an object in the Gantt Chart.

If you paste a media object such as a video clip or sound file into the Gantt Chart, it will appear as an icon. Double-clicking the icon typically is how you run the video clip or sound file.

If Project is the source or server, and you paste copies of selected cells from the Gantt Chart table into another application document as text, each row of task information would become a row of ordinary text in the document. But, if you copy the selection as an object, it will be displayed as a graphic figure in the client document.

In Figure 20.17 the same Project task rows are pasted first as text and then as a picture object into a Microsoft Word document. The task field text appears as an ordinary tab-separated list in Word. The picture of the tasks includes the Gantt Chart table cells along with the task bars and the timescale above the task bars. See the section "Placing Project Objects into Other Applications" later in this chapter for more options when placing Project objects in other application documents.

PART
VI

CH
20

Tasks pasted as text

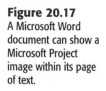

Figure 20.17
A Microsoft Word document can show a Microsoft Project image within its page of text.

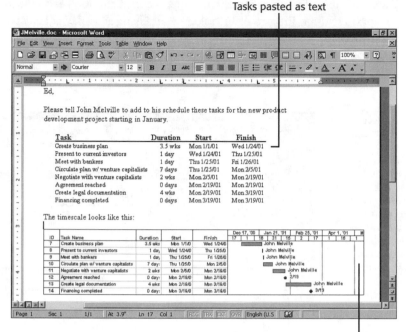

Tasks pasted as picture object

Inserting Objects

You can also use the <u>I</u>nsert, <u>O</u>bject command to place objects in a client document. This command can insert an existing file that was created by another (server) application into the client document. The inserted object may be linked or it may be embedded.

The <u>I</u>nsert, <u>O</u>bject command can also open a server application from within the client document to let you create a new embedded object that only exists within the client document. For example, you can insert an Excel spreadsheet into a Project document and place whatever data you would like into the spreadsheet using the Excel application's menu and toolbars. When you click on the Project workspace in the background, the object will remain embedded in Project and its data will exist only in the Project document. Likewise, from within Word or Excel you could insert a Project object—for example a Gantt Chart that you create on the fly. When you click outside the object, it will remain embedded in the Word or Excel document.

Placing Objects into Microsoft Project

You can paste or insert objects into Microsoft Project in four locations:

- In the graphics area of the Gantt Chart
- In the Notes box of the Task, Resource, or Assignment Information Forms

- In the special task Objects box in the Task Form or the resource Objects box on the Resource Form
- In the Header, Footer, or Legend of a view's Page Format dialog box

The following sections show you how to use objects in each of these locations. In the first two we will go into detail about pasting, inserting, and working with objects in the Gantt Chart. In the remaining sections we will not repeat all the detail but will look at the differences compared to placing objects in the Gantt Chart.

PASTING OBJECTS IN THE GANTT CHART

The Gantt Chart is the premier view in Microsoft Project. It can be enhanced by pasting Project drawings (see Chapter 7, "Viewing Your Schedule") or objects from other applications into the timescale area. To paste an object into the Gantt Chart, follow these steps:

1. Activate the source (the server application), select the source data, and copy it to the Clipboard with the Edit, Copy command.
2. Activate Project (the client application) and view the Gantt Chart.
3. Choose Edit, Paste Special to display the Paste Special dialog box (see Figure 20.18).

Figure 20.18
You can embed or link objects with the Paste Special dialog box.

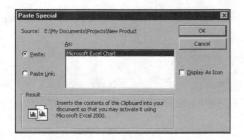

4. Choose Paste to embed the object or Paste Link to link it.
5. In the As box, you may have an option that includes the server application's name and/or you may have an option named Picture. Both choices produce picture images that look similar. The option with the server application's name will allow you to open the object in the server application—for instance, to edit or modify the object. The Picture option places a picture of the object into the Project document that can't be opened for editing.
6. Choose OK to paste the image.

Once the object appears in the Gantt Chart, you can move and resize it. If necessary, click the object to select it. Then drag it to a new position or drag its resizing handles to change its size. To remove the object, select it and press the Delete key.

PART

VI

CH

20

Tip from Tim and the Project Team

> Resizing a picture object (whether linked or not) leaves the same data displayed, and fonts for that data can appear distorted. To resize a picture object in the Gantt Chart without distorting the horizontal and vertical dimensions, hold down the Shift key as you drag one of the corner handles.

Caution

> You can't undo resizing or deleting of an object. Be sure to save the Project document before experimenting with either of these actions.

Tip from Tim and the Project Team

> If you have one or more objects placed in the Gantt Chart, it can sometimes be difficult to find them by merely scrolling the graphics area.
>
> Pressing the F6 key successively activates all the panes in the active project that are currently displayed, including the table pane in the Gantt Chart, the graphics pane of the Gantt Chart, and the panes at the bottom of the window if the window has been split. Press the F6 key until Project selects the graphics pane and scrolls the first object into view. The object will be selected and you will see its sizing handles. Press the Tab key to select other objects in that pane one at a time.

→ For more information on working with objects in the Gantt Chart, **see** "Adding Graphics and Text to Gantt Charts," **p. 275**

INSERTING OBJECTS IN THE GANTT CHART

In the preceding examples, the data in an object was created as part of a source (server) application document and then was copied and pasted into the target (client) application. You can also use the Insert Object command to place a linked or embedded copy of the entire source document into the client document as an object. Of course, if you embed a source document in Project, it will increase the Project document's file size and the embedded document will be cut off from updates to the original source document.

The Insert Object command also gives you the option of creating an object without using an existing file. You can create a new object using the formatting capabilities of server applications that support Microsoft OLE 2.0 or higher. The server application's interface will open from within Project to allow you to create the new data. On closing the server, the object will remain embedded in Project.

To insert an object, choose the Insert, Object command. Project will display the Insert Object dialog box. The default option button is Create New, which allows you to create a new, embedded object using one of the applications listed in the Object Type box. Choose Create from File if the data has already been created and saved to disk and you want to insert a linked or embedded copy of the source data.

As an illustration, suppose that you want to embed a new Excel worksheet object in the Gantt Chart that shows budgeted (baseline) and current gross margin data for a project (see Figure 20.19).

Worksheet object

Figure 20.19
Relevant cost and gross margin data can be displayed in the Gantt Chart as a worksheet object.

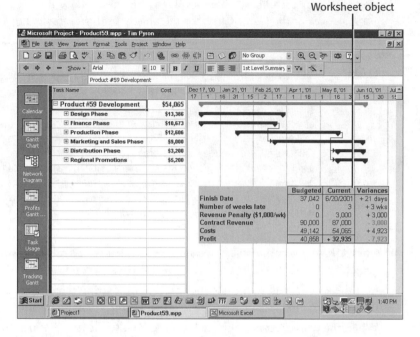

To create a new worksheet object, follow these steps:

1. Display a Gantt Chart view in the top pane.

2. Choose the Insert, Object command to display the Insert Object dialog box (see Figure 20.20). It takes a little time for this dialog box to appear because Project must prepare a list of all the server applications on your system that support OLE 2.0 or higher.

List of available server options

Figure 20.20
The Insert Object dialog box helps you create new objects or insert existing files as objects.

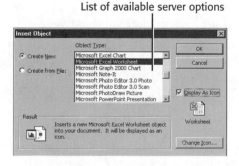

3. Choose Create New (it is selected by default).

4. Choose the server application you want to use from the list that appears in the Object Type list. For this example, we choose Microsoft Excel Worksheet.

5. Fill the check box for Display As Icon if you want to see just an icon in the Gantt Chart instead of the worksheet object. Once the object is inserted, you can double-click the

icon to display the object's contents. This is the best choice if there is little room in the graphics area of the Gantt Chart for the object. In this example, the check box is filled.

Tip from Tim and the Project Team

Even if you want the object to display as a mini-worksheet in the Gantt Chart, it is generally best to choose Display As Icon when you are initially inserting the object. After the data is entered and formatted, you can convert the object to display as a worksheet.

This is particularly true if you plan to build a complex embedded object, especially if the object will contain links to the field data in the Project document. If Display As Icon is selected, Project will initially open Excel in its own window for you to create the object. You will have full access to all Excel features and you can switch back and forth between Excel and Project easily with the Alt+Tab key combination. If Display As Icon is not selected, you will have to create the object in a small window within the graphics area of the Gantt Chart, where not all Excel menu commands will be available, and where switching back and forth between Project and Excel will be much more tedious.

6. Click OK to insert the object. Assuming you filled the Display As Icon check box, Project will open Excel in a new window for you to create the worksheet.

7. Edit the spreadsheet to include the data and formatting that you want to appear in the Gantt Chart.

   When the worksheet is completed, choose File, Close And Return To *filename* (where *filename* will be the name of the Project document in which you inserted the object). The icon for the object will be displayed in the Gantt Chart.

Once the object is embedded, you can double-click the icon to open or edit the data. You can also convert the object to display itself as a worksheet instead of an icon.

To convert the object by changing its display, follow these steps:

1. Select the object. If it is visible on your screen, simply click it. If it is not visible, use the F6 key to activate the first object in the graphics pane. If the object you want to convert is not the one selected, press the Tab key until the object you want is selected.

2. Choose the Edit, Worksheet Object, Convert command to display the Convert dialog box (see Figure 20.21). This command, at the bottom of the Edit menu, will be named for the type of object you have selected.

3. Clear the Display As Icon check box and click OK. The object will appear as a small worksheet.

The example above shows how to create a new object with the Insert, Object command. If a file already exists that you want to insert in the Gantt Chart as an object, follow these steps:

1. Display a Gantt Chart view in the top pane.

2. Choose the Insert, Object command to display the Insert Object dialog box.

3. Choose the Create from File option. The File text box will appear with a Browse button beneath to help you select the filename (see Figure 20.22).

Figure 20.21
Use the Convert command to change the display of an object from an icon to formatted data.

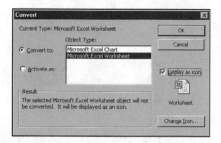

4. Either type the file's path and filename into the File box or use the Browse button to locate the filename.

5. Fill the Link check box if you want to inset a linked copy of the file's data. Leave the check box clear if you want to embed a copy of the file.

6. Fill the Display As Icon check box if you only want an icon to appear in the Gantt Chart.

7. Click OK to create the object.

Figure 20.22
Use the Insert Object dialog box to insert external document files as objects.

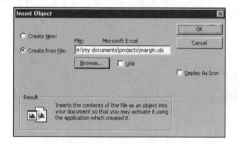

To open or edit an object, click the object to select it. At the bottom of the Edit menu, you will see a submenu for the object named for the object type. For example, the submenu for an object that originated as a worksheet might be titled Worksheet Object, and the submenu for a sound file might be titled Wave Sound Object. Depending on the format of the object, the submenu will contain one or more of these commands:

- **Edit**—This command opens the server application to allow you to edit the object. After editing, close the server application and you will return to Project.

- **Open**—This command is equivalent to the Edit command for text-based formats such as worksheets and documents. For media objects, this command displays a picture in the server application, plays the sound file, runs the video, and so on. Typically the media object is not open for editing.

- **Play**—This command appears for some media objects such as sound files and video. It plays the media data and then closes. For media objects, this is the default action when you double-click the object icon.

- **Convert**—This command only appears for some objects and can be used to change the Display As Icon choice for the object or to change the format of the object itself.

Note

You can use the Edit, Links command to manage linked objects just as described in the previous section on linking selected data.

If you want to format the object within Project, to attach it to a task bar for instance, use the techniques described in the section "Working with Drawing Objects in the Gantt Chart View" in Chapter 7.

PLACING OBJECTS IN THE NOTES FIELD

You can place objects into the Notes field for individual tasks, resources, or assignments (see Figure 20.23). The Notes field is the most obvious place to attach links to supporting documentation that is stored elsewhere on your computer, on your organization's network, or in an intranet folder. For example, you could insert into a note a group of objects, displayed as icons, that provide links to documents that define the scope, authorization, and budget for the project; or you could insert into a task note links to drawings or specifications for completing the task. By using links to external documents, you provide reliable access to relevant documentation.

Insert Object tool   Note text

Figure 20.23
The Notes field can display embedded and linked objects as formatted data or as icons.

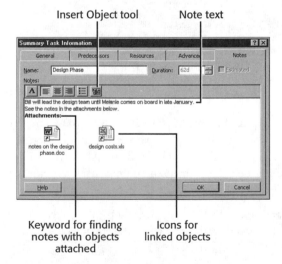

Keyword for finding notes with objects attached   Icons for linked objects

Caution

Objects placed in the Notes field for a Project summary task can be accidentally erased very easily. This note is also displayed as the Comments box on the Summary tab of the Properties dialog box (choose File, Properties). If you merely scroll the Comments box, or even click in it, and then close the dialog box with the OK button, all objects will be erased for the note.

For this reason you may want to create a milestone named Notes at the top or bottom of the task list and attach project-wide objects to that task.

If you display the links as icons, you will not increase the project file size by any substantial amount. If you display the linked object as formatted data, and especially if you embed the object, you may increase the file size of the project document substantially and thereby reduce the speed with which Project can open the file and process it. Furthermore, as the following Caution points out, a linked object in a note is not updated until you double-click the object to open the source document.

Caution

You will not find the linked objects you place in notes in the Links dialog box when you choose Edit, Links. The only way to update a linked object in a note is to double-click the object to open the source document.

Because linked objects in a note are not listed in the Links dialog box, if you change the filename or path to a linked object, you must delete the original link and place the object in the note again.

The only drawback to using the Notes field as a repository for links to supporting documentation is that there is no automatic way in Project to identify those notes that contain links to external documents. You will have to find the links on your own.

Tip from Tim and the Project Team

Since there is no filter or indicator to tell you if a note contains an object, you should adopt the habit of placing a keyword like Attachments: just before the inserted or pasted objects in a note. Then you can use the Edit, Find command to search the Notes field for those notes that contain the text Attachments:. You must place this keyword before any objects because the Find command stops searching a note when it encounters an object.

 You can paste objects into a note with the Paste or Paste Special commands on the shortcut menu for the Notes box. You can also insert objects in notes using the Insert Object tool that is displayed above the Notes box (refer to Figure 20.23). If you paste objects, you can only embed them—there is no paste-link option within notes. If you insert them, however, you have the choice of embedding or linking most objects.

To paste an object into the Notes box, follow these steps:

1. Copy the object to the Windows Clipboard from within the server application.
2. Switch to Microsoft Project, activate an appropriate view, and select the task, resource, or assignment record whose note you want to paste into.
 3. Click the Notes tool on the Standard toolbar. The Notes tab of the Information dialog box will be displayed, as in Figure 20.23.
4. Click in the Notes box at the location where you want to insert the object.
5. Display the shortcut menu (right-click) and choose the Paste command or the Paste Special command if it is available. The Paste command will immediately paste the object as a picture that cannot be opened by the server application once it has been pasted. If you are pasting a media object, like a sound wave file, the Paste command will paste an icon but the icon will not play the sound file. You will need to use the Paste Special command for media objects.

The Paste Special command will display the Paste Special dialog box (see Figure 20.24) which usually provides multiple formatting options in the As list box:

- The Picture option is usually the equivalent of the Paste command's action—a picture of the data in its original format. For media objects, this will simply be an icon that doesn't do anything.
- If there is an option that contains the name of the object's format, such as Microsoft Excel Worksheet or Wave Sound, you will be able to open the object using the server application to view and edit (in the case of a worksheet) or to play (in the case of a media object).
- If there is a Text option, the text that was copied to the Clipboard will be pasted into the note as regular text.

Figure 20.24
You can use the Paste Special command in the Notes box to embed an object in different ways.

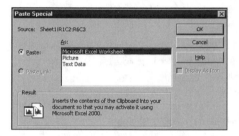

6. If you chose the Paste Special command, select the format for the object in the As list box.
7. Click the OK button to paste the object.
8. If you want to resize the object, click in the middle of the object to display the sizing handles around the object. Use the mouse to drag the sizing handles.
9. Choose OK to save the note.

Tip from Tim and the Project Team

The Notes box in the Information dialog box cannot be enlarged and you might find it too small for your tastes. You can increase the display size of task and resource notes (but not assignment notes) by viewing them in the Task Name Form or the Resource Name Form. These views can be displayed as full-screen views or in the bottom pane of a split window under a task or resource view.

For example, to work with task notes in a larger display, choose View, More Views, select the Task Name Form from the list of Views, and click the Apply button. Then choose Format, Details, Notes to display the Notes box. As you resize the view, you will resize the Notes box. Follow a similar process to work with resource notes in a larger display.

PLACING OBJECTS IN THE TASK OR RESOURCE OBJECTS BOX

Project has three standard task form views (the Task Form, the Task Details Form, and the Task Name Form) that can display an Objects box in which you can place objects that you want to associate with a task. Similarly, there are two standard resource form views (the

Resource Form and the Resource Name Form) that can display an Objects box for displaying objects that you associate with a resource. These forms are the only places you can view an Objects box onscreen. However, you can include the contents of the Objects boxes in custom reports (see Chapter 25, "Customizing Reports").

You can paste objects in the Objects box with either the Paste or Paste Special commands, and unlike pasting in notes, you can paste links to objects with the Paste Special command. You can also use the Insert Object command to place embedded or linked objects in an Objects box.

Project also has a task Objects field and a resource Objects field. If you display the Objects field in a table, it shows the number of objects that are stored in the Objects box for that task or resource. The main usage of the Objects field is in filters to identify those tasks or resources with objects in their Objects boxes. The standard filters Tasks With Attachments and Resources With Attachments select those tasks or resources whose Objects field has values greater than zero or whose Notes fields contain some text. You could make modified copies of these filters to focus just on those records that have objects stored in their Objects box.

In Figure 20.25, the Task Form is displayed beneath the Gantt Chart with the Objects box displayed in the details area. The gross margin worksheet that was used in previous examples is displayed in the Objects box.

The table in the Gantt Chart has been modified to display the Objects field. It shows that there are two objects attached to this resource. You would use the scrollbar next to the Objects box to see the next object.

Number of objects in this Objects box

Figure 20.25
The Objects field displays graphic or other objects that are attached to an individual task or resource.

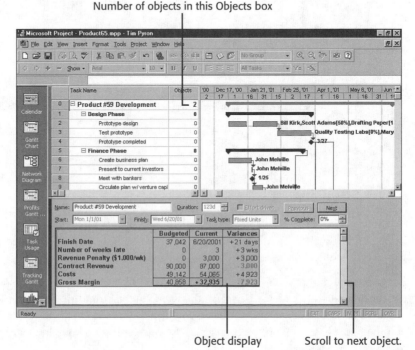

Object display   Scroll to next object.

To paste an object into an Objects field, follow these steps:

1. In the source (server) application, select the object and copy it to the Clipboard.

2. In Project, display one of the task or resource form views, depending on the type of record you want to paste the object into. Choose View, More Views and select the view name in the Views list box. Click the Apply button to display the form.

3. Choose Format, Details, Objects (or right-click anywhere outside a field box on the form and choose Objects from the shortcut menu).

4. Click in the Objects field at the bottom of the form to select it.

5. Choose Edit, Paste Special from the menu to display the Paste Special dialog box (see Figure 20.26).

Figure 20.26
The Paste Special options for the Objects box include linking to the source of the object.

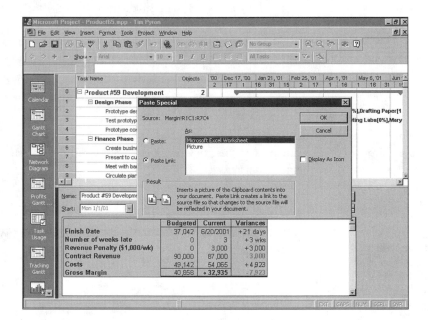

6. Choose Paste or Paste Link.

7. Choose the format option in the As list box.

8. Choose OK to finish pasting the object.

To insert an object in the Objects box, select the Objects box and choose Insert, Object to display the Insert Object dialog box, and use the dialog box options as described previously for inserting objects in notes and in the Gantt Chart.

You can place multiple objects in the Objects box. The first object you paste or insert will appear immediately and will be selected. When you place additional objects, they are inserted below the one that is currently selected and displayed. However, the selection will not change and the new object will not be displayed. Use the scrollbar or the down arrow to select and display the newly placed object.

Tip from Tim and the Project Team

> If you have multiple objects placed in an Objects box and would like to change the order in which they appear, use cut and paste to move objects in the stack. Display the object to be moved and choose the Edit, Cut command. Then select the object after which you want to place the cut object and choose the Edit, Paste or Paste Special command. If the object being moved is not formatted as a simple picture object, you must use the Paste Special command to retain its format.

Tip from Tim and the Project Team

> The Objects box scrollbar does not scroll through a single object, even if it is too large for the area it is displayed in. If you can't see the entire object, increase the size of the form. If you still can't see the entire object, open it in the server application. You cannot resize the objects that are pasted in the Objects box. If the object is pasted as a picture and you can't see all of it, you are out of luck.

If you want to delete an object in the Objects box, scroll to display that object and press the Delete key. The object will be deleted from the project document.

PLACING OBJECTS IN HEADERS, FOOTERS, AND LEGENDS

You can customize printed views and reports by placing graphics such as your organization's logo or a symbol for the project in the print header, footer, or legend area. In Figure 20.27, the tree graphic has been pasted into the header in the Gantt Chart Page Setup dialog box. You either paste a picture or insert a graphic file to create the object in this context, but you can only embed objects—they can't be linked.

Figure 20.27
Place objects like your logo in print headers, footers, or legends.

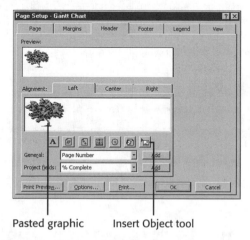

Pasted graphic   Insert Object tool

PART

VI

CH

20

To place a graphic object in a view or report's header, footer, or legend, you must first display the Page Setup dialog box for the view or report. For views, simply activate the view. For reports, follow these steps:

1. Choose View, Reports to display the Reports dialog box.

2. Select the Custom box and click Select to display the Custom Reports dialog box (in which all reports are listed).

3. Select the report in the Reports list and click Setup.

Note

You cannot define a legend for any of the reports, and the Project Summary report doesn't even allow you to create a header or footer.

Once the Page Setup dialog box is active, follow these steps to embed a picture:

1. If you are copying a picture, select the picture in its source and use the Copy command to place it on the Clipboard.

   If you are inserting a graphic file, you should create a copy of the graphic that is sized appropriately for the report. It can be awkward trying to resize pictures in the Page Setup dialog box.

2. Select the Header, Footer, or Legend tab as appropriate.

3. Select the Left, Center, or Right tab to position the picture on the page.

   The customized area of a legend occupies only the left portion of the legend. The position tabs position the picture within that area of the legend.

4. If pasting a picture, right-click in the alignment tab and select the Paste command from the shortcut menu (or press Ctrl+V).

Tip from Tim and the Project Team

Although the Paste Special command might be available on the shortcut menu, and it might offer to paste an object in the server application's format (which should let you edit the object from within the header, footer, or legend) the server-formatted objects tend to be very unstable—in fact, they can make the project file unstable. I recommend that you use the Paste command and place only simple pictures in headers, footers, and legends. At least make a backup of your project file before you try it.

If you are inserting a picture file, click the Insert Picture tool and browse to find the file. Once the file is selected, click the Insert button to place the image in the tab.

5. If you want to resize the object, click it to display sizing handles and use them to change the size.

6. When the picture is embedded, choose the OK button; or proceed to print by choosing the Print Preview or Print buttons.

PLACING PROJECT OBJECTS INTO OTHER APPLICATIONS

Microsoft Project has a number of distinctive graphical views that can be very effective when copied to the Clipboard and pasted into other applications. The views that can be copied include

- All the Gantt Chart views
- The Network Diagram and Detailed Network Diagram views
- The Calendar view
- Both of the Usage views (Task Usage and Resource Usage)
- The Resource Chart view
- Any of the sheet views (such as Task Sheet and Resource Sheet)

Note

Project provides no facility for copying the Relationship Diagram view or any of the form views. To copy these views, you must use the Windows Print Screen command or a third-party screen capture program.

You can copy these views with Project's Edit, Copy command or its Edit, Copy Picture command. If you want to paste a linked object in the other application, or if you want to embed a Project object that can be edited, you must use the Copy command. If you want to paste an unlinked picture of a Project view, you will do best to use the Copy Picture command. The following descriptions compare the results you get when you use the different commands:

- If you are content to paste a static, unlinked picture object, or if you need to create a .GIF file to include in a Web page, you should capture the object with the Copy Picture command. You can control precisely the date range to include in timescale views, and you can more easily resize the image without seriously distorting fonts.

- If you want the object you paste to be linked to the source document in Project, you must capture the object with the Copy command. You can paste the object as a linked picture object or as a linked Microsoft Project object. In practice there is very little difference between the two. Both can be updated to show changes in the timeline data for the tasks that are included in the original picture, and you can double-click either type of object to open the Project document that is the source of the link. However, there are limitations to this object type:

    You can't change the tasks or resources that are included in the original picture without deleting the object and starting over.

    You also have limited control over the date range that is included if the view contains a timescale. The Gantt Chart in particular uses graphic elements that extend before and after the start and finish dates for tasks (for example, summary task bars, linking lines, and bar text) and these often appear truncated in the final object.

- If you want total control over what is displayed in the object, capture the view with the Copy command and paste it as an unlinked Microsoft Project object. The data can't be updated, and the entire project is embedded in the other application (thus increasing file size dramatically). But, you have total control over what is displayed in the object image. You can change the view, use filters, change formats, and so forth.

USING THE COPY PICTURE COMMAND TO COPY A VIEW

The Copy Picture command has been improved in Project 2000 to provide more control over the way the object is prepared for display and to provide better picture quality. If the object looks like it might be too large to be displayed, the new Copy Picture Options dialog box offers you choices for the situation. The Copy Picture command is the best way to prepare a static picture object for insertion into other applications. It is also the only way to prepare a picture to be displayed by Web browsers (using the .GIF format).

You need to prepare the view in Project before making the copy, although the options in the Copy Picture dialog box offer additional control over what will be included in the image. In preparing to copy the view, prepare the screen using these guidelines:

- Whatever view you plan to copy, it is best to set it up so that it is contained in one screen. You can capture larger areas, but it is more difficult to get the results you want as the image gets larger.

- If the view has a table, you need to prepare the columns that are displayed and the rows that are selected.

  - Only the columns that are visible will be included in the picture. Therefore, you should arrange the display of columns as you want them in the picture.

  - The Copy Picture dialog box will give you the option of including just the rows that are visible on the screen, or including only the rows that you have selected. If you want to include selected rows, select at least one cell in each row you want to include. To include all rows, click any column heading to select all rows. If you select non-adjacent rows, the image will contain only the rows you selected. Note that selecting a summary task row does not include its subtasks in the image— they must also be selected.

- If the view has a timescale, you will get the best results by compressing the date range you want to include in the picture onto no more than two or three screens. However, you can create a picture that includes more screens of the timescale if you want, but the printed image can be no wider than 22 inches. You will have to zoom out the timescale to get a very large date range into the image successfully.

- If you are copying the Task Usage or Resource Usage view, be sure that the cells in the grid are at least 100% of their normal size. Otherwise, even though the cells are large enough for the values on the screen, you might see many cells filled with x's in the image indicating that the data can't be displayed. To fix the cell size, choose Format, Timescale and set the value in the Size box to 100% or greater.

- If you are copying the Calendar view, one of the Network Diagram views, or the Resource Graph view, Project will include only the current screen in the picture. Therefore, you should prepare the display that you want to fit onto one screen before capturing the picture.

The Copy Picture dialog box (see Figure 20.28) offers options that vary depending on the view you are copying. For all views you have choices about the format in which the picture is rendered:

- Choose For Screen if you are pasting the picture into another application just to be viewed onscreen.

- Choose For Printer if you are pasting the picture into an application for printing. The format of the picture will be determined by the printer you have selected in Project at the time you save the picture. If you change printers before you print, you should copy the picture again.

- Choose To GIF Image File if you plan to use the picture in a Web site display. The image will be saved in a GIF format file (a Graphics Interchange Format compressed bitmap) that the most widely used browsers can display with various controls. You must enter the path and filename for the file that is to be created. A Browse button is available if you want to search the directory structure or to search for a filename to replace. :

Figure 20.28
Use the Copy Picture dialog box to tailor the image you copy—what it includes and how it is rendered.

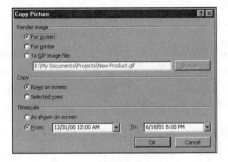

If the view you are copying includes a table display (which is true for the various Gantt Chart views, the Task and Resource Sheet views, and the Task and Resource Usage views), you will have the choice of including

- The Rows on Screen (just those visible when you take the picture)

- The Selected Rows (those in which you selected one or more cells before using the Copy Picture command)

If the view contains a timescale (which is true for the Gantt Charts and the Task and Resource Usage views), you will have the choice of

- Using the dates As Shown on Screen, which means that you can arrange the timescale onscreen as you want to see it in the picture, and then capture just that range of dates in a picture

- Using a range of dates that you specify in the From and To date boxes

Tip from Tim and the Project Team

When using Copy Picture with the Gantt Chart, it's best to include at least one time unit before and several time units after the actual date range you want to include. Many task bars contain graphic elements that extend beyond the start and finish date of the task. This is especially true for bar text that is displayed to the right of the task bar.

To copy the view to the Clipboard, follow these steps:

1. Set up the view you want to copy using the guidelines listed above.

 2. Choose the Edit, Copy Picture command or click the Copy Picture tool on the Standard toolbar to display the Copy Picture dialog box (refer to Figure 20.28).

3. Choose either For Screen, For Printer, or To GIF Image File. If you choose To GIF Image File, supply the path and filename for the GIF file in the text box.

4. If you are in a table display, choose Rows on Screen or Selected Rows.

5. If there is a timescale in the display, select either As Shown on Screen or From and To dates.

6. Choose OK to save the picture.

The maximum size for the picture is 22 inches by 22 inches. If the number of tasks you select or the date range you specify for the timescale might create a picture greater than 22 inches in either direction, Project will alert you with the Copy Picture Options dialog box (see Figure 20.29) that offers the following options:

- Choose Keep the Selected Range if you want to try the picture anyway.

- Choose Zoom Out the Timescale So the Picture Can Fit if you want Project to change the timescale units so that the date range will fit within the maximum dimensions.

- Choose Scale the Picture to 22 Inches in Width if you want Project to compress the date range to fit within 22 inches without changing the timescale units. Fill the Lock Aspect Ratio check box to keep the proportions of the picture the same during scaling.

- Choose Truncate the Picture to 22 Inches in Width and Project will use only the date range and rows in the table that will fit.

- Choose Cancel to start the Copy Picture command over and change the date range to be included.

In most cases you will get a better picture if you choose Cancel and manually adjust the timescale so the picture will fit. It might save you time to choose Zoom Out the Timescale So the Picture Can Fit and paste the picture to see what timescale unit is needed. Then manually zoom out the actual timescale and capture the picture again.

When you switch to the application where you plan to paste the picture, select the location for the picture and use the Edit, Paste command (or Ctrl+C). The Paste Special command is also available but it produces the same end result (pasting the picture as a picture object).

The object will appear with a border and resizing handles. If you drag the corner handles, the width and height of the object will change proportionally.

Figure 20.29
You must choose what to do when the picture is likely to be more than 22 inches in either dimension.

USING THE COPY COMMAND TO COPY A VIEW

When you copy a view to the Clipboard using the Edit, Copy command, there will be no dialog box with options for selecting what to copy. You must set up the screen exactly as you want the object to look when it is pasted in another application. The programmatic choices that you have all lie in the application where you paste the object using the Edit, Paste Special command. Consider the following when making your choices:

- If you want the object to be linked, you can paste it as a linked picture or as a linked Microsoft Project object. Since the display is the same, you should choose the Microsoft Project object because it adds slightly less to the file size in the other application.

- If the object can be unlinked, you will only use the unlinked Microsoft Project object, since the Copy Picture command produces better unlinked picture objects. The unlinked Microsoft Project object increases the file size in the other application by a considerable amount (by approximately the size of the Project document), but it allows you complete control over what is displayed in the other application.

To copy a view that will be pasted as a linked object, set up the view in Project to look the way you want it to look in the other application. Keep in mind that the Copy command generally copies only one screen (the exception is noted below). Use the following guidelines to set up the view:

- If the view contains a table (as does the Gantt Chart, the Usage views, and the Sheet views), only the columns that are visible on the screen will be included, but all rows that you select will be included. However, the rows must be adjacent or you will only be able to paste text instead of an object.

- If the view contains a timescale, the timescale in the object will always start with the earliest start date of any of the selected tasks and include one screen-width of the timescale. Therefore, you should scroll that earliest start date into view on your screen and compress the timescale to display exactly the date range you want covered in the object.

- When you copy the Network Diagram views or the Resource Graph, the object will only include the current screen; so, make sure that screen is exactly what you want in the object.

- The Calendar view can't be pasted as a linked object. Always use the Copy Picture command to paste a Calendar object.

PART

VI

CH

20

■ If you copy the Resource Usage view, the object will only include the table—the timephased data will not display or print. You must use the Copy Picture command if you want to display the Resource Usage view with its timephased data.

If you are copying a view that will be pasted as an unlinked Microsoft Project object, the setup of the screen is not too important because you can open the object and manage the display using the Project menu and toolbars.

When the view is prepared, execute the Copy command. Switch to the other application to paste the object. To paste a linked Microsoft Project object, choose Edit, Paste Special to display the Paste Special dialog box (see Figure 20.30). Choose Paste Link to keep the link to the Project document and choose Microsoft Project Document Object from the list of format types in the As box. Leave the Display As Icon check box unchecked. Then click OK to finish.

Figure 20.30
Use the Paste Special command to paste Microsoft Project objects into another application.

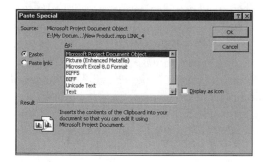

You can resize the object but you can't change what is displayed inside it. If the object contains part of a Gantt Chart, the timescale will change to reflect new dates when you update the link. Resize the object by dragging the sizing handle at the lower-right corner so that the proportions will remain unchanged. Otherwise, you may distort the fonts and graphic objects.

To paste the object as an unlinked Microsoft Project object, use the same commands listed previously except that you click the Paste Link button in the Paste Special dialog box.

Do not resize the unlinked object until you double-click it to activate it as a Microsoft Project object. When double-clicked, the object's border will change to a much thicker border with resizing handles, and the Microsoft Project menu and toolbars will appear. Use the resizing handles to change the overall size of the picture. Use the Project menu and toolbars to change the view if needed. When finished, click outside the object to return to the other application.

TROUBLESHOOTING

RESTORING THE DETAILS COLUMN HEADER

The column of row headers for the timephased data is not visible. What's wrong?

There are two reasons why Details column headers would disappear from the timephased data grid:

- You have split the window and placed another view in the bottom pane that contains timescaled data.

  If this is the case, either choose a different view for the bottom pane—one that doesn't use the timescale—or close the bottom pane altogether by choosing Window, Remove Split.

- You have turned off the display of the Details header column.

  To change this setting, right-click over the grid and choose Detail Styles from the context menu. Click the Usage Properties tab and select Yes in the pull-down list provided in the Display Details Header Column box. Click OK to close the dialog box.

THE EFFICIENT WAY TO CUSTOMIZE A TABLE

I want to modify the columns in a table, but when I do it also changes the table when it's displayed in other views. How can I avoid that?

The best way to make changes in a standard table is to make a copy of the table and customize the copy. The quickest way to do that is as follows:

1. Right-click over the gray-colored blank space above the row numbers to display the Tables shortcut menu. Select More Tables to display the More Tables dialog box. The table you are viewing will be selected.

2. Click the Copy button and Project will open the Table Definition dialog box with a copy of the table you were viewing. If you were already viewing a customized table, click the Edit button to refine it further in the Table Definition dialog box.

3. After making changes in the columns to be included in the table, click OK to save the table definition.

4. In the More Tables dialog box, click Apply to view the new table design.

RESTORING STANDARD TABLES THAT HAVE BEEN CUSTOMIZED

I customized a standard table without making a copy of it first. How can I restore the standard table and keep the customized version as a new table?

You need to do three things: Rename the customized version of the table, apply the renamed table to the view you designed it for, and copy the standard version of the table from the

Global template into the project. The quickest way to rename the table and apply it to its intended view is to follow these steps:

1. Display the view that contains the customized table.

2. Right-click the gray blank space above the row numbers to display the Table shortcut menu.

3. Select More Tables to display the More Table dialog box. The table name will be highlighted.

4. Click the Copy button to have Project create a copy of the customized table in the Table Definition dialog box.

5. Adjust the name of the table if you don't want to leave it named Copy of..., followed by the standard table's name.

6. Fill the Show In Menu if you want this table to appear on the Table menu. If you do add this copy to the menu, you should at least delete the ampersand (&) from the table name so that this copy and the original will not have the same hotkey on the menu.

→ For more details about defining tables, **see** "Using and Creating Tables," **p. 949**

7. Click the OK button to save the copy and return to the More Tables dialog box.

8. Click the Apply button to display the new table in the active view.

To restore the original version of the standard table, follow these steps:

1. Be sure that there is no view open that contains the table name you plan to copy from the Global template.

2. Display the Organizer by choosing Tools, Organizer.

3. Click on the Tables tab.

4. Select the standard table name in the list on the left (the list for the GLOBAL.MPT).

5. Click the Copy button to copy it to the list of tables on the right (the list for the active project).

6. When Project tells you that the table already exists in the active project, click Yes replace the table with the standard version from the template.

7. Click Close to close the Organizer.

PART **VII**

WORKING WITH VIEWS AND REPORTS

CHAPTER 21

USING THE STANDARD VIEWS, TABLES, AND FILTERS

In this chapter

EXPLORING THE STANDARD VIEWS

Views can be categorized in two different ways. The first logical breakdown of views is whether they display tasks or resources. All views focus on one or the other but not both. The next method of categorizing views is by their format. There are basically three different formats for views: sheets, forms, and graphs. The following list summarizes the predefined views using these category breakdowns. Graphical views are listed first, then sheets, then forms. The task views are listed in the column on the left while the resource views are listed on the right. The views marked with an asterisk must be accessed by choosing View, More Views:

View Type	Task Views	Resource Views
Graphical views	Calendar	Resource Graph
	Gantt Chart (Bar Rollup*, Detail Gantt*, Leveling Gantt*, Milestone Date Rollup*, Milestone Rollup*, PA_Expected Gantt*, PA_Optimistic Gantt*, PA_Pessimistic Gantt*, Tracking Gantt), Network Diagram, Descriptive Network Diagram, Relationship Diagram*	
Sheet views	Task Sheet*, Task Usage, PA_PERT Entry Sheet	Resource Sheet, Resource Usage
Form views	Task Form*, Task Details Form*, Task Name Form*	Resource Form*, Resource Name Form*
Combination	Task Entry*views	Resource Allocation*

The views listed with the Gantt Chart are fundamentally the same as the Gantt Chart, except they have a different table applied, and the bars are formatted differently. See the section "Exploring the Standard Tables," later in this chapter, for a discussion of these different tables.

The combination views are actually two standard views displayed on the same screen. They provide a unique combination of information that will be summarized at the end of the chapter.

The following sections will describe each of the views, with all the task views first and then the resource views.

THE CALENDAR

In the popular Calendar view (see Figure 21.1), tasks are displayed in a familiar calendar format. Each task is displayed as a bar that spans the days and weeks during which the task is scheduled to occur. For many people, it is easier to visualize a project when you can see it displayed in this familiar format.

Figure 21.1
The Calendar view displays tasks in a familiar format as you view, edit, or print your project.

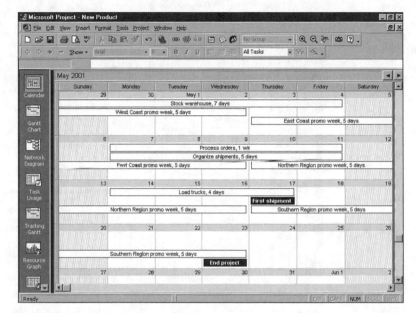

While it is possible to create a project using the calendar, it is not generally advisable to do so. Creating tasks on the calendar causes constraints to be applied to the tasks. This view can be very useful for reviewing the project plan, for editing a project after the initial design has taken place, and for printing.

→ To add tasks using the Calendar view, **see** "Inserting Tasks in Calendar View," **p. 287**

→ To learn more about constraints, **see** "Working with Task Constraints," **p. 234**

Quite often, the calendar displays too many tasks at once, and it becomes difficult to see what you want. Many filters can be applied to home in on particular categories of tasks—for example, tasks that are in progress, top-level tasks, or tasks using a particular resource. This last filter is very helpful when you want to give each resource a list of their respective tasks. Filters in general are discussed at the end of this chapter. Refer to the section "Moving Around in Calendar View" in Chapter 7, "Viewing Your Schedule," for more information about using filters specifically with the Calendar view.

THE GANTT CHART

The Gantt Chart, one of the most popular project management views, is actually a Task Sheet on the left side and a bar chart on the right (see Figure 21.2). The chart is a list of

PART

VII

CH

21

tasks displayed as bars overlaying a timescale. The length of the bars is determined by the duration of the tasks. The placement of the bars on the timescale is determined by the start and finish dates of the tasks. Dependency lines are drawn to show the predecessor and successor relationships between tasks.

Figure 21.2
The Gantt Chart draws bars on a timescale to show when tasks occur.

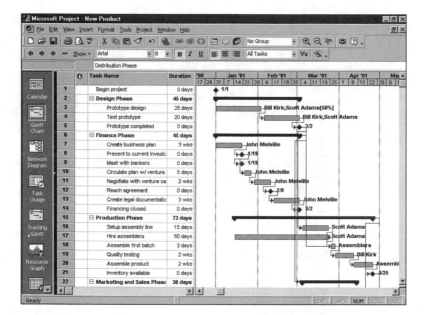

The Gantt Chart is useful during many stages of the project. During the initial planning stages of a project, you can enter tasks, make determinations about dependency relationships, and even assign resources. After the initial planning phase, you will probably need to crash the schedule, which basically means you want to reduce the amount of time taken to complete the whole project. The Gantt Chart is useful in immediately displaying the effect of your efforts. After the project is underway, the Gantt Chart offers practical displays of tasks that are in progress, behind, or ahead of schedule.

The options for formatting the Gantt Chart are so numerous that there is even a special automated tool, the Gantt Chart Wizard, which walks you through the process.

→ To learn more about how to format the Gantt Chart using the Gantt Chart Wizard, **see** "Using the Gantt Chart Wizard," **p. 912**

→ To reduce the overall time of a project, **see** "Strategies for Crashing the Schedule," **p. 527**

THE ROLLUP VIEWS

Several of the views based on the Gantt Chart view are grouped together because they are all rollup views. The technique of using rollups was discussed in greater detail in Chapter 12, "Reviewing the Project Plan." This section will describe the various predefined rollup views that are available, what information they provide, and how they are different from one another.

If you use outlining in your project task list, you can choose to display specified task names and/or dates on the summary task bar. This is useful when the outline level for that task is collapsed, but you would still like to see where that task falls along the summary task.

Figure 21.3 displays the value of using a collapsed outline with rollups. In this figure, the outline is collapsed, and milestones are set to roll up to the Gantt Chart. Milestones are special tasks that are used to show landmarks or turning points within your project. The rollup views use the Rollup table that includes a field called Text Above. Some of the milestones have the Text Above field set to Yes to stagger their titles. This feature can be enabled on an individual task by selecting that task and checking the option to Roll Up Gantt Bar to Summary from within the Task Information form, or it can be set for the project as a whole. This feature is enabled on the Format menu under Layout. It is called "Always Roll Up Gantt Bars."

Caution

A problem associated with rollups occurs when task names are long or the timescale is zoomed out to view a long time period—the text tends to overlap. Each of the rollup views uses the Rollup table to add a column in the Task Sheet called Text Above. This field offers a drop-down list with Yes and No as the options. When Yes is selected, the task name appears above the summary task bar, rather than below, which is the default.

→ To find out more about working with rolled-up tasks, **see** "Rolling Up the Task Bars," **p. 271**

Figure 21.3
Rollups can increase the level of detail available in a collapsed outline.

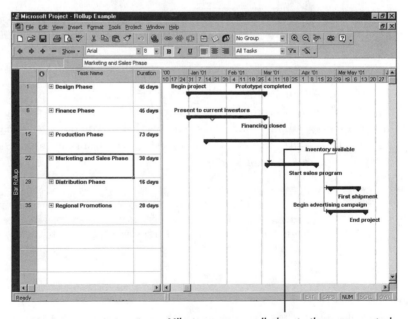

Milestone names rolled up to the summary task

Bar Rollup

If you roll up a task (rather than a milestone), the summary task bar will appear more like a task than a summary. This is useful when you want to highlight certain tasks when task details are not displayed. As shown in Figure 21.4, the rollup of the Quality Testing task emphasizes its importance.

Figure 21.4
The Bar Rollup view allows you to emphasize specific task details in a collapsed outline.

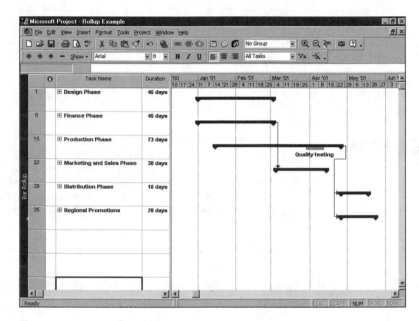

Milestone Date Rollup

The Milestone Date Rollup view is very similar to the Bar Rollup view. The difference is that the milestone dates roll up as well as their names. As shown in Figure 21.5, the names of the milestones appear above the summary task bar (you don't have to change the Text Above field) and the date appears below. Triangles only appear on the end of the summary task bar if you roll up a milestone to it.

Caution

Because all the rolled-up task names appear above the summary task bar, there is an increased likelihood that the task names will overlap. You might need to increase the span of the timescale, shorten the task names, or be more selective about which tasks are rolled up.

Milestone Rollup

The Milestone Rollup view is similar to the previous two rollup views. As displayed in Figure 21.6, when tasks are marked as Rolled Up, the task names only are rolled up, not the dates. There is a field in the Task Sheet called Text Above that allows you to choose from a drop-down list to have the text of the name appear above the summary task bar. If tasks are rolled up (rather than just milestones), only a triangle shows for them on the summary task bar, rather than a bar, as in the Bar Rollup view.

Figure 21.5
The Milestone Date Rollup view automatically puts names above the summary task bar and dates below.

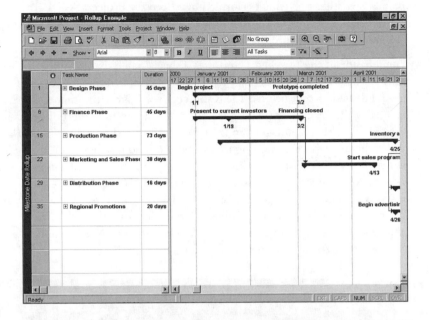

Figure 21.6
The Milestone Rollup view allows you to selectively place some rolled-up task names above the summary task bar and some below.

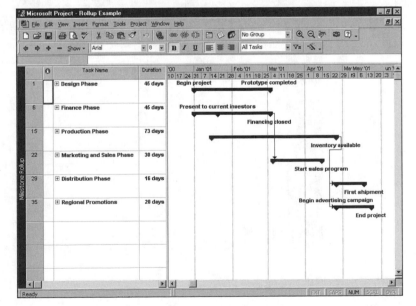

PART

VII

CH

21

THE LEVELING GANTT

Following the same general format of the Gantt Chart, the Leveling Gantt has been specifically formatted for use while resolving resource overallocation problems, either through manual leveling or leveling performed by Microsoft Project. See "Letting Project Level Overallocated Resources for You" in Chapter 11, "Resolving Resource Assignment Problems," for more information about leveling your project.

The left side of the Leveling Gantt uses a special table that includes the leveling delay field. This is where Project notes delays it calculates during automatic leveling, or where you can enter a delay in a task because the resource is too busy with other tasks. Several bars have been added for each task (see Figure 21.7). Extending to the left of each task is a very narrow delay bar that is drawn from the earliest date a task can start, known as the Early Start, to its scheduled start. Extending to the right of each task bar is another very narrow bar that depicts *free slack* (the amount of time that a task can be delayed without delaying any other tasks) that is drawn from the scheduled finish date to the amount of free slack. Using this bar, you can see how much a task can be delayed without causing a delay in the project. Assuming the default settings, a blue-colored bar shows the task as currently scheduled, while a green-colored bar shows the task before it was leveled. A dotted line shows where the task has been split as a result of leveling.

Figure 21.7
The Leveling Gantt allows for the input of, and shows the effect of, delaying tasks.

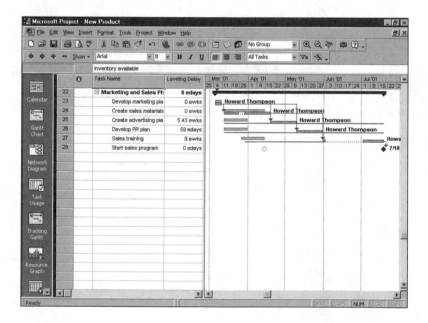

→ To learn more about leveling your project, **see** "Resolving Overallocations by Delaying Assignments,"
   p. 456

→ To learn more about resolving conflicts through splitting tasks, **see** "Splitting Individual Assignments,"
   p. 456

THE DETAIL GANTT

Based again on the same general format of the Gantt Chart, the Detail Gantt is very similar to the Leveling Gantt in that it shows where delays have been created as a result of leveling, whether performed by Project through automatic leveling or by you through manual leveling. The leveling table displays the leveling delay field. On the timescale portion of the Gantt Chart, additional bars are drawn to display how much a task can be delayed without causing the project to slip, how much a task has already been delayed, and where tasks have been split.

For example, in Figure 21.8 you can see that task 25 has been delayed for 5 weeks and could still be delayed a little over 10 more weeks without causing the project deadline to be missed. Work on one task can also be performed at two different times by splitting the task to accommodate other more pressing tasks assigned to the resource, as with task 24 and task 27.

The difference between the Detail Gantt and the Leveling Gantt is that the Detail Gantt does not show how the task was scheduled before it was delayed.

Figure 21.8
The Detail Gantt offers another view to keep track of tasks that have been delayed or that could be delayed to resolve resource overallocations.

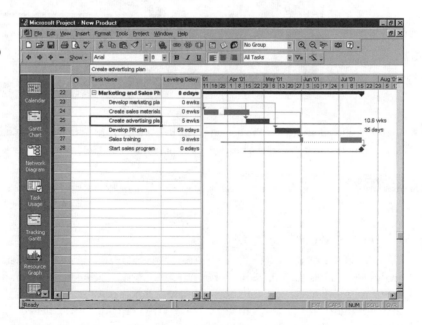

THE TRACKING GANTT

The Tracking Gantt is also based on the standard Gantt Chart and displays an additional gray bar, below the regular task bar, with the baseline information. The standard progress bars have been modified slightly; instead of a narrow black bar extending across the task bar, there are two equal-height bars for each task. The lower bar is gray and depicts baseline information. The top colored bar displays progress with a solid color and same color

PART

VII

CH

21

shading for the remaining work to be done for the task (see Figure 21.9). Text for the percent complete is included on the right side of all task bars. (For additional information on saving the baseline, see "Capturing the Baseline" in Chapter 16, "Tracking Work on the Project.")

Figure 21.9
The Tracking Gantt gives a snapshot of how the project is progressing.

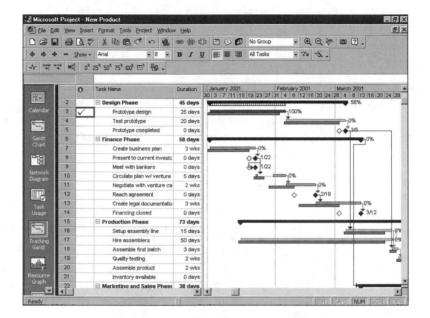

→ To learn more about viewing the baseline plan, **see** "Viewing the Tracking Gantt Chart," **p. 667**

→ To learn more about capturing a baseline for your project, **see** "Setting the Baseline or Plan," **p. 660**

Caution   The baseline bars will not display if the baseline has not been saved or has been cleared.

PERT ANALYSIS VIEWS

The PERT Analysis toolbar displays several special views that are associated with PERT analysis (which is the calculation of duration using a weighted average of best-case, worst-case, and most-likely-case duration estimates). The easiest way to access these views is through the PERT Analysis toolbar. These views are not initially listed with the other views when you go through View, More Views. They must first be accessed through the PERT Analysis toolbar, and then will display in the list of views.

→ To learn more about estimating durations, **see** "Project Extras: Letting Project Calculate Duration for You," **p. 202**

The PA_PERT Entry Sheet is the view where the user enters an optimistic estimation of duration, a pessimistic estimation of duration, and an estimate of the expected duration. The view is a sheet view that displays the PA_PERT Entry table. Project calculates the weighted average of the estimates and places the result in the Duration field.

 There are three special Gantt Chart views that you can display with the tools on the PERT Analysis toolbar. However, these views should not be used because they roll up the best case and worst case estimates for tasks into estimates for the project in a statistically unsound fashion. As a result they significantly exaggerate the best and worst case estimate of the duration of the project.

The Network Diagram

The Network Diagram, previously known as the PERT Chart, is another graphical view of a project, this time focusing on the dependency relationships between tasks. There is no reference to time at all, as in the Gantt Chart. As shown in Figure 21.10, the Network Diagram resembles a flow chart with boxes (nodes) for each task. Lines are drawn to illustrate predecessors and successors. The display in Figure 21.10 was created using the Zoom Out tool in the Standard toolbar. If you move the mouse pointer close to a task node, it zooms in to show a detailed view of that node. When you double-click a task node, the Task Information dialog box for that task is displayed. A new feature of this view includes outline symbols, which can be used to hide or display subtasks of summary tasks to see different levels of detail. In addition to being able to outline in this view, the Network Diagram can also be filtered to reflect only those tasks that meet certain criteria.

This view is primarily intended for use during the initial design phase of a project. It is here that you can ensure that the plan is logical.

Figure 21.10
The Network Diagram helps define the logic of predecessors and successors for the project plan.

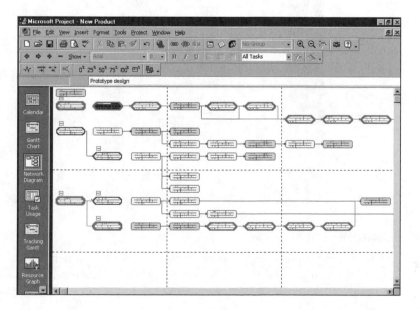

PART **VII**

CH **21**

→ For additional information about the Network Diagram, **see** "Working with the Network Diagram View," **p. 298**

→ For additional information about task dependencies, see "Modifying, Reviewing, and Removing Dependency Links," **p. 231**

Tip from Tim and the Project Team	You can also hide any summary tasks or field detail by using the Network Diagram toolbar.

THE DESCRIPTIVE NETWORK DIAGRAM

The Descriptive Network Diagram is almost identical to the Network Diagram. This view also focuses on the dependency relationships between tasks. However, the boxes that make up the Descriptive Network Diagram provide more detail information regarding the tasks they represent. As shown in Figure 21.11, the Descriptive Network Diagram illustrates the dependency relationships between tasks, while providing additional information about those tasks. As with the Network Diagram, if you move the mouse pointer close to the task node, it zooms in to show a detailed view of that node. This new feature includes outline symbols which can be used to hide or display subtasks of summary tasks, and can be used with task filters.

Figure 21.11
The Descriptive Network Diagram provides additional task information when analyzing task dependencies.

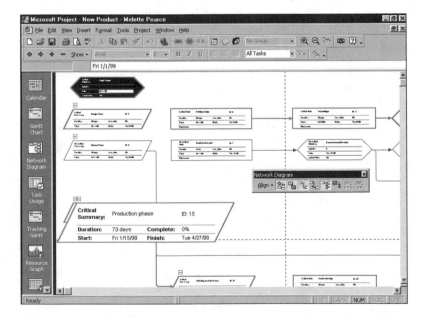

THE RELATIONSHIP DIAGRAM

The Relationship Diagram is a special kind of Network Diagram. This view has been previously referred to as the Task PERT view. As shown in Figure 21.12, the Relationship Diagram is typically displayed at the bottom of a task list (Task Sheet or Gantt Chart). It only shows the immediate predecessors and successors for the task selected in the top pane. This is a very useful view when examining the task dependencies of the project, particularly when making sure that every task is linked and that the links all make sense. For example, the dependencies for task 18 are much clearer in the Relationship Diagram view shown in the bottom pane than in the Gantt Chart in the top pane. The type of relationship is also displayed. For example, each of the tasks related to task 18 in Figure 21.12 has a finish-start (FS) relationship.

Figure 21.12
Use the Relationship Diagram to make sure that every task has at least one predecessor and successor and that all relationship links make sense.

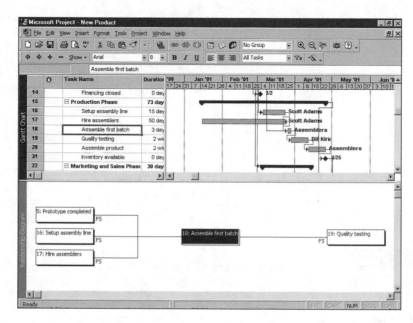

→ To learn more about working with task dependencies, **see** "Understanding Dependency Links," p. 209

Tip from Tim and the Project Team

When working with combination views, it might be useful to turn off the View bar. Point to a blank spot on the View bar, press the right mouse button, and choose View Bar. When this is done (as shown previously in Figure 21.12), the view name shows at the left edge of the view.

THE TASK SHEET

The Task Sheet view is a spreadsheet format of information. Tasks are displayed in rows with fields of information about those tasks displayed in columns. The fields (columns) that are displayed are determined by the table that has been applied. (See the section "Exploring the Standard Tables," later in this chapter, for more details about tables.) By choosing View, More Views, Task Sheet, you can use this view during many different phases of the project;

this is preferred by people who like working in a spreadsheet format rather than with a form or with a graphical view. Figure 21.13 displays the Task Sheet with the Entry table applied.

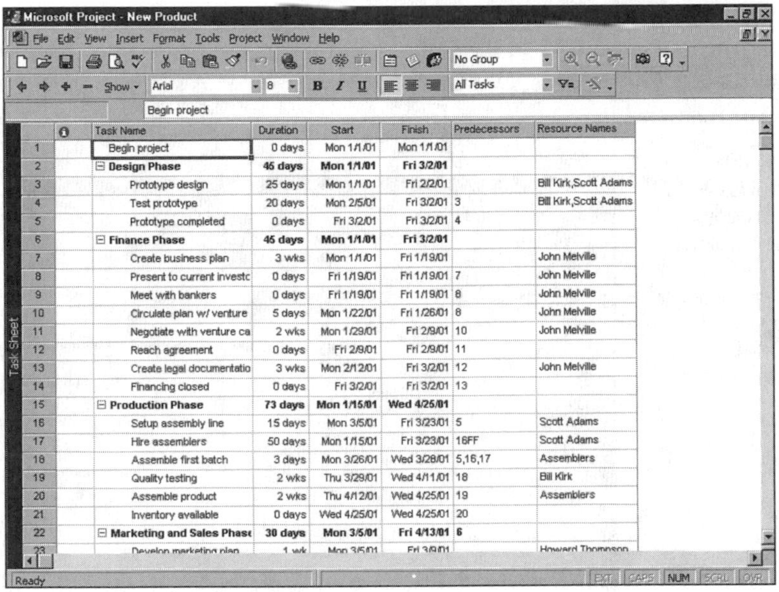

Figure 21.13
The Task Sheet with the Entry table applied enables the user to view a lot of detail information on one screen.

Caution

Don't change the start or finish dates in the Task Sheet when you see them. These are dates calculated by Project, and you might inadvertently create a constraint.

→ To learn more about conflicts caused by constraints, **see** "Working with Task Constraints," **p. 234**

TASK USAGE

The Task Usage view displays hours of work that are to be performed, laid out on a timescale. As shown in Figure 21.14, task 23 is a 1-week task assigned to Howard Thompson. In the timescale grid on the right side of the view, the task begins on Thursday with 8 hours of work, and continues through the following Wednesday, skipping the weekend. This view is primarily intended to be used for resource contouring, as discussed in detail in the section, "Contouring Resource Usage" of Chapter 9, "Understanding Resource Scheduling."

Figure 21.14
The Task Usage view displays exactly when work is scheduled to occur.

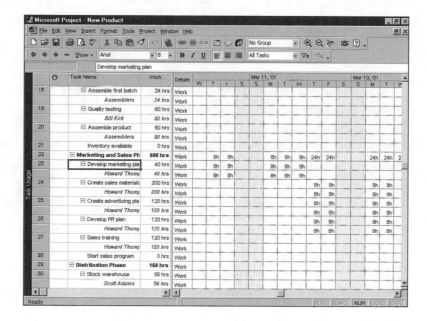

THE TASK FORM

In contrast with the Task Sheet, the Task Form presents basic information about only one task in a form format (see Figure 21.15). It is possible therefore to see more information about one task at a time than in a sheet view. The Task Form is often used in the bottom pane to display more detailed information about the selected task in the top pane. To view the Task Form in the bottom pane, choose Window, Split from a task view such as the Gantt Chart. Project will place the Task Form in the bottom pane by default. If displayed in a single-pane view by choosing View, More Views, Task Form, as in Figure 21.15, you can move from one task to another using the Previous and Next buttons.

The bottom portion of the form view can be set to display a variety of project details, such as predecessors and successors, resource schedule information, work hours, and cost, just to name a few. These options can be found by choosing Format, Details or by right-clicking anywhere in the form itself. It is also possible to create custom forms if the predefined ones do not meet your needs.

→ To learn about additional advantages of the Task Form, **see** "Using the Task Form for Tracking," **p. 683**

→ To learn how to enhance the Task Form, **see** "Formatting the Task and Resource Forms," **p. 927**

PART
VII

CH
21

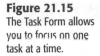

Figure 21.15
The Task Form allows you to focus on one task at a time.

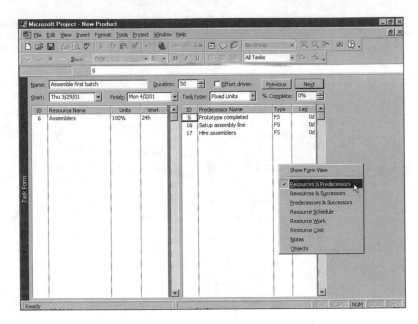

THE TASK DETAILS FORM

The Task Details Form shown in Figure 21.16 is similar in format to the Task Form but shows more detail. Notice in particular the options for Current, Baseline, and Actual Dates. You could use this form for tracking the progress of tasks already underway. Constraints are also displayed on this form, making them more obvious. As with the Task Form, open the Task Details Form by choosing View, More Views, Task Details Form. As with the Task Form, the bottom portion of the Task Details Form can display a variety of fields. To choose the fields to be displayed, select Format, Details from the main menu or right-click the form and choose an option from the shortcut menu.

THE TASK NAME FORM

The Task Name Form shown at the bottom of Figure 21.17 is, as its name implies, a simplified form that displays only the task name in the top portion of the form. The bottom portion of the form has the same formatting options as the Task Form and the Task Details Form. It is accessed by choosing View, More Views, Task Name Form. The Task Name Form is useful when used in the bottom pane of a combination view and you don't want to waste screen space with redundant information.

Figure 21.16
The Task Details Form is useful during scheduling and tracking.

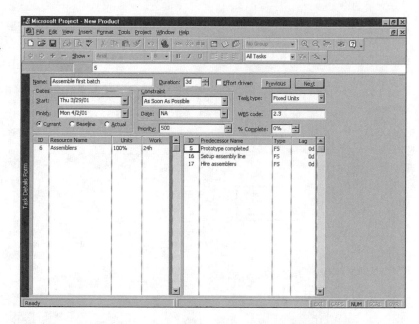

Figure 21.17
The simple Task Name Form doesn't distract the user with too much detail.

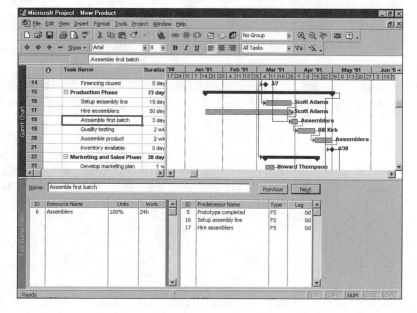

THE RESOURCE GRAPH

The Resource Graph is a graphical view displaying resource allocation over time (see the top pane in Figure 21.18). Found on the main <u>V</u>iew menu and on the View bar, it can be a single pane view by itself, or it can be used as part of a combination view, in either the top pane or the bottom pane. Used in conjunction with the Go To Next Overallocation button on the Resource Management toolbar, it can be very useful in determining when resources are overallocated, and by how much. For example, you can see in Figure 21.18 that, beginning the week of March 11, Howard Thompson has way too much to do.

Figure 21.18
The Resource Graph illustrates resource overallocations graphically on a timescale.

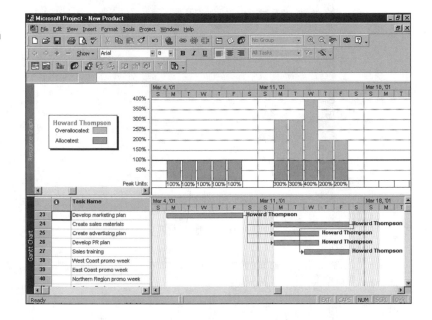

→ For more information on viewing resource conflicts, **see** "Displaying Overallocation," **p. 933**

→ For information on viewing the Resource Graph as part of a combination view, **see** "Creating a Combination View," **p. 948**

Tip from Tim and the Project Team

A very handy combination view is a view with the Resource Graph in the top pane and the Gantt Chart in the bottom pane (refer to Figure 21.18). With this combination view, after you have identified an overallocated resource and determined the time frame during which the overallocation occurs (the top pane), you can see which tasks the resource has been assigned to (the bottom pane).

RESOURCE USAGE

The Resource Usage view, accessed through the main <u>V</u>iew menu, is a sheet view listing resources on the left and their allocation to tasks on a timescale on the right (see Figure 21.19). This view displays similar information to the Resource Graph but in a different format, showing actual numbers rather than graphical representations of those numbers. Resources are listed on the left with the tasks assigned to them indented underneath. A symbol similar to the outline symbol in the task list allows you to hide or show the tasks assigned to the various resources. For example, in Figure 21.19 tasks for Scott Adams have been hidden; the plus symbol to the left of his name indicates that there is information not currently displayed. A diamond-shaped icon with an exclamation point displays in the Indicators column for the resources that need to be leveled. When you point to the icon, a message displays identifying the type of leveling setting that is required: day by day, week by week, and so on.

→ To learn more about resolving resource conflicts, **see** "Strategies for Eliminating Resource Overallocations," **p. 455**

The allocation information on the right side can be set to display hours of work, hours of overallocated work, cost, available time, and so on.

This view is primarily used when resolving overallocation problems. Much like the Resource Graph, it is useful when displayed in a combination view, particularly with the Gantt Chart in the bottom pane to display the tasks assigned to each resource.

Figure 21.19
Use the Resource Usage view when resolving overalloca-tion problems.

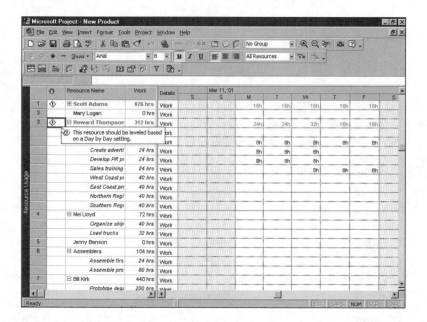

→ To learn about additional features of the Resource Usage View, **see** "Working with the Resource Usage View," **p. 449**

THE RESOURCE SHEET

The Resource Sheet shown in Figure 21.20 is a list of resource information displayed in familiar spreadsheet format. Accessed by choosing View, More Views, Resource Sheet, or using the View bar, it can be used to enter and edit data about resources whether they are work resources or material resources. Each resource is in a row with fields of resource data in columns. The Indicators column displays an icon for overallocated resources. The fields that are displayed depend on the table that has been applied. (See the section "Exploring the Standard Tables," later in this chapter, for more details.) This view is most often used for creating the initial resource pool.

PART

VII

CH

21

Figure 21.20
The Resource Sheet provides a spreadsheet format for entering and editing basic resource data.

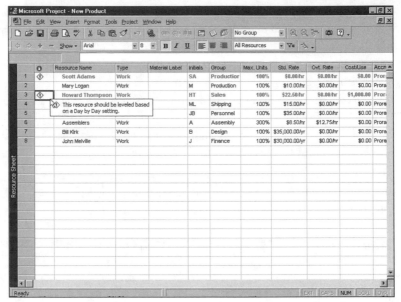

→ To learn more about setting up your resources, **see** "Defining the Resource Pool," **p. 322**

→ For additional information about how the Resource Sheet can aid in discovering resource conflicts, **see** "Identifying Resource Overallocations," **p. 444**

THE RESOURCE FORM

Displaying much the same information as the Resource Sheet, the Resource Form only shows one resource at a time, allowing you to focus on one at a time (see Figure 21.21). The information in the top portion of the Resource Form is the same as in the Resource Sheet. The bottom portion can be set to display a schedule of tasks to which the resource is assigned—the hours of work that are currently assigned, including overtime; costs associated with this resource; notes; and so on. You can find these choices by choosing Format, Details.

The Resource Form can be accessed by choosing View, More Views for display in a single or combination view. The top portion of the Resource Form can also be accessed by double-clicking a resource name in any view that displays it (see Figure 21.22). The form will appear this time as the Resource Information dialog box for easy viewing and editing.

Figure 21.21
Use the Resource Form to display both basic and detailed information about any resource.

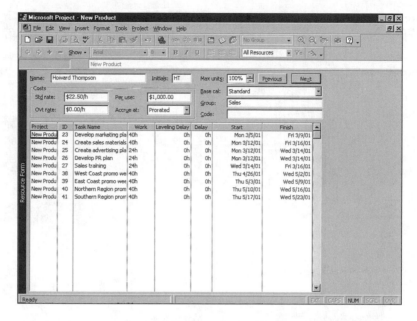

Figure 21.22
The top part of the Resource Form can be displayed by double-clicking any resource in any view.

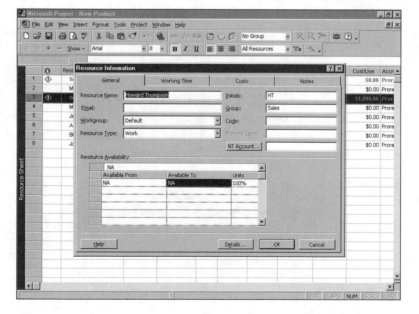

THE RESOURCE NAME FORM

Similar to the Task Name Form, the Resource Name Form is a simple form that only displays the Resource Name in the top portion (see Figure 21.23). The bottom portion can be formatted to display a variety of fields about resources by choosing Format, Details.

Figure 21.23
The Resource Name Form doesn't distract the user with too much detail.

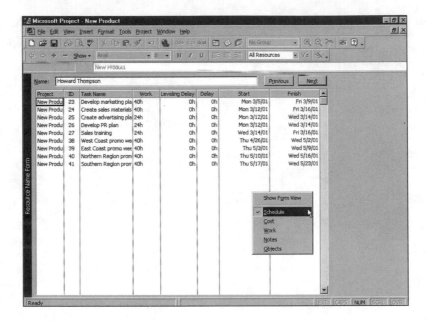

THE TASK ENTRY

The Task Entry view is actually a combination of two views already described—the Gantt Chart in the top pane and the Task Form in the bottom pane (see Figure 21.24). It is a useful view because you can see several different types of information at one time: tasks on a timescale at the top and detailed information about the selected task at the bottom. This view can be accessed in three ways: by choosing View, More Views, by clicking the Task Entry button on the Resource Management toolbar, or by merely splitting the window by choosing Window, Split when a Gantt Chart view is active. The Task Form is the default view that displays automatically when the window is split.

Caution

The Task Entry button runs the ResMgmt_TaskEntry macro that displays the Task Entry view and applies the Resource Schedule details for the Task Form in the bottom pane. That details selection will remain in place every time the window is split until a different details selection is applied.

Figure 21.24
The Task Entry view offers several different perspectives on your project.

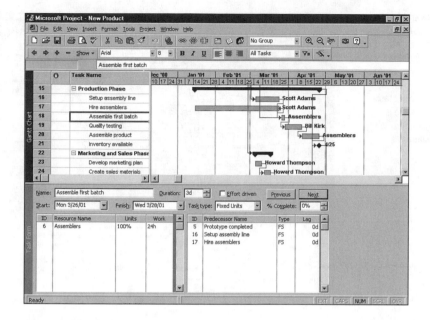

RESOURCE ALLOCATION

The Resource Allocation view is another predefined combination view using views that have already been described: the Resource Usage view at the top and the Leveling Gantt at the bottom (see Figure 21.25). The Resource Allocation view can be accessed by choosing View, More Views, Resource Allocation. As its name implies, this view was designed for resolving resource overallocations. In the top view, you determine which resources are overallocated, during what period of time, and to what degree. Then in the Gantt Chart at the bottom, you can determine which tasks are assigned to that resource. With this information, you can then make decisions about how to handle the overallocation. For example, in Figure 21.25 the top pane identifies the week of March 11 as a problem for Howard Thompson. The bottom pane identifies the tasks that Howard has assigned to him. Each of these tasks requires his full attention, causing the overallocation. With this information, you can make a wiser decision about how to handle the problem.

→ To learn more about resolving resource conflicts, **see** "Identifying Resource Overallocations," **p. 444**

This view can also be accessed in two ways: either by choosing View, More Views or by clicking the Resource Allocation View button on the Resource Management toolbar.

PART

VII

CH

21

Figure 21.25
Use the Resource Allocation view to see when and by how much a resource is overallocated, as well as what tasks the resource is assigned during that time period.

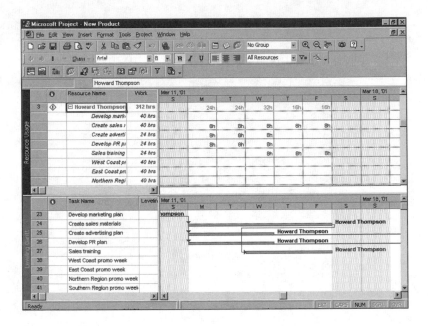

EXPLORING THE STANDARD TABLES

In the sheet views, the fields (columns) that are displayed are controlled by tables. You can choose different tables by choosing View, Table, More Tables. If you are in a task view, the list of task tables is displayed. If you are in a resource view, a list of resource tables is displayed. When you access the More Tables dialog box, you can view either the task or resource list of tables by choosing the appropriate option button in the top-left corner of the dialog box. The most commonly used tables are listed on the Table menu, but all tables are listed in the More Tables dialog box. You can only apply tables, however, for the appropriate view format; that is, you can only apply a task table when you are in a task view.

The following list displays all the predefined tables, with the task tables preceding the resource tables. Tables marked with an asterisk (*) must be accessed by choosing View, Table, More Tables.

Task Tables

- Cost
- Hyperlink
- Summary
- Usage
- Work
- Constraint Dates*
- Earned Value*

- Entry
- Schedule
- Tracking
- Variance
- Baseline*
- Delay*
- Export*

- PA_Expected Case*
- PA_PERT Entry*

- PA_Optimistic Case*
- PA_Pessimistic Case*
- Rollup Table*

Resource Tables

- Cost
- Hyperlink
- Usage
- Earned Value*
- Entry—Material Resource*

- Entry
- Summary
- Work
- Export*x
- Entry—Work Resource*

You can customize and even create your own tables. The purpose of this section is to describe each of the predefined tables that are included with Microsoft Project. The fields that are included in each table will be listed but not described in detail. You can, however, learn more about these fields through Microsoft Project's Help features that are discussed in "Using the Online Learning Aids" in Chapter 2, "Learning the Basics of Microsoft Project."

→ To create your own custom table, **see** "Using and Creating Tables," **p. 949**

THE TASK TABLES

By choosing View, Table, the most frequently used tables available for viewing task information will be displayed directly. There are a number of additional tables that can be accessed by choosing View, Table, More Tables. You can also edit, copy, and even create new tables in this dialog box. You must be in a task view before any of these tables are available.

THE COST TABLE

The Cost table is a task table that displays cost information about tasks. The fields that are displayed include ID, Name (titled Task Name), Fixed Cost, Fixed Cost Accrual, Cost, Baseline Cost, Cost Variance, Actual Cost, and Remaining Cost. This table is most useful when you are tracking a project and you need to see how costs are varying from what you had originally planned.

THE ENTRY TABLE

The Entry table is a task table and is used as the default for the Gantt Chart. It is particularly helpful during the data entry stage when creating your project. The fields that are displayed include ID, Indicators, Name (titled Task Name), Duration, Start, Finish, Predecessors, and Resource Names.

THE HYPERLINK TABLE

The Hyperlink table is a task table that allows you to create a hyperlink to a file on your own computer, a network in your organization, an intranet in your organization, or the

World Wide Web on the Internet. The fields that are displayed include ID, Indicators, Name (titled Task Name), Hyperlink, Hyperlink Address, and Hyperlink SubAddress.

→ To learn more about the power of hyperlinks, **see** "Navigating with Hyperlinks," **p. 568**

THE SCHEDULE TABLE

As its name implies, the Schedule table displays scheduling information about tasks. Fields that are included are ID, Name (titled Task Name), Start, Finish, Late Start, Late Finish, Free Slack, and Total Slack. *Free Slack* refers to the amount of time a task can be delayed without delaying its successor tasks, while *Total Slack* refers to the amount of time a task can be delayed without affecting the project's finish date. With this information, you can pinpoint tasks that can be adjusted when you are trying to reduce the overall duration of the project (crash the schedule). You know that you can delay noncritical tasks, but by how much? By providing the calculated values of free slack and total slack, you can tell how much a task can be delayed without it affecting related tasks or the project end date.

→ To learn more about reducing time within your project, **see** "Strategies for Crashing the Schedule," **p. 531**

THE SUMMARY TABLE

The Summary table provides basic task information. Fields displayed include ID, Name (titled Task Name), Duration, Start, Finish, Percent Complete, Cost, and Work. This view can be useful to management when printed as a summary of all the tasks that are part of the project.

THE TRACKING TABLE

The Tracking table provides a place to view or enter actual information on tasks as the project progresses. Fields that are displayed include ID, Name (titled Task Name), Actual Start, Actual Finish, Percent Complete, Actual Duration, Remaining Duration, Actual Cost, and Actual Work. Print the Task Sheet with this table applied and give to personnel who are not working in an office with a computer. The printout serves as their tracking tool. Notes taken on the printout can then be entered back into the file.

THE USAGE TABLE

The Usage table is used by the new Task Usage view and provides information about the hours of work incurred for each task. The fields that are displayed include ID, Indicators, Name (titled Task Name), Work, Duration, Start, and Finish.

THE VARIANCE TABLE

The Variance table is another task table that summarizes the difference between what was planned and what has actually happened in the project. Fields that are displayed include ID, Name (titled Task Name), Start, Finish, Baseline Start, Baseline Finish, Start Variance, and Finish Variance. For example, with the calculated variance fields it's possible to identify resources that start their tasks late but finish on time, or resources that start on time but finish late. These are two different kinds of resource problems and should be handled differently.

THE WORK TABLE

The Work table displays total hours of work required and performed for tasks. Fields that are displayed include ID, Name (titled Task Name), Work, Baseline Work, Work Variance, Actual Work, Remaining Work, and Percent Work Complete. This is useful information to have when you need to identify tasks that are requiring more time than originally expected, and tasks that are in trouble because of that. These tasks might need additional resources or different resources.

THE BASELINE TABLE

The Baseline table displays information about what you planned during the design phase of the project. As you enter actual information, Project continues calculating start and finish dates for the tasks that follow. Baseline dates are created at the time the baseline is set. Those dates will not be recalculated, but instead provide the comparison to what you planned. Fields that are displayed include ID, Name (titled Task Name), Baseline Duration, Baseline Start, Baseline Finish, Baseline Work, and Baseline Cost.

→ For additional information on capturing a baseline plan, **see** "Setting the Baseline or Plan," **p. 660**

THE CONSTRAINT DATES TABLE

Available only through the More Tables command, this task table is an invaluable tool for locating tasks that have had constraints applied, whether intentional or not. Fields that are displayed include ID, Name (titled Task Name), Duration, Constraint Type, and Constraint Date.

→ To learn more about resolving problems caused by constraints, **see** "Working with Task Constraints," **p. 234**

THE DELAY TABLE

The Delay table is used by the Detail and Leveling Gantt views, but you can use it directly if you want. It is helpful when you are trying to resolve overallocation problems. If you are using the Resource Leveling command, you can use this table to see where delays have been imposed on a task. If you are leveling resources on your own, this table offers a place to enter the delay information. This table is basically the Entry table with the Leveling Delay field added. Fields that are displayed include ID, Indicators, Name (titled Task Name), Leveling Delay, Duration, Start, Finish, Successors, and Resource Names.

→ To learn more about Resource Leveling, **see** "Resolving Overallocations by Delaying Assignments," **p. 456**

THE EARNED VALUE TABLE

The Earned Value table is used to compare actual progress against expected progress based on work completed by resources. It can also be used to predict whether a task will come in under budget based on costs incurred thus far. Most of the fields are calculated and include ID, Name (titled Task Name), BCWS (for Budgeted Cost of Work Scheduled), BCWP (for Budgeted Cost of Work Performed), ACWP (for Actual Cost of Work Performed), SV (for Schedule Variance), CV (for Cost Variance), Cost (titled EAC for Estimate at Completion), Baseline Cost (titled BAC for Budgeted at Completion), and VAC (for Variance at Completion).

→ For additional information on viewing your project's progress, **see** "Reviewing Progress Information at the Task Level," **p. 703**

THE EXPORT TABLE

The Export table is a task table that was designed with exporting to another application in mind. Most of the task fields, including many that are calculated, are displayed: ID, Unique ID, Name (titled Task Name), Duration, Type, Outline Level, Baseline Duration, Predecessors, Start, Finish, Early Start, Early Finish, Late Start, Late Finish, Free Slack, Total Slack, Leveling Delay, Percent Complete, Actual Start, Actual Finish, Baseline Start, Baseline Finish, Constraint Type, Constraint Date, Stop, Resume, Created, Work, Baseline Work, Actual Work, Cost, Fixed Cost, Baseline Cost, Actual Cost, Remaining Cost, WBS, Priority, Milestone, Summary, Rollup, Subproject File, and numerous customizable fields: Text 1–Text 10, Cost 1–Cost 3, Duration 1–Duration 3, Flag 1–Flag 10, Marked, Number 1–Number 5, Subproject File, Contact, Start 1–Start 5, and Finish 1–Finish 5.

→ To learn more about outside data sources that are supported by Microsoft Project, **see** "File Formats Supported by Microsoft Project 2000," **p. 761**

→ To learn more about exporting specific data from your project, **see** "Exchanging Selected Parts of a Project with Other Formats," **p. 774**

PERT ANALYSIS TABLES

There are four tables that are used in views that you display with the PERT Analysis toolbar. The tables are PA_Expected Case, PA_Optimistic Case, PA_Pessimistic Case, and PA_PERT Entry. As explained previously in the "PERT Analysis Views" section, the only one of those views you should use is the PA_PERT Entry Sheet and the PA_PERT Entry table which it displays. This table includes the task ID, Name, and Duration fields, plus the custom fields Duration1, Duration2, and Duration3, which are titled Optimistic Dur., Expected Dur., and Pessimistic Dur. in the table.

THE ROLLUP TABLE

The Rollup table is applied to the Rollup views to allow the user to control the title text of the rollup bar. It utilizes a Flag field as a way to capture a yes/no response for displaying the task name title above the summary bar. The fields that are displayed include ID, Indicators, Name (titled Task Name), Duration, Flag 10 (titled Text Above), Start, Finish, Predecessors, and Resource Names.

THE RESOURCE TABLES

When a Task Sheet is part of a view, the task tables described previously focus on task information. When a Resource Sheet view is displayed, the columns are also controlled by tables. Only the resource tables are available when you are in a resource view. The most commonly used tables are available directly by choosing View, Table; all resource tables are available when you choose View, Table, More Tables.

THE COST TABLE

There is also a Cost table for resources. Instead of calculating costs on a task-by-task basis, the Cost table for resources provides cost data by resource. Fields that are displayed include ID, Name (titled Resource Name), Cost, Baseline Cost, Cost Variance, Actual Cost, and Remaining Cost. This table can be helpful in determining which resources are the most and least expensive and which ones are over budget and under budget. When applied to the Resource Usage view, it is possible to see the cost information for the resource during the whole project, as well as broken down on a task-by-task basis.

THE RESOURCE ENTRY TABLE

Very similar to the Entry table for tasks, the Entry table for resources displays information about material resources as well as work resources that are usually gathered when the resource pool is being created. It is the default table used by the Resource Sheet. Fields that are displayed include ID, Indicators, Name (titled Resource Name), Type, Material Label, Initials, Group, Maximum Units, Standard Rate, Overtime Rate, Cost Per Use, Accrue At, Base Calendar, and Code.

→ For additional information on setting up resources, **see** "Defining the Resource Pool," **p. 322**

THE ENTRY—MATERIAL RESOURCES TABLE

2000 This resource table is based on the standard Entry table for defining resources. It specifically focuses on material or consumable resources, such as lumber or concrete, and omits fields that apply only to work resources. The fields that are displayed include ID, Indicators, Name (titled Resource Name), Type, Material Label, Initials, Group, Standard Rate, Cost Per Use, Accrue At, and Code. The Material Label field stores a unit of measurement, such as yards or gallons, that is associated with a particular resource. Each time this resource is assigned to a task, it is assigned in units corresponding to what is in the Material Label field.

→ To learn more about defining the resources for your project, **see** "Work Resources and Material Resources," **p. 315**

THE ENTRY—WORK RESOURCES TABLE

2000 This resource table is also taken from the standard Entry table for defining resources. It focuses on the work resources such as individuals or facilities where the resource cost and work schedules can vary based on the amount of work that the resource does on a task. It omits all fields that only relate to material resources and includes the fields ID, Indicators,

PART

VII

CH

21

Name (titled Resource Name), Type, Initials, Group, Maximum Units, Standard Rate, Overtime Rate, Cost Per Use, Accrue At, Base Calendar, and Code.

THE HYPERLINK TABLE

The Hyperlink table for resources is very similar to the Hyperlink table for tasks. It is used for storing hyperlink references to a file on your computer, a network, an organization's intranet, or even the World Wide Web on the Internet. The fields that are displayed include ID, Indicators, Name (titled Resource Name), Hyperlink, Hyperlink Address, and Hyperlink SubAddress.

THE SUMMARY TABLE

Similar to the Summary table for tasks, the Summary table for resources provides a synopsis of information about each resource in the pool. Fields that are displayed include ID, Name (titled Resource Name), Group, Max Units, Peak, Standard Rate, Overtime Rate, Cost, and Work. As with the Summary table for tasks, a useful printout for management would be the Resource Sheet with the Summary table applied.

THE USAGE TABLE

The Usage table provides information about the quantity of resources that are being used. Fields that are displayed include ID, Indicators, Name (titled Resource Name), and Work. With this table, it is very clear to see which resources are being over utilized and which are being under utilized. This is useful for resolving resource conflicts.

THE WORK TABLE

This resource table provides work information about each resource. Fields that are displayed include ID, Name (titled Resource Name), Percent Work Complete, Work (for total hours assigned), Overtime Work, Baseline Work (for planned work), Work Variance, Actual Work, and Remaining Work. From this table, you can tell a number of things about each resource. You can tell how much progress each of the resources have made on their assigned tasks, and how much work they have left to do. You can also tell how long they are working on tasks compared to how long it was planned, as well as how much of the work has been overtime, in some cases incurring overtime costs.

THE EARNED VALUE TABLE

Using traditional project management calculations, this resource table is useful for comparing work and costs that were budgeted to what the work is actually costing. All the values in this table are calculated. It is used for analysis only, not for entering or editing data. The fields that are displayed include ID, Name (titled Resource Name), BCWS (for Budgeted Cost of Work Scheduled), BCWP (for Budgeted Cost of Work Performed), ACWP (for Actual Cost of Work Performed), SV (for Schedule Variance), CV (for Cost Variance), Cost (titled EAC for Estimate at Completion), Baseline Cost (titled BAC for Budgeted at Completion), and VAC (for Variance at Completion).

THE EXPORT TABLE

Like the Export table for tasks, the Export table for resources provides a vehicle for resource information to be exported to other applications. Fields that are displayed include ID, Unique ID, Name (titled Resource Name), Initials, Max Units, Standard Rate, Overtime Rate, Cost Per Use, Accrue At, Cost, Baseline Cost, Actual Cost, Work, Baseline Work, Actual Work, Overtime Work, Group, Code, Text 1–Text 5, and Email Address.

→ To learn more about outside data sources supported by Microsoft Project, **see** "File Formats Supported by Microsoft Project 2000," **p. 761**

→ To learn more about exporting specific project data to other applications, **see** "Exchanging Selected Parts of a Project with Other Formats," **p. 774**

EXPLORING THE STANDARD FILTERS

As discussed, tables are a central building block of Microsoft Project. They determine which fields are displayed for tasks or resources. Filters are another major building block that determines which tasks or resources are displayed, depending on criteria that you provide.

All the views except the Relationship Diagram can have filters applied. All the standard views have been assigned the all-inclusive filter (All Tasks or All Resources).

Note Any view in the bottom pane of a combination view will not have any filters available. The bottom pane is already being filtered by virtue of being the bottom pane, which is always controlled by what is selected in the top pane.

→ For more information on applying filters, **see** "Filtering the Task or Resource List," **p. 510**

A *filter* helps you identify and display only the tasks or resources (depending on the view) that match one or more criteria. All other tasks or resources are temporarily hidden. If a filter is applied as a *highlight* filter, all tasks or resources are displayed, but those selected by the filter are displayed with highlight formatting features such as a different color, bold, italic, underline, and so on, as defined by choosing Format, Text Styles. Any filter can be applied as a highlight filter or a display-only filter.

→ To learn more about highlighting specific groups of tasks or resources, **see** "Formatting Text Displays for Categories of Tasks and Resources," **p. 894**

You define the criteria for a filter by specifying one or more field values that must be matched for a task or resource to be selected by the filter. For example, Microsoft Project maintains a field named Milestone for tasks, and automatically places the value Yes in the field if you define a task as a milestone; tasks that you don't mark as a milestone are given the value No in that field. The Milestone filter stipulates that the Milestone field must equal the value Yes.

In addition to these simple filters, there are special filters known as *interactive* filters that ask the user to supply the value or values to be searched for in the field. The Date Range filter, available by choosing Project, Filtered For, for example, asks the user to enter two dates and then displays all tasks that have a Scheduled Start or Finish date within this range of dates.

PART

VII

CH

21

Tip from Tim and the Project Team

Any of the filters on the Project, Filtered For menu command that contain an ellipsis are interactive filters.

You can also apply an existing filter by using the Filter list box on the Formatting toolbar.

Another type of filter, the *calculated* filter, determines which item to display by comparing the values in two fields in the database. For example, the Cost Overbudget filter compares the value in the Cost field (which is the total scheduled cost for a task) with the value in the Baseline Cost field for that same task. If the scheduled cost is greater than the planned cost, the filter selects the task.

Some filters use more than one test for selecting the items to display. For example, the In Progress Tasks filter selects all the tasks that have an Actual Start date recorded (the Actual Start field no longer displays NA) but do not have an Actual Finish date recorded (the Actual Finish field still displays NA). In this case, both conditions must be met for a task to be selected: The Actual Start must not have NA, and the Actual Finish must still have NA. This kind of criterion is usually called an *and* condition or criterion.

All Tasks

Another example of a filter that applies more than one test is the Tasks with Fixed Dates filter, which is accessed by either choosing Project, Filtered For, More Filters or by selecting it from the Filter list box on the Formatting toolbar. This filter locates all the tasks that either have constrained dates (the Constraint Type setting is not As Soon As Possible) or that already have an actual start date recorded (the Actual Start field no longer shows NA). This filter is useful for resolving scheduling problems caused by fixed dates. In this case, Project selects all the tasks that have a constraint imposed on them or that have already started and cannot be rescheduled. This type of criterion is called an *or* condition or criterion.

→ To learn more about resolving conflicts caused by constraints, **see** "Working with Task Constraints," **p. 234**

USING THE STANDARD FILTERS

Not every view can be filtered, and there are other limitations to using filters. The following points summarize these limitations:

- You can apply only task filters to task views and only resource filters to resource views.
- You cannot apply a filter to a bottom pane view. The reason is that the bottom pane view is already filtered: It displays only the tasks or resources that are associated with the item or items selected in the top pane.
- The Relationship Diagram cannot be filtered, but the standard filters are available for all other views.
- You cannot apply a highlight filter to a form. Using a filter as a highlight makes sense only for the views that display lists, because the purpose of a highlight is to make selected items stand out from the rest. Thus, only the views that contain a table can accept a highlight filter.

■ Each filter considers the entire set of tasks or resources for selections. Using the Filter drop-down list on the Standard toolbar or the standard filters on the Project, Filtered For menu, you cannot use successive filters to progressively narrow the set of selected tasks or resources. For example, if you filter the task list to show Milestones, and then you apply the Critical filter, you will see all critical tasks related, not just critical milestones. You must either create a filter, edit an existing one, or use the AutoFilter option to use more than one criterion at a time.

Tip from Tim and the Project Team

You can create successive filters using the AutoFilter feature covered in an upcoming section.

→ To learn how you can create your own filters, **see** "Creating Custom Filters," **p. 968**

Any view that can accept a filter can have one defined as part of the view: When the view is selected, the filter is automatically applied. All the standard views initially have the All Tasks or All Resources filters designated as part of the view definition.

→ To learn more about customizing your views through the use of filters, **see** "Selecting the Filter for the View," **p. 947**

DESCRIBING THE STANDARD FILTERS

The standard filters supplied with Microsoft Project provide standard selection criteria useful in many situations that you will encounter. You might never need to create your own filters. Tables 21.1 and 21.2 describe the standard task filters and resource filters, respectively.

Table 21.1 lists the filters that can be applied to task views. An asterisk (*) indicates that the filter is not found on the standard Project, Filtered For menu command, but is found instead on the More Filters menu. All filters are listed in the Filter list box on the Formatting toolbar as well.

TABLE 21.1 THE STANDARD TASK FILTERS

Filter Name	Purpose
All Tasks	Displays all tasks.
Completed Tasks	Displays tasks that are marked as 100% complete.
Confirmed*	Displays tasks for which the requested resources have agreed to take on the assignment.
Cost Greater Than…*	Displays a prompt asking for the cost to be used in a test for tasks that are greater than that cost.
Cost Overbudget*	Displays all tasks that have a scheduled cost greater than the baseline cost if the baseline cost is greater than 0.
Created After…*	Displays a prompt asking for a date to be used in a test for tasks that were created after that date.

PART

VII

CH

21

TABLE 21.1 CONTINUED

Filter Name	Purpose
Critical	Displays all critical tasks.
Date Range...	Displays a prompt asking for a range of dates to be used in a test for tasks that either start or finish within that range of dates.
In Progress Tasks*	Displays all tasks that have started but have not finished.
Incomplete Tasks	Displays all tasks that have a percent complete not equal to 100%.
Late/Overbudget Tasks Assigned To...*	Displays a prompt asking for a resource name to be used in a test for tasks assigned to that resource where the task's finish date is later than the baseline finish or the cost is greater than the baseline.
Linked Fields*	Displays all tasks that are linked to another application.
Milestones	Displays all milestones.
Resource Group...*	Displays all tasks assigned to the specified resource group.
Should Start By...*	Displays all tasks that should have started but have not started by a date supplied by the user.
Should Start/Finish By...*	Prompts for a range of dates which are used to display tasks that should have started by the beginning date or should have finished by the end date.
Slipped/Late Progress*	Displays tasks where the finish date is later than the baseline or the Budgeted Cost of Work Scheduled is greater than the Budgeted Cost of Work Performed.
Slipping Tasks*	Displays all tasks not finished and whose scheduled finish date is later than the planned finish date.
Summary Tasks	Displays all tasks that have subordinate tasks defined below them.
Task Range...	Displays all tasks that have ID numbers within a range specified by the user.
Tasks with a Task Calendar Assigned*	Displays all tasks that have been assigned a task-specific calendar.
Tasks with Attachments*	Shows tasks that have objects attached, such as a graph or a note in the Notes field.
Tasks with Deadlines*	Displays all tasks assigned a deadline date that works in conjunction with a task's constraint.
Tasks with Estimated Durations	Displays all tasks where the duration has been marked as estimated, denoted by a.? after the duration.
Tasks with Fixed Dates*	Displays all tasks that have a constraint other than As Soon As Possible or that have already started.

TABLE 21.1 CONTINUED

Filter Name	Purpose
Tasks/Assignments with Overtime*	Displays all tasks where overtime work has been assigned.
Top Level Tasks*	Displays all highest level summary tasks.
Unconfirmed*	Displays all tasks for which the requested resources have not yet committed to the task.
Unstarted Tasks*	Displays all tasks which have not yet started. For example, the Actual Start field is still set to NA.
Update Needed*	Displays all tasks that have incurred changes, such as revised start and finish dates or resource reassignments, and need to be sent for update or confirmation.
Using Resource in Date Range...*	Displays all tasks that use the resource named by the user during the range of dates also supplied by the user.
Using Resource...	Displays all tasks that use the resource named by the user.
Work Overbudget*	Displays all tasks where the actual hours of work performed are greater than what was planned (the baseline work).

Table 21.2 lists the filters that are available for resource views. Once again, an asterisk (*) marks filters not found on the standard Project, Filtered For menu command, but which are found instead on the More Filters menu.

TABLE 21.2 THE STANDARD RESOURCE FILTERS

Filter Name	Purpose
All Resources	Displays all resources. This is the default filter.
Confirmed Assignments*	Displays resources who have confirmed their task assignments.
Cost Greater Than...*	Displays resources where the cost is greater than the amount specified by the user.
Cost Overbudget	Displays all resources that have a cost that is greater than the baseline cost.
Date Range...*	Displays resources who have tasks that are occurring during a range of dates specified by the user.
Group...	Displays all resources that belong to the group specified by the user (which have the same entry in the Group field).
In Progress Assignments*	Displays resources who have tasks that are being worked on. For example, the tasks have an actual start date but no actual finish.
Linked Fields*	Displays all resources with fields that are linked to another application.

PART

VII

CH

21

TABLE 21.2 CONTINUED

Filter Name	Purpos
Overallocated Resources	Displays all resources that are overallocated. For example, resources that have too many hours of work assigned to them during some time period of the project.
Resource Range...	Displays all resources that have ID numbers within the range specified by the user.
Resources—Material	Displays consumable resources that are listed as Material in the Type field.
Resources—Work	Displays resources such as individuals or assets that are listed as Work in the Type field.
Resources with Attachments*	Displays resources that have objects attached or a note in the Notes field.
Resources/Assignments with Overtime*	Displays resources for whom some of the work assigned to them is incurred as overtime.
Should Start By...*	Displays resources assigned to tasks that have not started, where the calculated start falls after a date specified by the user.
Should Start/Finish By...*	Displays resources assigned to tasks that have not started, where the start or finish of the task falls between a date range specified by the user.
Slipped/Late Progress*	Displays resources with tasks assigned, where the finish date is later than the baseline or the Budgeted Cost of Work Scheduled is greater than the Budgeted Cost of Work Performed.
Slipping Assignments*	Displays resources with tasks assigned that are not finished and whose scheduled finish date is later than the planned finish date.
Unconfirmed Assignments*	Displays resources with tasks assigned for which a commitment has not yet been made.
Unstarted Assignments*	Displays all resources assigned to tasks that have not yet started but that have been confirmed. For example, the Actual Start field is still set to NA.
Work Complete*	Displays resources assigned to tasks that are 100% complete.
Work Incomplete*	Displays resources assigned to tasks that have started but are not 100% complete.
Work Overbudget	Displays all resources with scheduled work that is greater than the baseline work.

APPLYING A FILTER TO THE CURRENT VIEW

To apply a filter to a view, you can choose Project, Filtered For or use the Filter list box on the Formatting toolbar. If the filter that you want is on the Project, Filtered For menu, select the filter name, and it will be applied immediately. If the filter is not on the Project, Filtered For menu, first choose More Filters, and then choose the filter name from the complete list of filters in the More Filters entry list (see Figure 21.26). Choose the Apply button to apply the filter so that only filtered tasks or resources that satisfy the filter appear. If you want to apply the filter as a highlight filter (so that filtered items are highlighted and all other items remain displayed), choose the Highlight button instead of the Apply button.

Figure 21.26
The More Filters dialog box lists all filters that are available for both tasks and resources.

Tip from Tim and the Project Team

You can also apply filters as highlight filters by holding down the Shift key as you choose Project, Filtered For and select the filter name.

You can also apply a filter to the current view by selecting the filter name from the Filter list box on the Formatting toolbar (see Figure 21.27). When you select the filter name from the list, the filter is applied immediately. You cannot apply the filter as a highlight filter when using the Filter list box.

Figure 21.27
The Filter list box on the Formatting toolbar provides access to all filters.

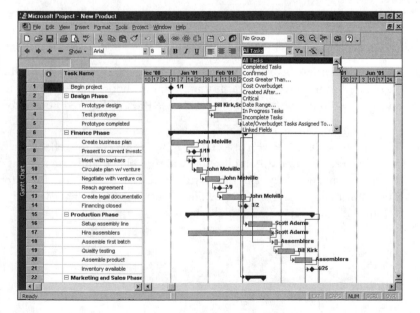

PART
VII

CH
21

Caution

When you apply a filter, all tasks or resources that satisfy the criteria at that moment are selected by the filter. If you change a value in a field, you might change how this value satisfies the filter criteria. The task or resource will continue to be displayed or highlighted, however, because the filter criteria are evaluated only at the moment the filter is applied. You might need to apply the filter again if you make significant changes in the project.

Tip from Tim and the Project Team

The filter does not automatically reflect changes to tasks or resources that would cause it to be included or not included in the filter. You can reapply the filter by pressing Ctrl+F3.

You can set a filter back to the default All Tasks or All Resources by pressing F3.

After you have finished using the filtered view, you can remove the filter by selecting the All Tasks filter or All Resources filter.

After you apply an interactive filter, a dialog box appears in which you must supply the values to be used for testing the tasks or resources. For example, Figure 21.28 shows the Using Resource filter dialog box. This filter will select all tasks assigned to the resource that you choose from the entry list.

Figure 21.28
The Using Resource filter dialog box allows you to choose from a list of available resources.

USING THE AUTOFILTER

 The AutoFilter in Microsoft Project is very similar to the AutoFilter feature in Microsoft Excel. To turn on the AutoFilter feature, you can choose the AutoFilter tool on the Formatting toolbar or from the menu, choose Project, Filtered For, AutoFilter.

 When enabled, the AutoFilter places a drop-down menu with AutoFilter values at the top of each table column (see Figure 21.29). To filter that column, choose an option from the drop-down menu. The column heading will turn blue to indicate that the column is filtered. You can apply a filter in this way to more than one column to perform successive filters. For example, in Figure 21.29 filters have been used to display only tasks assigned to John Melville that are starting this month.

Figure 21.29
Use the AutoFilter to easily narrow down a list of tasks or resources.

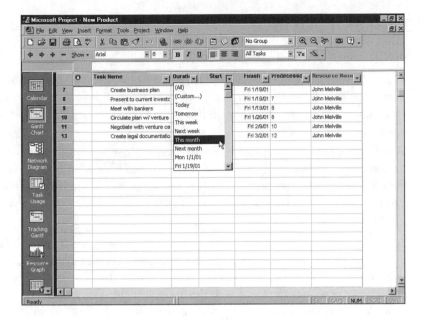

The Duration field has AutoFilter options for ranges less than one week, more than one week, and so on. Date fields have options for ranges as well—for example, this week, this month, next month, and so on (see Figure 21.29).

Each of the drop-down menus also has a custom option that allows you to create and save a filter with more than one condition, using either an *and* or an *or* condition (see Figure 21.30).

Figure 21.30
Create multiple condition fields that can be saved with the Custom AutoFilter option.

→ For additional information on creating your own specialized filters, **see** "Creating Custom Filters," **p. 968**

Tip from Tim and the Project Team

The keystrokes that reapply the filter (Ctrl+F3) and set a filter back to the default All Tasks or All Resources (F3) also work with the AutoFilter.

TROUBLESHOOTING

PROJECT 2000 ADOPTING PROJECT 98 VIEWS

Microsoft Project 2000 replaced the PERT Chart with the Network Diagram. However, when I open my project file, which was originally created in Microsoft Project 98, I show the PERT Chart as an available view on the View bar, as well as in the View menu. Why is this view being listed when it should no longer be there?

When working with a project file that was created in a previous version of Microsoft Project, any view, such as the PERT Chart, that had been even slightly changed while that file was open, will display as an available view when you bring that file into Microsoft Project 2000. This is because the Show in Menu option is checked for that view in Microsoft Project 98.

To remove such a view from the View bar, choose View, More Views, select the view from the list, and click the Edit button. From the View Definition dialog box, deselect the Show in Menu option. However, this only removes the view from being displayed on the View bar. The view will still be listed with the other available views when you go through the More Views menu. To remove the view entirely from the file, you will need to delete the view using the Organizer. The Organizer is a feature of Microsoft Project that allows you to delete, rename, or copy a file object such as a view or filter from one project to another. To access the Organizer, choose Tools, Organizer from the menu bar. From the Organizer, select the view that you want to remove and click the Delete button. More information about the features and benefits of the Organizer can be found in "Using the Organizer" in Chapter 4, "Working with Project Files."

CHAPTER 22

FORMATTING VIEWS

In this chapter

USING THE COMMON FORMAT OPTIONS IN THE STANDARD VIEWS

Views are basically broken down into three category types: sheets, forms, and graphical views. Views of the same type share similar customizing options. Sheet and graphical views all contain gridlines; therefore, you can use the Format, Gridlines command to change the appearance of the gridlines in all these views. Many graphical views also contain a timescale, so use the Format, Timescale command in all these views. Use the Format, Text Styles command to change the font, size, and color of text in all views.

Unlike tables and filters (described in the previous chapter), the options on the Format menu do not create named objects, but only change the look of the current view. Suppose you change the timescale on the Gantt Chart to show months instead of days. Until you change the timescale again, you see this format for the timescale each time you use the Gantt Chart. However, if you switch to another view that also has a timescale (the Resource Usage view, for example), you find that the timescale in that view does not incorporate the changes in the Gantt Chart timescale, but instead reflects the way the Resource Usage view was last displayed. These changes are saved with the project file only. If you change to another project file, you won't see the formatting changes you made in other files. You can borrow settings from another file or a template called GLOBAL.MPT that stores all your default settings using the Organizer.

➔ For more information on sharing views between files and templates, **see** "Organizing Views in Project Files," **p. 983**

SORTING THE TASKS OR RESOURCES IN A VIEW

Sorting is especially relevant for views that display tasks or resources in a table or list layout. But you also can sort the order in which tasks or resources appear in the form views as you scroll with the Next and Previous buttons. You can't sort the displayed items in the Relationship Diagram views, however.

The Sort command, on the Project menu, enables you to sort by a number of predefined fields, as well as a combination of up to three columns or fields that you specify. The predefined fields for sorting vary from one view to another. For example, in a resource view, predefined sort fields include By Cost, By Name, or By ID. The predefined fields in a task view include By Start Date, By Finish Date, By Priority, By Cost, and By ID. In addition, for both task and resource views, you can choose the Sort By option to specify other fields, a combination of fields, and the order of the sort.

For example, for resources, you might want to sort first by the group in which they are located. Then sort within each group by the standard rate the resources are paid—but in descending order, so that the highest paid are listed first within each group. If some of the people in the same group are paid the same standard rate, you also can alphabetize these people by name in ascending (normal) order.

To sort the entries in a view, choose Project, Sort. A cascading menu appears with the pre-defined sort fields (see Figure 22.1). If you choose from one of these, the tasks or resources are sorted immediately, but only by that one field and in ascending order. If you select the Sort By option, the Sort dialog box appears, offering more choices (see Figure 22.2).

Figure 22.1
The cascading sort list offers easy access for sorting tasks or resources.

Figure 22.2
The Sort dialog box offers more extensive options for sorting.

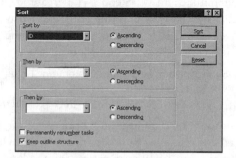

SELECTING THE SORT KEYS

Use the drop-down list arrow in the Sort By area to select the major sort field. Select the Ascending or Descending button to specify the sort order. If you want to further sort the list within the groups that are placed together by the first sort field, choose the two Then By fields, similarly indicating the sort order for each of these fields. In Figure 22.2, the Resource Sheet is being sorted by ID first, in ascending (normal) order. Within each group, the resources are being sorted by their Standard Rate of pay in descending (highest paying) order. Notice that the second Then By field is selected so that the resources earning the same standard rate are further sorted in ascending order by resource name.

SELECTING THE SORT OPERATION

After you define the fields to sort by, you need to indicate whether you want the tasks or resources to be permanently renumbered. Although the option to undo a sort is available, it is a good idea to save your project file before sorting, in case the Undo function is not available. For task views, you can also choose to keep all tasks under their summary tasks, but to sort subordinate tasks within their summary task, by marking the Keep Outline Structure check box. To sort all tasks without regard for their position within an outline, clear this box.

For resource views, there is also a check box for sorting the resources by the projects to which they are assigned. This is useful when you are using the same pool of resources for more than one project.

→ For more information on sharing a pool of resources, **see** "Sharing Resources Among Projects," **p. 751**

To sort the list immediately, choose the Sort button. To return the sort keys to the standard sort—by ID numbers only—choose the Reset button. Note that Reset does not display the original order of the list if Permanently Renumber Tasks was selected.

Choosing the Cancel button cancels all changes you made to the Sort dialog box and returns you to the workspace.

SORTING WITH CUSTOM OUTLINES

In addition to sorting on the predefined fields supplied with Project, you can also now sort your tasks or resources by custom outline and WBS codes you create. The method is exactly the same. Select Project, Sort, and then Sort By. Custom fields are also available in the drop-down list for sort keys. If a custom field has been renamed, both the generic field name and its alias appear in the list, each in its place alphabetically.

→ For more information on creating and using custom fields, **see** "Customizing Fields," **p. 956**

FORMATTING TEXT DISPLAYS FOR CATEGORIES OF TASKS AND RESOURCES

Most of the views enable you to choose special formatting options for displaying text. You can differentiate categories of tasks or resources by the font, type size, style, or color of text used to display the data. For example, you can format critical tasks to be displayed in red, or summary tasks to appear in bold. In table views, you can format the column headings. In timescale views, you can format the unit labels in the timescale. Text formatting also defines the appearance that highlight filters use to display items selected by the filter.

→ For more information on highlight filters, **see** "Exploring the Standard Filters," **p. 881**

To change the display of text for *categories* of tasks or resources in a view, choose Format, Text Styles. The Text Styles dialog box appears (see Figure 22.3). If the Text Styles command doesn't appear in the Format menu, you can't change the text display in this view. To change the text display for selected tasks or resources that don't fall into any particular category, see the section "Formatting Selected Text," later in this chapter.

Figure 22.3
Use the Text Styles dialog box to change text attributes for categories of tasks or resources.

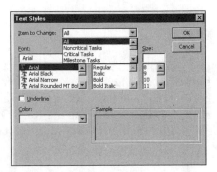

SELECTING THE ITEM TO CHANGE

From the Item to Change drop-down list, choose the item you want. Some items in the list take precedence over others when a task or resource falls into two or more categories. Here are the task items, listed in order of precedence (with the highest priority at the top):

- Highlighted Tasks (by a filter)
- Marked Tasks
- Summary Tasks
- Milestone Tasks
- Critical Tasks

Therefore, if a Milestone task is also a Critical task, the display is governed by the text format for Milestone tasks rather than for Critical tasks. If the same task is selected by a highlight filter, the task shows the Highlight display rather than either the Milestone or the Critical display.

Highlighted tasks refer to tasks selected by a highlight filter. Use Format, Text Styles (as described in this section) to determine how highlighted tasks or resources are displayed. Use the Project, Filtered For command with the Highlight option to display tasks or resources with the highlight format.

Tip from Tim and the Project Team

You can choose to highlight tasks selected by the filter rather than hide other tasks, by pressing the Shift key while choosing Project, Filtered For.

Marked tasks have the logical value Yes in the Marked field of the Project database. Use the Marked field to manually select tasks of interest without defining a filter or defining a custom field (or when there is no logical test that can be expressed for the filter). You can define any task table or custom form to display the Marked field for editing purposes. When you mark tasks, you can filter or use a special text format for them.

Milestone tasks have the logical value Yes in the Milestone field. The Milestone field is set to Yes when you enter a duration of zero for a task, but you can also designate any task as a Milestone task by checking the Mark Task as Milestone check box on the Advanced tab of the Task Information dialog box. Access the Task Information dialog box by double-clicking the task name or by choosing the Task Information tool on the Standard toolbar. You can also place the Milestone field in a table for editing purposes.

→ For more information on adding fields to a table, **see** "Using and Creating Tables," **p. 949**

The All item in the Item to Change drop-down list on the Text Styles dialog box enables you to easily make the same change in all items at once. If you make a change in the format options for the All item, this change is made for every other item in the selection list. You might use the All item initially, for example, to set an overall font type or size, leaving all other options clear. This procedure sets the same font type and size in all categories. You can then override the font and size on individual categories. If you later choose the All item again, however, and make a change in the font or point size, all categories change again and any manual override changes are lost.

The items listed after All are specific to tasks or resources, depending on which type of view is currently displayed. After those type-specific items are items that are specific features of the active view. When the Gantt Chart is the active view, for example, the first items listed deal with tasks: Critical, Noncritical, Milestone, and so on. After that, the item list includes Row & Column Titles (for the table part of the view), Major Timescale and Minor Timescale (for the unit measures at the top of the timescale), and Bar Text (for displaying field values next to the bars in the bar chart in the timescale). If the Task Usage view is active, an item row is added for formatting Assignment rows on the view.

CHANGING THE FONT

Use the Font scroll bar in the Text Styles dialog box to move through the list of font choices for the selected item. The fonts listed are the ones that have already been installed in Windows. After selecting the font, you might choose the size (in points) for the selected font from the Size list. You can use the scroll bar to move through the list or you might type in a desired point size if you have selected a TrueType font.

CHANGING THE TEXT STYLE

Select from the Font Style list to add bold or italic formatting or a combination of the two to the text. Choose Regular to clear a previous choice. Mark the Underline check box to turn on underlining.

Use the Color drop-down list to choose the color for the selected item's text. If you don't use a color printer, all the colors print as black (but with different shading on grayscale printers). The clear color option causes an item's text to be transparent in the display, although the row for the item still appears onscreen and on paper. The use of color onscreen is still useful, even if you use a black-and-white printer.

If all items in the Item to Change drop-down list have the same setting for one of the format features, this setting appears selected when the All item is selected. If all items use the same font, for example, you see the font name displayed when the All item is selected. If one or more items use a different font, however, the font name remains blank when you select the All item. The Underline check box is marked if all items apply that feature; the box is not marked if no items use the option; and the box is dimmed if at least one, but not all items use the feature.

FORMATTING SELECTED TEXT

There are two additional choices for formatting text: using the Format, Font command and using the Formatting toolbar. The choices available using Format, Font are the same as in the Text Styles dialog box, except that you don't have a choice for Item to Change. Changes that you make in this dialog box are made to any tasks that are *selected*, not to categories of tasks or resources.

The Formatting toolbar offers drop-down lists for changing the font and point size, as well as buttons for bold, italic, and underline. Additionally, there are three buttons for the alignment of selected text: left, center, and right.

 You can copy formatting options you've created for a single task or resource using the Format Painter button on the Standard toolbar. To use this button, select the task or resource with the format you want to copy. Click the Format Painter button. The mouse pointer changes to a cross with a paintbrush attached. Select the tasks or resources to which you want to apply the format. Formatting changes created using this button are the same as if you used the Formatting toolbar or the Format, Font command.

Use caution when using this button, however, because Undo is not available. If you change your mind about the format, you have to use the Formatting toolbar options or the Format, Font command to reset the changes you made.

Caution

The difference between using Format, Text Styles and using Format, Font (or the Formatting toolbar) is significant. When using the latter two options, you're making changes to selected text only, not to categories of tasks or resources. When additional tasks or resources belonging to a certain category are added, the formatting applied using the Format, Font command or the Formatting toolbar are not taken into account. Any text display changes are made only to selected tasks or resources.

FORMATTING GRIDLINES

Views that contain tables have gridlines between the rows and columns of the table and between the column and row titles. Views that have a timescale can have horizontal and vertical lines to separate the major and the minor timescale units. The Gantt Chart also can have gridlines between the bars in the bar chart. A very useful single gridline is the Current date that appears by default on several views, including Gantt Charts.

To change the display of gridlines, choose Format, Gridlines. The Gridlines dialog box appears. Figure 22.4 shows the Gantt Chart Gridlines dialog box.

Tip from Tim and the Project Team

You can also access the Gridlines dialog box by pointing to any blank area of the Gantt Chart and right-clicking. The Gridlines option appears on the shortcut menu.

Figure 22.4
Change the way lines appear using the Gridlines dialog box.

From the Line to Change list, choose the kind of gridline you want to change. The settings in the Normal box are applied to every line of the type that you choose unless a selection in the At Interval box also is active (in which case a different line and color appears at regular intervals). Only a few line categories can be given a distinguishing interval line type and color. Sheet Rows and Sheet Columns in table views, for example, can have intervals, and in the Gantt Chart and the Resource Usage views, rows and columns can have interval colors and line types.

Use the Type drop-down list in the Normal box to choose one of the five options (no line, solid, dotted, small dashes, and large dashes). Use the Color drop-down list arrow in the Normal box to choose a color. Select the At Interval line type and color if you want a distinguishing line (if available). Activate the At Interval Type and Color fields by choosing an interval. Choose 2 for every other, 3, or 4; or choose Other and type the interval number.

For most timescale views, you can define the style of the Current Date line. For table views, you can define the style of page break lines as seen onscreen (page break lines do not print). After you complete the procedure, click OK to accept the changes or click Cancel to return to your previous settings.

USING THE OUTLINE OPTIONS

Views that list tasks (the Gantt Chart and the Task Sheet) can display the tasks in ways that show information about their places in the outline structure. You can hide or display summary tasks, or indent subordinate tasks to show their level in the outline; outline numbers can be displayed next to each task; and summary tasks can be displayed either with or without a special symbol to show that these tasks have subordinate tasks.

→ For more information on controlling the task outline, **see** "Outlining the Task List," **p. 184**

To change the display of the outlined tasks, choose Tools, Options, and click the View tab. The Outline display default options are shown in Figure 22.5. Figure 22.6 shows the effects of each of these choices when they are marked.

Figure 22.5
Options for displaying outlines are on the View tab of the Options dialog box.

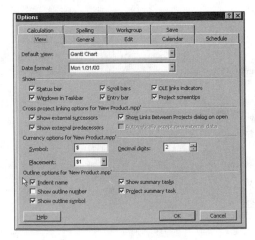

Note

Make sure you're in a view that can display outlines (Gantt Chart or Task Sheet) before accessing the Options dialog box. Otherwise the Outline Options section won't be available.

Figure 22.6
Outline display options are available on the View tab of the Options dialog box.

Outline symbol

Project summary task

First-level summary task

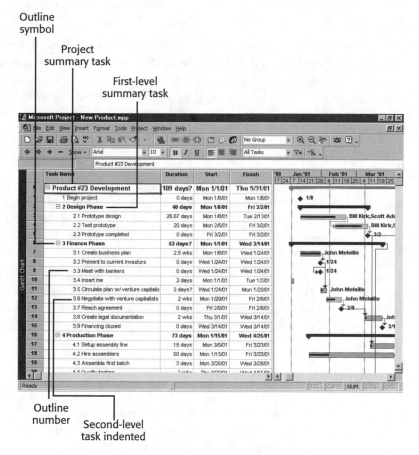

Outline number

Second-level task indented

If Show Summary Tasks is marked, you see the summary tasks included in the list of tasks. If the check box is not marked, the summary tasks do not appear in the list. If subtasks are currently hidden, they are also hidden. Notice also that the outlining commands on the Formatting toolbar are no longer available when summary tasks are not shown. If you clear the check box, you should clear the Indent Name check box also, so all the subordinate tasks align at the left margin. This is useful when you are linking tasks and you don't want to include the summary task in the link. It is also useful when applying a filter and then performing some action on all the tasks meeting the criteria of the filter. For example, this is useful when you want to mark all milestones to be rolled up to the summary task.

→ For more information on linking tasks, **see** "Understanding Dependency Links," **p. 209**

If Project Summary Task is marked, an additional summary task is displayed at the beginning of the task list that summarizes the entire project. This is useful when consolidating projects. (This topic is covered in Chapter 18, "Working with Multiple Projects.")

If the Indent Name box is marked, the tasks are indented to show their subordinate status. If the box is not marked, all tasks are aligned at the left margin.

If the Show Outline Number check box is marked, the task names are preceded by an outline number that identifies each task's place in the outline. The outline numbering is in the so-called legal style, with each task number including the related summary task numbers. This is the same number you see for WBS (Work Breakdown Structure) code in the Task Information dialog box on the Advanced tab unless a custom WBS has been created. If this box is not marked, you do not see the outline numbers.

→ For more information on Work Breakdown Structure codes, **see** "Using Custom WBS Codes," **p. 192**

If the Show Outline Symbol check box is marked, summary tasks are preceded by a plus (+) or a minus sign (–) depending on whether the subtasks for that summary task are hidden or shown. A plus sign indicates that the summary task has subtasks that are not currently being displayed, whereas the minus sign indicates that all tasks under the summary task are showing. If the Show Outline Symbol check box is not marked, no outline symbols are displayed.

Tip from Tim and the Project Team	When printing reports that include outlined tasks, you can save space by turning off the Indent Name option. If you do this, turn on the Show Outline Number option so that you can see your outline structure.

FORMATTING TIMESCALES

Views that display a timescale offer you the option of choosing the time units and the date formats for the timescale display. The timescale normally uses two levels of time units for clarity in interpreting the timescale. These levels are known as the *major units scale* and the *minor units scale*, either of which can be suppressed.

Tip from Tim and the Project Team	You can also use the View, Zoom command to zoom in on a variety of predefined time periods, including the entire project.

To change the timescale, choose Format, Timescale. The Timescale dialog box appears (see Figure 22.7).

Tip from Tim and the Project Team	You can also access the Timescale dialog box by double-clicking anywhere the timescale units are displayed or by right-clicking the timescale headings and choosing Timescale from the shortcut menu.

Figure 22.7
You can be very specific about how the time frame is displayed with the numerous options in the Timescale dialog box.

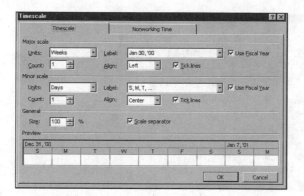

The Timescale dialog box provides areas for defining both the Major Scale and the Minor Scale. Below these areas is a sample display area that instantly shows you what the timescale looks like as you select different options.

CHANGING THE MAJOR SCALE

You define the major and minor scales separately. The only requirement is that the units selected for the major scale be at least as large as the units selected for the minor scale.

To change the Major Scale units, use the Units drop-down list to choose one of the options provided: Years, Half Years, Quarters, Months, Thirds of Months, Weeks, Days, Hours, and Minutes.

To include more than one time period within each major unit, choose the Count text box and enter a number other than 1. To have the major scale show fortnights (two weeks), for example, select Weeks as the Units and 2 for the Count. For the same effect, you also could select Days as the Unit and 14 for the Count. You can establish whatever kind of timescale you want to display for your project.

Note

If the major scale tick lines that separate the units of the major scale don't change in the sample area immediately after you change the count, you might need to select the Tick Lines check box twice to refresh the tick line display.

To choose the label to display in each major scale time unit, use the Label drop-down list. The list of options is extensive and depends on the units selected for the display. You can use three basic types of labels for any of the time units:

- **The specific time period named, such as the year, quarter number, month name or number, and day number**—Many choices are available, including abbreviations, full or partial specifications, numbers, and words. Figure 22.8 shows a partial list of options available for the Weeks unit.

Figure 22.8
Select a labeling option for the Weeks scale from the drop-down list.

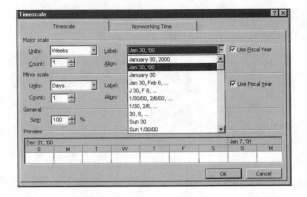

- **The number of the time period in the life of the project, starting from the beginning of the project or counting down from the end of the project**—These units are designated with either (From Start) or (From End) as part of the label definition. If the unit is Week 1 (From Start), for example, the time periods are labeled Week 1, Week 2, and so on, if you are counting from the beginning of the project. If you are counting down from the end of the project, the time periods are labeled Week 40, Week 39, and so on. This labeling scheme is useful in the early planning stages of a lengthy project, before specific start and finish dates are established or when a project file is used as a template.

→ For more information on using a file as a project template, **see** "Creating and Using Templates," **p. 124**

- **No label**—If minor scale labeling is sufficient, you can suppress any labeling of the major scale unit. You can't, however, avoid having a major timescale displayed.

> **Note**
> When working with a project that spans more than a single calendar year, be sure to include the year number in the label.

You can center, left-align, or right-align the time units labels. Use the Align drop-down list arrow to choose an alignment specification, or just type the specification. Also, you must mark the Tick Lines check box to display vertical separator tick lines between the major time units labels.

CHANGING THE MINOR SCALE

The Minor Scale options are virtually the same as the Major Scale options, with the following exceptions:

- *You can't have a minor scale unit that is larger than the major scale unit.* Specifically, the time span of the minor scale unit, including its count factor, can't be longer than the timescale of the major scale unit. You won't be notified of this until you choose OK, but you can see that there is a problem in the sample box at the bottom of the dialog box because it is blank.

■ *You can choose not to have a minor scale at all by choosing None in the Units drop-down list.* This display is useful when you want to show the big picture of a project without displaying too much distracting detail.

Otherwise, selecting the minor scale is identical to selecting the major scale.

P Additional settings are available in Project 2000 for displaying and labeling periods in a fis-
2000 cal year format. Both the major and minor timescale labels can reflect either calendar years (the default) or fiscal years. Set one or both of the Use Fiscal Year options on the Timescale dialog box. Also, to change the month that begins the fiscal year (so that Quarter 1 covers the months used by your organization in its reports), you must change the Fiscal Year Starts In option on the Calendar tab of the Options dialog box. (Choose Tools, Options to open this dialog box.) Using the drop-down list, change from the default, January, to the month you want to use. If you choose a month other than January, there is also a check box to indicate that you want to use the starting month for FY (fiscal year) numbering. Similarly, if you want the week to begin on a day other than Sunday (the default), you must change the Week Starts On item in the same location.

COMPLETING THE TIMESCALE DEFINITION

Notice the two options at the bottom of the Timescale tab in this dialog box; Size and Scale Separator. You use these options to adjust the overall look of the timescale.

To change the width of the timescale units displayed, choose the Size box and enter an adjustment percentage. For example, if the values in the Resource Usage view are too large to fit within the cells of the minor timescale units, type **120** or **150** to enlarge the unit space.

Likewise, if you are happy with your timescale settings but you just want to shrink the whole view down so more fits on the screen or on paper, choose a number smaller than 100%.

You can remove the horizontal line that separates the major scale labels from the minor scale labels. Just clear the Scale Separator check box.

After you enter all the changes, choose OK to put the new timescale format in place. The timescale changes affect only the display of the view that was active when you changed the timescale. Each timescale view has its own timescale format. For example, changes you make to the Gantt Chart timescale do not have any impact on the timescale in the Resource Usage view.

Caution

If you have customized your timescale settings, specifically the labels, when you use the Zoom In and Zoom Out buttons in the Standard toolbar, or apply a Zoom setting from the View menu, you lose your customized settings.

CHANGING THE DISPLAY OF NONWORKING TIME

Use the Nonworking Time tab in the Timescale dialog box to make changes to the way Nonworking Time is displayed on the Gantt chart. You can choose Format, Timescale and then click the Nonworking Time tab to bring it to the front. Alternatively, you can point at a blank spot on the timescale (not at a bar or a heading), press the right mouse button, and then choose Nonworking Time from the shortcut menu. Or, you can double-click the shaded working time if displayed. The choices on this tab are shown in Figure 22.9.

> **Caution**
>
> Don't confuse the shortcut menu for the body of the Gantt Chart with the shortcut menu for the timescale. The shortcut menu for the timescale provides a Change Working Time option that accesses the calendar and enables you to redefine what should be considered nonworking time. The shortcut menu for the body of the Gantt Chart provides a Nonworking Time option, which simply changes the way nonworking time is displayed.

Figure 22.9
Change the display of Nonworking Time on the Gantt Chart with the Timescale dialog box.

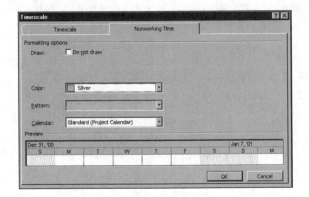

Choose the calendar for which you want the nonworking time displayed. The Standard calendar (which is the project calendar unless a different project calendar has been designated under the Project, Project Information command) is used by default. Use the drop-down list if you want to select an individual's resource calendar or an alternative base calendar. The options in the Draw section determine the way the bars are drawn when spanning nonworking time (evenings and weekends, for example). Nonworking time is shaded with a color and pattern of your choice. Whether this time is displayed depends on the Timescale format. For example, if your major timescale unit is set to Months, and the minor timescale unit is set to Weeks, you won't be able to see nonworking days, but you can see any complete weeks marked as nonworking time.

The options for where the shading is drawn include Behind Task Bars (the default), In Front of Task Bars (leaving a gap in the bars), or Do Not Draw. This last option effectively eliminates the shaded display of nonworking time altogether. Nonworking time is still displayed, but the display is no different from working time. Task bars that span nonworking time are simply longer than you might expect from their duration value.

Choosing the display of nonworking time in front of the task bars more clearly indicates that the tasks are not being worked on—over weekends, for example. The bars are longer not because their duration is longer, but because they span nonworking time.

USING PAGE BREAKS

Page breaks force the start of a new page when you print the view but have no effect on the screen display (other than an optional dashed line to indicate where the page break falls within the data). You can format the appearance of the page break line with the Format, Gridlines command.

To force a page break in the views that permit it, select any cell in the row below the intended page break. This row becomes the first row on the new page. Then choose Insert, Page Break.

To remove a page break, select the row below the page break and choose Insert, Remove Page Break.

To remove all page breaks from the view, select all tasks by clicking the Task or Resource Name column heading, or by clicking the Select All square above the ID column, before choosing the Insert, Remove All Page Breaks.

→ For more information on setting page breaks in views, **see** "Printing Views," **p. 541**

The page breaks that you have entered manually are honored by the Print command only if the Manual Page Breaks check box in the Print dialog box is marked. To print the report without using the manually inserted page breaks, clear this check box.

FORMATTING THE GANTT CHART

The Gantt Chart is one of the most important presentations in project management reporting. Therefore, many format choices are available for this presentation. You can either format it yourself or use the Gantt Chart Wizard.

REVIEWING THE FORMAT OPTIONS FOR THE GANTT CHART

The Format menu for Gantt Charts includes the following options: Font, Bar, Timescale, Gridlines, Gantt Chart Wizard, Text Styles, Bar Styles, and Layout. The options for Font, Timescale, Gridlines, and Text Styles were described in previous sections of this chapter. Refer to the appropriate sections for instructions on using these features. The following sections show you several ways to change the look of the bar chart in the timescale section of the Gantt Chart view.

USING THE BAR STYLES OPTIONS

One way to change the display of the bar chart section of the Gantt Chart view is to choose Format, Bar Styles. The Bar Styles dialog box appears (see Figure 22.10).

Figure 22.10
Use the Bar Styles dialog box to change the display of categories of task bars in the Gantt Chart.

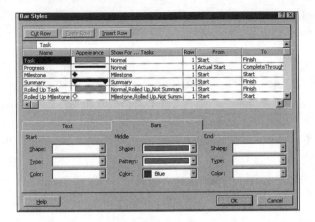

Tip from Tim and the Project Team

You can also open the Bar Styles dialog box by right-clicking a blank spot on the timescale portion of the Gantt Chart and choosing Bar Styles from the shortcut menu, or by double-clicking anywhere in the Gantt Chart background except at a specific bar.

The top half of the Bar Styles dialog box contains a definition table with rows for each of the bars and symbols that appear in the Gantt Chart. The bottom half of the dialog box contains two tabs. The Bars tab has drop-down lists for specifying the formatted look of the bars and symbols. You can specify the way a bar looks at the start, end, and in between. The Text tab has text boxes where text fields can be added in various locations around the bars. The second column in the table at the top of the dialog box displays a sample of the formatted look that you composed.

To insert a new bar within the table, select the row you plan to define the bar in and select the Insert Row button at the top of the dialog box.

To delete a bar from the definition, select the row that defines the bar and choose the Cut Row button. You can paste this definition into a new location; just select the new location and choose the Paste Row button. A blank row is inserted, and a copy of the row that you cut is placed in the new row.

To copy a row (for example, to create a bar that closely resembles a bar already defined), cut the row to be copied (use the Cut Row button) and immediately paste it back to the same location (use the Paste Row button). Then move to the location for the copy and paste the row again.

SUPPLYING THE BAR NAME

Use the first column of the definition table to enter a name for the bar. The bar name can be anything you choose and has no significance, except that the name appears in the legend next to the bar symbol when the Gantt Chart is printed.

DEFINING THE BAR APPEARANCE

The second column shows what the bar or symbol looks like when the Bars palette definition is applied. Change the look of the sample with the Start, Middle, and End sections on the Bars tab at the bottom of the dialog box.

You can define the Shape, Type, and Color of the start shape at the left edge of the bar. Use the Shape drop-down list to scroll the list for the shape you want. Use the first option, which is blank, if you don't want a symbol to mark the start of the bar. Use the Type drop-down list to choose Dashed, Framed, or Solid. Finally, use the Color drop-down list to choose a color.

In the Middle section, use the Shape drop-down list to view the options for the size and height of the bar itself. The list includes no bar at all, a full bar, a top half of a bar, a small bar in the center of the bar space, a bottom half of a bar, and heavy lines at the top, middle, and bottom of the bar space. These bar shapes can overlap. The Progress bar (the solid black center of the task bar when the *percent complete* is greater than zero), for example, is formed by displaying the thin center bar for the progress amount, and the full bar for the duration of the task. When you have multiple bars drawn for one task, the bars closer to the top of the dialog box are displayed first. Bars further down in the list in the dialog box are laid on top of the bars higher up in the list.

Use the Color drop-down list to choose the color of the bar. Use the Pattern drop-down list to choose the fill pattern or shading for the bar. The bar can show as an outline only, be solid, or have any one of nine fill patterns.

Tip from Tim and the Project Team

Bar colors can get lost when printing in black and white or when faxing a color printout. Change at least one bar style to a patterned appearance to help distinguish critical from noncritical tasks.

To select the shape for the end of the bar, follow the same procedure as for selecting the shape for the start of the bar. Use the Shape drop-down list to choose the shape, and the Type drop-down list to choose the type. Use the Color drop-down list to choose the color.

The Appearance column in the table at the top of the dialog box displays the effect of the choices. You must go through these steps for each bar or symbol that you place on the Gantt Chart. Before choosing any options at the bottom of this dialog box, make sure that the intended task is selected at the top.

SELECTING THE TASKS THAT DISPLAY THE BAR

Select the third column (Show For...Tasks) in the definition table at the top of the Bar Styles dialog box to define the categories of tasks for which the bar is displayed. When you click in this column, a drop-down list appears. Choose a bar category from the drop-down list or type the category. If you want to use two or more task categories, separate the task categories' names with commas (or the list separator character specified in Window's Control Panel, Regional Settings).

The drop-down list contains a large number of task types. All tasks fall into one of the first three categories: Milestone, Summary, or Normal (any task that is not a Milestone or a Summary task). You might use these three kinds of tasks in combination with the other types in the list to more narrowly define specific types of tasks—for example, Normal,Critical and Normal,Noncritical instead of just Normal (which includes both Critical and Noncritical). If a task falls into more than one category, it shows the formatting features of both categories. If one formatting feature overwrites another, the feature that is lowest in the definition table is applied last and remains visible in the display.

To select all tasks except the type named, you can place the word Not before the type name. Examples are Not Summary, Not Milestone, and Not Rolled Up.

The Rolled Up type refers to a special field for subordinate tasks that instructs Microsoft Project to show a representative bar or a symbol for the task on the Summary task bar. You designate tasks as Rolled Up tasks using the Task Information dialog box. The General tab has a check box for Roll Up Gantt Bar to Summary. Figure 22.11 illustrates the use of rollup symbols. Notice the mouse pointer is pointing at a diamond that represents a subtask milestone (task 13) that has been rolled up to the summary task. The Bar Styles settings required to produce this open diamond for a milestone are Diamond Shape, Framed Type, and Black Color.

Figure 22.11
Use rolled up dates to make summary tasks more descriptive.

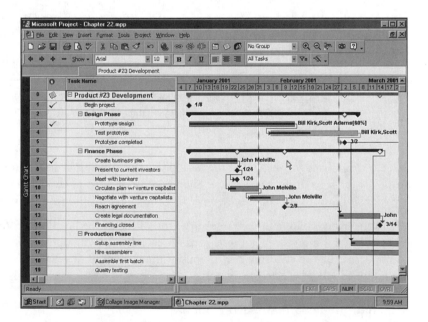

Each of the milestone tasks has been defined as a rolled up task, which means the Roll Up Gantt Bar to Summary check box on the Task Information dialog box is selected. The mouse pointer is pointing at one of the rollup symbols: a small diamond shape.

SELECTING THE ROW FOR THE BAR

You can place up to four rows of bars on the Gantt Chart for each task, or you can use the extra rows for displaying text. Notice in the dialog box in Figure 22.10 that the Progress bar is placed in Row 1 along with the Task bar. Because the shapes of the bars differ, the effect is to superimpose one over the other.

> **Caution**
>
> The order in which you list superimposed bars in the definition table is important. The bars in the Gantt Chart are drawn in the order listed in the definition table. If the Progress bar in this example were defined above the Normal bars, the Progress bar would be drawn before the Normal bars, and the larger Normal bars would hide the Progress bar.

DEFINING THE LENGTH OF THE BAR

The length and placement of every bar or symbol on the Gantt Chart is determined by entries in the From and To columns of the definition table at the top of the Bar Styles dialog box. You can use date fields or one of several measures of time (Percent Complete, Total Slack, Free Slack, Negative Slack, Actual Start, Late Start, and so on). Choose an entry from the drop-down list.

> **Caution**
>
> Choosing from the drop-down list for From and To requires a strong knowledge of what each of these dates represent. If you are not familiar with these, it might be easier to use the Gantt Chart Wizard.

> **Note**
>
> For a complete description of Project database fields, open the Help menu and choose Contents and Index. On the Welcome screen, select the Reference section. From the Reference screen, scroll to the "Reference content in Help" section and click "Fields reference." You can also check out the Microsoft 2000 Field Reference that is on the CD accompanying this book.

PLACING TEXT IN THE BAR CHART

On the Text tab of the Bar Styles dialog box is a column for designating a position next to the bar where data from one or more fields can be displayed. You can display field data at the left, right, top, and bottom of the bar, as well as inside the bar. You can't type literal text in these columns; you can only designate fields that contain text (including dates, durations, percentages, and other numeric values) to display the values in the selected fields. Thirty user-defined Text fields (Text1 through Text30) are available, in which you can type text in any list view that you want to display on the bar chart. For easy access when you want to enter text in these fields, either insert a column in an existing table or edit the table definition to include your custom fields.

→ For more information on displaying fields in tables, **see** "Using and Creating Tables," **p. 949**

Tip from Tim and the Project Team

Figure 22.12 shows the text columns and the selection that produces a display of Resource Initials next to the task to which they are assigned rather than a full Resource Name that often takes up too much room.

Figure 22.12
Use the Text tab of the Bar Styles dialog box to place text from fields around the bars of the Gantt Chart.

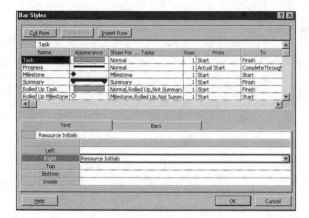

To select a field to be displayed beside a bar, select the bar row in the top of the Bar Styles dialog box, choose the Text tab on the dialog box, select the one of the five rows for the desired text position on the bar, and select the name from the drop-down list. Select OK to accept your changes or select Cancel to close the dialog box without implementing them.

Note   If you want to change the format of specific bars that don't fall into one of the categories available, choose Format, Bar. This command has the same options as the Bar Styles dialog box, but it only applies changes to the selected tasks.

CHANGING THE LAYOUT OF THE GANTT CHART

The Layout option on the Format menu accesses the Layout dialog box (shown in Figure 22.13), which offers a number of additional choices for the way bars are displayed on the Gantt Chart. This dialog box is also available by right-clicking the timescale side of the Gantt chart (not on a bar or timescale label) and choosing Layout from the shortcut menu. Although the primary focus of the Gantt Chart is a list of tasks occurring on a timeline, it's often helpful to see the dependency relationships between tasks. In the Links section of this dialog box, you can choose whether to have lines drawn to designate the dependency linkages between tasks, and if so you can choose between two styles of lines.

When dates are displayed as text around the bars, use the Date Format drop-down list to choose from a list of available formats. This won't change the default format for dates displayed elsewhere in the project. The first option on this list is Default, which returns you to the same format as specified on the View tab of the Options dialog box.

Figure 22.13
Use the Layout dialog box to further define the appearance of task bars on the Gantt Chart.

Use the Bar Height drop-down list to choose a size for the bars. Sizes vary from 6 to 24 points with a default of 12.

In previous versions of Project, each subtask that you wanted to be rolled up and represented symbolically on its summary task had to have the Roll Up Gantt Bar to Summary check box turned on, via the Task Information dialog box. Project 2000 provides an easier method for designating that all tasks should be rolled up and represented on summary tasks.

In the Layout dialog box, the Always Roll Up Gantt Bars option forces all tasks to behave as if the Roll Up Gantt Bar to Summary option has been turned on in the Task Information dialog box. Milestone indicators and bars connecting subtask start and finish dates are drawn on the respective summary tasks.

The companion option on the Layout dialog box, Hide Rollup Bars When Summary Expanded, eliminates the display of the summary bar itself when summary tasks are collapsed. The familiar black bar with down-pointing end shapes is not displayed under the rolled up bars and markers. In addition, when summary tasks are expanded and the subtasks are visible, there are no rollup indicators drawn on the summary task bars.

In Figure 22.14, the Layout options have been set to Always Roll Up Gantt Bars and to Hide Rollup Bars When Summary Expanded. Note the difference in appearance of the bars for summary tasks 2 and 6.

The Round Bars to Whole Days option determines how tasks with a duration less than the time period by the minor timescale are displayed. For example, if a task with a duration of 5 hours is displayed in a Gantt Chart with a minor timescale of days, and this box is cleared, then the bar displays a length of exactly five hours. If the Round Bars to Whole Days check box is marked, the bar extends to a full day. Only the display of the task is modified, the actual duration and calculated start and finish dates remain the same.

The Show Bar Splits check box instructs Project to display differently tasks that have been split. If this box is not checked, the task bar simply extends the duration of the task from start to finish, including the split. If this box is checked, it is very clear where work stopped and then resumed on the task.

The Show Drawings check box enables you to place graphics on the Gantt Chart.

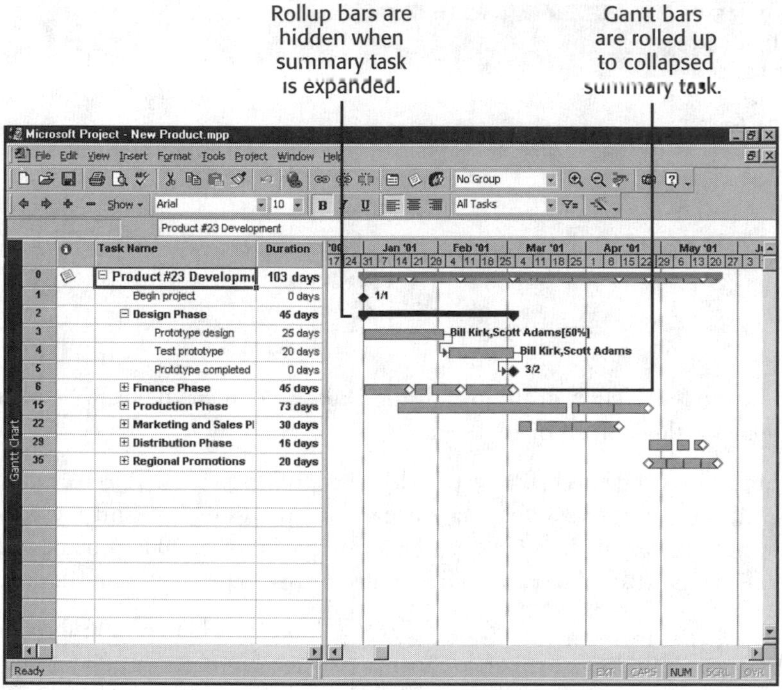

Rollup bars are
hidden when
summary task
is expanded.

Gantt bars
are rolled up
to collapsed
summary task.

Figure 22.14
New rollup behaviors
in Project 2000 pro-
duce cleaner Gantt
Chart appearance.

→ For more information on including drawn objects on a Gantt Chart, **see** "Adding Graphics and Text to Gantt Charts," **p. 275**

Choose OK to accept your changes or select Cancel to close the dialog box without implementing them.

USING THE GANTT CHART WIZARD

Microsoft Project includes a feature that makes formatting the bars on the Gantt Chart extremely easy. This automated feature walks you through the various formatting options, asking questions about how you would like to have the bars displayed. The options are basically the same as those already covered, but the wizard takes you through the process step by step. To access the Gantt Chart Wizard, you can choose Format, Gantt Chart Wizard; use the Gantt Chart Wizard button on the Formatting toolbar; or choose Gantt Chart Wizard from the Gantt Chart shortcut menu (accessed by right-clicking any blank area of the Gantt Chart).

You are initially presented with an introductory dialog box with a series of buttons at the bottom. Choose the Next button to see your first set of choices (see Figure 22.15). Notice that the title bar includes the step at which you are currently working. There are actually 14 separate steps, but you only see every step if you choose the Custom Gantt Chart. As you make your choices, you are taken to the next appropriate step, depending on your choice. Simply choose the desired option, and then choose the Next button to move to the next step. You can click Back, Cancel, or Finish at any time. If you are unsure as to the meaning of a particular option, click the Help button in the top-right corner (it appears as a question mark) and then click the option about which you have a question.

Figure 22.15
The Gantt Chart Wizard walks you through formatting options for the Gantt Chart.

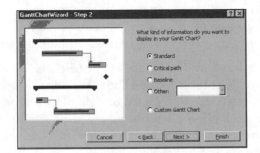

The first question you must answer involves selecting the basic way that tasks are displayed. Your choice here acts as a starting point for setting up the format of the bars on the Gantt Chart. The possible starting format options are as follows:

- **Standard**—Uses the same bars that are used in the default Gantt Chart.
- **Critical Path**—A helpful view to use when trying to reduce the total duration of the project (referred to as "crashing the schedule" in project management circles) or identifying those tasks that must be completed on time in order to meet the project deadline.
- **Baseline**—An appropriate choice when tracking a project already underway.
- **Other**—Offers a list of 13 pre-defined formats you can use as is or modify as desired.
- **Custom Gantt Chart**—Offers the most extensive choices and walks through all the choices for formatting one step at a time. These options include choices for the colors, patterns, and shapes of Critical, Normal, Summary, and Milestone tasks. You also have an option for adding bars for baseline information or slack. You can also choose to place text next to bars.

After you make your initial choice, you are prompted for the kind of text to display in and around the bars. Here again, you have a custom choice that allows for distinct definitions for the text formats of Normal, Summary, and Milestone tasks. The final question involves whether or not the link lines should be drawn to display dependency relationships between the task bars.

After you have made all your changes, the Gantt Chart Wizard does the rest. All you have to do is choose the Format It button and then choose the Exit Wizard button from the final dialog box that appears. You still have the option of making further changes using the techniques covered in previous sections.

FORMATTING THE CALENDAR

You can modify the display of the Calendar view in many ways to meet your specific needs. As with other views, you can use the Zoom command on the View menu, or you can use the Zoom In and Zoom Out buttons on the Standard toolbar to cycle through preset options for zooming. This is convenient if you have many tasks occurring at the same time.

A number of mouse methods are available for changing the height and width of the squares where the dates are displayed. Point to any vertical line in the calendar, and the mouse pointer changes to a double-headed arrow. Drag left or right to narrow or widen the column. Likewise, if you point to a horizontal line, the mouse pointer again changes to a double-headed arrow indicating that you can drag up or down to make the date box taller or shorter. This is particularly useful when you have more tasks on a given day than can be displayed at once.

The options that are available on the Format menu for the Calendar view include Timescale, Gridlines, Text Styles, Bar Styles, Layout, and Layout Now. The Text Styles and Gridlines options are the same as discussed in previous sections. The options for Timescale, Bar Styles, and Layout are unique to the Calendar view and are discussed in detail here.

FORMATTING THE TIMESCALE FOR THE CALENDAR

Display the Timescale dialog box by choosing Format, Timescale, or use the shortcut menu (right-click any spot other than a specific bar in the calendar portion of the view, not the headings). The Timescale dialog box has three tabs that offer choices for headings and titles, for additional data elements that can appear in the date boxes, and for applying shading on certain days.

The Week Headings tab is shown in Figure 22.16. Here you have numerous choices of labels for the month, the days of the week, and for each week. This figure shows a label for each week that counts down to the end of the project. Additionally, you can choose a 5- or 7-day week, and you can choose to show the previous and next month, much like printed calendars.

Figure 22.16
Customize the calendar display with the Week Headings tab on the Timescale dialog box.

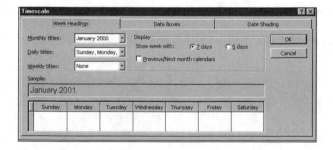

The Date Boxes tab, shown in Figure 22.17, enables you to place additional data elements in the top or bottom row of each individual date box. There are many choices here. The default setting omits a display for the bottom row and includes in the top row an overflow indicator and the date. The overflow indicator appears when all tasks scheduled to occur on a given day can't be displayed within the date box. When printing, overflow tasks appear on a separate page. A pattern and color can also be chosen for emphasis.

Figure 22.17
Customize each date box with additional information in the Date Boxes tab of the Timescale dialog box.

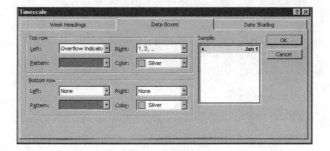

Finally, on the Date Shading tab (see Figure 22.18) you can shade a variety of categories of working or nonworking dates for the base calendar or individual resource calendars as specified in the Show Working Time For drop-down list. First, choose the type of date that you want to shade in the Exception Type list. Then choose a pattern and color from the drop-down lists at the bottom of the dialog box. A sample is displayed on the right as you make your choices. When you're finished making changes, click OK. You are returned to the Calendar view to see the effect of your formatting changes.

Figure 22.18
Indicate working and nonworking days on the Calendar view with options in the Date Shading tab of the Timescale dialog box.

SELECTING CALENDAR BAR STYLES OPTIONS

As with the Gantt Chart, you have control over how the bars in the calendar appear, including text that can be displayed as part of the bars. Access the Bar Styles dialog box by choosing Format, Bar Styles, or use the shortcut menu (right-click any spot other than a specific bar in the calendar portion of the view, not the headings) and select the Bar Styles option. The Bar Styles dialog box appears (see Figure 22.19).

Figure 22.19
The Bar Styles dialog box offers choices for changing the display of task bars in the Calendar view.

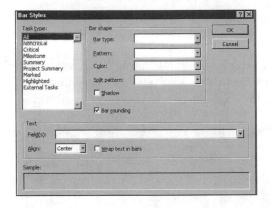

First, select the type of bar you want to modify in the Task Type list box. Then use the drop-down lists in the Bar Shape area to modify the Bar Type, Pattern, Color, and Split Pattern for the bar. You have a variety of choices for pattern and color. As for the bar type, you can have a bar or a simple line extending across the days of the task's duration. There are also choices of different displays for tasks that have split. If you choose a bar for the bar type, you can also apply a shadow for emphasis.

The Bar Rounding check box deals with tasks whose durations are not a whole day (for example, durations of a half day or a day and a half). If the check box is left marked, the bar on the calendar is rounded to a full day.

In the Text area, you can choose any number of fields to be displayed in the bar either by typing in their names (separated by commas) or by choosing them from the Field(s) drop-down list. If you want to have more than one field listed on the bar and you are choosing from the drop-down list, make sure to deselect the field name and type in a comma before selecting another field from the list. Otherwise, if you choose another field while the first field is still selected, the first field is replaced rather than added to. You can deselect a field name either by pressing the right arrow or by clicking with the mouse at the right end of the field name. Alignment options for the text of these fields can be centered, left, or right. When text is long, it might be useful to check the Wrap Text in Bars check box.

For all categories of tasks except All, a sample is displayed at the bottom of the dialog box to show you the effect of your choices. If All is the task type selected, and some, not all, of the task types have a check box option turned on, the check box is displayed with a gray shading. When all the task types have the check box turned on, there is a check mark in the check box. When none of the task types have the check box turned on, the check box is empty.

Choose the OK button when finished. You are returned to the calendar to see the effects of your changes.

Caution

Depending on your choices in the Bar Styles dialog box, you might see a message from the Planning Wizard indicating that some of the calendar bars have different heights. There are instructions for how to position those bars.

SETTING THE LAYOUT OPTIONS FOR THE CALENDAR VIEW

The Layout dialog box, as shown in Figure 22.20, can be accessed either by choosing Format, Layout or using the calendar shortcut menu. The options presented here determine the order of tasks displayed in each date box. The default is Use Current Sort Order. The alternative to this is Attempt to Fit as Many Tasks as Possible without regard for sorting. The check box for Show Bar Splits determines whether a task that has been split displays any differently than a regular task. By default when a task is split, a dotted outline is drawn during that portion of the task when work is not underway. The check box for Automatic Layout specifies that the settings in this dialog box are initiated automatically as tasks are edited, added, or deleted. When Automatic Layout is not selected, you must choose Layout Now from either the Format menu or from the calendar shortcut menu to apply the changes.

Figure 22.20
The Layout dialog box enables you to determine how and when tasks are sorted within each date box.

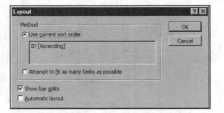

FORMATTING THE NETWORK DIAGRAM

In Project 2000, the new Network Diagram view includes many formatting enhancements. You can customize the Network Diagram by changing the shape, size, and borders of the nodes; by creating named data templates specifying fields to display within each node; and by applying layout characteristics of the task nodes. You can also change your perspective by zooming in or out to see more or less of the entire project and by applying a filter to the diagram. An overall description of the Network Diagram was included in the section "Working with the Network Diagram View" of Chapter 7, "Viewing Your Schedule." This section discusses the extensive formatting and layout possibilities for Network Diagrams.

REVIEWING THE FORMAT OPTIONS FOR THE NETWORK DIAGRAM

The Format menu for the Network Diagram view contains the options Box, Box Styles, and Layout. You can also use the Zoom option on the View menu or the Zoom In and Zoom Out buttons on the Standard toolbar.

The use of the Format menu to change the display of text was covered earlier in this chapter. The Zoom, Layout, and Layout Now commands were covered in previous sections but are summarized here for completeness. The Box Styles commands are covered in detail in the following sections.

USING THE BOX STYLES OPTIONS

You can customize the boxes that surround the nodes to display 10 node shapes, 4 border widths, and a variety of border colors. There are also options for background colors and patterns. Figure 22.21 shows the formatting options for box styles, borders, and colors.

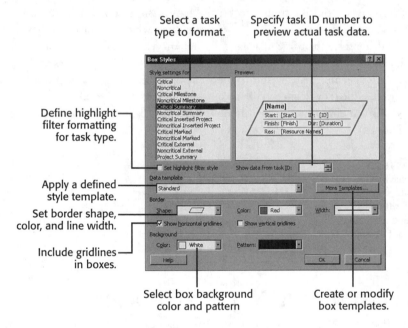

Figure 22.21
Formatting options for categories of tasks are set in the Box Styles dialog box.

Select a task type to format.

Specify task ID number to preview actual task data.

Define highlight filter formatting for task type.

Apply a defined style template.

Set border shape, color, and line width.

Include gridlines in boxes.

Select box background color and pattern

Create or modify box templates.

You can assign each shape one of 17 border colors. If you have a color printer or plotter, the use of color can be an effective tool. If you have a black-and-white printer, you can't distinguish one color from another.

The default box styles are assigned by types of tasks. Critical tasks, of any type such as a milestone or summary task, are outlined in red and have white backgrounds. Noncritical tasks are outlined in blue and have aqua backgrounds. The default shapes are rectangles for normal tasks, 4-sided parallelograms for summary tasks, and 6-sided boxes for milestones.

To assign border shapes, colors, and widths to tasks in the Network Diagram, follow these steps:

1. Choose Format, Box Styles or double-click an open space on the Network Diagram. The Box Styles dialog box appears (refer to Figure 22.21).

2. Change the node formatting for a category of tasks by choosing a task type from the Style Settings For list of task types.

3. In the Border section of the dialog box, use the Shape drop-down list to choose a predefined shape. The sample display Preview area shows the style you have selected.

Tip from Tim and the Project Team

To see how the style settings look with actual task information instead of the provided generic preview, enter a valid Task ID number in the Show Data from Task ID entry box below the Preview area.

4. Use the Color drop-down list to choose one of the available colors.

5. Use the Width drop-down list to choose one of four external border line widths.

6. Set the Show Horizontal Gridlines and Show Vertical Gridlines options to view or suppress cell dividers in the node.

7. By default, Project sets the formatting for boxes displayed in an applied highlight filter to be the same shape as non-highlighted nodes but with the background color changed to yellow. Turn on the Set Highlight Filter Style option to review or modify the highlight settings for node types.

8. After you make all the border selections, choose OK to accept the changes and close the dialog box.

USING DATA TEMPLATES FOR NETWORK DIAGRAM NODES

You can control the contents and the row and column layouts within each node by defining and applying data templates to the node types. Node definitions in a template include the following elements:

- Box cell layout of up to 16 cells in a 4-row×4-column grid

- Cell width sizing to increase readability

- Vertical and horizontal alignment settings for the contents of each cell

- Setting the number of lines of text to be displayed in cells up to a maximum of three

- Descriptive labels inserted in front of data in each cell

- Font size, style, and color options for each cell

- Fields that appear in each of up to 16 cell positions

- Date formats for Network Diagram displays

Initially, the contents and layout of all normal tasks, both critical and noncritical, are defined by the supplied Standard data template. This template displays seven fields of information in a 4-row×2-column grid: Name, ID, Start, Finish, Duration, %Complete, and Resource Names. In contrast, the Milestone template follows 3-row×1-column format and displays the task Name, task ID, and Start date.

To create additional Network Diagram data templates, follow these steps:

1. Display the Network Diagram Box Styles dialog box by viewing the Network Diagram; then double-clicking on the Network Diagram background, or right-clicking the diagram background and choosing Box Styles, or choosing Format, Box Styles.

2. In the Box Styles dialog box, choose the More Templates command button. The Data Templates dialog box appears, as shown in Figure 22.22.

Figure 22.22
Preview a generic sample of a data template or specify a valid task ID to view actual task values.

3. Choose the Import command button to bring in a box style template definition from within the current file or one that has already been created in another file. If needed, any second file must already be open to allow the import to take place.

4. To create a new data template, select New. To use an existing template as a starting point, select Copy or Edit.

Note

Note that you cannot edit the supplied Standard data template. If the standard definition is close to what you want, make a copy of the Standard template and edit the copy.

5. Set the options for the new template in the Data Template Definition dialog box, as seen in Figure 22.23.

6. Give the new template a name by typing in the Template Name entry area.

7. Choose the Cell Layout command button to display the Cell Layout dialog box (see Figure 22.24).

Type a name
for the template.

Open dialog box
to set row and
column layout.

Figure 22.23
Control cell layout
and individual cell
settings in the Data
Template Definition
dialog box.

Preview a generic
box or data from
a specific task.

Choose cell contents
from dropdown lists.

Formatting options
are set for each cell.

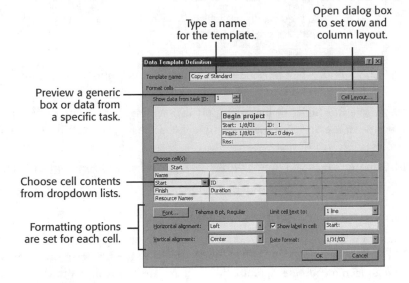

Figure 22.24
Adjust box grid and
cell width in the Cell
Layout dialog box.

8. In the Cell Layout dialog box, choose the number of rows and columns for the new diagram box. You can also expand or contract the setting for cell widths. (This setting can always be changed later.)

9. Also in the Cell Layout dialog box, make a selection for handling cells left blank. (In Figure 22.22, the standard data template contains a blank cell on row 1 in column 2. The Merge Blank Cells with Cell to the Left option is selected in the template definition, so the Name field appears to occupy two cells instead of one.)

10. Click OK when the cell layout is complete and you are ready to return to the Data Template Definition dialog box.

11. Again in the Data Template Definition dialog box, make selections for font, alignments, and number of text lines for *each individual cell*. Click each cell in the Choose Cell(s) area and make selections. Add a prefix label to any or all cells, and select a date format for date cells if desired.

Tip from Tim and the Project Team

To select and change settings for more than one cell at a time, click and drag, Shift+click, or Ctrl+click to select multiple cells.

12. Choose OK when finished with the template definition. Then choose Close in the Data Templates dialog box.

13. In the Box Styles dialog box, apply data template settings to nodes by choosing a task type in the Style Settings For list and choosing a Data Template from the drop-down list.

14. Choose OK when finished. Your changes are immediately reflected in the Network Diagram onscreen.

CONTROLLING THE NETWORK DIAGRAM LAYOUT

The layout in a network diagram is controlled by setting options in a Layout dialog box or by telling Project when to refresh the display with the Layout Now command. After the general layout is defined and applied, you can apply task filters to the diagram and hide tasks by collapsing summary tasks and applying outline level filtering.

SELECTING LAYOUT OPTIONS

The Layout command on the Network Diagram Format menu controls the overall look and feel of the Network Diagram, as opposed to the appearance and contents of individual network nodes. You can choose options for box layout order and spacing, style of box connection lines, color of link lines, diagram background style and color, drawing of task progress lines, and whether the diagram is laid out automatically or you have manual control of the box placements.

To set layout options for the Network Diagram, take the following steps:

1. Display the Layout dialog box shown in Figure 22.25 by viewing the Network Diagram and choosing Format, Layout.

Figure 22.25
Control the overall Network Diagram appearance through the Layout dialog box.

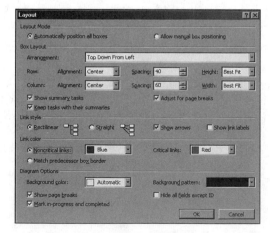

2. In the Layout Mode area, choose Automatically Position All Boxes to have Project maintain the onscreen layout or choose Allow Manual Box Positioning to allow click-and-drag movement of the boxes.

3. In the Box Layout area, use the drop-down lists and spinners to set Row Alignment, Spacing, and Height and also Column Alignment, Spacing, and Width. These settings are relative to other like elements; that is, a row alignment of Center positions all boxes on a single row so that the box horizontal centers form a straight line. Similarly, a column alignment of Left positions all boxes in a vertical column to display with left box edges aligned.

Note

Box sizes (height and width) might vary depending on data template settings applied to box types. See "Using Data Templates for Network Diagram Nodes," previously in this chapter.

4. The Arrangement drop-down list in the Box Layout area determines in what order Project draws the diagram. The standard, and default, arrangement is Top Down From Left. Figure 22.26 shows the Network Diagram for the beginning of the plan, drawn in Top Down From Left order. Most Network Diagrams (or PERT Charts) you've seen have been drawn this way.

Figure 22.26
The standard diagram arrangement is Top Down From Left, with rectilinear link lines and dotted page breaks displayed.

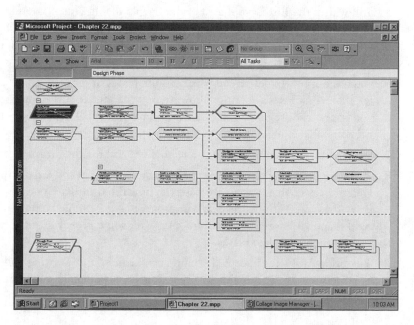

By comparison, Figure 22.27 illustrates how the top-left section of the Network Diagram would look if the arrangement option of Top Down by Week was applied. This figure is set to a custom zoom percentage of 40% (see "Using the Zoom Command," later in this chapter). Each column of nodes represents a week in the project; within columns boxes are in ID order.

Figure 22.27
A Top Down by Week
drawing of the
Network Diagram
gives a better repre-
sentation of the plan
over time.

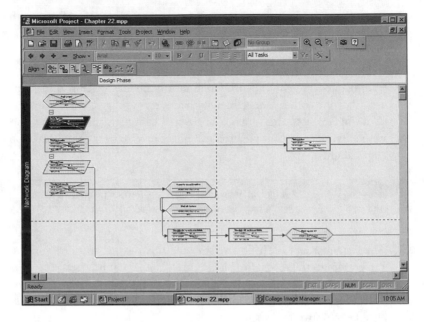

5. Still within the Box Layout area of the Layout dialog box, make selections to Show Summary Tasks, to Keep Tasks with Their Summaries when changing the layout arrangement, and to Adjust for Page Breaks so that boxes can't be split and printed partially on more than one page.

6. Choose options to determine whether lines between diagram boxes are Straight or Rectilinear (squared). Choose Show Arrows to indicate successor direction between nodes, and choose Show Link Labels to include a small dependency type label (FS, SS, FF, SF) on each link line.

7. Select color and pattern options for link lines and for the diagram display background.

8. Two very helpful options are available at the bottom of the Layout dialog box. Show Page Breaks enables you to see onscreen how the printing lays out without going to Print Preview. Turn on the Mark In-progress and Completed option to draw a left-to-right diagonal line across boxes for tasks with some progress and an additional diagonal line through completed tasks.

9. The Hide All Fields Except ID option can be helpful in viewing and printing the overall structure of the plan without displaying any task details (see Figure 22.28).

10. Click OK when all selections have been made.

Tip from Tim and the Project Team

Temporarily enlarge a box for easier viewing of its contents by moving the mouse pointer over the box and pausing.

Figure 22.28
Print a condensed schematic of the plan by hiding all fields except ID.

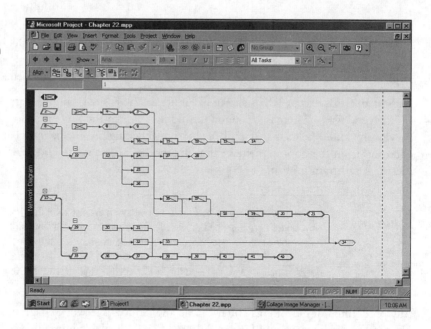

 The Network Diagram does not immediately reflect your new settings. Project must be instructed to redraw the diagram according to the new rules. To see the effect of the Layout settings, choose Format, Layout Now from the menu, right-click the diagram background and choose Layout Now, or select the Layout Now button on the Network Diagram toolbar.

Note You must select Layout Now for Project to incorporate your Layout dialog box changes onto the diagram screen display.

There is set logic behind each of the arrangement options in the Layout dialog box. When the standard Top Down From Left is selected, Project redraws the Network Diagram according to the following standard rules of node placement:

- Successor tasks are placed to the right of or below their predecessor tasks.
- Summary tasks are placed above and to the left of their subordinate tasks.
- Linked task nodes are connected with straight lines (diagonal lines if necessary), and an arrow is placed at the successor task's end of the line to indicate the direction of the relationship.

Other Arrangement options apply similar rules.

CONTROLLING BOXES IN THE VIEW

If the Allow Manual Box Positioning is turned on in the Layout dialog box, you can drag the boxes of the diagram around and reposition them for improved clarity. To reposition a node manually, place the mouse pointer over the edge of a node, hold until the mouse pointer shape changes to a four-pointed arrow, and then click and drag the border edge. You can also select the node and use Ctrl+ arrow keys to move it. The manual positioning stays in place until Layout Now is executed, even if the file is closed and reopened later.

 Hiding all fields except ID, as shown in Figure 22.28, is such a useful feature that it is accessible several ways. There is an option for hiding fields in the Layout dialog box, as discussed previously. Hide Fields is also available by right-clicking on the diagram background and choosing from the pop-up menu. A third method of access is the Hide Fields button on the Network Diagram toolbar.

Tip from Tim and the Project Team

A new Network Diagram toolbar is included with Project 2000. The Hide Fields and Layout Now buttons are described previously. Other commands available on toolbar buttons are Align (both vertically and horizontally), Show Summary Tasks (toggles display on or off), Show Progress Marks (toggles), Show Page Breaks, Show Link Labels, Straight Lines, and one command not available on the Layout menu—Layout Selection Now.

Any predefined or custom task filter can be applied to a Network Diagram view. After displaying the diagram, choose Project, Filtered For to display commonly used filters. Filtering was not possible in previous versions of Project.

Tip from Tim and the Project Team

Use custom outline codes as filter criteria to focus on a special selection of Network Diagram boxes.

Another method of controlling the Network Diagram display is by setting the outline detail level to be displayed. The Show button on the Formatting toolbar enables you to choose what levels of subtasks are displayed. You can also collapse and expand individual summary tasks on the screen by clicking the + or − symbol above each summary task.

→ For more information on creating a task outline, **see** "Outlining the Task List," **p. 184**

USING THE ZOOM COMMAND

 When viewing the Network Diagram, it's often helpful to change the perspective, either pulling back to see the big picture or moving in closer for a more detailed view. This feature is especially useful when you manually move the nodes around to redesign the chart. You can choose View, Zoom, use the shortcut menu, or click either the Zoom In or Zoom Out button on the Standard toolbar. You can zoom from 25% to 400%.

When you use the Zoom In and Zoom Out buttons, you are moved through the various preset zoom levels. When you use either the shortcut menu or the View menu, the Zoom dialog box appears. Choose any of the preset zoom values or enter a value of your own choice in the Custom text box. Figure 22.29 shows the 40% zoom setting used to display Figure 22.27.

Figure 22.29
Custom Zoom settings are particularly useful with Network Diagrams.

FORMATTING THE TASK AND RESOURCE FORMS

Like the other forms, the Task and Resource Forms can't be printed, and the formatting choices are limited. If the form is active in the top pane, you can view all resources with the form. Use the Next and Previous buttons to change the task or resource displayed in the form. If the form is active in the bottom pane, you can display only tasks or resources that are associated with the items selected in the top pane.

To display the Task or Resource Form, select the pane in which you want the form to appear, choose View, More Views, and then select Task or Resource Form from the More Views dialog box.

REVIEWING THE FORMAT OPTIONS FOR THE FORM VIEWS

The Resource and Task Forms have a limited number of format options. The Project menu for both the Resource and Task Form views provides a Sort option, and the Format menu provides a Details option that offers various entry field combinations that you can place at the bottom of the form.

When a form view is displayed full screen or as the top portion of a split screen, the Sort option changes the order in which resources or tasks appear when you use the Next and Previous buttons. If the form is displayed as the bottom portion of a split screen, applying a different sort order even when the form portion is active has no effect; in this case, the sort order applied to the top portion of the screen controls the behavior of Next and Previous buttons on the form.

To sort the resource or task list for display while using the form view, choose Project, Sort. Follow the same procedure for using the Sort dialog box (for all views), as described earlier in this chapter in "Sorting the Tasks or Resources in a View."

USING THE ENTRY FIELD OPTIONS

To select a different set of entry fields for the Task or Resource Form, you can choose other options by choosing Format, Details. These options are specific to form views and are described in this section.

Tip from Tim and the Project Team

You can also see a list of alternative formats for forms by right-clicking anywhere in a blank area of the form and choosing from the shortcut menu

The Resource Form and the Task Form have several detail options that are similar. In the Resource Form, the various tasks assigned to that resource are listed. Changing the details changes the display of the information about the tasks assigned. The Task Form focuses on a task and displays information about the resources assigned to the task. Therefore, changing the details in the Task Form changes the way the resource information is displayed about that task.

In the Task Form, to display fields for when work is scheduled as well as entry fields for imposing a delay either on the task itself or when the resource begins work on the task, choose Format, Details, Schedule. Notice the columns named Leveling Delay and Delay (see Figure 22.30). You can use the Delay field to delay the start of work on a task by the resource. The Leveling Delay field is a delay for the task itself and is the same field that appears on the Delay table on the Detail and Leveling Gantt Charts. The Delay field is a delay for the resource only. If the resource is the only one assigned to work on a task, the effect of a resource delay has the same effect on the schedule as the effect of a task delay: Both choices delay the start of the task. However, suppose several resources are assigned to a task and one of the resources needs to spend only the last several hours on the task (during the finishing stage, for example). The assignment of this resource to the task can be accompanied by a delay in when the resource begins work on the task, but does not result in a delay for the task.

Figure 22.30
With a Task Form view active, choose Format, Details, Schedule to display assigned resource scheduling fields.

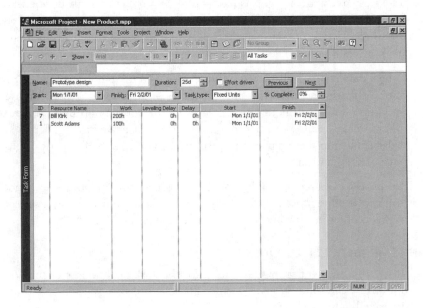

To display the cost fields for the resource for a task on the Task Form, apply the Resource Cost detail setting. To show on the Resource Form the cost contributions to each task that a resource has been assigned work, apply the Cost detail setting. Figure 22.31 shows the cost of each resource assigned to the Prototype Design task.

Figure 22.31
The Costs for each assigned resource on a task can be displayed on the Task Form.

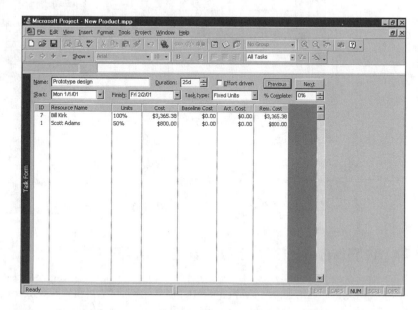

To display the fields for work on different tasks, choose Format, Details, Resource Work (for a Task Form) or Work (for a Resource Form). Use these versions of the forms to record the actual work and overtime spent on tasks by the resource.

Choose Format, Details, Notes to display the Notes field for the task or resource (see Figure 22.32).

Tip from Tim and the Project Team

In other views, such as a Gantt Chart, you can also attach a note to any selected task or resource by using the Task Notes button on the Standard toolbar, or by right-clicking any part of a task (the name, the ID, or the bar) and choosing Notes from the shortcut menu. On resource-oriented views, such as the Resource Sheet, the option changes to Resource Notes.

Choose Format, Details, Objects to display objects that were attached to the task or resource. For related information, see the section "Adding Graphics and Text to Gantt Charts" in Chapter 7.

Choosing Format, Details shows several additional choices for display in the Task Form. The standard display shows the Resources and Predecessors entry fields for the selected task. You also can choose to display Resources and Successors, or Predecessors and Successors.

Figure 22.32
Task Notes can be entered on the Task Form.

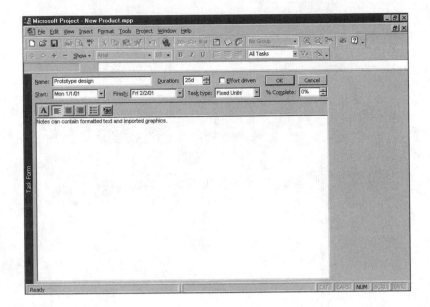

FORMATTING THE RESOURCE GRAPH

The Resource Graph shows values derived from the task assignments of one or more resources; these values are graphed along a timescale. To display the Resource Graph, choose View, Resource Graph or click the Resource Graph icon in the View bar. Figure 22.33 shows a histogram, or bar chart (in the lower pane), for the allocated and over-allocated task assignments for Scott Adams during the weeks of January 7 through February 11. The value measured in this example is the Peak Units, or percentage effort assigned during each time period (in this case, each week).

→ For more information about resources that are overallocated, **see** "Understanding How Resource Overallocations Occur," **p. 442**

→ For detailed information on the Resource Graph, **see** "The Resource Graph," **p. 867**

You can use the graph to show the following measurements for a resource in a time period on each task:

- Peak units
- Amount of work assigned
- Running total of work assigned to date
- Work overallocation of the resource
- Percent of effort currently allocated
- Effort in hours still available for assignments
- Cost of the assignments

- Running total of cost contribution to date
- Total work availability (does not reflect assignments)
- Total percentage availability (does not reflect assignments)

Figure 22.33
The Resource Graph showing peak units can be displayed below the Resource Usage View.

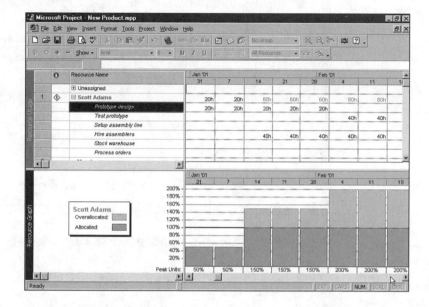

The graph can show these measurements for one resource, for a group of resources, or for the resource and the group together. The values can be for selected tasks or for all tasks during each time period.

If the Resource Graph is displayed in the bottom pane below a task view, the displayed values are for one resource only. You can show values for this resource's assignment to one task (the selected task) or to all tasks during each period measured on the timescale. Figure 22.34 shows the assignment bars for Howard Thompson for all tasks during each week. This figure provides a quick glimpse of the overassignment in terms of numbers of tasks assigned.

When the Resource Graph is in the top pane, or in the bottom pane but below a resource view, the values displayed are for all tasks and might be for one resource, for a group of resources, or for that one resource compared to the group of resources. If group data is displayed, the group is defined by the filter currently in use. If the All Resources filter (the default filter) is in use, for example, the data summarizes all resources for all tasks. Figure 22.35 shows the total costs associated with Howard Thompson's task assignments, relative to the total costs of all resource assignments in the project.

Figure 22.34
The Resource Graph below a task view shows bars for all task work in that period for a single resource.

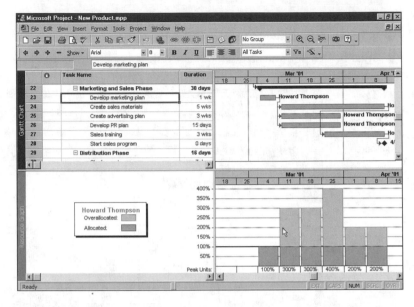

Figure 22.35
The Resource Graph displays costs associated with a single resource compared to the costs of all other resources.

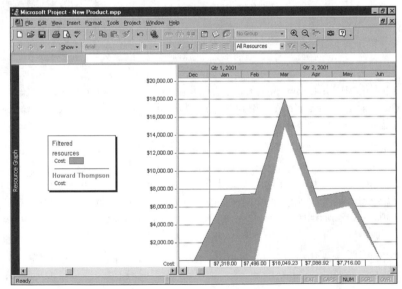

Table 22.1 summarizes the values displayed for different placement locations for the Resource Graph.

TABLE 22.1   VALUES SHOWN IN THE RESOURCE GRAPH

Location of Graph	Group Value	One Resource Value
Top pane or bottom pane below a resource view	Value is for all tasks for all filtered resources.	Value is for all tasks for the selected resource.
Bottom pane below a task view	Value is for one resource but for all tasks the tasks selected in.	Value is for one resource but for only the top pane.

REVIEWING THE FORMAT OPTIONS FOR THE RESOURCE GRAPH

As with other views, the Zoom command on the View menu is available for the Resource Graph and works as discussed previously in this chapter to modify the timeframes that are displayed. Likewise, the Zoom In and Zoom Out tools on the Standard toolbar can be used in this view.

The Format menu for the Resource Graph contains dialog box options described previously in this chapter for formatting the timescale (if the graph is not in a bottom pane), gridlines, and text styles. The Bar Styles dialog box, however, also offers features unique to the Resource Graph. These features are discussed in the following section.

The Format menu also provides a Details option. The choices on this list of calculated values control what information is displayed in the timescale portion of the Resource Graph. Because the Bar Styles dialog box options are based on these values, the Details options are described first.

SELECTING THE VALUES TO DISPLAY

The Format, Details menu displays a list of choices of what values are calculated and graphed in the Resource Graph.

Note
When work is chosen, the unit (hours, minutes, or days) is determined by the Work Is Entered In option on the Schedule tab of the Options dialog box. The display of costs is determined by the Currency Symbol, Currency Placement, and Currency Decimal Digits choices on the View tab in the same dialog box.

DISPLAYING PEAK UNITS

Peak Units measures the largest percentage of effort of a resource assigned at any moment during each time period on the graph. If the effort units exceeds the available number as set in Maximum Units on the Resource Sheet view, the excess is shown as an overallocation. An availability line shows the number of units available.

Note that peak units are measured in *effort assigned*, not work assigned. As such, Peak Units might mislead you when it shows an overallocation. Suppose a person is assigned full-time to two tasks during the same day. The peak units is 2, and because only one unit of a person is usually available per time period, the peak of 2 is an overallocation and is displayed as such. If each of the two tasks is a one-hour task, however, the person should have no problem completing both tasks during the day.

The Peak Units measurement is very useful, however, with multiple-unit resources in which the number of maximum units available is more than one. In these cases, the overallocation warning is more likely to be accurate.

DISPLAYING WORK

The Work choice on the Format, Details menu is measured in hours and is the number of units of each resource assigned to each task multiplied by the duration in hours of the tasks per time period displayed. For example, two programmers are assigned to work on a task that is estimated to take one 8-hour day. Project calculates this task to have 16 hours of Work.

The amount of work to be done by the resource is determined by the number of units of the resource, the resource calendar, and the resource availability contour during the time unit. If the total work for the time period exceeds the available amount of resource hours, the excess is shown as an overallocation.

DISPLAYING CUMULATIVE WORK

Another choice on the Format, Details menu is Cumulative Work. This is a measurement of the total work for the resource since the beginning of the project. This running total includes the work during the time period shown.

DISPLAYING OVERALLOCATION

The Overallocation value shows the overallocation of work for the resource for the time period. The Overallocation option shows just the amount of the overallocation, not any work hours that occurred during the normal work day. See the section, "Displaying Work," previously in this chapter, for the way Work is measured.

DISPLAYING PERCENT ALLOCATION

The Percent Allocation value is a measurement of the allocated work versus the available work. The Percent Allocation shows the amount of work as a percentage of the amount available. See the previous section, "Displaying Work," for the way in which Work is measured.

DISPLAYING AVAILABILITY

The Remaining Availability value is a measurement of the unallocated work for the resource during the time period. The Remaining Availability option shows the unused or unallocated work time that is still available. This is a useful option when you want to see who has some available time to work on tasks, or to see if you are available when new tasks are assigned to you. See the previous section "Displaying Work."

DISPLAYING COST

The Cost value is the scheduled cost of the resource work during the time period. If the resource cost is to be prorated (as defined in the Cost Accrual field on the Costs tab of the Resource Form), the costs appear in the time period when the work is done. If there is a Per Use Cost associated with a prorated resource, that cost is shown at the start of the task. If the resource cost is to accrue at the start or end of the task, the entire cost appears in the graph at the start or end of the task.

DISPLAYING CUMULATIVE COST

The Cumulative Cost display adds each period's cost to the preceding period's cumulative cost to show a running total of costs. You can use this measurement to show total cost over the life of the project if you use only the group graph and include all resources in the group (see "Using the Bar Styles Dialog Box," later in this chapter).

DISPLAYING WORK AVAILABILITY

The Work Availability display graphically presents the total number of hours a resource is available in a timeframe. This display is based on resource maximum units and the resource calendar. It does not reflect any work assignments that might exist in the period.

DISPLAYING UNIT AVAILABILITY

Unit Availability reflects the same information as the Work Availability detail option, but the resource availability is expressed in percentages.

USING THE BAR STYLES DIALOG BOX

The Bar Styles dialog box enables you to specify what type of graph you would like to display (bar, area, step, line, and so on), if any, as well as how it should look. It also enables you to specify whether you want to see groups or just selected resource information. When the Resource Graph is displayed, choose Format, Bar Styles to open the Bar Styles dialog box. A different Bar Styles dialog box appears for each of the value measurements just described. However, all these dialog boxes have the same layout and are used the same way. Figure 22.36 shows the Bar Styles dialog box for the Work value. As with all the Resource Graph Bar Styles dialog boxes, this dialog box has four main sections plus three options at the bottom of the box.

> **Note**
>
> The different areas of this dialog box that are available depend on the Details option that is set by choosing Format, Details.

Figure 22.36
Set the options for displaying work values on the Resource Graph in the Bar Styles dialog box.

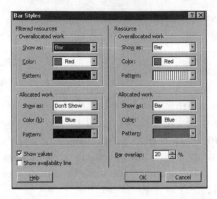

You use the two top sections to specify the display of overallocated amounts (if applicable), and the two bottom sections to specify the display of the allocated value up to the maximum available. The sections on the left side of the dialog box are for specifying the display of group data, and the sections on the right side are for specifying the display of one selected resource. Be aware that some of the values on the Details menu can display only two of the sections.

After the dialog box is closed, you might see multiple sets of double bars, and in some cases, each bar has an upper and a lower segment. The upper segment is the overallocation measurement. The lower segment is the allocation up to the overallocation level. Where you see pairs of bars, the left bar is the group measurement (again, note the similarity in the dialog box), and the right bar is the selected resource measurement. Recall that the resource group is defined by the filter that is applied when the Resource Graph is in the top pane or is a single pane. In this case, the group represents all resources because no filter has been applied.

Therefore, where you see a pair of bars in the graph (see Figure 22.37), the bar on the right (slightly in front) is the bar for the resource (Howard Thompson in this case), and the left bar (slightly behind) is the bar for the group (all resources in this case).

At the bottom of the graph, the work values are displayed in the time periods where the resource is allocated.

All these features are defined by the dialog box. (The graph in Figure 22.37 is defined by the settings in the dialog box in Figure 22.36.) The check box at the bottom is marked to show the values. The bars overlap by 20% to show that they are paired.

The shading patterns are determined by the selections in the four sections of the dialog box. For each section, you choose three features that determine how the value is represented. Use the Show As drop-down list to choose the general form of the representation. The Bar is the usual choice, but you also can use lines and areas. The choice Don't Show suppresses all representation of the value. Choose Color to select the color of the image, and choose Pattern for the pattern that fills the bar or area. (Notice that the underlined letters for these options are different in each section.)

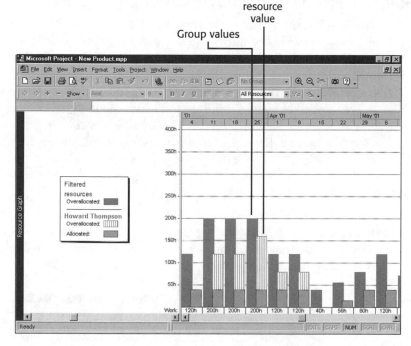

Figure 22.37
The Resource Graph demonstrates overallocation of a single resource compared to the entire resource pool.

You manage what is graphed by choosing what to display or not to display in each of the four sections of the dialog box. If you want to display only the values for the selected resource, with no representation of the group values, choose Don't Show from the Show As drop-down list for both sections on the left. If you want to show only the totals for all resources, choose Don't Show for both sections on the right. When you choose Overallocation on the Format, Details menu, the Bar Styles dialog box has both of the bottom sections dimmed to show that the sections are unneeded. When you finish making changes, choose OK to implement them or choose Cancel to ignore them.

To prepare the resource graph as shown in Figure 22.35, follow these steps:

1. Choose Format, Details, Cost.

2. Choose Format, Bar Styles.

3. In the Bar Styles dialog box in the Filtered Resources area, change the Show As option for the Resource cost (top left) to Area.

4. Set the Show As option for the selected Resource cost (top right) to Area. Choose a different color as well.

5. Click OK to close the dialog box.

6. Zoom the timescale to a major scale of quarters and a minor scale of months. You can use the Zoom Out button on the Standard toolbar or the Format, Timescale menu option to do this.

FORMATTING THE RESOURCE USAGE VIEW

The Resource Usage view shows the same data displayed in the Resource Graph, except that the values appear as number entries in a grid under the timescale. Figure 22.38 shows the Resource Usage view above the Resource Graph to demonstrate the similarity of the data presented. In both views, the value displayed is Work. The Format menu for the Resource Usage view includes text styles, formatting fonts, gridline formatting, and timescale formatting. As with the other views, sorting is also available on the Project menu, and page breaks can be inserted using the Insert menu. These are all topics covered previously in this chapter under their own headings. See those sections for information about using these format options.

CHOOSING THE DETAILS

The choices available by choosing Format, Details are some of the same value choices that were described under the Resource Graph: Work, Actual Work, Cumulative Work, Overallocation, Cost, and Remaining Availability. Select the value to display in the timescale grid by selecting one of these options.

Figure 22.38
Display work as data values and in graphic form by viewing the Resource Usage view over the Resource Graph.

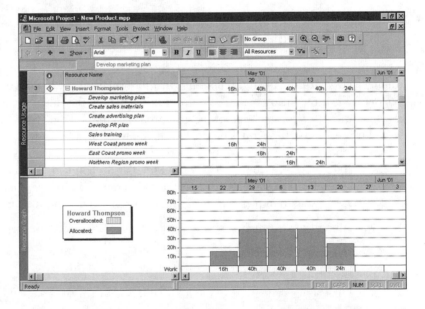

If the Resource Usage view is placed in the bottom pane under a task view, the only resources that are displayed are resources assigned to the task that you selected in the top pane. The values displayed next to the resource name are the total values for all tasks during the entire project. A breakdown of other tasks assigned to that resource are displayed under the resource name.

Figure 22.39 shows the Resource Usage view below the Gantt Chart. The values in the usage timescale table (in the same row as his name) show Work assigned to Howard Thompson for all tasks during each time period. Underneath his name and spread out across the timescale grid is a breakdown of the tasks that generated the totals. The values show that the resource is overallocated for a normal 40-hour work week, 8-hour work day.

Figure 22.39
View detail work breakdowns by task by displaying the Gantt Chart over the Resource Usage view.

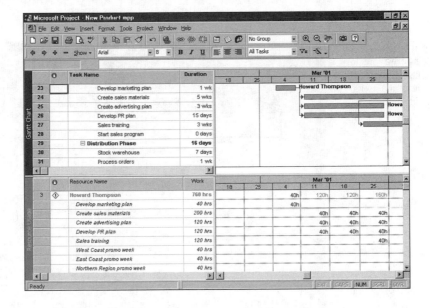

FORMATTING THE DETAIL STYLES

When the Resource Usage view is active, the Format menu contains an option for Detail Styles. Choosing this menu displays the dialog box displayed in Figure 22.40. Here you can choose from a wide variety of fields, and each might display a different font, background color, and pattern. From the Available Fields list on the left, simply select a field to be displayed and use the Show button. To remove a field from being displayed, select it from the Show These Fields list on the right and use the Hide button. To rearrange the order in which the fields are displayed, use the Move Up and Move Down buttons on the right side of the dialog box. The Usage Properties tab contains options for how the detail data should be aligned, and whether to display headings for the various columns and rows.

Figure 22.40
The Detail Styles dialog box offers many choices for how much detail to display in the timescale grid of the Resource Usage View.

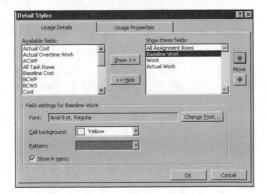

Figure 22.41 displays the additional rows of information for each task assigned to Howard Thompson. Not only are these additional rows useful for reviewing but you can enter data into many of the detail rows in this view. For example, this would be a handy place to enter actual information when you are tracking progress on your project.

Figure 22.41
Adding extra rows to the Task Usage view can make it a useful tracking tool.

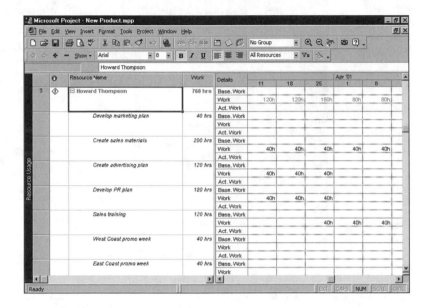

→ For more information on entering tracking data in the plan, **see** "Tracking Actual Performance and Costs," **p. 673**

FORMATTING THE TASK USAGE VIEW

The options for formatting the new Task Usage view are identical to the Resource Usage view. The main difference between the views is the focus. While the Resource Usage view is looking at the information from the perspective of the resource, the Task Usage view looks at each task, providing totals for various details and then a breakdown by each resource that is assigned to work on the task. As shown in Figure 22.42, the Prototype Design task has two resources assigned and each has his own hours and costs. Work and cost totals for the task, the related summary task, and the project are also shown.

Summary task totals ⎯

Project totals in this time period ⎯

Figure 22.42
Hours of work and
costs for those hours
of work can provide
useful information
when making deci-
sions about your
project.

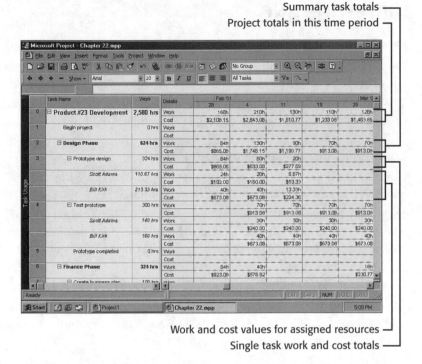

Work and cost values for assigned resources ⎯

Single task work and cost totals ⎯

FORMATTING THE SHEET VIEWS

The Task and Resource Sheets both display a table of field values for the list of tasks or
resources. The columns that are displayed on sheet views depend on the table applied to
the sheet. The Format menu for both the sheet views only includes options for changing
Font, Gridlines, and Text Styles. Also, as before, the Project menu has sort and filter
options, and the Insert menu offers a choice for inserting page breaks. These features were
discussed previously in this chapter under their own headings.

→ For more information on displaying table columns, **see** "Using and Creating Tables," **p. 949**

TROUBLESHOOTING

MISSING OUTLINE SYMBOLS

I'm working on a project that has an outline, but my outline symbols on the formatting toolbar are grayed out. Why can't I use them?

The Show Summary Tasks option has been turned off in the Options dialog box. The outlining tools will display again if you select Show Summary Tasks.

CONFIGURING MAJOR AND MINOR SCALES

I have set up the major and minor scale on my timescale exactly the way I like it but it's a little too small. Is there anything I can do without changing the setup?

Yes, simply change the 100% in the Size text box to a larger number. You might have to play with the number until you get the size right. Likewise, if your timescale is a little too big, change the Size number to 85 or 90% or whatever number gets the look you're after.

ADDING TEXT TO TASK BARS

I want to add text to the task bars but there's not enough room.

Add the text to a different row. You don't have to have a bar on the row; you can use it for text only.

Open the Bar Styles dialog box. Insert a row under the task type where you'd like to display text, such as under Normal,Noncritical. For Appearance, make the Start, Middle and End shapes blank. In the Row column, choose or type a 2. Move to the Text tab. Set the text position as inside and select the field to be printed.

FORMATTING THE TASK BAR

I would rather have information around the task bars than in columns on the left. Can I make that work?

Add the text around the bars as previously discussed. Then create and apply a table that only has one column in it, or position the vertical divider bar on the Gantt Chart so that only the left-most column is visible. You have to print at least one column but the information in the other columns can be placed around the task bars and covered by the divider bar.

CUSTOMIZING VIEWS, TABLES, FIELDS, AND FILTERS

In this chapter

CREATING NEW VIEWS

You can change the views that are available on the View menu or in the More Views dialog box by editing the standard views or creating new views. When creating a new view, you can save time by copying an existing view and making changes in the copy (leaving the original view undisturbed). If none of the standard views are satisfactory, you can create a new view from scratch.

Creating a new view by editing an existing one uses the same techniques as creating a view from scratch. After you are familiar with the basics, copying and editing views will be easy.

To start, choose View, More Views. The More Views dialog box appears (see Figure 23.1).

Figure 23.1
You can create new views or edit existing ones in the More Views dialog box.

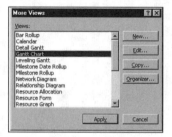

This dialog box has been used previously to change from one view to another. This section discusses three buttons on the right side of the dialog box: New, Edit, and Copy. The New button is used when you want to create a new view from scratch. The Edit button is used when you want to make changes to an existing view, overwriting the original. Finally, the Copy button is used when you want to make changes to an existing view but you don't want to overwrite the original. The steps are the same whether you choose New, Edit, or Copy. For this example, choose New. The Define New View dialog box appears as shown in Figure 23.2.

Tip from Tim and the Project Team

If you want to preserve the standard tables in their original form, use the Copy command rather than the Edit command and edit the copy of the table. You then will have both the original and the revised copies to use.

The purpose of the Define New View dialog box is to give you a place to indicate whether the new view will be a single-pane view or a combination view. A *combination view* is simply a display of two views: one in the top pane and one in the bottom pane (see Figure 23.3). Two commonly used combination views include the Task Entry view (the Gantt Chart over the Task Form) and the Resource Allocation view (Resource Usage over the Gantt Chart). Indeed, when two views are often used in combination to perform standard tasks, it is advantageous to save the view combination for easy access. The new view can even be displayed in the menu. See the upcoming section "Creating a Combination View" for step-by-step instructions.

Figure 23.2
Create a new view in the Define New View dialog box.

Figure 23.3
Use the View Definition dialog box to set up a new combination view.

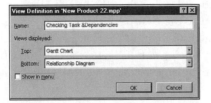

Before you can create a combination view, you must have created or determined which single pane views you want to display. To create a new single pane view, choose the New button from the More Views dialog box. When the Define New View dialog box appears, choose Single View. The View Definition dialog box appears (see Figure 23.4).

Figure 23.4
Create a new single pane view in the View Definition dialog box.

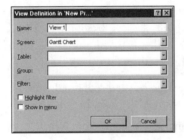

The View Definition dialog box has text boxes and check boxes for defining the following options:

- The Name of the new view
- The basic Screen or general view format used
- The Table used (if the chosen screen uses a table)
- The Group display setting to be used
- The Filter that should be used, and whether it is a highlight filter or a limited display filter
- Whether the new view name appears in the main View menu and on the View bar

Note If an existing view is copied, the Screen option cannot be changed.

ENTERING THE NAME OF THE VIEW

You should enter a name that readily identifies the features you are incorporating into the view. If the view is to appear on the View menu, you must mark the Show in Menu check box at the bottom of the dialog box. You can designate a letter to use to choose the view from the View menu using the keyboard rather than the mouse. Type an ampersand (&) before the chosen letter when you type the view name. When the view is displayed in the menu, this letter is underlined to indicate that this character is used to select the table. For example, if you enter **&Dependencies** in the Name text box, the Checking Task Dependencies view will appear on the menu as Checking Task Dependencies; you can type the letter **D** to select the view from the menu.

Note

Try to make sure that you designate a letter not already used by another view. If you choose a letter already being used by another menu command, you might have to press the letter twice to select the view.

SELECTING THE SCREEN

Microsoft Project provides a number of basic screens, used alone or in combination, to produce the standard views listed on the View menu and on the More Views dialog box. All views must use one of these basic, prefabricated screens.

You cannot change the screen assigned to one of the predefined views listed in the View menu. You can, however, create custom forms that resemble the basic screens.

→ For more information on creating custom forms, **see** "Using Custom Forms," **p. 1081**

Here are the basic screens:

Calendar	Resource Sheet
Gantt Chart	Resource Usage
Network Diagram	Task Details Form
Relationship Diagram	Task Form
Resource Form	Task Name Form
Resource Graph	Task Sheet
Resource Name Form	Task Usage

You can modify some of these screens extensively to customize a view; other screens, however, can be changed only in limited ways. You can create your own table to apply to the views that contain tables. In addition, you can create group definitions to control the list views and define a filter that will be attached to the view. Format choices can be customized in varying degrees for each of the views, and the format settings can be saved as part of the view. Refer to Chapter 22, "Formatting Views," for a refresher on formatting.

To define the screen on a new view, first select the Screen drop-down list from the View Definition dialog box, and then choose a screen from the list that appears.

SELECTING THE TABLE FOR THE VIEW

If the screen you choose displays a table of field columns, you must identify the table to use in the view. To select a table, select the Table drop-down list from the View Definition dialog box, and then choose a table name. The entry list contains all the tables included in the More Tables menu for the screen type (task or resource) that you have chosen. If you want to include a customized table, it must exist before you can use it in a view. See the section "Using and Creating Tables" later in this chapter.

SELECTING THE GROUP FOR THE VIEW

Views that display tables can also group the display by selected fields. The group must have already been defined to be displayed in the Group drop-down list. A selection of No Group displays the tasks or resources in the view in sorted or ID order. See the section "Creating Custom Groups" later in this chapter.

SELECTING THE FILTER FOR THE VIEW

All views have a filter attached, but it must be specified in the view definition. Select the Filter drop-down list to select one of the defined filters. In Figure 23.5, the Tasks With Fixed Dates filter is defined as a highlight filter for the view, which means that all tasks will be displayed, but tasks with fixed dates will be highlighted.

Figure 23.5
Completing the View
Definition dialog box.

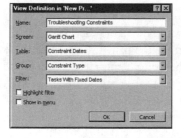

A highlight filter shows all tasks or resources. However, those selected by the filter are displayed with the highlight formatting (bold, italic, underline, and so on) as defined with the Format, Text Styles command for highlighted items.

If you want to filter by something other than the variables included with the standard filters, you must define the filter first before you can use it in a view. See the section "Creating Custom Filters" later in this chapter.

DISPLAYING THE VIEW NAME IN THE MENU

To display the view name in the View menu and on the View bar, mark the Show in Menu check box. All view names always appear in the More Views list.

SAVING THE VIEW DEFINITION

When you have finished using the View Definition dialog box, select the OK button to save your definition. You are returned to the More Views dialog box, where you can take one of the following actions:

- Select the Apply button to place the view onscreen immediately.
- Select the Close button to leave the current view onscreen, but save the view you have just defined.
- Select the New, Copy, or Edit button to continue working with the list of views.
- Select the Organizer button to save the newly defined view along with all other views to the global file. See the upcoming section "Organizing Views in Project Files" for more details.

CREATING A COMBINATION VIEW

If the view is a combination view (a view that defines other views to be placed in the top and bottom panes), the views for each pane must be defined before you can define the combination view. To define a combination view, access the More Views dialog box by choosing More Views from the View menu. Select the New button to display the Define New View dialog box (refer to Figure 23.2). Then, select the Combination View button. The View Definition dialog box that appears is designed for defining a combination view (refer to Figure 23.3).

In the Name field, enter a name for the view. Include an ampersand (&) in front of a letter to designate the selection letter for the view when the name appears on the menu. From the Top drop-down list, choose the view to place in the top pane. All single-pane views that have been defined are available for selection. From the Bottom entry list, choose the view to place in the bottom pane. All single-pane views can also appear in the bottom pane. Mark the Show in Menu check box if you want the view to appear on the View menu and on the View bar. Clear this check box if you want the view to appear in the More Views dialog box only.

To complete the view definition, select the OK button. Select the Apply button in the More Views dialog box to display the view immediately, or select the Close button to save the view but leave the screen unchanged. Figure 23.6 displays a new combination view that shows a customized Gantt Chart over the supplied Relationship Diagram view.

If you define a combination view that uses other customized views you have defined, and if these views use customized tables and filters you have defined, you must plan the order in which the customized components are developed. In other words, you must work from the bottom up. The following sequence is for the most complex case. In this example, you define a combination view that uses new views you have defined; these views use tables, groups, and filters you have defined that contain specific formatting changes you want to use.

1. Define all new tables you plan to use. It doesn't matter whether their names appear on the View, Table menu; they will be used automatically by the new view you are creating.

2. Define any custom groups you might want to see. The group name does not have to appear on the Project, Group By menu as long as it is a named group under More Groups.

3. Define any new filters you plan to use. These filters do not have to appear on the Project, Filtered For menu; appearing on the More Filters menu is sufficient.

4. Define the single-pane views you want to include in your combination view using the appropriate basic screens. Assign to these views the tables and filters you want the views to use.

5. Format each of the views with the special formatting options you want to use.

6. Define the combination view by naming the new customized views to be placed in the top and bottom panes. If you want to have this view directly available from the View menu, mark the Show in Menu check box. The definitions you have created are saved with the project file.

Figure 23.6
A newly created combination view enables you to focus on specific tasks.

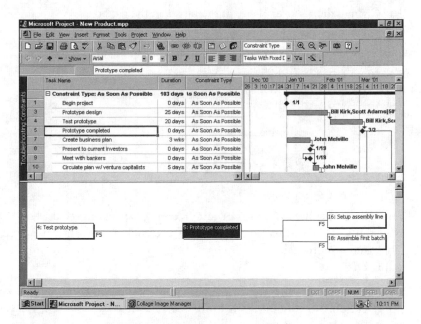

If you later decide that you want to use this view in another project file, you can copy it to a single project file or to GLOBAL.MPT—a template that makes views, tables, groups, and filters available to all project files. See the section "Organizing Views in Project Files" later in this chapter.

USING AND CREATING TABLES

This section shows you how to use the View, Table command to change the appearance and content of the column data in the sheet views. Tables are the building blocks of Microsoft

Project that control which fields are displayed in sheet views. This includes Gantt Charts because the left side of a Gantt Chart is actually a task sheet. Through the manipulation of tables, you can determine the data displayed in each column, the width of the column, the alignment of the data within the column, the title that appears at the top of the column, and the alignment of the column title. With the Table Definition dialog box, you can add new columns, delete columns, rearrange the order of columns, and make other changes in the definition of the table.

To change the display of a table, select View, Table and choose More Tables. The More Tables dialog box appears onscreen, with the currently displayed table highlighted (see Figure 23.7). You use this dialog box to perform the following procedures:

- Display a table that is not included on the main Table menu (several task and resource tables are available only from this dialog box).
- Create new tables, which can be based on existing tables.
- Change the features of any of the tables in the list box.
- Delete existing tables (through the Organizer).

Figure 23.7
The More Tables dialog box offers choices for customizing tables.

The names of either task tables or resource tables appear in the list box, depending on the view that was active when you chose the More Tables command. To switch between task tables and resource tables, choose one of the options, Task or Resource, at the top of the dialog box.

To apply a table to the current view, choose the desired table from the list and choose the Apply button. Note, however, that if the current view is a task view, you cannot display a resource table on this view.

To edit an existing table, choose the table from the list box and choose the Edit button. If you want to create a new table similar to an existing table, choose the original table from the list and choose the Copy button. To create a new table from scratch, choose the New button.

Whenever you choose the New, Copy, or Edit button, the Table Definition dialog box appears. If you choose New, the fields in the dialog box will be empty. If you choose either Edit or Copy, the fields will contain the values for the table you selected from the list box in the More Tables dialog box. Figure 23.8 illustrates a dialog box for a copy of the Entry table. The explanations that follow also apply when you are editing or creating new tables.

Figure 23.8
The Table Definition for a copy of the supplied Entry table.

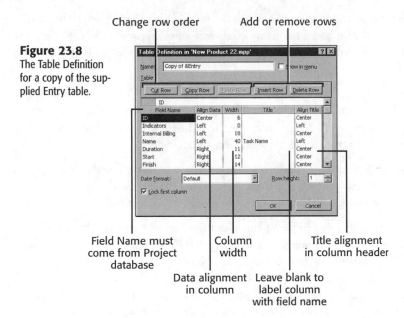

Change row order

Add or remove rows

Field Name must
come from Project
database

Column
width

Title alignment
in column header

Data alignment
in column

Leave blank to
label column
with field name

ENTERING A TABLE NAME

When you create a new table or edit a copy of another table, you will want to supply a new name for the table. If the table name is to appear on the Table menu, use an ampersand (&) before any character in the name to indicate that this character is used to select the table from the View, Table menu.

ADDING AND CHANGING THE COLUMNS IN THE TABLE

If you are starting with a new table, simply click on a space in the Field Name column and access the drop-down list at the right side of the column, as shown in Figure 23.9. Choose a field by scrolling through the list and selecting the one you want.

Figure 23.9
Use the list of Project database field names to choose the columns to display in a table.

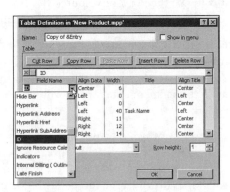

If you want to add more fields, move the cursor down to the next blank row, using the scroll bar on the right side of the dialog box if necessary. To insert a field between the existing fields, select the row below where you want to place the new field, and use the Insert Row button to insert a blank row.

To remove a field from the table, select any item (that is, Field Name, Width, and so on) in the row that contains the field to be deleted and use the Delete Row button. To replace a field with a new field, select the Field Name entry for the old field and select the new field from the drop-down list. This replaces the old field with the new field.

To rearrange the columns in your table, select the one you want to move and use the Cut Row button. Select the row below where you want the cut row to be moved and use the Paste Row button. You don't need to insert a blank row first.

When you use the drop-down list to choose a name from the Field Name list, the default Alignment and Width for the field are supplied automatically. However, you can change the alignment to Left, Center, or Right by typing this specification or by selecting the alignment from the drop-down list. Type a different Width for the field if you want a width other than the default. Use the Title column to supply a column name if you want one that is different from the field name. Leave the Title column blank if you want to use the field name as the displayed column title. The Title of a column can be aligned differently from the data displayed in the column. For example, you might want to center the title of a field over numeric data that is aligned right.

COMPLETING THE DEFINITION OF THE TABLE

At the top of the dialog box, the check box labeled Show in Menu must be marked if you want the table to appear on the View, Table menu (rather than just on the More Tables dialog box). The View, Table menu displays as many as 20 table names.

Mark the check box labeled Lock First Column if you want the first column of the table to remain onscreen at all times. As you scroll to the right in the table, if this box is checked, the first column will not scroll out of view. However, it is not editable when it is locked. In the standard sheet views, the first column is the task or resource ID. If the first column is locked, it will display on a gray background, as is typical with the ID column.

You can use the Date Format area to specify the format for date fields in the table. If you leave the Default entry in place, the date format selected through the Tools, Options command is used. Select the drop-down list to display the other date formats you can elect to use rather than the default format. The change in date format will not change your default or the date format used in other views.

The normal row height in a sheet view is 1, which means that one row of text is displayed for each task or resource row in the table. If the row height is greater than 1, long text entries in any column of the table automatically wrap if the width of the column is insufficient to display them on one line. Choose Row Height and enter the number of text lines to be displayed for each task. This row height is an initial setting only and can be changed graphically onscreen.

Note that all rows start out the same height and additional lines in cells take up space even if they are blank. With Microsoft Project 2000, individual rows can be of varying heights. To reset all rows to a consistent height, choose the Select All button on the top left of the sheet and drag a single row ID divider to the desired height.

Figure 23.10 shows the definition for a new table named Bid, which displays tasks with ID, Indicators, Name, Duration, Start, and Text1 with a Title set to the word "Comments". Note that the titles for several of the fields have been changed, and the Row Height has been changed to 3 to facilitate displaying the long text entries that might be found in the Text1 field.

PART

VII

CH

23

Tip from Tim and the Project Team

If you intend to use a name in the Title field for one of the custom fields (Text1–Text30, Number1–Number20, and so on), you can assign that title to the field permanently so that anywhere you display the custom field, the assigned title is displayed instead of the field name. See the section "Naming Custom Fields" later in this chapter.

Figure 23.10
The table definition for the Bid table.

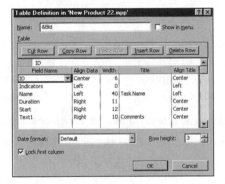

Figure 23.11 shows the Bid table (as defined in Figure 23.10) when applied to the Task Sheet view.

Tip from Tim and the Project Team

A very useful yet simple table is one with only one field, the task ID. Use this table in conjunction with a Gantt Chart that has the task names placed next to the task bars for a completely graphical view. It's much easier to read the task names when they are close to the task bars, and columns of text take up a lot of valuable space.

CHANGING TABLE FEATURES FROM THE VIEW SCREEN

Most of the features you define in the Table Definition dialog box can be changed from the view screen without having to go through the View, Table command. For example, you can access the Column Definition dialog box to insert, delete, or edit the definitions of columns directly in the table, without using the More Tables menu.

Figure 23.11
The Bid table applied to the Task Sheet view.

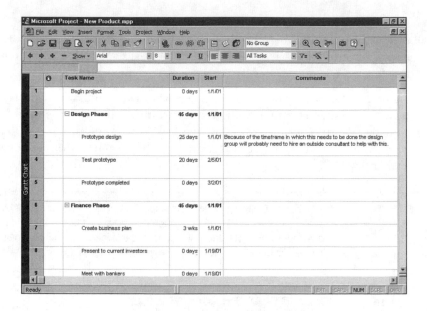

To change the definition of a column from the view screen, double-click the title of the column. The Column Definition dialog box appears, as shown in Figure 23.12, with the current column settings displayed in the selection fields. To redefine a column, change the selections in any of the following entry fields:

- Choose Field Name to view the list of field names, and then select a field from the list.

- Choose Title if you want a text title to appear at the head of the column instead of the field name.

- Choose Align Title to change the alignment for the column title and Align data to change the alignment for the data in column.

- Choose Width if you want to set the width of the column manually. Enter the width in number of characters. You also can use the Best Fit button to set the width to the widest entry in the column.

Figure 23.12
Double-click on a column title to display the Column Definition dialog box.

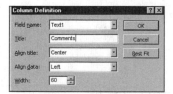

Complete the new definition of the column by choosing either OK or Best Fit. Choose OK if you want to apply the new column definition, including the Width setting. Choose Best Fit, however, if you want Microsoft Project to calculate the width needed to fully display both the title and the longest data value that initially goes into the column. The Best Fit button closes the dialog box and applies the new definition, but with the calculated column width.

To insert a new column, follow these steps:

1. Select the entire column currently located where the new column is to be placed. (Select a column by clicking on the column title.)

2. Either choose Insert, Column from the menu bar, right-click on the column title and choose Insert Column from the shortcut menu, or press the Insert (Ins) key. The Column Definition dialog box is displayed with values for the ID field supplied in the definition fields. Select the values for the new column, as previously described.

PART

VII

CH

23

The new column is inserted in front of the column that was selected. The selected column is moved right one position.

Two ways to remove a column from the table exist—by menu or by mouse. To remove a column using menu commands, first select the column (by selecting the column title). Then, either choose Hide Column from the Edit menu, right-click on the column title and choose Hide Column from the shortcut menu, or press the Delete key.

You can also adjust the column width directly on the view screen by using the mouse. Follow these steps:

1. Move the mouse pointer into the row at the top of the table where the column titles are displayed, and position the pointer on the right gridline of the column you want to adjust.

2. Drag the gridline to the right or left to adjust the column width.

3. Double-click the gridline to have Microsoft Project calculate and adjust the column width to the best fit for the data in the column. The width is set to the necessary space for a full display of the widest entry found in any row of the column.

Any column width you set using the mouse is automatically recorded in the Table Definition dialog box.

Hiding a column with a menu command such as Edit, Hide Column produces an effect different from hiding a column by dragging the column edge all the way to the left. A menu-hidden column can be retrieved only by inserting the column again or by editing the underlying table definition. A column hidden by dragging the column border can also be unhidden with the mouse. Move the mouse slowly to the column title gridline where the column is hidden; click and drag back to the right to reveal the hidden column.

In Project 2000, you also can change row heights with the mouse. Point to the bottom gridline in the first column (usually the ID column). When the mouse pointer changes to a double-headed arrow, drag up or down. This action adjusts the height for a single row, or for multiple rows if selected. To adjust all row heights at the same time, click the Select All area above the first column before adjusting row height.

> **Note**
> Be aware that changing row heights on a displayed table also changes the row heights in all other tables. Unlike column widths, unique row height settings aren't saved with the table definition.

If you want your modified table to appear when you select a view, you must define the view to include the table name. See the section "Creating New Views" earlier in this chapter for instructions on defining a view that displays a custom table.

CUSTOMIZING FIELDS

Even though Project 2000 includes an extensive database of predefined fields, every project has its own characteristics and requirements for data storage. The custom fields in Project provide reserved spaces that enable you to use a project file as a central data repository for your plan.

Perhaps you have an internal code for identifying every task on a project. This might be a cost code, work product code, or code provided by a customer to facilitate information exchange. These codes might actually be alphanumeric descriptive text that doesn't fit a pattern. Costs might also be associated with the project that are not easily included in the resource or fixed cost fields. Another requirement might be that you capture interim values Project is not set to automatically store, such as interim durations for a task or interim work values. It is also common to need to identify a status of a task other than %complete, such as approved/not approved. Project provides a variety of custom fields and field types to accommodate storing these and other types of specialized data.

A set of custom fields is provided for storing task information and another set for storing resource information. The names and lists of these fields are identical; the context of the use of a custom field (in a text-oriented view or a resource-oriented view) determines with which set you are working. Table 23.1 describes custom fields available for your use.

TABLE 23.1 CUSTOM FIELD LIST

Field Name	Data Description
Text1–Text30	Alphanumeric, up to 255 characters.
Number1–Number20	Any positive or negative number.
Cost1–Cost10	Formatted number values.
Date1–Date10	Any valid data value.
Duration1–Duration10	Any valid duration value (for example, 5d).
*Start1–Start10	Any valid date value.
*Finish1–Finsh10	Any valid date value.
Flag1–Flag20	Valid values are Yes/No only.
Outline Code1– Outline Code10	User-defined alphanumeric outline structures (new to Project 2000).

Caution

The task Start/Finish fields (flagged by * in Table 23.1) are used by Project when saving interim baselines for tasks. Use these fields for your own purposes only if you do not need them for baseline storage. Similar data can be stored in the custom Date fields.

→ The complete list of custom Project fields is available through online help. On the Help menu, select Contents and Index. Use the Answer Wizard to search for "custom fields," and then choose "Custom fields" from the displayed topic list.

In addition to providing the custom fields, Project enables you to create name aliases for the fields so that they appear with descriptive field names anywhere you use them. Also, custom fields can now calculate and store values as per formulas you create or import.

ACCESSING THE CUSTOM FIELDS

Custom field names will appear in any drop-down list in which the predefined fields are accessible. For example, when inserting a new column on a table, the field choices for the column will include all the custom field names, even if the fields have not been used for data storage.

Changes to a custom field, including its name and rollup behaviors, are made in the Customize Fields dialog box. Choose Tools, Customize, Fields to display the dialog box shown in Figure 23.13.

Figure 23.13
The Customize Fields dialog box gives you control over custom field behaviors.

In the Customize Fields dialog box, custom field names are listed by type. To work with a particular field, select the general type (Task or Resource) first. Then use the Type drop-down list to select a particular category of custom field (text, number, and so on). When the list of available fields of that category appears on the left side of the dialog box, click on one field of interest to begin changing custom settings.

NAMING CUSTOM FIELDS

Any place you use a custom field, like all fields, a name will be displayed for the field. Typically, field names are shown as column headings. You can temporarily rename the field with a more descriptive label by editing the column definition. You might want the data in Text1 to be displayed under a heading of "Dept Code," for example. However, edits made on a single table stay with that table definition. If you then display Text1 in another table, it will again be labeled Text1.

To avoid having to change the name labels for every display of a custom field, you can give the custom field an alias. Choose the Rename button in the Customize Fields dialog box and supply a more descriptive name for the field. In Figure 23.14, the Cost1 custom field has been renamed "Overhead" and both labels appear in the list of fields.

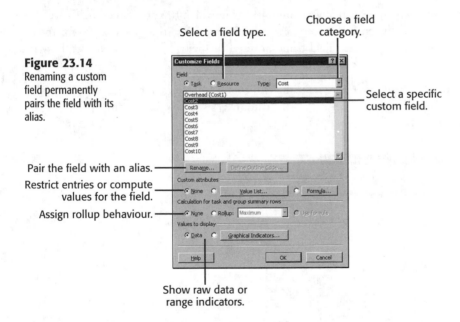

Select a field type.

Choose a field category.

Figure 23.14
Renaming a custom field permanently pairs the field with its alias.

Select a specific custom field.

Pair the field with an alias.

Restrict entries or compute values for the field.

Assign rollup behaviour.

Show raw data or range indicators.

After an alias is established, any place the custom field is used—before or after the field is renamed—the new name label will appear instead of the generic custom field name. Also, the custom field name/alias pair will appear together in drop-down field lists.

CREATING CALCULATED FIELDS

While tables in Project look similar to spreadsheets, it has not been possible to create and apply calculations or formulas to fields in previous versions of Project without developing macro code. Data in custom fields can now be derived from values in other fields in the project.

The Custom Attributes area of the Customize Fields dialog box enables you to specify value behaviors in custom fields. By default, all custom fields contain no entries and no formulas and can accept any valid entry for the field type. Use the Value List option to restrict entries in a field to a specified list of values, as shown in Figure 23.15.

Figure 23.15
Users can be restricted to entering values from a predefined list or the list can be allowed to grow.

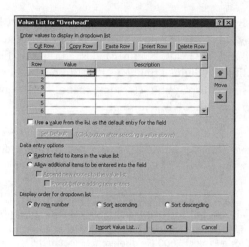

In the Value List dialog box, enter an acceptable value on as many rows as necessary, along with optional descriptions of the values to assist users in selection. Below the list you build is an option to Use a Value from the List as the Default Entry for the Field. Set the Data Entry Options to Restrict Field to Items in the Value List to prohibit unacceptable field entries, or choose to Allow Additional Items to Be Entered into the Field. You also can control the display order of the value list: By row number (the order they were entered), or in ascending or descending value order.

One additional option on the dialog box enables you to import a list of values that exist in another project file. The supplying file must be open and the incoming data must be located in a corresponding field type (cost into cost, text into text, and so on).

 A powerful new use of custom fields is the ability to define formulas for them that compute and populate values. Choosing the Formula option in the Custom Attributes area brings up the Formula dialog box for the field, as shown in Figure 23.16. This dialog box will look familiar to users of other Microsoft applications such as Access.

Figure 23.16
Create formulas for custom fields to compute new values of interest not provided in the Project database.

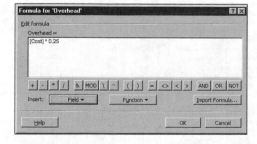

The formula in Figure 23.16 computes an overhead value for Cost1, which equals 25% of the task cost. A formula is built by typing directly into the Edit Formula area, by selecting fields and functions from the provided drop-down lists and operator buttons, or by choosing to import a formula previously created in another project file. The Insert Field drop-down list gives access to all the allowable Project fields. The fields are displayed in cascading menus of logical groups, such as Date fields, Number fields, and so on. The Function drop-down list displays all the possible predefined functions that can be used in custom field calculations. These functions also are displayed in cascading menus by groups, such as Date/Time functions, Conversion functions, and so on.

> **Note**
>
> Do not include the equal sign (=) in the Edit Formula area. Project adds it to any formula automatically.

→ A detailed discussion of custom field formulas and available functions is accessible through online help. On the Help menu, select Contents and Index. Use the Answer Wizard to search for "custom fields," and then choose "Work with custom field enhancements" from the displayed topic list. You can also consult the CD accompanying this book for a Project 2000 Field reference document.

To produce Figure 23.17, a customized cost table was created and applied to a Gantt Chart. The Cost column shows the normal total cost figure for each task as calculated by Project. The Overhead column contains values according to a formula for the Cost1 field and was renamed to the field alias, Overhead (refer to Figure 23.16). An additional cost field has been created: Cost2 has been renamed Cost with Overhead and assigned the simple formula [Cost] + [Overhead].

Figure 23.17
Add a calculated custom field to any task table.

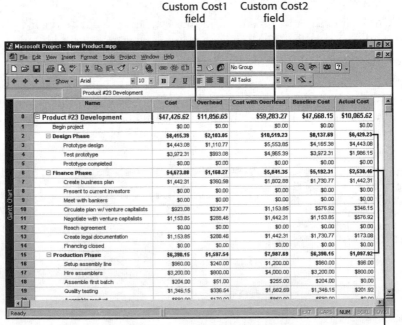

Custom Cost1 field   Custom Cost2 field

Summary tasks set to compute rather than rollup, sums for custom fields

CONTROLLING FIELD BEHAVIORS

For custom fields with values of any kind (text entries are not considered values), one more consideration should be taken into account when defining a field. The area in the Customize Fields dialog box labeled Calculation for Task and Group Summary Rows enables you to control custom field calculations for summary rows and for use in custom groups. By default, no value will be entered on summary or group rows for custom fields. Your options are to set the summary and group level fields to use the formula set for the field, or to set them to perform simple mathematical operations at the rollup level. The choices for math operations are Average, Maximum, Minimum, Sum, and Average First Sublevel. The Average First Level option, applicable to grouping, prevents a field value from being carried up in the calculations from very detailed groups into less detailed groups. In Figure 23.17, the summary and rollup behavior for both custom fields is set to Use Formula, forcing Project to calculate every value instead of summing individual task values.

CREATING INDICATOR FIELDS

For issues of confidentiality, or to avoid raw data overload, you might choose to display graphic symbols in a custom field instead of displaying the actual data values. The bottom of the Customize Fields dialog box offers options for Values to Display for each customized field. By default, the actual keyed-in or computed values are displayed. You can substitute a variety of symbols for ranges of the actual values.

In the Customize Fields dialog box, choose the Graphical Indicators command button to display the Graphical Indicators dialog box. Figure 23.18 shows the indicators dialog box set to display images instead of values for a third customized field, Cost3. This field has been renamed to Overhead Indicators and contains the formula =[Cost1] to simply copy all values from Overhead into this Cost3 field. The test section of the Graphical Indicators dialog box lists the logical tests and test values for ranges of Cost3 (Overhead Indicators) data. A low overhead value will display a flag; a medium overhead value will display a box; and a high overhead value will display a frowning face. Figure 23.19 illustrates the results of these settings.

Tip from Tim and the Project Team

If you have already created a set of tests, values, and corresponding images in another project file, or even in another custom field within the same file, import those settings instead of recreating them. Choose Import Indicator Criteria on the Graphical Indicators dialog box.

CREATING AND USING WBS CODE FORMATS

Many companies label and identify tasks by some structure other than the task numbering system in a project file. A code field in Project automatically creates a numbered structure for your use. This code field is called *WBS*, which stands for Work Breakdown Structure.

By default, the WBS code is an exact duplicate of the project's outline numbers. You can view both sets of numbers by customizing a table: Turn on the Show Outline Number option (under Tools, Options, View tab) and insert a column to display the WBS field. Figure 23.20 shows the result.

Figure 23.18
You can choose images from a predefined list and substitute them for actual values in custom fields.

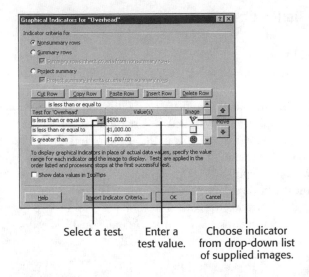

Select a test.   Enter a test value.   Choose indicator from drop-down list of supplied images.

Figure 23.19
A customized table displays both values and indicators for custom fields as set in Figure 23.18.

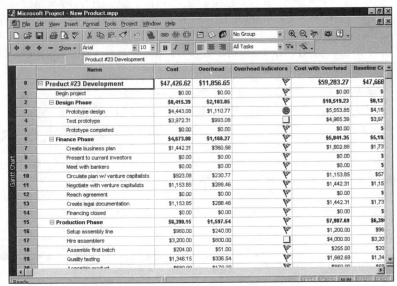

In previous versions of Project, you could key in to the WBS field any number or letter combination suitable for your company. You still can, but now you can control the user input to ensure an entered WBS code conforms to a correct pattern. To define a customized WBS code structure, start by choosing Project, WBS, Define Code. The WBS Code Definition dialog box will appear, as shown in Figure 23.21.

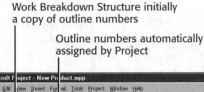

Work Breakdown Structure initially
a copy of outline numbers

Outline numbers automatically
assigned by Project

Figure 23.20
Turn on Outline
Numbers and add a
column for the WBS
code to compare the
two.

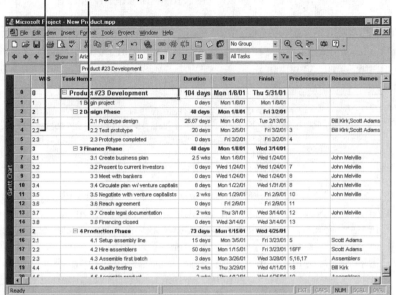

Figure 23.21
Create and preview a
customized Work
Breakdown Structure
code in the WBS
Code Definition dia-
log box.

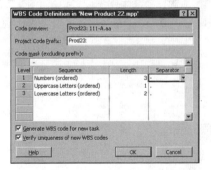

To create the code structure, fill in the Code Mask grid in the WBS Code Definition dialog
box. For each level in the numbering system, supply a Sequence type, a Length in characters for this portion of the structure, and a Separator character that will separate this part of
the code from the next level. A Sequence can be one of four types: Numbers (ordered so
that new tasks are assigned the next number in the sequence); Uppercase Letters and
Lowercase Letters (these also stay ordered); and Characters (in any order). For Length,
specify one to ten digits of letters for each level. The choices for level separator include a
period (.), a dash (-), an addition symbol (+), and a forward slash (/), but you can type in
your own separator symbol if you choose.

A code preview is provided at the top of the dialog box so you can verify the format as the code is defined. Also, if your WBS codes on a project must start with a prefix, such as a project number identifier, that can be entered in the Project Code Prefix area and will be added to the beginning of every WBS entry. To automatically generate a sequenced WBS code when a task is added to the plan, eliminating the data entry requirement, mark the Generate WBS Code for New Task option at the bottom of the WBS Code Definition dialog box. Whether the codes are entered manually or automatically, increase data integrity by turning on the Verify Uniqueness of New WBS Codes option.

Tip from Tim and the Project Team

Don't take the time to re-create WBS code masks for each new project. The WBS code definition can be copied to other files or the underlying Global template through the Organizer. See the section "Saving Other Custom Elements in the Global Template" later in this chapter.

In Figure 23.22, the custom WBS code has been created and displays automatically in the WBS field. Note tasks 11–13. They display all levels set up in the custom WBS code definition because they are three levels into the outline. These tasks were not entered in their current order: task 11 was created first, then 13, and then sometime later 12 was inserted. The WBS code is out of sequence for these tasks; it follows their creation order. The task outline numbers, however, are re-sequenced when new tasks are inserted.

Figure 23.22
Displaying the custom WBS code set in Figure 23.21.

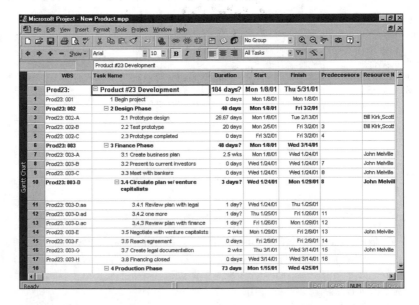

Tip from Tim and the Project Team

To display tasks in WBS code order, choose Project, Sort. Select the Sort By option. Select the WBS field in the Sort drop-down list and then click the Sort button.

CREATING AND USING CUSTOM OUTLINE FIELDS

You can create other coded numbering systems in addition to the automatic outline structure and a custom WBS code. Project provides 10 custom Outline Code fields for your use. Different people in your organization might have different coding and reporting requirements. In previous versions of Project, multiple structures were typically created in custom Text fields. The limitation with using Text fields for this purpose is the inability to control input so that it conforms to the outline code structure.

The steps to creating custom outline structures are a combination of the steps used in customizing fields and in creating a custom WBS code. The actual definition of the outline takes place through the Customize Fields dialog box. Specifications for an outline code include sequence, values, and separators, just as in defining a custom WBS code.

CREATING AN OUTLINE MASK

To create a custom outline code mask, follow these steps:

1. Choose Tools, Customize, Fields to display the Customize Fields dialog box (see Figure 23.23).

Figure 23.23
Open the Customize Fields dialog box to begin creating an outline code mask.

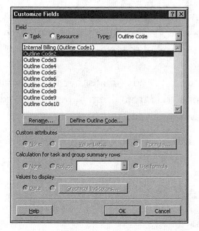

2. Select Task to display the custom fields for tasks.
3. Use the drop-down list in the Type box to select Outline Code. The 10 Outline Code fields will be displayed, and you must select the one you want to use.
4. You can optionally click the Rename button to assign the field an alias that will appear as the column heading. In the Rename Field dialog box, type in the alias you want to use and click OK. In Figure 23.23, Outline Code1 has been renamed as "Internal Billing," as indicated in the dialog box title.
5. Click the Define Outline Code button to display the Outline Code Definition dialog box in which you will create the mask (see Figure 23.24).

Figure 23.24
Defining an outline code is very similar to defining a custom WBS mask.

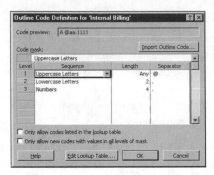

6. To create your own mask, click on the first blank row under the Sequence column in the Code Mask area. Use the pull-down arrow to choose Numbers, Uppercase Letters, Lowercase Letters, or Characters.

7. In the Length column, use the pull-down list to display the options for how many characters will be used for this part of the format. Choose Any if you want to be able to edit this part of the code and use a varying number of characters. Choose 1 through 10 to set a fixed number of characters for this section of the format.

8. In the Separator column, use the pull-down list to display the separator to use if another code follows this portion of the format. Choose from the period, hyphen, plus sign, or forward slash. You also can type in a symbol of your choosing.

You might have previously created an outline code, in another file or in another custom field in this file. Instead of creating an outline code from scratch, import an existing definition. To import an outline code definition, follow these steps:

1. Click the Import Outline Code button to display the Import Outline Code dialog box (see Figure 23.25).

Figure 23.25
Import an existing outline code mask from another file or from another field in the same file.

2. In the Import Outline Code dialog box, select the Project name in the drop-down list of open projects. You are allowed to import a code within a project file from one custom field to another of the same type.

3. Select Task or Resource to display the appropriate field names in the Field box.

4. Select the field name in the Field drop-down list of custom fields.

5. Click OK.

Click OK in the Outline Code Definition dialog box to complete the definition of the mask. If you already have the field displayed in the task view, you will see the new alias appear as the column heading.

CREATING AN OUTLINE CODE LOOKUP TABLE

You can define a value lookup table for users so that they are more accurate in entering the custom outline code. The logic is simply to type in an outline structure that fits your company's requirements. The steps for editing a lookup table are as follows:

1. Create an Outline Code mask as described previously.

2. In the Outline Code Definition dialog box, select Edit Lookup Table. The Edit Lookup Table dialog box will appear, as shown in Figure 23.26.

Figure 23.26
Reproduce your company's code structure in the outline code lookup table.

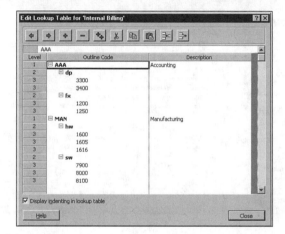

3. Type a list of valid entry codes in the Outline Code area. These entries are much easier to read and edit if the Display Indenting in Lookup Table option at the bottom of the dialog box is turned on.

4. Use the right arrow and left arrow outlining buttons on the provided toolbar to indent tasks to a higher-numbered level or outdent them to a lower-numbered level.

5. Use the standard Cut, Copy, and Paste buttons to assist you in editing the outline code.

6. Type an optional description of the codes to assist users if desired.

7. Click Close when finished. If any typed entries do not conform to the outline structure created before entering the Lookup Table area, a message warning will be displayed, indicating that an entry does not match the mask.

In the Outline Code Definition dialog box, two more settings enable you to further control data entry. Fill in the check box for Only Allow Codes Listed in the Lookup Table if you want to disallow any codes except those you list in a lookup table. Also fill the check box for Only Allow New Codes with Values in All Levels of Mask to force users to fill out codes completely if manual entries are being allowed.

USING CUSTOM OUTLINE CODES

Standard tables in Project do not include custom fields. You must modify a table to view the custom outline codes as well as other custom fields. See the section "Using and Creating Tables" earlier in this chapter.

In Figure 23.27, the Entry table has been modified to include the new custom outline code column that was renamed "Internal Billing." Notice the drop-down list in the column; the outline code settings demand that the user choose values from the lookup table.

Figure 23.27
Data entry is restricted to values from the outline code drop-down list.

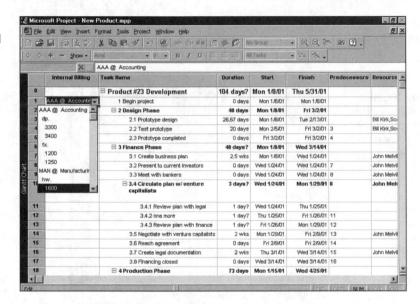

Figure 23.27 is the final result of several steps in our example, as listed in the following:

- Rename Outline Code1 to Internal Billing (Figure 23.23).
- Define the outline code (Figure 23.24).
- Create the Lookup Table (Figure 23.26)
- Display Internal Billing code on custom table (Figure 23.27).

MANAGING CUSTOM FIELDS

After you have created a custom WBS code or custom outline code field, you should copy it to the Global template to make it readily available for all your project documents based on the Global Template. See the section "Saving Other Custom Elements in the Global Template" later in this chapter for detailed instructions.

CREATING CUSTOM FILTERS

Before reading this section, be sure to read the section "Exploring the Standard Filters" in Chapter 21, "Using the Standard Views, Tables, and Filters." This section covers creating your own customized filters, including ones that prompt the user for input, calculate values, and allow multiple criteria to be entered. At the end of this section, the custom AutoFilter feature is discussed.

A good way to begin creating your own filters is to examine the definitions of the standard filters. To look at a filter definition, perform these steps:

1. Choose Project, Filtered For and select More Filters from the list.
2. Select a filter from the list (except the All Tasks or All Resources filter).
3. Choose the Edit button.

The Filter Definition dialog box appears. Figure 23.28 shows the Filter Definition box for the In Progress Tasks filter.

Figure 23.28
The Filter Definition dialog box for displaying tasks already underway.

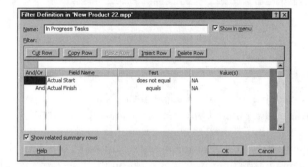

The In Progress Tasks filter applies two tests. The first test examines the Actual Start field to ensure that the value is *not equal* to NA (that is, a date has been entered so the task has been started), and the second test examines the Actual Finish field to see whether the value is NA (the task has not finished). The logical operator And has been entered in the And/Or field, meaning that both the first and the second conditions must be met for a task to be selected.

Figure 23.29 illustrates the interactive Should Start By filter. In this filter, the Start field is tested to see whether the Start date value falls before the entered value and whether the task is underway (Actual Start would still be NA if the task has not started). However, the filter is designed to prompt the user to supply the test start date at the time the filter is applied. Note that the *prompt* in the Values column is written within double quotation marks, and the *pause* for the user to enter a response is defined with the question mark. Prompts appear with a question mark immediately following the prompt. For multiple prompts, use a comma (or the list separator specified in the Options dialog box) to separate the values.

To define a filter, choose More Filters from the Project, Filtered For menu. If you want to create a new filter unlike any filter already defined, choose the New button. Otherwise, select an existing filter name from the Filters entry list if you want to edit or copy an existing filter. If you edit an existing filter, the original definition is lost; start by creating a copy with which to experiment. In all three cases—New, Edit, or Copy—the Filter Definition dialog box is displayed. The following sections show you how to develop an over-budget filter that displays all tasks over budget by at least $1,000.

Figure 23.29
The Filter Definition dialog box for the Should Start By filter illustrates a prompt used to get criteria from the user at the time the filter is run.

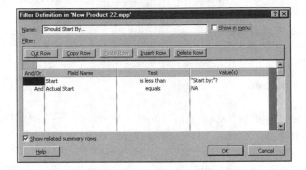

NAMING THE FILTER

Provide a name for the filter by typing a name in the Name field of the dialog box. If the filter name is to appear in the Filtered For menu, use an ampersand (&) before the letter that will be underlined (this letter is used to choose the filter from the menu). The check box labeled Show in Menu at the top of the dialog box must be selected for the filter name to appear in the menu and in the filter drop-down list on the Formatting toolbar.

In the example of the over-budget filter, enter the name as **O&ver Budget by 1000** (with v as the selection letter), and mark the Show in Menu box so that the filter is placed on the Filtered For menu (see Figure 23.30).

Figure 23.30
The finished Over Budget by $1,000 custom filter definition.

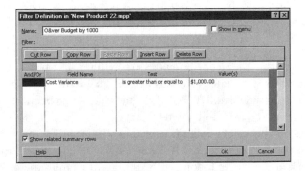

DEFINING THE FILTER CRITERIA

To define the criteria, you use the Filter area. For each test to be imposed on the database, you must fill in a row of this area. Each row must identify a Field Name, the nature of the Test to be conducted in the field, and the Value(s) to be looked for in the field. If multiple tests are to be imposed as part of the filter, the And/Or column must indicate the relationship of the criterion rows.

SELECTING THE FIELD NAME

Type the field name or select a field name from the drop-down list. In the example in Figure 23.30, the field name is Cost Variance.

SELECTING THE TEST

Select the cell in the Test column and use the drop-down list to view the tests you can select. Select the appropriate test or type the test phrase. In the example, the test is to be *greater than or equal to*, as indicated by the dialog box.

Table 23.2 describes the use of each of the items in the Test entry list.

TABLE 23.2   THE FILTER TEST OPTIONS

Test	Meaning and Example	Field Name	Value(s)
Equals	Field values must match value(s) exactly. Critical.	Critical Tasks	Yes
Does not equal	Field value must differ from Value(s) entry. Task has started.	Actual Start	NA
Is greater than	Field value must be greater than Value(s) entry. Task started after 8/1/97.	Actual Start	8/1/97
Is greater than or equal to	Field value must be greater than or equal to Value(s) entry. Budgeted cost $1000 or over.	Planned Cost	1000
Is less than	Field value must be less than Value(s) entry. Duration less than 1 day.	Duration	1d
Is less than or equal to	Field value must be less than or equal to Value(s) entry. Task finishes before 9/1/97.	Actual Finish	9/1/97
Is within	Field value must lie on or between the range of Value(s) entry. Duration is between 5 and 10 days.	Duration	5d,10d

TABLE 23.2 CONTINUED			
Test	**Meaning and Example**	**Field Name**	**Value(s)**
Is not within	Field value must lie outside the range of Value(s) entries. Tasks that are not in the middle of production.	% Complete	25%,75%
Contains	Field value must contain the string in Value(s). Resource assignment includes Mary Logan, among others.	Name (Resource)	Mary Logan
Does not contain	Field value must not contain the string in Value(s). Resource assignments include everyone except Mary Logan.	Name (Resource)	Mary Logan
Contains exactly	Field value must contain the exact string in Value(s). Resource assignment includes only Mary Logan.	Name (Resource)	Mary Logan

ENTERING THE VALUE(S)

To enter the test value, select the cell in the Value(s) column. The three options for specifying test values are type a value for the test, place a prompt for interactive filters, and use another field name for calculated filters. The drop-down list for this column is used for calculated filters and contains the names of the fields, with each field name automatically enclosed in square brackets as required by the calculated filters. In Figure 23.30, the value of 1000 was typed in (numeric formatting is allowed but not required).

COMPLETING THE FILTER DEFINITION

To edit a definition, use the Insert Row button to insert a blank row before the criterion rows you have selected. Use the Delete Row button to remove a criterion row from the definition.

If the filter is to appear in the Filtered For menu, be sure that the Show in Menu check box is selected. Mark the Show Related Summary Rows check box if you want the summary task for any task selected by the filter to also be displayed.

Choose the OK button to complete the definition and return to the More Filters dialog box. Choose the Apply or Highlight button to apply the filter immediately, or choose Close to save the filter definition but not apply the filter at this time.

USING MORE FILTER CRITERION TESTS

This section illustrates various types of filter criteria. These samples should help you design almost any kind of filter.

TESTING FOR LOGICAL VALUES

Many of the fields in the databases contain only the logical values Yes and No. For example, the Milestone field contains Yes for Milestone tasks and No for all other tasks. The standard filter for Milestone tasks looks for the value Yes in the appropriate field (see Figure 23.31).

PART

VII

CH

23

Figure 23.31
The Milestone task filter searches for the value Yes in the Project database Milestone field.

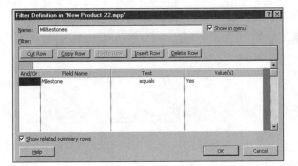

USING THE WITHIN AND NOT WITHIN TESTS

Use the Is Within test to look for values that lie within and include the upper and lower values in the Value(s) column. Use the Is Not Within test to identify values that fall outside a range of values. The range of values being used in the test is entered in the Value(s) column, with a comma separating the lower and upper values. In Figure 23.32, the Finish field is searched to find tasks that finish between 2/4/01 and 4/1/01, inclusive.

Figure 23.32
Filters can test for values within a specified range.

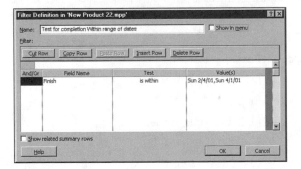

USING THE CONTAINS TEST

Some text fields (most notably, Resource Names, Predecessors, and Successors) can contain lists of entries separated by commas. The Resource Names field contains the list of all the resources assigned to a task, and the Predecessors field contains a list of all the predecessors to the task. These are really text fields. The Contains test examines the text to see whether a string of characters you enter in the Value(s) column is contained within the field contents. The Contains test is useful when you want to locate all the tasks whose names include a specified string of characters. Figure 23.33 shows a filter criterion that looks for the tasks whose names not only include the word "sales" but other words as well, either before or after sales. Note that the match is not case sensitive.

Figure 23.33
The Contains test in filters is useful for character searches.

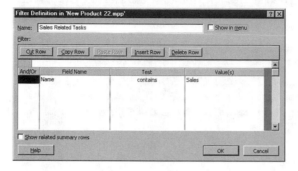

USING WILDCARDS IN A VALUE(S) STRING

Text field entries can be searched with wildcard characters in the search string. You must use only the Equals or Not Equals test for strings that include wildcards. The wildcard characters in Microsoft Project are similar to wildcard characters used in DOS—the asterisk (*) and the question mark (?).

A wildcard can match any character that falls in the same place as the wildcard in the search comparisons. Therefore, the test string ab?d is matched by any single character in the third position as long as the *a*, *b*, and *d* are in the right places. The asterisk represents any number of missing characters or no characters, whereas the question mark represents just one character. Note the following examples:

Test String with Wildcard	Possible Matches
f?d	f*a*d, f*b*d, f*c*d, f*d*d, f*e*d, f2d
f??d	f*in*d, fo*r*d, f*oo*d, f23d
f*d	fd, f*a*d, f*ee*d, f*ormatte*d
f*	f, f*1*, f*123*, f*ind this text*
12-?06	12-*A*06, 12-*1*06, 12-X06
12-*06	12-*A*06, 12-06, 12-*abc0*06

The filter in Figure 23.34 is defined to search the WBS field for entries that end in .1. This could conceivably produce a list of first steps under each summary task. For example, you might use this to assign a supervisor to the first step in any new summary task to get the work started.

Figure 23.34
A filter that finds WBS entries ending in .1, which will locate all first steps in this project.

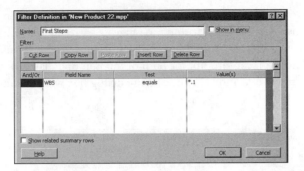

USING INTERACTIVE FILTERS

An *interactive filter* increases the versatility of a filter that must search for different values in a field from one time to the next. For example, the filter in Figure 23.35 is designed to locate tasks in which the word "sales" is included. To search for a different word, you must redefine the filter. You can, however, replace the specification of the word "sales" with instructions to ask the user for the word to be located. Then the filter can be used to locate the tasks containing the word of interest at the moment. This is similar to the Find feature, but is more useful because as a filter it can not only find the tasks with the specified word but also can hide all tasks that don't include the word or merely highlight the tasks that do include the word. Also, because it can be included on the menu and is automatically included on the filter drop-down list in the Formatting toolbar, it can be designed for use by people who aren't necessarily familiar with the software but can still use it to review project details.

Interactive filters are created by typing a message and a question mark in the Value(s) column of the filter definition. When the filter is applied, the message is displayed (in a dialog box) as a prompt for the user, and the question mark causes Microsoft Project to wait for the user to fill a blank that follows the message in the dialog box. For example, the message "What words are you looking for in task names?" is a suitable prompt. The entry in the Value(s) column of the filter definition would look like the entry in Figure 23.35.

Figure 23.35
An interactive filter prompts the user for input each time it is applied.

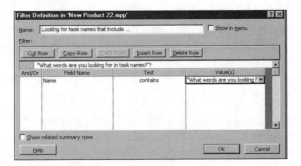

Another example would be a useful modification to the filter illustrated in Figure 23.32, which looks for Finish dates that fall within the range 2/4/01 and 4/1/01. You can replace both of these specific dates with prompts, as shown in Figure 23.36. If you are using an Is Within test with dates, you can prompt for both of them in one dialog box. Simply place a comma in between the two prompts. The resulting dialog box with prompts for this filter is shown in Figure 23.37.

Figure 23.36
An interactive filter with multiple prompts enables greater flexibility.

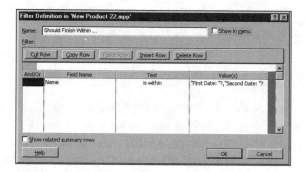

When an interactive filter is run, one or more dialog boxes will be presented for user input. In Figure 23.37, the input area for both the beginning and ending filter dates are contained in a single dialog box. You can present the user with two separate dialog boxes for input by making a simple change in the filter definition. In our example from Figure 23.36, replacing the comma between the Value(s) prompts with a semicolon would cause Project to prompt the user with one dialog box for the first date and then another box for the second date.

Figure 23.37
Two data entry prompts can be included in a single dialog box.

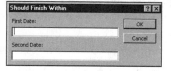

CREATING CALCULATED FILTERS

A *calculated filter* compares the value in one field of a task or resource with the value in another field for the same task or resource. For example, tasks that are over budget have in the Baseline Cost field a value that is less than the value in the Cost field (which is the currently scheduled cost). To filter over-budget tasks, the criterion needs to compare the Cost field with the Baseline Cost field (see Figure 23.38).

Remember, if you are entering a field name in the Value(s) column of the filter definition, the name must be placed in brackets. The drop-down list for the Value(s) column lists all the field names, which Microsoft Project automatically places within brackets.

Figure 23.38
Calculated filters compare values in the Project database fields.

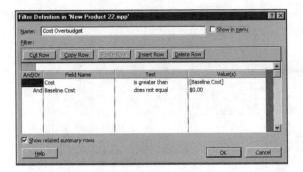

CREATING MULTIPLE CRITERIA FILTERS

If more than one test must be used to create the filter, each test is placed on its own row of the filter definition table. The first column (And/Or) is used to designate how each row is to be used with the row that follows it. If it is necessary that the tests on both rows be satisfied to satisfy the filter, the operator And is placed in the And/Or column. In the calculated filter in the previous example, two criteria had to be met: The Cost had to be greater than the Baseline Cost and the Baseline Cost had to be greater than $0 to match the comparison.

Another example would be a filter to locate all the critical milestones. This filter would need to test the Milestone field on one row and the Critical field on the next row. Because both requirements must be met, the And operator is placed in the And/Or column (see Figure 23.39). Only tasks calculated to be critical and specified as milestones will be selected by the filter.

Figure 23.39
Complex filters can contain more than one test.

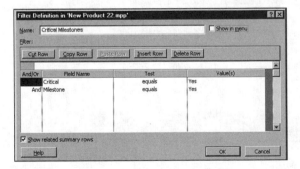

If, however, passing *either* of the tests is sufficient to satisfy the filter, the operator *Or* is placed in the And/Or column. If the Or operator is placed in this column in Figure 23.39, all critical tasks are selected (whether they are milestones or not), and all milestones are selected (whether they are critical tasks or not).

If more than two rows are used to define a filter, the tests are evaluated from the top down. Therefore, the first two rows are evaluated using the operator on the first row, and then the third row test is added using the operator on the second row, and so on—until all rows have been considered. For example, in Figure 23.40, the filter seeks to locate all the critical milestones as well as (or in addition to) all the tasks that include the word "Design."

Figure 23.40
Complex filters are evaluated in top-down order.

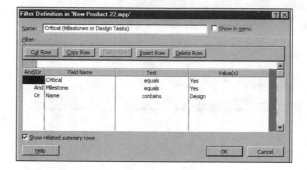

You also can group multiple criteria together to create more complex filters. For example, the Late/Overbudget Tasks Assigned To filter looks for tasks assigned to a resource (whose name is prompted for) and whose baseline has been set, as well as a finish that is later than planned or cost that is greater than planned. The first two rows must both be met and then either of the last two rows must be met.

To create a grouped series of criteria, select the And/Or field in a blank row between the two groups, choose either And or Or, and then move to the next row without entering any other criteria. Notice the shaded row in Figure 23.41.

Figure 23.41
Entering a condition on a blank row creates separate groups of criteria.

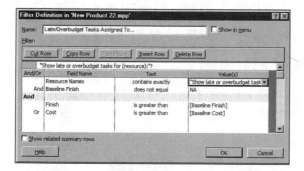

Supplied filters that include this grouping feature are Should Start/Finish By, Slipped/Late Progress, and Using Resource In Date Range.

CREATING CUSTOM FILTERS WITH AUTOFILTER

 A very easy way to create a custom filter is by using the Custom option on the AutoFilter list. First, turn on the AutoFilter feature by either choosing Project, Filtered For, AutoFilter or clicking the AutoFilter button on the Formatting toolbar. This displays an AutoFilter values drop-down list on each column heading. When you choose any of these, a menu will appear with a number of choices, including Custom. When you choose the Custom option, in this case from the Task Name field drop-down list, the dialog box in Figure 23.42 is displayed.

Figure 23.42
The Custom AutoFilter dialog box helps you create a custom filter.

The first field will be set to whatever column drop-down list you chose, and the test will depend on that field. For example, with a duration, or a start or finish date, the test will be Equals, while the task name field's test will be Contains. The drop-down list to the right of the field has a list of values from which you can choose, or you can type criteria as described in earlier sections. If multiple criteria exist, you can enter a second set and use either the And or Or option. When you choose OK, the filter will be applied. If you want to modify the criteria the next time you access the Custom option from the AutoFilter drop-down list, the previous criteria will still be there.

If the filter you create proves useful for future sessions, you can save it using the Save button in the Custom AutoFilter dialog box. When you choose this button, it takes you to the same Filter Definition dialog box used in earlier sections.

CREATING CUSTOM GROUPS

 Grouping tasks or resources is yet another way to display project data to meet your needs. In addition to sorting lists and filtering tasks for a narrow focus, grouping offers more control over displays and printouts. A key advantage to organizing tasks in groups is the ability to display subtotals for numeric data in the groups.

Project 2000 includes a number of predefined group definitions. Please read the section "Grouping the Task and Resource Lists" in Chapter 12, "Reviewing the Project Plan," for a description of groups and their application. This section focuses on creating custom groups to meet your specific needs. The method for creating a custom group is very similar to creating a custom filter; the logic behind grouping is very similar to sorting.

ACCESSING THE CUSTOM GROUPS

To define and format a custom group, the Group Definition dialog box must be displayed. Follow these steps to access the dialog box:

1. Choose Project, Group By.

2. Choose More Groups from the cascading menu.

3. Select an existing group name and click Edit or Copy to modify an existing group or to use a group as a starting point for the new group definition. To create a custom group from scratch, select New. The Group Definition dialog box will be displayed, as shown in Figure 23.43.

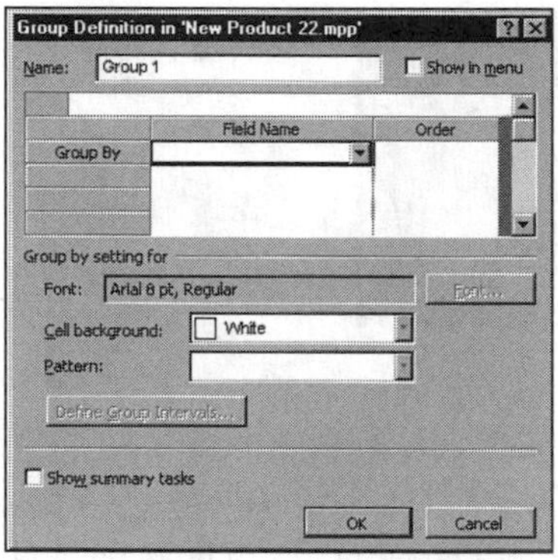

Figure 23.43
Groups are created or modified in the Group Definition dialog box.

4. Replace the generic Name, such as Group 1, with a descriptive name of your choosing.

5. To have the group name appear in the Group By cascading menu, turn on the Show in Menu option.

6. Complete the group definition as described in the following section.

Another access to the Group Definition dialog box is available directly off the Project, Group By cascading menu. Choose Customize Group By instead of More Groups. This method is a shortcut to the dialog box and enables you to experiment with group settings without saving a named group. However, any group you create in this way is *temporary* in that Microsoft Project holds the definition under the name of Custom Group. The Custom Group will then be displayed in the More Groups list, but you can't open this custom group for editing while in the More Groups list. You must access this temporary definition via Customize Group By to name it and to save it. When the data is displayed and summarized as required, choose Project, Group By, Customize Group By and select Save to name and permanently store the group definition.

SELECTING GROUPING FIELDS

The task or resource list might be grouped by up to 10 levels. Groups are created by selecting one or more fields from the database to create an outlined group structure. Groups are defined from the top down; that is, the first field in the definition represents the broadest group. Additional grouping fields refine the categorized lists into finer and finer detailed groupings.

To create the group structure, access the Group Definition dialog box. Select one field name for the Group By line and a sort order for the field (ascending or descending). For group refinements, move down one position and chose a Then By field (and its sort order). No preview area exists in this dialog box. Select OK when you are ready to return to the screen and view the results of your choices. Figure 23.44 illustrates a group definition designed to show how much of the budget will be committed at the end of a timeframe, with the time-frame in chronological order and the expenditures listed most costly first.

Figure 23.44
A custom group defi-nition to display cost obligations within time intervals.

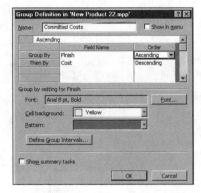

DEFINING GROUP INTERVALS

For some fields, the group interval is automatic. For example, if grouping on the Critical field, the only two possible values for Critical are yes and no. In other fields, particularly date fields, the group intervals are created logically but they might not match your require-ments. And in still other fields, such as costing data, a series of discrete or unique values exists, creating many groups with few entries in each.

The Group Definition dialog box includes an option to control how data is grouped. Within the dialog box, select a field name already specified on the Group By or Then By rows, and then choose Define Group Intervals. The Define Group Interval dialog box will be displayed, as shown in Figure 23.45. By default, every data type is set to be grouped on Each Value, from the earliest (or smallest) to the latest (or largest). The Group On drop-down list offers a choice of logical groupings for the data type. Date values can be grouped by intervals of minutes up to years; numeric data can be grouped in any intervals and can start the grouping in negative numbers; and text values can be grouped only by each value or by the first few characters.

Previous versions of Microsoft Project had no facility for viewing or printing subtotals for numeric data. Total values could be printed, but only through Show Totals options on reports. With the grouping feature, any numeric field displayed onscreen when a group is applied will show the group subtotals on the line with the group label. In Figure 23.46, the Cost column includes subtotals for groups of expenditures in intervals of $1,000 and sub-totals for all costs within each monthly timeframe.

Figure 23.45
The Finish field groups are set to display in monthly intervals.

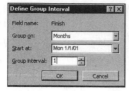

Second group level, by cost range
First group level, by month

Cost subtotal for first month

Cost subtotals for each range of cost values

Figure 23.46
Grouping includes subtotals for numeric data.

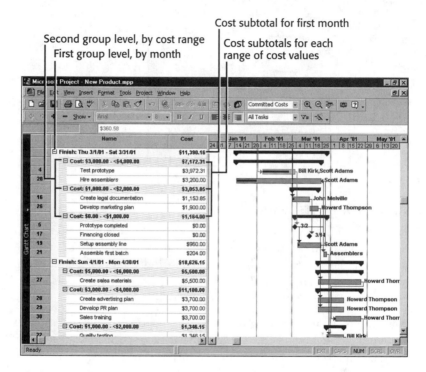

Tip from Tim and the Project Team

You can't change the value rollup behavior of standard fields for group displays. To see, for example, the average value for a group, you must create a calculated custom field (as described earlier in this chapter) and use a simple formula to set the custom field equal to a standard numeric field. In the Customize Fields dialog box, you can set the Calculation for Task and Group Summary Rows Rollup option to Average.

FORMATTING GROUP DISPLAYS

In addition to specifying field group internals, you can format the group displays. Each group level has its own settings for font size, background color, and pattern. Each group will display the task or resource detail information, plus a summary bar for the group. To avoid a display cluttered with multiple types of summary bars, turn off the Sho<u>w</u> Summary Tasks option.

SAVING CUSTOM GROUPS

Named custom group definitions are saved with the Project file. To make a group definition available to other files, use the Groups tab in the Organizer, as described later in this chapter.

ORGANIZING VIEWS IN PROJECT FILES

All the customized changes you make to the views—whether through defining views, tables, filters, or format specifications—are saved as part of the current project file. However, you can choose to make these customized views, tables, and filters available to other project files or to all projects. When they are available to all projects, the view definitions are stored in a global template. In Microsoft Project, this file is GLOBAL.MPT.

When you start Microsoft Project, GLOBAL.MPT loads with the project file. When you exit Project, all changes made to the views are saved only with the project file. Customized views created for one project file are not directly available to other project files. If you save the view data to the global file, however, these customized views can be made available across all project files that are tied to that global file.

To save the view changes to the GLOBAL.MPT file, follow these steps:

1. Choose <u>V</u>iew, <u>M</u>ore Views and select the <u>O</u>rganizer button.

2. The Organizer dialog box has tabs for each set of custom objects that can be copied between project files. The Views tab shows views available in the GLOBAL.MPT file on the left of the dialog box, and the right side shows a list of the customized and modified views available in the current project file along with any views used during this session of Project (see Figure 23.47). The other tabs follow the same format. Choose the tab that contains the customized objects (views, tables, filters, groups, and so on) you want to copy.

Figure 23.47
Use the Organizer to manage the storage of your custom views, tables, fields, filters, groups, and more.

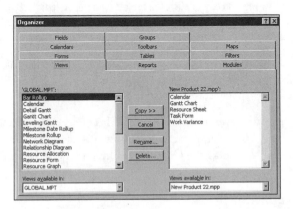

3. Select the view or views in the project file list that should also be in the global file and click the <u>C</u>opy button. This copies these view definitions from the project file over to the global file.

4. The Cancel button changes to Close after the copy is performed. Click the Close button to close the Organizer when you are finished copying the view definitions.

If you save the customized views in the global file, any time you create a new project based on that global file (which is the default), those views will be available.

Caution

When copying custom views to the GLOBAL.MPT or to other Project files, be sure you copy any custom filters, groups, or tables that are part of the custom view.

You also can use the Organizer to rename and delete views from the global or current project files. To delete a view (either customized or standard), perform the following steps:

1. Select the view in the view list from which it should be deleted—either the global file or the current project file.

2. Choose the Delete button.

3. Choose Yes to confirm the deletion or No to cancel the deletion.

4. The view will be gone from either the global file (which will affect all projects that used that view) or from the current project file only—depending on what was selected in step 1.

5. Click the Close button to complete the Organizer command.

If you don't want to copy an element to the GLOBAL.MPT file, but you want to use it in another project file, you can copy it from one file to another. First, be sure you open both files. Then, using the Organizer dialog box, choose both files from the drop-down lists at the bottom of the box—one on the left and one on the right. Choose the appropriate tab for the object you want and copy as specified previously.

Note

If you run a shared copy of Microsoft Project on a network, the GLOBAL.MPT file used by everyone might not be available to you for saving customized elements. In that case, storing your modifications becomes a matter of computing practices. You might choose to set aside one project file to be used as a holding vessel for storing and retrieving your personalized elements. In that case, copy objects between two open files, not between an open file and the GLOBAL.MPT template.

You can access the Organizer several ways. The most direct access to the Organizer is through Tools, Organizer. However, most dialog boxes in which you can customize named elements include a button to display the Organizer. These include the following:

- View, More Views
- View, Table, More Tables
- Project, Filtered For, More Filters
- Project, Group By, More Groups
- View, Reports, Custom

SAVING OTHER CUSTOM ELEMENTS IN THE GLOBAL TEMPLATE

2000 In this version of Microsoft Project, custom field names and definitions do not have to be recreated in each individual file. The Organizer now has a tab that enables copying and deleting of custom fields. The Re_n_ame button also appears to be available, but in fact, it can't be used when the Fields tab is active; an error message will be displayed. Similarly, you can use the Groups tab in the Organizer to copy, delete, and rename custom groups in the current file to the GLOBAL.MPT.

If you upgrade to Microsoft Project 2000 over an earlier version, the customized items in the old GLOBAL.MPT are automatically incorporated into the new template, while retaining any of the new features of the new version of Microsoft Project. The old template does not completely overwrite the old; they are merged.

TROUBLESHOOTING

RESTORING STANDARD VIEWS

I've already modified a standard view by editing it and now I want to get back the original.

Use the Organizer to copy the view definition you modified back into your project from the Global.MPT file. Be sure you rename your modified view first so that your work isn't overwritten.

CHANGING THE SCREEN TYPE FOR A VIEW

I want to change the basic screen type used for a view I created. How can I make this happen?

Instead of copying an existing view, you must create a brand new view. Use _V_iew, _M_ore Views to create a New view definition. You first might want to edit the view you were copying to begin with to see the settings that were used. Then, you can create a new view and enter those settings in the new definition.

FREEZING THE FIRST TABLE COLUMN

I'm working in a table with many columns, and when I scroll to the right side of the table, the task names disappear. Is there any way to lock them in place?

Yes, edit the table and move the task name field to the very first column. Make sure the _L_ock First Column check box is selected. The only problem with this arrangement is that you can't move your cursor into the column for editing. Edit your table in this way after your task names have been finalized or edit the table again and unlock the column.

CHAPTER 24

USING THE STANDARD REPORTS

In this chapter

ACCESSING THE STANDARD REPORTS

The Reports command on the View menu provides access to the Reports dialog box, which lists six groups of report formats: Overview, Current Activities, Costs, Assignments, Workload, and Custom (see Figure 24.1). Together, the first five groups contain 29 predefined summary, calendar, task, resource, and crosstab reports that are all set up and ready to print. The last report category, Custom, allows you to customize these reports or create your own reports. Chapter 25, "Customizing Reports," discusses how to tailor reports in Microsoft Project.

Figure 24.1
Use the 29 predefined reports to keep management and your project team informed of the status of all aspects of the project.

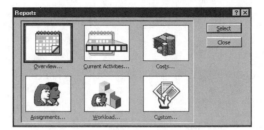

To select one of the report categories, either double-click the category button, or click the button once and choose Select.

After you select one of the category buttons in the Reports dialog box, another dialog box appears showing the actual reports that belong to that category. The Overview Reports category was selected, and the reports available in that category appear in Figure 24.2. To display one of the reports, you can either double-click the desired report button, or click it once and choose the Select button.

Figure 24.2
The Overview Reports category provides five different kinds of summary reports.

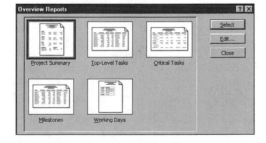

 When you select a report to display, you will see the report, based on your active project, in the Print Preview mode. To read the text of the report, you need to zoom in on the preview page. Use the magnifying glass button on the toolbar to zoom in, or position your mouse anywhere on the report. The mouse changes to a magnifying glass. Click to zoom in to that part of the report.

Most of the reports have headings at the top of the report. The information displayed comes from the properties entered for the project. Choose File, Properties to add or modify this information. Most common in the headings are the Title and Manager fields from the Properties information. Sometimes other fields or a date also are included in the heading.

THE OVERVIEW REPORTS CATEGORY

There are five different overview reports: Project Summary, Top-Level Tasks, Critical Tasks, Milestones, and Working Days. Together these reports display summary data over the life of the project. They are useful as documentation for presentations to management after the initial design period has been completed, as well as status reports while the project is underway.

THE PROJECT SUMMARY REPORT

The Project Summary report displays on one page the most significant project information. This report is useful for status meetings with your project team or senior management. Because the Variance and Remaining fields are calculated, this report is a good summary to have at the completion of the preliminary planning for your project, before work on the project actually begins.

PART

VII

CH

24

Best Practice Tips from Toby Brown, PMP

The Project Summary report is a printed report of the Project Statistics dialog box. Although the format is slightly different, all of the project elements displayed within this dialog box are included in this report. If the project manager continually monitors project performance by utilizing project statistics, this report format provides a quick way of generating written verification of the current status of the project.

There are six sections: Dates, Duration, Work, Costs, Status (both Task and Resource), and Notes (see Figure 24.3). The headings at the top of the report display the Title, Company, and Manager information that was entered into the Properties for the project. The date displayed comes from the Current Date option in the Project Information dialog box. Choose Project, Project Information to display the Project Information dialog box and adjust this date.

Figure 24.3
The Project Summary report provides a one-page overview of calculated project information. The top half of the report displays the report headings, the comparison of dates, and durations.

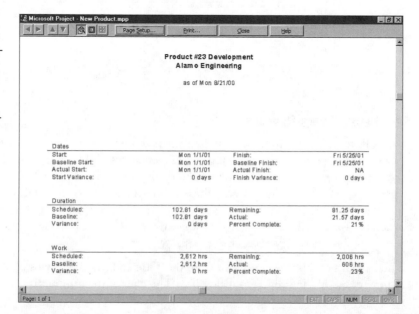

Tip from Tim and the Project Team

To change the heading for this report, simply change the information stored in the Properties. For example, if you want the name of your company to appear as the first line of the heading, choose File, Properties and then type the company name in the Title field of the Properties dialog box.

Comparisons can be made between what is currently scheduled, what the baseline indicates, and what actually happened.

The Task Status section displays the number of Tasks Not Yet Started, the number of Tasks in Progress, and the number of Tasks Completed in your project (see Figure 24.4). The number of overallocated resources you have also is given. Comments you enter on the Summary tab under the Properties dialog box appear in the Notes section.

Figure 24.4
This one report provides a consolidated status of your project. The bottom half of the Project Summary report compares Work, Costs, and a status of the Tasks and Resources.

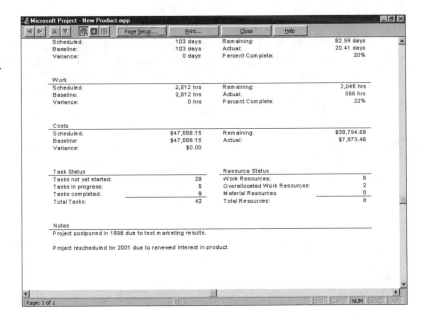

THE TOP-LEVEL TASKS REPORT

If you have used the outlining capability to create summary tasks in your project, the Top-Level Tasks report shows the highest level *summary* tasks. This report is used to focus on the major phases of the project, rather than individual tasks. Figure 24.5 shows a sample of this report. For each summary task, there is information about the Duration, Start, Finish, Percent Complete, Cost, and Work. These are rolled up (consolidated) values from the subordinate tasks, similar to the way they appear in the Gantt Chart view. If notes have been added to these summary tasks, they are printed out as well.

The heading of this report is taken from the Title and Manager fields entered into the Summary tab of the Properties dialog box. The date of the printout is also included in the heading.

Figure 24.5
Summary task information appears in bold in the Top-Level Tasks report.

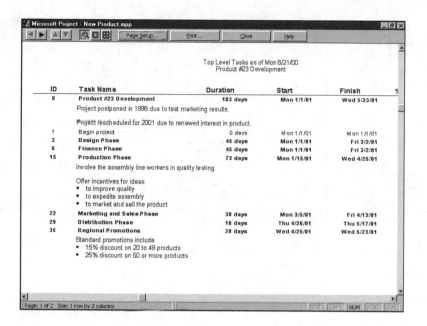

Tip from Tim and the Project Team

Make sure if you plan to use this report that you give your top-level summary tasks good descriptive names that clearly describe the tasks or phase they summarize. Otherwise, this report might be meaningless to the people who read it!

THE CRITICAL TASKS REPORT

When your project must finish by a set deadline, you need to focus on the critical tasks. Critical tasks are those tasks that, if delayed, will cause a delay in the finish date of your project. The Critical Tasks report displays all the critical tasks, categorized under their summary tasks, assuming that outlining (indenting and outdenting) has been used. For each task, there are columns for Duration, Start, Finish, Predecessors, and Resources. The indicator symbols seen in the table side of the Gantt Chart view are displayed next to the task ID. Refer to Chapter 2, "Learning the Basics of Microsoft Project," for more information on these indicators.

As shown in Figure 24.6, underneath the critical task name is a subchart that displays the successor tasks, along with the type of relationship and any lag or lead. Remember, Project displays leads as a negative number in the lag field. If notes have been added to the tasks, they are printed as well. The heading of the report includes the Title and Manager fields from the Summary tab of the Properties dialog box.

Figure 24.6
Focus on the tasks most important to your deadline with the Critical Tasks report.

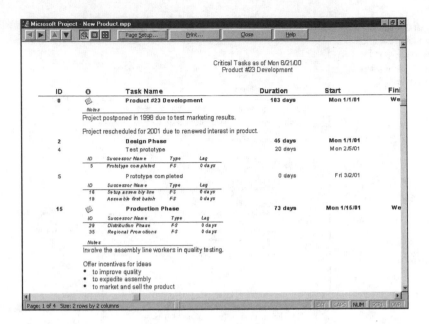

Caution

Critical tasks are not set in stone; they are dynamic and change depending on the changes you make to the project. When you make changes to the project, tasks that were not critical might become critical. After doing any kind of tinkering with your project design, make sure to reprint this report. The copy of the report you printed prior to the changes might no longer be accurate.

THE MILESTONES REPORT

Another way of concentrating on the major phases or turning points in the project is to focus on milestones. The Milestones report provides a columnar layout that includes Duration, Start, Finish, Predecessors, and Resource Names (see Figure 24.7). The indicators have been added to this report, providing additional information about the tasks. Milestones that have been completed are grouped together and listed first. The check mark indicator denotes which tasks have been completed. Those milestones that have not yet been reached are listed next. If notes have been added to the task, they are printed as well.

Best Practice Tips from Toby Brown, PMP

A milestone task is often used to indicate the completion of a project phase. These components of a well-established project are tied to the expected deliverables that occur when completing work within a project and are, therefore, often required for reporting purposes. Organizations tend to focus on bottom-line results, or rather the work product deliverables of a project, not just the work performed. The consideration of work performance occurs with earned value analysis, a report described later within this chapter.

Figure 24.7
Project does not create milestones to mark the major turning points in the project. You must add milestones to your project; milestones are tasks with 0 (zero) duration.

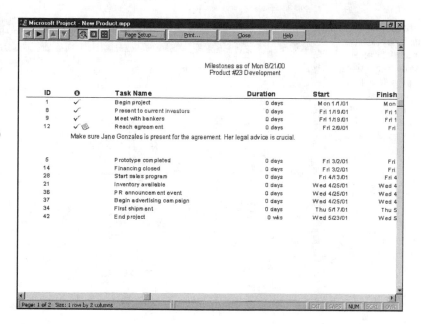

THE WORKING DAYS REPORT

The Working Days report provides a list of the working and nonworking times for each base calendar used in your project. Using this report is an excellent way to verify that the appropriate working hours have been established and that the holidays, and other nonworking times, are incorporated into your project. The information for each base calendar is printed on a separate page. Figure 24.8 shows information for the Standard base calendar. Figure 24.9 shows information for the Assemblers—AM base calendar.

Figure 24.8
Use this report to verify the base calendars you have created for the project.

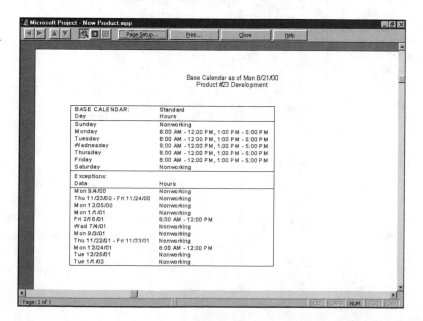

Figure 24.9
Create base calendars for groups of workers whose hours are significantly different from the normal hours. This figure displays the calendar for Assemblers who work a morning shift.

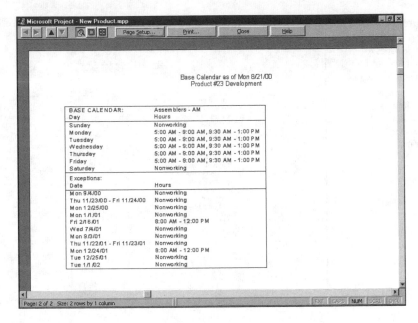

THE CURRENT ACTIVITY REPORTS CATEGORY

The next major category of reports focuses on tasks and provides you with a comprehensive status of the tasks as the project is underway. There are six reports in this category: Unstarted Tasks, Tasks Starting Soon, Tasks In Progress, Completed Tasks, Should Have Started Tasks, and Slipping Tasks (see Figure 24.10).

Figure 24.10
The Current Activity reports are useful primarily after your project has started; each focuses on specific groups of tasks.

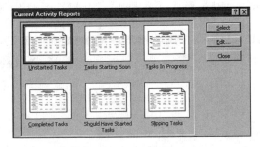

THE UNSTARTED TASKS REPORT

This report shows tasks for which no actual information has been entered, which means these tasks have not yet started. It specifically looks to see if the actual start date has been entered. In studying this report, you can focus your attention on tasks that have yet to start, making sure that materials are in place, resources are ready and available, and so on.

The Unstarted Tasks report is a columnar report that includes the following fields: ID, Task Name, Duration, Start, Finish, Predecessors, and Resource Names. In addition, underneath each task name is a subchart that includes the units of each resource assignment, the hours of work, and any delays (see Figure 24.11). If any notes have been added to tasks, they are printed here as well.

Figure 24.11
The Unstarted Tasks report provides a comprehensive list of tasks that have not begun–flagging those tasks that should have started and are behind schedule, as well as upcoming tasks you can verify are on schedule.

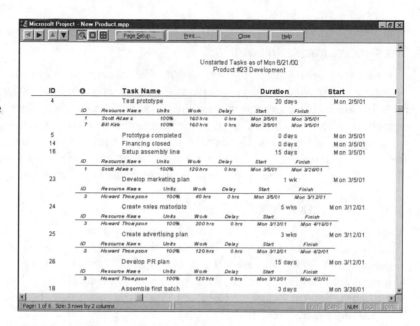

THE TASKS STARTING SOON REPORT

This report follows the exact same format as the Unstarted Tasks report but has an interactive filter as part of the definition of the report. Every time the report is run, the Date Range filter prompts you for a range of dates (see Figures 24.12 and 24.13). The tasks must occur within that range of dates to be included on the report.

Figure 24.12
Tasks must be scheduled to start after the date you enter in this prompt to be included in this report.

Figure 24.13
Tasks must be sched-uled to start before the date you enter in this prompt to be included in this report.

THE TASKS IN PROGRESS REPORT

A project manager often needs to know what tasks are currently underway so progress can be checked. The Tasks In Progress report displays all tasks that have a start date entered but no finish date. This is accomplished via the In Progress Tasks filter. The report is displayed in monthly intervals. The format is similar to the other task reports in the Current Activity category (see Figure 24.14). There are columns for ID, Task Name, Duration, Start, Finish, Predecessors, and Resource Names. Under the Task Name is a resource schedule that includes the units of the resource assignment, the hours of work, and any delays.

THE COMPLETED TASKS REPORT

A sense of accomplishment is often gained from seeing a list of tasks that have been finished. Using the Completed Tasks filter, this report displays tasks whose Percent Complete field has been set to 100%. Tasks are listed in monthly intervals with columns determined by the summary table (see Figure 24.15). The columns included are ID, Task Name, Duration, Start, Finish, Percent Complete, Cost, and Work. You can change the columns in this report by modifying the Summary table.

Figure 24.14
Only tasks that have started are included in this report. The indicators in the report are the same indicators that appear in the Gantt Chart view. The monthly intervals make the report easier to inter-pret.

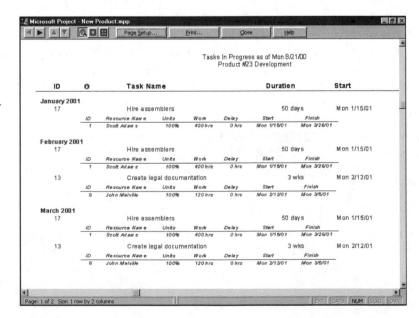

Figure 24.15
This report lists tasks by month. If a task starts in one month and finishes in another month, the task will appear in both months.

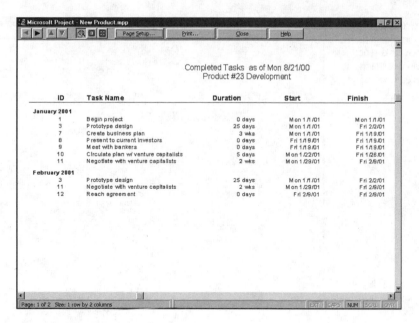

For more information on customizing tables, **see** "Using and Creating Tables," **p. 949**

THE SHOULD HAVE STARTED TASKS REPORT

A project manager needs to know at a moment's notice which tasks should have started but haven't. If you have forgotten to update the status of tasks that have begun, the Should Have Started Tasks report will be a good reminder for you. This report uses the Should Start By interactive filter to prompt the user for a date by which the tasks should begin. The date you enter appears in the report title. Tasks that should have started by that date but have not yet started (no actual Start date has been entered) are then displayed (see Figure 24.16). The date you enter is compared to the currently scheduled Start date, not the Baseline Start date.

Summary tasks for each subtask are included with columns determined by the Variance table. Columns include ID, Task Name, Start, Finish, Baseline Start, Baseline Finish, and Variance for Start and Finish. The Variance columns basically tell you how far behind you are for those tasks. Under each Task Name the successor name, relationship type, and any lag or lead is displayed. This way you can see other tasks that are going to be impacted by the delay in starting. If task notes have been added, they are displayed here as well. Because the preview of this report is zoomed in, not all the columns of information are displayed in Figure 24.16.

THE SLIPPING TASKS REPORT

It is equally important for a project manager to know which tasks have started but are not scheduled to complete on time, or within the duration that was originally planned. Perhaps additional resources or supervision are needed on these tasks. The Slipping Tasks report is based on the Slipping Tasks filter. As determined by this filter, slipping tasks have had a baseline set—the task has started but not finished—and the scheduled finish is later than the baseline (originally planned) finish date. Figure 24.17 shows this report.

Figure 24.16
Use the Should Have Started Tasks report to find those tasks that need immediate attention.

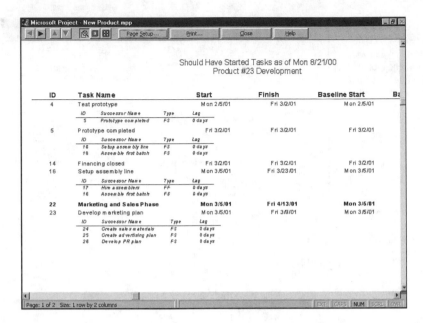

Caution

If you have added tasks after first saving the baseline, make sure to update the baseline again for the tasks you added and any tasks impacted by adding the new tasks, to make sure that all relevant tasks are displayed in this report. Only those tasks that are included in the baseline will be displayed in the report.

→   For more information on updating the baseline, **see** "Correcting the Baseline," **p. 664**

Tasks that meet the criteria of the filter are displayed in a columnar format with their summary tasks. The format is essentially the same as the Should Have Started Tasks report (refer to Figure 24.16). Columns are determined by the Variance table, which shows ID, Task Name, Start, Finish, Baseline Start, Baseline Finish, and Variance for Start and Finish. Under each Task Name is a subchart for successor information, including the relationship type, and any lag or lead that has been applied. If task notes have been added, they are displayed here as well. Because the preview of this report is zoomed in, not all the columns of information are displayed in Figure 24.17.

Figure 24.17
Slipping Tasks are tasks that are behind schedule, where the currently scheduled finish date has slipped beyond the baseline finish date for the tasks.

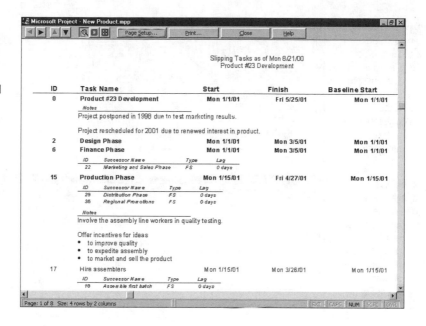

THE COST REPORTS CATEGORY

There are five reports in the Cost Reports category (see Figure 24.18). These include Cash Flow, Budget, Overbudget Tasks, Overbudget Resources, and Earned Value. These five reports together provide a broad range of cost data that is essential when trying to stay within a budget for a project.

Tip from Tim and the Project Team

Most of the reports in this category are based on tables in Project. You can modify the tables to remove any fields that you deem unnecessary for the report you need.

→ To remove fields from tables, **see** "Adding and Changing the Columns in the Table," **p. 951**

THE CASH FLOW REPORT

The Cash Flow report can be instrumental in managing how much money is needed and when the money is needed during the life of a project. This is a crosstab report based on the Task Cost table. It shows tasks in the first column and weekly periods of time in the remaining columns. The subsequent grid or spreadsheet that is created contains cost information (see Figure 24.19). The cost information is derived from resource usage costs and fixed costs associated with tasks. The report displays costs broken down into weekly increments. Tasks are displayed underneath their summary tasks. Each column (week) and row (task) is totaled. This allows you to see the total dollars required each week to finance the project, as well as the total cost for each task.

Figure 24.18
Keeping accurate track of the project budget is a significant concern for most project managers. The reports in the Cost Reports category provide quick access to budget information.

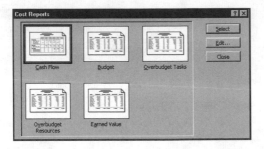

Figure 24.19
The weekly costs depicted in the Cash Flow report are based on when costs accrue at the start of the task, the completion of the task, or prorated throughout the duration of the task.

Cash Flow as of Mon 8/21/00
Product #23 Development

	12/31/00	1/7/01	1/14/01	1/21/01	1/28/01
Product #23 Development					
Begin project					
Design Phase					
Prototype design	$694.23	$867.79	$867.79	$867.79	$
Test prototype					
Prototype completed					
Finance Phase					
Create business plan	$494.51	$618.13	$618.13		
Present to current investors					
Meet with bankers					
Circulate plan w/ venture capitalists				$576.92	
Negotiate with venture capitalists					$
Reach agreement					
Create legal documentation					
Financing closed					
Production Phase					
Setup assembly line					
Hire assemblers			$320.00	$320.00	$
Assemble first batch					
Quality testing					
Assemble product					

Page: 1 of 8   Size: 2 rows by 4 columns

THE BUDGET REPORT

Using the Budget report, you can see which tasks are most expensive. These tasks will probably need closer management so that they don't go over budget. Secondly, you can see which tasks are going over budget based on actual information that has been entered.

The Budget report displays data from the Task Cost table. It shows a list of all tasks in a columnar format sorted by the total cost for the task, with most expensive tasks first (see Figure 24.20). Columns included from the Task Cost table include ID, Task Name, Fixed Cost, Fixed Cost Accrual, Total Cost, Baseline Cost, Variance, Actual, and Remaining. Each column is then totaled at the bottom so you can see actual totals, variances, and remaining dollars required. Because the preview of this report is zoomed in, not all the columns of information or totals are displayed in Figure 24.20.

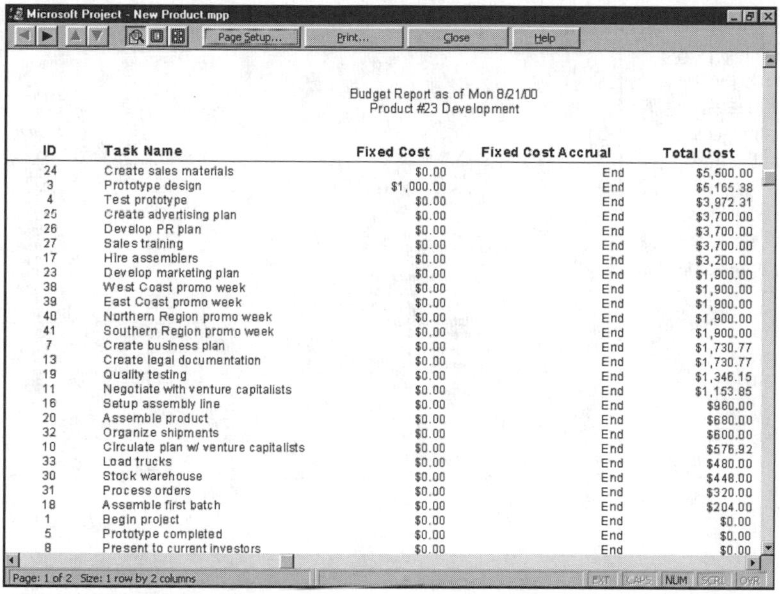

Budget Report as of Mon 8/21/00
Product #23 Development

ID	Task Name	Fixed Cost	Fixed Cost Accrual	Total Cost
24	Create sales materials	$0.00	End	$5,500.00
3	Prototype design	$1,000.00	End	$5,165.38
4	Test prototype	$0.00	End	$3,972.31
25	Create advertising plan	$0.00	End	$3,700.00
26	Develop PR plan	$0.00	End	$3,700.00
27	Sales training	$0.00	End	$3,700.00
17	Hire assemblers	$0.00	End	$3,200.00
23	Develop marketing plan	$0.00	End	$1,900.00
38	West Coast promo week	$0.00	End	$1,900.00
39	East Coast promo week	$0.00	End	$1,900.00
40	Northern Region promo week	$0.00	End	$1,900.00
41	Southern Region promo week	$0.00	End	$1,900.00
7	Create business plan	$0.00	End	$1,730.77
13	Create legal documentation	$0.00	End	$1,730.77
19	Quality testing	$0.00	End	$1,346.15
11	Negotiate with venture capitalists	$0.00	End	$1,153.85
16	Setup assembly line	$0.00	End	$960.00
20	Assemble product	$0.00	End	$680.00
32	Organize shipments	$0.00	End	$600.00
10	Circulate plan w/ venture capitalists	$0.00	End	$576.92
33	Load trucks	$0.00	End	$480.00
30	Stock warehouse	$0.00	End	$448.00
31	Process orders	$0.00	End	$320.00
18	Assemble first batch	$0.00	End	$204.00
1	Begin project	$0.00	End	$0.00
5	Prototype completed	$0.00	End	$0.00
8	Present to current investors	$0.00	End	$0.00

Figure 24.20
Use the Variance column to see which tasks have costs over or under what was planned in the baseline.

Tip from Tim and the Project Team

Most of the reports in this category are based on the Cost table in Project. You can modify the table to hide the Fixed Cost Accrual field because it is not as crucial as the other fields, especially when presenting status reports to senior management or the project team. Look ahead to Figure 24.21 for an example of this field removed from the Overbudget Tasks report (which is similar to the Budget report).

To hide a field in a table, simply resize the field so that it doesn't show in the Gantt Chart view. When you are finished printing the report, resize the column back to fit the text.

Caution

If you select the column and choose Edit, Hide Column, it is the same as deleting the column in the table. You will then have to edit the table definition to add the column back.

THE OVERBUDGET TASKS REPORT

The Overbudget Tasks report finds tasks whose Actual, or scheduled, cost is higher than the Baseline Cost. It does this by applying the Cost Overbudget filter to the Task Cost table. Tasks are displayed in order by variance. Tasks that are the most over budget are displayed first (see Figure 24.21). The columnar format is determined by the Task Cost table. Columns include ID, Task Name, Fixed Cost, Fixed Cost Accrual, Total Cost, Baseline Cost, Variance, Actual Cost, and Remaining Cost. Each column is then totaled. Because the preview of this report is zoomed in, not all the columns of information are displayed in Figure 24.21.

Figure 24.21

The Overbudget Tasks report helps pinpoint tasks that need the project manager's attention; the next step is to determine why the actual cost for a task was more than the budgeted cost.

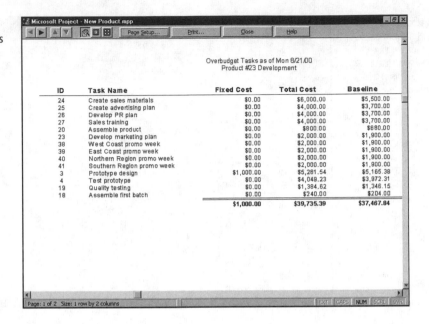

THE OVERBUDGET RESOURCES REPORT

The Overbudget Resources report follows a very similar format to the Overbudget Tasks report, with emphasis on resources rather than tasks (see Figure 24.22). This report checks the data in the Resource Cost table and pinpoints resources whose costs are higher than their baseline cost. Resources are working longer on tasks than was originally planned and are therefore costing more. The Cost Overbudget filter manages this.

The columnar format is controlled by the Resource Cost table, with ID, Resource Name, Cost, Baseline Cost, Variance, Actual Cost, and Remaining Cost included. Each column is then totaled. The resources that are the most over budget are listed first. Because the preview of this report is zoomed in, not all the columns of information are displayed in Figure 24.22.

THE EARNED VALUE REPORT

The Earned Value report is a cost comparison tool that utilizes data from the Earned Value table. It allows you to compare, with regards to cost, what is actually happening on each task in the project to what you expected to happen. The Current Date is used to calculate what costs have incurred and what costs you expected to incur when you originally planned the project. Actual Resource Costs and Fixed Costs are used to calculate the Percent Complete of each task, rather than what was entered for percentage completed. Then, you can compare if that matches the percentage completed of actual work done. For example, if a task is marked as 25% complete, and the actual cost so far is $300, you can calculate whether $300 is equal to 25% of the originally planned cost, the cost expected to be incurred by today for this task.

Figure 24.22
The Overbudget Resources report includes the actual costs incurred for the resources, as well as the costs planned for tasks these resources are assigned to, but have not yet started.

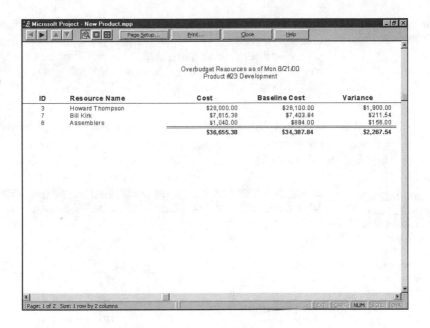

Note

Earned Value Analysis (EVA) was first developed by the U.S. Department of Defense in 1967 in response to contractors who often exaggerated their progress on Cost Reimbursable Contract projects. EVA allows the consideration of various project elements, including scope, cost, and schedule measurements, in order to determine what value has been earned to date within the project life cycle.

The format of the report is columnar with the columns determined by the Earned Value table (see Figure 24.23). Columns include the following:

- **Budgeted Cost of Work Scheduled (BCWS)**—Planned Cost multiplied by Percent Complete
- **Budgeted Cost of Work Performed (BCWP)**—The Baseline Cost multiplied by Planned Percent Complete
- **Actual Cost of Work Performed (ACWP)**—The cost of actual work performed plus fixed costs incurred
- **Schedule Variance (SV)**—The Budgeted Cost of Work Performed minus Budgeted Cost of Work Scheduled
- **Cost Variance (CV)**—The Budgeted Cost of Work Performed minus Actual Cost of Work Performed
- **Budgeted At Completion (BAC)**—The baseline cost of a task, which includes the cost of all resources assigned and any other fixed costs associated with the task
- **Estimate At Completion (EAC)**—The sum of actual costs incurred and remaining costs estimated for a task
- **Variance At Completion (VAC)**—The difference between the Baseline Cost and the scheduled cost

Note

Critical to the calculation of many of these items is the date used in performing the comparison. By default, Today's Date is used. This is the Current Date setting under the Project Information dialog box (choose Project, Project Information). If you prefer to use another date, change the Current Date setting.

All normal tasks are displayed, sorted by their IDs. Summary tasks are not displayed in this report. Because the preview of this report is zoomed in, not all the columns of information are displayed in Figure 24.23.

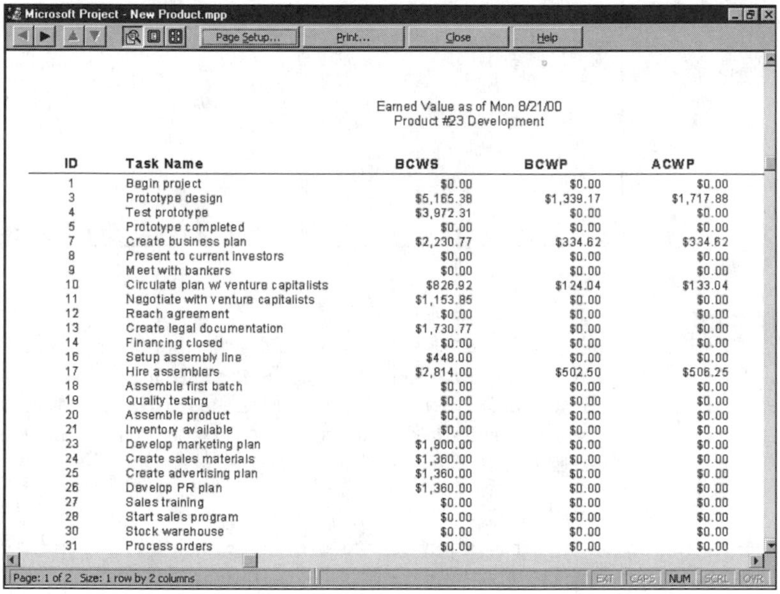

Earned Value as of Mon 8/21/00
Product #23 Development

ID	Task Name	BCWS	BCWP	ACWP
1	Begin project	$0.00	$0.00	$0.00
3	Prototype design	$5,165.38	$1,339.17	$1,717.88
4	Test prototype	$3,972.31	$0.00	$0.00
5	Prototype completed	$0.00	$0.00	$0.00
7	Create business plan	$2,230.77	$334.62	$334.62
8	Present to current investors	$0.00	$0.00	$0.00
9	Meet with bankers	$0.00	$0.00	$0.00
10	Circulate plan w/ venture capitalists	$826.92	$124.04	$133.04
11	Negotiate with venture capitalists	$1,153.85	$0.00	$0.00
12	Reach agreement	$0.00	$0.00	$0.00
13	Create legal documentation	$1,730.77	$0.00	$0.00
14	Financing closed	$0.00	$0.00	$0.00
16	Setup assembly line	$448.00	$0.00	$0.00
17	Hire assemblers	$2,814.00	$502.50	$506.25
18	Assemble first batch	$0.00	$0.00	$0.00
19	Quality testing	$0.00	$0.00	$0.00
20	Assemble product	$0.00	$0.00	$0.00
21	Inventory available	$0.00	$0.00	$0.00
23	Develop marketing plan	$1,900.00	$0.00	$0.00
24	Create sales materials	$1,360.00	$0.00	$0.00
25	Create advertising plan	$1,360.00	$0.00	$0.00
26	Develop PR plan	$1,360.00	$0.00	$0.00
27	Sales training	$0.00	$0.00	$0.00
28	Start sales program	$0.00	$0.00	$0.00
30	Stock warehouse	$0.00	$0.00	$0.00
31	Process orders	$0.00	$0.00	$0.00

Figure 24.23
The Earned Value report allows you to precisely track progress of resource costs compared to percentage of work completed.

THE ASSIGNMENT REPORTS CATEGORY

The Assignment category of reports displays information about the assignment of resources to tasks. There are four reports in this category with names that are fairly self-explanatory: Who Does What, Who Does What When, To-do List, and Overallocated Resources (see Figure 24.24).

THE WHO DOES WHAT REPORT

As the title indicates, the Who Does What report provides information about the resources working on your project and gives a comprehensive list of which tasks they are assigned to. The information in this report is displayed in a columnar format—based on the Usage table—which shows ID, Indicators, Resource Name, and the total Work (sometimes referred to as *effort*). Under each resource name in Figure 24.25, there is a subchart listing the tasks the resource is scheduled to work on, including the ID and Task Name, Units, Work, Delay, Start date, and Finish date. If task notes have been added, they are displayed here as well.

Figure 24.24
The Assignment Reports category includes reports that focus on resources and what they are scheduled to do.

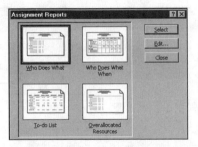

Figure 24.25
Indicators, such as the Resource Leveling indicators on Scott Adams and Howard Thompson, alert you that the resource's time is overallocated.

Resource leveling indicator

Notes indicator

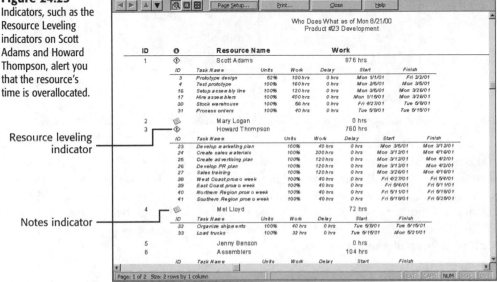

In this figure, the indicator symbols show that there are resource notes for Mary Logan and Mel Lloyd. Scott Adams and Howard Thompson have Resource Leveling indicators (shown as an exclamation warning).

THE WHO DOES WHAT WHEN REPORT

This report takes the Who Does What report one step further and breaks down work assignments by day. Using the Who Does What When report, a project manager would be able to quickly see what everyone is doing at any given time during the project, along with any overallocations. When shifting tasks from one resource to another, you also can see the resources that have time available.

This is a crosstab report that shows resources in the first column with each task that is assigned to them underneath (see Figure 24.26). The remaining columns display each daily time period for the remainder of the project. The resulting grid, or spreadsheet, calculates the hours of work that are assigned each day to each resource, by task.

Figure 24.26
The Who Does What When report lists the specific number of hours each day a resource is scheduled to work on the assigned tasks, and the total number of hours each day the resource is working on the project.

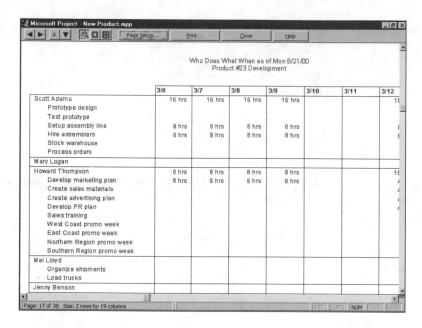

In this figure, Scott Adams is scheduled to work a total of 16 hours on 3/9—eight hours on Setup assembly line and eight hours on Hire Assemblers. This is an instance where his time is overallocated, as noted by the Resource Leveling (exclamation) indicator in Figure 24.25. Looking at the list of resources, Mary Logan, Mel Lloyd, and Jenny Benson are not working on this project on 3/9, and perhaps can be substituted for Scott Adams on one of these tasks, resolving his overallocation problem.

THE TO-DO LIST REPORT

The focus of this report is on tasks that are taking place during weekly time periods, rather than on resources as in the previous two reports. Each time the report is run, the Using Resource dialog box displays, prompting you to select a resource name (see Figure 24.27).

After choosing a resource from the drop-down list in the Using Resource dialog box, the report is run. The report displays only those tasks assigned to that resource (see Figure 24.28). Tasks are listed under a chronological listing of weeks. The columns that are included are determined by the Entry table: ID, indicators, Task Name, Duration, Start, Finish, Predecessors, and Resource Name. Because the preview of this report is zoomed in, not all the columns of information, including Resource Name, are displayed in Figure 24.28.

Tip from Tim and the Project Team

The title of the report does not indicate the name of the resource, because it appears as the last column in the printed report. To add the resource name to the header or footer of the report, modify the report by selecting the Page Setup button while previewing the report. For more information on print options, refer to Chapter 13, "Printing Views and Reports."

Figure 24.27
The To-do List report is a list of tasks generated for one resource. The Using Resource dialog box is actually a filter prompt where you indicate which resource the To-do List report is for.

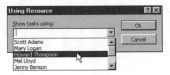

Figure 24.28
You can print a To-do List for each of your resources.

To Do List as of Mon 8/21/00
Product #23 Development

ID		Task Name	Duration	Start
Week of March 4				
23	✓ 🖉	Develop marketing plan	1 wk	Mon 3/5/01
Week of March 11				
23	✓ 🖉	Develop marketing plan	1 wk	Mon 3/5/01
24		Create sales materials	5 wks	Mon 3/12/01
25		Create advertising plan	3 wks	Mon 3/12/01
26		Develop PR plan	15 days	Mon 3/12/01
Week of March 18				
24		Create sales materials	5 wks	Mon 3/12/01
25		Create advertising plan	3 wks	Mon 3/12/01
26		Develop PR plan	15 days	Mon 3/12/01
Week of March 25				
24		Create sales materials	5 wks	Mon 3/12/01
25		Create advertising plan	3 wks	Mon 3/12/01
26		Develop PR plan	15 days	Mon 3/12/01
27		Sales training	3 wks	Mon 3/26/01
Week of April 1				
24		Create sales materials	5 wks	Mon 3/12/01
25		Create advertising plan	3 wks	Mon 3/12/01
26		Develop PR plan	15 days	Mon 3/12/01
27		Sales training	3 wks	Mon 3/26/01
Week of April 8				
24		Create sales materials	5 wks	Mon 3/12/01
27		Sales training	3 wks	Mon 3/26/01

Page: 1 of 4 Size: 2 rows by 2 columns

THE OVERALLOCATED RESOURCES REPORT

During the initial planning stages of the project, it is easy to assign too many tasks to valuable resources. The Overallocated Resources report lists all resources that are assigned to more hours of work than their calendar specifies. Underneath each resource is a subchart list of tasks to which they are assigned, the number of units of that resource that are assigned, the total number of hours of work, any delays that have been imposed, and the start and finish dates of the task (see Figure 24.29).

In this figure, Scott Adams and Howard Thompson are listed as the overallocated resources in this project.

With this information, the project manager can make some decisions about how to handle the overallocation: whether to hire additional help for the resource, reassign some tasks to other resources, or modify the resource's calendar.

→ For more information on how Microsoft Project finds allocation problems, **see** "Identifying Resource Overallocations," **p. 444**

→ For help in dealing with allocation problems, **see** "Strategies for Eliminating Resource Overallocations," **p. 455**

Figure 24.29
Use the Overallocated Resources report to help make decisions about resolving each resource's work overload.

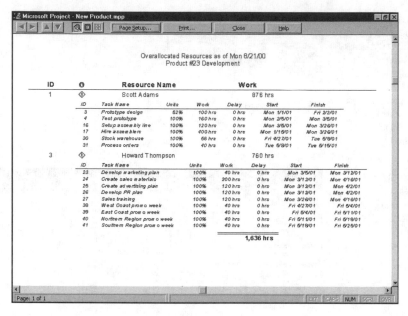

THE WORKLOAD REPORTS CATEGORY

The last category of reports contains crosstab reports that display information about how resources are being used (see Figure 24.30). The reports focus on how resources are being used, broken down by task or by resource. This category now includes two new reports that allow you to specify resource work or resource materials.

Figure 24.30
The Workload reports show how many hours each week a task will be worked on.

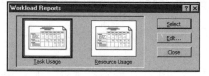

THE TASK USAGE REPORT

This crosstab report lists tasks, broken down by summary task, in the first column with the resources assigned to each task listed underneath. The remaining columns are weekly time increments. The resulting grid format displays the hours of work that each resource is assigned to work or the number of units of material resources being used (see Figure 24.31). Each week's hours are totaled at the bottom of the report; task and resource hours are totaled in the last column at the far right of the report.

THE RESOURCE USAGE REPORT

The Resource Usage report is another crosstab report that is very similar to the Task Usage report, except that its focus is on resources rather than tasks. Resources are listed in the first column, with the tasks that they are assigned underneath. The remaining columns are weekly increments during the life of the project. The resulting grid format displays the hours of work assigned to each resource during each week or the number of units of a material resource being used each week (see Figure 24.32). Each week is totaled at the bottom of the report; resource and task totals appear in the last column on the right of the report. When a project manager is juggling resources to accommodate overallocations or in an attempt to speed up the project, this report can be very useful in identifying resources that are not assigned to their full capacity.

Task Usage as of Mon 8/21/00
Product #23 Development

	2/11/01	2/18/01	2/25/01	3/4/01	3/11/01
Product #23 Development					
Begin project					
Design Phase					
Prototype design					
Scott Adams					
Bill Kirk					
Test prototype	72 hrs	80 hrs	80 hrs	8 hrs	
Scott Adams	36 hrs	40 hrs	40 hrs	4 hrs	
Bill Kirk	36 hrs	40 hrs	40 hrs	4 hrs	
Prototype completed					
Finance Phase					
Production Phase					
Setup assembly line				36 hrs	40 hrs
Scott Adams				36 hrs	40 hrs
Hire assemblers	36 hrs	40 hrs	40 hrs	40 hrs	40 hrs
Scott Adams	36 hrs	40 hrs	40 hrs	40 hrs	40 hrs
Assemble first batch					
Assemblers					
Glue (gallons)					
Quality testing					
Bill Kirk					

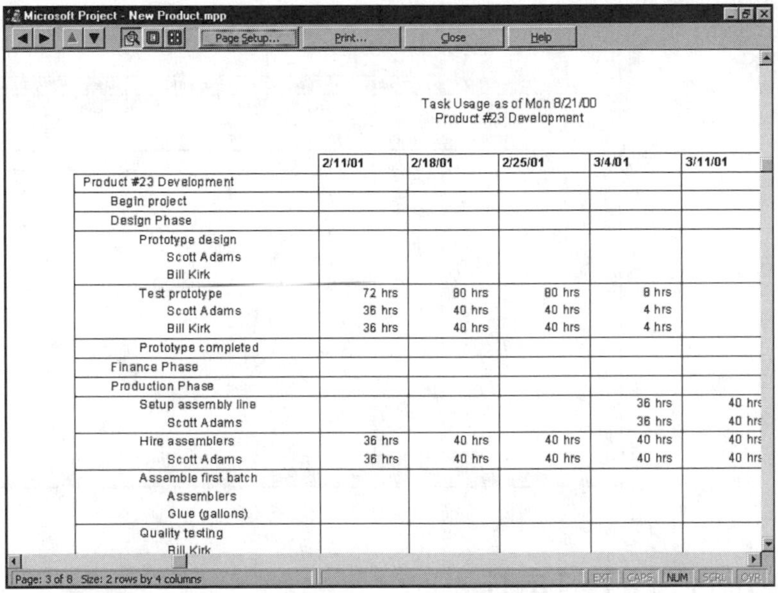

Figure 24.31
The Task Usage report displays all tasks, not just the subtasks, in a project. The focus of this report is on the hours worked on each task or the number of units of material resources used to complete each task.

Resource Usage as of Mon 8/21/00
Product #23 Development

	3/25/01	4/1/01	4/8/01	4/15/01	4/22/01
Scott Adams	8 hrs				5.5 hrs
Prototype design					
Test prototype					
Setup assembly line	4 hrs				
Hire assemblers	4 hrs				
Stock warehouse					5.5 hrs
Process orders					
Assemblers	24 hrs		7.5 hrs	37.5 hrs	35 hrs
Assemble first batch	24 hrs				
Assemble product			7.5 hrs	37.5 hrs	35 hrs
Glue (gallons)	25		46.88	234.38	218.75
Assemble first batch	25				
Assemble product			46.88	234.38	218.75
Bill Kirk	8 hrs	40 hrs	32 hrs		
Prototype design					
Test prototype					
Quality testing	8 hrs	40 hrs	32 hrs		
John Melville					
Create business plan					
Present to current investors					
Meet with bankers					

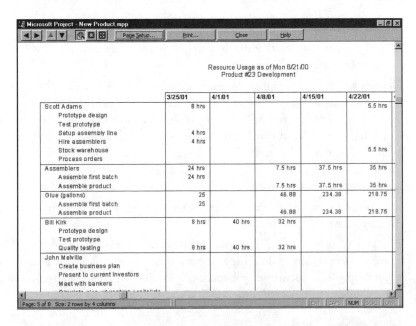

Figure 24.32
The order of the resources listed in the Resource Usage report is the order they appear in the Resource Sheet view. You can sort the Resource Sheet to display the resources in a different order.

In addition to the Resource Usage report, this version of Microsoft Project now includes two new reports: Resource Usage (work) and Resource Usage (material), the latter of which is shown in Figure 24.33. These reports look very similar to the Resource Usage report, but they target only resource work or material usage. These reports are available by selecting the Custom icon in the dialog box that appears when you select View, Reports in the menu bar.

Figure 24.33
The Resource Usage (material) report shows only the material resources used in your project.

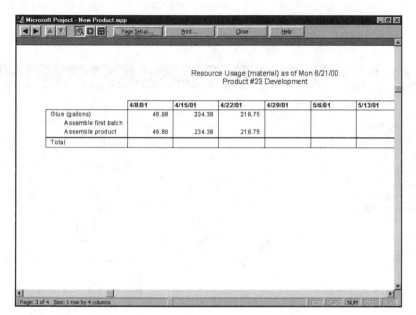

TROUBLESHOOTING

CHANGING COLUMN WIDTHS IN A REPORT

When I preview the report, several of the columns are too wide for the data being displayed. How can I reduce the width of the columns?

Identify which table supplies the data for the report by selecting the icon for the report in the Reports dialog box. Choose the Edit button. The Edit dialog box will show the name of the table used by the report. Close the dialog boxes and choose View, Table in the menu bar. Select the table on which your report is based. Change the width of the columns as needed. The new column widths will be used the next time you run the report.

WORK ASSIGNMENT REPORTS

As the project manager, I'd like to be able to see what everyone is responsible for each day. Can Project give me that type of report?

The Who Does What When report breaks down work assignments by day. It enables you to see what everyone is doing at any given time during the project—and more importantly, it can help you to identify any overallocations that exist and where best to redirect the responsibility to alleviate them.

Figure 24.34
Remove extra column width by changing the column width data in the Task Entry table.

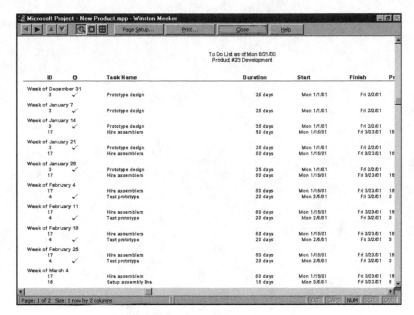

CHAPTER 25

CUSTOMIZING REPORTS

In this chapter

UNDERSTANDING REPORT CUSTOMIZATION IN MICROSOFT PROJECT

The Custom category in the Reports dialog box allows you to customize any of the existing predefined reports or to create your own reports. This chapter explores the range of options available to those who want to develop customized reports adapted to their project communication needs.

There are varying degrees of report customization available in Microsoft Project. Reports can be customized to change the way they look or the details of the information being presented. You can take an existing report and change the text formatting, the layout orientation, or the header and footer that appear when the report is printed. The details of the report can be altered by applying a different table or filter, or by choosing a different sort order for the report.

Most of the predefined reports available to you in Microsoft Project are variations of one of three basic report types: task list, resource list, and crosstab. There is a fourth report type, the monthly calendar report, that you can use for creating new reports but for which there are no predefined examples. There are also two unique predefined reports, the Project Summary report and the Base Calendar report, which are not based on any of the four report types previously mentioned.

The task, resource, and crosstab reports are the primary types used for reports in the Overview, Current Activities, Costs, Assignments, and Workload categories displayed in the Reports dialog box (see Figure 25.1). To access this dialog box, choose View, Reports.

Figure 25.1
The Reports dialog box lists the five categories of predefined reports and a sixth category for creating or modifying custom reports.

P
2000 There are 22 predefined reports available in Microsoft Project, which can be found in the five categories shown in Figure 25.1. These 22 reports can be accessed through the Custom category as well. The Custom category also includes three generic reports based on the task list, resource list, and crosstab report types that you can use to create custom reports. This version also includes two new resource reports: Resource (Material) and Resource (Work). They include a filter on the type of resource, material or work.

In Microsoft Project you can customize an existing report, create a custom report by making a copy of an existing report and make edit changes to the copy, or create a new report using one of the four report types previously listed.

CUSTOMIZING THE EXISTING REPORTS

There are two places you can customize an existing report: from within the specific category the report is listed or from within the Custom category. Chapter 24, "Using the Standard Reports," describes each of the standard, predefined reports if you are not familiar with these reports.

To change a report from within a specific category, double-click the category or click once on the category and choose Select. In Figure 25.2, the Assignments category has been selected. Choose the Overallocated Resources report. An Edit button within the category listing allows you to edit the contents of the report.

Figure 25.2
You can edit the content and level of detail while working in a category of reports.

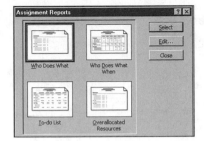

Selecting the Edit button shown in Figure 25.2 will display a dialog box with the editing changes you are allowed to make. The choices in this dialog box will differ depending on the type of report you are modifying. Figure 25.3 shows a sample dialog box used to make changes.

PART

VII

CH

25

Figure 25.3
The editing dialog box for the Overallocated Resources report. The choices displayed will vary depending on the type of report you are editing.

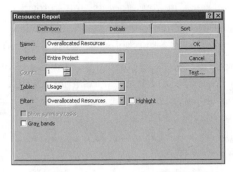

The editing choices listed here are the same as what would be available if you were editing the report through the Custom category (see "Customizing Specific Report Types," later in this chapter).

Tip from Tim and the Project Team

It is recommended that you do not customize the predefined reports, but instead make a copy of a report, using it as a basis for your new report. This way, the original report is left intact for you to use at a later time. If it is too late, see "Undoing Changes to a Predefined Report" later in this chapter.

USING THE CUSTOM CATEGORY OF REPORTS

The Custom category can be used to make content and level-of-detail changes to reports. All reports available within Project can be accessed through this category, as shown in Figure 25.4.

Figure 25.4
Use the Custom Reports dialog box to select a report to customize or to create a new report.

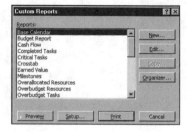

From the Custom category, you can do the following:

- Print one of the reports in the Reports list as the report is currently defined. Refer to Chapter 13, "Printing Views and Reports," for more information on printing reports.

- Set up the selected report before printing. (This is the same as the Page Setup function, which allows you to set up margins, headers, footers, and so forth.)

- Preview one of the reports before printing. With the Print Preview screen activated, you have the option of changing Page Setup before sending the report to the printer.

- Access the Organizer to copy customized reports to or from the Global template. This Organizer dialog box also allows you to delete reports from your Custom Reports list to keep your list current and uncluttered. Refer to Chapter 4, "Working with Project Files," for information on using the Organizer.

- Create a new report. The design must follow one of the four report types: task, resource, monthly calendar, or crosstab.

- Edit a report to change the table and filter used, and to change the details that are shown (for task and resource reports). You also can edit the column and row information (for crosstab reports), the sort order for presenting the details (for non-calendar reports), the text formatting used for parts of the report, and the use of border lines in the report. These changes become standard features of the named report.

- Copy an existing report and make modifications in the new report so that you have both the original and the new copy to use when needed.

The <u>N</u>ew and <u>C</u>opy buttons in the Custom Reports dialog box function almost identically to the <u>E</u>dit button. The only difference is that the end result for both <u>N</u>ew and <u>C</u>opy is a new report name to be added to the Custom Reports list. Use <u>N</u>ew to design a report from the ground up. Use <u>C</u>opy to use an existing report as a starting point for a new report. In all cases, the instructions begin at the Custom Reports dialog box.

After you've modified or created a report, you can print or preview your custom report directly from the Custom Reports dialog box by clicking the <u>P</u>rint or Previe<u>w</u> buttons.

Note

The <u>C</u>opy button is dimmed for the Base Calendar and Project Summary reports, because they can only be edited for simple text formatting changes.

CREATING REPORTS

You can create a new report either by copying an existing report and making changes to the copy or by designing an entirely new report "from scratch." Regardless of the method you choose to create a new report, after it is created, you will use the same methods for customizing the new report. What follows are the steps to create the new report. Other sections in this chapter discuss customizing the report after it has been created.

CREATING A NEW REPORT BASED ON AN EXISTING REPORT

One of the best and fastest ways to create a report is to start with one of the predefined Project reports that is similar to a report you need. By making a copy of the existing report, you take advantage of the features of that report, while leaving the original report unchanged for use in the future. Modifying a copy of an existing report is quick and convenient.

Tip from Tim and the Project Team

It is recommended that you use one of the predefined reports as a basis for your new report, because most of the work in creating the report has already been done. If none of the predefined reports are similar to what you are looking for, you will have to design a new report.

If you want to copy an existing report, follow these steps:

1. Choose <u>V</u>iew, <u>R</u>eports.
2. Double-click the C<u>u</u>stom category, or click once and choose <u>S</u>elect.
3. From the list in the Custom Report dialog box, choose the report you want to copy, and then choose the <u>C</u>opy button.
4. The report definition dialog box for that report will appear. The defined features will be identical to the original report. The only difference will be that the report name will be preceded by "Copy of." For example, the Critical Tasks report would be renamed "Copy of Critical Tasks."

5. In the Name box, enter a descriptive name for the report.

6. Complete the dialog box for the report type you have chosen to copy. Explicit instructions for making changes to the various types of Project reports are discussed in detail later in this chapter.

DESIGNING A NEW REPORT

Another method for creating a report is to design one from scratch. Use this method if none of the existing predefined reports are similar to the report you need. You must use this method if you want to create a monthly calendar report, because there are no predefined examples available for editing.

When you create a new report, you must select one of four report templates: Task, Resource, Monthly Calendar, or Crosstab.

- **Task**—A report that lists all the tasks (or optionally only those selected by a filter) and might include various details about each task. Any of the task fields can be added to this report by basing the report on a task table that includes that field.

- **Resource**—A report that lists all the resources (or optionally only those selected by a filter) and might include various details about each resource. Any of the resource fields can be added to this report by basing the report on a resource table that includes that field.

- **Monthly Calendar**—A monthly calendar that is similar to the Calendar view. This type of report is not included in the five predefined categories, but can be used to create a new report.

- **Crosstab**—A report in table format that shows cost or work summaries by time period for the project's tasks or for its resources. You choose whether tasks or resources will be listed in the rows; whether columns will cover days, weeks, months, or other time periods; and which cost or work value you want summed for each time period.

To create a new report, follow these steps:

1. Choose View, Reports.

2. Double-click the Custom category, or click once and choose Select.

3. Choose the New button.

4. You will see the Define New Report dialog box (shown in Figure 25.5) with the four basic types of reports listed. All new reports must be modeled after one of these types.

5. Choose a type and select OK.

6. The report definition dialog box for the report type you selected displays with the default settings (see Figure 25.6). A default report name, like Report 1, appears in the Name box.

Figure 25.5
When designing a new report, choose one of these four report types.

Figure 24.6
The report options in the definitions dialog box will vary, depending on the type of report selected. The Crosstab definitions dialog box is displayed here.

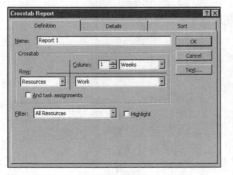

7. In the Name box, enter a descriptive name for the report.

8. Complete the dialog box for the report type you have chosen. Explicit instructions for customizing the various types of Project reports are discussed in detail later in this chapter.

USING THE COMMON CUSTOMIZATION CONTROLS

There are some custom options where the steps to make the changes are the same regardless of whether you are changing an existing predefined report, a copy of a report, or a newly created report. You can change the way reports look by changing the text format, page setup options, or order in which the information is sorted. The following sections describe some of the common custom options.

CONTROLLING PAGE BREAKS IN A REPORT

If your report is based on a particular view, Project will normally reflect the manual page breaks you have inserted in that view (using the Insert, Page Break command). You cannot put page breaks directly into a report.

If you want to print a draft copy of your report on as few pages as possible, you can tell Project to ignore page breaks by clearing the Manual Page Breaks box in the Print dialog box (see Figure 25.7).

FORMATTING TEXT IN A REPORT

Whenever you edit a report or design a new report, you will be presented with the definition dialog box for that report. While some of the options differ from report type to report type, you will always be able to format the way the text appears in the report. Choose the

Text button in the definitions dialog box. If the dialog box has multiple tabs, the Text button appears on each tab. Note that the text styles are automatically displayed when you edit the Project Summary report, because this is the only option you can customize on this report. In Figure 25.8, the Overallocated Resources report is being edited.

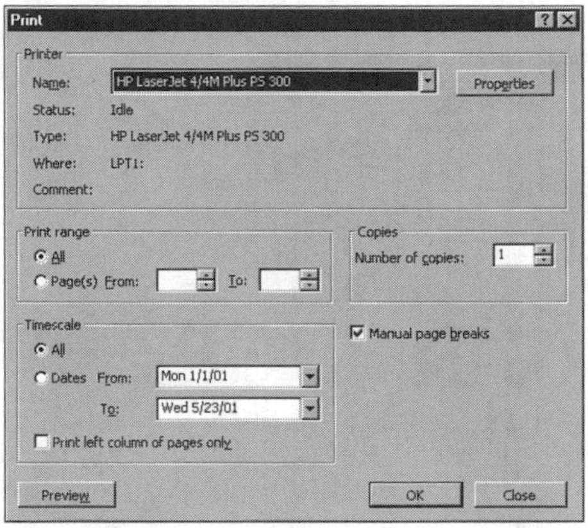

Figure 25.7
Choose File, Print to access the Print dialog box.

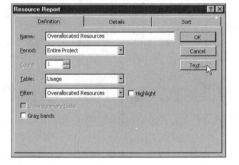

Figure 25.8
Use the Text button to customize the font styles used in a report.

The Text Styles dialog box (see Figure 25.9) appears after selecting the Text button in the definitions dialog box. This dialog box allows you to select special formatting for a category of tasks and resembles the dialog box that appears when you choose Format, Text Styles from the main menu. Use the Text Styles dialog box to make certain types of information stand out in your report by changing the size, font, or formatting of categories of text. The default format of each category is 8-point type with no distinguishing characteristics, unless specified in parentheses. By default, all the text will be changed unless you choose a specific type of information.

Specific information type choices depend on the type of report you are modifying.

When formatting text in a report, you will need to format the text separately for each individual report and separately from the text format shown in the current view. There is no connection between the text format in the view and the text format in the report. For example, even if summary tasks are shaded in your current Gantt view, they will not appear shaded in a task report unless you specify the Shade option in the Text Styles dialog box.

Figure 25.9
Use the Item to Change drop-down list to choose the text to format.

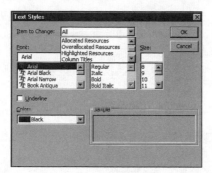

CHOOSING THE PAGE SETUP OPTIONS FOR A REPORT

While modifying your report, you might decide you'd prefer it to have different margins, or to display a different header. These changes are controlled by the page setup. To access the page setup options from the Custom Reports dialog box, choose the Setup button. If you are previewing the report, choose the Page Setup button at the top of the preview screen. No matter how you access the Page Setup dialog box, the options you have depend on the type of report you are modifying.

→ For additional information on how to change setup options, **see** "Changing the Page Setup," **p. 546**

CHANGING THE SORT ORDER FOR A REPORT

You can sort the order of the rows in all task, resource, and crosstab reports. From the definitions dialog box, select the Sort tab to access the Sort options for the report. The Sort tab in the Crosstab Report dialog box (shown in Figure 25.10) looks similar to the Sort By dialog box used with the Project, Sort, Sort By command. The options on the Sort tab allow you to sort by as many as three fields in the report. Each Sort By field may be sorted in Ascending or Descending order. For an explanation of the Text options, see "Formatting Text in a Report," earlier in this chapter.

When sorting the information in a report, there is no connection between the sort displayed in a view and the sort selected in a report. Therefore, you can print a report sorted by a specific field, such as Priority (for tasks) or Name (for resources), without affecting the task order in your current working view.

COLLAPSING TASK DETAIL IN A REPORT

There are two things that affect the level or type of tasks that appear in task, crosstab, or monthly reports—the outline level of the tasks and filters. If the outline is collapsed in the view when you print a report, the subordinate tasks that are hidden will not be displayed in the report. You must expand the outline before you print the report if you want all tasks to be displayed. However, the reports ignore any filter that might have been applied to the current view onscreen. You can select filters within the report definitions to be automatically applied regardless of the filter that might or might not be applied to the active view. Note, however, that subordinate tasks hidden by a collapsed outline at the time the report is print-ed are not included in the report, even though the defined filter usually selects these tasks. Collapsing an outline overrides the filter.

→ To learn more about hiding or showing subtasks, **see** "Collapsing and Expanding the Outline," **p. 186**

→ To learn more about filtering for specific tasks, **see** "Using Filters," **p. 512**

Figure 25.10
Change the sort order of the rows displayed in a report with the controls on the Sort tab.

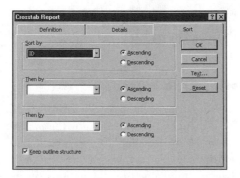

CUSTOMIZING SPECIFIC REPORT TYPES

There are five basic types of reports available in Microsoft Project: task list, resource list, monthly calendar, crosstab, and project summary. Of these reports, the task lists and resource lists have the most options for customization. In each case, you can select the columns of information to be displayed, the filter to be applied, and the amount of support-ing detail about the tasks or resources listed. The crosstab reports also are flexible in allow-ing you to select which task or resource detail you want to examine by given time period. Most of the task, resource, and crosstab reports allow the addition of gridlines and gray bands.

The monthly calendar and Project Summary reports are very specific types of reports. Each is addressed separately in sections later in this chapter.

All reports allow you to use text formatting to further organize the information for easier reading. You can edit reports to change the table and filter used and to change the details that are shown (for task and resource reports), the column and row information (for crosstab reports), the sort order for presenting the details (for non-calendar reports), and the use of border lines in the report.

CUSTOMIZING THE PROJECT SUMMARY REPORT

The Project Summary report is a specific predefined report listed under the Overview cate-gory, and the only one of its kind. This report cannot be copied. The only change you can make to this report is formatting the appearance of the text. Figure 25.11 shows a sample Project Summary report. The project name, company name, and project manager name fields that appear in the header are taken from the Title, Company, and Manager fields in the Properties dialog box. Any task notes added to the Project Summary Task or in the Comments field at the bottom of the Properties dialog box appear at the bottom of the Project Summary report. To enter or change the text for these project values, choose File, Properties. Then choose the Summary tab.

Figure 25.11
The Project Summary report cannot be customized beyond changing text fonts. The title rows are enhanced in this example.

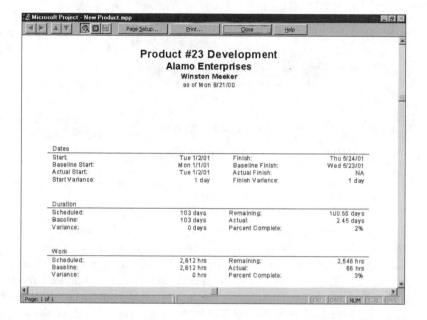

To change the formatting of the text for the Project Summary report, choose the report name from the Reports list in the Custom Reports dialog box. Then choose the Edit button. The Report Text dialog box is displayed. Figure 25.12 shows an example of this dialog box. Use the Item to Change drop-down list to choose the text you would like to format. Change the formats for the Project Name, Company Name, Manager Name, and Details. Select the OK button to return to the Custom Reports dialog box. The report in Figure 25.11 was printed with Times New Roman, 14-point text for the project name (New Product Development), 12-point text for the company name, and 10-point text for the project manager name and details.

CUSTOMIZING THE CALENDAR TYPE REPORTS

The two calendar reports, as shown in Table 25.1, are in fact the same report. Normally a report that is listed in one of the special categories also is listed in the Custom category. However, the Working Days report does not appear in the Custom category. Instead, the Base Calendar report is listed. These reports show the work days, non-working days, and work hours for each base calendar defined for the current file. Each base calendar will be printed on a separate page.

PART

VII

CH

25

Figure 25.12
Use the Report Text dialog box to format text styles in your Project Calendar reports.

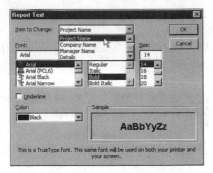

TABLE 25.1 PREDEFINED CALENDAR REPORTS

Report Name	Report Category
Base Calendar	Custom
Working Days	Overview

The only option in the Base Calendar report that can be changed is the text format for the Calendar Name and the Details of the report. To edit the Base Calendar report, choose Base Calendar from the Reports list in the Custom Reports dialog box. Then choose the Edit button. The Report Text dialog box appears as in the illustration for the Project Summary report (refer to Figure 25.12). Use the Item to Change drop-down list to choose the text you would like to format. Select the OK button to return to the Custom Reports dialog box. Then choose Print or Preview to proceed with printing the report. Refer to Chapter 13 for more information on print options. The Base Calendar report cannot be copied, nor can you use its format when creating a new report.

CUSTOMIZING TASK TYPE REPORTS

The task reports include all reports that are organized around tasks rather than resources and that are not crosstab reports. Table 25.2 lists all the task reports and the report category from the View Reports group in which they can be found.

TABLE 25.2 PREDEFINED TASK REPORTS

Report Name	Report Category
Budget	Costs
Completed Tasks	Current Activities
Critical Tasks	Overview
Earned Value	Costs
Milestones	Overview
Overbudget Tasks	Costs
Should Have Started Tasks	Current Activities

TABLE 25.2   CONTINUED

Report Name	Report Category
Slipping Tasks	Current Activities
Task	(Custom only)
Tasks in Progress	Current Activities
Tasks Starting Soon	Current Activities
Top-Level Tasks	Overview
Unstarted Tasks	Current Activities
To Do List	Assignments

Customizing a report can be accomplished either from the specific category to which the report belongs, or through the Custom category. For the purposes of this discussion, we will be accessing the reports from the Custom category list. When you have selected the report you would like to customize, choose Edit. The dialog box that appears is named for the report you selected. For example, if you selected the Task report to edit, the dialog box would be named Task Report (see Figure 25.13). There are three tabs in this dialog box: Definition, Details, and Sort. Though not all options are available for all reports, all the options available on each tab are discussed in the following sections.

Figure 25.13
The report editing dialog box is named for the report being edited—here the Task report.

CHANGING THE DEFINITIONS FOR A CUSTOM TASK REPORT

Select the Definition tab to see the current settings for the basic content of the report (the table, filter, and timescale). To change the columns of data to be displayed to the right of each task in the report, select the Table box and choose one of the tables from the drop-down list. The Table drop-down list displays all 16 of the standard task tables, plus any task tables created with the View, Tables command. If the standard task tables do not have the fields that you need for your custom report, you might want to create a custom table that includes the fields you choose. Then use the new custom table as the source table for your report.

→ For a list of the standard task tables and the fields these tables display, **see** "The Task Tables," **p. 875**

→ For help in creating your own custom tables, **see** "Using and Creating Tables," **p. 949**

You have the option of grouping tasks by time interval, but the default is to show the entire project with no intervals listed. To change the time period in the report, choose the Period box and choose Years, Quarters, Months, Weeks, or Days. You also can indicate how frequent the interval should be. Use the Count box to indicate if each interval should be displayed every other interval, every third interval, and so on.

For example, by default the Count is 1, which means each interval will display. If you choose Quarters in the Period box, the tasks will be grouped by quarter, with each quarter showing. If you change the Count to 2, you will only see labels for every other quarter (Quarter 1 and Quarter 3). The data for Quarter 2 will be displayed; it just won't have a label indicating when it begins. A better example of how the time grouping might be useful is if the resources are paid every two weeks. In this case, you might want a list of the related task assignments grouped by pay periods. Specifically, you need to set the Period to weeks and also set the Count box to 2. See Figure 25.15 for an example of a biweekly grouping.

Any filter that has been applied to the view has no impact on the filter that is used with the report. To filter the list of tasks, choose the Filter drop-down list and select a filter from the list. Remember that if you want to use a custom filter, you must create it first, using the Project, Filtered For command. If you choose an interactive filter, the interactive prompt appears each time you print or preview the report. As shown in Figure 25.14, the interactive Using Resource filter has been chosen.

To use the filter as a highlight filter only, check the Highlight check box. Tasks that meet the filter criteria are shaded. To display only the filtered resources, clear this check box.

Mark the Show Summary Tasks check box if you want to have each detail task shown with its summary tasks. This is useful if the detail task names are general, similar, or are duplicated within the same schedule. Having the detail tasks associated with a more descriptive summary task will explain them more fully for the reader of the report.

Mark the Gray Bands check box if you want gray horizontal lines to separate the time periods.

Figure 25.14 shows the Task Report dialog box with customized Definition options. Figure 25.15 displays the resulting report using the Task Report.

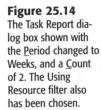

Figure 25.14
The Task Report dialog box shown with the Period changed to Weeks, and a Count of 2. The Using Resource filter also has been chosen.

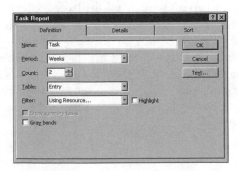

Figure 25.15
This is a preview of the customized task report, with the settings selected in Figure 25.14.

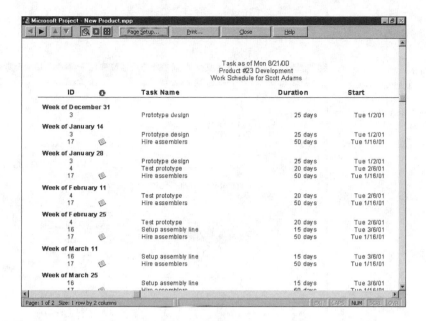

CHANGING THE DETAILS FOR A CUSTOM TASK REPORT

Some simple keystrokes can lift details about your tasks from your schedule to include in your report. The Details tab of your Task Report definition dialog box (see Figure 25.16) includes several categories of details that can be selected with check boxes.

Figure 25.16
You can include additional information in your report using the options on the Details tab of the Task Report dialog box.

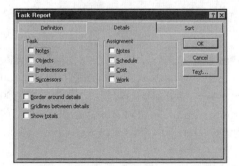

Depending on the Period indicated on the Definition tab, some of the detail options might not be available. These categories are explained in the following list:

- Under the Task heading, you can mark any of four boxes:
  - Select Notes to include notes you have written for any of your tasks (using the Notes icon on the Standard toolbar).
  - Select Objects if you want to include objects you have created using another Windows application, such as Microsoft Word or Excel. An example of an object might be a chart done in Microsoft Excel that shows the costs associated with a group of detail tasks under a summary task (see Figure 25.17).

→ For additional information on inserting objects, **see** "Placing Objects into Microsoft Project," **p. 828**

Figure 25.17
The Top Level Tasks report, with an Excel chart object displayed in the report.

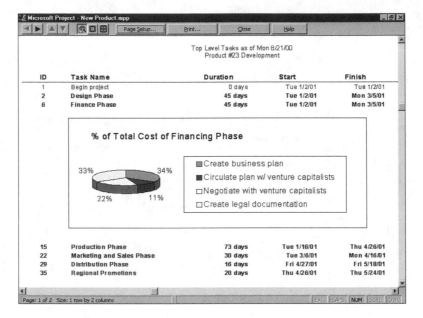

- Select the Predecessors check box if you want to include a list of the predecessor tasks with Type and Lag information under each task.
- Select the Successors check box if you want to include a list of the successor tasks with Type and Lag information under each task..

■ Under the Assignment heading, you can display many kinds of details about each resource by selecting any of the check boxes. Mark the Notes, Schedule, Cost, and Work check boxes to show details of the task assignments for the resource.

Three fields always appear onscreen for the Schedule, Cost, and Work detail sub-charts: Resource ID, Resource Name, and Units (of Resource Assigned). The following list shows the rest of the fields for each sub-chart:

Sub-chart	Fields
Notes	Assignment Notes
Schedule	Work (Scheduled Work), Delay, Start (Scheduled), Finish (Scheduled)
Cost	Cost (Scheduled Cost), Baseline Cost, Actual Cost, Remaining (Scheduled Cost)
Work	Work (Scheduled Work) Overtime Work, Baseline Work, Actual Work, Remaining Work (Scheduled)

If you choose two or three detail tables, Project will combine the fields into one table if the report has landscape as the orientation in the Setup options. The Work field will not be repeated if the Schedule and Worktables are combined.

- Add notes to an assignment to keep track of information specific to that assignment, such as the rate of work or scheduling assumptions. Notes must be added in Task Usage or Resource Usage views. These are a separate set of notes, not related to notes added to tasks or resources.

- If you want the detail sub-chart to be enclosed in border lines, mark the Border Around Details check box.

- If you want to see gridlines between each task, mark the Gridlines Between Details check box.

- Mark the Show Totals check box if you want to show totals at the bottom of the report for all columns in your table containing numeric information.

Tip from Tim and the Project Team

When displaying the details, it makes the report easier to read if a border surrounds the details; mark the Border Around Details option to display the border.

Figure 25.18 shows the Cost details surrounded by a border for all the tasks in the project.

Figure 25.18
A Task Report customized to show a sub-chart with Cost details. A border encloses the cost information.

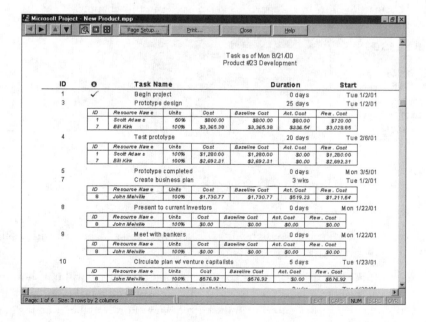

CHANGING THE TEXT FORMATTING IN A TASK REPORT

You can access the Text button from any of the tabs in the Task Report dialog box. The Text Styles dialog box (shown in Figure 25.19) allows you to select special formatting for a category of tasks and resembles the Format, Text Styles dialog box from the main menu. Use this dialog box to make certain types of information stand out in your report by changing the size, font, or formatting of categories of text. The default format of each category is 8-point type with no distinguishing characteristics, unless specified in parentheses.

The categories of tasks available for special formatting in Task Reports are as follows:

> All (default category)
>
> Noncritical Tasks
>
> Critical Tasks
>
> Milestone Tasks
>
> Summary Tasks (default is bold)
>
> Marked Tasks
>
> Highlighted Tasks (shaded)
>
> Column Titles (default is bold 9-point type)
>
> External Tasks
>
> Task Details (default is italic 7-point type)
>
> Totals

More specific information about formatting text in a report can be found in the section "Formatting Text in a Report," covered earlier in this chapter.

Figure 25.19
Use the Text Styles dialog box to format the text in the report. The Item to Change list box provides several choices of how to enhance the text.

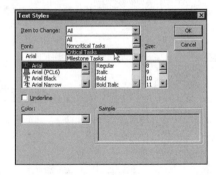

Figure 25.20 displays a task report with summary tasks formatted with a slightly larger font, and milestone tasks formatted in bold and italic.

Remember the text formatting you have altered in the view will not show up in the report. You will need to format the text separately for each individual task report and separately from the text format showing in the current view. For example, even if summary tasks are shaded in your current Gantt view, they will not appear shaded in a task report unless you specify the shading in the Text Styles box from the Task Report dialog box for the individual report.

Figure 25.20
Use text fonts to emphasize types of tasks in the report.

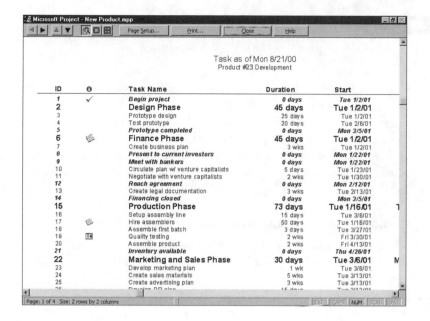

SORTING TASKS IN A TASK REPORT

The Sort tab is identical for all custom reports. See the section "Changing the Sort Order for a Report," earlier in this chapter, for more information.

After you have made the custom changes you want, select OK from any of the dialog box's three tabs to return to your Custom Reports dialog box. From there you can Preview or Print the report.

CUSTOMIZING RESOURCE TYPE REPORTS

The resource reports include all reports that are organized around resources. Table 25.4 lists all the resource reports and the category from the View Reports dialog box in which they can be found.

TABLE 25.4 PREDEFINED RESOURCE REPORTS

Report Name	Category
Resource	Custom
Resource (material)	Custom
Resource (work)	Custom
Who Does What	Assignments
Over-allocated Resources	Assignments
Overbudget Resources	Costs

Note

The Who Does What report is a crosstab report. Customizing crosstab reports is covered separately, later in this chapter.

Customizing a report can be accomplished either from the specific category the report belongs to or under the Custom category. We will be accessing the reports from the Custom category list in the following examples. When you have selected the report you would like to customize, choose Edit from the Custom dialog box. The Resource Report dialog box appears. There are three tabs in this dialog box: Definition, Details, and Sort. Although not all options are available for all reports, the options available on each tab are discussed in the following sections.

CHANGING THE DEFINITIONS FOR A CUSTOM RESOURCE REPORT

The Definition tab on the Resource Reports dialog box (shown in Figure 25.21) is similar to that for the task reports. The Table box lists the standard resource tables, including the new Hyperlink table, plus any custom resource tables created with the View, Tables command.

→ For a list of the standard resource tables and the fields these tables display, **see** "The Resource Tables," **p. 879**

Figure 25.21
The Definition tab of the Resource Report dialog box, shown with the default settings.

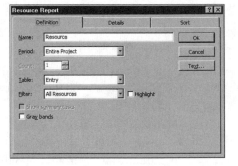

You can define a resource filter to use each time you print the report. To filter the list of resources, select the Filter drop-down list and then choose a filter from the list. If you choose an interactive filter, the interactive prompt appears each time you print the report. Remember that if you want to use a custom filter, you must create it first, using the Project, Filtered For command.

To use the filter as a highlight filter only, mark the Highlight check box; tasks that meet the Filter criteria are shaded. To display only the filtered resources, clear this check box.

To change the time period covered in each group in the report, choose the Period box and select one of these periods:

- Entire Project
- Years

- Half Years
- Quarters
- Months
- Thirds of Months (These are fixed dates on the first, eleventh, and twenty-first of each month.)
- Weeks
- Days

Using the Count box, you can stipulate that each time-period group includes multiple units of the time unit selected. If the resources are paid every two weeks, for example, you might want a list of those resources that worked during each pay period, along with their standard and overtime rates. In this case, you could apply a Custom Entry table, set the Period box to Weeks, and set the Count box to 2 (see Figure 25.22).

If you want to separate time periods with gray bands, mark the Gray Bands box.

Figure 25.22 displays the Resource Report dialog box with customized Definition options. A Custom Entry table, omitting the Resource Initials and Group fields, was used. Figure 25.23 displays the resulting report.

Figure 25.22
Use the Resource Report dialog box to customize the table, period, or filter used in the report.

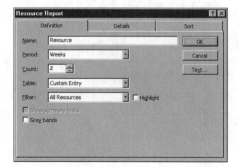

CHANGING THE DETAILS FOR A CUSTOM RESOURCE REPORT

Changing the details included in a custom resource report is much like changing details in a custom task report. The Details tab of the Resource Report definition dialog box gives you many options. Figure 25.24 shows the Resource Report dialog box with the Details tab selected.

Note

Unless you selected the time period Entire Project on the Definition tab, the following check boxes on the Details tab will be dimmed: Resource Notes and Objects; Assignment Notes, Cost, and Work; and Show Totals.

Figure 25.23
This report shows each resource that is scheduled to work each pay period (every two weeks), along with its rates.

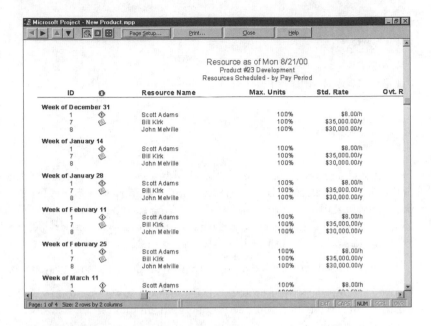

Figure 25.24
Use the Details tab of the Resource Report dialog box to select additional information you want to appear in the report.

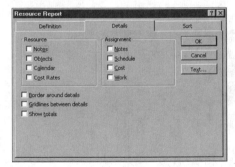

You can customize the following details:

- Select the Details tab to select the task and resource details to be included with each task. The options shown on the Details tab for resource reports (refer to Figure 25.24) vary slightly from those shown for task reports. Figure 25.25 shows a resource report with details information included.

- Under the Resource heading, you can mark one of four boxes:

  Select Notes to include notes you have written for any of your resources (using the Notes button on the Standard toolbar).

  Select Objects if you want to represent data you have created using another Windows application, such as Microsoft Word or Excel. An example of an object might be a Microsoft Excel graph of work hours assigned for a group of resources assigned to a group of tasks.

→ For additional information on inserting objects, **see** "Placing Objects into Microsoft Project," **p. 828**

Figure 25.25
Detail options in a resource report showing calendar and schedule information.

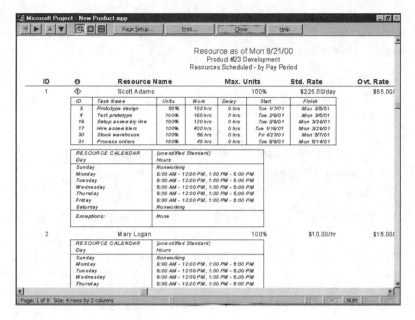

Select Calendar if you want to include resource calendars in the report.

Select Cost Rates if you want to see the cost rate tables for each resource. Refer to Chapter 8, "Defining Resources and Costs," for more information on how they are used.

- Under the Assignment heading, you can display many kinds of details about each resource (refer to Figure 25.25). Mark the Notes, Schedule, Cost, and Work check boxes to show details of the task assignments for the resource. The fields for each task assigned are the same as those listed under resource details on the Task Reports.

  Add notes to an assignment to keep track of information specific to that assignment, such as the rate of work or scheduling assumptions. Notes must be added in Task Usage or Resource Usage views. These are a separate set of notes, not related to notes added to tasks or resources.

- If you want the detail tables to be enclosed in border lines, mark the Border Around Details check box.

- To see gridlines separating the resources, mark the Gridlines Between Details box.

- Mark the Show Totals check box if you want to show totals at the bottom of the report for all columns in your table containing numeric information.

CHANGING THE TEXT FORMATTING IN A RESOURCE REPORT

You can access the Text button from any of the tabs in the Resource Report dialog box. The Text Styles dialog box allows you to select special formatting for a category of resources and resembles the dialog box that appears when you choose Format, Text Styles from the main menu. Use this box to make certain types of information stand out in your report by changing the size, font, or formatting of certain categories of text. The default format of each category is 8-point type with no distinguishing characteristics, unless specified in parentheses in the following list. Categories of resources available for special formatting in Resource Reports are the following:

All (default category)
Allocated Resources
Overallocated Resources
Highlighted Resources (shaded)
Column Titles (default is bold 9-point type)
Resource Details (default is italic 7-point type)
Totals

The "Formatting Text in a Report" section, earlier in this chapter, covers specific steps to format the text.

Remember the text formatting you have altered in the view is not related to the text formatting in the report. You will need to format the text separately for each individual task report and separately from the text format showing in the current view. For example, even if overallocated resources are highlighted in your current Resource Sheet view, they will not appear highlighted in a resource report unless you specify the format for highlighted text in the Text Styles dialog box.

SORTING TASKS IN A RESOURCE REPORT

The Sort tab on the Resource Report dialog box is identical for all custom reports. See the section "Changing the Sort Order for a Report," earlier in this chapter, for more information.

After you have made the custom changes you want, select OK from any of the dialog box's three tabs to return to your Custom Reports dialog box. From there, you can Preview or Print the report.

CUSTOMIZING CROSSTAB TYPE REPORTS

Crosstab reports show cost amounts or work hours by task or resource in a grid format by selected time period. Table 25.6 lists the predesigned crosstab reports available for customizing.

TABLE 25.6   PREDEFINED CROSSTAB REPORTS

Report Name	Category
Crosstab	Custom
Who Does What When	Assignments
Weekly Cash Flow	Costs
Resource Usage	Workload
Resource Usage (material)	Workload
Resource Usage (work)	Workload
Task Usage	Workload

If you would like to customize one of Project's predefined crosstab reports, it is recommended that you make a copy of the report first, and then customize the copy. This leaves the standard report intact.

You can customize a report either from the specific category the report belongs to or under the Custom category. From the Custom category list, select the crosstab report you would like to customize and choose Edit. The Crosstab Report dialog box appears. There are three tabs in this dialog box: Definition, Details, and Sort. Not all options are available for all reports.

CHANGING THE DEFINITIONS FOR A CUSTOM CROSSTAB REPORT

Selecting the type of information to be displayed in your crosstab report is done through the Definition tab of the Crosstab Report dialog box. Select the Definition tab to display the Definition box for crosstab reports (see Figure 25.26).

Figure 25.26
The Definition tab on the Crosstab Report dialog box provides a unique way to display project information.

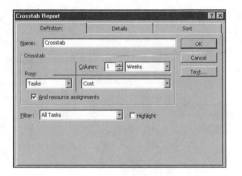

The Definition tab allows you to indicate whether you want to list tasks or resources down your rows by selecting one of the two in the Row box. The available information to include in the grid for your row information depends on whether you are working with Tasks or Resources. Table 25.7 outlines these options.

TABLE 25.7   CROSSTAB ROW AND COLUMN ALTERNATIVES

Row Choice	Options
Tasks	Actual Cost
	Actual Overtime Work
	Actual Work
	ACWP (Actual Cost of Work Performed)
	Baseline Cost
	Baseline Work
	BCWP (Budgeted Cost of Work Performed)

TABLE 25.7 CONTINUED

Row Choice	Options
	BCWS (Budgeted Cost of Work Scheduled)
	Cost (Scheduled)
	Cumulative Cost (Scheduled, Time-phased)
	Cumulative Work (Scheduled, Time-phased)
	CV (Cost Variance)
	Fixed Cost
	Overtime Work (Scheduled)
	Regular Work (Scheduled)
	SV (Schedule Variance)
	Work (Scheduled)
Resources	Actual Cost
	Actual Overtime Work
	Actual Work
	ACWP (Actual Cost of Work Performed)
	Baseline Cost
	Baseline Work
	BCWS (Budgeted Cost of Work Scheduled)
	Cost (Scheduled)
	Cumulative Cost (Scheduled, Time-phased)
	Cumulative Work (Scheduled, Time-phased)
	CV (Cost Variance)
	Overallocation
	Overtime Work (Scheduled)
	Peak Units
	Percent Allocation
	Regular Work (Scheduled)
	Remaining Availability
	SV (Schedule Variance)
	Unit Availability
	Work (Scheduled)
	Work Availability

After you select the information to appear in the Row and Column fields, you also might select the time period represented by each column in the grid with the Column section. Figure 25.27 shows a crosstab report that lists monthly cumulative work by resources.

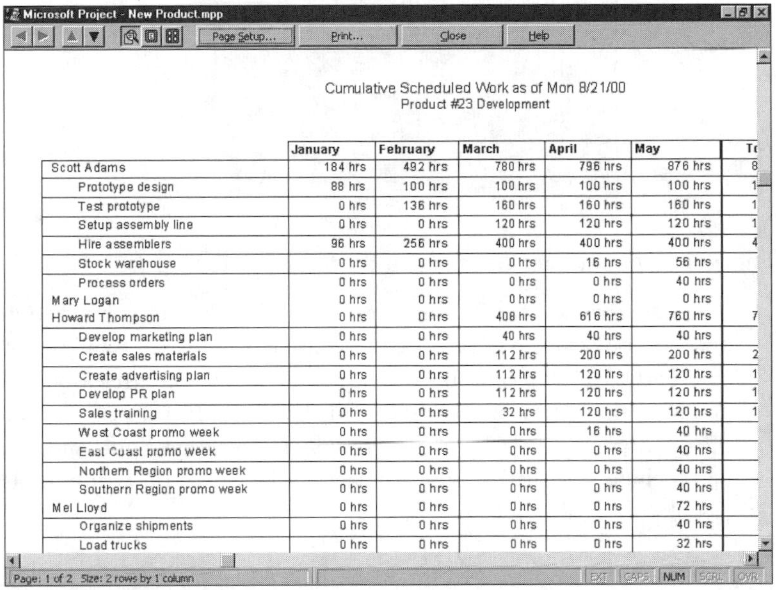

Cumulative Scheduled Work as of Mon 8/21/00
Product #23 Development

	January	February	March	April	May	To
Scott Adams	184 hrs	492 hrs	780 hrs	796 hrs	876 hrs	8
Prototype design	88 hrs	100 hrs	100 hrs	100 hrs	100 hrs	1
Test prototype	0 hrs	136 hrs	160 hrs	160 hrs	160 hrs	1
Setup assembly line	0 hrs	0 hrs	120 hrs	120 hrs	120 hrs	1
Hire assemblers	96 hrs	256 hrs	400 hrs	400 hrs	400 hrs	4
Stock warehouse	0 hrs	0 hrs	0 hrs	16 hrs	56 hrs	
Process orders	0 hrs	0 hrs	0 hrs	0 hrs	40 hrs	
Mary Logan	0 hrs	0 hrs	0 hrs	0 hrs	0 hrs	
Howard Thompson	0 hrs	0 hrs	408 hrs	616 hrs	760 hrs	7
Develop marketing plan	0 hrs	0 hrs	40 hrs	40 hrs	40 hrs	
Create sales materials	0 hrs	0 hrs	112 hrs	200 hrs	200 hrs	2
Create advertising plan	0 hrs	0 hrs	112 hrs	120 hrs	120 hrs	1
Develop PR plan	0 hrs	0 hrs	112 hrs	120 hrs	120 hrs	1
Sales training	0 hrs	0 hrs	32 hrs	120 hrs	120 hrs	1
West Coast promo week	0 hrs	0 hrs	0 hrs	16 hrs	40 hrs	
East Coast promo week	0 hrs	0 hrs	0 hrs	0 hrs	40 hrs	
Northern Region promo week	0 hrs	0 hrs	0 hrs	0 hrs	40 hrs	
Southern Region promo week	0 hrs	0 hrs	0 hrs	0 hrs	40 hrs	
Mel Lloyd	0 hrs	0 hrs	0 hrs	0 hrs	72 hrs	
Organize shipments	0 hrs	0 hrs	0 hrs	0 hrs	40 hrs	
Load trucks	0 hrs	0 hrs	0 hrs	0 hrs	32 hrs	

Figure 25.27
This figure represents a crosstab report showing cumulative work by resources with task assignments.

Part VII
Ch 25

As with resource and task reports, you can select a filter. If you choose to list tasks as your row information, you will be presented with your list of task filters in the Filter box. If you choose to list resources as your row information, you will see your list of resource filters in the Filter box. Remember that if you want to use a custom filter, you must create it first, using the Project, Filtered For command.

→ For additional information on creating your own filters, **see** "Creating Custom Filters," **p. 968**

If you are listing resources in your rows and want to include details on assigned tasks for each resource, check the And Task Assignments box. The box changes its label to And Resource Assignments if you choose Tasks as your Row information, and it will list all assigned resources for the tasks listed in your report. Figure 25.27 shows monthly cumulative work by resources with task assignments included.

Changing the Details for a Custom Crosstab Report

Adding details to a custom crosstab report is done through the same Details tab available in the custom report dialog box for task and resource reports. However, the details you add to a crosstab report differ somewhat from task and resource reports because the type of information shown in a crosstab report is primarily numeric rather than descriptive. Figure 25.28 shows the Details tab for a crosstab report with all details selected, except gridlines between resources assigned to the same task.

Figure 25.28
The Details tab of the Crosstab Report dialog box is notably different from the Task Report and the Resource Report dialog boxes.

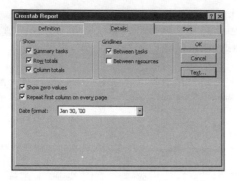

The Details options are described in the following list:

- The Show section allows you to print Ro<u>w</u> Totals and <u>C</u>olumn Totals by checking the appropriate boxes. If both boxes are checked, an overall total is printed at the intersection of the row and column totals. If you chose to list tasks as your Ro<u>w</u> information, you have the option of showing <u>S</u>ummary Tasks. If you select resources for your Ro<u>w</u> information, the <u>S</u>ummary Tasks option will be grayed out. Summary task information will include information from all detail tasks even if they are not displayed on the report (see Figure 25.29).

Figure 25.29
Task crosstab report showing scheduled weekly work with most details displayed.

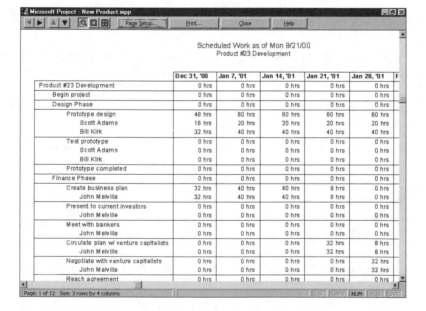

- You can show horizontal gridlines between your tasks or resources by clicking the appropriate box in the Gridlines section.

- The Show <u>Z</u>ero Values box allows you to show or suppress 0s for the grid box representing a time period when the time period's value is 0.

- Check the Repeat First Column on Every Page option when your crosstab report extends to more than one page horizontally, and you want the row titles in the first column to repeat on every page.

- The Date Format box allows you to specify the date as it will appear along the top of your grid, representing your time period.

CHANGING THE TEXT FORMATTING AND SORTING IN A CROSSTAB REPORT

You can access the Text button from any of the tabs in the Crosstab Report dialog box. The Text Styles dialog box allows you to select special formatting and resembles the Format, Text Styles dialog box from the main menu. Use formatting to make certain types of information stand out in your report by changing the size, font, or formatting of certain categories of text. The default format of each category is 8-point type with no distinguishing characteristics, unless specified in parentheses. Choose Item to Change to select the text you want to format.

The "Formatting Text in a Report" section, earlier in this chapter, covers specific steps to format the text.

Remember the text formatting you have altered in the view is not related to the text formatting in the report. You will need to format the text separately for each individual task report and separately from the text format showing in the current view.

The Sort tab for this dialog box is identical for all custom reports. See the section "Changing the Sort Order for a Report," earlier in this chapter, for more information.

After you have made the custom changes you want, select OK from any of the dialog box's three tabs to return to your Custom Reports dialog box. From there you can Preview or Print the report.

CUSTOMIZING THE MONTHLY CALENDAR TYPE REPORT

Microsoft Project offers the option of a monthly calendar report for those who want to report task information in a calendar format. This is not a report available in any other category but Custom, and must be designed from scratch.

The monthly calendar report offers fewer formatting options than the Calendar view but can be customized to print any individual's resource calendar (something the Calendar view cannot do). The resource calendar for each individual resource can be customized through the Tools, Change Working Time command from the menu.

→ For help on changing a resource's available time, **see** "Working Time," **p. 335**

The monthly calendar report is accessed only by clicking the New button from the Custom Reports dialog box. After that, select Monthly Calendar from the Define New Report dialog box, and select OK (see Figure 25.30).

Figure 25.30
The Define New Report dialog box is the only place you can find the monthly calendar report.

The Monthly Calendar Report Definition dialog box offers you choices for filtering, which base or resource calendar to display, and how to display and label tasks (see Figure 25.31).

Figure 25.31
The Monthly Calendar Report Definition dialog box, shown with the default settings.

You can choose any base or resource calendars to use for displaying the working and non-working days on the report. The advantage of this report over the Calendar view is that it prints any individual's resource calendar, reflecting his or her working and non-working days. To select the calendar to use for the report, choose the Calendar box, and then choose one of the base or resource calendars from the drop-down list.

You can apply one of the filters from the Filter drop-down list to limit the tasks displayed. You might apply the Using Resource filter, for example, to print a calendar to distribute to a certain resource, showing the tasks and dates when the resource is scheduled to work on the project.

To make the filter a highlight filter only, mark the Highlight check box. All tasks will be displayed, but the filtered tasks are displayed with the format chosen for Highlighted Tasks (see the text choices in the last item in the following list). If you select an interactive filter, the interactive prompt appears each time you preview or print the report.

The remaining options on the Monthly Calendar Report Definition dialog box regulate the display of the data, as shown in the following list:

- To distinguish working and non-working days on the calendar, mark the Gray Nonworking Days check box.
- If you decide to display bars for the tasks, you can choose to display breaks in the bars (from one week or month to the next) with dotted or solid lines at the bar ends. Mark the Solid Bar Breaks check box if you want solid lines. For dotted lines, leave the check box unmarked.

- If you want a gray band to separate the dates in the list, mark the Print Gray Bands check box.

- To show tasks as bars or lines that stretch across the calendar for the duration of the task, mark the Bars or Lines option button. To show the scheduled start and stop dates for tasks on the calendar, mark the Start/Finish Dates option button.

- Mark the check boxes for ID number, Name, and Duration if you want to include these field values in the label for the task. You can use any combination of these three values.

- If more tasks are assigned on a day than will fit on the calendar, an asterisk is displayed beside the day number, and the unprinted tasks appear in a list at the end of the report. The list is sorted by date.

- Choose the Text button to designate different text formats for parts of the report. You can select unique formats for different kinds of tasks (Noncritical, Critical, Milestone, Summary, Marked, and Highlighted) and for the labels in the calendar.

After you finish defining the monthly calendar report, select the OK button to return to the Custom Reports dialog box. You then can Print or Preview the report immediately or use the Close button to save the list of reports and print later.

Figure 25.32 shows an example of the settings in the Monthly Calendar Report Definition dialog box for a monthly calendar report filtered to show only the tasks assigned to Howard Thompson. The report also is defined to use the resource calendar for Howard Thompson. Figure 25.33 shows the resulting report, previewing the month of April 2001.

Figure 25.32
The Monthly Calendar Report Definition dialog box, customized to show a particular resource calendar and filter.

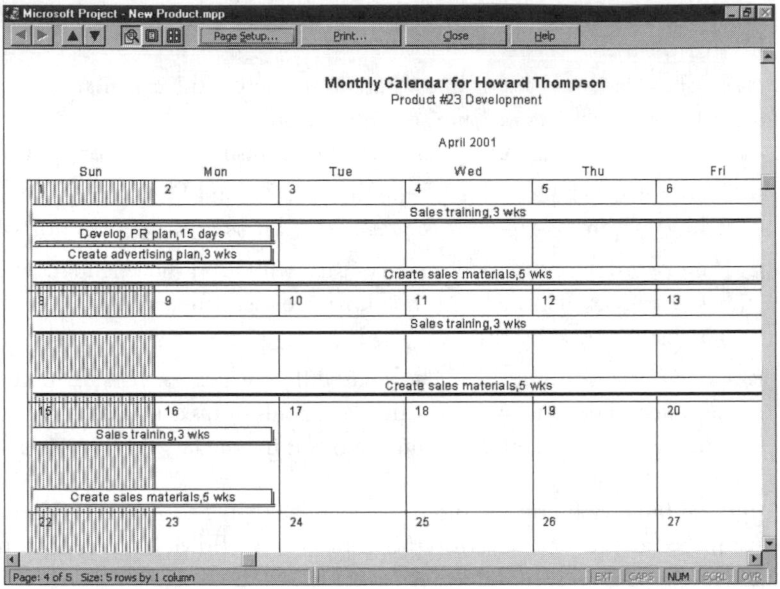

Figure 25.33
The monthly calendar report for an individual resource.

SAVING AND SHARING YOUR CUSTOM REPORTS

All the reports are saved with your project file, so remember to save your file if you have customized reports—even if you have not changed your task or resource information. If you want to make your custom reports available to all your project files or to other people sharing the same copy of Microsoft Project, you must copy these reports into the global template file, GLOBAL.MPT, with the Organizer. You can access the Organizer from the Custom Reports dialog box. All reports in the GLOBAL.MPT template file are available to all users of Microsoft Project sharing that GLOBAL.MPT file.

→ For additional information on the Organizer, **see** "Using the Organizer," **p. 128**

TROUBLESHOOTING

UNDOING CHANGES TO A PREDEFINED REPORT

I've modified one of the existing reports. I want to keep my modified report, but also want the original report available to use later. What should I do?

Access the Custom category of reports, through View, Reports. Using the Copy button in the Custom Reports dialog box, make a copy of the report you modified and rename it. Then using the Organizer button from the Custom Reports dialog box, access the Global template. Copy the report from the Global template to your project file. You now have your modified report and have reset the original report. For more information on using the Organizer and the Global template, see Chapter 4.

APPLYING FILTERS TO REPORTS

When I apply a task filter before running a report, Project ignores the filter and shows all the tasks anyway.

Any filter that has been applied to the view has no impact on the filter that is used with the report. Instead of filtering the view, you should customize the report design to include the filter.

DISTRIBUTING REPORTS BASED ON CUSTOM TABLES

I created a report based on a custom table and copied it into another user's file with the Organizer. But they get an error whenever they run the report stating that the "table...on which it is based has been deleted." Did I do something wrong?

When you use the Organizer to copy the custom report over to another file, you also must copy the custom table used by that report to the other file as well. Without the custom table, the custom report has no data source.

PART VIII

CUSTOMIZING AND PROGRAMMING MICROSOFT PROJECT 2000

CHAPTER 26

CUSTOMIZING TOOLBARS, MENUS, AND FORMS

In this chapter

ALTERING THE PERSONALIZED MENU AND TOOLBAR BEHAVIOR

The toolbars and menus in Microsoft Project provide an efficient means for you to interact with the projects you design. As you have discovered, commands on both the toolbars and menus are organized to group together the tasks you perform most often. You may also have discovered that while most of the toolbars and menus provide you with the commands you need, other commands might be unavailable or buried so deeply on a menu that they aren't convenient to use. Project provides a number of different features that enable you to customize the user interface to make your work easier and more efficient.

 Realizing that people use a handful of commands frequently, other commands occasionally, and some commands not at all, Microsoft has revamped the behavior of the menus and toolbars in Project 2000.

> **Note**
> Microsoft uses a rather complex formula for determining when to promote and demote items from prominence in the personalized menus—the computation involves the number of times the application is launched and how many successive launches a given feature goes unused. As you use commands, the ones you use more frequently appear on the menu, and ones you don't use at all get suppressed. The end result is that what you use most frequently ends up on the abbreviated personalized menus.

The personalized menus and toolbars are designed to increase your productivity. If you prefer to see the full set of toolbar icons and menu commands, you have several choices:

- You can change the toolbar option settings to display both the full Standard and Formatting toolbars, as they used to be displayed in previous versions of Project.

- You can double-click the menus to see the full list of commands, or you can permanently turn off the setting that hides menu commands you don't use frequently.

ADJUSTING THE MENU BEHAVIOR

If you want to see the full list of commands every time you click a menu, you can adjust the menu behavior in the Customize dialog box. Right-click a menu or toolbar, and choose Customize from the shortcut menu. In the Customize dialog box, click the Options tab (shown in Figure 26.1).

> **Note**
> You can also gain access to the Customize dialog box by selecting Tools, Customize, Toolbars or View, Toolbars, Customize.

Remove the check from the Menus Show Recently Used Commands First option and click Close to turn off the personalized menus. Making this change affects the menu behavior in all applications, not just the menu behavior in Project.

Figure 26.1
Personalized menus are turned on by default in Project 2000.

You can also customize the items that appear on the application menus (discussed later in this chapter).

ADJUSTING THE TOOLBAR BEHAVIOR

When you first open Project 2000, the Standard and Formatting toolbars share one line at the top of the window (see Figure 26.2). Initially, most of the Standard toolbar is displayed, and only a small part of the Formatting toolbar. There is a *move handle* in front of each toolbar with which you can move or adjust each toolbar. The mouse pointer changes to a four-headed arrow when positioned on the move handle. You can drag the Formatting toolbar move handle to the left to see more of the Formatting toolbar. However, to make room for these buttons, some of the buttons on the Standard toolbar will be hidden.

Note

You can also use the move handle to reposition a toolbar. If you drag a toolbar to the edge of the application window or to a place next to another docked toolbar, it becomes docked at that position.

Each toolbar has a set of default buttons that it displays. Although the Standard and Formatting toolbars share one line, there isn't enough space to show all the default buttons on both toolbars.

The buttons you use most frequently are displayed on the toolbar; the buttons you use least frequently are hidden—hence the name *personalized toolbars*. You access the hidden buttons through the More Buttons drop-down list at the end of the toolbar (refer to Figure 26.2). When you click a hidden button, that button is added to the toolbar. To make room for the button, however, one of the buttons that has *not* been used recently is placed on the More Buttons list.

If you want to see all the buttons on the Standard and Formatting toolbars, you can display the toolbars on separate rows. The easiest way to do this is to drag the move handle of the Formatting toolbar so that it is positioned beneath the Standard toolbar.

Figure 26.2
Both toolbars appear on one line at first.

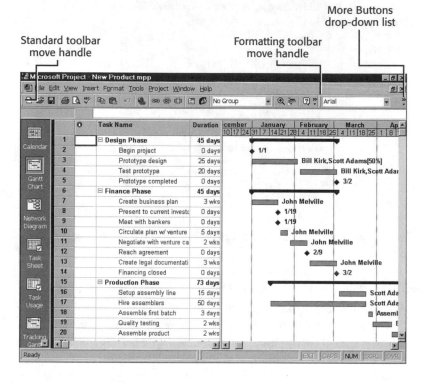

Alternatively, you can right-click any toolbar and choose Customize. On the Options tab, remove the check from the Standard and Formatting Toolbars Share One Row option and click Close.

> **Note**
>
> This setting is application specific; it does not change the appearance of the toolbars in the other Office programs.

QUICKLY CUSTOMIZING PERSONALIZED TOOLBARS

 If you have the Standard and Formatting toolbars sharing one line, there is a quick way to customize those toolbars. In addition to listing the active—but hidden—buttons, the More Buttons drop-down list also has an Add or Remove Buttons option to quickly customize a toolbar—a nice improvement in Project 2000.

When you click the Add or Remove Buttons drop-down list, the default buttons appear. There may be an arrow button at the top or bottom to see additional toolbar buttons. Figure 26.3 shows the list of buttons for the Standard toolbar in Project.

Buttons with check marks are from the default set of buttons associated with the toolbar. If you see a button grayed on the list, this indicates it is a button that is not part of the default set of buttons associated with the toolbar. It is a button that has been manually added to the toolbar through the Customize dialog box (the procedures to do this are discussed later in this chapter).

Figure 26.3
Click the Reset Toolbar option to display the original set of default buttons on the toolbar.

Scroll up to see additional toolbar buttons.

Button included in the toolbar's default set

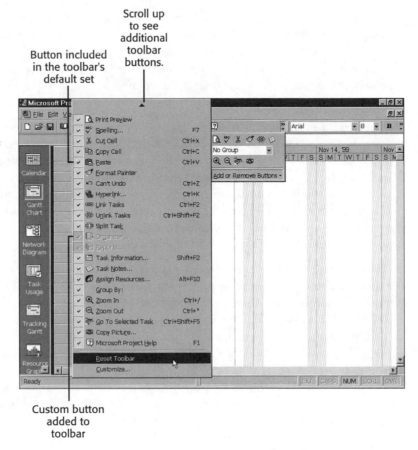

Custom button added to toolbar

CUSTOMIZING TOOLBARS AND MENUS

Buttons displayed on the toolbars provide shortcuts for executing menu commands. The menu commands used most frequently are attached to specific buttons and positioned on toolbars according to the types of tasks they perform. For example, the second button on the Standard toolbar in Microsoft Project displays a picture of a file folder opening. Clicking the button displays the Open dialog box, from which you choose a file to open. You would get the same result if you selected the Open command from the File menu. Because opening a file is a task you could conceivably perform frequently, Microsoft Project included a button on the Standard toolbar to reduce the number of steps you need to perform.

Microsoft has standardized its toolbars across applications so that those tasks common to all applications remain constant in their presentation on toolbars. As a result, after you become accustomed to using toolbar buttons in one application, you will recognize them in other applications. The Open button, for example, is available on the Standard toolbar of other Microsoft applications.

As you continue to work with Microsoft Project, you will find that some of the buttons on the toolbars are vital to the way you work, while others you use rarely. This is often determined by the type of work you do. In addition, you might find that there are tasks you perform frequently for which there are no toolbar buttons available. You can customize toolbars to remove the buttons you rarely use and replace them with buttons to help perform those tasks you do more frequently.

Each button on a toolbar runs a *macro*—a series of steps designed to perform a task. The example of clicking the Open button to display the Open dialog box (described earlier) runs a macro that contains the two steps required to perform the same task using the menus. When you create simple macros to perform tasks you use most frequently, you can assign them to toolbar buttons. For example, if you were to create a simple macro designed to turn on the Project Summary task, you can assign a toolbar button to run the macro and include the button on a toolbar. After it's assigned to a toolbar, all you have to do is click the toolbar button to perform the function.

In previous chapters, you may have created special views, tables, forms, or filters and found that they were stored as part of the project in which you created them. When you need to use them in another project, you have to copy them into the new project file or to the GLOBAL.MPT. Customizing toolbars and menus is different because toolbars and menus are part of the *application* file rather than a *project* file. As a result, changing the toolbars and menus makes the changes available to all projects you create or edit on your computer. They are stored as part of the GLOBAL.MPT file automatically. You can still copy them from the GLOBAL.MPT file to a project file when you want to include them in a file you are sending to someone else, or when you want to copy them to a different computer. Otherwise, copying them is not necessary.

REVIEWING THE BUILT-IN TOOLBARS

Microsoft Project 2000 includes 10 built-in toolbars that group tasks by type. Two of these toolbars appear by default when you start Microsoft Project. You can display any of the remaining eight toolbars as you need them. Of the 13 toolbars, there is one new toolbar added for Microsoft Project 2000—Network Diagram.

The two default toolbars are

- **Standard toolbar**—It provides access to the main Microsoft Project features. Buttons on the left end of this toolbar are found on the Standard toolbars of other Microsoft applications. Buttons on the right end of the toolbar are specific to Microsoft Project.

- **Formatting toolbar**—Buttons on this toolbar give you access to outlining, filters, and text formatting features. Many of the buttons on the right end of this toolbar are found on the Formatting toolbars of other Microsoft applications. Buttons on the left of this toolbar are frequently found on Outlining toolbars of other Microsoft applications.

The eleven additional toolbars included with Microsoft Project are

- **Analysis toolbar**—Provides access to the Adjust Dates macro. This macro is used when you need to adjust all dates in your project relative to a new start. Any tasks with constraints will also be adjusted.

- **Custom Forms toolbar**—Contains many of the buttons needed to customize tasks or resource information entry screens.

- **Database Upgrade Utility toolbar**—With this utility you can upgrade your Microsoft Project 98 database (.mpd), Microsoft Access (.mdb), or any supported ODBC-compliant database projects to the Microsoft Project 2000 database format.

- **Drawing toolbar**—Provides access to graphic drawing tools for drawing figures and text boxes in the Gantt Chart.

- **PERT Analysis toolbar**—Contains buttons which can display several different Gantt Charts (Optimistic, Expected, Pessimistic), the PERT Entry Form, and the PERT Entry Sheet.

- **Resource Management toolbar**—Provides access to tools for resolving resource over-allocations.

- **Tracking toolbar**—Provides access to the commands necessary to track progress and reschedule work on uncompleted tasks.

- **Visual Basic toolbar**—Displays buttons for recording, running, and editing macros.

- **Web toolbar**—Displays buttons that activate your World Wide Web browser, keep a list of your favorite Web sites, and assist you in moving through Web pages.

- **Workgroup toolbar**—Provides tools you can use to share project information with others in your workgroup.

- **Network Diagram toolbar**—Displays analysis tools for use with the Network Diagram view (which replaces the PERT Chart view). This toolbar provides quick access to several viewing options in the Network Diagram view as well as access to several useful commands such as Layout Now.

Many toolbar buttons are easy to identify and their use is self-explanatory. The purpose of some buttons, however, is difficult to determine. To help identify these buttons, point to the button and pause briefly. The purpose of the button appears in the form of a *ScreenTip*. When you need a more detailed description of a button, click the What's This? command from the Help menu, and then click the button for which you need more information. A definition of the button appears.

DISPLAYING TOOLBARS

Project enables you to show and hide toolbars using two different procedures. Perhaps the more efficient means is by selecting a toolbar from the Toolbar shortcut menu. Another way to select toolbars is through the View, Toolbars command. The procedures for displaying toolbars using both approaches are explained in the following sections.

PART

VIII

CH

26

The Toolbar shortcut menu contains a listing of all toolbars, as well as a command that lets you customize toolbars. To activate the shortcut menu, position the mouse pointer over one of the toolbars and click the right mouse button (see Figure 26.4). Notice that the Standard and Formatting toolbars have check marks next to them. These check marks indicate that the toolbars are currently displayed, or *active*. Other toolbars do not contain check marks, indicating that they are inactive.

Figure 26.4
The Toolbar shortcut menu lists all toolbars and identifies the toolbars that are displayed by a check mark. The menu can be used to display or hide individual toolbars.

Choose a toolbar that isn't checked to display the toolbar. If you choose a toolbar that is already active, the check mark disappears, thereby hiding the toolbar.

As an alternative, you can show and hide toolbars by selecting Toolbars from the View menu. The toolbar choices are identical to those shown in Figure 26.4.

POSITIONING TOOLBARS ON THE SCREEN

Most toolbars are set to position themselves at a docking location at the top of the screen. Each toolbar you activate docks beneath the other active toolbars in the order in which you activate them. When a toolbar is displayed, however, you can move it from the top of the screen to a new position. Toolbars can be *docked* at the sides or bottom of the screen or *floated* in a small window of their own in the middle of the screen. Toolbars that have combination boxes (buttons with a text box and an entry-list arrow) can be floated or docked at the top or bottom of the screen. The Group drop-down box on the Standard toolbar and the Font drop-down box on the Formatting toolbar are examples of combination (or combo) boxes. When docked on the sides of the screen, the combo boxes are not displayed. To reposition a toolbar, click the move handle bar that appears on the left edge of the toolbar or any separator bar in the toolbar. As you drag, the toolbar changes shape to fit the active position. When you have the toolbar placed where you want it, release the mouse button. Figure 26.5 identifies the move handle and the separator bars, and shows a docked and floating toolbar.

Notice that the floating toolbar has a title bar and a Close button. You can click the Close button to hide a floating toolbar or drag the title bar to dock it.

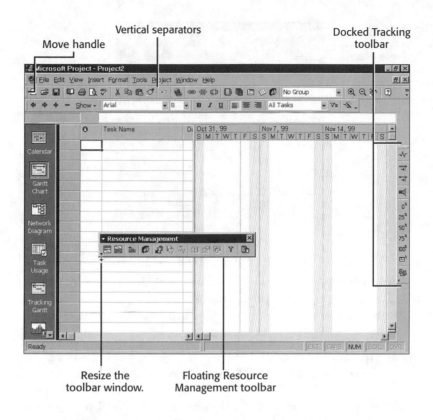

Vertical separators

Move handle

Docked Tracking toolbar

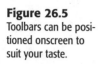

Figure 26.5
Toolbars can be positioned onscreen to suit your taste.

Resize the toolbar window.

Floating Resource Management toolbar

Tip from Tim and the Project Team

You also can double-click the toolbar background to make it float as a window in the middle of the screen. Double-click the title of a floating toolbar to return it to its docked position.

Floating toolbars can be resized in the same way you resize other windows. Position the mouse pointer on a border of the toolbar window (refer to Figure 26.5). The mouse pointer changes to a double-headed arrow. Drag to resize the toolbar.

USING THE CUSTOMIZE DIALOG BOX

Before you can create a new toolbar or customize an existing toolbar, you must display the Customize dialog box (see Figure 26.6). From the Customize dialog box, you can create new toolbars, add buttons or remove buttons from any active toolbar, resize combo boxes, rearrange the order of the buttons on a toolbar, and establish toolbar options, such as deactivating the setting, in which the Standard and Formatting toolbars share one row. If you are customizing a toolbar, the toolbar you want to customize must be active.

There are three ways to display the Customize dialog box. Use one of the following:

- Right-click any toolbar and choose Customize from the Toolbar shortcut menu.

- Choose View, Toolbars, Customize.

- Choose Tools, Customize, and select Toolbars from the cascading menu.

Figure 26.6
Use the Customize
dialog box to create
new toolbars or to
change the buttons
that appear on the
existing toolbars.

The Customize dialog box displays the custom choices on three tabs:

- **Tool<u>b</u>ars**—You can choose to display or hide a toolbar by marking or unmarking the toolbar name. New toolbars can be created, renamed, or deleted, and toolbars you have customized can be reset to display their original buttons.

- **<u>C</u>ommands**—Using the button categories, you can add a tool to a toolbar.

- **<u>O</u>ptions**—From this tab you can enlarge the tool button size, control what is displayed in the toolbar button ToolTip, and control how the menus are animated.

When the Customize dialog box appears in front of toolbars you want to customize, drag the colored title bar of the Customize dialog box to move it to a different location.

CUSTOMIZING TOOLBARS

Most of the toolbars included with Microsoft Project contain the commands that people need to complete the most frequently accessed tasks. As discussed earlier in this chapter, however, they are not necessarily designed to contain commands for the tasks *you* perform most often. As a result, it is sometimes necessary to customize a toolbar by removing commands you seldom use and adding commands for tasks you use frequently.

Before you can customize a toolbar, the toolbar you want to customize must be activated. The Customize dialog box then needs to be accessed. From the Customize dialog box, choose the <u>C</u>ommands tab (see Figure 26.7) to add buttons or remove buttons from any active toolbar.

The <u>C</u>ommands tab displays a list of Categories of tools on the left. Whenever you select a category, the corresponding Comman<u>d</u>s appear in the list box on the right. In Figure 26.7, the File category is selected.

To see the description of a command (which is used as the ToolTip), select a command and choose Descri<u>p</u>tion. In Figure 26.8 the [Task/Resource Notes] command from the Project category has been selected. You must click the Description button to see the command description.

Figure 26.7
Use the Commands tab in the Customize dialog box to change the buttons that appear on the active toolbars.

Figure 26.8
You can find out more about commands by displaying their descriptions.

The Modify Selection button is used to change the command buttons on the toolbars. It is active when you select a command on a toolbar, not when the command is selected in the Commands list box. You can also activate Modify Selection when you right-click a button on a toolbar.

Commands you add to the toolbars might or might not have corresponding icon buttons. Those that do not have icon buttons will be displayed as text buttons.

ADDING AND REMOVING COMMAND BUTTONS

When you locate the command button you want to add to a toolbar, all you have to do is drag the button from the Commands list on to the desired toolbar. By positioning the button between two existing buttons, the button drops into place and existing buttons move to accommodate it. If there are too many buttons on the toolbar, those at the far right end begin to wrap to a new line for the toolbar. To remove a button from a toolbar, simply drag it off its toolbar and release it in the center of the screen away from other toolbars.

PART

VIII

CH

26

To add buttons to a toolbar, follow these steps:

1. Display the toolbar you want to edit.

2. Right-click any toolbar and choose <u>C</u>ustomize from the Toolbar shortcut menu, or choose <u>V</u>iew, <u>T</u>oolbars, <u>C</u>ustomize. The Customize dialog box appears.

3. Select the <u>C</u>ommands tab.

4. Choose the category containing the desired command.

5. Click the command and drag it into any position on the toolbar. When dragging a command to a toolbar, your mouse pointer changes to the shape of a white arrow with a gray box on the tip of the arrow and an X on the stem of the arrow. When you move the mouse pointer into the toolbar, it becomes a thick capital I.

6. Repeat steps 4–5 until all buttons have been added to the desired toolbars.

   In Figure 26.9, the Close button and Properties button from the File category have been added to the Standard toolbar. A third tool (Page Setup) is being added, as can be seen by the mouse pointer shape.

7. Close the Customize dialog box.

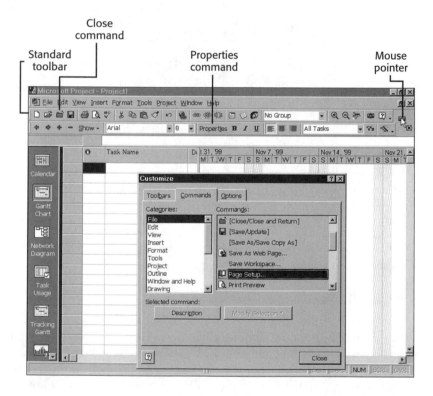

Figure 26.9
Commands can be added to any active toolbar. Some appear as icons, while others display as text.

Tip from Tim and the Project Team

Microsoft Project makes it easy to insert a button on a toolbar that executes a macro you have created. The category All Macros on the Commands tab of the Customize dialog box lists every macro in Project, including the ones you create. Simply drag the macro name to the desired toolbar. The name of the macro appears as a button on the toolbar. You can create an image for that button instead of having the macro name appear on the toolbar.

→ For more information on creating your own customized command buttons, **see** "Customizing Command Buttons," **p. 1066**

→ To learn how to take advantage of macros with Project, **see** Chapter 27, "Introduction to Visual Basic Macros with Project 2000," **p. 1095**

One very nice feature of the toolbars is that if you add more buttons than can be displayed on a single toolbar line, those buttons at the far right end begin to wrap to a new line for the toolbar. The grouping of the buttons determines how many buttons wrap. See the section "Grouping Command Buttons," later in this chapter, for more information on setting and changing groups. Naturally, the more toolbars (or lines to a toolbar) there are displayed, the smaller the viewable area of your screen will become.

You might find that there are certain command buttons that you never use and decide to remove them from the toolbar to make room for other buttons. To remove buttons from existing toolbars, follow these steps:

1. Display the toolbar you want to edit.

   Right-click any toolbar and choose Customize from the Toolbar shortcut menu, or choose View, Toolbars, Customize. The Customize dialog box appears.

3. From the toolbar, select the button that you want to remove. A heavy black border indicates which button is selected.

4. Drag the button off the toolbar; release it anywhere *away* from other existing toolbars. When dragging a command off a toolbar, your mouse pointer changes to the shape of a white arrow with a gray box on the tip of the arrow and an X on the stem of the arrow.

5. Repeat steps 3–4 until all desired buttons are removed.

6. Close the Customize dialog box.

MOVING COMMAND BUTTONS

You can rearrange the commands on the toolbar by dragging buttons to different locations. When you select a button to move it, a heavy border indicates the button is selected. As you move the button, the mouse pointer changes to a thick capital I. To move buttons, the Customize dialog box must be active.

When you want to move a button from one toolbar to another, you can remove it from one and add it to the other using procedures described in the previous section. Or, simply drag the button from one toolbar to the other. When moving buttons from one toolbar to another, both toolbars must be displayed and the Customize dialog box must be active.

GROUPING COMMAND BUTTONS

Command buttons on the toolbars are organized by groups. Vertical separator bars distinguish one group from another. To add a separator bar in front of the active command button, right-click the button which will begin the new group. A list of command-button display options appears. Figure 26.10 shows the Properties button selected on the Standard toolbar and the list of options.

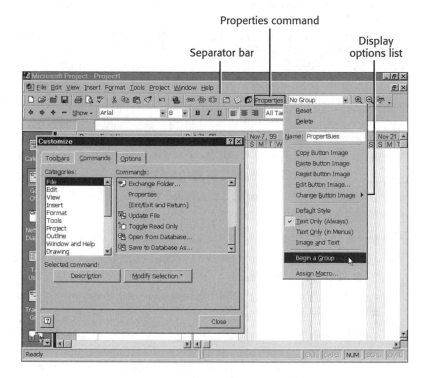

Figure 26.10
You can change the display of command buttons on toolbars.

> **Note**
>
> You can also activate the list of display options by selecting the button on the toolbar and clicking the Modify Selection button on the Commands tab of the Customize dialog box. The Modify Selection button is only active when you select a button on a toolbar, not when the command is selected in the Commands list box.

While the Customize dialog box is active, you can add a vertical separator bar in front of the active button, allowing you to group similar commands together. To add a separator bar, click Begin a Group. A separator bar will appear in front of the selected button. You can remove a separator bar from a button by right-clicking the button on the toolbar, and selecting Begin a Group again. Check marks that appear in front of options indicate options that are active.

RESIZING COMBO BOXES

Combination (or *combo*) boxes are two-part boxes that combine a text box with a drop-down list arrow that can be used to select valid options. These boxes appear frequently in dialog boxes and on toolbars. For example, on the Formatting toolbar there are combo boxes for Font, Font Size, and Filter. The width of the text box portion of the combo boxes can be changed while the Customize dialog box is active.

To widen or shorten the width of a combo box, follow these steps:

1. Display the toolbar containing the combo box and display the Customize dialog box. You can have any tab in the Customize dialog box active to resize a combo box.

2. Select the combo box in the toolbar. A heavy black border appears around the combo box, indicating that it is selected.

3. Position the mouse pointer over one side of the combo box. The mouse pointer changes to a two-headed dark arrow (see Figure 25.11).

Figure 26.11
The mouse is set to resize the Font combo box by dragging the edge of the text box.

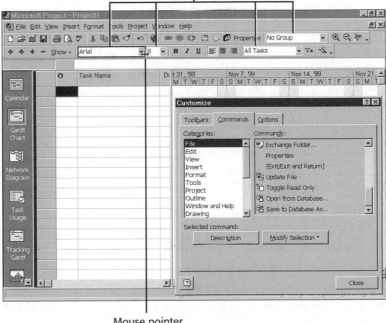

Combo boxes

Mouse pointer

PART

VIII

CH

26

4. Drag the edge of the combo box to the desired size.

5. Repeat steps 2–4 for each combo box you want to size.

6. Close the Customize dialog box.

CREATING NEW TOOLBARS

Sometimes the buttons you use most frequently are on several different toolbars. Instead of having four or five toolbars displayed, which reduces the space available on the screen to display your project document, you might want to have one or two toolbars that contain most (if not all) of the command buttons you use. At other times, you might want to customize an existing toolbar without affecting the original toolbar. Microsoft Project enables you to create new toolbars on which you can store the buttons you use most frequently without affecting the buttons currently available on other toolbars.

When the toolbar you want to create contains many of the same buttons available on an existing toolbar, you can make a copy of the existing toolbar, give it a unique name, and add the buttons you use most frequently. Alternatively, you can start with a blank toolbar and create a completely new collection of buttons.

If you want to make a copy of an existing toolbar and modify it, you must make the copy in the Organizer before using the Customize dialog box. If you want to create a blank toolbar, you can start from the Customize dialog box.

CREATING A TOOLBAR BY COPYING AN EXISTING TOOLBAR

When an existing toolbar contains many of the buttons you want to include on your new toolbar, making a copy of the existing toolbar is a good starting point. Copying the existing toolbar reduces the number of buttons you have to place on the new toolbar.

→ You cannot create a copy of a toolbar from within the Customize dialog box. To copy a toolbar, you will have to access the Organizer, **see** "Using the Organizer," **p. 128**

To create a copy of a toolbar, follow these steps:

1. From the menu bar choose Tools, Organizer.
2. Select the Toolbars tab in the Organizer. On the left side of the dialog box is the GLOBAL.MPT, on the right side of the dialog box is your active file.
3. Select the name of the toolbar you want to copy from the GLOBAL.MPT, and choose Copy.
4. The toolbar name will appear in your active file, listed on the right.
5. Select the toolbar name you just made a copy of on the right (in your active file) and choose Rename. The Rename dialog box will appear.
6. In the Rename dialog box, type in the new name for the copied toolbar and choose OK.

    Make sure the name you type is not a name used by another toolbar. For example, if you copied the Tracking toolbar, rename the copy My Tracking or Custom Tracking to differentiate it from the original Tracking toolbar.
7. Select the toolbar you just renamed (on the right) and choose Copy to place the copy with the new name in the GLOBAL.MPT. This makes the new toolbar available in all your projects, not just your active project.
8. Select the toolbar on the right (in your active file) and choose Delete. This removes it from the active file. It is not needed there because it is in your GLOBAL.MPT.

9. Close the Organizer.

10. Access the Customize dialog box. Use the techniques outlined in the previous sections to modify the copied toolbar for your needs.

BUILDING A NEW TOOLBAR

Creating a new toolbar from scratch creates an empty floating toolbar window that you must fill with the command buttons you want to add to the new toolbar.

To build a new toolbar, follow these steps:

1. Right-click any toolbar and choose Customize from the Toolbar shortcut menu, or choose View, Toolbars, Customize. The Customize dialog box appears.

2. From the Toolbars tab, choose New to open the New Toolbar dialog box. Project assigns a generic number sequentially to each new toolbar and identifies the toolbar with a generic name, such as Custom 1.

3. Type the new toolbar name. Toolbar names must be unique and are limited to any combination of 50 characters and spaces.

4. Choose OK.

The new toolbar name appears in the list on the Toolbars tab, while the new empty toolbar appears inside the dialog box (see Figure 26.12). Select the Commands tab and drag command buttons onto the toolbar to create the collection you desire. The toolbar will enlarge as you add command buttons. As is true with all toolbars, you can dock the toolbar or leave it floating.

New custom
toolbar

Figure 26.12
Drag buttons you
want to include on
the new custom tool-
bar.

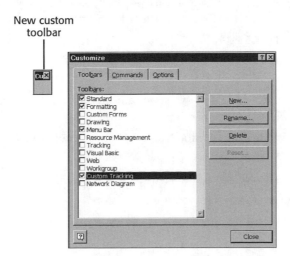

DELETING A USER-DEFINED TOOLBAR

Toolbars installed with the Microsoft Project software remain a part of the application even after you customize them. As a result, they can be reset, but they cannot be deleted.

However, new toolbars you create, referred to as *user-defined toolbars*, can be deleted. To delete a user-defined toolbar, follow these steps:

1. Right-click any toolbar and choose Customize from the Toolbar shortcut menu, or choose View, Toolbars, Customize. The Customize dialog box appears.

2. From the Toolbars tab, select the toolbar you want to delete.

Note

If the Delete button is not active, you have selected a toolbar that is installed with the Microsoft Project software. These toolbars can be reset, but not deleted.

3. Choose Delete. A warning dialog box appears asking you to confirm the deletion of the toolbar.

4. Choose OK to delete the toolbar.

5. Choose Close to close the Customize dialog box.

RESTORING THE BUILT-IN TOOLBARS

Changes you make to the built-in toolbars as you customize might become out of date and may not fit every project you create. As a result, you may want to restore the default buttons to a toolbar. Microsoft Project includes a feature that makes restoring toolbars quick and easy.

Caution

Resetting a toolbar removes *all* customized changes you have made to that toolbar—not just the most recent changes. If you have placed custom buttons on a toolbar that you plan to reset, you will lose the custom buttons. To avoid this, drag the custom buttons to another toolbar if you want to preserve them.

To restore the default set of command buttons to the built-in toolbars, follow these steps:

1. Right-click any toolbar and choose Customize from the Toolbar shortcut menu, or choose View, Toolbars, Customize. The Customize dialog box appears.

2. From the Toolbars tab, select the toolbar you want to restore to its default settings.

3. Choose Reset.

4. Choose OK from the warning box to restore the toolbar.

5. Repeat steps 2–4 for each toolbar you want to restore.

6. Close the Customize dialog box.

CUSTOMIZING COMMAND BUTTONS

Some of the commands available in the Customize dialog box have no button image associated with them. When the command is added to a toolbar, only the name of the command is displayed.

Additionally, there will be times when no command button is available for a task you perform frequently, and it might be necessary for you to create a macro to record the steps of such a task. After you have created the macro, the name of the macro is listed on the Commands tab of the Customize dialog box. As with other commands, no button image is associated with the macro command. When the command is added to a toolbar, only the name of the macro is displayed.

When you want to add a new command to a toolbar that will perform a custom function, you'll probably want a button image that carries a distinctive design so that you won't confuse it with other buttons on the toolbar. You can add one of the available images to a command button that doesn't have an image, or design your own image for the command button by using the button display options.

ACCESSING THE BUTTON DISPLAY OPTIONS

To modify the command button images, you need to access the list of button display options. To see these options, you must first display the toolbar that contains the command button you want to change and then display the Customize dialog box (the quickest way to display the Customize dialog box is to right-click any toolbar and choose Customize). After you have the toolbar and dialog box displayed, choose one of the following methods to see the button display options list:

- Right-click the button you want to modify.

- Select the button you want to modify. Select the Commands tab in the Customize dialog box and choose the Modify Selection button.

CUSTOMIZING THE BUTTON FACE

The Customize dialog box enables you to copy an existing design from one button to another, or access the Editor dialog box where you can customize a button design. If another button carries a design that resembles the one you want to use on the new button, you can copy the design from the button to the Clipboard and then paste it on the blank button. Copying the design does not copy the function of the original button to the new button. After you paste the design on the blank button, you can then modify the design to customize it for the new button. You can also create a design from scratch.

CHANGING A BUTTON IMAGE USING AN IMAGE FROM THE LIBRARY

Project contains a library of images from which you can select an image to apply to a button that doesn't have an image, or to choose a different image for a button that already has an image. Figure 26.13 shows the image library available in Microsoft Project.

To change a button image to one of the existing images, follow these steps:

1. Right-click any toolbar and choose Customize from the Toolbar shortcut menu, or choose View, Toolbars, Customize. The Customize dialog box appears.

2. If necessary, go to the Toolbars tab and display the toolbar that contains the command to change the button image.

3. Right-click the button on the toolbar you want to change. A heavy black border indicates the button is selected and the list of button display options appears.

Note
You can also click the Commands tab in the Customize dialog box and click the Modify Selection button to see the list of button display options.

4. From the list of button display options, choose Change Button Image. A submenu of button choices appears.

Some of these images are generic, but others can be used by Project or other Microsoft programs.

5. Choose an image from the list.

6. Close the Customize dialog box.

Figure 26.13
Click the Change Button Image option to display the list of images from the library.

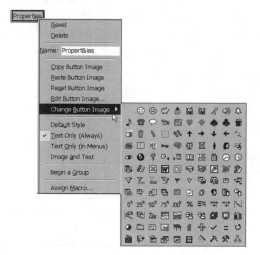

COPYING A BUTTON IMAGE

To copy the design of an existing toolbar button to another button, follow these steps:

1. Right-click any toolbar and choose Customize from the Toolbar shortcut menu, or choose View, Toolbars, Customize. The Customize dialog box appears.

2. Position the mouse pointer over the button on the toolbar containing the design you want to copy and click the right mouse button. The list of button display options appears.

3. Choose Copy Button Image to copy the design to the Clipboard.

4. Point to the button to which you want to apply the design and right-click the mouse.

5. Choose Paste Button Image to place the design on the new button.

6. Close the Customize dialog box.

DESIGNING A NEW BUTTON IMAGE

When a command has a blank button image, you can design your own image for the command.

1. Display the Customize dialog box and point to the toolbar button you want to edit.

2. Right-click the command button to see the button display options list . Choose Edit Button Image. The Button Editor dialog box displays.

The procedures for editing an existing image are described in the next section.

EDITING THE BUTTON IMAGE

After you choose a button image from the library or copy an image from another button, you might want to edit the picture. If the image was copied, changing the picture so that it differs from the design of a button used to perform a different task will help you identify both buttons. To edit the picture you must use the Button Editor dialog box. In Figure 26.14 the design assigned to the Paste button is selected as the design for a new command button (Paste Special), and will be edited so that it isn't confused with the Paste button that appears on the Standard toolbar.

Figure 26.14
The Paste image is selected as a starting point for building a new image. Use the Button Editor to create or modify a button image.

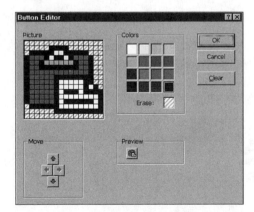

PART

VIII

CH

26

After selecting the design for the button, the Button Editor dialog box is opened so that the selected design can be customized (refer to Figure 26.14). The button design appears enlarged so that individual pixels can be identified in the Picture box. You can then change the location of each pixel in the image using the mouse to achieve the desired design.

To open the Button Editor, follow these steps:

1. Right-click the button you want to edit; the button display options list appears.
2. Choose Edit Button Image to open the Button Editor dialog box.
3. Verify that the button you want to customize is selected.

The Colors box is your palette for selecting colored pixels for your design. The Move arrows help you position the picture on the button by moving it one row or column at a time. The Preview area shows you how the current picture appears.

To change the picture, use any of the following techniques:

- To change the color of any pixel, click a color in the Colors box and then click the pixel, or drag the color across a group of pixels.

- To erase or clear pixels, click the erase box and then click all pixels you want to clear, drag the pointer across pixels you want to clear, or click a pixel a second time to clear the existing color.

- To reposition the picture on the button, clear an area along the edge toward which you want to move the design and then click the desired move arrow button.

- To clear the picture canvas and start a new image from scratch, choose Clear.

- To cancel changes and start over, choose Cancel or press Esc.

When you are finished modifying the button, choose OK. The new design now appears on the new button. Figure 26.15 shows the finished picture that will be assigned to the Paste Special button.

Figure 26.15
This figure shows the finished picture for the Paste Special button.

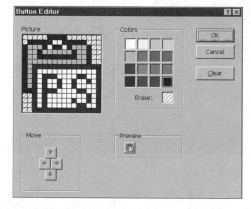

CHANGING THE ATTRIBUTES OF A BUTTON

After you have added a command button to a toolbar or modified the button image, you might decide to change the command associated with that button. The command that is executed when the button is clicked is identified in the Command drop-down list on the

Customize Tool dialog box. Figure 26.16 shows the command for the Open button on the Standard toolbar.

Figure 26.16
All the commands in Project are listed in the Command drop-down list.

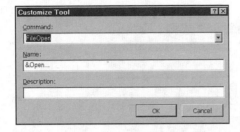

When you click the Command drop-down list, you will see all the Microsoft Project commands (including forms and macros) that you can assign to a button. For example, to assign a macro to a button, select the Macro command that displays the desired macro in double quotes from the Command drop-down list. Similarly, to designate the button to activate a custom form, you would choose the Form command that includes the desired form name in double quotes.

→ To learn more about macros and Microsoft Project, **see** Chapter 27 "Introduction to Visual Basic Macros with Project 2000," **p. 1095**

You can access the Customize Tool dialog box directly from the Project window, without having to go through the Customize dialog box. To change the attributes of a toolbar button, follow these steps:

1. If you need to create a button (including a button for a macro), see the section "Adding and Removing Command Buttons," earlier in this chapter.

2. Press the Ctrl key and click the button you want to change. The Customize Tool dialog box appears. In Figure 26.17, a macro named ProjectSummary was created and assigned to a new button.

3. Choose the Command drop-down list arrow and scroll through the commands to find the one you need. Commands are listed in alphabetical order and are grouped by type on the list. As a result, you might have to scroll through the list to find the command you need.

4. Choose OK.

ENTERING THE DESCRIPTION

Descriptions for many commands installed with Microsoft Project automatically appear in the Description field of the Customize Tool dialog box when you choose a command from the Command drop-down list. When you assign a command to a toolbar button, this description is set to appear in the status bar at the bottom of the screen when you use the button. When no description appears, you can create your own description. In addition, you can edit existing descriptions to meet your needs, when necessary. Each description can include up to 80 characters. Macros that you create will have a default description that identifies the macro name, the date it was created, and by whom. Figure 26.17 previously showed a custom description for the ProjectSummary macro.

Figure 26.17
Macros automatically appear in the list of commands that can be assigned to a button.

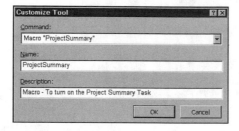

CUSTOMIZING THE MENU BAR

A *menu* is a collection of commands that pertains to a particular topic or action. So the File menu is a collection of commands that perform actions with your documents—opening, closing, saving, printing, and so forth. Likewise, underneath a menu on the menu bar, are submenus. So any command that has a pointing triangle is considered a menu. In Figure 26.18, the complete Edit menu is active. Within the Edit menu there are three other built-in menus—Fill, Clear, and Object.

Figure 26.18
The Edit menu contains three other built-in menus: Fill, Clear, and Object.

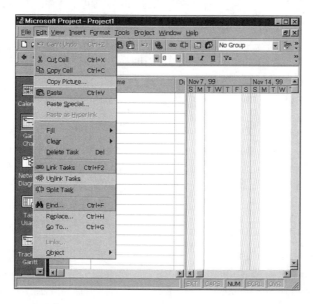

A *command* is a specific action within an application; for example, Save As is a command. When describing a command, most people and reference books (such as the one you are now reading) typically identify a command by stating the menu followed by the command. So, although technically it is the Save As command, you will often see it referred to as the

File, Save As command. Identifying the menu as well as the command simply provides additional clarity when referring to a command.

Project, like Office, treats the menu bar as just another toolbar. Customizing the menu bar is performed much in the same way you customize a toolbar, by dragging commands on and off the menu bar. You can create new menus, add commands to the menus, rearrange commands, and remove commands from the menus just as you do with the toolbars. By default, the menu bar is docked at the top of the screen, but like toolbars, it can be moved and docked at the side or bottom of the screen, or left floating in the middle of the screen.

In previous versions of Project, customizing menus provided an efficient means for accessing tasks performed most often. Commands used frequently were moved to the tops of menus or placed together on a new separate menu. With the introduction of the personalized toolbars and menus feature in Project 2000, the need to relocate commands to the tops of menus has diminished. By design, this feature displays the commands you use frequently on the menu and hides the commands you rarely or never use. You can see the full list of commands by double-clicking the menu or by pausing on the menu (which displays the full list after a slight delay).

→ To change the new behavior of the menus and toolbars back to the way they used to work, **see** "Altering the Personalized Menu and Toolbar Behavior," **p. 1050**

There still remain several reasons for customizing the menu bar: to make commands buried too deep in the menu system more accessible and to create new menus.

Note

In earlier chapters, you learned how to create custom views, tables, forms, or filters and found that they are stored as part of the project in which you created them. When you need to use them in another project, you have to copy them into the new project file. Customizing menus is different because menus are part of the *application* file rather than a *project* file. As a result, changing them makes them available to all projects you create or edit on your computer. They are stored as part of the GLOBAL.MPT file that is used as a basis for all projects you create or open on your machine. You can still copy them from the GLOBAL.MPT file to a project file when you want to include them in a file you are sending to someone else, or when you want to copy them to a different computer. Otherwise, copying them is not necessary.

PART
VIII

CH
26

Customizing menus offers a wide range of possibilities. You might simply want to attach commands to existing menus. Items such as frequently used views, tables, filters, and macros can be attached to existing menus quite easily. Procedures for adding these features are included in the chapter in which they were created. When you want to change the name of a menu bar item or create a new menu bar item, you are, in effect, creating a custom menu bar. The next few sections focus on editing menu bar items for existing menu bars and creating new menu bars.

To add commands to a menu, follow the steps outlined in the sections earlier in this chapter for adding commands to toolbars. These next few sections focus in on customizing options that are unique to menus.

→ To learn more about the steps for altering the appearance of the toolbars and menus, or to add new commands to toolbars and menus, **see** "Customizing Toolbars," **p. 1058**

ADDING VIEWS TO THE VIEW MENU

The list of views on the View menu contains a short list of the most widely used views in Project. However, there are many other views available under the View, More Views command. If there is a view you use frequently from the More Views list, you can add it to the View menu for quicker access. Likewise, if you have created a custom view that you want easy access to, you can have it appear on the View menu. When a view is listed on the View menu, it will also be listed on the View bar.

> **Note**
>
> Adding a view to the View menu is a setting you select for that particular view in the Views dialog box, and cannot be done through the Customize dialog box.

To add a view to the View menu, follow these steps:

1. Choose View, More Views to display the More Views dialog box.
2. Select the view you want displayed on the View menu. In Figure 26.19 the Resource Allocation view is selected.
3. Click Edit to display the View Definition dialog box (shown in Figure 26.20) for the selected view.
4. Mark the Show in Menu check box and click OK.
5. The More Views dialog box displays once again. Repeat steps 2–4 until you have changed this setting for all the views you want displayed in the View menu.
6. Click Close to close the More Views dialog box.

Figure 26.19
The More Views dialog box lists all the views available in Project, both built-in views and views you have created.

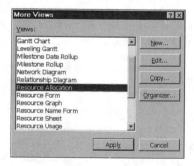

ADDING NEW MENUS TO THE MENU BAR

You can add new menus either directly on the menu bar, or as a submenu along with the commands underneath a menu. To accomplish this, you must have the Customize dialog box displayed.

Figure 26.20
The View Definition dialog box varies slightly for single pane views. The dialog box shown in this figure is for a combination view—where one view appears in the top half of the screen and a separate view appears in the bottom half of the screen.

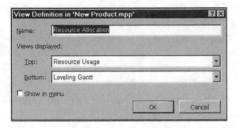

To add a new menu, follow these steps:

1. Right-click any toolbar and choose <u>C</u>ustomize from the Toolbar shortcut menu, or choose <u>V</u>iew, <u>T</u>oolbars, <u>C</u>ustomize. The Customize dialog box appears.

2. Select the <u>C</u>ommands tab.

3. Scroll down the list of Categories and select New Menu. The only option in the Comman<u>d</u>s list is New Menu.

4. Drag the New Menu command to the place on the menu bar where you want to insert the new menu.

   • **Inserting a new menu directly on the menu bar**—When you drag the New Menu command to the menu bar, a thick capital I symbol appears on the menu bar. Release the mouse when this symbol is in the correct location on the menu bar where you want the new menu to appear.

   • **Inserting a new menu underneath an existing menu**—Drag the New Menu command to the menu bar, next to the menu you want to place it under. When the list of commands on that menu appears, drag the mouse down to the exact position between the existing commands where you want the new menu to appear. Release the mouse.

RENAMING MENUS AND COMMANDS

After you have added the new menu, you will want to name the menu and add commands to it. To name the menu, right-click the menu name to see the list of display options. In the <u>N</u>ame text box, replace the default name with the name you want to use for the menu. Press Enter to accept the name change. To rename a submenu, click the main menu. Then right-click the newly inserted menu to change the name.

Most menus and commands have a keyboard *hotkey* that can be used to activate the menu or command via the keyboard instead of the mouse. These hotkeys are represented by the underscored letter in the menu. For example, the hotkey for the <u>F</u>ile menu is F, the underscored letter. Hotkeys are designated in the <u>N</u>ame text box using an ampersand (&) in front of the letter that is to be used as the hotkey. For the <u>F</u>ile menu, this appears in the <u>N</u>ame text box as &File. Likewise, the <u>F</u>ormat menu name appears as F&ormat in the <u>N</u>ame text box.

PART

VIII

CH

26

Caution

You must make certain that the letter you are using for the hotkey is not already being used by another menu or command. For the menu bar, you only need to look at the other menu names, not the commands under neither those menus. So if you are adding a new menu to the menu bar, the letters F, E, V, I, O, T, P, W, H are already used by the File, Edit, View, Insert, Format, Tools, Project, Window, and Help menus.

If you are adding a menu or command to an existing menu, you only need to look at the words on that specific menu to make sure you are not using duplicate letters. So if you are adding a new custom view to the View menu, you will only need to look at the words on that specific menu to avoid duplicate hotkeys.

ADDING ITEMS TO THE MENU BAR

You can add commands, other menus, and special items to the existing or new menu bar commands. You add items to menus using the same basic techniques for adding buttons to toolbars. Simply select the category and item you want to add and drag it onto the menu bar. By positioning the command between two existing commands, the new item drops into place. When you drag the item to a menu, a capital I indicates the position of the command. Figure 26.21 shows the Go To Next Overallocation command being added to a new menu.

→ To learn how to customize the commands that appear on menus, **see** "Adding and Removing Command Buttons," **p. 1059**

Figure 26.21
Drag commands from the Customize dialog box to the new menu.

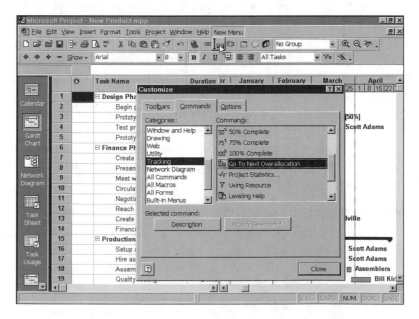

The following is a list of several different types of items you can add to a new menu bar:

- **Commands**—Any command can be added to the new menu. Choose the command from either the category in which the command is listed, or from the All Commands category listed toward the bottom of the list. All Commands is an alphabetical listing of every command in Project.

- **Built-in Menus**—Other built-in menus can be added to the new menu. Choose the Built-in Menus category for a complete listing of menus that are installed with Microsoft Project.

- **Special Items**—There are many other items that appear in menus aside from commands and menus. These are often grouped in lists. For example, on the View menu you see lists of different types of views, while in the Window menu, you see a list of your open project files.

Additionally, there is a category in the Customize dialog box called Special Items that lists collections of items that you might want to add to a menu. These Special Items are

- **Task Views**—Only task views marked to display in menus.

- **Resource Views**—Only resource views marked to display in menus.

- **Views**—All views (task and resource) marked to display in menus, identical to the list that appears in the View menu.

- **Tables**—All tables marked to display in menus, identical to the list that appears in the View, Tables menu.

- **Filters**—All filters marked to display in menus, identical to the list that appears in the Project, Filter For menu.

- **Sorts**—All sorts marked to display in menus, identical to the list that appears in the Project, Sort menu.

- **Macros**—All macros, identical to the list that appears in the Tools, Macro, Macros menu.

- **Custom Forms**—All custom forms available from the Custom Forms toolbar.

- **Form View Formats**—All Format Detail options when a form-type view is active. For example, if you split the screen when the Gantt Chart view is displayed, the Task Form view appears in the lower split. You can choose Format, Details to change the information that appears in the form, such as *Resources and Predecessors* or *Resource Work*.

- **Toolbars**—All toolbars, identical to the list that appears in the View, Toolbars menu.

- **Recently Used Files**—The list of files you have worked with recently, identical to the list that appears at the bottom of the File menu. The maximum number of files that can be listed is nine, and is controlled through the General tab under Tools, Options.

- **Windows**—The list of your open files, identical to the list that appears at the bottom of the Window menu.

- **OLE Actions**—A list of actions you can take with objects that have been linked or embedded.

- **Groups**—All groups marked to display in menus, identical to the list that appears in the Project, Group By menu.

PART

VIII

CH

26

REMOVING AND RESTORING MENUS AND COMMANDS

If you no longer use a menu or particular command, you can remove it from the menu bar. To remove menus or commands from a particular menu, you simply drag it off the menu bar. Use these steps to remove a menu or a command:

1. Display the Customize dialog box.

2. Select the menu or menu command that you want to remove from the menu bar. A heavy black border indicates which item is selected.

3. Drag the menu or command off the menu bar, being careful to release it away from the toolbars. When dragging a command off the menu bar, your mouse pointer changes to the shape of a white arrow with a gray box on the tip of the arrow and an X on the stem of the arrow.

4. Repeat steps 2–3 until all desired menus or commands are removed.

5. Close the Customize dialog box.

If you have customized a menu and removed some of the default commands from menus, you can restore the standard Project menus and commands to their original settings by restoring the menu bar.

Caution

Restoring the menu bar will remove any custom menus you have created.

To restore the menu bar, follow these steps:

1. Display the Customize dialog box.

2. Select the Toolbars tab.

3. Choose Menu Bar from the list of toolbars.

4. Choose Reset. A warning message appears to confirm resetting the menu bar.

5. Choose OK.

6. Close the Customize dialog box.

MOVING MENUS AND COMMANDS

The order of the menu commands on the menu bar can be rearranged by dragging the menu name to a different location. You can also reorder the commands within a particular menu. When you select a menu or command name to move, a heavy border indicates the name is selected. Hold and drag the name to its new location. As you move the name, the mouse pointer changes to a thick capital I. When this line is in the new location, release the mouse button.

Note

When rearranging the order of the menus or commands, the Customize dialog box must be active.

CHANGING THE ATTRIBUTES OF A MENU OR COMMAND

Each menu item has a set of attributes, or display options, that you can change. One of these options is the name that appears on the menu, discussed in the earlier section "Renaming Menus and Commands."

Another attribute is whether these items are separated in groups. Horizontal bars in the menus distinguish one group from another. The way you designate a group is by selecting the command that will be the first command in the group. When you right-click that command, the list of display options appears on a shortcut menu. To add a horizontal separator bar, click Begin a Group. A check mark appears in front of the option to indicate a separator bar has been added. You remove a separator bar from a menu item by selecting the item and removing the check mark.

As with many of the actions you take customizing menus and toolbar, the Customize dialog box must be displayed to change the display options for menus and commands.

MANAGING TOOLBARS WITH THE ORGANIZER

Toolbars are global objects in Microsoft Project and are attached to the application in general rather than to a specific project. As a result, toolbars are stored as part of the GLOBAL.MPT template and are available for all projects you create, review, or edit. Changes you make to the various toolbars are also stored in the GLOBAL.MPT template. Toolbars not included in the GLOBAL.MPT file are not available for any project. Generally, this is not a problem because the toolbars you create or edit are automatically attached to the GLOBAL.MPT template stored in the computer on which they were created.

→ To learn more about how useful this template is, **see** "The GLOBAL.MPT," **p. 125**

However, there might be times when you create a custom toolbar or edit an existing toolbar and want to copy it to another computer system, such as a laptop or a home computer. At other times you might want to include a special toolbar as part of a file you are sending to a coworker.

When you need to include a special toolbar with a particular project file, you can use the Organizer to copy the toolbar. The Organizer also provides options for renaming and deleting toolbars.

→ To learn all about how to work with the Organizer, **see** "Using the Organizer," **p. 128**

To rename a toolbar, follow these steps:

1. From the menu bar, choose Tools, Organizer.
2. Select the Toolbars tab in the Organizer. On the left side of the dialog box is the GLOBAL.MPT; on the right side of the dialog box is your active Project file. Typically there are no toolbars listed in your active file (see Figure 26.22).
3. Select the name of the toolbar you want to rename from the GLOBAL.MPT, and choose Copy.
4. The toolbar name will appear in your active file, listed on the right.

5. Select the toolbar name you just made a copy of on the right (in your active file) and choose Rename. The Rename dialog box appears (see Figure 26.23).

6. In the Rename dialog box, type in the new name for the copied toolbar and choose OK.

   Make sure the name you type is not a name used by another toolbar. For example, if you copied the Tracking toolbar, rename the copy My Tracking or Custom Tracking to differentiate it from the original Tracking toolbar.

7. Close the Organizer.

Figure 26.22
The Toolbars tab of the Organizer dialog box shows the named toolbars, which are stored in the GLOBAL.MPT file.

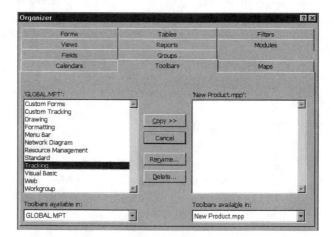

Figure 26.23
Provide a new name for a toolbar in the Rename dialog box.

Toolbars that are attached to project files can't be displayed directly from the project. When you want to make a toolbar available on a different system, you can copy it to a project and then copy it from the project into the GLOBAL.MPT template on the other system. To copy a toolbar into a project file, follow these steps:

1. Open the project to which you want to copy the toolbar.

2. Choose Tools, Organizer. The Organizer dialog box opens.

3. Select the toolbar you want to copy from those available in the GLOBAL.MPT list on the left. You can select multiple toolbars by dragging the mouse or by pressing the Ctrl key as you click additional toolbars.

Tip from Tim and the Project Team

If the project file you want to use doesn't already appear above the box on the right side of the Toolbars tab on the Organizer dialog box, select it from the Toolbars Available In drop-down list.

4. Choose <u>C</u>opy to copy all selected toolbars to the project file.

5. Click the Close button or press Esc to close the Organizer dialog box.

Figure 26.24 shows that a copy of the toolbar Custom Resource Management has been placed in the New Product.mpp project file.

Figure 26.24
Toolbars copied into a project file can't be displayed, but they can be copied into GLOBAL.MPT templates on other computers.

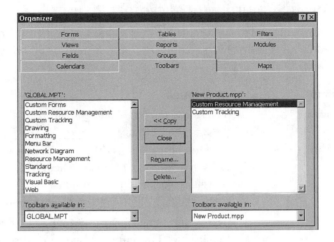

USING CUSTOM FORMS

Custom forms are pop-up data entry forms that resemble dialog boxes. These forms give you quick access to *fields*—pieces of information—that are not displayed on the current view. Using a custom form enables you to access a field containing the information you need without changing views, and enter the same value into multiple task and resource fields. This section identifies some of the features available for using custom forms and reviews the procedures for accomplishing these tasks.

Project comes equipped with a number of different forms that you can use to perform some of the most common tasks. You can, for example, use the Update Task form when you need to track the progress of a Project task. You can edit built-in forms by moving information around, but you can't add additional fields or delete fields. As a result, you might want to design your own custom forms. The Custom Form Editor, which is one of the server applications in Windows, is used to create custom forms.

Because custom forms are designed for editing and viewing tasks and resources, you can attach them to toolbar buttons, to a menu, or to shortcut keys (Ctrl+*letter*). You cannot place a custom form in a pane and then use the form to scroll through the task list or resource list. The task(s) or resource(s) selected when you activate the form are affected by any entries you make. When you select the OK or Cancel button on the form, the form is removed from display.

Because you have to display the form for each new task or resource, these forms are inappropriate as a primary vehicle for original data entry. To provide continued access to fields

PART
VIII

CH
26

not included in a standard view, it would be more efficient to create a view that incorporates a custom table. You can then design and display the custom view in the Task or Resource Sheet view.

→ For guidelines in creating custom views, **see** "Using the Standard Views, Tables, and Filters," **p. 851**

REVIEWING THE FORMS SUPPLIED WITH MICROSOFT PROJECT

Microsoft Project includes eight custom task forms and four custom resource forms. Each of these predefined forms is designed to accomplish a specific task, as described in the following table:

Task Forms	**Description**
Cost Tracking	Tracks costs for tasks and percent completed, and compares costs to the baseline.
Earned Value	Examines calculations of comparative cost variances for tasks, based on the planned, scheduled, and actual duration, as well as work and cost amounts.
Entry	Edits the Task Name, Dates, Duration, and Rollup fields.
PERT Entry	Tracks duration estimates—Optimistic, Expected, and Pessimistic. This information can be displayed in a table.
Schedule Tracking	Tracks the duration and percentage completed and displays scheduled task dates and variances.
Task Relationships	Displays the list of predecessors and successors for the selected task(s).
Tracking	Tracks the duration and dates for tasks. This is the form that appears when you select the Tracking button on the toolbar.
Work Tracking	Tracks duration and views the calculated work tracking fields.
Resource Forms	**Description**
Cost Tracking	Displays total cost for a resource (for all tasks).
Entry	Identifies the resource name, initials, group, rate, and maximum available units.
Summary	Reports the overall cost and work tracking variances.
Work Tracking	Tracks percent of work completed and compares it to the baseline.

USING CUSTOM FORMS

Each custom form that comes with Project is attached to the Tools menu. To make the form more accessible, you might want to attach the form to a toolbar button or a shortcut key. Procedures for using the menus to access a form, and for attaching forms to toolbar buttons and keyboard shortcuts, are described in this section.

USING THE MENU TO DISPLAY A FORM

When you want to display or edit information for one task or resource, select the task or resource before displaying the form. When you want to display or edit information for multiple tasks or resources, select all tasks and resources before displaying the form. Remember that entries made to the form when multiple tasks or resources are selected affect all selected tasks or resources.

To display a custom form with the menu, follow these steps:

1. Select the task(s) or resource(s) you want to edit.
2. Choose Tools, Customize, Forms. The Customize Forms dialog box appears (see Figure 26.25). If a task is selected, the task forms are listed. If a resource is selected, the resource forms are listed.

Figure 26.25
Select a task or resource form from the Customize Forms dialog box.

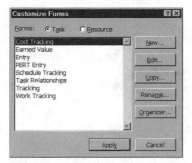

3. Select the desired form from the Forms list.
4. Choose Apply.
5. Edit or view field values for selected task(s) or resource(s).
6. Choose OK.

ASSIGNING A SHORTCUT KEY TO DISPLAY A FORM

To make a form you use frequently more accessible, you might want to assign it to a shortcut key. To assign a shortcut key to a custom form, follow these steps:

1. Choose Tools, Customize, Forms to open the Customize Forms dialog box.
2. Select the form you want to assign to a shortcut key from the Forms list.
3. Choose Rename. The Define Custom Form dialog box appears (see Figure 26.26). You can use this dialog box to change the name of the form or to change the shortcut key assignment.

Figure 26.26
Use the Define Custom Form dialog box to rename a form or assign it a new shortcut key.

4. Select the <u>K</u>ey box and type the letter that you want to use to activate the custom form. Numbers cannot be used. This letter, used with the Ctrl key, will display the form.

Tip from Tim and the Project Team

The letters are not case sensitive, so typing an upper- or lowercase letter makes no difference.

Caution

Be careful to avoid shortcut keys already assigned to other tasks. The shortcut keys already assigned include: B (Bold), C (Edit, Copy), D (Fill Down), F (Edit, Find), I (Italics), N (File, New), O (File, Open), P (File, Print), S (File, Save), U (Underline), V (Edit, Paste), X (Edit, Cut), and Z (Edit, Undo). When you select one of these characters, you will be warned that it's reserved for use with Project and you will be instructed to select a different character.

5. Choose OK to save the key assignment.

To use the shortcut key, first select the task or resource for which you want to display the form, and then press the shortcut letter while holding down the Ctrl key.

ASSIGNING A TOOLBAR BUTTON TO DISPLAY A FORM

To assign a form to a toolbar button, you have to access the Customize Tool dialog box. You can access the Customize Tool dialog box directly from the Project window, without displaying the Customize dialog box first. To assign a form to a toolbar button, follow these steps:

1. If you need to create a button to use to access a form, see the previous section in this chapter, "Adding and Removing Command Buttons."

2. Press the Ctrl key and click the button you want to use to display the form. The Customize Tool dialog box appears (see Figure 26.27).

3. Click the <u>C</u>ommand drop-down list box and scroll the Form commands to find the form name you want to access through the toolbar button.

Tip from Tim and the Project Team

You also can type **Form *form name***, where *form name* is the name that appears in the list of Custom Forms.

4. Choose the <u>D</u>escription text box and type the description you want to display on the status bar when you click the button.

5. Choose OK to save the button definition.

Figure 26.27
Use the Customize Tool dialog box to designate a form to be displayed when you click a toolbar button.

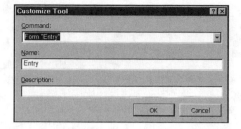

After you assign a toolbar button to a form, select the task or resource for which you want to view the form and click the assigned button.

CREATING A NEW CUSTOM FORM

When the custom forms that come with Microsoft Project do not contain the fields of data and information you need, you can create your own custom form or modify existing forms so that it includes the fields you need. As you found when you created custom toolbars, you can create a new custom form by copying an existing form and modifying it to meet your needs, or you can create a new custom form from scratch. The Custom Form Editor enables you to add fields to a custom form and modify the appearance of existing fields by sizing them or repositioning them on the form. You can also use the Custom Form Editor to set the placement of the form on the screen when you activate it.

Many of the procedures you used to create custom toolbars and menu bars can be used to create a custom form. You can assign a name to the form and identify the fields of information you want to include on the form. When you create a form from scratch, the Custom Form Editor (see Figure 26.28) displays a small outline of a dialog box in the center of the screen. Each custom form, by default, includes an OK button and a Cancel button. These buttons are positioned on the right side of the dialog box. You select and add the information to the form that you need.

Figure 26.28
The initial form contains only the OK and Cancel buttons. Add text, fields, and group boxes to complete the form.

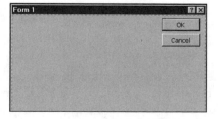

When you create a new form by customizing a copy of an existing form, the existing form is positioned in the Custom Form Editor screen. Figure 26.29 displays a Copy of Entry form in the Custom Form Editor screen.

PART

VIII

CH

26

Figure 26.29
A copy of an existing form can also be used to create a new form. The copy displays the existing form information, which you can edit for the new form.

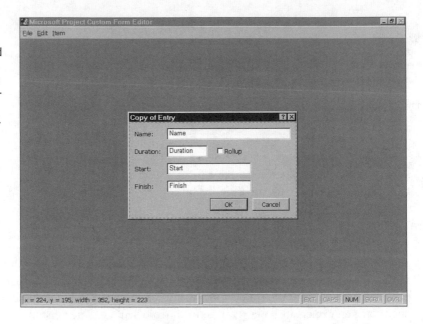

OPENING THE CUSTOM FORM EDITOR

Regardless of which approach you want to use to create a new custom form, you will need to open the Custom Form Editor. To display the Custom Form Editor, follow these steps:

1. Choose Tools, Customize, Forms. The Customize Forms dialog box appears.

2. Choose New to create a new form, or select a form from the list and choose Copy to base the new form on an existing form.

3. Type a name for the custom form in the Name field of the Define Custom Form dialog box.

4. Assign a shortcut key letter in the Key field, if desired.

5. Choose OK.

SIZING AND POSITIONING THE DIALOG BOX

You can use the mouse to resize the Form dialog box using the same procedures to size windows or other dialog boxes. Drag the borders or corners of the box to any desired dimension within the Custom Form Editor window. To reposition the form in the window, drag the title bar until the form is properly positioned. To change the position or size settings for the dialog box, follow these steps:

1. Choose Tools, Customize, Forms to display the Customize Forms dialog box. Select the form you want to edit.

2. Choose Edit to display the Microsoft Custom Form Editor.

3. Select the dialog box outline by clicking once anywhere on the box, or choose Edit, Select Dialog.

4. Double-click the Form dialog box or choose Edit, Info to display the Form Information dialog box (see Figure 25.30).

Figure 26.30
The Form Information dialog box can be used to position or resize the form.

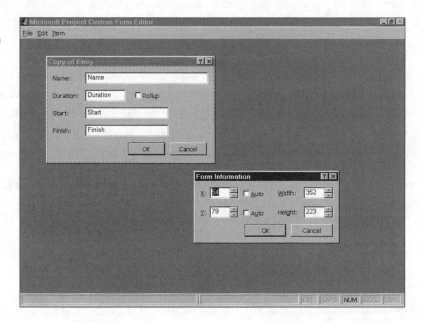

5. Enter values in the X and Y text boxes if you want to set the horizontal and vertical positions of the dialog box manually.

Note

The values in the X and Y boxes refer to the resolution values used in the screen display. A value of 1 in the X text box places the box at the left edge of the screen. A value of 100 places the left edge of the box 100 pixels from the left of the screen. If your screen resolution is 800 pixels wide, then a value of 400 would place the left edge of the box at the center of the screen. Similarly, the values in the Y box locate the top edge of the form relative to the top of the screen. Select the Auto check boxes to center the form on the Microsoft Project screen.

6. Enter values in the Width and Height check boxes to set the dimensions of the form.

After you adjust the size of the Form dialog box, you might want to move or reposition existing items on the form. Each item that you place on the form can be positioned and sized by changing the settings in the Item Information dialog box, or you can drag the item to a new position.

PLACING ITEMS ON THE FORM

Fields that contain pieces of information, text, borders, groups, buttons, and check boxes are examples of *items* that you might include on forms. Most forms automatically include OK and Cancel buttons. You can place additional items on forms using commands from the Item menu. As you add each item, you will want to position the item on the form and might need to adjust the size of the form to accommodate all form items. In the following activities, you will add items to the blank form pictured earlier in Figure 26.28.

Placing Text on the Form

Text items are labels; they identify the information contained on a form. For example, to identify a resource name on a custom form, you would include the word Resource on the form beside the text box that identifies the resource.

When you add a text item to a form, a text box containing the word Text is outlined as a placeholder on the form. To replace the default word Text with the information you want to display on the form, select the word Text and type the desired text. The text placeholder is sized according to the width of the form. As a result, if the text you want to add to the form does not fit into the text placeholder, you will need to adjust the size of the form, reposition items on the form, and drag the text placeholder to accommodate the message. After you complete the text entry, you can reposition, size, or delete the text item. When it is positioned and complete, click a neutral area of the form to deselect the text item.

The position of a selected text item appears in the status bar. You can use these position indicators to position the text item, or double-click the text item to display the Item Information dialog box and specify the location of the item. You can also select the text item and then choose Info from the Edit menu.

Figure 26.31 shows the first text item that was added to the blank form. Use the mouse to drag the text item to another location.

Figure 26.31
A new text item contains generic text that you can replace with more meaningful text. Then you can move it to a new location or size it as needed.

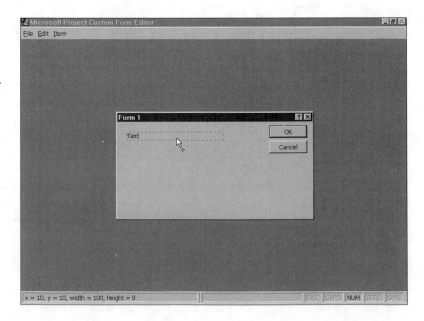

To add a text item to a form, follow these steps:

1. Choose Tools, Customize, Forms to display the Customize Forms dialog box and select the form you want to edit.
2. Choose Edit to display the Microsoft Custom Form Editor.
3. Choose Item, Text. A new text placeholder appears on the custom form.
4. Select the default text and type the desired text.
5. Reposition or size the text placeholder to accommodate the text and form.

PLACING FIELD VALUES ON THE FORM

Custom forms are created to report information about a specific task or resource in an active project. Therefore, they need to be designed to display information from the project file. To do this, you need to add a Field item to the form. Field items access project information and display it in the Customize Forms dialog box so that you can review project information. In addition, you might want to allow users to edit information directly to the project file using the custom form. When you want to restrict editing, you can designate that the field be displayed as Read Only, so it can't be edited by selecting and marking the Show as Static Text check box. You can reposition the field item or resize the display of a field item using the same techniques used to reposition and size text items.

To add a field value item to a custom form, follow these steps:

1. Display the form in the Custom Form Editor window.
2. Choose Item, Fields. The Item Information dialog box appears.
3. Select a field from the Field drop-down list. Because the list includes fields of information contained in the project, placing a field in the form will pull the information from the project and report the information for the selected task or resource each time you activate the custom form.
4. Choose Show as Static Text to prevent users from editing the field in the form, if desired.
5. Choose OK. The field item appears on the form as displayed in Figure 26.32. The field item that appears in the example is designed to display the duration of the selected task.
6. Reposition or size the field item as needed.

PLACING A GROUP BOX ON THE FORM

Group boxes allow you to create sections on a custom form so that you can group related information. A group box provides a boundary line around fields on the form, and you can add fields to a form and place them inside the group box. The same basic procedures are used to add a group box to a form that you used to add a text item to a form. You can then name the group box to summarize the relationship of the fields it contains. Enter the text that you want displayed at the top of the group box while the new group item is still selected, and then use the mouse to position the group box at the desired location. You might need to adjust the size of the form dialog box to accommodate a group box. Positioning it on top of existing items hides other items from view.

Figure 26.32
Place a field item on a form to access information from the project.

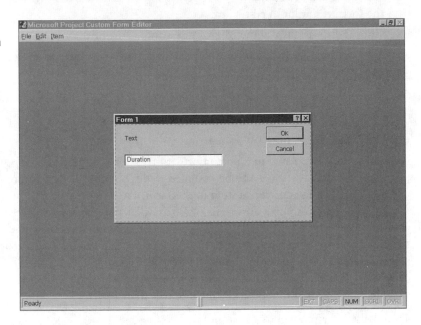

To add a group box to a custom form, follow these steps:

1. Display the form in the Custom Form Editor window.

2. Choose Item, Group Box. A new group box placeholder appears on the custom form and displays the default name Group.

3. Press Backspace to remove the default group name and type the desired group name, or double-click the placeholder and type the desired group name in the Text field of the Item Information dialog box.

4. Reposition or size the group box placeholder to accommodate the information you plan to place in it and the form. Figure 26.33 displays a group box added to the new custom form.

Most items that can be added to a custom form can be included in a group box. To add items to the group box, use these steps:

1. Add a group box to the custom form.

2. Add the desired items to the form and move them into the group box, positioning them as desired.

3. Adjust the size of the group box as required.

Figure 26.33
Group boxes are used to provide visual orientation. Place the group item and then move other items into it.

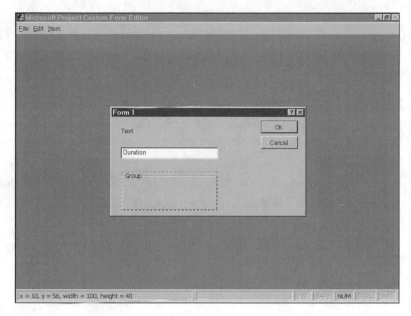

PLACING BUTTONS ON THE FORM

Two different types of buttons can be added to custom forms: the OK button and the Cancel button. Each form can contain only one of each type of button, and these are added by default when you create a custom form. You can delete the buttons if desired, or move them to a new location on the form. If you add a new button that already appears on the form, it simply replaces the original button on the form. Use the same procedures to place a button on the form that you used to place other items on custom forms:

1. Display the form in the Custom Form Editor window.
2. Choose Item, Button.
3. Select the desired button type.
4. Choose OK.
5. Reposition or resize the buttons as desired.

SAVING THE FORM

To save the form and continue working on it, choose Save from the File menu. After the form is complete, choose File, Exit. If unsaved changes exist, you are prompted to save the form again before exiting.

RENAMING, EDITING, AND COPYING CUSTOM FORMS

Forms you create are attached to the project in which they were created. Therefore, to use a form in another project, you need to copy the form to the project. The Customize Forms dialog box provides access to the Organizer so that you can use the same techniques to copy custom forms to another project that you used to copy toolbars and menu bars to a project. You can also use the Organizer to delete custom forms or rename them. The Customize Forms dialog box can be used to edit an existing form, to make a copy of a custom form, or to rename a form.

Renaming Custom Forms

You can rename a custom form using both the Customize Forms dialog box and the Organizer. To change the name of a form using the Customize Forms dialog box, use these steps:

1. Choose Tools, Customize, Forms to display the Customize Forms dialog box.
2. Select the form you want to rename in the Custom Forms list.
3. Choose Rename.
4. Type the new name for the form in the Name field of the Define Custom Form dialog box.
5. Choose OK to save the form using the new name.

Editing a Custom Form

You can edit an existing custom form when you need to add or remove items but don't want to create a completely new form. Editing an existing form places it in the Custom Form Editor window, and you can use techniques described earlier in this section to add and remove items.

To change the design of a form, follow these steps:

1. Choose Tools, Customize, Forms to display the Customize Forms dialog box.
2. Select the form you want to edit in the Custom Forms list.
3. Choose Edit. The Custom Form Editor opens and displays the form for you to edit.
4. Add and remove items following procedures described earlier in this section.

Managing Forms with the Organizer

Custom forms are created and saved in the project file that is active when you create the form. You can use the Organizer to copy a custom form to another project file or to the GLOBAL.MPT template so that it's available for every project. You can also use the Organizer to delete custom forms and to rename them.

To display the Organizer, follow these steps:

1. Choose Tools, Customize, Forms to display the Custom Forms dialog box.
2. Choose Organizer. The Forms tab of the Organizer dialog box is automatically displayed.

→ To learn more about the techniques and procedures you can use to rename, delete, and copy forms, see "Using the Organizer," p. 128

TROUBLESHOOTING

REMOVING TOOLBAR BUTTONS

I can't remove a button from the toolbar. What am I doing wrong?

Be sure the Customize dialog box is open whether you are adding or removing toolbar buttons. Otherwise, clicking the button automatically performs the commands of the macro that are attached to the button. When the Customize dialog box is open, Project knows you're working with the toolbars rather than issuing commands using the toolbar buttons.

DISAPPEARING CUSTOM TOOLBARS

I customized my toolbars at the office, but when I open a project on my system at home the default toolbars appear. Where are my customized toolbars?

The toolbars you customize are attached to the application on the system you were using when you customized them. Actually, they are attached to the GLOBAL.MPT on your system. To install them on your machine at home, you need to copy the GLOBAL.MPT file on your machine at work to a disk and replace the GLOBAL.MPT file on your home system with the one you copied from the office computer.

WORKING WITH GROUP BOXES

When I move an item into a group box, the text box doesn't move with it. Is that really how it's supposed to work?

Correct. You have to move each piece of data and each item separately into a group box.

MAKING YOUR CUSTOM FORMS WORK

I created a custom form but now I can't figure out how to use it. How can I make it work?

You can display the form from the Customize Forms dialog box by selecting the form and choosing Apply. This, however, takes away the advantage of creating the form in the first place. As a result, you will probably want to assign the custom form to a menu, to a shortcut keystroke, or to a toolbar button to make accessing it more efficient.

MISSING CUSTOM FORMS?

I created a custom form but when I created a new project, it wasn't there. Where is it?

Custom forms are stored with the project for which they were created. To use them in other projects, you need to use the Organizer to copy the form to the GLOBAL.MPT so that it's available for all projects.

CHAPTER 27

INTRODUCTION TO VISUAL BASIC MACROS WITH PROJECT 2000

In this chapter *by Rod Gill – www.projectlearning.com*

WHY USE VISUAL BASIC MACROS?

Visual Basic for Applications macros enable you to automate your work. A VBA macro is simply text created either by recording it or by manually entering the instructions via the Visual Basic Editor (VBE) that are then interpreted by Project when you run the macro.

For example, instead of manually printing a series of reports, waiting for each to complete before you manually start the next, you can automate the process and leave the macro to remember what has to be done, how to do it, and the format it should be in. A macro can also turn a job that only someone skilled in the use of Project can do into one that anyone can do by opening a Project file and pressing a specific keystroke combination. Thus, automation using Visual Basic macros can save you time and allow delegation of what would otherwise be advanced work to the less skilled.

Visual Basic for Applications (VBA) is a version of BASIC that comes built in to all current Office products. Office 97 and Project 98 had VBA 5; Project and Office 2000 both have VBA 6. Each new release has more productive ways of helping you code more quickly and accurately.

→ Macros are stored either in your Project files or in the GLOBAL.MPT file. To learn more about working with the GLOBAL.MPT file, **see** "The GLOBAL.MPT," **p. 125**

Macros have many uses beyond printing your reports. Using macros to format views for specific purposes can also save much time. Instead of manually having to make changes, you can run a prerecorded macro to perform them for you. Other uses for VBA macros include

- **Importing data into Project and generating a Project plan**—Take a look at the macro called ImportProject, which imports data from an Excel spreadsheet and builds a plan (see Chapter 28, "Developing Visual Basic Macros").

- **Sharing Project reports with people who don't have Project**—When it comes to reports in Project, they either are views, which aren't available in electronic form for people without Project, or are printed, hard-copy reports. These aren't always the ideal way of sharing data about your project plans. In this case, a macro that exports data to Excel to allow people to further format it or email it is a very powerful and useful tool. This can be accomplished with the ProfitLossReport macro in Chapter 28.

- **Utilizing email to update the project team**—While the Workgroup and Project Central functionality are very useful, they don't work across the Internet. Having a macro to create and send details of all selected tasks via email would save time and help improve communications. See Chapter 28 for the macro EmailData, as an example of how to email data from your project file via Microsoft Outlook.

- **Exporting and importing time sheet information**—Because the Task and Resource time sheets allow reports and input of data on a day-by-day basis, Project lends itself to being directly linked to time sheet applications. ExportWorkData is a macro example of how you can export data by time (see Chapter 28).

  The CD that comes with this book has an example of a time sheet system—Project Program Manager. In fact, the full version of Project Program Manager comes complete with all code, making it a great source of working code for you to learn from.

Anything you can do manually in Project, you can automate in VBA. In fact, anything you can do manually in any other Office product, you can have VBA perform for you from within Project. You can also use VBA in other Office applications to control Project. What this means is that you can create a solution using whichever Office application is most suitable. Where one Office program on its own might not be able to perform the complex tasks you need to accomplish, you can use two or more programs and "glue" them together using VBA. This is being recognized as an increasingly useful tool for many organizations, because powerful solutions can be created in a fraction of the time it would take to develop them from scratch using traditional programming tools.

An example of this is using Microsoft Project to manage the information for your projects and Excel for some of the reports. This provides a solution with Project's strengths as a planning tool and Excel's power to manipulate and present numerical data. A VBA macro would be the glue that reads the relevant data, exports it to Excel before formatting it, and leaves it ready for printing or emailing. Chapter 28 has a working example of this type of system.

WHAT YOU NEED TO KNOW ABOUT VBA

To create successful VBA Macros, first you need to know what Project 2000 can and can't do. This is already clear to you if you've read all the previous chapters or are fairly familiar with Project 2000. You also need to have an understanding of how to record macros and how to use the Visual Basic Editor (VBE) environment.

When you're comfortable with that, it's vital that you understand how Project VBA interacts with Project 2000—how it accesses project data and how it performs actions such as printing, editing tasks, managing resources and assignments, and so on.

The great news is that if you already know how to program in VBA for any of the other Office programs (or the many third-party programs that have a licensed version of VBA in them), you're already one step ahead. In fact you can probably just skim through this chapter as a refresher and move on to Chapter 28. If this is your first experience with Visual Basic macros, this chapter will prepare you to use VBA for not only Project, but other applications as well.

Once you've mastered recording Visual Basic macros, you should try your hand at writing your own code to take advantage of the power and usefulness of VBA programming that just recording on its own cannot deliver.

By the time you have read and digested this chapter and the information in Chapter 28, you will have a working knowledge of how to create macros (by recording and writing them manually). You should then be able to take that knowledge and move farther into using VBA if you so desire. To help you tackle the basics, you'll see plenty of examples. Any vocabulary you run across, that you aren't already familiar with, are technical words that are important for you to know to facilitate your understanding and to better use the comprehensive help system built into Project 2000.

RECORDING VBA MACROS FOR PROJECT

Recording a macro works well for simple tasks such as printing a particular view or report. It is also useful when you want to see how Project records an action when programming larger, more complex macros. Beyond that, recording complete macros becomes less productive because the more complex the task, the more manual coding you will need to do. By learning to code manually, your programming will be done more quickly and effectively. Recorded macros might work properly when run immediately, but are likely to produce undesirable results when run the next day, week, or month.

For example, typical things that change and can stop a recorded macro are blank tasks or resources being added, extra tasks or resources being added or deleted, names being changed, and project files that need to be open being closed, or closed ones being open and changing dates. All these changes can be managed, but only by manually editing the recorded macro. As you become more experienced, you will find yourself writing more and more of your code and recording less and less. Until then, it's best that you use macro recording to automate simple tasks and give you sample code to get you started and to show you how to code some of the many Project commands. With that in mind, let's take a look at how to create basic macros.

RECORDING AND SAVING A MACRO

Even if you have a view specifically for printing, it is amazing how often you can forget to return to the standard Gantt Chart and change the Gantt Chart—Print view settings by mistake. So, one easy way to guarantee that the correct view is printed—with the correct table, filter, and timescale selected—is to record a macro of you going through the steps to manually print. After this has been recorded, in the future when you want to print, all you need to do is run the macro.

STEP 1: PREPARING TO RECORD YOUR MACRO

When you prepare to create your macro, you need to keep in mind what your end result is going to be. In some cases, what you want to produce might not actually exist yet in its entirety within Project. For example, if you want to create a macro that will display a non-standard view or report, you need to create those elements first. While you could do all the formatting and reformatting in the macro, any change to how you want the final result to look would then require re-recording it. As you learned earlier in the chapter, the more complex the macro, the greater the chance of getting something wrong—a key to useful recorded macros you can use over and over is simplicity.

Tip from Tim and the Project Team

For easier printing, copy the Gantt Chart and call it Gantt Chart—Print. Format this view exactly as you want to see it on paper. After you've printed the Gantt Chart, swap back to the standard Gantt Chart to continue working. It will save you a lot of time formatting and reformatting!

Create a Gantt Chart—Print view now in any Project plan that you want to work with. You will use it in a macro example for step 2.

→ To learn more about creating custom views, **see** "Creating New Views," **p. 944**

→ To copy the Gantt Chart—Print view, or other views your create, to the GLOBAL.MPT file so that it can be used by all your Project files, **see** "Creating and Using Templates," **p. 124**

Before recording anything, make sure that you have created any views, tables, and filters you need to apply in the macro. If this macro needs to work for several Project files, then these views, tables, and filters need to be copied to the Organizer. Have a clear idea of what the end result needs to look like. If you're not completely clear, it's often a good idea to have a dry run.

→ For more information about working with the Organizer in Project, **see** "Using the Organizer," **p. 128**

You will find it confusing to read a macro where half the code involves doing and then redoing various actions. For example, if, when you are recording, it takes you several attempts to find the right table and filter, the result is likely to be messy when replayed. Practice all the actions in advance of actually recording the macro, perhaps jotting down view and filter names. Rehearsing before you begin recording your macro will help so that you can record your macro cleanly with the minimum number of steps required.

Tip from Tim and the Project Team

Write a brief script (a script here is simply a list of the steps that you will follow) for more complex macros. For example, your script might be: Select Gantt Chart—Print view, select Cost table, select Monthly timescale, preview whole project.

STEP 2: RECORDING YOUR MACRO

After you have prepared everything you need to be able to record the entire macro, choose Tools, Macro, Record Macro to display the Record Macro window (see Figure 27.1).

Figure 27.1
The Record macro dialog box edited and ready to start recording.

The macro name must start with a letter. It can contain letters, numbers, and the underscore character, but no spaces. A good technique when you are naming macros is to capitalize the first letter of each word, as in PrintGanttChart.

Next, you can assign a shortcut key. You should do this only for macros you will use frequently. A shortcut key allows you to run a macro by pressing Ctrl plus a letter. Because of the shortcuts built into Project already, the only shortcut keys available are A, E, J, L, M, Q, T, and Y.

In Figure 27.1, you should notice that This Project is designated as the place to store the macro. It's a good rule of thumb to always record your macros into your current project file. After you have them working, you can then copy the macros to the Organizer for use in other project plans. Following this guideline will help prevent you from having a build-up of little-used or broken macros in the GLOBAL.MPT file.

The Record Macro dialog box also gives you the option to enter a description for your macro. While it's tempting to leave the description empty, you can use this space to enter a meaningful description that explains to you, and others, what this macro does and who wrote it. In most cases, the time spent entering a description will be saved many times down the road.

The last two sections you see in the Record Macro box in Figure 27.1 are Row References and Column References. Although we aren't concerned about these sections in our current example, it's helpful for you to understand what they control. For example, if the macro you record entails moving down one row, and you want the macro to record always moving down one row, regardless of which row you started in, keep the Row References setting on Relative. On the other hand, if you want to record going to a specific task, you should either select Absolute (ID) or, when recording your macro, press F5 (Goto) to go to the task you want. As for the Column References setting, by default moving from column to column is always in absolute mode. This is due to the frequency of wanting to go to specific information rather than moving over to the next column.

Now put to use what you've just learned. Record a macro called PrintGanttChart that selects the Gantt Chart—Print view, applies the table Cost and the filter All Tasks, and then changes the timescale to Monthly. Finally, your macro should preview the view and return to the standard Gantt Chart. To create this type of macro, follow these steps:

1. Choose Tools, Macro, Record Macro.
2. Enter the name **PrintGanttChart**.
3. Select This Project as the destination to save the resulting macro and click OK.
4. Now select Gantt Chart—Print view, the Cost table, the filter All Tasks (even if it is already selected; otherwise, displaying All Tasks won't be recorded). Be sure to format the timescale, as required.
5. Perform any other formatting that will enhance the printout and then select Print Preview.
6. Close the preview and view the standard Gantt Chart to finish the macro. Now you just need to stop the recording, so move on to step 3.

STEP 3: COMPLETING YOUR MACRO

With everything done that you want recorded, stop your macro recording session by choosing Tools, Macro, Stop Recorder. The macro is now saved in your active project. If you didn't select the This Project option in the initial Record Macro dialog box, the default location where your macro will be recorded is the Global file. If you realize that you saved it in the Global file, but want it in your current project, you can move it using the Organizer (see "Working with the Organizer" in Chapter 3, "Setting Up a New Project Document"). Macros saved in the project file aren't saved until the project file itself is saved. Macros recorded into the Global file aren't saved until you exit Project.

Tip from Tim and the Project Team	The Global file isn't actually saved until you exit Project, so it's in your best interest to exit Project and then restart it after you have successfully recorded a useful macro and saved it in the GLOBAL.MPT file. If your PC crashes or loses power, the Global file along with your precious macro—won't be saved if you haven't exited Project normally.
	If you are running Project over a network, your GLOBAL.MPT file is often in a read-only directory, preventing your GLOBAL.MPT file from being updated. Copy the GLOBAL.MPT file from the read-only directory (usually the program directory on your server) to a directory you have write permission for (for example, your C: drive or personal directory on the network). If you run Project from the Start Programs menu, then in Windows Explorer find the directory `C:\Windows\Start Menu\Programs`. Right-click the Project 2000 shortcut and select Properties. If you run Project from the Office toolbar, right click the Project icon and select Properties from there. In the Shortcut Start In box, enter the directory where you saved your copy of the GLOBAL.MPT file. When you start Project, it looks in the directory nominated by the Start In field for the GLOBAL.MPT file. If it's not there, Project looks in the program directory.

Tip from Tim and the Project Team	If you need to go to a particular task to perform some action, first make sure that the Task Name is unique within the project, and use Edit, Find to find the task name. If you go to a task ID, there is a good chance that someone will add or delete a task causing the task ID to change and end your macro's usefulness.

RUNNING YOUR MACROS

Now that you've recorded your macro, it's time to try running it. To run your macro, choose Tools, Macro, Macros (or press Alt+F8).

In the Macros dialog box, your macro name will appear with the project filename, an exclamation mark (!), and then the macro name if it's stored in your project file. If it's in the GLOBAL.MPT file, just the macro name appears in the list. Click the name of the macro you want to run, and then click the Run button.

Tip from Tim and the Project Team	To run a macro that's in another file, open that file and all its macros will appear on the macro list as well.

RUNNING YOUR MACROS FROM A TOOLBAR

Frequently run macros can usefully be added to a toolbar as icons. To add a button that runs a macro for you, follow these instructions:

1. Select Tools, Customize, Toolbars to display the Customize window.

2. With the Commands tab selected, scroll down the Categories list to All Macros.

3. Click and drag your macro from the Commands list to wherever you want it on any visible toolbar.

4. With the macro button on the toolbar still selected, click Modify Selection.

5. Edit the button's name to change the text, if you desire.

6. Click the Change Button Image option and select an image.
   Click Modify Selection again and then Default.
   Your macro button should now only show the image you selected.

7. Click Close to finish adding a macro button.

To remove a button from a toolbar, select Tools, Customize, Toolbars, and then drag the button down off the toolbar until a small x appears next to the mouse pointer.

THE VISUAL BASIC EDITOR

By default the Visual Basic Editor (VBE) has four screen areas. All these areas can be closed to free up more room for the other windows. By choosing Tools, Options and then the Docking tab, you can uncheck the different windows so that they can float around or be arranged in any way you like. However, leaving them docked is usually the most useful way because it automatically gives the windows that need it (especially the code window) the most space (see Figure 27.2).

THE PROJECT EXPLORER

This area is similar in look to Windows Explorer, but instead of seeing folders you will see Project objects and modules. To display the Project Explorer, choose View, Project Explorer (Ctrl+R).

Sometimes, depending on how you last left VBE, nothing might be displayed. Display the Project Explorer and then navigate to the module you want. You should double-click it to display its code.

THE PROPERTIES WINDOW

The Properties window's most likely use for you is to rename modules to more meaningful names. To display the Properties window, click View, Properties Window (F4).

To change the name of a module, click it in the Project Explorer and then edit the Name property in the Properties window. By default the first module with a recorded macro in it is Module1, then Module2, and so on.

Figure 27.2
The Visual Basic Editor showing the code of a recorded macro.

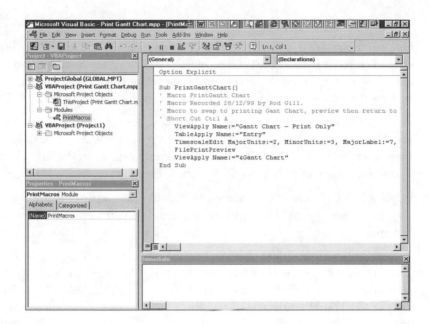

The same default naming convention applies when inserting a module manually with Insert, Module.

THE CODE WINDOW

The largest area is the code window. If this is blank for you, display the Project Explorer (Ctrl+R) and navigate to the module with your macro and either double-click it or click View, Code (F7).

Note that in the bottom-left corner of the code window are two small icons. Hover your mouse over them and the left one is called Procedure view and the right one Full Module view. Procedure view only shows one routine or function at a time. In fact, to begin with you might only see the statement Option Explicit (explained later in this chapter).

Press Page Down on the keyboard twice to view the first routine, and Page Down again when you are at the bottom of the code of that routine to view the next subroutine, and so on.

Alternatively, use Ctrl+Down to go from routine to routine (Ctrl+Page Up to move up through the routines) or select the name of the routine you want from the Procedure drop-down list at the top right of the code window.

Subroutines can be recorded and then edited in this code window or manual typed into it. As your experience levels grow, you will find you do less and less recording and more manual entry. This is because you will get to an end result quicker and with more intelligible code.

PART
VIII

CH
27

THE IMMEDIATE WINDOW

One of the most time-consuming parts of writing a macro is the time spent getting your code to do just what you want and no more! The Immediate window is an excellent tool for that phase of development—usually called the debugging stage. To display the Immediate window if it isn't already visible, select View, Immediate Window (Ctrl+G).

Try clicking anywhere in the Immediate Window, typing **?5*5**, and then pressing the Enter key. The question mark is a shorthand notation for print. After pressing Enter, the Immediate Window evaluates any functions or calculations on the current line and displays the answer on the next. In this case, you should see the answer 25.

While it is useful to have a calculator available like this, more typically you will want to display the contents of variables or to create some code that works and then copy it to the code window.

Try entering **?activeproject.name** and pressing Enter. This time the answer is evaluated as the name of the active project. After you had typed **?activeproject** and the fullstop, did you notice the drop-down list that appeared? It contained all the valid instructions that can follow the activeproject statement. The fullstop acts as a separator between parts of your statement. In this case it marked the divide between activeproject and its Name instruction (or as you will learn soon, its Name property). Try some of the other instructions, such as HoursPerDay, FullName, NumberOfTasks, and NumberOfResources. Some of the words are actions relevant to projects; others, such as the examples just mentioned, are descriptions—defined in VBA as properties and described more in Chapter 28.

Tip from Tim and the Project Team

> If there is something you don't know how to write manually in Visual Basic, record it. Save the macro to the active Project file; after you have copied the code to where you want it, you can use the Project Explorer to remove the module created by the recording process.

MAKING MACROS AVAILABLE TO ALL PROJECTS

You can make a macro available to all other projects without the project it was saved in having to be open. You simply need to copy the module it's in to the GLOBAL.MPT file using the Organizer. By default, the module your first macro is saved in is called Module1. It is a good idea to rename this to something more meaningful—PrintMacros would be good for the PrintGanttChart macro. Many macros can be written in each module.

→ To can learn specific details about Project's Organizer, **see** "Using the Organizer," **p. 128**

Figure 27.3 shows the Organizer with the Modules tab selected. Notice that the default module name is Module1, then Module2, and so on. Obviously these names aren't meaningful. You can either change the name here in the Organizer or in the Visual Basic Editor. To do so, display the Project Explorer (Ctrl+R) and the Properties window (F4). Click the module name, expanding the tree if necessary, and then rename it in the Properties window. Use meaningful names, such as PrintMacros. If you record a macro you no longer want to keep, the <u>D</u>elete button will delete a module for you. Be careful that there aren't any other macros saved in the module first.

Figure 27.3
The Organizer with the Modules tab selected, ready to rename Module1 and copy it to the GLOB-AL.MPT file.

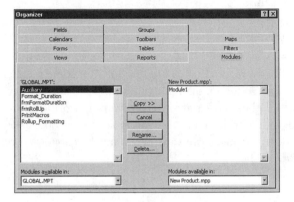

Tip from Tim and the Project Team

As you collect useful macros in the GLOBAL.MPT file, it might save you much heartache if you make sure it gets backed up regularly. An even better idea is to always keep the original projects with their macros separate, and backed up, so that if the GLOBAL.MPT file ever gets over-written or deleted, the macros can be recopied to the new GLOBAL.MPT file.

CREATING A FILTERING MACRO

As an example to help you explore the VBE, a macro to filter tasks for the next two weeks only is a good exercise. Open a project file to record the following macro, or open "Chap27/Filter.mpp" from the CD. Perform the following steps to create the macro:

1. Choose <u>T</u>ools, <u>M</u>acro, <u>R</u>ecord Macro.
2. Enter a macro name of **FilterNextTwoWeeks**.
3. Select to store the macro in This Project.
4. You can edit the description if you wish and assign a shortcut key.
5. Choose OK.
6. Click <u>P</u>roject, <u>F</u>iltered For and then the <u>D</u>ate Range filter or select Date Range from the drop-down list of filters on the Formatting toolbar.
7. Enter today's date and choose OK.
8. Enter a date for two weeks time and choose OK.
9. Click <u>T</u>ools, <u>M</u>acro, Stop <u>R</u>ecorder to end the recording.
10. Choose <u>T</u>ools, <u>M</u>acro, <u>V</u>isual Basic Editor or press Alt+F11 to display VBE.

If the code window doesn't show the macro you recorded, make sure the Project Explorer is visible by pressing Ctrl+R. Double-click first the Modules folder and then the Module1 module to display your code, or click the Filter module to display the already recorded version in Filter.Mpp.

Its code should look like this:

```
Sub FilterNextTwoWeeks()
FilterApply Name:="Date Range..."
End Sub
```

This is a classic example of a macro that will only work after some manual intervention because every time the macro is run, the filter will prompt for the start and end dates. These have not been recorded. Other classics are macros that only work while a coded date is current, or until tasks are added or deleted. While designing your code, always remember that data will change and that your macro must handle as much change as is reasonably possible.

To make your macro always work from the current day for two weeks, edit the code to look like this:

```
Sub FilterNextTwoWeeks()
'This macro takes a basic filter and automates it by using
'the Date function which always returns today's date.
'Adding 14 to Date produces a date two weeks (14 days) into
'the future.
FilterApply Name:="Date Range...", Value1:=Date, Value2:=Date + 14
End Sub
```

The added rows are comment rows. Anything to the right of a single quote (') is ignored by Project. The comment quote can be at the beginning of a line, or after some code. They are great for explaining what's going on. You might remember which code does what now, but only a week or two after first writing it, it's easy to forget what your original intent and function might have been for the code.

When you look closely at the newly written code you've revised, you'll see that what has changed is the Value1:= and Value2:= portion of the row that has been added to the FilterApply statement. FilterApply in Project VBA is a method. Another way of describing it is an action. It does something—in this case, it applies the filter Date Range. FilterApply is followed by a space and then a series of what are called *parameters*. A parameter is a piece of information needed by the method for it to do its work. When recording the macro, Project remembers and includes the name of the filter, but not the dates. When the Value1 and Value2 parameters are not coded, Project prompts you for the required information—in this case, the start and end dates. If you click the word FilterApply and press F1 for help, you will note that there are only Value1 and Value2, so don't create a filter with more than two prompts. Clicking on any method and searching help tells you which parameters you need, which are optional, and what their names are. You will also note that if you type the statement, the Visual Basic Editor (VBE) displays the names and sequence of parameters for you.

For Project to understand that the word Value1 is a parameter and not something else, it is followed by := (a colon and an equal sign). Parameter names aren't compulsory, but if you don't type them, you must get the paramaters in the right sequence and you can't miss any.

Keep in mind that each parameter is separated by a comma. By having , , (two commas), you create a placeholder and Project skips to the next parameter (unnecessary if parameter names are used).

There are various methods, like sort, where there are numerous parameters and you usually only need one or two. Using parameter names is good practice because it makes the command easier to understand and allows you to enter only the parameters needed. It also makes your code easier to read and therefore easier to follow the logic of the code.

You now know that FilterApply is a method and it is followed by a space and a series of parameters. The FilterApply method is coded in something called a subroutine, which always has a clear start and finish. A subroutine starts with a statement such as the following:

```
Sub FilterNextTwoWeeks()
```

The Sub statement defines the name of a macro and is short for Subroutine. It also defines the start of the macro, which is always ended by the statement

```
End Sub
```

What comes between these two statements (Sub and End Sub) is what the next chapter covers.

USING HELP TO UNDERSTAND YOUR CODE

Click your mouse anywhere on the word FilterApply and press F1 for Help. You can do this for anything that is a word built in to Project VBA. Help will appear and tell you all about what you clicked on (see Figure 27.4).

Figure 27.4
The FilterApply help window is complete with See Also and Example words, which you can click for further online help information.

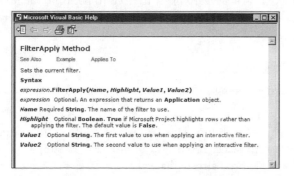

Help describes the method FilterApply, gives the syntax for it, and then explains all about each parameter. Take a look in Figure 27.4 at the Applies To hyperlink. It can be useful to read the objects this particular method can be applied to.

Note that Value is an optional string. First, this means that, depending what you do with the other parameters, it might not be needed at all. Second, it must be in the form of a string.

A *string* is anything that is text and is delimited by double quotes ("). Spaces, numbers, characters (!@#$), and so on, are all permissible. You have, however, just entered Date and Date+14. Both these are dates and are of a data type called Date, not String. The code has worked because Project has automatically converted the Date format to a string. This might not always work, and future versions might not do the automatic conversion reliably.

A safer way to adjust your code is to use CStr(Date) and CStr(Date+14) to force conversion of the dates to strings. CStr is in blue, which means it's a *reserved word*—it has a special meaning in VBA. Date is a built-in *function*. A function is a piece of code, either provided already in VBA (as is the CStr function) or created by you. CStr converts whatever is in the parentheses into a string. CStr is short for Convert to String. Try using Help to read up on data type conversion (enter **data type conversion** into Help's Answer Wizard).

Date on its own produces a date type, not a string. In Excel, for those of you who are familiar with it, have you formatted a cell to Date, Number, Currency, or just General? This is much the same. A date can be the number of days since 1900, it can be a date with all sorts of date calculations that can be done on it,(add two months to a date or subtract 14 days, and so forth), or it can be converted to a string (by using CStr()).

By looking in Help, you have learned that the value must be a string and that by using CStr we can convert the Date function into a string. Read up on the other data conversion functions. You will need to use some of them sooner or later.

Also try clicking the Contents tab in Help, followed by the Functions book and then the D-G book. Click some of the other Date functions. Be sure to click the Example keyword (in blue), which appears for most topics, for examples of using each function. Dates are frequently used in Project, so you are very likely to need to perform calculations on them and manipulate them in various ways. The Date functions are the tools that enable you to do this.

Testing Your Filtering Macro

Now that you've created a macro to filter tasks for the next two weeks only, you need to test it out.

The best place from which to run the macro is Project itself, not the Visual Basic Editor. Go to the Windows task bar and select Project (or use Alt+F11 to swap between VBE and Project). Open a project plan you already have that has tasks that are running now and have in the past and/or will in the future.

If you don't have current tasks in the project you have open, running the macro will hide all tasks.

Tip from Tim and the Project Team | F3 will display the filter All Tasks and show you all the tasks again after the macro or applying a filter manually has hidden some of them.

Press Alt+F8, which is a shortcut for Tools, Macro, Macros, and double-click the Filter!FilterNextTwoWeeks macro to run it. (The name of the project the macro is saved in appears before the macro name with a ! separator.)

When you need to test more complex macros, you will be able to step through your code one instruction at a time. You will also be able to insert a breakpoint so that code will stop at nominated places, test individual instructions, and edit them before continuing.

MACRO VIRUS PROTECTION ISSUES

Having completed the exercise to preview Gantt Chart—Print, save and close the Project file you recorded the macro into, and then open it again. This makes sure the macro is saved. It's also a good thing to do before testing, so if running the macro scrambles your data you can close (without saving changes) and then reopen the file and continue working.

When you reopen your Project file, what you are more than likely to see is demonstrated in Figure 27.5. As part of Microsoft's security policy, all Office programs (including Project) have a security certificate. With the medium security setting (default), you are warned when a file you are opening has a macro in it. Given the epidemic of Outlook and Word viruses in the world, this is a useful feature. Since there are no known macro viruses for Project as of mid 2000, it can only be a matter of time before some appear.

Figure 27.5
This dialog box appears when you open a file with one or more macros.

By selecting Tools, Macro, Security from Project, you can nominate High, Medium or Low security. Medium is the default and the best setting for you to keep. As you can read from this dialog box, Medium setting will display this alert if the macro has not been authenticated. You can then choose to Disable or Enable macros.

High security will always disable unsigned macros. There are two ways to get a security certificate for your macros: Either buy one from certificate providers over the Internet (there is an annual fee that varies according to the number of people using the certificate and the level of security desired) or create your own using a utility that comes with Office Premium.

CREATING YOUR OWN DIGITAL CERTIFICATE

To prevent this macro message from appearing every time without setting security to its lowest level, you need to create or purchase your own digital certificate. To create your own certificate, you must install and use a digital certificate program (Selfcert.exe) provided with Microsoft Office 2000 Premium.

Run the Office 2000 Setup program (you might need to insert the Office 2000 Disk 1 CD in your CD drive). On the opening screen in the Setup program, expand Office Tools and choose Digital Signature for VBA projects. Click the arrow next to it and select Run from My Computer before continuing. Setup should then install Selfcert.exe. If you installed Project from a Network setup, Selfcert.exe may already be in the Office program directory on the server. (If all else fails, don't forget to check with your Network Administrator.)

Start Selfcert.exe (use Windows Explorer to double-click the file—typically it's in the `Program Files\Microsoft Office\Office` directory).

Because digital certificates you create yourself aren't issued by a formal certification authority, macro projects you digitally sign by using them are considered self-signed projects. Highest security settings do not allow you to run macros signed by certificates created with Selfcert.exe. For high-level security, you need to get a formal certificate, but this involves an annual cost. With the default Medium security setting, self-signed certificates work fine.

Enter your name and your organization's name as you want them to appear on the certificate and the Security Warning window (see Figure 27.6) and then choose OK.

Figure 27.6
What you see after running SelfCert.exe. Enter your name and organization and then click OK.

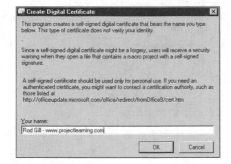

SIGNING YOUR OWN MACROS

Open the project with your macro and then go to the VBE (Alt+F11). After you're there, select Tools, Digital Signature. As you see in Figure 27.7, the Choose button is what you use to make the selection from all the certificates available.

To sign your own macro, select the Choose button and then the certificate you created in SelfCert.exe. You can also see details of the chosen certificate here or remove a certificate from a file.

Figure 27.7
Signing your own
macros.

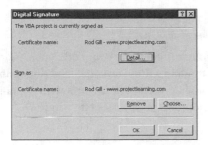

Next time you open your project file, the Disable/Enable message window will have an option to view your certificate details and the option to select Always Trust Macros from This Source. Clicking it will prevent the message from displaying again for all files signed with your certificate.

This method is exactly the same in VBA for all other Office programs. Resave your project file, and then close and open it to test the certificate. Select Tools, Macro, Security and set High Security. Close and reopen your project file and try to run a macro. Return to Medium level security when you have finished.

PUTTING IT ALL TOGETHER

As a useful exercise, try recording a macro to create a .Gif file, and then include it in the Save As Web Page command. In the Visual Basic Editor, click the EditCopyPicture command and press F1 to read all about default values for the FromDate and ToDate parameters. Note that deleting the recorded FromDate and ToDate parameters means that the .Gif file will always go from the earliest to latest dates visible on the Gantt Chart at the time of running the macro.

Remember to edit the "Export to HTML using standard template" map to get it to include the .Gif file if that hasn't already been done before in your active project.

You have now learned to record a macro, save the project file with a self-signed digital certificate, and use the Visual Basic Editor. You have recorded, edited, and run your first macro. In the next chapter you will learn how to write your own code to accomplish things within Project that can't be recorded with keystrokes.

TROUBLESHOOTING

CONTINUALLY GROWING MACROS

When I look at my macro in the VBE, it still appears to have rows added to it. Am I doing something wrong?

If you swap to the VBE editor and notice that the macro you are recording is still growing (rows have been added to the bottom of it), you have probably forgotten to select Tools, Macro, Stop Recorder.

VISUAL BASIC EDITOR IS BLANK

Yikes! I've opened VBE and the code window is blank.

It's likely that you haven't got the module containing your code open. Select View, Project Explorer, and then double-click the module with your code. If in doubt about which is the correct module, double-click every module whose name starts with Module—for example, Module1, and so on. Your code should now appear in a code window.

MULTIPLE OPEN CODE WINDOWS

I have two code windows open, but where is the second one?

Just like in other Microsoft programs, you can have more than one window open. Either use the Window menu to swap between your open windows, or press Ctrl+F6. Alternatively, you can double-click the module name in the Project Explorer to see the code in the other module.

VIEWING MORE CODE

With the Project Explorer and Properties windows open, it's hard to read longer lines of code. What can I do?

Sometimes it helps if you can see as much code as possible, and it saves having to scroll too much. In the top-right corner of every window, there is a small cross. Click it to close that window. You can close the Project Explorer, Properties, and Immediate windows to display the maximum possible amount of code.

GLOBAL.MPT FILE PROBLEMS

When I close my project after recording a macro, I get an error message saying Project couldn't save the GLOBAL.MPT file.

On many networks, Project is installed in a directory that is then protected as Read Only for all users. If you choose to have your macro saved in the Global file, you have two choices for the GLOBAL.MPT file. The file must either be write enabled, or you need to make a copy of the GLOBAL.MPT file and save it in the directory named by the Start In property of the shortcut you use to start Project. The error message is therefore typically encountered on network installations. Another alternative is to always save macros in Project files, not the Global file itself.

CHAPTER 28

DEVELOPING VISUAL BASIC MACROS

In this chapter

by Rod Gill – www.projectlearning.com

GETTING STARTED WITH VISUAL BASIC MACROS

Rather than describe what all the individual building blocks of a macro are, this chapter is going to build some useful macros you can take advantage of in your Project use and explain things as you build them. Project 2000's Help is very comprehensive, so you will be guided to relevant help along the way.

> **Note**
>
> You'll discover that many of the common support questions asking for VBA help in the Microsoft newsgroups are answered in this chapter.

Remember, a great way to start is to build up bits of your macros by recording and then editing them to create the finished product. If you need anything specific explained, you can click it with your mouse in the code window and press F1 for help.

One of the basic tasks writers of macros need to do is to loop through each task and do something with them. In this chapter, you will look at two simple macros with loop examples. The first one shows how to concatenate a task name and its summary task name into the Text1 field so that it can be displayed next to the task bar in the Gantt Chart. You also learn how to concatenate the contents of two different fields, also into Text1. Both of these are often requested for reporting purposes, so learning to automate these steps will prove beneficial.

Tip from Tim and the Project Team

> Whenever you have a new macro to write, break down the job into components small enough that you can work out how to do just that part on its own. This technique is sometimes called *chunking* or a *top-down* approach. Instead of trying to do the whole thing at once, break your process down into parts that are small and simple enough to do. Then slowly build up the final solution with these components until you're completely finished.

THE TASKSUMMARYNAME MACRO

This macro will expose you to loops, objects, properties, and variables. As already suggested, loops are one of the most common things you will need to code into your macros. Objects are the things you will be controlling and changing. Examples of objects are projects, tasks, resources, assignments, and so on.

Properties belong to objects and help describe them. Properties can be changed and then affect how you see the object. For example, a Task object has a name property. Change the name property, and the text in the Gantt Chart changes to reflect the change to its name property.

Variables are temporary in nature and exist purely to help you make things happen. If you want to loop through all tasks and count how many tasks of a certain type there are, you will use a variable to store the count. You also need variables to refer to objects and to construct loops, as you will see next.

Very often, projects have a set of tasks repeated numerous times with only the summary task details changing. There is then the need to have some way of having a new description for the tasks that includes their summary task name. This first sample macro does that, creating a composite name in the custom field Text1.

The following chunks are key components of the solution you will be building:

- Name and set up the macro.
- Define some variables to use.
- Create a mechanism to loop through all tasks.
- Test for a blank task row.
- Test for outline level 1 and summary tasks. (They will be simply copied across on their own.)
- Get the task's name and its summary task name.
- Concatenate the two and save in Text1.
- Add an "I've finished" message and a count of the number of nonblank tasks worked on.

NAMING AND CONFIGURING THE TASKSUMMARYNAME MACRO

This is something you will need to do for every application. To create the TaskSummaryName macro, follow these instructions:

1. First, open a Project file of your own.
2. Press Alt+F11 to show the VBE.
3. Click Insert, Module to add a module to your Project file.
4. Type the code in Listing 28.1.

If you prefer not to type the code, open "Chap28/Text1Macro.Mpp" from the CD and press Alt+F11 to open the Visual Basic Editor (VBE).

LISTING 28.1 THE TASKSUMMARYNAME MACRO

```
Sub TaskSummaryName()
Dim T As Task              'Task Variables start = Nothing
Dim TaskCount As Integer   'Integer variables start as 0 (zero)

For Each T In ActiveProject.Tasks
    If Not (T Is Nothing) Then        'Is this Task blank?
        If T.OutlineLevel > 1 And T.Summary = False Then
            T.Text1 = T.OutlineParent.Name & ": " & T.Name
        Else
            T.Text1 = T.Name
        End If
        TaskCount = TaskCount + 1    'Increment the count
    End If
Next T
MsgBox "Macro finished" & vbCrLf & vbCrLf & TaskCount & _
    " Tasks worked on"
End Sub
```

PART VIII

CH 28

Notice the rows with a ' (single quote). Remember that they denote a comment in the code. Everything to the right of a quote is ignored by Project.

As you type this code, you will notice some of the power features of Visual Basic. When you pressed Enter after typing in the Sub statement (first line), VBE automatically adds an End Sub statement—the one we want at the end. All code between the Sub and End Sub is kept together. (Sub is short for *Subroutine*.)

After typing Dim T As, a drop-down list will appear to display all possible entries you can type next. Typing T for Task is enough to uniquely select Task. Press the Tab, Enter, or space key to have VBE fill in the rest of the command for you. This will happen all through your code. Whenever there is a limited set of commands, VBE displays that list. It is a fantastic help because you no longer need to remember commands, spelling, different options, and so on. It increases your code writing speed by up to 20% or more.

Tip from Tim and the Project Team

Type everything (except the variable names in the Dim statement) in lowercase. When you move the cursor off the row you've just typed, Project capitalizes your code. If you type activeprojct (missed the last e), it would be very obvious. Insert the missing e, move the cursor down a row, and ActiveProject capitalizes itself—providing instant proof of correct spelling (remember, computers have an IQ of zero, so you need to be very specific with your code—one mistyped character can stop the program from working properly).

DEFINING SOME VARIABLES TO USE

When doing more complex calculations on a calculator, using the memory function saves writing temporary results down and then reentering them. When programming, you will often need to temporarily save information to use later. You might also refer to a piece of information several times that requires a lengthy piece of code to read. Do this once and save it for easy referral later. Using variables, you can do all this and more. Create them by declaring the variables at the start of the macro with a Dim statement (short for *Dimension* statement).

Dim STATEMENTS

You might also hear people say, "declare the variable." By declaring variables (with Dim statements), you are telling Project what variables you need, what they are to be called, and what information they can and cannot hold. Dim T As Task instructs Project to reserve a small piece of memory in the PC and refer to it by using the name T. You could use Tsk or any other name in place of T. As a standard, you can always call a variable that refers to a task T (or whatever name you prefer). The goal is to help make your code more readable.

In our example, As Task means that T will only be used to point to a Task object in Project. It will cause an error if you try to use T for referencing a resource, or for storing a count, or anything else. (Typists often used to have a stand for their copy with a ruler to mark the line they were at. Similarly, the T variable in your code can be used to mark which task you are working on.)

`Dim TaskCount As Integer` tells Project to reserve some memory for a counter we have called `TaskCount`, and it will count the number of tasks that are worked on.

Click the word `Integer` and press F1 to open Help. Note that the maximum value `Integer` can hold is 32,767. While it is big enough for what you want, it might not always be, especially because it can't handle decimal places. In Help, click the See Also words (they should be blue) and then double-click the Data Type Summary option. Now you can see all the different types of variables you can use to store numbers. Keep in mind that `Long` is an alternative to `Integer` for numbers up to 2 billion or `Single` for numbers that have decimal places. When handling numbers that are guaranteed to be less than 32,767, use `Integer` because it uses less memory and is processed faster.

In looking at the example, assuming that `TaskCount` is a variable to hold a number, what is `T`? `T` is a variable used to point to a task in the project plan and then access all information related to that task.

Option Explicit

Have you noticed the `Option Explicit` statement as the very first row in your module? What this does is force every variable you use to be declared using a `Dim` statement. Without the `Option Explicit` statement, you can use variables without having a `Dim`.

So why `Dim` each variable? Let's say you have a variable called `TaskCount` for counting the number of tasks you work on. If you type the name as `TskCount` (missed the a) by mistake, then with `Option Explicit`, Project will detect that `TskCount` hasn't been declared and will let you know so you can correct the typing error. Without `Option Explicit` you will now have two variables and `TaskCount` can end up with the wrong value, a classic mistake that can take many frustrating hours to discover and correct.

If `Option Explicit` isn't displayed at the top of your modules, you can force `Option Explicit` in each module by making sure that Require Variable Declaration is turned on in the Editor tab under Tools, Options while in VBE. It is strongly recommended that `Option Explicit` does appear at the top of every module. The time spent typing the `Dim` statements will be saved many times over once you start testing.

OBJECTS

`T` is an example of an object variable, it points to an object, in this case a Task object.

Close Help, click the word `ActiveProject`, and again press F1 for Help.

Click the Contents tab and scroll up the list of topics on the left until you get to the top. Click the book "Microsoft Project Visual Basic Reference" and then the topic "Microsoft Project Objects." This shows you the hierarchy of all objects in Project. You will need to become very familiar with it. Take a look at Figure 28.1 to see the Project Object Model.

Figure 28.1
The Project Object Model as seen in Help.

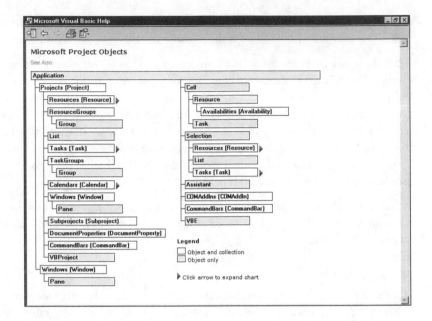

Notice the red triangle against the Resources, Tasks and other objects. Click the triangle and you will see the related objects.

The top object is Application, which represents Project 2000 itself. In this hierarchy, each object has properties, and all properties belong to objects and help describe them. There are usually many properties for each object. For example, one property of the Application object is `ActiveProject`. It provides a pointer to the active project in the form of a Project object. `ActiveProject` itself has properties—one is `Name`. The code `ActiveProject.Name` will always return the filename of the project. A full stop is always used to separate an object from the property. When typing the full stop, Project will display all valid properties for you—a fantastic programming aid.

`ActiveProject` is particularly useful because you can always use it to refer to the active project, meaning that your macros can work with any project. The alternative is to code your macro to work with a specific project file, which isn't so flexible.

Notice that Tasks comes under the Project object in Figure 28.1. A Task is an object representing everything about a single task in Project. When it comes to Project objects, Tasks represent a collection of objects. `ActiveProject.Tasks` represents every task in the current project plan.

`ActiveProject.Resources` represents every resource in the active project and is another collection; typically plural objects are collections. To work with a single object in a collection, there are two popular ways: `ActiveProject.Tasks(ID)` and `ActiveProject.Tasks("Task Name")`. Using the ID is useful not only when the information you have is the ID number, but to loop forward or backward through all tasks. Using the Task Name works well, provided each task name is unique. If they aren't, only the first task by that name is ever found.

CREATING A MECHANISM TO LOOP THROUGH ALL TASKS

`For Each T In ActiveProject.Tasks` says that, for each task in the collection of tasks, it is the beginning of a loop. In turn, `T` will point to every task in the active Project file. Every code line from the `For Each` line to the `Next T` line will be run for each and every task. You won't have to do anything else to make it happen.

TESTING FOR A BLANK TASK ROW

Project macros can often come to a grinding halt when they encounter a blank task row in the Project plan. To make your code survive them and pass them by, test each task to see if it's blank and only process the task if it's not blank.

```
If Then Else
If Not (T Is Nothing) Then        'Is this Task blank?
```

`T` is an object variable. If it points to an empty row in your Gantt Chart, it will have the value `Nothing`. (`Nothing` is a special, testable condition that all object variables have if they are not pointing to a valid object.) The previous row of code is an `If` statement—it allows you to ask questions and have the code do different things depending on the answer.

Close Help if it's still open, click the word `If`, and press F1 again. Read Help on the `If Then Else` statement.

In our example, we test for `Not (T Is Nothing)`. Only if `T` is not `Nothing` will the code underneath be executed. In our example, if `T` is equal to `Nothing`, we don't want to do anything other than move to the next task—we only want code executed if the opposite is true. If `T` is equal to something, every instruction until the `End If` is carried out.

Note that, in Listing 28.1, the code is indented. This is not required, but it makes the code much more structured in appearance and easier to understand. It's recommended that you always indent `If` statements and loops, such as `For Each`, for increased readability.

TESTING FOR OUTLINE LEVEL 1 AND SUMMARY TASKS

To test for the outline level and whether or not the current task is a summary task or not, you will need to know and use some more properties.

SOME TASK PROPERTIES

```
If T.OutlineLevel > 1 And T.Summary = False Then
```

In our macro we only want to concatenate (combine together) the task name and its summary task's name if the current task is not itself a summary task and it's not a top-level task. `T.OutlineLevel` is a `Task` property that returns the task level. A project summary task is level 0; all main tasks are level 1 and so on down. This property shows exactly the same information for each task that is displayed in the Outline Level Task field.

In our macro code, `T.Summary` is a *flag* property. A flag is an indicator that is only ever True or False. Please note that the task and resource `FlagN` fields display as Yes or No in Project—Yes indicates True, and No indicates False.

If T.Summary returns True, that task is a summary task. While this property is read only because it is set internally by Project, most properties can be changed as well as read. Click on a property and then press F1 (Help) to find out whether it's read only.

```
For Each T In ActiveProject.Tasks
    If Not (T Is Nothing) Then        'Is this Task blank?
        If T.OutlineLevel > 1 And T.Summary = False Then
            T.Text1 = T.OutlineParent.Name & ": " & T.Name
```

Now we indent again and the next line, T.Text1 = T.OutlineParent.Name & ": " & T.Name, is only executed if the current task is not Nothing, is not a summary task, and has an Outline Level > 1. Make sure you understand the logic and how the code in the snippet above controls it.

CHANGING INFORMATION IN A PROJECT

```
T.Text1 = T.OutlineParent.Name & ": " & T.Name
```

T.Text1 refers to the Text1 field in the active project for the task that is currently pointed to by T. And T.OutlineParent.Name returns the name of the summary task this task sits under.

CONCATENATING THE TWO AND SAVING IN TEXT1

The & (ampersand) is the concatenation command. The summary task name will have ": " and then the name of the task (T.Name) appended to it.

You can change any of the active task's information by having "T.", then the field name (spelled the same way as in Project, but any spaces removed), followed by = and the information to put in. For example, take a look at this code from our macro:

```
Else
    T.Text1 = T.Name
End If
```

Else means that if the condition in the If expression above is not met (returns False), what follows the Else is executed instead. In this example, if T were either a summary or first-level task, the macro would duplicate the task name.

End If represents the end of the If statement.

ADDING AN "I'VE FINISHED" MESSAGE

When a macro finishes, it is user friendly to display a message so that the user knows that the macro is finished and whether or not it ran successfully. It can also be interesting and useful to see counts of tasks or resources worked on.

KEEPING A COUNT

```
TaskCount = TaskCount + 1      'Increment the count
```

Number variables always start at zero. This code simply adds 1 to itself. Each time it's run, the counter increments by 1. At the end of the macro, this counter will be used for the final message.

`Next T` makes up the following line of code and marks the end of the loop. When Project reaches this statement, it automatically returns to the `For Each` line, sets `T` to point to the next task, and then processes all the code again. If the last task has already been processed, the line following the `Next T` statement is executed.

DISPLAYING A MESSAGE

```
MsgBox "Macro finished" & vbCrLf & vbCrLf & TaskCount & _
    " Tasks worked on"
```

Note the " _" (space underscore) at the end of the first line. It means this instruction is continued on the next line.

Click the word `MsgBox` and press F1 for Help so you can read about what this powerful function can do for you. (You'll use it again later.) This time `Msgbox` concatenates the different parts of the message together and displays the default OK button.

If you add `,vbInformation` at the end, an information icon is added to the pop-up message and the code will look like this:

```
MsgBox "Macro finished" & vbCrLf & vbCrLf & TaskCount & _
    " Tasks worked on", vbInformation
```

`VbCrLf` is a *constant*—a fixed number or text string. This one creates a carriage return and line feed so that the two parts of the message are separated by a blank line. Constants that start with `vb` are common to VBA for all Office applications. Constants starting with `pj` are unique to Project VBA only.

After the `MsgBox` line in Listing 28.1, the macro halts until the user chooses the OK button. The `End Sub` statement is next, completing your TaskSummaryName macro.

DEBUGGING YOUR CODE

There are two parts to the debugging. First, create valid code that Project can recognize (all code needs to be typed correctly and in an appropriate syntax), and second, have code that does what you want when it's run.

SYNTAX CHECKING

When you enter code and move the cursor off a line, Project automatically verifies the line for correct syntax. For example, if you omit `Then` from the end of an `If` statement, Project generates an immediate compile error with the message `Expected Then or GoTo`. This feature of Project eliminates many errors that might otherwise be hard to find, before you even start testing.

TESTING YOUR CODE

Another description for testing is "debugging." One explanation for this term is that in the early days of the first mainframe computers (complete with valves and other ancient technologies), it is rumored that in an important demonstration to a major client, a computer wouldn't run. The cause of the problem was a family of spiders that had set up shop between valves and shorted them out. There was a bug in the system!

After you have developed your code, there are many, many reasons why it might not run as expected. You will need to debug it before it will work to your satisfaction.

In the VBE, click anywhere on the For Each instruction line and select Debug, Toggle Breakpoint, or press F9. This will highlight that row of code in red. Next, select Run, Run Sub/UserForm, or press F5. This will execute the subroutine the cursor is in. Your red line will now be yellow to indicate that it is the next instruction to be executed. Project stops executing the code once it reaches your breakpoint.

Press F8 once. This makes Project single-step through the code. The For Each statement is red again and the first If statement is yellow. Next, hover your mouse over T in (T Is Nothing). You will see a tool tip with T = 1 in it. This means Task ID 1 is the current active task (each object has a default property; the default property for a task object is its ID). Click and drag with your mouse to select T Is Nothing, and then move the mouse over the selected (blue) area. Now the tool tip says T Is Nothing = False. Finally, hover your mouse over each property (OutlineLevel, Summary, OutlineParent.Name, and so on) and see what values they have.

Next in your code test, press Ctrl+G. This will activate the Immediate window and place the cursor there. You can use this to investigate all the properties of any active object. It can also be used to test any single lines of code to assist you in getting them right and deciphering exactly what is happening. For example, if T is pointing to each task in turn, find out which task it's pointing to when stopped at a specific breakpoint by typing **?T.Name** or **?T.Id** in the Immediate window and then pressing Enter. The name or ID of the task pointed to by T will be displayed.

Your next step in testing the code is to type **?T.Name** and press the Enter key. The ? is short-hand for Debug.Print. The value of the task's name will appear in the next row. The ? allows you to have the value of any variable or property printed to the Immediate window. A line without the ? is used to execute a statement. Remember the task name displayed by ?T.Name and, in a blank line, type **T.Name="Test"** and press Enter. Now scroll back to and click on the ?T.Name line and press Enter again. The task name should now be Test.

Press Alt+Tab to return to Project 2000 and confirm that the task name has changed to Test. Alt+Tab back to the VBE and reset the task name using another T.Name= line in the Immediate window.

When testing your code, you can also try typing **?Activecell.Task.Name**. Activecell can be very useful, but it only has a few properties. By using the Task property in this example, you can access all the task information for the task in the selected row.

Other common and very useful properties of tasks that you need to work with are Work and Duration. In the Immediate window, go down to a blank row and type **?T.Duration** and press Enter. The answer will be a rather large number that looks nothing like what you see in the Duration column of Project 2000.

Project stores all Duration and Work values in minutes. To convert to days, divide by 60 and then by the number of hours per day in <u>T</u>ools, <u>O</u>ptions, Calendar tab. The default number of hours per day is 8, so `?T.Duration/60/8` will display the correct number of days' duration.

Tip from Tim and the Project Team

`ActiveProject.HoursPerDay` will give you the number of hours per day to use in the formula instead of 8. Try typing `?T.Duration/60/ActiveProject.HoursPerDay` in the Immediate window to confirm this.

You have already learned that the variable `T` is `Nothing` until the `For Each` loop when it points to each task in turn. You also need to be aware that the variable has no value at all in the Immediate window if the macro hasn't stopped at a breakpoint.

If you type `?T.Name` in the Immediate window when the code hasn't stopped at a breakpoint, an error is generated. `T` only points to a task once the `For Each T In ActiveProject.Tasks` statement has been executed. After `End Sub` is reached, `T` has no value, and any attempt to use it in the Immediate window will fail.

You should now be starting to get a good idea of how objects and properties relate to each other. Remember that if you want more information on a property or object, click it and press F1 for Help.

When the code has stopped at a breakpoint, notice that, in the gray border on the left of the Visual Basic Editor, the yellow line has a yellow arrow and the breakpoint has a red spot. Click the red spot to toggle the breakpoint off or on, or click anywhere on the line's code and press F9 again.

You can also click and drag the yellow arrow to move the yellow line (changing which line will be executed next). Try moving it back to the `For Each` row. Press F8 again and again and watch the code being stepped through. At any time you can press F5 to have it run continuously to the next breakpoint or the end of the subroutine, whichever comes first.

Enter a line like `Set T=ActiveProject.Tasks(1)` into the Immediate window and press Enter, and the line is executed. This is a good way to get a line of code working properly before copying it back to the editing pane.

Remember that by clicking on any instruction and pressing F9, the code can be made to stop. You then hover your mouse over any variable for a tip on what its value is, or use `?` to print values in the Immediate window. You can also single-step through the code to see exactly what is happening, correcting the code as you go. And you can also use Alt+Tab to swap between the VBE and Project (or any other program you are controlling from Project VBA) to look at what the code has done.

THE SEND AN EMAIL MACRO

While it is useful to loop through every task in a project, sometimes you might only want to loop through tasks that have been selected before running the macro. In this example, the macro only loops through every task that has been selected and creates a simple email based on the task names and assigned resources.

Workgroup and Project Central functionality allows this; however, they don't work over the Internet. This macro you will create uses Microsoft Outlook to send an email over the Internet and creates a simple structure that you can use to expand and create quite sophisticated messages.

To create this macro, you will build the following components:

- Connect to Outlook
- Create a new mail message
- Accept an address and subject
- Create the message
- Send the message

NAMING AND CONFIGURING THE EMAIL MACRO

To run this macro, you need to select one or more tasks in any project file, have Microsoft Outlook 98 or 2000 installed on your PC, and then run the macro (Tools, Macro, Macros).

To view the code, open "Chapter 28/Email Task Details.mpp" from the CD and press Alt+F11. Alternatively, you could type the code in Listing 28.2 into a new module.

If you do type your own code, you will also have to create a link to the Outlook Object Library. Follow these steps:

1. In the VBE, select Tools, References.
2. Scroll down the list until you find Microsoft Outlook.
3. Click the box so a tick appears in it and then click OK.

Now your Outlook code typed into Project will be able to control anything in Outlook.

LISTING 28.2 THE SEND AN EMAIL MACRO

```
Sub EmailData()
Dim T As Task
Dim A As Assignment
Dim OlApp As Outlook.Application
Dim msg As Outlook.MailItem
Dim msgBody As String

On Error Resume Next
Set OlApp = GetObject(, "Outlook.Application")
If OlApp Is Nothing Then
  Set OlApp = CreateObject("Outlook.Application")
    If OlApp Is Nothing Then
        MsgBox "Can't find Outlook"
        Exit Sub
    End If
```

```
End If
Set msg = OlApp.CreateItem(olMailItem)    'Create new message
msg.To = InputBox("Enter Email address to send details to")
msg.Subject = InputBox("Enter Subject for new email")
msgBody = "These are the Task details as of " & _
    Format(Date, "Short Date") & vbCrLf
For Each T In ActiveSelection.Tasks
    msgBody = msgBody & "Task Name: " & T.Name & " Start: " _
        & T.Start & " Finish: " & T.Finish & vbCrLf
    msgBody = msgBody & "Task Notes: " & T.Notes & vbCrLf
    For Each A In T.Assignments
        msgBody = msgBody & A.ResourceName & " Work=" & _
            A.Work / 60 & "h" & vbCrLf   'Work stored as minutes
    Next
    msgBody = msgBody & vbCrLf 'Create blank line
Next T

msg.Body = msgBody      'Add text to message
msg.Send                'Send to Outbox
If Err.Number <> 0 Then
    MsgBox Err.Description, vbOKOnly + vbCritical
End If
End Sub
```

The following sections will explain in detail all parts of the code that you might not be familiar with yet. Anything (such as statements, objects, and properties) that was covered in the SummaryTaskName example previously in this chapter won't be covered again in this example. Remember, for the macro to run, you need Outlook (2000 or 98, although 97 might work as well) installed.

CONNECTING TO OUTLOOK

```
Dim OlApp As Outlook.Application
Dim msg As Outlook.MailItem
```

The first line here defines OlApp as a variable that will represent the Outlook application itself. Through it you will be able to access any and all information and capabilities of Outlook.

The next line, msg As Outlook.MailItem, defines a variable msg that will point to and represent everything to do with the new email message you are about to create.

```
On Error Resume Next
Set OlApp = GetObject(, "Outlook.Application")
If OlApp Is Nothing Then
    Set OlApp = New Outlook.Application
    If OlApp Is Nothing Then
        MsgBox "Can't find Outlook"
        Exit Sub
    End If
    OlApp.Visible=True
End If
```

`On Error Resume Next` is an instruction that tells Project that if an error occurs, it should continue running with the next statement. This leaves the onus on you to test for errors and handle them as you go.

```
Set OlApp = GetObject(, "Outlook.Application")
```

This is a powerful instruction because it sets the `OlApp` variable to point to any running instance of the Outlook application. If, however, Outlook isn't running, `OlApp` will be left with its default value of `Nothing`. The next line, the `If` statement, tests for this. If `OlApp` is equal to `Nothing`, the next line is executed, which creates a new instance of Outlook. If that fails as well, the final action is to display the message "Can't find Outlook" and exit the subroutine. If the new instance of Outlook starts properly, it starts hidden. The `OlApp.Visible=True` line sets the `Visible` property for the hidden instance of Outlook to `True`, making it visible and displaying an icon on the Windows task bar.

CREATING A NEW MAIL MESSAGE

```
Set msg = OlApp.CreateItem(olMailItem)   'Create new message
```

`Msg` is an object (in this case, a `MailItem` object), and like all other objects, it is always made to point to its target using the `set` instruction. `OlApp.CreateItem(olMailItem)` is a method that creates a new Outlook item (the `olMailItem` constant specifically specifies a Mail item), and sets the object `msg` to point to it. (See Help for other Outlook objects that can be created by clicking on `CreateItem` and pressing F1 for Help.)

ACCEPTING AN ADDRESS AND SUBJECT

```
msg.To = InputBox("Enter Email address to send details to")
msg.Subject = InputBox("Enter Subject for new email")
```

Just like filling in details for a new message manually, you need to provide an address and subject. The `Inputbox` function prompts the user for this information and puts the entered text into the `.To` and `.Subject` properties.

You might be wondering what a function is and how it differs from a method or subroutine. A *method* is similar to an action—it does something. A *subroutine* is used to write code that does something specific. A *function* can also do things—it can hold any code a `Sub` can, but specifically, it returns a value. The first example in the `msg.to =` line returns the email address of the person the mail is to be sent to so it can be stored in the `.To` property.

> **Note**
>
> InputBox, like MsgBox, is a very useful and commonly used function. Make sure you read everything about what it can and can't do in Help.

CREATING THE MESSAGE

```
msgBody = "These are the Task details as of " & _
    Format(Date, "Short Date") & vbCrLf
```

MsgBody is a variable defined as a string. You are going to use it to build up the message before storing it in the message. The first step is to create the initial line that has the introductory message followed by the Format function. (The Format function is another very useful tool to know and use.) Format(Date, "Short Date") creates a string filled with today's date formatted as per the Regional settings in the Windows Control Panel. Help shows you examples of some of the numerous custom formats you can create using Format().

Note that the msgBody = lines end with an & vbCrLf. VbCrLf is a Visual Basic constant and it does the same thing in Visual Basic for all applications. The constant adds a carriage return/line feed combination to the end of the string—the equivalent of pressing the Enter key to create a new paragraph in Outlook.

```
For Each T In ActiveSelection.Tasks
    msgBody = msgBody & "Task Name: " & T.Name & " Start: " & _
        T.Start & " Finish: " & T.Finish & vbCrLf
        msgBody = msgBody & "Task Notes: " & T.Notes & vbCrLf
```

For Each T In ActiveSelection.Tasks is another common instruction. ActiveSelection lets you work with all the selected cells in the active project. The .Tasks property specifically chooses the tasks selected. This instruction will loop once for each task in the selected cells of the active project.

In the macro code, msgBody = msgBody & is how you concatenate one string onto another. In this example, you are appending the text Task Name: followed by the name of the task (using T.Name). The following code adds lines for the start and finish dates and task notes. If Rich Text Format notes are entered, then this method will only read the text, not the formatting.

```
For Each A In T.Assignments
    msgBody = msgBody & A.ResourceName & " Work=" & _
        A.Work / 60 & "h" & vbCrLf  'Work stored as minutes
Next A
msgBody = msgBody & vbCrLf  'Create blank line
```

Just as For Each T in ActiveSelection.Tasks looped through every task, For Each A in T.Assignments will loop through each assignment for the current task. A is defined as an assignment. One of its properties is ResourceName and another is Work, allowing you to build up the rest of the message by appending each new piece to the end of the msg variable holding it all.

Work and all other Work-related properties, including ActualWork and Duration, are stored as a number of minutes. Therefore, A.Work / 60 calculates the number of hours of work.

The final line, msgBody = msgBody & vbCrLf, simply creates a blank line after the last assignment, leaving a space before returning for the next task.

SENDING THE MESSAGE

```
msg.Body = msgBody       'Add text to message
msg.Send                 'Send to Outbox
If Err.Number <> 0 Then
    MsgBox Err.Description, vbOKOnly + vbCritical
End If
```

The first two instructions in this code snippet are easy to comprehend. They copy the contents of the msgBody variable into the body of the email message and then send the message. You should note that .Body is a read/write property and .Send is a method that performs an action.

However, it isn't good practice to just end the macro there. For example, if an invalid To address was entered, Outlook won't send the message. You need to test for any errors and then warn the user of them. Err is an object that holds all information regarding the last error that happened. If Err.Number equals 0, there has been no error. On the other hand, if Err.Number is not equal to 0, Err.Description returns a string description of what has gone wrong. The MsgBox function is best used to display that message. In this macro, the vbOKOnly + vbCritical Visual Basic constants (the same ones work in all other Office products) change the MsgBox display to show a critical icon and only an OK button, not OK and Cancel buttons.

A good exercise for you is to single-step through this code to watch how it works (use F8 to single-step after putting the cursor anywhere in the subroutine). Before single-stepping through the code, click on the variable msgBody and press Shift+F9. This displays the current value of msgBody (which at this stage will be "<Out of Context>." Click the Add button and most of the Immediate window will be replaced with a Watches window. Now, you can single-step through the code and watch the variable msgBody build up as you go. You can add numerous variables to the window and see what happens to them. (To remove a variable from the window, click on it and press the Delete key.)

As an exercise in expanding the Send an Email macro, try adding your name and organization to the end of the message.

THE IMPORTPROJECT MACRO

Let's say you have an Excel spreadsheet full of data and you want to build a plan from it. This is a common problem for Project VBA developers. Solving it will introduce you to controlling Excel from within Project, creating links between tasks, indenting them to create summary tasks, and then assigning resources. A typical occurrence is a basic list of tasks for a project created by mainframe production or enterprise control software that can be exported to Excel. The next problem you face is getting that data into Project.

For this macro to work, you will need Excel 97 or 2000 actively running with a spreadsheet having the following columns: Task ID, Task Name, Duration in Days, Outline Level, Predecessor, Resource Name, and Work in Hours. (Open "Chap28/Project Information.xls" for an example.) These are the basic building blocks for the ImportProject macro:

- Connect to the active workbook in Excel
- Set the project start date
- Point to the first task
- Create tasks
- Indent tasks

- Add any predecessors
- Add a resource if not already added
- Assign a resource and workload

NAMING AND CONFIGURING THE IMPORTPROJECT MACRO

Follow these instructions to name and set up this macro:

1. Open a Project file of your own.
2. Press Alt+F11 to show the VBE.
3. Click Insert, Module to add a module to our project file.
4. Open "Chap28/Import Project Data from Excel.Mpp" from the CD and press Alt+F11 to open the VBE and view this code.
   Or type the code in Listing 28.3.

LISTING 28.3   THE IMPORTPROJECT MACRO

```
Sub ImportProject()
Dim xlApp As Excel.Application
Dim xlBook As Excel.Workbook
Dim xlTask As Excel.Range
Dim T As Task
Dim R As Resource
Dim Ts As Tasks
Dim Rs As Resources
Dim Level As Integer

On Error Resume Next

'First point to Excel and then the active Workbook
Set xlApp = GetObject(, "Excel.Application")
If xlApp Is Nothing Then
    MsgBox "Excel isn't running. Please open Project " & _
        "Information.xls and start again"
    Exit Sub
End If

Set xlBook = xlApp.ActiveWorkbook

'TaskStart is the named header cell in Excel
Set xlTask = xlApp.Range("TaskStart")

'Set Project Start Date
ActiveProject.ProjectStart = _
    CDate(xlApp.Range("ProjectStartDate"))

'Point to the first task
Set xlTask = xlTask.Offset(1, 0)     'Offset uses row, column
Set Ts = ActiveProject.Tasks         'Point to Tasks Collection
Set Rs = ActiveProject.Resources     'Same for Resources
```

PART **VIII**

CH **28**

LISTING 28.3   CONTINUED

```
'Loop until an empty cell is reached.
Do Until IsEmpty(xlTask)
    'Add Task to end of project then point to it.
    Set T = Ts.Add(xlTask.Range("B1"))
    Level = xlTask.Range("D1")

    'Loop INdenting task until it reaches correct level
    Do Until T.OutlineLevel >= Level
        T.OutlineIndent
    Loop

    'Loop OUTdenting task until it reaches correct level
    Do Until T.OutlineLevel <= Level
        T.OutlineOutdent
    Loop

    'If the task is a summary task it won't have a duration
    If Not IsEmpty(xlTask.Range("C1")) Then
        'Store Duration as minutes
        T.Duration = xlTask.Range("C1") * 60 * 8
    End If

    'If Predecessors cell not empty, set up link
    If Not IsEmpty(xlTask.Range("E1")) Then
        T.Predecessors = CStr(xlTask.Range("E1"))
    End If

'If unsuccessful pointing to the resource, then need to add it
    Set R = Nothing
    Set R = Rs(xlTask.Range("F1").Text)
    If R Is Nothing Then
        Set R = Rs.Add(CStr(xlTask.Range("F1")))
    End If

    'Assign Resource to Task
    T.Assignments.Add ResourceID:=R.ID, _
      Units:=(xlTask.Range("G1") / (T.Duration / 60))

    'Point to next task - down 1 row
    Set xlTask = xlTask.Offset(1, 0)
Loop

'Edit Goto also moves timescale to show selected task
Application.EditGoTo 1

End Sub
```

> **Caution**
>
> This macro only handles one resource. The predecessor column must be in exactly the same format as the predecessor column in Project.

Some of this macro should be self-explanatory after the previous two examples in this chapter, so the following sections focus only on what might be new to you.

Remember, to run the macro successfully, Excel must be running with the Chap28/Project Information.Xls, or a similarly structured file, open.

CONNECTING TO THE ACTIVE WORKBOOK IN EXCEL

As suggested in Chapter 27, "Introduction to Visual Basic Macros with Project 2000," Project VBA can control anything in another Office program—in this case, Excel. One of the power features of VBA is the ability to see drop-down lists of relevant objects, methods, and properties as you type. You can get the same thing for Excel objects, methods, and properties by setting up a reference to an Excel Object Library. The Excel Object Library is installed automatically as part of the Excel installation process, even for minimal installations.

To link to Excel from Project, go to the VBE and select <u>T</u>ools, <u>R</u>eferences. Scroll down the list until you find Microsoft Excel and select its box. The location of this file is saved in the Registry for each PC, so if you copy your project file to a PC with Excel installed in a different location, your Project macro will still work.

Project 2000 enables you to link to Excel 8 (Excel 97) or Excel 9 (Excel 2000). Obviously, if you reference Excel 97, you won't be able to program Excel 2000 features.

```
Dim xlApp As Excel.Application
```

Type **Dim xlApp As Excel** and then a full stop, and Project displays all objects or other items relevant to Excel. `Excel.Application` refers to the Excel application, the top-level object for Excel.

```
Set xlApp = GetObject(, "Excel.Application")
```

`GetObject` is a VBA function that gets an object for the application named in the parameter. In this case, it looks for an Excel application that is already running. If it's found, Project points `xlApp` to it. You can then use `xlApp` to access anything in Excel.

```
If xlApp Is Nothing Then
```

If `xlApp` equals `Nothing`, the search for a running copy of Excel failed. The code will display an error and exit the `Sub`.

```
Set xlBook = xlApp.ActiveWorkbook
```

This section of the code points `xlBook` at the active workbook in Excel, which contains your project data.

```
Set xlTask = xlApp.Range("TaskStart")
```

The most robust way of coding with Excel is to name a cell and then refer to it. `XlApp.Range("TaskStart")` refers to the cell named TaskStart and returns an Excel Range object that is set to the `xlTask` variable. To name a cell in Excel, first select the cell, then either type the name into the Address box or choose <u>I</u>nsert, Name, Define and type the name there.

SETTING THE PROJECT START DATE

```
ActiveProject.ProjectStart = _
    CDate(xlApp.Range("ProjectStartDate"))
```

Although this section of the macro is on two lines, the space and underscore (_) at the end of the first line say the next line is a continuation of the first. Sometimes lengthy lines of code can be developed, forcing you to scroll left and right to read the whole line on the screen. By using a continuation character to break the line into two, you help make the code easier to read and understand.

.ProjectStart is a property that allows you to read or write the project start date. CDate(xlApp.Range("ProjectStartDate")) gets the contents of the cell named ProjectStartDate and converts it to a date. The result is saved in ActiveProject.ProjectStart, setting the start date of the project.

POINTING TO THE FIRST TASK

```
Set xlTask = xlTask.Offset(1, 0)      'Offset uses row, column
Set Ts = ActiveProject.Tasks          'Point to Tasks Collection
Set Rs = ActiveProject.Resources      'Same for Resources
```

XlTask.Offset(1,0) is an instruction to Excel to point to the cell 1 row down and 0 cells to the right from the cell xlTask currently points to.

The Set Ts and Set Rs instructions point Ts and Rs to all existing tasks and resources.

CREATING TASKS AND RESOURCES

```
Set T = Ts.Add(CStr(xlTask.Offset(0, 1)))
Level = xlTask.Offset(0,3)
```

Add is a standard method for a collection. By default it adds a new task to the end of the project. The first parameter provides the task name; in this case, the name is the contents of the cell pointed to by the cell 0 (zero) cells down and 1 to the right. (Excel statements that require a row and column number or offset are always in Row/Column sequence). Note the use of CStr to convert the contents to the string required by Add for the task name.

If you read Help, you should find that the Add method returns a pointer to the newly created task or resource. You can use the same approach to set your task variable T to the newly created object. To make the statement work, you should note that, instead of a space separating the first parameter from the method Add, there is an open round bracket with a matching closing round bracket at the end. This is because Add is acting as a function as well as a method; it adds a task and returns a pointer to it. The parentheses are part of the required syntax for a function.

INDENTING TASKS

T.OutlineIndent and T.OutlineOutdent are two methods that either indent or outdent a task relative to the task that precedes it.

Because any task can be further indented by one level or at the top level (Outline Level = 1), and because a new task added to the end of a project automatically has the same outline level as the preceding task, you must test for the need to indent and outdent.

ADDING ANY PREDECESSORS

```
If Not IsEmpty(xlTask.Offset(0, 4)) Then
    T.Predecessors = CStr(xlTask.Offset(0, 4))
End If
```

IsEmpty tests for whether a given cell is empty. In this case, if it isn't empty, there is a predecessor.

T.Predecessors is a Task property for predecessors in the form of a string exactly as seen in the Predecessor column of the Task Entry table (default table in the Gantt Chart view). Read the value from Excel and the task link(s) are done.

ADDING A RESOURCE IF NOT ALREADY ADDED

```
Set R = Nothing
Set R = Rs(xlTask.Offset(0, 5).Text)
If R Is Nothing Then
    Set R = Rs.Add(CStr(xlTask.Offset(0, 5)))
End If
```

By setting R = Nothing, if the attempt to point to the resource named in Excel fails, it can't exist already in Project, so Project adds it.

ASSIGNING A RESOURCE AND WORKLOAD

```
T.Assignments.Add ResourceID:=R.ID, _
    Units:=(xlTask.Offset(0,6) / (T.Duration / 60))
```

By the time this statement is executed, T refers to the current task and R to the resource for it. Assignments is another collection and again the Add method will be used to add an assignment. In this instance, you are adding an assignment to a task. Given that T.Assignments.Add already provides the task, the first parameter needs to be a resource ID. You can also provide a units value. Remember that units is equal to Work divided by Duration; that xlTask.Offset(0,6) points to column G, which holds hours of work, and, that Duration values are stored in Project as a number of minutes (dividing by 60 therefore calculates a number of hours).

The ImportProject macro finishes with Application.EditGoTo 1, which is the same as selecting Edit, Go To, or pressing F5. The result is that Task ID 1 is selected and the timescale moves to display the start of the Task 1 bar on the Gantt Chart.

This is a fun macro to single-step through because you can use Alt+Tab to swap back to Project 2000 to see the results as you go.

PART

VIII

CH

28

THE PROFITLOSSREPORT MACRO

The ProfitLossReport macro will produce a report showing the cost of running a project and the billable value of it, all in Excel.

The chunks of the ProfitLossReport macro are

- Point to Excel
- Write titles and format
- Write project-level summary task costs
- Export tasks, baseline costs, and client cost
- Set Rate B for all assignments
- Write cost of work to Excel and generate profit margin

Open "Chap28/Profit Loss Report.Mpp" from the CD and press Alt+F11 to open the VBE and view this code.

Or, type the code in Listing 28.4 into a new, empty module after adding a reference to Excel as you did for the ImportProject example earlier in this chapter.

LISTING 28.4 THE PROFITLOSSREPORT MACRO

```
Sub ProfitLossReport()
Dim xlApp As Excel.Application
Dim xlBook As Excel.Workbook
Dim xlRng As Excel.Range
Dim T As Task
Dim R As Resource
Dim A As Assignment

'If an error occurs continue to next statement
'Without this On Error command code stops if an error occurs
On Error Resume Next

'Assume Excel may or may not be running.
'First try to find a running copy of Excel
Set xlApp = GetObject(, "Excel.Application")

'If there isn't one, xlApp will still be Nothing
If xlApp Is Nothing Then
    'Excel not found, start a new copy
    Set xlApp = New Excel.Application

    'Excel starts without being on Task Bar
    xlApp.Visible = True    'Make visible on Task Bar
End If
AppActivate "Microsoft Excel"

'Create new Workbook. Add method returns a pointer
'to the new workbook
Set xlBook = xlApp.Workbooks.Add
```

LISTING 28.4   CONTINUED

```
'Set Rng to point to A1 in first sheet
Set xlRng = xlApp.ActiveCell

'Write and format Title
xlRng = "Profit Loss Report for " & ActiveProject.Name
xlRng.Range("A2") = "As of " & Format(Date, "mmmm d yyyy")
xlRng.Range("A1:A2").Font.Bold = True
xlRng.Font.Size = 14

'Move xlRng below titles
Set xlRng = xlRng.Offset(3, 0)

'Create column titles and format
xlRng.Offset(0, 0) = "Task Name"
xlRng.Offset(0, 1) = "Baseline Cost"
xlRng.Offset(0, 2) = "Client Billed $"
xlRng.Offset(0, 3) = "Variance"
xlRng.Offset(0, 4) = "Cost of work $"
xlRng.Offset(0, 5) = "Margin"
With xlRng.EntireRow
    .Font.Bold = True
    .WrapText = True
    .HorizontalAlignment = xlHAlignCenter
    .VerticalAlignment = xlVAlignCenter
    .AutoFit
End With
xlRng.EntireColumn.ColumnWidth = 25
Set xlRng = xlRng.Offset(1, 0)   'Point to next row

'Write Project Summary Data
With ActiveProject.ProjectSummaryTask
    xlRng = .Name
    xlRng.Offset(0, 1) = .BaselineCost
    xlRng.Offset(0, 2) = .Cost
    xlRng.Offset(0, 3) = .CostVariance
    xlRng.EntireRow.Font.Bold = True
    Set xlRng = xlRng.Offset(1, 0)   'Point to next row
End With

'Loop thru every Task export name, Baseline Cost, Cost, Var
'Bold rows with Summary Tasks
For Each T In ActiveProject.Tasks
    If Not (T Is Nothing) Then
        xlRng = T.Name
        xlRng.Offset(0, 1) = T.BaselineCost
        xlRng.Offset(0, 2) = T.Cost
        xlRng.Offset(0, 3) = T.CostVariance
        If T.Summary = True Then
            xlRng.EntireRow.Font.Bold = True
        End If
        Set xlRng = xlRng.Offset(1, 0)   'Point to next row
    End If
Next T

'Loop thru resource assignments changing Rate to plan B
```

LISTING 28.4   CONTINUED

```
'This will change the cost to represent the cost of the work
For Each R In ActiveProject.Resources
    For Each A In R.Assignments
        A.CostRateTable = 1      'Set Plan B
    Next A
Next R

'Write Project Summary Data
Set xlRng = xlApp.ActiveSheet.Range("A5")
xlRng.Offset(0, 4) = ActiveProject.ProjectSummaryTask.Cost
xlRng.Offset(0, 5).FormulaR1C1 = "=rc[-3]-rc[-1]"
xlRng.Range("B1:F1").NumberFormat = "$#,##0;[Red]$#,##0"
Set xlRng = xlRng.Offset(1, 0)  'Point to next row

'Loop Writing Cost rate and margin formula to Excel
For Each T In ActiveProject.Tasks
    xlRng.Offset(0, 4) = T.Cost
    xlRng.Offset(0, 5).FormulaR1C1 = "=rc[-3]-rc[-1]"
    xlRng.Range("B1:F1").NumberFormat = "$#,##0;[Red]$#,##0"
    Set xlRng = xlRng.Offset(1, 0)  'Point to next row
Next T

'Loop thru resource assignments changing the
'Rate back to the Standard Rate
For Each R In ActiveProject.Resources
    For Each A In R.Assignments
        A.CostRateTable = 0            'Set Plan A
    Next
Next R

End Sub
```

WRITING DATA TO EXCEL

```
'Set Rng to point to A1 in first sheet
Set xlRng = xlApp.ActiveCell
'Write and format Title
xlRng = "Profit Loss Report for " & ActiveProject.Name
xlRng.Range("A2") = "As of " & Format(Date, "mmmm d yyyy")
xlRng.Range("A1:A2").Font.Bold = True
xlRng.Font.Size = 14
```

`Set xlRng = xlApp.ActiveCell` gets the `xlRng` variable to point to the active cell in Excel. By default a new workbook opens with the cursor in A1 (to point to a specific cell in Excel, use `xlApp.Range("A1")`).

In Listing 28.4, `xlRng.Range("A2")` hasn't been covered so far. If `xlRng` points to A1, `xlRng.Range("A2")` points to A2. However, if `xlRng` points to A4, `xlRng.Range("A2")` points to A5. The `.Range("A2")` part is always relative to what's on the left. The same effect can be achieved using the `Offset` property.

`Format(Date, "mmmm d yyyy")` is a very useful function that you can use in VBA for any program. It creates a string (text) by taking whatever is in the first parameter for `Format`—in this case, Date—and formatting it as specified by the second parameter. The possibilities are exactly the same as those for custom formats in Excel. Click the word Format and then press F1 for full help. The Examples hyperlink in the Help topic for this function is very useful.

A lot of what follows in this section is already familiar to you after having walked through the previous macros in this chapter. If you have trouble understanding the code in Listing 28.4, first read the line-by-line comments, and then click any row that is confusing and press F9 to add a breakpoint. Run the macro from the Profit Loss Report.Mpp project and when the code stops at the breakpoint, single-step through the code to see what each instruction does. Remember you can use Alt+Tab to swap between VBE and Excel to do this, and then return to execute the next instruction (F8 runs a single step).

```
For Each R In ActiveProject.Resources
    For Each A In R.Assignments
        A.CostRateTable = 1        'Set Rate B
    Next A
Next R
```

By default all assignments use the standard rate (Cost Table A in the Resource Information dialog box) to calculate its cost. A good way of arranging the project is to use the standard rate to hold the charge-out rates for each resource and Rate B for the cost rate. In Project 2000's Resource view, double-click each resource to see its Resource Information dialog box and then click the Costs tab. From there, you can select the B Tab and enter the actual rate that particular resource costs your organization.

The previous code loops through every resource's assignments, setting it to use Rate B (VBA uses 0 for Rate A, 1 for Rate B, and so on).

Alternatively, you could loop through every task and then each task's assignments. Because there are almost always fewer resources than tasks, and many tasks don't have assignments, the way this macro does it is usually faster.

```
xlRng.Offset(0, 5).FormulaR1C1 = "=rc[-3]-rc[-1]"
```

This is the last row that might be new to you. In Excel there are two ways of referencing a cell. The first is the familiar A1, B1 format. The second is the R1C1 format, where R is a Row number and C is a Column number. R3C3 refers to address C3. R[1]C is different. R[1] means down one row from the current row (-1 is up one row) and C on its own means same Column (or Row for R on its own).

"=rc[-3]-rc[-1]" means type a formula =cell 3 columns to left, this row minus cell one column to left, this row. The power of this notation is that this formula will work for any row, where =C5—E5 will only produce the desired result in row 5. In addition, it is the only format to use if you ever want to enter a formula to more than one cell at a time.

```
xlRng.Range("B1:F1").NumberFormat = "$#,##0;[Red]$#,##0"
```

If xlRng points to A10, .Range("B1:F1") selects B10:F10—it's relative to where xlRng is pointing. The rest of the statement simply sets the number format to any type you like as if you selected it in the Format, Cells command in Excel.

Finally, the standard rate is set again for all assignments and the job is finished.

A good learning technique is to take a macro that works and modify it. Try adding two columns to show Actual Cost and Remaining Cost for each task. Another exercise is to store the current cost rate table number in the Number1 field at the beginning of the macro before forcing Rate A for each assignment, and then restoring it at the end of the macro. This will fully restore the plan to how it was and makes sure the macro can handle some assignments starting on a rate other then the standard rate.

THE EXPORTWORKDATA MACRO

Another very common task you might want to code is the export of weekly hours of work from an open project file to Excel. Having your reports in Excel is useful because users can then format and adjust the report to suit their needs, and because they can then email it to others or print it. You can also email them the report rather than printing it and carrying or mailing it to them.

The ExportWorkData macro will also be easy for you to edit to export Actual Work, or many other fields, or make the export by Day or Month instead of by Week.

The most important tool to learn in this example is reading data for a task by time. If you look at a Resource or Task Usage view in Project, the techniques used in this macro will let you read any piece of information in the timescaled part of the screen.

Learning to modify this macro will provide you with a very powerful reporting tool that solves numerous requests for information from users.

These are the chunks of this macro that will be new to you:

- Create a blank report in Excel
- Get timescaled data
- Write data to Excel
- Create subtotals

Open "Chap28/Time Scaled Data.Mpp" from the CD and press Alt+F11 to open the VBE and view this code.

Or, type the code in Listing 28.5 into a new, empty module after adding a reference to Excel as you did for the ImportProject example.

LISTING 28.5   THE EXPORTWORKDATA MACRO

```
Sub ExportWorkData()
Dim xlApp As Excel.Application
Dim xlBook As Excel.Workbook
Dim xlRng As Excel.Range
Dim Proj As Project
Dim T As Task
Dim TSV As TimeScaleValues
Dim WeekNumber As Integer
```

LISTING 28.5   CONTINUED

```
Dim DatesAdded As Boolean     'Start value=False

'If an error occurs continue to next statement
'Without this On Error command code stops if an error occurs
On Error Resume Next

'Assume Excel may or may not be running.
'First try to find a running copy of Excel
Set xlApp = GetObject(, "Excel.Application")

'If there isn't one, xlApp will still be Nothing
If xlApp Is Nothing Then
    'Excel not found, start a new copy
    Set xlApp = New Excel.Application

    'Excel starts without being on Task Bar
    xlApp.Visible = True     'Make visible on Task Bar
End If
AppActivate "Microsoft Excel"

'Create new Workbook. Add method returns a pointer
'to the new workbook
Set xlBook = xlApp.Workbooks.Add

'Set Rng to point to A1 in first sheet
Set xlRng = xlApp.ActiveCell

'Write and format Title
Set Proj = ActiveProject     'Using Proj is slightly faster
xlRng = "Weekly Work Report for " & Proj.Name
xlRng.Range("A2") = "As of " & Format(Date, "mmmm d yyyy")
xlRng.Range("A1:A2").Font.Bold = True
xlRng.Font.Size = 14

'Move xlRng below titles
Set xlRng = xlRng.Offset(3, 0)

'Create column titles and format
xlRng = "Task Name"
With xlRng.EntireRow
    .Font.Bold = True
    .WrapText = True
    .HorizontalAlignment = xlHAlignCenter
    .VerticalAlignment = xlVAlignCenter
    .AutoFit
End With
xlRng.EntireColumn.ColumnWidth = 35
Set xlRng = xlRng.Offset(1, 0)   'Point to next row

'Loop thru every Task exporting weekly work
'Bold rows with Summary Tasks
For Each T In Proj.Tasks
    If Not (T Is Nothing) Then
        xlRng = T.Name
```

PART

VIII

CH

28

LISTING 28.5   CONTINUED

```
              'Get Time Scaled Data
              Set TSV = T.TimeScaleData(Proj.ProjectStart, _
                  Proj.ProjectFinish, pjTaskTimescaledWork, _
                  pjTimescaleWeeks, 1)

              'If first Task then add dates to title row
              If DatesAdded = False Then
                  For WeekNumber = 1 To TSV.Count
                      xlRng.Offset(-1, WeekNumber) = _
                          TSV(WeekNumber).EndDate
                  Next
                  xlRng.Offset(-1, 0).EntireRow.NumberFormat = _
                      "Short Date"
                  DatesAdded = True
              End If
              For WeekNumber = 1 To TSV.Count
                  xlRng.Offset(0, WeekNumber) = _
                      TSV(WeekNumber).Value / 60
              Next
              If T.Summary = True Then
                  xlRng.EntireRow.Font.Bold = True
              End If
              Set xlRng = xlRng.Offset(1, 0)  'Down 1 rows
          End If
      Next

      'Format Data
      xlRng.Offset(-1, 0).CurrentRegion.Offset(1, 0).NumberFormat = _
          "0.00\h;;"

      End Sub
```

CREATING A BLANK REPORT IN EXCEL

None of this code is new, simply a variation on everything you have learned before. If you are not sure on any statement, click it and press F1 for Help. Then you can single-step through the code (using F8) and swap to Excel to see the result of each line.

GETTING TIMESCALED DATA

```
Dim TSV As TimeScaleValues
```

TimeScaleValues is a collection of data about a task, a resource, or an assignment. This data is *timephased* or *timescaled* which means that for the data you want to see (work, actual work, cost, and so on) there will be a value for each time period (defined by you). Each object in the collection represents one time period and each of these time-period-based objects has a value.

Tsv is a variable that can be pointed to any collection of timescaled data—basically at any timescaled information viewable in the Resource or Task Usage views in Project.

```
Set TSV = T.TimeScaleData(Proj.ProjectStart, _
    Proj.ProjectFinish, pjTaskTimescaledWork, _
    pjTimescaleWeeks, 1)
```

TimeScaleData is the method that will collect any timephased data you want. Click it and press F1 for help to read the technical details of the method. This is a line of code that merits you typing it in, rather than copying it or using the example file. If you have opened the example file, create a new line underneath this statement and type it in. As you do, take note of all the options in the lists that appear as you type. They will show you exactly what possibilities exist.

This TimeScaleData line gets the work on a week-by-week basis from the project's start to finish. You can substitute your own date range if you want.

The first two parameters of TimeScaleData are named StartDate and EndDate. While self explanatory, it is worth knowing that they will be rounded up and down to suit the timescale. If you enter the same date for both parameters and it's for a Wednesday, the date is automatically reduced to the start of the week for StartDate and the end of the week for EndDate.

You might also need to be careful because, even though an end date is correct, the date's time by default will be for 1 minute past midnight. To get the last day included in day-by-day timescales, add one day to the EndDate value (for example, Date + 1).

The third parameter is called Type. In Listing 28.5, it is type pjTaskTimescaledWork that reads the work from the work row of the Task or Resource Usage views.

The next parameter is TimeScaleUnit - pjTimescaleWeeks in our example. Again you can enter whatever value you can select manually in a Usage view. The last parameter is Count, which allows you to read values for every 4-week period or any multiple of the selected time period. For a full list of all possible options for each parameter, click on the TimeScaleData code and press F1 for Help.

WRITING DATA TO EXCEL

```
If DatesAdded = False Then
```

This code is a new, useful tool for you. In this instance, you need to add the Week Ending dates for each week in the top row, but only once. DatesAdded has been declared as a Boolean variable. Boolean variables can only be True or False and they always default to False. This line tests for that. If DatesAdded is False, the code inside the If statement is executed. Because the last statement is DatesAdded = True, the code won't run a second time.

```
For WeekNumber = 1 To TSV.Count
    xlRng.Offset(-1, WeekNumber) = TSV(WeekNumber).EndDate
```

TSV is actually a collection of objects, each of which holds information about one time slice of data. To access the information for any time slice, simply use TSV(1) for the first time slice of data, or TSV(2), and so on. As with all collections, Count is a property and allows you to know how many there are. It makes for very easy loop control because TSV.Count provides the largest number WeekNumber needs to reach.

Click the TSV(WeekNumber).EndDate statement and press F9 to create a breakpoint, and then run the macro. When code stops at this line, press Ctrl+G to enter the Immediate window.

PART
VIII
CH
28

Type **?TSV(1)** and then a full stop. Look down the list at everything you can access for a time slice. Select StartDate and press Enter, and then type **?TSV(1).EndDate** and press Enter before trying other properties.

```
xlRng.Offset(0, WeekNumber) = TSV(WeekNumber).Value / 60
```

The Value property provides the minutes of work for the current time slice—divide by 60 to get the number of hours.

```
xlRng.Offset(-1, 0).CurrentRegion.Offset(1, 0).NumberFormat _
= "0.00\h;;"
```

When the loop through each task finishes, xlRng points to the first blank row under the last task. Offset(-1,0) points back to the last row. In Excel, CurrentRegion is the same as pressing Ctrl+*—it selects everything until a blank row or column is reached. Because we don't want to change the format of the header row of dates, the final .Offset(1,0) moves the whole selection down. Try removing parts of this instruction and see what happens.

That's it! You have now created a report, nicely formatted, in Excel, using up-to-date information in Project. The basic structure can be reused many times. All you need to do is change the parameters (date ranges, the time units, and the type of information required, for example), use Cost instead of Work, and you have another report.

In the ExportWorkData macro, you have only read timescaled data. By using tsv(1)=60, you can make the first time slice have the value of 60 minutes. Now you can set any value you can read in the Usage views using VBA.

For further information on programming Excel, use the VBA help within Excel.

Note

For some additional information on using Excel VBA, take a look at Chapter 30, "Creating Interactive Excel Applications with VBA," in *Special Edition Using Microsoft Excel 2000*.

THE PROJECT_OPEN EVENT

It can often be useful to have some code run automatically—for example, when you open a project file. You can accomplish this by using an event. An event is something that is used in most other Office applications as well. In this section you will learn about the Open event. There are basically two types of events as far as Project 2000 is concerned: project-level events and events related to things inside a project—such as tasks. The difference between the two event types is that Project 2000 has project-level events readily and easily available to you for coding. The other events take a bit more work.

An event like the File Open event occurs every time a file is opened and is generated by Project 2000 itself. If you provide code for this event, it will be run every time a file is opened.

Open "Chap28/Open and Delete Events.Mpp" from the CD. You should see a message pop up, as displayed by the Open Event code shown in Figure 28.2.

To create this Event code in your own project file, do the following:

1. Open the project you want to work with.
2. View the VBE by pressing Alt+F11. Make sure the Project Explorer is showing (press Ctrl+R if not).
3. Navigate to the ThisProject object and right-click it. This should produce the situation shown in Figure 28.2.
4. Click the View Code command from the shortcut menu to display code for project-level events.
5. There are two drop-down lists at the top of every code window; the left one for this window is the Object list. From the drop-down list, select Project. The right list is the Procedure list; from here you should now see a list of all project-level events. Select Open.
6. The following code will now appear. Enter whatever code you want in this Sub. (The Open and Delete Events.Mpp file on the CD has a simple MsgBox statement.)

```
Private Sub Project_Open(ByVal pj As Project)
End Sub
```

The pj As Project part of the code provides a Project object. That way you can get at the name of the project file and all other project information, since in some circumstances the ActiveProject property won't produce the result you might expect.

The Open event could be used to add extra menus to assist users and the BeforeClose event can remove them when the project is closed.

Figure 28.2
Creating the Project_Open event. To get this view, right-click the ThisProject folder.

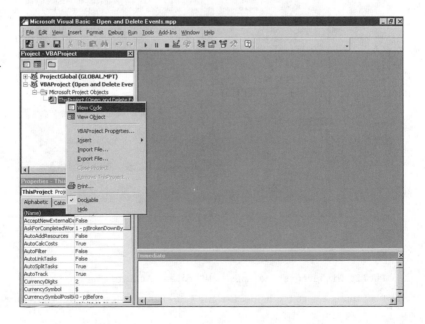

THE PROJECTBEFORETASKDELETE EVENT

This section shows you how to develop code that runs when a task is deleted. The process is more involved, but provided all steps are carried out in sequence, you will find it reliable. What this event does is ensure that, when you press the Delete key to delete any task in your project file, the code in this event will be run first. The code can cancel the event and therefore the delete. At last, accidentally pressing the Delete key need no longer remove a day's work!

A task is only part of a project and is therefore not a project-level event created as the Project_Open event is. Follow the instructions below to create the ProjectBeforeTaskDelete event. Be sure not to miss anything or change the sequence.

1. Go to the VBE (press Alt+F11) and insert a new class module. In Figure 28.3 you see that the Properties window has been used to rename the class from Class1 to DeleteClass (remember this name for step 4). A class module is different from a standard module in that it is used to group together all logical methods and properties for a new object or class that you might develop. It has its own events and properties associated with it and its biggest advantage is the easy-to-understand-and-use end result and the ease with which its code can be reused in other macros.

Figure 28.3
Finished DeleteClass code.

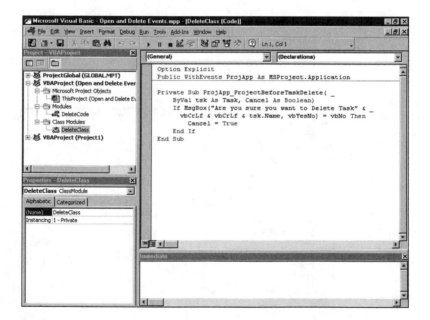

2. In the class module, enter

```
Public WithEvents ProjApp As MSProject.Application
```

ProjApp is a variable name; use any valid name you want, but remember it for step 6.

WithEvents can only be used in a Dim statement in a class module. It says that the variable defined is created to respond to events generated by the object defined after the As part, which in this case is the MSProject application itself.

3. Create a new module (renamed from Module1 to DeleteCode in Figure 28.4).

Figure 28.4
Finished DeleteCode module contents.

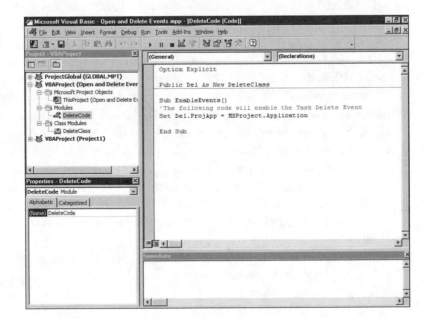

4. In the module, enter

```
Public Del As New DeleteClass
```

Del is a variable. DeleteClass refers to the class module name entered in step 1. They can both have other names, but make sure that you make the names the same for the other steps; otherwise, the events won't work.

You also need some code that will "start" the event. The code in the DeleteCode module is

```
Sub EnableEvents()
    Set Del.ProjApp = MSProject.Application
End Sub
```

The procedure EnableEvents must be run before the Delete event (and the other events) can be enabled. The best tactic is therefore to call EnableEvents from the Project_Open event so it automatically runs every time the project file is opened.

5. Switch back to the DeleteClass class module using the Window menu or Ctrl+F6.

6. You can either type the procedure name and parameters, or you can select from the Class module window. The procedure name is

```
ProjApp_ProjectBeforeTaskDelete(ByVal tsk As Task, Cancel As Boolean)
```

PART
VIII

CH
28

To select this from the window, however, do the following:

From the Object drop-down list (top of the class module window on the left side), choose ProjApp (or whatever the variable name is you defined in step 2).

In the Procedure drop-down list (top right side), select the event that you want. This will place the procedure into your class module. This is less complex than it looks and is very useful.

`ProjApp_ProjectBeforeTaskDelete` represents the Project application with events enabled and the name of the event. All event names are specific and cannot be changed. `tsk` is a Task object that points to the task that is being deleted. Using `tsk`, you can test anything to do with the task before deciding whether or not it should be deleted.

`Cancel` is a flag that has a default value of False. If left at that, when the procedure finishes, the deletion of the task continues. If the code sets `Cancel` to True, the deletion is cancelled and nothing changes.

7. Finally, add a call to `EnableEvents` in the Open event (use the Window menu or Ctl+F6 to swap to the Project_Open event code). By having a statement that is simply the name of a `Sub` procedure (in this case, `EnableEvents`), that procedure will be run and code execution will then continue from the line following. The Open event could now look like Figure 28.5.

Test the code. Close the project, saving changes, and then reopen it. Now try deleting a task and see what happens. You should get the "Are you sure…" message if you are deleting a task in any open project.

When you are confident with what you've got, try some of the other events.

Figure 28.5
Final Project_Open event code.

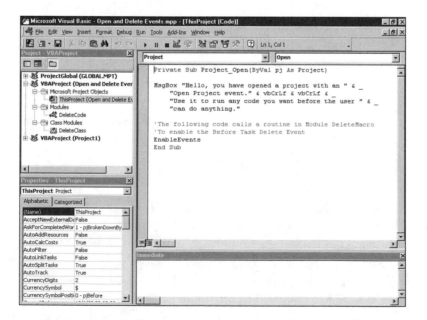

WRITING VBA CODE THAT WILL WORK NEXT MONTH

It was suggested that the best code to write is code that will keep on working long after you originally wrote it. You have already seen a number of techniques that make this happen. For example, code that loops from task ID 1 to 100 in a project with 100 tasks will have problems if more tasks are added—the extra tasks will be missed. The following techniques all support code survival:

- `For Each T in ActiveProject.Tasks` guarantees that every task will be processed. Alternatively use the `ActiveProject.Tasks.Count` property to make sure that every task is processed.

- Testing for empty tasks—even if your plan doesn't have them—is also good, because you never know when an empty task might be added (see the TaskSummaryName macro discussed previously in this chapter).

- Not having fixed dates is another good survival technique. Wherever possible, use the `Date` function to return the current day's date and then adjust the date as needed. For example, `Date + 14` gave you the date two weeks into the future (refer to the FilterNextTwoWeeks macro in Chapter 27).

- Outputting reports to Excel means that one-off changes in requirements can be handled manually in Excel without needing macro changes (take a look at the ProfitLossReport macro).

- Applying specific views and tables can help, because if the user wants a slightly different view, they need only reformat the view for the macro to keep working (as discussed in Chapter 27). If all formatting is in the macro, any format changes will require macro edits.

The bottom-line rule is to look at your project and try to define all changes that are legitimate—such as task changes, for example—and confirm that your macro can handle them.

WHERE TO NEXT

If you have grasped all the concepts introduced in these two chapters and have made variations of the code work, you are well on your way to successfully coding your own macros for Project 2000 VBA.

The most important thing to do now is practice. Remember to write down the basic building blocks for the application you want to write. Break them down again until you can understand and work on each in turn, so assembling your final code.

Be sure to make heavy use of the Help system built into Project and other Office programs. You might find it hard to discover just what you need the first time, but persevere. When you're in Help, go to the Contents tab and explore all the topics for "Getting Started with Microsoft Project Visual Basic" and the "Microsoft Project Visual Basic Reference," especially the code examples.

PART
VIII
CH
28

Support and help is never far away in today's world. Microsoft has a large number of newsgroups, two of which are `microsoft.public.project` and `microsoft.public.project.vba` on the `msnews.microsoft.com` news server. Make full use of them to help you. Then after you gather confidence, you can try your hand at helping other people with some of the simpler questions and then the harder ones. It's a great way to explore new areas and learn as you go. Take a look at Figure 28.6 for good Help topics to read.

Figure 28.6
Good Help topics to read. Also, browse through the methods, objects, and properties and make sure you look at all the code examples. Some of them will be very useful for you.

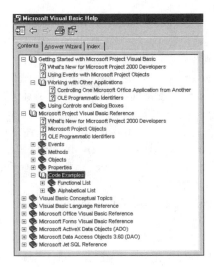

TROUBLESHOOTING

FINDING THE SAME TASK WHEN IDs AND NAMES CHANGE

I have made all task names unique within my project. But during the week users often edit task descriptions or insert and delete tasks and I can't get my macro to return to the original tasks. What can I do?

Project has a field not usually displayed called Unique ID. This provides a unique ID for every project. Use this to reference a task and unless that task is deleted, you can always return to it.

```
Dim TaskUID as Long
TaskUID=T.UniqueId
EditGoto ActiveProject.Tasks.UniqueID(TaskUID).Id
```

This code records the Unique ID for a task pointed to by the task variable T. The `EditGoto` statement then jumps the cursor to the task whose unique ID was stored in `TaskUID`.

CODE TO CONTROL ANOTHER APPLICATION

I've copied the code from one of the example projects that came with the book and I keep getting a compile error. Am I doing something wrong?

You have probably forgotten to add a reference to the other program. In the VBE in Project select Tools, References, and click the Microsoft Excel Object Library (or that for whichever program you want to control).

In Excel, go to its VBE and select Tools References and choose the Microsoft Project Object Library.

PART

IX

APPENDIXES

REVIEWING THE BASICS OF PROJECT MANAGEMENT

In this appendix   *by Toby Brown, PMP*

UNDERSTANDING PROJECT MANAGEMENT

Regardless of your experience with Microsoft Project, a review of the basics of project management will assist you with planning and executing a successful project plan. Although this is not meant to be a replacement for experience or schooling within the discipline, this short appendix will introduce you to the basics of what you must consider when building a plan. Look to it as a review, or even a primer, of many of the factors you should consider prior to embarking upon a project.

Further detail beyond that which is explained here can be found in *A Guide to the Project Management Body of Knowledge* (PMBOK Guide). The PMBOK Guide is a publication developed and maintained by the Project Management Institute (PMI). Recognized as the authoritative Guide to project management, the PMBOK guide was deemed the ANSI standard for project management in November 1999. The Guide is available for purchase or you can download it for free directly from PMI's Web site, www.pmi.org. Once there, you can navigate to the publications page and download a copy, or you can go directly to the document at http://www.pmi.org/publictn/pmboktoc.htm.

After filling out a form agreeing to terms and conditions of use of the PMBOK Guide, it can be downloaded for free. You should realize that the Guide is over 175 pages, so it might be easier to order a copy from the PMI bookstore link instead (www.pmibookstore.org) or by calling (412) 741-6206. The cost of a pre-printed copy is $26.35 for PMI members and $32.95 for nonmembers.

Note

Throughout this appendix, you'll see references to chapters and page numbers in the PMBOK Guide. Look to those places for additional information or clarification of the material being presented.

DEFINING A PROJECT

Organizations and companies approach the required work to be performed from two distinct viewpoints. Their efforts generally involve either the management of the operations of the company, or project-related activities, which are distinct efforts to fulfill strategic initiatives and to further the objects or strategic mission. Although there are numerous characteristics shared between the two, including work being performed by associates usually limited in their available time, there are unmistakable differences. A project is usually defined as "a temporary endeavor undertaken to create or enhance a unique product, service, or system" (see the PMBOK Guide, p. 4).

Characteristics of a project include

- A temporary, unique, and one-time effort.
- Proactive (versus reactive), integrative (versus isolated), and preventive (versus corrective).

- One or many defined objectives or deliverables.
- A defined start and finish.
- The consumption of constrained or finite resources.

Temporary means that the effort has a definite start and finish. *Unique* means that the final product is different from all other similar products, services, or systems. Although many of your projects can, in fact, include an element of repetition, each project is considered to have a unique deliverable accomplished through distinctly defined efforts.

Projects are performed for all sorts of reasons, but usually they are to address one or more of the following: a market demand, a business need, a customer request, a technological advance, or a legal requirement. Many of these factors are often considered the fixes to problems, taking advantage of opportunities, or for the fulfillment of some necessary business requirement. For whatever the reason, an organization must decide how it wants to get the work done, on time and on budget (see the PMBOK Guide, p. 49).

THE ART OF PROJECT MANAGEMENT

Project management is typically defined as the application of knowledge, skills, tools, and techniques to project-related activities (see the PMBOK Guide, p. 6). To do so, it usually means fulfilling the requirements while balancing competing demands among scope, time, cost, and quality. The obvious expectations are usually ascertained right from the beginning of the project and provide the basis for proceeding with the project. However, equally important to the project manager are the unspoken or nondefined expectations. In fact, many customers (the users of the final product of the project) sometimes don't know what they want until well into project planning. Attempting to identify these customer wants from the beginning, and incorporating their fulfillment as part of the project plan, is part of the art of managing projects.

Regardless of how proficient you become with project management software, the reality is that a tool like Microsoft Project will not make you a better project manager any more than Microsoft Word will make you a better writer. Project management is a skill as well as an art form, fast becoming recognized as a necessary element of any company wanting to move forward in business. In fact, it's an area of study with many secondary schools now offering a master's degree or certificate with a project management emphasis. Also, the PMP certificate, a rigorous certification program offered through the Project Management Institute (PMI), now offers application standards and testing requirements to demonstrate competency within the discipline.

Many organizations are now adopting management by projects. These organizations are implementing management systems to specifically facilitate project management. In fact, project-based organizations will typically derive their revenue by primarily performing their projects for others, so they must become experts at accounting, tracking, and reporting on multiple simultaneous projects (see the PMBOK Guide, p. 17).

Regardless of your position within a company, your education level at this point within the discipline, or the current maturity of the organization in terms of *projectized-efforts*, no tool or certification is going to replace experience. The fact remains that with each project being a unique endeavor, only those who have some knowledge of what needs to happen will make the best project managers. In fact, performance-based pay is no longer an unfamiliar method of compensation, recognizing the contributions of the talent within an organization.

Note

Projectized efforts is a current buzzword in project management to characterize an organization in terms of how it operates. In other words, how significant is project management within the company—does it operate by projects and is it a significant portion of its revenue and defined purpose?

BALANCING COMPETING DEMANDS

Project managers walk a fine line to ensure balance among four distinct variables: scope, cost, quality, and time. A change in any one of these four will have an impact on one or more of the remaining three. Many project managers think of this in terms of the good, fast, or cheap argument. In aligning the four competing demands with the three areas of trade-off, we tend to group them this way: Scope and quality encompass good. In other words, you could go out and buy a brand new car, but it might only be the base model. In this case, we might not think of the car as good, because it doesn't have all the bells and whistles. (In actuality, we should recognize the difference between quality and grade, but we won't for this example.) The project scope should be directly tied to the features and functions of the final product. In fact, changes of scope in a well-defined project are typically at the expense of content or quality. Removal of content in a project usually means the removal of features or functions in the interest of time. Issues of quality arise when we attempt to cut corners to complete the work, frequently to meet a newly imposed earlier deadline.

The element of time is a variable of how fast you want the deliverable. Compromises of good (scope and quality) and cheap (increased costs) are common for the sake of speedy delivery. When money is no object, we expect the project to be more timely and delivered at a higher quality with more features.

The formula suggests that any two of the three "competing demands" can be realized by compromising on the third element. A summary of this would be as follows:

- You can have it cheap and fast, but it might not be very good (either complete or high quality—scope/quality together become the variable or trade-off while maintaining costs and time).

- You can have it fast and good, but it probably won't be very cheap (money is then considered no concern, so cost becomes the variable or trade-off while maintaining scope/quality and time).

- You can have it good and cheap, but it might take longer to deliver. (A willingness to wait to obtain the best indicating time is not an issue. It then becomes the variable or trade-off while maintaining scope/quality and cost.)

The trade-off, occurring with any one of the three elements at any time within the project, is necessary to ensure successful delivery at predetermined expectations and is the final objective of every project manager. Bottom-line results with a strong sense of purpose are now the standard by which projectized organizations, whose day-to-day operations are performed by projects, now operate.

THE SCIENCE OF PROJECT MANAGEMENT: THE NINE KNOWLEDGE AREAS

The knowledge areas of project management describe important considerations for project success. These processes have been organized into nine distinct knowledge areas: Managing Integration, Managing Scope, Managing Time, Managing Costs, Managing Quality, Managing Human Resources, Managing Communication, Managing Risk, and Managing Procurement. A summary of each knowledge area is provided for your benefit.

MANAGING INTEGRATION

Project Integration Management (see the PMBOK Guide, Chapter 4) includes the processes required to ensure that the various elements of the project are properly coordinated. It involves making tradeoffs among competing objectives and alternatives to meet or exceed stakeholder needs and expectations. Although all project management processes are integrative, to some extent, the processes described in the Integration Management section of the PMBOK Guide are primarily integrative.

There are three major processes to integration. They include

- **Project plan development**—Taking the results of other planning processes and putting them into a consistent, coherent document.
- **Project plan execution**—Carrying out the project plan by performing the activities included therein.
- **Overall change control**—Coordinating changes across the entire project.

These processes interact with each other and with other defined processes in the other knowledge areas as well. The processes, tools, and techniques used to integrate project management are the focus of this knowledge area.

MANAGING SCOPE

Project Scope Management includes the processes required to ensure that the project includes all the work required, and only the work required, to complete the project successfully (see the PMBOK Guide, Chapter 5).

It includes five defined processes:

- **Initiation**—Committing the organization to start a project or the next phase of a project.
- **Scope Planning**—Developing a written scope statement as the basis for future project decisions.

- **Scope Definition**—Subdividing the major project deliverables into smaller, more manageable parts.
- **Scope Verification**—Formalizing acceptance of the project scope.
- **Scope Change Control**—Controlling changes to project scope.

In the overall project context, the term *scope* can refer to the following:

- Product scope defines the features and functions of deliverables, which are to be included in the developed product or service.
- Project scope defines the work that must be performed to derive the expected deliverables of the project.

The development of project scope is the focus of scope management. Designation of product scope depends on the application area as part of the project lifecycle. The completion of each is measured against different standards. Completion of product scope is measured against the requirements called for in the initial design specifications of the product, while completion of project scope is measured against the established plan or baseline. Both types of scope management should be incorporated to ensure that the result of the project offers delivery of the expected product.

MANAGING TIME

Project time management includes the processes required for timely completion of the project (see the PMBOK Guide, Chapter 6). There are five major processes identified for doing so. They include

- **Activity Definition**—Identifying the specific activities that must be performed to produce the various project deliverables.
- **Activity Sequencing**—Identifying and documenting inter-dependencies among the activities.
- **Activity Duration Estimating**—Estimating the number of work periods needed to complete individual activities.
- **Schedule Development**—Analyzing activity sequences, activity durations, and resource requirements to create the project schedule.
- **Schedule Control**—Controlling changes to the project schedule.

With many projects, activity definition, sequencing, and duration estimating—along with schedule development—happen as a single process. However, the PMBOK Guide chapter on time management clearly defines the role of each one. Project uses the term *task*, but there is currently no consensus within the profession about the relationship between activities and tasks. Regardless, the focus should be on how to break the work into management pieces, not the naming convention used.

MANAGING COSTS

"Finance is the art of passing currency from hand to hand until it finally disappears." Robert W. Sarnoff (1918–1997), American communications industry executive

Project Cost Management includes the processes required to ensure that the project is completed within the approved budget (see the PMBOK Guide, Chapter 7). The major processes include

- **Resource Planning**—Determining what resources (the people, equipment, and materials or supplies) and how much of each should be used.
- **Cost Estimating**—Arriving at an estimate of approximate costs for the resources that are used.
- **Cost Budgeting**—Allocating the overall cost estimate to the individual work elements.
- **Cost Control**—Controlling changes to the projected budget.

On many projects, resource planning, cost estimating, and cost budgeting are performed as a single process. Cost control, however, requires an examination of project costs after work is actually performed.

In general, cost management is concerned with the required resources that need to be deployed and should also consider the needs of the individual project stakeholders and their measurement criteria. Consideration should be given to not only the measurements of costs used, but also when applied.

MANAGING QUALITY

"People forget how fast you did a job—but they remember how well you did it." Howard W. Newton (1903–1951), American industrialist

Project Quality Management includes the processes to ensure that the project will satisfy the needs for which it was undertaken (see the PMBOK Guide, Chapter 8). It includes the activities of the overall management function that designate the quality policy, objectives, and responsibilities and implements them by processes such as quality planning, quality control, quality assurance, and quality improvement, each defined within the quality system.

The three major quality processes include

- **Quality Planning**—Identifying which quality standards are relevant to the project and determining how to satisfy them.
- **Quality Assurance**—Evaluating overall project performance on a regular basis to provide confidence that the project will satisfy the relevant quality standards.
- **Quality Control**—Monitoring specific project results to determine if they comply with the relevant quality standards and identifying ways to eliminate causes of unsatisfactory performance.

The approach to quality within this chapter intends to conform to the ISO 9000 and 10,000 series of standards and Guidelines. Consideration is also given to proprietary measurements of quality by Deming, Juran, Crosby, and other nonproprietary Guidelines such as Total Quality Management (TQM), Continuous Improvement, and others.

Quality assurance inspections need to be defined within every project. Failure to do so increases project risk and can have negative consequences for project stakeholders. Methods for quality considerations typically include customer satisfaction (for conformance to specs and fitness for use), prevention over inspection (avoiding mistakes is less costly than fixing them), management responsibility and accountability (ensuring resource availability), and processes within phases (a repeated inspection element at set intervals during the project lifecycle).

By initiating quality improvement methodologies, the performing organization improves not only the quality of the final product, but also the methods by which the project is managed.

MANAGING HUMAN RESOURCES

> "*Put your personnel work first because it is the most important.*" General Robert E. Wood (1879–1969) President, Sears, Roebuck & Company

Project Human Resources Management includes the processes required to make the most effective use of the people involved with the project (see the PMBOK Guide, Chapter 9). It includes all the project stakeholders—the sponsors, customers, individual contributors, and others.

The three major processes of this knowledge area include

- **Organizational Planning**—Identifying, documenting, and assigning project roles, responsibilities, and reporting relationships.
- **Staff Acquisition**—Getting the human resources required and assigned to work on the project.
- **Team Development**—Developing individual and group skills to enhance project performance.

There is a great deal of information published for dealing with people in a work environment. Topics include assistance with leading, communicating, and negotiating, as well as general management skills. From a leadership standpoint, human resources management includes techniques for delegating, motivating, coaching, and mentoring. Information with regards to group interaction, team building, and conflict resolution is also available. Basic management concepts such as performance appraisal, recruitment, employee retention, labor relations, and health and safety compliance are all part of managing a project effort.

The temporary nature of projects adds another dimension to managing the people assigned to a project team. This type of transitory work requires greater sensitivity for selecting appropriate management techniques.

MANAGING COMMUNICATION

> "*It is a luxury to be understood.*" Ralph Waldo Emerson (1803–1882), American essayist and poet

Project Communications Management includes the processes required to ensure timely and appropriate generation, collection, dissemination, storage, and ultimate disposition of project-related information (see the PMBOK Guide, Chapter 10). It provides the critical links among people, ideas, and information that are necessary for success. Everyone involved in the project must understand how the communications they are involved in as individuals affect the project as a whole.

There are four major processes defined for communications management. They include

- **Communications Planning**—Determining the information and communication needs of the project stakeholders: Who needs what information, when they will need it, and how it will be given to them.

- **Information Distribution**—Making needed information available to the stakeholders of the project in a timely manner.

- **Performance Reporting**—The collection and dissemination of relevant performance information. This includes status reporting, progress measurement, and forecasting.

- **Administrative Closure**—Generating, gathering, and disseminating information to formalize a phase or project completion.

General communication skills as a management concept are related to, but not necessarily the same as, project communications management. General communication tends to encompass a broader subject and involves much more than a narrow scope of project management. Such applications include choices of sender-receiver models (feedback loops, barriers to overcome, and so on), selection of media types (written versus oral communication methods), various writing styles, presentation techniques, and management meeting styles.

Managing Risk

> "*Take calculated risks. That is quite different from being rash.*" General George S. Patton (1885–1945), U.S. Army

Project Risk Management includes the processes concerned with identifying, analyzing, and responding to project risk (see the PMBOK Guide, Chapter 11). It includes maximizing the results of positive events and minimizing the consequences of adverse events.

There are four defined processes for risk:

- **Risk Identification**—Determining which risks are likely to affect the project and documenting the characteristics of each.

- **Risk Quantification**—Evaluating risks and risk interactions to assess the range of possible project outcomes.

- **Risk Response Development**—Defining enhancement steps for opportunities and responses to threats.

- **Risk Response Control**—Responding to changes in risk over the course of the project.

Different areas of application often use different names for the processes outlined previously. Risk identification and quantification are often combined into a single process and called *risk analysis* or *assessment*. A developed response to risk is frequently called *response planning* or *risk mitigation*. Finally, risk response development and response control can also be combined into a single process called *risk management*.

MANAGING PROCUREMENT

Project Procurement Management includes the processes required in acquiring the goods and services from outside the performing organization (see the PMBOK Guide, Chapter 12). The information is presented from the perspective of the buyer in the buyer/seller relationship, and assumes that the seller is external to the performing organization. Most of the text is equally applicable to formal agreements entered into with other areas of the performing organization.

There are six defined processes for procurement management:

- **Procurement Planning**—Determining what needs to be procured and when.
- **Solicitation Planning**—The documentation of product requirements and identifying potential sources.
- **Solicitation**—Obtaining quotes, bids, offers, or proposals as needed. Often referred to as an RFP (Request For Proposal) or RFQ (Request For Quote).
- **Source Selection**—Selecting services or products from potential sellers.
- **Contract Administration**—Maintaining the relationship with the seller.
- **Contract Closeout**—Completion and settlement of a contract, and securing final resolution of any remaining open items.

PUTTING IT ALL TOGETHER

So how do you frame 37 processes within five process groups and nine knowledge areas? Within the PMBOK Guide to Project Management resides a description of each of the 37 processes, the nine knowledge areas, and the five process groups of the iterative process model of Project Management. Putting the processes within the context of each knowledge area is detailed in Table A.1.

TABLE A.1 PROJECT MANAGEMENT PROCESS AND KNOWLEDGE AREAS

Process Group/ Knowledge Area	Initiating	Planning	Executing	Controlling	Closing
Integration Management (PMBOK) Guide Ch.4		Project Plan Development	Project Plan Execution	Overall Change Control	

TABLE A.1 CONTINUED

Process Group Knowledge Area	Initiating	Planning	Executing	Controlling	Closing
Scope Management (PMBOK Guide Ch. 5)	Initiation	Scope Planning Scope Definition	Scope Verification	Scope Change Control	
Time Management (PMBOK Guide Ch. 6)		Activity Definition Activity Sequencing Activity Duration Estimating Schedule Development		Schedule Control	
Cost Management (PMBOK Guide Ch. 7)		Resource Planning Cost Estimating Cost Budgeting		Cost Control	
Quality Management (PMBOK Guide Ch. 8)		Quality Planning	Quality Assurance	Quality Control	
Human Resources Management (PMBOK Guide Ch. 9)		Organizational Planning Staff Acquisition	Team Development		
Communications Management (PMBOK Guide Ch. 10)		Communications Planning	Information Distribution	Performance Reporting	Administrative Closure
Risk Management (PMBOK Guide Ch. 11)		Risk Identification Risk Quantification Risk Response		Risk Response Control	

Table A.1 Continued

Process Group/ Knowledge Area	Initiating	Planning	Executing	Controlling	Closing
Procurement Management		Procurement Planning	Solicitation		Contract Closeout
(PMBOK Guide Ch. 12)		Solicitation Planning	Source Selection		
			Contract Admin.		

Project Management Versus Other Management Methodologies

There are many strategies within organizations for getting the work done. In practice, general management can be broken down into four distinct approaches: strategic, operations, crisis, and project. In order to understand how project management fits as a function within an organization, it is important to define and differentiate each approach and area of focus. Along with a description of each management methodology, there is a metaphor for describing each method. If various management techniques are considered to get from point A to point B, a mode of transportation serves well as a descriptor of each management style.

Strategic management implements the overall strategic plan and direction for the on-going work of the organization. It is for the purpose of proactively achieving a long-range vision or mission to be fulfilled. It also addresses the overall business strategy and how to deliver it. Mostly performed at an executive or high level of the organization, you can remember strategic management as a Lear jet screaming across the sky.

Operations management focuses on the on-going, day-to-day work of an organization. Its purpose is to proactively maintain the status quo. Operations serve to keep the fire going, so to speak. With this in mind, it's not hard to picture a steam engine moving down the tracks. The metaphor works additionally well when you think of the railroad tracks as representing the status quo: the way the company has always operated in the past and the way it is expected to continue to function in the future. Concerned with keeping the engine going, operations management is the fundamental component for keeping the place running smoothly.

Crisis management is a mode many of us operate in at one time or another. It focuses on fighting fires by fixing operations when they breaks or malfunctions. It is meant to be a temporary assignment performed as a reaction to a current situation. Because we are frequently called to tend to emergencies as part of working within an office, a fire truck serves well to describe assistance to these efforts. Additionally, because rarely is someone given the official title of crisis manager, and everyone is expected to drop everything on occasion, a volunteer fire department is created within every company. No one is exempt should an emergency arise.

Finally, *project management* works to change the status quo in a temporary, proactive way. In doing so, it attempts to fulfill the strategic plan or mission set at the executive level, improve the operations of the organization, and avoid reactive crises by managing and mitigating risks. Like a tall ship of many years ago, the attempt is often to take advantage of prevailing opportunities and to take an appropriate tack to overcome difficulties in steering directly to a desired objective.

WORKING WITH MULTIPLE PROJECTS

Certain types of endeavors are closely related to projects. A *program* is often defined as a series of projects that are managed in a coordinated way to realize benefits not available from managing the projects separately. Many programs include elements of on-going operations, such as the NASA space program. Additionally, programs often involve a series of repeated undertakings, such as a fundraising program, to maintain a nonprofit organization, or membership drives, continually performed by many organizations.

In some corporations, program and project management are treated as synonyms. In others, programs are considered subsets of projects. Within others, smaller, more manageable subprojects are sometimes rolled up into larger, comprehensive master projects. Contracted companies that are external to the performing organization often work subprojects.

Examples of subprojects might include a single phase of a project—for example, the installation of plumbing or electrical fixtures in a house—component parts of a modular software package, or the high-volume manufacturing of consumer goods from concept to store delivery. Because an outsourced vendor often performs subprojects, they are often considered a procured service from the perspective of the performing organization, with each one providing a unique deliverable (see the PMBOK Guide, p. 10).

PROJECT STAKEHOLDERS

The project stakeholders, according to the PMBOK Guide, are the key "individuals and organizations who are actively involved in the project, or whose interests may be positively or negatively affected as a result of project execution or successful project completion" (see the PMBOK Guide, p. 15). The key stakeholders in every project include

- The *customer* is the individual or organization who will use the product of the project or benefits directly from the project deliverable or deliverables.

- The *performing organization* is the enterprise whose employees are most directly involved in performing the work of the project.

- The *sponsor* is the individual or group within the performing organization who provides the financial resources, in case or in kind, for the project. Another name for the sponsor is the *financier*. Not to be confused with the customer, the sponsor finances the project from the beginning until paid back by the customer at the end of the project or during the project life cycle.

- The *project manager* is the individual responsible for managing the project.

A way to think about and remember this could be to consider a project as a movie production:

> The customer would be the audience.
>
> The performing organization would be the actors and actresses.
>
> The sponsor would be the producer.
>
> The project manager would be the director.

THE DECISION ELEMENTS OF PROJECT MANAGEMENT

When given the authority, the project manager makes many decisions during the life of a project. The various organizational structures provide different levels of autonomy to make or influence these decisions. There are five defined decision elements, which are the manageables of a project manager, impacting their ability to make things happen. These decision elements include

- **People**—Who can we utilize to help do the work of the project?
- **Time**—How much time is used and when is work scheduled?
- **Money**—How much can be spent and what are the budget implications for executing the work?
- **Quality**—How good is the final product?
- **Tools and Techniques**—Other than resources, what else can be used to get the job done?

THE ITERATIVE PROCESS MODEL OF PROJECT MANAGEMENT

The iterative project management processes can be organized into five groups, which are connected by the results that each one produces (see the PMBOK Guide, p. 28). The processes are

> **Initiating**—Understanding when a new project, or new phase of a project, should begin and committing the performing organization to do so. The two most important deliverables of the initiating process include creation of the project charter and identifying the project manager.
>
> **Planning**—Developing and maintaining a workable scheme to address the business need for which the project was undertaken. With 19 of the 37 process groups established for planning, the majority of project management is planning. But that is not to say that project management is only planning.
>
> **Executing**—The coordination of people as well as other resources to carry out the plan. The majority of the project's budget will be expended during the execution of the project plan.

Controlling—The consistent monitoring and measurement of progress, and taking corrective action when necessary to meet project objectives. Controlling requires the project team to step back from the work and evaluate what has been accomplished. Often it is necessary to implement changes to the plan in order to bring expected future performance (schedule) back in line with the plan (baseline).

Closing—Formal acceptance of the product of the project or project phase and bringing it to an orderly end. Evaluation of lessons learned becomes a valuable input to starting a similar project, which is why a project debriefing is so important.

Take a look at how to roll everything together by following these process groups.

INITIATING—UNDERTAKING A PROJECT

The Initiation process commits the performing organization to start the next phase of a project or simply recognizes that a new project should begin or an existing project should continue into its next phase. It also ties the project to the ongoing work of the performing organization.

COMMUNICATING THE OBJECTIVE

Projects are performed for all sorts of reasons, but usually they are to address one or more of the following: a market demand, a business need, a customer request, a technological advance, or a legal requirement. Many of these factors are often considered the fixes to problems, taking advantage of opportunities, or fulfilling some necessary business requirement. Regardless, the point is that the company must decide how they want to get the work done.

> *"Right up front, tell people what you're trying to accomplish and what you're willing to sacrifice to accomplish it."* Lee Iacocca, former chairman, Chrysler Corporation

Communicating the objective or the reason the project is being undertaken is important to all the stakeholders of the project. By doing so, the project manager is attempting to communicate four important elements:

- The business reason as to why the project was undertaken
- A description of the product (the product of the project)
- Any constraints that might be encountered—barriers or obstacles which might interfere with the ability to fulfill the objective(s) of the project
- Any obvious assumptions—anything that can be taken for granted as being factual, but might not be true.

ISSUING THE PROJECT CHARTER

The *Project Charter* is a document that formally recognizes the existence of a project. It should include, either directly or by reference to other documents: 1) The business need or reason the project was undertaken (sometimes referred to as the *Mission Statement*) and 2) The product description (or product of the project).

The charter should be issued by management external to the project. It is used to give authority to the project manager to utilize and assign resources to project tasks or activities. When a project is performed under contract, the signed documents can serve as the project charter. This document legitimizes the existence of a project and acts as the work permit to proceed. The charter is recognized by all project stakeholders as the right to continue with the project.

PLANNING—DEFINING A PROJECT

"Plans are nothing; planning is everything." Dwight D. Eisenhower (1890–1969), U.S. Army general and president of the United States

Planning is of major importance on a project, because, by definition, it involves creating something unique. Another way of thinking of this is that you are heading into uncharted waters and so you should have a plan to navigate through them safely. Defining the scope of the project includes the processes required to ensure that the project includes all the work required to complete the project successfully.

THE DEVELOPMENT OF THE PROJECT PLAN*

In defining the steps and techniques necessary to build a project management plan, there are two distinct elements that must be defined: definition of the product/service and definition of the project management controls. In defining the products and services, the stakeholders need to arrive at a consensus of the acceptance criteria for delivery of the project product. By level-setting these expectations, the performing organization of the project understands the client expectations in terms of the acceptance or sign-off criteria upon the perceived completion of the project.

In addition to project deliverables, it is also the responsibility of the project team to establish the project management controls. These quality assurance procedures ensure effective delivery of the required products and services, and management of risk, communications, and procurement tasks, in addition to controlling changes to scope, time, and cost constraints. Doing so significantly enhances the capability to realize project goals.

In terms of defining the work of the project, proceed with the development of a comprehensive *Work Breakdown Structure* or WBS for the products and services to be created. This evaluation process requires a systematic breakdown of how to proceed with the project. It includes discovery, definition, design, development, and deployment activities and phases.

Additionally, the activities or tasks required to perform project management controls must be defined as part of the project plan. These controls are administered to incorporate consideration for the uncertainties and inevitable changes that will (not might) occur. This is where many organizations usually stumble. They do not plan for uncertainty, manage change, or schedule time for communication and milestone inspection.

The "Development of the Project Plan" information is provided with the assistance of MaryGrace T. Allenchey, PMP, chair of Project Management Institute's Certification Board Center, and a vice president with PMSI-Project Mentors.

With a combination of both the defined products/services and associated WBS, along with the defined project management controls and associated WBS, the sequencing of the activities to build the network diagram is the next step. With each activity having an estimated effort, a PERT analysis for each task can be calculated. This process is the application of the formula: Best Case + (4 x Most Likely) + Worst Case, divided by 6, to each activity in the plan.

Completing this effort takes the project team into an iterative process for building the plan. Conceptually, the iterative process means that it might be repeated numerous times as the project is built. The sequence of activities is as follows:

1. Determine the task duration by using the WBS and applying the resource requirement.
2. Define the critical path with consideration for linkages, task durations, and resource assignments.
3. Assign the resources (based on skill) to each task.
4. Define the schedule with consideration of the project calendar and resource availability.

After completing this process, the effort can focus on cost definitions, based on resource assignments along with the necessary fixed costs, which provides a budget estimate for the work effort. This budget estimate is (with an accuracy of –10 to +25%) better than the order of magnitude estimate (with an accuracy of –50 to +75%) based solely on experience, because it is based on a bottom-up estimating process.

Last, due process would include a risk management plan to identify, assess, quantify, and respond to project risks. Updating the plan with these considerations requires a certain expertise in how to apply these processes. Regardless, even an inexperienced project manager can quickly evaluate an established schedule in terms of critical tasks and the possible effect of slippage along the critical path.

When finished, consideration should then be given to the completeness of the plan. Has everything been included? Has anything been left out? Anything missed presents opportunities for *scope creep*, a contributing factor to missed project dates and cost overruns. Repeated evaluation should be completed prior to project plan execution.

Finally, you need to obtain *buy-in* from all project stakeholders, including the customer, project manager, sponsor, and any others on the project team. It was once said, "People tend to support the ideas that they themselves create." Successful project plan execution must have the commitment of all the players. It is essential for success.

EXECUTING—DOING THE WORK

> *"Plan your work and work your plan."* Anonymous

Project Plan Execution is the only core process of the executing process group. This is where the defined work is performed and the schedule is deployed. It incorporates not only the project plan, but also any supporting details, organizational policies, and corrective action to achieve the objective(s). The outputs of this process group include work results and change requests. *Work results* are the outcomes of activities performed to accomplish the project. *Change requests* are for the purpose of expanding or contracting project scope, and are often identified while the work of the project is being done.

CONTROLLING—TRACKING PROJECT PERFORMANCE

"It is a bad plan that admits of no modification." Publilus Syrus (first century BC), Latin writer of mimes

Controlling the project is to ensure that the project objectives are being met by monitoring and measuring progress and taking corrective action whenever necessary. *Variance analysis*, which is the process of comparing actual performances with planned performance, is part of the controlling process. Additionally, it includes evaluation of possible alternatives and taking appropriate corrective action as needed.

It is often said that you "expect what you inspect." Change management considers *configuration management* as a documented procedure used to apply technical and administrative direction to the project team along with inspection of the functional and physical characteristics. Controlling the project requires taking a step back from the work in progress so that you can see if the project is progressing according to plan. If not, a change management control needs to be deployed.

Performance reporting, also a component of the controlling process, involves the collection and dissemination of performance information. It is specifically used to provide stakeholders with information about how resources are being deployed to achieve project objectives.

CLOSING—COMPLETING THE CLOSE-OUT

"Hindsight is an exact science." Guy Bellamy, American journalist and writer

Formal acceptance of the project or phase and bringing it to an orderly end is the process of closing. To complete the close out of a project, there must be consideration to three administrative components, including any performance measurement documentation, documentation of the product of the project, and any other project records. By using various performance reporting tools and techniques, the closing of a project will include project records for archive, formal acceptance of the project, and lessons learned for any future projects to be performed.

Project archives typically include a complete set of indexed project records. Any project-specific or program-wide historical databases should be updated, and if done under contract involving significant expenditures of procurement, special attention should be given to the financial records during project execution. Formal acceptance includes notice and documentation that there has been acceptance of the product and that the contract has been completed.

Finally, a lessons-learned evaluation examines the causes of variances and the reasoning behind corrective actions that were taken. These should be well documented so that they become part of the historical database of the performing organization. These types of records can act as a template for how a future similar project should be planned and executed, ensuring a greater amount of success with fewer corrections.

BEFORE "SETTING SAIL"

The Iterative processes of Project Management (repeated during the life cycle of the project and/or during any one phase of the project—Initiating, Planning, Executing, Controlling, and Closing) frames the fundamentals of carrying out a project. By applying this process model, the project manager, regardless of experience, will significantly increase his or her chances of carrying out a project plan successfully.

Following the Initiating phase, which creates the project charter, a majority of a project manager's time (often estimated to be 7–10% of the total project duration) will be spent on planning. In fact, 19 of the 37 processes previously outlined are in planning. While Microsoft Project can significantly assist in developing the scope of the project, other tools and techniques should be used prior to developing a time-driven schedule. These distinct products of project management planning can include a scope statement (or statement of work), supporting detail, a scope management plan, a comprehensive WBS, a precedence diagram (or Network diagram), a resource assignment matrix for staff acquisition, a cost budget, a quality management plan, a risk management plan and, finally, a procurement plan if goods or services need to be obtained from outside the performing organization. Each of these deliverables is derived through careful planning of the project. (For further information, refer to the PMBOK Guide for a clear description of each one.)

RULES OF THUMB

As an aid in developing your plan within Microsoft Project, the following rules of thumb can assist in putting together a project schedule.

DEFINING THE WORK

Name each activity as a clear call to action. To do so, it is best to express a task activity in verb-noun format. Examples include Disassemble Computers, Distribute Boxes, Move Warehouse, and Assemble Furniture.

Every work task within a project should meet all of the following criteria. As a general rule, each activity should be

- **Definable**—It should have a definite start and finish time and date.
- **Assignable**—It should be able to be completed by a resource within the project.
- **Significant**—It should be important to the plan. Otherwise, we refer to it as *outside of scope*.

ESTIMATING DURATIONS

Once you've created your task list, you are ready to enter a duration for each activity. Before entering a duration, you need to know an estimate of how long you believe it will take to complete the task.

ENTERING MILESTONES

Milestones are sub-goals or checkpoints within your project. They are often used to indicate a significant event during the project, as well as to measure the progress of the project. Sometimes milestone tasks are included to indicate project or phase deliverables, quality checkpoints (Q gates), phase exits, or kill points within a project.

Milestones are usually listed in past-tense noun-verb format, sometimes referred to as *event format*, and are entered just like regular tasks except that the duration is entered as zero. Examples include Computers Disassembled, Boxes Distributed, Warehouse Moved, and Furniture Assembled.

All projects, at a minimum, should have two milestones indicating the start and completion of a project.

LINKING TASKS

When modeling a project, it is suggested that all tasks (with the exception of the start and finish milestones and summary tasks, which are not linked at all) have a predecessor and successor. A task that is missing either a predecessor or successor is referred to as a *Hanger* or a *Dangle*; it is an unintended break in the dependency relationships and, therefore, a break in the overall workflow of the project.

NAMING RESOURCES

Resources within a project are the people, equipment, and supplies necessary to complete a task. Any consumable that is required to successfully complete the project could be listed as part of the resource pool. Money and time are not considered resources and are, therefore, not listed in the resource pool. Instead, Microsoft Project is used to track these elements of the project.

Note Resources should be listed in the resource pool in noun format. Examples include Design Engineer, Warehouse Worker, or Electrician.

Every activity should be considered as if only one resource is assigned to do the work. Otherwise, the duration of the task needs to be reconsidered with the addition of each new resource assigned to the task.

You should assign resources if you want to

- Track the amount of work performed by people assigned to the project
- Track the equipment used to work on tasks within the project

- Monitor the work levels of resources and time in which they work
- Ensure that the resources with the proper skill sets are available when necessary
- Establish and keep track of resource cost estimates
- Develop a more accurate estimate of the project completion date
- Indicate who is accountable or responsible for each task

NEXT STEPS

As you continue to build your project within Microsoft Project, remember to keep the basics of project management in mind. It will expedite the planning process and help to alleviate many of the problems often encountered while planning.

Project management—following the completion of a schedule and the baselining of the plan—is, in fact, risk management. A project manager will have to work diligently to ensure that a well-defined project will be completed without compromises to scope, schedule, costs, and quality. Careful risk assessment, quantification, response, and control are the keys to successful project plan completion, on time and under budget.

MICROSOFT PROJECT 2000 SHORTCUT KEYS

Most shortcut keys emulate menu commands or other actions in Project. They are listed in Table B.1 by the function they perform. In some cases the shortcut key executes a shortened version of the menu command or a special function that is related to the menu command.

TABLE B.1 SHORTCUT KEYS FOR MICROSOFT PROJECT 2000

Activity/Function	Shortcut Key
Working with Menus	
Activate/deactivate the menu and toolbars	Alt or F10
Change the active toolbar	Ctrl+Tab, Ctrl+Shift+Tab
Activate the application control menu	Alt+- (hyphen)
Activate the Windows control menu	Alt+spacebar
Using Help	
Activate the Office Assistant	F1
Activate context-sensitive Help pointer	Shift+F1
Using File Operations	
Open a file	Ctrl+O
New document	Ctrl+N or F11
Save	Ctrl+S
Save As	F12 or Alt+F2
Print	Ctrl+P
Close document	Ctrl+F4
Exit Microsoft Project	Alt+F4
Updating Calculations	
Turn Auto Calculate on/off	Ctrl+F9
Calculate all open projects	F9
Calculate active project	Shift+F9
Update links to external sources (DDE)	Alt+F9
Searching	
Find command (Edit menu)	Ctrl+F or Shift+F5
Repeat Find	Shift+F4
Replace (Edit menu)	Ctrl+H
Go To command (Edit menu)	Ctrl+G or F5
Go to next resource overallocation	Alt+F5

TABLE B.1 CONTINUED

Activity/Function	Shortcut Key
Selecting Cells in Either Tables or Timephased Data	
Move the selection to the last row	Ctrl+↓
Move the selection to the first row	Ctrl+↑
Extend the selection to the last row	Ctrl+Shift+↓
Extend the selection down one row	Shift+↓
Extend the selection to the first row	Ctrl+Shift+↑
Extend the selection up one row	Shift+↑
Extend the selection left	Shift+←
Extend the selection right	Shift+→
Extend the selection down one page	Shift+Page Down
Extend the selection up one page	Shift+Page Up
Move the selection right one page	Ctrl+Page Down
Move the selection left one page	Ctrl+Page Up
Move within a selection down one cell	Enter
Move within a selection up one cell	Shift+Enter
Move within a selection right one cell	Tab
Move within a selection left one cell	Shift+Tab
Go to the first cell in the next block of nonadjacent selected cells	Ctrl+Tab
Go to the first cell in the previous block of nonadjacent selected cells	Ctrl+Shift+Tab
Extend the selection to include the entire column	Ctrl+spacebar
Extend the selection to include the entire row	Shift+spacebar
Extend the selection to all rows and columns	Ctrl+Shift+spacebar
Reduce the selection to a single cell	Shift+Backspace
Turn on/off the Extend Selection mode	F8
Turn on/off the Add To Selection mode	Shift+F8
Selecting Cells in Tables	
Move the selection to the first column in a row	Ctrl+←
Move the selection to the last column in a row	Ctrl+→
Select the first cell in a row	Home
Move the selection to the first row, first column	Ctrl+Home
Extend the selection to the first cell in a row	Shift+Home
Extend the selection to the first cell of the first row	Ctrl+Shift+Home
Select the last cell in a row	End

PART

IX

APP

B

TABLE B.1 CONTINUED

Activity/Function	Shortcut Key
Move the selection to the last row, last column	Ctrl+End
Extend the selection to the last cell in a row	Shift+End
Extend the selection to the last cell of the last row	Ctrl+Shift+End

Selecting Cells in Timephased Data

Move the selection to the start of the calendar	Ctrl+←
Move the selection to the end of the calendar	Ctrl+→
Move to a row's cell at the start of a project	Home
Extend the selection to the start of a project	Shift+Home
Move to a row's cell at the end of a project	End
Extend the selection to end of project	Shift+End

Editing

Insert task or resource	Insert or Ctrl++ (on number pad)
Delete task, resource, or assignment	Delete or Ctrl+- (on number pad)
Clear or reset contents of the selection	Ctrl+Delete
Activate the entry bar to edit a field value	F2
Turn on/off the Overtype mode when the entry bar is active	Insert
Delete previous word in the Edit bar	Ctrl+Backspace
Delete next word in the Edit bar	Ctrl+Delete
Display list in field with list control arrow	Alt+↓
Copy selection	Ctrl+C or Ctrl+Insert
Cut selection	Ctrl+X or Shift+Delete
Paste	Ctrl+V or Shift+Insert
Undo editing	Ctrl+Z
Insert Hyperlink	Ctrl+K
Fill Down	Ctrl+D
Fill Right	Ctrl+R
Spelling command (Tools menu)	F7

TABLE B.1 CONTINUED

Activity/Function	Shortcut Key
Working with Outlines	
Show all tasks	Alt+Shift+*
Show subtasks for selection	Alt+Shift++
Hide subtasks	Alt+Shift+-
Indent task in outline	Alt+Shift+→
Outdent task in outline	Alt+Shift+←
Linking Tasks	
Link Tasks command (Edit menu)	Ctrl+F2
Unlink Tasks command (Edit menu)	Ctrl+Shift+F2
Formatting Text	
Font (Bold)	Ctrl+B
Font (Italic)	Ctrl+I
Font (Underlined)	Ctrl+U
Working with Timescales	
Gantt Chart: scroll one minor time unit left	Alt+←
Gantt Chart: scroll one minor time unit right	Alt+→
Gantt Chart: go to the start of the project	Alt+Home
Gantt Chart: go to the end of the project	Alt+End
Gantt Chart: scroll one screen left	Alt+Page Up
Gantt Chart: scroll one screen right	Alt+Page Down
Scroll to the selected task in a timescale	Ctrl+Shift+F5
Zoom in	Ctrl+/
Zoom out	Ctrl+*
Managing Views	
Activate the next pane in a combination view	F6
Activate the split bar	Shift+F6
Select the first details area at the bottom of a form	Alt+1
Select the second details area at the bottom of a form	Alt+2

TABLE B.1 CONTINUED

Activity/Function	Shortcut Key
Sorting, Grouping, and Filtering	
Remove filter (apply All Tasks/All Resources filter)	F3
Reapply current filter	Ctrl+F3
Remove sort or grouping (sort by ID number)	Shift+F3
Reapply current sort order or grouping	Ctrl+Shift+F3
Displaying Special Tools	
Display the Information dialog box (Task, Resource, Assignment)	Shift+F2
Display the Column Definition dialog box	Alt+F3
Display the Assign Resources dialog box	Alt+F10
Display the macros dialog box	Alt+F8
Display the Visual Basic Editor	Alt+F11
Working with Windows	
Activate the next document window	Ctrl+F6
Activate the previous document window	Ctrl+Shift+F6
New window (Window menu)	Alt+Shift+F1 or Shift+F11
Maximize the document window	Ctrl+F10
Restore the document window	Ctrl+F5
Move the document window	Ctrl+F7
Size the document window	Ctrl+F8
Activate the previous application window	Alt+Shift+Esc
Move the previous application window to the top	Alt+Shift+Tab
Move the next application window to the top	Alt+Tab
Activate the next application window	Alt+Esc

COMPANION PRODUCTS FOR MICROSOFT PROJECT 2000

In this appendix

As Microsoft Project has become the leading project management software product in the world, the number of add-on and companion products that extend or enhance Microsoft Project has grown rapidly. Many of the vendors who offer these products are Solution Provider partners with Microsoft.

To introduce you to the wealth of additional functionality that these products offer to Microsoft Project users, a number of the vendors were contacted and offered the opportunity to describe their products and services in this appendix. The text was provided by the vendors. No warranty, guarantee, or product endorsement is intended by the authors or by Que in including these products. However, we feel confident that you will find merit in each of these products for some, if not all, of your project management needs.

PRODUCT DESCRIPTIONS AND VENDOR INFORMATION

The products included in this appendix are all designed to be used with Microsoft Project. In most cases, these products rely on Project to do all the scheduling calculations. Some of the companion products provide a front end that guides you in the planning process and helps you reap special advantages from using Microsoft Project. Other products add special features to the Microsoft Project menu and toolbars, such as specialized views and reports, or aids to learning and using Project.

Some vendors offer multiple products. The listing is organized alphabetically by vendor, with all products for the vendor listed together.

ATLAS BUSINESS SOLUTIONS

Vendor:	Atlas Business Solutions, Inc.
Address:	3330 Fiechtner Drive SW Fargo, ND 58106-9013
Phone:	800-874-8801 or 701-235-5226
Fax:	701-280-0842
Web:	www.abs-usa.com

Visual Staff Scheduler PRO 4.0—VSS PRO is the number-one employee-scheduling software solution. Used by more than 20,000 businesses worldwide, no other tool can help you get your work schedules done faster, better, or easier! The VSS PRO software contained on the companion CD to this book is a full 30-day version (single-user).

CRITICAL TOOLS

Vendor:	Critical Tools, Inc.
Address:	8004 Bottlebrush Drive Austin, TX 78750
Phone:	512-342-2232
Fax:	512-342-2234
Web:	www.criticaltools.com

PERT Chart EXPERT 1.5—PERT Chart EXPERT is Microsoft Project add-on software that allows you to create presentation-quality PERT charts (also known as Network Diagrams or Precedence diagrams) directly from your Microsoft Project plans. PERT Chart EXPERT contains extensive PERT charting capabilities unlike those found in Microsoft Project's PERT chart. Create Timescaled PERT charts; view PERT charts grouped by Resource, Summary Level, or other custom grouping fields; use the Microsoft Project filters to create filtered PERT charts; automatically hide summary tasks in a PERT chart; and more. PERT Chart EXPERT integrates seamlessly with Microsoft Project (Project 4.x, Project 98, and Project 2000). The demo version of PERT Chart EXPERT on this CD is only compatible with Project 2000. Visit the Critical Tools Web site at www. criticaltools.com for more information on the PERT Chart EXPERT software and to download any updated demos that might be available since the release of this publication.

WBS Chart for Project 3.2—WBS Chart for Project is Microsoft Project add-on software that allows you to plan and display your projects using a tree-style diagram known as a Work Breakdown Structure (WBS) chart. WBS charts display the structure of a project showing how the project is broken down into summary and detail levels. Plan new projects with WBS Chart for Project using an intuitive top-down approach, or display existing Microsoft Project plans in an easy-to-understand diagram.

WBS Chart for Project integrates seamlessly with Microsoft Project (Project 4.x, Project 98, and Project 2000). (There is a demo version of WBS Chart for Project on the CD accompanying this book. It is only compatible with Project 2000.) Visit the Web site at www.criticaltools.com for more information on the WBS Chart for Project software and to download any updated demos that might be available since the release of this publication.

PART

IX

APP

C

KIDASA SOFTWARE

Vendor:	KIDASA Software, Inc.
Address:	1114 Lost Creek Blvd., Suite 300 Austin, TX 78746
Phone:	512-328-0167
Fax:	512-328-0247
Web:	www.kidasa.com

Milestones, Etc. 5.01—Milestones, Etc. is an easy-to-use project management and scheduling program that enables you to quickly create Gantt, Milestone, and Timeline charts. Importing and exporting to Microsoft Project is supported.

EXPERIENCE IN SOFTWARE

Vendor:	Experience in Software
Address:	2000 Hearst Avenue, Suite 202 Berkeley, CA 94709-2176

Phone: 510-644-0694

Fax: 510-644-3823

Web: www.experienceware.com

Project KickStart 2.05—Project KickStart is the fast, easy way to plan and organize your projects. The software's seven step-icons quickly guide you through the process of building a strategic plan. You'll consider project goals, obstacles, resources, and other big-picture issues. Use the Project KickStart hot-link icon to transfer your plan into Microsoft Project. Project data will appear in MS Project's Task column ready for scheduling.

PROJECT LEARNING LTD.

Vendor: Project Learning Ltd.

Address: 73A Park Rise, Campbells Bay
                          Auckland, 1003
                          New Zealand

Phone: +64 9 4787629

Fax: +64 21 695109

Web: www.projectlearning.com

Project Program Manager—A Project for Windows companion product that works seamlessly with native Project files to report on resource needs across multiple projects. It will report on resource work by week or month, by name, by skill, by team, by department, and more. It also includes a time sheet system that records times against current project tasks and then seamlessly updates the tasks in their project files. For any organization working with multiple projects, this project management information system will save much time and effort.

PROJECT ASSISTANTS

Vendor: Project Assistants, Inc.

Address: 2503 Silverside Road, Suite 200
                          Wilmington, DE 19803-0323

Phone: 302-529-5700

Fax: 302-529-703

Web: www.projectassistants.com

Project Commander 2000 3.0—Project Commander combines Microsoft Project's powerful project management engine with a comprehensive and easy-to-use set of functions that make planning, tracking, analyzing, and reporting a snap. Here are a few of the many powerful features:

- Use Project Commander Central to perform your most important Project Management functions from a single, intuitive interface. There's no need to worry about where to double-click, secondary click, split the screen, or apply views, tables, and filters to get to your most critical project data.

- Use the powerful Task Checklist feature to create a to-do list for the tasks in your project. Eliminate all those extra tasks that make managing your project a project in itself!

- Capture and report on important issues with the easy-to-use Issue Log feature, seamlessly integrated within the familiar Microsoft Project desktop.

With Project Commander's enhanced Web reporting capabilities, you'll be sharing your most important data on the Internet in no time.

ProjectSynchronizer 2000 1.0—ProjectSynchronizer allows you to easily distribute all your organization's standard views, tables, filters, reports, toolbars, modules, and settings to all your Project users directly from your network, intranet, or even the Internet. Just add your organization's standard environment to an .mpp file, and ProjectSynchronizer will ensure that each Project user receives all your latest updates each time they start up Project.

TeamWork 2000 2.0—Project-centric process management. TeamWork 2000 provides all the benefits of process management while working directly within Microsoft Project. You start by building a customized work plan template in Microsoft Project. Incorporate and automate your organization's methodologies as you easily link tasks to all the intellectual assets required to perform the task—detailed methodology steps, Microsoft Word or other document templates, multimedia files such as PowerPoint presentations, hot links to Internet URLs, Excel spreadsheets, Access databases, faxes, and email communications. The only limit is your imagination.

PROJECTEXCHANGE

Vendor:	ProjectExchange
Address:	549 Columbian Street Weymouth, MA 02190
Phone:	781-340-4400
Fax:	781-340-4401
Web:	www.projectexchange.com

ProjectExchange Family—The ProjectExchange family of products consists of ProjectExplorer, WebTime, and ResourceXchange. They provide project management, time tracking, and resource planning capabilities over the World Wide Web, reducing your organization's cost of ownership and providing a more efficient enterprise-wide work management solution. ProjectExchange helps to improve team utilization, increase knowledge sharing, and improve multi-project reporting capabilities.

PART

IX

APP

C

UTILITY PRODUCT DESCRIPTIONS AND VENDOR INFORMATION

The products in this section are some of the utility products or programs that you might find quite useful in your Project use.

ADOBE SYSTEMS

Vendor:	Adobe Systems
Address:	345 Park Avenue San Jose, CA 95110-2704
Phone:	408-536-6000
Fax:	408-537-6000
Web:	www.adobe.com

Acrobat Reader 4.0—The free Adobe Acrobat Reader allows you to view, navigate, and print PDF files across all major computing platforms. Acrobat Reader is the free viewing companion to Adobe Acrobat and to Acrobat Capture software.

IPSWITCH

Vendor:	IPSwitch, Inc.
Address:	81 Hartwell Ave. Lexington, MA 02421
Phone:	781-676-5700
Fax:	781-674-2828
Web:	www.ispwitch.com

WS_FTP Pro 6.01—Quickly and easily upload and manage your Web site, download graphics and games, and transfer files with the world's most popular FTP client for Windows.

WINZIP COMPUTING

Vendor:	WinZip Computing, Inc.
Address:	PO Box 540 Mansfield, CT 06268
Fax:	860-429-3542
Web:	www.winzip.com

WinZip 7.0—WinZip brings the convenience of Windows to the use of Zip files and other archive and compression formats. The optional wizard interface makes unzipping easier than ever. WinZip features built-in support for popular Internet file formats, including TAR, gzip, Unix compress, UUencode, BinHex, and MIME. ARJ, LZH, and ARC files are supported via external programs. WinZip interfaces to most virus scanners.

GLOSSARY

Accrual method   Determines when the cost for a resource is recognized as incurred. By default, costs are prorated over the duration of the task, but you can also have them recognized at the start or finish of a task.

Actual   Tasks or assignments in the project that have actually happened, in whole or in part, and have been recorded as actual dates, duration, work, and/or cost. Contrasts with planned (scheduled or predicted) activities. Includes recorded data for tasks, resources, and assignments.

Actual cost   The cost that has actually been incurred for a task, resource, or assignment.

Actual cost of work performed (ACWP)   Shows actual costs incurred for work by a resource up to the project status date (or to today's date if no status date is defined).

Actual duration   The amount of time that work on a task has actually been in progress. Project uses this value to calculate the remaining duration using the formula Remaining Duration = Duration – Actual Duration.

Actual work   The amount of time that work has actually been performed on a task. Project uses this value to calculate the remaining work using the formula Remaining Work = Work – Actual Work.

Allocation   The percentage of a resource's available work for a time period that is assigned to a single task; or the sum of all such percentages for the time period.

ASCII   American Standard Code for Information Interchange that is used for exchanging text data among different computer programs and platforms.

Assignment   A specific resource scheduled to work on a specific task.

Assignment delay   An amount of time between the start of the task and the start of one or more assignments to the task that need to start later than other assignments for functional (nonleveling) reasons.

Assignment units   The amount of a resource that is assigned to a task. For work resources, whether units are shown in percentage or decimal format, the units' number represents a multiple of the hours on the resource calendar that are to be devoted to an assignment. For material resources, the assignment units are always in decimal format and show either a fixed amount of the resource that will be consumed by the task or a variable rate of consumption per unit of duration time.

Assignment view   A view that shows the resources assigned to each task as well as the total and time-phased work and cost information for each assignment. The two assignment views are the Task Usage and Resource Usage views.

Authentication   The process of identifying a Microsoft Project Central user and confirming that the user has access privileges.

AutoFilter   Provides a drop-down menu of all entries found in a column. Click an entry on the menu and the display will be filtered to show only rows that contain that value in the filtered column. Turn AutoFilter on and off with the AutoFilter tool on the Formatting toolbar.

Base calendar   A calendar used as the primary calendar for the entire project, as the base for multiple resources that have the same working and nonworking time, or as a task calendar.

Baseline   A copy of the scheduled dates, work, and cost data that is used for comparison purposes when tracking project progress. Usually the baseline is created by copying the schedule just before work begins on the project.

Baseline cost   The cost of assignments and tasks as shown in the baseline plan. The baseline cost is a snapshot of the cost at the time when the baseline plan was saved. Tracking and comparing baseline costs against actual costs can help you track cost performance and calculate earned value information.

Break mode   The temporary suspension of a running program or macro while in the VBA development environment. In break mode, you can examine, debug, reset, step, or continue to run the program or macro.

Budget   The estimated cost as shown in the baseline cost.

Budget at completion (BAC)   The cost amount in the baseline.

Budgeted cost of work performed (BCWP)   How much of the budgeted amount should have been spent by a specific date in the project, theoretically, calculated by multi-plying the budgeted (baseline) costs for the coverage period by the percentage of the planned work that actually took place during the period.

Budgeted cost of work scheduled (BCWS)   An earned value field that shows how much of the cumulative budgeted or baseline cost for a task, assignment, or resource should have been incurred up to the status date or today's date.

Calculated field   A field that you cannot enter data into directly and in which the value is determined by Microsoft Project, based on information in other fields. For example, the task field Critical is given the value 'Yes' if the task is a critical task.

Calculated filter   A filter that compares values in two fields for a task or resource as a basis for selecting the task or resource.

Calculated or entered field   A field which will be calculated by Project (see *Calculated field*) unless you enter a value yourself.

Code mask   A format you can define for a WBS code or a custom outline code. A mask defines the sequence and number of letters or numbers required for each outline level as well as the symbols separating the levels.

Collapsed outline   A view of the task outline where the subtasks for one or more of the summary tasks are hidden from view. Collapsing detail rows lets you focus on the major phases. You can also collapse or hide the indented listing of assignments under tasks or resources in the Task Usage and Resource Usage views. See also *Expanded outline*.

Combination view   A view that is composed of two component views in separate panes. The bottom-pane view always shows details of the selection in the top-pane view.

Consolidated project   A project file (also called a master project) that has one or more other projects (see subprojects) inserted into it as summary tasks. The subprojects can retain links to their source projects, and changes to the inserted projects in the consolidated file can be passed on to the source file.

Constraint   A limitation set on the scheduling of the start or finish of a task. Normally, in fixed start-date projects, all tasks are scheduled to start and finish as soon as possible; in fixed finish-date projects they're scheduled as late as possible. Constraints can be placed on the start or on the finish of a task. They can be expressed as Must Start On, Must Finish On, Start No Earlier Than, Finish No Earlier Than, Start No Later Than, or Finish No Later Than.

Container   The document in which an OLE object that was created in another program or document resides.

Contour   The name for variable patterns of distribution of assigned work over time. By default, Project schedules resource units (and work) at the same rate each time period until the assignment is completed. By applying a contour, you can have Project schedule more units at different times during the assignment to better reflect actual work patterns. The term is derived from the shape that a bar chart would have if you charted the work per period against a timescale. Predefined contour options include flat, back-loaded, front-loaded, late-peak, early-peak, double-peak, bell, and turtle.

Cost   The total scheduled cost for a task, resource, resource assignment, or project. Includes fixed cost and resource cost.

Cost performance index (CPI)   The ratio of budgeted, or baseline, costs of work performed to actual costs of work performed (calculated using the earned value fields BCWP and ACWP). Some analysts use the cumulative CPI (which is the sum of the BCWP for all tasks divided by the sum of the ACWP for all tasks) to predict whether a project will go over budget and by how much.

Cost Rate table   A table that you can define for a resource containing the resource's standard cost rates, overtime rates, and per-use rates, with the dates within which each set of those rates is effective. You can define up to five different tables for each resource to represent different types of tasks the resource might be assigned to and for which you want to charge different cost levels.

Cost variance (CV)   An earned value field that subtracts the actual cost of work performed (ACWP) from the budgeted cost of work performed (BCWP) on a task. If positive, the actual cost is currently under the budgeted (or baseline) amount; if negative, the cost is currently over budget.

Crash   To compress a project's overall duration. Crashing a project might require assigning additional resources to tasks or redefining the scope of the project.

Critical path   A sequence of tasks, each of which must finish on schedule for the project to finish on time. The critical path is the longest sequence of tasks in the project.

Critical path method (CPM)   A method of calculating the ending date and total duration of a project based on individual task durations and their dependencies.

Critical task   A task which, if its finish date were delayed, would delay the finish of the project. The linked critical tasks make up the critical path.

Cross-Project links   Dependency relationships or links between tasks that are in different projects. In a project with links to a task in another project, the external task is represented by a placeholder copy or surrogate that can be formatted and linked but not edited. See also *External task*.

CSV file format   The comma-separated values file format is an ASCII text format commonly used for exchanging data between different computer programs and platforms. Each field of a task or resource record is separated by a list-separator character, usually a comma or semicolon. Each task or resource record ends with a carriage return and linefeed.

Cumulative cost performance index (CPI)   In earned value analysis, the sum of all the budgeted costs of work performed (BCWP) for all tasks divided by the sum of all the actual costs of work performed (ACWP) for all tasks. The Cumulative CPI is used by some analysts to predict whether a project will go over budget and by how much. If the ratio is greater than one, the project is under budget; if less than one, it is over budget.

Currency Rate field   A field type where the content is a rate of pay (for example, $10 per hour). Examples include the Standard Rate and Overtime Rate fields.

Current date line   A (usually) dotted vertical line in the chart portion of a Gantt Chart or Resource Graph that indicates the current date.

Deliverable   A tangible and measurable result, outcome, or item that must be produced to complete a project or part of a project. The project team and project stakeholders should agree on the deliverables before the project begins.

Dependency relationship   General term that describes the relationship between a dependent task and its predecessor. See also *Predecessor*, *Successor*, and *Lead time*.

Dependent task   A task whose scheduled start or finish date must be set to coincide with or be linked to the scheduled start or finish date of some other task (its predecessor).

Divider bar   The vertical bar that separates different panes in a view.

Driving resource   One resource among multiple resources that are assigned to a task whose work takes the longest duration to complete. The duration for the task is driven by the time needed by this resource to complete its work.

Duration field   A field type that contains time amounts. Examples include the Work, Duration, and Delay fields. A duration field value includes a number and the unit of time the number represents (such as minute, hour, day, week, or month).

Dynamic data exchange (DDE)   A protocol for inserting linked data into a container document that actually resides in another document. When the information changes in the source document, it can be updated in the container automatically.

Early finish date   The earliest date that a task could finish, considering the start of the project, the early finish dates of tasks it's linked to, constraints, and any leveling delay.

Earned value   A method of analysis for measuring project performance indicating how much of the budget should have been spent, considering the proportion of the work that has been done so far. The term is also applied to the Budgeted Cost of Work Performed (BCWP).

Effort-driven task   A task whose total work (effort) is reapportioned among all resources when the list of resources assigned to the task is increased or decreased, thus decreasing or increasing the task duration while keeping the total work constant. Tasks are effort driven by default.

Elapsed duration   The actual clock time (not the working calendar time) that elapses between the start and finish of a task. This time is based on a 24-hour day and a 7-day week.

Embedded object   Data in a container document (the client document) that is created and formatted by another application. Once embedded, the object resides only in the container file. When you double-click an embedded object, it opens in the application it was created in (the server program).

Embedding   Placing an OLE object in a container document. You can edit an embedded object from within the container document using the application with which it is associated. See also *Object linking and embedding*.

Estimate at completion (EAC)   The earned value field that shows the total scheduled cost (the Cost field value) for a task, resource, or assignment. This includes costs already incurred plus scheduled costs for the remaining duration.

Exception   Instance where a task or resource calendar differs from the calendar on which it is based. An example would be a resource's vacation time.

Expanded outline   An outline view in which all the subtasks or indented rows are displayed. See also *Collapsed outline*.

Expected duration   In the PERT Analysis for estimating duration, the expected duration is the most likely duration estimate. See also *Optimistic duration*, *Pessimistic duration*, and *Weighted duration*.

Export/Import map   See *Import/Export map*.

Exporting   Saving Project data to another file format such as Microsoft Excel or Access.

External dependency   A dependency link between a task in the active project and one in another project.

External predecessor   A predecessor for a task in the active project that is actually a task in another project file. The external task is represented in the active project by a ghost task.

External successor   A successor for a task in the active project that is actually a task in another project file. The external task is represented in the active project by a ghost task.

External task   A placeholder or surrogate copy of a task from another project file that is linked to one or more tasks in the active project file. You can format and link to external tasks, but you must open the project they reside in to edit them.

Fill handle   A small black square in the corner of the selection border of a cell in a table or sheet view. The pointer changes to a black cross when you point to the fill handle. Drag the fill handle to copy the contents of the selection to cells above or below the selection.

Filter   A criterion or set of criteria that is applied to all tasks or resources to differentiate those that meet the criteria from those that do not. A filter can operate in two ways: It can hide all tasks that fail to match the filter criteria or it can show all tasks but highlight those that match the criteria.

Fixed consumption rate   A fixed quantity of a material resource that is assigned to be used or consumed in an assignment. The rate is fixed with respect to task duration or assignment length. See also *Variable consumption rate*.

Fixed cost   Fixed costs are assigned directly to tasks and remain constant regardless of task duration. Fixed Cost is added to Resource Cost to yield (total) Cost.

Fixed date tasks   Tasks that have constrained dates or that already have a recorded Actual Start Date and cannot be rescheduled by Microsoft Project.

Fixed duration task   A task for which you can change the duration, but Project is prevented from recalculating the duration if you change the work or the assigned units or resources. See also *Fixed work task* and *Fixed units task*.

Fixed task   A term used in earlier versions of Microsoft Project for fixed duration tasks. A task whose duration will not be affected by increasing or decreasing the quantity of resources assigned to do work on the task. See also *Resource-driven task*.

Fixed units task   A type of task (the default type) for which you can change the assigned units, but Project will not recalculate units if you change the assigned work or the task duration. See also *Fixed work task* and *Fixed duration task*.

Fixed work task   A task type for which you can change the assigned work, but Project will not recalculate the work when you change the assigned units or the task duration. See also *Fixed duration task* and *Fixed units task*.

Flexible constraint   A constraint that will not create a conflict between the constraint and expansion of duration for the task's predecessors (in a fixed start-date project) or successors (in a fixed finish-date project).

Form   A view of project data that gives you detailed information about only one task or resource at a time. The data is typically arranged on multiple rows or in groupings to help clarify the field relationships.

Free slack   In projects scheduled from a fixed start date, the amount of time a task can be delayed without delaying its successor tasks. For a task without successors, free slack is the amount of time the task can be delayed without delaying the finish date of the project. Project does not calculate free slack in projects scheduled from a fixed finish date.

Gantt bar   The horizontal graphical bar on the chart portion of the Gantt Chart view that connects the start and finish of a task.

Ghost task   The surrogate task information for an external task that is a predecessor or successor to a task in the active project. The default display is a dimmed task bar and dimmed text in the Gantt Chart view.

Global template   The GLOBAL.MPT file that is the template for new project files and contains all the views, tables, filters, import/export maps, macro modules, and so forth that a new file should contain.

Graphics area   Areas in Project views that can display objects from another document or program. Objects can be pictures, text, or media (such as sound or video), and they can be embedded or linked. The graphics areas include the chart portion of a Gantt Chart view; the task, resource, and assignment notes, headers, footers, and legends in views; headers and footers in reports; and the Objects box in a task form or resource form. See *Object linking and embedding* and *Object*.

Graphics Interchange Format (GIF) file   A compressed file format for graphics that Web browsers can display and that is used for transmitting images across the Internet.

Group   To sort and combine tasks or resources based on specific criteria. For example, you might group tasks by $5,000 cost ranges, or by stage of progress. Grouping is not to be confused with the resource field named Group, although resource grouping can use the values in the Group field.

Group resource   A single resource name that refers to a team or group of resource units, such as a group of trucks, or a group of painters. Also called a resource set in Microsoft Project.

Highlighting filter   Filters normally hide all but the task or resource records that match the filter criteria. Applying the filter as a highlighting filter causes Project to highlight the selected tasks or resources while still displaying all records.

HTML   An acronym for Hypertext Markup Language, the formatting convention for presenting text and graphics on the World Wide Web. HTML format uses tags that are embedded in the text to specify formatting of the text.

Hyperlink   A text reference or link to another file or a location within a file that allows you to open the other file (and go to the specified location if provided) by merely clicking the hyperlink. Hyperlinks are displayed by default in blue, underlined text, with the color changing after the hyperlink is used the first time.

Hyperlink address   The address of the hyperlink's destination file.

Hyperlink representation   The descriptive text (initially in blue, underlined font) that you click to activate a hyperlink.

Hyperlink Subaddress   The optional location within the file named in a hyperlink.

Import/Export map   A table showing what data you want to exchange with another application and which Project fields should be paired with the specific data locations in the other application.

Importing   Opening a file from another format to copy data into Microsoft Project. When you import data, you choose or create an import/export map that defines the project fields into which the imported data should be copied.

Indicators   Icons that are displayed in the Indicators field in a table and which represent at a glance the status of various information fields for a task or resource, whether those fields are displayed in the table or not.

Indicators field   A read-only field that displays icons to convey at a glance the status of various fields for an assignment, resource, or task. For example, a notepad icon indicates that there is text in the Notes field for that row.

Inflexible constraint   A constraint that might create a conflict between the constraint and the expansion of duration for the task's predecessors (in a fixed start-date project) or successors (in a fixed finish-date project).

Inserted project   Subprojects are inserted into a master (consolidated) project file, and are thus also called inserted projects. The inserted project appears as a summary task in the master project.

Integer List field   A type of field whose content is a list of integers separated by the list separator character (typically a comma). The Predecessors and Successors fields are examples.

Interactive filter   A filter that first prompts the user for one or more values that are then used in selecting the tasks or resources to display in a view.

Interim plan   A set of baseline start and finish dates that you can save at interim points in the life of planning or tracking your project. You can compare an interim plan with the baseline plan or current plan to monitor project progress or slippage.

Late finish date   The latest date that a task can finish considering the finish of the project, the late finish date of successor tasks, and any leveling delay.

Lead time   An amount of time by which a dependent task can be scheduled to overlap or anticipate the scheduled start or finish of its predecessor task.

Leveling   The process of delaying tasks to level out the demands on resources so that the resources are no longer overallocated.

Leveling delay   An amount of time that an assignment or task is to be delayed past the originally scheduled start date to free resources for other assignments. The Level Now command inserts values in the Leveling Delay field.

Link line   The line that appears between two tasks on the Gantt Chart or Network Diagram to indicate a dependency relationship between tasks.

Link type   The type of dependency relationship between two tasks. The four dependency types are Finish-to-start (FS), Finish-to-finish (FF), Start-to-start (SS), Start-to-finish (SF).

Linked project   A project that contains tasks with dependency ties to tasks in other project files. A link to a task in another project is represented by displaying a ghost task to represent the external task.

Linked tasks   Tasks that have a dependency relationship.

Linking   1. Defining a dependency relationship between tasks. 2. Linking an OLE object to its source so that it can be updated. See also *Object linking and embedding*.

List separator character   The character that is used to separate items on a list when they are typed on the same line. Defined in the Control Panel's Regional Settings applet in Windows.

Macro   An automated list of instructions that you create to replicate an operation or command. Macros are maintained with Visual Basic.

MAPI   Messaging Application Programming Interface is the Microsoft program that coordinates sending user messages from one application to another.

Master project   A project that contains one or more summary tasks that are links to other projects (subprojects) and whose duration, work, and costs are a summary of the entire duration, work, and cost of the subprojects they represent.

Material resource   A resource, such as supplies or parts, that is consumed during the work on a task. See also *Work resource*.

Maximum units   A percentage or decimal number that represents how many hours of work can be scheduled for a resource for each hour it has available on the calendar during the current date (as entered in the Resource Availability table on the Resource Information dialog box). The maximum units can be different for different time periods. See also *Unit availability*.

Message rule   A set of criteria for updating a project file with the information in Microsoft Project Central workgroup messages.

Microsoft Project Central   A companion product that is distributed with Project 2000 to enable workgroup members and stakeholders to collaborate in planning and tracking the project using the Internet or an intranet.

Microsoft Project database format (.MPD)   A file format with the extension .mpd that can store all information for multiple projects. This format is useful for archiving all project information in a central location to facilitate cross-project analysis and reporting, as well as for security purposes. The Microsoft Project database format replaces the old MPX file format as the standard interchange format for project data. The Microsoft Project 2000 database format is the same as the Microsoft Access 2000 format, and the data can be read or modified by any application that can read Access 2000 files.

Microsoft Project Workspace file format   A file you can save that merely remembers all the open files on your workspace at the moment.

Microsoft Visual Basic for Applications (VBA)   See *Visual Basic for Applications*.

Microsoft Windows user account   All the information that defines a user to Microsoft Project Central, including the username and any required password, membership in groups, and the rights and permissions associated with the user.

Module   The location in Project where VBA macros are stored. Modules in the Global.mpt file are available to any project and can be used to store universal macros and procedures.

MPD file format   See *Microsoft Project database format*.

MPX file format   The Microsoft Project Exchange (MPX) file format is a record-based ASCII text format that was formerly used to exchange project data between different versions of Microsoft Project and between Project and other project management applications.

Multiple critical paths   Microsoft Project displays, by default, only one critical path in a schedule. You can, however, change this behavior so that Microsoft Project displays separate critical paths for all nonconvergent parallel sequences of activities.

Noncritical task   A task whose finish can be delayed up to a point without delaying the project, as defined by the existence of slack time. See also *Total slack*.

Nonworking time   Hours or days in a calendar when Microsoft Project should not schedule work. Nonworking time can include lunch breaks, weekends, vacations, sick leave, and holidays, for example.

Note   Documentation that you can attach to a task, resource, or assignment. You can type formatted text into the Note field, and you can also insert hyperlinks to external documents or objects derived from other applications.

Null field   In the Task Usage and Resource Usage views, the rows contain both task and assignment records or resource and assignment records. The columns display fields that do not always have meaning for both types of records in the rows. For example, in the Resource Usage view the column for Actual Finish shows the finish date of an assignment but must display NA on the resource rows because there is no Actual Finish field in the resource table. In cases like these the field has a null value on some rows and will display an uneditable zero, NA, or blank.

Object   In OLE, information such as a chart or text that is generated and formatted by one application but displayed in documents managed by another application.

Object linking and embedding (OLE)   A mechanism that allows information such as a chart or text (the object) that is in the file format of one application to be displayed in a document (the container) that is formatted by a different application. Linking allows the object that is stored in a container document to be updated whenever the source information is changed in the source document. Embedding allows the object's information to be stored entirely within the container and to be edited from within the container using the program in which the information was created.

Objective The quantifiable criteria that must be met for the project to be considered successful. Objectives must include, at least, cost, schedule, and quality measures. Unquantified objectives (for example, customer satisfaction) increase the risk that the project won't be considered to have met them.

Objects box An area that you can display on task or resource forms to insert and display linked or embedded objects.

ODBC Open Database Connectivity is an industry-wide interface, based on the SQL Access Group specifications that Microsoft announced in December 1991. The ODBC driver defines access to different database sources so that a user can work with data from different sources.

OLE See *Object linking and embedding*.

OLE server The application or document that creates and formats an OLE object that is used in another (container) program or document.

Operator A device used in filters to link multiple criteria. If multiple criteria must all be met to satisfy the filter, the AND operator is used. If meeting any one of the multiple criteria will satisfy the filter, the OR operator is used.

Optimistic duration In the PERT Analysis for estimating duration, the optimistic duration is the estimate of the shortest likely duration. See also *Expected duration*, *Pessimistic duration*, and *Weighted duration*.

Organizer A dialog box that allows you to rename, delete, and copy views, tables, filters, groups, reports, calendars, forms, toolbars, Import/Export maps, and Visual Basic for Applications modules between projects and GLOBAL.MPT.

Outdenting Moving a task to the left in the Task Name field, thus promoting it to a higher outline level.

Outline A structured presentation in Microsoft Project, similar in function to the traditional Work Breakdown Structure that allows tasks or activities to be grouped under summary tasks to show functional relationships. Detailed, subordinate subtasks are indented under their summary tasks to produce a traditional outline appearance. See also *Work Breakdown Structure*.

Outline code Custom codes you define for tasks or resources that allow you to sort them in different ways to show different hierarchies than the WBS codes or outline numbers. You can create up to 10 sets of custom outline codes in your project to represent various organizational hierarchies such as accounting cost codes for tasks and job codes for resources.

Outline level The number of levels a task is indented from the top level of the outline. You can indent to more than 65,000 levels in Microsoft Project. Top-level tasks are those at the first outline level.

Outline number   Numbers in the legal numbering format that indicate the exact position of a task in the outline. For example, a task with an outline number of 2.3 indicates that it's the third subtask under the second top-level summary task. Project places these outline numbers in the WBS field as the default WBS codes.

Overallocation   The situation where a resource is assigned more work during a time period than the resource is capable of delivering.

Overtime   The amount of work on an assignment scheduled outside the assigned resource's regular working hours, and charged at the resource's overtime rate, usually for the purpose of shortening the duration of the task.

Path   A sequence of all folder names from the root of the storage medium to a file's current folder, separated by backslash characters (\) in Microsoft Windows.

Peak units   The highest level of units that are assigned for a resource during a given period of time.

Per-use cost   A fee you can define for the use of a resource that is independent of the duration of the task and that is added to the hourly costs (both standard and overtime). For work resources, the added cost is the defined per-use cost amount multiplied by the units of the resource that are assigned to the task. For material resources, the added cost is the defined per-use cost amount itself, regardless of the units assigned.

Percent complete   A measurement of the actual duration that has been completed on a task. It is calculated as the ratio of actual duration to scheduled duration. You can enter this value, or Project will calculate it for you if you enter actual duration.

Percent work complete   The percentage of total scheduled work on a task that has been completed. You can enter this value or Project will calculate it for you if you enter actual work.

PERT analysis   Program Evaluation and Review Technique analysis is a procedure for estimating the probable duration of a task based on the weighted average of an optimistic estimation, a pessimistic estimation, and the most likely estimation of duration.

PERT Chart   The name of the view in previous versions of Microsoft Project that was the forerunner of the Network Diagram in Project 2000.

Pessimistic duration   In the PERT Analysis for estimating duration, the pessimistic duration is the estimate of the longest likely duration. See also *Optimistic duration*, *Expected duration*, and *Weighted duration*.

Phase   A major group of activities or tasks in a project that are subsumed under a summary task to represent the whole group.

Pivot table   An interactive crosstab table in Microsoft Excel that quickly summarizes large amounts of data. You can interactively switch its rows and columns to see different summaries of the source data, filter the data by displaying different pages, or display the details for areas of interest.

Pixel   A point of light that makes up a computer image.

Places bar   The bar on the left side of dialog boxes, such as those for the Open and Save As commands, that contains shortcuts to the History, My Documents, Desktop, Favorites, and Web folders.

Plan   A schedule of start and finish dates and work and cost information. A baseline plan is the finalized plan prior to starting the project that you save and use to monitor project progress. The current plan is the current schedule. An interim plan is a set of dates you can save during the project to compare to the baseline plan, the current plan, and to other interim plans.

Predecessor   If the scheduled start or finish of task A is determined by the scheduled start or finish of task B, then B is the predecessor task for task A. Predecessor is a potentially confusing term because in common usage the word suggests chronological precedence, when the important point is that the scheduling of task A is dependent on the scheduled date for task B. See also *Dependency relationship* and *Successor*.

Progress bar   A bar in the Gantt Chart that overlays the task bar to show how much of the task has been completed.

Progress line   A vertical line displayed in the Gantt Chart view that is anchored on a progress line date that you specify and that draws attention to tasks that are behind or ahead of schedule as of that date. Tasks with bars that lie to the left of the progress line should have started and be complete up to the progress line date. If the task is behind schedule, the progress line branches to the left to the start of the task (if no actual progress is recorded) or to the end of the task progress bar. If the task is ahead of schedule, the progress line branches to the right to actual completion bar for the task.

Project calendar   The base calendar that is used to schedule tasks in a project. It is superceded by resource calendars for those tasks with assignments and by task calendars for those tasks that have them assigned.

Project Network Diagram   A view that shows a Network Diagram with boxes for tasks and lines connecting them to show dependencies between the tasks. This view replaces the PERT Chart found in previous version of Microsoft Project.

Project Summary report   A one-page overview of project information, which includes the project start and finish dates, duration, work, and costs (along with variances for those values). It also includes a breakdown of the number of tasks in various states of completion as well as the number of work and material resources and the number of overallocated resources.

Project summary task   A summary task that Project can display to sum the duration, work, and costs of all tasks in a project. When displayed, the project summary task appears at the top of the project, its ID number is 0, and it presents the project's timeline from start to finish. The project summary task is not displayed by default.

Reschedule tasks   A Microsoft Project command that you can use when part of the work on a task has been completed but the remainder must be rescheduled to a later time.

Resource calendar   A calendar that shows the working days and hours for a specific resource. It is created by defining a base calendar as a starting reference and then listing all the exceptions to the base calendar.

Resource conflict   The conflict that results when a resource is scheduled to do more work in a given time period than the resource is available to deliver.

Resource cost   The sum of all costs for a task that are based on resource assignments. Resource cost includes the cost of work resources (the product of the hours of work multiplied by the cost rate per hour for the resource, both standard and overtime) as well as the cost per use for the resource if defined. Resource cost also includes the cost of the material resources consumed. Resource Cost and Fixed Cost add up to (total) Cost. See also *Fixed cost*.

Resource group   Resources that have some characteristic in common and that have a group name. The resource field named Group is used to enter the names of groups to which a resource belongs for filtering, grouping, sorting, or reporting purposes. Not to be confused with group resources, which are resources with maximum units in excess of 100%. See also *Group resource*.

Resource pool   The list of resources that are available for assignment to tasks. A project can have its own resource pool, or it might use the resource pool that is already defined in another project file.

Resource sharing   Use of the same resources in more than one project file. When one project uses the resources listed in another project, the file that is borrowing the resources is the sharing file, and the file contributing its resources is the resource pool.

Resource type   Project recognizes two resource types: work resources and material resources. Work resources, such as people and equipment, provide their time and effort but are not consumed by a task. Material resources are consumed when assigned to a task.

Resource usage   A view that shows how many hours a resource is scheduled to work within each time period.

Resource view   A view that displays resource record data (see *Task view*). The standard resource views include the Resource Sheet, Resource Graph, Resource Form, Resource Allocation, and Resource Usage views.

Resource-driven scheduling   A scheduling method that revises a task's duration based on changes in the amount of work the task requires and the number of resource units assigned to it.

Resource-driven task   A task whose duration is driven or determined by the number of resource units assigned to the task and the amount of work they are assigned to complete. Similar to effort-driven tasks, but the latter term is restricted in Microsoft Project to designate tasks where changing the number of named resources assigned to the task, not just the units assigned, leads to changes in duration. See also *Fixed task* and *Fixed duration task*.

Resources   The people, equipment, facilities, materiel, and contractors used to complete the work of the project.

Risk management plan   A document that identifies risks and their probabilities and usually includes a contingency plan.

Roll up   In general, to add details about a task, resource, or assignment to a summary record. For example, to include the cost of a task in the cost of its summary task. Also, to display a marker on a summary task bar in a Gantt Chart to show a date for one of the subtasks.

RTF field   A field type that can hold text in Rich Text Format. The task, resource, and assignment Note fields are the RTF field, and they can contain formatted text, including bulleted lists, and objects formatted by other applications.

S-curve graph   A graph that is plotted using cumulative timephased data (such as BCWP and Cumulative Cost) to show earned value information. This graph is plotted when you use the Analyze Timescaled Data in Excel Wizard, located on the Analysis toolbar.

Schedule   Often called the current plan. The current set of actual (already completed) and predicted (yet to be completed) dates, durations, resource assignments, and costs for the project. Duration, Start, and Finish show values for the current schedule.

Schedule performance index (SPI)   The ratio of work performed to work scheduled (as measured by BCWP/BCWS), which is often used to estimate the project completion date.

Schedule variance (SV)   The difference between the budgeted cost of work actually performed (BCWP) and the budgeted cost of work scheduled (BCWS) for the same period. A positive SV indicates that the project costs are ahead of schedule.

Scheduled costs   The currently scheduled cost of tasks, resources, assignments, and the entire project, which Project displays in the Cost field as cost or total cost. The scheduled or current cost is kept up to date with cost adjustments you make and with the project's progress. When tracking costs, the scheduled or current cost represents the actual cost incurred to date plus the remaining cost for tasks, resources, assignments, or the project.

Scope   The products and/or services the project exists to provide.

Shared file   A project file using resources that are defined in another file.

Shared resource   A resource that is available for assignment in more than one project file, whether in a resource pool that is shared by multiple files or listed separately in multiple files.

Sheet   A view of project data that is designed like a spreadsheet with rows and columns of cells containing field values. Each row specifies an individual task, resource, or assignment record. Each column displays a field of information for the records.

Shortcut menu   A menu (sometimes called a context menu) that you access by pointing to a part of the screen and clicking the secondary mouse button. Project has a large number of shortcut menus that save time and make it easier for you to work with your project files.

Single pane view   A view that uses only one pane, as opposed to a dual pane or combination view that has a split window with separate views in the top pane and bottom pane.

Sizing handle   A small black square that appears at each corner and along the sides of the rectangular border that surrounds a selected object that you drag to change the size of the object.

Slack   Total slack is the amount of time by which a task can be delayed without delaying the finish of the project. Free slack is even more restrictive: It is the amount of time a task can be delayed without delaying the schedule for any other task.

Slippage   A measure of the amount of time by which a task's scheduled start or finish is behind its baseline (planned) start or finish dates.

Slippage bar   A bar in a Gantt view (like the Detail Gantt view) that connects the baseline start of a task and the currently scheduled start of the task to show the extent to which the start has slipped.

Sorting   Changing the order in which task, resource, and assignment rows are displayed in a table.

Source   The original location of pasted, inserted, imported, or exported information. The source can be another view in the same document or another document from the same or a different application.

Split task   A task whose scheduled work is interrupted by one or more periods of inactivity, usually to accommodate work on other tasks with higher priority.

Stakeholders   Individuals and organizations who have an involvement or interest in the project.

Standard rate   A base rate you assign to resources and that Project uses to calculate resource cost totals. For work resources this rate is the cost of an hour of work. For material resources it is the cost of one unit of the resource.

Start date   The date when a task is scheduled to begin.

Static picture   A graphical object, often from another document or program, that is not linked to the document or program in which the information was created.

Static text   Text that cannot be edited.

Status date   A date that you set for reporting the time, cost, or performance condition of a project. If the status date is not set, Project uses the current date.

Status report   A report from a workgroup member describing the status of his assigned work.

Subphase   A phase or summary task that is indented under another phase or summary task.

Subproject   A project file that is inserted as a summary task in a consolidated project file. The consolidated project file uses the start and finish dates of the subproject as the start and finish dates of the summary task that represents the subproject. The subproject schedule is fitted into the consolidated project schedule by defining links between subproject summary tasks or between individual tasks in different subprojects. See also *Consolidated project*.

Subtask   A task that is indented under, and summarized by, a summary task.

Successor   In a dependency relationship, the dependent task is called the successor task, and the task it depends on is called the predecessor task. The tasks might actually overlap in time, however, and you shouldn't assume that the successor task comes after the predecessor task. See also *Predecessor*.

Summary recurring task   The summary task that is automatically created to summarize the individual tasks that represent a recurring activity (such as a weekly meeting).

Summary task   A task that encompasses and summarizes the duration, work, and costs of other tasks (called subtasks) Can also represent an entire subproject that has been inserted into a consolidated project.

Supplier   An outside contractor, vendor, or other agency that serves as a resource for completing a project.

Tab-delimited text format   A file format that is commonly used to exchange data between environments and in which each field of a task or resource record is separated by a list-separator character, usually the tab. Each task or resource record ends with a carriage return/line feed.

Task   An activity that is essential to the completion of the project and that has an observable start and finish. A normal task represents an essential job or operation that must be completed for a project to be completed. Milestones and summary tasks are special types of tasks.

Task calendar   A base calendar that you assign to an individual task to control the scheduling of the task. If there are resources assigned to the task, by default Project schedules the task assignments during periods that are working times on both the task calendar and the resource calendar. However, you also have the option to ignore the resource calendars and schedule the resources during the working time on the task calendar.

Task delegation   The situation in which one workgroup member assigns a task to another workgroup member in Microsoft Project Central. When a task is delegated to another workgroup member, that workgroup member actually does the work on the task, although the person who delegates the task has the option of reviewing and approving status and actuals on the task before forwarding them to the project manager.

Task dependency   The situation where the scheduled start or finish of a task is tied to, and changes with, the scheduled start or finish of another task (its predecessor). If a task's schedule is tied to a predecessor, it is itself then called a successor task, although the better term would be dependent task.

Task ID   A number that Microsoft Project automatically assigns to a task as you add it to the project. The Task ID reflects the task's position in the order of tasks and will change if you move a task to another position in the order. See also *Unique ID*.

Task list   The list of activities shown in the table displayed in the sheet portion of a view like the Gantt Chart.

Task report   A report that is organized around the tasks in a project. Assignment data can be added and summed by task.

Task view   A view of the project data that is organized around the task records. The standard task views include the Gantt Chart, Calendar, Task Sheet, Task Forms, and Network Diagram.

TeamAssign command   Notifies resources by email or Microsoft Project Central that the project manager wants to assign the resource to a task.

TeamStatus command   Sends a request to assigned resources asking for an update on the status of the assigned work.

TeamUpdate command   Sends a notice to all assigned resources whose assignment schedule has changed.

Template   A Microsoft Project file format for a file that will be used as the starting point for new schedules. Typically, the template contains a list of tasks and/or resources that will be repeated in future projects.

Text List field   A field whose content is a list of text items separated by the list separator character, typically a comma. Examples include the resource Group, resource Initials and Resource Names fields.

Timephased   Task, resource, or assignment information that is distributed into the time periods you select for display or for reporting. You can review timephased information, such as work or costs, in fields on the right side of the Task Usage and Resource Usage views.

Timescale   An area in a view that marks chronological dates along the top of the view and shows data for tasks or resources placed in the appropriate time periods.

Timesheet   The form where workgroup members specify the specific status of tasks so that the status information can be sent to the project manager.

Total cost   The calculated cost of a project, task, resource, or assignment over the life of the project. The field name is Cost.

Total slack   The amount of time a task finish date can be delayed without delaying the finish date of the project.

UNC   Acronym for Universal Naming Convention addresses, which are used to identify the location of a file that resides on a network server. UNC addresses begin with two back-slash characters (\\) followed by the server name, the share name (if any), and full path to the file.

Unique ID   A unique number that Microsoft Project automatically assigns to a task, resource, or assignment when it is created and that never changes even when the ID number changes due to changing the order of the records.

Unit availability   A number that shows how many units of a resource are available during a given date range. Whether displayed in percentage or decimal units, it shows the number of hours that can be scheduled for a resource for each hour on the calendar. Unit availability is entered in the Resource Availability table on the Resource Information dialog box.

URL   Acronym for Uniform Resource Locator, which is a standard for locating an object on the Internet, such as a file or newsgroup. It is also used to specify the target of a hyper-link.

Variable consumption rate   A quantity of a material resource that is to be consumed for each unit of duration time in an assignment. See also *Fixed consumption rate*.

Variable cost   Costs that vary with the duration of the task and the number of hours of work.

Variance   The difference between the baseline and currently scheduled data. Variances can be calculated for dates, work, or costs.

Variance at completion (VAC)   The earned value field that shows the difference between the baseline cost (BAC) and the scheduled cost (EAC).

View bar   A screen element of Project that is displayed on the left of the Project window. The View Bar contains icons for all the views that appear in the View menu that can be clicked to switch to that view.

Visual Basic for Applications (VBA)   A complete programming language that you can use to automate your work in Microsoft Project, as well as to automate interactions between Microsoft Project and other applications that run under Windows and NT and that have implemented Visual Basic for Applications.

Web server   A program running on a machine that allows remote users to request Internet-based files from it. In the case of Microsoft Project, Microsoft Project Central can be integrated with the Web server to allow remote connection to the project schedule through a Web browser.

WebInbox   The message center in Microsoft Project in which a workgroup manager can view messages from workgroup members who are using Microsoft Project Central. The workgroup manager can automatically update the project schedule based on the responses of workgroup members.

Weighted duration   A calculated duration that the PERT Analysis places in the Duration field. It is the weighted average of the expected, pessimistic, and optimistic dates and durations. By default, the PERT analysis calculation gives heaviest weight (4) to the expected duration, and the lightest weight (1 each) to the pessimistic and optimistic durations.

"What-if" scenario   Changing values in a project schedule to see the effect on target values such as overall cost or finish date.

Work   The amount of time that all units of a resource spend on a task assignment. For example, if two electricians work 8 hours on an assignment, the work for this assignment would be 16 hours. The assignment work value can be summed to show the total amount of time all resources spend on a task, or the total amount of time a resource spends on all tasks.

Work Breakdown Structure (WBS)   A method of organizing a project by which tasks are grouped into a hierarchical structure featuring major phase groups, with subgroups at many levels, that allow you to quickly group activities for schedules or cost reports. Tasks are assigned a default WBS code that identifies the group, subgroups, and individual tasks within each group; alternatively, you can create your own coding system.

Work resource   People and equipment resources that spend time completing a task. Work resources are not themselves consumed by a task, although their available time is. See also *Material resource*.

Workgroup   A group composed of a manager and other members who are working on the same project. The manager assigns the other members to work on tasks, and can communicate with the members about assignments in Microsoft Project via email or using Microsoft Project Central, the Internet, or an intranet.

Workgroup manager   The manager in a workgroup who creates and maintains the project schedule and who uses workgroup messages to assign tasks to the workgroup members.

Workgroup members   The individuals in a workgroup who receive workgroup messages from the workgroup manager.

Workgroup messages   Messages that the workgroup manager and workgroup members send through Microsoft Project Central or email to assign, modify, or update the tasks of a project.

Working Days report   A report that shows the normal working times for base calendars used in the project along with nonworking time exceptions.

Working time   The days and hours on a calendar during which work on tasks can be scheduled.

INDEX

H